THE SECOND BOOK OF MOSES,

EXODUS

PART II
(Chapters 19-40)

VOLUME 4

THE
PREACHER'S
OUTLINE & SERMON
BIBLE®

THE SECOND BOOK OF MOSES, CALLED

EXODUS

PART II
(Chapters 19-40)

VOLUME 4

THE
PREACHER'S
OUTLINE & SERMON
BIBLE®

OLD TESTAMENT

KING JAMES VERSION

Leadership Ministries Worldwide
PO Box 21310
Chattanooga, TN 37424-0310

Please address all requests for information or permission to:
Leadership Ministries Worldwide
PO Box 21310
Chattanooga, TN 37424-0310
Ph.# (423) 855-2181   FAX (423) 855-8616   E-Mail outlinebible@compuserve.com
http://www.outlinebible.org

Library of Congress Catalog Card Number: 96-75921
International Standard Book Number: 1-57407-050-9

Printed in the United States of America

Publisher &
Distributor

DEDICATED:

To all the men and women of the world
who preach and teach the Gospel of our
Lord Jesus Christ
and
To the Mercy and Grace of God.

• Demonstrated to us in Christ Jesus our Lord.

> "In whom we have redemption through His
> blood, the forgiveness of sins, according to the
> riches of His grace." (Eph. 1:7)

• Out of the mercy and grace of God His Word has
flowed. Let every person know that God will have
mercy upon him, forgiving and using him to fulfill His
glorious plan of salvation.

> "For God so loved the world, that he gave his only
> begotten Son, that whosoever believeth in him should
> not perish, but have everlasting life. For God sent not
> his Son into the world to condemn the world; but that
> the world through him might be saved." (Jn 3:16-17)

> "For this is good and acceptable in the sight of God
> our Saviour; who will have all men to be saved,
> and to come unto the knowledge of the truth." (I Tim. 2:3-4)

The Preacher's Outline and Sermon Bible®
is written for God's people to use
in their preparation for preaching and teaching.

OUR VISION, PASSION & PURPOSE:

• To share the Word of God with the world.
• To help the believer, both minister and layman alike, in his understanding,
preaching, and teaching of God's Word.
• To do everything we possibly can to lead men, women, boys, and girls to
give their hearts and lives to Jesus Christ and to secure the eternal life
which He offers.
• To do all we can to minister to the needy of the world.
• To give Jesus Christ His proper place, the place which the Word gives
Him. Therefore — No work of Leadership Ministries Worldwide
will ever be personalized.

9/96

OUTLINE BIBLE RESOURCES

This material, like similar works, has come from imperfect man and is thus susceptible to human error. We are nevertheless grateful to God for both calling us and empowering us through His Holy Spirit to undertake this task. Because of His goodness and grace **The Preacher's Outline & Sermon Bible®** - New Testament is complete in 14 volumes, and the Old Testament volumes release periodically. **The Minister's Handbook** is available and *OUTLINE* Bible materials are releasing electonically on **POSB-CD** and our **Web site**.

God has given the strength and stamina to bring us this far. Our confidence is that, as we keep our eyes on Him and grounded in the undeniable truths of the Word, we will continue working through the Old Testament volumes and the second series known as **The Teacher's Outline & Study Bible.** The future includes helpful *Outline Bible* books and **Handbook** materials for God's dear servants.

To everyone everywhere who preaches and teaches the Word, we offer this material firstly to Him in whose name we labor and serve, and for whose glory it has been produced.

Our daily prayer is that each volume will lead thousands, millions, yes even billions, into a better understanding of the Holy Scriptures and a fuller knowledge of Jesus Christ the incarnate Word, of whom the Scriptures so faithfully testify.

> As you have purchased this volume, you will be pleased to know that a small portion of the price you have paid has gone to underwrite and provide similar volumes in other languages (Russian, Korean, Spanish and others yet to come) — To a preacher, pastor, lay leader, or Bible student somewhere around the world, who will present God's message with clarity, authority, and understanding beyond their own. *Amen.*

For information and prices, kindly contact your *OUTLINE* Bible bookseller or:

LEADERSHIP
MINISTRIES
WORLDWIDE

P.O. Box 21310, 515 Airport Road, Suite 107
Chattanooga, TN 37424-0310
(423) 855-2181 FAX (423) 855-8616
E-Mail - outlinebible@compuserve.com
Web site: www.outlinebible.org

 Publisher & Distributor of...

Materials Published & Distributed by **LEADERSHIP MINISTRIES WORLDWIDE:**

- **THE PREACHER'S OUTLINE & SERMON BIBLE®** - [POSB] - **NEW TESTAMENT**

Volume 1	St. Matthew I (chapters 1-15)
Volume 2	St. Matthew II (chapters 16-28)
Volume 3	St. Mark
Volume 4	St. Luke
Volume 5	St. John
Volume 6	Acts
Volume 7	Romans
Volume 8	1 & 2 Corinthians (1 volume)
Volume 9	Galatians - Colossians (1 volume)
Volume 10	1 Thessalonians - Philemon (1 volume)
Volume 11	Hebrews -James (1 volume)
Volume 12	1 Peter-Jude (1 volume)
Volume 13	Revelation
Volume 14	Master Outline & Subject Index
	FULL SET — 14 Volumes:

- **THE PREACHER'S OUTLINE & SERMON BIBLE®** - [POSB] - **OLD TESTAMENT**

Volume 1	Genesis I (chapters 1-11)
Volume 2	Genesis II (chapters 12-50)
Volume 3	Exodus I (chapters 1-18)
Volume 4	Exodus II (chapters 19-40)

  Subsequent O.T. volumes about every 6-8 months until the OT is completed.

- **THE PREACHER'S OUTLINE & SERMON BIBLE®** - English **SOFTBOUND SET**

  PerfectBound 14 Vol. Set for leadership training, missionaries, overseas church leaders - Lightweight/Affordable

- **The Minister's Personal Handbook** - **What the Bible Says...to the Minister**

  12 Chapters — 127 Subjects — 400 Pages — Over 18,000 in use

  • More than 400 verses from OT and NT dealing with God's minister and servant; all assembled in the unique *Outline* style. Features God's Word for His chosen and called servants who minister the Word.

- **What the Bible Says to the Minister About FALSE TEACHING**

  80 page booklet from The Minister's Handbook - Great Gift or Study Book

- **Translations of POSB N.T. Volumes and Minister's Handbook:** <u>Limited Quantities</u>

  Russian — Spanish — Korean • *Future: Hindi, Taligu, Asia Project (1997) & 6 others*
  — Contact us for specific Language and Prices —

- **THE TEACHER'S OUTLINE & STUDY BIBLE • New Testament •**

  Minimum of 17 lessons/book; 205 pages • Verse Study • Student Journal • Quantity Discounts

- **CD-ROM - WORD***search* **4™ - w/KJV** (+ 8 optional versions) - **Win3.1/95 & STEP**

  Complete N.T. (14 vols) on 1 disc; PLUS...30 Bible study tool options on the same disk!

+ **All these great Volumes & Materials are also available at affordable prices to qualifying overseas preachers, evangelists, and church leaders by contacting:**

• *Your OUTLINE Bible Bookseller, or...*

LEADERSHIP MINISTRIES WORLDWIDE
PO Box 21310
Chattanooga, TN 37424-0310
(423) 855-2181 (9-5 Eastern Time)   FAX (423) 855-8616 (24 hrs)
E•Mail - outlinebible@compuserve.com. — www.outlinebible.org *[Free downloads!]*

ACKNOWLEDGMENTS AND BIBLIOGRAPHY (1)

Every child of God is precious to the Lord and deeply loved. And every child as a servant of the Lord touches the lives of those who come in contact with him or his ministry. The writing ministry of the following servants have touched this work, and we are grateful that God brought their writings our way. We hereby acknowledge their ministry to us, being fully aware that there are so many others down through the years whose writings have touched our lives and who deserve mention, but the weaknesses of our minds have caused them to fade from memory. May our wonderful Lord continue to bless the ministry of these dear servants, and the ministry of us all as we diligently labor to reach the world for Christ and to meet the desperate needs of those who suffer so much.

THE REFERENCE WORKS

Archer, Gleason L. Jr. *A Survey of Old Testament Introduction*. Chicago, IL: Moody Bible Institute of Chicago, 1974.

Baker's Dictionary of Theology. Everett F. Harrison, Editor-in-Chief. Grand Rapids, MI: Baker Book House, 1960.

Brown, Francis. *The New Brown-Driver-Briggs-Gesenius Hebrew-English Lexicon*. Peabody, MA: Hendrickson Publishers, 1979.

Cruden's Complete Concordance of the Old & New Testament. Philadelphia, PA: The John C. Winston Co., 1930.

Dake's Annotated Reference Bible, The Holy Bible. Finis Jennings Dake. Lawrenceville, GA: Dake Bible Sales, Inc., 1963.

Elwell, Walter A., Editor. *The Evangelical Dictionary of Theology*. Grand Rapids, MI: Baker Book House, 1984.

Encyclopedia of Biblical Prophecy. J. Barton Payne. New York, NY: Harper & Row, Publishers, 1973.

Funk & Wagnalls Standard Desk Dictionary. Lippincott & Crowell, Publishers, 1980, Vol.2.

Geisler, Norman. *A Popular Survey of the Old Testament*. Grand Rapids, MI: Baker Book House, 1977.

Good News Bible. Old Testament: © American Bible Society, 1976. New Testament: © American Bible Society, 1966, 1971, 1976. Collins World.

Good, Joseph. *Rosh HaShanah and the Messianic Kingdom to Come*. Pt. Arthur, TX: Hatikva Ministries, 1989.

Harrison, Roland Kenneth. *Introduction to the Old Testament*. Grand Rapids, MI: Eerdmans Publishing Company, 1969.

Josephus, Flavius. *Complete Works*. Grand Rapids, MI: Kregel Publications, 1981.

Kelley, Page H. *Exodus: Called for Redemptive Mission*. January Bible Study. Nashville, TN: Convention Press, 1977.

Kohlenberger, John R. III. *The Interlinear NIV Hebrew-English Old Testament*. Grand Rapids, MI: Zondervan Publishing House, 1987.

Life Application® Bible. Wheaton, IL: Tyndale House Publishers, Inc., 1991.

Lindsell, Harold and Woodbridge, Charles J. *A Handbook of Christian Truth*. Westwood, NJ: Fleming H. Revell Company, A Division of Baker Book House, 1953.

<u>ACKNOWLEDGMENTS AND BIBLIOGRAPHY</u> (2)

Lipis, Joan R. *Celebrate Passover Haggadah*. San Francisco, CA: Purple Pomegranate Productions, 1993.

Living Quotations For Christians. Edited by Sherwood Eliot Wirt and Kersten Beckstrom. New York, NY: Harper & Row, Publishers, 1974.

Lockyer, Herbert. *All the Books and Chapters of the Bible*. Grand Rapids, MI: Zondervan Publishing House, 1966.

Lockyer, Herbert. *All the Men of the Bible*. Grand Rapids, MI: Zondervan Publishing House, 1958.

Lockyer, Herbert. *The Women of the Bible*. Grand Rapids, MI: Zondervan Publishing House, 1967.

Martin, Alfred. *Survey of the Scriptures*, Part I, II, III. Chicago, IL: Moody Bible Institute of Chicago, 1961.

McDowell, Josh. *Evidence That Demands A Verdict*, Vol.1. San Bernardino, CA: Here's Life Publishers, Inc., 1979.

Miller, Madeleine S. & J. Lane. *Harper's Bible Dictionary*. New York, NY: Harper & Row Publishers, 1961.

Nave's Topical Bible. Orville J. Nave. Nashville, TN: The Southwestern Company. Copyright © by J.B. Henderson, 1921.

Nelson's Expository Dictionary of the Old Testament. Merrill F. Unger & William White, Jr. Nashville, TN: Thomas Nelson Publishers, 1980.

New American Standard Bible, Reference Edition. La Habra, CA: The Lockman Foundation, 1975.

New International Version Study Bible. Grand Rapids, MI: Zondervan Bible Publishers, 1985.

New Living Translation, Holy Bible. Wheaton, IL: Tyndale House Publishers, Inc., 1996.

NIV Exhaustive Concordance. (Grand Rapids, MI: Zondervan Corporation, 1990).

Orr, William. *How We May Know That God Is*. Wheaton, IL: Van Kampen Press, No date given.

Owens, John Joseph. *Analytical Key to the Old Testament,* Vols.1, 2, 3. Grand Rapids, MI: Baker Book House, 1989.

Pilgrim Edition, Holy Bible. New York, NY: Oxford University Press, 1952.

Ridout, Samuel. *Lectures on the Tabernacle*. New York, NY: Loizeaux Brothers, Inc., 1914.

Roget's 21st Century Thesaurus, Edited by Barbara Ann Kipfer. New York, NY: Dell Publishing, 1992.

Rosen, Ceil and Moishe. *Christ In The Passover*. Chicago, IL: Moody Press, 1978.

Slemming, C.W. *Made According To Pattern*. Fort Washington, PA: Christian Literature Crusade, 1983.

Soltau, Henry W. *The Holy Vessels And Furniture Of The Tabernacle*. Grand Rapids, MI: Kregel Publications, 1971.

Soltau, Henry W. *The Tabernacle The Priesthood And The Offerings*. Grand Rapids, MI: Kregel Publications, 1972.

Stone, Nathan J. *Names of God*. Chicago, IL: Moody Press, 1944.

Strong's Exhaustive Concordance of the Bible. James Strong. Nashville, TN: Thomas Nelson, Inc., 1990.

Strong, James. *The Tabernacle Of Israel*. Grand Rapids, MI: Kregel Publications, 1987.

The Amplified Bible. Scripture taken from THE AMPLIFIED BIBLE, Old Testament copyright © 1965, 1987 by the Zondervan Corporation. The Amplified New Testament copyright © 1958, 1987 by The Lockman Foundation. Used by permission.

The Hebrew-Greek Key Study Bible, New International Version. Spiros Zodhiates, Th.D., Executive Editor. Chattanooga, TN: AMG Publishers, 1996.

The Holy Bible in Four Translations. Minneapolis, MN: Worldwide Publications. Copyright © The Iversen-Norman Associates: New York, NY, 1972.

The Interlinear Bible, Vol.1, 2, & 3, Translated by Jay P. Green, Sr. Grand Rapids, MI: Baker Book House Company, 1976.

The International Standard Bible Encyclopaedia, Edited by James Orr. Grand Rapids, MI: Eerdmans Publishing Company, 1939.

The NASB Greek/Hebrew Dictionary and Concordance. (La Habra, CA: The Lockman Foundation, 1988).

The New Compact Bible Dictionary, Edited by T. Alton Bryant. Grand Rapids, MI: Zondervan Publishing House, 1967. Used by permission of Zondervan Publishing House.

The New Scofield Reference Bible, Edited by C.I. Scofield. New York, NY: Oxford University Press, 1967.

The New Thompson Chain Reference Bible. Indianapolis, IN: B.B. Kirkbride Bible Co., Inc., 1964.

The Open Bible. Nashville, TN: Thomas Nelson Publishers, 1975.

The Zondervan Pictorial Encyclopedia of the Bible, Vol.1. Merrill C. Tenney, Editor. Grand Rapids, MI: Zondervan Publishing House, 1982.

Theological Wordbook of the Old Testament, Edited by R. Laird Harris. Chicago, IL: Moody Bible Institute of Chicago, 1980.

Vine's Complete Expository Dictionary of Old and New Testament Words. W.E. Vine, Merrill F. Unger, William White, Jr. Nashville, TN: Thomas Nelson Publishers, 1985.

Webster's Seventh New Collegiate Dictionary. Springfield, MA: G. & C. Merriam Company, Publishers, 1971.

Wilson, William. *Wilson's Old Testament Word Studies*. McLean, VA: MacDonald Publishing Company, No date given.

Wood, Leon. *A Survey of Israel's History*. Grand Rapids, MI: Zondervan Publishing House, 1982.

Young's Analytical Concordance to the Bible. Robert Young. Grand Rapids, MI: Eerdmans Publishing Company, No date given.

Young, Edward J. *An Introduction to the Old Testament*. Grand Rapids, MI: Eerdmans Publishing Company, 1964.

Zehr, Paul M. *Glimpses of the Tabernacle*. Lancaster, PA: Mennonite Information Center, 1976.

ACKNOWLEDGMENTS AND BIBLIOGRAPHY (4)

THE COMMENTARIES

Barclay, William. *The Letters to the Philippians, Colossians, and Thessalonians.* "Daily Study Bible Series." Philadelphia, PA: Westminster Press, Began in 1953.

Barclay, William. *The Old Law & The New Law.* Philadelphia, PA: The Westminster Press, 1972.

Barnes' Notes, Exodus to Esther. F.C. Cook, Editor. Grand Rapids, MI: Baker Book House, No date given.

Bush, George. *Commentary on Exodus.* Grand Rapids, MI: Kregel Publications, 1993.

Bush, George. *Exodus.* Minneapolis, MN: Klock & Klock Christian Publishers, Inc., 1981.

Childs, Brevard S. *The Book of Exodus.* Philadelphia, PA: The Westminster Press, 1974.

Cole, R. Alan. *Exodus.* "The Tyndale Old Testament Commentaries." Downers Grove, IL: Inter-Varsity Press, 1973.

Dunnam, Maxie. *Mastering the Old Testament*, Vol.2. Dallas, TX: Word Publishing, 1987.

Durham, John I. *Understanding the Basic Themes of Exodus.* Dallas, TX: Word, Inc., 1990.

Durham, John I. *Word Biblical Commentary, Exodus.* Waco, TX: Word, Inc., 1987.

Ellison, H.L. *Exodus.* Philadelphia, PA: The Westminster Press, 1982.

Fretheim, Terence E. *Exodus, Interpretation.* Louisville, KY: John Knox Press, 1991.

Gaebelein, Frank E. *The Expositor's Bible Commentary*, Vol.2. Grand Rapids, MI: Zondervan Publishing House, 1990.

Gill, John. *Gill's Commentary*, Vol.1. Grand Rapids, MI: Baker Book House, 1980.

Hayford, Jack W., Executive Editor. *Milestones to Maturity.* Nashville, TN: Thomas Nelson Publishers, 1994

Henry, Matthew. *Matthew Henry's Commentary*, 6 Volumes. Old Tappan, NJ: Fleming H. Revell Co., No date given.

Heslop, W.G. *Extras from Exodus.* Grand Rapids, MI: Kregel Publications, 1931.

Hewitt, Thomas. *The Epistle to the Hebrews.* "Tyndale New Testament Commentaries." Grand Rapids, MI: Eerdmans Publishing Co., Began in 1958.

Huey, F.B. Jr. *A Study Guide Commentary, Exodus.* Grand Rapids, MI: Zondervan Publishing House, 1977.

Hyatt, J.P. *The New Century Bible Commentary, Exodus.* Grand Rapids, MI: Eerdmans Publishing Company, 1971.

Keil-Delitzsch. *Commentary on the Old Testament*, Vol.1. Grand Rapids, MI: Eerdmans Publishing Company, No date given.

Life Change Series, Exodus. Colorado Springs, CO: NavPress, 1989.

Maclaren, Alexander. *Expositions of Holy Scripture*, 11 Vols. Grand Rapids, MI: Eerdmans Publishing Company, 1952-59.

McGee, J. Vernon. *Thru The Bible*, Vol.1. Nashville, TN: Thomas Nelson Publishers, 1981.

Meyer, F.B. *Devotional Commentary on Exodus*. Grand Rapids, MI: Kregel Publications, 1978.

Napier, B. Davie. *Exodus*. "The Layman's Bible Commentary," Vol.3. Atlanta, GA: John Knox Press, 1963.

Pink, Arthur. *Gleanings in Exodus*. Chicago, IL: Moody Bible Institute of Chicago, Moody Press, No date given.

Pink, Arthur W. *The Ten Commandments*. Grand Rapids, MI: Baker Books, 1994.

Reapsome, James. *Exodus*. Downers Grove, IL: InterVarsity Press, 1989.

Salmond, S.D.F.. *The Epistle to the Ephesians*. "The Expositor's Greek Testament," Vol.3. Grand Rapids, MI: Eerdmans Publishing Co., 1970.

Sarna, Nahum M. *Exploring Exodus*. New York, NY: Schocken Books Inc., 1986.

Strauss, Lehman. *Devotional Studies in Galatians & Ephesians*. Neptune, NJ: Loizeaux Brothers, 1957.

The Biblical Illustrator, Exodus. Edited by Joseph S. Exell. Grand Rapids, MI: Baker Book House, 1964.

The Epistle of Paul to the Ephesians. "Tyndale New Testament Commentaries." Grand Rapids, MI: Eerdmans, No date listed.

The Interpreter's Bible, 12 Vols. New York, NY: Abingdon Press, 1956.

The Pulpit Commentary. 23 Volumes. Edited by H.D.M. Spence & Joseph S. Exell. Grand Rapids, MI: Eerdmans Publishing Company, 1950.

Thomas, W.H. Griffith. *Through the Pentateuch Chapter by Chapter*. Grand Rapids, MI: Eerdmans Publishing Company, 1957.

Wuest, Kenneth S.. *Ephesians and Colossians*. "Word Studies in the Greek New Testament," Vol.1. Grand Rapids, MI: Eerdmans Publishing Co., 1966.

Youngblood, Ronald F. *Exodus*. Chicago, IL: Moody Press, 1983.

OTHER SOURCES

Anderson, Norman. *Issues of Life and Death*. Downers Grove, IL: InterVarsity Press, 1977.

Briscoe, Stuart. *The Ten Commandments*. Wheaton, IL: Harold Shaw Publishers, 1986.

Geisler, Norman. *Ethics: Alternatives and Issues*. Grand Rapids, MI: Zondervan, 1971.

McGee, J. Vernon. *Love Liberation and the Law*. Nashville, TN: Thomas Nelson Publishers, 1995.

Olford, Stephen. *The Tabernacle, Camping With God*. Neptune, NJ: Loizeaux Brothers, 1971.

Rogers, Adrian. *Ten Secrets For A Successful Family*. Wheaton, IL: Crossway Books, 1996.

Sell, Charles M.. *Family Ministry*. Grand Rapids, MI: Zondervan Corporation, 1981.

MISCELLANEOUS ABBREVIATIONS

&	=	And
Arg.	=	Argument
Bckgrd.	=	Background
Bc.	=	Because
Circ.	=	Circumstance
Concl.	=	Conclusion
Cp.	=	Compare
Ct.	=	Contrast
Dif.	=	Different
e.g.	=	For example
Et.	=	Eternal
Govt.	=	Government
Id.	=	Identity or Identification
Illust.	=	Illustration
K.	=	Kingdom, K. of God, K. of Heaven, etc.
No.	=	Number
N.T.	=	New Testament
O.T.	=	Old Testament
Pt.	=	Point
Quest.	=	Question
Rel.	=	Religion
Resp.	=	Responsibility
Rev.	=	Revelation
Rgt.	=	Righteousness
Thru	=	Through
V.	=	Verse
Vs.	=	Verses
Vs.	=	Versus

TABLE OF CONTENTS

The
Preacher's
Outline
&
Sermon
Bible®

*Woe is unto me, if I
preach not the gospel*
(I Cor. 9:16).

THE SECOND BOOK OF MOSES, CALLED

EXODUS

INTRODUCTION

I. AUTHOR

Moses, the great lawgiver and deliverer of Israel. Moses was the great leader who led Israel from Egyptian bondage and through the *wilderness wanderings*.

1. The internal evidence of Scripture--Scripture itself--strongly points to Moses being the author of Exodus. The force of this claim can be clearly seen by simply glancing down through the following Scriptures.

   a. The Old Testament points toward Moses being the author.

> "And the LORD said unto Moses, Write this *for* a memorial in a book, and rehearse *it* in the ears of Joshua: for I will utterly put out the remembrance of Amalek from under heaven" (Ex. 17:14).

> "And Moses wrote all the words of the LORD, and rose up early in the morning, and builded an altar under the hill, and twelve pillars, according to the twelve tribes of Israel" (Ex. 24:4).

> "And he took the book of the covenant, and read in the audience of the people: and they said, All that the LORD hath said will we do, and be obedient" (Ex. 24:7).

> "And the LORD said unto Moses, Write thou these words: for after the tenor of these words I have made a covenant with thee and with Israel" (Ex. 34:27).

> "These *are* the journeys of the children of Israel, which went forth out of the land of Egypt with their armies under the hand of Moses and Aaron. And Moses wrote their goings out according to their journeys by the commandment of the LORD: and these *are* their journeys according to their goings out" (Num. 33:1-2).

> "And Moses wrote this law, and delivered it unto the priests the sons of Levi, which bare the ark of the covenant of the LORD, and unto all the elders of Israel" (Dt. 31:9).

> "Only be thou strong and very courageous, that thou mayest observe to do according to all the law, which Moses my servant commanded thee: turn not from it *to* the right hand or *to* the left, that thou mayest prosper whithersoever thou goest. This book of the law shall not depart out of thy mouth; but thou shalt meditate therein day and night, that thou mayest observe to do according to all that is written therein: for then thou shalt make thy way prosperous, and then thou shalt have good success" (Josh. 1:7-8).

> "As Moses the servant of the LORD commanded the children of Israel, as it is written in the book of the law of Moses, an altar of whole stones, over which no man hath lift up *any* iron: and they offered thereon burnt offerings unto the LORD, and sacrificed peace offerings" (Josh. 8:31).

   b. The New Testament points toward Moses being the author.

> "For Moses said, Honour thy father and thy mother; and, Whoso curseth father or mother, let him die the death" (Mk.7:10).

> "And as touching the dead, that they rise: have ye not read in the book of Moses, how in the bush God spake unto him, saying, I [am] the God of Abraham, and the God of Isaac, and the God of Jacob?" (Mk.12:26).

> "And when the days of her purification according to the law of Moses were accomplished, they brought him to Jerusalem, to present him to the Lord; (As it is written in the law of the Lord, Every male that openeth the womb shall be called holy to the Lord)" (Lk.2:22-23).

   c. Jesus Christ Himself said that Moses was the author.

> "And they said, Moses suffered to write a bill of divorcement, and to put her away. And Jesus answered and said unto them, For the hardness of your heart he wrote you this precept" (Mk.10:4-5).

> "And he said unto them, These [are] the words which I spake unto you, while I was yet with you, that all things must be fulfilled, which were written in the law of Moses, and [in] the prophets, and [in] the psalms, concerning me" (Lk.24:44).

> "For had ye believed Moses, ye would have believed me: for he wrote of me. But if ye believe not his writings, how shall ye believe my words?" (Jn.5:46-47).

> "Did not Moses give you the law, and [yet] none of you keepeth the law? Why go ye about to kill me?" (Jn.7:19).

2. The external evidence also strongly points to Moses being the author of Exodus.

   a. Tradition--both Jewish and Christian tradition-- has been unanimous in holding that Moses is the author of Exodus. In fact, tradition is strong, very strong, that Moses wrote the entire Pentateuch (Genesis, Exodus, Leviticus, Numbers, Deuteronomy).

   b. Archeology also points to Moses being the author. The author certainly lived during the day when Exodus was written. What shows us this? The facts we find in the Pentateuch, facts describing such matters as...

- customs
- conduct
- geography
- history
- events
- places
- names

F.B. Huey says this:

> "Archaeological discoveries have confirmed the accuracy of customs, events, and names that are found in the Pentateuch and suggest that the author was not writing hundreds of years after the event."[1]

3. The qualifications of Moses point to his being the author of Exodus.

   a. Moses had the education to write Exodus. He was well educated in "all the wisdom of the Egyptians" (Acts 7:22). Moreover, he was obviously well prepared by God to take both the written and oral testimony of his forefathers and write Exodus. (See Introduction, Author--Genesis for more discussion.)

   b. Moses was well acquainted with all that happened in the Book of Exodus. He knew all about Egypt, Midian, the desert, and the Sinai Peninsula. He knew all about the customs, conduct, geography, events, places, and people. He knew because he was there.

   c. Moses had the time to write Exodus. He lived and walked through the desert with the Israelites for forty years, forty long years. In forming the slaves into a nation of people, he was bound to know the importance of recording their history for future generations.

   d. Moses was God's appointed deliverer, the founding father of the nation Israel. Moses was a man of destiny, a man appointed by God to take a worn out body of slaves and form them into a nation of people. In building the nation, he was bound to record the events and history of the Israelites.

Just think for a moment: being the great deliverer of Israel, it would have been most unusual--so unusual it would have been foolish--for him not to record the events and history of what was happening. In fact, keep in mind, he was building an impoverished body of people into a nation. He knew this. It would be must unreasonable to think Moses was not recording the events for posterity, to help give structure--building blocks, a foundation--to the nation

In addition to all the above, if we believe that God inspired ("breathed") the Holy Scriptures, one fact comes to the forefront: God would have led men from the earliest days of human history to record His plan of redemption. Therefore to the believer, there is no question: God appointed men from the very beginning of human history, appointed them to write the Holy Scriptures. And as they wrote, God inspired (God breathed) the words of Scripture (2 Tim.3:16).

As seen, the evidence is strong: Moses wrote the great Book of Exodus. No other person has ever been suggested that can rival Moses. It would be difficult to reject all the evidence that points to Moses and suggest that some *unknown, nameless* person wrote Exodus. The only reasonable and honest conclusion is to say what Scripture indicates: Moses wrote Exodus. (See Introduction--Genesis for more discussion.)

II. DATE

Probably some time between 1446-1406 B.C.

1. Moses lived 120 years (Dt.34:7).
2. Moses spent 40 years in Egypt (Acts 7:22-23).
3. Moses spent 40 years in Midian (Ex.2:15).
4. Moses spent 40 years leading Israel through the wilderness experiences (Dt.8:2f).

Now, we know with some accuracy when Moses lived:

> **"And it came to pass in the four hundred and eightieth year after the children of Israel were come out of the land of Egypt, in the fourth year of Solomon's reign over Israel, in the month Zif, which is the second month, that he began to build the house of the LORD" (1 Ki.6:1).**

The fourth year of Solomon's reign was about 966 B.C.; therefore, Moses led Israel out of Egypt around 1446 B.C. (480 years before Solomon's 4th year as king (NIV Study Bible, p.2, 84). Based upon this information, Moses' life would be dated as follows:

⇒ Moses in Egypt 1526-1486 B.C.
⇒ Moses in Midian 1486-1446 B.C.
⇒ Moses leading Israel through the wilderness 1446-1406 B.C.

Moses had access to the records and writings of Israel, and he personally led Israel through their wilderness wanderings. Moses unquestionably wrote at least four books of the Pentateuch during this period: Exodus, Leviticus, Numbers, and Deuteronomy). Genesis was either written during the same period of wilderness wandering or during Moses' latter years in Egypt or during his forty years in Midian. Apparently, he did what many great men have done down through history, he kept a diary of the events and compiled his notes into the various books as he found time. Remember, as the future prince of Egypt, Moses would have been taught the importance of writing and recording history.

Note two other significant points:

1. Moses was spiritually mature during the wilderness wanderings. He had the spiritual maturity necessary for the Holy Spirit to inspire him to write Exodus.

---

[1] F.B. Huey. *Exodus.* (Grand Rapids, MI: Zondervan Publishing House, 1977), p.8.

2. It was during the wilderness wanderings that God dealt with Moses time and again face to face (so to speak). God is the real Author of the Holy Scriptures. Therefore in the final analysis, the name of a human author has little if any bearing upon the value of the Scripture. Knowing the name of the human author is of secondary importance.

III. TO WHOM WRITTEN

Israel in particular and the human race in general.

1. Exodus was written to give Israel a record of its history and law and to instruct the people how they were to live, serve, and worship God.

2. Exodus was written to all people of all generations...

- to give us an example and warning about how not to live.

> **"Now all these things happened unto them for examples: and they are written for our admonition [warning], upon whom the ends of the world are come" (1 Cor.10:11).**

- to teach us so that through the Scripture we might be encouraged and have great hope.

> **"For whatsoever things were written aforetime were written for our learning, that we through patience and comfort of the scriptures might have hope" (Ro.15:4).**

IV. PURPOSE

There are at least three purposes for the Book of Exodus.

1. The *historical purpose*: to give the Israelites a permanent record of their history and law and a record of how they were to serve and worship God. Historically, Exodus was written...

a. To teach Israel their God-given purpose, the very reason God had chosen them to be His people (Ex.1:1-22).
- To teach Israel that there was only one living and true God, one God who had created and purposed all things (Is.43:10-13).
- To teach Israel its roots, that they had actually been chosen by God Himself through Abraham, appointed to be *the chosen line* of God's people.
- To teach Israel that *the promised seed*, the Savior, was to be sent into the world through them. They were *the chosen line* through whom God was going to save the world. Salvation--*the promised seed*--was to come through Israel.
- To teach Israel that they were to receive *the promised land*, the land of Canaan, and that God would be faithful to His Word and give them *the promised land*.

b. To always remind Israel of their glorious deliverance from slavery to Egypt, glorious deliverance by the mighty hand of God (Ex.2:1-13:16).

c. To teach Israel the great laws upon which their nation was to be built and governed (Ex.19:1-40:38).

d. To teach Israel how they must believe and follow God...
- in facing and conquering the trials and enemies of life.
- in seeking after the promised land (Ex.13:17-18:27).

e. To teach Israel how they were to serve and worship God (Ex.19:1-40:38).

2. The *doctrinal or spiritual purpose*:

a. To teach that the great promise of God, the promise of the *promised seed*, did take place: a great nation of people was born of Abraham's seed, the people who were to give birth to the *promised seed and Savior*, the Lord Jesus Christ (Ex.1:6-7).

b. To teach the wonderful nature of God, the great doctrines of...
- God's love, mercy, and grace (Ex.3:7-10; 6:5-9).
- God's election, predestination, foreordination, and foreknowledge (Ex.6:6-9).
- God's power and sovereignty (Ex.1:1-18:27).
- God's justice and judgment (Ex.7:8-14:31; 17:8-16).
- God's faithfulness (Ex.1:1-40:38).
- God's salvation and redemption (Ex.1:1-40:38).
- God's holiness (Ex.3:1-10; 19:1-40:38).
- God's care, guidance, provision, and protection (Ex.1:1-40:38).

c. To teach that salvation is based solely upon the blood of the lamb: that a person must hide behind the blood of the lamb...
- to be delivered from judgment
- to begin a *new life*
- to be given the hope of the promised land (a symbol of heaven) (Ex.12:1-13:16; cp. Heb.11:13-16, 24-29)

d. To teach the law of God and to make a covenant--an agreement--with man to keep His law (Ex.19:1-40:38).

e. To teach the terrible depravity of man, the true condition of man's heart...
- that man is a sinner, a transgressor of God's law.
- that man breaks God's heart time and again, no matter how good God is to him (Ex.1:1-40:38).

f. To teach the desperate need of man for a mediator: that man desperately needs a mediator to approach God for him (Ex.1:1-40:38).

g. To teach the service and worship of God: to spell out how man is to serve and worship God (Ex.1:1-40:38).

h. To teach the absolute necessity of the Priesthood, that man needs a High Priest, a Mediator, an Intercessor, to represent him before God (Ex.1:1-40:38).

3. The *Christological or Christ-centered purpose*: to teach that certain things point to Jesus Christ as the Savior of the world:

a. That the great deliverer Moses pictures the need of man for an even greater Deliverer, a Deliverer who can save man from the world (Egypt), its enslavements, and from the judgment to come.

"The LORD thy God will raise up unto thee a Prophet [Deliverer] from the midst of thee, of thy brethren, like unto me; unto him ye shall hearken" (Dt.18:15).

b. That the Passover lamb pictures the need of man for the Lamb of God who takes away the sin of the world.

"The next day John seeth Jesus coming unto him, and saith, Behold the Lamb of God, which taketh away the sin of the world" (Jn.1:29).

c. That the shed blood of the lamb without blemish pictures the need for man to escape the judgment of God by hiding behind the blood of the perfect Lamb of God, the Lord Jesus Christ.

"For if the blood of bulls and of goats, and the ashes of an heifer sprinkling the unclean, sanctifieth to the purifying of the flesh: How much more shall the blood of Christ, who through the eternal Spirit offered himself without spot to God, purge your conscience from dead works to serve the living God?" (Heb.9:13-14; cp. Ro.5:8-9).

d. That the manna, the bread from heaven, pictures the Lord Jesus Christ who is the Bread of Life (Jn.6:32-33; 6:48-51; 6:58).

"And Jesus said unto them, I am the bread of life: he that cometh to me shall never hunger; and he that believeth on me shall never thirst" (Jn.6:35).

e. That the law of God and man's inability to obey God's law in all its points (perfection) pictures the great need of man for an advocate, an intercessor, a mediator. Jesus Christ is our advocate, and He is also the propitiation (the sacrifice) for our sins.

"My little children, these things write I unto you, that ye sin not. And if any man sin, we have an advocate with the Father, Jesus Christ the righteous: And he is the propitiation for our sins: and not for ours only, but also for the sins of the whole world" (1 Jn.2:1-2; cp. 1 Tim.2:5; Heb.8:6; 9:15, 24; 12:24).

f. That the priesthood of Israel and the high priest, Aaron, pictures the need of man for a perfect mediator, a perfect High Priest, who can approach God for man. The perfect High Priest is the Lord Jesus Christ.

"Wherefore he is able also to save them to the uttermost that come unto God by him, seeing he ever liveth to make intercession for them. For such an high priest became us, who is holy, harmless, undefiled, separate from sinners, and made higher than the heavens; Who needeth not daily, as those high priests, to offer up sacrifice, first for his own sins, and then for the people's: for this he did once, when he offered up himself" (Heb.7:25-27; cp. Heb.2:17; 4:14-15; 9:11).

g. That the tabernacle--"God's royal tent" (NIV), God's "portable temple" (Geisler)-- pictures that man can enter God's holy presence only as God dictates, only through a prepared High Priest and Mediator, the Lord Jesus Christ.

"Now of the things which we have spoken this is the sum: We have such an high priest, who is set on the right hand of the throne of the Majesty in the heavens; A minister of the sanctuary, and of the true tabernacle, which the Lord pitched, and not man" (Heb.8:1-2; cp. Heb.9:11; 2:17; 4:14-15; 7:25-27).

V. SPECIAL FEATURES

1. Exodus is "The Great Book of Israel's Exodus." The word *Exodus* means "departure," "going out," exiting out," "a road out," or "a way out." The word *Exodus* is the Latin word translated from the Greek Bible "exodos." The exodus (deliverance, departure) of Israel is the greatest event in all the Old Testament, and it points to the greatest event in the New Testament, the cross of Christ.

2. Exodus is "The Great Book of Continuation." It continues the story of Genesis, the first book of the Bible. In fact, note Ex.1:6-7, where a period of about 400 years is covered. Two brief verses cover the whole history of the Israelites from Joseph to Moses. The point is this: Exodus picks up where Genesis left off. Exodus continues the *great history of redemption* that God began to write in Genesis. Exodus is one of the most important books in all the Word of God.

3. Exodus is "The Great Book of Hebrew History." Nowhere in Scripture can the reader find such a detailed record of Israel's history. From sensing the pain and suffering of enslavement over to rejoicing for their great deliverance from Pharaoh's grasp, the reader is given an inside look at how the Israelites experienced life as the people of God. Being God's elect meant the Israelites needed to keep God's Law, and they needed to know how to approach and worship Him. The major events in the history of the Hebrew people are herein covered: their slavery, deliverance, wilderness experiences, receiving the Law and the instructions to build the Tabernacle.

4. Exodus is "The Great Book of Salvation, Redemption, and Deliverance." God is seen...
- saving His people from Egyptian slavery (Ex.1:1-11:10).
- redeeming His people from the judgment of death through the Passover Lamb (Ex.12:1-13:16).

- delivering His people through the trials of the wilderness wanderings: delivering them through six terrible trials as they journeyed toward the promised land (Ex.13:17-18:27).

5. Exodus is "The Great Book of God's Power and Sovereignty." God is the *Lord of History*. He is sovereign over history: the nations of this world and the affairs of men are ruled over by God.

- It was God's sovereign power that chose one man, Abraham, to give birth to a whole new race of people, a race that was to be God's witness to the world.
- It was God's sovereign power that caused Abraham's family of seventy plus people to be enslaved so they could multiply into a population of over two million. If they had not been enslaved, they would most likely have been scattered and never stayed together as one race of people, not all two plus million.
- It was God's sovereign power that launched the plagues of judgment upon Egypt and rescued the Israelites from slavery.
- It was God's sovereign power that protected and provided for His people during their wilderness wanderings.
- It was God's sovereign power that gave the law and the worship instructions to Israel and began to mold them into a nation.

6. Exodus is "The Great Book of Hope." For over four-hundred years, Egypt had become Israel's home. When they first came to Egypt, they came at the invitation of Pharaoh and lived in Goshen. Now, another Pharaoh who did not know nor remember Joseph ruled them with an iron fist. The *promised land* seemed to be only a distant dream, void of any reality. For the Israelites, life had become hopeless. But God still had a plan, a covenant, a promise to keep. In a land where hope was non-existent, hope took the form of a baby who floated down the Nile River in an ark. That baby grew up to be God's vessel of hope. As an adult, Moses became the physical embodiment of Israel's hope. Moses' leadership provided the basis for hope in:

a. God's great faithfulness and deliverance (Ex. 1:1-22).
b. God's ability to send a deliverer (Ex. 2:1-7:7).
c. God's power over Pharaoh's power (Ex. 7:8-11:10).
d. God passing over them in judgment (the great Passover) (Ex. 12:1-13:16).
e. God's supernatural guidance by day and by night (Ex. 13:17-22).
f. God's provision of food and water (Ex. 13:16-18:27).
g. God's protection from their enemies (Ex. 17:8-16).
h. God's promise to take them to a special place, the *promised land* (Ex. 3:8).

7. Exodus is "The Great Book of Liberty and Freedom." The reader sees how an entire race of slaves was set free: how they were given the glorious rights of all men, the right to life, liberty, and justice for all. The reader sees how God set His impoverished people free and formed them into a nation.

8. Exodus is "The Great Book Covering a Nation's Birth." The birth of Israel occurs in Exodus. God is seen taking a family of seventy people and causing them to multiply into a population of over two million, all within a period of about 430 years. And most of the growth took place while they were brutally enslaved by Egypt. Exodus shows God taking this body of impoverished slaves, delivering them and forming them into a great nation of people, a nation governed by the laws given by God Himself.

9. Exodus is "The Great Book of Law." The laws that were to take an impoverished group of slaves and form them into a nation are given in Exodus. Moreover, the great law that God gave to govern all men, the *Ten Commandments*, is covered in Exodus. Exodus covers...

- the Ten Commandments (Ex.20:1-26).
- the Moral or Civil Law of Israel (Ex.21:1-23:19).

10. Exodus is "The Great Book of the Mosaic Covenant." God lays down in Exodus the law by which Israel is to live and the Ten Commandments which are to govern all men. And God formulates the agreement that is to be signed and sealed within the heart of man.

"Now therefore, if ye will obey my voice indeed, and keep my covenant, then ye shall be a peculiar treasure unto me above all people: for all the earth is mine: And ye shall be unto me a kingdom of priests, and an holy nation. These are the words which thou shalt speak unto the children of Israel" (Ex.19:5-6).

"But ye are a chosen generation, a royal priesthood, an holy nation, a peculiar people; that ye should show forth the praises of him who hath called you out of darkness into his marvellous light: Which in time past were not a people, but are now the people of God: which had not obtained mercy [through Christ], but now have obtained mercy" (1 Pt.2:9-10).

11. Exodus is "The Great Book Demonstrating God's Judgment." In launching the ten plagues of judgment upon Egypt, God demonstrated for all generations a terrifying fact: a day of justice is coming. God is going to judge the ungodliness and unrighteousness of men.

12. Exodus is "The Great Book of *Christian Experience*" or "The Great Book of the *Believer's Pilgrimage*." Exodus covers Israel's deliverance from bondage through the power of God and the blood of the Passover lamb. It also covers the beginning of Israel's journey through the *wilderness wanderings*. This is...

- a picture of the believer being delivered by the blood of the Lord Jesus Christ, the Lamb of God.
- a picture of the believer as he journeys through the wilderness of this world on his way to the promised land of heaven.

13. Exodus is "The Great Book of the Wilderness Wanderings." Once the Israelites were delivered from Egypt, the people began a new life...

- a new life journeying away from their old life as slaves to Egypt (symbolizing the world).
- a new life journeying to the promised land of God.

INTRODUCTION

This is what is known as the *wilderness wanderings* of Israel, the new life Israel had as free people, the new life of marching through the wilderness of this world to the promised land of God.

14. Exodus is "The Great Book of God's Care, Guidance, Provision, and Protection." From the opening to the ending page, God is seen looking after and taking care of His people. In the pages of Exodus, He demonstrates and proves...

- His care
- His guidance
- His provision
- His protection

15. Exodus is "The Great Book of Conquest and Victory." God is seen conquering the terrible enemies of Israel including...

- the Egyptian army that entrapped them at the Red Sea.
- the Amalekites who secretly attacked and slaughtered the stragglers: the maimed, the sick, the aged, the children.
- the impossible trials and obstacles that confronted them.

God triumphed over all the enemies of His people. God gave victory to the Israelites.

16. Exodus is "The Great Book of Worship." Explicit instructions on how God wanted His people to worship are given through the model of the Tabernacle. With these blueprints, God charged Moses to follow the instructions exactly as God had revealed. And this Moses did. Moses prepared a place where men could approach and worship God exactly as God dictated.

17. Exodus is "The Great Book of Family Life." Beginning with the first chapter of Exodus, the record of Israel's family tree introduces the important role of the family. It is significant to note that the building-block for any vibrant civilization is the family unit: fathers, mothers, sons, daughters, grandparents, aunts, uncles, nephews, and nieces. In the book of Exodus, great detail is given to emphasize the family:

a. Jacob's family and extended family were seventy in number, not counting Joseph (Ex. 1:5).
b. The names of Jacob's sons are listed (Ex. 1:2-5).
c. Joseph's generation died, all the family members who first lived in Egypt (Ex. 1:6).
d. Jacob's children, the children of Israel, rapidly grew into a large population (Ex. 1:7).
e. The children of Israel were considered a threat to the stability of the new Pharaoh's regime (Ex. 1:8-11).
f. Every member of the Israelite family became a slave, without exception (Ex. 1:11-14).
g. The midwives took a moral stand for the unborn male babies. They refused to obey Pharaoh's evil instructions to kill the children (Ex. 1:15-22).
h. Moses was born in a home where the mother was a courageous believer, a woman who risked her life in order to protect her son (Ex. 2:1-3).
i. In God's sovereignty, Pharaoh's daughter adopted Moses and allowed his mother to assist in raising him (Ex. 2:5-10).
j. Moses met a young woman (Zipporah) in Midian after escaping from Pharaoh, and he married her (Ex. 2:21).
k. Moses' father-in-law was Jethro, the priest of Midian (Ex. 3:1).
l. Moses had two sons, Gershom and Eliezer (Ex. 2:22; 18:4).
m. Moses had a brother (Aaron) and a sister (Miriam) (Ex. 4:14; 15:20).
n. The Passover meal was to be celebrated by each family; it was to be family-centered (Ex. 12:3-4).

18. Exodus is "The Great Book of Transparency." It is a book that does not hide the failures of its main characters. Remember, it was:

a. Moses who killed an Egyptian (Ex. 2:12).
b. Israel who wrongly placed their trust in Egypt (see outline--Ex. 2:23).
c. Moses who was a reluctant prophet, offering arguments and excuses against serving God (Ex. 3:11-4:17).
d. Moses' wife, Zipporah, who objected to circumcising their son (Ex. 4:25-26).
e. Moses who had to be chastised by God almost to the point of death, chastised because he failed to circumcise his son according to the covenant (Ex. 4:24).
f. The leaders of Israel who blamed Moses and Aaron for their troubles (Ex. 5:20-21).
g. Moses who questioned God for allowing evil to fall upon His people (Ex. 5:22).
h. Moses who questioned God's wisdom in sending him to deliver the Israelites (Ex. 5:22).
i. Moses who blamed himself for bringing trouble upon Israel (Ex. 5:23).
j. Israel who complained, grumbled, and murmured against Moses at Marah (Ex. 15:22-27).
k. Israel who sinned by grumbling and failing to believe God (Ex. 16:1-36).
l. Israel who trusted more in Moses than they did in God (Ex. 17:1-7).
m. Israel who built and then worshipped the golden calf (Ex. 32:1-35).

19. Exodus is "The Great Book of Theological Themes" (see <u>Purpose</u>, pt.2).

20. Exodus is "The Great Book of Types, Symbols, and Pictures." A vast wealth of Biblical types, symbols, and pictures can be drawn from the pages of Exodus. There are many historical facts that have a practical meaning for today's believer. (See <u>Types Chart</u>, pt. VI.--Introduction.)

VI. TYPES, SYMBOLS, AND PICTURES
THE BOOK OF EXODUS
Part II
(Chapters 19-40)

What is a biblical type or symbol? Simply put, a *biblical type* is a "foreshadowing" of what was to come at a later time in history. Through a person, place or thing, a biblical type points toward a New Testament fulfillment.

In addition to Biblical types, there are what we may call *biblical pictures*. A biblical picture is a lesson that we can see in the Scriptures <u>without distorting the truth</u>. The study of biblical types and pictures is a valuable study in that it helps us apply the truth of Scripture to our lives. Scripture itself tells us this:

"Now all these things happened unto them for examples: and they are written for our admonition, upon whom the ends of the world are come" (1 Cor.10:11).

"For whatsoever things were written aforetime were written for our learning, that we through patience and comfort of the scriptures might have hope" (Ro.15:4).

GENERAL OUTLINE

PERSON/PLACE/THING	PAGE #	SCRIPTURE, OUTLINE AND DISCUSSION
(1) The Sabbath (Ex.20:8)	122	Ex.20:8-11; (D.S.#2, 3, 4)
(2) The Law (Ex.24:12)	262	Ex.24:12-18
(3) Badger (sea cow) skins (Ex.25:5)	273-274	Ex.25:3-7; 26:1-14
(4) Onyx stones (Ex.25:7)	274	Ex.25:3-7
(5) Acacia wood (Ex.25:10)	284	Ex.25:3-7
(6) The Ark or Chest (Ex.25:10-22; 40:20)	284-286	Ex.25:10-22; 26:31-35; 30:1-6; 31:1-11; 35:10-20; 37:1-5; 37:10-16; 37:25-29
(7) Gold (Ex.25:17)	286	Ex.25:3-7
(8) The Mercy Seat (Ex.25:17-21; 25:22)	286-288	Ex.25:17-21; 25:21-22; 26:31-35; 30:1-6; 31:1-11; 35:10-20; 37:6-9
(9) The Table of Showbread (Ex.25:23-30; 40:22-23)	293	Ex.25:23-30; 26:31-35; 30:22-33; 31:1-11; 35:10-20; 37:10-16
(10) The Gold Lampstand (Ex.25:31-40; 40:24)	298-300	Ex.25:31-39; 26:31-35; 27:20-21; 30:22-33; 31:1-11; 35:10-20; 37:17-24
(11) Fine threaded linen (Ex.26:1)	313	Ex.25:3-7; 26:1-14; 26:31-35; 26:36-37; 27:9-19; 36:8-13; 36:35-36; 36:37-38; 38:9-20
(12) Blue (Ex.26:1)	313	Ex.25:3-7
(13) The Inner Curtains in the Sanctuary (Ex.26:1-6; 36:8-9)	314-315	Ex.26:1-14; 35:10-20; 36:8-13
(14) Goat Hair Covering (Ex.26:7)	315	Ex.25:3-7; 26:1-14; 35:21-29; 36:14-19
(15) Ram skins dyed red (Ex.26:14)	315-316	Ex.25:3-7; 26:1-14; 35:21-29; 36:14-19
(16) The Framework of the Tabernacle (the posts, bases, boards, and crossbars) (Ex.26:15-30; 36:31-33)	316	Ex.26:15-30; 36:20-34
(17) The Inner Curtain or Veil (Ex.26:31-35; 36:35-36)	317-319	Ex.26:31-35; 35:10-20; 36:35-36
(18) The Outer Veil or Curtain Door (The Holy Place: The First Room or Outer Sanctuary) (Ex.26:36-37; 36:37-38)	319-320	Ex.26:36-37; 35:10-20; 36:37-38
(19) The Horns of the Altar (Ex.27:2)	328-330	Ex.27:1-8; 30:1-10; 37:25-29; 38:1-7;
(20) Brass (bronze or copper) (Ex.27:2-3)	330	Ex.25:3-7; 26:36-37; 27:1-8; 30:17-21
(21) The Courtyard Walls (Ex.27:9-19)	331	Ex.27:9-19; 35:10-20; 36:20-34; 38:9-20
(22) The Door or Gate (Ex.27:16)	331-332	Ex.27:9-19; 35:10-20
(23) Oil for light (Ex.27:20-21)	332	Ex.25:3-7; 27:20-21
(24) The Sash (Ex.28:4; 39:29)	343-344	Ex.28:1-5; 39:27-29
(25) Purple (Ex.28:5-6)	344	Ex.25:3-7

VII. TIMELINE OF SUBJECTS, CHARACTERS, & EVENTS

DIVISION VI. THE LAW AND THE PROMISES OF GOD (THE MOSAIC COVENANT) (PART 1): GOD'S GREAT CALL, THE CALL TO TOTAL COMMITMENT (Exodus 19:1-25)		
THE EVENT	THE SCRIPTURE	PRACTICAL APPLICATION
The Setting and Basis for the Covenant: At the Base of Mount Sinai	Exodus 19:1-25	God's Great Call, the Call to Total Commitment

"Now therefore, if ye will obey my voice indeed, and keep my covenant, then ye shall be a peculiar treasure unto me above all people: for all the earth is mine" (Ex.19:5).

DIVISION VII. THE LAW AND THE PROMISES OF GOD (THE MOSAIC COVENANT) (PART 2): THE TEN COMMANDMENTS--NECESSARY LAWS TO GOVERN MAN AND SOCIETY (Exodus 20:1-26)		
THE EVENT	THE SCRIPTURE	PRACTICAL APPLICATION
The Great Basis of the Ten Commandments	Exodus 20:1-2	The Person and Work of God Himself

"And God spake all these words, saying, I am the LORD thy God, which have brought thee out of the land of Egypt, out of the house of bondage" (Ex.20:1-2).

EXODUS CHRONOLOGY OF MAIN CHARACTERS AND EVENTS		
	Chapter 19	Chapter 20
AT THE BASE OF MOUNT SINAI	*God's great call to Israel*	
MOSES RECEIVES THE TEN COMMANDMENTS		*The Basis of all Morality, 20:1-26*
MOSES RECEIVES THE CIVIL AND RELIGIOUS LAWS OF ISRAEL		
THE CLIMATIC ADOPTION OF THE LAW		
MOSES RECEIVES THE BLUEPRINTS FOR THE TABERNACLE AND ITS PRIESTHOOD		
THE GOLDEN CALF AND MOSES' GREAT INTERCESSION		
THE TABERNACLE, ITS CONSTRUCTION AND DEDICATION		
THE GLORY OF GOD FILLS THE TABERNACLE		

DIVISION VII. THE LAW AND THE PROMISES OF GOD (THE MOSAIC COVENANT) (PART 2): THE TEN COMMANDMENTS-- NECESSARY LAWS TO GOVERN MAN AND SOCIETY (continued) (Exodus 20:1-26)		
THE EVENT	THE SCRIPTURE	PRACTICAL APPLICATION
The Ten Commandments, The Laws Governing Man's Duty to God (Part 1): Commandment One	Ex.20:3	Concerns God's Being--Never Believe in False Gods
The Ten Commandments, The Laws Governing Man's Duty to God (Part 2): Commandment Two	Ex.20:4-6	Concerns God's Worship--Never Make Nor Worship False Gods
The Ten Commandments, The Laws Governing Man's Duty to God (Part 3): Commandment Three	Ex.20:7	Concerns God's Name--Never Misuse God's Name; Never Use Profanity or Vulgarity
The Ten Commandments, The Laws Governing Man's Duty to God (Part 4): Commandment Four	Ex.20:8-11	Concerns God's Day--Never Fail to Observe the Sabbath, to Keep it Holy

"Thou shalt have no other gods before me" (Ex.20:3).

EXODUS CHRONOLOGY OF MAIN CHARACTERS AND EVENTS		
		Chapter 20
AT THE BASE OF MOUNT SINAI		
MOSES RECEIVES THE TEN COMMANDMENTS		*The Basis of all Morality, 20:1-26*
MOSES RECEIVES THE CIVIL AND RELIGIOUS LAWS OF ISRAEL		
THE CLIMATIC ADOPTION OF THE LAW		
MOSES RECEIVES THE BLUEPRINTS FOR THE TABERNACLE AND ITS PRIESTHOOD		
THE GOLDEN CALF AND MOSES' GREAT INTERCESSION		
THE TABERNACLE, ITS CONSTRUCTION AND DEDICATION		
THE GLORY OF GOD FILLS THE TABERNACLE		

DIVISION VII. THE LAW AND THE PROMISES OF GOD (THE MOSAIC COVENANT) (PART 2): THE TEN COMMANDMENTS-- NECESSARY LAWS TO GOVERN MAN AND SOCIETY (continued) (Exodus 20:1-26)		
THE EVENT	**THE SCRIPTURE**	**PRACTICAL APPLICATION**
The Ten Commandments, The Laws Governing Man's Duty to Others (Part 1): Commandment Five	Ex.20:12	**Concerns the Family-- Never Dishonor Parents**
The Ten Commandments, The Laws Governing Man's Duty to Others (Part 2): Commandment Six	Ex.20:13	**Concerns Man's Life--Never Kill**
The Ten Commandments, The Laws Governing Man's Duty to Others (Part 3): Commandment Seven	Ex.20:14	**Concerns Man's Family--Never Commit Adultery or Immorality**
The Ten Commandments, The Laws Governing Man's Duty to Others (Part 4): Commandment Eight	Ex.20:15	**Concerns Man's Property-- Never Steal**
The Ten Commandments, The Laws Governing Man's Duty to Others (Part 5): Commandment Nine	Ex.20:16	**Concerns Man's Word and Character**
The Ten Commandments, The Laws Governing Man's Duty to Others (Part 6): Commandment Ten	Ex.20:17	**Concerns Our Neighbor's Property--Never Covet**
The Purposes for the Law	Ex.20:18-26	**Why God Gave the Ten Commandments and the Law**

"And all the people saw the thunderings, and the lightnings, and the noise of the trumpet, and the mountain smoking...And they said unto Moses, Speak thou with us, and we will hear: but let not God speak with us, lest we die" (Ex.20:18-19).

EXODUS CHRONOLOGY OF MAIN CHARACTERS AND EVENTS		
		Chapter 20
AT THE BASE OF MOUNT SINAI		
MOSES RECEIVES THE TEN COMMANDMENTS		*The Basis of all Morality, 20:1-26*
MOSES RECEIVES THE CIVIL AND RELIGIOUS LAWS OF ISRAEL		
THE CLIMATIC ADOPTION OF THE LAW		
MOSES RECEIVES THE BLUEPRINTS FOR THE TABERNACLE AND ITS PRIESTHOOD		
THE GOLDEN CALF AND MOSES' GREAT INTERCESSION		
THE TABERNACLE, ITS CONSTRUCTION AND DEDICATION		
THE GLORY OF GOD FILLS THE TABERNACLE		

DIVISION VIII. THE LAW AND THE PROMISES OF GOD (THE MOSAIC COVENANT) (PART 3): THE CIVIL AND RELIGIOUS LAWS OF ISRAEL--HELPFUL PRINCIPLES TO GOVERN MAN AND SOCIETY (Exodus 21:1-24:18)		
THE EVENT	THE SCRIPTURE	PRACTICAL APPLICATION
The Civil Law of Israel is Given	Ex.21:1-32	The Laws Governing Human Rights
The Civil Law of Israel is Given	Ex.21:33-22:15	The Laws Governing Property Rights
The Civil Law of Israel is Given	Ex.22:16-31	The Laws Governing Social and Moral Obligations

"Now these are the judgments [laws] which thou shalt set before them" (Ex.21:1).

EXODUS CHRONOLOGY OF MAIN CHARACTERS AND EVENTS		
	Chapter 21	Chapter 22
AT THE BASE OF MOUNT SINAI		
MOSES RECEIVES THE TEN COMMANDMENTS		
MOSES RECEIVES THE CIVIL AND RELIGIOUS LAWS OF ISRAEL	*Rules to live by, justice for all, 21:1-32*	• *Ownership of property, 21:33-22:15* • *Community standards, 22:16-31*
THE CLIMATIC ADOPTION OF THE LAW		
MOSES RECEIVES THE BLUEPRINTS FOR THE TABERNACLE AND ITS PRIESTHOOD		
THE GOLDEN CALF AND MOSES' GREAT INTERCESSION		
THE TABERNACLE, ITS CONSTRUCTION AND DEDICATION		
THE GLORY OF GOD FILLS THE TABERNACLE		

DIVISION VIII. THE LAW AND THE PROMISES OF GOD (THE MOSAIC COVENANT) (PART 3): THE CIVIL AND RELIGIOUS LAWS OF ISRAEL--HELPFUL PRINCIPLES TO GOVERN MAN AND SOCIETY (continued) (Exodus 21:1-24:18)		
THE EVENT	**THE SCRIPTURE**	**PRACTICAL APPLICATION**
The Civil Law of Israel is Given	Ex.23:1-9	**The Laws Governing Justice and Mercy In Court and Among Neighbors**
The Religious Law of Israel is Given	Ex.23:10-19	**The Laws Governing Religion: The Sabbath and Religious Feasts**
The Conclusion of the Law, the Mosaic Covenant	Ex.23:20-33	**The Rewards of Obedience**
The Climatic Adoption of the Law, the Mosaic Covenant	Ex.24:1-18	**The Great Duty of Believers After Receiving the Law, the Word of God**

"And Moses came and told the people all the words of the LORD, and all the judgments [laws]: and all the people answered with one voice, and said, All the words which the LORD hath said will we do. And Moses wrote all the words of the LORD, and rose up early in the morning, and builded an altar under the hill, and twelve pillars, according to the twelve tribes of Israel" (Ex.24:3-4).

EXODUS CHRONOLOGY OF MAIN CHARACTERS AND EVENTS		
	Chapter 23	**Chapter 24**
AT THE BASE OF MOUNT SINAI		
MOSES RECEIVES THE TEN COMMANDMENTS		
MOSES RECEIVES THE CIVIL AND RELIGIOUS LAWS OF ISRAEL	• *Administration of fair laws, 23:1-9* • *Following the right religion, 23:10-19* • *The rewards of obedience, 23:20-33*	
THE CLIMATIC ADOPTION OF THE LAW		*The great duty of believers after receiving the Word of God, 24:1-18*
MOSES RECEIVES THE BLUEPRINTS FOR THE TABERNACLE AND ITS PRIESTHOOD		
THE GOLDEN CALF AND MOSES' GREAT INTERCESSION		
THE TABERNACLE, ITS CONSTRUCTION AND DEDICATION		
THE GLORY OF GOD FILLS THE TABERNACLE		

VII. TIMELINE OF SUBJECTS, CHARACTERS, & EVENTS

DIVISION IX. THE TABERNACLE, ITS BLUEPRINT AND PRIESTHOOD: THE TRUE WAY TO APPROACH AND WORSHIP GOD (Exodus 25:1-31:18)		
THE EVENT	THE SCRIPTURE	PRACTICAL APPLICATION
The Materials Needed to Construct the Tabernacle	Ex.25:1-9	God's Call to Stewardship, to Give From a Willing Heart
The Ark or Chest and Mercy Seat of God	Ex.25:10-22	The Symbol of the Very Throne and Presence of God
The Table of Showbread	Ex.25:23-30	The Symbol of God Himself as the Bread of Life
The Gold Lampstand	Ex.25:31-40	The Symbol of God Himself as the Light of the World
The Tabernacle Itself	Ex.26:1-37	The Symbol of God Dwelling Among His People and of Man's Need to Approach God Exactly as God Dictates

"And let them make me a sanctuary; that I may dwell among them. According to all that I show thee, after the pattern [blueprint] of the tabernacle, and the pattern of all the instruments thereof, even so shall ye make it" (Ex.25:8-9).

EXODUS CHRONOLOGY OF MAIN CHARACTERS AND EVENTS		
	Chapter 25	Chapter 26
AT THE BASE OF MOUNT SINAI		
MOSES RECEIVES THE TEN COMMANDMENTS		
MOSES RECEIVES THE CIVIL AND RELIGIOUS LAWS OF ISRAEL		
THE CLIMATIC ADOPTION OF THE LAW		
MOSES RECEIVES THE BLUEPRINTS FOR THE TABERNACLE AND ITS PRIESTHOOD	*The Lord's plans for the Ark, Mercy Seat, Table of Showbread, & Lampstand, 25:10-40*	*The Lord's plans for the Tabernacle itself, 26:1-37*
THE GOLDEN CALF AND MOSES' GREAT INTERCESSION		
THE TABERNACLE, ITS CONSTRUCTION AND DEDICATION		
THE GLORY OF GOD FILLS THE TABERNACLE		

14

DIVISION IX. THE TABERNACLE, ITS BLUEPRINT AND PRIESTHOOD: THE TRUE WAY TO APPROACH AND WORSHIP GOD (continued) (Exodus 25:1-31:18)		
THE EVENT	THE SCRIPTURE	PRACTICAL APPLICATION
The Altar of Burnt Offering, the Court of the Tabernacle, and the Lampstand	Ex.27:1-21	All Symbolizing the True Way to Approach God
The Garments of the Priests	Ex.28:1-43	The Symbol of Bringing Dignity and Honor to the Name of God

"And thou shalt command the children of Israel, that they bring thee pure oil olive beaten for the light, to cause the lamp to burn always. In the tabernacle of the congregation without the vail, which is before the testimony, Aaron and his sons shall order it from evening to morning before the LORD: it shall be a statute for ever unto their generations on the behalf of the children of Israel" (Ex.27:20-21).

"And thou shalt make holy garments for Aaron thy brother for glory and for beauty. And thou shalt speak unto all that are wise hearted, whom I have filled with the spirit of wisdom, that they may make Aaron's garments to consecrate him, that he may minister unto me in the priest's office" (Ex.28:2-3).

EXODUS CHRONOLOGY OF MAIN CHARACTERS AND EVENTS		
	Chapter 27	Chapter 28
AT THE BASE OF MOUNT SINAI		
MOSES RECEIVES THE TEN COMMANDMENTS		
MOSES RECEIVES THE CIVIL AND RELIGIOUS LAWS OF ISRAEL		
THE CLIMATIC ADOPTION OF THE LAW		
MOSES RECEIVES THE BLUEPRINTS FOR THE TABERNACLE AND ITS PRIESTHOOD	The Lord's plans for the Altar of Burnt Offering & the Courtyard, 27:1-21	The Lord's plans for the Garments of the Priests, 28:1-43
THE GOLDEN CALF AND MOSES' GREAT INTERCESSION		
THE TABERNACLE, ITS CONSTRUCTION AND DEDICATION		
THE GLORY OF GOD FILLS THE TABERNACLE		

VII. TIMELINE OF SUBJECTS, CHARACTERS, & EVENTS

DIVISION IX. THE TABERNACLE, ITS BLUEPRINT AND PRIESTHOOD: THE TRUE WAY TO APPROACH AND WORSHIP GOD (continued) (Exodus 25:1-31:18)		
THE EVENT	**THE SCRIPTURE**	**PRACTICAL APPLICATION**
The Dedication, Consecration, and Ordination of the Priests	Ex.29:1-46	God's Qualifications for Leadership
The Altar of Incense	Ex.30:1-10	The Symbol of the Prayers and Communion of God's People Ascending to God
Other Instructions for the Tabernacle	Ex.30:11-38	The Symbols of Spiritual Health and Maturity

"And I will dwell among the children of Israel, and will be their God. And they shall know that I am the LORD their God, that brought them forth out of the land of Egypt, that I may dwell among them: I am the LORD their God" (Ex.29:45-46).

"And thou shalt put it before the vail that is by the ark of the testimony, before the mercy seat that is over the testimony, where I will meet with thee" (Ex.30:6).

EXODUS CHRONOLOGY OF MAIN CHARACTERS AND EVENTS		
	Chapter 29	**Chapter 30**
AT THE BASE OF MOUNT SINAI		
MOSES RECEIVES THE TEN COMMANDMENTS		
MOSES RECEIVES THE CIVIL AND RELIGIOUS LAWS OF ISRAEL		
THE CLIMATIC ADOPTION OF THE LAW		
MOSES RECEIVES THE BLUEPRINTS FOR THE TABERNACLE AND ITS PRIESTHOOD	*God's qualifications for spiritual leadership, 29:1-46*	*The Lord's plans for the Altar of Incense, Bronze Wash Basin, & Anointing Oil, 30:1-38*
THE GOLDEN CALF AND MOSES' GREAT INTERCESSION		
THE TABERNACLE, ITS CONSTRUCTION AND DEDICATION		
THE GLORY OF GOD FILLS THE TABERNACLE		

VII. TIMELINE OF SUBJECTS, CHARACTERS, & EVENTS

DIVISION IX. THE TABERNACLE, ITS BLUEPRINT AND PRIESTHOOD: THE TRUE WAY TO APPROACH AND WORSHIP GOD (continued) (Exodus 25:1-31:18)		
THE EVENT	THE SCRIPTURE	PRACTICAL APPLICATION
Other Instructions for the Tabernacle	Ex.31:1-18	Three Great Charges Given to Man

"See, I have called by name Bezaleel the son of Uri, the son of Hur, of the tribe of Judah: And I have filled him with the spirit of God, in wisdom, and in understanding, and in knowledge, and in all manner of workmanship" (Ex.31:2-3).

DIVISION X. THE GOLDEN CALF AND MOSES' GREAT INTERCESSION: THE BREAKING AND RENEWAL OF THE COVENANT BETWEEN GOD AND ISRAEL (Exodus 32:1-34:35)		
THE EVENT	THE SCRIPTURE	PRACTICAL APPLICATION
The Golden Calf--The Breaking of the Covenant Between God and Man	Ex.32:1-35	A Picture of Man's Corrupt Heart and Rebellion Against God

"And it came to pass, as soon as he came nigh unto the camp, that he saw the calf, and the dancing: and Moses' anger waxed hot, and he cast the tables out of his hands, and brake them beneath the mount. And he took the calf which they had made, and burnt it in the fire, and ground it to powder, and strawed it upon the water, and made the children of Israel drink of it" (Ex.32:19-20).

EXODUS CHRONOLOGY OF MAIN CHARACTERS AND EVENTS		
	Chapter 31	Chapter 32
AT THE BASE OF MOUNT SINAI		
MOSES RECEIVES THE TEN COMMANDMENTS		
MOSES RECEIVES THE CIVIL AND RELIGIOUS LAWS OF ISRAEL		
THE CLIMATIC ADOPTION OF THE LAW		
MOSES RECEIVES THE BLUEPRINTS FOR THE TABERNACLE AND ITS PRIESTHOOD	*Three great charges given to man, 31:1-18*	
THE GOLDEN CALF AND MOSES' GREAT INTERCESSION		*A picture of man's sinful, corrupt heart, 32:1-35*
THE TABERNACLE, ITS CONSTRUCTION AND DEDICATION		
THE GLORY OF GOD FILLS THE TABERNACLE		

DIVISION X. THE GOLDEN CALF AND MOSES' GREAT INTERCESSION: THE BREAKING AND RENEWAL OF THE COVENANT BETWEEN GOD AND ISRAEL (continued) (Exodus 32:1-34:35)		
THE EVENT	THE SCRIPTURE	PRACTICAL APPLICATION
The Threat of Separation From God and Moses' Great Intercession	Ex.33:1-23	The Essentials for Repentance and Renewal After Sinning
The Renewal of the Covenant Between God and Man	Ex.34:1-35	The Steps to Starting Over

"And it came to pass, as Moses entered into the tabernacle, the cloudy pillar descended, and stood at the door of the tabernacle, and the LORD talked with Moses. And all the people saw the cloudy pillar stand at the tabernacle door: and all the people rose up and worshipped, every man in his tent door. And the LORD spake unto Moses face to face, as a man speaketh unto his friend. And he turned again into the camp: but his servant Joshua, the son of Nun, a young man, departed not out of the tabernacle" (Ex.33:9-11).

EXODUS CHRONOLOGY OF MAIN CHARACTERS AND EVENTS		
	Chapter 33	Chapter 34
AT THE BASE OF MOUNT SINAI		
MOSES RECEIVES THE TEN COMMANDMENTS		
MOSES RECEIVES THE CIVIL AND RELIGIOUS LAWS OF ISRAEL		
THE CLIMATIC ADOPTION OF THE LAW		
MOSES RECEIVES THE BLUEPRINTS FOR THE TABERNACLE AND ITS PRIESTHOOD		
THE GOLDEN CALF AND MOSES' GREAT INTERCESSION	*The five essentials for restoration after sinning, 33:1-23*	*The steps to starting over, 34:1-35*
THE TABERNACLE, ITS CONSTRUCTION AND DEDICATION		
THE GLORY OF GOD FILLS THE TABERNACLE		

VII. TIMELINE OF SUBJECTS, CHARACTERS, & EVENTS

DIVISION XI. THE TABERNACLE, ITS CONSTRUCTION AND DEDICATION: THE PEOPLE OBEY GOD (Exodus 35:1-40:38)		
THE EVENT	THE SCRIPTURE	PRACTICAL APPLICATION
The Preparations for Building the Tabernacle	Ex.35:1-35	The Call to Give Sacrificially
The Construction of the Tabernacle	Ex.36:1-38	The Excitement of Building for God

"And they came, every one whose heart stirred him up, and every one whom his spirit made willing, and they brought the LORD'S offering to the work of the tabernacle of the congregation, and for all his service, and for the holy garments" (Ex.35:21).

EXODUS CHRONOLOGY OF MAIN CHARACTERS AND EVENTS		
	Chapter 35	Chapter 36
AT THE BASE OF MOUNT SINAI		
MOSES RECEIVES THE TEN COMMANDMENTS		
MOSES RECEIVES THE CIVIL AND RELIGIOUS LAWS OF ISRAEL		
THE CLIMATIC ADOPTION OF THE LAW		
MOSES RECEIVES THE BLUEPRINTS FOR THE TABERNACLE AND ITS PRIESTHOOD		
THE GOLDEN CALF AND MOSES' GREAT INTERCESSION		
THE TABERNACLE, ITS CONSTRUCTION AND DEDICATION	*Sacrificial giving, 35:1-35*	*The excitement of building for God, 36:1-38*
THE GLORY OF GOD FILLS THE TABERNACLE		

VII. TIMELINE OF SUBJECTS, CHARACTERS, & EVENTS

DIVISION XI. THE TABERNACLE, ITS CONSTRUCTION AND DEDICATION: THE PEOPLE OBEY GOD (continued) (Exodus 35:1-40:38)		
THE EVENT	**THE SCRIPTURE**	**PRACTICAL APPLICATION**
The Building of the Furnishings For the Tabernacle (Part 1)	Ex.37:1-29	Learning the Only Way to Approach God
The Building of the Furnishings For the Tabernacle (Part 2)	Ex.38:1-31	Learning the Only Way to Approach God

"And Bezaleel the son of Uri, the son of Hur, of the tribe of Judah, <u>made all that the LORD commanded Moses</u>" (Ex.38:22).

EXODUS CHRONOLOGY OF MAIN CHARACTERS AND EVENTS		
	Chapter 37	**Chapter 38**
AT THE BASE OF MOUNT SINAI		
MOSES RECEIVES THE TEN COMMANDMENTS		
MOSES RECEIVES THE CIVIL AND RELIGIOUS LAWS OF ISRAEL		
THE CLIMATIC ADOPTION OF THE LAW		
MOSES RECEIVES THE BLUEPRINTS FOR THE TABERNACLE AND ITS PRIESTHOOD		
THE GOLDEN CALF AND MOSES' GREAT INTERCESSION		
THE TABERNACLE, ITS CONSTRUCTION AND DEDICATION	*The Ark, Mercy Seat, Table of Showbread, Lampstand, & Altar of Incense are made, 37:1-29*	*The Altar of Burnt Offering, Bronze Wash Basin, & the Courtyard are made, 38:1-20*

DIVISION XI. THE TABERNACLE, ITS CONSTRUCTION AND DEDICATION: THE PEOPLE OBEY GOD (continued) (Exodus 35:1-40:38)		
THE EVENT	**THE SCRIPTURE**	**PRACTICAL APPLICATION**
The Making of the Garments For the Priests	Ex.39:1-43	**Being Clothed in Righteousness**
The Assembly and Dedication of the Tabernacle, the Center of Worship	Ex.40:1-38	**Experiencing the Presence of the Lord**

"Then a cloud covered the tent of the congregation, and the glory of the LORD filled the tabernacle. And Moses was not able to enter into the tent of the congregation, because the cloud abode thereon, and the glory of the LORD filled the tabernacle" (Ex.40:34-35).

EXODUS CHRONOLOGY OF MAIN CHARACTERS AND EVENTS		
	Chapter 39	**Chapter 40**
AT THE BASE OF MOUNT SINAI		
MOSES RECEIVES THE TEN COMMANDMENTS		
MOSES RECEIVES THE CIVIL AND RELIGIOUS LAWS OF ISRAEL		
THE CLIMATIC ADOPTION OF THE LAW		
MOSES RECEIVES THE BLUEPRINTS FOR THE TABERNACLE AND ITS PRIESTHOOD		
THE GOLDEN CALF AND MOSES' GREAT INTERCESSION		
THE TABERNACLE, ITS CONSTRUCTION AND DEDICATION	*Being clothed in righteousness, 39:1-43*	*Experiencing the presence of the Lord, 40:1-38*
THE GLORY OF GOD FILLS THE TABERNACLE		*The awesome glory of the Lord, 40:34-38*

A BRIEF CHRONOLOGY OF THE MAIN CHARACTERS AND EVENTS OF EXODUS

Part II
(Chapters 19-40)

	Chapter 19	Chapter 20
THE SETTING & BASIS FOR THE COVENANT: AT THE BASE OF MOUNT SINAI	*God's great call to Israel, 19:1-25*	
THE TEN COMMANDMENTS		*The basis of all morality, 20:1-26*
	Chapter 21-23	**Chapter 24**
THE CIVIL AND RELIGIOUS LAWS OF ISRAEL	*Rules to live by, justice for all, 21:1-23:33*	
THE CLIMATIC ADOPTION OF THE LAW		*The great duty of believers after receiving the Law, the Word of God, 24:1-18*
	Chapter 25-30	**Chapter 31**
THE TABERNACLE, ITS BLUEPRINT AND PRIESTHOOD	*Learning the true way to approach & worship God, 25:1-30:38*	
THE THREE GREAT CHARGES GIVEN TO MAN		*The charge...* • *to build the Tabernacle* • *to keep the Sabbath Day* • *to keep the Ten Commandments, 31:1-18*
	Chapter 32-34	**Chapter 35-40**
THE GOLDEN CALF AND MOSES' GREAT INTERCESSION	*The breaking and renewal of the covenant between God and Israel, 32:1-34:35*	
THE TABERNACLE, ITS CONSTRUCTION AND DEDICATION		*The people obey God, 35:1-40:38*

OUTLINE OF EXODUS
Part II
(Chapters 19-40)

THE PREACHER'S OUTLINE & SERMON BIBLE® is *unique*. It differs from all other Study Bibles & Sermon Resource Materials in that every Passage and Subject is outlined right beside the Scripture. When you choose any *Subject* below and turn to the reference, you have not only the Scripture, but you discover the Scripture and Subject *already outlined for you--verse by verse*.

For a quick example, choose one of the subjects below and turn over to the Scripture, and you will find this marvelous help for faster, easier, and more accurate use.

In addition, every point of the Scripture and Subject is *fully developed in a Commentary with supporting Scripture* at the bottom of the page. Again, this arrangement makes sermon and lesson preparation much easier and faster.

Note something else: The Subjects of Exodus have titles that are both Biblical and *practical*. The practical titles sometimes have more appeal to people.

A suggestion: For the quickest overview of EXODUS, first read *all the major titles* (VI, VII, VIII, etc.), then come back and read the subtitles.

OUTLINE OF EXODUS
Part II
(Chapters 19-40)

VI.   **THE LAW AND THE PROMISES OF GOD (THE MOSAIC COVENANT) (PART 1): GOD'S GREAT CALL--THE CALL TO TOTAL COMMITMENT, 19:1-25**

VII. **THE LAW AND THE PROMISES OF GOD (THE MOSAIC COVENANT) (PART 2): THE TEN COMMANDMENTS--NECESSARY LAWS TO GOVERN MAN AND SOCIETY, EX.20:1-26**
A.   The Great Basis of the Ten Commandments: The Person and Work of God Himself, Ex.20:1-2
B.   The Ten Commandments, The Laws Governing Man's Duty to God (Part 1): Commandment One Concerns God's Being--Never Believe in False Gods, Ex.20:3
C.   The Ten Commandments, The Laws Governing Man's Duty to God (Part 2): Commandment Two Concerns The Worship of God--Never Make Nor Worship False Gods, Ex.20:4-6
D.   The Ten Commandments, The Laws Governing Man's Duty to God (Part 3): Commandment Three Concerns God's Name--Never Misuse God's Name; Never Use Profanity or Vulgarity, Ex.20:7
E.   The Ten Commandments, The Laws Governing Man's Duty to God (Part 4): Commandment Four Concerns *God's Day*--Never Fail to Observe the Sabbath, to Keep it Holy, Ex.20:8-11
F.   The Ten Commandments, The Laws Governing Man's Duty To Others (Part 1): Commandment Five Concerns the Family--Never Dishonor Parents, Ex.20:12
G.   The Ten Commandments, The Laws Governing Man's Duty To Others (Part 2): Commandment Six Concerns Man's Life--Never Kill, Ex.20:13
H.   The Ten Commandments, The Laws Governing Man's Duty To Others (Part 3): Commandment Seven Concerns Man's Family--Never Commit Adultery or Immorality, Ex.20:14
I.   The Ten Commandments, The Laws Governing Man's Duty To Others (Part 4): Commandment Eight Concerns Man's Property--Never Steal, Ex.20:15
J.   The Ten Commandments, The Laws Governing Man's Duty To Others (Part 5): Commandment Nine Concerns Man's Word and Character--Never Lie, Ex.20:16
K.   The Ten Commandments, The Laws Governing Man's Duty To Others (Part 6): Commandment Ten Concerns Man's Desires and Security--Never Covet, Ex.20:17
L.   The Purposes For the Law: Why God Gave the Ten Commandments and the Law, Ex.20:18-26

OUTLINE OF EXODUS

VIII. **THE LAW AND THE PROMISES OF GOD (THE MOSAIC COVENANT) (PART 3): THE CIVIL AND RELIGIOUS LAWS OF ISRAEL--HELPFUL PRINCIPLES TO GOVERN MAN AND SOCIETY, EX.21:1-24:18**

    A.   The Laws Governing Human Rights, Ex.21:1-32

    B.   Laws Governing Property Rights, Ex.21:33-22:15

    C.   Laws Governing Social and Moral Obligations, Ex.22:16-31

    D.   Laws Governing Justice and Mercy In Court and Among Neighbors, Ex.23:1-9

    E.   Laws Governing Religion: The Sabbath and Religious Feasts, Ex. 23:10-19

    F.   The Conclusion of the Law, the Mosaic Covenant: The Rewards of Obedience, Ex. 23:20-33

    G.   The Climactic Adoption of the Law, the Mosaic Covenant: The Great Duty of Believers After Receiving the Law, the Word of God, Ex.24:1-18

IX. **THE TABERNACLE, ITS BLUEPRINT AND PRIESTHOOD: THE TRUE WAY TO APPROACH AND WORSHIP GOD, EX.25:1-31:18**

    A.   The Materials Needed to Construct the Tabernacle: God's Call to Stewardship, to Give from a Willing Heart, 25:1-9

    B.   The Ark or Chest of God: the Symbol of the Very Throne and Presence of God, 25:10-22

    C.   The Table of Showbread: The Symbol of God Himself as the Bread of Life, 25:23-30

    D.   The Gold Lampstand, the Symbol of God Himself as the Light of the World, 25:31-40

    E.   The Tabernacle Itself: The Symbol of God Dwelling Among His People and of Man's Need to Approach God Exactly as God Dictates, Ex.26:1-37

    F.   The Altar of Burnt Offering, The Court of the Tabernacle, and The Lampstand: All Symbolizing the True Way to Approach God, Ex. 27:1-21

    G.   The Garments of the Priests: The Symbol of Bringing Dignity and Honor to the Name of God, Ex. 28:1-43

    H.   The Dedication, Consecration, and Ordination of the Priests: God's Qualifications for Leadership, Ex.29:1-46

    I.   The Altar of Incense: The Symbol of the Prayers and Communion of God's People Ascending to God: Ex.30:1-10

    J.   Other Instructions for the Tabernacle: Symbolizing Spiritual Health and Maturity, Ex.30:11-38

    K.   Other Instructions For the Tabernacle: Three Great Charges Given to Man, Ex.31:1-18

X. **THE GOLDEN CALF AND MOSES' GREAT INTERCESSION: THE BREAKING AND RENEWAL OF THE COVENANT BETWEEN GOD AND ISRAEL, Ex.32:1-34:35**

    A.   The Golden Calf--The Breaking of the Covenant Between God and Man : A Picture of Man's Corrupt Heart and Rebellion Against God, Ex.32:1-35

    B.   The Threat of Separation From God and Moses' Great Intercession: The Essentials for Repentance & Renewal After Sinning, Ex.33:1-23

    C.   The Renewal of the Covenant Between God and Man: The Steps to Renewal, Ex.34:1-35

XI. **THE TABERNACLE, ITS CONSTRUCTION AND DEDICATION: THE PEOPLE OBEY GOD, Ex.35:1-40:38**

    A.   The Preparations for Building the Tabernacle: The Call to Give Sacrificially, Ex.35:1-35

    B.   The Construction of the Tabernacle: The Excitement of Building for God, Ex.36:1-38

    C.   The Building of the Furnishings For the Tabernacle (Part 1): Learning the Only Way to Approach God, Ex.37:1-29

    D.   The Building of the Furnishings For the Tabernacle (Part 2): Learning the Only Way to Approach God, Ex.38:1-31

    E.   The Making of the Garments For the Priests: Being Clothed in Righteousness, Ex.39:1-43

    F.   The Assembly and Dedication of the Tabernacle, the Center of Worship: Experiencing the Presence of the Lord, Ex.40:1-38

THE LAW AND THE PROMISES OF GOD (THE MOSAIC COVENANT) (PART 1): GOD'S GREAT CALL--THE CALL TO TOTAL COMMITMENT, 19:1-25

(19:1-25) **DIVISION OVERVIEW--Law, The--Covenant, Mosaic**: the Bible now begins to cover the law of God, the great Mosaic Covenant. The law of God lays the groundwork for all that follows in the Old Testament. For this reason, the law needs to be looked at as a whole before it is studied in detail. The following discussion gives an overall view of this most important subject: *The Law of God, the Great Mosaic Covenant*. However before beginning, note that the following overview covers the entire Mosaic Covenant (chapters 19-24). The Mosaic Covenant is being split into three Divisions because of the importance of the Ten Commandments and the need to handle them in a separate division. The three Divisions are:

VI.   THE LAW AND THE PROMISES OF GOD (THE MOSAIC COVENANT) (PART 1): GOD'S GREAT CALL--THE CALL TO TOTAL COMMITMENT, 19:1-25
VII.   THE LAW AND THE PROMISES OF GOD (THE MOSAIC COVENANT) (PART 2): THE TEN COMMANDMENTS--NECESSARY LAWS TO GOVERN MAN AND SOCIETY, EX.20:1-26
VIII.   THE LAW AND THE PROMISES OF GOD (THE MOSAIC COVENANT) (PART 3): THE CIVIL AND RELIGIOUS LAWS OF ISRAEL--HELPFUL PRINCIPLES TO GOVERN MAN AND SOCIETY, EX.21:1-24:18

1. The Mosaic covenant is sometimes called "the law," "the law of God," or "the law of Moses." In addition, the covenant is sometimes divided into three different systems or types of laws:
   ⇒ *The moral law*: referring to the ten commandments.
   ⇒ *The ceremonial law*: referring to the commandments governing the religious and sacrificial system.
   ⇒ *The civil law*: referring to the laws governing the daily lives of people (the Israelites).
2. The covenant of the law spells out the duty of God's people: obedience. God has always demanded only one thing of believers: obedience. Both Old and New Testament believers are given the same charge: obey God. Norman L. Geisler says this:

> "Duty follows deliverance. Complete redemption involved more than getting Israel out of Egypt. It also involved getting 'Egypt' (i.e., the world) out of them. Not unlike believers of today, the Israelites often lusted for the things of Egypt (16:3) instead of fulfilling their duty. Their duty was to follow God's law in order to receive God's blessing."[1]

3. The covenant was conditional (Ex.19:5-6). The Israelites had to obey God in order to receive the blessings and promises of the covenant. What was to be Israel's response in the coming centuries? Failure. The rest of the Old Testament is primarily...
   • a record of Israel's gross disobedience to God.
   • a record of the prophets' denunciation of Israel's sin.
   • a record of the warning of coming judgment upon all the disobedient of this earth, upon both the Jew and the Gentile.
   • a record of a people failing to become what God wanted them to become.
   • a record of a people failing to do what God wanted them to do.
(The idea for the above statements was gleaned from F.B. Huey, Jr., Exodus.[2])
4. Both the Old Testament and the New Testament tell us why God gave the law. There were at least nine purposes. (See outline and notes--Ex.20:18-26; Ro.3:19-20; 7:7-13; Gal.3:1-4:7 for more discussion.)
   a. The law was given to mark believers, to mark them as the true followers of God, as being God's holy and treasured people.

> "Now therefore, if ye will obey my voice indeed, and keep my covenant, then ye shall be a peculiar treasure unto me above all people: for all the earth is mine: And ye shall be unto me a kingdom of priests, and an holy nation. These are the words which thou shalt speak unto the children of Israel" (Ex.19:5-6).

---

[1]   Norman L. Geisler. *A Popular Survey of the Old Testament*. (Grand Rapids, MI: Baker Book House, 1977), p.58.
[2]   F.B. Huey, Jr. *Exodus*, p.81.

"He showeth his word unto Jacob, his statutes and his judgments unto Israel. He hath not dealt so with any nation: and as for his judgments, they have not known them. Praise ye the LORD" (Ps.147:19-20).

"My brethren, my kinsmen according to the flesh: Who are Israelites; to whom pertaineth the adoption, and the glory, and the covenants, and the giving of the law, and the service of God, and the promises; Whose are the fathers, and of whom as concerning the flesh Christ came, who is over all, God blessed for ever. Amen" (Ro.9:3ᵇ-5).

b. The law was given to mark believers as the priests, the true witnesses and servants of God upon earth.

"Now therefore, if ye will obey my voice indeed, and keep my covenant, then ye shall be a peculiar treasure unto me above all people: for all the earth is mine: And ye shall be unto me a kingdom of priests, and an holy nation. These are the words which thou shalt speak unto the children of Israel" (Ex.19:5-6).

"But ye shall be named the Priests of the LORD: men shall call you the Ministers of our God: ye shall eat the riches of the Gentiles, and in their glory shall ye boast yourselves" (Is.61:6).

"Ye also [all believers], as lively stones, are built up a spiritual house, an holy priesthood, to offer up spiritual sacrifices, acceptable to God by Jesus Christ" (1 Pt.2:5).

c. The law was given to show man that he is sinful, that he is far short of God's glory, that he is not perfect.

"Moreover the law entered, that the offence might abound. But where sin abounded, grace did much more abound" (Ro.5:20).

"What shall we say then? Is the law sin? God forbid. Nay, I had not known sin, but by the law: for I had not known lust, except the law had said, Thou shalt not covet" (Ro.7:7).

"Wherefore then serveth the law? It was added because of transgressions, till the seed should come to whom the promise was made; and it was ordained by angels in the hand of a mediator" (Gal.3:19).

"Knowing this, that the law is not made for a righteous man, but for the lawless and disobedient, for the ungodly and for sinners, for unholy and profane, for murderers of fathers and murderers of mothers, for manslayers, For whoremongers, for them that defile themselves with mankind, for menstealers, for liars, for perjured persons, and if there be any other thing that is contrary to sound doctrine" (1 Tim.1:9-10).

"For the law having a shadow of good things to come, and not the very image of the things, can never with those sacrifices which they offered year by year continually make the comers thereunto perfect" (Heb.10:1).

"As it is written, There is none righteous, no, not one....Now we know that what things soever the law saith, it saith to them who are under the law: that every mouth may be stopped, and all the world may become guilty before God. Therefore by the deeds of the law there shall no flesh be justified in his sight: for by the law is the knowledge of sin" (Ro.3:10, 19-20).

d. The law was given to show man that he can never be justified by the law, never be perfected by the law, never keep the law perfectly. In fact, he comes ever so short of keeping the law, ever so short of perfection.

"Therefore by the deeds of the law there shall no flesh be justified in his sight: for by the law is the knowledge of sin" (Ro.3:20).

"For the law having a shadow of good things to come, and not the very image of the things, can never with those sacrifices which they offered year by year continually make the comers thereunto perfect" (Heb.10:1).

"For all have sinned, and come short of the glory of God" (Ro.3:23).

e. The law was given to show man that he needs a Savior, a Savior who can deliver him from the curse and penalty of the law.

"For as many as are of the works of the law are under the curse: for it is written, Cursed is every one that continueth not in all things which are written in the book of the law to do them. But that no man is justified by the law in the sight of God, it is evident: for, The just shall live by faith. And the law is not of faith: but, The man that doeth them shall live in them. Christ hath redeemed us from the curse of the law, being made a curse for us: for it is written, Cursed is every one that hangeth on a tree" (Gal.3:10-13).

"But when the fulness of the time was come, God sent forth his Son, made of a woman, made under the law, To redeem them that were under the law, that we might receive the adoption of sons. And because ye are sons, God hath sent forth the Spirit of his Son into your hearts, crying, Abba, Father" (Gal.4:4-6; cp. Gal.1:4).

"Therefore by the deeds of the law there shall no flesh be justified in his sight: for by the law is the knowledge of sin. But now the righteousness of God without the law is manifested, being witnessed by the law and the prophets; Even the righteousness of God which is by faith of Jesus Christ unto all and upon all them that believe: for there is no difference" (Ro.3:20-22).

"For all have sinned, and come short of the glory of God; Being justified freely by his grace through the redemption that is in Christ Jesus" (Ro.3:23-24).

"There is therefore now no condemnation to them which are in Christ Jesus, who walk not after the flesh, but after the Spirit. For the law of the Spirit of life in Christ Jesus hath made me free from the law of sin and death. For what the law could not do, in that it was weak through the flesh, God sending his own Son in the likeness of sinful flesh, and for sin, condemned sin in the flesh: That the righteousness of the law might be fulfilled in us, who walk not after the flesh, but after the Spirit" (Ro.8:1-4).

"Knowing that a man is not justified by the works of the law, but by the faith of Jesus Christ, even we have believed in Jesus Christ, that we might be justified by the faith of Christ, and not by the works of the law: for by the works of the law shall no flesh be justified" (Gal.2:16).

"For I through the law am dead to the law, that I might live unto God" (Gal.2:19).

"For the law made nothing perfect, but the bringing in of a better hope [in Christ] did; by the which we draw nigh unto God" (Heb.7:19).

f. The law was given to show man that he needs a mediator to approach God. God appointed Moses to be the mediator between Himself and Israel, but Moses was only a type of the promised *Mediator and Prophet*, the Lord Jesus Christ...
- who was to be *raised up* by God Himself
- who was to be the very *Prophet* of God Himself
- who was to be the *Savior and Messiah* of the world
- who was to be the *High Priest* of God Himself

"The LORD thy God will raise up unto thee a <u>Prophet</u> from the midst of thee, of thy brethren, like unto me; unto him ye shall hearken; According to all that thou desiredst of the LORD thy God in Horeb in the day of the assembly, saying, Let me not hear again the voice of the LORD my God, neither let me see this great fire any more, that I die not. And the LORD said unto me, They have well spoken that which they have spoken. I will raise them up a Prophet from among their brethren, like unto thee, and will put my words in his mouth; and he shall speak unto them all that I shall command him. And it shall come to pass, that whosoever will not hearken unto my words which he shall speak in my name, I will require it of him" (Dt.18:15-19).

"Then those men, when they had seen the miracle that Jesus did, said, This is of a truth <u>that prophet</u> that should come into the world" (Jn.6:14).

"Repent ye therefore, and be converted, that your sins may be blotted out, when the times of refreshing shall come from the presence of the Lord; And he shall send Jesus Christ, which before was preached unto you: Whom the heaven must receive until the times of restitution of all things, which God hath spoken by the mouth of all his holy prophets since the world began. For Moses truly said unto the fathers, A <u>prophet</u> shall the Lord your God raise up unto you of your brethren, like unto me; him shall ye hear in all things whatsoever he shall say unto you" (Acts 3:19-22).

"Wherefore he is able also to save them to the uttermost that come unto God by him, seeing he ever liveth to make intercession for them. For such an high priest became us, who is holy, harmless, undefiled, separate from sinners, and made higher than the heavens" (Heb.7:25-26).

g. The law was given to be a guide (a schoolmaster or guardian), a guide who would lead people to Christ.

"Wherefore the law was our schoolmaster to bring us unto Christ, that we might be justified by faith" (Gal.3:24).

h. The law was given to arouse people to seek both life and the promised land.

"Now therefore hearken, O Israel, unto the statutes and unto the judgments, which I teach you, for to do them, <u>that ye may live, and go in and possess the land</u> which the LORD God of your fathers giveth you. Ye shall not add unto the word which I command you, neither shall ye diminish ought from it, that ye may keep the commandments of the LORD your God which I command you" (Dt.4:1-2).

"Ye shall observe to do therefore as the LORD your God hath commanded you: ye shall not turn aside to the right hand or to the left. Ye shall walk in all the ways which the LORD your God hath commanded you, that ye may live, and that it may be well with you, and that ye may prolong your days <u>in the land which ye shall possess</u>" (Dt.5:32-33).

i. The law was given to show man how to live a peaceful and productive life upon earth, how to be at peace with God and man and to live a life that overflows with the blessings of God. Note the commandments, how each...
  - leads either to peace with God or peace with man
  - leads to a productive and fruitful life upon earth

    Commandment 1: Never believe in false gods.
    Commandment 2: Never make nor worship false gods.
    Commandment 3: Never misuse God's name; never use vulgarity.
    Commandment 4: Keep the Sabbath day holy.
    Commandment 5: Honor your father and mother.
    Commandment 6: Never kill.
    Commandment 7: Never commit adultery or immorality.
    Commandment 8: Never steal.
    Commandment 9: Never lie or speak falsely against anyone.
    Commandment 10: Never covet anything that belongs to a neighbor—his house, wife, servant, workers, animals, or anything else.

5. Scripture tells us seven things that the law (the Mosaic covenant) cannot and does not do.
  a. The law does not replace nor void the great promises of God, the great promises of the Abrahamic covenant...
    - the promise of the promised land (heaven)
    - the promise of the promised seed, meaning both the promise of a great nation of believers and the promise of the Savior and Messiah of the world.

    Note how clearly this is stated by Scripture: the law does not replace nor void the great promises given to Abraham and his seed (believers of all generations):

    > "For the promise, that he should be the heir of the world, was not to Abraham, or to his seed, through the law, but through the righteousness of faith. For if they which are of the law be heirs, faith is made void, and the promise made of none effect: Because the law worketh wrath: for where no law is, there is no transgression. Therefore it is of faith, that it might be by grace; <u>to the end the promise might be sure to all the seed</u>; not to that only which is of the law, but to that also which is of the faith of Abraham; who is the father of us all" (Ro.4:13-16).

    > "Christ hath redeemed us from the curse of the law, being made a curse for us: for it is written, Cursed is every one that hangeth on a tree: <u>That the blessing of Abraham</u> might come on the Gentiles through Jesus Christ; that we might receive the promise of the Spirit through faith" (Gal.3:13-14).

    > "Brethren, I speak after the manner of men; Though it be but a man's covenant, yet if it be confirmed, no man disannulleth, or addeth thereto. Now to Abraham and his seed were the promises made. He saith not, And to seeds, as of many; but as of one, And to thy seed, which is Christ. And this I say, that the covenant, that was confirmed before of God in Christ, the law, which was four hundred and thirty years after, cannot disannul, that it should make the promise of none effect. For if the inheritance be of the law, it is no more of promise: but God gave it to Abraham by promise" (Gal.3:15-18).

  b. The law could not be a permanent covenant; it was only a temporary covenant until Christ came.

    > "Wherefore then serveth the law? It was added because of transgressions, till the seed should come to whom the promise was made; and it was ordained by angels in the hand of a mediator" (Gal.3:19).

    > "But the scripture hath concluded all under sin, that the promise by faith of Jesus Christ might be given to them that believe" (Gal.3:22).

    > "But before faith came, we were kept under the law, shut up unto the faith which should afterwards be revealed. Wherefore the law was our schoolmaster to bring us unto Christ, that we might be justified by faith. But after that faith is come, we are no longer under a schoolmaster. For ye are all the children of God by faith in Christ Jesus. For as many of you as have been baptized into Christ have put on Christ. There is neither Jew nor Greek, there is neither bond nor free, there is neither male nor female: for ye are all one in Christ Jesus. And if ye be Christ's, then are ye Abraham's seed, and heirs according to the promise" (Gal.3:23-29).

  c. The law cannot save a person because no person can keep the law.

    > "But that no man is justified by the law in the sight of God, it is evident: for, The just shall live by faith" (Gal.3:11).

    > "Therefore by the deeds of the law there shall no flesh be justified in his sight: for by the law is the knowledge of sin" (Ro.3:20).

d. The law cannot make a person perfect.

> **"For the law made nothing perfect, but the bringing in of a better hope did; by the which we draw nigh unto God" (Heb.7:19, cp. Heb.7:11-18).**

e. The law cannot justify a person from sin.

> **"Be it known unto you therefore, men and brethren, that through this man is preached unto you the forgiveness of sins: And by him all that believe are justified from all things, from which ye could not be justified by the law of Moses" (Acts 13:38-39).**
>
> **"Now we know that what things soever the law saith, it saith to them who are under the law: that every mouth may be stopped, and all the world may become guilty before God. Therefore by the deeds of the law there shall no flesh be justified in his sight: for by the law is the knowledge of sin. But now the righteousness of God without the law is manifested, being witnessed by the law and the prophets; Even the righteousness of God which is by faith of Jesus Christ unto all and upon all them that believe: for there is no difference: For all have sinned, and come short of the glory of God; Being justified freely by his grace through the redemption that is in Christ Jesus: Whom God hath set forth to be a propitiation through faith in his blood, to declare his righteousness for the remission of sins that are past, through the forbearance of God; To declare, I say, at this time his righteousness: that he might be just, and the justifier of him which believeth in Jesus. Where is boasting then? It is excluded. By what law? of works? Nay: but by the law of faith. Therefore we conclude that a man is justified by faith without the deeds of the law" (Ro.3:19-28).**

f. The law cannot make us righteous, cannot impute righteousness to man.

> **"Therefore by the deeds of the law there shall no flesh be justified in his sight: for by the law is the knowledge of sin. But now the righteousness of God without the law is manifested, being witnessed by the law and the prophets; Even the righteousness of God which is by faith of Jesus Christ unto all and upon all them that believe: for there is no difference" (Ro.3:20-22).**
>
> **"For he hath made him to be sin for us, who knew no sin; that we might be made the righteousness of God in him" (2 Cor.5:21).**
>
> **"I do not frustrate the grace of God: for if righteousness come by the law, then Christ is dead in vain" (Gal.2:21).**
>
> **"Who his own self bare our sins in his own body on the tree, that we, being dead to sins, should live unto righteousness: by whose stripes ye were healed" (1 Pt.2:24).**

g. The law cannot give life to man.

> **"Is the law then against the promises of God? God forbid: for if there had been a law given which could have given life, verily righteousness should have been by the law" (Gal.3:21).**

6. The law is compared to several things throughout Scripture.
   a. The law is compared to a *mirror* because it reveals a person's sins.

> **"But be ye doers of the word, and not hearers only, deceiving your own selves. For if any be a hearer of the word, and not a doer, he is like unto a man beholding his natural face in a glass: For he beholdeth himself, and goeth his way, and straightway forgetteth what manner of man he was. But whoso looketh into the perfect law of liberty, and continueth therein, he being not a forgetful hearer, but a doer of the work, this man shall be blessed in his deed" (Jas.1:22-25).**

   b. The law is compared to a *yoke*, to the bondage of a yoke, because a person cannot keep the law, not perfectly.

> **"For what the law could not do, in that it was weak through the flesh, God sending his own Son in the likeness of sinful flesh, and for sin, condemned sin in the flesh" (Ro.8:3).**
>
> **"Stand fast therefore in the liberty wherewith Christ hath made us free, and be not entangled again with the yoke of bondage" (Gal.5:1).**

   c. The law is compared to a school guardian because it leads us to Christ, leads us to see our great need for a Savior.

> **"But before faith came, we were kept under the law, shut up unto the faith which should afterwards be revealed. Wherefore the law was our schoolmaster to bring us unto Christ, that we might be justified by faith. But after that faith is come, we are no longer under a schoolmaster. For ye are all the children of God by faith in Christ Jesus. For as many of you as have been baptized into Christ have put on Christ. There is neither Jew nor Greek, there is neither bond nor free, there is neither male nor female: for ye are all one in Christ Jesus. And if ye be Christ's, then are ye Abraham's seed, and heirs according to the promise. Now I say,**

That the heir, as long as he is a child, differeth nothing from a servant, though he be lord of all; But is under tutors and governors until the time appointed of the father. Even so we, when we were children, were in bondage under the elements of the world: But when the fulness of the time was come, God sent forth his Son, made of a woman, made under the law, To redeem them that were under the law, that we might receive the adoption of sons. And because ye are sons, God hath sent forth the Spirit of his Son into your hearts, crying, Abba, Father. Wherefore thou art no more a servant, but a son; and if a son, then an heir of God through Christ" (Gal.3:23-4:7).

d. The law is compared to *letters written on stones* in contrast to the law of love written on our hearts by God's Spirit.

"But if the ministration of death, written and engraven in stones, was glorious, so that the children of Israel could not stedfastly behold the face of Moses for the glory of his countenance; which glory was to be done away" (2 Cor.3:7).

e. The law is compared to a *shadow* in contrast to the reality and fulfillment we have in Christ.

"For the law having a shadow of good things to come, and not the very image of the things, can never with those sacrifices which they offered year by year continually make the comers thereunto perfect" (Heb.10:1).

"Blotting out the handwriting of ordinances that was against us, which was contrary to us, and took it out of the way, nailing it to his cross; And having spoiled principalities and powers, he made a show of them openly, triumphing over them in it. Let no man therefore judge you in meat, or in drink, or in respect of an holyday, or of the new moon, or of the sabbath days: Which are a shadow of things to come; but the body is of Christ" (Col.2:14-17).

7. The relationship of Jesus Christ to the law is of critical importance.
   a. Jesus Christ obeyed the law; He never transgressed the law, not even once. He was without sin.

"For it became him, for whom are all things, and by whom are all things, in bringing many sons unto glory, to make the captain of their salvation <u>perfect</u> through sufferings" (Heb.2:10

"For we have not an high priest which cannot be touched with the feeling of our infirmities; but was in all points tempted like as we are, yet <u>without sin</u>" (Heb.4:15).

"And being made perfect, he became the author of eternal salvation unto all them that obey him" (Heb.5:9).

"For such an high priest became us, who is holy, harmless, undefiled, separate from sinners, and made higher than the heavens" (Heb.7:26).

"For the law maketh men high priests which have infirmity; but the word of the oath, which was since the law, maketh the Son, who is consecrated for evermore" (Heb.7:28).

"Which of you convinceth me of sin? And if I say the truth, why do ye not believe me?" (Jn.8:46).

"For he hath made him to be sin for us, who <u>knew no sin</u>; that we might be made the righteousness of God in him" (2 Cor.5:21).

"But with the precious blood of Christ, as of a lamb without blemish and without spot" (1 Pt.1:19).

"Who did no sin, neither was guile found in his mouth" (1 Pt.2:22).

   b. Jesus Christ declared that He came to fulfill the law, not to destroy it.

"Think not that I am come to destroy the law, or the prophets: I am not come to destroy, but to fulfil" (Mt.5:17).

Christ said He was neither contradicting nor destroying the law nor standing against it. He was fulfilling and completing the law, embracing, keeping, and obeying the commandments with all His heart and life. There are several ways in which Jesus Christ fulfilled the law.

⇒ Before Christ, the law described how God wanted man to live. The law was the ideal, the words that told man what he was to do. But Christ fulfilled and completed the law; that is, God gave man more than just mere words to describe how He wants man to live. He gave man the Life, the Person who perfectly pictures and demonstrates the law before the world's very eyes. Jesus Christ is the Picture, the Living Example, the Pattern, the Demonstration of life as it is to be lived. He is the Perfect Picture of *God's Will and Word*, the Ideal Man, the Representative Man, the Pattern for all men.

"And <u>the Word</u> was made flesh, and dwelt among us, (and we beheld his glory, the glory as of the only begotten of the Father,) full of grace and truth" (Jn.1:14).

⇒ Before Christ, the law was only words and rules. It could only inject the idea of behavior into the mind of a person. It had no spirit, no life, no power to enable a person to do the law. But Christ fulfilled and completed the law. He was *Spirit and Life*, so He was able to put spirit and life to the words and rules of the law. He was able to live the life described by the words and rules. As such, He was able to inject both the idea and the power to behave into a person's mind and life. It is now His life that sets the standard and the rule for the believer; it is His Spirit and life that gives the believer power to obey.

> **"There is therefore now no condemnation to them which are in Christ Jesus, who walk not after the flesh, but after the Spirit. For the law of the <u>Spirit of life</u> in Christ Jesus hath made me free from the law of sin and death. For what the law could not do, in that it was weak through the flesh, God sending his own Son in the likeness of sinful flesh, and for sin, condemned sin in the flesh: that the righteousness of the law might be fulfilled in us, who walk not after the flesh, but after the Spirit" (Ro.8:1-4).**

⇒ Before Christ, the law stated only the rule and the principle of behavior. It did not explain the rule nor the spirit behind the rule. Neither did the law give the full meaning of the rule. The law always had to have an interpreter. But Christ fulfilled and completed the law. He explained the rule and the spirit behind the rule. He interpreted the law. He gave the law its real and full meaning.

> **"But before faith came, we were kept under the law, shut up unto the faith which should afterwards be revealed. Wherefore the law was our schoolmaster to bring us unto Christ, that we might be justified by faith" (Gal.3:23-24.)**

⇒ Before Christ, the law demanded perfect righteousness; it demanded a perfect life. But man failed at certain points. Man just could not obey the law perfectly; he fell short of perfect righteousness. But Christ fulfilled and completed the law. He kept the law in *every detail*. He secured the *perfect righteousness* demanded by the law. He fulfilled all the requirements, all the types, and all the ceremonies of the law--perfectly. As such, He became the Perfect Man, the Ideal Man, the Representative Man for all men. As the Ideal Man, He simply embraced all men; He embodied the righteousness that man must now have.

> **"For he hath made him to be sin for us, who <u>knew no sin</u>; that we might be made the righteousness of God in him" (2 Cor.5:21).**

⇒ Before Christ, the law demanded punishment for disobedience. If a man broke the law, he was to be punished. But Christ fulfilled and completed the law. In fact, He went to the farthest point possible in fulfilling the law. He paid the maximum price and showed the ultimate love. He bore the punishment of the law for every man's disobedience; He took the punishment of the law upon Himself. As the Ideal Man, He not only embodies the righteousness that must cover all men, He also frees all men from the penalty of the law. And He makes them sons of God. (Cp. Ro.8:15-17; Gal.3:13-14; 4:1-7.)

> **"For God sent not his Son into the world to condemn the world; but that the world through him might be saved" (Jn.3:17).**
> **"Who his own self bare our sins in his own body on the tree, that we, being dead to sins, should live unto righteousness: by whose stripes ye were healed" (1 Pt.2:24).**

DIVISION VI

THE LAW AND THE PROMISES OF GOD (THE MOSAIC COVENANT) (PART 1): GOD'S GREAT CALL--THE CALL TO TOTAL COMMITMENT, 19:1-25

1. The setting & basis for the covenant
a. The time: Took place in the third month after Israel's deliverance from Egyptian slavery (a symbol of redemption)
b. The place: Israel was camped at the base of Mt. Sinai

c. The persons
1) The LORD spoke to Moses, His mediator
2) Moses spoke to the people
3) The people heard the message of God
d. The basis for the covenant: The LORD's great deliverance--He freed His people as though He carried them on eagles' wings

2. The call to obedience[DSI]
a. The call was conditional: If obey
b. The results, the promises
1) If obey, they would be God's treasured people
2) If obey, they would be a kingdom of priests
3) If obey, they would be a holy nation

c. The response to God's call
1) Moses called the elders together & shared all the LORD had commanded

2) The people committed themselves to obey the Lord: To keep all His commandments

3) The LORD gave great assurance to His dear servant: God promised to come to Moses in a special manifestation of His presence--so the people would believe Moses then & for all time

3. The call to sanctification
a. Means being clean, pure--totally set apart to God
b. Was symbolized by the washing of clothes

VI. THE LAW & THE PROMISES OF GOD (THE MOSAIC COVENANT) (PART 1): GOD'S GREAT CALL-- THE CALL TO TOTAL COMMITMENT, 19:1-25

In the third month, when the children of Israel were gone forth out of the land of Egypt, the same day came they into the wilderness of Sinai.
2 For they were departed from Rephidim, and were come to the desert of Sinai, and had pitched in the wilderness; and there Israel camped before the mount.
3 And Moses went up unto God, and the LORD called unto him out of the mountain, saying, Thus shalt thou say to the house of Jacob, and tell the children of Israel;
4 Ye have seen what I did unto the Egyptians, and how I bare you on eagles' wings, and brought you unto myself.
5 Now therefore, if ye will obey my voice indeed, and keep my covenant, then ye shall be a peculiar treasure unto me above all people: for all the earth is mine:
6 And ye shall be unto me a kingdom of priests, and an holy nation. These are the words which thou shalt speak unto the children of Israel.
7 And Moses came and called for the elders of the people, and laid before their faces all these words which the LORD commanded him.
8 And all the people answered together, and said, All that the LORD hath spoken we will do. And Moses returned the words of the people unto the LORD.
9 And the LORD said unto Moses, Lo, I come unto thee in a thick cloud, that the people may hear when I speak with thee, and believe thee for ever. And Moses told the words of the people unto the LORD.
10 And the LORD said unto Moses, Go unto the people, and sanctify them to day and to morrow, and let them wash their clothes,

11 And be ready against the third day: for the third day the LORD will come down in the sight of all the people upon mount Sinai.
12 And thou shalt set bounds unto the people round about, saying, Take heed to yourselves, that ye go not up into the mount, or touch the border of it: whosoever toucheth the mount shall be surely put to death:
13 There shall not an hand touch it, but he shall surely be stoned, or shot through; whether it be beast or man, it shall not live: when the trumpet soundeth long, they shall come up to the mount.
14 And Moses went down from the mount unto the people, and sanctified the people; and they washed their clothes.
15 And he said unto the people, Be ready against the third day: come not at your wives.
16 And it came to pass on the third day in the morning, that there were thunders and lightnings, and a thick cloud upon the mount, and the voice of the trumpet exceeding loud; so that all the people that was in the camp trembled.
17 And Moses brought forth the people out of the camp to meet with God; and they stood at the nether part of the mount.
18 And mount Sinai was altogether on a smoke, because the LORD descended upon it in fire: and the smoke thereof ascended as the smoke of a furnace, and the whole mount quaked greatly.
19 And when the voice of the trumpet sounded long, and waxed louder and louder, Moses spake, and God answered him by a voice.
20 And the LORD came down upon mount Sinai, on the top of the mount: and the LORD called Moses up to the top of the mount; and Moses went up.
21 And the LORD said unto Moses, Go down, charge the people, lest they break through unto the LORD to gaze, and many of them perish.

---

4. The call to reverence & to fear God's holy presence
a. God called the people to prepare to meet Him: He was to appear on Mt. Sinai
b. God demanded that His holy presence be respected
1) Demonstrated by setting boundaries around Mt. Sinai & prohibiting anyone from touching the mount: Symbolizing His holiness

2) Demonstrated by the severe punishment executed against those who touched the mountain, who did not honor God's holiness

c. God demanded that the people sanctify themselves (v.10): They followed through with their personal sanctification (v.14)
d. God demanded that the people totally focus upon Him & their need for sanctification: They abstained from sexual relations

5. The call to approach God only through His appointed mediator
a. God descended upon Mt. Sinai
1) There was a violent storm: Thunder & lightning, a dense, thick cloud, & the blast of a loud trumpet
2) The people were stricken with fear & trembling
b. The mediator between God & man is an absolute essential: Moses, God's appointed mediator, brought the people to God
c. The reasons
1) Because the LORD is holy: He descended in fire
• Smoke bellowed up as from a fiery furnace
• The whole mount shook & trembled violently
• The trumpet blast grew louder & louder

2) Because God speaks only through His appointed mediator

3) Because God's Holy presence must be reverenced: Violators will perish

| 4) Because even the priests were unclean: The very people who were supposed to be closest to God had to be cleansed or face judgment
5) Because the very earth itself was unclean: The very place where God's presence is demonstrated & symbolized must be sanctified | 22 And let the priests also, which come near to the LORD, sanctify themselves, lest the LORD break forth upon them.
23 And Moses said unto the LORD, The people cannot come up to mount Sinai: for thou chargedst us, saying, Set bounds about the mount, and sanctify it. | 24 And the LORD said unto him, Away, get thee down, and thou shalt come up, thou, and Aaron with thee: but let not the priests and the people break through to come up unto the LORD, lest he break forth upon them.
25 So Moses went down unto the people, and spake unto them. | 6) Because everyone must approach God through God's appointed mediator: Violators will be judged
• God appointed Moses & Aaron
• All others were warned
d. Moses obeyed: He went to the people & warned them |

DIVISION VI

THE LAW AND THE PROMISES OF GOD (THE MOSAIC COVENANT) (PART 1): GOD'S GREAT CALL-- THE CALL TO TOTAL COMMITMENT, 19:1-25

(19:1-25) **Introduction**: picture the Israelites at the foot of Mt. Sinai, over three million people camped at the foot of the mountain. Remember, it had been only three months since the miraculous deliverance from Egypt, only three months since God had delivered His people from four hundred years of Egyptian slavery. In the minds of the Israelites, the Promised Land was only a few more days away. Once they arrived, they could then get on with their lives.

But in the words of Norman Geisler:

"Duty follows deliverance. Complete redemption involved more than getting Israel out of Egypt. It also involved getting 'Egypt' (i.e., the world) out of them."[1]

How was God going to get "Egypt" (the spirit of the world) out of His people? Two things were necessary. First, God had to give them His law. God had to...
• describe how they were to live
• tell them what to do and what not to do
• spell out exactly how life was meant to be lived

Second, God had to give them His very own presence--a special manifestation--to help them obey His commandments, to guide them as they journeyed throughout life to the promised land of God.

Simply stated, God had to issue a call to His people, a call to enter a *covenant* with Him. That *covenant* was the law of God, the great commandments of God that are known as the Mosaic Covenant. F.B. Huey says this:

"Chapters 19-24 of Exodus (along with Genesis 3) have frequently been called the most important chapters of the Old Testament. In these chapters is found the account of the covenant that God made with Israel at Mount Sinai. The covenant was conditioned upon Israel's obedience to laws which were given to the people at Sinai. The rest of the Old Testament contains the story of how Israel responded to the demands of this covenant relationship. Unfortunately, it is largely a story of disobedience, unheeded warnings of the prophets, and punishment. The history of Israel in Old Testament times has been called a 'history of failure'--failure to be the people that God wanted them to be."[2]

Believers must know this one fact: the call of God is demanding. God's call is...
• to a life of obedience
• to a life of trust
• to a life of self-denial
• to a life of faith and assurance
• to a life of commitment

This is the great lesson of this passage of Scripture. It is the lesson of: *The Law and the Promises of God (The Mosaic Covenant) (Part 1): God's Great Call--A Call to Total Commitment,* Ex.19:1-25.
1. The setting and basis for the covenant (v.1-4).
2. The call to obedience (v.5-9).
3. The call to sanctification (v.10).
4. The call to reverence and to fear God's holy presence (v.11-16).
5. The call to approach God only through His appointed mediator (v.16-25).

1 (19:1-4) **Law, The--Covenant--Israel**: there was the setting for the covenant. Note these facts about the setting.

1. The covenant was given in the third month after Israel's deliverance from Egyptian slavery (v.1). It was given three months after the very day of their deliverance. This means that the covenant with God was made just seven weeks or about fifty days after God had delivered them from the world of Egyptian slavery to serve Him.
2. The place where Israel set up camp was at the base of Mount Sinai, the mountain that is called the mountain of God (see Deeper Study # 1--Ex.3:1 for more discussion). The Israelites actually camped at Mt. Sinai for almost a year. All the

---

[1] Norman L. Geisler. *A Popular Survey of the Old Testament*, p.58.
[2] F.B. Huey, Jr. *Exodus*, p.81.

events from this point on through Numbers 10:10 took place before Israel left Mt. Sinai and continued their march to the promised land (Num.10:11-13).

    3. The persons involved in the covenant or agreement were threefold (v.3).
- ⇒ There was the *LORD*. The LORD gave the covenant to His people through Moses, His appointed mediator.
- ⇒ There was *Moses*. Moses was God's appointed spokesman, God's appointed mediator between Himself and the people.
- ⇒ There were *the people*. The people were to hear the message of God and approach God through His appointed mediator, Moses, and they were to agree to the covenant.

    Note how God referred to the people: He called them "the house of Jacob," reminding them of their low, humble beginnings, and then He called them the "children of Israel." Why this sudden switch in titles? Remember Jacob's all night wrestling experience with God? Jacob had wrestled in prayer with God all night, until finally, sometime in the early morning hours, he surrendered and made a permanent commitment to serve God with all his heart. (See outline and notes--Gen.32:22-32 for more discussion.) It was at that time that God changed Jacob's name to Israel, which means *he who strives and prevails with God*. God was no doubt arousing His people to think of this great event in Jacob's life. God was challenging His people to be the "children of Israel," the nation of people who would surrender and commit themselves to serve God with all their hearts, the people who would truly *strive and prevail with God*.

    4. The basis for the covenant was God's great deliverance of His people. God had delivered His people from enslavement, gloriously saved and redeemed them from the evil world of the Egyptians. And God was now leading them to the *promised land*.

    Note the graphic picture describing God's glorious deliverance: He had freed and led His people as though He had carried them on eagles' wings. It is said that eagles do carry their young on their wings. This is explained by Scripture itself:

> **"As an eagle stirreth up her nest, fluttereth over her young, spreadeth abroad her wings, taketh them, beareth them on her wings: So the LORD alone did lead him [Israel], and there was no strange god with him" (Dt.32:11-12).**

    The picture being painted is that of an eagle soaring upon the currents of the wind, bearing its young upon its wings, the picture of...
- protection and security
- speed and swiftness
- provision and supply
- care and affection

    God had done all this and so much more for His dear people, all since He had delivered them from their enslavement. He had saved them time and again...
- by forcing the Egyptians to free them from their enslavement.
- by miraculously leading them through the Red Sea and drowning the Egyptian army that was pursuing them.
- by leading them with the cloud by day and the pillar of fire by night.
- by providing water for them out in the middle of the desert.
- by supplying their need for food day by day through the manna and the quails.
- by protecting them from the Amalekites who viciously attacked them, seeking to wipe them from the face of the earth.

    God's people lacked nothing as they journeyed through the wilderness of the desert. The LORD was guiding and meeting all their needs day by day. It was as though they were being carried along on the wings of an eagle.

    The point is this: it had been fifty days since God had saved and redeemed Israel from the evil world of Egypt. For fifty long days God had been guiding and delivering His people through trial after trial. Now, it was time for God's people to make a commitment to Him...
- a life-long agreement
- a life-long covenant

    This is, as stated above, the great subject of this portion of Scripture...
- the great covenant which God wanted signed and sealed with His people.
- the great covenant under which God wanted His people to live.
- the great covenant that was to establish Israel as a nation ruled by God.

2 (19:5-9) **Obedience--Believers, Nature of--Rewards**: there was the call to obedience. In one word, God told His people what He expected of them: *obedience*. He had saved and delivered them; now He expected them to follow Him, to keep His covenant, to obey His commandments.

    Note that God referred to the covenant as "My covenant" (v.5). The covenant was not to be a covenant between equals. God and man were not to sit down together and work out an agreement between themselves. The covenant of law about to be given to man was God's covenant, the covenant of the LORD God Himself. The laws of the covenant came from the mind and heart of God--not man. They were the laws that God knew man needed, the laws that would bless man and bless the relationship between God and man. Note two significant facts.

    1. The covenant of law was conditional (Ex.19:5-6). The covenant was just like the covenant of a king (a lord, a master) that was being given to his subjects for their benefit. If they kept the covenant, they would be greatly blessed; if they broke the covenant, they would be condemned.

    2. God made three great promises to His people if they obeyed His covenant, His laws.

EXODUS 19:1-25

a. God's people would be special "treasures" (sequallah) to Him. The Hebrew means select, choice, prized, precious, something held dear. The person who obeys God, who keeps God's commandment, is....
- God's *personal possession*
- God's *precious treasure*
- God's *choice property*

Note that God was not to be the property of Israel, but Israel was to be the property of God. Israel was to be obedient to God, available for God to lead and direct as He knew best.

Note another fact as well: all the earth is the Lord's (v.5). That is, He is the Sovereign Lord and Majesty of the entire universe: He could have chosen any people to be His holy and treasured people, His priests and witnesses upon earth. But He chose Israel. Scripture tells us why:

> **"The LORD did not set his love upon you, nor choose you, because ye were more in number than any people; for ye were the fewest of all people: But because the LORD loved you, and because he would keep the oath which he had sworn unto your fathers, hath the LORD brought you out with a mighty hand, and redeemed you out of the house of bondmen, from the hand of Pharaoh king of Egypt" (Dt.7:7-8).**

Simply stated, God chose and delivered Israel from the world of Egyptian slavery...
- because Israel was the fewest in number of all people: God could thereby more clearly demonstrate His sovereignty, power, and grace.
- because He loved Israel.
- because He was faithful to His oath, His promise to give the promised land and the promised seed to the forefathers (Abraham, Isaac, and Jacob). (See Deeper Study # 1, Promised Land--Ex.2:24; Deeper Study # 2, Promised Seed--Ex.1:6-7 for more discussion.)

> **"For thou art an holy people unto the LORD thy God: the LORD thy God hath chosen thee to be a special people unto himself, above all people that are upon the face of the earth" (Dt.7:6).**
> **"For the LORD'S portion is his people; Jacob is the lot of his inheritance" (Dt.32:9).**
> **"For the LORD hath chosen Jacob unto himself, and Israel for his peculiar treasure" (Ps.135:4).**
> **"And they shall be mine, saith the LORD of hosts, in that day when I make up my jewels; and I will spare them, as a man spareth his own son that serveth him" (Mal.3:17).**
> **"Who gave himself for us, that he might redeem us from all iniquity, and purify unto himself a peculiar people, zealous of good works" (Tit.2:14).**
> **"But ye are a chosen generation, a royal priesthood, an holy nation, a peculiar people; that ye should show forth the praises of him who hath called you out of darkness into his marvellous light" (1 Pt.2:9).**

b. God's people would be a "kingdom of priests" to Him (v.6). The idea is that of both *kings and priests*. The person who obeys God becomes both a king and priest to God.

The promise is clear: the *obedient* person is victorious over all the enemies of life as he marches to the promised land. The obedient person stands as a priest before God; therefore, when he needs help, he has open access, an open door into God's presence. He cries to God for help and God helps him. Moreover, as a priest, the obedient person is God's witness (His missionary) to the unbelievers of the world.

> **"By whom also we have access by faith into this grace wherein we stand, and rejoice in hope of the glory of God" (Ro.5:2).**
> **"For we have not an high priest which cannot be touched with the feeling of our infirmities; but was in all points tempted like as we are, yet without sin. Let us therefore come boldly unto the throne of grace, that we may obtain mercy, and find grace to help in time of need" (Heb.4:15-16).**
> **"Ye also, as lively stones, are built up a spiritual house, an holy priesthood, to offer up spiritual sacrifices, acceptable to God by Jesus Christ" (1 Pt.2:5).**
> **"But ye are a chosen generation, a royal priesthood, an holy nation, a peculiar people; that ye should show forth the praises of him who hath called you out of darkness into his marvellous light" (1 Pt.2:9).**
> **"But ye shall be named the Priests of the LORD: men shall call you the Ministers of our God" (Is.61:6).**
> **"Blessed and holy is he that hath part in the first resurrection: on such the second death hath no power, but they shall be priests of God and of Christ, and shall reign with him a thousand years" (Rev.20:6).**

c. God's people would be a "holy nation" of people (v.6). The word "holy" means to be sanctified, separate, different, pure, righteous within and without, totally consecrated to God and His mission upon earth.

Thought 1. Think for a moment about what has just been studied: concentrate upon the great promises just made by God. If we obey God and keep His commandments, we become...

- the "personal possession" of God
- the "precious treasure" of God
- the "choice property" of God
- a king to God
- a priest to God
- a holy--sanctified, pure, righteous, consecrated--people to God

"For thou art an holy people unto the LORD thy God: the LORD thy God hath chosen thee to be a special people unto himself, above all people that are upon the face of the earth" (Dt.7:6).

"For thou art an holy people unto the LORD thy God, and the LORD hath chosen thee to be a peculiar [treasured] people unto himself, above all the nations that are upon the earth" (Dt.14:2).

"What? know ye not that your body is the temple of the Holy Ghost which is in you, which ye have of God, and ye are not your own? For ye are bought with a price: therefore glorify God in your body, and in your spirit, which are God's" (1 Cor.6:19-20).

"Ye also, as lively stones, are built up a spiritual house, an holy priesthood, to offer up spiritual sacrifices, acceptable to God by Jesus Christ" (1 Pt.2:5).

"And hath made us kings and priests unto God and his Father; to him be glory and dominion for ever and ever. Amen" (Rev.1:6).

"And hast made us unto our God kings and priests: and we shall reign on the earth" (Rev.5:10).

3. The response to God's call was positive, a resounding commitment to obey God (v.7-9). Note what happened.
   a. Moses called the elders together and shared all that the LORD had commanded (v.7).
   b. The people--with deep conviction and sincerity of heart--committed themselves to God's covenant, to obey Him and keep His commandments (v.8). Note: they did not yet know the terms of the covenant. The laws of God had not yet been spelled out. Nevertheless, the people had learned that God loved and cared for them; therefore, they knew that His commandments would be holy, just, and good (Ro.7:12). They were in essence committing themselves to God personally, declaring that they would trust and follow Him. They would go wherever He led, do whatever He commanded.

   Now, how do we know that this was what happened, that their commitment was made out of deep conviction and sincerity of heart? Because Scripture says so:

   "And the LORD heard the voice of your words, when ye spake unto me; and the LORD said unto me, I have heard the voice of the words of this people, which they have spoken unto thee: they have well said all that they have spoken. O that there were such an heart in them, that they would fear me, and keep all my commandments always, that it might be well with them, and with their children for ever!" (Dt.5:28-29).

   c. Note the great assurance given by the LORD to His dear servant Moses. The LORD promised to give him a *special manifestation* of God's presence. Why? So that people would believe Moses, both people who lived then and people of all time (v.9). What was the special manifestation? Right there on Mt. Sinai, every time God spoke to Moses, an astounding cosmic spectacle took place:
   ⇒ A dense, pitch black cloud hung over the mountain
   ⇒ Thunder roared
   ⇒ Lightning flashed
   ⇒ God's voice pierced and boomed forth from the cloud

   Again, God's purpose was to stir the people to believe Moses, to believe his testimony that the Ten Commandments and laws had come from God. They were truly the commandments of God.

   "Now all these things happened unto them for ensamples: and they are written for our admonition, upon whom the ends of the world are come" (1 Cor.10:11).

   "For whatsoever things were written aforetime were written for our learning, that we through patience and comfort of the scriptures might have hope" (Ro.15:4).

   "All scripture is given by inspiration of God, and is profitable for doctrine, for reproof, for correction, for instruction in righteousness" (2 Tim.3:16).

   "For the prophecy came not in old time by the will of man: but holy men of God spake as they were moved by the Holy Ghost" (2 Pt.1:21).

   "The statutes of the LORD are right, rejoicing the heart: the commandment of the LORD is pure, enlightening the eyes" (Ps.19:8).

   "I have chosen the way of truth: thy judgments have I laid before me" (Ps.119:30).

   "Behold, I have longed after thy precepts: quicken me in thy righteousness" (Ps.119:40).

   "Thy words were found, and I did eat them; and thy word was unto me the joy and rejoicing of mine heart: for I am called by thy name, O LORD God of hosts" (Jer.15:16).

   "Ye shall not add unto the word which I command you, neither shall ye diminish ought from it, that ye may keep the commandments of the LORD your God which I command you" (Dt.4:2).

   "What thing soever I command you, observe to do it: thou shalt not add thereto, nor diminish from it" (Dt.12:32).

DEEPER STUDY # 1

(19:5-6) Mosaic Covenant--Abrahamic Covenant--Believer, Life and Walk: the Mosaic covenant is a continuation of God's covenant with His people, a continuation of the Abrahamic covenant. Remember, in ancient history the whole world had forsaken God. Few if any people were totally following God (see outlines and notes--Gen.11:10-32). Thus God had chosen one man and given him the great promises of God. That man was Abraham. God called Abraham to forsake the world, to believe God, and to seek the great promises of God. If Abraham forsook the world and believed God, diligently seeking God's promises, then God would fulfill the promises in the lives of Abraham's descendents. There were three great promises given to Abraham:

⇒ the promise of the promised land, the land of Canaan (a symbol of heaven).
⇒ the promise that Abraham would be a blessing to all the nations of the earth, meaning that the Savior and Messiah of the world would come through his descendents and bless the whole world.
⇒ the promise of the promised seed, meaning both a multitude of descendents who would become a great nation of people and the promised seed of the Messiah (cp. Gal.3:16).

That great nation of people was Israel. There at Mt. Sinai, God was ready to expand and enlarge His covenant given to Abraham.

⇒ God called Abraham to believe Him and to seek the great promises of God.
⇒ God called Israel to obey Him and to become two things: the holy people of God and His witnesses to the world.

Simply stated, the Mosaic covenant was simply a continuation of the Abrahamic covenant. The following chart shows both the connection and the additional items of the Mosaic covenant.

The call/challenge	The promises
Abrahamic Covenant (Gen.12:1-3; Acts 3:12; Gal.3:6-8; Gal.3:16)	⇒ God's people would inherit the promised land ⇒ God's people would be a blessing to the entire world, meaning that the Messiah and Savior of the world would come through his descendents and bless the whole world ⇒ God's people would bear the promised seed, both a great nation of people and the Savior and Messiah

The call/challenge	The promises
Mosaic Covenant (Ex.19:5-6)	⇒ God's people would become the special people of God ⇒ God's people would become a holy nation, marked as the true followers of the only living and true God, a nation set apart to follow God in all righteousness and godliness ⇒ God's people would become a kingdom of priests, the witnesses of God to the world

Note this significant fact: the Abrahamic covenant pictures *salvation* and the Mosaic covenant pictures the *believers' life and walk*.

1. The Abrahamic covenant pictures salvation: if a person forsakes the world, believes God, and diligently seeks the promises of God...
 • he inherits the promised land
 • he blesses the world by possessing Christ, by following Christ, and by offering Christ to the world
 • he *bears seed*, a number of spiritual descendents who become believers

2. The Mosaic covenant pictures the believer's life and walk: if a person obeys God...
 • he becomes a special person, a valuable treasure to the Lord, a person marked as a follower of the only living and true God
 • he becomes a holy person, a member of the holy nation of God
 • he becomes a king and a priest to God, a witness for God to the whole world

Another significant fact needs to be noted at this point: Scripture refers to the Mosaic Covenant as the "old" or "first" covenant. The "old covenant" is often contrasted with the "new covenant" established by Christ. Ronald Youngblood says this about the two covenants:

"Our Bible is divided into two Testaments: Old and New. The word for 'testament' can also be translated 'covenant,' a term that implies significant and intimate relationship between two parties (whether collective or individual). Many Scripture passages compare and contrast the 'old' or 'first' covenant with the 'new covenant' (see, for example, Jer.31:31-34; Heb.9:15-22). Although the Bible (particularly the Old Testament) describes many covenants in detail, the terms *old covenant* and *first covenant* always refer to the one we are about to study, the Mosaic (Sinaitic) covenant (see especially 2 Cor.3:14-15; Heb.9:15-20), the most important of the older covenants. The Old Testament, then, is basically the story of redemption ratified by the 'old covenant' (the Mosaic covenant), and the New Testament is basically the story of redemption ratified by the 'new covenant' (instituted by Jesus during the Last Supper; see Luke 22:20). Both covenants become effective only through the shedding of blood (Exod.24:8; Matt.26:28)."[3]

---

[3] Ronald F. Youngblood. *Exodus.* (Chicago, IL: Moody Press, 1983), p.90-91.

3 (19:10) **Sanctification--Consecration--Set Apart--Separation--Purity**: there was the call to sanctification. The word "sanctification" means to be consecrated, totally given over to God; to be separated from the pollutions of the world and committed to God and His service; to be pure, clean, righteous, holy before God.

Note how the people were to *sanctify* and *consecrate* themselves: they were to wash their clothes. While washing and cleaning their clothes, they were to be meditating upon *sanctification*, upon asking God to cleanse them from the sins and pollutions of this world.

The point is this: God was preparing His people to receive His covenant, preparing His people to make a total commitment to Him. One of the first steps to commitment is *sanctification or consecration*. Before God could give His covenant to His people, before the people could be totally committed to God, they had to be *sanctified, consecrated*: cleansed from all sin, from all the pollutions and contaminations of this world.

> "For I *am* the LORD your God: ye shall therefore sanctify yourselves, and ye shall be holy; for I *am* holy: neither shall ye defile yourselves with any manner of creeping thing that creepeth upon the earth" (Lev. 11:44).
>
> "And Joshua said unto the people, Sanctify yourselves: for to morrow the LORD will do wonders among you" (Josh. 3:5).
>
> "Sanctify them through thy truth: thy word is truth" (Jn.17:17).
>
> "And for their sakes I sanctify myself, that they also might be sanctified through the truth" (Jn. 17:19).
>
> "Husbands, love your wives, even as Christ also loved the church, and gave himself for it; That he might sanctify and cleanse it with the washing of water by the word" (Eph.5:25-26).
>
> "For this is the will of God, *even* your sanctification, that ye should abstain from fornication: That every one of you should know how to possess his vessel in sanctification and honour" (1 Th.4:3-4).
>
> "And the very God of peace sanctify you wholly; and *I pray God* your whole spirit and soul and body be preserved blameless unto the coming of our Lord Jesus Christ" (1 Th.5:23).
>
> "Let no man despise thy youth; but be thou an example of the believers, in word, in conversation [behavior, conduct], in charity, in spirit, in faith, in purity" (1 Tim.4:12).
>
> "But sanctify the Lord God in your hearts: and *be* ready always to *give* an answer to every man that asketh you a reason of the hope that is in you with meekness and fear" (1 Pt.3:15).

4 (19:11-16) **Holiness, of God--Reverence--Fear, of God--Awe--Sex--Sanctification**: there was the call to reverence and to fear God's holy presence. God is holy; that is, God is totally different, separated and set apart from everything else. He is set apart in person, being, purity, righteousness, and perfection from the universe and from all that is in the universe. God is totally different and set apart. He is the Sovereign Lord and Majesty of the universe, the Creator and Sustainer of all that is or has ever been or ever will be. God is Light--pure Light--before whom no person or thing could ever stand apart from His will, not without being consumed. Note how God called His people to reverence and to fear His holy presence.

1. God demanded that the people be ready to meet Him. Why? His holy presence was to descend down upon Mt. Sinai on the third day in the sight of all the people (v.11).

2. God demanded that His holy presence be acknowledged and respected (v.12-13). How?
   ⇒ Boundaries were to be set around the mountain, and the people were not to cross the boundaries (v.12). The boundary pictured the *great distance* between God and man, the *great gulf* that separates God and man. Any person who crossed the boundary--any person who violated and did not reverence and fear God's holy presence--was to be executed, put to death (v.13).

3. God had demanded that the people *sanctify* and *consecrate* themselves. Note that they followed through with His demand: they washed their clothes, obviously asking God to cleanse their hearts while they washed their clothes (v.14).

4. God demanded that the people focus totally upon Him. Note how He secured their full attention: they had to abstain from sexual relations during the three days of preparation for God's descent from the mountain (v.15).

> **Thought 1**. God is holy. Consequently, one of the great duties of man is that we reverence and fear His holiness. Any person who curses and denies God is going to face a holy and just God some day. But in addition, any person who shows disrespect and irreverence--who does not fear God in all His majestic being and holiness--will also face a holy, just God in the day of judgment.
>
> God is so high above man that we cannot even conceive the distance that separates us. Our understanding of God--even with the revelation of Scripture and of the Lord Jesus Christ--amounts to no more than a thimble full of water compared to the seas of the earth. Think about the universe--how vast and enormous--yet God's presence and power extend out beyond the universe.
>
> Man must reverence and fear God. If not, we can expect nothing but the terrifying wrath of the holy, just God. God is love, yes; Jesus Christ showed us that God is love. But the cross, where Jesus Christ bore the sins of the world because of God's holiness and justice, shows us that God dwells in perfect holiness and perfect justice. If God's holiness judged His very own Son for the sins of the world, then no person must ever think that God's holiness will not judge him.
>
> > "Who *is* like unto thee, O LORD, among the gods? who *is* like thee, glorious in holiness, fearful *in* praises, doing wonders?" (Ex.15:11).
> >
> > "And when he had consulted with the people, he appointed singers unto the LORD, and that should praise the beauty of holiness, as they went out before the army, and to say, Praise the LORD; for his mercy *endureth* for ever" (2 Chron.20:21).
> >
> > "God reigneth over the heathen: God sitteth upon the throne of his holiness" (Ps.47:8).

"God is greatly to be feared in the assembly of the saints, and to be had in reverence of all *them that are* about him" (Ps.89:7).

"O worship the LORD in the beauty of holiness: fear before him, all the earth" (Ps.96:9).

"And an highway shall be there, and a way, and it shall be called The way of holiness; the unclean shall not pass over it; but it *shall be* for those: the wayfaring men, though fools, shall not err *therein*" (Is.35:8).

"There is no fear of God before their eyes" (Ro.3:18).

"Having therefore these promises, dearly beloved, let us cleanse ourselves from all filthiness of the flesh and spirit, perfecting holiness in the fear of God" (2 Cor.7:1).

"Submitting yourselves one to another in the fear of God" (Eph. 5:21).

"Wherefore we receiving a kingdom which cannot be moved, let us have grace, whereby we may serve God acceptably with reverence and godly fear" (Heb.12:28).

5 (19:16-25) **Mediator--Gulf, Between God and Man--Nature**: there was the call to approach God only through His appointed mediator. The memorable day now happened; the appointed day for the glory of God's presence to descend upon the mountain now arrived.

1. The glory of God's presence descended upon Mt. Sinai. The people trembled before God: they stood in awe, reverence, and fear, astounded at the spectacle they were witnessing (v.16). It all happened in the morning, probably early morning. Apparently, the most spectacular storm imaginable was taking place upon the mountain. The storm was filled with the loudest roar and rumble of thunder imaginable and the brightest flashes of lightning ever seen. Most of the people had probably been awakened by the rumble of thunder and the bright flashes of lightning. Scripture describes the scene best: in the morning there was...

- thunder and lightning
- a thick cloud upon the mountain
- the loud blast of a trumpet
- all the people trembling

The storm was so ferocious that no person dared approach the mountain. Everyone was stricken with a deep sense of awe: a cosmic event was taking place; a spectacular stormy cloud was descending upon the mountain. Standing there witnessing what Moses had been telling them--that God was going to descend upon the mountain in three days--everyone was stricken not only with awe and reverence, but with a dreadful sense of fear.

2. This points to the need for a mediator between God and man. A mediator was an absolute essential (v.17). The Israelites would not approach the mountain, not without Moses, not with sharp lightning flashing every second and thunder roaring so loudly that the earth itself shook under its rumblings. People who live in areas where thunderstorms are a common happening know how dangerous such storms are. Just imagine the most spectacular thunderstorm ever to occur upon earth: it took place when the glory of God's holy presence descended upon Mt. Sinai.

The point is this: there was a great gulf between God's holy presence and man. The laser-like brightness of God's holiness would have consumed any person who dared to approach God. God was clearly demonstrating the truth of His holiness and the utter necessity for man to approach Him through a mediator. (See note, pt.4--Ex.19:11-16 for more discussion.) The only way any Israelite could approach God was through His appointed mediator, Moses. A mediator between God and man is an absolute essential.

MT. SINAI or MT. HOREB [4]

---

[4] *Life Application* ® Bible (c) 1988, 1989, 1990, 1991 by Tyndale House Publishers, Inc., Wheaton, IL 60189. Used by permission. All rights reserved.

3. Note that six reasons are given why man must approach God through His appointed mediator (v.18-25).
   a. A mediator is necessary because of God's holy presence (v.18). Note that a volcanic eruption and an earthquake are being described. Both heaven and earth were involved in the spectacular display of God's holy presence descending upon Mt. Sinai. Again, picture the scene as the people drew near and stood at the foot of the mountain. There was the most violent storm ever seen raging around the mountain:
      ⇒ the deep roar and rumbling of constant thunder (v.16).
      ⇒ the brightest, sharpest, and most spectacular flashes of lightning, no doubt flashing every second or two in a continuous display of light (v.16).
      ⇒ a dense, pitch black cloud hung over the mountain (v.16). Fire and smoke blazed up out of the mountain as though blazing out of a huge fiery furnace (18).
      ⇒ the whole mountain was shaking and trembling violently (v.18).
      ⇒ the continuous blast of the trumpet was growing louder and louder (v.19).

      The people were just as we would be if faced with the most violent thunderstorms, life-threatening earthquakes, or volcanic eruptions: they were trembling and stricken with a terrifying fear. But the experience was teaching them a valuable lesson: God is holy and righteous as well as good and loving.
      ⇒ God expects His law, His commandments, to be kept.
      ⇒ God has the power to judge and punish men if man does not obey Him and keep His commandments.
      ⇒ God can never be approached unless God allows man to approach Him.

   b. A mediator is necessary because God speaks only through His appointed mediator (v.20). Note that Moses alone was called by God to come up the mountain.
   c. A mediator is necessary because the holy presence of God must be reverenced (v.21). When the people saw Moses walk up the mountain into the raging storm, some of them apparently became so exited over the possibility of experiencing the glory of God that they were about to rush up the mountain behind Moses. Note what would have happened: they would have been stricken dead. God's presence and holiness are to be reverenced and respected. The only person who can enter God's presence--the mediator--is the person appointed by Him.
   d. A mediator is necessary because even the priests were unclean and worthy of judgment (v.22). Unless they were sanctified or consecrated, they too would be stricken dead. No person, not even priests, must ever approach God by any means other than through the mediator God has appointed.
   e. A mediator is necessary because the very earth itself was unclean (v.23). Note that the mountain itself had to be set apart as holy unto God. A boundary had to be set around the mountain and the land given over totally to God. No person was to cross the boundary, no person except God's appointed mediator.
   f. A mediator is necessary because everyone must approach God through His appointed mediator (v.24). Note that God told Moses to bring Aaron up the mountain with him. Why? God was soon to set Aaron and his tribe apart as the priests of Israel. Calling him up to the mountain with Moses would set him apart in the eyes of the people. Note that anyone other than God's appointed mediator would be killed if they violated God's holy presence.

   Thought 1. God calls every person to approach Him through His appointed mediator. For Israel, that mediator was Moses. For us, the mediator is the Lord Jesus Christ, the Son of God Himself. Since the coming of the promised seed--the Savior and Messiah of the world, the Son of God Himself--no person can approach God except through His Son, the Lord Jesus Christ.

   "Jesus saith unto him, I am the way, the truth, and the life: no man cometh unto the Father, but by me" (Jn.14:6).
   "Neither is there salvation in any other: for there is none other name under heaven given among men, whereby we must be saved" (Acts 4:12).
   "Wherefore then *serveth* the law? It was added because of transgressions, till the seed should come to whom the promise was made; *and it was* ordained by angels in the hand of a mediator. Now a mediator is not *a mediator* of one, but God is one" (Gal. 3:19-20).
   "For *there is* one God, and one mediator between God and men, the man Christ Jesus" (1 Tim.2:5).
   "But now hath he obtained a more excellent ministry, by how much also he is the mediator of a better covenant, which was established upon better promises" (Heb. 8:6).
   "And for this cause he is the mediator of the new testament, that by means of death, for the redemption of the transgressions *that were* under the first testament, they which are called might receive the promise of eternal inheritance" (Heb. 9:15).
   "And to Jesus the mediator of the new covenant, and to the blood of sprinkling, that speaketh better things than *that of* Abel" (Heb.12:24).
   "My little children, these things write I unto you, that ye sin not. And if any man sin, we have an advocate [mediator] with the Father, Jesus Christ the righteous" (1 Jn.2:1).

THE LAW AND THE PROMISES OF GOD (THE MOSAIC COVENANT) (PART 2): THE TEN COMMANDMENTS--NECESSARY LAWS TO GOVERN MAN AND SOCIETY, 20:1-26

(20:1-26) **DIVISION OVERVIEW--Commandments, The Ten**: the most important document ever written is *the Ten Commandments*. The influence of the Ten Commandments upon nations and societies could never be measured; indeed the importance of the Ten Commandments can never be overstressed. For this reason, the Ten Commandments need to be looked at as a whole before they are studied in detail. The <u>Preacher's Outline & Sermon Bible</u>® outlines and discusses each commandment separately for those who wish to preach or teach a series on the Ten Commandments. For those who wish to preach or teach just two or perhaps three messages on the Ten Commandments, the following overall outline is given as an aid.

1. **The basis of the 10 commandments**
   a. God's existence: "And God"
   b. God's Word: "God spoke," (v.1)
   c. God's name: The LORD
   d. God's relationship with man: "Your God"
   e. God's salvation, deliverance
2. **Com. 1 concerns** *God's being*: **Have no other gods** *whatsoever*
3. **Com. 2 concerns** *God's worship*: **Do not make, worship, or serve any idol whatsoever**
   a. The commandment forbids the making of any idols: Things in heaven, earth, or water
   b. The reasons
      1) God is a jealous God
      2) The influence & result of idolatry is passed down from fathers to children

      3) The influence of loving & obeying God lasts for a thousand generations

4. **Com. 3 concerns** *God's name*: **Do not misuse the LORD'S name**
   a. He is the LORD your God
   b. He will hold you accountable
5. **Com. 4 concerns** *God's day*: **Keep the Sabbath day holy**
   a. The commandment:
      1) Work for six days
      2) Rest & worship on the

A. The Ten Commandments (Part 1): The Laws Governing Man's Duty to God, Ex.20:1-11

And God spake all these words, saying,
2 I am the LORD thy God, which have brought thee out of the land of Egypt, out of the house of bondage.
3 Thou shalt have no other gods before me.
4 Thou shalt not make unto thee any graven image, or any likeness of any thing that is in heaven above, or that is in the earth beneath, or that is in the water under the earth:
5 Thou shalt not bow down thyself to them, nor serve them: for I the LORD thy God am a jealous God, visiting the iniquity of the fathers upon the children unto the third and fourth generation of them that hate me;
6 And showing mercy unto thousands of them that love me, and keep my commandments.
7 Thou shalt not take the name of the LORD thy God in vain; for the LORD will not hold him guiltless that taketh his name in vain.
8 Remember the sabbath day, to keep it holy.
9 Six days shalt thou labour, and do all thy work:
10 But the seventh day is

the sabbath of the LORD thy God: in it thou shalt not do any work, thou, nor thy son, nor thy daughter, thy manservant, nor thy maidservant, nor thy cattle, nor thy stranger that is within thy gates:
11 For in six days the LORD made heaven and earth, the sea, and all that in them is, and rested the seventh day: wherefore the LORD blessed the sabbath day, and hallowed it.

B. The Ten Commandments (Part 2): The Law Governing Man's Duty To Others, Ex.20:12-17

12 Honour thy father and thy mother: that thy days may be long upon the land which the LORD thy God giveth thee.
13 Thou shalt not kill.
14 Thou shalt not commit adultery.
15 Thou shalt not steal.
16 Thou shalt not bear false witness against thy neighbour.
17 Thou shalt not covet thy neighbour's house, thou shalt not covet thy neighbour's wife, nor his manservant, nor his maidservant, nor his ox, nor his ass, nor any thing that is thy neighbour's.

seventh day
b. The reasons
   1) Because the 7th day is the Lord's: No work whatsoever is to be done on the Sabbath, not by anyone

   2) Because the Lord created the universe in six days, & then rested on the seventh day
   3) Because the Lord blessed the seventh day & made it holy

1. **Com. 5 concerns** *man's parents*: **Honor your father & mother**
   a. Helps one to live longer
   b. Helps one to inherit the promised land
2. **Com. 6 concerns** *man's life*
3. **Com. 7 concerns** *man's family*: **Forbids adultery**
4. **Com. 8 concerns** *man's property*
5. **Com. 9 concerns** *man's word*: **Forbids lying or speaking falsely against anyone**
6. **Com. 10 concerns** *man's desires & security*: **Forbids coveting anything that belongs to your neighbor—his house, wife, servant, workers, animals, or anything else**

	C. The Purposes For the Law: Why God Gave the Ten Commandments & the Law, Ex.20:18-26		
1. To reveal the glorious majesty & holiness of God: Showing that a great barrier--a great gulf--exists between man and God	18 And all the people saw the thunderings, and the lightnings, and the noise of the trumpet, and the mountain smoking: and when the people saw it, they removed, and stood afar off.	22 And the LORD said unto Moses, Thus thou shalt say unto the children of Israel, Ye have seen that I have talked with you from heaven. 23 Ye shall not make with me gods of silver, neither shall ye make unto you gods of gold.	**4. To teach that God alone is the LORD:** He alone has truly revealed Himself, has spoken to man from heaven
2. To reveal man's need for a mediator, for a person who can approach God in behalf of man **3. To test man** a. To see if man will walk in the fear & reverence of God b. To see if man will truly obey God & not sin c. To see if man will trust the mediator appointed by God	19 And they said unto Moses, Speak thou with us, and we will hear: but let not God speak with us, lest we die. 20 And Moses said unto the people, Fear not: for God is come to prove you, and that his fear may be before your faces, that ye sin not. 21 And the people stood afar off, and Moses drew near unto the thick darkness where God was.	24 An altar of earth thou shalt make unto me, and shalt sacrifice thereon thy burnt offerings, and thy peace offerings, thy sheep, and thine oxen: in all places where I record my name I will come unto thee, and I will bless thee. 25 And if thou wilt make me an altar of stone, thou shalt not build it of hewn stone: for if thou lift up thy tool upon it, thou hast polluted it. 26 Neither shalt thou go up by steps unto mine altar, that thy nakedness be not discovered thereon.	**5. To teach how God alone is to be approached & worshipped** a. No idolatry: No gods whatsoever are to be made or worshipped b. No pageantry: 1) The altar of worship was to be of earth: A non-showy, non-costly material provided (created) by God alone 2) The altar of worship was to be made of natural, undressed stones: A material provided by God, not defiled & polluted by man c. No unrefined behavior: The altar was not to have steps that would expose a person's nakedness (symbolized self-righteousness, man ascending up to God)

1.   The Ten Commandments have influenced the world and the civil laws of nations more than any other document ever devised. Maxie Dunnam says this:

"I doubt if any document has influenced Western culture to the degree that the Ten Commandments have. In Western civilization, they have a position of inescapable significance. For Jews, Roman Catholics, and Protestants, this is the only formulation of religious principles held in common. In many Christian churches, knowledge of the Ten Commandments is a requirement for membership. The civil law of many lands has rootage in this covenant law of God given at Sinai"[1]

2.   The Ten Commandments are called by several names throughout the Bible.
   a.   In the Old Testament the Ten Commandments are referred to as…
      •   The *Ten Commandments* or *Ten Words* (the literal translation of the Hebrew) or the *Decalogue* (the literal Greek term for the Ten Commandments).

   "And he was there with the LORD forty days and forty nights; he did neither eat bread, nor drink water. And he wrote upon the tables the words of the covenant, the Ten commandments" (Ex.34:28).
   "And he declared unto you his covenant, which he commanded you to perform, even Ten commandments [ten words, decalogue]; and he wrote them upon two tables of stone" (Dt.4:13).
   "And he wrote on the tables, according to the first writing, the Ten commandments, which the LORD spake unto you in the mount out of the midst of the fire in the day of the assembly: and the LORD gave them unto me" (Dt.10:4).

      •   The Words of the covenant.

   "And he was there with the LORD forty days and forty nights; he did neither eat bread, nor drink water. And he wrote upon the tables the words of the covenant, the Ten commandments" (Ex.34:28).

      •   The Words spoken by the LORD (Jehovah, Yahweh)

   "And God spake all these words, saying" (Ex.20:1).
   "And the LORD said unto Moses, Write thou these words: for after the tenor of these words I have made a covenant with thee and with Israel" (Ex.34:27).
   "These words the LORD spake unto all your assembly in the mount out of the midst of the fire, of the cloud, and of the thick darkness, with a great voice: and he added no more. And he wrote them in two tables of stone, and delivered them unto me" (Dt.5:22).

---

[1]   Maxie Dunnam. *Mastering The Old Testament, Volume 2: Exodus.* (Dallas, TX: Word Publishing, 1987), p.247.

"And I will write on the tables the words that were in the first tables which brakest, and thou shalt put them in the ark" (Dt.10:2)

- The testimony of God

"As the LORD commanded Moses, so Aaron laid it up before the Testimony, to be kept" (Ex.16:34).
"And thou shalt put into the ark the testimony which I shall give thee" (Ex.25:16).

- The two tablets of stone

"And the LORD said unto Moses, Come up to me into the mount, and be there: and I will give thee tables of stone, and a law, and commandments which I have written; that thou mayest teach them" (Ex.24:12).
"And he gave unto Moses, when he had made an end of communing with him upon mount Sinai, two tables of testimony, tables of stone, written with the finger of God" (Ex.31:18).
"And Moses turned, and went down from the mount, and the two tables of the testimony were in his hand: the tables were written on both their sides; on the one side and on the other were they written. And the tables were the work of God, and the writing was the writing of God, graven upon the tables" (Ex.32:15-16).
"And the LORD delivered unto me two tables of stone written with the finger of God; and on them was written according to all the words, which the LORD spake with you in the mount out of the midst of the fire in the day of the assembly" (Dt.9:10).
"And I took the two tables, and cast them out of my two hands, and brake them before your eyes" (Dt.9:17).

b. In the New Testament the Ten Commandments are simply referred to as "commandments":

"And he said unto him, Why callest thou me good? [there is] none good but one, [that is], God: but if thou wilt enter into life, keep the commandments. He saith unto him, Which? Jesus said, Thou shalt do no murder, Thou shalt not commit adultery, Thou shalt not steal, Thou shalt not bear false witness, Honour thy father and [thy] mother: and, Thou shalt love thy neighbour as thyself" (Mt.19:17-19).
"Honour thy father and mother; (which is the first commandment with promise;)" (Eph.6:2).

3. The Bible does not number the Ten Commandments; consequently, they are numbered differently by different commentators.
⇒ The verses concerning God and idols, verses 3-6, are combined as one commandment by some commentators (primarily Lutherans and Roman Catholics). When these are combined, the commandment concerning coveting (v.17) is usually split into two commandments. The first sentence of verse 17 is counted as the ninth commandment, and the rest of the verse is counted as the tenth commandment. The ninth and tenth commandments would then look like this:
   9. Thou shalt not covet thy neighbour's house
   10. Thou shalt not covet thy neighbour's wife, nor his manservant, nor his maidservant, nor his ox, nor his ass, nor any thing that is thy neighbour's.

4. The Ten Commandments are repeated in the New Testament.
   1. Commandment 1 concerning God's being: have no other gods whatsoever (Acts 14:15; 1 Cor.10:14; 1 Jn.5:21)
   2. Commandment 2 concerning God's worship: do not make, worship, nor serve any idol whatsoever (Acts 17:29; Ro.1:22-23; 1 Jn.5:21; 1 Cor.10:7, 14).
   3. Commandment 3 concerning God's name: do not misuse the LORD'S name (Jas.5:12; Mt.5:33-37; 6:5-9).
   4. Commandment 4 concerning God's day: keep the Sabbath day holy. This is not repeated anywhere in the New Testament, but Christ observed the Sabbath and New Testament believers kept the LORD's Day (Mk.1:21; 6:2; Lk.4:16; Acts 17:2; 18:4; Heb.10:25).
   5. Commandment 5 concerning man's parents: honor your father and mother (Mt.19:18-19; Eph.6:1-4).
   6. Commandment 6 concerning man's life: prohibits murder (1 Jn.3:15; Mt.5:21-22; 19:18-19).
   7. Commandment 7 concerning man's family: forbids adultery (Mt.5:27-28; 19:18-19; 1 Cor.5:1-13; 6:9-20; Heb.13:4).
   8. Commandment 8 concerning man's property: prohibits stealing (Mt.19:18-19; Eph.4:28; 2 Th.3:10-12; Jas.5:1-4).
   9. Commandment 9 concerning man's word: forbids lying or speaking falsely against anyone (Mt.19:18-19; Col.3:9; Eph.4:25).
   10. Commandment 10 concerning man's security: forbids coveting anything that belongs to your neighbor--his house, wife, servant, workers, animals, or anything else (Mt.19:18-19; Eph.5:3; Lk.12:15-21).

5.   The New Testament gives several summaries of the commandments.

> **"He saith unto him, Which? Jesus said, Thou shalt do no murder, Thou shalt not commit adultery, Thou shalt not steal, Thou shalt not bear false witness, Honour thy father and [thy] mother: and, Thou shalt love thy neighbour as thyself" (Mt.19:18-19; cp. Mk.10:18-19; Lk.18:18-19).**

> **"Owe no man any thing, but to love one another: for he that loveth another hath fulfilled the law. For this, Thou shalt not commit adultery, Thou shalt not kill, Thou shalt not steal, Thou shalt not bear false witness, Thou shalt not covet; and if there be any other commandment, it is briefly comprehended in this saying, namely, Thou shalt love thy neighbour as thyself. Love worketh no ill to his neighbour: therefore love is the fulfilling of the law" (Ro.13:8-10).**

6.   It is important to note the form of the Ten Commandments, just how they are written. Note these facts:
   a.   The Ten Commandments are stated as *moral absolutes*. They absolutely must be kept. There is no equivocation and no conditions attached to the commandments--no *ifs, ands,* or *buts.* The commandments are to be kept.
   b.   The Ten Commandments are written in the second person singular, *"you."* This means that the Ten Commandments apply to you, the individual, as well as to you, a community or society of people.
   c.   The commandments fall into a natural division:
      ⇒ The first four commandments concern *man's relationship to God.*
      ⇒ The next six commandments concern *man's relationship to others.*

7.   Eight of the Ten Commandments are stated negatively, and two commandments are stated positively. Note that the eight negative commandments imply the positive and the two positive commandments imply the negative. The commandments even arouse the mind to immediately think of the opposite statement. This was obviously the very reason God stated the commandments so simply. A double focus or imprint is made upon the mind, both a negative and positive emphasis when the commandments are read.
   a.   "You shall have no other gods before me" (Ex.20:3) implies that "you shall believe and follow the only living and true God, the LORD Himself."
   b.   "You shall not make for yourself [worship] any graven image [idol]" (Ex.20:4-6) implies that "you shall worship only the LORD, Him and Him alone."
   c.   "You shall not take the name of the LORD your God in vain" (Ex.20:7) implies that "you shall always honor the name of the LORD your God."
   d.   "Remember the Sabbath day to keep it holy" (Ex.20:8-11) implies that "you shall not neglect nor abuse the Sabbath day."
   e.   "Honor you father and your mother" (Ex.20:12) implies that "you shall not mistreat your father and mother."
   f.   "You shall not kill" (Ex.20:13) implies that "you shall respect and reverence life."
   g.   "You shall not commit adultery" (Ex.20:14) implies that "you shall be sexually moral and faithful."
   h.   "You shall not steal" (Ex.20:15) implies that "you shall be honest."
   i.   "You shall not bear false witness" (Ex.20:16) implies that "you shall never lie."
   j.   "You shall not covet (Ex.20:17) implies that "you shall be content with that you have."

8.   Jesus Christ taught that the Ten Commandments are timeless and universal laws: they are given to all people of all nations for all time. Everyone is to keep the Ten Commandments. The Ten Commandments are to underlie all civil laws of a nation.
   How about Christian believers: Are we required to keep the Ten Commandments? Are we not saved by grace and not by law? Yes, we are saved by grace, but the Ten Commandments are still binding upon us. Jesus Christ made this clear time and again.
   a.   Jesus Christ declared that He came to fulfill the law, not destroy (abolish) it.

> **"Think not that I am come to destroy the law, or the prophets: I am not come to destroy, but to fulfil" (Mt.5:17).**

   What does this mean? It means that Jesus Christ embraced the law, kept and fulfilled it. As such, He embodies the law and so much more. Therefore, the person who follows Jesus Christ embraces and keeps the Ten Commandments. For example, the person who follows Jesus Christ does not steal, nor kill, nor commit adultery, nor break any of the other commandments.
   The person who follows Jesus Christ focuses upon Jesus Christ not the law. He looks to Christ, focuses upon Him, seeking to live a righteous and godly life just as Christ lived a righteous and godly life. By so doing, the believer keeps the law and fulfills it. In fact, when the believer follows Jesus Christ, he keeps the Ten Commandments and a whole lot more. (See notes--Mt.5:17-18; Deeper Study # 2--Mt.5:17 for more discussion. Also see note, pt.2--Ex.20:3.)
   b.   Jesus Christ condensed the law in one simple statement:

> **"Therefore all things whatsoever ye would that men should do to you, do ye even so to them: for this is the law and the prophets" (Mt.7:12).**

   c.   Jesus Christ said that love is the basis of the law, that the law can be summarized in two commandments:

> **"Then one of them, which was a lawyer, asked him a question, tempting him, and saying, Master, which is the great commandment in the law? Jesus said unto him, Thou shalt love the Lord thy God with all thy heart, and with all thy soul, and with all thy mind.**

This is the first and great commandment. And the second [is] like unto it, Thou shalt love thy neighbour as thyself. On these two commandments hang all the law and the prophets" (Mt.22:35-40).

"And thou shalt love the LORD thy God with all thine heart, and with all thy soul, and with all thy might" (Dt.6:5).

"Thou shalt not avenge, nor bear any grudge against the children of thy people, but thou shalt love thy neighbour as thyself: I am the LORD" (Lev.19:18).

    d.   Jesus Christ enlarged the commandment to love our neighbors: He declared that His followers must love one another just as He loved them. How did Christ love us? Sacrificially, even to the point of dying for us.

"A new commandment I give unto you, That ye love one another; as I have loved you, that ye also love one another. By this shall all [men] know that ye are my disciples, if ye have love one to another" (Jn.13:34-35).

"This is my commandment, That ye love one another, as I have loved you. Greater love hath no man than this, that a man lay down his life for his friends" (Jn.15:12-13).

"These things I command you, that ye love one another" (Jn.15:17).

"And walk in love, as Christ also hath loved us, and hath given himself for us an offering and a sacrifice to God for a sweetsmelling savour" (Eph.5:2).

"Hereby perceive we the love of God, because he laid down his life for us: and we ought to lay down our lives for the brethren. But whoso hath this world's good, and seeth his brother have need, and shutteth up his bowels of compassion from him, how dwelleth the love of God in him? My little children, let us not love in word, neither in tongue; but in deed and in truth" (1 Jn.3:16-18).

The International Standard Bible Encyclopaedia says this:

"'Thou shalt love' is the first word and the last in the teaching of Our Lord. His teaching is positive rather than negative, and so simple that a child can understand it. For the Christian, the Decalogue [the Ten Commandments] is no longer the highest summary of human duty. He must ever read it with sincere respect as one of the great monuments of the love of God in the moral and religious education of mankind; but it has given place to the higher teaching of the Son of God."[2]

    e.   Jesus Christ declared that a person proves his love by obeying the commandments:

"He that hath my commandments, and keepeth them, he it is that loveth me: and he that loveth me shall be loved of my Father, and I will love him, and will manifest myself to him" (Jn.14:21).

"Jesus answered and said unto him, If a man love me, he will keep my words: and my Father will love him, and we will come unto him, and make our abode with him" (Jn.14:23).

"For this is the love of God, that we keep his commandments: and his commandments are not grievous" (1 Jn.5:3).

"Here is the patience of the saints: here are they that keep the commandments of God, and the faith of Jesus" (Rev.14:12).

9.   Jesus Christ obeyed the commandments, obeyed them perfectly. He was without sin; He never transgressed the commandments, not even once.

"And he made his grave with the wicked, and with the rich in his death; because he had done no violence, neither was any deceit in his mouth" (Is.53:9).

"Which of you convinceth me of sin? And if I say the truth, why do ye not believe me?" (Jn.8:46).

"For he hath made him to be sin for us, who knew no sin; that we might be made the righteousness of God in him" (2 Cor.5:21).

"For we have not an high priest which cannot be touched with the feeling of our infirmities; but was in all points tempted like as we are, yet without sin" (Heb.4:15).

"For such an high priest became us, who is holy, harmless, undefiled, separate from sinners, and made higher than the heavens" (Heb.7:26).

"Forasmuch as ye know that ye were not redeemed with corruptible things, as silver and gold, from your vain conversation received by tradition from your fathers; But with the precious blood of Christ, as of a lamb without blemish and without spot" (1 Pt.1:18-19).

"Who did no sin, neither was guile found in his mouth" (1 Pt.2:22).

10.   Jesus Christ expects us--all believers--to obey the Ten Commandments. He even expects believers to go beyond the Ten Commandments and do far more than just the rules laid down by the commandments. Note what He had to say about each of the commandments.

---

[2]   *The International Standard Bible Encyclopaedia*, Vol.V. (Grand Rapids, MI: Eerdmans Publishing Co., 1939), p.2946-2947.

a. Commandment 1: Jesus Christ declared that there is *only One LORD GOD* of the universe, and that we are to love Him with all our hearts, souls, and minds.

> **"Then one of them, which was a lawyer, asked him a question, tempting him, and saying, Master, which is the great commandment in the law? Jesus said unto him, Thou shalt love the Lord thy God with all thy heart, and with all thy soul, and with all thy mind. This is the first and great commandment. And the second [is] like unto it, Thou shalt love thy neighbour as thyself. On these two commandments hang all the law and the prophets"** (Mt.22:35-40).

b. Commandment 2: Jesus Christ declared that *God is Spirit*. Consequently, all the images of gods, whether created by the hands of people or simply existing in the imaginations of people, are but dead, helpless and false gods.

> **"God [is] a Spirit: and they that worship him must worship [him] in spirit and in truth"** (Jn.4:24).

c. Commandment 3: Jesus Christ declared that man is not to swear.

> **"But I say unto you, Swear not at all; neither by heaven; for it is God's throne: Nor by the earth; for it is his footstool: neither by Jerusalem; for it is the city of the great King. Neither shalt thou swear by thy head, because thou canst not make one hair white or black. But let your communication be, Yea, yea; Nay, nay: for whatsoever is more than these cometh of evil"** (Mt.5:34-37).

d. Commandment 4: Jesus Christ faithfully worshipped on the Sabbath, and He declared that we are to worship the LORD our God and Him alone.

> **"Then saith Jesus unto him, Get thee hence, Satan: for it is written, Thou shalt worship the Lord thy God, and him only shalt thou serve"** (Mt.4:10).
> **"And he came to Nazareth, where he had been brought up: and, as <u>his custom was</u>, he went into the synagogue on the sabbath day, and stood up for to read"** (Lk.4:16).

e. Commandment 5: Jesus Christ declared that man is always to honor father and mother even above vows and offerings and that man is never to curse father and mother.

> **"For God commanded, saying, Honour thy father and mother: and, He that curseth father or mother, let him die the death. But ye say, Whosoever shall say to [his] father or [his] mother, [It is] a gift, by whatsoever thou mightest be profited by me; And honour not his father or his mother, [he shall be free]. Thus have ye made the commandment of God of none effect by your tradition"** (Mt.15:4-6).

Jesus Christ also declared that the fifth commandment governing the honor of parents must be obeyed. He insisted that a person had to honor his father and mother in order to inherit eternal life.

> **"And when he was gone forth into the way, there came one running, and kneeled to him, and asked him, Good Master, what shall I do that I may inherit eternal life? And Jesus said unto him, Why callest thou me good? [there is] none good but one, [that is], God. Thou knowest the commandments, Do not commit adultery, Do not kill, Do not steal, Do not bear false witness, Defraud not, <u>Honour thy father and mother</u>"** (Mk.10:17-19).

f. Commandment 6: Jesus Christ declared that the law governing murder goes much deeper than the act itself: it covers the deep-seated feelings of unjustified anger.

> **"Ye have heard that it was said by them of old time, Thou shalt not kill; and whosoever shall kill shall be in danger of the judgment: But I say unto you, That whosoever is angry with his brother without a cause shall be in danger of the judgment: and whosoever shall say to his brother, Raca, shall be in danger of the council: but whosoever shall say, Thou fool, shall be in danger of hell fire"** (Mt.5:21-22).

Jesus Christ also declared that the sixth commandment governing murder must be obeyed: "Do not kill."

> **"Thou knowest the commandments, Do not commit adultery, <u>Do not kill</u>, Do not steal, Do not bear false witness, Defraud not, Honour thy father and mother"** (Mk.10:19).

g. Commandment 7: Jesus Christ declared that the law governing adultery goes much deeper than the act itself: it covers the feelings of lust within the human heart.

> **"Ye have heard that it was said by them of old time, Thou shalt not commit adultery: But I say unto you, That whosoever looketh on a woman to lust after her hath committed adultery with her already in his heart. And if thy right eye offend thee, pluck it out, and cast [it] from thee: for it is profitable for thee that one of thy members should perish, and not**

[that] thy whole body should be cast into hell. And if thy right hand offend thee, cut it off, and cast [it] from thee: for it is profitable for thee that one of thy members should perish, and not [that] thy whole body should be cast into hell. It hath been said, Whosoever shall put away his wife, let him give her a writing of divorcement: But I say unto you, That whosoever shall put away his wife, saving for the cause of fornication, causeth her to commit adultery: and whosoever shall marry her that is divorced committeth adultery" (Mt.5:27-32).

Jesus Christ also declared that the seventh commandment must be obeyed: "Do not commit adultery."

"Thou knowest the commandments, <u>Do not commit adultery</u>, Do not kill, Do not steal, Do not bear false witness, Defraud not, Honour thy father and mother" (Mk.10:19).

h. Commandment 8: Jesus Christ declared that the eighth commandment governing stealing must be obeyed: "Do not defraud."

"Thou knowest the commandments, Do not commit adultery, Do not kill, Do not steal, Do not bear false witness, <u>Defraud not</u>, Honour thy father and mother" (Mk.10:19).

i. Commandment 9: Jesus Christ not only upheld the ninth commandment against bearing false witness, He enlarged it to include…
   • evil thoughts
   • blasphemy
   • idle words

"Wherefore I say unto you, All manner of sin and <u>blasphemy</u> shall be forgiven unto men: but the blasphemy [against] the [Holy] Ghost shall not be forgiven unto men" (Mt.12:31).
"But I say unto you, That every <u>idle word</u> that men shall speak, they shall give account thereof in the day of judgment" (Mt.12:36).
"For out of the heart proceed evil thoughts, murders, adulteries, fornications, thefts, <u>false witness</u>, <u>blasphemies</u>" (Mt.15:19).
"Thou knowest the commandments, Do not commit adultery, Do not kill, Do not steal, <u>Do not bear false witness</u>, Defraud not, Honour thy father and mother" (Mk.10:19).

j. Commandment 10: Jesus Christ warned people against covetousness.

"And he said unto them, Take heed, and beware of covetousness: for a man's life consisteth not in the abundance of the things which he possesseth" (Lk.12:15; cp. v.16-21).

11. The Ten Commandments are meant for all people of all generations. They are not just religious records or archives limited to a particular sect of people. God's law has been placed in the heart, in the very conscience of every man, woman, and child--no matter what a person may claim. God has stamped a sense of morality deep into man's inner-most being. God's Word declares this fact:

"Which show the work of the law written in their hearts, their conscience also bearing witness, and their thoughts the mean while accusing or else excusing one another)" (Ro.2:15).

How the Ten Commandments are Outlined and Discussed

The Ten Commandments are being outlined as the Scripture dictates. But remember, several of the Ten Commandments are forcefully stated in one brief sentence. Because of this, in addition to the Scripture Outline, certain outline points of commandment two are being adopted for all the commandments. This is being done to help us in studying and understanding the commandments.

Moreover, our purpose is to give an overall discussion of the Ten Commandments, not to limit our discussion just to the brief statement of the commandment. Our purpose is to cover the full teaching of Scripture about each of the commandments. This is done with the conviction and hope that this study will be of far greater value to God's dear servants as they preach and teach His Holy Commandments to a society and world that is rapidly becoming lawless, immoral, perverted, and desensitized, losing all sense of conscience, all sense of right and wrong. Some or all of the following outline points are discussed for each of the Ten Commandments.
1. Who is to obey this commandment?
2. How long was this commandment to be in force? (Note: this point or question is sometimes combined with point one.)
3. What is forbidden by this commandment? or What is the charge of this commandment?
4. What is the decision demanded or required by this commandment?

In addition to these points, three <u>Deeper Studies</u> are included for each commandment:
⇒ A Deeper Study on *The Biblical Consequences of Breaking This Commandment.*
⇒ A Deeper Study on *The Biblical Benefits of Keeping This Commandment.*
⇒ A Deeper Study on *Jesus Christ and His Teaching Concerning This Commandment.*

DIVISION VII

THE LAW AND THE PROMISES OF GOD (THE MOSAIC COVENANT) (PART 2): THE TEN COMMANDMENTS--NECESSARY LAWS TO GOVERN MAN AND SOCIETY, 20:1-26

A. The Great Basis of the Ten Commandments: The Person and Work of God Himself, Ex.20:1-2

B. The Ten Commandments, The Laws Governing Man's Duty to God (Part 1): Commandment One Concerns God's Being--Never Believe in False Gods, Ex.20:3

C. The Ten Commandments, The Laws Governing Man's Duty to God (Part 2): Commandment Two Concerns The Worship of God--Never Make Nor Worship False Gods, Ex.20:4-6

D. The Ten Commandments, The Laws Governing Man's Duty to God (Part 3): Commandment Three Concerns God's Name--Never Misuse God's Name; Never Use Profanity or Vulgarity, Ex.20:7

E. The Ten Commandments, The Laws Governing Man's Duty to God (Part 4): Commandment Four Concerns *God's Day*--Never Fail to Observe the Sabbath, to Keep it Holy, Ex.20:8-11

F. The Ten Commandments, The Laws Governing Man's Duty To Others (Part 1): Commandment Five Concerns the Family--Never Dishonor Parents, Ex.20:12

G. The Ten Commandments, The Laws Governing Man's Duty To Others (Part 2): Commandment Six Concerns Man's Life--Never Kill, Ex.20:13

H. The Ten Commandments, The Laws Governing Man's Duty To Others (Part 3): Commandment Seven Concerns Man's Family--Never Commit Adultery or Immorality, Ex.20:14

I. The Ten Commandments, The Laws Governing Man's Duty To Others (Part 4): Commandment Eight Concerns Man's Property--Never Steal, Ex.20:15

J. The Ten Commandments, The Laws Governing Man's Duty To Others (Part 5): Commandment Nine Concerns Man's Word and Character--Never Lie, Ex.20:16

K. The Ten Commandments, The Laws Governing Man's Duty To Others (Part 6): Commandment Ten Concerns Man's Desires and Security--Never Covet, Ex.20:17

L. The Purposes For the Law: Why God Gave the Ten Commandments and the Law, Ex.20:18-26

The Ten Commandments

And God spake all these words, saying, I am the LORD thy God...

I Thou shalt have no other gods before me

II Thou shalt not make unto thee any graven image

III Thou shalt not take the name of the LORD thy God in vain

IV Remember the sabbath day, to keep it holy

V Honour thy father and thy mother

VI Thou shalt not kill

VII Thou shalt not commit adultery

VIII Thou shalt not steal

IX Thou shalt not bear false witness against thy neighbour

X Thou shalt not covet

EXODUS XX

The Ten Commandments

You hold in your hands the most important document in all of history, a document that was given to the world by God Himself. Down through history, the Ten Commandments have influenced people and societies more than any other single document. The importance of the Ten Commandments can never be overstated. The Ten Commandments are...

- The pattern for a righteous society, for establishing fair and just laws within society.

    "Keep therefore and do them; for this is your wisdom and your understanding in the sight of the nations, which shall hear all these statutes, and say, Surely this great nation is a wise and understanding people" (Dt.4:6).
    "Righteousness exalteth a nation: but sin is a reproach to any people" (Pr.14:34).
    "Wherefore the law is holy [set apart, consecrated by God as His very special laws], and the commandment holy, and just, and good [for society]" (Ro.7:12).

- The basic laws that will govern lawlessness, that will bring about a safe, orderly, peaceful, and just society.

    "Knowing this, that the law is not made for a righteous man, but for the lawless and disobedient, for the ungodly and for sinners, for unholy and profane, for murderers of fathers and murderers of mothers, for manslayers, For whoremongers, for them that defile themselves with mankind, for menstealers, for liars, for perjured persons, and if there be any other thing that is contrary to sound doctrine" (1 Tim.1:9-10).

- The means that God uses to bring us to Christ.

    "Wherefore the law was our schoolmaster to bring us unto Christ, that we might be justified by faith" (Gal.3:24).

- The main laws that are to be taught and learned by every citizen, family, and child.

    "And thou shalt love the LORD thy God with all thine heart, and with all thy soul, and with all thy might. And these words, which I command thee this day, shall be in thine heart: And thou shalt teach them diligently unto thy children, and shalt talk of them when thou sittest in thine house, and when thou walkest by the way, and when thou liest down, and when thou risest up" (Dt.6:5-7).

	VII. THE LAW AND THE PROMISES OF GOD (THE MOSAIC COVENANT) (PART 2): THE TEN COMMANDMENTS--NECESSARY LAWS TO GOVERN MAN AND SOCIETY, EX.20:1-26
	A. The Great Basis of the Ten Commandments: The Person & Work of God Himself, Ex.20:1-2
1. God's existence: "And God"	And God spake all these words, saying,
2. God's Word: "God spoke"	
3. God's name: The LORD[DS1]	2 I am the LORD thy God, which have brought thee out of the land of Egypt, out of the house of bondage.
4. God's relationship with man: "Your God"	
5. God's salvation, deliverance, & redemption: "Brought you out"	

DIVISION VII

THE LAW AND THE PROMISES OF GOD (THE MOSAIC COVENANT) (PART 2): THE TEN COMMANDMENTS--NECESSARY LAWS TO GOVERN MAN AND SOCIETY, EX.20:1-26

A. **The Great Basis of the Ten Commandments: The Person and Work of God Himself, Ex.20:1-2**

Introduction (20:1-2): What is the basis of morality? Who can be absolutely sure what is right or wrong? The world offers various opinions. Is it left up to man to formulate his own values, his own system of morality and ethics? Unfortunately there are many voices in the world today who believe anything goes, ideas that encourage...

- taking what a person wants
- saying what a person wants
- doing what a person wants
- believing what a person wants

The result has been tragic: man is losing control of society and the world; sin and evil are sweeping the world, running rampant, out of control, the sin and evil of...

- lawlessness
- drugs
- alcohol
- abuse
- violence
- murder
- immorality

At times, the problems of sin and evil seem insurmountable. Humanly there seems to be no answer to the problems of society; the situation seems almost hopeless. But note: there is good news. The solution for a world that has gone berserk does not lie with man. Thousands of years ago, God gave man a plan for order within society, a plan that was to guide man down through the centuries, a plan that will work today as much as it would have worked in ancient history. What is that plan? The *Ten Commandments*. The Ten Commandments will work within any generation--if man will just institute and enforce them. God's *Ten Commandments* can bring order to the world. How can we say this? Because the Ten Commandments were given by God Himself. The Ten Commandments are not based upon...

- the prejudices and morality of men
- the latest popularity polls
- the worldly desires of people
- the purposes of government

The basis of the Ten Commandments has been set in stone, in the Rock of Ages, in the One who is the Alpha and Omega, the Beginning and the End, the First and the Last. The basis of the Ten Commandments is God Himself. Therefore, the Ten Commandments work. They work because God knows man, knows exactly what man needs to live a fulfilled and orderly life. The Ten Commandments are based upon God Himself, upon His person and work, upon His knowledge of what man needs, upon His understanding and wisdom. This is the great focus of our study: *The Great Basis of the Ten Commandments: The Person and Work of God Himself*, Ex.20:1-2.

1. God's existence: "And God" (v.1).
2. God's Word: "God spoke" (v.1).
3. God's Name: the LORD (Yahweh) (v.2).
4. God's relationship with man: "Your God" (v.2).
5. God's salvation, deliverance, and redemption: "Brought you out" (v.2).

1 (20:1) **God, the Existence of--Sovereignty**: the first basis of the Ten Commandments is God's existence, His eternal existence. God exists. And God created the world and gave His commandments to the people He had created. Note the words "And God." The existence of God is declared. His existence is not argued or debated. There is no attempt to prove God's existence. Scripture assumes that everyone is *thoughtful and honest, thoughtful and honest* enough to know and acknowledge that God exists. Therefore, Scripture declares without any hesitation or explanation, "And God"; that is, God exists. Consequently, because God exists, He is bound to show man how to live; He is bound to give His commandments to the people He created. This is what the Ten Commandments are: they are the commandments of God Himself, the commandments that tell us how to live. The Ten Commandments are to be the *basic laws* of society, the *basic laws* that govern human relationships and the relationship between God and man. And they are to *govern* man down through history, *govern* every generation and every society of man.

God Himself is the Person who worked out and spoke forth the Ten Commandments. God Himself is the source of the Ten Commandments. God Himself--His existence, His eternal existence--is the basis of the Ten Commandments. The Ten Commandments exist because God Himself exists, and He wants us to know how to live.

Thought 1. What does it mean to us that God is the basis, the source, the One who has given us the Ten Commandments? It means that the Ten Commandments are true; the Ten Commandments should be the basic laws that govern our lives and our society. The Ten Commandments...
- are the basic laws that show us how to live
- are the basic laws that can help us live a fruitful and productive life
- are the basic laws that can help us live together in love, joy, and peace

> **"In the beginning God created the heaven and the earth" (Gen.1:1).**
>
> **"Ye shall not add unto the word which I command you, neither shall ye diminish ought from it, that ye may keep the commandments of the LORD your God which I command you" (Dt.4:2).**
>
> **"Hear, O Israel: The LORD our God is one LORD: And thou shalt love the LORD thy God with all thine heart, and with all thy soul, and with all thy might. And these words, which I command thee this day, shall be in thine heart: And thou shalt teach them diligently unto thy children, and shalt talk of them when thou sittest in thine house, and when thou walkest by the way, and when thou liest down, and when thou risest up" (Dt.6:4-7).**
>
> **"And he said, LORD God of Israel, there is no God like thee, in heaven above, or on earth beneath, who keepest covenant and mercy with thy servants that walk before thee with all their heart" (1 Ki.8:23).**

2 (20:1) **God--Communicating**: the second basis of the Ten Commandments is God's Word, the fact that God speaks to man, that God communicates with man. What a glorious truth this is: God speaks to us. Despite our rejection of Him-- our denial, cursing, and rebellion--God cares for us. Therefore, He has communicated with us, telling us how to live. Note how this verse reads:

> **"And God spake all these words, saying"**

Men try to make false gods speak and sometimes even claim that they do speak, but they are mistaken. They are deceived and are making deceptive claims. False gods cannot speak. Scripture declares:

> **"They [idols] *are* upright as the palm tree, but speak not: they must needs be borne, because they cannot go. Be not afraid of them; for they cannot do evil, neither also *is it* in them to do good" (Jer.10:5).**
>
> **"That which may be known of God is manifest in them; for God hath showed it unto them. For the invisible things of him from the creation of the world are clearly seen, being understood by the things that are made, even his eternal power and Godhead; so that they are without excuse: Because that, when they knew God, they glorified him not as God, neither were thankful; but became vain in their imaginations, and their foolish heart was darkened" (Ro.1:19-21).**

The LORD God, the only true and living God, has chosen to speak to us. Moreover, He has chosen to speak in a way that can be clearly understood. How has God chosen to speak?
⇒ Through His written Word, the Holy Scripture
⇒ Through the Living Word, the Lord Jesus Christ, the Son of God Himself

The present passage of Scripture covers how God has given us part of the written Word, in particular the Ten Commandments. God Himself spoke and gave the law to man. God did not leave man in the dark, wondering how he is to live. Man does not have to stumble around in the dark groping and grasping after the truth, wondering how to live and bring peace and reconciliation to the world, wondering how to please God and become acceptable to Him. God has spoken to man and declared His Word to man; but more than just speaking, God has seen to it that His law is written down for man. God has spoken and given His law in the most permanent way possible: in *written form*. God has communicated with man, given man the Holy Law of God in written form, so that man will always have access to the Ten Commandments, will always know how to relate and live in peace and reconciliation.

Thought 1. God has spoken to us, telling us how to live. Note what Scripture declares:
1) God has given us the written Word of God.

"For whatsoever things were written aforetime were written for our learning, that we through patience and comfort of the scriptures might have hope" (Ro.15:4).

"Now all these things happened unto them for ensamples: and they are written for our admonition, upon whom the ends of the world are come" (1 Cor.10:11).

"All scripture is given by inspiration of God, and is profitable for doctrine, for reproof, for correction, for instruction in righteousness" (2 Tim.3:16).

"For the prophecy came not in old time by the will of man: but holy men of God spake as they were moved by the Holy Ghost" (2 Pt.1:21).

2) God has given us the *living Word of God*, the Lord Jesus Christ Himself. God did not just give us the written Word of God, but He sent His own Son to demonstrate and show us how to live out His Word.

"In the beginning was the Word, and the Word was with God, and the Word was God. The same was in the beginning with God. All things were made by him; and without him was not any thing made that was made. In him was life; and the life was the light of men. And the light shineth in darkness; and the darkness comprehended it not" (Jn.1:1-5).

"And the Word was made flesh, and dwelt among us, (and we beheld his glory, the glory as of the only begotten of the Father,) full of grace and truth" (Jn.1:14).

"God, who at sundry times and in divers manners spake in time past unto the fathers by the prophets, Hath in these last days spoken unto us by his Son, whom he hath appointed heir of all things, by whom also he made the worlds" (Heb.1:1-2).

"That which was from the beginning, which we have heard, which we have seen with our eyes, which we have looked upon, and our hands have handled, of the Word of life; (For the life was manifested, and we have seen it, and bear witness, and show unto you that eternal life, which was with the Father, and was manifested unto us;) That which we have seen and heard declare we unto you, that ye also may have fellowship with us: and truly our fellowship is with the Father, and with his Son Jesus Christ" (1 Jn.1:1-3).

"And this is his commandment, That we should believe on the name of his Son Jesus Christ, and love one another, as he gave us commandment" (1 Jn.3:23).

3 (20:2) **God, Name of--Jehovah**: the third basis of the Ten Commandments is God's name. (See Deeper Study # 1--Ex.20:2 for more discussion.) Note that the name of God is the LORD (Jehovah - Yahweh).
* The name of God means that He is the great I AM: "I AM THAT I AM." God is the Essence, Force, and Energy of Being, the Self-existent One (see Deeper Study # 1--Ex.3:14-15 for more discussion).
* The name of God means that He is the God of salvation, deliverance, and redemption.
* The name of God means that He is the God of revelation. (See Deeper Study # 1--Jn.6:20 for more discussion.)

God's very name means that He is the Source of all being; that He created man; that He loves man; that He saves, delivers, and redeems man; that He reveals and unveils the truth to man; that He reveals the truth of God and of the world to man. This is what the Ten Commandments (the law of God) are: the revelation of a loving God seeking to help man, showing man how to live. The very name of God tells us this. God's name is the basis, the very reason, the Ten Commandments are given to us. The name of God tells us that the LORD Himself loves us: He saves, delivers, and redeems us. He reveals the truth to us, showing us how to live and relate to Him and to one another. This He has done in the Ten Commandments. Simply stated, the LORD God loves us and wants us to know how to live; therefore, He gave us the Ten Commandments.

"And God said unto Moses, I AM THAT I AM: and he said, Thus shalt thou say unto the children of Israel, I AM hath sent me unto you. And God said moreover unto Moses, Thus shalt thou say unto the children of Israel, The LORD God of your fathers, the God of Abraham, the God of Isaac, and the God of Jacob, hath sent me unto you: this is my name for ever, and this is my memorial unto all generations" (Ex.3:14-15).

"Hear, O Israel: The LORD our God is one LORD: And thou shalt love the LORD thy God with all thine heart, and with all thy soul, and with all thy might. And these words, which I command thee this day, shall be in thine heart: And thou shalt teach them diligently unto thy children, and shalt talk of them when thou sittest in thine house, and when thou walkest by the way, and when thou liest down, and when thou risest up" (Dt.6:4-7).

"For the LORD is our judge, the LORD is our lawgiver, the LORD is our king; he will save us" (Is.33:22).

"Hearken unto me, my people; and give ear unto me, O my nation: for a law shall proceed from me, and I will make my judgment to rest for a light of the people. My righteousness is near; my salvation is gone forth, and mine arms shall judge the people; the isles shall wait upon me, and on mine arm shall they trust" (Is.51:4-5).

DEEPER STUDY # 1
(20:2) **God, Existence of--I AM--Names, of God**: because of the length of this Deeper Study, it is being placed at the end of this commentary to keep from breaking the flow. Please see Deeper Study # 1 after Major Point # 5.

4 (20:2) **God--Relationship**: the fourth basis of the Ten Commandments is God's relationship with man. Note that God is said to be the LORD *your* God. God is not far off in outer space someplace, unreachable, unapproachable. God is near, near enough for us to speak to Him. In fact, God wants us to speak with Him; God wants to develop a relationship with us, a personal, loving relationship. This is the reason God gave us the Ten Commandments. He is the great Creator and Father of mankind. Therefore, He gave us the commandments to nourish the relationship between Him and the people He created. He gave us the Ten Commandments to guide us into a closer relationship with Him.

> "Now therefore, if ye will obey my voice indeed, and keep my covenant, then ye shall be a peculiar treasure unto me above all people: for all the earth is mine: And ye shall be unto me a kingdom of priests, and an holy nation. These are the words which thou shalt speak unto the children of Israel" (Ex.19:5-6).
> "O that there were such an heart in them, that they would fear me, and keep all my commandments always, that it might be well with them, and with their children for ever!" (Dt.5:29).
> "He that hath my commandments, and keepeth them, he it is that loveth me: and he that loveth me shall be loved of my Father, and I will love him, and will <u>manifest</u> myself to him" (Jn.14:21).
> "Jesus answered and said unto him, If a man love me, he will keep my words: and my Father will love him, and we will come unto him, and make our abode with him" (Jn.14:23).
> "Wherefore come out from among them, and be ye separate, saith the Lord, and touch not the unclean thing [keep God's commandments]; and I will receive you, And will be a Father unto you, and ye shall be my sons and daughters, saith the Lord Almighty" (2 Cor.6:17-18).

5 (20:2) **God, Our Savior--Deliverance--Salvation**: the fifth basis of the Ten Commandments is God's salvation, deliverance, and redemption. Note that God Himself rescued Israel from the evil place of bondage, the land of Egypt (a symbol of the world). God gave us the Ten Commandments to save us from the evil and lawlessness of this world, evil and lawlessness such as...

- covetousness and greed
- lying
- stealing
- adultery
- murder

- abuse
- violating the Sabbath, the day of rest and worship
- cursing God
- false worship
- unbelief, denial of God

Evil and lawlessness have always swept the world in places where the Ten Commandments were not present or followed. The commandments help us only if we keep them. This is the reason God demands one thing above all else: *obedience*. God is our Savior and Deliverer. He wants us out of harm's way, living like we should, living in peace and reconciliation, both with Him and with one another. Therefore, He gave us the Ten Commandments. God's salvation, deliverance, and redemption are the bases of the Ten Commandments.

> "O that there were such an heart in them, that they would fear me, and keep all my commandments always, that it might be well with them, and with their children for ever!" (Dt.5:29).
> "But the salvation of the righteous is of the LORD: he is their strength in the time of trouble" (Ps.37:39).
> "Behold, God is my salvation; I will trust, and not be afraid: for the LORD JEHOVAH is my strength and my song; he also is become my salvation" (Is.12:2).
> "And it shall be said in that day, Lo, this is our God; we have waited for him, and he will save us: this is the LORD; we have waited for him, we will be glad and rejoice in his salvation" (Is.25:9).
> "The LORD thy God in the midst of thee is mighty; he will save, he will rejoice over thee with joy; he will rest in his love, he will joy over thee with singing" (Zeph.3:17).
> "This book of the law shall not depart out of thy mouth; but thou shalt meditate therein day and night, that thou mayest observe to do according to all that is written therein: for then thou shalt make thy way prosperous, and then thou shalt have good success" (Josh.1:8).
> "For the grace of God that bringeth salvation hath appeared to all men, Teaching us that, denying ungodliness and worldly lusts, we should live soberly, righteously, and godly, in this present world; Looking for that blessed hope, and the glorious appearing of the great God and our Saviour Jesus Christ" (Tit.2:11-13).

DEEPER STUDY #1

THE GREAT "I AM'S" OF GOD AND CHRIST

(20:2) **God, Existence of--I AM--Names, of God**: there is only one living and true God, only one Creator and Sovereign Majesty of the universe, the LORD God Himself (Jehovah, Yahweh).

One of the great declarations in Holy Scripture is the revelation of God Himself as the great I AM. When God says "I AM"...

- He is linking His holy Name with historical events
- He is associating His Name with what He has done in the past or plans to do in the future
- He is defining His character, what He stands for and what He stands against
- He is declaring His sovereign existence

Note that God's very existence is defined by who God says He is. His very words testify of His existence: "I AM THAT I AM." A careful study of the Word of God will warm the heart of the believer who longs to know Him intimately, who desires to know God as the great I AM.

GOD SAYS...	SCRIPTURE REFERENCE
I AM your shield I AM your very great reward	*"After these things the word of the LORD came unto Abram in a vision, saying, Fear not, Abram: <u>I am thy shield, and thy exceeding great reward</u>"* (Gen.15:1).
I AM the LORD	*"And he said unto him, <u>I am the LORD</u> that brought thee out of Ur of the Chaldees, to give thee this land to inherit it"* (Gen.15:7). *"And God spake unto Moses, and said unto him, <u>I am the LORD</u>"* (Ex.6:2). *"Wherefore say unto the children of Israel, <u>I am the LORD</u>, and I will bring you out from under the burdens of the Egyptians, and I will rid you out of their bondage, and I will redeem you with a stretched out arm, and with great judgments: And I will take you to me for a people, and I will be to you a God: and ye shall know that I am the LORD your God, which bringeth you out from under the burdens of the Egyptians. And I will bring you in unto the land, concerning the which I did swear to give it to Abraham, to Isaac, and to Jacob; and I will give it you for an heritage: <u>I am the LORD</u>"* (Ex.6:6-8). *"The LORD spake unto Moses, saying, <u>I am the LORD</u>: speak thou unto Pharaoh king of Egypt all that I say unto thee. And Moses said before the LORD, Behold, I am of uncircumcised lips, and how shall Pharaoh hearken unto me?"* (Ex.6:29-30). *"And the Egyptians shall know that <u>I am the LORD</u>, when I stretch forth mine hand upon Egypt, and bring out the children of Israel from among them"* (Ex.7:5). *"Thus saith the LORD, In this thou shalt know that <u>I am the LORD</u>: behold, I will smite with the rod that is in mine hand upon the waters which are in the river, and they shall be turned to blood"* (Ex.7:17). *"And that thou mayest tell in the ears of thy son, and of thy son's son, what things I have wrought in Egypt, and my signs which I have done among them; that ye may know how that <u>I am the LORD</u>"* (Ex.10:2). *"For I will pass through the land of Egypt this night, and will smite all the firstborn in the land of Egypt, both man and beast; and against all the gods of Egypt I will execute judgment: <u>I am the LORD</u>"* (Ex.12:12). *"And I will harden Pharaoh's heart, that he shall follow after them; and I will be honoured upon Pharaoh, and upon all his host; that the Egyptians may know that <u>I am the LORD</u>. And they did so"* (Ex.14:4). *"And the Egyptians shall know that <u>I am the LORD</u>, when I have gotten me honour upon Pharaoh, upon his chariots, and upon his horsemen"* (Ex.14:18). *"Ye shall therefore keep my statutes, and my judgments: which if a man do, he shall live in them: <u>I am the LORD</u>"* (Lev.18:5). *"None of you shall approach to any that is near of kin to him, to uncover their nakedness: <u>I am the LORD</u>"* (Lev.18:6).
I AM the Almighty God	*"And when Abram was ninety years old and nine, the LORD appeared to Abram, and said unto him, <u>I am the Almighty God</u>; walk before me, and be thou perfect"* (Gen.17:1). *"And God said unto him, <u>I am God Almighty</u>: be fruitful and multiply; a nation and a company of nations shall be of thee, and kings shall come out of thy loins"* (Gen.35:11).
I AM the God of Bethel	*"<u>I am the God of Bethel</u>, where thou anointedst the pillar, and where thou vowedst a vow unto me: now arise, get thee out from this land, and return unto the land of thy kindred"* (Gen.31:13).
I AM the God of your fathers: • the God of Abraham • the God of Isaac • the God of Jacob	*"And the LORD appeared unto him the same night, and said, <u>I am the God of Abraham thy father</u>: fear not, for I am with thee, and will bless thee, and multiply thy seed for my servant Abraham's sake"* (Gen.26:24). *"And, behold, the LORD stood above it, and said, <u>I am the LORD God of Abraham thy father</u>, and the God of Isaac: the land whereon thou liest, to thee will I give it, and to thy seed"* (Gen.28:13). *"And he said, <u>I am God, the God of thy father</u>: fear not to go down into Egypt; for I will there make of thee a great nation"* (Gen.46:3). *"Moreover he said, <u>I am the God of thy father, the God of Abraham, the God of Isaac, and the God of Jacob</u>. And Moses hid his face; for he was afraid to look upon God"* (Ex.3:6). *"Saying, <u>I am the God of thy fathers</u>, the God of Abraham, and the God of Isaac, and the God of Jacob. Then Moses trembled, and durst not behold"* (Acts 7:32).

GOD SAYS...	SCRIPTURE REFERENCE
I AM THAT (WHO) I AM	*"And God said unto Moses, I AM THAT I AM: and he said, Thus shalt thou say unto the children of Israel, I AM hath sent me unto you"* (Ex.3:14).
I AM the LORD your God	*"And I will take you to me for a people, and I will be to you a God: and ye shall know that I am the LORD your God, which bringeth you out from under the burdens of the Egyptians"* (Ex.6:7). *"I have heard the murmurings of the children of Israel: speak unto them, saying, At even ye shall eat flesh, and in the morning ye shall be filled with bread; and ye shall know that I am the LORD your God"* (Ex.16:12). *"I am the LORD thy God, which have brought thee out of the land of Egypt, out of the house of bondage"* (Ex.20:2). *"For I am the LORD your God: ye shall therefore sanctify yourselves, and ye shall be holy; for I am holy: neither shall ye defile yourselves with any manner of creeping thing that creepeth upon the earth. For I am the LORD that bringeth you up out of the land of Egypt, to be your God: ye shall therefore be holy, for I am holy"* (Lev.11:44-45) *"Speak unto the children of Israel, and say unto them, I am the LORD your God"* (Lev.18:2). *"Ye shall do my judgments, and keep mine ordinances, to walk therein: I am the LORD your God"* (Lev.18:4).
I AM the LORD in the midst of the earth (I, the LORD, am in this land)	*"And I will sever in that day the land of Goshen, in which my people dwell, that no swarms of flies shall be there; to the end thou mayest know that I am the LORD in the midst of the earth"* (Ex.8:22).
I AM the LORD... • who heals you • who sanctifies you, who makes you holy • who hallows you, who makes you holy • who has made all things • who teaches you to profit (teaches what is best for you • who leads you (directs you) in the way you should go • who does not change	*"And said, If thou wilt diligently hearken to the voice of the LORD thy God, and wilt do that which is right in his sight, and wilt give ear to his commandments, and keep all his statutes, I will put none of these diseases upon thee, which I have brought upon the Egyptians: for I am the LORD that healeth thee"* (Ex.15:26). *"Speak thou also unto the children of Israel, saying, Verily my sabbaths ye shall keep: for it is a sign between me and you throughout your generations; that ye may know that I am the LORD that doth sanctify you"* (Ex.31:13). *"Neither shall ye profane my holy name; but I will be hallowed among the children of Israel: I am the LORD which hallow you"* (Lev.22:32). *"Thus saith the LORD, thy redeemer, and he that formed thee from the womb, I am the LORD that maketh all things; that stretcheth forth the heavens alone; that spreadeth abroad the earth by myself"* (Is.44:24). *"Thus saith the LORD, thy Redeemer, the Holy One of Israel; I am the LORD thy God which teacheth thee to profit, which leadeth thee by the way that thou shouldest go"* (Is.48:17). *"For I am the LORD, I change not; therefore ye sons of Jacob are not consumed"* (Mal.3:6).
I AM gracious (compassionate)	*"For that is his covering only, it is his raiment for his skin: wherein shall he sleep? and it shall come to pass, when he crieth unto me, that I will hear; for I am gracious"* (Ex.22:27).
I AM the LORD their God	*"And they shall know that I am the LORD their God, that brought them forth out of the land of Egypt, that I may dwell among them: I am the LORD their God"* (Ex.29:46). *"So the house of Israel shall know that I am the LORD their God from that day and forward"* (Ezk.39:22). *"And I will strengthen the house of Judah, and I will save the house of Joseph, and I will bring them again to place them; for I have mercy upon them: and they shall be as though I had not cast them off: for I am the LORD their God, and will hear them"* (Zech.10:6).
I AM holy	*"For I am the LORD your God: ye shall therefore sanctify yourselves, and ye shall be holy; for I am holy: neither shall ye defile yourselves with any manner of creeping thing that creepeth upon the earth. For I am the LORD that bringeth you up out of the land of Egypt, to be your God: ye shall therefore be holy, for I am holy"* (Lev.11:44-45).
I AM the LORD Your God who brought you up out of the land of Egypt... • to be your God • to give you the land of Canaan • to deliver you from the house of bondage	*"For I am the LORD your God: ye shall therefore sanctify yourselves, and ye shall be holy; for I am holy: neither shall ye defile yourselves with any manner of creeping thing that creepeth upon the earth. For I am the LORD that bringeth you up out of the land of Egypt, to be your God: ye shall therefore be holy, for I am holy"* (Lev.11:44-45).

GOD SAYS...	SCRIPTURE REFERENCE
I AM the LORD Your God who brought you up out of the land of Egypt... (cont.) • to fill your mouth • to know that there is no Savior beside me	*"I am the LORD your God, which brought you forth out of the land of Egypt, to give you the land of Canaan, and to be your God"* (Lev.25:38). *"I am the LORD thy God, which brought thee out of the land of Egypt, from the house of bondage"* (Dt.5:6). *"I am the LORD thy God, which brought thee out of the land of Egypt: open thy mouth wide, and I will fill it"* (Ps.81:10). *"Yet I am the LORD thy God from the land of Egypt, and thou shalt know no god but me: for there is no saviour beside me"* (Hos.13:4).
I AM your share and your inheritance among the children of Israel	*"And the LORD spake unto Aaron, Thou shalt have no inheritance in their land, neither shalt thou have any part among them: I am thy part and thine inheritance among the children of Israel"* (Num.18:20).
I AM a worm (a prophesy of the suffering Messiah)	*"But I am a worm, and no man; a reproach of men, and despised of the people"* (Ps.22:6).
I AM poured out like water (a prophesy of the suffering Messiah)	*"I am poured out like water, and all my bones are out of joint: my heart is like wax; it is melted in the midst of my bowels"* (Ps.22:14).
I AM God	*"Be still, and know that I am God: I will be exalted among the heathen, I will be exalted in the earth"* (Ps.46:10). *"Hear, O my people, and I will speak; O Israel, and I will testify against thee: I am God, even thy God"* (Ps.50:7). *"I have declared, and have saved, and I have showed, when there was no strange god among you: therefore ye are my witnesses, saith the LORD, that I am God"* (Is.43:12).
I AM the rose of Sharon, the lily of the valley (beautiful, sweet, fragrant, worthy to be sought, cherished, & desired, easily accessible)	*"I am the rose of Sharon, and the lily of the valleys"* (Song 2:1).
I AM your God	*"Fear thou not; for I am with thee: be not dismayed; for I am thy God: I will strengthen thee; yea, I will help thee; yea, I will uphold thee with the right hand of my righteousness"* (Is.41:10).
I AM... • the LORD • the Holy One of Israel • the Creator of Israel • your Savior, your King	*"For I am the LORD thy God, the Holy One of Israel, thy Saviour: I gave Egypt for thy ransom, Ethiopia and Seba for thee"* (Is.43:3). *"I am the LORD, your Holy One, the creator of Israel, your King"* (Is.43:15).
I, even I, AM the LORD	*"I, even I, am the LORD; and beside me there is no saviour"* (Is.43:11).
I, even I, AM He... • who blots out your transgressions & remembers them no more • who makes alive, heals, and delivers • who comforts you	*"See now that I, even I, am he, and there is no god with me: I kill, and I make alive; I wound, and I heal: neither is there any that can deliver out of my hand"* (Dt.32:39). *"I, even I, am he that blotteth out thy transgressions for mine own sake, and will not remember thy sins"* (Is.43:25). *"I, even I, am he that comforteth you: who art thou, that thou shouldest be afraid of a man that shall die, and of the son of man which shall be made as grass"* (Is.51:12).
I AM the First; I AM the Last	*"Thus saith the LORD the King of Israel, and his redeemer the LORD of hosts; I am the first, and I am the last; and beside me there is no God"* (Is.44:6).
I AM the LORD, and there is no other	*"I am the LORD, and there is none else, there is no God beside me: I girded thee, though thou hast not known me: That they may know from the rising of the sun, and from the west, that there is none beside me. I am the LORD, and there is none else"* (Is.45:5-6). *"For thus saith the LORD that created the heavens; God himself that formed the earth and made it; he hath established it, he created it not in vain, he formed it to be inhabited: I am the LORD; and there is none else"* (Is.45:18). *"Look unto me, and be ye saved, all the ends of the earth: for I am God, and there is none else"* (Is.45:22).
I AM God, and there is none like (beside) Me	*"Remember the former things of old: for I am God, and there is none else; I am God, and there is none like me"* (Is.46:9). *"Therefore hear now this, thou that art given to pleasures, that dwellest carelessly, that sayest in thine heart, I am, and none else beside me; I shall not sit as a widow, neither shall I know the loss of children"* (Is.47:8).
I AM the LORD your God who divided (churned up) the sea	*"But I am the LORD thy God, that divided the sea, whose waves roared: The LORD of hosts is his name"* (Is.51:15).

GOD SAYS...	SCRIPTURE REFERENCE
I AM merciful	*"Go and proclaim these words toward the north, and say, Return, thou backsliding Israel, saith the LORD; and I will not cause mine anger to fall upon you: for **I am merciful**, saith the LORD, and I will not keep anger for ever"* (Jer.3:12).
I AM (your husband) married unto you (spiritually united as God and follower)	*"Turn, O backsliding children, saith the LORD; for **I am married unto you**: and I will take you one of a city, and two of a family, and I will bring you to Zion"* (Jer.3:14).
I AM full of the fury (wrath) of the LORD; I AM weary of holding back my judgment	*"Therefore **I am full of the fury of the LORD; I am weary with holding in**: I will pour it out upon the children abroad, and upon the assembly of young men together: for even the husband with the wife shall be taken, the aged with him that is full of days"* (Jer.6:11).
I AM the LORD who exercises... • lovingkindness • judgment (justice) • righteousness	*"But let him that glorieth glory in this, that he understandeth and knoweth me, that **I am the LORD which exercise lovingkindness, judgment, and righteousness**, in the earth: for in these things I delight, saith the LORD"* (Jer.9:24).
I AM with you to rescue, save, and deliver you	*"And I will make thee unto this people a fenced brasen wall: and they shall fight against thee, but they shall not prevail against thee: for **I am with thee to save thee and to deliver thee**, saith the LORD"* (Jer.15:20).
I AM against you (the oppressor)	*"Behold, **I am against thee**, O inhabitant of the valley, and rock of the plain, saith the LORD; which say, Who shall come down against us? or who shall enter into our habitations?"* (Jer.21:13). *"Therefore thus saith the Lord GOD; Because ye have spoken vanity, and seen lies, therefore, behold, I am against you, saith the Lord GOD"* (Ezk.13:8).
I AM against the prophets... • who steal My words from his neighbor • who speak wrongly in God's name • who prophesy false dreams	*"Therefore, behold, **I am against the prophets**, saith the LORD, that steal my words every one from his neighbour. Behold, **I am against the prophets**, saith the LORD, that use their tongues, and say, He saith. Behold, **I am against them that prophesy false dreams**, saith the LORD, and do tell them, and cause my people to err by their lies, and by their lightness; yet I sent them not, nor commanded them: therefore they shall not profit this people at all, saith the LORD"* (Jer.23:30-32).
I AM a Father to Israel	*"They shall come with weeping, and with supplications will I lead them: I will cause them to walk by the rivers of waters in a straight way, wherein they shall not stumble: for **I am a father to Israel**, and Ephraim is my firstborn"* (Jer.31:9).
I AM the LORD, the God of all mankind	*"Behold, **I am the LORD, the God of all flesh**: is there any thing too hard for me?"* (Jer.32:27).
I AM against your magic charms	*"Wherefore thus saith the Lord GOD; Behold, **I am against your pillows [magic charms]**, wherewith ye there hunt the souls to make them fly, and I will tear them from your arms, and will let the souls go, even the souls that ye hunt to make them fly"* (Ezk.13:20).
I AM profaned (blasphemed, defiled, desecrated) among them (the priests)	*"Her priests have violated my law, and have profaned mine holy things: they have put no difference between the holy and profane, neither have they showed difference between the unclean and the clean, and have hid their eyes from my sabbaths, and **I am profaned among them**"* (Ezk.22:26).
I AM the LORD God (the Sovereign LORD)	*"And they shall recompense your lewdness upon you, and ye shall bear the sins of your idols: and ye shall know that **I am the Lord GOD**"* (Ezk.23:49). *"Thus Ezekiel is unto you a sign: according to all that he hath done shall ye do: and when this cometh, ye shall know that **I am the Lord GOD**"* (Ezk.24:24).
I AM against Pharaoh, (the evil) king of Egypt	*"Therefore thus saith the Lord GOD; Behold, **I am against Pharaoh king of Egypt**, and will break his arms, the strong, and that which was broken; and I will cause the sword to fall out of his hand"* (Ezk.30:22).
I AM against the [false] shepherds	*"Thus saith the Lord GOD; Behold, **I am against the shepherds**; and I will require my flock at their hand, and cause them to cease from feeding the flock; neither shall the shepherds feed themselves any more; for I will deliver my flock from their mouth, that they may not be meat for them"* (Ezk.34:10).
I AM for you (concerned for you)	*"For, behold, **I am for you**, and I will turn unto you, and ye shall be tilled and sown"* (Ezk.36:9).

GOD SAYS...	SCRIPTURE REFERENCE
I AM their inheritance I AM their possession	"And it shall be unto them for an inheritance: _I am their inheritance: and ye shall give them no possession in Israel: I am their possession_" (Ezk.44:28).
I AM God, and not man	"I will not execute the fierceness of mine anger, I will not return to destroy Ephraim: for _I am God, and not man_; the Holy One in the midst of thee: and I will not enter into the city" (Hos.11:9).
I AM with you	"Then spake Haggai the LORD'S messenger in the LORD'S message unto the people, saying, _I am with you_, saith the LORD" (Hag.1:13).
I AM jealous for Jerusalem and for Zion	"So the angel that communed with me said unto me, Cry thou, saying, Thus saith the LORD of hosts; _I am jealous for Jerusalem_ and for Zion with a great jealousy" (Zech.1:14).
I AM displeased (angry) with the heathen that feel secure	"And _I am very sore displeased with the heathen that are at ease_: for I was but a little displeased, and they helped forward the affliction" (Zech.1:15).
I AM a great King	"But cursed be the deceiver, which hath in his flock a male, and voweth, and sacrificeth unto the LORD a corrupt thing: for _I am a great King_, saith the LORD of hosts, and my name is dreadful among the heathen" (Mal.1:14).
I AM well pleased	"And lo a voice from heaven, saying, This is my beloved Son, in whom _I am well pleased_" (Mt.3:17).

JESUS CHRIST SAYS...	SCRIPTURE REFERENCE
I AM meek (gentle) and lowly (humble) in heart	"Take my yoke upon you, and learn of me; for _I am meek and lowly in heart_: and ye shall find rest unto your souls" (Mt.11:29).
I AM the God... • of Abraham • of Isaac • of Jacob	"..._I am the God of Abraham_, and the God of _Isaac_, and the God of _Jacob_? God is not the God of the dead, but of the living" (Mt.22:32).
I AM with you always	"Teaching them to observe all things whatsoever I have commanded you: and, lo, _I am with you alway_, even unto the end of the world. Amen" (Mt.28:20).
I AM	"And Jesus said, _I am_: and ye shall see the Son of man sitting on the right hand of power, and coming in the clouds of heaven" (Mk.14:62).
I AM among you as One who serves	"For whether is greater, he that sitteth at meat, or he that serveth? is not he that sitteth at meat? but _I am among you as he that serveth_" (Lk.22:27).
I AM the Bread of Life	"And Jesus said unto them, _I am the bread of life_: he that cometh to me shall never hunger; and he that believeth on me shall never thirst" (Jn.6:35). "I am that bread of life" (Jn.6:48).
I AM the Bread that came down from heaven	"The Jews then murmured at him, because he said, _I am the bread which came down from heaven_" (Jn.6:41).
I AM the Living Bread	"_I am the living bread_ which came down from heaven: if any man eat of this bread, he shall live for ever: and the bread that I will give is my flesh, which I will give for the life of the world" (Jn.6:51).
I AM from Him	"Then cried Jesus in the temple as he taught, saying, Ye both know me, and ye know whence I am: and I am not come of myself, but he that sent me is true, whom ye know not. But I know him: for _I am from him_, and he hath sent me" (Jn.7:28-29).
I AM the Light of the world	"Then spake Jesus again unto them, saying, _I am the light of the world_: he that followeth me shall not walk in darkness, but shall have the light of life" (Jn.8:12). "As long as I am in the world, _I am the light of the world_" (Jn.9:5)
I AM not alone; I am with the Father	"And yet if I judge, my judgment is true: for _I am not alone_, but I and the Father that sent me" (Jn.8:16).
I AM one that bears witness of Myself	"_I am one that bear witness of myself_, and the Father that sent me beareth witness of me" (Jn.8:18).
I AM from above I AM not of this world	"And he said unto them, Ye are from beneath; _I am from above_: ye are of this world; _I am not of this world_" (Jn.8:23).
I AM He (the One I Claim to be)	"I said therefore unto you, that ye shall die in your sins: for if ye believe not that _I am he_, ye shall die in your sins" (Jn.8:24).

JESUS CHRIST SAYS...	SCRIPTURE REFERENCE
I AM in the world	"As long as *I am in the world*, I am the light of the world" (Jn.9:5).
I AM the Door (Gate)	"Then said Jesus unto them again, Verily, verily, I say unto you, *I am the door of the sheep*" (Jn.10:7). "*I am the door*: by me if any man enter in, he shall be saved, and shall go in and out, and find pasture" (Jn.10:9).
I AM the Good Shepherd	"*I am the good shepherd*: the good shepherd giveth his life for the sheep" (Jn.10:11).
I AM the Son of God	"Say ye of him, whom the Father hath sanctified, and sent into the world, Thou blasphemest; because I said, *I am the Son of God?*" (Jn.10:36).
I AM the Resurrection and the Life	"Jesus said unto her, *I am the resurrection, and the life*: he that believeth in me, though he were dead, yet shall he live" (Jn.11:25).
I AM Master (Teacher) and Lord	"Ye call me Master and Lord: and ye say well; for so *I am*" (Jn.13:13).
I AM... • the way • the truth • the life	"Jesus saith unto him, *I am the way*, the *truth*, and the *life*: no man cometh unto the Father, but by me" (Jn.14:6).
I AM in the Father	"Believest thou not that *I am in the Father*, and the Father in me? the words that I speak unto you I speak not of myself: but the Father that dwelleth in me, he doeth the works. Believe me that *I am in the Father*, and the Father in me: or else believe me for the very works' sake" (Jn.14:10-11).
I AM the Vine	"*I am the true vine*, and my Father is the husbandman" (Jn.15:1). "*I am the vine*, ye are the branches: He that abideth in me, and I in him, the same bringeth forth much fruit: for without me ye can do nothing" (Jn.15:5).
I AM a King	"Pilate therefore said unto him, Art thou a king then? Jesus answered, Thou sayest that *I am a king*. To this end was I born, and for this cause came I into the world, that I should bear witness unto the truth. Every one that is of the truth heareth my voice" (Jn.18:37).
I AM Jesus	"And he said, Who art thou, Lord? And the Lord said, *I am Jesus* whom thou persecutest: it is hard for thee to kick against the pricks" (Acts 9:5).
I AM Jesus of Nazareth	"And I answered, Who art thou, Lord? And he said unto me, *I am Jesus of Nazareth*, whom thou persecutest" (Acts 22:8).
I AM Alpha and Omega, the Beginning and the Ending, the First and the Last	"*I am Alpha and Omega, the beginning and the ending*, saith the Lord, which is, and which was, and which is to come, the Almighty" (Rev. 1:8). "And when I saw him, I fell at his feet as dead. And he laid his right hand upon me, saying unto me, Fear not; *I am the first and the last*" (Rev.1:17). "I am Alpha and Omega, the beginning and the end, the first and the last" (Rev.22:13).
I AM He who lives (the Living One) I AM alive for evermore, for ever and ever	"*I am he that liveth*, and was dead; and, behold, *I am alive for evermore*, Amen; and have the keys of hell and of death" (Rev.1:18).
I AM the Root and offspring of David, the Bright Morning Star	"I Jesus have sent mine angel to testify unto you these things in the churches. I am the root and the offspring of David, and the bright and morning star" (Rev.22:16).

	B. The Ten Commandments, The Laws Governing Man's Duty to God (Part 1): Commandment One Concerns God's Being-- Never Believe in False Gods, Ex.20:3
Commandment 1: Have no other gods *whatsoever*^{DS1}	3 Thou shalt have no other gods before me.

DIVISION VII

THE LAW AND THE PROMISES OF GOD (THE MOSAIC COVENANT) (PART 2): THE TEN COMMANDMENTS--NECESSARY LAWS TO GOVERN MAN AND SOCIETY, EX.20:1-26

B. The Ten Commandments, The Laws Governing Man's Duty to God (Part 1): Commandment One Concerns God's Being--Never Believe in False Gods, Ex.20:3

(20:3) **Introduction**: God is; God exists. There is a Creator of the universe: the one true and living God. He is the LORD GOD Himself (Jehovah, Yahweh). He created all that is, including man. Therefore, God cares for man: He cares about man's welfare, what happens to man as he walks throughout life day by day. But God cares about something else as well: God cares about what man thinks of Him. What people think about God determines their eternal fate. God wants, even longs, for us all to live with Him eternally. This is the reason God gave us this first commandment:

"Thou shalt have no other gods before me" (Ex.20:3).

But the great tragedy is this: not all of us will live with God eternally. Why? Because many do not live with God now.
1. There are some who deny God: they just do not believe that God is, that God exists.
⇒ Some persons are secularists, people who believe that this physical world is all that exists.
⇒ Still others are evolutionists, people who believe that man has evolved to be the ultimate being of this earth, evolved to be the god of this earth.
⇒ Other persons are humanists, people who believe that man--his knowledge, his science, his technology-- determines the destiny of man and of all else in this world.

Now if a person denies God, he naturally does not live with God, not now nor will he in the future. He has cut himself off from God. This commandment is directed to the atheists, secularists, humanists, and evolutionists.

"Thou shalt have no other gods before me"--not this secular world and universe and certainly not man himself who is ever so frail, so frail that his life is as a vapor that appears for just a brief time and then vanishes ever so quickly.

2. There are some people who question God's existence: God may exist, but He may not exist. There may be a God behind the universe, but there may not be. They just do not know, not for sure. How could they ever know? They are skeptical toward God. They are agnostics.
Now, if a person questions God's existence, he naturally does not live with God, not now nor will he in the future. This commandment is directed to the agnostic:

"Thou shalt have no other gods before me"--not man's questioning and reasoning ability, not his science, technology, nor exploratory abilities.

3. There are other people who believe in many gods, believe that the destiny of man and his world are in the hands of many powers and authorities throughout the universe (polytheism). This commandment is directed to all who believe in many gods. There is only one true and living God.

"Thou shalt have no other gods before me" (Ex.20:3).

4. There are many people--many, many people--who believe in one god and only in one god. But that god is not the true and living God, not the God and Father of our Lord Jesus Christ. Many people, especially within industrialized nations, say that the god worshipped by the Moslems, Buddhists, Christians, and others is the same god, that we all just call god by different names. But this is not true, not according to Scripture, not according to the Father of our Lord Jesus Christ.
The Father of our Lord Jesus Christ claims to be the only living and true God. He declares that this is the very reason He sent His Son, Jesus Christ, into the world: to reveal Himself--to reveal the truth to us--that there is only one true and

living God. And this is the key belief: the god most people believe in is not the God and Father of our Lord Jesus Christ. He and He alone is the true and living God. He and He alone is the One who sent Jesus Christ to reveal the truth of Himself and the world to us.

This commandment is directed to those who believe in only one god, but who believe that he is the god of all people and religions of the earth.

"Thou shalt have no other gods before me" (Ex.20:3).

As stated above, God loves all people and longs for all to live with Him eternally. But so many of us are mistaken about God; so many of us deny, question, and have wrong images of God; so many of us tragically reject the Father of our Lord Jesus Christ. And all who reject the Father of our Lord Jesus Christ reject the only living and true God. And if we reject Him, we doom ourselves to be separated forever from God. This is the reason God gives us the first great commandment: to warn us, to warn us that there is only one true and living God.

"Thou shalt have no other gods before me" (Ex.20:3).

This is the first of the Ten Commandments: *Commandment One Concerns God's Being--Never Believe in False Gods*, 20:3.
1.   Who is to obey the commandment (v.3)?
2.   How long was the commandment to be in force (v.3)?
3.   What is forbidden by the commandment (v.3)?
4.   What is the decision required by this commandment (v.3)?

1 (20:3) **Obedience--Commandments, The Ten**: Who is to obey this commandment? "You." Note the word "you." The first commandment is personal. The commandment is addressed to each person, each individual. Keep in mind that God is the Sovereign LORD and Majesty of the universe, the only living and true God. His commandments are, therefore, bound to be addressed to every person throughout the universe. No person--believer or unbeliever--would ever be exempt from the commandments given by the Sovereign Lord and God of the universe. Every person is required to obey God's commandments.

You yourself are personally responsible; *you yourself* are held accountable to obey this commandment.

> **"Now therefore, <u>if ye will obey</u> my voice indeed, and keep my covenant, then ye shall be a peculiar treasure unto me above all people: for all the earth is mine: And ye shall be unto me a kingdom of priests, and an holy nation" (Ex.19:5-6).**
> **"This day the LORD thy God hath commanded thee to do these statutes and judgments: thou shalt therefore keep and do them with all thine heart, and with all thy soul" (Dt.26:16).**
> **"This book of the law shall not depart out of thy mouth; but thou shalt meditate therein day and night, that thou mayest observe to do according to all that is written therein: for then thou shalt make thy way prosperous, and then thou shalt have good success" (Josh.1:8).**
> **"Not every one that saith unto me, Lord, Lord, shall enter into the kingdom of heaven; but he that doeth the will of my Father which is in heaven" (Mt.7:21).**

2 (20:3) **Obedience--Commandments, The Ten**: How long was this commandment to be in force? Was it given by God to Israel alone, or was it given through Israel to the whole world? At least three facts show us that this commandment is to be obeyed by all people of all generations, to be obeyed as long as the universe stands.

First, God is the LORD (Jehovah, Yahweh), the Sovereign Majesty of the universe, the only living and true God (cp. v.2). There is no other God, not a living God, not a true God. You can search throughout the whole world--travel throughout the entire universe--and you will never find another true and living God. There is only one Creator and Sustainer of the universe: the LORD God Himself (cp. v.1-2). He is; He exists. The LORD God always has existed, is now existing, and always will exist. Therefore, as long as God exists and as long as the universe stands--as long as there are generations of people--God will command and demand: "You shall have no other gods before me" (v.3).

Second, Jesus Christ Himself told us that the Ten Commandments are meant for all generations of people.

> **"Think not that I am come to destroy the law, or the prophets: I am not come to destroy, but to <u>fulfil</u>" (Mt.5:17).**

Jesus Christ declared that He *fulfilled* the law: He completed and perfected the law. He never failed to keep the law, not even in one minute point. Therefore, He fulfilled the demands of the law perfectly. The point is this: by fulfilling the law, Jesus Christ embraces the law. He embodies, encompasses, integrates, and contains the law within His very being. The law of God is part of the very being of Jesus Christ, of God Himself.

When a person looks at Jesus Christ, he sees the law of God in all its perfection. True, he sees more, much more. The person sees within Jesus Christ the very embodiment and perfection of love, mercy, compassion, joy, peace, longsuffering, gentleness, goodness, faithfulness, meekness, control, power, and justice. The person sees all that God Himself is. But in addition to all this, when the person sees Jesus Christ, he sees the law of God embodied within the very being of Jesus Christ. Therefore, when a person gives his life to follow Jesus Christ, that person follows the law of God and all else that Christ is.

Now, how long was this commandment to be in force? How many generations are to obey this commandment? As long as God loves the world and as long as Jesus Christ is the Savior of the world, people are to obey this commandment. All generations of people are to follow Christ and obey Him. They are to obey all that Christ is, which includes the Ten Commandments--the Ten Commandments plus so much more.

"O that there were such an heart in them, that they would fear me, and keep all my commandments <u>always</u>, that it might be well with them, and with their children for ever!" (Dt.5:29).

"Hear, O Israel: The LORD our God is one LORD: And thou shalt love the LORD thy God with all thine heart, and with all thy soul, and with all thy might. And these words, which I command thee this day, shall be in thine heart: And thou shalt teach them diligently unto thy children, and shalt talk of them when thou sittest in thine house, and when thou walkest by the way, and when thou liest down, and when thou risest up" (Dt.6:4-7).

"Be ye therefore very courageous to keep and to do all that is written in the book of the law of Moses, that ye turn not aside therefrom to the right hand or to the left" (Josh.23:6).

"For verily I say unto you, Till heaven and earth pass, one jot or one tittle shall in no wise pass from the law, till all be fulfilled" (Mt.5:18).

"Heaven and earth shall pass away: but my words shall not pass away" (Lk.21:33).

3 (20:3) **Obedience--Commandments, The Ten**: What is forbidden by this first commandment, "You shall have no other gods before me" (v.3)? How is this commandment broken, violated? This commandment concerns God's being. God is declaring that He alone is the *Supreme Being*, the absolute authority of the universe. There is no other *supreme being*, no other god who created and who rules and reigns over the universe. He alone is the LORD, the only living and true God, the only living and true Creator. Note that God makes three stringent demands, three clear requirements in this commandment.

1. Man is to have no other gods, none whatsoever (v.3).

a. Man is not to set himself up as a god. Man is not to believe that he himself nor any other being or energy in the universe is the ultimate source of the universe.
  ⇒ Man is not to deny God, declaring there is no God (atheism).
  ⇒ Man is not to question God, saying God may exist but He also may not exist (agnosticism).
  ⇒ Man is not to declare that man himself is the supreme being, the ultimate authority of his world (humanism).
  ⇒ Man is not to look to science and technology as the ultimate power in life (secularism).
  ⇒ Man is not to hold that his own knowledge and reasoning ability are the ultimate control of the universe.
  ⇒ Man is not to believe that the spirit of man (the combined spirit of all men) is the ultimate energy of the universe.
  ⇒ Man is not to proclaim some impersonal mass, energy, or gas in the universe as *the force* behind all things.

b. Man is not to believe that other beings, animals, or material things are God. Man is not to look in the sky above nor in the earth below nor in the sea and its depths and declare that something therein is God.
  ⇒ Man is not to look at the sky and declare the heavenly bodies and beings to be the supreme force of the universe: not the sun, moon, stars, angels, principalities, powers nor any other creature of any world or any dimension of being.
  ⇒ Man is not to look at the earth nor at some material substance of the earth and declare it to be God.
  ⇒ Man is not to look upon animals as some god, no matter what the animal is.
  ⇒ Man is not to consider the physical mass nor energy nor gases that comprise the basic substance of things as a god: not the atoms, protons, neutrons, nor whatever the most minute building-block of existence may be.

c. Man is not to believe in many gods (polytheism). There is only one living and true God, only one true Creator, only one LORD and Majesty of the universe (monotheism). Therefore, man is to have no other gods whatsoever. All other so-called gods are nothing more than...
  • things created by the imaginations and thoughts of people
  • things called gods by people
  • things that are lifeless and powerless
  • things that are only images made out of metal, wood, stone, chemicals, or dirt

2. God also makes a second demand of man: "You shall have no other gods <u>before me</u>" (v.3). The words "before me" (alpamaya) mean literally *before my face, against my face, in hostility toward me, in my presence, in my sight*. It means that man...
  • is to set no god *before* the LORD God.
  • is to set no god *beside* the LORD God.
  • is to set no god *in the presence* of the LORD God.
  • is to set no god *in the face* of the LORD God.

The great nineteenth century commentator George Bush makes several excellent statements that tell us exactly what the first commandment means:
  ⇒ "[Creating idols] may be done mentally as well as manually. There may be idolatry without idols."
  ⇒ "[This commandment] forbids the making of any other objects [as gods] whether persons or things, real or imaginary."
  ⇒ "[Our] supreme regard, reverence, esteem, affection, and obedience [is due] God alone."
  ⇒ "God is the fountain of happiness, and no intelligent being can be happy but through him...[consequently] whoever seeks for supreme happiness in the creature instead of the Creator is guilty of a violation of this command."[1]

---

[1] George Bush. *Exodus*. (Minneapolis, MN: Klock & Klock Christian Publishers, Inc., 1981), p.260.

If we set up anything that is a rival interest in our hearts and minds, anything that absorbs the love and service which belongs only to the true God, then that thing becomes another god. Whatever the heart clings to, that becomes our god. Consequently...

- the proud man who idolizes himself makes himself a god.
- the ambitious man who pays homage to popular applause makes his ambition and the praise of men his god.
- the covetous person who craves money and things makes a god out of money and things.
- the greedy person who hoards possessions makes possessions his god.
- the immoral person who craves sex makes sex his god.
- the glutton who craves food makes eating his god.
- the doting lover--whether husband, wife, mother or father--who sets his supreme affection on the person loved instead of upon God makes that person his god.[2]

3. God also makes a third demand of us: man is to know and acknowledge the only true and living God. There is one true and living God, the LORD God Himself.

    a. God declares that people who think there is no God are wrong (atheists). I AM the LORD God, the true and living God. *Atheists* may deny God, and *agnostics* may question if God really exists, but God is forceful in His declaration.

        ⇒ "I AM--I AM the LORD Your God" (v.2).

        "The fool hath said in his heart, There is no God" (Ps.14:1).

    b. No other object and no other being is ever to be set up as a so-called 'god.' Taking ideas or objects and beings and calling them God is forbidden, absolutely forbidden.

        ⇒ The LORD Himself (Jehovah, Yahweh) emphatically declares:

        "I am the LORD: that is my name: and my glory will I not give to another, neither my praise to graven images" (Is.42:8).

        ⇒ The great apostle Paul declared:

        "For though there be [many] that are called gods, whether in heaven or in earth, (as there be gods many, and lords many,) But to us there is but one God, the Father, of whom are all things" (1 Cor.8:5-6).

We make a god out of anything that we esteem or love, fear or serve more than God. Again, whatever the heart clings to, that is a person's god. It may be oneself. Frankly, many people focus upon pleasing and satisfying themselves. They live by their own values and are concerned primarily with their own feelings, comfort, desires, and pleasures. They simply live like they want and do their own thing. They have exalted themselves to be their own god. Other people make gods out of...

• heavenly bodies	• images	• recognition	• family	• the latest style of clothing
• science	• money	• fame	• sex	• cars, trucks
• force, energy	• property	• career	• food	• sports
• animals	• position	• power	• pleasure	• recreation

A god can be anything or any person. Man's first allegiance, first loyalty, first devotion is to be to the LORD God. The LORD God is to be first in a man's life; He is to be enthroned in the heart of man. Man is to know and acknowledge that there is one God and one God alone. The first commandment of the LORD is to be obeyed:

"You shall have no other gods before me" (v.3)

Thought 1. Note several points.

1) The so called gods of heaven and earth are nothing more than the creation of man's imagination and hands.

    "Their idols are silver and gold, the work of men's hands. They have mouths, but they speak not: eyes have they, but they see not: They have ears, but they hear not: noses have they, but they smell not: They have hands, but they handle not: feet have they, but they walk not: neither speak they through their throat. They that make them are like unto them; so is every one that trusteth in them" (Ps.115:4-8).

    "To whom then will ye liken God? or what likeness will ye compare unto him? The workman melteth a graven image, and the goldsmith spreadeth it over with gold, and casteth silver chains. He that is so impoverished that he hath no oblation chooseth a tree that will not rot; he seeketh unto him a cunning workman to prepare a graven image, that shall not be moved" (Is.40:18-20).

    "Assemble yourselves and come; draw near together, ye that are escaped of the nations: they have no knowledge that set up the wood of their graven image, and pray unto a god that cannot save" (Is.45:20).

---

[2] The idea for this paragraph was also taken from George Bush, *Exodus*, p.260.

"Thus saith the LORD, Learn not the way of the heathen, and be not dismayed at the signs of heaven; for the heathen are dismayed at them. For the customs of the people are vain: for one cutteth a tree out of the forest, the work of the hands of the workman, with the axe. They deck it with silver and with gold; they fasten it with nails and with hammers, that it move not. They are upright as the palm tree, but speak not: they must needs be borne, because they cannot go. Be not afraid of them; for they cannot do evil, neither also is it in them to do good" (Jer.10:2-5).

"Professing themselves to be wise, they became fools, And changed the glory of the uncorruptible God into an image made like to corruptible man, and to birds, and fourfooted beasts, and creeping things" (Ro.1:22-23).

"Ye know that ye were Gentiles, carried away unto these dumb idols, even as ye were led" (1 Cor.12:2).

2) There is only one true and living God, the LORD Himself (Jehovah, Yahweh).

"Unto thee it was showed, that thou mightest know that the LORD he is God; there is none else beside him" (Dt.4:35).

"Hear, O Israel: The LORD our God is one LORD: And thou shalt love the LORD thy God with all thine heart, and with all thy soul, and with all thy might" (Dt.6:4-5).

"Wherefore thou art great, O LORD God: for there is none like thee, neither is there any God beside thee, according to all that we have heard with our ears" (2 Sam.7:22).

"O LORD, there is none like thee, neither is there any God beside thee, according to all that we have heard with our ears" (1 Chron.17:20).

"That men may know that thou, whose name alone is JEHOVAH, art the most high over all the earth" (Ps.83:18).

"For thou art great, and doest wondrous things: thou art God alone" (Ps.86:10).

"Ye are my witnesses, saith the LORD, and my servant whom I have chosen: that ye may know and believe me, and understand that I am he: before me there was no God formed, neither shall there be after me. I, even I, am the LORD; and beside me there is no saviour" (Is.43:10-11).

"Thus saith the LORD the King of Israel, and his redeemer the LORD of hosts; I am the first, and I am the last; and beside me there is no God" (Is.44:6).

"For thus saith the LORD that created the heavens; God himself that formed the earth and made it; he hath established it, he created it not in vain, he formed it to be inhabited: I am the LORD; and there is none else" (Is.45:18).

"Look unto me, and be ye saved, all the ends of the earth: for I am God, and there is none else" (Is.45:22).

"And the scribe said unto him, Well, Master, thou hast said the truth: for there is one God; and there is none other but he" (Mk.12:32).

"And Jesus answered him, The first of all the commandments [is], Hear, O Israel; The Lord our God is one Lord" (Mk.12:29).

"As concerning therefore the eating of those things that are offered in sacrifice unto idols, we know that an idol is nothing in the world, and that there is none other God but one. For though there be that are called gods, whether in heaven or in earth, (as there be gods many, and lords many,) But to us there is but one God, the Father, of whom are all things, and we in him; and one Lord Jesus Christ, by whom are all things, and we by him" (1 Cor.8:4-6).

"One God and Father of all, who is above all, and through all, and in you all" (Eph.4:6).

"For there is one God, and one mediator between God and men, the man Christ Jesus" (1 Tim.2:5).

3) There is only one sovereign Creator who meets the needs of man.

"In the beginning God created the heaven and the earth" (Gen.1:1).

"Thou, even thou, art LORD alone; thou hast made heaven, the heaven of heavens, with all their host, the earth, and all things that are therein, the seas, and all that is therein, and thou preservest them all; and the host of heaven worshippeth thee" (Neh.9:6).

"He stretcheth out the north over the empty place, and hangeth the earth upon nothing" (Job 26:7).

"By the word of the LORD were the heavens made; and all the host of them by the breath of his mouth" (Ps.33:6).

"Of old hast thou laid the foundation of the earth: and the heavens are the work of thy hands" (Ps.102:25).

"For as I passed by, and beheld your devotions, I found an altar with this inscription, TO THE UNKNOWN GOD. Whom therefore ye ignorantly worship, him declare I unto you. God that made the world and all things therein, seeing that he is Lord of heaven and earth, dwelleth not in temples made with hands; Neither is worshipped with men's hands, as though he needed any thing, seeing he giveth to all life, and breath, and all things; And hath made of one blood all nations of men for to dwell on all the face of the earth, and hath determined the times before appointed, and the bounds of their habitation; That they should seek the Lord, if haply they might feel after him, and find him, though he be not far from every one of us: For in him we live, and move, and have our being; as certain also of your own poets have said, For we are also his offspring. Forasmuch then as we are the offspring of God, we ought not to think that the Godhead is like unto gold, or silver, or stone, graven by art and man's device. And the times of this ignorance God winked at; but now commandeth all men every where to repent: Because he hath appointed a day, in the which he will judge the world in righteousness by that man whom he hath ordained; whereof he hath given assurance unto all men, in that he hath raised him from the dead" (Acts 17:23-31).

"Through faith we understand that the worlds were framed by the word of God, so that things which are seen were not made of things which do appear" (Heb.11:3).

Thought 2. The very first commandment says, "You shall have no other gods *before me*" (v.3). Note the words "*before me*." This suggests at least two facts:
1) If we set some so-called god "*before God*," He knows it. We cannot hide the fact from Him.
2) If we set a god "*before Him*," His anger is aroused.

"If we have forgotten the name of our God, or stretched out our hands to a strange god; Shall not God search this out? for he knoweth the secrets of the heart" (Ps.44:20-21).

"I am the LORD: that is my name: and my glory will I not give to another, neither my praise to graven images" (Is.42:8).

"For the wrath of God is revealed from heaven against all ungodliness and unrighteousness of men, who hold the truth in unrighteousness" (Ro.1:18).

4 (20:3) **Obedience; Commandments, The Ten**: What is the decision required by this commandment?
1. The decision can be stated positively:
   a. We must acknowledge that there is only one living and true God and serve Him with our whole heart.

"And thou, Solomon my son, know thou the God of thy father, and serve him with a perfect heart and with a willing mind: for the LORD searcheth all hearts, and understandeth all the imaginations of the thoughts: if thou seek him, he will be found of thee; but if thou forsake him, he will cast thee off for ever" (1 Chron.28:9).

"Thou hast avouched the LORD this day to be thy God, and to walk in his ways, and to keep his statutes, and his commandments, and his judgments, and to hearken unto his voice" (Dt.26:17).

"For though there be that are called gods, whether in heaven or in earth, (as there be gods many, and lords many,) But to us there is but one God, the Father, of whom are all things, and we in him; and one Lord Jesus Christ, by whom are all things, and we by him. Howbeit there is not in every man that knowledge" (1 Cor.8:5-7).

   b. We must turn to the LORD and be saved, for He alone is God.

"Look unto me, and be ye saved, all the ends of the earth: for I am God, and there is none else" (Is.45:22).

   c. We must love the LORD our God (Jehovah, Yahweh) with all our hearts.

"Hear, O Israel: The LORD our God is one LORD: And thou shalt love the LORD thy God with all thine heart, and with all thy soul, and with all thy might" (Dt.6:4-5).

   d. We must seek to walk before God and be blameless.

"And when Abram was ninety years old and nine, the LORD appeared to Abram, and said unto him, I am the Almighty God; walk before me, and be thou perfect" (Gen.17:1).

"But this thing commanded I them, saying, Obey my voice, and I will be your God, and ye shall be my people: and walk ye in all the ways that I have commanded you, that it may be well unto you" (Jer.7:23).

   e. We must sanctify the LORD in our hearts, set Him apart as holy and fear Him.

"Sanctify the LORD of hosts himself; and let him be your fear, and let him be your dread" (Is.8:13).

   f. We must realize that we cannot serve two masters; we cannot serve God and money.

"No man can serve two masters: for either he will hate the one, and love the other; or else he will hold to the one, and despise the other. Ye cannot serve God and mammon" (Mt.6:24).

2. The decision can be stated negatively: we must have no other gods whatsoever; we must never believe in false gods, none whatsoever.

> **"Thou shalt have no other gods before me"** (Ex.20:3).
> **"Take heed to yourselves, that your heart be not deceived, and ye turn aside, and serve other gods, and worship them"** (Dt.11:16).
> **"Little children, keep yourselves from idols. Amen"** (1 Jn.5:21).

Thought 1. The decision demanded by God is clear: we are not to have any other gods, none whatsoever. There is only one true and living God. We are to believe *in Him and in Him alone*.

> **"And he believed in the LORD; and he counted it to him for righteousness"** (Gen.15:6).
> **"And they rose early in the morning, and went forth into the wilderness of Tekoa: and as they went forth, Jehoshaphat stood and said, Hear me, O Judah, and ye inhabitants of Jerusalem; Believe in the LORD your God, so shall ye be established; believe his prophets, so shall ye prosper"** (2 Chron.20:20).
> **"For God so loved the world, that he gave his only begotten Son, that whosoever believeth in him should not perish, but have everlasting life"** (Jn.3:16).
> **"Then said they unto him, What shall we do, that we might work the works of God? Jesus answered and said unto them, This is the work of God, that ye believe on him whom he hath sent"** (Jn.6:28-29).
> **"And this is his commandment, That we should believe on the name of his Son Jesus Christ, and love one another, as he gave us commandment"** (1 Jn.3:23).

THE BIBLICAL CONSEQUENCES OF HAVING
OTHER GODS, OF BELIEVING IN OTHER GODS

DEEPER STUDY # 1

(20:3) Commandments, The Ten--Obedience--Judgment: What are the consequences of breaking this commandment? This passage does not cover the consequences. The reason is seen in the first two verses (20:1-2). The motivation for keeping the Ten Commandments is not to be fear of the judgment of God. The reason for keeping the commandments is to be the love of God, the glorious salvation and deliverance He has provided. Note what God says:

> **"I am the LORD thy God, which have brought thee out of the land of Egypt, out of the house of bondage"** (v.2).

The Israelites were to keep the Ten Commandments because God had delivered them out of Egypt, out of slavery and bondage. Remember, Egypt is a picture of the world, and Israel's slavery to Egypt is a picture of man's enslavement to the world, to its bondages of sin and death. But God loves us; therefore, He has provided salvation for us in Christ Jesus our Lord. It is this--the love of God--that is to compel us to keep His commandments. But having said this, there are other reasons for obeying the commandments. And, as mentioned, these are covered in other Scriptures. Our purpose in discussing the Ten Commandments is to give an overall discussion. For this reason, we are including the consequences for breaking the commandments in a Deeper Study for each of the commandments.

1. There are the consequences upon God.

   a. The person who does not follow God cuts the heart of God: causes pain and hurt for Him.

> **"And the LORD said unto Samuel, Hearken unto the voice of the people in all that they say unto thee: for they have not rejected thee, but they have rejected me, that I should not reign over them"** (1 Sam.8:7).
> **"But my people would not hearken to my voice; and Israel would none of me"** (Ps. 81:11).
> **"The Lord is not slack concerning his promise, as some men count slackness; but is longsuffering to us, not willing that any should perish, but that all should come to repentance"** (2 Pt.3:9).

   b. The person who does not follow God causes the name of God to be blasphemed.

> **"Thou that makest thy boast of the law, through breaking the law dishonourest thou God? For the name of God is blasphemed among the Gentiles through you, as it is written"** (Ro.2:23-24).

c. The person who does not follow God lives a life that is detestable to God.

"They profess that they know God; but in works they deny *him,* being abominable [detestable], and disobedient, and unto every good work reprobate [worthless, NASB]" (Tit.1:16).

2. There are the consequences upon oneself, one's day to day life.

a. The person who does not follow God follows after dumb, lifeless idols, man-made gods that can never help him.

"Shall a man make gods unto himself, and they *are* no gods?" (Jer.16:20).
"Ye know that ye were Gentiles, carried away unto these dumb idols, even as ye were led" (1 Cor.12:2).

b. The person who does not follow God exchanges a life of glory for a life that does not profit, a life that is worthless.

"Hath a nation changed *their* gods, which *are* yet no gods? but my people have changed their glory for *that which* doth not profit" (Jer.2:11).

c. The person who does not follow God experiences a life of emptiness and trouble, missing out on the spiritual rest and peace of God.

"Let us labour therefore to enter into that rest, lest any man fall after the same example of unbelief" (Heb.4:11).
"For all this they sinned still, and believed not for his wondrous works. Therefore their days did he consume in vanity, and their years in trouble" (Ps.78:32-33).

d. The person who does not follow God lives a life of hopelessness.

"That at that time ye were without Christ, being aliens from the commonwealth of Israel, and strangers from the covenants of promise, having no hope, and without God in the world" (Eph.2:12).

e. The person who does not follow God lives a life that is enslaved to sin.

"Howbeit then, when ye knew not God, ye did service unto them which by nature are no gods. But now, after that ye have known God, or rather are known of God, how turn ye again to the weak and beggarly elements, whereunto ye desire again to be in bondage?" (Gal.4:8-9).

f. The person who does not follow God lives a hypocritical life, a life that denies the truth.

"Having a form of godliness, but denying the power thereof: from such turn away" (2 Tim.3:5).
"For the wrath of God is revealed from heaven against all ungodliness and unrighteousness of men, who hold the truth in unrighteousness; Because that which may be known of God is manifest in them; for God hath showed it unto them. For the invisible things of him from the creation of the world are clearly seen, being understood by the things that are made, even his eternal power and Godhead; so that they are without excuse: Because that, when they knew God, they glorified him not as God, neither were thankful; but became vain in their imaginations, and their foolish heart was darkened. Professing themselves to be wise, they became fools, And changed the glory of the uncorruptible God into an image made like to corruptible man, and to birds, and fourfooted beasts, and creeping things" (Ro.1:18-23).

g. The person who does not follow God defiles his mind and conscience.

"Unto the pure all things are pure: but unto them that are defiled and unbelieving is nothing pure; but even their mind and conscience is defiled" (Tit.1:15).

h. The person who does not follow God experiences the most illogical life that can be lived: the life of a fool.

"The fool hath said in his heart, *There is* no God. They are corrupt, they have done abominable works, *there is* none that doeth good" (Ps.14:1).

i. The person who does not follow God will have no root and will fall away when temptation comes.

"Those by the way side are they that hear; then cometh the devil, and taketh away the word out of their hearts, lest they should believe and be saved. They on the rock *are they,* which, when they hear, receive the word with joy; and these have no root, which for a while believe, and in time of temptation fall away" (Lk.8:12-13).

j. The person who does not follow God places his faith only in signs and wonders.

> **"Then said Jesus unto him, Except ye see signs and wonders, ye will not believe" (Jn.4:48).**

k. The person who does not follow God is blinded in his mind, unable to see the saving light of the gospel of Christ.

> **"In whom the god of this world hath blinded the minds of them which believe not, lest the light of the glorious gospel of Christ, who is the image of God, should shine unto them" (2 Cor.4:4).**

l. The person who does not follow God lives a life of ungodly lusts, a life that mocks God and His Son, the Lord Jesus Christ.

> **"How that they told you there should be mockers in the last time, who should walk after their own ungodly lusts" (Jude 1:18).**
> **"Knowing this first, that there shall come in the last days scoffers, walking after their own lusts, And saying, Where is the promise of his coming? for since the fathers fell asleep, all things continue as they were from the beginning of the creation. For this they willingly are ignorant of, that by the word of God the heavens were of old, and the earth standing out of the water and in the water" (2 Pt.3:3-5).**
> **"Then certain philosophers of the Epicureans, and of the Stoicks, encountered him. And some said, What will this babbler say? other some, He seemeth to be a setter forth of strange gods: because he preached unto them Jesus, and the resurrection" (Acts 17:18).**
> **"And they [the ungodly] say, How doth God know? and is there knowledge in the most High? Behold, these are the ungodly, who prosper in the world; they increase in riches" (Ps.73:11-12).**

3. There are the consequences of judgment.

a. The person who does not follow God will not inherit the kingdom of God.

> **"Know ye not that <u>the unrighteous</u> shall not inherit the kingdom of God? Be not deceived: neither fornicators, nor <u>idolaters</u>, nor adulterers, nor effeminate, nor abusers of themselves with mankind, Nor thieves, nor covetous, nor drunkards, nor revilers, nor extortioners, shall inherit the kingdom of God" (1 Cor.6:9-10).**

b. The person who does not follow God displeases God and arouses His anger and wrath.

> **"He that believeth on the Son hath everlasting life: and he that <u>believeth not</u> the Son shall not see life; but the wrath of God abideth on him" (Jn.3:36).**
> **"I said therefore unto you, that ye shall die in your sins: for if ye <u>believe not</u> that I am *he,* ye shall die in your sins" (Jn.8:24).**
> **"Well; because of unbelief they were broken off, and thou standest by faith. Be not highminded, but fear" (Ro.11:20).**
> **"That they all might be damned who believed not the truth, but had pleasure in unrighteousness" (2 Th.2:12).**
> **"I will therefore put you in remembrance, though ye once knew this, how that the Lord, having saved the people out of the land of Egypt, afterward <u>destroyed them that believed not</u>" (Jude 1:5).**

c. The person who does not follow God is broken off, separated, cut loose, turned away from by God.

> **"Well; because of <u>unbelief</u> they were broken off, and thou standest by faith. Be not highminded, but fear" (Ro.11:20).**
> **"And the word of the LORD came unto me, saying, Son of man, these men have set up their idols in their heart, and put the stumblingblock of their iniquity before their face: should I be inquired of at all by them? Therefore speak unto them, and say unto them, Thus saith the Lord GOD; Every man of the house of Israel that setteth up his idols in his heart, and putteth the stumblingblock of his iniquity before his face, and cometh to the prophet; I the LORD will answer him that cometh according to the multitude of his idols; That I may take the house of Israel in their own heart, because they are all estranged from me through their idols" (Ezk.14:2-5).**

d. The person who does not follow God experiences the judicial judgment of God: God gives him over to his sin, to reap what he sows. (See <u>Deeper Study # 1</u>--Jn.12:39-41; note--Ro.1:24 for more discussion.)

> **"And even as they did not like to retain God in *their* knowledge, <u>God gave them over to a reprobate</u> [depraved] <u>mind</u>, to do those things which are not convenient" (Ro.1:28).**

e. The person who does not follow God shall not enter heaven, no matter what he professes and has done in the name of God.

> "Not every one that saith unto me, Lord, Lord, shall enter into the kingdom of heaven; but he that doeth the will of my Father which is in heaven. Many will say to me in that day, Lord, Lord, have we not prophesied in thy name? and in thy name have cast out devils? and in thy name done many wonderful works? And then will I profess unto them, I never knew you: depart from me, ye that work iniquity" (Mt.7:21-23).

f. The person who does not follow God shall face the fierce judgment of God and perish.

> "He that rejecteth me, and receiveth not my words, hath one that judgeth him: the word that I have spoken, the same shall judge him in the last day" (Jn.12:48).
> "But the heavens and the earth, which are now, by the same word are kept in store, reserved unto fire against the day of judgment and perdition of ungodly men" (2 Pt.3:7).
> "And Enoch also, the seventh from Adam, prophesied of these, saying, Behold, the Lord cometh with ten thousands of his saints, To execute judgment upon all, and to convince all that are ungodly among them of all their ungodly deeds which they have ungodly committed, and of all their hard speeches which ungodly sinners have spoken against him" (Jude 1:14-15).
> "How shall I pardon thee for this? thy children have forsaken me, and sworn by them that are no gods: when I had fed them to the full, they then committed adultery, and assembled themselves by troops in the harlots' houses. They were as fed horses in the morning: every one neighed after his neighbour's wife. Shall I not visit for these things? saith the LORD: and shall not my soul be avenged on such a nation as this?" (Jer.5:7-9).
> "The ungodly are not so: but are like the chaff which the wind driveth away. Therefore the ungodly shall not stand in the judgment, nor sinners in the congregation of the righteous. For the LORD knoweth the way of the righteous: but the way of the ungodly shall perish" (Ps.1:4-6).

g. The person who does not follow God shall face the terrible experience of dying in his sins and going to hell.

> "I said therefore unto you, that ye shall die in your sins: for if ye believe not that I am he, ye shall die in your sins" (Jn.8:24).
> "But the fearful, and unbelieving, and the abominable, and murderers, and whoremongers, and sorcerers, and idolaters, and all liars, shall have their part in the lake which burneth with fire and brimstone: which is the second death" (Rev.21:8).

h. The person who does not follow God is deluded and damned.

> "And for this cause God shall send them strong delusion, that they should believe a lie: That they all might be damned who believed not the truth, but had pleasure in unrighteousness" (2 Th.2:11-12).

i. The person who does not follow God causes God to hide his face from him.

> "And he said, I will hide my face from them, I will see what their end shall be: for they are a very froward generation, children in whom is no faith" (Dt.32:20).

j. The person who does not follow God brings judgment upon his children.

> "And the LORD saith, Because they have forsaken my law which I set before them, and have not obeyed my voice, neither walked therein; But have walked after the imagination of their own heart, and after Baalim, which their fathers taught them: Therefore thus saith the LORD of hosts, the God of Israel; Behold, I will feed them, even this people, with wormwood, and give them water of gall to drink. I will scatter them also among the heathen, whom neither they nor their fathers have known: and I will send a sword after them, till I have consumed them" (Jer.9:13-16).
> "Ahaziah the son of Ahab began to reign over Israel in Samaria the seventeenth year of Jehoshaphat king of Judah, and reigned two years over Israel. And he did evil in the sight of the LORD, and walked in the way of his father, and in the way of his mother, and in the way of Jeroboam the son of Nebat, who made Israel to sin: For he served Baal, and worshipped him, and provoked to anger the LORD God of Israel, according to all that his father had done" (1 Ki.22:51-53).
> "He [Ahaziah] also walked in the ways of the house of Ahab: for his mother was his counseller to do wickedly. Wherefore he did evil in the sight of the LORD like the house of Ahab: for they were his counsellers after the death of his father to his destruction" (2 Chron.22:3-4).
> "But I said unto their children in the wilderness, Walk ye not in the statutes of your fathers, neither observe their judgments, nor defile yourselves with their idols: I am the LORD your God; walk in my statutes, and keep my judgments, and do them; And hallow my sabbaths; and they shall be a sign between me and you, that ye may know that I am the LORD your God. Notwithstanding the children rebelled against me: they walked not in my statutes, neither kept my judgments to do them, which if a man do, he shall even live in them; they polluted my sabbaths: then I

said, <u>I would pour out my fury upon them</u>, to accomplish my anger against them in the wilderness" (Ezk.20:18-21).

"Thus saith the LORD; For three transgressions of Judah, and for four, I will not turn away the punishment thereof; because they have despised the law of the LORD, and have not kept his commandments, and their lies caused them to err, after the which their fathers have walked" (Amos 2:4).

THE BIBLICAL BENEFITS OF KEEPING THIS COMMANDMENT: NEVER HAVE OTHER GODS, NEVER BELIEVE IN FALSE GODS

DEEPER STUDY #2
(20:3) <u>Commandments, The Ten--Benefits--Obedience</u>: What are the benefits of keeping this commandment? The LORD (Jehovah, Yahweh) is the only living and true God. Consequently, He is bound to pour out the richest blessings imaginable upon the person who keeps this commandment, upon the person who truly believes and follows Him.

1. The person who believes God--genuinely believes God--will be saved, never condemned, through God's Son, the Lord Jesus Christ.

"For God so loved the world, that he gave his only begotten Son, that whosoever believeth in him should not perish, but have everlasting life. For God sent not his Son into the world to condemn the world; but that the world through him might be saved. <u>He that believeth on him is not condemned</u>: but he that believeth not is condemned already, because he hath not believed in the name of the only begotten Son of God" (Jn.3:16-18).

"For the wages of sin is death; but the gift of God is eternal life through Jesus Christ our Lord" (Ro.6:23).

"That if thou shalt confess with thy mouth the Lord Jesus, and shalt believe in thine heart that God hath raised him from the dead, thou shalt be saved. For with the heart man believeth unto righteousness; and with the mouth confession is made unto salvation" (Ro.10:9-10).

"For by grace are ye saved through faith; and that not of yourselves: it is the gift of God: Not of works, lest any man should boast. For we are his [God's] workmanship, created in Christ Jesus unto good works, which God hath before ordained that we should walk in them" (Eph.2:8-10).

2. The person who believes God will be redeemed, never condemned.

"The LORD redeemeth the soul of his servants: and none of them that trust in him shall be desolate [condemned]" (Ps.34:22).

3. The person who believes God will escape the wrath of God and live forever, live eternally with God and with His Son, the Lord Jesus Christ.

"He that believeth on the Son hath everlasting life: and he that believeth not the Son shall not see life; but the wrath of God abideth on him" (Jn.3:36).

"Verily, verily, I say unto you, He that heareth my word, and believeth on him that sent me, hath everlasting life, and shall not come into condemnation; but is passed from death unto life" (Jn.5:24).

"Jesus said unto her, I am the resurrection, and the life: he that believeth in me, though he were dead, yet shall he live" (Jn.11:25).

"Let not your heart be troubled: ye believe in God, believe also in me. In my Father's house are many mansions: if [it were] not [so], I would have told you. I go to prepare a place for you" (Jn.14:1-2).

"That if thou shalt confess with thy mouth the Lord Jesus, and shalt believe in thine heart that God hath raised him from the dead, thou shalt be saved" (Ro.10:9).

"They that trust in the LORD *shall be* as mount Zion, *which* cannot be removed, *but* abideth for ever" (Ps.125:1).

4. The person who believes God will be justified: God will count his faith for righteousness.

"Therefore it is of faith, that it might be by grace; to the end the promise [of eternal life] might be sure to all the seed; not to that only which is of the law, but to that also which is of the faith of Abraham; who is the father of us all, (As it is written, I have made thee a father of many nations,) before him whom he believed, even God, who quickeneth the dead, and calleth those things which be not as though they were" (Ro.4:16-17).

"Now it was not written for his sake alone, that it was imputed to him; But for us also, to whom it shall be imputed, if we believe on him that raised up Jesus our Lord from the dead; Who was delivered for our offences, and was raised again for our justification" (Ro.4:23-25).

5. The person who believes God--genuinely believes--will be a member of God's family, His treasured possession, and receive unbelievable reward.

> "Now therefore, if ye will obey my voice indeed, and keep my covenant, then ye shall be a peculiar treasure unto me above all people: for all the earth is mine" (Ex.19:5).
>
> "This day the LORD thy God hath commanded thee to do these statutes and judgments: thou shalt therefore keep and do them with all thine heart, and with all thy soul. Thou hast avouched the LORD this day to be thy God, and to walk in his ways, and to keep his statutes, and his commandments, and his judgments, and to hearken unto his voice: And the LORD hath avouched thee this day to be his peculiar people, as he hath promised thee, and that thou shouldest keep all his commandments; And to make thee high above all nations which he hath made, in praise, and in name, and in honour; and that thou mayest be an holy people unto the LORD thy God, as he hath spoken" (Dt.26:16-19).

6. The person who believes God will come to know God personally, in an intimate way.

> "That I may know him [Jesus Christ], and the power of his resurrection, and the fellowship of his sufferings, being made conformable unto his death" (Ph.3:10).
>
> "Unto thee it was showed, that thou mightest know that the LORD he is God; there is none else beside him" (Dt.4:35).
>
> "Ye are my witnesses, saith the LORD, and my servant whom I have chosen: that ye may know and believe me, and understand that I am he: before me there was no God formed, neither shall there be after me" (Is.43:10).
>
> "Jesus answered them, and said, My doctrine is not mine, but his that sent me. If any man will do his will, he shall know of the doctrine, whether it be of God, or [whether] I speak of myself" (Jn.7:16-17).

7. The person who believes God will live in perfect peace, assurance, and confidence as he walks throughout life, as he trusts God and keeps his mind upon Him.

> "Thou wilt keep *him* in perfect peace, *whose* mind *is* stayed *on thee:* because he trusteth in thee" (Is.26:3).
>
> "Therefore being justified by faith, we have peace with God through our Lord Jesus Christ" (Ro.5:1).

8. The person who believes God will be given the strength of God day by day, even the everlasting strength of God Himself.

> "Trust ye in the LORD for ever: for in the LORD JEHOVAH *is* everlasting strength" (Is.26:4).

9. The person who believes God will be secure through the trials and temptations of life, safe from all the enemies.

> "The fear of man bringeth a snare: but whoso putteth his trust in the LORD shall be safe" (Pr.29:25).
>
> "Who shall separate us from the love of Christ? shall tribulation, or distress, or persecution, or famine, or nakedness, or peril, or sword? Nay, in all these things we are more than conquerors through him that loved us. For I am persuaded, that neither death, nor life, nor angels, nor principalities, nor powers, nor things present, nor things to come....Nor height, nor depth, nor any other creature, shall be able to separate us from the love of God, which is in Christ Jesus our Lord" (Ro.8:35, 37-39).

10. The person who believes God will be looked after and taken care of by God.

> "Commit thy way unto the LORD; trust also in him; and he shall bring *it* to pass" (Ps.37:5).
>
> "Casting all your care upon him; for he careth for you" (1 Pt.5:7).
>
> "But seek ye first the kingdom of God, and his righteousness; and all these things shall be added unto you" (Mt.6:33).

11. The person who believes God will be guided and directed by God.

> "Trust in the LORD with all thine heart; and lean not unto thine own understanding. In all thy ways acknowledge him, and he shall direct thy paths" (Pr.3:5-6).

12. The person who believes God will experience the love and power of God: all things will work out for good.

> "And we know that all things work together for good to them that love God, to them who are the called according to his purpose" (Ro.8:28).

13. The person who believes God overcomes the world.

> "For whatsoever is born of God overcometh the world: and this is the victory that overcometh the world, even our faith. Who is he that overcometh the world, but he that believeth that Jesus is the Son of God?" (1 Jn.5:4-5).

14. The person who believes God overcomes the temptations of the devil.

> "Above all, taking the shield of faith, wherewith ye shall be able to quench all the fiery darts of the wicked" (Eph.6:16).

15. The person who believes God is given the righteousness and justification of God.

> "But now the righteousness of God without the law is manifested, being witnessed by the law and the prophets; Even the righteousness of God which is by faith of Jesus Christ unto all and upon all them that believe: for there is no difference: For all have sinned, and come short of the glory of God; Being justified freely by his grace through the redemption that is in Christ Jesus" (Ro.3:21-24).
> "And be found in him, not having mine own righteousness, which is of the law, but that which is through the faith of Christ, the righteousness which is of God by faith" (Ph.3:9; cp. 2 Cor.5:21).
> "But let him that glorieth glory in this, that he understandeth and knoweth me, that I am the LORD which exercise lovingkindness, judgment, and righteousness, in the earth: for in these things I delight, saith the LORD" (Jer.9:24).

16. The person who believes God receives what he asks in prayer.

> "And all things, whatsoever ye shall ask in prayer, believing, ye shall receive" (Mt.21:22).

17. The person who believes God will be greatly rewarded by God.

> "But without faith *it is* impossible to please *him*: for he that cometh to God must believe that he is, and *that* he is a rewarder of them that diligently seek him" (Heb.11:6).

18. The person who believes God will experience the glorious goodness and blessings of God.

> "*Oh* how great *is* thy goodness, which thou hast laid up for them that fear thee; *which* thou hast wrought for them that trust in thee before the sons of men!" (Ps.31:19).

DEEPER STUDY # 3
JESUS CHRIST AND HIS TEACHING CONCERNING <u>FALSE GODS</u>
"Thou shalt have no other gods before me" (Ex.20:3).

THE TEACHING OF CHRIST	THE BELIEVER'S RESPONSE
1. Jesus Christ declared that there is *only one true and living God, One Sovereign LORD and Majesty* of the universe, and that we are to love Him with all our hearts, souls, and minds.	1) We are to know and acknowledge the only true and living God, Him and Him alone.
	2) We must not believe nor follow any false gods, none whatsoever.
	3) We are...
	• to set no false god *before* the LORD God
	• to set no false god *beside* the LORD God
	• to set no false god "in the presence" of the LORD God
	• to set no false god in the face of the LORD God
"Then one of them, *which was* a lawyer, asked *him a question*, tempting him, and saying, Master, which *is* the great commandment in the law? Jesus said unto him, Thou shalt love the Lord thy God with all thy heart, and with all thy soul, and with all thy mind. This is the first and great commandment. And the second *is* like unto it, Thou shalt love thy neighbour as thyself. On these two commandments hang all the law and the prophets" (Mt.22:35-40).	"Ye *are* my witnesses, saith the LORD, and my servant whom I have chosen: that ye may know and believe me, and understand that I *am* he: before me there was no God formed, neither shall there be after me" (Is.43:10).
	"Thus saith the LORD the King of Israel, and his redeemer the LORD of hosts; I *am* the first, and I *am* the last; and beside me *there is* no God" (Is.44:6).
	"Fear ye not, neither be afraid: have not I told thee from that time, and have declared *it*? ye *are* even my witnesses. Is there a God beside me? yea, *there is* no God; I know not *any*" (Is.44:8).
	"I *am* the LORD, and *there is* none else, *there is* no God beside me: I girded thee, though thou hast not known me" (Is.45:5).
	"For thus saith the LORD that created the heavens; God himself that formed the earth and made it; he hath established it, he created it not in vain, he formed it to be inhabited: I *am* the LORD; and *there is* none else" (Is.45:18).

THE TEACHING OF CHRIST	THE BELIEVER'S RESPONSE
	"Remember the former things of old: for I *am* God, and *there is* none else; *I am* God, and *there is* none like me" (Is.46:9). "One God and Father of all, who *is* above all, and through all, and in you all" (Eph.4:6). "For *there is* one God, and one mediator between God and men, the man Christ Jesus" (1 Tim.2:5).
2. Jesus Christ declared that God exists by proclaiming that He is the Son of God Himself. "He that believeth on him is not condemned: but he that believeth not is condemned already, because he hath not believed in the name of the only begotten Son of God" (Jn.3:18). "Verily, verily, I say unto you, The hour is coming, and now is, when the dead shall hear the voice of the Son of God: and they that hear shall live" (Jn.5:25).	⇒ We must believe in the Son of God in order to be saved. "For God so loved the world, that he gave his only begotten Son, that whosoever believeth in him should not perish, but have everlasting life" (Jn.3:16). "But these are written, that ye might believe that Jesus is the Christ, the Son of God; and that believing ye might have life through his name" (Jn.20:31). "And lo a voice from heaven, saying, This is my beloved Son, in whom I am well pleased" (Mt.3:17).
3. Jesus Christ declared that God exists by proclaiming that He was One with the Father. "I and *my* Father are one" (Jn.10:30).	1) The only way to have a relationship with the Father is to believe in the Son of God. 2) We must trust in Christ and believe His Word: He and the Father are One. "If I do not the works of my Father, believe me not. But if I do, though ye believe not me, believe the works: that ye may know, and believe, that the Father is in me, and I in him" (Jn.10:37-38). "Believest thou not that I am in the Father, and the Father in me? the words that I speak unto you I speak not of myself: but the Father that dwelleth in me, he doeth the works" (Jn.14:10). "And now I am no more in the world, but these are in the world, and I come to thee. Holy Father, keep through thine own name those whom thou hast given me, that they may be one, as we *are*" (Jn.17:11). "And the glory which thou gavest me I have given them; that they may be one, even as we are one" (Jn.17:22).
4. Jesus Christ declared that God exists by proclaiming His own pre-existence with the Father. "Jesus said unto them, Verily, verily, I say unto you, Before Abraham was, I am" (Jn.8:58). "And now, O Father, glorify thou me with thine own self with the glory which I had with thee before the world was" (Jn.17:5).	1) Because Jesus Christ is God, the believer must... • worship Christ as he would worship God • obey Christ as he would obey God • serve Christ as he would serve God • honor Christ as he would honor God • believe Christ as he would believe God 2) Because Jesus Christ is God, we have a God who is our... • Lord • Savior • Master • Creator • Provider • Intercessor • Great High Priest • Sacrificial Lamb of God • Coming King and Lord of lords "In the beginning was the Word, and the Word was with God, and the Word was God. The same was in the beginning with God. All things were made by him; and without him was not any thing made that was made" (Jn.1:1-3). "I am Alpha and Omega, the beginning and the end, the first and the last" (Rev.22:13).
5. Jesus Christ declared that God exists by proclaiming the love of God. "For God so loved the world, that he gave his only begotten Son, that whosoever believeth in him should	⇒ The most glorious truth is that God gave His one and only Son, His only begotten Son. This is the most remarkable proof of God's love. It magnifies and shows how great His love really is. "Then they that were in the ship came and worshipped him, saying, Of a truth thou art the Son of God" (Mt.14:33).

THE TEACHING OF CHRIST	THE BELIEVER'S RESPONSE
not perish, but have everlasting life" (Jn.3:16).	"While he yet spake, behold, a bright cloud overshadowed them: and behold a voice out of the cloud, which said, This is my beloved Son, in whom I am well pleased; hear ye him" (Mt.17:5). "The beginning of the gospel of Jesus Christ, the Son of God" (Mk.1:1). "And I saw, and bare record that this is the Son of God" (Jn.1:34). "Say ye of him, whom the Father hath sanctified, and sent into the world, Thou Blasphemest; because I said, I am the Son of God?" (Jn.10:36). "She saith unto him, Yea, Lord: I believe that thou art the Christ, the Son of God, which should come into the world" (Jn.11:27). "Whosoever shall confess that Jesus is the Son of God, God dwelleth in him, and he in God" (1Jn.4:15).
6. Jesus Christ declared that God exists by proclaiming that a person can live eternally with God. "For God so loved the world, that he gave his only begotten Son, that whosoever believeth in him should not perish, but have everlasting life" (Jn.3:16). "Verily, verily, I say unto you, He that heareth my word, and believeth on him [God] that sent me, hath everlasting life, and shall not come into condemnation; but is passed from death unto life" (Jn.5:24).	⇒ God was willing to give the thing most dear to His heart in order to save the world. Note this: God even planned to give His Son throughout eternity. "Him, being delivered by the <u>determinate counsel and foreknowledge of God</u>, ye have taken, and by wicked hands have crucified and slain: Whom God hath raised up, having loosed the pains of death: because it was not possible that he should be holden of it" (Acts 2:23-24). "And was there until the death of Herod: that it might be fulfilled which was spoken of the Lord by the prophet, saying, Out of Egypt have I called my son" (Mt.2:15). "And the angel answered and said unto her, The Holy Ghost shall come upon thee, and the power of the Highest shall overshadow thee: therefore also that holy thing which shall be born of thee shall be called the Son of God" (Lk.1:35)
7. Jesus Christ declared that God exists by teaching that the person who rejects the Son of God will bear the terrible judgment and wrath of God. "But whosoever shall deny me before men, him will I also deny before my Father which is in heaven" (Mt.10:33). "But he that denieth me before men shall be denied before the angels of God" (Lk.12:9). "He that believeth on the Son hath everlasting life: and he that believeth not the Son shall not see life; but the wrath of God abideth on him" (Jn.3:36). "He that believeth on him is not condemned: but he that believeth not is condemned already, because he hath not believed in the name of the only begotten Son of God" (Jn.3:18).	1) Man's eternal fate hinges on believing that God exists. "That whosoever believeth in him should not perish, but have eternal life. For God so loved the world, that he gave his only begotten Son, that whosoever believeth in him should not perish, but have everlasting life" (Jn.3:15-16). "That if thou shalt confess with thy mouth the Lord Jesus, and shalt believe in thine heart that God hath raised him from the dead, thou shalt be saved" (Ro.10:9). 2) We must believe on the Son in order to guarantee everlasting life. "Verily, verily, I say unto you, He that heareth my word, and believeth on him that sent me, hath everlasting life, and shall not come into condemnation; but is passed from death unto life" (Jn.5:24). "Jesus said unto her, I am the resurrection, and the life: he that believeth in me, though he were dead, yet shall he live" (Jn.11:25). "But these are written, that ye might believe that Jesus is the Christ, the Son of God; and that believing ye might have life through his name" (Jn.20:31). "And that from a child thou hast known the holy scriptures, which are able to make thee wise unto salvation through faith which is in Christ Jesus" (2 Tim.3:15). "Whosoever believeth that Jesus is the Christ is born of God: and every one that loveth him that begat loveth him also that is begotten of him" (1 Jn.5:1). 3) We are never to be ashamed of our relationship with Jesus Christ. Christ has done far too much for us to deny Him, to ever be ashamed of Him. "For I am not ashamed of the gospel of Christ: for it is the power of God unto salvation to every one that believeth; to the Jew first, and also to the Greek" (Ro.1:16). "As it is written, Behold, I lay in Sion a stumblingstone and rock of offence: and whosoever believeth on him shall not be ashamed" (Ro.9:33). "According to my earnest expectation and *my* hope, that in nothing I shall be ashamed, but *that* with all boldness, as always, *so* now also Christ shall be magnified in my body, whether *it be* by life, or by death" (Ph.1:20). "Yet if *any man suffer* as a Christian, let him not be ashamed; but let him glorify God on this behalf" (1 Pt.4:16).

THE TEACHING OF CHRIST	THE BELIEVER'S RESPONSE
	"And now, little children, abide in him; that, when he shall appear, we may have confidence, and not be ashamed before him at his coming" (1 Jn.2:28).
8. Jesus Christ declared the existence of God when He prayed to His Father, the LORD God Himself (Jehovah, Yahweh).	1) We must focus and direct our prayers to the only living and true God, to the Father of the Lord Jesus Christ, to Him and Him alone.
	2) We must never pray nor seek help from false gods, gods that are nothing more than the imaginations of men.
"These words spake Jesus, and lifted up his eyes to heaven, and said, Father, the hour is come; glorify thy Son, that thy Son also may glorify thee" (Jn.17:1).	"At that time Jesus answered and said, I thank thee, O Father, Lord of heaven and earth, because thou hast hid these things from the wise and prudent, and hast revealed them unto babes" (Mt.11:25).
"And now, O Father, glorify thou me with thine own self with the glory which I had with thee before the world was" (Jn.17:5).	"Then said Jesus, Father, forgive them; for they know not what they do. And they parted his raiment, and cast lots" (Lk.23:34).
"And now I am no more in the world, but these are in the world, and I come to thee. Holy Father, keep through thine own name those whom thou hast given me, that they may be one, as we *are*" (Jn.17:11).	"Then they took away the stone from the place where the dead was laid. And Jesus lifted up his eyes, and said, Father, I thank thee that thou hast heard me" (Jn.11:41).
"Father, I will that they also, whom thou hast given me, be with me where I am; that they may behold my glory, which thou hast given me: for thou lovedst me before the foundation of the world. O righteous Father, the world hath not known thee: but I have known thee, and these have known that thou hast sent me" (Jn.17:24-25).	"Ye have not chosen me, but I have chosen you, and ordained you, that ye should go and bring forth fruit, and *that* your fruit should remain: that whatsoever ye shall ask of the Father in my name, he may give it you" (Jn.15:16).
	"And in that day ye shall ask me nothing. Verily, verily, I say unto you, Whatsoever ye shall ask the Father in my name, he will give *it* you. Hitherto have ye asked nothing in my name: ask, and ye shall receive, that your joy may be full" (Jn.16:23-24).

	C. The Ten Commandments, The Laws Governing Man's Duty to God (Part 2): Commandment Two Concerns The Worship of God--Never Make Nor Worship False Gods, Ex.20:4-6	the earth beneath, or that is in the water under the earth: 5 Thou shalt not bow down thyself to them, nor serve them: for I the LORD thy God am a jealous God, visiting the iniquity of the fathers upon the children unto the third and fourth generation of them that hate me; 6 And showing mercy unto thousands of them that love me, and keep my commandments.
1. Who is to obey this commandment? You **2. How long was this commandment to be in force? Forever** **3. What is forbidden by this**	4 Thou shalt not make unto thee any graven image, or any likeness of any thing that is in heaven above, or that is in	**commandment?** a. Prohibits the making of idols b. Prohibits the worship of idols c. Prohibits covetousness (cp. Col.3:5) **4. Why did God give this commandment**[DS1]**?** a. Because God is a jealous God b. Because the influence of idolatry is passed down from parents to children c. Because the influence of loving God lasts for generations **5. What is the decision required by this commandment? Obedience**

DIVISION VII

THE LAW AND THE PROMISES OF GOD (THE MOSAIC COVENANT) (PART 2): THE TEN COMMANDMENTS--NECESSARY LAWS TO GOVERN MAN AND SOCIETY, EX.20:1-26

C.   The Ten Commandments, The Laws Governing Man's Duty to God (Part 2): Commandment Two Concerns The Worship of God--Never Make Nor Worship False Gods, Ex.20:4-6

(20:4-6) Introduction: there is only one true and living God, the Sovereign LORD and Majesty of the universe. He is the great Creator and Sustainer of the universe. He is the LORD God (Jehovah, Yahweh) of heaven, the Father of the LORD Jesus Christ. As the Lord God, the Creator of all people, He has one major concern: how people worship Him. This is the concern of this commandment, the worship of God by man. Every person upon earth worships something. The great tragedy is that most people worship falsely. They worship something other than the only true and living God. They worship false gods...

- the false gods created by the imagination of people
- the false gods of science and technology
- the false gods made of wood, stone, metal, and other materials--all formed into the image of idols
- the false gods of self, money, sex, pleasure, houses, lands, and the other possessions of this earth
- the false gods of the state and government, of its power to feed, protect, and take care of man
- the false gods of natural law, of the basic forces of the universe, of believing that energy or force itself is the controlling power of the universe and of life

The false gods worshipped by people are innumerable. Every person has an image of what the *supreme* authority of the universe is, an image of the supreme being of the universe, an image of that to which he should give his life. To what should we give our lives? What should we be worshipping? The demand of this commandment is that we give our lives to the only true and living God, that we worship Him and Him alone.

Note what worship is:
⇒ Worship is the heart reaching out to God (drawing near God for His love and care) and the giving of one's heart to God in praise, thanksgiving, service, and witness.

This is exactly what God demands:
⇒ that we reach out to Him, draw near Him for His love and care
⇒ that we give ourselves (sacrificially) to God in praise, thanksgiving, service, and witness

This is the subject of this great commandment: *Commandment Two Concerns The Worship of God--Never Make Nor Worship False Gods*, 20:4-6.
1.   Who is to obey this commandment? You (v.4).
2.   How long was this commandment to be in force? Forever (v.4).
3.   What is forbidden by this commandment (v.4-5)?
4.   Why did God give this commandment (v.5-6)?
5.   What is the decision required by this commandment? Obedience (v.6).

1   **(20:4) Commandments, The Ten--Obedience**: Who is to obey this commandment? Note the very first word of the commandment: "You." God addresses this commandment to "you." "You" are personally responsible to Him, responsible to obey His commandment. But you are not only *responsible* to obey: you are held *accountable* to obey by God. The idea is just this: If you disobey God, you will be held accountable and judged by God.
   Now, who is to obey this commandment?
⇒   "You," you personally.
⇒   "You" are *responsible* to obey this commandment.
⇒   "You" are held *accountable* to obey. And if you disobey the commandment, you will be judged.

"The soul that sinneth, it shall die" (Ezk.18:20).
"This day the LORD thy God hath commanded thee to do these statutes and judgments: thou shalt therefore keep and do them with all thine heart, and with all thy soul" (Dt.26:16).
"For this ye know, that no whoremonger, nor unclean person, nor covetous man, who is an **idolater**, hath any inheritance in the kingdom of Christ and of God. Let no man deceive you with vain words: for because of these things cometh the wrath of God upon the children of disobedience" (Eph.5:5-6).

2 (20:4) **Commandments, The Ten--Obedience**: How long was this commandment to be in force? Was it given to Israel alone, or was it given through Israel to all people of all generations? Note the commandment: You shall not make nor worship any idol whatsoever (v.4-5). God Himself spoke these words (v.1), a commandment that forbids--absolutely forbids--the making and worshipping of anything other than God Himself.

God is the great Creator, the Sovereign Lord and Majesty of the universe. This means that He and He alone is to be *acknowledged and worshipped* by His creation. In fact, the Creator would never tolerate His subjects (creation) worshipping anything or anyone other than Himself.

How long is this commandment in force? It is in force as long as God's creation stands, as long as the universe exists. This commandment was in force when it was first given by God, and the commandment is still in force today. It will be in force throughout all eternity. No person is ever to worship anything other than the LORD God Himself.

You and your descendants are under the force of this commandment. All people of all generations are to obey this commandment.

"Take heed to yourselves, that your heart be not deceived, and ye turn aside, and serve other gods, and worship them" (Dt.11:16).
"This day the LORD thy God hath commanded thee to do these statutes and judgments: thou shalt therefore keep and do them with all thine heart, and with all thy soul" (Dt.26:16).
"O worship the LORD in the beauty of holiness: fear before him, all the earth" (Ps.96:9).
"I am the LORD: that is my name: and my glory will I not give to another, neither my praise to graven images" (Is.42:8).
"Then saith Jesus unto him, Get thee hence, Satan: for it is written, Thou shalt worship the Lord thy God, and him only shalt thou serve" (Mt.4:10).
"Not every one that saith unto me, Lord, Lord, shall enter into the kingdom of heaven; but he that doeth the will of my Father which is in heaven" (Mt.7:21).
"Blessed are they that do his commandments, that they may have right to the tree of life, and may enter in through the gates into the city" (Rev.22:14).

3 (20:4-5) **Commandments, The Ten--Obedience--Disobedience--Worship--Idolatry**: What is forbidden by this commandment? "You shall not make any idol nor worship any false god--none whatsoever." How is this commandment broken? How is it violated? Scripture says that this commandment forbids at least three things.

1. This commandment prohibits the *making* of any idol whatsoever; therefore, the commandment is broken and violated by making idols (v.4).
   a. To make an image of anything for worship is wrong. Note the verse: We must not build an image of anything for worship, not an image of anything in the sky above nor that is in the earth beneath, nor that is in the water upon the earth. Nothing in the universe is ever to have an image made of it, not for worship.
   Note that the entire universe is covered; even the unseen world of heaven is covered. No idol of anything is ever to be made...
   - not of heavenly creatures: angels, demons, devils, or imaginary gods
   - not of heavenly bodies such as the sun, moon, or stars
   - not of earthly creatures such as cows, elephants, or man
   - not of water creatures such as fish, crocodiles, or sea animals

   The making of any idol whatsoever is forbidden--absolutely forbidden. God emphatically declares, "You shall never make an idol of anything, not ever--not of anything."
   b. This commandment also forbids the making of an image of God Himself; He is an heavenly being (v.4). Note that "no image or form or likeness of anything in heaven is to be made" (v.4). God is in heaven, in the spiritual world or dimension of being; therefore, no image is to be made of God.
   c. A question needs to be asked at this point: What about images such as pictures, crucifixes, statues, and other symbols that are used to stir our memories to pray and worship? Is this commandment speaking against such images? There is a tendency within human nature to focus upon that which is seen instead of upon the unseen, a tendency to fix our attention upon the seen object instead of upon God. Reason and honesty--especially *honesty*--demands that we acknowledge this fact. Consequently, if we use visible objects to arouse us to pray and worship, there is great danger...
   - that a pure and spiritual worship of God will fade, deteriorate, and be degraded.
   - that the physical object will become more valued and receive more of our attention than God. Why? Because God is spiritual and unseen, and the physical object is seen.

William Barclay has an excellent statement on idolatry. Note carefully what he says:

"[Idolatry] began because men found it difficult to worship a god they could not see. So they said to themselves, 'We will make something which will represent the god and that will make it easier to think of the god.' In the first instance the idol was never meant to be the god; it was meant only to stand for the god.

"We can perhaps understand it, if we think of it this way. Suppose we have a friend whom we have not seen for a very long time, and suppose we sit down to write a letter to that friend, and suppose we find the letter hard to write, because we have been separated for so long. In such a situation it might well help if we took a photograph of the friend and put it where we could see it, and wrote, as it were, looking at the photograph. The photograph would bring our friend nearer to our mind. At first that is what an idol was meant to do.

"The trouble was that men began to worship the idol instead of the god it stood for; men began to worship the symbol instead of the reality it was supposed to represent. It is not really difficult to see how idolatry began, and it is not really so silly as it looks. For all that, we may well be saying, 'I am not likely to do a thing like that.' But perhaps we are more likely to do it than we think.

"Take a very small thing first of all. Quite a lot of people carry some kind of lucky mascot, some kind of charm. Some carry a lucky penny or a lucky sign of the zodiac, or, for instance, if they go on a journey, they take a St. Christopher sign to avoid accidents. That is really idolatry, for it is believing that in some way the carrying of a little bit of metal or plastic can have an effect on their lives.

"But there is something much more serious than that. The real essence of idolatry is that a man worships a thing instead of God.

"There is no doubt at all that there is a great deal of that today. People assess their success in life by the number of things which they possess. We think a man a success if he has a big motor car, or an elaborate television set or record-player, or if he can go every year for a Continental holiday.

"This is obviously wrong."[1]

Arthur W. Pink gives a thought-provoking statement on idolatry that is well worth quoting:

"This commandment strikes against a desire, or should we say a disease, which is deeply rooted in the human heart, namely, to bring in some aids to the worship of God, beyond those which He has appointed--material aids, things which can be perceived by the senses. Nor is the reason for this difficult to find: God is incorporeal, invisible, and can be realized only by a spiritual principle, and since that principle is dead in fallen man, he naturally seeks that which accords with his carnality. But how different is it with those who have been quickened by the Holy Spirit. No one who truly knows God as a living reality needs any images to aid his devotions; none who enjoys daily communion with Christ requires any pictures of Him to help him to pray and adore, for he conceives of Him by faith and not by fancy."[2]

Now, having said this, the commandment does not forbid artistic talent, that is, the making of sculptures, pictures, statues, and crucifixes for the purpose of the fine arts. The commandment strikes against making and using images and idols...
- for the purpose of worship
- for the purpose of controlling our lives and looking after us

This steals our hearts away from the only living and true God.

Thought 1. Adrian Rogers has an excellent illustration dealing with making an image or likeness of God for the purpose of worship and prayer:

"Idolatry is wrong because it gives a distorted or false picture of God. An idol is a material thing, and no idol can represent the invisible, spiritual God. Jesus said in John 4:24, 'God is a Spirit.' I know the King James Version includes the indefinite article, but the literal translation is, God is spirit.' That is, spirit is His very essence.

"No wonder, then, that Jesus went on to say, 'They that worship him must worship him in spirit and in truth.' What material thing could possibly represent spirit? God is a circle whose center is everywhere and whose circumference is nowhere. God is spirit. There is nowhere where God is not, and no material thing can represent Him.

"There's nothing you can compare God to or with. There's nothing that says, 'This is what God is totally like.' God Himself asked, 'To whom then will ye liken me, or shall I be equal?' (Isaiah 40:25). We can say one man is like another man, one chair is like another chair, one piano like another piano, and so on. But there's only one God. You can't compare Him to anything or anyone....

"Suppose a woman walks into a room and finds her husband embracing another woman. He sees his wife out of the corner of his eye and says, 'Now wait a minute, honey. Don't get the wrong idea here. Let me tell you what I was doing. This woman is so beautiful, she reminded me of you. I was really just thinking of you when I was embracing her.'

"There's not a woman in America who would buy that, including my wife, Joyce! And God doesn't buy it either when we worship something else and say, 'Now, Lord, wait a minute. Don't get the wrong idea here. I was only worshiping this thing because it reminds me of You. I'm really worshiping You.'

"No, you really aren't. That's what the Second Commandment is all about."[3]

[1] William Barclay. *The Old Law and the New Law*. (Philadelphia, PA: The Westminster Press, 1972), p.11-13.
[2] Arthur W. Pink. *The Ten Commandments*. (Grand Rapids, MI: Baker Books, 1994), p.21-22.
[3] Adrian Rogers. *Ten Secrets For A Successful Family*. (Wheaton, IL: Crossway Books, 1996), p.44-45.

Thought 2. There is only one true image of God, only one *image* that is acceptable to God.[4]
1) Jesus Christ is the visible image of the invisible God.

> **"[God] who hath delivered us from the power of darkness, and hath translated us into the kingdom of his dear Son: In whom we have redemption through his blood, even the forgiveness of sins: Who is the <u>image</u> of the invisible God, the firstborn of every creature" (Col.1:13-15).**

2) Jesus Christ is the express image, the exact representation, of God's person.

> **"God, who at sundry times and in divers manners spake in time past unto the fathers by the prophets, Hath in these last days spoken unto us by his Son, whom he hath appointed heir of all things, by whom also he made the worlds; Who being the brightness of his glory, and the <u>express image</u> of his person, and upholding all things by the word of his power, when he had by himself purged our sins, sat down on the right hand of the Majesty on high" (Heb.1:1-3).**

3) Jesus Christ is the very form, the very nature, of God.

> **"Who, being in the <u>form</u> of God, thought it not robbery to be equal with God" (Ph.2:6).**

4) Jesus Christ is the fulness of the Godhead bodily.

> **"For in him dwelleth all the fulness of the Godhead bodily. And ye are complete in him, which is the head of all principality and power" (Col.2:9-10).**

5) Jesus Christ is the image to whom we are to be conformed.

> **"For whom he did foreknow, he also did predestinate to be conformed to the image [likeness, NIV] of his Son, that he might be the firstborn among many brethren" (Ro.8:29).**

6) Jesus Christ is the image to which we shall be gloriously and eternally made (transformed).

> **"Beloved, now are we the sons of God, and it doth not yet appear what we shall be: but we know that, when he shall appear, we shall be like him; for we shall see him as he is" (1 Jn.3:2).**

7) Jesus Christ is the very nature and revelation of God Himself.

> **"If ye had known me, ye should have known my Father also: and from henceforth ye know him, and have seen him. Philip saith unto him, Lord, show us the Father, and it sufficeth us. Jesus saith unto him, Have I been so long time with you, and yet hast thou not known me, Philip? he that hath seen me hath seen the Father; and how sayest thou [then], Show us the Father? Believest thou not that I am in the Father, and the Father in me? the words that I speak unto you I speak not of myself: but the Father that dwelleth in me, he doeth the works" (Jn.14:7-10).**

2. This commandment prohibits the *worship* of any false god whatsoever, prohibits the worship of anything other than God Himself (v.5).
  a. This strikes a death blow against one of the most common ideas and claims of people: that all religions worship the same god, that no matter what we may call god and no matter what religion we follow, we all worship the same *supreme being*.
    Remember the first commandment: there are no other gods; there is only one true and living God (v.5). Therefore, if we create a god within our own minds--if we worship something else, some other so-called god, if we treat something else as a god--we misrepresent the truth. No matter how large our religion may become, even if billions of people followed, our worship would be a lie. It would be wrong; it would be sinful behavior. Our idea of God would be inaccurate, incomplete, and false. And false worship is a gross insult to the *only* living and true God, to the *only* Sovereign Lord and Majesty of the universe.
    ⇒ It is wrong to worship things in the sky such as the sun, moon, and stars; wrong to trust and use the zodiac and other so-called *fortune-tellers* to guide one's life.
    ⇒ It is wrong to worship things in the earth such as man, cows, elephants, and other animals.
    ⇒ It is wrong to worship things in the water such as fish, crocodiles, and so-called sea creatures.
    ⇒ It is wrong to worship false messiahs and saviors.
    ⇒ It is wrong to engage in the false worship of anything.

    Simply stated, it is wrong to worship the image of God created by man's imagination, wrong to picture what we think God is like and wrong to worship our image of God. God has revealed Himself, revealed exactly who He is and what He is like, in the Lord Jesus Christ and in the Holy Scripture. It is the Lord God revealed by Jesus Christ and the Holy Scripture that we are to picture and worship. We are to worship the *LORD God of revelation*--

---

[4] These points are taken from the Sunday School material: *Ten Overlooked Principles in Building Successful Families* which is derived from Adrian Rogers' *Ten Secrets For A Successful Family*.

the LORD God *revealed by Jesus Christ*--worship Him and Him alone. (See note, pt.2--Ex.20:1; also see outline and note--Jn.14:4-7; 14:8-14.)

b. This commandment also strikes a death blow against what was mentioned earlier, that of using images of heavenly beings for worship and prayer (v.5). God does not accept any worship that comes to Him through an idol. God is Spirit, not physical and material. God is invisible, not visible to the naked eye. Therefore, to worship an image of God is to misrepresent God, and misrepresentation of God is a lie, is sinful behavior. It is a gross insult to the Sovereign Lord of the universe.

⇒ It is wrong to worship any physical or visible image of God, wrong to worship any idol or anything else upon earth, even wrong to worship an invisible image of God created within the imagination of man.

⇒ It is even wrong to worship religious rituals; our worship and passion should be only for God Himself.

"To whom then will ye liken me, or shall I be equal? saith the Holy One" (Is.40:25)

God is Spirit. He has no physical form that can be seen with the human eye. Therefore, God is not to be worshipped through physical, visible objects. When God is worshipped in some visible form, the glory of the invisible God is degraded. Why? Because God is Spirit, omnipotent and omnipresent Spirit, the all-powerful and all-knowing Sovereign of the Universe, the Creator of all things that are in heaven and earth, both visible and invisible. God cannot be bottled up; His glory cannot be formed and sculpted into any image whatsoever. No imagination of man can picture God. Man's thoughts, descriptions, and images of God are totally incomplete and inadequate. As Spirit, He is out beyond the universe, surrounding and embracing the universe. No planet or star--no heavenly body--extends out beyond God's presence and knowledge.

As stated, God is Spirit and they that worship Him must worship Him in Spirit and in truth. The Scripture emphatically declares:

"God [is] a Spirit: and they that worship him must worship [him] in spirit and in truth" (Jn.4:24).

"For the invisible things of him from the creation of the world are clearly seen, being understood by the things that are made, even his eternal power and Godhead; so that they are without excuse: Because that, when they knew God, they glorified him not as God, neither were thankful; but became vain in their imaginations, and their foolish heart was darkened. Professing themselves to be wise, they became fools, And changed the glory of the uncorruptible God into an image made like to corruptible man, and to birds, and fourfooted beasts, and creeping things. Wherefore God also gave them up to uncleanness through the lusts of their own hearts, to dishonour their own bodies between themselves: Who changed the truth of God into a lie, and worshipped and served the creature more than the Creator, who is blessed for ever. Amen" (Ro.1:20-25).

"Little children, keep yourselves from idols. Amen" (1 Jn.5:21).

"Ye shall make you no idols nor graven image, neither rear you up a standing image, neither shall ye set up any image of stone in your land, to bow down unto it: for I am the LORD your God" (Lev.26:1).

"Take ye therefore good heed unto yourselves; for ye saw no manner of similitude [form] on the day that the LORD spake unto you in Horeb out of the midst of the fire: Lest ye corrupt yourselves, and make you a graven image, the similitude of any figure, the likeness of male or female, The likeness of any beast that is on the earth, the likeness of any winged fowl that flieth in the air, The likeness of any thing that creepeth on the ground, the likeness of any fish that is in the waters beneath the earth: And lest thou lift up thine eyes unto heaven, and when thou seest the sun, and the moon, and the stars, even all the host of heaven, shouldest be driven to worship them, and serve them, which the LORD thy God hath divided unto all nations under the whole heaven" (Dt.4:15-19).

"Take heed to yourselves, that your heart be not deceived, and ye turn aside, and serve other gods, and worship them" (Dt.11:16).

3. This commandment prohibits *covetousness*, prohibits craving after and seeking anything more than one craves after and seeks God (v.5, cp. Col.3:5). Scripture emphatically declares...

• "Covetousness...is idolatry" (Col.3:5).

Covetousness is craving and desiring something so much that a person makes it the primary thing in his life. The object becomes the first thing in a person's life, the major craving, the longing desire of the person's heart and life. A person can covet and make an idol out of anything:

⇒ sex	⇒ girlfriend	⇒ money	⇒ position	⇒ ritual
⇒ drugs	⇒ boyfriend	⇒ fame	⇒ business	⇒ ceremony
⇒ alcohol	⇒ recreation	⇒ power	⇒ job	⇒ crucifix or cross
⇒ family	⇒ sports	⇒ pornography	⇒ country	

A person's god or idol is that which he puts first in his life, that which he desires and craves the most, that to which he gives his life: his primary thoughts, energy, time, and money. Note what God said about man during the last days of human history:

⇒ they would be lovers of self (2 Tim.3:2)
⇒ they would be lovers of pleasure (2 Tim.3:4)
⇒ their god would be their stomachs (Ph.3:19)

"(For many walk, of whom I have told you often, and now tell you even weeping, that they are the enemies of the cross of Christ: Whose end is destruction, <u>whose God is their belly</u>, and whose glory is in their shame, who mind earthly things)" (Ph.3:18-19).

"This know also, that in the last days perilous times shall come. For men shall be <u>lovers of their own selves</u>, covetous, boasters, proud, blasphemers, disobedient to parents, unthankful, unholy, Without natural affection, trucebreakers, false accusers, incontinent, fierce, despisers of those that are good, Traitors, heady, highminded, <u>lovers of pleasures</u> more than lovers of God; Having a form of godliness, but denying the power thereof: from such turn away" (2 Tim.3:1-5).

Thought 1. Maxie Dunnam has a practical comment on this commandment that is well worth quoting at length:

"God is unseen, a Spirit and Power invisible to our eyes. So, we need settings, symbols, places of worship to be vivid reminders of God. The problem comes when the symbol, the reminder, becomes a substitute, when it becomes an idol and takes the place of God.

"There's a dramatic story of this in Numbers 21. In their wandering through the wilderness, the people of Israel were attacked and tortured by fiery serpents. Moses, on the instruction of God, made a bronze serpent and set it up on a pole. Those who had been bitten looked at the bronze serpent and were healed. Not much is made of that story as it is found in Numbers 21:6-9, but centuries later we find that bronze serpent making another brief appearance. This time, we find King Hezekiah breaking the serpent in pieces, because the people had been burning incense to it (2 Kings 18:4). What had happened? What Moses had used as a reminder of God's power prevailing over the poison of the serpents, bit by bit, had become a god itself.

"This has happened in Christian history in relation to the cross and the crucifix. That which is to be a reminder of the love of the cross, meant to help men and women in looking at it to fix their hearts and minds on the One who bled and died there, becomes regarded with superstitious reverence. The cross, or the crucifix, becomes a holy thing. The symbol is identified and confused with the reality for which it stands.

"The core lesson is this: whenever anyone or anything usurps the place that God should have in our lives, we're guilty of idolatry.

"For most of us, that would not be a graven image such as a cross or a crucifix. But how easily money becomes an idol. We allow money--how we get it and how we use it--to edge God out of the number one place in our lives.

"I've seen love in marriage distorted to the point that it usurps God's place in our lives. I've certainly seen love of country distorted to the point that it blinds people to God's call to justice and righteousness.

"The making of idols usually means making the means an end. This happens all the time in the church. I know some people who do that with the Bible. The Bible itself becomes an idol. Listen carefully to people who passionately crusade, in their words, to 'save the Bible.' Look at their lives. We can angrily wage a war to protect the inerrancy of the Bible, and appear to be righteous in the cause, and still lose our souls. That's the problem Jesus was addressing when He said, 'Not everyone who says to Me, "Lord, Lord," will enter the Kingdom of Heaven, but those who do the will of My heavenly Father.'

"In all sorts of ways, we have committed the sin of idolatry by making the means an end. Even in our worship, we turn the liturgy, our means of worshipping God, into an end itself, so that the means and methods of worship become more important than the worship itself. We need to even look at...our spiritual disciplines. Spiritual discipline is for the purpose of facilitating our relationship to God. We pray and worship and study Scripture, sometimes we fast, to be open to God, to cultivate Christ's presence. But to make these disciplines ends in themselves, to make them the measurement of how holy we are, is making discipline a fetish. Not only are we in danger of turning others off when we zealously exaggerate these disciplines, they become idols."[5]

Thought 2. J. Vernon McGee also has an excellent application on this commandment.

"Some people may feel that this passage does not apply to us today. Colossians 3:5 tells us that '...covetousness...is idolatry.' Anything that you give yourself to, especially in abandonment, becomes your 'god.' Many people do not worship Bacchus, the cloven-footed Greek and Roman god of wine and revelry of long ago, but they worship the bottle just the same. There are millions of alcoholics in our country right now. The liquor interests like to tell us about how much of the tax burden they carry, when actually they do not pay a fraction of the bill for the casualties they cause by their product. A lot of propaganda is being fed to this generation and large groups of people are being brainwashed. Whether or not folk recognize it, they worship the god Bacchus.

"Other people worship Aphrodite, that is, the goddess of sex. Some people worship money. Anything to which you give your time, heart, and soul, becomes your God. God says that we are not to have any gods before Him."[6]

"**Wherefore should the heathen say, Where is now their God? But our God is in the heavens: he hath done whatsoever he hath pleased. Their idols are silver and gold, the work of men's hands. They have mouths, but they speak not: eyes have they, but they see not: They have ears, but they hear not: noses have they, but they smell not: They have hands, but they handle not:**

---

[5] Maxie Dunnam. *Mastering the Old Testament, Volume 2: Exodus*, p.255-256.
[6] J. Vernon McGee. *Thru The Bible*, Vol.1. (Nashville, TN: Thomas Nelson Publishers, 1981), p.267.

feet have they, but they walk not: neither speak they through their throat. They that make them are like unto them; so is every one that trusteth in them" (Ps.115:2-8).

"They [idols] are upright as the palm tree, but speak not: they must needs be borne, because they cannot go. Be not afraid of them; for they cannot do evil, neither also is it in them to do good" (Jer.10:5).

4 (20:5-6) **Testimony--Influence--Sin, Results--Children--Parents**: Why did God give this commandment? God gave this commandment for at least three reasons. (See Deeper Study # 1--Ex.20:4-6 for more discussion.)

1. First, God prohibits the worship of idols because He is a jealous God. The Hebrew word for *jealous* means to be red in the face. This means that God loves and cares for man. God does not want people living in error and following false gods that can do absolutely nothing to help them throughout life. Therefore, God is jealous of man, jealous--hot in the face--against anything that turns people away from the truth and from God Himself.

Note this fact: Scripture declares that idolatry is *spiritual adultery*; therefore, the displeasure of God against idolatry is rightly called jealous.[7] Jealousy means that God has a sensitive nature, a nature of love. God is jealous of anything or anyone who threatens to take away the honor, recognition, or reverence that is due Him. Therefore, if a person gives his primary devotion, his primary attention, honor, time, energy, effort, or money to anything other than God Himself, he commits spiritual adultery against God. He turns away from God to something else. The result: God becomes jealous, red-hot against any person who is unfaithful to Him. Man must never forget: God does not tolerate unfaithfulness; He will never allow a rival to replace Him. Note what Scripture says:

⇒ God's jealousy will not allow His glory and honor ever to be transferred to another.

"I am the LORD: that is my name: and my glory will I not give to another, neither my praise to graven images" (Is.42:8).
"For mine own sake, even for mine own sake, will I do it: for how should my name be polluted? and I will not give my glory unto another" (Is.48:11).

⇒ God declares that His very name is Jealous; therefore, He absolutely will not tolerate the worship of any other god.

"But ye shall destroy their altars, break their images, and cut down their groves: For thou shalt worship no other god: for the LORD, whose name is Jealous, is a jealous God" (Ex.34:13-14).

⇒ God's jealousy arouses His anger against those who deny and hate Him.

"(For the LORD thy God is a jealous God among you) lest the anger of the LORD thy God be kindled against thee, and destroy thee from off the face of the earth" (Dt.6:15).

⇒ God's jealousy will judge all those who oppose Him.

"The LORD will not spare him [the idolater], but then the anger of the LORD and his jealousy shall smoke against that man, and all the curses that are written in this book shall lie upon him, and the LORD shall blot out his name from under heaven" (Dt.29:20; cp. 1 Ki.14:22; Ps.79:5; Is.42:13; Is.59:17; Ezk.5:13; 16:38; 23:25; 36:5).
"God is jealous, and the LORD revengeth; the LORD revengeth, and is furious; the LORD will take vengeance on his adversaries, and he reserveth wrath for his enemies" (Nah.1:2).
"Neither their silver nor their gold shall be able to deliver them in the day of the LORD'S wrath; but the whole land shall be devoured by the fire of his jealousy: for he shall make even a speedy riddance of all them that dwell in the land" (Zeph.1:18; cp. Zeph.3:8).
"He that overcometh shall inherit all things; and I will be his God, and he shall be my son. But the fearful, and unbelieving, and the abominable, and murderers, and whoremongers, and sorcerers, and idolaters, and all liars, shall have their part in the lake which burneth with fire and brimstone: which is the second death" (Rev.21:7-8).

⇒ God's jealousy, His zeal, will vindicate His true people, His true followers.

"For out of Jerusalem shall go forth a remnant, and they that escape out of mount Zion: the zeal of the LORD of hosts shall do this" (2 Ki.19:31).
"Of the increase of his government and peace there shall be no end, upon the throne of David, and upon his kingdom, to order it, and to establish it with judgment and with justice from henceforth even for ever. The zeal of the LORD of hosts will perform this" (Is.9:7; cp. Is.26:11).
"Therefore thus saith the Lord GOD; Now will I bring again the captivity of Jacob, and have mercy upon the whole house of Israel, and will be jealous for my holy name" (Ezk.39:25).
"Then will the LORD be jealous for his land, and pity his people" (Joel 2:18; Zech.1:14).
"Thus saith the LORD of hosts; I was jealous for Zion with great jealousy, and I was jealous for her with great fury" (Zech.8:2).

---

[7] Matthew Henry. *Matthew Henry's Commentary*, Vol. 1. (Old Tappan, NJ: Fleming H. Revell Co., A Division of Baker Book House, No date given), p.359.

⇒ God's jealousy demands total allegiance, loyalty, and devotion.

> "For thou shalt worship no other god: for the LORD, whose name is Jealous, is a jealous God" (Ex.34:14).
> "And Joshua said unto the people, Ye cannot serve the LORD: for he is an holy God; he is a jealous God; he will not forgive your transgressions nor your sins" (Josh.24:19).

2. Second, God prohibits the worship of idols because the influence of idolatry is passed down from the parents to their children. If a person's worship is false, he leads his children and grandchildren into false worship. What he does greatly influences and affects his family.

We must never forget this one fact: the human race is a living organism. What one person does affects other persons. This is clearly seen in acts of love, care, benevolence, war, lawlessness, drunkenness, drugs, immorality--in all the acts of behavior. The closer a person is to others, the more the person's actions affect them. People influence people, and the point of this verse is that parents influence children, greatly influence them. A mother who is a drug addict is likely to lead her children to use drugs. A father who loves and puts sports before God leads his children to love and put things before God.

Note that Scripture uses the word "hate" (v.5). If parents deny and *hate* God and worship idols, the children will be greatly influenced to deny and *hate* God and worship idols. Consequently, God's judgment falls upon the children for generations. The result and consequences of idolatry are terrible. The worship of idols, just like all other behavior, influences the children of a family. Children are conditioned, heavily influenced by the behavior of their parents and their surroundings. Therefore, if a parent worships idols, most likely the children will worship idols. And all idolaters shall be judged by God. Therefore, the sin of idolatry and the judgment upon idolatry are passed down from generation to generation. Terrible consequences! All due to the *sins of the fathers and mothers*, especially the evil sin of idolatry.

This is what is known as the *judicial judgment of God*, a judgment that is justly deserved. (See Deeper Study # 1-- Jn.12:39-41; note--Ro.1:24 for more discussion.) If a parent sows the seed of idolatry, he is usually going to bear children who will be greatly influenced by his behavior. The children will deny and hate God and worship the idols of man. But note: this does not mean that God holds a child guilty for the sins of his parents. God is not talking about the guilt of sin. He is talking about the results, the consequences of sin. Every person shall bear the judgment and punishment for his own sin. No person will ever be judged and punished for the sins of others.

> "The fathers shall not be put to death for the children, neither shall the children be put to death for the fathers: every man shall be put to death for his own sin" (Dt.24:16).

Thought 1. God punishes sin, the sins of all people for all generations. God executes justice upon the sins of the fathers and the sins of the children. No generation of sin ever escapes the judgment of God.

> "[God] now commandeth all men every where to repent: Because he hath appointed a day, in the which he will judge the world in righteousness by that man whom he hath ordained; whereof he hath given assurance unto all men, in that he hath raised him from the dead" (Acts 17:30-31).
> "And to you who are troubled rest with us, when the Lord Jesus shall be revealed from heaven with his mighty angels, In flaming fire taking vengeance on them that know not God, and that obey not the gospel of our Lord Jesus Christ: Who shall be punished with everlasting destruction from the presence of the Lord, and from the glory of his power" (2 Th.1:7-9).
> "And Enoch also, the seventh from Adam, prophesied of these, saying, Behold, the Lord cometh with ten thousands of his saints, To execute judgment upon all, and to convince all that are ungodly among them of all their ungodly deeds which they have ungodly committed, and of all their hard speeches which ungodly sinners have spoken against him" (Jude 14-15).
> "Behold, it is written before me: I will not keep silence, but will recompense, even recompense into their bosom, Your iniquities, and the iniquities of your fathers together, saith the LORD, which have burned incense upon the mountains, and blasphemed me upon the hills: therefore will I measure their former work into their bosom" (Is.65:6-7).
> "Then shalt thou say unto them, Because your fathers have forsaken me, saith the LORD, and have walked after other gods, and have served them, and have worshipped them, and have forsaken me, and have not kept my law; And ye have done worse than your fathers; for, behold, ye walk every one after the imagination of his evil heart, that they may not hearken unto me: Therefore will I cast you out of this land into a land that ye know not, neither ye nor your fathers; and there shall ye serve other gods day and night; where I will not show you favour" (Jer.16:11-13).
> "I the LORD search the heart, I try the reins, even to give every man according to his ways, and according to the fruit of his doings" (Jer.17:10).
> "Behold, all souls are mine; as the soul of the father, so also the soul of the son is mine: the soul that sinneth, it shall die" (Ezk.18:4).

3. Third, God prohibits the worship of idols because the influence of a loving and obedient parent lasts forever, for a thousand generations. Note that the sin and punishment of idolatry is passed down for three or four generations, but the love and obedience of parents is passed down to their children for *thousands of generations*. This is what is known as Hebrew parallelism: it does not mean thousands of people, but thousands of generations. Note exactly what the verse says:

God's mercy is shown to thousands of those who love and obey Him, shown for thousands of generations. Parents who love God and keep God's commandments...

- will influence their children for thousands of generations
- will have the mercy of God showered upon thousands of their children for thousands of generations

This shows the awesome influence of parents upon their children and the absolute necessity for loving and obeying God. Judgment will fall upon those who disobey this commandment--fall upon both the parents and their children for three or four generations. But God's mercy will be showered upon those who obey this commandment, be showered upon thousands of children for thousands of generations.

However, note a most significant fact: God's mercy is showered only upon the obedient, only upon those who love God and keep His commandments, the very commandments He is spelling out in this passage.

> "And the LORD was with Jehoshaphat, because he walked in the first ways of his father David, and sought not unto Baalim" (2 Chron.17:3).
> "And he [Uzziah] did that which was right in the sight of the LORD, according to all that his father Amaziah did" (2 Chron.26:4).
> "Train up a child in the way he should go: and when he is old, he will not depart from it" (Pr.22:6).
> "When I call to remembrance the unfeigned faith that is in thee [Timothy], which dwelt first in thy grandmother Lois, and thy mother Eunice; and I am persuaded that in thee also" (2 Tim.1:5).

5 (20:5-6) **Decision--Obedience**: What is the decision required by this commandment? Obedience. God shows love to all who love Him and keep His commandments.

> "He that hath my commandments, and keepeth them, he it is that loveth me: and he that loveth me shall be loved of my Father, and I will love him, and will manifest myself to him" (Jn.14:21).
> "If ye keep my commandments, ye shall abide in my love; even as I have kept my Father's commandments, and abide in his love....Ye are my friends, if ye do whatsoever I command you" (Jn.15:10, 14).

1. The commandment can be stated positively:
   a. We must choose this day whom we will serve, the false gods of this earth or the LORD Himself (Jehovah, Yahweh).

   > "Now therefore fear the LORD, and serve him in sincerity and in truth: and put away the gods which your fathers served on the other side of the flood, and in Egypt; and serve ye the LORD. And if it seem evil unto you to serve the LORD, choose you this day whom ye will serve; whether the gods which your fathers served that were on the other side of the flood, or the gods of the Amorites, in whose land ye dwell: but as for me and my house, we will serve the LORD" (Josh.24:14-15).
   > "And Elijah came unto all the people, and said, How long halt ye between two opinions? if the LORD be God, follow him: but if Baal [false god], then follow him" (1 Ki.18:21).

   b. We must remember this day the LORD our Creator, bow down and worship Him and Him alone as our Maker.

   > "O come, let us worship and bow down: let us kneel before the LORD our maker. For he is our God; and we are the people of his pasture, and the sheep of his hand" (Ps.95:6-7).
   > "Remember now thy Creator in the days of thy youth, while the evil days come not, nor the years draw nigh, when thou shalt say, I have no pleasure in them" (Eccl.12:1).

   c. We must honor the LORD as our Father.

   > "Wherefore come out from among them, and be ye separate, saith the Lord, and touch not the unclean thing; and I will receive you, And will be a Father unto you, and ye shall be my sons and daughters, saith the Lord Almighty" (2 Cor.6:17-18).

   d. We must worship God in Spirit and in truth.

   > "God [is] a Spirit: and they that worship him must worship [him] in spirit and in truth" (Jn.4:24).

   e. We must trust the LORD and keep our minds upon the LORD.

   > "Thou wilt keep him in perfect peace, whose mind is stayed on thee: because he trusteth in thee. Trust ye in the LORD for ever: for in the LORD JEHOVAH is everlasting strength" (Is.26:3-4).

f. We must meditate upon the LORD.

"When I remember thee upon my bed, and meditate on thee in the night watches" (Ps.63:6).

g. We must pray and rejoice in everything.

"Be careful for nothing; but in every thing by prayer and supplication with thanksgiving let your requests be made known unto God. And the peace of God, which passeth all understanding, shall keep your hearts and minds through Christ Jesus" (Ph.4:6-7).

h. We must give thanks in the name of Christ for everything.

"Giving thanks always for all things unto God and the Father in the name of our Lord Jesus Christ" (Eph.5:20).
"Be careful for nothing; but in every thing by prayer and supplication with thanksgiving let your requests be made known unto God" (Ph.4:6).

i. We must rejoice in the LORD and be glad.

"Be glad in the LORD, and rejoice, ye righteous: and shout for joy, all ye that are upright in heart" (Ps.32:11).

j. We must delight ourselves in the LORD.

"Delight thyself also in the LORD; and he shall give thee the desires of thine heart" (Ps.37:4).

k. We must assemble ourselves together to worship the LORD.

"Not forsaking the assembling of ourselves together, as the manner of some is; but exhorting one another: and so much the more, as ye see the day approaching" (Heb.10:25).

l. We must guard our steps when we go to the house of God, guard ourselves and make sure we listen.

"Keep thy foot when thou goest to the house of God, and be more ready to hear, than to give the sacrifice of fools: for they consider not that they do evil" (Eccl.5:1).
"And ye shall know the truth, and the truth shall make you free" (Jn.8:32).
"Sanctify them through thy truth: thy word is truth" (Jn.17:17).

m. We must continue to study and preach God's Word, pray, observe the Lord's Supper, and fellowship together.

"And they continued stedfastly in the apostles' doctrine and fellowship, and in breaking of bread, and in prayers" (Acts 2:42).
"Preach the word; be instant in season, out of season; reprove, rebuke, exhort with all longsuffering and doctrine" (2 Tim.4:2).

n. We must baptize all new believers in the name of the Father.

"Go ye therefore, and teach all nations, baptizing them in the name of the Father, and of the Son, and of the Holy Ghost" (Mt.28:19).

2. The commandment can be stated negatively:
a. We must not worship any other god, no other god whatsoever. We must never worship anything other than the LORD God Himself, the only living and true God.

"Thou shalt not make unto thee any graven image, or any likeness of any thing that is in heaven above, or that is in the earth beneath, or that is in the water under the earth" (Ex.20:4).
"Take heed to yourselves, that your heart be not deceived, and ye turn aside, and serve other gods, and worship them" (Dt.11:16).
"Wherefore, my dearly beloved, flee from idolatry" (1 Cor.10:14).
"Little children, keep yourselves from idols. Amen" (1 Jn.5:21).

b. We must not set the poor example of a false worship for our children. We must not mislead our children into the worship of false religion and false idols; we must not lead our children to worship anything other than the LORD God Himself, the only living and true God.

"Only take heed to thyself, and keep thy soul diligently, lest thou forget the things which thine eyes have seen, and lest they depart from thy heart all the days of thy life: but teach them thy sons, and thy sons' sons" (Dt.4:9).

"And he did evil in the sight of the LORD, and walked in the way of his father, and in the way of his mother, and in the way of Jeroboam the son of Nebat, who made Israel to sin" (1 Ki.22:52).

"And thou, Solomon my son, know thou the God of thy father, and serve him with a perfect heart and with a willing mind: for the LORD searcheth all hearts, and understandeth all the imaginations of the thoughts: if thou seek him, he will be found of thee; but if thou forsake him, he will cast thee off for ever" (1 Chron.28:9).

"He also walked in the ways of the house of Ahab: for his mother was his counseller to do wickedly" (2 Chron.22:3).

"Train up a child in the way he should go: and when he is old, he will not depart from it" (Pr.22:6).

"But have walked after the imagination of their own heart, and after Baalim, which their fathers taught them" (Jer.9:14).

"And she, being before instructed of her mother, said, Give me here John Baptist's head in a charger" (Mt.14:8).

c. We must remove and destroy all false worship.

"But thus shall ye deal with them; ye shall destroy their altars, and break down their images, and cut down their groves, and burn their graven images with fire" (Dt.7:5).

"Ye shall defile also the covering of thy graven images of silver, and the ornament of thy molten images of gold: thou shalt cast them away as a menstruous cloth; thou shalt say unto it, Get thee hence" (Is.30:22).

d. We must mortify, put to death, all false worship.

"Mortify therefore your members which are upon the earth; fornication, uncleanness, inordinate affection, evil concupiscence, and covetousness, which is idolatry" (Col.3:5).

e. We must recognize that an idol is nothing, that there is only one true and living God.

"As concerning therefore the eating of those things that are offered in sacrifice unto idols, we know that an idol is nothing in the world, and that there is none other God but one. For though there be that are called gods, whether in heaven or in earth, (as there be gods many, and lords many,) But to us there is but one God, the Father, of whom are all things, and we in him; and one Lord Jesus Christ, by whom are all things, and we by him. Howbeit there is not in every man that knowledge: for some with conscience of the idol unto this hour eat it as a thing offered unto an idol; and their conscience being weak is defiled" (1 Cor.8:4-7).

THE BIBLICAL CONSEQUENCES OF A FALSE WORSHIP, OF WORSHIPPING IDOLS AND FALSE GODS, OF WORSHIPPING SOMETHING OTHER THAN THE ONLY LIVING AND TRUE GOD

DEEPER STUDY # 1
(20:4-6) **Commandments, The Ten--Sin, Results--Disobedience--Worship, False--Idolatry--Judgment**: What are the consequences of breaking this commandment, the consequences of worshipping false idols or gods, the consequences of worshipping something other than God Himself? What are the consequences of false worship?

1. The person who follows a false worship will not inherit the kingdom of God.

"Now the works of the flesh are manifest, which are *these;* Adultery, fornication, uncleanness, lasciviousness, Idolatry, witchcraft, hatred, variance, emulations, wrath, strife, seditions, heresies, Envyings, murders, drunkenness, revellings, and such like: of the which I tell you before, as I have also told *you* in time past, that they which do such things shall not inherit the kingdom of God" (Gal.5:19-21).

"Know ye not that the unrighteous shall not inherit the kingdom of God? Be not deceived: neither fornicators, nor idolaters, nor adulterers, nor effeminate, nor abusers of themselves with mankind, Nor thieves, nor covetous, nor drunkards, nor revilers, nor extortioners, shall inherit the kingdom of God" (1 Cor.6:9-10).

2. The person who follows a false worship is an idolater.

"Now these things [the Old Testament] were our examples, to the intent we should not lust after evil things, as they also lusted. Neither be ye idolaters, as *were* some of them; as it is written, The people sat down to eat and drink, and rose up to play. Neither let us commit fornication, as some of them committed, and fell in one day three and twenty thousand. Neither let us tempt Christ, as some of them also tempted, and were destroyed of serpents. Neither murmur ye, as some of them also murmured, and were destroyed of the destroyer" (1 Cor.10:6-10).

3. The person who follows a false worship serves a false religion or god.

"For all the gods of the people *are* idols: but the LORD made the heavens" (1 Chron.16:26).
"For they served idols, whereof the LORD had said unto them, Ye shall not do this thing" (2 Ki.17:12).

4. The person who follows a false worship is only worshipping the work of his own hands.

"Their land also is full of idols; they <u>worship</u> the work of their own hands, that which their own fingers have made" (Is.2:8).
"To whom will ye liken me, and make *me* equal, and compare me, that we may be like? They lavish gold out of the bag, and weigh silver in the balance, *and* hire a goldsmith; and he maketh it a god: they fall down, yea, they worship. They bear him upon the shoulder, they carry him, and set him in his place, and he standeth; from his place shall he not remove: yea, *one* shall cry unto him, yet can he not answer, nor save him out of his trouble" (Is.46:5-7).

5. The person who follows a false worship is only following the rituals and teachings of men.

"He answered and said unto them, Well hath Esaias prophesied of you hypocrites, as it is written, This people honoureth me with *their* lips, but their heart is far from me. Howbeit in vain do they worship me, teaching *for* doctrines the commandments of men. For laying aside the commandment of God, ye hold the tradition of men, *as* the washing of pots and cups: and many other such like things ye do. And he said unto them, Full well ye reject the commandment of God, that ye may keep your own tradition" (Mk.7:6-9).

6. The person who follows a false worship fails to experience the power of God.

"[People] having a form of godliness, but denying the power thereof: from such turn away" (2 Tim.3:5).

7. The person who follows a false worship is detestable to God and unfit for doing anything good.

"They profess that they know God; but in works they deny *him,* being abominable [detestable], and disobedient, and unto every good work reprobate" (Tit.1:16).

8. The person who follows a false worship is a fool: he shows that his thinking is futile, his mind confused, and his heart darkened.

"For the wrath of God is revealed from heaven against all ungodliness and unrighteousness of men, who hold the truth in unrighteousness; Because that which may be known of God is manifest in them; for God hath showed *it* unto them. For the invisible things of him from the creation of the world are clearly seen, being understood by the things that are made, *even* his eternal power and Godhead; so that they are without excuse: Because that, when they knew God, they glorified *him* not as God, neither were thankful; but became vain in their imaginations, and their foolish heart was darkened....Who changed the truth of God into a lie, and worshipped and served the creature more than the Creator, who is blessed for ever. Amen" (Ro.1:18-21, 25).

9. The person who follows a false worship is seduced and carried away.

"Ye know that ye were Gentiles, carried away unto these dumb idols, even as ye were led" (1 Cor.12:2).
"For false Christs and false prophets shall rise, and shall show signs and wonders, to seduce, if *it were* possible, even the elect" (Mk.13:22).

10. The person who follows a false worship will cry out for help, but there will be no help.

"They that make a graven image *are* all of them vanity; and their delectable things shall not profit; and they *are* their own witnesses; they see not, nor know; that they may be ashamed. <u>Who hath formed a god, or molten a graven image *that* is profitable for nothing?</u> Behold, all his fellows shall be ashamed: and the workmen, they *are* of men: let them all be gathered together, let them stand up; *yet* they shall fear, *and* they shall be ashamed together. The smith with the tongs both worketh in the coals, and fashioneth it with hammers, and worketh it with the strength of his arms:

yea, he is hungry, and his strength faileth: he drinketh no water, and is faint. The carpenter stretcheth out *his* rule; he marketh it out with a line; he fitteth it with planes, and he marketh it out with the compass, and maketh it after the figure of a man, according to the beauty of a man; that it may remain in the house. He heweth him down cedars, and taketh the cypress and the oak, which he strengtheneth for himself among the trees of the forest: he planteth an ash, and the rain doth nourish *it.* Then shall it be for a man to burn: for he will take thereof, and warm himself; yea, he kindleth *it,* and baketh bread; yea, he maketh a god, and worshippeth *it;* he maketh it a graven image, and falleth down thereto. He burneth part thereof in the fire; with part thereof he eateth flesh; he roasteth roast, and is satisfied: yea, he warmeth *himself,* and saith, Aha, I am warm, I have seen the fire: And the residue thereof he maketh a god, *even* his graven image: he falleth down unto it, and worshippeth *it,* and prayeth unto it, and saith, Deliver me; for thou *art* my god. They have not known nor understood: for he hath shut their eyes, that they cannot see; *and* their hearts, that they cannot understand. And none considereth in his heart, neither *is there* knowledge nor understanding to say, I have burned part of it in the fire; yea, also I have baked bread upon the coals thereof; I have roasted flesh, and eaten *it:* and shall I make the residue thereof an abomination? shall I fall down to the stock of a tree? He feedeth on ashes: a deceived heart hath turned him aside, that he cannot deliver his soul, nor say, *Is there* not a lie in my right hand?" (Is.44:9-20).

"They are vanity, and the work of errors: in the time of their visitation they shall perish." (Jer.10:15).

"Then shall the cities of Judah and inhabitants of Jerusalem go, and cry unto the gods unto whom they offer incense: but they shall not save them at all in the time of their trouble" (Jer.11:12).

"What profiteth the graven image that the maker thereof hath graven it; the molten image, and a teacher of lies, that the maker of his work trusteth therein, to make dumb idols?" (Hab.2:18).

11. The person who follows a false worship becomes a hater of God.

"And even as they did not like to retain God in their knowledge, God gave them over to a reprobate mind, to do those things which are not convenient; Being filled with all unrighteousness, fornication, wickedness, covetousness, maliciousness; full of envy, murder, debate, deceit, malignity; whisperers, Backbiters, haters of God, despiteful, proud, boasters, inventors of evil things, disobedient to parents, Without understanding, covenantbreakers, without natural affection, implacable, unmerciful" (Ro.1:28-31).

12. The person who follows a false worship will face severe punishment.

"And to you who are troubled rest with us, when the Lord Jesus shall be revealed from heaven with his mighty angels, In flaming fire taking vengeance on them that know not God, and that obey not the gospel of our Lord Jesus Christ: Who shall be punished with everlasting destruction from the presence of the Lord, and from the glory of his power" (2 Th.1:7-9).

"Then said I unto them, Cast ye away every man the abominations of his eyes, and defile not yourselves with the idols of Egypt: I *am* the LORD your God. But they rebelled against me, and would not hearken unto me: they did not every man cast away the abominations of their eyes, neither did they forsake the idols of Egypt: then I said, I will pour out my fury upon them to accomplish my anger against them in the midst of the land of Egypt" (Ezk.20:7-8).

"They have deeply corrupted *themselves* [by false worship], as in the days of Gibeah: *therefore* he will remember their iniquity, he will visit [punish them for] their sins" (Hos.9:9).

"Therefore, behold, the days come, that I will do judgment upon the graven images of Babylon: and her whole land shall be confounded, and all her slain shall fall in the midst of her" (Jer.51:47).

13. The person who follows a false worship will face the judicial judgment of God.

"Wherefore God also gave them up to uncleanness through the lusts of their own hearts, to dishonour their own bodies between themselves: Who changed the truth of God into a lie, and worshipped and served the creature more than the Creator, who is blessed for ever. Amen"(Ro. 1:24-25, cp. 18-25).

14. The person who follows a false worship will be judged because he ensnares and deludes others.

"Hear ye this, O priests; and hearken, ye house of Israel; and give ye ear, O house of the king; for judgment *is* toward you, because ye have been a snare on [the people of] Mizpah, and a net spread upon [the people of] Tabor....They will not frame their doings to turn unto their God: for the spirit of whoredoms *is* in the midst of them, and they have not known the LORD" (Hos.5:1, 4).

"Listen to this, you priests and all of Israel's leaders; listen, all you men of the royal family: You are doomed! For you have deluded the people with idols at Mizpah and Tabor" (Hos.5:1 LIVING BIBLE).

15. The person who follows a false worship will turn people away from the truth and bring about their destruction.

> "For the time will come when they will not endure sound doctrine; but after their own lusts shall they heap to themselves teachers, having itching ears; And they shall turn away *their* ears from the truth, and shall be turned unto fables" (2 Tim.4:3-4).
>
> "They [Israel and Judah] have dealt treacherously against the LORD [worshipping false gods]: for they have begotten strange children [who worship false gods]: now shall a month devour them with their portions" (Hos.5:7).
>
> "They have dealt treacherously against the LORD, For they have borne illegitimate children. Now the new moon will devour them with their land" (Hos.5:7, NASB).
>
> "They [Israel] have set up kings, but not by me [God] : they have made princes, and I knew *it* not: of their silver and their gold have they made them idols, that they may be cut off" (Hos.8:4).
>
> "They [Israel] set up kings without my [God] consent; they choose princes without my approval. With their silver and gold they make idols for themselves to their own destruction" (Hos.8:4 NIV).
>
> "Your eyes have seen what the Lord did because of Baal-peor: for all the men that followed Baal-peor, the Lord thy God hath destroyed them from among you" (Dt.4:3).

16. The person who follows a false worship will see all of his human efforts come to ruin.

> "For Israel hath forgotten his Maker, and buildeth temples [to worship false gods]; and Judah hath multiplied fenced cities: but I will send a fire upon his cities, and it shall devour the palaces thereof" (Hos.8:14).

17. The person who follows a false worship dishonors God and brings shame upon the witness of God.

> "Thou that makest thy boast of the law, through breaking the law dishonourest thou God? For the name of God is blasphemed among the Gentiles through you, as it is written" (Ro.2:23-24).
>
> "Many will say to me in that day, Lord, Lord, have we not prophesied in thy name? and in thy name have cast out devils? and in thy name done many wonderful works? And then will I profess unto them, I never knew you: depart from me, ye that work iniquity" (Mt.7:22-23).
>
> "Therefore by the deeds of the law there shall no flesh be justified in his sight: for by the law is the knowledge of sin" (Ro.3:20).
>
> "Knowing that a man is not justified by the works of the law, but by the faith of Jesus Christ, even we have believed in Jesus Christ, that we might be justified by the faith of Christ, and not by the works of the law: for by the works of the law shall no flesh be justified" (Gal.2:16).

18. The person who follows a false worship will face God's wrath.

> "Mortify therefore your members which are upon the earth; fornication, uncleanness, inordinate affection, evil concupiscence, and covetousness [greed], which is idolatry: For which things' sake the wrath of God cometh on the children of disobedience" (Col.3:5-6).

19. The person who follows a false worship has no hope and is without God in this world, without His care.

> "That at that time ye were without Christ, being aliens from the commonwealth of Israel, and strangers from the covenants of promise, having no hope, and without God in the world" (Eph.2:12).

20. The person who follows a false worship turns away from the LORD, the only living and true God.

> "And I will visit upon her the days of Baalim, wherein she burned incense to them, and she decked herself with her earrings and her jewels, and she went after her lovers, and forgat me, saith the LORD" (Hos.2:13).
>
> "For the wrath of God is revealed from heaven against all ungodliness and unrighteousness of men, who hold the truth in unrighteousness; Because that which may be known of God is manifest in them; for God hath showed it unto them. For the invisible things of him from the creation of the world are clearly seen, being understood by the things that are made, even his eternal power and Godhead; so that they are without excuse: Because that, when they knew God, they glorified him not as God, neither were thankful; but became vain in their imaginations, and their foolish heart was darkened....Who changed the truth of God into a lie, and worshipped and served the creature more than the Creator, who is blessed for ever. Amen" (Ro.1:18-21, 25).

21. The person who follows a false worship will be sentenced to hell.

> "But the fearful, and unbelieving, and the abominable, and murderers, and whoremongers, and sorcerers, and idolaters, and all liars, shall have their part in the lake which burneth with fire and brimstone: which is the second death" (Rev.21:8).

THE BIBLICAL BENEFITS OF KEEPING THIS COMMANDMENT:
NEVER TO MAKE NOR WORSHIP FALSE GODS

DEEPER STUDY #2

(20:4-6) <u>Commandments, The Ten--Benefits of Keeping--False Worship--Obedience</u>: What are the benefits of keeping this commandment? The greatest blessings imaginable are heaped upon the person who worships the LORD God and Him alone.

1. The person who worships God--truly worships Him--will be saved.

   "Ye worship ye know not what: we know what we worship: for salvation is of the Jews. But the hour cometh, and now is, when the true worshippers shall worship the Father in spirit and in truth: for the Father seeketh such to worship him. God [is] a Spirit: and they that worship him must worship [him] in spirit and in truth" (Jn.4:22-24).

2. The person who worships God--truly worships Him--will escape the judgment of God.

   "Not forsaking the assembling of ourselves together, as the manner of some is; but exhorting one another: and so much the more, as ye see the day approaching. For if we sin wilfully after that we have received the knowledge of the truth, there remaineth no more sacrifice for sins, But a certain fearful looking for of judgment and fiery indignation, which shall devour the adversaries" (Heb.10:25-27).

3. The person who worships God--truly worships Him--will receive the peace of God that passes all understanding.

   "Be careful for nothing; but in every thing by prayer and supplication with thanksgiving let your requests be made known unto God. And the peace of God, which passeth all understanding, shall keep your hearts and minds through Christ Jesus" (Ph.4:6-7).
   "Thou wilt keep him in perfect peace, whose mind is stayed on thee: because he trusteth in thee" (Is.26:3).

4. The person who worships God--truly worships Him--will receive the *spiritual rest* of God.

   "O come, let us worship and bow down: let us kneel before the LORD our maker. For he is our God; and we are the people of his pasture, and the sheep of his hand. To day if ye will hear his voice, Harden not your heart, as in the provocation, and as in the day of temptation in the wilderness: When your fathers tempted me, proved me, and saw my work. Forty years long was I grieved with this generation, and said, It is a people that do err in their heart, and they have not known my ways: Unto whom I sware in my wrath that they should not enter into my rest" (Ps.95:6-11).
   "There remaineth therefore a rest to the people of God. For he that is entered into his rest, he also hath ceased from his own works, as God did from his. Let us labour therefore to enter into that rest, lest any man fall after the same example of unbelief" (Heb.4:9-11).

5. The person who worships God--truly worships Him--is filled with the joy of life.

   "And they worshipped him, and returned to Jerusalem with great joy" (Lk.24:52).
   "Speaking to yourselves in psalms and hymns and spiritual songs, singing and making melody in your heart to the Lord; Giving thanks always for all things unto God and the Father in the name of our Lord Jesus Christ" (Eph.5:19-20).
   "Thou wilt show me the path of life: <u>in thy presence</u> *is* fulness of joy; at thy right hand *there are* pleasures for evermore" (Ps.16:11).

6. The person who worships God--truly worships Him--will enjoy and abide in the presence of the Lord.

   "Surely goodness and mercy shall follow me all the days of my life: and I will dwell in the house of the Lord for ever" (Ps.23:6).
   "Lord, I have loved the habitation of thy house, and the place where thine honour dwelleth" (Ps.26:8).
   "One thing have I desired of the Lord, that will I seek after; that I may dwell in the house of the Lord all the days of my life, to behold the beauty of the Lord, and to enquire in his temple" (Ps.27:4).
   "Blessed is the man whom thou choosest, and causest to approach unto thee, that he may dwell in thy courts: we shall be satisfied with the goodness of thy house, even of thy holy temple" (Ps.65:4).
   "My soul longeth, yea, even fainteth for the courts of the Lord: my heart and my flesh crieth out for the living God" (Ps.84:2).

"For a day in thy courts is better than a thousand. I had rather be a doorkeeper in the house of my God, than to dwell in the tents of wickedness" (Ps.84:10).
"I was glad when they said unto me, Let us go into the house of the Lord" (Ps.122:1).

7. The person who worships God--truly worships Him--will receive the desires of his heart.

"Delight thyself also in the LORD; and he shall give thee the desires of thine heart" (Ps.37:4).

8. The person who worships God--truly worships Him--will be delivered from sorrow and trouble and surrounded by mercy.

"Many sorrows shall be to the wicked: but he that trusteth in the LORD, mercy shall compass him about. Be glad in the LORD, and rejoice, ye righteous: and shout for joy, all ye that are upright in heart" (Ps.32:10-11).

9. The person who worships God--truly worships Him--will be delivered through the temptations and trials of this life.

"Wherefore in all things it behoved him to be made like unto his brethren, that he might be a merciful and faithful high priest in things pertaining to God, to make reconciliation for the sins of the people. For in that he himself hath suffered being tempted, he is able to succour them that are tempted" (Heb.2:17-18).
"For we have not an high priest which cannot be touched with the feeling of our infirmities; but was in all points tempted like as we are, yet without sin. Let us therefore come boldly unto the throne of grace, that we may obtain mercy, and find grace to help in time of need" (Heb.4:15-16).

10. The person who worships God--truly worships Him--will be assured of God's resurrection power.

"And Abraham said unto his young men, Abide ye here with the ass; and I and the lad will go yonder and worship, and come again to you....And it came to pass after these things, that God did tempt Abraham, and said unto him, Abraham: and he said, Behold, here I am. And he said, Take now thy son, thine only son Isaac, whom thou lovest, and get thee into the land of Moriah; and offer him there for a burnt offering upon one of the mountains which I will tell thee of. And Abraham rose up early in the morning, and saddled his ass, and took two of his young men with him, and Isaac his son, and clave the wood for the burnt offering, and rose up, and went unto the place of which God had told him. Then on the third day Abraham lifted up his eyes, and saw the place afar off. And Abraham said unto his young men, Abide ye here with the ass; and I and the lad will go yonder and worship, and come again to you. And Abraham took the wood of the burnt offering, and laid it upon Isaac his son; and he took the fire in his hand, and a knife; and they went both of them together. And Isaac spake unto Abraham his father, and said, My father: and he said, Here am I, my son. And he said, Behold the fire and the wood: but where is the lamb for a burnt offering? And Abraham said, My son, God will provide himself a lamb for a burnt offering: so they went both of them together. And they came to the place which God had told him of; and Abraham built an altar there, and laid the wood in order, and bound Isaac his son, and laid him on the altar upon the wood. And Abraham stretched forth his hand, and took the knife to slay his son. And the angel of the LORD called unto him out of heaven, and said, Abraham, Abraham: and he said, Here am I. And he said, Lay not thine hand upon the lad, neither do thou any thing unto him: for now I know that thou fearest God, seeing thou hast not withheld thy son, thine only son from me. And Abraham lifted up his eyes, and looked, and behold behind him a ram caught in a thicket by his horns: and Abraham went and took the ram, and offered him up for a burnt offering in the stead of his son. And Abraham called the name of that place Jehovah-jireh: as it is said to this day, In the mount of the LORD it shall be seen" (Gen.22:5; 22:1-14).
"By faith Abraham, when he was tried, offered up Isaac: and he that had received the promises offered up his only begotten son, Of whom it was said, That in Isaac shall thy seed be called: Accounting that God was able to raise him up, even from the dead; from whence also he received him in a figure" (Heb.11:17-19).
"For if we believe that Jesus died and rose again, even so them also which sleep in Jesus will God bring with him" (1 Th.4:14).

11. The person who worships God--truly worships Him--will remember God's deliverance and salvation

"But the LORD, who brought you up out of the land of Egypt with great power and a stretched out arm, him shall ye fear, and him shall ye worship, and to him shall ye do sacrifice" (2 Ki.17:36).
"But if not, be it known unto thee, O king, that we will not serve thy gods, nor worship the golden image which thou hast set up....Then Nebuchadnezzar spake, and said, Blessed be the God of Shadrach, Meshach, and Abednego, who hath sent his angel, and delivered his servants that trusted in him, and have changed the king's word, and yielded their bodies, that they might not serve nor worship any god, except their own God" (Dan.3:18, 28).

"And you hath he quickened, who were dead in trespasses and sins; Wherein in time past ye walked according to the course of this world, according to the prince of the power of the air, the spirit that now worketh in the children of disobedience: Among whom also we all had our conversation in times past in the lusts of our flesh, fulfilling the desires of the flesh and of the mind; and were by nature the children of wrath, even as others. But God, who is rich in mercy, for his great love wherewith he loved us, Even when we were dead in sins, hath quickened us together with Christ, (by grace ye are saved;)" (Eph.2:1-5).

12. The person who worships God--truly worships Him--will be used by God to bring the lost to Christ.

"And when the day of Pentecost was fully come, they were all with one accord in one place. And suddenly there came a sound from heaven as of a rushing mighty wind, and it filled all the house where they were sitting. And there appeared unto them cloven tongues like as of fire, and it sat upon each of them. And they were all filled with the Holy Ghost, and began to speak with other tongues, as the Spirit gave them utterance. And there were dwelling at Jerusalem Jews, devout men, out of every nation under heaven....But Peter, standing up with the eleven, lifted up his voice, and said unto them, Ye men of Judaea, and all ye that dwell at Jerusalem, be this known unto you, and hearken to my words....Then they that gladly received his word were baptized: and the same day there were added unto them about three thousand souls" (Acts 2:1-5, 14, 41).
"Go, stand and speak in the temple to the people all the words of this life" (Acts 5:20).
"And at midnight Paul and Silas prayed, and sang praises unto God: and the prisoners heard them. And suddenly there was a great earthquake, so that the foundations of the prison were shaken: and immediately all the doors were opened, and every one's bands were loosed. And the keeper of the prison awaking out of his sleep, and seeing the prison doors open, he drew out his sword, and would have killed himself, supposing that the prisoners had been fled. But Paul cried with a loud voice, saying, Do thyself no harm: for we are all here. Then he called for a light, and sprang in, and came trembling, and fell down before Paul and Silas, And brought them out, and said, Sirs, what must I do to be saved? And they said, Believe on the Lord Jesus Christ, and thou shalt be saved, and thy house" (Acts 16:25-31).
"Come and hear, all ye that fear God, and I will declare what he hath done for my soul" (Ps.66:16).
"I will mention the lovingkindnesses of the LORD, and the praises of the LORD, according to all that the LORD hath bestowed on us, and the great goodness toward the house of Israel, which he hath bestowed on them according to his mercies, and according to the multitude of his lovingkindnesses" (Is.63:7).
"Then they that feared the LORD spake often one to another: and the LORD hearkened, and heard it, and a book of remembrance was written before him for them that feared the LORD, and that thought upon his name" (Mal.3:16).

13. The person who worships God--truly worships Him--can worship God in spirit no matter where he is, any time and any place.

"Our fathers worshipped in this mountain; and ye say, that in Jerusalem is the place where men ought to worship. Jesus saith unto her, Woman, believe me, the hour cometh, when ye shall neither in this mountain, nor yet at Jerusalem, worship the Father. Ye worship ye know not what: we know what we worship: for salvation is of the Jews. But the hour cometh, and now is, when the true worshippers shall worship the Father in spirit and in truth: for the Father seeketh such to worship him. God is a Spirit: and they that worship him must worship him in spirit and in truth" (Jn.4:20-24).
"For we are the circumcision, which worship God in the spirit, and rejoice in Christ Jesus, and have no confidence in the flesh" (Ph.3:3).

14. The person who worships God--truly worships Him--will have the wonderful opportunity of laying his crown at the feet of Christ, his LORD and Savior.

"The four and twenty elders fall down before him that sat on the throne, and worship him that liveth for ever and ever, and cast their crowns before the throne, saying, Thou art worthy, O Lord, to receive glory and honour and power: for thou hast created all things, and for thy pleasure they are and were created" (Rev.4:10-11).

15. The person who worships God--truly worships Him--will experience a strong bond and fellowship with other believers.

"And they continued stedfastly in the apostles' doctrine and fellowship, and in breaking of bread, and in prayers" (Acts 2:42).
"And they, continuing daily with one accord in the temple, and breaking bread from house to house, did eat their meat with gladness and singleness of heart" (Acts 2:46)
"That which we have seen and heard declare we unto you, that ye also may have fellowship with us: and truly our fellowship is with the Father, and with his Son Jesus Christ" (1 Jn.1:3).

DEEPER STUDY # 3

JESUS CHRIST AND HIS TEACHING
CONCERNING THE WORSHIP OF GOD

"Thou shalt not make unto thee any graven image, or any likeness of any thing that is in heaven above, or that is in the earth beneath, or that is in the water under the earth: Thou shalt not bow down thyself to them, nor serve them: for I the LORD thy God am a jealous God, visiting the iniquity of the fathers upon the children unto the third and fourth generation of them that hate me; And showing mercy unto thousands of them that love me, and keep my commandments" (Ex.20:4-6).

THE TEACHING OF CHRIST	THE BELIEVER'S RESPONSE
1. Jesus Christ declared that He would worship only the LORD God, Him and Him alone. Christ refused to engage in false worship. "If thou therefore wilt worship me, all shall be thine. And Jesus answered and said unto him, Get thee behind me, Satan: for it is written, Thou shalt worship the Lord thy God, and him only shalt thou serve" (Lk.4:7-8).	1) The believer must worship the LORD God, Him and Him alone. "Give unto the LORD the glory *due* unto his name: bring an offering, and come before him: worship the LORD in the beauty of holiness" (1 Chron.16:29). "My soul longeth, yea, even fainteth for the courts of the LORD: my heart and my flesh crieth out for the living God" (Ps.84:2). "O come, let us worship and bow down: let us kneel before the LORD our maker" (Ps.95:6). "O worship the LORD in the beauty of holiness: fear before him, all the earth" (Ps.96:9). "Exalt ye the LORD our God, and worship at his footstool; *for* he *is* holy" (Ps.99:5). 2) The believer absolutely must never engage in false worship. "Turn ye not unto idols, nor make to yourselves molten gods: I *am* the LORD your God" (Lev.19:4). "Ye shall make you no idols nor graven image, neither rear you up a standing image, neither shall ye set up *any* image of stone in your land, to bow down unto it: for I *am* the LORD your God" (Lev.26:1). "For all the gods of the nations *are* idols: but the LORD made the heavens" (Ps.96:5). "What profiteth the graven image that the maker thereof hath graven it; the molten image, and a teacher of lies, that the maker of his work trusteth therein, to make dumb idols?" (Hab.2:18). "Wherefore, my dearly beloved, <u>flee from idolatry</u>" (1 Cor.10:14). "Little children, keep yourselves from idols. Amen" (1 Jn.5:21). "Mortify [put to death] therefore your members which are upon the earth; fornication, uncleanness, inordinate affection, evil concupiscence, and covetousness, which is <u>idolatry</u>" (Col.3:5). "Notwithstanding I have a few things against thee, because thou sufferest that woman Jezebel, which calleth herself a prophetess, to teach and to seduce my servants to commit fornication, and to eat things sacrificed unto idols" (Rev.2:20). "For they themselves show of us what manner of entering in we had unto you, and how ye <u>turned to God from idols to serve the living and true God</u>" (1 Th.1:9).
2. Jesus Christ declared that the Father seeks true worshippers, those who worship Him in spirit and in truth. "Our fathers worshipped in this mountain; and ye say, that in Jerusalem is the place where men ought to worship. Jesus saith unto her, Woman, believe me, the hour cometh, when ye shall neither in this mountain, nor yet at Jerusalem, worship the Father. Ye worship ye know not what: we know what we worship: for salvation is of the Jews. But the hour cometh, and now is, when the true worshippers shall	1) Our worship of God must be true and genuine, not fake or hypocritical. "My little children, let us not love in word, neither in tongue; but in deed and in truth. And hereby we know that we are of the truth, and shall assure our hearts before him" (1 Jn.3:18-19). "He answered and said unto them, Well hath Esaias prophesied of you hypocrites, as it is written, This people honoureth me with their lips, but their heart is far from me" (Mk.7:6). 2) We must worship God in spirit. "Then he answered and spake unto me, saying, This is the word of the LORD unto Zerubbabel, saying, Not by might, nor by power, but by my spirit, saith the LORD of hosts" (Zech.4:6). "And be not drunk with wine, wherein is excess; but be filled with the Spirit; Speaking to yourselves in psalms and hymns and spiritual songs, singing and making melody in your heart to the Lord" (Eph.5:18-19).

THE TEACHING OF CHRIST	THE BELIEVER'S RESPONSE
worship the Father in spirit and in truth: for the Father seeketh such to worship him. God is a Spirit: and they that worship him must worship him in spirit and in truth" (Jn.4:20-24).	3) We must worship God in truth. "The LORD is nigh unto all them that call upon him, to all that call upon him in truth" (Ps.145:18). "Jesus saith unto him, I am the way, the truth, and the life: no man cometh unto the Father, but by me" (Jn.14:6). "And I will pray the Father, and he shall give you another Comforter, that he may abide with you for ever; *Even* the Spirit of truth; whom the world cannot receive, because it seeth him not, neither knoweth him: but ye know him; for he dwelleth with you, and shall be in you" (Jn.14:15-17). 4) We must worship God continually and consistently. "Rejoice in the Lord alway: *and* again I say, Rejoice" (Ph..4:4). "...I will bless the LORD at all times: his praise *shall* continually *be* in my mouth" (Ps.34:1).
3. Jesus Christ declared that there is only one true image of God, only one *image* that is acceptable to God: Jesus Christ, the very Image and Revelation of God Himself: "If ye had known me, ye should have known my Father also: and from henceforth ye know him, and have seen him. Philip saith unto him, Lord, show us the Father, and it sufficeth us. Jesus saith unto him, Have I been so long time with you, and yet hast thou not known me, Philip? he that hath seen me hath seen the Father; and how sayest thou *then*, Show us the Father? Believest thou not that I am in the Father, and the Father in me? the words that I speak unto you I speak not of myself: but the Father that dwelleth in me, he doeth the works" (Jn.14:7-10).	1) We must believe that Jesus Christ is the visible image, the very nature, of the invisible God. "Who hath delivered us from the power of darkness, and hath translated *us* into the kingdom of his dear Son: In whom we have redemption through his blood, *even* the forgiveness of sins: Who is the image of the invisible God, the firstborn of every creature" (Col.1:13-15). 2) We must believe that Jesus Christ is the express image, the exact representation, of God's person. "God, who at sundry times and in divers manners spake in time past unto the fathers by the prophets, Hath in these last days spoken unto us by *his* Son, whom he hath appointed heir of all things, by whom also he made the worlds; Who being the brightness of *his* glory, and the express image of his person, and upholding all things by the word of his power, when he had by himself purged our sins, sat down on the right hand of the Majesty on high" (Heb.1:1-3). 3) We must believe that Jesus Christ is God: the very form, the very nature, of God. "Who, being in the form of God, thought it not robbery to be equal with God" (Ph.2:6). 4) We must believe that Jesus Christ is the fulness of the Godhead, the fulness of God in a human body. "For in him dwelleth all the fulness of the Godhead bodily. And ye are complete in him, which is the head of all principality and power" (Col.2:9-10). 5) We must believe that Jesus Christ is the image to whom we are to be conformed. "For whom he did foreknow, he also did predestinate *to be* conformed to the image of his Son, that he might be the firstborn among many brethren" (Ro.8:29). 6) We must believe that Jesus Christ is the image to which we shall be gloriously and eternally made (transformed). "Beloved, now are we the sons of God, and it doth not yet appear what we shall be: but we know that, when he shall appear, we shall be like him; for we shall see him as he is" (1 Jn.3:2).
4. Jesus Christ displayed great humility in His worship of God, falling on His face before His Heavenly Father. "And he went a little farther, and	1) We must approach God with great humility, acknowledging that we have nothing to offer Him yet need everything from Him. "For I know that in me (that is, in my flesh,) dwelleth no good thing: for to will is present with me; but *how* to perform that which is good I find not" (Ro.7:18).

THE TEACHING OF CHRIST	THE BELIEVER'S RESPONSE
fell on his face, and prayed, saying, O my Father, if it be possible, let this cup pass from me: nevertheless not as I will, but as thou *wilt*" (Mt.26:39).	2) We must be willing to put aside all pride and humble ourselves before God's mighty hand. "And Moses and Aaron went from the presence of the assembly unto the door of the tabernacle of the congregation, and they fell upon their faces: and the glory of the Lord appeared unto them" (Num.20:6). "And he said, Nay; but as captain of the host of the Lord am I now come. And Joshua fell on his face to the earth, and did worship, and said unto him, What saith my lord unto his servant?" (Josh.5:14). "So Ahab went up to eat and to drink. And Elijah went up to the top of Carmel; and he cast himself down upon the earth, and put his face between his knees" (1 Ki.18:42). "And Jehoshaphat bowed his head with his face to the ground: and all Judah and the inhabitants of Jerusalem fell before the Lord, worshipping the Lord" (2 Chron.20:18). 3) We must humble ourselves before God and cast our care upon Him, trusting that He has our greatest good in mind. "Likewise, ye younger, submit yourselves unto the elder. Yea, all *of you* be subject one to another, and be clothed with humility: for God resisteth the proud, and giveth grace to the humble. Humble yourselves therefore under the mighty hand of God, that he may exalt you in due time: Casting all your care upon him; for he careth for you" (1 Pt.5:5-7).
5. Jesus Christ made it His custom to worship God with other believers on the Sabbath. "And he came to Nazareth, where he had been brought up: and, as his custom was, he went into the synagogue on the sabbath day, and stood up for to read" (Lk.4:16). "Now about the midst of the feast Jesus went up into the temple, and taught" (Jn.7:14).	1) We must never forsake our worship of God, not even for a brief time. "And he came to Nazareth, where he had been brought up: and, as his custom was, he went into the synagogue on the sabbath day, and stood up for to read" (Lk.4:16). "And they worshipped him, and returned to Jerusalem with great joy: And were continually in the temple, praising and blessing God. Amen" (Lk.24:52-53). "And they, continuing daily with one accord in the temple, and breaking bread from house to house, did eat their meat with gladness and singleness of heart" (Acts 2:46). 2) We must assemble together... • for worship • for prayer • for the study of God's Word • for ministry and witnessing "And when he was departed thence, he went into their synagogue" (Mt.12:9). "And they went into Capernaum; and straightway on the sabbath day he entered into the synagogue, and taught" (Mk.1:21). "But when they departed from Perga, they came to Antioch in Pisidia, and went into the synagogue on the sabbath day, and sat down" (Acts 13:14). "Now Peter and John went up together into the temple at the hour of prayer, *being* the ninth *hour*" (Acts 3:1). 3) We must assemble together often and never forsake our coming together. Genuine believers need each other--the presence, fellowship, strength, encouragement, care, and love of one another. "Not forsaking the assembling of ourselves together, as the manner of some is; but exhorting one another: and so much the more, as ye see the day approaching" (Heb.10:25). "Blessed *are* they that dwell in thy house: they will be still praising thee. Selah" (Ps.84:4).

	D. The Ten Commandments, The Laws Governing Man's Duty to God (Part 3): Commandment Three Concerns God's Name--Never Misuse God's Name; Never Use Profanity or Vulgarity, Ex.20:7

Commandment 3: Never dishonor God's name; never use profanity or vulgarity
    a. He is the LORD your God
    b. He will hold you accountable
	7 Thou shalt not take the name of the LORD thy God in vain; for the LORD will not hold him guiltless that taketh his name in vain.

DIVISION VII

THE LAW AND THE PROMISES OF GOD (THE MOSAIC COVENANT) (PART 2): THE TEN COMMANDMENTS--NECESSARY LAWS TO GOVERN MAN AND SOCIETY, EX.20:1-26

D. **The Ten Commandments, The Laws Governing Man's Duty to God (Part 3): Commandment Three Concerns God's Name--Never Misuse God's Name; Never Use Profanity or Vulgarity, Ex.20:7**

(20:7) **Introduction--Cursing--Profanity--Swearing--Tongue--Speech--Vulgarity**: profanity and vulgarity are sweeping the earth. Cursing, swearing, foul and filthy talk, polluted and distasteful language--even using God's name in vain--all forms of profanity and vulgarity are flowing from the mouth of man. Words that expose a prejudicial and disrespectful heart and that degrade others are even peppering the daily conversation of people.

Unfortunately, man's language has always included *gutter talk*. But today, *gutter talk*--profanity--seems to be running rampant. Profanity is becoming more and more accepted by society. Profanity is becoming one of the most prevailing sins and 'popular' vices of the world. This is the subject covered by this commandment, a subject that must be heeded or else the very foundation of society--human language with all the emotions it arouses--will collapse. Simply stated, profanity is a creeping paralysis that will destroy civilization. How could profanity and vulgarity possibly have such a devastating effect upon society? Because civilization is bound together by the civility and decency of human language and by God's grace being poured out upon mankind. Profanity will cause civilization to disintegrate into verbal attacks that lead to personal violence and lawlessness. Profanity--foul, dirty cursing and indecent, prejudicial, and damning talk--destroys human language and arouses emotions and reactions that cause people to strike out against fellow citizens. Thereby civil and decent societies are corrupted and civilizations destroyed--all because human language lost its decency and civility; all because profanity paralyzed the growth and development of human relationships. This is the subject of this great commandment: *Commandment Three Concerns God's Name--Never Misuse God's Name; Never Use Vulgarity*, 20:7.

1. Who is to obey this commandment? You (v.7).
2. How long was this commandment to be in force? Forever (v.7).
3. What is forbidden by this commandment (v.7)?
4. Why did God give this commandment (v.7)?
5. What is the decision required by this commandment? Obedience (v.7).

1 (20:7) **Commandments, The Ten--Obedience--Profanity--Vulgarity--Cursing--Swearing**: Who is to obey this commandment? You. It is a *personal* commandment: a commandment given to you individually. How you use God's name--how you treat God's name--is of vital concern to God. He is the great Creator, the Sovereign LORD and Majesty, the Supreme Ruler and Judge of the universe; therefore, His name is always to be honored, praised, and worshipped. Because of His person--who He is--God demands and insists that you never--no, never--misuse His name.

⇒ *You* must never curse nor abuse His name.
⇒ *You* must never use His name in a frivolous or insincere way.
⇒ *You* must never take the name of the LORD God in vain.

This commandment is directed to *you*. It is directed to me. It is directed to every human being upon the earth.

> **"But above all things, my brethren, swear not, neither by heaven, neither by the earth, neither by any other oath: but let your yea be yea; and your nay, nay; lest ye fall into condemnation" (Jas.5:12).**

2 (20:7) **Commandments, The Ten--Obedience--Cursing--Language, Foul**: How long was this commandment to be in force? As long as people live. No person who has ever lived, who is living now, or who ever will live is ever to misuse God's name. The true and living God is *God Almighty*, the Sovereign LORD and Majesty of the universe, the *Ruler and Judge* of all people. Therefore, any person is a fool to misuse God's name...
- a fool to curse God
- a fool to use God's name in any abusive way or in any frivolous or insincere way

No person of any generation or period of history--as long as God lives, as long as God exists, from everlasting to everlasting--is to misuse or take God's name in vain. This is what God demands; this is one of the ways we are to relate to God. This commandment is in force as long as we live and as long as God exists, forever.

> **"And all people of the earth shall see that thou art called by the name of the LORD; and they shall be afraid of thee" (Dt.28:10).**
> **"Sanctify [set apart] the LORD of hosts himself; and let him be your fear, and let him be your dread" (Is.8:13).**

3 (20:7) **Commandments, The Ten--Obedience--Cursing--Swearing--Tongue--Language, Foul--Name, of God--God, Name of**: What is forbidden by the third commandment: "You shall never misuse, never take the name of the Lord God in vain" (v.7)? How is this commandment broken or violated?

The Hebrew word "vain" (lassaw) means empty, meaningless, thoughtless, senseless, frivolous, worthless, groundless. It means using God's name in a thoughtless and insincere way. The root of the word (shawu) has the idea of a vapor that fades and vanishes away, a vapor that is meaningless and worthless.[1] It also has the idea of a tempest, a storm, a tornado that is erratic, that jumps here and there, that causes destruction and devastation, that is totally senseless and destructive.[2]

How does a person misuse the Lord's name? There are at least four ways that a person misuses God's name or takes God's name in vain.

1. A person misuses God's name or takes God's name in vain by *profanity and vulgarity*. This commandment forbids profanity.
   a. Profanity is the cursing, abusive, bitter, blasphemous use of God's name or of any of God's creation. By creation is meant everything within the universe. Thus taking God's name in vain, misusing God's name, includes all uses of vulgarity and profanity: the use of foul, distasteful slang words, and even words such as damn, hell, darn, and other such words.

   What do such words have to do with misusing God's name? Very simply, when we use profanity, we are profaning and cursing something in creation. And no person has the right to profane and curse anything in God's creation. We must never forget this one fact:
   ⇒ The earth is the Lord's: He is the great Creator and Sustainer of everything within the universe. He is the Sovereign LORD and Majesty of the universe itself and of everything within the universe. All creation exists because of God, and all creation stands to the praise of God's name. Therefore, to profane or curse anything in creation is to take God's name in vain. To use profanity--to profane and curse anything--is destructive, totally senseless and worthless.

   b. Profanity is a terrible thing when it curses God Himself or uses His name to swear. Using God's name is an insult cast in His face and will result in terrible judgment upon the profane curser.

   Remember, a person's name stands for the person. When a person's name is mentioned, if we know the person, our thoughts immediately picture him: who he is and what he is, his nature, character, behavior, and beliefs. We have an immediate image of the person, the kind of person he is.

   This is especially true with God. God is holy and righteous. He is loving, kind, and gracious. God is the great Creator and Sustainer of the universe, the sovereign LORD and Majesty of all. Moreover, God is the great Redeemer, the Savior of mankind. He is God Almighty, the Most High God, the LORD God of the universe, whose name is set above the heavens, and whose name is called Wonderful, Counselor, the Mighty God, the Everlasting Father, the Prince of Peace (Is.9:6).

   God's name is holy. God's name is different from all other names, set apart from all other names. God's name is above, before, and over all other names. God's name is higher than the heavens, far above every name that is named, in both heaven and earth, visible and invisible.

   The point is this: God's holy name should arouse us to stand in awe before Him, never to curse Him. God's holy name should stir us to reverence and adore Him, even fear and tremble before Him. The last thing any person should ever do is misuse God's name:
   ⇒ use His name as a curse word
   ⇒ use His name in a vulgar, disgusting way
   ⇒ use His name in a profane way

Thought 1. Profanity is like a storm, a terrible, terrifying tempest that is destructive and totally senseless and worthless. Profanity is a prevailing sin that is sweeping our nation and world today. Profanity is rapidly becoming so

---

[1] William Wilson. *Wilson's Old Testament Word Studies*. (McLean, VA: MacDonald Publishing Company, No date given), p.465.
[2] James Strong. *Strong's Exhaustive Concordance of the Bible*. (Nashville, TN: Thomas Nelson, Inc., 1990), 7723.

acceptable that it is a part of everyday conversation. The terrible danger of profanity has been forgotten. The danger is tragically ignored and even denied. Nevertheless, the danger is a true fact: profanity is a creeping paralysis...

- that destroys the source of respect between people, between the citizens of a diverse society and nation
- that destroys the moral strength and esteem of a people for one another and for their nation
- that corrupts the language of a nation and people
- that destroys the ability of a people to continue to grow, build, advance, enhance, enlarge, and increase the quality of their lives, society, and nation.

Profanity will destroy a nation by corrupting the language and respect of people for one another. Over time, profanity will attack and destroy everything held dear by society. Note how a foul mouth destroys:

> "And ye shall not swear by my name falsely, neither shalt thou profane the name of thy God: I am the LORD" (Lev.19:12).
> "His mouth is full of cursing and deceit and fraud: under his tongue is mischief and vanity. He sitteth in the lurking places of the villages: in the secret places doth he murder the innocent: his eyes are privily set against the poor....He hath said in his heart, God hath forgotten: he hideth his face; he will never see it" (Ps.10:7-8, 11).
> "Their throat is an open sepulchre; with their tongues they have used deceit; the poison of asps is under their lips: Whose mouth is full of cursing and bitterness: Their feet are swift to shed blood: Destruction and misery are in their ways: And the way of peace have they not known: There is no fear of God before their eyes" (Ro.3:13-18).
> "But above all things, my brethren, swear not, neither by heaven, neither by the earth, neither by any other oath: but let your yea be yea; and your nay, nay; lest ye fall into condemnation" (Jas.5:12).

2. A person misuses God's name by *false swearing*. Perjury--lying under oath--is wrong. Calling upon God to witness to a lie is misusing God's name. False swearing may take place before a neighbor, a business partner, a wife or husband, a judge or jury. Tragically, when we are called upon to swear or take an oath to verify that we are telling the truth, far too often we lie: we swear falsely.

> "Again, ye have heard that it hath been said by them of old time, Thou shalt not forswear thyself, but shalt perform unto the Lord thine oaths: But I say unto you, Swear not at all; neither by heaven; for it is God's throne: Nor by the earth; for it is his footstool: neither by Jerusalem; for it is the city of the great King. Neither shalt thou swear by thy head, because thou canst not make one hair white or black. But let your communication be, Yea, yea; Nay, nay: for whatsoever is more than these cometh of evil" (Mt.5:33-37).
> "If a soul sin, and commit a trespass against the LORD, and lie unto his neighbour in that which was delivered him to keep, or in fellowship, or in a thing taken away by violence, or hath deceived his neighbour; Or have found that which was lost, and lieth concerning it, and sweareth falsely; in any of all these that a man doeth, sinning therein" (Lev.6:2-3).

3. A person misuses God's name by using His name in some *irreverent way*, in some frivolous, dishonoring, or light way. How does a person do this? *Reverence* is the key word. When God's name is used, it is always to be in a reverent way. God's name is never to be used in any irreverent way whatsoever.
   a. All the little sayings that use God's name in an irreverent or careless way are wrong:

⇒ God Almighty	⇒ God damn
⇒ Sweet Jesus	⇒ God or Jesus Christ or Christ (by themselves, when spoken carelessly)
⇒ Lord have mercy	⇒ The Man upstairs
⇒ Oh God	⇒ Somebody up there

   Any use of God's name that is not reverent--that is not in prayer, praise, witness, or worship--is wrong.
   b. All the flippant joking about God, the frivolous, humorous stories that use God's name, are wrong.
   c. All the prayers that carelessly and repetitiously use God's name in a *thoughtless* and *meaningless* way are wrong: "Lord do this; Lord do that," "Lord bless" and "Lord help."
      God's name is sacred: it is holy, righteous, and pure. God's name is the name of the Omnipresent, Omnipotent, Omniscient God. God's name is to be worshipped and praised--always reverenced--never used in a thoughtless, meaningless, flippant, frivolous way; never used in a dishonoring or light way. God's name is never to be misused, never to be taken in vain.

> "But fornication, and all uncleanness, or covetousness, let it not be once named among you, as becometh saints; Neither filthiness, nor foolish talking, nor jesting [crude, rude, foul, dirty joking], which are not convenient: but rather giving of thanks" (Eph.5:3-4).

Thought 1. Adrian Rogers, in his book Ten Secrets for a Successful Family, says this: "When you use...profanity, it shows two things: an empty head and a wicked heart. You see, profanity reveals a feeble mind trying to express itself. But it also reveals a wicked heart truly expressing itself. 'Out of the abundance of the heart the mouth speaketh,' Jesus said in Matthew 12:34....A profane mouth reveals a profane heart!"[3] Or, as Vance Havner once said, "What's down in the well comes up in the bucket!"

---

[3] Adrian Rogers. *Ten Secrets For A Successful Family*, p.60.

4. A person misuses God's name by *hypocrisy*. This commandment prohibits using God's name hypocritically, forbids claiming the name of the Lord in a hypocritical way. A hypocrite....
- is a person who professes the name of God but lives for self and the world
- is a person who uses God's name to manipulate people (to get what he wants)
- is a person who uses God's name to secure support for projects that are not necessarily God's will (for example, politicians or religious leaders)
- is a person who uses God's name to secure followers, to deceive people

"Not every one that saith unto me, Lord, Lord, shall enter into the kingdom of heaven; but he that doeth the will of my Father which is in heaven. Many will say to me in that day, Lord, Lord, have we not prophesied in thy name? and in thy name have cast out devils? and in thy name done many wonderful works? And then will I profess unto them, I never knew you: depart from me, ye that work iniquity" (Mt.7:21-23).

"And why call ye me, Lord, Lord, and do not the things which I say?" (Lk.6:46).

"Hear ye this, O house of Jacob, which are called by the name of Israel, and are come forth out of the waters of Judah, which swear by the name of the LORD, and make mention of the God of Israel, but not in truth, nor in righteousness" (Is.48:1).

Thought 1. In the early days of American history, the great general George Washington took a strong stand against profanity. He wrote in his orderly book of August 3, 1776: "The General is sorry to be informed that the foolish and wicked practice of profane swearing, a vice hitherto little known in the American army, is growing into fashion...He hopes the officers will, by example as well as influence, endeavor to check it, and that both they and the men will reflect that we can have little hope of the blessing of heaven on our arms if we insult it by our impiety and profanity."[4]

4 (20:7) **Commandments, The Ten--Judgment-- Cursing--Swearing--Sin, Results**: Why did God give this commandment? Why does God forbid vulgarity? Why must we never misuse God's name, never swear, curse, nor damn anything upon earth, never damn anything in creation? Two reasons are given within the commandment itself.

1. First, you must not use vulgarity or misuse God's name for a very clear reason: because the LORD is *your* God (v.2, 7). If you have accepted Christ as your Savior, then the LORD has saved you from Egypt, from the enslavements and bondages of this earth (v.2). He has saved you from sin, shame, and death. He has saved you from the bondages of the flesh, from...
- adultery and immorality
- drunkenness and carousing
- false worship and idolatry
- hatred and strife
- jealousy and envy
- wild living and sensuality
- cursing and lying
- sorcery and witchcraft
- anger and division
- selfish ambition and greed

And on and on. God has saved you from all this to a life of love, joy, and peace. Moreover, He has saved you from death and the judgment to come. He has saved you from hell itself. You are going to live forever, eternally with Him. The LORD is now your God. How could you ever misuse His name?

Now note: if you have never accepted Christ, then all the above can be yours. God will save you from the enslavements and bondages of this earth and give you life eternal. The point is this: the drive and energy of your heart must be not to misuse the name of the LORD God, the Savior of the world. The drive and energy of your life must be to stand in awe of His name: to praise, worship, serve, and bear testimony to His name

"Enter into his gates with thanksgiving, and into his courts with praise: be thankful unto him, and bless his name" (Ps.100:4).

"Sanctify the LORD of hosts himself; and let him be your fear, and let him be your dread" (Is.8:13).

"For thus saith the high and lofty One that inhabiteth eternity, whose name is Holy; I dwell in the high and holy place, with him also that is of a contrite and humble spirit, to revive the spirit of the humble, and to revive the heart of the contrite ones" (Is.57:15).

"And being found in fashion as a man, he humbled himself, and became obedient unto death, even the death of the cross. Wherefore God also hath highly exalted him, and given him a <u>name</u> which is above every name: That at the name of Jesus every knee should bow, of things in heaven, and things in earth, and things under the earth: And that every tongue should confess that Jesus Christ is Lord, to the glory of God the Father" (Ph.2:8-11).

"By him therefore let us offer the sacrifice of praise to God continually, that is, the fruit of our lips giving thanks to his name" (Heb.13:15).

"But ye are a chosen generation, a royal priesthood, an holy nation, a peculiar people; that ye should show forth the praises of him who hath called you out of darkness into his marvellous light" (1 Pt.2:9).

2. Second, you must not use vulgarity, must not misuse God's name for a terrifying reason: because the LORD holds you accountable if you misuse His name. The word "guiltless" (waqah) means that God will not count us clear or free from blame. He will not count us clean or pure, innocent or guiltless. God will not acquit us, not let us go unpunished.

---

[4] J. Vernon McGee. *Love Liberation and the Law.* (Nashville, TN: Thomas Nelson Publishers, 1995), p.38-39.

A man may curse God or swear falsely to his wife or neighbor or even to some jury, and he may not be corrected or punished. But God knows that the man cursed His name or lied, and Scripture is clear: God will punish him. God will avenge the person who insulted His great and glorious name. In fact, note what Scripture says: the person who curses and misuses God's name stands as an *enemy of God*.

"Thine enemies take thy name in vain" (Ps.139:20).

⇒ The person who uses profanity openly declares that he is the sworn enemy of the high and holy God. This person is condemned; God shall avenge His name and judge the *curser*.

⇒ The person who swears falsely deliberately declares that he is the sworn enemy of the true and righteous God. The person is condemned; God shall avenge His name and judge the *false swearer*.

⇒ The person who uses God's name in an irreverent way, who is careless and thoughtless in the use of God's name, will not be guiltless. He shall be condemned. God shall avenge His name and judge the *irreverent person*.

⇒ The person who uses God's name hypocritically stands as the sworn enemy of God. The hypocrite is condemned. God shall avenge His name and severely judge the *hypocrite*.

⇒ The bold sinner--the person who misuses God's name--must appear before God and give an account for his cursing and lying and for his irreverent use of God's holy name. If a person curses God, he curses the name of the high and lofty One, the name of the LORD God Himself, the only living and true God, the only holy name that could have saved him from death and judgment to come. God shall avenge His name and judge the *bold sinner*.

"As he loved cursing, so let it come unto him: as he delighted not in blessing, so let it be far from him" (Ps.109:17).

"And I will come near to you to judgment; and I will be a swift witness against the sorcerers, and against the adulterers, and <u>against false swearers</u>, and against those that oppress the hireling [hired laborer] in his wages, the widow, and the fatherless, and that turn aside the stranger from his right, and fear not me, saith the LORD of hosts" (Mal.3:5).

"And to you who are troubled rest with us, when the Lord Jesus shall be revealed from heaven with his mighty angels, In flaming fire taking vengeance on them that know not God, and that obey not the gospel of our Lord Jesus Christ" (2 Th.1:7-8).

"And as it is appointed unto men once to die, but after this the judgment" (Heb.9:27).

"But the heavens and the earth, which are now, by the same word are kept in store, reserved unto fire against the day of judgment and perdition of <u>ungodly men</u>" (2 Pt.3:7).

"And Enoch also, the seventh from Adam, prophesied of these, saying, Behold, the Lord cometh with ten thousands of his saints, To execute judgment upon all, and to convince all that are ungodly among them of all their ungodly deeds which they have ungodly committed, and of all their hard speeches which ungodly sinners have spoken against him" (Jude 14-15).

"But the fearful, and unbelieving, and the abominable, and murderers, and whoremongers, and sorcerers, and idolaters, and all <u>liars</u> [cursers, false swearers], shall have their part in the lake which burneth with fire and brimstone: which is the second death" (Rev.21:8).

5 (20:7) **Decision--Obedience**: What is the decision required by this commandment? Obedience! Simply stated, we must obey God's commandments.

1. Note that the commandment can be stated positively: Honor God's name--always. This was exactly what Christ Himself said. In fact, He said that we were to pray every day for God's name to be *hallowed* (Mt.6:9).

2. Note also that the commandment can be stated negatively: you shall not misuse God's name, shall not take His name in vain.

What decision is demanded by this commandment? We must not curse and swear; we must turn to God for salvation and forgiveness. We must...
- quit cursing and swearing
- quit using God's name in irreverent and thoughtless ways
- quit using God's name hypocritically

Note what Scripture says about this commandment and God's name.

1. We must not misuse God's name, never take God's name in vain. This is one of the Ten great Commandments.

"Thou shalt not take the name of the LORD thy God in vain; for the LORD will not hold him guiltless that taketh his name in vain" (Ex.20:7).

2. We must never swear falsely, not by God's name: we must not profane His name.

"And ye shall not swear by my name falsely, neither shalt thou profane the name of thy God: I am the LORD" (Lev.19:12).

3. We must fear God's name.

> **"If thou wilt not observe to do all the words of this law that are written in this book, that thou mayest fear this glorious and fearful name, THE LORD THY GOD; Then the LORD will make thy plagues wonderful [fearful]" (Dt.28:58-59).**

4. We must not use God's name hypocritically nor have a hypocritical tongue.

> **"Hear ye this, O house of Jacob, which are called by the name of Israel, and are come forth out of the waters of Judah, which swear by the name of the LORD, and make mention of the God of Israel, but not in truth, nor in righteousness" (Is.48:1).**
> **"Therewith bless we God, even the Father; and therewith curse we men, which are made after the similitude of God. Out of the same mouth proceedeth blessing and cursing. My brethren, these things ought not so to be. Doth a fountain send forth at the same place sweet water and bitter? Can the fig tree, my brethren, bear olive berries? either a vine, figs? so can no fountain both yield salt water and fresh" (Jas.3:9-12).**

5. We must not love false oaths.

> **"And let none of you imagine evil in your hearts against his neighbour; and love no false oath: for all these are things that I hate, saith the LORD" (Zech.8:17).**

6. We must never swear; rather we must speak directly, never swearing nor using oaths.

> **"But I say unto you, Swear not at all; neither by heaven; for it is God's throne: Nor by the earth; for it is his footstool: neither by Jerusalem; for it is the city of the great King. Neither shalt thou swear by thy head, because thou canst not make one hair white or black. But let your communication be, Yea, yea; Nay, nay: for whatsoever is more than these cometh of evil" (Mt.5:34-37).**
> **"But above all things, my brethren, swear not, neither by heaven, neither by the earth, neither by any other oath: but let your yea be yea; and your nay, nay; lest ye fall into condemnation" (Jas.5:12).**

7. We must swear only by the God of Truth.

> **"That he who blesseth himself in the earth shall bless himself in the God of truth; and he that sweareth in the earth shall swear by the God of truth" (Is.65:16).**

8. We are to believe on God's name, not curse His name.

> **"But as many as received him, to them gave he power to become the sons of God, even to them that believe on <u>his name</u>" (Jn.1:12).**
> **"For whosoever shall call upon the name of the Lord shall be saved" (Ro.10:13).**

9. We are to walk in the name of the LORD our God, not curse Him.

> **"For all people will walk every one in the name of his god, and we will walk in the name of the LORD our God for ever and ever" (Mic.4:5).**

10. We are to proclaim the name of God to people, bear testimony to His name.

> **"But sanctify the Lord God in your hearts: and be ready always to give an answer to every man that asketh you a reason of the hope that is in you with meekness and fear" (1 Pt.3:15).**
> **"Ye are my witnesses, saith the LORD, and my servant whom I have chosen: that ye may know and believe me, and understand that I am he: before me there was no God formed, neither shall there be after me" (Is.43:10).**
> **"Then I said, I will not make mention of him, nor speak any more in his name. But his word was in mine heart as a burning fire shut up in my bones, and I was weary with forbearing, and I could not stay" (Jer.20:9).**

11. We must praise God's name, not curse His name.

> **"Praise the LORD; for the LORD is good: sing praises unto his name; for it is pleasant" (Ps.135:3).**

12. We must hallow God's name, set God's name far above all names.

> **"After this manner therefore pray ye: Our Father which art in heaven, Hallowed be thy name" (Mt.6:9).**
> **"Sanctify them through thy truth: thy word is truth" (Jn.17:17).**

13. We must not misuse God's name by making a false, hypocritical profession.

"Not every one that saith unto me, Lord, Lord, shall enter into the kingdom of heaven; but he that doeth the will of my Father which is in heaven. Many will say to me in that day, Lord, Lord, have we not prophesied in thy name? and in thy name have cast out devils? and in thy name done many wonderful works? And then will I profess unto them, I never knew you: depart from me, ye that work iniquity" (Mt.7:21-23).
"And why call ye me, Lord, Lord, and do not the things which I say?" (Lk.6:46).

THE BIBLICAL CONSEQUENCES OF OF MISUSING
GOD'S NAME, OF TAKING GOD'S NAME IN VAIN

DEEPER STUDY #1
(20:7) <u>Commandments, The Ten--Sin, Results--Disobedience--Cursing--Profanity--Swearing--Judgment</u>: What are the consequences of breaking this particular commandment, the consequences of misusing God's name?

"Thou shalt not take the name of the LORD thy God in vain."

What happens to the person who uses profanity and blasphemes God? What happens to the person who damns things and curses things to hell, who has a foul, filthy, degrading and distasteful mouth? God's name is holy and it must be treated as such. No foul mouthed person, no person who misuses God's name, can escape these terrible consequences.

1. There are the consequences upon God.
   a. The person who misuses God's name, who uses profanity, blasphemes the name of the LORD.

   "Do not they blaspheme that worthy name by the which ye are called?" (Jas.2:7).
   "And the Israelitish woman's son blasphemed the name *of the LORD,* and cursed. And they brought him unto Moses: (and his mother's name *was* Shelomith, the daughter of Dibri, of the tribe of Dan:)" (Lev.24:11).

   b. The person who misuses God's name, who uses profanity, profanes or abuses God's name.

   "And I will sanctify my great name, which was <u>profaned among the heathen</u>, which ye have profaned in the midst of them; and the heathen shall know that I *am* the LORD, saith the Lord GOD, when I shall be sanctified in you before their eyes" (Ezk.36:23).

2. There are the consequences upon oneself, the day to day consequences.

   a. The person who misuses God's name, who uses profanity, shows that he does not know God, that he is wicked and unrighteous.

   "As it is written, There is none righteous, no, not one: There is none that understandeth, there is none that seeketh after God. They are all gone out of the way, they are together become unprofitable; there is none that doeth good, no, not one. Their throat is an open sepulchre; with their tongues they have used deceit; the poison of asps is under their lips: Whose mouth is full of cursing and bitterness" (Ro.3:10-14).
   "The wicked in his pride doth persecute the poor: let them be taken in the devices that they have imagined....His mouth is full of cursing and deceit and fraud: under his tongue is mischief and vanity" (Ps.10:2, 7).
   "But unto the wicked God saith, What hast thou to do to declare my statutes, or that thou shouldest take my covenant in thy mouth? Seeing thou hatest instruction, and castest my words behind thee....Thou givest thy mouth to evil, and thy tongue frameth deceit. Thou sittest and speakest against thy brother; thou slanderest thine own mother's son" (Ps.50:16-17, 19-20).

   b. The person who misuses God's name, who uses profanity, shows that he is a hypocrite.

   "Then began he [Peter] to curse and to swear, saying, I know not the man. And immediately the cock crew" (Mt.26:74).
   "Therewith bless we God, even the Father; and therewith curse we men, which are made after the similitude of God. Out of the same mouth proceedeth blessing and cursing. My brethren, these things ought not so to be" (Jas.3:9-10).

c. The person who misuses God's name, who uses profanity, is a fool.

"He that hideth hatred *with* lying lips, and he that uttereth a slander, *is* a fool" (Pr.10:18).

d. The person who misuses God's name, who uses profanity, has a throat like an open grave, a throat that bears the stinking smell of death.

"For *there is* no faithfulness in their mouth; their inward part *is* very wickedness; their throat *is* an open sepulchre; they flatter with their tongue" (Ps.5:9).

"Their throat *is* an open sepulchre; with their tongues they have used deceit; the poison of asps *is* under their lips" (Ro.3:13).

e. The person who misuses God's name, who uses profanity, shows that he has an evil heart.

"O generation of vipers, how can ye, being evil, speak good things? for out of the abundance of the heart the mouth speaketh" (Mt.12:34).

"*The words* of his mouth were smoother than butter, but war *was* in his heart: his words were softer than oil, yet *were* they drawn swords" (Ps.55:21).

f. The person who misuses God's name, who uses profanity, will have a testimony, a reputation, that is marked by malice and deception.

"Let all bitterness, and wrath, and anger, and clamour, and evil speaking, be put away from you, with all malice" (Eph.4:31).

"Wherefore laying aside all malice, and all guile, and hypocrisies, and envies, and all evil speakings" (1 Pt.2:1).

"For he that will love life, and see good days, let him refrain his tongue from evil, and his lips that they speak no guile" (1 Pt.3:10).

g. The person who misuses God's name, who uses profanity, will be deceived and have a vain, useless, empty religion.

"If any man among you seem to be religious, and bridleth not his tongue, but deceiveth his own heart, this man's religion *is* vain" (Jas.1:26).

h. The person who misuses God's name, who uses profanity, will defile his body.

"And the tongue *is* a fire, a world of iniquity: so is the tongue among our members, that it defileth the whole body, and setteth on fire the course of nature; and it is set on fire of hell" (Jas.3:6).

i. The person who misuses God's name, who uses profanity, will be found out, he will be exposed, even though he took every caution to be discreet and secretive.

"Curse not the king, no not in thy thought; and curse not the rich in thy bedchamber: for a bird of the air shall carry the voice, and that which hath wings shall tell the matter" (Eccl. 10:20).

j. The person (believer) who misuses God's name, who uses profanity, shall be disciplined by the church.

"Of whom is Hymenaeus and Alexander; whom I have delivered unto Satan, that they may learn not to blaspheme" (1 Tim.1:20).

k. The person who misuses God's name, who uses profanity, curses people who are made in God's image.

"For oftentimes also thine own heart knoweth that thou thyself likewise hast cursed others" (Eccl.7:22).

"Therewith bless we God, even the Father; and therewith curse we men, which are made after the similitude [likeness] of God. Out of the same mouth proceedeth blessing and cursing. My brethren, these things ought not so to be" (Jas.3:9-10).

"An hypocrite with *his* mouth destroyeth his neighbour: but through knowledge shall the just be delivered" (Pr.11:9).

"Take ye heed every one of his neighbour, and trust ye not in any brother: for every brother will utterly supplant, and every neighbour will walk with slanders" (Jer.9:4).

"Speak not evil one of another, brethren. He that speaketh evil of *his* brother, and judgeth his brother, speaketh evil of the law, and judgeth the law: but if thou judge the law, thou art not a doer of the law, but a judge" (Jas.4:11).

1. The person who misuses God's name, who uses profanity, will be held accountable for every idle word in the day of judgment.

> "O generation of vipers, how can ye, being evil, speak good things? for out of the abundance of the heart the mouth speaketh. A good man out of the good treasure of the heart bringeth forth good things: and an evil man out of the evil treasure bringeth forth evil things. But I say unto you, That every idle word that men shall speak, they shall give account thereof in the day of judgment" (Mt.12:34-36).

m. The person who misuses God's name, who uses profanity, will suffer the reciprocal judgment of God: suffer the very curse he pronounced and uttered.

> "As he loved cursing, so let it come unto him: as he delighted not in blessing, so let it be far from him. As he clothed himself with cursing like as with his garment, so let it come into his bowels like water, and like oil into his bones" (Ps.109:17-18).

3. There are the consequences of judgment.

a. The person who misuses God's name, who uses profanity, will face the judgment of God and not inherit the kingdom of God.

> "Neither filthiness [obsenity], nor foolish talking, nor jesting [coarse joking], which are not convenient: but rather giving of thanks. For this ye know, that no whoremonger, nor unclean person, nor covetous man, who is an idolater, hath any inheritance in the kingdom of Christ and of God" (Eph.5:4-5).
> "Whoso privily slandereth his neighbour, him will I cut off: him that hath an high look and a proud heart will not I suffer" (Ps.101:5).
> "Behold, ye trust in lying words, that cannot profit. Will ye steal, murder, and commit adultery, and swear falsely, and burn incense unto Baal, and walk after other gods whom ye know not....And I will cast you out of my sight, as I have cast out all your brethren, even the whole seed of Ephraim" (Jer.7:8-9, 15).
> "For the land is full of adulterers; for because of swearing the land mourneth; the pleasant places of the wilderness are dried up, and their course is evil, and their force is not right. For both prophet and priest are profane; yea, in my house have I found their wickedness, saith the LORD. Wherefore their way shall be unto them as slippery ways in the darkness: they shall be driven on, and fall therein: for I will bring evil upon them, even the year of their visitation, saith the LORD" (Jer.23:10-12).

b. The person who misuses God's name, who uses profanity, will be declared guilty and condemned.

> "Thou shalt not take the name of the LORD thy God in vain; for the LORD will not hold him guiltless that taketh his name in vain" (Ex.20:7).
> "But above all things, my brethren, swear not, neither by heaven, neither by the earth, neither by any other oath: but let your yea be yea; and your nay, nay; lest ye fall into condemnation" (Jas.5:12).

c. The person who misuses God's name, who uses profanity, will bear the curse of his profanity and be destroyed by his very own words.

> "As he loved cursing, so let it come unto him: as he delighted not in blessing, so let it be far from him" (Ps.109:17).
> "He that keepeth his mouth keepeth his life: but he that openeth wide his lips shall have destruction" (Pr.13:3).
> "Whoso keepeth his mouth and his tongue keepeth his soul from troubles" (Pr.21:23).

d. The person who curses his father or mother shows that he is not cleansed and will be condemned and face the terrible wrath of God.

> "Whoso curseth his father or his mother, his lamp shall be put out in obscure darkness" (Pr.20:20).
> "There is a generation that curseth their father, and doth not bless their mother. There is a generation that are pure in their own eyes, and yet is not washed from their filthiness" (Pr.30:11-12).
> "For the sin of their mouth and the words of their lips let them even be taken in their pride: and for cursing and lying which they speak. Consume them in wrath, consume them, that they may not be: and let them know that God ruleth in Jacob unto the ends of the earth. Selah" (Ps.59:12-13).

THE BIBLICAL BENEFITS OF KEEPING THIS COMMANDMENT: OF NOT MISUSING GOD'S NAME, OF NOT TAKING GOD'S NAME IN VAIN

DEEPER STUDY #2

(20:7) Commandments, The Ten; Benefits of Keeping; Proper Use of God's Name; Obedience: What are the benefits of keeping this commandment? What happens to the person who does not misuse nor take God's name in vain? The person who uses God's name correctly will be greatly blessed.

1. The person who uses God's name correctly will be saved.

> "For whosoever shall call upon the name of the Lord shall be saved" (Ro.10:13).
> "But as many as received him, to them gave he power to become the sons of God, even to them that believe on his name" (Jn.1:12).
> "Seek ye the LORD while he may be found, call ye upon him while he is near: Let the wicked forsake his way, and the unrighteous man his thoughts: and let him return unto the LORD, and he will have mercy upon him; and to our God, for he will abundantly pardon" (Is.55:6-7).

2. The person who uses God's name correctly will confess and bow at the name of His Son, Jesus Christ.

> "Wherefore God also hath highly exalted him, and given him a name which is above every name: That at the name of Jesus every knee should bow, of things in heaven, and things in earth, and things under the earth; And that every tongue should confess that Jesus Christ is Lord, to the glory of God the Father" (Ph.2:9-11).

3. The person who uses God's name correctly will be filled with God's Spirit, walking about with joy.

> "And be not drunk with wine, wherein is excess; but be filled with the Spirit; Speaking to yourselves in psalms and hymns and spiritual songs, singing and making melody in your heart to the Lord" (Eph.5:18-19).

4. The person who uses God's name correctly will walk in light.

> "Who is among you that feareth the LORD, that obeyeth the voice of his servant, that walketh in darkness, and hath no light? let him trust in the name of the LORD, and stay upon his God" (Is.50:10).

5. The person who uses God's name correctly will be heard, helped, and strengthened in the day of trouble.

> "The LORD hear thee in the day of trouble; the name of the God of Jacob defend thee; Send thee help from the sanctuary, and strengthen thee out of Zion; Remember all thy offerings, and accept thy burnt sacrifice; Selah" (Ps.20:1-3).
> "The LORD is nigh unto all them that call upon him, to all that call upon him in truth. He will fulfil the desire of them that fear him: he also will hear their cry, and will save them" (Ps.145:18-19).
> "For there is no difference between the Jew and the Greek: for the same Lord over all is rich unto all that call upon him" (Ro.10:12).

6. The person who uses God's name correctly will be safe and secure.

> "The name of the LORD is a strong tower: the righteous runneth into it, and is safe" (Pr.18:10).

7. The person who uses God's name correctly will have his prayers answered.

> "After this manner therefore pray ye: Our Father which art in heaven, Hallowed be thy name" (Mt.6:9).
> "Call unto me, and I will answer thee, and show thee great and mighty things, which thou knowest not" (Jer.33:3).

8. The person who uses God's name correctly will have a mouth filled with praise and honor.

> "Let my mouth be filled *with* thy praise *and with* thy honour all the day" (Ps.71:8).

9. The person who uses God's name correctly will know how to help others with a special word of encouragement.

> "The Lord God hath given me the tongue of the learned, that I should know how to speak a word in season to him that is weary: he wakeneth morning by morning, he wakeneth mine ear to hear as the learned" (Is.50:4).

DEEPER STUDY # 3

JESUS CHRIST AND HIS TEACHING CONCERNING GOD'S NAME

"Thou shalt not take the name of the LORD thy God in vain; for the LORD will not hold him guiltless that taketh his name in vain" (Ex.20:7).

THE TEACHING OF CHRIST	THE BELIEVER'S RESPONSE

1. Jesus Christ declared that a person misuses God's name by false swearing.
 	
"**Again, ye have heard that it hath been said by them of old time, Thou shalt not forswear thyself, but shalt perform unto the Lord thine oaths: But I say unto you, Swear not at all; neither by heaven; for it is God's throne: Nor by the earth; for it is his footstool: neither by Jerusalem; for it is the city of the great King. Neither shalt thou swear by thy head, because thou canst not make one hair white or black. But let your communication be, Yea, yea; Nay, nay: for whatsoever is more than these cometh of evil**" (Mt.5:33-37).
	1) We must never swear to make a promise we cannot keep.
	2) Perjury--lying under oath--is wrong. All misuse of God's name that calls upon Him to witness to a lie is misusing God's name. The false swearing may take place...
	   • before a neighbor
	   • before a business partner
	   • before a wife or husband
	   • before a judge or jury
	   • before any person
	
	"**But above all things, my brethren, swear not, neither by heaven, neither by the earth, neither by any other oath: but let your yea be yea; and** *your* **nay, nay; lest ye fall into condemnation**" (Jas.5:12).
	"**If a man vow a vow unto the LORD, or swear an oath to bind his soul with a bond; he shall not break his word, he shall do according to all that proceedeth out of his mouth**" (Num.30:2).
	"**When thou shalt vow a vow unto the LORD thy God, thou shalt not slack to pay it: for the LORD thy God will surely require it of thee; and it would be sin in thee**" (Dt.23:21).
	"**Thou shalt make thy prayer unto him, and he shall hear thee, and thou shalt pay thy vows**" (Job 22:27).
	"**Offer unto God thanksgiving; and pay thy vows unto the most High**" (Ps.50:14).
	"**Vow, and pay unto the LORD your God: let all that be round about him bring presents unto him that ought to be feared**" (Ps.76:11).
	"**When thou vowest a vow unto God, defer not to pay it; for** *he hath no pleasure in fools: pay that which thou hast vowed*" (Eccl.5:4).

2. Jesus Christ declared that God's Name is holy, set apart from all other names. "**After this manner therefore pray ye: Our Father which art in heaven, Hallowed be thy name**" (Mt.6:9).	1) God's name is much too precious to be used flippantly. His name is a <u>refuge for man</u>, not a cesspool to be filled with foul language. "**I will say of the LORD,** *He is* **my refuge and my fortress: my God; in him will I trust**" (Ps.91:2). "**Wherefore God also hath highly exalted him, and given him a name which is above every name: That at the name of Jesus every knee should bow, of things in heaven, and things in earth, and things under the earth; And that every tongue should confess that Jesus Christ is Lord, to the glory of God the Father**" (Ph. 2:9-11). 2) God's name is to be hallowed, set apart as holy. "**And he said unto them, When ye pray, say, Our Father which art in heaven, Hallowed be thy name. Thy kingdom come. Thy will be done, as in heaven, so in earth**" (Lk.11:2). "**Speak unto Aaron and to his sons, that they separate themselves from the holy things of the children of Israel, and that they profane not my holy name in those things which they hallow unto me: I am the LORD**" (Lev.22:2). 3) God's name is to be feared. "**If thou wilt not observe to do all the words of this law that are written in this book, that thou mayest fear this glorious and fearful name, THE LORD THY GOD**" (Dt.28:58). 4) God's name is to be a strong tower into which the believer can run. "**The name of the LORD is a strong tower: the righteous runneth into it, and is safe**" (Pr.18:10).

3. Jesus Christ declared that God's name must be glorified and honored. "Father, glorify thy name. Then came there a voice from heaven, *saying,* I have both glorified *it,* and will glorify *it* again" (Jn.12:28).	⇒ We must always seek to glorify and honor God's name… • in everything we do • in everything we say • in everything we think "Let your light so shine before men, that they may see your good works, and glorify your Father which is in heaven" (Mt.5:16). "And call upon me in the day of trouble: I will deliver thee, and thou shalt glorify me" (Ps.50:15). "Now the God of patience and consolation grant you to be likeminded one toward another according to Christ Jesus: That ye may with one mind *and* one mouth glorify God, even the Father of our Lord Jesus Christ" (Ro.15:5-6). "Ye that fear the LORD, praise him; all ye the seed of Jacob, glorify him; and fear him, all ye the seed of Israel" (Ps.22:23). "I will praise thee, O Lord my God, with all my heart: and I will glorify thy name for evermore" (Ps.86:12). "What? know ye not that your body is the temple of the Holy Ghost *which is* in you, which ye have of God, and ye are not your own? For ye are bought with a price: therefore glorify God in your body, and in your spirit, which are God's" (1 Cor.6:19-20).
4. Jesus Christ declared that God's name must not be abused by the hypocrisy of self-righteous men [professing believers]. "Even so ye also outwardly appear righteous unto men, but within ye are full of hypocrisy and iniquity" (Mt.23:28).	1) We must not misuse God's name by professing (blessing) God and then using profanity. "Out of the same mouth proceedeth blessing and cursing. My brethren, these things ought not so to be" (Jas. 3:10). 2) We must not misuse God's name by living a hypocritical life, claiming to know God but refusing to obey Him. "He that saith, I know him, and keepeth not his commandments, is a liar, and the truth is not in him" (1 Jn.2:4). "They profess that they know God; but in works they deny him, being abominable, and disobedient, and unto every good work reprobate" (Tit.1:16). 3) We must not misuse God's name by judging others in the name of God when we are ever so short ourselves. "Either how canst thou say to thy brother, Brother, let me pull out the mote that is in thine eye, when thou thyself beholdest not the beam that is in thine own eye? Thou hypocrite, cast out first the beam out of thine own eye, and then shalt thou see clearly to pull out the mote that is in thy brother's eye" (Lk.6:42).

	E. The Ten Command-ments, The Laws Governing Man's Duty to God (Part 4): Commandment Four Concerns *God's Day*—Never Fail to Observe the Sabbath, to Keep it Holy, Ex.20:8-11	Sabbath of the LORD thy God: in it thou shalt not do any work, thou, nor thy son, nor thy daughter, thy manservant, nor thy maidservant, nor thy cattle, nor thy stranger that is within thy gates:	the Sabbath: No work whatsoever is to be done on the Sabbath, not by anyone under your authority, including animals and strangers
1. Who is to obey this commandment?	**8** Remember the Sabbath day, to keep it holy.	**11** For in six days the LORD made heaven and earth, the sea, and all that in them is, and rested the seventh day: wherefore the LORD blessed the Sabbath day, and hallowed it.	**3. Why did God give this commandment?** a. Because the 7th day is to be a day of rest: The Lord's example b. Because the 7th day is to be a day of worship: The Lord blessed it & made it holy
2. What is the charge of this com.? a. You *shall work* for six days b. You *shall not do any work* on	**9** Six days shalt thou labor, and do all thy work:		
	10 But the seventh day is the		

DIVISION VII

THE LAW AND THE PROMISES OF GOD (THE MOSAIC COVENANT) (PART 2): THE TEN COMMANDMENTS--NECESSARY LAWS TO GOVERN MAN AND SOCIETY, EX.20:1-26

E. The Ten Commandments, The Laws Governing Man's Duty to God (Part 4): Commandment Four Concerns *God's Day*--Never Fail to Observe the Sabbath, to Keep it Holy, Ex.20:8-11

(20:8-11) **Introduction--Sabbath--Sunday--Worship**: work, rest, and worship--these are three of the basic essentials of human life. Listen to them again:

⇒ work
⇒ rest
⇒ worship

Man needs all three. God made man to work, to rest, and to worship. This is what the Sabbath is all about. God Himself divided time into seven days. Holy Scripture declares that God created the universe in six days and then rested on the seventh day (Gen.2:1-3).

Man is to work for six days, but after working six days, he is to take the seventh day and use it to rest and worship. God Himself set the day aside for us. God loves and cares for us, and He knows what we need. We need a full day every week for rest and relaxation and for worship--so much so that God made it one of the ten great laws that are to govern human life. This is the subject of this great commandment: *Commandment Four Concerns God's Day—Never Fail to Observe the Sabbath, to Keep it Holy,* 20:8-11.

1. Who is to obey this commandment? How long was this commandment to be in force (v.8)?
2. What is the charge of this commandment (v.9-10)?
3. Why did God give this commandment (v.11)?
4. What is the decision required by this commandment (v.11)?

[1] (20:8) **Commandments, The Ten--Obedience--Sabbath--Sunday--Worship**: Who is to obey this commandment? This is the longest of the Ten Commandments, four verses, almost one-third of the fifteen verses that cover the Ten Commandments (v.3-17). And note: all four verses dealing with the Sabbath declare that it is *you* who is to keep this commandment. Note the emphasis, the force of the language toward *you*:

⇒ Verse 8: the imperative *you--You* are to remember the Sabbath day, to keep it holy.
⇒ Verse 9: *You* are to labor and do all your work in six days.
⇒ Verse 10: *You* are not to do any work on the Sabbath day, nor is your family, nor is any slave or employee for whom you are responsible.
⇒ Verse 11: the understood *you--You* are to follow God's example and set the Sabbath day aside, use it as a day of rest and worship.

How long was this commandment to be in force? Note the word "remember" (zakar). God is charging us to remember something that had taken place in the past. What? Long before the Sabbath was included in the Ten Commandments, the Sabbath day had been instituted as a day of rest and worship. Verse 11 tells us when: at creation, right after God had created the universe (see outline and notes--Gen.2:1-3 for more discussion).

The point is this: the Sabbath day was not given to Israel alone; the Sabbath day was given to every nation and people upon earth. The Sabbath day was instituted by God at creation, long before the Ten Commandments were ever given, long before Israel was ever formed as a people or nation. The Sabbath day was given to all people for rest and worship. A day of rest and worship--one day out of every seven--is the God-given right of every man, woman, and child upon earth. This commandment applies to every generation of people, to every person, so long as the earth stands.

> **"And he said unto them, The Sabbath was made for man, and not man for the Sabbath"** (Mk.2:27).

"Let us hold fast the profession of our faith without wavering; (for he is faithful that promised;) And let us consider one another to provoke unto love and to good works: Not forsaking the assembling of ourselves together, as the manner of some is; but exhorting one another: and so much the more, as ye see the day approaching" (Heb.10:23-25).

"For in six days the LORD made heaven and earth, the sea, and all that in them is, and rested the seventh day: wherefore the LORD blessed the Sabbath day, and hallowed it [for all people]" (Ex.20:11).

2 (20:9-10) **Commandments, The Ten--Obedience--Sabbath--Sunday--Work--Worship**: What is the charge of the fourth commandment? "Remember the Sabbath day, to keep it holy." Several facts need to be noted.

1. The word "remember" (zakar) is imperative, a strong, strong imperative: "You must remember--remember to the point of *keeping* and *observing*--the day of rest and worship." When the Ten Commandments are repeated in Deuteronomy, the Hebrew word is translated "keep" or "observe":

"**Keep** the Sabbath day to sanctify it, as the LORD thy God hath commanded thee" (Dt.5:12).

2. The Hebrew word "Sabbath" does not mean the seventh day (Saturday) as so many people think. The word "Sabbath" (shabbath) means to rest, to repose, to cease. It means to cease from work, to rest from work.

This is significant, for God is charging us to keep the Sabbath, the day of rest and worship. He is not specifying a particular day of the week when man is to worship and rest. God simply says, work six days and then rest on the seventh day.

a. This fact is important for industrialized and technological societies. Why? Because so many people *have* to work on Saturday or on Sunday, on the day set aside by their religion as the day of worship and rest. In many cases, factories cannot shut down their huge furnaces, boilers, and machines without damaging them mechanically. They have to be operated continually; therefore, thousands upon thousands of people have to work on Saturday and Sunday. The same is true with many service industries and other businesses.

Thought 1. When businesses have to operate seven days a week, what are the employees of these businesses to do about worship and rest? Two very practical things must be done throughout the remaining generations of history:
⇒ The church must provide other services through the week for worship and rest, provide them for people who have to work on Saturday or Sunday.
⇒ People who work on the regular day of worship and rest must still worship God and rest at the alternate services and days scheduled by the church.

"Not forsaking the assembling of ourselves together, as the manner of some is; but exhorting one another: and so much the more, as ye see the day approaching" (Heb.10:25).
"And they went into Capernaum; and straightway on the sabbath day he [Jesus Christ] entered into the synagogue, and taught" (Mk.1:21).
"And he came to Nazareth, where he had been brought up: and, as his custom was, he went into the synagogue on the sabbath day, and stood up for to read" (Lk.4:16).
"But when they departed from Perga, they came to Antioch in Pisidia, and went into the synagogue on the sabbath day, and sat down" (Acts 13:14).

b. When the law was given by Moses, the Jews set aside the seventh day, Saturday, as their day of worship and rest. Today, others follow their practice. But the largest body of Christian believers have switched their day of worship and rest from the last day of the week to the first day of the week, from Saturday to Sunday. Why?
⇒ Because Jesus Christ burst loose from the bonds of death on the first day of the week. Believers wish to celebrate His glorious resurrection and the great hope of their salvation on the very day He arose.
⇒ Because the first day of the week is called "the Lord's day" (Rev.1:10). Believers wish to worship on the Lord's day.
⇒ Because the early followers of Christ switched their day of worship and rest to the first day of the week. The tradition has continued down through the centuries.

"And upon the first day of the week, when the disciples came together to break bread, Paul preached unto them, ready to depart on the morrow; and continued his speech until midnight" (Acts 20:7).
"Upon the first day of the week let every one of you lay by him in store, as God hath prospered him, that there be no gatherings when I come" (1 Cor.16:2).

3. The Sabbath, the day of rest and worship, is to be kept *holy* (v.8. See Deeper Study # 1--Ex.20:8 for discussion.)
4. Note that two clear instructions are given by God, two demands, two "you shalls" concerning the Sabbath commandment:
⇒ You *shall* work six days, but only for six days (v.9).
⇒ You *shall not* do any work on the seventh day (v.10).

a. You shall work six days, but *only* six days a week (v.9). This commandment declares that man is to work, to work diligently. From the very beginning of creation, God commanded man to work.

⇒ God told Adam (man) to dress and keep the Garden of Eden, to develop and maintain it.

"And the LORD God took the man, and put him into the garden of Eden to dress it and to keep it" (Gen.2:15).

⇒ Scripture clearly says that a man must work if he is to eat and meet his needs.

"For even when we were with you, this we commanded you, that if any would not work, neither should he eat. For we hear that there are some which walk among you disorderly, working not at all, but are busybodies. Now them that are such we command and exhort by our Lord Jesus Christ, that with quietness they work, and eat their own bread" (2 Th.3:10-12).

⇒ Scripture also says that a person should look after his own affairs and work with his own hands.

"And that ye study to be quiet, and to do your own business, and to work with your own hands, as we commanded you" (1 Th.4:11).

What about people who have enough money, so much that they do not have to work? They have worked hard and earned huge amounts of money, or have inherited large estates or won a large sum. Does this commandment apply to them? Yes. No person is ever to sit idle nor live an extravagant lifestyle, wasting and hoarding wealth. Scripture warns us: we are responsible to meet the needs of the world. Every person is to work as long as he lives, helping to conquer the evils of this earth--all the ravaging and destructive forces that bring suffering and destruction to man:

⇒ hunger ⇒ loneliness
⇒ thirst ⇒ emptiness
⇒ disease ⇒ death, both physical and spiritual

"Jesus said unto him, If thou wilt be perfect, go [and] sell that thou hast, and give to the poor, and thou shalt have treasure in heaven: and come [and] follow me. But when the young man heard that saying, he went away sorrowful: for he had great possessions. Then said Jesus unto his disciples, Verily I say unto you, That a rich man shall hardly enter into the kingdom of heaven. And again I say unto you, It is easier for a camel to go through the eye of a needle, than for a rich man to enter into the kingdom of God" (Mt.19:21-24).

"And he spake a parable unto them, saying, The ground of a certain rich man brought forth plentifully: And he thought within himself, saying, What shall I do, because I have no room where to bestow my fruits? And he said, This will I do: I will pull down my barns, and build greater; and there will I bestow all my fruits and my goods. And I will say to my soul, Soul, thou hast much goods laid up for many years; take thine ease, eat, drink, [and] be merry. But God said unto him, [Thou] fool, this night thy soul shall be required of thee: then whose shall those things be, which thou hast provided? So [is] he that layeth up treasure for himself, and is not rich toward God" (Lk.12:16-21).

What about the people who are lazy and slothful, people who do not give an honest day's work or else shun work altogether? Again, Scripture warns the lazy and slothful.

"Yet a little sleep, a little slumber, a little folding of the hands to sleep: So shall thy poverty come as one that travelleth, and thy want as an armed man" (Pr.6:10-11).

"For the drunkard and the glutton shall come to poverty: and drowsiness shall clothe a man with rags" (Pr.23:21).

"He that tilleth his land shall have plenty of bread: but he that followeth after vain persons shall have poverty enough" (Pr.28:19).

Man is to work six days a week. God created man with a nature that must work. There is within man a restlessness, a drive, an energy to be active, to work and achieve and conquer. Man never experiences complete fulfillment and satisfaction unless he works and senses that he achieves something worthwhile. If man does not direct his energy into profitable work, then he directs it to worthless or even destructive activities: to lawlessness, gangs, mobs, war, sex, alcohol, drugs, over-eating--all to the damage of others or himself. It is this--a lack of work and a lack of sensing fulfillment and satisfaction--that causes so much lawlessness and problems for society.

But note this fact: man is to work six days a week, but *only* six days a week.

b. You shall not do any work on the seventh day, none whatsoever (v.10). Note how strongly God expects this commandment to be obeyed: no person is to work seven days a week...

- not you (male or female)
- not your son or daughter
- not your slaves (employees)
- not your animals
- not even a stranger

Thought 1. The fourth commandment was given for our good. Without the Sabbath rest, we would soon break our bodies down. We would be constantly weary, worn out, and burned out. Productivity would soon decline. This has been proven time and again in dictatorial nations and slave markets that have demanded constant, unbroken work with no rest for its labor force. Productivity declined sharply, as well as health, physical strength, and mental alertness and ability.

Resting one day a week is an absolute essential for the human body. Business and labor, individuals and groups--we all must protect our bodies and the productivity of our society and economies. How? By obeying God's fourth commandment: Remember the Sabbath day; keep it holy--do not work on the Sabbath. Allow our bodies and minds to rest one day a week.

> **"For in six days the LORD made heaven and earth, the sea, and all that in them is, and rested the seventh day: wherefore the LORD blessed the sabbath day, and hallowed it" (Ex.20:11).**
>
> **"Six days thou shalt do thy work, and on the seventh day thou shalt rest: that thine ox and thine ass may rest, and the son of thy handmaid, and the stranger, may be refreshed" (Ex.23:12).**
>
> **"Ye shall keep the sabbath therefore; for it is holy unto you" (Ex.31:14).**

DEEPER STUDY # 1

(20:8) <u>Holy</u> (qados): means sanctified, separated, set apart, devoted, dedicated, consecrated, hallowed, honored, made sacred. It means to be pure, clean, and free from all pollution and defilement, totally free from sin and evil. It means to be totally different and distinct from anything else, from all that is in the world with all its corruption.[1]

The Sabbath, the day of worship and rest...
- is to be a day sanctified, set apart, devoted, dedicated, and consecrated to God, for worship and rest.
- is to be a day hallowed, honored, and made sacred in obedience to God and His command.
- is to be a day that <u>focuses our minds</u> upon living pure and clean lives, lives that are free from all pollution and defilement, lives that are totally free from sin and evil.
- is to be a day that is totally different and distinct from all other days of the world and their busy schedules.

> **"Exalt the LORD our God, and worship at his holy hill; for the LORD our God is holy" (Ps.99:9).**
>
> **"Wherefore come out from among them, and be ye separate, saith the Lord, and touch not the unclean thing; and I will receive you, And will be a Father unto you, and ye shall be my sons and daughters, saith the Lord Almighty. Having therefore these promises, dearly beloved, let us cleanse ourselves from all filthiness of the flesh and spirit, <u>perfecting holiness</u> in the fear of God" (2 Cor.6:17-7:1).**
>
> **"Follow peace with all men, and holiness, without which no man shall see the Lord" (Heb.12:14).**
>
> **"Because it is written, Be ye holy; for I am holy" (1 Pt.1:16).**
>
> **"Who shall not fear thee, O Lord, and glorify thy name? for thou only art holy: for all nations shall come and worship before thee; for thy judgments are made manifest" (Rev.15:4).**

---

3 (20:11) <u>Sabbath--Sunday--Commandment, The Ten</u>: Why did God give this commandment? God gives two strong reasons why the Sabbath is to be kept.

1. Man needs a day of rest: he needs to rest and relax one day out of every seven (v.11^a). The LORD Himself created the earth in six days and then rested on the seventh day (Gen.2:1-3). The Lord showed man that there is a natural flow to life. For example, there is the natural flow of birth and growth, aging and dying, inhaling and exhaling air. On and on the list could go. But for the present point, there is the natural flow of day and night and of work and sleep. God knows this; He created the natural flow to life. Therefore, He knows that man must by nature rest as well as work. He knows that a person cannot just go on working day after day and week after week without a break from the routine. The human body could never stand up under such pressure. This is one of the major reasons for the Sabbath, that man might have a break in his normal work routine, that he might have a day given over to rest and relaxation.

2. Now note why the seventh day is to be a day of worship (v.11^b): because the LORD Himself blessed the Sabbath day and made it holy. He Himself set it apart as a special day, as a day when man would focus upon worshipping and honoring God. (See <u>Deeper Study # 1</u>, Ex.20:8--for more discussion.)

Thought 1. The Sabbath day is only a shadow--a picture, a type, a symbol--of the Lord Jesus Christ. This is exactly what Scripture says:

> **"Let no man therefore judge you in meat, or in drink, or in respect of an holyday, or of the new moon, or of the <u>sabbath day</u>: Which are a shadow of things to come; but the body is of Christ" (Col.2:16-17).**

---

[1] Harris, Archer, Waltke. *Theological Wordbook of the New Testament.* (Chicago, IL: Moody Bible Institute of Chicago, 1980), p.786-789.
Vine, Unger, White. *Vine's Complete Expository Dictionary of Old and New Testament Words.* (Nashville, TN: Thomas Nelson Publishers, 1985), p.113-114.
Francis Brown. *The New Brown-Driver-Briggs-Gesenius Hebrew-English Lexicon.* (Peabody, MA: Hendrickson Publishers, 1979), p.872-873.

The Sabbath rest and worship point to the Lord Jesus Christ; the Sabbath is a picture of the perfect rest and worship that Jesus Christ brings to man. The Sabbath gives man a day to rest and worship, but Jesus Christ gives man rest itself, a complete and perfect rest and a perfect worship, the perfect assurance that we are acceptable to God.

1) Jesus Christ gives us the rest of salvation and deliverance, rest from the burden of sin.

   "Come unto me, all [ye] that labour and are heavy laden, and I will give you rest" (Mt.11:28).

2) Jesus Christ gives us the rest of freedom, rest from the bondages and enslavements to sin.

   "Who his own self bare our sins in his own body on the tree, that we, being dead to sins, should live unto righteousness: by whose stripes ye were healed" (1 Pt.2:24).

3) Jesus Christ gives us rest from condemnation.

   "There is therefore now no condemnation to them which are in Christ Jesus, who walk not after the flesh, but after the Spirit....For what the law could not do, in that it was weak through the flesh, God sending his own Son in the likeness of sinful flesh, and for sin, condemned sin in the flesh" (Ro.8:1, 3).

4) Jesus Christ gives us the rest of conquest and victory, the glorious liberty of living a life above the terrible trials and sufferings of this world.

   "But the natural man receiveth not the things of the Spirit of God: for they are foolishness unto him: neither can he know them, because they are spiritually discerned" (1 Cor.2:14).
   "For whatsoever is born of God overcometh the world: and this is the victory that overcometh the world, even our faith. Who is he that overcometh the world, but he that believeth that Jesus is the Son of God?" (1 Jn.5:4-5).

5) Jesus Christ gives us the rest of guidance.

   "Lo, I am with you alway, [even] unto the end of the world. Amen" (Mt.28:20).
   "Howbeit when he, the Spirit of truth, is come, he will guide you into all truth" (Jn.16:13).
   "There hath no temptation taken you but such as is common to man: but God is faithful, who will not suffer you to be tempted above that ye are able; but will with the temptation also make a <u>way to escape</u>, that ye may be able to bear it" (1 Cor.10:13).

6) Jesus Christ gives us the rest of provision.

   "But seek ye first the kingdom of God, and his righteousness; and all these things shall be added unto you" (Mt.6:33).
   "The LORD is my shepherd; I shall not want. He maketh me to lie down in green pastures: he leadeth me beside the still waters. He restoreth my soul: he leadeth me in the paths of righteousness for his name's sake. Yea, though I walk through the valley of the shadow of death, I will fear no evil: for thou art with me; thy rod and thy staff they comfort me. Thou preparest a table before me in the presence of mine enemies: thou anointest my head with oil; my cup runneth over. Surely goodness and mercy shall follow me all the days of my life: and I will dwell in the house of the LORD for ever" (Ps.23:1-6).

7) Jesus Christ gives us the rest of assurance, the assurance of security and protection.

   "Who shall separate us from the love of Christ? shall tribulation, or distress, or persecution, or famine, or nakedness, or peril, or sword?...Nay, in all these things we are more than conquerors through him that loved us. For I am persuaded, that neither death, nor life, nor angels, nor principalities, nor powers, nor things present, nor things to come, Nor height, nor depth, nor any other creature, shall be able to separate us from the love of God, which is in Christ Jesus our Lord" (Ro.8:35, 37-39).

8) Jesus Christ gives us the rest of a fruitful life, the rest of satisfaction and fulfillment.

   "I am come that they might have life, and that they might have [it] more abundantly" (Jn.10:10).

9) Jesus Christ gives us the rest of eternal life.

   "In my Father's house are many mansions: if [it were] not [so], I would have told you. I go to prepare a place for you. And if I go and prepare a place for you, I will come again, and receive you unto myself; that where I am, [there] ye may be also" (Jn.14:2-3).

10) Jesus Christ gives us the rest of the human soul.

> **"Take my yoke upon you, and learn of me; for I am meek and lowly in heart: and ye shall find rest unto your souls" (Mt.11:29).**

11) Jesus Christ gives us the rest of peace and rest from anxiety.

> **"Peace I leave with you, my peace I give unto you: not as the world giveth, give I unto you. Let not your heart be troubled, neither let it be afraid" (Jn.14:27).**
>
> **"These things I have spoken unto you, that in me ye might have peace. In the world ye shall have tribulation: but be of good cheer; I have overcome the world" (Jn.16:33).**
>
> **"Be careful for nothing; but in every thing by prayer and supplication with thanksgiving let your requests be made known unto God. And the peace of God, which passeth all understanding, shall keep your hearts and minds through Christ Jesus" (Ph.4:6-7).**
>
> **"Casting all your care upon him; for he careth for you" (1 Pt.5:7).**

4 (20:11) **Decision--Sabbath--Sunday--Commandment, The Ten--Obedience**: What is the decision required by this commandment? Obedience! People from every nation must obey the charge to remember the Sabbath and keep the Sabbath holy. The fourth commandment is stated positively: we are to...

- remember the Sabbath day
- keep it holy
- work for six days of the week
- rest on the seventh day
- follow God's example and set the Sabbath day aside and use it as a day of rest and worship

The fourth commandment requires a personal choice, a choice that will greatly improve our lives if we will obey God and keep the commandment. Note the teaching of Scripture, the decisions demanded by this commandment:

1. We must follow the Lord's example and worship one day a week, consistently and regularly.

> **"And he [Jesus Christ] came to Nazareth, where he had been brought up: and, as his custom was, he went into the synagogue on the sabbath day, and stood up for to read" (Lk.4:16).**

2. We must not forsake our worship, the assembling together with other believers.

> **"Not forsaking the assembling of ourselves together, as the manner of some is; but exhorting one another: and so much the more, as ye see the day approaching" (Heb.10:25).**

3. We are to bring our offerings to the Lord on the day of worship.

> **"Upon the first day of the week let every one of you lay by him in store, as God hath prospered him, that there be no gatherings when I come" (1 Cor.16:2).**

4. We must not fail to worship regularly lest others criticize our testimony for Christ.

> **"One man esteemeth one day above another: another esteemeth every day alike. Let every man be fully persuaded in his own mind. He that regardeth the day, regardeth it unto the Lord; and he that regardeth not the day, to the Lord he doth not regard it. He that eateth, eateth to the Lord, for he giveth God thanks; and he that eateth not, to the Lord he eateth not, and giveth God thanks" (Ro.14:5-6).**

5. We must work six days and then rest and worship on the Sabbath.

> **"Remember the sabbath day, to keep it holy. Six days shalt thou labour, and do all thy work: But the seventh day is the sabbath of the LORD thy God: in it thou shalt not do any work, thou, nor thy son, nor thy daughter, thy manservant, nor thy maidservant, nor thy cattle, nor thy stranger that is within thy gates" (Ex.20:8-10).**

6. We must keep the Sabbath, not just do what we want or feel like doing on the Sabbath.

> **"Ye shall fear every man his mother, and his father, and keep my sabbaths: I am the LORD your God" (Lev.19:3).**
>
> **"If thou turn away thy foot from the sabbath, from doing thy pleasure on my holy day; and call the sabbath a delight, the holy of the LORD, honourable; and shalt honour him, not doing thine own ways, nor finding thine own pleasure, nor speaking thine own words: Then shalt thou delight thyself in the LORD; and I will cause thee to ride upon the high places of the earth, and feed thee with the heritage of Jacob thy father: for the mouth of the LORD hath spoken it" (Is.58:13-14).**

7. We must rejoice and be glad on the Sabbath, for it is the day the Lord has made.

"This is the day which the LORD hath made; we will rejoice and be glad in it" (Ps.118:24).

THE BIBLICAL CONSEQUENCES OF FAILING
TO KEEP THE SABBATH, TO KEEP IT HOLY

DEEPER STUDY #2

(20:8-11) Commandments, The Ten--Obedience--Judgment--Sabbath: What are the consequences of breaking this commandment? After creating the world in six days, God rested. He did not rest because He was tired and needed relaxation. God spent the seventh day resting in order to establish the Sabbath as a day of rest and worship for man. God set the pattern: man is to follow God's pattern, to obey His commandment to remember the Sabbath day and keep it holy. The very fact that God Himself rested on the Sabbath means that the day is of major importance: God expects man to observe the Sabbath, to keep it holy. God, in His infinite wisdom, knew that those who were made in His image needed to rest and worship one day a week. This is a commandment that God fully expects His people to obey. This is made perfectly clear throughout Scripture. Severe consequences fall upon people who do not keep the Sabbath, the day of rest and worship.

1. The person who does not keep the Sabbath willingly disobeys God, stubbornly refuses to do what God has commanded. The man who *consistently* breaks this commandment, who never keeps the Sabbath (never worships God nor rests) puts his soul in grave, eternal danger. This person shows that he does not really believe God and will not inherit the kingdom of God.

> **"And let us consider one another to provoke unto love and to good works: Not forsaking the assembling of ourselves together, as the manner of some *is;* but exhorting *one another:* and so much the more, as ye see the day approaching. <u>For if we sin wilfully after that we have received the knowledge of the truth, there remaineth no more sacrifice for sins,</u> But a certain fearful looking for of judgment and fiery indignation, which shall devour the adversaries. He that despised Moses' law died without mercy under two or three witnesses: Of how much sorer punishment, suppose ye, shall he be thought worthy, who hath trodden under foot the Son of God, and hath counted the blood of the covenant, wherewith he was sanctified, an unholy thing, and hath done despite unto the Spirit of grace? For we know him that hath said, Vengeance *belongeth* unto me, I will recompense, saith the Lord. And again, The Lord shall judge his people. *It is* a fearful thing to fall into the hands of the living God" (Heb.10:24-31).**

> **"But the house of Israel rebelled against me in the wilderness: they walked not in my statutes, and they despised my judgments, which if a man do, he shall even live in them; and my sabbaths they greatly polluted: then I said, I would pour out my fury upon them in the wilderness, to consume them" (Ezk.20:13).**

2. The person who does not keep the Sabbath displeases God and shall face the judgment of God.

   a. The violators of the Sabbath faced the judgment of God in the Old Testament.

> **"Ye shall keep the sabbath therefore; for it is holy unto you: every one that defileth it shall surely be put to death: for whosoever doeth any work therein, that soul shall be cut off from among his people" (Ex.31:14).**

> **"And while the children of Israel were in the wilderness, they found a man that gathered sticks upon the sabbath day. And they that found him gathering sticks brought him unto Moses and Aaron, and unto all the congregation. And they put him in ward, because it was not declared what should be done to him. And the LORD said unto Moses, The man shall be surely put to death: all the congregation shall stone him with stones without the camp" (Num.15:32-35).**

> **"Thou hast despised mine holy things, and hast profaned my sabbaths....And I will scatter thee among the heathen, and disperse thee in the countries, and will consume thy filthiness out of thee" (Ezk.22:8, 15).**

   b. The violators of the Sabbath faced the judgment of God in the New Testament.

> **"Not forsaking the assembling of ourselves together, as the manner of some is; but exhorting one another: and so much the more, as ye see the day approaching. For if we sin wilfully after that we have received the knowledge of the truth, there remaineth no more sacrifice for sins, But a certain fearful looking for of judgment and fiery indignation, which shall devour the adversaries. He that despised Moses' law died without mercy under two or three witnesses: Of how much sorer punishment, suppose ye, shall he be thought worthy, who hath trodden under foot the Son of God, and hath counted the blood of the covenant, wherewith he was sanctified, an unholy thing, and hath done despite unto the Spirit of grace?" (Heb.10:25-29).**

3. The person who does not keep the Sabbath breaks the clear commandment of God.

> **"And it came to pass, that there went out some of the people on the seventh day for to gather [manna], and they found none. And the LORD said unto Moses, How long refuse ye to keep my commandments and my laws?" (Ex.16:27-28).**

"Remember the sabbath day, to keep it holy" (Ex.20:8).
"Not forsaking the assembling of ourselves together, as the manner of some is; but exhorting one another: and so much the more, as ye see the day approaching" (Heb.10:25).

4. The person who does not keep the Sabbath profanes, desecrates, violates, and even ignores what God has called holy.

"Ye shall keep the sabbath therefore; for it is holy unto you" (Ex.31:14).
"Thou hast despised mine holy things, and hast profaned my sabbaths" (Ezk.22:8).
"Then I contended with the nobles of Judah, and said unto them, What evil thing is this that ye do, and profane the sabbath day? Did not your fathers thus, and did not our God bring all this evil upon us, and upon this city? yet ye bring more wrath upon Israel by profaning the sabbath. And it came to pass, that when the gates of Jerusalem began to be dark before the sabbath, I commanded that the gates should be shut, and charged that they should not be opened till after the sabbath: and some of my servants set I at the gates, that there should no burden be brought in on the sabbath day" (Neh.13:15-19).

5. The person who does not keep the Sabbath pollutes or desecrates the worship of God.

"Little children, keep yourselves from idols. Amen" (1 Jn.5:21).
"Because they had not executed my judgments, but had despised my statutes, and had polluted my sabbaths, and their eyes were after their fathers' idols" (Ezk.20:24).
"Moreover this they have done unto me: they have defiled my sanctuary in the same day, and have profaned my sabbaths" (Ezk.23:38).

6. The person who does not keep the Sabbath loses out on the worship and fellowship with other believers.

"And they continued stedfastly in the apostles' doctrine and fellowship, and in breaking of bread, and in prayers" (Acts 2:42).
"Not forsaking the assembling of ourselves together, as the manner of some is; but exhorting one another: and so much the more, as ye see the day approaching" (Heb.10:25).
"But if we walk in the light, as he is in the light, we have fellowship one with another, and the blood of Jesus Christ his Son cleanseth us from all sin" (1 Jn.1:7).
"I am a companion of all them that fear thee, and of them that keep thy precepts" (Ps.119:63).

7. The person who does not keep the Sabbath gives occasion for others to judge and criticize him.

"Let no man therefore judge you in meat, or in drink, or in respect of an holyday, or of the new moon, or of the sabbath days: Which are a shadow of things to come; but the body is of Christ" (Col.2:16-17).
"Who art thou that judgest another man's servant? to his own master he standeth or falleth. Yea, he shall be holden up: for God is able to make him stand. One man esteemeth one day above another: another esteemeth every day alike. Let every man be fully persuaded in his own mind. He that regardeth the day, regardeth it unto the Lord; and he that regardeth not the day, to the Lord he doth not regard it. He that eateth, eateth to the Lord, for he giveth God thanks; and he that eateth not, to the Lord he eateth not, and giveth God thanks. For none of us liveth to himself, and no man dieth to himself. For whether we live, we live unto the Lord; and whether we die, we die unto the Lord: whether we live therefore, or die, we are the Lord's" (Ro.14:4-8).
"Let us not therefore judge one another any more: but judge this rather, that no man put a stumblingblock or an occasion to fall in his brother's way" (Ro.14:13).

8. The person can observe the Sabbath but fail to keep the Sabbath holy as God dictates: he can become legalistic and rigid; he can stress the keeping of the Sabbath over meeting the needs of people.

"And, behold, there was a man which had [his] hand withered. And they asked him, saying, Is it lawful to heal on the sabbath days? that they might accuse him. And he said unto them, What man shall there be among you, that shall have one sheep, and if it fall into a pit on the sabbath day, will he not lay hold on it, and lift [it] out? How much then is a man better than a sheep? Wherefore it is lawful to do well on the sabbath days. Then saith he to the man, Stretch forth thine hand. And he stretched [it] forth; and it was restored whole, like as the other" (Mt.12:10-13).
"And the ruler of the synagogue answered with indignation, because that Jesus had healed on the sabbath day, and said unto the people, There are six days in which men ought to work: in them therefore come and be healed, and not on the sabbath day. The Lord then answered him, and said, [Thou] hypocrite, doth not each one of you on the sabbath loose his ox or [his] ass from the stall, and lead [him] away to watering? And ought not this woman, being a daughter of Abraham, whom Satan hath bound, lo, these eighteen years, be loosed from this bond on the sabbath day?" (Lk.13:14-16).

THE BIBLICAL BENEFITS OF KEEPING THIS COMMANDMENT:
TO REMEMBER THE SABBATH AND TO KEEP IT HOLY

DEEPER STUDY #3

(20:8-11) <u>Commandments, The Ten--Sabbath--Blessings--Obedience</u>: when God requires something from His people, it is always for their good. Always. The same is true concerning the Sabbath. For our own good, we are to remember the Sabbath and keep it holy.

1. The person who keeps the Sabbath and trusts God will find rest, both physical and spiritual rest.

> "Six days thou shalt do thy work, and on the seventh day thou shalt rest: that thine ox and thine ass may rest, and the son of thy handmaid, and the stranger, may be refreshed" (Ex.23:12).
> "There remaineth therefore a rest to the people of God. For he that is entered into his rest, he also hath ceased from his own works, as God did from his. Let us labour therefore to enter into that rest, lest any man fall after the same example of unbelief" (Heb.4:9-11).

2. The person who follows God will keep the Sabbath and live a sanctified life, a life set apart by God.

> "Speak thou also unto the children of Israel, saying, Verily my sabbaths ye shall keep: for it is a sign between me and you throughout your generations; that ye may know that I am the LORD that doth sanctify you" (Ex.31:13).

3. The person who obeys God and who keeps the Sabbath will be given an everlasting name.

> "For thus saith the LORD unto the eunuchs [committed believers] that keep my sabbaths, and choose *the things* that please me, and take hold of my covenant; Even unto them will I give in mine house and within my walls a place and a name better than of sons and of daughters: I will give them an everlasting name, that shall not be cut off" (Is.56:4-5).

4. The person who loves the Lord and who keeps the Sabbath will inherit God's holy mountain (heaven) and experience the joy of having his prayers answered.

> "Also the sons of the stranger, that join themselves to the LORD, to serve him, and to love the name of the LORD, to be his servants, every one that keepeth the sabbath from polluting it, and taketh hold of my covenant; Even them will I <u>bring to my holy mountain</u>, and <u>make them joyful in my house of prayer</u>: their burnt offerings and their sacrifices *shall be* accepted upon mine altar; for mine house shall be called an house of prayer for all people" (Is.56:6-7).

5. The person who follows the Lord and keeps the true spirit of the Sabbath will do acts of mercy and good on the Sabbath day.

> "And, behold, there was a man which had *his* hand withered. And they asked him, saying, Is it lawful to heal on the sabbath days? that they might accuse him. And he said unto them, What man shall there be among you, that shall have one sheep, and if it fall into a pit on the sabbath day, will he not lay hold on it, and lift *it* out? How much then is a man better than a sheep? Wherefore it is lawful to do well on the sabbath days. Then saith he to the man, Stretch forth thine hand. And he stretched *it* forth; and it was restored whole, like as the other" (Mt.12:10-13).
> "And Jesus answering spake unto the lawyers and Pharisees, saying, Is it lawful to heal on the sabbath day? And they held their peace. And he took *him,* and healed him, and let him go; And answered them, saying, Which of you shall have an ass or an ox fallen into a pit, and will not straightway pull him out on the sabbath day? And they could not answer him again to these things" (Lk.14:3-6).

6. The person who keeps the Sabbath will be able to enjoy the special day that was made for him.

> "And he said unto them, The sabbath was made for man, and not man for the sabbath: Therefore the Son of man is Lord also of the sabbath" (Mk.2:27-28).

7. The person who truly follows the Lord and who keeps the Sabbath will be filled with joy and be victorious throughout life.

> "If thou turn away thy foot from the sabbath, from doing thy pleasure on my holy day; and call the sabbath a delight, the holy of the LORD, honourable; and shalt honour him, not doing thine own ways, nor finding thine own pleasure, nor speaking thine own words: Then shalt thou delight thyself in the LORD; and I will cause thee to ride upon the high places of the earth, and feed thee with the heritage of Jacob thy father: for the mouth of the LORD hath spoken it" (Is.58:13-14).

DEEPER STUDY # 4

JESUS CHRIST AND HIS TEACHING CONCERNING THE SABBATH DAY

"Remember the sabbath day, to keep it holy. Six days shalt thou labour, and do all thy work:
But the seventh day is the sabbath of the LORD thy God: in it thou shalt not do any work, thou, nor thy son,
nor thy daughter, thy manservant, nor thy maidservant, nor thy cattle, nor thy stranger that is within thy gates:
For in six days the LORD made heaven and earth, the sea, and all that in them is, and rested the seventh day:
wherefore the LORD blessed the sabbath day, and hallowed it" (Ex.20:8-11).

THE TEACHING OF CHRIST	THE BELIEVER'S RESPONSE
1. Jesus Christ declared that He is the Lord of the Sabbath. **"For the Son of man is Lord even of the sabbath day" (Mt.12:8).** **"Therefore the Son of man is Lord also of the sabbath" (Mk.2:28).**	⇒ Jesus Christ is the Source and LORD of the Sabbath. As the Source and LORD of the Sabbath, Jesus Christ wants us to know that He and He alone has the right... • to determine how the Sabbath is to be used • to determine how we are to rest on the Sabbath • to determine how we are to worship God on the Sabbath **"For *in* six days the LORD made heaven and earth, the sea, and all that in them *is,* and rested the seventh day: wherefore the LORD blessed the sabbath day, and hallowed it" (Ex.20:11).** **"But I say unto you, That in this place is [one] greater than the temple. But if ye had known what [this] meaneth, I will have mercy, and not sacrifice, ye would not have condemned the guiltless. For the Son of man is Lord even of the sabbath day" (Mt.12:6-8).** **"And the ruler of the synagogue answered with indignation, because that Jesus had healed on the sabbath day, and said unto the people, There are six days in which men ought to work: in them therefore come and be healed, and not on the sabbath day. The Lord then answered him, and said, [Thou] hypocrite, doth not each one of you on the sabbath loose his ox or [his] ass from the stall, and lead [him] away to watering? And ought not this woman, being a daughter of Abraham, whom Satan hath bound, lo, these eighteen years, be loosed from this bond on the sabbath day? And when he had said these things, all his adversaries were ashamed: and all the people rejoiced for all the glorious things that were done by him" (Lk.13:14-17).** **"And it came to pass, as he went into the house of one of the chief Pharisees to eat bread on the sabbath day, that they watched him. And, behold, there was a certain man before him which had the dropsy. And Jesus answering spake unto the lawyers and Pharisees, saying, Is it lawful to heal on the sabbath day? And they held their peace. And he took him, and healed him, and let him go; And answered them, saying, Which of you shall have an ass or an ox fallen into a pit, and will not straightway pull him out on the sabbath day?" (Lk.14:1-5).**
2. Jesus Christ declared that the Sabbath was made for man and not man for the Sabbath. **"And it came to pass, that he went through the corn fields on the sabbath day; and his disciples began, as they went, to pluck the ears of corn. And the Pharisees said unto him, Behold, why do they on the sabbath day that which is not lawful?...And he said unto them, The sabbath was made for man, and not man for the sabbath" (Mk.2:23-24, 27).**	⇒ We must never be rigid and inflexible in what we allow and disallow on the Sabbath, so rigid that we bind ourselves to a life of legalism instead of grace (cp. 1 Sam.6:1-6). **"At that time Jesus went on the sabbath day through the corn; and his disciples were an hungred, and began to pluck the ears of corn, and to eat. But when the Pharisees saw *it,* they said unto him, Behold, thy disciples do that which is not lawful to do upon the sabbath day. But he said unto them, Have ye not read what David did, when he was an hungred, and they that were with him; How he entered into the house of God, and did eat the showbread, which was not lawful for him to eat, neither for them which were with him, but only for the priests?" (Mt.12:1-4).** **"*There is* therefore now no condemnation to them which are in Christ Jesus, who walk not after the flesh, but after the Spirit" (Ro.8:1).** **"Stand fast therefore in the liberty wherewith Christ hath made us free, and be not entangled again with the yoke of bondage" (Gal.5:1).**

3. Jesus Christ declared that it is sometimes a necessity to work on the Sabbath.
 	
"And it came to pass on the second sabbath after the first, that he went through the corn fields; and his disciples plucked the ears of corn, and did eat, rubbing *them* in *their* hands" (Lk.6:1).
"Then said Jesus unto them, I
	1) When businesses have to operate seven days a week, what are the employees of these businesses to do about worship and rest? Two very practical things must be done throughout the remaining generations of history:
	  a) The church must provide other services through the week for worship and rest, provide them for people who have to work Saturday or Sunday.
	  b) People who work on the regular day of worship and rest must still worship God and rest at the alternative services and days scheduled by the church.

THE TEACHING OF CHRIST	THE BELIEVER'S RESPONSE
will ask you one thing; Is it lawful on the sabbath days to do good, or to do evil? to save life, or to destroy *it?* And looking round about upon them all, he said unto the man, Stretch forth thy hand. And he did so: and his hand was restored whole as the other" (Lk.6:9-10).	"Not forsaking the assembling of ourselves together, as the manner of some *is;* but exhorting *one another:* and so much the more, as ye see the day approaching" (Heb.10:25). "And he came to Nazareth, where he had been brought up: and, as his custom was, he went into the synagogue on the sabbath day, and stood up for to read" (Lk.4:16). "But when they departed from Perga, they came to Antioch in Pisidia, and went into the synagogue on the sabbath day, and sat down" (Acts 13:14). 2) There are many people who have to work on Sunday: ⇒ medical workers ⇒ policemen ⇒ firemen ⇒ pastors ⇒ missionaries ⇒ industrial maintenance workers ⇒ media personnel (television, radio, newspapers, etc.) ⇒ professional athletes And so on. As demanding as these professions are, every person still needs a day in the week for worship and rest. We must never get so busy that we forget the LORD. God knows us better than we do; therefore He knows how easily we slip into bad habits. God will not strike us down and kill us if we fail to keep the Sabbath but we will be destroying ourselves. "And it came to pass, *that* there went out *some* of the people on the seventh day for to gather, and they found none. And the LORD said unto Moses, How long refuse ye to keep my commandments and my laws?" (Ex.16:27-28). "Ye shall keep the sabbath therefore; for it *is* holy unto you: every one that defileth it shall surely be put to death: for whosoever doeth *any* work therein, that soul shall be cut off from among his people" (Ex.31:14). "But the house of Israel rebelled against me in the wilderness: they walked not in my statutes, and they despised my judgments, which *if* a man do, he shall even live in them; and my sabbaths they greatly polluted: then I said, I would pour out my fury upon them in the wilderness, to consume them" (Ezk.20:13). "Thou hast despised mine holy things, and hast profaned my sabbaths" (Ezk.22:8).

ADDITIONAL NOTES ABOUT JESUS CHRIST AND THE SABBATH

1. Jesus Christ gives us the rest of... *SALVATION AND DELIVERANCE*	⇒ The believer must trust, rest in Jesus Christ for salvation and deliverance. "Behold, God *is* my salvation; I will trust, and not be afraid: for the LORD JEHOVAH *is* my strength and *my* song; he also is become my salvation" (Is.12:2). "The LORD *is* my light and my salvation; whom shall I fear? the LORD *is* the strength of my life; of whom shall I be afraid?" (Ps.27:1). "But the salvation of the righteous *is* of the LORD: *he is* their strength in the time of trouble" (Ps.37:39). "For the Son of man is come to seek and to save that which was lost" (Lk.19:10). "Who gave himself for our sins, that he might deliver us from this present evil world, according to the will of God and our Father" (Gal.1:4). "Wherefore he is able also to save them to the uttermost that come unto God by him, seeing he ever liveth to make intercession for them" (Heb.7:25).
2. Jesus Christ gives us the rest of... *ASSURANCE*	⇒ The believer must trust, rest in Jesus Christ for assurance. "My sheep hear my voice, and I know them, and they follow me: And I give unto them eternal life; and they shall never perish, neither shall any [man] pluck them out of my hand. My Father, which gave [them] me, is greater than all; and no [man] is able to pluck [them] out of my Father's hand" (Jn.10:27-29). "Being confident of this very thing, that he which hath begun a good

	work in you will perform *it* until the day of Jesus Christ" (Ph.1:6).
	"For I know whom I have believed, and am persuaded that he is able to keep that which I have committed unto him against that day" (2 Tim.1:12).
	"Let us draw near with a true heart in full assurance of faith, having our hearts sprinkled from an evil conscience, and our bodies washed with pure water" (Heb.10:22).
	"Now unto him that is able to keep you from falling, and to present *you* faultless before the presence of his glory with exceeding joy, To the only wise God our Saviour, *be* glory and majesty, dominion and power, both now and ever. Amen" (Jude 1:24-25).
3. Jesus Christ gives us the rest of... *SECURITY*	⇒ The believer must trust, rest in Jesus Christ for security. "When thou liest down, thou shalt not be afraid: yea, thou shalt lie down, and thy sleep shall be sweet" (Pr.3:24). "When thou passest through the waters, I *will be* with thee; and through the rivers, they shall not overflow thee: when thou walkest through the fire, thou shalt not be burned; neither shall the flame kindle upon thee" (Is.43:2). "Who shall separate us from the love of Christ? *shall* tribulation, or distress, or persecution, or famine, or nakedness, or peril, or sword?...Nay, in all these things we are more than conquerors through him that loved us. For I am persuaded, that neither death, nor life, nor angels, nor principalities, nor powers, nor things present, nor things to come, Nor height, nor depth, nor any other creature, shall be able to separate us from the love of God, which is in Christ Jesus our Lord" (Ro.8:35, 37-39). "Nevertheless the foundation of God standeth sure, having this seal, The Lord knoweth them that are his. And, Let every one that nameth the name of Christ depart from iniquity" (2 Tim.2:19). "So that we may boldly say, The Lord is my helper, and I will not fear what man shall do unto me" (Heb.13:6).
4. Jesus Christ gives us the rest of... *PROVISION*	⇒ The believer must trust, rest in Jesus Christ for provision, for his daily bread and every other human need. "Behold the fowls of the air: for they sow not, neither do they reap, nor gather into barns; yet your heavenly Father feedeth them. Are ye not much better than they?" (Mt.6:26). "But seek ye first the kingdom of God, and his righteousness; and all these things shall be added unto you" (Mt.6:33). "But my God shall supply all your need according to his riches in glory by Christ Jesus" (Ph. 4:19). "Thou preparest a table before me in the presence of mine enemies: thou anointest my head with oil; my cup runneth over" (Ps.23:5). "For since the beginning of the world *men* have not heard, nor perceived by the ear, neither hath the eye seen, O God, beside thee, *what* he hath prepared for him that waiteth for him" (Is.64:4). "Bring ye all the tithes into the storehouse, that there may be meat in mine house, and prove me now herewith, saith the LORD of hosts, if I will not open you the windows of heaven, and pour you out a blessing, that *there shall* not *be room* enough *to receive it*" (Mal.3:10).
5. Jesus Christ gives us the rest of... *CONQUEST AND VICTORY*	⇒ The believer must trust, rest in Jesus Christ for conquest and victory over sin and death. "These things I have spoken unto you, that in me ye might have peace. In the world ye shall have tribulation: but be of good cheer; I have overcome the world" (Jn.16:33). "Nay, in all these things we are more than conquerors through him that loved us" (Ro.8:37). "There hath no temptation taken you but such as is common to man: but God *is* faithful, who will not suffer you to be tempted above that ye are able; but will with the temptation also make a way to escape, that ye may be able to bear *it*" (1 Cor.10:13). "Now thanks *be* unto God, which always causeth us to triumph in Christ, and maketh manifest the savour of his knowledge by us in every place" (2 Cor.2:14). "(For the weapons of our warfare *are* not carnal, but mighty through God to the pulling down of strong holds;) Casting down imaginations, and every high thing that exalteth itself against the knowledge of God, and bringing into captivity every thought to the obedience of Christ" (2 Cor.10:4-5).

	"For whatsoever is born of God overcometh the world: and this is the victory that overcometh the world, *even* our faith. Who is he that overcometh the world, but he that believeth that Jesus is the Son of God?" (1 Jn.5:4-5). "Through thee will we push down our enemies: through thy name will we tread them under that rise up against us" (Ps.44:5). "And ye shall tread down the wicked; for they shall be ashes under the soles of your feet in the day that I shall do *this,* saith the LORD of hosts" (Mal.4:3).
6. Jesus Christ gives us the rest of... *A FULFILLED LIFE*	⇒ The believer must trust, rest in Jesus Christ for a fulfilled life. "...I am come that they might have life, and that they might have it more abundantly" (Jn.10:10). "And God is able to make all grace abound toward you; that ye, always having all sufficiency in all things, may abound to every good work" (2 Cor.9:8). "Now unto him that is able to do exceeding abundantly above all that we ask or think, according to the power that worketh in us" (Eph.3:20). "For I am now ready to be offered, and the time of my departure is at hand. I have fought a good fight, I have finished *my* course, I have kept the faith: Henceforth there is laid up for me a crown of righteousness, which the Lord, the righteous judge, shall give me at that day: and not to me only, but unto all them also that love his appearing" (2 Tim.4:6-8). "And God gave Solomon wisdom and understanding exceeding much, and largeness of heart, even as the sand that *is* on the sea shore" (1 Ki.4:29).
7. Jesus Christ gives us the rest of... *ETERNAL LIFE*	⇒ The believer must trust, rest in Jesus Christ for eternal life. "Then shall the King say unto them on his right hand, Come, ye blessed of my Father, inherit the kingdom prepared for you from the foundation of the world" (Mt.25:34). "For God so loved the world, that he gave his only begotten Son, that whosoever believeth in him should not perish, but have everlasting life" (Jn.3:16). "Labour not for the meat which perisheth, but for that meat which endureth unto everlasting life, which the Son of man shall give unto you: for him hath God the Father sealed" (Jn.6:27). "And I give unto them eternal life; and they shall never perish, neither shall any man pluck them out of my hand" (Jn.10:28). "In hope of eternal life, which God, that cannot lie, promised before the world began" (Tit.1:2). "Keep yourselves in the love of God, looking for the mercy of our Lord Jesus Christ unto eternal life" (Jude 1:21). "Surely goodness and mercy shall follow me all the days of my life: and I will dwell in the house of the LORD for ever" (Ps.23:6).
8. Jesus Christ gives us the rest of... *THE HUMAN SOUL*	⇒ The believer must trust, rest in Jesus Christ for the eternal fate of his soul. "And fear not them which kill the body, but are not able to kill the soul: but rather fear him which is able to destroy both soul and body in hell" (Mt.10:28). "Take my yoke upon you, and learn of me; for I am meek and lowly in heart: and ye shall find rest unto your souls" (Mt.11:29). "In a moment, in the twinkling of an eye, at the last trump: for the trumpet shall sound, and the dead shall be raised incorruptible, and we shall be changed. For this corruptible must put on incorruption, and this mortal *must* put on immortality. So when this corruptible shall have put on incorruption, and this mortal shall have put on immortality, then shall be brought to pass the saying that is written, Death is swallowed up in victory. O death, where *is* thy sting? O grave, where *is* thy victory? The sting of death *is* sin; and the strength of sin *is* the law. But thanks *be* to God, which giveth us the victory through our Lord Jesus Christ" (1 Cor.15:52-57). "And I saw thrones, and they sat upon them, and judgment was given unto them: and *I saw* the souls of them that were beheaded for the witness of Jesus, and for the word of God, and which had not worshipped the beast, neither his image, neither had received *his* mark upon their foreheads, or in their hands; and they lived and reigned with Christ a thousand years" (Rev.20:4).

9. Jesus Christ gives us the rest of...	⇒ The believer must trust, rest in Jesus Christ for peace, a perfect rest from all anxiety.
PEACE, THE REST FROM ANXIETY	"Peace I leave with you, my peace I give unto you: not as the world giveth, give I unto you. Let not your heart be troubled, neither let it be afraid" (Jn.14:27).
	"These things I have spoken unto you, that in me ye might have peace. In the world ye shall have tribulation: but be of good cheer; I have overcome the world" (Jn.16:33).
	"But the fruit of the Spirit is love, joy, <u>peace</u>, longsuffering, gentleness, goodness, faith" (Gal.5:22).
	"Grace and peace be multiplied unto you through the knowledge of God, and of Jesus our Lord" (2 Pt.1:2).
	"For he [Jesus Christ] is our peace, who hath made both one, and hath broken down the middle wall of partition *between us*" (Eph.2:14).
	"Be careful for nothing; but in every thing by prayer and supplication with thanksgiving let your requests be made known unto God. And the peace of God, which passeth all understanding, shall keep your hearts and minds through Christ Jesus" (Ph.4:6-7).
	"And let the peace of God rule in your hearts, to the which also ye are called in one body; and be ye thankful" (Col.3:15).
	"Therefore being justified by faith, we have peace with God through our Lord Jesus Christ" (Ro.5:1).
	"And the very God of peace sanctify you wholly; and *I pray God* your whole spirit and soul and body be preserved blameless unto the coming of our Lord Jesus Christ" (1 Th.5:23).
	"Casting all your care upon him; for he careth for you" (1 Pt.5:7).
	"Thou wilt keep *him* in perfect peace, *whose* mind *is* stayed *on thee*: because he trusteth in thee" (Is.26:3).

TYPES, SYMBOLS, AND PICTURES
(Exodus 20:8-11)

Historical Term	Type or Picture (Scriptural Basis for Each)	Life Application for Today's Believer	Biblical Application for Today's Believer
The Sabbath (Ex.20:8-11)	*The word "sabbath" means rest; therefore, the Sabbath is a symbol of the rest that comes only from having a relationship with Jesus Christ.* "Remember the sabbath day, to keep it holy. Six days shalt thou labour, and do all thy work: But the seventh day *is* the sabbath of the LORD thy God: *in it* thou shalt not do any work, thou, nor thy son, nor thy daughter, thy a personservant, nor thy maidservant, nor thy cattle, nor thy stranger that *is* within thy gates: For *in* six days the LORD made heaven and earth, the sea, and all that in them *is*, and rested the seventh day: wherefore the LORD blessed the sabbath day, and hallowed it" (Ex.20:8-11).	⇒ The Sabbath is a picture of the perfect rest that Jesus Christ brings to a person. The Sabbath gives a person a day to rest and worship, but... • Jesus Christ gives a person rest itself, a complete rest, a perfect rest of mind and soul. • Jesus Christ gives a person the perfect assurance that we are acceptable to God. A person is to be faithful to worship and rest on the Sabbath, as God has ordained. It is only through obedience to God's command that we are able to receive the perfect rest that only God can give.	*"There remaineth therefore a rest to the people of God. For he that is entered into his rest, he also hath ceased from his own works, as God did from his. Let us labour therefore to enter into that rest, lest any man fall after the same example of unbelief" (Heb.4:9-11).* *"Come unto me, all ye that labour and are heavy laden, and I will give you rest" (Mt.11:28).* *"But they that wait upon the LORD shall renew their strength; they shall mount up with wings as eagles; they shall run, and not be weary; and they shall walk, and not faint" (Is.40:31).* *"For the Son of man is Lord even of the sabbath day" (Mt.12:8; cp. Mk. 2:27-28).*

	F. The Ten Commandments, The Laws Governing Man's Duty To Others (Part 1): Commandment Five Concerns the Family—Never Dishonor Parents, Ex.20:12
Commandment 5 concerns *man's family*: Honor your father & mother	12 Honour thy father and thy mother: that thy days may be long upon the land which the LORD thy God giveth thee.

DIVISION VII

THE LAW AND THE PROMISES OF GOD (THE MOSAIC COVENANT) (PART 2): THE TEN COMMANDMENTS--NECESSARY LAWS TO GOVERN MAN AND SOCIETY, EX.20:1-26

F.   The Ten Commandments, The Laws Governing Man's Duty To Others (Part 1): Commandment Five Concerns the Family--Never Dishonor Parents, Ex.20:12

(20:12) Introduction--Children--Family--Parents--Society--Commandments, The Ten: the family is of vital importance, for the family was the first institution formed upon earth. God created the first man and woman, Adam and Eve, and they became man and wife; then Eve bore a son. Thereby, the first family was formed, created as the most important institution, as the foundation of all human life and development that was to follow. It is the family that forms the community, society, and government of nations. It is not enough for men and women to exist. Men and women must become fathers and mothers. They must give birth to children or else everything human eventually ceases to exist:

⇒ Human life would stop.
⇒ Human society would stop.
⇒ Human government would stop.

The family--father, mother, and child--is the most important institution, the very foundation of society, communities, and nations. As goes the family, so goes society.

The point: every generation must give attention to the family and strengthen it if the human race is to survive. Today, we are fools if we do not strengthen our families, do not strengthen them for our generation and for future generations. The very survival of society and civilization depends upon strong families, upon fathers, mothers, and children who honor and respect one another. For this reason, we must give attention and fight against the evils of men, the evils that destroy us all...

- selfishness
- disrespect
- disobedience
- rebellion
- withdrawal
- coldness
- bitterness
- revenge
- hatred
- hostility
- abuse
- murder
- adultery
- immorality
- indulgence
- license
- alcohol, drugs
- gambling
- irresponsibility
- greed
- materialism
- ungodliness
- unbelief
- lawlessness

God established the primacy and importance of the family forever when He created the first man and the first woman. He reinforces the primacy of the family with this great commandment: "Honor your father and your mother" (v.12). This is the subject of the present commandment: *Commandment Five Concerns the Family--Never Dishonor Parents*, 20:12.

1. Who is to obey this commandment? You (v.12).
2. How long was this commandment to be in force? Forever (v.12).
3. What is the charge of this commandment (v.12)?
4. There are two great promises attached to this commandment (v.12).
5. What is the decision required by this commandment? Obedience (v.12).

1 (20:12) **Commandment, The Ten--Parents--Children--Family--Believers, Duty--Obedience:** Who is to obey this commandment? Who is to obey his father and his mother? Everyone of us. Just think for a moment: every person upon earth has, or has had in the past, a father and mother! God commands us--everyone of us--to honor and respect our fathers and mothers. What about abusive parents? They will be discussed in a later point, but for now the point is this: God expects us, He commands us, to honor and respect our fathers and mothers. As the verse says, "Honor your father and your mother" (v.12).

2 (20:12) **Commandment, The Ten--Family--Parents--Children--Obedience:** How long was this commandment to be in force? Was it meant for Israel alone, meant only for the ancient world? Or has there always been a need for children to honor and respect their parents? How about today? Is there a need today for us to honor our fathers and mothers?

The answer is obvious. In fact, each of the Ten Commandments meets a very specific need of man, a desperate need that has to be met or else man and society will be destroyed. Glance quickly at each of the commandments and this fact is clearly seen.

The point is just this: God loves man and has determined that man must be saved not destroyed. Therefore, God has reached out to man and given man the Ten Commandments to govern his life and community.

If the family disintegrated, then all the great virtues of life to keep him from destroying himself would soon disappear: honor, respect, concern, responsibility, decency, love, joy, peace--true love, joy, and peace. When the great virtues are weakened, community and society are weakened. How long then is the fifth commandment to be in force? How many generations of people are to honor their parents? As long as men and women and children live upon earth, we are to honor and obey our parents.

> **"Children, obey your parents in the Lord: for this is right. Honour thy father and mother; (which is the first commandment with promise;) That it may be well with thee, and thou mayest live long on the earth" (Eph.6:1-3).**

3 (20:12) **Commandment, The Ten--Obedience--Children--Parents--Family--Father--Mother**: What is the charge of this commandment, "Honor your father and your mother"? The first four commandments covered our duty to God. But once we have done our duty to God, note what our very next duty is: to honor our parents.

⇒ The divine order is just this: God first, then our parents.

Note six points about the charge of this commandment.

1. The Hebrew word *honor* (kabed) means that we are to respect, esteem, and highly regard our parents. There is even the idea of reverence in the word *honor*: we are to *reverence* our parents. The Greek word for *honor* (timao) pictures exactly what is meant: it means that we are to esteem and value our parents as precious (Amplified Bible); to show them respect, reverence, kindness, and obedience. Matthew Henry says that in practical terms, the commandment means we are to...

- respect our parents, reverence them
- obey our parents
- submit to the rebukes, instructions, and corrections of our parents
- listen to our parents' advice, direction, and concern
- comfort our parents[1]

Thought 1. What does God mean by *honoring our parents*? Scripture tells us:

⇒ To honor means to obey and respect our parents.

> **"For Moses said, Honour thy father and thy mother; and, Whoso curseth father or mother, let him die the death" (Mk.7:10).**
> **"Children, obey your parents in the Lord: for this is right. Honour thy father and mother; (which is the first commandment with promise;) That it may be well with thee, and thou mayest live long on the earth" (Eph.6:1-3).**
> **"Children, obey your parents in all things: for this is well pleasing unto the Lord" (Col.3:20).**
> **"Honour thy father and thy mother: that thy days may be long upon the land which the LORD thy God giveth thee" (Ex.20:12).**
> **"Honour thy father and thy mother, as the LORD thy God hath commanded thee; that thy days may be prolonged, and that it may go well with thee, in the land which the LORD thy God giveth thee" (Dt.5:16).**
> **"For God commanded, saying, Honour thy father and mother: and, He that curseth father or mother, let him die the death" (Mt.15:4).**

⇒ To honor means to listen to the instructions of our parents; to obey the instructions, never forsaking them.

> **"My son, hear the instruction of thy father, and forsake not the law of thy mother" (Pr.1:8).**
> **"Hear, ye children, the instruction of a father, and attend to know understanding....Hear, O my son, and receive my sayings; and the years of thy life shall be many. I have taught thee in the way of wisdom; I have led thee in right paths. When thou goest, thy steps shall not be straitened [hampered, NIV]; and when thou runnest, thou shalt not stumble. Take fast hold of instruction; let her not go: keep her; for she is thy life" (Pr.4:1, 10-13).**
> **"My son, keep thy father's commandment, and forsake not the law of thy mother" (Pr.6:20).**

⇒ To honor means to listen to our parents and never despise them when they are old.

> **"Hearken unto thy father that begat thee, and despise not thy mother when she is old" (Pr.23:22).**

---

[1] Matthew Henry. *Matthew Henry's Commentary*, p. 361-362.

⇒ To honor means to be wise, never foolish.

> "A wise son maketh a glad father: but a foolish son is the heaviness of his mother" (Pr.10:1).
> "A wise son maketh a glad father: but a foolish man despiseth his mother" (Pr.15:20).

⇒ To honor means to have a testimony of pure and right behavior.

> "Even a child is known by his doings, whether his work [behavior, conduct] be pure, and whether it be right" (Pr.20:11).

⇒ To honor means to respect and reverence our parents when they are elderly.

> "Ye shall fear every man his mother, and his father, and keep my sabbaths: I am the LORD your God" (Lev.19:3).
> "Thou shalt rise up before the hoary [gray] head, and honour the face of the old man, and fear thy God: I am the LORD" (Lev.19:32).
> "And Elihu the son of Barachel the Buzite answered and said, I am young, and ye are very old; wherefore I was afraid, and durst not show you mine opinion" (Job 32:6).
> "Hearken unto thy father that begat thee, and despise not thy mother when she is old" (Pr.23:22).

⇒ To honor means to accept the true faith of our parents, their belief in God's Son, the Lord Jesus Christ.

> "When I call to remembrance the unfeigned faith that is in thee, which dwelt first in thy grandmother Lois, and thy mother Eunice; and I am persuaded that in thee also" (2 Tim.1:5).
> "And that from a child thou hast known the holy scriptures, which are able to make thee wise unto salvation through faith which is in Christ Jesus" (2 Tim.3:15).

⇒ To honor means to respect our parents so much that it carries over to others, honoring and respecting all persons.

> "Rebuke not an elder, but intreat him as a father; and the younger men as brethren" (1 Tim.5:1).

2. Note that mothers are to be honored just as much as fathers, and fathers just as much as mothers: "[Children] honor your father and your mother" (v.12). Mothers and fathers are placed on equal footing. God Himself honors and respects mothers as much as fathers and charges all children to honor each equally.

3. Note that every person within the family is mentioned: the child, mother, and father. If our mothers and fathers are living, we are to honor and respect them. But note this fact as well: every person in the world, whether young or old (adult), is the child of some father and mother. Thus if every child showed honor and respect to his parents, then every person upon earth would be showing honor and respect to one another. Honor and respect would catch aflame and spread throughout the world.

The implication is clear: the families of the earth and the world as a whole are to be filled with honor and respect. Honor and respect are to flood the hearts and lives of our families. If so, then honor and respect will flow out and flood society and civilization. The whole world will be filled with honor and respect. This is God's will; this is one of the main reasons God has given this commandment.

Note: the family is the basic unit of society, the very foundation of society. If honor and respect control the behavior of the family, it will help to control the behavior of our communities and society. God wants *honor and respect* to be the prevailing force flowing out from the hearts of people to one another. God knows:

⇒ if we honor and respect one another, then peace and love will prevail upon the earth.
⇒ if we honor and respect one another, then the behavior of men will be controlled.
⇒ if we honor and respect one another, there will be no lawlessness and selfishness. There will be only honor and respect for all people--for all the parents and children of the earth.

Thought 1. William Barclay makes three points that should stir us to keep this commandment, to always honor our parents:

> "With the fifth commandment we come right home, for the fifth commandment is 'Honour your father and your mother' (Exodus 20:12). Of all the commandments this should be the easiest to obey.
> "i. It should be easy to obey this commandment because it is natural to do so. This commandment is, as it were, built into the very structure of life. It is not a commandment which we find only in the Bible. There never was a society of any kind in which this commandment was not accepted as binding. In ancient Greece, for instance, Solon the great law-giver laid it down that, if a son did not support his parents in their old age, when they needed support, he should lose his rights as a citizen. The Greeks believed that to honour parents is part of the basic duty of every citizen of the state. Anyone who has good parents and who does not realise the duty of honouring them is an unnatural person. Nature itself demands that we keep this commandment.
> "ii. It is a duty of gratitude to keep this commandment. It was our parents who brought us into this world, and we owe them our lives. Of all living creatures man takes longest to become able to support and look after himself.

"There is a long time when we cannot get ourselves a home or food or clothes, and when we are entirely dependent on our parents; and there is a considerable part of that time when we are so helpless, that a blow would kill us, and, even if nothing was done to us, and we were just alone, we would certainly die. We ought to find it easy to keep this commandment, if only as a matter of gratitude to those to whom we literally owe the fact that we came into the world, and that we survived through the years when we were quite unable to help ourselves, or to get the things necessary to keep body and soul together.

"Apart from that purely physical side of life, many of us owe a great deal to the care and the love and even to the sacrifice of our parents to give us a good start in life....We ought to be grateful that in many, many homes the parents do without things and plan and save so that their children should have a chance to do well in life. Of all faults, ingratitude is the ugliest and the most hurting, and not to keep this commandment is to be guilty of ingratitude.

"iii. To honour our parents is a matter of common sense. They have walked the journey of life before us, and therefore they know the dangers and the pitfalls in the way. If you are going on a journey through what is to you an unknown country, a map and a guide-book will be very useful, but most useful of all will be the advice and the experience of one who has already travelled that way.

"When parents advise their child to do or not to do something, he should understand that it is not because they wish to show their authority or because they are killjoys or because they are old-fashioned, it is because out of their experience they know that the thing is right or wrong, safe or dangerous.

"The man who will not listen to the voice of experience will certainly end in trouble--and he will deserve all that is coming to him....

"It is sensible to listen to what our parents tell us, because they have an experience of life that we do not yet possess."[2]

4. Note that this commandment emphasizes one of the great lessons of life, that we learn by example. Children are to learn to honor their parents. How? By the parents showing honor to their parents. The commandment charges all children to honor their parents. Even if they are adults and parents themselves, the adult child is to honor and respect his parents. Parents are to create an atmosphere of honor and respect in the home. By so doing, the parent teaches--sets an example-- for his child to honor him. This commandment stresses the awesome importance of parents setting the right example before their children.

> **"In all things showing thyself a pattern of good works: in doctrine showing uncorruptness, gravity, sincerity" (Tit.2:7).**
>
> **"Train up a child in the way he should go: and when he is old, he will not depart from it" (Pr.22:6).**

God makes it clear: parents have the obligation to teach this commandment and all the other commandments to their children.

> **"And thou shalt teach them [the commandments] diligently unto thy children, and shalt talk of them when thou sittest in thine house, and when thou walkest by the way, and when thou liest down, and when thou risest up" (Dt.6:7).**
>
> **"And, ye fathers, provoke not your children to wrath: but bring them up in the nurture and admonition of the Lord" (Eph.6:4).**

5. What about parents who neglect their children or who abuse their children? Are children to honor and respect parents who are evil, who live in sin and abuse them? The Preacher's Outline & Sermon Bible® (N.T. Vol.9) has an excellent comment on this point that is quoted at length because of its importance:

> **"Children obey your parents in the Lord: for this is right" (Eph.6:1).**

"Children are to obey their parents. The word 'obey' (hupakouo) means to submit to; to comply with; to hearken; to heed; to follow the directions or guidance of some instruction. When a parent guides and directs a child, the child is to obey the parent. But what about the problems that are so repulsively evident in society: the problems of parental abuse--the problems of physical abuse, sexual abuse, and mental abuse? Is a child to obey a parent when the parent is so devilishly wrong? No! A thousand times no!

"To obey means to obey *in the Lord*. Note the command again: 'Children, obey your parents <u>in the Lord</u>.' The phrase 'in the Lord' means at least two things.

a. "There is a limit to the child's obedience. When a parent is not acting in the Lord, he is not to be obeyed. The Lord has nothing whatsoever to do with the filth of unrighteousness and abuse of precious children. If a child can break away and free himself from such parental corruption, he has every right to be freed from his parent. The Lord came to set men free from the abuse and the filth of sin, not to enslave men to it, and especially not to enslave children to it.

"One of the most severe warnings ever issued in all of history was issued by the Lord Jesus to adults who abuse children:

> **"And whosoever shall offend one of these little ones that believe in me, it is better for him that a millstone were hanged about his neck, and he were cast into the sea. And if thy hand offend thee [by abusing a child], cut it off: it is better for thee to enter into life maimed, than**

---

[2] William Barclay. *The Old Law & The New Law*, p.24-26.

having two hands to go into hell, into the fire that never shall be quenched: where their worm dieth not, and the fire is not quenched. And if thy foot offend thee [by abusing a child], cut it off: it is better for thee to enter halt into life, than having two feet to be cast into hell, into the fire that never shall be quenched: where their worm dieth not, and the fire is not quenched. And if thine eye offend thee [by lusting after a child], pluck it out: it is better for thee to enter into the kingdom of God with one eye, than having two eyes to be cast into hell fire: where their worm dieth not, and the fire is not quenched" (Mk.9:42-48).

"The abusing parent had better heed, for one of the things that God will not tolerate--absolutely not tolerate-- is the abuse of a child. We must proclaim the Word of God: children are to obey their parents, but they are to obey only if the parents' desire and instructions are *in the Lord*. If a parent is beating a child black and blue or sexually abusing a child, the child should go to some other adult he feels close to and ask for help. And ministers of the Lord--ministers who are called to proclaim Christ and to do what they can to bring His righteousness to earth--must teach the truth from the pulpits of the world.

b. "The phrase 'in the Lord' also tells why the child is to obey his parents. 'Children, obey your parents in the Lord'--obeying your parents is right; it is of the Lord; it pleases the Lord; therefore, obey them. When they guide and instruct you, follow them (cp. Col.3:20).

"Lehman Strauss points out that obedience is the first law of the universe--that the law of obedience regulates everything in the world: the stars, the planets, the seasons. Even man himself tries to govern the world by the law of obedience. He wants obedience in the state, at work, at play, and at home.[3] The point is simply this: the law of obedience is the very nature of things, at the very core of the universe and of man's life and behavior upon earth. Therefore, it is to be expected that God would command children to obey their parents. Children are to obey-- obey because it pleases the Lord and it is the right thing to do.

"Note the emphasis here; it is striking. Children are not told to obey parents because it pleases the parent, but because it pleases the Lord. Pleasing one's parents is, of course, a reason for obeying them. But the *first* reason for obeying parents is that it pleases the Lord. The child is to know the Lord to such a degree that he is continually thinking about the Lord and about pleasing Him. The child is to walk so closely with the Lord that his mind is constantly upon the Lord--upon what he can do to please the Lord. When the child so knows the Lord, then obeying his parents will become an automatic response."[4]

"For Moses said, Honour thy father and thy mother; and, Whoso curseth father or mother, let him die the death" (Mk.7:10).
"Children, obey your parents in the Lord: for this is right" (Eph.6:1).
"Children, obey your parents in all things: for this is well pleasing unto the Lord" (Col.3:20).
"My son, hear the instruction of thy father, and forsake not the law of thy mother" (Pr.1:8; cp. Pr.6:20; 23:22).
"My son keep my words, and lay up my commandments with thee" (Pr.7:1).
"A wise son maketh a glad father: but a foolish son is the heaviness of his mother" (Pr.10:1).
"Even a child is known by his doings, whether his work be pure, and whether it be right" (Pr.20:11).
"Remember now thy Creator in the days of thy youth, while the evil days come not, nor the years draw nigh, when thou shalt say, I have no pleasure in them" (Eccl.12:1).

6. What about abusive children, children who abuse their parents? Again, The Preacher's Outline & Sermon Bible® (N.T. Vol.9) has an excellent statement covering this point:

"To obey parents means to honor one's father and mother. The word 'honor' (timao) means to 'esteem and value as precious' (The Amplified New Testament); to show respect, reverence, kindness, courtesy, and obedience.[5] Scripture is not speaking to any certain age child. It is speaking to all of us who are children with parents still living. We are to honor our fathers and mothers: *to esteem and value them as precious*--to respect and reverence them. Tragically, this is a rarity today. Too often a child's response to his parent is that of...

- talking back
- cutting the parent
- ignoring the parent
- grumbling
- disregarding instructions
- speaking disrespectfully
- not listening
- acting like a 'know it all'
- calling the parent a cute but *disrespectful* name

"In addition to these, there is the dishonor of delinquency, crime, drugs, alcohol, and the abuse of property; and the list could go on and on. And when it comes to adult children with aged parents, there is the dishonor of neglect, the ignoring of their needs and the shuffling of them to the side and failing to adequately care for them. Too many adult children forget how much their parents have done for them--bringing them into the world and taking care of them for years. Too many children forget the rich experience and knowledge that their parents have gained through the years and that could be put to great use in meeting community and world needs. And even if the parents failed to be and to do all they should have, we as Christian children are instructed to honor them as followers of the Lord Jesus Christ."[6]

3 Lehman Strauss. *Devotional Studies in Galatians & Ephesians*. (Neptune, NJ: Loizeaux Brothers, 1957), p.212.
4 *Galatians, Ephesians, Philippians, Colossians*, Vol.9. "The Preacher's Outline & Sermon Bible"®, p.219-220.
5 Kenneth S. Wuest. *Ephesians and Colossians*. "Word Studies in the Greek New Testament," Vol.1. (Grand Rapids, MI: Eerdmans Publishing Co., 1966), p.136.
6 *Galatians, Ephesians, Philippians, Colossians*, Vol.9. "The Preacher's Outline & Sermon Bible"®, p.219-220.

"Children, obey your parents in the Lord: for this is right" (Eph.6:1).

"But if any widow have children or nephews, let them learn first to show piety at home, and to requite [repay, pay back] their parents: for that is good and acceptable before God....But if any provide not for his own, and specially for those of his own house, he hath denied the faith, and is worse than an infidel" (1 Tim.5:4, 8).

"Whoso curseth his father or his mother, his lamp shall be put out in obscure darkness" (Pr.20:20).

"The eye that mocketh at his father, and despiseth to obey his mother, the ravens of the valley shall pick it out, and the young eagles shall eat it" (Pr.30:17).

"Honour thy father and thy mother: that thy days may be long upon the land which the Lord thy God giveth thee" (Ex.20:12).

"Ye shall fear every man his mother, and his father, and keep my sabbaths: I am the Lord your God" (Lev.19:3).

"Thou shalt rise up before the hoary [gray] head, and honor the face of the old man, and fear thy God: I am the LORD" (Lev.19:32).

"Cursed be he that setteth light by his father or his mother: and all the people shall say, Amen" (Dt.27:16).

Thought 1. Maxie Dunnam warns us about making a "cult of the child" within society, showing how this attitude teaches children to be disrespectful and disobedient.

> "I'm concerned about the extreme to which we have gone with the cult of the child during the past thirty or forty years in the United States. To be sure, we needed to give more attention to children. The adage 'Children are to be seen and not heard' was a caricature of children treated as wards and, in the extreme in many cultures, as chattel. So we needed to get away from that. But as is so often the case, the pendulum swung too far. We reared our children to be self-centered. We ordered our worlds around not only their needs, but their whims. Our thinking about discipline was distorted. We spared the rod and spoiled the child. There was no center of authority around which the child could order his life, no clear guidelines or directions, no well-defined values. And so respect was diminished, especially at the point of children listening and being obedient. This was not so much the child's fault as the parent's default."[7]

4 (20:12) **Commandments, The Ten--Parents--Children--Family**: note the two great promises attached to this commandment. Every person should seek ever so diligently to lay hold of these promises.

1. The person who honors his parents will live an extended life upon earth (v.12^b). Common sense tells us this. A tension-filled home--a home full of arguments, bickering, abuse, and divisiveness--causes all kinds of physical and emotional problems, shortening the life of family members. Whereas a home filled with love, joy, and peace strengthens the health and emotional stability of a person, thereby adding years to a person's life.

God knows what He is talking about; He knows exactly what He is promising. If the Israelites would teach their children to honor their parents, then generations of Israelite homes would be filled with love, joy, and peace. Maxie Dunnam has an excellent thought on the importance of the family to Israel that sets a dynamic example for every civilization:

> "I believe one of the primary reasons Judaism has survived across the years is precisely its family structure. The Jews survived the Holocaust and thousands of years of anti-Semitism because the Jewish family had a sense of identity and a sense of order. It doesn't matter where the family is on the Sabbath, when the Sabbath comes, they stop and pray. It didn't matter what Hitler and all the powers of Nazism said, when Passover came it was time to tell the story, even if the family was gathered in a concentration camp and there were no candles to light. There was a sense of order and identity that gave them roots and strength and perspective and discipline. At the heart of that family structure was a reverence for parents, a high regard, a respect, an esteem for the older members of the family. The elderly were honored and cared for."[8]

2. The person who honors his parents will inherit *the promised land* (v.12^c). This was a glorious promise to the Israelites: if they would honor their parents, they would have a long reign in *the promised land*. But the converse is implied as well: if they dishonored their parents, they would live for only a short time in *the promised land*.

Note how *the promised land* is tied to honoring one's parents. This does not mean that a person who honors his parents will necessarily inherit eternal life. God does not use this commandment (to honor our parents) to set up a merit system to reach the promised land of heaven. What God means is this: a person who truly follows and honors God will obey God: he will keep this commandment; he will honor his parents. And because he believes and obeys God, he will inherit the promised land.

Thought 1. In practical terms, Scripture tells us exactly what God means by this commandment.
1) To honor our parents means to respect and to reverence our parents.
2) To honor our parents means to obey our parents.

---

[7] Maxie Dunnam. *Mastering the Old Testament, Volume 2: Exodus*, p.261-262.
[8] ibid., p.261.

"Children, obey your parents in the Lord: for this is right. Honour thy father and mother; (which is the first commandment with promise;) That it may be well with thee, and thou mayest live long on the earth" (Eph.6:1-3).
"Children, obey your parents in all things: for this is well pleasing unto the Lord" (Col.3:20).

5 (20:12) **Decision--Commandments, The Ten--Parents--Children--Family**: What is the decision required by this commandment? Obedience! Simply stated, obedience. Without a doubt, many of the world's problems--perhaps most-- would be solved if the fifth commandment were obeyed. The fifth commandment is stated positively: we are to honor our fathers and our mothers. Note the teaching of Scripture, the decisions demanded by this commandment:

1. We are to honor our parents because it is the right thing to do.

"Children, obey your parents in the Lord: for this is right" (Eph.6:1).
"Children, obey your parents in all things: for this is well pleasing unto the Lord" (Col.3:20).

2. We are to honor our parents because it helps to extend our lives and makes things go better (far better than a tension-filled home).

"Honour thy father and thy mother, as the LORD thy God hath commanded thee; that thy days may be prolonged, and that it may go well with thee, in the land which the LORD thy God giveth thee" (Dt.5:16; cp. 1 Pt.3:10-12).

3. We are to honor our parents because it is one of God's ten great commandments.

"Honour thy father and thy mother: that thy days may be long upon the land which the LORD thy God giveth thee" (Ex.20:12).

4. We are to fear, reverence, and respect our parents.

"Ye shall fear every man his mother, and his father, and keep my sabbaths: I am the LORD your God" (Lev.19:3).

5. We are to obey our parents "in the Lord."

"Children, obey your parents in the Lord: for this is right" (Eph.6:1).

6. We are to keep and follow the teaching of our parents.

"My son, keep thy father's commandment, and forsake not the law of thy mother: Bind them continually upon thine heart, and tie them about thy neck. When thou goest, it shall lead thee; when thou sleepest, it shall keep thee; and when thou awakest, it shall talk with thee. For the commandment is a lamp; and the law is light; and reproofs of instruction are the way of life: To keep thee from the evil woman, from the flattery of the tongue of a strange woman" (Pr.6:20-24).

7. We are to heed the Christian witness of our parents.

"When I call to remembrance the unfeigned faith that is in thee, which dwelt first in thy grandmother Lois, and thy mother Eunice; and I am persuaded that in thee also" (2 Tim.1:5).
"And that from a child thou hast known the holy scriptures, which are able to make thee wise unto salvation through faith which is in Christ Jesus" (2 Tim.3:15).

8. We are to honor our parents even when we become adults.

"And Joseph brought them out from between his knees, and he bowed himself with his face to the earth" (Gen.48:12).
"Bath-sheba therefore went unto king Solomon, to speak unto him for Adonijah. And the king rose up to meet her, and bowed himself unto her, and sat down on his throne, and caused a seat to be set for the king's mother; and she sat on his right hand" (1 Ki.2:19).
"Hearken unto thy father that begat thee, and despise not thy mother when she is old" (Pr.23:22).

9. We are to follow the example of Christ in obeying and subjecting ourselves to our parents.

"And he went down with them, and came to Nazareth, and was subject unto them: but his mother kept all these sayings in her heart" (Lk.2:51).

10. We are to provide for our parents when they become aged.

"If any man or woman that believeth have widows, let them relieve them, and let not the church be charged; that it may relieve them that are widows indeed" (1 Tim.5:16).

11. We are not to deify our parents or family.

>"He that loveth father or mother more than me is not worthy of me: and he that loveth son or daughter more than me is not worthy of me" (Mt.10:37).

12. We must not follow in the steps of evil parents as some have done in the past.

>"Ahaziah the son of Ahab began to reign over Israel in Samaria the seventeenth year of Jehoshaphat king of Judah, and reigned two years over Israel. And he did evil in the sight of the LORD, and walked in the way of his father, and in the way of his mother, and in the way of Jeroboam the son of Nebat, who made Israel to sin" (1 Ki.22:51-52).
>"Forty and two years old was Ahaziah when he began to reign, and he reigned one year in Jerusalem. His mother's name also was Athaliah the daughter of Omri. He also walked in the ways of the house of Ahab: for his mother was his counseller to do wickedly" (2 Chron.22:2-3).
>"And she, being before instructed of her mother [Herodias], said, Give me here John Baptist's head in a charger" (Mt.14:8).

THE BIBLICAL CONSEQUENCES OF FAILING TO HONOR YOUR FATHER AND YOUR MOTHER

DEEPER STUDY #1
(20:12) **Commandments, The Ten--Obedience--Judgment**: What are the consequences of breaking this commandment?

>"Honour thy father and thy mother" (Ex.20:12).

This commandment is stated in the positive: it is a gracious invitation by God to obey. If a person obeys, God promises to bless him mightily. But if the person breaks this commandment, he faces terrible consequences.

1. A person who does not honor his parents--*consistently*, over the course of time--is in serious jeopardy of affecting his eternal destiny. The man who is marked by the deeds of the sinful nature cannot and will not honor his parents. Scripture says this person will not inherit the kingdom of God.

>"Now the works of the flesh are manifest, which are *these;* Adultery, fornication, uncleanness, lasciviousness, Idolatry, witchcraft, hatred, variance, emulations, wrath, strife, seditions, heresies, Envyings, murders, drunkenness, revellings, and such like: of the which I tell you before, as I have also told *you* in time past, that they which do such things shall not inherit the kingdom of God" (Gal.5:19-21).
>"And even as they did not like to retain God in *their* knowledge, God gave them over to a reprobate mind, to do those things which are not convenient; Being filled with all unrighteousness, fornication, wickedness, covetousness, maliciousness; full of envy, murder, debate, deceit, malignity; whisperers, Backbiters, haters of God, despiteful, proud, boasters, inventors of evil things, disobedient to parents, Without understanding, covenantbreakers, without natural affection, implacable, unmerciful: Who knowing the judgment of God, that they which commit such things are worthy of death, not only do the same, but have pleasure in them that do them" (Ro.1:28-32).
>"This know also, that in the last days perilous times shall come. For men shall be lovers of their own selves, covetous, boasters, proud, blasphemers, disobedient to parents, unthankful, unholy, Without natural affection, trucebreakers, false accusers, incontinent, fierce, despisers of those that are good, Traitors, heady, highminded, lovers of pleasures more than lovers of God; Having a form of godliness, but denying the power thereof: from such turn away. For of this sort are they which creep into houses, and lead captive silly women laden with sins, led away with divers lusts, Ever learning, and never able to come to the knowledge of the truth. Now as Jannes and Jambres withstood Moses, so do these also resist the truth: men of corrupt minds, reprobate concerning the faith" (2 Tim.3:1-8).

2. A person who does not honor his parents brings the full judgment of God upon himself.

>"And he that smiteth his father, or his mother, shall be surely put to death" (Ex.21:15).
>"The eye that mocketh at his father, and despiseth to obey his mother, the ravens of the valley shall pick it out, and the young eagles shall eat it" (Pr.30:17).
>"For every one that curseth his father or his mother shall be surely put to death: he hath cursed his father or his mother; his blood shall be upon him" (Lev.20:9).
>"Not every one that saith unto me, Lord, Lord, shall enter into the kingdom of heaven; but he that doeth the will of my Father which is in heaven" (Mt.7:21).

3. A person who does not honor his parents fills the home with hatred.

>"For the son dishonoureth the father, the daughter riseth up against her mother, the daughter in law against her mother in law; a man's enemies *are* the men of his own house" (Mic.7:6).

"Better *is* a dry morsel, and quietness therewith, than <u>an house full of sacrifices *with* strife</u>. A wise servant shall have rule over a son that causeth shame, and shall have part of the inheritance among the brethren" (Pr.17:1-2).

"*As* coals *are* to burning coals, and wood to fire; <u>so *is* a contentious man to kindle strife</u>" (Pr.26:21).

4. A person who does not honor his parents causes his parents to become heavy in spirit and broken-hearted.

"<u>And the king [David] was much moved, and went up to the chamber over the gate, and wept</u>: and as he went, thus he said, O my son Absalom, my son, my son Absalom! <u>would God I had died for thee</u>, O Absalom, my son, my son!" (2 Sam.18:33. Absalom had committed insurrection against his father and been killed.)

"A wise son maketh a glad father: but <u>a foolish son *is* the heaviness of his mother</u>" (Pr.10:1).

5. A person who does not honor his parents shames and disgraces his parents.

"He that wasteth *his* father, *and* chaseth away *his* mother, is <u>a son that causeth shame, and bringeth reproach</u>" (Pr.19:26).

"The rod and reproof give wisdom: but <u>a child left *to himself* bringeth his mother to shame</u>" (Pr.29:15).

6. A person who does not honor his parents will cause his parents to suffer great sorrow and regret, losing their joy.

"He that begetteth a fool *doeth it* to his sorrow: and the father of a fool hath no joy" (Pr.17:21).

7. A person who does not honor his parents is marked by destruction.

"Whoso robbeth his father or his mother, and saith, It *is* no transgression; <u>the same *is* the companion of a destroyer</u>" (Pr.28:24).

8. A person who does not honor his parents has the haunting testimony of a fool.

"He that begetteth a fool *doeth it* to his sorrow: and the father of a fool hath no joy" (Pr.17:21).

"<u>A foolish son *is* the calamity of his father</u>: and the contentions of a wife *are* a continual dropping" (Pr.19:13).

9. A person who curses his father and mother is not cleansed from his filth.

"There is a generation that curseth their father, and doth not bless their mother....[those who] are pure in their own eyes, and yet is not washed from their filthiness" (Pr.30:11-12).

THE BIBLICAL BENEFITS OF KEEPING THIS COMMANDMENT: TO HONOR YOUR FATHER AND YOUR MOTHER

DEEPER STUDY #2

(20:12) <u>Commandments, The Ten--Benefits of Honoring Father and Mother--Children--Parents--Obedience</u>: What are the benefits of keeping this commandment? There are wonderful blessings in store for those who keep this commandment.

1. A person who honors his parents will make his father glad.

"A wise son maketh a glad father: but a foolish man despiseth his mother" (Pr.15:20).

2. A person who honors his parents helps to extend his life and makes things go better (far better than a tension-filled home).

"Honour thy father and thy mother, as the LORD thy God hath commanded thee; that thy days may be prolonged, and that it may go well with thee, in the land which the LORD thy God giveth thee" (Dt.5:16).

"That it may be well with thee, and thou mayest live long on the earth" (Eph.6:3).

3. A person who honors his parents will greatly influence his own children to do what is right.

"And he did that which was right in the sight of the LORD, and walked in all the way of David his father, and turned not aside to the right hand or to the left" (2 Ki.22:2).

4. A person who honors his parents will gain wisdom and understanding from parents who have experienced life.

"Hear, ye children, the instruction of a father, and attend to know understanding" (Pr.4:1).

5. A person who honors his parents will learn how to discern between good and bad company.

"Whoso keepeth the law is a wise son: but <u>he that is a companion of riotous men</u> shameth his father" (Pr.28:7).

6. A person who honors his parents will appreciate the discipline his parents applied during his childhood.

"The rod and reproof give wisdom: but a child left to himself bringeth his mother to shame" (Pr.29:15).

7. A person who honors his parents will have a good testimony to show the world.

"Even a child is known by his doings, whether his work *be* pure, and whether *it be* right" (Pr.20:11).

8. A person who honors his parents will be in a right relationship with God and man.

"Children, obey your parents in the Lord: for this is right" (Eph.6:1).

9. A person who honors his parents will inherit the promised land of heaven.

"Honour thy father and thy mother: that thy days may be long upon the land [promised land, a symbol of heaven] which the LORD thy God giveth thee" (Ex.20:12).
"Honour thy father and mother; (which is the first commandment with promise;)" (Eph.6:2).

10. A person who honors his parents will always have God's care, even if his parents fail him.

"When my father and my mother forsake me, then the LORD will take me up" (Ps.27:10).

11. A person who honors his parents will be blessed as he keeps God's commandments.

"Now therefore hearken unto me, O ye children: for blessed *are they that* keep my ways" (Pr.8:32).

12. A person who honors his parents will most likely come to know Christ and the truth of the Scriptures.

"When I call to remembrance the unfeigned faith that is in thee, which dwelt first in thy grandmother Lois, and thy mother Eunice; and I am persuaded that in thee also" (2 Tim.1:5).
"And that from a child thou hast known the holy scriptures, which are able to make thee wise unto salvation through faith which is in Christ Jesus" (2 Tim.3:15).

DEEPER STUDY # 3

JESUS CHRIST AND HIS TEACHING
CONCERNING <u>MAN'S PARENTS</u>

"Honour thy father and thy mother: that thy days may be long upon the land which the LORD thy God giveth thee" (Ex.20:12).

THE TEACHING OF CHRIST	THE BELIEVER'S RESPONSE
1. Jesus Christ declared that children are to honor their parents. **"For God commanded, saying, Honour thy father and mother: and, He that curseth father or mother, let him die the death" (Mt.15:4).** **"Thou knowest the commandments, Do not commit adultery, Do not kill, Do not steal, Do not bear false witness, <u>Honour thy father and thy mother</u>" (Lk.18:20).**	1) Scripture is clear. There should be no misunderstanding: we are to honor and obey our parents. **"And it shall be, if he say unto thee, I will not go away from thee; because he loveth thee and thine house, because he is well with thee" (Dt.15:16).** **"Children, obey your parents in the Lord: for this is right" (Eph.6:1).** **"Children, obey your parents in all things: for this is well pleasing unto the Lord" (Col.3:20).**

THE TEACHING OF CHRIST	THE BELIEVER'S RESPONSE
2. Jesus Christ declared that it is wrong to break God's commandment (honor your father and mother). "But he answered and said unto them, Why do ye also transgress the commandment of God by your tradition? For God commanded, saying, Honour thy father and mother: and, He that curseth father or mother, let him die the death. But ye say, Whosoever shall say to [his] father or [his] mother, [It is] a gift, by whatsoever thou mightest be profited by me; And honour not his father or his mother, [he shall be free]. Thus have ye made the commandment of God of none effect by your tradition. [Ye] hypocrites, well did Esaias prophesy of you, saying, This people draweth nigh unto me with their mouth, and honoureth me with [their] lips; but their heart is far from me. But in vain they do worship me, teaching [for] doctrines the commandments of men" (Mt.15:3-9).	1) We must never ignore the needs of our parents by twisting God's Word to excuse us from our duty to take care of them. 2) We must pledge total obedience to God's Word and honor our parents... • no matter how unpopular it is to do so • no matter how much it goes against the grain of society • no matter how much help and care they need "He answered and said unto them, Well hath Esaias prophesied of you hypocrites, as it is written, This people honoureth me with [their] lips, but their heart is far from me. Howbeit in vain do they worship me, teaching [for] doctrines the commandments of men. For laying aside the commandment of God, ye hold the tradition of men, [as] the washing of pots and cups: and many other such like things ye do" (Mk.7:6-8). "Making the word of God of none effect through your tradition, which ye have delivered: and many such like things do ye" (Mk.7:13). "Children, obey your parents in the Lord: for this is right. Honour thy father and mother; (which is the first commandment with promise;) That it may be well with thee, and thou mayest live long on the earth" (Eph.6:1-3). "But whoso looketh into the perfect law of liberty, and continueth therein, he being not a forgetful hearer, but a doer of the work, this man shall be blessed in his deed" (Jas.1:25). "Thou shalt rise up before the hoary [gray] head, and honour the face of the old man, and fear thy God: I am the LORD" (Lev.19:32). "O that there were such an heart in them, that they would fear me, and keep all my commandments always, that it might be well with them, and with their children for ever!" (Dt.5:29). "And if thou wilt walk in my ways, to keep my statutes and my commandments, as thy father David did walk, then I will lengthen thy days" (1 Ki.3:14). "Hearken unto thy father that begat thee, and despise not thy mother when she is old" (Pr.23:22).
3. Jesus Christ declared that in the case of marriage, a man must leave his parents and cleave to his wife. "For this cause [starting another home] shall a man leave his father and mother, and cleave to his wife" (Mk.10:7).	1) A man shall cleave to his wife and create a new family distinct from the family of his parents. 2) A man leaves his father and mother. The union between husband and wife is to gain primacy over the union between parent and child. Leaving is a permanent act; cleaving is also a permanent act. "Therefore shall a man leave his father and his mother, and shall cleave unto his wife: and they shall be one flesh" (Gen.2:24). "What therefore God hath joined together, let not man put asunder" (Mk.10:9). "For the woman which hath an husband is bound by the law to her husband so long as he liveth; but if the husband be dead, she is loosed from the law of her husband" (Ro.7:2). "And unto the married I command, yet not I, but the Lord, Let not the wife depart from her husband: But and if she depart, let her remain unmarried, or be reconciled to her husband: and let not the husband put away his wife" (1 Cor.7:10-11).
4. Jesus Christ declared that the person who loved his parents or anyone else in his family more than Christ was not worthy of Christ. "He that loveth father or mother more than me is not worthy of me: and he that loveth son or daughter more than me is not worthy of me" (Mt.10:37).	1) We must love God supremely, putting Him before all others, even before our families (cp. Mt.6:33). 2) A man's decision to follow Christ, no matter the sacrifice to his family, is a wise decision; in fact, it is the only reasonable decision (Ro.12:1-2). "If any man come to me, and hate not his father, and mother, and wife, and children, and brethren, and sisters, yea, and his own life also, he cannot be my disciple" (Lk.14:26). "Anyone who wants to be my follower must love me far more than he does his own father, mother, wife, children, brothers, or sisters--yes, more than his own life--otherwise he cannot be my disciple" (Lk.14:26, LIVING BIBLE). "Jesus said unto him, Thou shalt love the Lord thy God with all thy heart, and with all thy soul, and with all thy mind. This is the first and great commandment" (Mt.22:37-38). "I beseech you therefore, brethren, by the mercies of God, that ye present your bodies a living sacrifice, holy, acceptable unto God, which is your reasonable service. And be not conformed to this world: but be ye transformed by the renewing of your mind, that ye may prove what is that good, and acceptable, and perfect, will of God" (Ro.12:1-2).

	G. The Ten Command-ments, The Laws Governing Man's Duty To Others (Part 2)—Commandment Six Concerns Man's Life--Never Kill, Ex.20:13
Com. 6 concerns *man's life*	13 Thou shalt not kill.

DIVISION VII

THE LAW AND THE PROMISES OF GOD (THE MOSAIC COVENANT) (PART 2): THE TEN COMMANDMENTS--NECESSARY LAWS TO GOVERN MAN AND SOCIETY, EX.20:1-26

G.   The Ten Commandments, The Laws Governing Man's Duty To Others (Part 2): Commandment Six Concerns Man's Life--Never Kill, Ex.20:13

(20:13) **Introduction--Media--Murder--Violence--Lawlessness**: murder, lawlessness, and violence are sweeping the earth. Hundreds of thousands of people are being murdered and slaughtered year after year. The value of human life is almost worthless in some societies.

* Society after society considers human beings, even young children, to be nothing more than chattel property, laborers existing only for the ruling class and the wealthy.
* Society after society allows the constant barrage of violence and lawlessness to be shown in films and other media, shown even to small children--despite the undesirable impression printed upon the human mind and its terrible consequences.

People have become desensitized and hardened to lawlessness, violence, and killing. The front pages of newspapers and news reports of television and radio are usually filled with terrible crimes. In addition, the entertainment industry--television, movies, video games, music, books, magazines--focuses upon lawlessness, violence, and killing as well as immorality.

The point is this: life is pictured as cheap by both the media and the entertainment industry of society. The mind of a person is bombarded by act after act of lawlessness, violence, and killing every day of his life--if he reads the newspaper, watches television, listens to the radio, or picks up a magazine.

Think about what has just been said: every day of a person's life is filled with images and thoughts of lawlessness, violence, and killing if he reads the newspaper, watches television, listens to the radio, or picks up a magazine.

No wonder we have become desensitized and hardened to violence and murder. No wonder life is so cheap and means so little to so many people. No wonder so many have become lawless and violent. No wonder so many assault and kill. We just see and hear so much about violence and killing every day of our lives.

This is the important subject of this commandment, a commandment so desperately needed: *Commandment Six Concerns Man's Life--Never Kill*, 20:13.

1. Who is to obey this commandment? How long was this commandment to be in force (v.13)?
2. What is forbidden by this commandment (v.13)?
3. What is the decision required by this commandment (v.13)?

1 (20:13) **Commandments, The Ten--Murder--Killing**: Who is to obey this commandment? How long was this commandment to be in force? Was it only to govern Israel and the ancient world? Was murder--lawlessness and violence--only a problem in the ancient world? The answer is obvious. One of the most terrible social ills down through history has been murder and the lawlessness and violence that surround murder. God gave this commandment to govern civilization, the societies of every generation of man. God gave this commandment to make communities and streets safe, our homes and businesses secure.

Now, who is to keep this commandment: "You shall not murder" (v.13)? *You*! The commandment is forceful; it is directed to *you* personally, to every person upon this earth: "*You* shall not murder." The motives and emotions that arouse a person to murder--the desires, passions, greed, anger, wrath, revenge--are all to be put down and controlled. *You*--all of us--are responsible to obey this commandment. *You* are to control the anger, passions, and greed of your flesh when they are aroused. *You* are to obey the sixth great commandment of God: "*You* shall not murder" (v.13).

2 (20:13) **Commandments, The Ten--Man--Murder--Killing--Violence--Lawlessness--Obedience**: What is forbidden by this commandment: "You shall not murder" (v.13)? How is this commandment broken or violated? Before actually looking at what the commandment forbids, note why God gave the commandment.

1. The purpose for this commandment is to preserve life: to teach people the sanctity of human life, that they are to honor and hold human life in the highest esteem. Man is created in the image and likeness of God; therefore, man's life is of infinite value to God (Gen.1:26-27). Man is...

* God's *master creation*
* God's *royal masterpiece*
* God's *precious possession*
* God's *priceless property*

Why is man to be so highly esteemed? As stated, because man is created in the *image and likeness* of God. God demands that human life be valued above all the wealth in the world (Mt.16:26; Mk.8:36). The sanctity of human life is to be honored above all else.

> **"And God said, Let us make man in our image, after our likeness: and let them have dominion over the fish of the sea, and over the fowl of the air, and over the cattle, and over all the earth, and over every creeping thing that creepeth upon the earth. So God created man in his own image, in the image of God created he him; male and female created he them" (Gen.1:26-27).**

> **"And surely your blood of your lives will I require; at the hand of every beast will I require it, and at the hand of man; at the hand of every man's brother will I require the life of man. Whoso sheddeth man's blood, by man shall his blood be shed: for in the <u>image of God</u> made he man. And you, be ye fruitful, and multiply; bring forth abundantly in the earth, and multiply therein" (Gen.9:5-7).**

> **"For what shall it profit a man, if he shall gain the whole world, and lose his own soul?" (Mk.8:36; cp. Mt.16:26).**

2. Now, what is forbidden by this commandment: "You shall not murder" (v.13)? The Hebrew word for *kill* or *killing* (rasah) means premeditated, planned, deliberate, intentional, unauthorized murder.

This commandment is broken either by a planned murderous attack upon a person(s) or by a rash, reckless attack. This commandment forbids the taking of a life because a person is...

• angry	• passionate	• lusting
• bitter	• vengeful	• coveting
• violent	• selfish	• rebelling
• uncontrolled	• stealing	

Murder for such reasons as these is wrong and must always be counted wrong. This is the only way to make our community, society, and civilization safe and secure. The terrifying evils of this earth--lawlessness, violence, and murder--must not be allowed. We must always agree with God's Holy Word: murder for such reasons as anger, robbery, and violence must always be counted wrong and be punished.

But there are also other forms of murder that are just as wrong as lifting one's own hand to kill another person. All over the world, there are people who commit murder...

- by forcing people to work in conditions that will injure or eventually kill them, that lead to their premature death
- by forcing people to live in horrible conditions, so horrible that the environment or lack of basic necessities eventually kills them
- by selling and hooking people on drugs, drugs that eventually enslave and kill the addicts

Man must control and punish the lawless, the violent, and the murderers who roam his streets and in many cases sit in the plush offices of authority and rule. Evil men must be stopped and taught to obey this commandment or else our civilization can never survive. Lawlessness, violence, and murder must be stamped out. We can have safe streets and parks, unlocked doors, and the freedom to move about at night only if we obey this commandment. We will have a satisfying and fruitful life only if we heed this commandment: "You shall not murder [live lawless and violent lives]" (v.13).

But even the above are not the only kinds of murder forbidden by God. The spirit of lawlessness, violence, and murder so sweep through the societies and history of man that at least two other types of murder need to be discussed. (See <u>Deeper Study # 1</u>, <u>Abortion</u>--Ex.20:13; <u>Deeper Study # 2</u>, <u>Suicide</u>--Ex.20:13 for discussion.)

3. Note this fact: this commandment is not a blanket commandment against all killing. God's Word clearly says that the taking of life is justified, understandable, and allowed...

- as capital punishment (Gen.9:6)
- in a justified war (Dt.13:15; 1 Sam.15:3; 2 Sam.10:1f)
- in cases of adultery (Lev.20:10). This may seem harsh to society today, but this commandment and penalty were given to protect and preserve the family. The very survival of Israel depended upon the family being preserved as the basic unit of society. Loyalty to the family taught the Israelites to be loyal to the nation as a whole.
- in the defense of ourselves, for example, when a thief breaks into our home (Ex.22:2)
- in accidental killing (Dt.19:5)
- in killing animals for food (Gen.9:3)

4. What is the ultimate cause, the basic source, of murder? Scripture says that the underlying cause and source of murder is twofold:

a. Satan, the devil, is the arch-enemy of God and man: he seeks to tempt and arouse people to live greedy and selfish lives, lives of lawlessness, violence, and murder.

> **"Ye are of [your] father the devil, and the lusts of your father ye will do. He was a murderer from the beginning, and abode not in the truth, because there is no truth in him. When he speaketh a lie, he speaketh of his own: for he is a liar, and the father of it" (Jn.8:44).**

b. Lust--the unregulated urges of man's heart--drives some people to rob, assault, and kill. Some people allow the lust of their soul--greed and covetousness--to drive them to lawlessness, violence, and murder.

"But every man is tempted, when he is drawn away of his own lust, and enticed. Then when lust hath conceived, it bringeth forth sin: and sin, when it is finished, bringeth forth death" (Jas.1:14-15).

"From whence come wars and fightings among you? come they not hence, even of your lusts that war in your members? Ye lust, and have not: ye kill, and desire to have, and cannot obtain: ye fight and war, yet ye have not, because ye ask not. Ye ask, and receive not, because ye ask amiss, that ye may consume it upon your lusts" (Jas.4:1-3).

5. What will be the eternal judgment of God upon the murderer? Death, spiritual and eternal death.

"For the wages of sin is death" (Ro.6:23).

"For to be carnally minded is death" (Ro.8:6).

"Now the works of the flesh are manifest, which are these; Adultery, fornication, uncleanness, lasciviousness, Idolatry, witchcraft, hatred, variance, emulations, wrath, strife, seditions, heresies, Envyings, murders, drunkenness, revellings, and such like: of the which I tell you before, as I have also told you in time past, that they which do such things shall not inherit the kingdom of God" (Gal.5:19-21).

"But every man is tempted, when he is drawn away of his own lust, and enticed. Then when lust hath conceived, it bringeth forth sin: and sin, when it is finished, bringeth forth death" (Jas.1:14-15).

"But the fearful, and unbelieving, and the abominable, and murderers, and whoremongers, and sorcerers, and idolaters, and all liars, shall have their part in the lake which burneth with fire and brimstone: which is the second death" (Rev.21:8).

"The soul that sinneth, it shall die" (Ezk.18:4).

6. Can a murderer be saved and forgiven for his sin of murder? Scripture says "yes," a resounding "yes." But the murderer must confess his sin and repent, turning away from the life of sin. He must genuinely give his heart and life to Jesus Christ and live for Jesus Christ.

"I tell you, Nay: but, except ye repent, ye shall all likewise perish" (Lk.13:3).

"Repent ye therefore, and be converted, that your sins may be blotted out, when the times of refreshing shall come from the presence of the Lord" (Acts 3:19).

"Let the wicked forsake his way, and the unrighteous man his thoughts: and let him return unto the LORD, and he will have mercy upon him; and to our God, for he will abundantly pardon" (Is.55:7).

"But if the wicked will turn from all his sins that he hath committed, and keep all my statutes, and do that which is lawful and right, he shall surely live, he shall not die" (Ezk.18:21).

"Then Peter said unto them, Repent, and be baptized every one of you in the name of Jesus Christ for the remission of sins, and ye shall receive the gift of the Holy Ghost" (Acts 2:38).

"For the wages of sin is death; but the gift of God is eternal life through Jesus Christ our Lord" (Ro.6:23).

"For to be carnally minded is death; but to be spiritually minded is life and peace" (Ro.8:6).

7. Jesus Christ taught that this commandment means far more than just prohibiting the killing of people. He enlarged the meaning to include both the anger that is aroused within the heart and the lawless motives that drive a person to kill others.

"Ye have heard that it was said by them of old time, Thou shalt not kill; and whosoever shall kill shall be in danger of the judgment: But I say unto you, That whosoever is angry with his brother without a cause shall be in danger of the judgment: and whosoever shall say to his brother, Raca, shall be in danger of the council: but whosoever shall say, Thou fool, shall be in danger of hell fire" (Mt.5:21-22).

Note what Christ is saying: He is saying that man has a problem. Man misreads God's law. Man interprets God's law to say what he wishes it to say. Man applies it only to the outward act, in this case to the act of murder. Man fails to look inward--within himself--to the cause (see note--Mt.5:17-18; Deeper Study # 2--Mt.5:17; note--Mk.7:14-23).

Murder is deeper than just an outward act. It is an inward act: an act of anger, bitterness, enmity. Murder is born from within, from an uncontrolled spirit, from an unregulated urge, from an inner anger. Anger itself is the real sin, the sin that breaks the law of God. Anger is...

- bitterness and enmity
- indignation and wrath
- striking out against a person
- a disappointment or hatred of oneself
- rage and fury
- an uncontrolled spirit
- desiring a person's hurt
- envying and killing a person's happiness
- slandering and destroying a person's image (who is created in God's image)

The growth of anger is dangerous. Unresolved anger will fester. It can become uncontrolled and give birth to murder. There are three steps in the growth of anger given by Christ.

a. The anger that broods, that is selfish. It harbors malice; it will not forget; it lingers; it broods; it wills revenge and sometimes seeks revenge.

b. The anger that holds contempt (raca). It despises; it ridicules; it arrogantly exalts self and calls another person empty and useless. This is an anger that is full of malice. It despises and scorns (raca). It arises from pride--a proud wrath (Pr.21:24). Such feelings or anger walk over and trample a person. It says that whatever ill comes upon a person is deserved.

c. The anger that curses. It seeks to destroy a man and his reputation morally, intellectually, and spiritually.

There is a justified anger. In fact, the believer must be an angry person--angry with those who sin and do wrong, who are unjust and selfish in their behavior. However, a justified anger is always disciplined and controlled; it is always limited to those who do wrong either against God or against others. The distinguishing mark between justified and unjustified anger is that a justified anger is never selfish; it is never shown because of what has happened to oneself. It is an anger that is purposeful. The believer knows that he is angry for a legitimate reason, and he seeks to correct the situation in the most peaceful way possible (see notes--Eph.4:26-27; Ro.12:18; Jn.2:14-17. Also see Deeper Study # 1--Jn.2:14.)

> "Be ye angry, and sin not: let not the sun go down upon your wrath" (Eph.4:26).
> "If it be possible, as much as lieth in you, live peaceably with all men" (Ro.12:18).
> "And the Jews' passover was at hand, and Jesus went up to Jerusalem, and found in the temple those that sold oxen and sheep and doves, and the changers of money sitting: and when he had made a scourge of small cords, he drove them all out of the temple, and the sheep, and the oxen; and poured out the changer's money, and overthrew the tables" (Jn.2:13-16).

Thought 1. Anger is cast against many. Too often hurt feelings exist between those who are supposed to be the closest: husband and wife, parent and child, neighbor and friend, employer and employee. The Lord is clear about the matter: we must never allow anger to take hold of us without just cause.

> "But now ye also put off all these; anger, wrath, malice, blasphemy, filthy communication out of your mouth" (Col.3:8).
> "Wherefore, my beloved brethren, let every man be swift to hear, slow to speak, slow to wrath" (Jas.1:19).
> "Whosoever hateth his brother is a murderer: and ye know that no murderer hath eternal life abiding in him" (1 Jn.3:15).
> "Cease from anger, and forsake wrath: fret not thyself in any wise to do evil" (Ps.37:8).
> "He that is soon angry dealeth foolishly; and a man of wicked devices is hated" (Pr.14:17).
> "He that is slow to anger is better than the mighty; and he that ruleth his spirit than he that taketh a city" (Pr.16:32).
> "The discretion of a man deferreth his anger; and it is his glory to pass over a transgression" (Pr.19:11).
> "Be not hasty in thy spirit to be angry: for anger resteth in the bosom of fools" (Eccl.7:9).

Thought 2. There are reasons why people get angry and develop feelings against others:
⇒ To seek revenge and to hurt
⇒ To show ego or authority
⇒ To reveal passion or secure some end
⇒ To show hurt, resentment, or bitterness
⇒ To express disagreement or displeasure
⇒ To correct a wrong (a justified anger)
⇒ To give warning

Thought 3. It is a serious matter to hold feelings against another person--a very, very serious matter. There is (1) the *danger of judgment,* (2) the *danger of having to come before earthly courts*, and (3) the *danger of hell fire*. Violence is to be judged--not only before the councils of the world but before the councils of God.

DEEPER STUDY # 1

(20:13) Abortion--Children--Pregnancy--Unborn, The--Murder--Ministry: abortion, the killing of unborn babies, is one of the major indictments against the human race down through the centuries. The sanctity of life has been and still is under lethal attack. Tragically, the tide of public opinion usually runs counter to the clear commandment of God, "You shall not kill." Because abortion is legal in so many societies and is so prevalent, it is being discussed at length here.

1. What does the Bible say about the creation of man and the fetus or unborn baby in the womb?

> "So God created man in his own image, in the image of God created he him; male and female created he them" (Gen.1:27).
> "This is the book of the generations of Adam. In the day that God created man, in the likeness of God made he him" (Gen.5:1).
> "Did not he that made me in the womb make him? and did not one fashion us in the womb?" (Job 31:15).
> "Thy hands have made me and fashioned me: give me understanding, that I may learn thy commandments" (Ps.119:73).
> "For thou hast possessed my reins: thou hast covered me in my mother's womb. I will praise thee; for I am fearfully and wonderfully made: marvellous are thy works; and that my soul knoweth right well. My substance was not hid from thee, when I was made in secret, and curiously wrought in

the lowest parts of the earth. Thine eyes did see my substance, yet being unperfect; and in thy book all my members were written, which in continuance were fashioned, when as yet there was none of them" (Ps.139:13-16).

"As thou knowest not what is the way of the spirit, nor how the bones do grow in the womb of her that is with child: even so thou knowest not the works of God who maketh all" (Eccl.11:5).

"Then the word of the LORD came unto me, saying, Before I formed thee in the belly I knew thee; and before thou camest forth out of the womb I sanctified thee, and I ordained thee a prophet unto the nations" (Jer.1:4-5).

"Now the birth of Jesus Christ was on this wise: When as his mother Mary was espoused to Joseph, before they came together, she was found with child of the Holy Ghost. Then Joseph her husband, being a just man, and not willing to make her a public example, was minded to put her away privily. But while he thought on these things, behold, the angel of the Lord appeared unto him in a dream, saying, Joseph, thou son of David, fear not to take unto thee Mary thy wife: for that which is conceived in her is of the Holy Ghost" (Mt.1:18-20).

2. What does the medical profession say about the fetus or unborn child in the mother's womb? The excellent Bible teacher Stuart Briscoe says this:

"Physicians have given us a wide variety of suggestions about when the fetus becomes human. Seven of them are outlined by Oliver O'Donavan and quoted in Norman Anderson's *Issues of Life and Death*.[1]

"   1.   The first group says the fetus becomes fully human at the point of conception. Among those some would say 'the point of conception' rather unguardedly, while others would describe it not as a moment, but a process that we cannot accurately measure. But both would agree that, whenever it takes place, the child becomes invested with the divine image.

"   2.   Others claim that the problem with the first theory is that 50 percent of all impregnated ova disappear in the natural course of events. If that is the case, then 50 percent of unborn, unformed, unimplanted ova have the divine image and simply drift off into eternity without having existed in any sense that is meaningful to us. These people state that the person starts to be formed at implantation; before that it has no meaningful existence at all.

"   3.   A third group says the fetus becomes human when it takes human shape. They say it will measure at least three centimeters, which will happen between forty-five and forty-nine days after conception.

"   4.   Still another group claims the fetus becomes human at animation. Old-time theologians used to try to figure out when the body got the soul and when the soul left. They thought of the body having a soul, as opposed to thinking that humans are body, soul, and spirit. When it came to animation, people believed--and in some circumstances still do believe--that a time exists when the fetus becomes ensouled. To give you an idea how things have changed, Aristotle said that took place twenty-five to forty days after conception for the male, but fifty to eighty days after conception for the female.

"   5.   A fifth way of thinking says the fetus becomes human at viability--the point at which it could survive without its mother. We have a problem with this today because with our rapidly advancing technology the fetus's viability point changes all the time. Supreme Court Justice Sandra Day O'Connor said, 'Fetal viability in the first trimester of pregnancy may be possible in the not too distant future.' If that happens, it will make the Supreme Court's ruling palpable nonsense.

"   6.   Another set of people would try to get the problem out of the way simply by declaring the fetus human at birth, not before. If so, how do you take into account the biblical passages we've considered?

"   7.   Finally, some would claim that the fetus becomes fully human one year after birth. They say that at this stage the human child is comparable to all other animals at the moment of birth, because human children are much more helpless than other animals."[2]

3. Now, when does the unborn child become a human being? When is the fetus made in the image of God? Having looked at what the Bible says and at what different people in the medical profession say, when does the fetus actually become human? Stuart Briscoe gives an excellent discussion of this question as well.

"All this speculation leaves us in a great, big fog--because when we look at Scripture, medical science, and our knowledge, we find it very difficult to pinpoint the moment the unborn becomes a human made in the image of God.

"Because of this difficulty, people argue about whether the fetus is a person, is fully human, is subhuman, or is potentially human. Those in favor of aborting call it subhuman. They would compare it to an appendix--simply a pile of useless tissue, lacking importance. In the light of Scripture, we cannot accept this position under any circumstances.

"Despite the complexity of the issue and the degree of uncertainty that surrounds it, if we allow the fetus to go full term, it will become a human being. Therefore under no circumstances should we feel comfortable in agreeing to any callous or careless interference with that. If I cannot categorically say when something is made in God's image, I'm not even going to get close to tampering with it. It would seem we need to take that minimal position at the very least."[3]

---

[1]   Stuart Briscoe. *The Ten Commandments*. (Wheaton, IL: Harold Shaw Publishers, 1986), p.96-98.
[2]   Norman Anderson. *Issues of Life and Death*. (Downers Grove, IL: InterVarsity Press, 1977).
[3]   Stuart Briscoe. *The Ten Commandments*, p.98.

4. What about the mother whose life is in danger if she bears the child? Or whose unborn child is due to rape or incest? Or who had an abortion without any knowledge of what God says about the mother? Are we as believers to minister to them? Again, Stuart Briscoe's discussion of this point is so excellent that it is well worth quoting at length:

"If we are in favor of life, we must favor not only the life of the unborn, but also that of the mother. We need to express concern for the mother, her physical well-being, her emotional situation, and her spiritual state.

"We need to care for the young woman whom we tell, 'In having an abortion, you murdered something made in the image of God.'
⇒ "What will that do to her emotions?
⇒ "How does that affect her spiritually?
⇒ "How can she look the world in the face again?

"If we aggressively go after women who have had abortions, we may well drive them to the point of emotional breakdown or even suicide. Among those who have experienced abortions, there exists a high incidence of depression and an increasingly high level of suicide. It seems to me that if we call ourselves prolife, we must be prolife for the unborn and the born as well. We've got to be for the fetus and for the mother, which complicates the abortion issue quite dramatically.

"In some cases that means we must balance out the rights of the unborn against those of the living.
⇒ "The Roman Catholics have arrived at a simple answer for this: They see the rights of the fetus as the primary ones.
⇒ "Those in the feminist tradition and with more liberal thinking call that nonsense, saying the rights of the living are far more important than the rights of the potentially living.
⇒ "Others who grapple with the Word of God ask, 'How do we put these together?'

"Can we countenance abortion on demand? Emphatically no! Can we ban abortion, period, for all circumstances and conditions? It would seem to me that by doing so we could get ourselves in situations where we cannot adequately deal with the needs for the life of the mother and the life of the unborn. Some people would probably agree that if the mother has a very major medical problem, and carrying the child threatens her life, action needs to be taken. To balance this out, let me quote a British physician: 'In forty years of gynecological and obstetric practice, I can only remember a handful of occasions in which the mother's life was in danger because of the birth of the fetus.' We need to bear that in mind.

"I believe we must uphold the sanctity of life for both the born and the unborn. I believe we must take that position. If we wish to take a stand for the rights of the unborn, potentially made in the image of God, we must be ready at the same time to care for those who have had abortions and feel depression and overwhelming guilt and who might commit suicide. We need to cultivate compassion for both. When we persuade women not to abort the unborn, we should be prepared to help with the steps of the pregnancy that follow. But we also need to aid those who need forgiveness--we must help human lives in many dimensions, not only in the right to be born"[4]

DEEPER STUDY # 2

(20:13) <u>Suicide--Murder--Ministry</u>: suicide is viewed differently by different people and societies. For example...
- Can a Christian believer commit suicide? Become so despondent, depressed, and discouraged that he takes his own life?
- Can a person be justified if he is so heroic that he undertakes a suicide mission for his nation or for some great cause? This has happened often down through history. The Japanese kamikaze pilots of the Second World War are a prime example. In fact, many of the surviving men who have fought in war would know of men who gave themselves to undertake suicidal missions.

One thing is sure: a deliberate suicide *to escape* this life with all its trials and problems is a desperate crime, a crime that should never be committed. Suicide happens, happens far too often, but it is never the answer. God has stamped His image upon every human life, and no person should ever destroy himself. There are three strong reasons why a person should never commit suicide.

1. God forbids murder, and suicide is the murdering of oneself.

"**Thou shalt not kill**" (Ex.20:13).
"**For this, Thou shalt not commit adultery, Thou shalt not kill, Thou shalt not steal, Thou shalt not bear false witness, Thou shalt not covet; and if there be any other commandment, it is briefly comprehended in this saying, namely, Thou shalt love thy neighbor <u>as thyself</u>**" (Ro.13:9).
"**But let none of you suffer as a murderer, or as a thief, or as an evildoer, or as a busybody in other men's matters**" (1 Pt.4:15).

2. The person destroys the very image of God that is stamped upon his or her life.

"**So God created man in his own image, in the image of God created he him; male and female created he them**" (Gen.1:27).

---

4   Stuart Briscoe. *The Ten Commandments*, p.98-100.

3. Jesus Christ, God's very own Son, loves and cares for us. He helps us *conquer* and *overcome* whatever problems confront us, no matter how terrible. He will give us wisdom and show us how to *conquer* the problem.

> "For in that he himself hath suffered being tempted, he is able to succour them that are tempted" (Heb.2:18).
> "For we have not an high priest which cannot be touched with the feeling of our infirmities; but was in all points tempted like as we are, yet without sin. Let us therefore come boldly unto the throne of grace, that we may obtain mercy, and find grace to help in time of need" (Heb.4:15-16).
> "There hath no temptation taken you but such as is common to man: but God is faithful, who will not suffer you to be tempted above that ye are able; but will with the temptation also make a way to escape, that ye may be able to bear it" (1 Cor.10:13).
> "If any of you lack wisdom, let him ask of God, that giveth to all men liberally, and upbraideth not; and it shall be given him" (Jas.1:5).

Now, having said the above, what should our attitude (and the church's attitude) be toward suicidal people and their families? To the genuine Christian believer, the answer is obvious: we are to minister to them. We are to seek out and help all who hurt and face desperate problems and circumstances. Note what has just been said: we are not to sit around waiting for hurting people to cross our paths. We are to actively seek out, find, and help hurting people. This is the call of every Christian believer and the mission of the church. Christ made this perfectly clear.

> "Even as the Son of man came not to be ministered unto, but to minister, and to give his life a ransom for many" (Mt.20:28; cp. Lk.4:18).
> "Let this mind be in you, which was also in Christ Jesus: Who, being in the form of God, thought it not robbery to be equal with God: But made himself of no reputation, and took upon him the form of a servant, and was made in the likeness of men" (Ph.2:5-7; cp. Lk.4:18).
> "For the Son of man is come to seek and to save that which was lost" (Lk.19:10; cp. Jn.20:21).
> "Peace [be] unto you: as [my] Father hath sent me, even so send I you" (Jn.20:21).

3 (20:13) **Obedience--Decision--Commandment, The Ten**: What is the decision required by this commandment? How can lawlessness, violence, and murder be eliminated from society? What can we do to make our streets and homes safe, to feel free and secure to walk about in a neighborhood?

1. We must not live a life of hypocrisy: we must hate what is evil and cleave to what is good; we must become actively involved in stamping out violence, lawlessness, and murder.

> "Let love be without dissimulation [hypocrisy]. Abhor that which is evil; cleave to that which is good" (Ro.12:9).

2. We must teach the sanctity of life and the brotherhood of man:
   ⇒ Teach that we are all created in the image of God and that we all bear that image.

> "So God created man in his own image, in the image of God created he him; male and female created he them" (Gen.1:27).

   ⇒ Teach that we are to love our neighbor as ourselves.

> "And the second [is] like unto it, Thou shalt love thy neighbor as thyself" (Mt.22:39).
> "This is my commandment, That ye love one another, as I have loved you" (Jn.15:12).
> "For this, Thou shalt not commit adultery, Thou shalt not kill, Thou shalt not steal, Thou shalt not bear false witness, Thou shalt not covet; and if there be any other commandment, it is briefly comprehended in this saying, namely, Thou shalt <u>love thy neighbor</u> as thyself. Love worketh no ill to his neighbor: therefore love is the fulfilling of the law" (Ro.13:9-10).
> "Seeing ye have purified your souls in obeying the truth through the Spirit unto unfeigned love of the brethren, see that ye love one another with a pure heart fervently" (1 Pt.1:22).

3. We must conquer anger when it first arises within our hearts and minds:
   a. By not giving way to a vicious, vengeful anger.

> "Ye have heard that it was said by them of old time, Thou shalt not kill; and whosoever shall kill shall be in danger of the judgment: But I say unto you, That whosoever is angry with his brother without a cause shall be in danger of the judgment: and whosoever shall say to his brother, Raca, shall be in danger of the council: but whosoever shall say, Thou fool, shall be in danger of hell fire" (Mt.5:21-22).
> "Be ye angry, and sin not: let not the sun go down upon your wrath: Neither give place to the devil" (Eph.4:26-27).

   b. By not allowing egotistical pride to take a foothold in our lives, for pride breeds contention (anger).

> "Only by pride cometh contention: but with the well advised is wisdom" (Pr.13:10).

c. By not making friends with a hot tempered person, a person who is easily angered.

> "Make no friendship with an angry man; and with a furious man thou shalt not go: Lest thou learn his ways, and get a snare to thy soul" (Pr.22:24-25).

4. We must make sure that justice is executed, that the lawless, violent, and murderous are justly punished.

> "Whoso sheddeth man's blood, by man shall his blood be shed: for in the image of God made he man" (Gen.9:6).
> "And thine eye shall not pity; but life shall go for life, eye for eye, tooth for tooth, hand for hand, foot for foot" (Dt.19:21).
> "He that smiteth a man, so that he die, shall be surely put to death" (Ex.21:12).

THE BIBLICAL CONSEQUENCES OF KILLING ANOTHER PERSON

DEEPER STUDY #3

(20:13) <u>Commandments, The Ten--Obedience--Judgment</u>: What are the consequences of breaking this commandment?

> "Thou shalt not kill."

These four words have behind them the eternal force of the One who is the Author of life. Life is sacred. The sanctity of life has and always will remain unchanged in the eyes of God. Those who break this commandment will face the Righteous Judge who will hold them completely accountable for murder. No murderer can escape these terrible consequences.

1. The person who murders another person will suffer the wrath of God.

> "For the wrath of God is revealed from heaven against all ungodliness and unrighteousness of men, who hold the truth in unrighteousness....Being filled with all unrighteousness, fornication, wickedness, covetousness, maliciousness; full of envy, <u>murder</u>, debate, deceit, malignity; whisperers" (Ro.1:18, 29).

2. The person who murders another person will be judged and will not inherit the kingdom of God. He will not inherit eternal life.

> "Now the works of the flesh are manifest, which are these; Adultery, fornication, uncleanness, lasciviousness, Idolatry, witchcraft, hatred, variance, emulations, wrath, strife, seditions, heresies, Envyings, <u>murders</u>, drunkenness, revellings, and such like: of the which I tell you before, as I have also told you in time past, that they which do such things shall not inherit the kingdom of God" (Gal.5:19-21).
> "Whosoever hateth his brother is a murderer: and ye know that no murderer hath eternal life abiding in him" (1 Jn.3:15).

3. The person who kills another person is to face civil court, sentencing, imprisonment, the death penalty, or some other form of retribution.

> "For rulers are not a terror to good works, but to the evil. Wilt thou then not be afraid of the power? do that which is good, and thou shalt have praise of the same: For he is the minister of God to thee for good. But if thou do that which is evil, be afraid; for he beareth not the sword in vain: for he is the minister of God, a revenger to execute wrath upon him that doeth evil" (Ro.13:3-4).
> "And he that killeth any man shall surely be put to death" (Lev.24:17).
> "Then ye shall appoint you cities to be cities of refuge for you; that the slayer may flee thither, which killeth any person at unawares" (Num 35:11).
> "The revenger of blood himself shall slay the murderer: when he meeteth him, he shall slay him. But if he thrust him of hatred, or hurl at him by laying of wait, that he die; Or in enmity smite him with his hand, that he die: he that smote him shall surely be put to death; for he is a murderer: the revenger of blood shall slay the murderer, when he meeteth him. But if he thrust him suddenly without enmity, or have cast upon him any thing without laying of wait, Or with any stone, wherewith a man may die, seeing him not, and cast it upon him, that he die, and was not his enemy, neither sought his harm: Then the congregation shall judge between the slayer and the revenger of blood according to these judgments: And the congregation shall deliver the slayer out of the hand of the revenger of blood, and the congregation shall restore him to the city of his refuge, whither he was fled: and he shall abide in it unto the death of the high priest, which was anointed with the holy oil" (Num.35:19-25).

4. The person who kills another person destroys a person made in the image of God.

> "Whoso sheddeth man's blood, by man shall his blood be shed: for in the image of God made he man" (Gen.9:6).

5. The person who kills another person shows that he is defiled and has an evil heart.

> "For out of the heart proceed evil thoughts, murders, adulteries, fornications, thefts, false witness, blasphemies: These are [the things] which defile a man" (Mt.15:19-20).

6. The person who murders another person causes the loss of someone's loved one, a mother, father, sister, brother, son, daughter, or close friend.

> "Then Herod, when he saw that he was mocked of the wise men, was exceeding wroth, and sent forth, and slew all the children that were in Bethlehem, and in all the coasts thereof, from two years old and under, according to the time which he had diligently inquired of the wise men. Then was fulfilled that which was spoken by Jeremy the prophet, saying, In Rama was there a voice heard, lamentation, and weeping, and great mourning, Rachel weeping [for] her children, and would not be comforted, because they are not" (Mt.2:16-18).
>
> "And they stoned Stephen, calling upon God, and saying, Lord Jesus, receive my spirit. And he kneeled down, and cried with a loud voice, Lord, lay not this sin to their charge. And when he had said this, he fell asleep....And devout men carried Stephen *to his burial,* and made great lamentation over him" (Acts 7:59-60; 8:2).

THE BIBLICAL BENEFITS OF KEEPING THIS COMMANDMENT: NOT TO KILL ANOTHER PERSON

DEEPER STUDY #4

(20:13) **Commandments, The Ten--Benefits of Keeping--Life--Murder--Obedience**: the person who obeys this commandment and does not kill another person has made a decision to value life. The contrast is stark between a culture that allows or executes the innocent and helpless and a culture that honors and protects the sacredness of human life. Those who really love, defend, and protect life benefit an entire community, nation, and world. What are the benefits when God's people speak out against murder? What are the benefits to believers who respect the sanctity of life?

1. The person who belongs to the LORD and respects the sanctity of life will not kill but will walk in the Spirit and bear the fruit of the Spirit.

> "Now the works of the flesh are manifest, which are *these;* Adultery, fornication, uncleanness, lasciviousness, Idolatry, witchcraft, hatred, variance, emulations, wrath, strife, seditions, heresies, Envyings, <u>murders</u>, drunkenness, revellings, and such like: of the which I tell you before, as I have also told *you* in time past, that they which do such things shall not inherit the kingdom of God. <u>But the fruit of the Spirit</u> is love, joy, peace, longsuffering, gentleness, goodness, faith, Meekness, temperance: against such there is no law. And they that are Christ's have crucified the flesh with the affections and lusts. If we live in the Spirit, let us also walk in the Spirit" (Gal.5:19-25).

2. The person who follows God and respects the sanctity of life will have a sacrificial love for his brother.

> "We know that we have passed from death unto life, because we love the brethren. He that loveth not *his* brother abideth in death. Whosoever hateth his brother is a murderer: and ye know that no murderer hath eternal life abiding in him. Hereby perceive we the love *of God,* because he laid down his life for us: and we ought to lay down *our* lives for the brethren" (1 Jn.3:14-16).

3. The person who belongs to the LORD and respects the sanctity of life will have great love for his friends, willing to die if necessary.

> "Greater love hath no man than this, that a man lay down his life for his friends" (Jn.15:13).

4. The person who shares in the glorious salvation of God and respects the sanctity of life will experience a true urgency, a keen sense of the times, a sober perspective, an understanding about how fragile life can be.

> "Whereas ye know not what *shall be* on the morrow. For what *is* your life? It is even a vapour, that appeareth for a little time, and then vanisheth away" (Jas.4:14).
>
> "As for man, his days are as grass: as a flower of the field, so he flourisheth. For the wind passeth over it, and it is gone; and the place thereof shall know it no more" (Ps.103:15-16).
>
> "The voice said, Cry. And he said, What shall I cry? All flesh is grass, and all the goodliness thereof is as the flower of the field: The grass withereth, the flower fadeth: because the spirit of the LORD bloweth upon it: surely the people is grass" (Is.40:6-7).
>
> "I, even I, am he that comforteth you: who art thou, that thou shouldest be afraid of a man that shall die, and of the son of man which shall be made as grass" (Is.51:12).
>
> "For all flesh is as grass, and all the glory of man as the flower of grass. The grass withereth, and the flower thereof falleth away" (1 Pt.1:24).

5. The person who knows the truth and respects the sanctity of life will live in the truth and not be deceived by the original murderer, Satan.

"Ye are of your father the devil, and the lusts of *your* father ye will do. He was a murderer from the beginning, and abode not in the truth, because there is no truth in him. When he speaketh a lie, he speaketh of his own: for he is a liar, and the father of it" (Jn.8:44).

6. The person who truly respects the sanctity of life will understand that the only way to save his life is to give it away to Christ.

"For whosoever will save his life shall lose it: but whosoever will lose his life for my sake, the same shall save it. For what is a man advantaged, if he gain the whole world, and lose himself, or be cast away [eternally]?" (Lk.9:24-25).

7. The person who follows God and respects the sanctity of life will enjoy abundant life, life in Jesus Christ.

"The thief [Satan] cometh not, but for to steal, and to kill, and to destroy: I am come that they might have life, and that they might have *it* more abundantly" (Jn.10:10).

8. The person who respects the sanctity of life will be saved from doing Satan's will (to destroy human life).

"The thief [Satan] cometh not, but for to steal, and to kill, and to destroy: I am come that they might have life, and that they might have *it* more abundantly" (Jn.10:10).

9. The person who fully and completely respects the sanctity of life respects the life of the baby who is still in the womb of the mother.

"For thou hast possessed my reins: thou hast covered me in my mother's womb. I will praise thee; for I am fearfully *and* wonderfully made: marvellous *are* thy works; and *that* my soul knoweth right well. My substance was not hid from thee, when I was made in secret, *and* curiously wrought in the lowest parts of the earth. Thine eyes did see my substance, yet being unperfect; and in thy book all *my members* were written, *which* in continuance were fashioned, when as yet there was none of them" (Ps.139:13-16).
"Before I formed thee in the belly I knew thee; and before thou camest forth out of the womb I sanctified thee, *and* I ordained thee a prophet unto the nations" (Jer.1:5).
"And it came to pass, that, when Elisabeth heard the salutation of Mary, the babe leaped in her womb; and Elisabeth was filled with the Holy Ghost: And she spake out with a loud voice, and said, Blessed *art* thou among women, and blessed *is* the fruit of thy womb" (Lk.1:41-42).

DEEPER STUDY # 5

JESUS CHRIST AND HIS TEACHING CONCERNING MURDER

"Thou shalt not kill" (Ex.20:13).

THE TEACHING OF CHRIST	THE BELIEVER'S RESPONSE

1. Jesus Christ declared that murder is not only an outward act but also an attitude. Murder occurs within the hearts of men.
 	
"Ye have heard that it was said by them of old time, Thou shalt not kill; and whosoever shall kill shall be in danger of the judgment: But I say unto you, That whosoever is angry with his brother without a cause shall be in danger of the judgment: and whosoever shall say to his brother, Raca, shall be in danger of the council: but whosoever shall say, Thou fool, shall be in danger of hell fire" (Mt.5:21-22).
	1) Murder is not only an outward act; it is also inward. It is born within a person's heart and mind. It is...
	  • anger
	  • bitterness
	  • enmity
	  We must never allow anger to take hold of us without just cause. Reconciliation is urgent while there is still time. We must not allow our relationships to sour beyond repair. Life is far too short to allow our anger to make us bitter and unforgiving. We must forgive others.
	2) Anger that goes unresolved will allow a spirit of murder to enter the human heart.
	
	"Be ye angry, and sin not: let not the sun go down upon your wrath" (Eph.4:26).
	"If a man say, I love God, and hateth his brother, he is a liar: for he that loveth not his brother whom he hath seen, how can he love God whom he hath not seen? And this commandment have we from him, That he who loveth God love his brother also" (1 Jn.4:20-21).
	"For out of the heart proceed evil thoughts, murders, adulteries, fornications, thefts, false witness, blasphemies" (Mt.15:19).
	"For from within, out of the heart of men, proceed evil thoughts, adulteries, fornications, murders" (Mk.7:21).

THE TEACHING OF CHRIST	THE BELIEVER'S RESPONSE
2. Jesus Christ declared that Satan is the source of murder, that he is the arch-enemy of God and man, that he was a murderer from the beginning. "Ye are of your father the devil, and the lusts of *your* father ye will do. He was a murderer from the beginning, and abode not in the truth; because there is no truth in him. When he speaketh a lie, he speaketh of his own: for he is a liar, and the father of it" (Jn.8:44).	⇒ We must not reject the truth and follow in the murderous steps of Satan. Satan is a murderer in three senses: 1) He was behind the first murder: the man Cain killing his brother (Gen.4:8). 2) He was behind the sin of Adam, which brought death to the whole human race. He is the murderer, the one who caused the death of men (Ro.5:12). 3) He is behind the murder of human life and behind the loss of man experiencing real life here on earth. The devil destroys life and all abundant living when he can: all love, joy, peace, patience, gentleness, goodness, faith, meekness, and discipline. "The thief cometh not, but for to steal, and to kill, and to destroy...." (Jn.10:10). "But <u>let none of you suffer as a murderer</u>, or as a thief, or as an evil doer, or as a busybody in other men's matters" (1 Pt.4:15). "<u>Whosoever hateth his brother is a murderer</u>: and ye know that no murderer hath eternal life abiding in him" (1 Jn.3:15). "Be sober, be vigilant; because your adversary the devil, as a roaring lion, walketh about, seeking whom he may devour" (1 Pt.5:8). "Then Satan answered the LORD, and said, Doth Job fear God for nought? Hast not thou made an hedge about him, and about his house, and about all that he hath on every side? thou hast blessed the work of his hands, and his substance is increased in the land. But put forth thine hand now, and touch all that he hath, and he will curse thee to thy face" (Job 1:9-11).
3. Jesus Christ declared that some of His disciples would be murdered by family members because of their allegiance to Him. "And the brother shall deliver up the brother to death, and the father the child: and the children shall rise up against *their* parents, and cause them to be put to death. And ye shall be hated of all *men* for my name's sake: but he that endureth to the end shall be saved" (Mt.10:21-22).	1) A believer's own family can become his greatest persecutor, even his murderer. Why? There are three reasons: a) Because of the believer's commitment to Christ and His righteousness. b) Because of the family's orthodox religion or church. c) Because of the believer's commitment to live for Christ. Such an active witness is sometimes an embarrassment to a family. 2) Nothing hurts more than having our own family oppose us when we make a decision to follow Christ. When our families oppose and persecute us, it hurts deeply. "If the world hate you, ye know that *it hated* me before it hated you. If ye were of the world, the world would love his own: but because ye are not of the world, but I have chosen you out of the world, therefore the world hateth you. Remember the word that I said unto you, The servant is not greater than his lord. If they have persecuted me, they will also persecute you; if they have kept my saying, they will keep yours also" (Jn.15:18-20). "And he said unto them, Verily I say unto you, There is no man that hath left house, or parents, or brethren, or wife, or children, for the kingdom of God's sake, Who shall not receive manifold more in this present time, and in the world to come life everlasting" (Lk.18:29-30).
4. Jesus Christ declared that evil men will kill believers, *thinking* that they are doing God a service. "They shall put you out of the synagogues: yea, the time cometh, that whosoever killeth you will think that he doeth God service" (Jn.16:2).	1) The believer is warned that religious extremists will persecute and murder the followers of Christ. 2) The believer can stumble and fall over persecution. Persecution can... • cause a believer to question his beliefs • cause a believer to weaken and return to the way of false religion • silence a believer and his witness • cause a believer to deny Jesus 3) The believer must take comfort in God's great promises to His persecuted people. "Blessed are ye, when *men* shall revile you, and persecute *you,* and shall say all manner of evil against you falsely, for my sake. Rejoice, and be exceeding glad: for great *is* your reward in heaven: for so persecuted they the prophets which were before you" (Mt.5:11-12). "And they departed from the presence of the council, rejoicing that they were counted worthy to suffer shame for his name" (Acts 5:41). "And if children, then heirs; heirs of God, and joint-heirs with Christ; if so be that we suffer with *him,* that we may be also glorified together" (Ro.8:17). "Choosing rather to suffer affliction with the people of God, than to enjoy the pleasures of sin for a season" (Heb.11:25). "But the God of all grace, who hath called us unto his eternal glory by Christ Jesus, after that ye have suffered a while, make you perfect, stablish,

THE TEACHING OF CHRIST	THE BELIEVER'S RESPONSE
	strengthen, settle *you*" (1 Pt.5:10). "Yea, and all that will live godly in Christ Jesus shall suffer persecution. But evil men and seducers shall wax worse and worse, deceiving, and being deceived" (2 Tim.3:12-13).
5. Jesus Christ declared that His people would be the victims of great violence and murder in the last days. "For nation shall rise against nation, and kingdom against kingdom: and there shall be famines, and pestilences, and earthquakes, in divers places. All these *are* the beginning of sorrows. Then shall they deliver you up to be afflicted, and shall kill you: and ye shall be hated of all nations for my name's sake. And then shall many be offended, and shall betray one another, and shall hate one another. And many false prophets shall rise, and shall deceive many. And because iniquity shall abound, the love of many shall wax cold. But he that shall endure unto the end, the same shall be saved. And this gospel of the kingdom shall be preached in all the world for a witness unto all nations; and then shall the end come" (Mt.24:7-14).	⇒ The believer must expect persecution. He must remember that Christ foretold that he would be persecuted. Remembering keeps the believer from being caught off guard and stumbling. The believer is to *prepare* for persecution by *thinking through* what he will do when he is... <table><tr><td>• ridiculed</td><td>• attacked</td></tr><tr><td>• criticized</td><td>• slandered</td></tr><tr><td>• opposed</td><td>• tortured</td></tr><tr><td>• questioned</td><td>• imprisoned</td></tr><tr><td>• abused</td><td>• martyred</td></tr></table> "Remember the word that I said unto you, The servant is not greater than his lord. If they have persecuted me, they will also persecute you; if they have kept my saying, they will keep yours also" (Jn.15:20). "But these things have I told you, that when the time shall come, ye may remember that I told you of them. And these things I said not unto you at the beginning, because I was with you" (Jn.16:4). "But the God of all grace, who hath called us unto his eternal glory by Christ Jesus, after that ye have suffered a while, make you perfect, stablish, strengthen, settle *you*. To him *be* glory and dominion for ever and ever. Amen" (1 Pt.5:10-11).
6. Jesus Christ declared that religious hypocrites are related to the sons of those who murdered God's prophets. "Woe unto you, scribes and Pharisees, hypocrites! because ye build the tombs of the prophets, and garnish the sepulchres of the righteous, And say, If we had been in the days of our fathers, we would not have been partakers with them in the blood of the prophets. Wherefore ye be witnesses unto yourselves, that ye are the children of them which killed the prophets. Fill ye up then the measure of your fathers...how can ye escape the damnation of hell? Wherefore, behold, I send unto you prophets, and wise men, and scribes: and *some* of them ye shall kill and crucify; and *some* of them shall ye scourge in your synagogues, and persecute *them* from city to city: That upon you may come all the righteous blood shed upon the earth, from the blood of righteous Abel unto the blood of Zacharias son of Barachias, whom ye slew between the temple and the altar. Verily I say unto you, All these things shall come upon this generation" (Mt.23:29-36).	⇒ We must have no part in crucifying the Body of Christ all over again. We must not in any way be associated with verbal abuse against any of God's people, not with... • slander • gossip • smearing • scolding • insults "*Saying,* Touch not mine anointed, and do my prophets no harm" (Ps.105:15). "Whoso privily [secretly] slandereth his neighbour, him will I cut off: him that hath an high look and a proud heart will not I suffer" (Ps.101:5). "An hypocrite with *his* mouth destroyeth his neighbour: but through knowledge shall the just be delivered" (Pr.11:9). "Thou shalt not go up and down as a talebearer among thy people: neither shalt thou stand against the blood of thy neighbour: I am the Lord" (Lev.19:16). "A talebearer revealeth secrets: but he that is of a faithful spirit concealeth the matter" (Pr.11:13). "He that covereth a transgression seeketh love; but he that repeateth a matter separateth very friends" (Pr.17:9). "The words of a talebearer are as wounds, and they go down into the innermost parts of the belly" (Pr.18:8). "He that goeth about as a talebearer revealeth secrets: therefore meddle not with him that flattereth with his lips" (Pr.20:19). "Where no wood is, there the fire goeth out: so where there is no talebearer, the strife ceaseth" (Pr.26:20).

	H. The Ten Command- ments, The Laws Gov- erning Man's Duty To Others (Part 3): Com- mandment Seven Con- cerns Man's Family— Never Commit Adultery or Immorality, Ex.20:14
Commandment 7 concerns *man's family*: Forbids adultery	14 Thou shalt not commit adultery.

DIVISION VII

THE LAW AND THE PROMISES OF GOD (THE MOSAIC COVENANT) (PART 2): THE TEN COMMANDMENTS--NECESSARY LAWS TO GOVERN MAN AND SOCIETY, EX.20:1-26

H. **The Ten Commandments, The Laws Governing Man's Duty To Others (Part 3): Commandment Seven Concerns Man's Family--Never Commit Adultery or Immorality, Ex.20:14**

(20:14) **Introduction--Adultery--Immorality--Sin**: How serious a problem is adultery? In just a moment we shall see that this commandment refers to all forms of immorality. In light of that, how serious a problem is immorality in our society? Most authorities and polls tell us that...
- adultery is prevalent
- pregnany among unwed mothers is on a sharp rise
- premarital sex is becoming commonplace, the accepted practice among the young
- sex among unmarried adults--young and old alike--is accepted and even expected by the vast majority of people

Is there a cesspool of immorality in society today? Most honest and thinking observers of history would say that immorality is a very serious problem today. Why? Because it threatens the family, the very foundation of society and civilization. The family is the primary place where trust, loyalty, and love are to be taught and demonstrated. If a person will not be faithful and loyal to his family, how can he be trusted to be faithful and loyal to his nation, society, and civilization? It is far easier to be loyal to that which can be physically seen, such as one's family, than for that which is only an ideal such as nation, society, and civilization. Immorality strikes at the very foundation of society, the family. It tears apart the family and causes hurt, suffering, strain, shame, guilt, secrecy, destitution, distrust, disloyalty, and unfaithfulness. Moreover, immorality and adultery teach that certain behavior is acceptable: selfishness, unfaithfulness, distrust, disloyalty, secrecy, irresponsibility, and on and on.

This is the reason God gave us this commandment: to preserve our lives, to preserve the great qualities that bring peace, love, and trust to our lives, qualities that build a healthy mind and heart. This is the great subject of this commandment, a much needed subject: *Commandment Seven Concerns Man's Family--Never Commit Adultery or Immorality*, 20:14.
1. Who is to obey this commandment? How long was this commandment to be in force (v.14)?
2. What is forbidden by this commandment (v.14)?
3. What is the decision required by this commandment (v.14)?

1 (20:14) **Commandments, The Ten--Adultery--Immorality--Sin**: Who is to obey this commandment? How long is this commandment to be in force? Was this commandment to govern only the ancient world or is there still a need for the commandment: "You shall not commit adultery, immorality"? It is almost ridiculous to ask if this commandment governing immorality is needed today. Keep in mind that this is one of the ten great commandments of God. God has created man and God knows that man has some very basic needs, needs that have to be controlled or else they will run wild and destroy man and his world. One of these needs is the need for sex. God created man as a sexual being primarily to build a close bond between husband and wife (holding the family together) and to repopulate the earth. God knows that man's sexual drive is strong, very strong. God has created the drive to be strong to make sure the great qualities of life are nourished (love, joy, peace, trust, faithfulness, unity) and that the earth is always repopulated. But God also knows that man has to control his drive: man has to keep his drive within bounds, within very specific limits. Therefore, God commands man: "You shall not commit adultery; you shall not commit acts of immorality against marriage and the family."

Who is to obey this commandment? And how long is this commandment to be in force? You are to obey, and the commandment is in force as long as man lives, as long as man is to repopulate the earth.

> "Thou shalt not commit adultery" (Ex.20:14).
> "Flee fornication [all forms of sex outside of marriage]. Every sin that a man doeth is without the body; but he that commiteth fornication sinneth against his own body" (1 Cor.6:18).
> "For this is the will of God, even your sanctification, that ye should abstain from fornication: That every one of you should know how to possess his vessel in sanctification and honour; Not in the lust of concupiscence, even as the Gentiles which know not God" (1 Th.4:3-5).

2 (20:14) **Commandments, The Ten--Adultery--Immorality--Sex, Illicit--Morality--Marriage**: What is forbidden by this seventh commandment, "You shall not commit adultery" (v.14)? How is this commandment broken, violated?

1. Adultery (naap) or *adulterate* means to debase, to corrupt oneself sexually, to make oneself impure sexually, to have sex outside of marriage. What God is saying is simple, unqualified, and irrevocable: "You shall not commit adultery: you shall not debase yourself, corrupt yourself, nor make yourself impure sexually. You shall not have sex outside of marriage."

   a. Scripture teaches that a person becomes sexually impure in at least three ways:
     ⇒ A person has sex with someone other than his or her spouse. This is what is commonly called *adultery*.
     ⇒ A person has sex before marriage. This is called *fornication*. Fornication refers to any sexual immorality, either before marriage or after marriage.
     ⇒ A person fantasizes and lusts after a person other than his or her spouse, allows his mind and heart to be set upon another person.

   b. Note that the sin of adultery embraces all that leads up to the act of sex, not just the sexual act itself. Adultery is far more than just being sexually unfaithful in marriage. This commandment forbids any immoral thought or act...
     • that makes a person impure for marriage
     • that spots or dirties a person's marriage
     • that causes a person to lose his or her virginity
     • that keeps a person from being able to offer himself or herself as a pure virgin when married
   Illicit sex is a violation against the marriage to be. Illicit sex dirties, corrupts, spots, and makes a person impure either before or after marriage.

   c. The thought life of a person is important when dealing with adultery. Adultery is committed in the heart long before the act is committed. Always keep in mind that God's law is spiritual; therefore His law deals with the thoughts of our mind and heart. This commandment forbids committing adultery in the heart. A person is...
     • not to prostitute his thoughts and imaginations
     • not to allow impure, lustful thoughts
     • not to indulge in illicit fantasies

2. The meaning of adultery was expanded by the Lord Jesus Christ, by God's Son Himself. Christ taught that this commandment means far more than just committing the act of adultery. He enlarged the commandment to include thoughts and lusts, to include the second look when a person is dressed to sexually attract or expose his or her body.

> "Ye have heard that it was said by them of old time, Thou shalt not commit adultery: But I say unto you, That whosoever <u>looketh</u> on a woman to lust after her hath committed adultery with her already in his heart. And if thy right eye offend thee, pluck it out, and cast [it] from thee: for it is profitable for thee that one of thy members should perish, and not [that] thy whole body should be cast into hell. And if thy right hand offend thee, cut it off, and cast [it] from thee: for it is profitable for thee that one of thy members should perish, and not [that] thy whole body should be cast into hell" (Mt.5:27-30).

3. Now, what causes adultery and immorality? There are no doubt many causes, but we can perhaps summarize them all under the following five categories.
   a. Immorality is caused by corrupt moral standards or a lack of moral standards.
     ⇒ Some people have never been taught nor are they aware that sex outside of marriage is wrong in the sight of God. Their society has become so corrupted down through the ages that belief in the true and living God has been lost as well as the sanctity of sex and marriage.
   b. Immorality is caused by lax or liberal moral standards, or by a selfish, worldly, immoral lifestyle. These people either ignore or deny God's commandment, choosing to live as they wish.
   c. Immorality is caused by the need for companionship, attention, or love or by the need for appreciation or fulfillment. Many people reach out to others because of these very basic needs. This is especially true during marriage when a husband or wife fails to meet these needs in his or her spouse.
   d. Immorality is caused by anger, hostility, or the seeking of revenge. A host of behaviors can anger a person and arouse him to commit adultery, such things as coldness, indifference, neglect, a biting tongue, harshness, selfishness.
   e. Immorality is caused by poor ego strength or by an inflated ego, by a lack of self-esteem or self-worth, by a need to feel important, or by the challenge and conquest of the affair. The most intimate thing a person can give to another is his or her body. Therefore, sex is a challenge or conquest for many people; it is an ego booster, an act that either builds a person's feelings of importance or adds to his or her trophy case of conquests.

Sex is a very normal, natural act, a most precious and cherished act given by God. God has built the desire for sex into the very nature of man. In fact, sex is the most intimate experience God has chosen for man to nourish the great virtues of life and to propagate the human race. But the depraved, sinful heart of man has corrupted sex, so much so that man has developed a sex-crazed society. In very practical terms, immorality is caused...
     • by ignoring or denying God and His Word
     • by ignoring right vs. wrong
     • by lack of teaching and training
     • by unsatisfying, inadequate sex with a spouse
     • by coldness, the alienation of husband or wife
     • by living in a dream or fantasy world due to such things as pornography, films, or suggestive music

- by not guarding relationships, by getting too close and becoming attracted to a person
- by not guarding against loneliness, emptiness, or the disappointment in one's spouse or loved one

4. Now, why does God forbid adultery? Prohibit immorality? What is God's purpose, His reason for giving this commandment? Keep in mind what is stated above: the experience of sex is a gift to man, a gift given by God. God created sex for man, and even went so far as to make sex...
- a part of man's very nature
- the very way man is to propagate the human race

Note what this means: if man failed to have sex, the human race would cease to be. Human life would become extinct within a few generations. God so intertwined sex within man's nature that man must have sex. All this is to say one thing: sex is of critical importance to God. God not only approves of sex: He is the Giver and Creator of the experience of sex. But He put boundaries and limits around sex. Sex was created for marriage, for the home, and only for marriage and the home. This leads us to the purposes for sex, the reasons why God gave this seventh commandment.

a. God gave the seventh commandment to preserve man, to protect and safeguard the value of the individual, the sanctity of man's body and spirit. When a man and woman lie together, they are never more vulnerable, never more exposed. Lying together, their bodies and spirits are more exposed than at any other time. God intended sex to be one of the most intimate, warm, precious, and growing experiences of human life. Sex was created so that two people could grow together, could nourish and nurture each other in...

- love
- joy
- peace
- trust

- loyalty
- perseverance
- attractiveness
- attention

- care
- security
- self-esteem
- a sense of fulfillment

On and on the list could go; but note all the wonderful, positive, and strong qualities that sex is supposed to bring between two people. This is the reason God gave the seventh commandment: "You shall not commit adultery" (v.13). These things are so important for a healthy personality that God did something: He ordained that one man and one woman were to give their lives to one another, that they were to focus upon sharing and developing the wonderful qualities in the other. God ordained marriage. Sex outside marriage never develops these qualities. Illicit sex always causes problems...

- guilt
- jealousy
- a sense of being used
- unwanted pregnancies
- broken marriages
- insecurity
- a false sense of security

- unhappiness
- disease
- a cheapening of sex
- broken trust
- selfishness
- loss of self-esteem
- loss of respect for others

- loss of respect by others
- dissolution of the family
- problem children
- emotional problems
- disloyalty
- loss of affection and relationships
- a lack of fulfillment

The point: God gave the seventh commandment to preserve the value of human life, the sanctity of man's body and spirit.

b. God gave the seventh commandment to preserve the family and the human race, society itself. The family is the basic unit of any society; therefore, the family has to be protected and preserved for society to survive. This was true for Israel and it is true for us, no matter what our generation. When husbands and wives are living in love and are faithful to each other, the great qualities of life are learned and taught: loyalty, trust, commitment, love, joy, and peace. These are the very qualities that grow and develop fruitful lives, families, and nations. No family, society, or nation can survive without these great qualities.

God demands the *sanctity of marriage*. God demands that husbands and wives be pure and faithful to one another, that they love one another and never commit adultery: "You shall never commit adultery, never commit any act of immorality."

"**Thou shalt not commit adultery**" (Ex.20:14).
"**Flee fornication [all forms of sex outside of marriage]. Every sin that a man doeth is without the body; but he that commiteth fornication sinneth against his own body**" (1 Cor.6:18).
"**Abstain from fornication**" (1 Th.4:3).
"**Abstain from fleshly lusts, which war against the soul**" (1 Pt.2:11).

3 (20:14) <u>Commandments, The Ten--Adultery--Immorality--Sex, Illicit--Purity--Morality--Marriage</u>: What is the decision required by this commandment? Obedience! Very simply, we must never commit adultery, never commit an immoral act. We must live pure, holy lives. But how? How can we guard ourselves and keep from committing sexual sin in a sex-crazed society--a society that uses sex to sell products, provide entertainment, pleasure, recreation, and clothing for day to day dress? Scripture says the following:

1. Never take a second look. And if you can prevent the first look, *never* look. As someone has said, we cannot keep the birds from flying over our heads, but we can prevent them from roosting there.

"**But I say unto you, That whosoever looketh on a woman to lust after her hath committed adultery with her already in his heart**" (Mt.5:28).

2. Flee temptation; flee the very appearance of evil. We must always flee at the very first offer, the very first sight, the very first thought, the very first urge (desire).

"**Abstain from all appearance of evil**" (1 Th.5:22).

3. Flee immorality--abstain totally.

> **"Flee fornication [all forms of illicit sex]" (1 Cor.6:18).**
> **"For this is the will of God, even your sanctification, that ye should <u>abstain from fornication</u>: That every one of you should know how to possess his vessel in sanctification and honour; Not in the lust of concupiscence, even as the Gentiles which know not God" (1 Th.4:3-5).**

4. Never touch the unclean thing.

> **"Wherefore come out from among them, and be ye separate, saith the Lord, and touch not the unclean thing; and I will receive you, And will be a Father unto you, and ye shall be my sons and daughters, saith the Lord Almighty" (2 Cor.6:17-18).**

5. Never talk about immorality, not even once.

> **"But fornication, and all uncleanness, or covetousness, let it not be once named among you, as becometh saints; Neither filthiness, nor foolish talking, nor jesting, which are not convenient: but rather giving of thanks" (Eph.5:3-4).**

6. Never give any part of your body over to sin.

> **"Neither yield ye your members [body parts] as instruments of unrighteousness unto sin: but yield yourselves unto God, as those that are alive from the dead, and your members as instruments of righteousness unto God" (Ro.6:13).**

7. Never let sin control your body.

> **"Let not sin therefore reign in your mortal body, that ye should obey it in the lusts thereof" (Ro.6:12, cp. v.11-13).**

8. Do not love the world nor the things of the world.

> **"Love not the world, neither the things that are in the world. If any man love the world, the love of the Father is not in him. For all that is in the world, the lust of the flesh, and the lust of the eyes, and the pride of life, is not of the Father, but is of the world" (1 Jn.2:15-16).**

9. Live a crucified life, a life sacrificed totally to Christ.

> **"I am crucified with Christ: nevertheless I live; yet not I, but Christ liveth in me: and the life which I now live in the flesh I live by the faith of the Son of God, who loved me, and gave himself for me" (Gal.2:20).**
> **"And he said to [them] all, If any [man] will come after me, let him deny himself, and take up his cross daily, and follow me" (Lk.9:23).**

10. Sacrifice and commit your body totally to Jesus Christ.

> **"I beseech you therefore, brethren, by the mercies of God, that ye present your bodies a living sacrifice, holy, acceptable unto God, which is your reasonable service. And be not conformed to this world: but be ye transformed by the renewing of your mind, that ye may prove what is that good, and acceptable, and perfect, will of God" (Ro.12:1-2).**

11. Put the sinful acts of the body to death.

> **"Likewise reckon ye also yourselves to be dead indeed unto sin, but alive unto God through Jesus Christ our Lord" (Ro.6:11).**
> **"For if ye live after the flesh, ye shall die: but if ye through the Spirit do mortify the deeds of the body, ye shall live" (Ro.8:13).**

12. Discipline yourself--strenuously so--in order to control your body.

> **"But I keep under my body, and bring it into subjection: lest that by any means, when I have preached to others, I myself should be a castaway" (1 Cor.9:27).**

13. Be filled with the Spirit of God, bearing His character and His character alone.

> **"And be not drunk with wine, wherein is excess; but be filled with the Spirit" (Eph.5:18).**

14. Guard your spirit.

> "**Take heed to your spirit, and let none deal treacherously against the wife of his youth**" (Mal.2:15).

15. Glorify God in your body.

> "**Flee fornication. Every sin that a man doeth is without the body; but he that committeth fornication sinneth against his own body. What? know ye not that your body is the temple of the Holy Ghost which is in you, which ye have of God, and ye are not your own? For ye are bought with a price: therefore glorify God in your body, and in your spirit, which are God's**" (1 Cor.6:18-20).

16. Captivate and subject every thought to obey Christ.

> "**Casting down imaginations, and every high thing that exalteth itself against the knowledge of God, and bringing into captivity every thought to the obedience of Christ**" (2 Cor.10:5).

17. Listen to God's Word: hide His Word in your heart and live by it.

> "**Wherewithal shall a young man cleanse his way? by taking heed thereto according to thy word....Thy word have I hid in mine heart, that I might not sin against thee**" (Ps.119:9, 11).

THE BIBLICAL CONSEQUENCES OF COMMITTING ADULTERY

DEEPER STUDY #1

(20:14) **Commandments, The Ten--Obedience--Judgment--Adultery**: What are the consequences of breaking this commandment--not to commit adultery? It is clear that there is no such thing as a private sin. The sins of one man will affect the lives of many. This is especially true when adultery is committed. Adultery is a gross act of betrayal; adultery is a hideous crime against everyone: God, oneself, and others. Those who commit adultery will face severe judgment, both now and in the future. The consequences should cause any man or woman contemplating this sin to seriously weigh the pleasure of the fleeting experience against the terrible harm it causes.

1. The person who commits adultery (sexual immorality) and never repents will forfeit eternal life; he will not inherit the kingdom of God.

> "**Know ye not that the unrighteous shall not inherit the kingdom of God? Be not deceived: neither fornicators, nor idolaters, <u>nor adulterers</u>, nor effeminate, nor abusers of themselves with mankind, Nor thieves, nor covetous, nor drunkards, nor revilers, nor extortioners, <u>shall inherit the kingdom of God</u>. And such were some of you: but ye are washed, but ye are sanctified, but ye are justified in the name of the Lord Jesus, and by the Spirit of our God**" (1 Cor.6:9-11).

2. The person who commits adultery (sexual immorality) and never repents will eventually die in his sin and face the severe judgment of God.

> "**Marriage is honourable in all, and the bed undefiled: but whoremongers and adulterers God will judge**" (Heb.13:4).
> "**But the fearful, and unbelieving, and the abominable, and murderers, and whoremongers, and sorcerers, and idolaters, and all liars, shall have their part in the lake which burneth with fire and brimstone: which is the second death**" (Rev.21:8).
> "**And the man that committeth adultery with another man's wife, even he that committeth adultery with his neighbour's wife, the adulterer and the adulteress shall surely be put to death**" (Lev.20:10).

3. The person who commits adultery (sexual immorality) and never repents destroys his soul.

> "***But* whoso committeth adultery with a woman lacketh understanding: <u>he *that* doeth it destroyeth his own soul</u>**" (Pr.6:32).

4. The person who commits adultery (sexual immorality) and never repents loses the battle for his soul.

> "**Dearly beloved, I beseech you as strangers and pilgrims, abstain from fleshly lusts, which war against the soul**" (1 Pt.2:11).

5. The person who commits adultery (sexual immorality) and never repents will suffer the judicial judgment of God. (See notes--Jn.12:39-41; Ro.1:24 for more discussion.)

"Wherefore God also gave them up to uncleanness through the lusts of their own hearts, to dishonour their own bodies between themselves....For this cause God gave them up unto vile affections: for even their women did change the natural use into that which is against nature: And likewise also the men, leaving the natural use of the woman, burned in their lust one toward another; men with men working that which is unseemly, and receiving in themselves that recompence of their error which was meet. And even as they did not like to retain God in their knowledge, God gave them over to a reprobate mind, to do those things which are not convenient" (Ro.1:24, 26-28).

6. The person who committed adultery under the law of the Old Testament was put to death.

"And the man that committeth adultery with *another* man's wife, *even he* that committeth adultery with his neighbour's wife, the adulterer and the adulteress shall surely be put to death" (Lev.20:10).

7. The person who commits adultery (sexual immorality) and never repents injures and devastates people, destroys the unity of a family.

"And it came to pass in an eveningtide, that David arose from off his bed, and walked upon the roof of the king's house: and from the roof he saw a woman washing herself; and the woman was very beautiful to look upon. And David sent and inquired after the woman. And one said, Is not this Bath-sheba, the daughter of Eliam, the wife of Uriah the Hittite? And David sent messengers, and took her; and she came in unto him, and he lay with her; for she was purified from her uncleanness: and she returned unto her house. And the woman conceived, and sent and told David, and said, I am with child....And it came to pass in the morning, that David wrote a letter to Joab, and sent it by the hand of Uriah. And he wrote in the letter, saying, Set ye Uriah in the forefront of the hottest battle, and retire ye from him, that he may be smitten, and die. And it came to pass, when Joab observed the city, that he assigned Uriah unto a place where he knew that valiant men were. And the men of the city went out, and fought with Joab: and there fell some of the people of the servants of David; and Uriah the Hittite died also....And when the wife of Uriah heard that Uriah her husband was dead, she mourned for her husband. And when the mourning was past, David sent and fetched her to his house, and she became his wife, and bare him a son. But the thing that David had done displeased the LORD" (2 Sam.11:2-5, 14-17, 26-27; cp. 2 Sam.12:1f).

8. The person who commits adultery (sexual immorality) and never repents lives a worldly, fleshly life, not a spiritual life.

"Love not the world, neither the things that are in the world. If any man love the world, the love of the Father is not in him. For all that is in the world, the lust of the flesh, and the lust of the eyes, and the pride of life, is not of the Father, but is of the world" (1 Jn.2:15-16).

9. The person who commits adultery (sexual immorality) and never repents shows that he has a corrupted heart [thought-life] and that he lacks self-control.

"But I say unto you, That whosoever looketh on a woman to lust after her hath committed adultery with her already in his heart" (Mt.5:28).
"Lust not after her beauty in thine heart; neither let her take thee with her eyelids" (Pr.6:25).

10. The person who commits adultery (sexual immorality) and never repents becomes enslaved to a sinful lifestyle.

"Know ye not, that to whom ye yield yourselves servants to obey, his servants ye are to whom ye obey; whether of sin unto death, or of obedience unto righteousness?" (Ro.6:16).
"For they that are after the flesh do mind the things of the flesh; but they that are after the Spirit the things of the Spirit" (Ro.8:5).
"Having eyes full of adultery, and that cannot cease from sin; beguiling unstable souls: an heart they have exercised with covetous practices; cursed children" (2 Pt.2:14).

11. The person who commits adultery (sexual immorality) and never repents sins against his own body. The person creates all kinds of problems for himself--emotionally, mentally, and physically.

"Flee fornication. Every sin that a man doeth is without the body; but he that committeth fornication sinneth against his own body" (1Cor.6:18).

12. The person who commits adultery (sexual immorality) and never repents lives a secretive life.

"The eye also of the adulterer waiteth for the twilight, saying, No eye shall see me: and disguiseth his face" (Job 24:15).

13. The person who commits adultery (sexual immorality) and never repents attacks the precious symbolism between Christ and His bride, the church.

> "For *as* a young man marrieth a virgin, *so* shall thy sons marry thee: and *as* the bridegroom rejoiceth over the bride, *so* shall thy God rejoice over thee" (Is.62:5).
> "Husbands, love your wives, <u>even as Christ also loved the church</u>, and gave himself for it" (Eph.5:25).
> "For I am jealous over you with godly jealousy: for I have espoused you to one husband, that I may present *you as* a chaste virgin to Christ" (2 Cor.11:2).
> "Let us be glad and rejoice, and give honour to him: for the marriage of the Lamb is come, and his wife hath made herself ready" (Rev.19:7).
> "And I John saw the holy city, new Jerusalem, coming down from God out of heaven, prepared as a bride adorned for her husband" (Rev.21:2).
> "And the Spirit and the bride say, Come. And let him that heareth say, Come. And let him that is athirst come. And whosoever will, let him take the water of life freely" (Rev.22:17).

THE BIBLICAL BENEFITS OF NOT COMMITTING ADULTERY

DEEPER STUDY #2
(20:14) <u>Commandments, The Ten--Adultery--Benefits of Keeping--Marriage--Obedience</u>: there are many wonderful benefits for those who keep this commandment.

1. A person who is sexually faithful and who trusts Jesus Christ as his Savior will have a life that is washed, sanctified, and justified in the name of Jesus Christ.

> "Know ye not that the unrighteous shall not inherit the kingdom of God? Be not deceived: neither fornicators, nor idolaters, nor <u>adulterers</u>, nor effeminate, nor abusers of themselves with mankind....<u>And such were some of you</u>: but ye are washed, but ye are sanctified, but ye are justified in the name of the Lord Jesus, and by the Spirit of our God" (1Cor. 6:9, 11).

2. A person who has a pure heart is sexually faithful and will see God.

> "Blessed *are* the pure in heart: for they shall see God" (Mt.5:8).

3. A person who is sexually faithful gains the wonderful experience of being joined together as one flesh, of being spiritually united to one husband or wife.

> "Therefore shall a man leave his father and his mother, and shall cleave unto his wife: and they shall be one flesh" (Gen.2:24).
> "For this cause shall a man leave his father and mother, and cleave to his wife" (Mk.10:7).
> "What therefore God hath joined together, let not man put asunder" (Mk.10:9).

4. A person who is sexually faithful and who follows God will never lose the presence of God (David's prayer after committing adultery).

> "Cast me not away from thy presence; and take not thy holy spirit from me" (Ps.51:11).

5. A person who is sexually faithful and shares in the glorious salvation of God will have his prayers answered.

> "Likewise, ye husbands, dwell with *them* according to knowledge, <u>giving honour unto the wife</u>, as unto the weaker vessel, and as being heirs together of the grace of life; <u>that your prayers be not hindered</u>" (1 Pt.3:7).

6. A person who knows the Lord and is sexually faithful receives the very special favor of the Lord.

> "*Whoso* findeth a wife findeth a good *thing,* and obtaineth favour of the LORD" (Pr.18:22).

7. A person who is sexually faithful protects his body from certain emotional, mental, and physical problems.

> "Flee fornication. Every sin that a man doeth is without the body; but he that commiteth fornication sinneth against his own body" (1 Cor.6:18).

8. A person who is sexually faithful gains self-control, the control over his body.

> "But the fruit of the Spirit is love, joy, peace, longsuffering, gentleness, goodness, faith, Meekness, temperance [self-control]: against such there is no law" (Gal.5:22-23).
> "But the fruit of the Spirit is love, joy, peace, patience, kindness, goodness, faithfulness, gentleness, <u>self-control</u>; against such things there is no law" (Gal.5:22-23, NASB).

9. A person who knows God and is sexually faithful protects his body as the temple of God's Spirit and glorifies God.

"What? know ye not that your body is the temple of the Holy Ghost which is in you, which ye have of God, and ye are not your own? For ye are bought with a price: therefore glorify God in your body, and in your spirit, which are God's" (1 Cor.6:19-20).

10. A person who is sexually faithful will win the war that is going on in his soul.

"Dearly beloved, I beseech you as strangers and pilgrims, abstain from fleshly lusts, which war against the soul" (1 Pt.2:11).

11. A person who is sexually faithful has integrity before God and man.

"I made a covenant with mine eyes; why then should I think upon a maid?" (Job 31:1).

12. A person who is sexually faithful enjoys a commitment that lasts for a lifetime.

"For the woman which hath an husband is bound by the law to her husband so long as he liveth; but if the husband be dead, she is loosed from the law of her husband" (Ro.7:2).
"And unto the married I command, yet not I, but the Lord, Let not the wife depart from her husband: But and if she depart, let her remain unmarried, or be reconciled to her husband: and let not the husband put away his wife" (1Cor.7:10-11).

13. A person who is sexually faithful will have an honorable and undefiled marriage.

"Marriage is honourable in all, and the bed undefiled: but whoremongers and adulterers God will judge" (Heb.13:4).

14. A person who is sexually faithful enjoys giving and receiving love.

"Let the husband render unto the wife due benevolence [his marital duty]: and likewise also the wife unto the husband [her marital duty]. The wife hath not power of her own body, but the husband: and likewise also the husband hath not power of his own body, but the wife" (1 Cor.7:3-4).

15. A person who knows God and is sexually faithful has a most glorious experience, that of walking in *Biblical* submission to the LORD.

"Wives, submit yourselves unto your own husbands, as unto the Lord" (Eph.5:22).
"Likewise, ye wives, be in subjection to your own husbands; that, if any obey not the word, they also may without the word be won by the conversation of the wives" (1 Pt.3:1).

16. A person who gives his life to Christ and is sexually faithful enjoys a most wonderful experience, that of sharing in the sacrificial love of Christ Himself.

"Husbands, love your wives, even as Christ also loved the church, and gave himself for it" (Eph.5:25).

17. A person who is sexually faithful helps to preserve the unity and spirit of the family.

"Therefore shall a man leave his father and his mother, and shall cleave unto his wife: and they shall be one flesh" (Gen.2:24).
"What therefore God hath joined together, let not man put asunder" (Mk.10:9).
"For this cause shall a man leave his father and mother, and shall be joined unto his wife, and they two shall be one flesh" (Eph.5:31).

18. A person who knows God and is sexually faithful will have a fruitful family.

"Thy wife shall be as a fruitful vine by the sides of thine house: thy children like olive plants round about thy table" (Ps.128:3).

19. A person who is sexually faithful will always be given a way of escape.

"There hath no temptation taken you but such as is common to man: but God is faithful, who will not suffer you to be tempted above that ye are able; but will with the temptation also make a way to escape, that ye may be able to bear it" (1 Cor.10:13).

DEEPER STUDY # 3

JESUS CHRIST AND HIS TEACHING
CONCERNING ADULTERY AND MAN'S FAMILY
"Thou shalt not commit adultery" (Ex.20:14).

THE TEACHING OF CHRIST	THE BELIEVER'S RESPONSE
1. Jesus Christ declared that God commanded man not to commit adultery. "He saith unto him, Which? Jesus said, Thou shalt do no murder, Thou <u>shalt not commit adultery</u>, Thou shalt not steal, Thou shalt not bear false witness" (Mt.19:18; cp. Mk.10:19; Lk.18:20).	⇒ Scripture is forceful: no person is to commit adultery nor any other immoral act. "Thou shalt not commit adultery" (Ex.20:14). "Flee fornication [all forms of sex outside marriage]" (1 Cor.6:18). "For this is the will of God, even your sanctification, that ye <u>should abstain from fornication</u>: That every one of you should know how to possess his vessel in sanctification and honour; Not in the lust of concupiscence, even as the Gentiles which know not God" (1 Th.4:3-5).
2. Jesus Christ declared that the real meaning of adultery and all sexual immorality… • is a deliberate look • is a desire, a lust, a passion • begins in the heart "Ye have heard that it was said by them of old time, Thou shalt not commit adultery: But I say unto you, That whosoever looketh on a woman to lust after her hath committed adultery with her already in his heart" (Mt.5:27-28).	1) The wrong use of sex is sin. In the right context, sex is a part of man's nature… • that nourishes and expresses an intimate love • that creates life 2) The purpose for this law is threefold: a) To assure respect and protection for families and neighbors. God will take vengeance upon those who destroy families through adultery. "Abstain from all appearance of evil" (1 Th.5:22). "For this is the will of God, even your sanctification, that ye should abstain from fornication: that every one of you should know how to possess his vessel in sanctification and honour; not in the lust of concupiscence, even as the Gentiles which know not God: that no man go beyond and defraud his brother in any matter: because that the <u>Lord is the avenger</u> of all such, as we also have forewarned you and testified" (1 Th.4:3-6). "And the man that committeth adultery with *another* man's wife, *even he* that committeth adultery with his neighbour's wife, the adulterer and the adulteress shall surely be put to death" (Lev.20:10). b) To protect a man from eternal judgment, the judgment of perishing in hell. "Know ye not that the unrighteous shall not inherit the kingdom of God? Be not deceived: neither fornicators, nor idolaters, nor <u>adulterers</u>, nor effeminate, nor abusers of themselves with mankind, Nor thieves, nor covetous, nor drunkards, nor revilers, nor extortioners, <u>shall inherit the kingdom of God</u>" (1 Cor.6:9-10). "For all the law is fulfilled in one word, *even* in this; Thou shalt love thy neighbour as thyself. But if ye bite and devour one another, take heed that ye be not consumed one of another. *This* I say then, Walk in the Spirit, and ye shall not fulfil the lust of the flesh. For the flesh lusteth against the Spirit, and the Spirit against the flesh: and these are contrary the one to the other: so that ye cannot do the things that ye would. But if ye be led of the Spirit, ye are not under the law. Now the works of the flesh are manifest, which are *these*; <u>Adultery</u>, fornication, uncleanness, lasciviousness, Idolatry, witchcraft, hatred, variance, emulations, wrath, strife, seditions, heresies, Envyings, murders, drunkenness, revellings, and such like: of the which I tell you before, as I have also told *you* in time past, that <u>they which do such things shall not inherit the kingdom of God</u>" (Gal.5:14-21). "But the fearful, and unbelieving, and the abominable, and murderers, and whoremongers, and sorcerers, and idolaters, and all liars, shall have their part in the lake which burneth with fire and brimstone: which is the second death" (Rev.21:8). "But whoso committeth adultery with a woman lacketh understanding: <u>he that doeth it destroyeth his own soul</u>" (Pr.6:32). "Marriage *is* honourable in all, and the bed undefiled: but whoremongers and <u>adulterers God will judge</u>" (Heb.13:4). c) To protect a man from sinning against his own body, from damaging his body emotionally, mentally, and physically.

THE TEACHING OF CHRIST	THE BELIEVER'S RESPONSE
	"Flee fornication [all forms of illicit sex]. Every sin that a man doeth is without the body; but he that committeth fornication sinneth against his own body" (1 Cor.6:18). "For this is the will of God, *even* your sanctification, that ye should abstain from fornication [all forms of illicit sex]: That every one of you should know how to possess his vessel [body] in sanctification and honour; Not in the lust of concupiscence, even as the Gentiles which know not God" (1 Th.4:3-5).
3. Jesus Christ declared that the source of adultery and sexual immorality is the human heart. "For out of the heart proceed evil thoughts, murders, <u>adulteries</u>, <u>fornications</u>, thefts, false witness, blasphemies" (Mt.15:19).	1) Adultery and all sexual immorality is an affliction that arises within the human heart. Men and women are powerless to resist this destructive sin unless they walk in the Spirit of God. And the spiritual walk must last for a lifetime, for sex is exalted throughout society as the summit of human experience; therefore, it is looked upon as acceptable even outside marriage. 2) The best choice a person can make when tempted to commit a sexual sin is... a) control the eyes: look away b) control the mind: focus on something else c) walk or even run away: flee from the temptation d) whisper a prayer for strength e) consider the consequences "Know ye not that the unrighteous shall not inherit the kingdom of God? Be not deceived: neither fornicators, nor idolaters, <u>nor adulterers</u>, nor effeminate, nor abusers of themselves with mankind, Nor thieves, nor covetous, nor drunkards, nor revilers, nor extortioners, <u>shall inherit the kingdom of God</u>" (1 Cor.6:9-10). "But I say unto you, That whosoever looketh on a woman to lust after her hath committed adultery with her already in his heart" (Mt.5: 28). "Keep thy heart with all diligence; for out of it *are* the issues of life" (Pr.4:23). "For as he thinketh in his heart, so *is* he: Eat and drink, saith he to thee; but his heart *is* not with thee" (Pr.23:7). "A good man out of the good treasure of his heart bringeth forth that which is good; and an evil man out of the evil treasure of his heart bringeth forth that which is evil: for of the abundance of the heart his mouth speaketh" (Lk.6:45).
4. Jesus Christ declared that the sin of divorce may cause others to fall into adultery and sexual immorality. "But I say unto you, That whosoever shall put away his wife, saving for the cause of fornication [sexual immorality], <u>causeth her to commit adultery</u>: and whosoever shall marry her that is divorced committeth adultery" (Mt.5:32). "And I say unto you, Whosoever shall put away his wife, except *it be* for fornication, and shall marry another, committeth adultery: and <u>whoso marrieth her which is put away doth commit adultery</u>" (Mt.19:9).	⇒ The great tragedy of fornication (sexual immorality) or adultery is that it breaks the union and attachment between husband and wife. The union and attachment and all that goes with it--faith, hope, love, trust, assurance, confidence, and strength--are broken. If the husband and wife are not believers, then the physical union and the mental union of the marriage are broken. If they are believers, then all three unions are broken: the physical, mental, *and spiritual*. "What therefore God hath joined together, let not man put asunder" (Mk.10:9). "And unto the married I command, yet not I, but the Lord, Let not the wife depart from her husband: But and if she depart, let her remain unmarried, or be reconciled to her husband: and let not the husband put away his wife" (1Cor.7:10-11). "Let thy fountain be blessed: and <u>rejoice with the wife of thy youth</u>" (Pr.5:18). "Husbands, love your wives, even as Christ also loved the church, and gave himself for it" (Eph.5:25). "Likewise, ye wives, *be* in subjection to your own husbands; that, if any obey not the word, they also may without the word be won by the conversation [behavior, conduct] of the wives" (1 Pt.3:1). "Know ye not that the unrighteous shall not inherit the kingdom of God? Be not deceived: neither fornicators, nor idolaters, nor <u>adulterers</u>, nor effeminate, nor abusers of themselves with mankind....<u>And such were some of you</u>: but ye are washed, but ye are sanctified, but ye are justified in the name of the Lord Jesus, and by the Spirit of our God" (1 Cor. 6:9, 11). "Marriage *is* honourable in all, and the bed undefiled: but whoremongers and adulterers God will judge" (Heb.13:4). "Dearly beloved, I beseech you as strangers and pilgrims, abstain from fleshly lusts, which war against the soul" (1 Pt.2:11). "Let thy fountain be blessed: and rejoice with the wife of thy youth" (Pr.5:18). "Let the husband render unto the wife due benevolence: and likewise also

THE TEACHING OF CHRIST	THE BELIEVER'S RESPONSE
	the wife unto the husband. The wife hath not power of her own body, but the husband: and likewise also the husband hath not power of his own body, but the wife" (1 Cor.7:3-4).
5. Jesus Christ declared that adultery and sexual immorality are not unforgivable sins and that people can turn away from a life of sin.	1) We must always confess and repent of our sins.

5. Jesus Christ declared that adultery and sexual immorality are not unforgivable sins and that people can turn away from a life of sin.

"And the scribes and Pharisees brought unto him a woman taken in adultery; and when they had set her in the midst, They say unto him, Master, this woman was taken in adultery, in the very act. Now Moses in the law commanded us, that such should be stoned: but what sayest thou? This they said, tempting him, that they might have to accuse him. But Jesus stooped down, and with *his* finger wrote on the ground, *as though he heard them not.* So when they continued asking him, he lifted up himself, and said unto them, He that is without sin among you, let him first cast a stone at her. And again he stooped down, and wrote on the ground. And they which heard *it*, being convicted by *their own* conscience, went out one by one, beginning at the eldest, *even* unto the last: and Jesus was left alone, and the woman standing in the midst. When Jesus had lifted up himself, and saw none but the woman, he said unto her, Woman, where are those thine accusers? hath no man condemned thee? She said, No man, Lord. And Jesus said unto her, Neither do I condemn thee: go, and sin no more" (Jn.8:3-11).

1) We must always confess and repent of our sins.

"Repent therefore of this thy wickedness, and pray God, if perhaps the thought of thine heart may be forgiven thee" (Acts 8:22).
"If we confess our sins, he is faithful and just to forgive us *our* sins, and to cleanse us from all unrighteousness" (1 Jn.1:9).
"Let the wicked forsake his way, and the unrighteous man his thoughts: and let him return unto the LORD, and he will have mercy upon him; and to our God, for he will abundantly pardon" (Is.55:7).
"But if the wicked will turn from all his sins that he hath committed, and keep all my statutes, and do that which is lawful and right, he shall surely live, he shall not die" (Ezk.18:21).

2) We must never lose hope that Jesus Christ will lift us out of sin. He will wash us, sanctify us, and justify us.

"For he hath made him to be sin for us, who knew no sin; that we might be made the righteousness of God in him" (2 Cor.5:21).
"Nay, ye do wrong, and defraud, and that *your* brethren. Know ye not that the unrighteous shall not inherit the kingdom of God? Be not deceived: neither fornicators, nor idolaters, nor <u>adulterers</u>, nor effeminate, nor abusers of themselves with mankind, Nor thieves, nor covetous, nor drunkards, nor revilers, nor extortioners, shall inherit the kingdom of God. And such were some of you: but ye are <u>washed</u>, but ye are <u>sanctified</u>, but ye are <u>justified</u> in the name of the Lord Jesus, and by the Spirit of our God" (1 Cor.6:8-11).
"Who his own self bare our sins in his own body on the tree, that we, being dead to sins, should live unto righteousness: by whose stripes ye were healed" (1 Pt.2:24).
"And he is the propitiation [sacrifice, covering] for our sins: and not for ours only, but also for *the sins of* the whole world" (1 Jn.2:2).
"Herein is love, not that we loved God, but that he loved us, and sent his Son *to be* the propitiation for our sins" (1 Jn.4:10).

3) We must not accept Satan's condemnation, for God forgives the repentant sinner, forgives us no matter how terrible our sin.

"*There is* therefore now no condemnation to them which are in Christ Jesus, who walk not after the flesh, but after the Spirit. For the law of the Spirit of life in Christ Jesus hath made me free from the law of sin and death" (Ro.8:1-2).
"He hath not dealt with us after our sins; nor rewarded us according to our iniquities. For as the heaven is high above the earth, *so* great is his mercy toward them that fear him. As far as the east is from the west, *so* far hath he removed our transgressions from us. Like as a father pitieth *his* children, *so* the LORD pitieth them that fear him. For he knoweth our frame; he remembereth that we *are* dust" (Ps.103:10-14).
"Who forgiveth all thine iniquities; who healeth all thy diseases" (Ps.103:3).

4) We must not abuse God's grace and fall back into a life-style of sin.

"What shall we say then? Shall we continue in sin, that grace may abound? God forbid. How shall we, that are dead to sin, live any longer therein?" (Ro.6:1-2).
"For if after they have escaped the pollutions of the world through the knowledge of the Lord and Saviour Jesus Christ, they are again entangled therein, and overcome, the latter end is worse with them than the beginning. For it had been better for them not to have known the way of righteousness, than, after they have known *it,* to turn from the holy commandment delivered unto them. But it is happened unto them according to the true proverb, The dog *is* turned to his own vomit again; and the sow that was washed to her wallowing in the mire" (2 Pt.2:20-22).

	I. The Ten Command-ments, The Laws Gov-erning Man's Duty To Others (Part 4): Com-mandment Eight Con-cerns Man's Property--Never Steal, Ex.20:15
Com. 8 concerns *man's property*	15 Thou shalt not steal.

DIVISION VII

THE LAW AND THE PROMISES OF GOD (THE MOSAIC COVENANT) (PART 2): THE TEN COMMANDMENTS--NECESSARY LAWS TO GOVERN MAN AND SOCIETY, EX.20:1-26

I. The Ten Commandments, The Laws Governing Man's Duty To Others (Part 4): Com-mandment Eight Concerns Man's Property--Never Steal, Ex.20:15

(20:15) **Introduction--Commandments, The Ten--Stealing**: think for a moment. What is *the crime* most often committed within your community? The nation? Around the world? Probably stealing. So many people steal that stealing has become a very commonplace crime of society. If the thief does not assault or kill the victim, he is simply called a *common thief.* Thievery, robbery, and swindling have become epidemic, contributing to the lawlessness within society. And stealing is such a terrible epidemic that it threatens the very foundation of society itself. Just think of...

- government leaders who steal and misuse funds
- employees who steal from their employer
- employers who steal through unfair prices and wages
- dishonest athletes and famous people who steal
- acquaintances and neighbors who steal and are dishonest
- people who steal by living extravagant and indulgent lifestyles, hoarding and banking when so many are in such desperate need throughout the world
- people who steal by taking so much of the earth's wealth and resources

Stealing shows a disrespect for property and for human life. Stealing leads to more and more lawlessness, sometimes even assault and murder. Stealing always creates some havoc, and it can cause devastation. Stealing can bankrupt families, companies, communities, and even nations. Stealing always causes loss, loss for both the victim and the thief. The victim, of course, loses whatever object (physical or otherwise) is stolen; but in addition, the loss can be very painful and some-times irreplaceable. The thief, though frequently undetected by men, always loses his reputation, integrity, and character before God; and eventually, unless he repents and turns from his sin, he loses his soul.

This is the subject of this important commandment: *Commandment Eight Concerns Man's Property--Never Steal,* 20:15.
1. Who is to obey this commandment? How long was this commandment to be in force (v.15)?
2. What is forbidden by this commandment (v.15)?
3. What is the decision required by this commandment (v.15)?

1 (20:15) **Commandments, The Ten--Stealing--Responsibility**: Who is to obey this commandment? How long was this commandment to be in force? Was it only for the people of ancient times or is it for us today as well? Stealing has been a problem for society as long as man has been on the earth, a serious problem. God gave this commandment because He cares for man, so much so that He wants to protect everything that concerns man, both his life and his property. Frankly, it would be foolish to suggest that God was concerned for the people and property of the ancient world but is un-concerned with the people and property of our day.

Note the verse: "You shall not steal." This commandment is directed to you and to every person who will ever live. It was wrong to steal in the ancient world, a terrible violation against man and God, and it is wrong to steal today. This commandment is in force today as much as it was in force for Israel:

> "**Thou shalt not steal**" (**Ex.20:15**).
> "**Let him that stole steal no more**" (**Eph.4:28**).

2 (20:15) **Commandments, The Ten--Property--Stealing--Theft**: What is forbidden by this commandment, "You shall not steal"? How is this commandment violated, broken?
1. **Stealing** (ganab) means to take and keep something that belongs to another person. William Barclay says:

> "[Stealing] *is a 'natural' sin. It is human nature to want what we have not got; and the desire may turn to action; and, when it does, a man may steal. We do not need to argue about the rightness of this commandment. Everyone agrees that stealing is wrong.*"[1]

---

[1] William Barclay. *The Old & The New Law,* p.37.

God has made man a working being, a being who must work, produce, achieve, accomplish, and possess. The desire to move ahead and progress is planted within man by God. This is the reason we desire things that we do not have. The desire is normal and natural; it is God-given. But the legitimate way to fulfill that desire is to work for what we want and can achieve in life. The illegitimate way to fulfill the desire is to steal. When we act out our desire and take something that does not belong to us--take it either secretly or by force--it is stealing.

2. Note that stealing is a *heart problem*: the cause, the source of stealing, is found in the human heart. Stealing begins with a desire, a passion, a lust, an urge, a coveting within man. When the desire is planted--when it conceives and it is carried out--the person steals. This is exactly what God says:

> "But every man is tempted, when he is drawn away of his own lust, and enticed. Then when lust hath conceived, it bringeth forth sin: and sin, when it is finished, bringeth forth death" (Jas.1:14-15).

Thought 1. Note an excellent example of coveting--of desiring and lusting--in Scripture.

> "When I saw among the spoils a goodly Babylonish garment, and two hundred shekels of silver, and a wedge of gold of fifty shekels weight, then I coveted them, and took them; and, behold, they are hid in the earth in the midst of my tent, and the silver under it" (Josh.7:21).

Thought 2. Arthur W. Pink[2] points out the following:
1) Stealing was the first sin committed by the human race: Eve took of the forbidden fruit.

> "And when the woman saw that the tree was good for food, and that it was pleasant to the eyes, and a tree to be desired to make one wise, she took of the fruit thereof, and did eat, and gave also unto her husband with her; and he did eat" (Gen.3:6).

2) Stealing was the first recorded sin committed by Israel after entering Canaan: Achan stole the spoils of war.

> "When I saw among the spoils a goodly Babylonish garment, and two hundred shekels of silver, and a wedge of gold of fifty shekels weight, then I coveted them, and took them; and, behold, they are hid in the earth in the midst of my tent, and the silver under it" (Josh.7:21).

3) Stealing was the first sin to defile the early church: Ananias and Sapphira kept back some of the money from the sale of their property, money that was to be given to the church.

> "But a certain man named Ananias, with Sapphira his wife, sold a possession, And kept back part of the price, his wife also being privy to it, and brought a certain part, and laid it at the apostles' feet. But Peter said, Ananias, why hath Satan filled thine heart to lie to the Holy Ghost, and to keep back part of the price of the land?" (Acts 5:1-3).

3. God's purpose for commanding people not to steal can be simply stated: it is to protect a person's property and his right to own property, to preserve peace among neighbors and within society. Stealing causes loss--sometimes terrible loss--to the victim. And stealing always leads to hard feelings, broken relationships, and sometimes revenge. This commandment protects a person's right...
- to feed, house, clothe, and provide for himself and his family
- to own property
- to reap and keep the property and rewards of his labor
- to secure enough goods and money to help meet the desperate needs of the poor, the suffering, and the lost of this world

> "Let him that stole steal no more: but rather let him labour, working with his hands the thing which is good, that he may have to give to him that needeth" (Eph.4:28).
> "For even when we were with you, this we commanded you, that if any would not work, neither should he eat. For we hear that there are some which walk among you disorderly, working not at all, but are busybodies. Now them that are such we command and exhort by our Lord Jesus Christ, that with quietness they work, and eat their own bread" (2 Th.3:10-12).

4. Now, how is this commandment broken, violated? Stealing is so common and so costly to society that the way people go about stealing needs to be studied. Moreover, stealing is not only a sin against society and the people stolen from, stealing is a sin against God. Stealing condemns a person to death, eternal death--unless the person repents and turns to God. For this reason, the various forms of stealing need to be looked at in some detail. A person breaks God's commandment, a person steals...
- by robbing a person, store, company, organization or bank
- by shoplifting
- by loafing on the job
- by not paying bills
- by keeping something borrowed
- by failing to pay debts
- by not paying due taxes
- by false or deceptive advertising
- by keeping an overpayment or excessive refund check, or over-shipment of goods
- by overcharging or price-gouging: charging unfair prices
- by not paying fair and just wages
- by not giving a full day's work on the job
- by unjustly extending business trips at company expense
- by manipulating information or stocks for personal gain
- by abusing sick days
- by arriving at work late or leaving work early without permission

[2] Arthur W. Pink. *The Ten Commandments*, p.54.

- by stealing the reputation and character of another through lies, gossip, or rumor
- by taking away a person's right to justice (Is.10:1-3)

- by taking things from one's employer
- by making unauthorized phone calls
- by padding expense reports

- by stealing and enslaving people for work and profit
- by breaking the rules or cheating to win something, a game or a prize

All acts of stealing are wrong, but there is one form of stealing that is most serious and damning, that of robbing God:
⇒ A person robs God by failing to pay his tithes and offerings to God.

"Even from the days of your fathers ye are gone away from mine ordinances, and have not kept them. Return unto me, and I will return unto you, saith the LORD of hosts. But ye said, Wherein shall we return? Will a man rob God? Yet ye have robbed me. But ye say, Wherein have we robbed thee? In tithes and offerings" (Mal.3:7-8).

⇒ A person robs God by living a hypocritical, inconsistent life. When a person professes to believe and follow God, then fails to follow through, he robs God and other men of a *godly testimony*.

"What? know ye not that your body is the temple of the Holy Ghost which is in you, which ye have of God, and ye are not your own? For ye are bought with a price: therefore glorify God in your body, and in your spirit, which are God's" (1 Cor.6:19-20).

⇒ A person robs God by living for self and the world, by choosing not to live for God. God is the great Creator of man; therefore, man owes his life--all he is and has--to God. When a person chooses to live like he wants, he steals his life from God.

"I beseech you therefore, brethren, by the mercies of God, that ye present your bodies a living sacrifice, holy, acceptable unto God, which is your reasonable service. And be not conformed to this world: but be ye transformed by the renewing of your mind, that ye may prove what is that good, and acceptable, and perfect, will of God" (Ro.12:1-2).
"Love not the world, neither the things that are in the world. If any man love the world, the love of the Father is not in him. For all that is in the world, the lust of the flesh, and the lust of the eyes, and the pride of life, is not of the Father, but is of the world" (1 Jn.2:15-16).

Thought 1. This commandment against stealing is broken when property is taken, no matter how little and insignificant the item may be. F.B. Huey again has an excellent comment on the breaking of this commandment.

"The spirit of this commandment can be broken in ways other than taking the property of another violently or covertly. The employee who takes paper clips, postage stamps, stationery, etc., from his employer for personal use, the taxpayer who falsifies his tax return, the friend who borrows money or even a cup of sugar without intent of returning it, the shopkeeper who uses dishonest scales or engages in any kind of fraudulent business practice, the student who takes credit for work that was done by someone else, the employee who loafs on the job but accepts full wages, or the nation that takes the land of another by war--all violate this commandment."[3]

Maxie Dunnam also has an excellent application on this commandment:

"One of the tragedies of our day is how the justice system treats crimes of stealing. Poor people, with no money to hire legal defense, waste away in prisons for stealing a car or a television, while officers of huge corporate organizations preside in posh board rooms, though it is proven they have manipulated the stock market. Television gives us almost daily reports of defense contract 'cost overrides' that steal millions of tax dollars....Ours is a society 'on the take,' and stealing is one of our most blatant sins....
"Apart from the obvious ways of seeing this commandment broken, we should think of the more subtle ways we break it.
- by not giving our employers a full day for the pay we receive
- by stealing the good name of another with malicious gossip
- by remaining silent, thus stealing from another the word that might preserve reputation and/or undergird character
- by failing to give to others the support, praise, and credit they're due."[4]

3 (20:15) **Commandments, The Ten--Stealing--Decision**: What is the decision demanded by this commandment?
1. Scripture is very forceful in telling us exactly what not to do:
   a. We must never steal, not even once.

"Thou shalt not steal" (Ex.20:15).

---
[3] F.B. Huey, Jr. *Exodus*, p.91.
[4] Maxie Dunnam, *Mastering the Old Testament, Volume 2: Exodus*, p.265-266.

b. We must never withhold tithes and offerings from God.

> **"Will a man rob God? Yet ye have robbed me. But ye say, Wherein have we robbed thee? In tithes and offerings. Ye are cursed with a curse: for ye have robbed me, even this whole nation. Bring ye all the tithes into the storehouse, that there may be meat in mine house, and prove me now herewith, saith the LORD of hosts, if I will not open you the windows of heaven, and pour you out a blessing, that there shall not be room enough to receive it" (Mal.3:8-10).**

c. We must never cheat our brother in anything.

> **"That no man go beyond and defraud his brother in any matter: because that the Lord is the avenger of all such, as we also have forewarned you and testified" (1 Th.4:6).**

d. We must never steal people: the enslavement of people takes away a person's right to his own life.

> **"And he that stealeth a man, and selleth him, or if he be found in his hand, he shall surely be put to death" (Ex.21:16).**

2. Scripture is also very forceful in telling us exactly <u>what to do</u>:
   a. We must practice the golden rule: be honest, fair, and just with all people; treat others as we would want to be treated.

   > **"Recompense to no man evil for evil. Provide things honest in the sight of all men" (Ro.12:17).**
   > **"Therefore all things whatsoever ye would that men should do to you, do ye even so to them: for this is the law and the prophets" (Mt.7:12).**

   b. We must love our neighbor as ourselves.

   > **"Master, which is the great commandment in the law? Jesus said unto him, Thou shalt love the Lord thy God with all thy heart, and with all thy soul, and with all thy mind. This is the first and great commandment. And the second [is] like unto it, Thou shalt love thy neighbour as thyself" (Mt.22:36-39).**

   c. We must be temperate, controlled in all things.

   > **"And every man that striveth for the mastery is temperate in all things. Now they do it to obtain a corruptible crown; but we an incorruptible" (1 Cor.9:25).**

   d. We must learn to be content with what we have; learn that we brought nothing into this world and we can carry nothing out.

   > **"For we brought nothing into this world, and it is certain we can carry nothing out. And having food and raiment let us be therewith content" (1 Tim.6:7-8).**
   > **"Let your conversation [behavior, conduct, life] be without covetousness; and be content with such things as ye have: for he hath said, I will never leave thee, nor forsake thee" (Heb.13:5).**

   e. We must channel our desires toward eternal, heavenly treasures, not toward the temporary things of the earth.

   > **"Set your affection on things above, not on things on the earth" (Col.3:2).**

   f. We must quit stealing and go to work: we must even work long and hard in order to earn more so that we can earn enough to help others.

   > **"Let him that stole steal no more: but rather let him labour, working with his hands the thing which is good, that he may have to give to him that needeth" (Eph.4:28).**

   g. We must realize this astounding truth: what we measure to others will be measured to us.

   > **"Give, and it shall be given unto you; good measure, pressed down, and shaken together, and running over, shall men give into your bosom. For with the same measure that ye mete withal it shall be measured to you again" (Lk.6:38).**

   h. We must learn the phenomenal, unbelievable promise of God: that we are not to get things by stealing, but by prayer and hard work.

   > **"Let him that stole steal no more: but rather let him labour, working with his hands the thing which is good, that he may have to give to him that needeth" (Eph.4:28).**
   > **"Ye have not, because ye ask not" (Jas.4:2).**

160

i. We must learn to work hard and trust God for the necessities of life. Stealing shows that we fail to trust God and His care for us.

"But seek ye first the kingdom of God, and his righteousness; and all these things [clothing, food, shelter] shall be added unto you" (Mt.6:33).

"But my God shall supply all your need according to his riches in glory by Christ Jesus" (Ph.4:19).

"For we hear that there are some which walk among you disorderly, working not at all, but are busybodies. Now them that are such we command and exhort by our Lord Jesus Christ, that with quietness they work, and eat their own bread" (2 Th.3:11-12).

j. We must realize that stealing is a terrible sin: the thief shall face the terrifying judgment and condemnation of God.

"Not every one that saith unto me, Lord, Lord, shall enter into the kingdom of heaven; but he that doeth the will of my Father which is in heaven. Many will say to me in that day, Lord, Lord, have we not prophesied in thy name? and in thy name have cast out devils? and in thy name done many wonderful works? And then will I profess unto them, I never knew you: depart from me, ye that work iniquity" (Mt.7:21-23).

"And as it is appointed unto men once to die, but after this the judgment" (Heb.9:27).

"For what shall it profit a man, if he shall gain the whole world, and lose his own soul? Or what shall a man give in exchange for his soul?" (Mk.8:36-37).

"And I will say to my soul, Soul, thou hast much goods laid up for many years; take thine ease, eat, drink, [and] be merry. But God said unto him, [Thou] fool, this night thy soul shall be required of thee: then whose shall those things be, which thou hast provided? So [is] he that layeth up treasure for himself, and is not rich toward God" (Lk.12:19-21).

"That no man go beyond and defraud his brother in any matter: because that the Lord is the avenger of all such, as we also have forewarned you and testified" (1 Th.4:6).

"Woe unto them that decree unrighteous decrees, and that write grievousness which they have prescribed; To turn aside the needy from judgment, and to take away the right from the poor of my people, that widows may be their prey, and that they may rob the fatherless! And what will ye do in the day of visitation, and in the desolation which shall come from far? to whom will ye flee for help? and where will ye leave your glory?" (Is.10:1-3).

k. We must realize that stealing is a terrible sin. Stealing causes loss for the victim, perhaps something frivolous (jewelry, a television, a stereo, etc.) or perhaps something he needs (money, food, a job, or even his life) all because the thief acted on a desire of the heart and took what did not belong to him. The commandment against stealing is one of the ten basic commandments of God:

"Thou shalt not steal" (Ex.20:15).

THE BIBLICAL CONSEQUENCES OF STEALING

DEEPER STUDY #1
(20:15) **Commandments, The Ten--Obedience--Judgment--Steal--Rob:** What are the consequences of breaking this commandment--not to steal, not to rob another person? We live in a world where people have little respect for the property of others. Even when devastating tragedies strike (such as hurricanes), people race each other to see how much they can steal before the authorities restore order. God hates the sin of stealing because of the direct association with the greatest thief of all, Satan himself. The Scriptures expose Satan for what he is--a thief.

"The thief [Satan] cometh not, but for to steal, and to kill, and to destroy: I am come that they might have life, and that they might have *it* more abundantly" (Jn.10:10).

God has spared no judgment for the thief of all thieves. Likewise, God will give every thief his just due. Anyone who breaks this holy commandment will suffer serious consequences. A thief would do well to heed this strong warning, a warning that will punish any violator who would dare break this commandment.

1. The person who steals, and is committed to a life of crime, will not inherit the kingdom of God.

"Know ye not that the unrighteous shall not inherit the kingdom of God? Be not deceived: neither fornicators, nor idolaters, nor adulterers, nor effeminate, nor abusers of themselves with mankind, Nor thieves, nor covetous, nor drunkards, nor revilers, nor extortioners, shall inherit the kingdom of God" (1 Cor.6:9-10).

2. The person [Adam and Eve] who stole from God in the garden of Eden died.

> "And the LORD God commanded the man, saying, Of every tree of the garden thou mayest freely eat: But of the tree of the knowledge of good and evil, thou shalt not eat of it: for in the day that thou eatest thereof thou shalt surely die" (Gen.2:16-17).

3. The person who steals defiles himself, makes himself unclean.

> "For out of the heart proceed evil thoughts, murders, adulteries, fornications, thefts, false witness, blasphemies: These are *the things* which defile a man" (Mt.15:19-20).

4. The person who steals angers God and provokes His wrath.

> "But the children of Israel committed a trespass in the accursed thing: for Achan, the son of Carmi, the son of Zabdi, the son of Zerah, of the tribe of Judah, took of the accursed thing: and the anger of the LORD was kindled against the children of Israel" (Josh.7:1).
> "A false balance *is* abomination to the LORD: but a just weight *is* his delight" (Pr.11:1).
> "Divers [differing] weights, *and* divers [differing] measures, both of them *are* alike abomination to the LORD" (Pr.20:10).
> "Woe unto him that buildeth his house by unrighteousness, and his chambers by wrong; *that* useth his neighbour's service without wages, and giveth him not for his work" (Jer.22:13).

5. The person who steals places his life in mortal danger.

> "The getting of treasures by a lying tongue *is* a vanity tossed to and fro of them that seek death" (Pr.21:6).

6. The person who steals shows that he has forgotten God.

> "In thee have they taken gifts to shed blood; thou hast taken usury and increase, and thou hast greedily gained of thy neighbours by extortion, and hast forgotten me, saith the Lord GOD" (Ezk.22:12).

7. The person who steals follows in the steps of God's adversary, Satan himself.

> "The thief [Satan] cometh not, but for to steal, and to kill, and to destroy: I am come that they might have life, and that they might have *it* more abundantly" (Jn.10:10).

8. The person who steals causes heartache and sometimes painful suffering for others.

> "And it came to pass, when David and his men were come to Ziklag on the third day, that the Amalekites had invaded the south, and Ziklag, and smitten Ziklag, and burned it with fire; And had taken the women captives, that *were* therein: they slew not any, either great or small, but carried *them* away, and went on their way. So David and his men came to the city, and, behold, it was burned with fire; and their wives, and their sons, and their daughters, were taken captives. Then David and the people that *were* with him lifted up their voice and wept, until they had no more power to weep" (1 Sam.30:1-4).

9. The person who steals causes economic hardship for the victim.

> "Thou shalt not defraud thy neighbour, neither rob *him*: the wages of him that is hired shall not abide with thee all night until the morning" (Lev.19:13).

10. The person who steals the wife or husband of another causes families to be torn apart.

> "A foolish woman *is* clamorous: *she is* simple, and knoweth nothing. For she sitteth at the door of her house, on a seat in the high places of the city, To call passengers who go right on their ways: Whoso *is* simple, let him turn in hither: and *as for* him that wanteth understanding, she saith to him, Stolen waters are sweet, and bread *eaten* in secret is pleasant. But he knoweth not that the dead *are* there; *and that* her guests *are* in the depths of hell" (Pr.9:13-18).

11. The person who steals will eventually lose everything and prove that he is a fool.

> "As the partridge sitteth *on eggs,* and hatcheth *them* not; *so* he that getteth riches, and not by right, shall leave them in the midst of his days, and at his end shall be a fool." (Jer.17:11).

12. The person who steals is to make restitution. He is held accountable by God to make restitution.

> "If a man shall steal an ox, or a sheep, and kill it, or sell it; he shall restore five oxen for an ox, and four sheep for a sheep" (Ex.22:1).
> "If a man shall deliver unto his neighbour money or stuff to keep, and it be stolen out of the man's house; if the thief be found, let him pay double" (Ex.22:7).
> "And if it be stolen from him, he shall make restitution unto the owner thereof" (Ex.22:12).

13. The person who steals from the poor will become poor himself.

> "He that oppresseth the poor to increase his *riches, and* he that giveth to the rich, *shall* surely *come* to want" (Pr.22:16).

14. The person who steals tithes and offerings--who does not give his tithes and offerings to God--robs God.

> "Will a man rob God? Yet ye have robbed me. But ye say, Wherein have we robbed thee? In tithes and offerings" (Mal.3:8).

THE BIBLICAL BENEFITS OF KEEPING THIS COMMANDMENT: DO NOT STEAL

DEEPER STUDY #2

(20:15) <u>Commandments, The Ten--Benefits of Keeping--Obedience</u>: What would the world be like if everyone kept this commandment? If there was no theft upon earth? The benefits and blessings of honesty would be unlimited.

1. A person who is honest and lives for God will have the constant presence and care of God.

> "Let your conversation [behavior, conduct] be without covetousness; and be content with such things as ye have: for he hath said, I will never leave thee, nor forsake thee" (Heb.13:5).

2. A person who follows God and is honest will escape many problems and sorrows.

> "But they that will be rich fall into temptation and a snare, and into many foolish and hurtful lusts, which drown men in destruction and perdition. For the love of money is the root of all evil: which while some coveted after, they have erred from the faith, and pierced themselves through with many sorrows" (1 Tim.6:9-10).

3. A person who belongs to the LORD and is honest will walk in righteousness and live in security.

> "He that walketh uprightly walketh surely: but he that perverteth his ways [steals] shall be known" (Pr.10:9).

4. A person who follows God and is honest will learn to be content.

> "Not that I speak in respect of want: for <u>I have learned</u>, in whatsoever state I am, therewith <u>to be content</u>. I know both how to be abased, and I know how to abound: every where and in all things I am instructed both to be full and to be hungry, both to abound and to suffer need" (Ph.4:11-12).
> "But godliness with contentment is great gain. For we brought nothing into this world, and it is certain we can carry nothing out. And having food and raiment let us be therewith content" (1 Tim.6:6-8).

5. A person who is honest and follows the LORD will be freed from vanity and deceit.

> "Two things have I required of thee; deny me them not before I die: Remove far from me vanity and lies: give me neither poverty nor riches; feed me with food convenient for me: Lest I be full, and deny thee, and say, Who is the LORD? or lest I be poor, and <u>steal</u>, and take the name of my God in vain" (Pr.30:7-9).

6. A person who is honest and fears the LORD will be better off than a person with great treasure.

> "Better is little with the fear of the LORD than great treasure and trouble therewith" (Pr.15:16).

7. A person who is honest will have labor that is profitable.

> "Wealth gotten by vanity [dishonest money] shall be diminished: but he that gathereth by labour shall increase" (Pr.13:11).

8. A person who is honest and knows the LORD labors with his own hands, helping those in need.

> "Let him that stole steal no more: but rather let him labour, working with *his* hands the thing which is good, that he may have to give to him that needeth" (Eph.4:28).

9. A person who is honest before the LORD shares in the glorious salvation of God: he does not have to steal some other way into God's presence, some other door into eternal life.

> "Verily, verily, I say unto you, He that entereth not by the door into the sheepfold, but climbeth up some other way, the same is a thief and a robber" (Jn.10:1).

10. A person who lives a righteous life is honest and will be delivered from death.

> "Treasures of wickedness profit nothing: but righteousness delivereth from death" (Pr.10:2).
> "But they that will be rich fall into temptation and a snare, and into many foolish and hurtful lusts, which drown men in destruction and perdition....But thou, O man of God, flee these things; and follow after righteousness, godliness, faith, love, patience, meekness. Fight the good fight of faith, lay hold on eternal life, whereunto thou art also called, and hast professed a good profession before many witnesses" (1 Tim.6:9, 11-12).

11. A person who loves God is honest and earns eternal treasures that are safely stored in heaven.

> "Lay not up for yourselves treasures upon earth, where moth and rust doth corrupt, and where thieves break through and steal: But lay up for yourselves treasures in heaven, where neither moth nor rust doth corrupt, and where thieves do not break through nor steal" (Mt.6:19-20).

13. A person who belongs to the LORD and is honest bears a strong witness for the Lord.

> "Not purloining [stealing], but showing all good fidelity; that they may adorn the doctrine of God our Saviour in all things" (Tit.2:10).

DEEPER STUDY # 3

JESUS CHRIST AND HIS TEACHING CONCERNING STEALING
"Thou shalt not steal" (Ex.20:15).

THE TEACHING OF CHRIST	THE BELIEVER'S RESPONSE
1. Jesus Christ declared that God commanded man not to steal. "He saith unto him, Which? Jesus said, Thou shalt do no murder, Thou shalt not commit adultery, Thou **shalt not steal**, Thou shalt not bear false witness" (Mt.19:18; cp. Mk.10:19; Lk.18:20).	1) Scripture is clear: stealing is wrong. "Thou shalt not steal" (Ex.20:15). "Thou shalt not defraud thy neighbour, neither rob him" (Lev.19:13). "Let him that stole steal no more" (Eph.4:28). 2) A person who steals and never repents by turning to God will not inherit the kingdom of God. "Know ye not that the unrighteous shall not inherit the kingdom of God? Be not deceived: neither fornicators, nor idolaters, nor adulterers, nor effeminate, nor abusers of themselves with mankind, Nor **thieves**, nor covetous, nor drunkards, nor revilers, nor extortioners, **shall inherit the kingdom of God**" (1 Cor.6:9-10).
2. Jesus Christ declared that Satan is a thief and the source behind all stealing. "The thief [Satan] cometh not, but for to steal, and to kill, and to destroy..." (Jn.10:10).	1) Satan is a subtle destroyer of God's people. Satan is the one who tempts men to steal what is not theirs. "Now the serpent was more subtil than any beast of the field which the LORD God had made. And he said unto the woman, Yea, hath God said, Ye shall not eat of every tree of the garden? And the woman said unto the serpent, We may eat of the fruit of the trees of the garden: But of the fruit of the tree which *is* in the midst of the garden, God hath said, Ye shall not eat of it, neither shall ye touch it, lest ye die. And the serpent said unto the woman, Ye shall not surely die: For God doth know that in the day ye eat thereof, then your eyes shall be opened, and ye shall be as gods, knowing good and evil. And when the woman saw that the tree *was* good for food, and that it *was* pleasant to the eyes, and a tree to be desired to make *one* wise, she took of the fruit thereof, and did eat, and gave also unto her husband with her; and he did eat" (Gen.3:1-6).

THE TEACHING OF CHRIST	THE BELIEVER'S RESPONSE
	2) Satan is crafty. He fills the hearts of careless and unprotected men with an unquenchable desire for more and more. "But the children of Israel committed a trespass in the accursed thing: for Achan, the son of Carmi, the son of Zabdi, the son of Zerah, of the tribe of Judah, took of the accursed thing: and the anger of the LORD was kindled against the children of Israel" (Josh.7:1). "And it came to pass, as we went to prayer, a certain damsel possessed with a spirit of divination met us, which brought her masters much gain by soothsaying: The same followed Paul and us, and cried, saying, These men are the servants of the most high God, which show unto us the way of salvation. And this did she many days. But Paul, being grieved, turned and said to the spirit, I command thee in the name of Jesus Christ to come out of her. And he came out the same hour. And when her masters saw that the hope of their gains was gone, they caught Paul and Silas, and drew them into the marketplace unto the rulers" (Acts 16:16-19). "But none of these things move me, neither count I my life dear unto myself, so that I might finish my course with joy, and the ministry, which I have received of the Lord Jesus, to testify the gospel of the grace of God. And now, behold, I know that ye all, among whom I have gone preaching the kingdom of God, shall see my face no more. Wherefore I take you to record this day, that I am pure from the blood of all men. For I have not shunned to declare unto you all the counsel of God" (Acts 20:24-27). "For Demas hath forsaken me, having loved this present world, and is departed unto Thessalonica; Crescens to Galatia, Titus unto Dalmatia" (2 Tim.4:10).

3. Jesus Christ declared that there is no security in storing the world's treasures because thieves steal them or else they waste away or decrease in value.
 	
"Lay not up for yourselves treasures upon earth, where moth and rust doth corrupt, and where thieves break through and steal: But lay up for yourselves treasures in heaven, where neither moth nor rust doth corrupt, and where thieves do not break through nor steal" (Mt.6:19-20).
	1) We are to place no confidence in earthly riches: they will not last.
	2) We are to collect heavenly riches because…
	  • they will give meaning and purpose to life
	  • they will escape corruption
	  • they cannot be stolen by anyone
	3) We are to have a pure heart in order to…
	  • grasp the true treasure, the treasure in heaven
	  • protect ourselves from the consequences of greed and covetousness
	4) We are to love Christ with an undivided and uncompromising devotion.
	
	"For what is a man profited, if he shall gain the whole world, and lose his own soul? or what shall a man give in exchange for his soul?" (Mt.16:26).
	"For the love of money is the root of all evil: which while some coveted after, they have erred from the faith, and pierced themselves through with many sorrows" (1 Tim.6:10).
	"Better is little with the fear of the LORD than great treasure and trouble therewith" (Pr.15:16).
	"But seek ye first the kingdom of God, and his righteousness; and all these things shall be added unto you. Take therefore no thought for the morrow: for the morrow shall take thought for the things of itself. Sufficient unto the day is the evil thereof" (Mt.6:33-34).

4. Jesus Christ declared that man's craving for material possessions (the cares of this life and the lure of wealth) will leave him with an empty life, an unfruitful life.
 	
"And some [seed] fell among thorns; and the thorns sprung up, and choked them….He also that received seed among the thorns is he that heareth the word; and the care of this world, and the deceitfulness of riches, choke the word, and he becometh unfruitful" (Mt.13:7, 22).
	1) We must not be deceived and ensnared by the cares of the world. Note their effect on a person:
	  a) They prick and prick away at the Word.
	  b) They entangle a person in the world and the things of the world (2 Tim.2:3-4).
	  c) They irritate, aggravate, trouble, and hinder a person from pursuing his task.
	  d) They keep a person's mind on the cares of the world, not on God and the things of the Word or Spirit (Ro.8:5-8; 2 Cor.10:3-5).
	2) We must not crave wealth or we will become deceived…
	  • by becoming self-confident and self-dependent
	  • by becoming overly comfortable, extravagant, and indulgent
	  • by becoming consumed with thoughts of keeping what we have and passionately finding more
	  • by becoming secure in a false idea of what it means to be blessed by God
	
	"For we brought nothing into *this* world, *and it is* certain we can carry nothing out" (1 Tim.6:7).
	"But they that will be rich fall into temptation and a snare, and *into* many

THE TEACHING OF CHRIST	THE BELIEVER'S RESPONSE
	foolish and hurtful lusts, which drown men in destruction and perdition" (1 Tim.6:9). "And the cares of this world, and the deceitfulness of riches, and the lusts of other things entering in, choke the word, and it becometh unfruitful" (Mk.4:19). "Then said Jesus unto his disciples, Verily I say unto you, That a rich man shall hardly enter into the kingdom of heaven. And Jesus looked round about, and saith unto his disciples, How hardly shall they that have riches enter into the kingdom of God! And the disciples were astonished at his words. But Jesus answereth again, and saith unto them, Children, how hard is it for them that trust in riches to enter into the kingdom of God! It is easier for a camel to go through the eye of a needle, than for a rich man to enter into the kingdom of God" (Mk.10:23-2).5 "And again I say unto you, It is easier for a camel to go through the eye of a needle, than for a rich man to enter into the kingdom of God" (Mt.19:23-24). "Your gold and silver is cankered; and the rust of them shall be a witness against you, and shall eat your flesh as it were fire. Ye have heaped treasure together for the last days" (Jas.5:3). "Wilt thou set thine eyes upon that which is not? for *riches* certainly make themselves wings; they fly away as an eagle toward heaven" (Pr.23:5). "As the partridge sitteth *on eggs,* and hatcheth *them* not; *so* he that getteth riches, and not by right, shall leave them in the midst of his days, and at his end shall be a fool" (Jer.17:11).
5. Jesus Christ declared: ⇒ if a man cheats a little, he will not be honest with greater responsibilities. ⇒ if a man is not faithful with the money of other people, he cannot be trusted with his own money. ⇒ a man cannot serve God and money--he must chose whom he will serve. ⇒ if a man cannot be trusted with worldly wealth, he cannot be trusted with the true riches of heaven. ⇒ unless a man is faithful in small matters he will not be faithful in large ones. "He that is faithful in that which is least is faithful also in much: and he that is unjust in the least is unjust also in much. If therefore ye have not been faithful in the unrighteous mammon, who will commit to your trust the true *riches?* And if ye have not been faithful in that which is another man's, who shall give you that which is your own? No servant can serve two masters: for either he will hate the one, and love the other; or else he will hold to the one, and despise the other. Ye cannot serve God and mammon" (Lk.16:10-13).	1) We must be found faithful in handling possessions, for our faithfulness determines what we will be trusted with eternally. 2) Money and possessions are the least trust given to a person. They are nothing compared to spiritual riches, to true heavenly riches. We must desire true and lasting treasure more than anything else. 3) A person serves one of two masters, either God or the things and riches of the world. He gives himself either to one or the other: a) He focuses himself upon the things and riches of the world or upon God. b) He turns himself over to the things and riches of the world or to God. c) He thinks primarily upon the things of the world or upon God. d) He gives his time, energy, and effort to the things of the world or to God. e) He allows his worldly pursuits to control him, or Christ to control his pursuits. "And if it seem evil unto you to serve the LORD, choose you this day whom ye will serve; whether the gods which your fathers served that *were* on the other side of the flood, or the gods of the Amorites, in whose land ye dwell: but as for me and my house, we will serve the LORD" (Josh.24:15). "Then Jesus beholding him loved him, and said unto him, One thing thou lackest: go thy way, sell whatsoever thou hast, and give to the poor, and thou shalt have treasure in heaven: and come, take up the cross, and follow me" (Mk.10:21). "Draw nigh to God, and he will draw nigh to you. Cleanse *your* hands, *ye* sinners; and purify *your* hearts, *ye* double minded" (Jas.4:8). "See, I have set before thee this day life and good, and death and evil" (Dt.30:15). "...How long halt ye between two opinions? if the LORD *be* God, follow him: but if Baal, *then* follow him. And the people answered him not a word" (1 Ki.18:21).

	J. The Ten Commandments, The Laws Governing Man's Duty To Others (Part 5): Commandment Nine Concerns Man's Word & Character--Never Lie, Ex.20:16
Com. 9 concerns *man's word & character:* Forbids lying or speaking falsely against anyone	16 Thou shalt not bear false witness against thy neighbour.

DIVISION VII

THE LAW AND THE PROMISES OF GOD (THE MOSAIC COVENANT) (PART 2): THE TEN COMMANDMENTS--NECESSARY LAWS TO GOVERN MAN AND SOCIETY, EX.20:1-26

J.   The Ten Commandments, The Laws Governing Man's Duty To Others (Part 5): Commandment Nine Concerns Man's Word and Character--Never Lie, Ex.20:16

(20:16) **Introduction--Commandments, The Ten--Lying**: lying--bearing false testimony against people--is common to all of us. We have all lied. Sometime in the past we have all...

- told a little white lie
- twisted the truth
- told a half-truth
- gossiped, not really knowing the truth
- discredited someone
- slandered someone

- sought to escape blame by skirting around the truth
- tried to place blame elsewhere by failing to come forth with the truth
- cast a suggestive hint or insinuated an untruth about someone
- boasted or exaggerated the truth in order to boost ourselves
- raised an eyebrow, shrugged a shoulder, or made some motion to indicate something untrue or to keep from disclosing the truth

Scripture emphatically declares: "All men are liars" (Ps.116:11). Lying is so common that it is condoned, accepted, and even expected by many people. But lying is not ever justified. Silence sometimes is, but not lying, not answering dishonestly. Leaders, both business and political, can say or promise anything and people either accept or overlook their twisting of the truth. A person's character, his word and integrity, seem to matter little. Making false claims and promises has become a way of life. There is a feeling that a person just cannot survive nor get ahead unless he twists the truth to boost himself. Telling the truth and being honest have fallen by the wayside.

Lying--bearing false witness--threatens the very foundation of society. Nothing can survive when it is filled with lies, not for long: not families, friendships, businesses, clubs, schools, churches, communities, governments. Any organization or group will collapse in the wake of mistrust and broken, severed relationships.

This is the great concern of the ninth commandment, the concern for truth, that we build our lives upon truth: build our families, friendships, businesses, clubs, schools, churches, communities, and governments upon truth. *Commandment Nine Concerns Man's Word and Character: Never Lie* (v.16).

1. Who is to obey this commandment (v.16)?
2. What is forbidden by this commandment (v.16)?
3. What is the decision required by this commandment (v.16)?

1 (20:16) **Commandments, The Ten--Lying--Obedience**: Who is to obey this commandment? Some commentators say that this commandment was initially given to govern testimony in legal courts, to make absolutely sure that no one ever lied or gave a false testimony in court. There is no question, this commandment does govern a person who gives evidence in court: his testimony must always be true. But the commandment is much broader than this: it covers far more than just legal testimony. God is declaring that no person is ever to lie against a neighbor, not on any occasion. We must never bear a false witness *against* a neighbor, and we must never bear false witness *to* a neighbor. We must always tell the truth, the whole truth, and nothing but the truth.

> "Wherefore putting away lying, speak every man truth with his neighbour: for we are members one of another" (Eph.4:25).
> "Lie not one to another" (Col.3:9).
> "Thou shalt not bear false witness against thy neighbour" (Ex.20:16).
> "Thou shalt not raise a false report: put not thine hand with the wicked to be an unrighteous witness" (Ex.23:1).

Was this commandment given to govern only the ancient Israelites, only those who lived before Christ came? Was lying a problem only for the ancient world? Or, is lying still a serious problem? The answer is obvious. This commandment is needed today as much as it was needed by the ancient world. God's concern for righteousness upon the earth is as strong today as it has ever been. "You shall not bear false witness: you shall never lie"--this commandment was given to *you. You* are not to lie, not ever.

"These six things doth the LORD hate: yea, seven are an abomination unto him: A proud look, a <u>lying tongue</u>, and hands that shed innocent blood, An heart that deviseth wicked imaginations, feet that be swift in running to mischief, A <u>false witness that speaketh lies</u>, and he that soweth discord among brethren" (Pr.6:16-19).

"But I say unto you, That every idle word that men shall speak, they shall give account thereof in the day of judgment. For by thy words thou shalt be justified, and by thy words thou shalt be condemned" (Mt.12:36-37).

2 (20:16) <u>Commandments, The Ten--Lying--Testimony, False--Witness, False--Deception--Perjury--Tongue--Speech, False</u>: What is forbidden by this commandment? How is this commandment broken, violated: "You shall not lie--never bear false witness against your neighbor" (v.15)?

1. This commandment is broken by lying, by telling any untruth of any kind. Man's concept of lying is this: "If I lie, it is justifiable, but if you lie to me, it is unforgivable." But to God, lying is lying. The word "lying" (sheqer) means that which is false, untrue. It is untruthfulness, deception, misrepresentation, exaggeration.

Note how Scripture itself defines a false witness:

⇒ A false witness is a person who breathes out lies.

"A faithful witness will not lie: but a false witness will <u>utter lies</u>" (Pr.14:5).
"A false witness shall not be unpunished, and he that <u>speaketh lies</u> shall not escape" (Pr.19:5).

⇒ A false witness is a person who shares a false report.

"Thou shalt not raise a <u>false report</u>: put not thine hand with the wicked to be an unrighteous witness" (Ex.23:1).

⇒ A false witness is a person who deceives.

"He that speaketh truth showeth forth righteousness: but a false witness <u>deceit</u>" (Pr.12:17).

As pointed out in note one, when some people look at the ninth commandment, they think of a courtroom scene and think that lying against someone in court is what is being forbidden. But as the Scriptures above show, *bearing false witness* means far more than just not lying against someone in court. *Bearing* false witness means any kind of lying. Hosea 4:2 clearly shows this. When Hosea charged the people with breaking several of the commandments, he did not charge them with bearing false witness in court. He charged them with lying in their day-to-day affairs:

"Hear the word of the LORD, ye children of Israel: for the LORD hath a controversy with the inhabitants of the land, because there is no truth, nor mercy, nor knowledge of God in the land. By swearing, and <u>lying</u>, and killing, and stealing, and committing adultery, they break out, and blood toucheth blood" (Hos.4:1-2).

2. There are several forms or kinds of lies, and they must be diligently guarded against.
   a. There is slander: thinking something bad about a person and sharing it; misrepresenting something about someone; tearing down the reputation and life of a person by spreading bad news about him.

"Whoso privily [secretly] slandereth his neighbour, him will I cut off: him that hath an high look and a proud heart will not I suffer" (Ps.101:5).
"He that hideth hatred with lying lips, and <u>he that uttereth a slander, is a fool</u>" (Pr.10:18).

   b. There is rumor or gossip or tale-bearing: spreading little or big tales, idle or active tales, whether imagined or real; spreading the evil news that one has imagined in his mind or has heard.

"And withal they learn to be idle, wandering about from house to house; and not only idle, but <u>tattlers</u> also and <u>busybodies</u>, <u>speaking things</u> which they ought not" (1 Tim.5:13).
"But let none of you suffer as a murderer, or as a thief, or as an evildoer, or as a <u>busybody</u> in other men's matters" (1 Pt.4:15).
"Thou shalt not go up and down as a <u>talebearer</u> among thy people" (Lev.19:16).
"A talebearer revealeth secrets: but he that is of a faithful spirit concealeth the matter" (Pr.11:13).
"A froward man soweth strife: and a <u>whisperer</u> separateth chief friends" (Pr.16:28).
"Where no wood is, there the fire goeth out: so where there is no <u>talebearer</u>, the strife ceaseth" (Pr.26:20).

   c. There are suggestive hints or insinuations: arousing a bad impression about someone; stirring the idea that something might possibly be true; planting in the mind the possibility of something improper or indecent.

"Thou shalt not <u>raise</u> a false report: put not thine hand with the wicked to be an unrighteous witness" (Ex.23:1).

"Take ye heed every one of his neighbor, and trust ye not in any brother: for every brother will utterly **supplant**, and every neighbor will walk with slanders" (Jer.9:4).

d. There is deception: thinking or wanting something to be true, accepting it as true and sharing it; tricking oneself and others into thinking something is true; deceiving oneself and others by accepting bad news as true when the truth is really not known; causing oneself and others to believe bad news.

"He that speaketh truth showeth forth righteousness: but a false witness deceit" (Pr.12:17).
"Be not a witness against thy neighbor without cause; and deceive not with thy lips" (Pr.24:28).

e. There are false charges and criticism: accusations made against a person to a third party; sharing the faults and failures of a person with someone other than the person himself; talking about the weaknesses and failures of a person with someone else; condemning, blaming, and censoring a person with others.

"Blessed are ye, when men shall revile you, and persecute you, and shall say all manner of evil against you **falsely**, for my sake. Rejoice, and be exceeding glad: for great is your reward in heaven: for so persecuted they the prophets which were before you" (Mt.5:11-12).
"Having a good conscience; that, whereas they speak evil of you, as of evildoers, they may be ashamed that **falsely accuse** your good conversation in Christ" (1 Pt.3:16).
"For I have heard the slander of many: fear was on every side: while they took counsel together against me, they devised to take away my life" (Ps.31:13).

f. There is exaggeration and blown up flattery: stretching the truth about a person; excessively praising someone; falsely representing someone; painting a false picture of a person.

"Let me not, I pray you, accept any man's person; neither let me give flattering titles unto man" (Job 32:21).
"He that goeth about as a talebearer revealeth secrets: therefore meddle not with him that flattereth with his lips" (Pr.20:19).
"A lying tongue hateth those that are afflicted by it; and a flattering mouth worketh ruin" (Pr.26:28).
"He that rebuketh a man, afterward shall find more favor than he that flattereth with the tongue" (Pr.28:23).
"A man that flattereth his neighbor spreadeth a net for his feet" (Pr.29:5).
"The LORD shall cut off all flattering lips, and the tongue that speaketh proud things" (Ps.12:3).
"But as we were allowed of God to be put in trust with the gospel, even so we speak; not as pleasing men, but God, which trieth our hearts. For neither at any time used we **flattering words**, as ye know, nor a cloke of covetousness; God is witness" (1 Th.2:4-5).
"He that saith unto the wicked, Thou art righteous; him shall the people curse, nations shall abhor him" (Pr.24:24).

g. There are innumerable ways in which we lie, such as...
- perjury
- propaganda
- boasting
- telling half-truths
- breaking vows
- twisting the truth to protect oneself
- shifting blame
- seeking to discredit someone
- sharing a convenient lie
- making up an excuse
- seeking to escape responsibility or punishment
- raising an eyebrow, shrugging the shoulder, or snickering--doing anything that indicates something is untrue or that disavows knowledge of the truth

3. A lie has at least three terrible effects upon people.
   a. Lying misrepresents the truth. It camouflages and hides the truth. The person lied to does not know the truth; therefore, he has to act or live upon a lie. If the lie is serious, it can be very damaging:
   ⇒ A lie about a business deal can cost money and cause terrible loss.
   ⇒ A lie about loving someone can stir emotions that lead to destruction.
   ⇒ A lie about the salvation of the gospel can cost a person the hope of eternal life.
   b. Lying deceives a person. It leads a person astray. A person deceives...
   - to get what he wants
   - to seduce someone
   - to cover up or hide something
   - to cause harm or hurt

The point to see is that lying is a deception, and deception eventually causes misunderstanding, disappointment, bewilderment, helplessness, emotional upheaval, loss, and sometimes immorality and destruction.

c. Lying builds a wrong relationship, a relationship built upon sinking sand. Two people cannot possibly be friends or live together if the relationship is based upon lies. Lying destroys...

- confidence
- assurance
- security
- love
- trust
- hope

4. Four facts need to be noted about lying or bearing false witness.
   a. False witness is usually shared with loved ones and good friends, with people we feel can be trusted. Therefore, we always feel that our loved ones and friends can be trusted with the *bad news*. However, what is overlooked is that our loved ones and friends have good friends whom they feel can be trusted. And so the bad news is spread further and further afield; more damage and hurt is done to people and to the cause of Christ. God knows this is the way people are. This is the reason God forbids His people from sharing failure, whether true or untrue, except in dealing with the person involved with the issue.
   b. Bearing tales about a person, whether true or untrue, always hurts the person. The person being talked about has a heart just like we do: a heart that is subject to being cut and hurt and suffering pain. Therefore, when tales are shared, we are eventually going to cause pain and hurt, sometimes a great deal of pain, to the person and his loved ones. (Imagine how God feels about this.)

   > "All that hate me whisper together against me: against me do they devise my hurt" (Ps.41:7).
   > "The words of a talebearer are as wounds, and they go down into the innermost parts of the belly" (Pr.18:8).
   > "A man that beareth false witness against his neighbor is a maul [hammer], and a sword, and a sharp arrow" (Pr.25:18).

   c. The person who bears tales, giving false witness, shall be judged by God, no matter who he is.

   > "Being filled with all unrighteousness...deceit...whisperers, backbiters....Who knowing the judgment of God, that they which commit such things are worthy of death, not only do the same, but have pleasure in them that do them" (Ro.1:29-30, 32).
   > "Whoso privily [secretly] slandereth his neighbour, him will I cut off: him that hath an high look and a proud heart will not I suffer" (Ps.101:5).
   > "A false witness shall not be unpunished; and he that speaketh lies shall perish" (Pr.19:9).

   d. If a person truly loves, he will not bear false witness about anyone. If there is a problem or some questionable report, he will deal with the person himself, seeking to restore him to the faith. Note: love does not deal with a person in harshness, downgrading him, but in love and tenderness and in *strength*, being guided by the Holy Spirit of God.

   > "Brethren, if a man be overtaken in a fault, ye which are spiritual, restore such an one in the spirit of meekness; considering thyself, lest thou also be tempted. Bear ye one another's burdens, and so fulfil the law of Christ" (Gal.6:1-2).
   > "I have seen his ways, and will heal him: I will lead him also, and restore comforts unto him and to his mourners" (Is.57:18).
   > "Set a watch, O LORD, before my mouth; keep the door of my lips" (Ps.141:3).

5. The source of lies and lying is Satan. He was the first ever to lie; therefore, he is called the father of lies. The person who lies follows in the footsteps of Satan and is called by Scripture a "child of the devil."

   > "Ye are of [your] father the devil, and the lusts of your father ye will do. He was a murderer from the beginning, and abode not in the truth, because there is no truth in him. When he speaketh a lie, he speaketh of his own: for he is a liar, and the father of it" (Jn.8:44).

6. The source of truth is God. Note Scripture declares time and again that God is the God of truth.

   > "God is not a man, that he should lie; neither the son of man, that he should repent: hath he said, and shall he not do it? or hath he spoken, and shall he not make it good?" (Num.23:19).
   > "He is the Rock, his work is perfect: for all his ways are judgment: a God of truth and without iniquity, just and right is he" (Dt.32:4).
   > "And now, O Lord GOD, thou art that God, and thy words be true, and thou hast promised this goodness unto thy servant" (2 Sam.7:28).
   > "Happy is he that hath the God of Jacob for his help, whose hope is in the LORD his God: Which made heaven, and earth, the sea, and all that therein is: which keepeth truth for ever" (Ps.146:5-6).
   > "That he who blesseth himself in the earth shall bless himself in the God of truth; and he that sweareth in the earth shall swear by the God of truth; because the former troubles are forgotten, and because they are hid from mine eyes" (Is.65:16).
   > "God forbid: yea, let God be true, but every man a liar; as it is written, That thou mightest be justified in thy sayings, and mightest overcome when thou art judged" (Ro.3:4).

**"In hope of eternal life, which God, that cannot lie, promised before the world began"
(Tit.1:2).**

"Wherein God, willing more abundantly to show unto the heirs of promise the immutability of his counsel, confirmed it by an oath: That by two immutable things, in which it was impossible for God to lie, we might have a strong consolation, who have fled for refuge to lay hold upon the hope set before us" (Heb.6:17-18).

7. The very foundation or basis of society is truth. Families, businesses, organizations, clubs, neighbors, or communities in any society will disintegrate and collapse unless the members are truthful with one another. If we lie and deceive one another, the consequences are hurtful, damaging, and often devastating. Wrong decisions are made and wrong actions are taken. Lies and deception--bearing false witness--are often what cause...

- divorce
- job loss
- unemployment
- severed relationships
- pain and hurt

- failure
- bankruptcy
- collapse
- vengeance
- retaliation

- abuse
- accident
- suffering
- imprisonment
- death

8. A critical question needs to be asked when dealing with lying or telling the truth. Should we ever tell the truth bluntly or harshly? In a court of law, the truth must always be spoken straight to the point: directly and straightforward. But when dealing in personal face-to-face relationships, we should not intentionally cause pain, hurt, embarrassment, or shame. We should never wound a person with a blunt, harsh statement, not with the truth. Truth is to be spoken in love and kindness not in harshness and ugliness.

"But speaking the truth in love, may grow up into him in all things, which is the head, even Christ" (Eph.4:15).

"Let all bitterness, and wrath, and anger, and clamour, and evil speaking, be put away from you, with all malice: And be ye kind one to another, tenderhearted, forgiving one another, even as God for Christ's sake hath forgiven you" (Eph.4:31-32).

Thought 1. William Barclay has an excellent statement on this point:

"When we speak about telling the truth, one special point arises. Must we always tell the truth baldly and bluntly? For instance, if a person has played a game or sung a song or given some kind of performance, and not done very well, must we say that he was no good, or is there any harm in the polite compliment which will encourage him, even if it is not strictly true? Must we tell the truth, even when it is unpleasant and when it might hurt?

"Someone has given us a valuable rule about this. There are three questions we should always ask about anything we say about anyone else, or to anyone else. The first question is: *Is it true?* And, of course, if it is not true, then it must not be said at all. The second question is: *Is it necessary?* If it is necessary, it will have to be said, but there are not many times when politeness and courtesy need to be disregarded. The third question is: *Is it kind?* It is hardly ever a duty to be unkind. There are ways and ways of telling the truth. You can tell it in a way that is deliberately designed to wound and hurt; there are people who take a delight in seeing other people wince when something is said. On the other hand, it was said of Florence Allshorn, a great teacher, that, when she had some criticism to make, she always made it, as it were, with her arm round your shoulder. She spoke the truth; she said what was necessary; but she took care to say it kindly and in a way that would help and not hurt. And that is the best rule of all."[1]

3 **(20:16) Commandments, The Ten--Lying--Decision**: What is the decision required by this commandment? Obedience! Telling the truth is not an option. We must learn to conquer and overcome lying, to guard, prevent, and keep ourselves from lying. Scripture tells us:

1. We must obey God; keep His commandment: never bear false witness nor deceive a neighbor.

"Thou shalt not bear false witness against thy neighbour" (Ex.20:16).
"Keep thy tongue from evil, and thy lips from speaking guile" (Ps.34:13).
"Be not a witness against thy neighbour without cause; and deceive not with thy lips" (Pr.24:28).

2. We must never spread a false report nor help a wicked person by lying for him.

"Thou shalt not raise a false report: put not thine hand with the wicked to be an unrighteous witness" (Ex.23:1).

3. We must never bear false witness, but rather we are to love one another.

"Owe no man any thing, but to love one another: for he that loveth another hath fulfilled the law. For this, Thou shalt not commit adultery, Thou shalt not kill, Thou shalt not steal, Thou shalt not bear false witness, Thou shalt not covet; and if there be any other commandment, it is briefly comprehended in this saying, namely, Thou shalt love thy neighbour as thyself. Love worketh no ill to his neighbour: therefore love is the fulfilling of the law" (Ro.13:8-10).

---

[1] William Barclay. *The Old Law & The New Law*, p.43-44.

4. We must always speak the truth, but we are to speak it in love.

> "But speaking the truth in love, [that we] may grow up into him in all things, which is the head, even Christ" (Eph.4:15).
> "These are the things that ye shall do; Speak ye every man the truth to his neighbour; execute the judgment of truth and peace in your gates" (Zech.8:16).

5. We must teach every living person, especially our children and the youth of the world, the Word of God, the Ten Commandments.

> "And these words, which I command thee this day, shall be in thine heart: And thou shalt teach them diligently unto thy children, and shalt talk of them when thou sittest in thine house, and when thou walkest by the way, and when thou liest down, and when thou risest up" (Dt.6:6-7).
> "All scripture is given by inspiration of God, and is profitable for doctrine, for reproof, for correction, for instruction in righteousness" (2 Tim.3:16).
> "Wherefore laying aside all malice, and all guile [deception], and hypocrisies, and envies, and all evil speakings [slander, lying], As newborn babes, desire the sincere milk of the word, that ye may grow thereby" (1 Pt.2:1-2).

6. We must put away lying--put away all falsehood--and speak only the truth.

> "Sanctify them through thy truth: thy word is truth" (Jn.17:17).
> "Wherefore putting away lying [falsehood], speak every man truth with his neighbour: for we are members one of another" (Eph.4:25).

7. We must put off the old man of lying and put on the new man of righteousness.

> "Lie not one to another, seeing that ye have put off the old man with his deeds; And have put on the new man [of righteousness], which is renewed in knowledge after the image of him that created him" (Col.3:9-10).

8. We must stop all corrupt, unwholesome talk and slander (a type of lying); we must be kind and forgiving of one another.

> "Let no corrupt communication [unwholesome talk] proceed out of your mouth, but that which is good to the use of edifying, that it may minister grace unto the hearers....Let all bitterness, and wrath, and anger, and clamour, and evil speaking [slander], be put away from you, with all malice: And be ye kind one to another, tenderhearted, forgiving one another, even as God for Christ's sake hath forgiven you" (Eph.4:29, 31-32).
> "Wherefore laying aside all malice, and all guile, and hypocrisies, and envies, and all evil speakings" (1 Pt.2:1).

9. We must be diligent--stand guard--keep our tongues from deception and lying.

> "Keep thy tongue from evil, and thy lips from speaking guile" (Ps.34:13).
> "Whoso keepeth his mouth and his tongue keepeth his soul from troubles" (Pr.21:23).
> "Take ye heed every one of his neighbour, and trust ye not in any brother: for every brother will utterly supplant, and every neighbour will walk with slanders" (Jer.9:4).

10. We must pray, ask God to guard our tongues from lying.

> "Set a watch, O LORD, before my mouth; keep the door of my lips" (Ps.141:3).

THE BIBLICAL CONSEQUENCES OF BEARING FALSE WITNESS [LYING] AGAINST YOUR NEIGHBOR

DEEPER STUDY #1

(20:16) **Commandments, The Ten--Obedience--Judgment--Lying**: What are the consequences of bearing false witness, of lying? When this commandment is broken, the false words dig deep into the heart. Damaging words often do more harm than a physical blow. The person who breaks this commandment becomes a willing partner of the "father of all lies" and "the accuser" of believers, of those who truly follow God.

> "Ye are of your father the devil, and the lusts of your father ye will do. He was a murderer from the beginning, and abode not in the truth, because there is no truth in him. When he speaketh a lie, he speaketh of his own: for he is a liar, and the father of it" (Jn.8:44).

"And I heard a loud voice saying in heaven, Now is come salvation, and strength, and the kingdom of our God, and the power of his Christ: for the accuser of our brethren is cast down, which accused them before our God day and night" (Rev.12:10).

1. The person who lies--consistently lies--will not inherit the kingdom of God: he will be sentenced to hell.

"But the fearful, and unbelieving, and the abominable, and murderers, and whoremongers, and sorcerers, and idolaters, and all liars, shall have their part in the lake which burneth with fire and brimstone: which is the second death" (Rev.21:8).

"And there shall in no wise enter into it any thing that defileth, neither whatsoever worketh abomination, or maketh a lie: but they which are written in the Lamb's book of life" (Rev.21:27).

"Blessed *are* they that do his commandments, that they may have right to the tree of life, and may enter in through the gates into the city. For without [the heavenly city] *are* dogs, and sorcerers, and whoremongers, and murderers, and idolaters, and whosoever loveth and maketh a lie [practices falsehood]" (Rev.22:14-15).

2. The person who lies and does not repent will not escape: he shall face the judgment of God and perish.

"Thou shalt destroy them that speak leasing [tell lies]: the LORD will abhor the bloody and deceitful man" (Ps.5:6).

"The LORD shall cut off all flattering lips, and the tongue that speaketh proud things" (Ps.12:3).

"A false witness shall not be unpunished, and he that speaketh lies shall not escape" (Pr.19:5).

"A false witness shall not be unpunished, and he that speaketh lies shall perish" (Pr.19:9).

"And I will come near to you to judgment; and I will be a swift witness against the sorcerers, and against the adulterers, and against false swearers, and against those that oppress the hireling in his wages, the widow, and the fatherless, and that turn aside the stranger from his right, and fear not me, saith the LORD of hosts" (Mal.3:5).

3. The person who lies will be separated from God.

"Whoso privily slandereth his neighbour, him will I cut off: him that hath an high look and a proud heart will not I suffer" (Ps.101:5).

"He that worketh deceit shall not dwell within my house: he that telleth lies shall not tarry in my sight" (Ps.101:7).

4. The person who lies sins against God.

"If a soul sin, and commit a trespass against the LORD, and lie unto his neighbour in that which was delivered him to keep, or in fellowship, or in a thing taken away by violence, or hath deceived his neighbour; Or have found that which was lost, and lieth concerning it, and sweareth falsely; in any of all these that a man doeth, sinning therein" (Lev.6:2-3).

5. The person who lies rebels against God and ignores His law.

"That this is a rebellious people, lying children, children that will not hear the law of the LORD" (Is.30:9).

"But thou shalt say unto them, This is a nation that obeyeth not the voice of the LORD their God, nor receiveth correction: truth is perished, and is cut off from their mouth" (Jer.7:28).

6. The person who lies forgets God.

"This is thy lot, the portion of thy measures from me, saith the LORD; because thou hast forgotten me, and trusted in falsehood" (Jer.13:25).

7. The person who lies perverts the Word of God.

"And the burden of the LORD shall ye mention no more: for every man's word shall be his burden; for ye have perverted the words of the living God, of the LORD of hosts our God" (Jer.23:36).

8. The person who lies about following God is a hypocrite: he flatters God, but his own heart betrays his true feelings.

"And they remembered that God *was* their rock, and the high God their redeemer. Nevertheless they did flatter him with their mouth, and they lied unto him with their tongues. For their heart was not right with him, neither were they stedfast in his covenant" (Ps.78:35-37).

9. The person who lies follows after the father of lies, Satan.

"Ye are of [your] father the devil, and the lusts of your father ye will do. He was a murderer from the beginning, and abode not in the truth, because there is no truth in him. When he speaketh a lie, he speaketh of his own: for he is a liar, and the father of it" (Jn.8:44).

"But Peter said, Ananias, why hath Satan filled thine heart to lie to the Holy Ghost, and to keep back part of the price of the land? Whiles it remained, was it not thine own? and after it was sold, was it not in thine own power? why hast thou conceived this thing in thine heart? thou hast not lied unto men, but unto God" (Acts 5:3-4).

10. The person who lies is a fool.

"He that hideth hatred with lying lips, and he that uttereth a slander, is a fool" (Pr.10:18).

11. The person who lies will be turned into a fool by God.

"[God] frustrateth the tokens of the liars, and maketh diviners mad; that turneth wise men backward, and maketh their knowledge foolish" (Is.44:25).

"Causing the omens of boasters to fail, Making fools out of diviners, Causing wise men to draw back, And turning their knowledge into foolishness" (Is.44:25, NASB).

"I am the one who shows what liars all false prophets are, by causing something else to happen than the things they say. I make wise men give opposite advice to what they should and make them into fools" (Is.44:25, LIVING PARAPHRASE).

12. The person who lies will have a life marked by deceit.

"He that speaketh truth showeth forth righteousness: but a false witness deceit" (Pr.12:17).

"Be not a witness against thy neighbour without cause; and deceive not with thy lips" (Pr.24:28).

"Being filled with all unrighteousness, fornication, wickedness, covetousness, maliciousness; full of envy, murder, debate, deceit, malignity; whisperers, Backbiters, haters of God, despiteful, proud, boasters, inventors of evil things, disobedient to parents, Without understanding, covenantbreakers, without natural affection, implacable, unmerciful" (Ro.1:29-31).

"What then? are we better than they? No, in no wise: for we have before proved both Jews and Gentiles, that they are all under sin; As it is written, There is none righteous, no, not one: There is none that understandeth, there is none that seeketh after God. They are all gone out of the way, they are together become unprofitable; there is none that doeth good, no, not one. Their throat is an open sepulchre; with their tongues they have used deceit; the poison of asps is under their lips: Whose mouth is full of cursing and bitterness: Their feet are swift to shed blood: Destruction and misery are in their ways: And the way of peace have they not known: There is no fear of God before their eyes. Now we know that what things soever the law saith, it saith to them who are under the law: that every mouth may be stopped, and all the world may become guilty before God. Therefore by the deeds of the law there shall no flesh be justified in his sight: for by the law is the knowledge of sin" (Ro.3:9-20).

"Thou givest thy mouth to evil, and thy tongue frameth deceit" (Ps.50:19).

"Thou lovest evil more than good; and lying rather than to speak righteousness....Thou lovest all devouring words, O thou deceitful tongue" (Ps.52:3-4).

13. The person who lies only deceives himself; he has an empty religion.

"If any man among you seem to be religious, and bridleth not his tongue, but deceiveth his own heart, this man's religion is vain" (Jas.1:26).

14. The person who lies causes discord among people.

"A false witness that speaketh lies, and he that soweth discord among brethren" (Pr.6:19).

15. The person who lies destroys the reputations and lives of people.

"An hypocrite with his mouth destroyeth his neighbour: but through knowledge shall the just be delivered" (Pr.11:9).

16. The person who lies will have a reputation of being a gossip, of being mean and malicious, and sometimes evil.

"A man that beareth false witness against his neighbour is a maul [hammer], and a sword, and a sharp arrow" (Pr.25:18).

17. The person who lies will have a life marked by a critical spirit that is quick to judge the actions of others.

> "Speak not evil one of another, brethren. He that speaketh evil of his brother, and judgeth his brother, speaketh evil of the law, and judgeth the law: but if thou judge the law, thou art not a doer of the law, but a judge" (Jas.4:11).

18. The person who lies causes hatred and ruin in the lives of many.

> "A lying tongue hateth those that are afflicted by it; and a flattering mouth worketh ruin" (Pr.26:28).
> "A lying tongue hates those it crushes, And a flattering mouth works ruin" (Pr.26:28, NASB).

19. The person who lies causes the corruption of society.

> "In transgressing and lying against the LORD, and departing away from our God, speaking oppression and revolt, conceiving and uttering from the heart words of falsehood. And judgment is turned away backward, and justice standeth afar off: for truth is fallen in the street, and equity cannot enter. Yea, truth faileth; and he that departeth from evil maketh himself a prey: and the LORD saw it, and it displeased him that there was no judgment" (Is.59:13-15).
> "Take ye heed every one of his neighbour, and trust ye not in any brother: for every brother will utterly supplant, and every neighbour will walk with slanders. And they will deceive every one his neighbour, and will not speak the truth: they have taught their tongue to speak lies, and weary themselves to commit iniquity" (Jer.9:4-5).

20. The person who lies causes God's people to make wrong decisions.

> "Behold, I am against them that prophesy false dreams, saith the LORD, and do tell them, and cause my people to err by their lies, and by their lightness; yet I sent them not, nor commanded them: therefore they shall not profit this people at all, saith the LORD" (Jer.23:32).

21. The person who lies causes wickedness to spread to others.

> "If a ruler hearken to lies, all his servants are wicked" (Pr.29:12).
> "If a ruler pays attention to falsehood, All his ministers *become* wicked" (Pr.29:12, NASB).

22. The person who lies will become enslaved to many sins.

> "And even as they did not like to retain God in their knowledge, God gave them over to a reprobate mind, to do those things which are not convenient; Being filled with all unrighteousness, fornication, wickedness, covetousness, maliciousness; full of envy, murder, debate, deceit, malignity; whisperers, Backbiters, haters of God, despiteful, proud, boasters, inventors of evil things, disobedient to parents" (Ro.1:28-30).

23. The person who lies will have a life marked by destruction and defilement.

> "And the tongue is a fire, a world of iniquity: so is the tongue among our members, that it defileth the whole body, and setteth on fire the course of nature; and it is set on fire of hell" (Jas.3:6).

THE BIBLICAL BENEFITS OF KEEPING THIS COMMANDMENT:
DO NOT LIE, DO NOT BEAR FALSE WITNESS AGAINST YOUR NEIGHBOR

DEEPER STUDY #2
(20:16) **Commandments, The Ten--Benefits of Keeping--Obedience--Truthfulness**: What are the benefits of keeping this commandment? Our word is our bond. If a man's word is trusted, Scripture declares he will be greatly blessed.

1. A person who tells the truth and shares in the glorious salvation of God will receive blessings and righteousness from the Lord.

> "He that hath clean hands, and a pure heart; who hath not lifted up his soul unto vanity, nor sworn deceitfully. He shall receive the blessing from the LORD, and righteousness from the God of his salvation" (Ps.24:4-5).

2. A person who tells the truth and belongs to the LORD will derive joy from God's Word.

> "I hate and abhor lying: but thy law do I love" (Ps.119:163).

3. A person who tells the truth and follows God will be delivered.

> "The words of the wicked are to lie in wait for blood: but the mouth of the upright shall deliver them" (Pr.12:6).

4. A person who tells the truth and belongs to the LORD will be assured of his eternity.

> "The lip of truth shall be established for ever: but a lying tongue is but for a moment" (Pr.12:19).

5. A person who tells the truth and follows God will not be brought to shame.

> "A righteous man hateth lying: but a wicked man is loathsome, and cometh to shame" (Pr.13:5).

6. A person who tells the truth and obeys God can be counted on to be a faithful witness.

> "A faithful witness will not lie: but a false witness will utter lies" (Pr.14:5).
> "A true witness delivereth souls: but a deceitful witness speaketh lies" (Pr.14:25).

7. A person who tells the truth and is a true believer in Jesus Christ will be trusted to put his words into action.

> "My little children, let us not love in word, neither in tongue; but in deed and in truth" (1 Jn.3:18).

8. A person who tells the truth and who trusts in Christ as his Savior proves to others that the Spirit of truth lives in his heart.

> "And I will pray the Father, and he shall give you another Comforter, that he may abide with you for ever; Even the Spirit of truth; whom the world cannot receive, because it seeth him not, neither knoweth him: but ye know him; for he dwelleth with you, and shall be in you" (Jn.14:16-17).

9. A person who tells the truth and has saving faith in Christ will be able to speak the truth in love, right from his heart.

> "But speaking the truth in love, may grow up into him in all things, which is the head, even Christ" (Eph.4:15).
> "And the woman said to Elijah, Now by this I know that thou art a man of God, and that the word of the LORD in thy mouth is truth" (1 Ki.17:24).
> "LORD, who shall abide in thy tabernacle? who shall dwell in thy holy hill? He that walketh uprightly, and worketh righteousness, and speaketh the truth in his heart. He that backbiteth not with his tongue, nor doeth evil to his neighbour, nor taketh up a reproach against his neighbour" (Ps.15:1-3).

10. A person who tells the truth and has been gloriously saved by Jesus Christ will appear righteous, not deceitful, before the world.

> "He that speaketh truth showeth forth righteousness: but a false witness deceit" (Pr.12:17).

11. A person who tells the truth and follows God walks without shame before God.

> "But he that doeth truth cometh to the light, that his deeds may be made manifest, that they are wrought in God" (Jn.3:21).

12. A person who tells the truth and trusts in Christ as his Savior will strive to have a disciplined mind focused on the truth.

> "Finally, brethren, whatsoever things are true, whatsoever things are honest, whatsoever things are just, whatsoever things are pure, whatsoever things are lovely, whatsoever things are of good report; if there be any virtue, and if there be any praise, think on these things" (Ph.4:8).

13. A person who tells the truth and follows God will not need to twist God's Word to justify his behavior or lifestyle.

> "Study to show thyself approved unto God, a workman that needeth not to be ashamed, rightly dividing the word of truth" (2 Tim.2:15).

14. A person who tells the truth and lives a righteous life will live in God's presence both now and forever.

> "LORD, who shall abide in thy tabernacle? who shall dwell in thy holy hill? He that walketh uprightly, and worketh righteousness, and speaketh the truth in his heart" (Ps.15:1-2; cp. v.3-5).

DEEPER STUDY # 3

JESUS CHRIST AND HIS TEACHING
CONCERNING MAN'S WORD AND LYING
"Thou shalt not bear false witness against thy neighbour" (Ex.20:16).

THE TEACHING OF CHRIST	THE BELIEVER'S RESPONSE
1. Jesus Christ declared that God commanded man not to lie. "He saith unto him, Which? Jesus said, Thou shalt do no murder, Thou shalt not commit adultery, Thou shalt not steal, <u>Thou shalt not bear false witness</u>," (Mt.19:18; cp. Mk.10:19; Lk.18:20).	⇒ Scripture is clear: lying is wrong. "Thou shalt not bear false witness against thy neighbour" (Ex.20:16). "Thou shalt not raise a false report: put not thine hand with the wicked to be an unrighteous witness" (Ex.23:1). "These six things doth the LORD hate: yea, seven are an abomination unto him: A proud look, a <u>lying tongue</u>, and hands that shed innocent blood, An heart that deviseth wicked imaginations, feet that be swift in running to mischief, A false witness that speaketh lies, and he that soweth discord among brethren" (Pr.6:16-19). "Wherefore putting away lying, speak every man truth with his neighbour: for we are members one of another" (Eph.4:25).
2. Jesus Christ declared that men are responsible for every word they speak and will give an account in the day of judgment. "But I say unto you, That every idle word that men shall speak, they shall give account thereof in the day of judgment" (Mt.12:36).	1) A man's words expose his true nature: what he is like beneath the surface. 2) A man's words expose what he is down deep within his heart: his motives, desires, and ambitions. 3) A man's words expose his true character: good or bad, kind or cruel. 4) A man's words expose his mind, what he thinks: pure or impure thoughts, clean or dirty thoughts. 5) A man's words expose his spirit, what he believes and pursues: the legitimate or illegitimate, the intelligent or ignorant, the true or false, the beneficial or wasteful. "Whoso privily slandereth his neighbour, <u>him will I cut off</u>: him that hath an high look and a proud heart will not I suffer" (Ps.101:5). "Being filled with all unrighteousness...<u>deceit</u>...<u>whisperers</u>, <u>backbiters</u>" (Ro.1:29-30). "But the fearful, and unbelieving, and the abominable, and murderers, and whoremongers, and sorcerers, and idolaters, and all liars, shall have their part in the lake which burneth with fire and brimstone: which is the second death" (Rev.21:8).
3. Jesus Christ declared that Satan is the father of lies, and that the liar has a life that marks him as a child of the devil. "Ye are of your father the devil, and the lusts of your father ye will do. He was a murderer from the beginning, and abode not in the truth, because there is no truth in him. When he speaketh a lie, he speaketh of his own: for he is a liar, and the father of it" (Jn.8:44).	⇒ Anything that is not true is false—whether a lie, thoughts, ideas, words, or acts. Lying is of the devil and exposes a person to be a child of the devil. A person is certainly not of God if he is lying. His father is not the Father of Jesus Christ. "But Peter said, Ananias, why hath Satan filled thine heart to <u>lie to the Holy Ghost</u>, and to keep back part of the price of the land? Whiles it remained, was it not thine own? and after it was sold, was it not in thine own power? why hast thou conceived this thing in thine heart? thou hast not <u>lied</u> unto men, <u>but unto God</u>" (Acts 5:3-4). "I have not written unto you because ye know not the truth, but because ye know it, and that no lie is of the truth. Who is a liar but he that denieth that Jesus is the Christ? He is antichrist, that denieth the Father and the Son. Whosoever denieth the Son, the same hath not the Father: *(but) he that acknowledgeth the Son hath the Father also*" (1 Jn.2:21-23). "A false witness shall not be unpunished, and he that speaketh lies shall not escape" (Pr.19:5). "But the fearful, and unbelieving, and the abominable, and murderers, and whoremongers, and sorcerers, and idolaters, and <u>all liars</u>, shall have their part in the lake which burneth with fire and brimstone: which is the second death" (Rev.21:8).
4. Jesus Christ declared that our words will either justify or condemn us. "For by thy words thou shalt be justified, and by thy words thou shalt be condemned" (Mt.12:37).	⇒ The same law stated by Christ is common to man. A man is judged to be guilty or not guilty based upon the testimony of his words. • Words that are kind, gracious, loving, edifying, and profitable will testify for us and justify us in the day of judgment. • Words that are ugly, dirty, filthy, angry, spiteful, gossiping, grumbling, and murmuring will testify against us and condemn us in the day of judgment.

THE TEACHING OF CHRIST	THE BELIEVER'S RESPONSE
	"He that hideth hatred with lying lips, <u>and he that uttereth a slander, is a fool</u>" (Pr.10:18). "Death and life *are* in the power of the tongue: and they that love it shall eat the fruit thereof" (Pr.18:21). "A false witness shall not be unpunished, and he that speaketh lies shall perish" (Pr.19:9). "And the tongue is a fire, a world of iniquity: so is the tongue among our members, that <u>it defileth the whole body,</u> and setteth on fire the course of nature; and it is set on fire of hell" (Jas.3:6). "Speak not evil one of another, brethren. He that speaketh evil of his brother, and judgeth his brother, speaketh evil of the law, and judgeth the law: but if thou judge the law, thou art not a doer of the law, but a judge" (Jas.4:11).
5. Jesus Christ declared that men will slander and speak evil of His people. **"Blessed are ye, when *men* shall revile you, and persecute *you,* and shall say all manner of evil against you falsely, for my sake. Rejoice, and be exceeding glad: for great *is* your reward in heaven: for so persecuted they the prophets which were before you" (Mt.5:11-12).**	1) What is to be the believer's attitude toward persecution? ⇒ It is *not* to be retaliation, pride, spiritual superiority ⇒ It *is* to be joy and gladness 2) The persecuted are promised great rewards: a) The Kingdom of Heaven—*now*. The persecuted believer experiences... • a special honor (Acts 5:41) • a special consolation (2 Cor.1:5) • a special closeness, a glow of the Lord's presence (see note-- 1 Pt.4:14). • a greater witness for Christ (2 Cor.1:4-6) b) The Kingdom of Heaven—*eternally* (Heb.11:35f; 1 Pt.4:12-13; see note Mt.19:23-24) "For I have heard the slander of many: fear *was* on every side: while they took counsel together against me, they devised to take away my life" (Ps.31:13). "Having a good conscience; that, whereas they speak evil of you, as of evildoers, they may be ashamed that falsely accuse your good conversation in Christ" (1 Pt.3:16). "Yea, and all that will live godly in Christ Jesus shall suffer persecution" (2 Tim.3:12). "Beloved, think it not strange concerning the fiery trial which is to try you, as though some strange thing happened unto you: But rejoice, inasmuch as ye are partakers of Christ's sufferings; that, when his glory shall be revealed, ye may be glad also with exceeding joy. If ye be reproached for the name of Christ, happy *are ye;* for the spirit of glory and of God resteth upon you: on their part he is evil spoken of, but on your part he is glorified" (1 Pt.4:12-14). "Marvel not, my brethren, if the world hate you" (1 Jn.3:13).

	K. The Ten Commandments, The Laws Governing Man's Duty To Others (Part 6): Commandment Ten Concerns Man's Desires & Security—Never Covet, Ex.20:17
Commandment 10 concerns *man's desires & security*: Forbids coveting anything that belongs to a neighbor—his house, wife, servant, workers, animals, or anything else	17 Thou shalt not covet thy neighbour's house, thou shalt not covet thy neighbour's wife, nor his manservant, nor his maidservant, nor his ox, nor his ass, nor any thing that is thy neighbour's.

DIVISION VII

THE LAW AND THE PROMISES OF GOD (THE MOSAIC COVENANT) (PART 2): THE TEN COMMANDMENTS--NECESSARY LAWS TO GOVERN MAN AND SOCIETY, EX.20:1-26

K.   The Ten Commandments, The Laws Governing Man's Duty To Others (Part 6): Commandment Ten Concerns Man's Desires and Security--Never Covet, Ex.20:17

(20:17) **Introduction--Covet--Desire--Lust**: covetousness is a sin given little attention. Few sermons are ever preached and few lessons ever taught on covetousness. And there are even fewer books written on the subject. This is surprising, for covetousness is one of the most prevailing evils of society. Simply stated, covetousness is a predominant desire or thought, a desire or thought that craves, lusts, and yearns, that just eats away at the human heart. It is covetousness...

- that craves the things of the world, the things a person does not have
- that craves the things of others

Covetousness can and often does enslave the human soul: it often destroys a person or causes the destruction of other people. Covetousness is what causes and leads to so many of the other sins:

⇒ A person covets a woman and commits adultery.
⇒ A person covets money or property and steals or kills.
⇒ A person covets recognition and acceptance, or he seeks to escape suspicion; therefore, he lies.
⇒ A person feels unattractive, unhealthy, inadequate, or poor and he covets what someone else has to the point of wishing that something bad would happen to the person

Covetousness is terribly destructive. It is a desire or thought that will gnaw away at the mind until it consumes a person. A covetous thought or desire left unchecked can be so consuming that it almost forces a person to act. In such covetous moments, only the power of God can enable us to withstand the temptation. Only God can keep us from reaching out and taking what is not ours. Covetousness is a sin of the human heart that causes so many of the problems within society.

This is the critical importance of this commandment: *Commandment Ten Concerns Man's Desires and Security--Never Covet*, 20:17.

1.   Who is to obey this commandment? How long was this commandment to be in force (v.17)?
2.   What is forbidden by this commandment (v.17)?
3.   What is the decision required by this commandment (v.17)?

1 (20:17) **Commandments, The Ten--Covetousness--Desire--Lust--Craving**: Who is to obey this commandment? How long was this commandment to be in force? Beyond question, covetousness is the most serious infection that corrupts man's heart. Covetousness always has been and always will be the prevailing sin of man's heart. Before man ever carries out any sin, covetousness--the desire, the lust, the thought--is aroused within his heart. Man covets, desires, lusts to sin; and then he carries out the act of sin.

The point is clear and forceful: as long as man exists and God rules over the earth, there will be a need for this tenth commandment, a need for man to heed the demand of God: "You shall not covet" (v.17).

Now, who is to obey this commandment? Note the verse: "You." Everyone of us. Every generation of man is to obey this commandment.

> **"Thou shalt not covet thy neighbour's house, thou shalt not covet thy neighbour's wife, nor his manservant, nor his maidservant, nor his ox, nor his ass, nor any thing that is thy neighbour's" (v.17).**

2 (20:17) **Commandments, The Ten--Covetousness--Desire--Lust--Sin--Security**: What is forbidden by this commandment, "You shall not covet"? How is this commandment broken, violated? Commandment ten concerns man's security. This commandment forbids coveting anything that belongs to our neighbor: his house, wife, servant, workers, animals, or anything else. A man should be able to live in peace and feel secure. He should not have to worry about someone coveting and stealing what he has. God wants man to feel secure and protected. God wants man to know that his wife and family, his property and possessions, his joy and anything else he has is secure and protected against the covetousness and theft of people.

1. The Hebrew word for *covet* (hamad) means to desire, crave, want, long for, thirst for, yearn for, lust after. *Coveting* is a neutral word; that is, coveting can be good as well as bad, legitimate as well as illegitimate.

   a. The Bible clearly says that there is a legitimate covetousness, that God has planted within man certain inalienable desires, desires that we are entitled to, desires that are good. We all have legitimate desires for love, joy, and peace; legitimate desires to be secure, successful, fulfilled, and satisfied.

   ⇒ The Bible says that every good and perfect gift comes from God Himself. This being so, we should actually *seek after* and *covet* good and perfect gifts.

   "Every good gift and every perfect gift is from above, and cometh down from the Father of lights, with whom is no variableness, neither shadow of turning" (Jas.1:17).

   ⇒ The Bible says that the excellent qualities of life and the best gifts of God are to be coveted.

   "Blessed [are] they which do <u>hunger and thirst</u> after righteousness: for they shall be filled" (Mt.5:6).
   "But <u>covet earnestly</u> the best gifts: and yet show I unto you a more excellent way" (1 Cor.12:31).
   "The fear of the LORD is clean, enduring for ever: the judgments of the LORD are true and righteous altogether. More to be <u>desired</u> are they than gold, yea, than much fine gold: sweeter also than honey and the honeycomb" (Ps.19:9-10).

   ⇒ The Bible even says that God gives us the ability to get wealth and that we should work so diligently that we can actually earn enough to meet the needs of others.

   "Let him that stole steal no more: but rather let him labour, working with his hands the thing which is good, that he may have to give to him that needeth" (Eph.4:28).

   b. The Bible clearly says there is an illegitimate covetousness, that man commits evil when he desires another person's wife or property, or any other possession belonging to the person.

   "Thou shalt not covet thy neighbour's house, thou shalt not covet thy neighbour's wife, nor his manservant, nor his maidservant, nor his ox, nor his ass, nor any thing that is thy neighbour's" (Ex.20:17).
   "But fornication, and all uncleanness, or <u>covetousness</u>, let it not be once named among you, as becometh saints" (Eph.5:3).
   "Mortify [put to death] therefore your members which are upon the earth; fornication, uncleanness, inordinate affection, evil concupiscence, and <u>covetousness</u>, which is idolatry" (Col.3:5).

2. Covetousness is an inward sin, a sin of the heart and mind: it is a *desire*, a *thought* within the heart and mind. This commandment differs from the other commandments in this very fact, differs rather significantly: covetousness is not the outward sin; it is the inward *desire* and *thought* that leads to the outward sin.

Remember, the first nine commandments dealt primarily with outward acts, with such acts as lying, stealing, and killing. But this tenth commandment deals with the human heart, with inward feelings, desires, thoughts, and attitudes. But note: the first nine commandments *also involved* the desires and thoughts of a person. Before a person ever lies, steals, or kills, the desire or thought to take such action arises in his heart and mind. The desire to do something always precedes the actual act. A man commits immorality because he desires a person. A woman steals because she either desires the thing stolen or the excitement of stealing. In dealing with the first nine commandments, we discussed this fact, the fact that the evil forbidden was aroused first of all in the heart and mind of a person, that the evil was basically a heart problem.

This is the very reason God has covered coveting last, listed it as the tenth commandment. Coveting (desire, lust, the covetous thought) is the first thing that happens before a person commits the outward sin. The sin is *aroused* within the heart before it is committed; the evil act is *thought about* before it is done. This commandment underlies all the commandments: coveting--the desire or thought--takes place within the human heart and mind before any of the nine commandments are publicly or secretly committed. Before a person ever commits the sinful act, he desires and thinks about what someone else has, his...

- house
- wife
- servant
- livestock

- horse
- vehicle
- property
- money

- clothing
- appearance
- personality
- looks

- position
- power
- recognition
- job

- promotion
- opportunity
- influence

The list could go on ad infinitum. We commit the sin of covetousness when our *hearts and minds* are set on some possession, so set that we...

- crave, long, and lust after it
- are consumed with getting it
- give ourselves over to pursuing it
- give top priority and first attention to it
- focus our hearts, minds, energy, and time to securing it

Covetousness is being so consumed with getting something that we become gripped and enslaved by it. Our hearts become focused upon *a possession, a thing, something other than God*. This is the reason Scripture declares that covetousness is idolatry:

"For this ye know, that no whoremonger, nor unclean person, nor covetous man, who is an idolater, hath any inheritance in the kingdom of Christ and of God" (Eph.5:5).

Thought 1. Maxie Dunnam has an excellent application on this commandment:

"Most of us are guilty of looking at others, comparing ourselves to them, and seeing ourselves come out on the short end. We torture ourselves in this fashion, drive ourselves to depression by self-pity, thinking we deserve more. When we find ourselves jealous of what life is for someone else, dreaming of how happy we would be if we were in someone else's situation, it's a dead giveaway that we are falling into the subtle, seductive hands of covetousness.

"How often do we convince ourselves that other people always get the breaks and not us? How recently have we thought that we were deprived of opportunity? We look at our peers, friends our own age, and see where they are in life, and we're plagued with the notion that they had far more opportunity than we did.

"You probably have not associated that with coveting, but whatever name you give it, it is exactly that, and it is destructive....

"We convince ourselves that we have a sort of cosmic right to an equal share of the good things of life. That's a fallacious idea, and it plays folly in our lives. There's no equality to being in the right place at the right time.

"There is no cosmic right that is ours to have an equal share of what everybody else has. If you're prone to leaning in that direction, consider how you would feel if you were averaged out with the world's two billion starving people. You see, we always want to be averaged up and not down."[1]

Thought 2. Matthew Henry has a very graphic application:

"'O that such a man's house were mine! Such a man's wife mine! Such a man's estate mine!' This is certainly the language of discontent at our own lot, and envy at our neighbour's; and these are the sins principally forbidden here."[2]

Thought 3. The covetous life has been described as follows by an unnamed author:

"The passion to possess is an ugly sin no matter how we look at it. But when the object of our passion belongs to some one else, as the Tenth Commandment says "thy neighbor", this sin takes on an even uglier hue. When we covet something "out there", something that is available and waiting to be claimed, we limit most of the destruction to ourselves. But, when we covet that which belongs to others, we bring those people into the situation, and jeopardize our attitudes toward them and our relationships with them.

"Someone may covet a starting position on a sports team or another individual's job. This person, consumed with envy, may scheme and wish for his nemesis to be hurt, or miss a deadline, or lose an account, in order to claim his position. Or, what about coveting someone else's spouse? This person berates their own mate, feeds discontent with insensitive comparisons, and undermines another's marriage with subtle (or, not-so-subtle) advances. Some selfish siblings count the days to their parents' death as they covet the inheritance money.

"Coveting what belongs to another person is a serious offense on two counts. First, it indicates our lack of love for our neighbor, our relative, our friend, or whoever owns what we desire. The first and great commandment has to do with love; but, covetousness stands in direct opposition to love. When we place our affections on an inheritance, we remove our love from the person who's bequeathing it to us. When we see our neighbor's wife as the object of our desire, we begin to view our neighbor as the object of our disdain. When we scheme to get someone else's job, we reveal our calloused, insensitive heart. When we wish another person illness, injury, or bad fortune, we make it clear that the ONLY person we care about is 'NUMBER ONE', ourselves. When we covet what belongs to someone else, we displace the owner. In our minds, we kick him out of the game, or out of the job, or out of the marriage."[3]

3 (20:17) **Commandments, The Ten--Covetousness--Decision--Desire--Lust**: What is the decision required by this commandment? Note that covetousness is not a material or physical thing. We cannot see nor touch covetousness--only the results of it. Covetousness is an arousal, a passion that arises within our hearts and minds: it involves thoughts, desires, cravings, attitudes, longings, lusts. And these inward feelings and thoughts are far more difficult to control than outward acts. Nevertheless, this is exactly what God demands. He expects a strong decision, a clear cut decision: that we *never covet*. This is the tenth and final great commandment of God: "You shall not covet" (20:17).

1. We must stamp out the very first thought or urge to covet (desire or lust). The excellent commentator Arthur Pink says this:

---

[1]   Maxie Dunnam. *Mastering the Old Testament, Volume 2: Exodus,* p.267-268.
[2]   Matthew Henry. *Matthew Henry's Commentary,* Vol. 1, p.362-363.
[3]   SS literature. get info. p.6-7

"[Covetousness] is the first film or shadow of an evil thought, the imperfect embryo of a sin before it is shaped in us or has any lineaments or features. This is what the Scripture refers to as 'every imagination of the thoughts' of the human heart. Such imaginations are expressly declared to be 'evil' (Gen.6:5). Such are the first risings of our corrupt nature toward those sins which are pleasing to our sensual inclinations. They are to be steadfastly watched, hated, and resisted. They are to be stamped upon as the sparks of a dangerous fire, for as soon as they begin to stir within us they pollute our souls. Just as the breathing upon a mirror sullies it, leaving a dimness there, so the very first breathings of an evil desire or thought within one's breast defile the soul."[4]

2. We must not covet (desire, lust) the things of this world.

> **"Thou shalt not covet thy neighbour's house, thou shalt not covet thy neighbour's wife, nor his manservant, nor his maidservant, nor his ox, nor his ass, nor any thing that is thy neighbour's" (Ex.20:17).**
> **"Neither shalt thou desire thy neighbour's wife, neither shalt thou covet thy neighbour's house, his field, or his manservant, or his maidservant, his ox, or his ass, or any thing that is thy neighbour's" (Dt.5:21).**
> **"Now these things were our examples, to the intent we should not lust after evil things, as they also lusted" (1 Cor.10:6).**
> **"Love not the world, neither the things that are in the world. If any man love the world, the love of the Father is not in him. For all that is in the world, the lust of the flesh, and the lust of the eyes, and the pride of life, is not of the Father, but is of the world" (1 Jn.2:15-16).**

3. We must beware and guard against the very first urging and thought of covetousness.

> **"And he said unto them, Take heed, and beware of covetousness: for a man's life consisteth not in the abundance of the things which he possesseth" (Lk.12:15).**
> **"Casting down imaginations, and every high thing that exalteth itself against the knowledge of God, and bringing into captivity every thought to the obedience of Christ" (2 Cor.10:5).**

4. We must put to death the arousal and growth of covetousness (desires, lusts) in our hearts.

> **"Mortify therefore your members which are upon the earth; fornication, uncleanness, inordinate affection, evil concupiscence, and covetousness, which is idolatry" (Col.3:5).**

5. We must not covet (lust, crave) after women.

> **"Lust not after her beauty in thine heart; neither let her take thee with her eyelids" (Pr.6:25).**
> **"But I say unto you, That whosoever looketh on a woman to lust after her hath committed adultery with her already in his heart" (Mt.5:28).**

6. We must not fellowship with a covetous person.

> **"But now I have written unto you not to keep company, if any man that is called a brother be a fornicator, or covetous, or an idolater, or a railer, or a drunkard, or an extortioner; with such an one no not to eat" (1 Cor.5:11).**

7. We must not envy sinners, no matter who they are or what they have.

> **"Let not thine heart envy sinners: but be thou in the fear of the LORD all the day long" (Pr.23:17).**
> **"Be not thou envious against evil men, neither desire to be with them" (Pr.24:1).**

8. We must covet (desire, long for) only the good things of life.

> **"But covet earnestly the best gifts: and yet show I unto you a more excellent way" (1 Cor.12:31).**
> **"Wherefore, brethren, covet to prophesy, and forbid not to speak with tongues" (1 Cor.14:39).**

9. We must not seek first the things of this earth, but rather seek first the kingdom of God and His righteousness.

> **"But seek ye first the kingdom of God, and his righteousness; and all these things shall be added unto you" (Mt.6:33).**

10. We must not lay up treasure upon earth, but rather lay up treasure in heaven.

> **"Lay not up for yourselves treasures upon earth, where moth and rust doth corrupt, and where thieves break through and steal: But lay up for yourselves treasures in heaven, where neither moth nor rust doth corrupt, and where thieves do not break through nor steal" (Mt.6:19-20).**

---

[4] Arthur Pink. *The Ten Commandments*, p.64.

11. We must walk in the Spirit of God not in the lusts of the flesh.

> "This I say then, Walk in the Spirit, and ye shall not fulfill the lust [covetousness, desires] of the flesh" (Gal.5:16).

12. We must pray and seek God for the things we need and want, not covet them.

> "Ye lust [covet, desire], and have not: ye kill, and desire to have, and cannot obtain: ye fight and war, yet ye have not, because ye ask not" (Jas.4:2).

13. We must not attempt to serve (covet, long after) both God and money.

> "No servant can serve two masters: for either he will hate the one, and love the other; or else he will hold to the one, and despise the other. Ye cannot serve God and mammon. And the Pharisees also, who were covetous, heard all these things: and they derided him" (Lk.16:13-14).

14. We must be content with what we have.

> "Let your conversation be without covetousness; and be content with such things as ye have: for he hath said, I will never leave thee, nor forsake thee. So that we may boldly say, The Lord is my helper, and I will not fear what man shall do unto me" (Heb.13:5-6).

The Preacher's Outline & Sermon Bible® in its commentary on Hebrews 13:5-6 says this:

1. "Covetousness" (aphilarguros) means loving money or possessions. A person can love money, property, estates, houses, cars--anything on earth. Thomas Hewitt points out that the Greek word for "conversation" (tropos) means *manner of life*, or *the way of thought and life*.[5] The believer's very thoughts are to be free from covetousness. His thoughts are to be focused upon Christ and the glorious hope of eternity, not upon this passing world and its possessions. The believer is to have no secret lust for the things of this world.

2. A believer is to be content with what he has. This does not mean that a believer is not to improve himself, nor that he is not to work and make money and be wise in investments. Scripture teaches the very opposite: we are to work and invest and make money. We are to make enough so that we can meet the needs of the world. What this passage means is that we are to be...

- satisfied with our lot in life: our ability, capacity, job, position, opportunities, and on and on
- satisfied with the home, possessions, clothing, goods and everything else we have, whether it is little or nothing
- satisfied with our present condition

Again, this does not mean that we do not plan and focus upon improving everything around us--ranging from our personal possessions over to the world's economy and environment. Believers are to work and labor more diligently than anyone else in the world. But while we labor, we know...

- God never leaves us nor forsakes us (Job 1:5)
- God is our helper, and we are secure no matter what men may do to us (Ps.118:6)

Even if the world's economy and peace collapsed, believers--true believers--would be secure in God. God provides for His dear followers until He is ready to take them home to heaven (Mt.6:33). Matthew Henry sums it up well:

> "This promise contains the sum and substance of all the promises. I will never, no, never leave thee, nor ever forsake thee. Here are no fewer than five negatives heaped together, to confirm the promise; the true believer shall have the gracious presence of God with him in life, at death, and for ever."[6]

THE BIBLICAL CONSEQUENCES OF COVETING
ANYTHING THAT BELONGS TO YOUR NEIGHBOR

DEEPER STUDY #1

(20:17) **Commandments, The Ten--Obedience--Judgment--Covet-Coveting--Lust**: What are the consequences of coveting? The person who breaks this commandment totally disregards trust in God's provision. Instead of being content with what God has provided, this person...

• wants more	• sees more	• needs more
• desires more	• craves more	• wishes for more
• envies more	• longs for more	• lusts for more
• thirsts for more	• hungers for more	• requires more

The person who habitually breaks this commandment will never be satisfied. His flesh and his sinful nature will always long for more. God clearly warns: there are bitter consequences for breaking this commandment.

---

5   Thomas Hewitt. *The Epistle to the Hebrews.* "Tyndale New Testament Commentaries." (Grand Rapids, MI: Eerdmans Publishing Co., Began in 1958), p.206.

6   Matthew Henry. *Matthew Henry's Commentary*, Vol.6, p.962.

1. There are the consequences upon God.
   a. The covetous person rejects God: His care, His kingdom, and His righteousness.

   > "But <u>seek ye first</u> the kingdom of God, and his righteousness; and all these things shall be added unto you" (Mt.6:33).
   > "Let your conversation be without covetousness; and be content with such things as ye have: for he hath said, I will never leave thee, nor forsake thee" (Heb.13:5).

   b. The covetous person becomes an enemy of God.

   > "(For many walk, of whom I have told you often, and now tell you even weeping, that they are the enemies of the cross of Christ: Whose end is destruction, whose God is their belly, and whose glory is in their shame, who mind earthly things)" (Ph.3:18-19).
   > "Ye adulterers and adulteresses, know ye not that the friendship of the world is enmity with God? <u>whosoever therefore will be a friend of the world is the enemy of God</u>" (Jas.4:4).

2. There are the consequences upon one's family and others.
   a. The covetous person sometimes ruins lives and families, causing terrible pain, suffering, and division.

   > "And he said, Thy brother came with subtilty, and hath taken away thy blessing. And he said, Is not he rightly named Jacob? for he hath supplanted me these two times: he took away my birthright; and, behold, now he hath taken away my blessing. And he said, Hast thou not reserved a blessing for me? And Isaac answered and said unto Esau, Behold, I have made him thy lord, and all his brethren have I given to him for servants; and with corn and wine have I sustained him: and what shall I do now unto thee, my son? And Esau said unto his father, Hast thou but one blessing, my father? bless me, even me also, O my father. And Esau lifted up his voice, and wept. And Esau hated Jacob because of the blessing wherewith his father blessed him: and Esau said in his heart, The days of mourning for my father are at hand; then will I slay my brother Jacob" (Gen.27:35-38, 41).
   > "And it came to pass in an eveningtide, that David arose from off his bed, and walked upon the roof of the king's house: and from the roof he saw a woman washing herself; and the woman was very beautiful to look upon. And David sent and inquired after the woman. And one said, Is not this Bath-sheba, the daughter of Eliam, the wife of Uriah the Hittite? And David sent messengers, and took her; and she came in unto him, and he lay with her; for she was purified from her uncleanness: and she returned unto her house. And the woman conceived, and sent and told David, and said, I am with child....And it came to pass in the morning, that David wrote a letter to Joab, and sent it by the hand of Uriah. And he wrote in the letter, saying, Set ye Uriah in the forefront of the hottest battle, and retire ye from him, that he may be smitten, and die. And it came to pass, when Joab observed the city, that he assigned Uriah unto a place where he knew that valiant men were. And the men of the city went out, and fought with Joab: and there fell some of the people of the servants of David; and Uriah the Hittite died also....And when the wife of Uriah heard that Uriah her husband was dead, she mourned for her husband. And when the mourning was past, David sent and fetched her to his house, and she became his wife, and bare him a son. But the thing that David had done displeased the LORD" (2 Sam.11:2-5, 14-17, 26-27).

   b. The covetous person sometimes oppresses people and steals from them.

   > "And they covet fields, and take them by violence; and houses, and take them away: so they oppress a man and his house, even a man and his heritage" (Mic.2:2).
   > "And Jacob was wroth, and chode with [admonished, reproached] Laban: and Jacob answered and said to Laban, What is my trespass? what is my sin, that thou hast so hotly pursued after me? Whereas thou hast searched all my stuff, what hast thou found of all thy household stuff? set it here before my brethren and thy brethren, that they may judge betwixt us both. This twenty years have I been with thee; thy ewes and thy she goats have not cast their young, and the rams of thy flock have I not eaten. That which was torn of beasts I brought not unto thee; I bare the loss of it; of my hand didst thou require it, whether stolen by day, or stolen by night. Thus I was; in the day the drought consumed me, and the frost by night; and my sleep departed from mine eyes. Thus have I been twenty years in thy house; I served thee fourteen years for thy two daughters, and six years for thy cattle: and thou hast <u>changed my wages ten times</u>. Except the God of my father, the God of Abraham, and the fear of Isaac, had been with me, surely thou hadst sent me away now empty. God hath seen mine affliction and the labour of my hands, and rebuked thee yesternight" (Gen.31:36-42).

   c. The covetous person causes grief for his entire family because of his pursuit of dishonest money.

   > "<u>He that is greedy of gain troubleth his own house</u>; but he that hateth gifts [bribes] shall live" (Pr.15:27).

d. The covetous person sometimes enslaves other people for money.

> "**And the patriarchs, moved with envy, sold Joseph into Egypt: but God was with him**" **(Acts 7:9).**

e. The covetous person sometimes seeks to make a profit in sinful and evil ways.

> "**And it came to pass, as we went to prayer, a certain damsel possessed with a spirit of divination met us, which brought her masters much gain by soothsaying: The same followed Paul and us, and cried, saying, These men are the servants of the most high God, which show unto us the way of salvation. And this did she many days. But Paul, being grieved, turned and said to the spirit, I command thee in the name of Jesus Christ to come out of her. And he came out the same hour. And when her masters saw that the hope of their gains was gone, they caught Paul and Silas, and drew them into the marketplace unto the rulers**" (Acts 16:16-19).
>
> "**For a certain** *man* **named Demetrius, a silversmith, which made silver shrines for Diana, brought no small gain unto the craftsmen; Whom he called together with the workmen of like occupation, and said, Sirs, ye know that by this craft we have our wealth. Moreover ye see and hear, that not alone at Ephesus, but almost throughout all Asia, this Paul hath persuaded and turned away much people, saying that they be no gods, which are made with hands**" (Acts 19:24-26).

3. There are the consequences upon oneself, one's day to day life.
   a. The covetous person sometimes becomes an adulterer.

> "**But I say unto you, That** whosoever looketh on [covets] **a woman to lust after her hath committed adultery with her already in his heart. And if thy right eye offend thee, pluck it out, and cast it from thee: for it is profitable for thee that one of thy members should perish, and not that thy whole body should be cast into hell**" (Mt.5:28-29).
>
> "**And it came to pass in an eveningtide, that David arose from off his bed, and walked upon the roof of the king's house: and from the roof he saw a woman washing herself; and the woman was very beautiful to look upon. And David sent and inquired after the woman. And one said, Is not this Bath-sheba, the daughter of Eliam, the wife of Uriah the Hittite? And David sent messengers, and took her; and she came in unto him, and he lay with her; for she was purified from her uncleanness: and she returned unto her house**" (2 Sam.11:2-4).

b. The covetous person becomes an idolater, one who refuses to acknowledge God as Lord and Master.

> "**Mortify therefore your members which are upon the earth; fornication, uncleanness, inordinate affection, evil concupiscence, and** covetousness, which is idolatry" **(Col.3:5).**

c. The covetous person is greedy and will suffer many sorrows and much grief.

> "**So are the ways of every one that is greedy of gain; which taketh away the life of the owners thereof**" **(Pr.1:19).**
>
> "**For the love of money is the root of all evil: which while some coveted after, they have erred from the faith, and pierced themselves through with many sorrows**" (1 Tim.6:10).

d. The covetous person is unsatisfied, unfulfilled, and unhappy.

> "**Yea,** *they are* **greedy dogs** *which* **can never have enough, and they** *are* **shepherds** *that* **cannot understand: they all look to their own way, every one for his gain, from his quarter**" (Is.56:11).
>
> "**Then I returned, and I saw vanity under the sun. There is one** *alone,* **and** *there is* **not a second; yea, he hath neither child nor brother: yet** *is there* **no end of all his labour; neither is his eye satisfied with riches; neither** *saith he,* **For whom do I labour, and bereave my soul of good? This** *is* **also vanity, yea, it** *is* **a sore travail**" (Eccl.4:7-8).
>
> "He that loveth silver shall not be satisfied with silver; **nor he that loveth abundance with increase: this is also vanity**" (Eccl.5:10).
>
> "**All the labour of man is for his mouth, and** yet the appetite is not filled" (Eccl.6:7).

e. The covetous person has a warped perspective on the value of material things.

> "**And he said unto them, Take heed, and beware of covetousness: for** a man's life consisteth not in the abundance of the things which he possesseth" (Lk.12:15).

f. The covetous person is misguided, placing his trust in accumulated riches and wealth.

> "**They that trust in their wealth, and boast themselves in the multitude of their riches; None** *of* *them* **can by any means redeem his brother, nor give to God a ransom for him**" (Ps.49:6-7).

"Be not thou afraid when one is made rich, when the glory of his house is increased; For when he dieth he shall carry nothing away: his glory shall not descend after him" (Ps.49:16-17).

"Lo, *this is* the man *that* made not God his strength; but trusted in the abundance of his riches, *and* strengthened himself in his wickedness" (Ps.52:7).

"Riches profit not in the day of wrath: but righteousness delivereth from death" (Pr.11:4).

"He that trusteth in his riches shall fall: but the righteous shall flourish as a branch" (Pr.11:28).

g. The covetous person does not receive the answers to his prayers.

"From whence *come* wars and fightings among you? *come they* not hence, *even* of your lusts that war in your members? Ye lust, and have not: ye kill, and desire to have, and cannot obtain: ye fight and war, yet ye have not, because ye ask not. Ye ask, and receive not, because ye ask amiss, that ye may consume *it* upon your lusts" (Jas.4:1-3).

h. The covetous person is envious of the prosperity of the wicked.

"But as for me, my feet were almost gone; my steps had well nigh slipped. For I was envious at the foolish, *when* I saw the prosperity of the wicked" (Ps.73:2-3).

i. The covetous person will become sick from what he covets.

"Hast thou found honey? eat so much as is sufficient for thee, lest thou be filled therewith, and vomit it" (Pr.25:16).

j. The covetous person is a hypocrite.

"And they come unto thee as the people cometh, and they sit before thee as my people, and they hear thy words, but they will not do them: for with their mouth they show much love, *but* their heart goeth after their covetousness" (Ezk.33:31).

k. The covetous person is doomed to a life of unfruitfulness.

"And these are they which are sown among thorns; such as hear the word, And the cares of this world, and the deceitfulness of riches, and the lusts of other things entering in, choke the word, and it becometh unfruitful" (Mk.4:18-19).

l. The covetous person is worldly and carnal, a prisoner to the flesh, enslaved and given over to his lust and filled with coveteousness.

"And even as they did not like to retain God in *their* knowledge, God gave them over to a reprobate mind, to do those things which are not convenient; Being filled with all unrighteousness, fornication, wickedness, covetousness, maliciousness; full of envy, murder, debate, deceit, malignity; whisperers" (Ro.1:28-29).

"But they that will be rich fall into temptation and a snare, and into many foolish and hurtful lusts, which drown men in destruction and perdition" (1 Tim.6:9).

"Lust not after her beauty in thine heart; neither let her take thee with her eyelids" (Pr.6:25).

4. There are the consequences of judgment.
   a. The covetous person is deceived and will not inherit the kingdom of God.

"Nay, ye do wrong, and defraud, and that *your* brethren. Know ye not that the unrighteous shall not inherit the kingdom of God? Be not deceived: neither fornicators, nor idolaters, nor adulterers, nor effeminate, nor abusers of themselves with mankind, Nor thieves, nor covetous, nor drunkards, nor revilers, nor extortioners, shall inherit the kingdom of God" (1 Cor.6:8-10).

"For this ye know, that no whoremonger, nor unclean person, nor covetous man, who is an idolater, hath any inheritance in the kingdom of Christ and of God" (Eph.5:5).

b. The covetous person will face the severe judgment of God.

"(For many walk, of whom I have told you often, and now tell you even weeping, that they are the enemies of the cross of Christ: Whose end is destruction, whose God is their belly, and whose glory is in their shame, who mind earthly things)" (Ph.3:18-19).

"And shall receive the reward of unrighteousness, *as* they that count it pleasure to riot in the daytime. Spots *they are* and blemishes, sporting themselves with their own deceivings while they feast with you; Having eyes full of adultery, and that cannot cease from sin; beguiling unstable souls: an heart they have exercised with covetous practices; cursed children....For if after they have escaped the pollutions of the world through the knowledge of the Lord and Saviour Jesus Christ, they are again entangled therein, and overcome, the latter end is worse with them than the beginning. For it had been better for them not to have known the way of righteousness, than, after they have known it, to turn from the holy commandment delivered unto them" (2 Pt.2:13-14, 20-21).

c. The covetous person is a castaway who will lose his soul.

"For what is a man profited, if he shall gain the whole world, and lose his own soul? or what shall a man give in exchange for his soul?" (Mt.16:26; cp. Mk.8:36-37).
"For what is a man advantaged, if he gain the whole world, and lose himself, or be cast away?" (Lk.9:25).
"And he said unto them, Take heed, and beware of covetousness: for a man's life consisteth not in the abundance of the things which he possesseth. And he spake a parable unto them, saying, The ground of a certain rich man brought forth plentifully: And he thought within himself, saying, What shall I do, because I have no room where to bestow my fruits? And he said, This will I do: I will pull down my barns, and build greater; and there will I bestow all my fruits and my goods. And I will say to my soul, Soul, thou hast much goods laid up for many years; take thine ease, eat, drink, [and] be merry. But God said unto him, [Thou] fool, this night thy soul shall be required of thee: then whose shall those things be, which thou hast provided? So [is] he that layeth up treasure for himself, and is not rich toward God" (Lk.12:15-21).

d. The covetous person is to be disciplined by the church, cut off from Christian fellowship.

"But now I have written unto you not to keep company, if any man that is called a brother be a fornicator, or covetous, or an idolater, or a railer, or a drunkard, or an extortioner; with such an one no not to eat" (1 Cor.5:11).

e. The covetous person is lost, passing away without God.

"For all that is in the world, the lust of the flesh, and the lust of the eyes, and the pride of life, is not of the Father, but is of the world. And the world passeth away, and the lust thereof: but he that doeth the will of God abideth for ever" (1 Jn.2:16-17).

THE BIBLICAL BENEFITS OF NOT COVETING ANYTHING THAT BELONGS TO YOUR NEIGHBOR

DEEPER STUDY #2
(20:17) Commandments, The Ten; Benefits--Obedience; Covet - Coveting: What are the benefits of keeping this commandment, the benefits of not coveting, of being content with what we have? Scripture declares the following: it is human nature to want more and more, to crave what is not ours, to desire things that will make our lives more comfortable. When God provides these things, it is a blessing. When man seeks these things outside of God's will, it is coveting. There are many great promises that can be claimed by the person who is content in the LORD and does not covet.

1. A person who is content in the LORD and truly seeks the LORD will have everything he needs.

"But seek ye first the kingdom of God, and his righteousness; and all these things shall be added unto you" (Mt.6:33).
"But my God shall supply all your need according to his riches in glory by Christ Jesus" (Ph.4:19).

2. A person who is content in the LORD and faithful will have plenty of God's provisions.

"I will abundantly bless her provision: I will satisfy her poor with bread" (Ps.132:15).
"Honour the LORD with thy substance, and with the firstfruits of all thine increase: So shall thy barns be filled with plenty, and thy presses shall burst out with new wine" (Pr.3:9-10).
"For the seed shall be prosperous; the vine shall give her fruit, and the ground shall give her increase, and the heavens shall give their dew; and I will cause the remnant of this people to possess all these things" (Zech.8:12).

3. A person who is content in the LORD and lives a righteous life will be blessed, even when the hard times come.

"Behold, the eye of the LORD is upon them that fear him, upon them that hope in his mercy; To deliver their soul from death, and to keep them alive in famine" (Ps.33:18-19).
"The LORD knoweth the days of the upright: and their inheritance shall be for ever. They shall not be ashamed in the evil time: and in the days of famine they shall be satisfied" (Ps.37:18-19).

4. A person who is content in the LORD will find pleasures and be satisfied forevermore.

"Thou wilt show me the path of life: in thy presence *is* fulness of joy; at thy right hand *there are* pleasures for evermore" (Ps.16:11).

"And ye shall eat in plenty, and be satisfied, and praise the name of the LORD your God, that hath dealt wondrously with you: and my people shall never be ashamed" (Joel 2:26).

5. A person who is content in the LORD and continually seeks the LORD will prosper in all he does (keeping in mind that prosperity in God's eyes and man's eyes are sometimes two entirely different things).

"Keep therefore the words of this covenant, and do them, that ye may prosper in all that ye do" (Dt.29:9).

"Then shalt thou prosper, if thou takest heed to fulfil the statutes and judgments which the Lord charged Moses with concerning Israel: be strong, and of good courage; dread not, nor be dismayed" (1 Chron.22:13).

"And they rose early in the morning, and went forth into the wilderness of Tekoa: and as they went forth, Jehoshaphat stood and said, Hear me, O Judah, and ye inhabitants of Jerusalem; Believe in the Lord your God, so shall ye be established; believe his prophets, so shall ye prosper" (2 Chron.20:20).

"And he sought God in the days of Zechariah, who had understanding in the visions of God: and as long as he sought the Lord, God made him to prosper" (2 Chron.26:5).

"And in every work that he began in the service of the house of God, and in the law, and in the commandments, to seek his God, he did it with all his heart, and prospered" (2 Chron.31:21).

"And he shall be like a tree planted by the rivers of water, that bringeth forth his fruit in his season; his leaf also shall not wither; and whatsoever he doeth shall prosper" (Ps.1:3).

6. A person who is content and obedient in the LORD will be greatly blessed and have much success.

"And all these blessings shall come on thee, and overtake thee, if thou shalt hearken unto the voice of the Lord thy God" (Dt.28:2).

"This book of the law shall not depart out of thy mouth; but thou shalt meditate therein day and night, that thou mayest observe to do according to all that is written therein: for then thou shalt make thy way prosperous, and then thou shalt have good success" (Josh.1:8).

"Many, O LORD my God, *are* thy wonderful works *which* thou hast done, and thy thoughts *which are* to us-ward: they cannot be reckoned up in order unto thee: *if* I would declare and speak *of them,* they are more than can be numbered" (Ps.40:5).

"Many, O LORD my God, are the wonders which Thou hast done, And Thy thoughts toward us; There is none to compare with Thee; If I would declare and speak of them, They would be too numerous to count" (Ps.40:5, NASB).

"A faithful man shall abound with blessings: but he that maketh haste to be rich shall not be innocent" (Pr.28:20).

"Bring ye all the tithes into the storehouse, that there may be meat in mine house, and prove me now herewith, saith the Lord of hosts, if I will not open you the windows of heaven, and pour you out a blessing, that there shall not be room enough to receive it" (Mal.3:10).

7. A person who is content in the LORD will find that his job promotion and positions come from the Lord.

"So now it was not you that sent me hither, but God: and he hath made me a father to Pharaoh, and lord of all his house, and a ruler throughout all the land of Egypt" (Gen.45:8).

"The Lord maketh poor, and maketh rich: he bringeth low, and lifteth up" (1 Sam.2:7).

"Now therefore so shalt thou say unto my servant David, Thus saith the Lord of hosts, I took thee from the sheepcote, from following the sheep, to be ruler over my people, over Israel" (2 Sam.7:8).

"Go, tell Jeroboam, Thus saith the Lord God of Israel, Forasmuch as I exalted thee from among the people, and made thee prince over my people Israel" (1 Ki.14:7).

"For promotion *cometh* neither from the east, nor from the west, nor from the south. But God is the judge: he putteth down one, and setteth up another" (Ps.75:6-7).

"And he changeth the times and the seasons: he removeth kings, and setteth up kings: he giveth wisdom unto the wise, and knowledge to them that know understanding" (Dan.2:21).

8. A person who is content in the LORD will be rewarded for his faithfulness and for having the right priorities.

"And he said unto him, Well thou good servant: because thou hast been faithful in a very little, have thou authority over ten cities" (Lk.19:17).

"For ye have need of patience, that, after ye have done the will of God, ye might receive the promise" (Heb.10:36).

"By faith Moses, when he was come to years, refused to be called the son of Pharaoh's daughter; Choosing rather to suffer affliction with the people of God, than to enjoy the pleasures of sin for a season; Esteeming the reproach of Christ greater riches than the treasures in Egypt: for he had respect unto the recompence of the reward" (Heb.11:24-26).

"And God said to Solomon, Because this was in thine heart, and thou hast not asked riches, wealth, or honour, nor the life of thine enemies, neither yet hast asked long life; but hast asked wisdom and knowledge for thyself, that thou mayest judge my people, over whom I have made thee king: Wisdom and knowledge is granted unto thee; and I will give thee riches, and wealth, and honour, such as none of the kings have had that have been before thee, neither shall there any after thee have the like" (2 Chron.1:11-12).

9. A person who is content in the LORD will, if needed, experience God's miraculous care and provision.

"Yea, forty years didst thou sustain them in the wilderness, so that they lacked nothing; their clothes waxed not old, and their feet swelled not" (Neh.9:21).

10. A person who is content in the LORD is a recipient of God's grace: he receives what he does not deserve.

"And I have given you a land for which ye did not labour, and cities which ye built not, and ye dwell in them; of the vineyards and oliveyards which ye planted not do ye eat" (Josh.24:13).

11. A person who is content in the LORD personally knows the Source of his supply.

"Then answered I them, and said unto them, The God of heaven, he will prosper us; therefore we his servants will arise and build: but ye have no portion, nor right, nor memorial, in Jerusalem" (Neh.2:20).

"But my God shall supply all your need according to his riches in glory by Christ Jesus" (Ph.4:19).

12. A person who is content in the LORD knows that everything belongs to God.

"The earth is the LORD's, and the fulness thereof; the world, and they that dwell therein" (Ps.24:1).

13. A person who is content in the LORD has a firm faith in God's ability to provide for his needs.

"O fear the LORD, ye his saints: for there is no want to them that fear him" (Ps.34:9).

"I have been young, and now am old; yet have I not seen the righteous forsaken, nor his seed begging bread" (Ps.37:25).

"God hath spoken once; twice have I heard this; that power belongeth unto God. Also unto thee, O Lord, belongeth mercy: for thou renderest to every man according to his work" (Ps.62:11-12).

14. A person who is content in the LORD understands that life and material possessions are temporal.

"And said, Naked came I out of my mother's womb, and naked shall I return thither: the LORD gave, and the LORD hath taken away; blessed be the name of the LORD" (Job 1:21).

15. A person who is content in the LORD *learns* to be content no matter the circumstances and problems.

"Not that I speak in respect of want: for I have learned, in whatsoever state I am, *therewith* to be content. I know both how to be abased, and I know how to abound: every where and in all things I am instructed both to be full and to be hungry, both to abound and to suffer need" (Ph.4:11-12).

"But godliness with contentment is great gain. For we brought nothing into this world, and it is certain we can carry nothing out. And having food and raiment let us be therewith content" (1 Tim.6:6-8).

16. A person who obeys the LORD is content in the LORD and has his prayers answered.

"And whatsoever we ask, we receive of him [contentment], because we keep his commandments, and do those things that are pleasing in his sight" (1 Jn.3:22).

DEEPER STUDY # 3

JESUS CHRIST AND HIS TEACHING CONCERNING <u>MAN'S SECURITY</u>

"Thou shalt not covet thy neighbour's house, thou shalt not covet thy neighbour's wife, nor his manservant, nor his maidservant, nor his ox, nor his ass, nor any thing that is thy neighbour's" (Ex.20:17).

THE TEACHING OF CHRIST	THE BELIEVER'S RESPONSE
1. Jesus Christ declared that man should never defraud (cheat) his neighbor, i.e., never covet anything of his neighbor. "Thou knowest the commandments, Do not commit adultery, Do not kill, Do not steal, Do not bear false witness, <u>Defraud not</u>, Honour thy father and mother" (Mk.10:19).	⇒ Scripture is clear: covetousness is wrong. We must never covet: we must never cheat our neighbor out of anything. "Thou shalt not covet thy neighbour's house, thou shalt not covet thy neighbour's wife, nor his manservant, nor his maidservant, nor his ox, nor his ass, nor any thing that is thy neighbour's" (Ex.20:17). "Take heed, and beware of covetousness" (Lk.12:15). "But fornication, and all uncleanness, or covetousness, let it not be once named among you" (Eph.5:3). "Let your conversation [behavior, conduct] be without covetousness" (Heb.13:5).
2. Jesus Christ declared that man should beware of coveteousness because man's life is more than accumulating material things. "And he said unto them, Take heed, and beware of covetousness: for a man's life consisteth not in the abundance of the things which he possesseth" (Lk.12:15).	1) We must be content with what God has provided for us. 2) Within the heart of every man is the desire to have more and more. God has promised to provide everything that His people *need*. The greedy or coveteous man is unwilling to wait for God to provide; consequently, his passion for more is never quenched. "Not that I speak in respect of want: for I have learned, in whatsoever state I am, *therewith* to be content. I know both how to be abased, and I know how to abound: every where and in all things I am instructed both to be full and to be hungry, both to abound and to suffer need. I can do all things through Christ which strengtheneth me" (Ph.4:11-13). "*Let your* conversation [behavior, conduct] *be* without covetousness; *and be* content with such things as ye have: for he hath said, I will never leave thee, nor forsake thee. So that we may boldly say, The Lord *is* my helper, and I will not fear what man shall do unto me" (Heb.13:5-6). "Ye lust, and have not: ye kill, and desire to have, and cannot obtain: ye fight and war, yet ye have not, because ye ask not. Ye ask, and receive not, because ye ask amiss, that ye may consume it upon your lusts" (Jas.4:2-3). "(For many walk, of whom I have told you often, and now tell you even weeping, that they are the enemies of the cross of Christ: Whose end is destruction, whose God is their belly, and whose glory is in their shame, who mind earthly things)" (Ph.3:18-19). "Love not the world, neither the things that are in the world. If any man love the world, the love of the Father is not in him. For all that is in the world, the lust of the flesh, and the lust of the eyes, and the pride of life, is not of the Father, but is of the world" (1 Jn.2:15-16).

3. Jesus Christ declared that a man who covets (lusts, craves) after beauty in his heart has committed adultery and sexual immorality.
 	
"But I say unto you, That whosoever looketh on a woman to lust after her hath committed adultery with her already in his heart" (Mt.5:28).
	1) Coveting and lusting after a woman can never be justified. Sex is never right when a person covets another person to whom he or she is not married.
	2) The Bible does not teach that sex is wrong. But the Bible does teach that sex outside of marriage is wrong, and the wrong use of sex is sin. Sex has been given by God for at least three reasons.
	  a) Sex causes a person to be attracted to another person. Therefore, sexual attraction is one of the major tools that brings about marriage (Gen.2:18, 21-25).
	  b) Sex is a tool with which to love. Sex, properly rooted and expressed in God, is one of the deepest and richest involvements and expressions of love (Eph.5:28-32).
	  c) Sex creates life. God has given man the privilege of being sub-creators of life--under Him (Gen.1:29).
	2) Adultery is often said to be sexual unfaithfulness by a married person. This is true, but it is much more. Man's idea of adultery is shattered by Christ (see <u>Deeper Study # 5</u>--Mt.19:9). Christ says adultery is not only the actual act, but adultery is committed by any one of five acts:
	  a) A deliberate look.
	  b) Passion within the heart: desiring and lusting.
	  c) The actual act of sex with someone other than one's own spouse.
	  d) Divorce relationships (Mt.5:32; 19:9-11; Mk.10:11-12; Lk.16:18).
	  e) Spiritual unfaithfulness toward God or apostasy from God (Mt.12:39; 16:4; Mk.8:38; Jas.4:4; cp. Ezk.16:15f; 23:43f).

THE TEACHING OF CHRIST	THE BELIEVER'S RESPONSE
	"Lust not after her beauty in thine heart; neither let her take thee with her eyelids" (Pr.6:25). "Ye adulterers and adulteresses, know ye not that the friendship of the world is enmity with God? whosoever therefore will be a friend of the world is the enemy of God" (Jas.4:4). "Know ye not that the unrighteous shall not inherit the kingdom of God? Be not deceived: neither fornicators, nor idolaters, nor adulterers, nor effeminate, nor abusers of themselves with mankind, Nor thieves, nor covetous, nor drunkards, nor revilers, nor extortioners, shall inherit the kingdom of God" (1 Cor.6:9-10). "And it came to pass in an eveningtide, that David arose from off his bed, and walked upon the roof of the king's house: and from the roof he saw a woman washing herself; and the woman was very beautiful to look upon. And David sent and enquired after the woman. And one said, Is not this Bath-sheba, the daughter of Eliam, the wife of Uriah the Hittite? And David sent messengers, and took her; and she came in unto him, and he lay with her; for she was purified from her uncleanness: and she returned unto her house" (2 Sam.11:2-4).
4. Jesus Christ declared that we must not seek the things of this earth, but rather seek first the kingdom of God and His righteousness. "But seek ye first the kingdom of God, and his righteousness; and all these things shall be added unto you" (Mt.6:33).	1) Only God can meet the need of the heart that cries out for more and more. Things will never satisfy us. 2) When we die and pass on into the spiritual world, we can take nothing with us because we have no strength, no energy, no power, no way for our spirits to carry away material possessions. "For what shall it profit a man, if he shall gain the whole world, and lose his own soul? Or what shall a man give in exchange for his soul?" (Mk.8:36-37). "For we brought nothing into this world, and it is certain we can carry nothing out" (1 Tim.6:7). "A faithful man shall abound with blessings: but he that maketh haste to be rich shall not be innocent" (Pr.28:20). "Yea, they are greedy dogs which can never have enough, and they are shepherds that cannot understand: they all look to their own way, every one for his gain, from his quarter" (Is.56:11). "Then I returned, and I saw vanity under the sun. There is one alone, and there is not a second; yea, he hath neither child nor brother: yet is there no end of all his labour; neither is his eye satisfied with riches; neither saith he, For whom do I labour, and bereave my soul of good? This is also vanity, yea, it is a sore travail" (Eccl.4:7-8). "He that loveth silver shall not be satisfied with silver; nor he that loveth abundance with increase: this is also vanity" (Eccl.5:10).

5. Jesus Christ declared that we must not lay up treasure upon earth, but rather lay up treasure in heaven.
 	
"Lay not up for yourselves treasures upon earth, where moth and rust doth corrupt, and where thieves break through and steal: But lay up for yourselves treasures in heaven, where neither moth nor rust doth corrupt, and where thieves do not break through nor steal" (Mt.6:19-20).
	1) It is easier to covet earthly things than heavenly things for four reasons.
	  a) They are seen and can be handled.
	  b) They are sought by most people, and other people influence us. A person is either worldly minded or heavenly minded (Ro.8:5-7).
	  c) They are to varying degrees necessary for life.
	  d) They are present, ever before us, and can be possessed right now.
	2) The things on earth are insecure for three reasons:
	  a) They can be stolen, eaten up, or destroyed.
	  b) They do not last; they waste away.
	  c) A person cannot take a single thing with him when he passes from this world into the next.
	
	"Hast thou found honey? eat so much as is sufficient for thee, lest thou be filled therewith, and vomit it" (Pr.25:16).
	"And the cares of this world, and the deceitfulness of riches, and the lusts of other things entering in, choke the word, and it becometh unfruitful" (Mk.4:19).
	"For all that is in the world, the lust of the flesh, and the lust of the eyes, and the pride of life, is not of the Father, but is of the world. And the world passeth away, and the lust thereof: but he that doeth the will of God abideth for ever" (1 Jn.2:16-17).
	"Thou wilt show me the path of life: in thy presence is fulness of joy; at thy right hand there are pleasures for evermore" (Ps.16:11).

		22 And the LORD said unto Moses, Thus thou shalt say unto the children of Israel, Ye have seen that I have talked with you from heaven. 23 Ye shall not make with me gods of silver, neither shall ye make unto you gods of gold.	4. To teach that God alone is the LORD: He alone has truly revealed Himself, has spoken to man from heaven
	L. The Purposes For the Law: Why God Gave the Ten Commandments & the Law, Ex.20:18-26		
1. To reveal the glorious majesty & holiness of God: Showing that a great barrier--a great gulf--exists between man and God	18 And all the people saw the thunderings, and the lightnings, and the noise of the trumpet, and the mountain smoking: and when the people saw it, they removed, and stood afar off.		**5. To teach how God alone is to be approached & worshipped** a. No idolatry: No gods whatsoever are to be made or worshipped b. No pageantry
2. To reveal man's need for a mediator, for a person who can approach God on behalf of man	19 And they said unto Moses, Speak thou with us, and we will hear: but let not God speak with us, lest we die.	24 An altar of earth thou shalt make unto me, and shalt sacrifice thereon thy burnt offerings, and thy peace offerings, thy sheep, and thine oxen: in all places where I record my name I will come unto thee, and I will bless thee.	1) The altar of worship was to be of earth: A non-showy, non-costly material provided (created) by God alone 2) The altar of worship was to be made of natural, undressed stones: A material provided by God, not defiled & polluted by man
3. To test man a. To see if man will walk in the fear & reverence of God b. To see if man will truly obey God & not sin c. To see if man will trust the mediator appointed by God	20 And Moses said unto the people, Fear not: for God is come to prove you, and that his fear may be before your faces, that ye sin not. 21 And the people stood afar off, and Moses drew near unto the thick darkness where God was.	25 And if thou wilt make me an altar of stone, thou shalt not build it of hewn stone: for if thou lift up thy tool upon it, thou hast polluted it. 26 Neither shalt thou go up by steps unto mine altar, that thy nakedness be not discovered thereon.	c. No immodest behavior: The altar was not to have steps that would expose a person's nakedness (symbolized self-righteousness, man ascending up to God)

DIVISION VII

THE LAW AND THE PROMISES OF GOD (THE MOSAIC COVENANT) (PART 2): THE TEN COMMANDMENTS--NECESSARY LAWS TO GOVERN MAN AND SOCIETY, EX.20:1-26

L.   The Purposes For the Law: Why God Gave the Ten Commandments and the Law, Ex.20:18-26

(20:18-26) **Introduction**: Scripture is clear: God gave the Ten Commandments as the basic law to govern all people. But why? Why exactly did God give the Ten Commandments to the world? What were His purposes? What did God have in mind? What were His reasons for instituting the Ten Commandments to be the basic law for all men to obey?

We must understand God's reasons, His purposes for giving the Ten Commandments, in order to gain the greatest benefit from them. A careful study of the present passage tells us why God gave the law. Five very specific purposes can be gleaned from the experience of Israel right after receiving the Ten Commandments. This is the all-important subject of this Scripture: *The Purposes For the Law: Why God Gave the Ten Commandments and the Law*, Ex.20:18-26.

1.   To reveal the glorious majesty and holiness of God: showing that a great barrier--a great gulf--exists between man and God (v.18).
2.   To reveal man's need for a mediator, for a person who can approach God on behalf of man (v.19).
3.   To test man (v.20-21).
4.   To teach that God alone is the LORD: He alone has truly revealed Himself, has spoken to man from heaven (v.22).
5.   To teach how God alone is to be approached and worshipped (v.23-26).

1️⃣ (20:18) **Law--Commandments, The Ten--Holiness, of God--Majesty, of God--Glory, of God**: Why did God give the Ten Commandments to man? First, to reveal the glorious majesty and holiness of God's person, to reveal that a great barrier--a great gulf--exists between man and God. Remember what had happened: God's holy presence had descended to the top of Mt. Sinai in what was probably the most spectacular, terrifying storm and cloud ever witnessed upon earth. Note the glorious description: there was...

- thunder and lightning
- the constant blast of a loud trumpet
- a flaming fire that engulfed the mountain (19:18)
- a cloud of bellowing smoke that arose as though from a huge volcanic eruption (19:18)
- the violent quaking of the mountain that never stopped trembling (19:18)

The people reacted just as any of us would: they withdrew from the foot of the mountain; they shrunk back from God's holy presence. They feared for their lives; feared lest the holy presence of God strike out at them (v.19). Obviously, they were sensing a great gulf between the holy presence of God and their own sinful, human nature. They sensed a deep, terrifying distance between the majesty and holiness of God's person and their own human condition, a condition of weakness, failure, shortcoming, and sinfulness. They knew that the majesty of God being displayed upon the mountain, the majesty they were witnessing, could strike them dead at any moment (v.19). Thus they shrunk back and withdrew from God's holy presence.

This was the very point that God wished to convey to the people: He is the very embodiment of *majestic glory and holiness*. There is a great gulf--a chasm, an abyss, a terrifying separation--between Himself and man, between what He Himself is and what man is. Again, God is the very embodiment of *majestic glory and holiness*; therefore, the very law of God--the Ten Commandments, the very *words* which God spoke--were holy and glorious (Ro.7:12, 14, 16). The law of God and the Ten Commandments were the very expression of God's being. Therefore, people were to obey God's law or else face the terrifying glory and holiness of God.

Thought 1. This was the first reason God gave the law: to reveal His majestic glory and holiness, that there is a *great gulf*, a terrifying separation between God and man.

"But your iniquities have <u>separated</u> between you and your God, and your sins have hid his face from you, that he will not hear" (Is.59:2).
"But we are all as an unclean thing, and all our righteousnesses are as filthy rags; and we all do fade as a leaf; and our iniquities, like the wind, have <u>taken us away</u>" (Is.64:6).
"And there is none that calleth upon thy name, that stirreth up himself to take hold of thee: for thou hast <u>hid thy face</u> from us, and hast consumed us, because of our iniquities" (Is.64:7).
"And beside all this, between us [in heaven] and you [in hell] there is a <u>great gulf</u> fixed: so that they which would pass from hence to you cannot; neither can they pass to us, that [would come] from thence" (Lk.16:26).
"For all have sinned, and <u>come short</u> of the glory of God" (Ro.3:23).
"If we say that we have no sin, we deceive ourselves, and the truth is not in us" (1 Jn.1:8).
"And GOD saw that the wickedness of man was great in the earth, and that every imagination of the thoughts of his heart was only evil continually" (Gen.6:5).
"Who can say, I have made my heart clean, I am pure from my sin?" (Pr.20:9).

2 (20:19) **Mediator--Law, The--Commandments, The Ten--Approach, To God--Salvation**: Why did God give the Ten Commandments to man? To reveal man's need for a *mediator*, for a person who can approach God for man, a person who can represent man before God. Apparently, the people had heard the booming voice of God speaking out from the cloud covering the mountain. Scripture suggests that God's booming voice actually spoke and gave the Ten Commandments directly to the people:

"The LORD <u>talked with you face to face</u> in the mount out of the midst of the fire" (Dt.5:4).
"These words <u>the LORD spake</u> unto all your assembly in the mount out of the midst of the fire, of the cloud, and of the thick darkness, with a great voice: and he added no more. And he wrote them in two tables of stone, and delivered them unto me. And it came to pass, when ye heard the voice out of the midst of the darkness, (for the mountain did burn with fire,) that ye came near unto me, even all the heads of your tribes, and your elders; And ye said, Behold, the LORD our God hath showed us his glory and his greatness, and we have <u>heard his voice</u> out of the midst of the fire: we have seen this day that God doth talk with man, and he liveth. Now therefore why should we die? for this great fire will consume us: if we hear the voice of the LORD our God any more, then we shall die. For who is there of all flesh, that hath heard the voice of the living God speaking out of the midst of the fire, as we have, and lived? Go thou near, and hear all that the LORD our God shall say: and speak thou unto us all that the LORD our God shall speak unto thee; and we will hear it, and do it" (Dt.5:22-27).

Two terrifying events were happening: the people were witnessing the awesome sight of God's glory and majesty, and they were actually hearing the booming voice of God Himself declare the Ten Commandments. Both struck a deep sense of unworthiness in the people. They became keenly aware of the vast difference--the enormous gulf--between God and man, the vast difference...
• between God's holy nature and man's sinful nature
• between God's awesome power and man's helplessness before that power
• between what God is like and what man is like

The sight of God's majestic glory and the hearing of God's booming voice revealed a startling fact to the people: there was a *great gulf* between man and God and the people sensed the *gulf* deeply. They were so aware of God's holiness and their sinfulness--so aware of the vast difference between God's awesome person and their humanity--that they did not want God to speak directly to them, not anymore. They obviously feared some pronouncement of judgment upon them (v.19).

The point is this: they sensed the need for a mediator, for a person to approach God for them, a person who could represent them before God. They wanted God's messenger to be their mediator: they wanted Moses to approach God, to receive God's message, and then to bring God's message back to them. Note what the people promised: they would hear and obey the word of God (v.19).

This great sense and need for a mediator led to one of the great promises in Scripture, the promise of God's Perfect Mediator, the Lord Jesus Christ. As God's Perfect Mediator, Jesus Christ was to stand before God for all people of all ages. Note what Moses himself was later to proclaim to the people:

"The LORD thy God will raise up unto thee a Prophet from the midst of thee, of thy brethren, like unto me; unto him ye shall hearken; According to all that thou desiredst of the LORD thy God in Horeb [Mt. Sinai] in the day of the assembly, saying, Let me not hear again the voice of the

LORD my God, neither let me see this great fire any more, that I die not. And the LORD said unto me, They have well spoken that which they have spoken. I will raise them up a Prophet from among their brethren, like unto thee, and will put my words in his mouth; and he shall speak unto them all that I shall command him. And it shall come to pass, that whosoever will not hearken unto my words which he shall speak in my name, I will require it of him" (Dt.18:15-19).

Thought 1. The law--that is, our failure to keep the law--shows how far short we come, how far away we are from God. The law shows our great need for a mediator, for someone to approach God and to intercede for us. That Someone, that Person, is Jesus Christ. Jesus Christ is our mediator, the person who approaches God for us.

"For there is one God, and one mediator between God and men, the man Christ Jesus; Who gave himself a ransom for all, to be testified in due time" (1 Tim.2:5-6).
"Forasmuch then as the children are partakers of flesh and blood, he also himself likewise took part of the same; that through death he might destroy him that had the power of death, that is, the devil; And deliver them who through fear of death were all their lifetime subject to bondage. For verily he took not on him the nature of angels; but he took on him the seed of Abraham. Wherefore in all things it behoved him to be made like unto his brethren, that he might be a merciful and faithful <u>high priest</u> [mediator] in things pertaining to God, to make reconciliation for the sins of the people" (Heb.2:14-17).
"Wherefore he is able also to save them to the uttermost that come unto God by him, seeing he ever liveth [as the mediator] to make intercession for them" (Heb.7:25).
"But now hath he obtained a more excellent ministry, by how much also he is the mediator of a better covenant, which was established upon better promises" (Heb.8:6).
"And for this cause he is the mediator of the new testament, that by means of death, for the redemption of the transgressions that were under the first testament, they which are called might receive the promise of eternal inheritance" (Heb.9:15).

3 (20:20-21) **Test - Testing--Obedience**: Why did God give the Ten Commandments to man? To test man. Note the word *fear*: two kinds of fear are mentioned in this verse:
⇒ A *tormenting fear* (yare): the fear that defeats a person, that keeps a person from acting and doing what he should.
⇒ A *respectful, honoring fear* (yirah): the fear of God that arouses a person to reverence and obey God.

Moses encouraged the people not to be gripped with a tormenting fear of God. God was not out to destroy them but to test them. God had actually given them the Ten Commandments to test them (v.20).

Remember, the people had earlier promised to do all that the LORD had said. They had made a strong profession and commitment to the LORD. Remember what had happened:

"And Moses came and called for the elders of the people, and laid before their faces all these words which the LORD commanded him. And all the people answered together, and said, All that the LORD hath spoken we will do. And Moses returned the words of the people unto the LORD" (Ex.19:7-8).

Now the LORD was going to use the Ten Commandments to test the people:
⇒ To see if the people would truly walk in the fear and reverence of God. He had given the people a glimpse of the majestic glory and holiness of God. Would they keep the sight before their minds and obey the commandments, the commandments given by the Lord of glory and holiness?
⇒ To see if the people would truly obey God and not sin, not break the Ten Commandments.
⇒ To see if the people would trust the mediator appointed by God (v.21). Note that Moses approached the cloud and thick darkness where God was. He was God's appointed mediator to represent the people before God. Would the people trust and follow him as they journeyed to the promised land?

Thought 1. Did Israel pass the test of God? Tragically, no. Israel did what so many have done down through the ages: promised to obey God and failed to follow through.
1) Many have rejected God: refused to walk in the fear and reverence of God.
2) Many have disobeyed the Ten Commandments and lived in sin.
3) Many have rejected God's appointed mediator, the Lord Jesus Christ.

"Now therefore, if ye will obey my voice indeed, and keep my covenant, then ye shall be a peculiar treasure unto me above all people: for all the earth is mine" (Ex.19:5).
"Beware of him, and obey his voice, provoke him not; for he will not pardon your transgressions: for my name is in him" (Ex.23:21).
"Behold, I set before you this day a blessing and a curse; A blessing, if ye obey the commandments of the LORD your God, which I command you this day: And a curse, if ye will not obey the commandments of the LORD your God, but turn aside out of the way which I command you this day, to go after other gods, which ye have not known" (Dt.11:26-28).

"Ye shall walk after the LORD your God, and fear him, and keep his commandments, and obey his voice, and ye shall serve him, and cleave unto him" (Dt.13:4).

"And the people said unto Joshua, The LORD our God will we serve, and his voice will we obey" (Josh.24:24).

"And Samuel said, Hath the LORD as great delight in burnt offerings and sacrifices, as in obeying the voice of the LORD? Behold, to obey is better than sacrifice, and to hearken than the fat of rams" (1 Sam.15:22).

"For the time is come that judgment must begin at the house of God: and if it first begin at us, what shall the end be of them that obey not the gospel of God?" (1 Pt.4:17).

4 (20:22) **Revelation, of God--Word of God--Commandments, The Ten**: Why did God give the Ten Commandments to man? To teach that God alone is the LORD: He alone has truly revealed Himself, has truly spoken to man from heaven. Remember, God's name--the LORD--means the LORD of salvation, deliverance, redemption, and revelation.

Think for a moment about all the so-called gods declared and worshipped by people. No matter who the so-called gods are, there is only one LORD, only one true and living God who can save, deliver, and redeem people, who can reveal Himself. Who is He? Note this verse:

"And the LORD said unto Moses, Thus thou shalt say unto the children of Israel, Ye have seen that I have talked with you from heaven" (v.22).

The LORD truly revealed Himself; He "has talked with you [man] from heaven" (v.22). The LORD is the only living and true God who has spoken to man and given man the Ten Commandments.

Thought 1. The point is clear: God revealed Himself; He came down upon Mt. Sinai and gave the Ten Commandments to prove that He alone is the LORD who can save and redeem man. Man must, therefore, obey the LORD; man must do what the LORD says to be saved and redeemed.

"Not every one that saith unto me, Lord, Lord, shall enter into the kingdom of heaven; but he that doeth the will of my Father which is in heaven" (Mt.7:21).

"And to you who are troubled rest with us, when the Lord Jesus shall be revealed from heaven with his mighty angels, In flaming fire taking vengeance on them that know not God, and that obey not the gospel of our Lord Jesus Christ" (2 Th.1:7-8).

"Blessed are they that do his commandments, that they may have right to the tree of life, and may enter in through the gates into the city" (Rev.22:14).

"Now therefore, if ye will obey my voice indeed, and keep my covenant, then ye shall be a peculiar treasure unto me above all people: for all the earth is mine" (Ex.19:5).

"This day the LORD thy God hath commanded thee to do these statutes and judgments: thou shalt therefore keep and do them with all thine heart, and with all thy soul" (Dt.26:16).

"But if ye will not obey the voice of the LORD, but rebel against the commandment of the LORD, then shall the hand of the LORD be against you, as it was against your fathers" (1 Sam.12:15).

"For if the word spoken by angels was stedfast, and every transgression and disobedience received a just recompense of reward; How shall we escape, if we neglect so great salvation; which at the first began to be spoken by the Lord, and was confirmed unto us by them that heard him" (Heb.2:2-3).

5 (20:23-26) **Worship--Approach, To God**: Why did God give the Ten Commandments and the law to man? To teach how God is to be approached and worshipped. Note three instructions spelled out by God.

1. There is to be no idolatry in worship: no so-called *imaginary* gods are to be made or worshipped (v.23). This, of course, would include the gods of man's imagination, the gods that men dream up. There is only one true and living God, the Father of the Lord Jesus Christ. He alone is to be worshipped. No other so-called gods are to be worshipped.

2. Worship is not to be full of pageantry, not to be ostentatious, flashy, or showy: the altar was to be made of earth, the plainest and simplest material of all (v.24). The altar of earth was, of course, to be a temporary center of worship until the tabernacle was erected. Note: if an altar of stone were to be built, only undressed stones were to be used. The stone was not to be touched by any tool of man. Touching it with any tool or giving any shape to the stone was considered by God to be a defilement (v.25). The point being made was that worship was to be totally free of any ostentation or flashiness. Worship was not to be showy, not even the focus of worship, which was the altar. Nothing was to distract from the people's worship.

3. Worship was to involve no unrefined or disrespectful behavior, none whatsoever: the altar was to have no steps (v.26). In ancient times, it was the common practice to build high altars with steps leading up to the top of the altars. As the priest climbed the steps of the altar, his nakedness was often exposed to the people standing at the bottom of the altar. God was declaring that there was to be no disrespectful behavior, no immoral behavior ever associated or conducted in the worship services of His people.

Note this fact as well: altars of that day were built high, symbolizing that man was ascending up to God, offering himself and his offering to the false god. But God forbids this, forbids it for four reasons:

⇒ Man cannot climb up in righteousness: he has no righteousness to offer up to God.
⇒ Man cannot ascend up to God. God has to descend down to man (reveal Himself to man).
⇒ Man cannot climb up and break through to heaven; he cannot enter the spiritual world; God has to enter the physical world.
⇒ Man cannot climb man-made steps and reach God; the mediator of God has to stand before God for man.

Thought 1. Three lessons are clearly seen in this point.

1) We must never approach and worship any person nor any false god dreamed up by man. There is only one true and living God, the Father of the Lord Jesus Christ. He and He alone is the one true and living God; consequently, He and He alone is to be approached and worshipped.

> "Take heed to yourselves, that your heart be not deceived, and ye turn aside, and serve other gods, and worship them" (Dt.11:16).
>
> "But unto the place which the LORD your God shall choose out of all your tribes to put his name there, even unto his habitation shall ye seek, and thither thou shalt come" (Dt.12:5).
>
> "Let all the earth fear the LORD: let all the inhabitants of the world stand in awe of him" (Ps.33:8).
>
> "I am the LORD: that is my name: and my glory will I not give to another, neither my praise to graven images" (Is.42:8).
>
> "Little children, keep yourselves from idols. Amen" (1 Jn.5:21).

2) We must never worship God for show--with a spirit of ostentation or flashiness.

> "Therefore when thou doest [thine] alms, do not sound a trumpet before thee, as the hypocrites do in the synagogues and in the streets, that they may have glory of men. Verily I say unto you, They have their reward" (Mt.6:2).
>
> "And when thou prayest, thou shalt not be as the hypocrites [are]: for they love to pray standing in the synagogues and in the corners of the streets, that they may be seen of men. Verily I say unto you, They have their reward" (Mt.6:5).
>
> "Moreover when ye fast, be not, as the hypocrites, of a sad countenance: for they disfigure their faces, that they may appear unto men to fast. Verily I say unto you, They have their reward" (Mt.6:16).
>
> "But all their works they do for to be seen of men: they make broad their phylacteries, and enlarge the borders of their garments" (Mt.23:5).

3) We must never be disrespectful nor irreverent in our worship; we must never pollute nor defile our worship.

> "And he said, Draw not nigh hither: put off thy shoes from off thy feet, for the place whereon thou standest is holy ground" (Ex.3:5).
>
> "Ye shall keep my sabbaths, and reverence my sanctuary: I am the LORD" (Lev.19:30).
>
> "And the captain of the LORD'S host said unto Joshua, Loose thy shoe from off thy foot; for the place whereon thou standest is holy. And Joshua did so" (Josh.5:15).
>
> "God is greatly to be feared in the assembly of the saints, and to be had in reverence of all them that are about him" (Ps.89:7).
>
> "Keep thy foot when thou goest to the house of God, and be more ready to hear, than to give the sacrifice of fools: for they consider not that they do evil" (Eccl.5:1).
>
> "And the Jews' passover was at hand, and Jesus went up to Jerusalem, And found in the temple those that sold oxen and sheep and doves, and the changers of money sitting: And when he had made a scourge of small cords, he drove them all out of the temple, and the sheep, and the oxen; and poured out the changers' money, and overthrew the tables; And said unto them that sold doves, Take these things hence; make not my Father's house an house of merchandise" (Jn.2:13-16).
>
> "But if I tarry long, that thou mayest know how thou oughtest to behave thyself in the house of God, which is the church of the living God, the pillar and ground of the truth" (1 Tim.3:15).
>
> "But the LORD is in his holy temple: let all the earth keep silence before him" (Hab.2:20).

DIVISION VIII

THE LAW AND THE PROMISES OF GOD (THE MOSAIC COVENANT) (PART 3): THE CIVIL AND RELIGIOUS LAWS OF ISRAEL-- HELPFUL PRINCIPLES TO GOVERN MAN AND SOCIETY, 21:1-24:18

(21:1-24:18) **DIVISION OVERVIEW--Israel, Laws of--Civil Law--Religious Law--Culture--Obedience**: the civil and religious laws of Israel are now covered, one after another. Legal statement after legal statement, legal case after legal case is given. Note these facts:

1. The principles covered by the laws can be applied to the experiences and legal situations of all societies, both ancient and modern. True, these laws deal with ancient Israelite society, not with the societies of other nations nor with the societies of future history (modern society). Simply stated, these laws may govern something that does not exist today or govern some event that does not happen today. Nevertheless, the principles can be applied to the experiences and legal cases of all societies.

2. The laws listed here were only *the Basic Laws, the Guiding Laws, the Foundational Laws* of Israel. They were to be used as guiding principles to apply to the multitude of legal cases and experiences of human life. This is seen in that the laws given to Israel were often illustrated by an example or a particular legal case. The example was just that, an example or case that was to be used by the judge to apply to a multitude of experiences. This same approach to justice can be seen in the Constitution of the U.S. in that the Constitution covers only the basic principles that are to govern the free nation. The judges are to apply the basic laws to the multitude of cases that are brought into their courts.

3. The civil and religious laws of Israel and of any other nation can be dry, boring, and uninteresting. Moreover, the question can be reasonably asked, Of what use is it for believers today to read, preach, and teach the ancient laws of Israel? The Preacher's Outline & Sermon Bible® is aware of this point; therefore, two new things are being done to help make this section of Scripture more meaningful to share with God's people:

⇒ An additional feature is being used throughout this section to help the reader.
⇒ A great amount of practical application is being given.

Hopefully, this will better enable us to learn and apply the lessons of these laws to our own lives. Once we have personally learned the lessons, we can then build a far better society for ourselves and our children.

4. The broad range of experiences and legal situations that the Israelite citizen faced day by day are covered in these laws. Situations from every perspective are addressed. There are...
- laws that govern slavery
- laws that govern capital offenses
- laws that govern bodily injuries
- laws that govern the relationship between family members, both children and parents
- laws that govern kidnapping
- laws that govern compensation and restitution
- laws that govern the protection of the weak and helpless
- laws that govern property damage
- laws that govern theft of personal property
- laws that govern the social responsibility between unmarried men and women
- laws that govern the pagan religious practices of the world (sorcery, idolatry, etc)
- laws that govern the protection and dignity of foreigners, resident aliens, immigrants, travelers, or strangers
- laws that govern fire and burning control
- laws that govern deposits and loans
- laws that govern morality
- laws that govern animal control
- laws that govern the respect for government its leaders and rulers

By simply glancing at these different laws, the modern believer can appreciate a wonderful fact: God gave His people a full range of legal examples to govern their lives as they marched to the promised land, examples that are applicable to any and every society.

5. The law was given so God's people could live in security and peace. God gave the law to unify and mold His people into a nation. God already knew what history has shown man: that a nation without laws, or a nation that does not enforce its laws, quickly slips into chaos and anarchy. Thus God gave the law to His people so the nation of Israel would have a firm foundation to govern their relationships with one another and with God.

6. The laws were given by God in order to mold a community of people into law-abiding citizens. The citizen who lives by God's law bears a very special mark: the mark of responsible citizenship to community, society, and nation.

"By the blessing of the upright the city is exalted: but it is overthrown by the mouth of the wicked" (Pr.11:11).

"Righteousness exalteth a nation: but sin *is* a reproach to any people" (Pr.14:34).

"Take away the wicked *from* before the king, and his throne shall be established in righteousness" (Pr.25:5).

7. The laws that God gave to Israel were founded upon His great love and compassion for people. For example, slaves were valued as people who were made in the image of God and slaves were cared for and protected. Moreover, God's love and compassion limited the scope of retaliation against criminals. Life was just too valuable to waste on tempers that overreacted, that caused death and destruction.

The love and compassion of God made it possible for the Israelites to live in peace, secure in the fact that the law was a deterrent to crime and that justice was going to be enforced--both for the victim and for the offender.

8. The laws that God gave to Israel were a totally new concept to the world. Remember, the Israelites had just been slaves themselves, subject to the unpredictable, insane dictates of Pharaoh and his cruel taskmasters. At any given moment, the Israelite could have been struck down for no reason at all. Justice in Egypt was dispensed at random and was completely unpredictable. God's people were at the mercy of men who did not know the LORD God of Israel and did not care about pleasing or displeasing Him. The Egyptian masters were not interested in how the Israelites felt nor in what they needed. Egyptian law did not care about personal rights. But God did, and He provided for His people a system of justice that was guaranteed by the very Word of God itself. For the first time in history, a people were given a form of government that would protect the rights of everyone in true justice, peace, security, and understanding--if the people would just follow God and seek to live in the Promised Land of God. God established a *theocracy*, a government that recognized Him as the Sovereign King, and provided a "Declaration of Independence" for His people. The establishment of these laws and form of government was only a foreshadowing of things to come. One day in the future, God's Son, the Lord Jesus Christ, the King of kings and Lord of lords, will return to earth and establish His eternal kingdom. The Scriptures declare this fact: Jesus Christ will rule forever and ever in perfect justice.

"He shall be great, and shall be called the Son of the Highest: and the Lord God shall give unto him the throne of his father David: And he shall reign over the house of Jacob for ever; and of his kingdom there shall be no end" (Lk.1:32-33).

"But unto the Son *he saith,* Thy throne, O God, *is* for ever and ever: a sceptre of righteousness *is* the sceptre of thy kingdom" (Heb.1:8).

"Of the increase of *his* government and peace *there shall be* no end, upon the throne of David, and upon his kingdom, to order it, and to establish it with judgment and with justice from henceforth even for ever. The zeal of the LORD of hosts will perform this" (Is.9:7).

"I make a decree, That in every dominion of my kingdom men tremble and fear before the God of Daniel: for he is the living God, and stedfast for ever, and his kingdom *that* which shall not be destroyed, and his dominion *shall be even* unto the end" (Dan.6:26).

9. The one thing above all else to look for in studying the civil laws of Israel is this: the *spirit and principle* underlying the laws. Note three facts:
  a. The nation that would work out its laws based upon the spirit and principles of God's laws (given to the Israelites) would be one of the greatest societies in history, a society that would be...
     • just and equitable
     • safe and secure
     • protected and supported (cared for)
     • compassionate and merciful
  b. The spirit and principles lying behind the laws of God could change society if they were written into the laws of a nation. How can this be said? Because the spirit and principles are based upon...
     • true justice and protection
     • true mercy and compassion
  c. A society that would base its laws upon the principles of God's law would be a righteous community. What is a righteous community? The righteous society is a neighborhood, a city, a nation where the *laws of a nation and of God* are applied with *justice toward every person*. The Scripture promises great benefits to the righteous society.

THE BENEFITS TO A RIGHTEOUS SOCIETY

⇒ God will exalt the nation that diligently listens to His voice.

"And it shall come to pass, if thou shalt hearken diligently unto the voice of the LORD thy God, to observe *and* to do all his commandments which I command thee this day, that the LORD thy God will set thee on high above all nations of the earth" (Dt.28:1).

⇒ God will bless the nation who claims Him. He will claim them for His very own inheritance.

"Blessed *is* the nation whose God *is* the LORD: *and* the people *whom* he hath chosen for his own inheritance" (Ps.33:12).

⇒ God will exalt a righteous nation.

"Righteousness exalteth a nation: but sin *is* a reproach to any people" (Pr.14:34).

⇒ God will bless the city that is filled with righteous people.

"When it goeth well with the righteous, the city rejoiceth: and when the wicked perish, *there is* shouting. By the blessing of the upright the city is exalted: but it is overthrown by the mouth of the wicked" (Pr.11:10-11).

⇒ God will protect the city that trusts in Him.

"Except the LORD build the house, they labour in vain that build it: except the LORD keep [protect] the city, the watchman waketh *but* in vain" (Ps.127:1).

⇒ God will make a righteous nation a great nation.

"Keep [the laws] therefore and do *them;* for this *is* your wisdom and your understanding in the sight of the nations, which shall hear all these statutes, and say, Surely this great nation *is* a wise and understanding people. For what nation *is there so* great, who *hath* God *so* nigh unto them, as the LORD our God *is* in all *things that* we call upon him *for?* And what nation *is there so* great, that hath statutes and judgments *so* righteous as all this law, which I set before you this day?" (Dt.4:6-8).

⇒ God will spare a society from judgment if righteousness is found within its borders.

"And the LORD said, If I find in Sodom fifty righteous within the city, then I will spare all the place for their sakes" (Gen.18:26).
"Peradventure there shall lack five of the fifty righteous: wilt thou destroy all the city for *lack of* five? And he said, If I find there forty and five, I will not destroy *it*....And he said, Oh let not the Lord be angry, and I will speak yet but this once: Peradventure ten shall be found there. And he said, I will not destroy it for ten's sake" (Gen.18:28,32).

DIVISION VIII

THE LAW AND THE PROMISES OF GOD (THE MOSAIC COVENANT) (PART 3): THE CIVIL AND RELIGIOUS LAWS OF ISRAEL-- HELPFUL PRINCIPLES TO GOVERN MAN AND SOCIETY, 21:1-24:18

A. The Laws Governing Human Rights, Ex.21:1-32

B. The Laws Governing Property Rights, Ex.21:33-22:15

C. The Laws Governing Social and Moral Obligations, Ex.22:16-31

D. The Laws Governing Justice and Mercy In Court and Among Neighbors, Ex.23:1-9

E. The Laws Governing Religion: The Sabbath and Religious Feasts, Ex. 23:10-19

F. The Conclusion of the Law, the Mosaic Covenant: The Rewards of Obedience, Ex. 23:20-33

G. The Climactic Adoption of the Law, the Mosaic Covenant: The Great Duty of Believers After Receiving the Law, the Word of God, Ex.24:1-18

VIII. THE LAW AND THE PROMISES OF GOD (THE MOSAIC COVENANT) (PART 3): THE CIVIL AND RELIGIOUS LAWS OF ISRAEL--HELPFUL PRINCIPLES TO GOVERN MAN & SOCIETY, 21:1-24:18

A. The Laws Governing Human Rights, Ex.21:1-32

1. **The charge of God: Set these laws before the people**

2. **Laws governing the Hebrew male slave (employee)**
   a. Freedom assured: After six years
   b. Marriage protected: The wife of a slave was also to be freed if he was married when enslaved
   c. Workers assured for the master: If the wife had been given by the master, the wife & children were to be the master's if the slave chose to leave
   d. Security & love guarded for the slave
      1) Given the right to stay out of love for his master & family
      2) Given the right to a secure future, to a slave-master contract, sealed before judges
         • His ear was pierced
         • He pledged to serve his master forever

3. **Laws governing the Hebrew female sold as a slave**
   a. Protection assured: Not ever to be sent out alone
   b. Provision & security protected
      1) If she displeased her husband (master)
         • Was to be redeemed, sold back to her father
         • Was never to be sold to foreigners
      2) If she was given to the master's son: To be given the rights of a daughter
      3) If a second wife was taken[DS1]
         • The first was still to be provided for & treated fairly
         • The first was to be freed without any charge--if not treated fairly

4. **Laws governing violence**
   a. Deliberate murder: The criminal deserves the death penalty

Now these are the judgments which thou shalt set before them.
2 If thou buy an Hebrew servant, six years he shall serve: and in the seventh he shall go out free for nothing.
3 If he came in by himself, he shall go out by himself: if he were married, then his wife shall go out with him.
4 If his master have given him a wife, and she have born him sons or daughters; the wife and her children shall be her master's, and he shall go out by himself.
5 And if the servant shall plainly say, I love my master, my wife, and my children; I will not go out free:
6 Then his master shall bring him unto the judges; he shall also bring him to the door, or unto the door post; and his master shall bore his ear through with an aul; and he shall serve him for ever.
7 And if a man sell his daughter to be a maidservant, she shall not go out as the menservants do.
8 If she please not her master, who hath betrothed her to himself, then shall he let her be redeemed: to sell her unto a strange nation he shall have no power, seeing he hath dealt deceitfully with her.
9 And if he have betrothed her unto his son, he shall deal with her after the manner of daughters.
10 If he take him another wife; her food, her raiment, and her duty of marriage, shall he not diminish.
11 And if he do not these three unto her, then shall she go out free without money.
12 He that smiteth a man, so that he die, shall be surely put to death.

13 And if a man lie not in wait, but God deliver him into his hand; then I will appoint thee a place whither he shall flee.
14 But if a man come presumptuously upon his neighbour, to slay him with guile; thou shalt take him from mine altar, that he may die.
15 And he that smiteth his father, or his mother, shall be surely put to death.
16 And he that stealeth a man, and selleth him, or if he be found in his hand, he shall surely be put to death.
17 And he that curseth his father, or his mother, shall surely be put to death.
18 And if men strive together, and one smite another with a stone, or with his fist, and he die not, but keepeth his bed:
19 If he rise again, and walk abroad upon his staff, then shall he that smote him be quit: only he shall pay for the loss of his time, and shall cause him to be thoroughly healed.
20 And if a man smite his servant, or his maid, with a rod, and he die under his hand; he shall be surely punished.
21 Notwithstanding, if he continue a day or two, he shall not be punished: for he is his money.
22 If men strive, and hurt a woman with child, so that her fruit depart from her, and yet no mischief follow: he shall be surely punished, according as the woman's husband will lay upon him; and he shall pay as the judges determine.
23 And if any mischief follow, then thou shalt give life for life,
24 Eye for eye, tooth for tooth, hand for hand, foot for foot,
25 Burning for burning, wound for wound, stripe for stripe.
26 And if a man smite the eye of his servant, or the eye of his maid, that it perish; he shall let him go free for his eye's sake.
27 And if he smite out his manservant's tooth, or his maidservant's tooth; he shall let him go free for his tooth's sake.

b. Accidental death: The person to be allowed to live in a city of refuge[DS2]

c. Premeditated murder: The criminal deserves the death penalty

d. Murder of parents: The criminal deserves the death penalty
e. Kidnapping: The criminal deserves the death penalty

f. Cursing parents: The person deserves the death penalty

g. Injury due to a quarrel or fight

   1) The attacker was to pay for all medical costs--until the person had completely recovered
   2) The attacker was to pay for all lost time & lost income from employment
h. Beating a slave
   1) If the slave died, the master was to be punished

   2) If the slave did not die, the master was not to be punished

i. Injury to a pregnant woman
   1) If the injury caused a premature birth, the offender was to pay whatever the husband demanded & the court allowed

   2) If the woman was seriously injured, the offender was to be equally punished, but no more: The punishment was to be limited to a life for a life, an eye for an eye[DS3]

j. Striking a slave: If permanently injured, he was to be freed
   1) If his eye was destroyed, he was to be freed
   2) If his tooth was knocked out, he was to be freed

5. Laws governing animal control
a. The non-violent animal that killed a person
  1) The animal: To be killed
  2) The owner: Not held responsible
b. The violent animal that killed a person because the owner did not keep it penned
  1) The animal: To be killed
 	
  2) The owner: Was to be
	28 If an ox gore a man or a woman, that they die: then the ox shall be surely stoned, and his flesh shall not be eaten; but the owner of the ox shall be quit.
	29 But if the ox were wont to push with his horn in time past, and it hath been testified to his owner, and he hath not kept him in, but that he hath killed a man or a woman; the ox shall be stoned, and his owner also shall be put to
		death.
		30 If there be laid on him a sum of money, then he shall give for the ransom of his life whatsoever is laid upon him.
		31 Whether he have gored a son, or have gored a daughter, according to this judgment shall it be done unto him.
		32 If the ox shall push a manservant or a maidservant; he shall give unto their master thirty shekels of silver, and the ox shall be stoned.
			executed or to pay a ransom if preferred by the injured family
			
			3) The same law applied if an animal killed a child
			
			c. The violent animal that killed a slave
			  1) The animal: To be killed
			  2) The owner: To pay a fee

DIVISION VIII

THE LAW AND THE PROMISES OF GOD (THE MOSAIC COVENANT) (PART 3): THE CIVIL AND RELIGIOUS LAWS OF ISRAEL--HELPFUL PRINCIPLES TO GOVERN MAN AND SOCIETY, 21:1-24:18

A. The Laws Governing Human Rights, Ex.21:1-32

(21:1-32) **Introduction**: What is the color of your skin? What is your nationality? What is your economic status? Are you poor, rich, or middle income? No matter who you are or where you are, you have certain rights; but tragically, in far too many places, the rights are few. The reason so many people live under rulers who grant few rights is because we live in a world of...

- sin
- selfishness
- broken promises
- injustice
- lying
- tyranny
- deception
- moral decline
- crime

The world is full of evil and sinful behavior. This is the very reason God gave these laws to Israel. God knew that men would never have the power to live together if there were no laws, no rules on how people should treat each other. This is the reason God established rules that would help His people live in a world filled with law-breakers. God gave these laws to teach us all to respect the rights of others. And if there is a need in the world, it is the need for us all...

- to respect, honor, esteem, and appreciate one another
- to be kind, considerate, and compassionate to one another

A people who will study God's laws governing human rights and apply the *spirit and principles* of the laws to their own society will become a nation respected and loved by the people of the earth--all because the nation highly esteems and respects the human rights of its citizens. This is the subject of the present passage: *The Laws Governing Human Rights*, Ex.21:1-7.

1. The charge of God: set these laws before the people (v.1).
2. Laws governing the Hebrew male slave (employee) (v.2-6).
3. Laws governing the Hebrew female sold as a slave (v.7-11).
4. Laws governing violence (v.12-27).
5. Laws governing animal control (v.28-32).

1 (21:1) **Israel, Law of--Obedience--Law, Civil**: there was the charge of God: set these laws before the people (v.1). Remember, judges had been set up throughout the land to help in settling civil disputes between the people (Ex.18:15). Now God is giving the laws that Moses and the judges were to use in governing the people. The laws are more accurately called "judgments" (mispatim), for they are the laws that were being given to *judge* civil disputes. The civil dispute required a judgment to be made by the judge, a judgment that would settle the dispute. Note the point being made by the Scripture in this particular verse:

THE CHARGE OF GOD:
SET THESE LAWS BEFORE THE PEOPLE

OUTLINE	SCRIPTURE
	A. The Laws Governing Human Rights, Ex.21:1-7
1. The charge of God: Set these laws before the people	Now these are the judgments which thou shalt set before them.

Thought 1. Note the force of this charge. God was not making suggestions to the people, suggestions that they may or may not obey. Neither was God giving a list of rules that might or might not help the people if they chose to behave a certain way. There was no hesitation or equivocation on God's part in giving these laws. God was clear, direct, straightforward: "These are the judgments [laws] that you shall set before the people" (v.1).

Note another fact as well: the commandments of God are never complex or hard to understand. The law of the Lord is always direct and to the point, clearly set forth and easy to understand. It is, therefore, the responsibility of believers to study and learn exactly what God commands. God tells us exactly how He expects us to live, tells us how to live full and rich lives as citizens of the earth. We must, therefore, study and learn God's Word, search out His commandments and learn how to live as He commands.

"Study to show thyself approved unto God, a workman that needeth not to be ashamed, rightly dividing the word of truth" (2 Tim.2:15).
"All scripture is given by inspiration of God, and is profitable for doctrine, for reproof, for correction, for instruction in righteousness" (2 Tim.3:16).
"Blessed are the undefiled in the way, who walk in the law of the LORD" (Ps.119:1).
"Wherewithal shall a young man cleanse his way? by taking heed thereto according to thy word. With my whole heart have I sought thee: O let me not wander from thy commandments. Thy word have I hid in mine heart, that I might not sin against thee" (Ps.119:9-11).
"Open thou mine eyes, that I may behold wondrous things out of thy law" (Ps.119:18).

2 (21:2-6) **Slavery--Bondage--Laws, of Israel**: there were the laws governing Hebrew slavery. Slavery has been a part of society since the earliest days of human history. Every generation has witnessed the enslavement of millions of people. Men of power, the rulers and the wealthy of the world, have always sought more and more of everything:

⇒ more power
⇒ more recognition
⇒ more honor
⇒ more wealth
⇒ more property
⇒ more land
⇒ more possessions
⇒ more pleasure
⇒ more fame

One of the easiest ways to gain more of these things is through slave-labor. Slave-labor is cheap labor. Slave-labor means more for the slave owner, whether the owner is the ruler of a nation, the Board of a corporation, a wealthy individual, or a crime syndicate.

In the ancient world, the entire economy of the world was based upon slavery. Slavery was the very way of life, the fiber and fabric of society itself. When nations conquered people in war, the people were enslaved by the conquering nation. The economy of that day was not a monetary economy (based upon money), but a *goods or materials* economy. That is, people swapped labor for housing, food, clothes. The poor people (the have-nots) of the earth had no way to survive apart from becoming the slave-laborers of the rulers and the wealthy of society. They received housing, food, and clothing by becoming the slaves of the powerful of the earth, by selling their labor (themselves) to the rulers and wealthy. As stated, this was just the way of life in the ancient world, the way the peoples of the earth lived and formed the society of their day. The very economy of the world--the trading of goods, merchandise, possessions--was based upon slavery. As in any society, there were both good and evil slave owners. However, as history has proven, the vast majority of slave owners exposed the evil of the human heart. The rulers and wealthy of the world took advantage of slave-labor...

- housing the slaves in run-down, dilapidated shanties
- paying few if any wages
- giving little attention to medical treatment
- forcing the people to struggle for food and clothing
- demanding exhaustive labor
- giving little attention to working conditions and the environment
- mistreating through abuse, violence, and rape

The one fact to remember above all others in dealing with slavery is this: most people in the ancient world had to hire themselves out as slaves in order to survive. They just had no other way to secure housing, food, and clothing--the very basic necessities of life. This is the background that must be looked at when studying this particular law governing Hebrew slaves. When this background is understood, the purpose of God in giving this particular law is clearly seen. God set out to correct the terrible evil of human slavery throughout the world. This is seen throughout the entire Old Testament and the New Testament as well. (See note--Eph.6:5-9 for more discussion.) However, in correcting the evil of slavery, keep one clear fact in mind: God could not demand the elimination of slavery all at once. This act would have caused terrible pain and suffering for the majority of people in the world.

⇒ Slaves would have immediately lost the housing, food, clothing, and what little income if any they were receiving from their owners.
⇒ The rulers and wealthy of the earth would have reacted by law or violence against any slave who demanded that he be freed because he was following the commandment of the LORD God.

Very simply, if God had given a clear-cut commandment that all slavery was to be eliminated, the ancient world would have been thrown into a terrifying revolution and holocaust. Multiplied millions of people--any mass of slaves who attempted to follow the command of God--would have been slaughtered by the armies of the rulers and wealthy of the earth. This is the reason God moved progressively--ever so slowly, but progressively--in demanding that slavery be eliminated from the face of the earth.

Now, note what God did in the present passage dealing with slavery. God demanded that all slaves be treated with care and compassion. Safeguards were set up to protect any Hebrew who was enslaved by another Israelite. Note exactly what the law says, how clearly the compassion of God is spelled out for the slaves of the earth. Keep in mind that this was the first time in human history that compassion for human slaves was written into the laws of a nation.

LAWS GOVERNING THE HEBREW MALE SLAVE (EMPLOYEE)

OUTLINE	SCRIPTURE	SCRIPTURE	OUTLINE
2. Laws governing the Hebrew male slave (employee) a. Freedom assured: After six years b. Marriage protected: The wife of a slave was also to be freed if married when enslaved c. Workers assured for the master: If the wife had been given by the master, the wife & children were to be the master's if the slave chose to	2 If thou buy an Hebrew servant, six years he shall serve: and in the seventh he shall go out free for nothing. 3 If he came in by himself, he shall go out by himself: if he were married, then his wife shall go out with him. 4 If his master have given him a wife, and she have born him sons or daughters; the wife and her children shall be her master's, and he	shall go out by himself. 5 And if the servant shall plainly say, I love my master, my wife, and my children; I will not go out free: 6 Then his master shall bring him unto the judges; he shall also bring him to the door, or unto the door post; and his master shall bore his ear through with an aul; and he shall serve him for ever.	leave d. Security & love guarded for the slave 1) Given the right to stay out of love for his master & family 2) Given the right to a secure future, to a slave-master contract, sealed before judges • His ear was pierced • He pledged to serve his master forever

Again, note the great tenderness and mercy of God, the great care and compassion being set in the concrete laws of the nation. The Israelites who had just recently been freed from four hundred years of slavery were to treat all future Hebrew slaves with great care and compassion:

⇒ No Hebrew was ever to be enslaved for more than six years (v.2). This probably referred to the year of Jubilee which was to be commemorated every seven years by the nation of Israel (Lev.25:10; 25:28; 27:17; Num.36:4; Ezk.46:17). During the year of Jubilee all slaves were to be freed. This means that no Hebrew was ever enslaved for more than six years, and that many would have served far fewer years, depending upon what year they were enslaved prior to the year of Jubilee.

⇒ If the slave had no place to go--no housing, no way to feed and clothe himself, no way to earn a livelihood--he could choose to remain and continue as an employee (slave) of the master. The slave was never to be forced to leave and struggle for survival.

⇒ If the slave were married when he was enslaved, he was to take his wife and children with him (v.3).

⇒ If the slave had secured a wife after being enslaved, he was not allowed to take his wife or children with him (v.4). But again, he could choose to remain with his family and with his master out of love for them.

3 (21:7-11) **Law, Civil--Slavery--Women, Treatment of--Dowry**: there were the laws governing the Hebrew female sold (dowry) for marriage. It was a common custom in the ancient world for the poor to sell their children to the wealthy. A host of reasons caused this custom to evolve within the society of the ancient world:

⇒ extreme poverty
⇒ being a slave oneself due to the conquests of war or to the struggle for survival
⇒ hoping that one's daughter would marry into a family of wealth

Children, especially young girls, were often treated as little more than chattel (movable property). This was especially true in the barbarian nations of the ancient world. As with the Hebrew male slaves, God showed great compassion for the female slaves. God wanted His people to be compassionate and to take care of any person of dire poverty and destitution. Note the care of God written into the law governing any daughter who is sold to be a servant:

LAWS GOVERNING THE HEBREW FEMALE SOLD AS A SLAVE

OUTLINE	SCRIPTURE	SCRIPTURE	OUTLINE
3. Laws governing the Hebrew female sold as a slave a. Protection assured: Not ever to be sent out alone b. Provision & security protected 1) If she displeased her husband (master) • Was to be redeemed, sold back to her father • Was never to be sold to foreigners	7 And if a man sell his daughter to be a maidservant, she shall not go out as the menservants do. 8 If she please not her master, who hath betrothed her to himself, then shall he let her be redeemed: to sell her unto a strange nation he shall have no power, seeing he hath dealt deceitfully with her.	9 And if he have betrothed her unto his son, he shall deal with her after the manner of daughters. 10 If he take him another wife; her food, her raiment, and her duty of marriage, shall he not diminish. 11 And if he do not these three unto her, then shall she go out free without money.	2) If she was given to the master's son: To be given the rights of a daughter 3) If a second wife was taken[DSI] • The first was still to be provided for & treated fairly • The first was to be freed without any charge--if not treated fairly

1. Protection for the Hebrew female was assured (v.7). Note the distinction between the male and the female servant: the woman servant was to be treated much differently than the man. The man was to be freed after six years, but not the woman, not if she was to be dismissed all alone, by herself, out into the world. She was not to be alone out in the world fending for herself, struggling for survival in a male dominated world.

2. The female's provision and security was protected (v.8-11). This particular law deals with the female who had been sold for marriage, usually to become a concubine or secondary wife. Again, note the care and compassion, the protection and safeguard written into the law. Three situations are covered.

a. If she displeased her husband, if they could not get along together and he felt the need to dismiss her, she was to be redeemed (v.8). This means that the husband (master) was to try to find another man to buy her or else he was to return her to her father without demanding repayment of the dowry (cp. v. 11). Note that the woman could never be sold to a foreigner. Her father and mother had sold her only on the basis of her being married to a Hebrew. This expectation was to be honored. Both the young woman and her parents--despite their extreme poverty--were to be treated fairly and justly: their expectations and hopes were to be fulfilled, or else she was to be returned to her parents. Care and compassion were to be shown her.
b. If the young woman had been bought to be married to the master's son, she was to be given the rights of a daughter, raised and elevated to the status of a family member (v.9). She was to be loved and cared for just as any of the other daughters in the master's family. Again, note how God is taking these laws and beginning to break down the hardness of the human heart and the harsh customs of that day and time.
c. If the husband married the young woman himself and then later took another wife, she was never to be treated as chattel property, never mistreated as so many of the barbarian nations mistreated their women, never dismissed and sent out to fend and struggle for survival in a male dominated world. The husband (master) was still to provide the necessities of life for his first wife: her food, her clothing, her housing--all of her marital rights. If he failed to provide for her, she was to be freed, returned to her father and family at once (v.11). She was to be a free woman with the right of marrying someone else, and no portion of the dowry that the husband had paid for her was to be returned.

Thought 1. This law shows the deep care and compassion of God for the oppressed people of the earth. God cares for the oppressed women of the earth, even for those who are the most oppressed: those who have been enslaved for prostitution or hard labor; those who have been abused or violently mistreated. No matter how terrible the woman's circumstances, God cares and His heart reaches out in compassion to her. God will never allow one of His female servants to go it alone, to be forsaken by Him. Even if others abandon her, God will not. God will remain her faithful and eternal Helper, a far greater helper than even a husband.

> **"For thy Maker is thine husband; the LORD of hosts is his name; and thy Redeemer the Holy One of Israel; The God of the whole earth shall he be called" (Is.54:5).**

Thought 2. It is the man's responsibility to care for the woman. In many societies men have forgotten God's charge. Nevertheless, the charge of God is clear: Scripture even says that God Himself will be as a husband to the wife who is deserted by her husband--if she will just allow God to be her redeemer (Savior) (Is.54:5).
- The husband is to cleave to his wife.

> **"Therefore shall a man leave his father and his mother, and shall cleave unto his wife: and they shall be one flesh" (Gen.2:24).**

- The husband is to love his wife just as much as Christ loved the church.

> **"Husbands, love your wives, even as Christ also loved the church, and gave himself for it" (Eph.5:25).**

- The husband is to know what his wife needs--emotionally, sexually, physically, and spiritually.

> **"Likewise, ye husbands, dwell with them according to knowledge, giving honour unto the wife, as unto the weaker vessel, and as being heirs together of the grace of life; that your prayers be not hindered" (1 Pt.3:7).**

- The husband is to honor the woman.

> **"Likewise, ye husbands, dwell with them according to knowledge, giving honour unto the wife, as unto the weaker vessel, and as being heirs together of the grace of life; that your prayers be not hindered" (1 Pt.3:7).**

Thought 3. It is the man's responsibility to treat all women fairly. All too often women are denied things that are rightfully theirs, just because of their gender. Many women...
- are not given respect
- are sexually harassed
- are not given promotions at work
- are the subject of offensive and vulgar jokes
- are not paid fair wages

> **"Withhold not good from them to whom it is due, when it is in the power of thine hand to do it" (Pr.3:27).**
> **"Let nothing be done through strife or vainglory; but in lowliness of mind let each esteem other better than themselves. Look not every man on his own things, but every man also on the things of others" (Ph.2:3-4).**
> **"But if ye have respect to persons, ye commit sin, and are convinced of the law as transgressors" (Jas.2:9).**

Thought 4. Today, we live in a world where behavior toward women has become...
- obnoxious...crude...and rude
- ill-mannered...arrogant...and disrespectful
- obscene...lewd...and annoying
- offensive...sarcastic...and insulting
- vulgar...crass...and slanderous

This law clearly shows that women are not to be mistreated and abused. They are to be respected, cared for, and looked after. Christian men who are true believers are to defend the women of the world. Instead of following the world's example, God has set in place a much more honorable way. It is the way of edification, of reaching women for Christ and building them up in the eyes of the world.

"**Let us therefore follow after the things which make for peace, and things wherewith one may edify [build up] another**" (Ro.14:19).
"**Let every one of us please his neighbour for his good to edification**" (Ro.15:2).
"**Let no corrupt communication proceed out of your mouth, but that which is good to the use of edifying, that it may minister grace unto the hearers**" (Eph.4:29).

DEEPER STUDY # 1

(21:10) **Marriage--Fidelity--Monogamy--Polygamy**: Why did God allow the Hebrew men to take a second wife? This is totally inconsistent with the clear teachings of Scripture--one man and one wife. How can this apparent contradiction be explained?

God only tolerated polygamy, that is, having more than one wife; He has never condoned polygamy as godly behavior. Biblical scholar Norman Geisler has stated this point very well.

"There is ample evidence, even within the Old Testament, that polygamy was not God's ideal for man. That monogamy (marriage to only one wife) was His ideal for man is obvious from several perspectives.
⇒ God made only one wife for Adam, thus setting the ideal precedent for the race.
⇒ Polygamy is first mentioned as part of the wicked Canaanite civilization (Gen. 4:23).
⇒ God clearly forbade the kings of Israel (leaders were the persons who became polygamists) saying, 'And he shall not multiply wives for himself, lest his heart turn away again' (Deut. 17:17).
⇒ The saints who became polygamists paid for their sins....'Now King Solomon loved many foreign women...and his wives turned away his heart' (1 Kings 11:1,3).
⇒ Polygamy is usually situated in the context of sin in the O. T. Abraham's marriage of Hagar was clearly a carnal act of unbelief (Gen. 16:1f). David was not at a spiritual peak when he added Abigail and Ahinoam as his wives (1 Sam. 25:42-43), nor was Jacob when he married Leah and Rachel (Gen. 29:23, 38).
⇒ The polygamous relation was less than ideal. It was one of jealousy among the wives. Jacob loved Rachel more than Leah (Gen. 29:31). Elkanah's one wife was considered a 'rival' or adversary by the other, who 'used to provoke her sorely, to irritate her...' (1 Sam. 1:6).
⇒ When polygamy is referred to, the conditional, not the imperative, is used. 'If he takes another wife to himself, he shall not diminish her food, her clothing, or her marital rights' (Exod. 21:10). Polygamy is not the moral ideal, but the polygamist must be moral."[1]

Charles M. Sell further expounds upon the monogamous principle in his book, <u>Family Ministry</u>:

"...Walter Wegner, a professor of Old Testament...provides convincing evidence...that throughout her history Israel's ideal for marriage was monogamy. He points first to the prototype of Adam and Eve, which was clearly monogamous. And, he explains, the Old Testament proposes a one-husband and one-wife pattern, even though Israel's actions did not always match God's plan.
"In particular, the prophets, who cover half a millennium of Israel's life, affirm monogamy in their messages. Using the marriage relationship as a metaphor of God's relationship to Israel, Hosea is a shining example of love and faithfulness to one's partner in marriage."[2]

Christian marriage is a relationship ordained by God. Man does not have permission to experiment with marriage...
- by switching partners
- by having sex outside of marriage
- by entertaining adulterous thoughts
- by promoting divorce and remarriage as inevitable and socially acceptable.

A Christian marriage requires a total commitment to the marriage partner. Anything less than total commitment is no commitment at all!

"Marriage is an exclusive relationship. The total unity of persons--physically, emotionally, intellectually, and spiritually--comprehended by the concept 'one flesh' eliminates polygamy as an option. One cannot relate wholeheartedly in this way to more than one person at a time."[3]

---

[1] Norman Geisler. *Ethics: Alternatives and Issues*. (Grand Rapids, MI: Zondervan, 1971), p.204-205. (Quote outlined by us for simplicity.)
[2] Charles M. Sell. *Family Ministry*. (Grand Rapids, MI: Zondervan Corporation, 1981), p.53.
[3] Walter A. Elwell, Editor. *The Evangelical Dictionary of Theology*. (Grand Rapids, MI: Baker Book House, 1984), p.694.

> "And [Jesus Christ] said, For this cause shall a man leave father and mother, and shall cleave to his wife: and they twain shall be one flesh?" (Mt. 19:5).
> "A bishop then must be blameless, the husband of one wife, vigilant, sober, of good behaviour, given to hospitality, apt to teach" (1 Tim.3:2).
> "Let the deacons be the husbands of one wife, ruling their children and their own houses well" (1 Tim.3:12).

4 (21:12-27) **Law, Civil--Violence--Murder--Kidnapping--Cursing--Pregnancy--Arguing--Quarreling**: there were the laws governing violence. No society can survive if its people are lawless, if lawlessness is allowed to run rampant. And no civilization can survive anarchy, leaders and citizens who do not enforce the law. When the law of the land is scorned and the people move beyond the boundaries of civilized behavior, chaos rules the day. God knows this; therefore, it was imperative that the following laws be established. God's people--those who believe and follow Him--are to be the most law abiding citizens in their community.

LAWS GOVERNING VIOLENCE

OUTLINE	SCRIPTURE	SCRIPTURE	OUTLINE
4. **Laws governing violence** a. Deliberate murder: The criminal deserves the death penalty b. Accidental death: The person to be allowed to live in a city of refuge[DS2]	12 He that smiteth a man, so that he die, shall be surely put to death. 13 And if a man lie not in wait, but God deliver him into his hand; then I will appoint thee a place whither he shall flee.	20 And if a man smite his servant, or his maid, with a rod, and he die under his hand; he shall be surely punished. 21 Notwithstanding, if he continue a day or two, he shall not be punished: for he is his money.	h. Beating a slave 1) If the slave died, the master was to be punished 2) If the slave did not die, the master was not to be punished
c. Premeditated murder: The criminal deserves the death penalty	14 But if a man come presumptuously upon his neighbour, to slay him with guile; thou shalt take him from mine altar, that he may die.	22 If men strive, and hurt a woman with child, so that her fruit depart from her, and yet no mischief follow: he shall be surely punished, according as the woman's husband will lay upon him; and he shall pay as the judges determine.	i. Injury to a pregnant woman 1) If the injury caused a premature birth, the offender was to pay whatever the husband demanded & the court allowed
d. Murder of parents: The criminal deserves the death penalty	15 And he that smiteth his father, or his mother, shall be surely put to death.		
e. Kidnapping: The criminal deserves the death penalty	16 And he that stealeth a man, and selleth him, or if he be found in his hand, he shall surely be put to death.	23 And if any mischief follow, then thou shalt give life for life,	2) If the woman was seriously injured, the offender was to be equally punished, but no more: the punishment was to be limited to a life for a life, an eye for an eye[DS3]
f. Cursing parents: The person deserves the death penalty	17 And he that curseth his father, or his mother, shall surely be put to death.	24 Eye for eye, tooth for tooth, hand for hand, foot for foot,	
g. Injury due to a quarrel or fight	18 And if men strive together, and one smite another with a stone, or with his fist, and he die not, but keepeth his bed:	25 Burning for burning, wound for wound, stripe for stripe. 26 And if a man smite the eye of his servant, or the eye of his maid, that it perish; he shall let him go free for his eye's sake.	j. Striking a slave: If permanently injured, he was to be freed 1) If his eye was destroyed, he was to be freed
1) The attacker was to pay for all medical costs--until the person had completely recovered 2) The attacker was also to pay for all lost time & lost income from employment	19 If he rise again, and walk abroad upon his staff, then shall he that smote him be quit: only he shall pay for the loss of his time, and shall cause him to be thoroughly healed.	27 And if he smite out his manservant's tooth, or his maidservant's tooth; he shall let him go free for his tooth's sake.	2) If his tooth was knocked out, he was to be freed

1. Deliberate murder was to be dealt with severely (v.12, 14). Why? Because of the sanctity of human life and the eternal value of a human soul. God demands true, equitable justice: *"Whoso sheddeth man's blood, by man shall his blood be shed" (Gen.9:6ᵃ)*.

Remember: God had already made it perfectly clear how He felt about murder. This He did in the Ten Commandments. The sixth commandment clearly says, *"Thou shalt not kill [murder]" (Ex.20:13)*. Murder maliciously destroys life, life that has been created in God's image. Failing to bring the full force of the law upon this heinous crime is a mockery of God's clear commandment.

Thought 1. Murder is not only an outward act, it is also inward. It is anger, bitterness, enmity. Murder is born within the human heart. Christ Himself declared:

> "Ye have heard that it was said by them of old time, Thou shalt not kill; and whosoever shall kill shall be in danger of the judgment: But I say unto you, That whosoever is angry with his brother without a cause shall be in danger of the judgment: and whosoever shall say to his brother,

Raca, shall be in danger of the council: but whosoever shall say, Thou fool, shall be in danger of hell fire" (Mt.5:22).

2. Those who committed manslaughter or caused an accidental death were allowed to flee to a city of refuge (v.13). It is important to note the distinction that God makes between deliberate, premeditated murder and accidental death. In accidental death, the loss of life was entirely a misfortune: it was unplanned and unintentional, without any forethought or knowledge that the accident was going to happen (cp. Num.35:22-23; Dt.19:4-5). (See Deeper Study #2 for more information about the cities of refuge.)

Thought 1. In a fallen world, accidents happen. Sometimes the accidents cause the death of loved ones (v.13). When we lose a loved one, our only hope rests in God. God is our refuge and strength. He loves and cares for us, and He will take care of us, even in the most painful and grieving experiences of life.

"And we know that all things work together for good to them that love God, to them who are the called according to his purpose" (Ro.8:28).
"The LORD is my strength and my shield; my heart trusted in him, and I am helped: therefore my heart greatly rejoiceth; and with my song will I praise him" (Ps.28:7).
"But I am poor and needy; yet the Lord thinketh upon me: thou art my help and my deliverer; make no tarrying, O my God" (Ps.40:17).
"Fear thou not; for I am with thee: be not dismayed; for I am thy God: I will strengthen thee; yea, I will help thee; yea, I will uphold thee with the right hand of my righteousness" (Is.41:10).

3. Premeditated murderers were to suffer the death penalty without any exception whatsoever (v.14). Life is sacred: no price can be placed upon life. Life is the most valuable possession upon earth: its worth cannot be measured. Life has supreme value, unlimited value. Therefore, if a person deliberately planned or premeditated the murder of someone, he was to be executed. Even if the murderer fled to the worship center, to the very altar of God Himself for refuge, he was not to be spared. He was to be dragged away from the altar to pay the penalty for his terrible evil, his violent and malicious wrath. The evil, violent murderer was never to be allowed refuge nor given safety. Why? So that he would never have another chance to kill (v.14). Pure justice was demanded: he was to be executed for his act of murder.

Thought 1. Premeditated murder is not just a random act of violence. It is the most dastardly evil imaginable. It has been...
- thought out
- planned ahead
- rehearsed in the mind time and time again

"**For out of the heart** proceed evil thoughts, **murders**, adulteries, fornications, thefts, false witness, blasphemies" (Mt.15:19).

Every premeditated murder has always begun in the human heart; thus man is given a stern warning...
- to carefully guard his heart

"Keep thy heart with all diligence; for out of it are the issues of life" (Pr.4:23).

- to know the true condition of his heart

"The heart is deceitful above all things, and desperately wicked: who can know it?" (Jer.17:9).

- to control what comes out of his heart

"But those things which proceed out of the mouth come forth from the heart; and they defile the man" (Mt.15:18).

Thought 2. Many people hide behind religion when they get into trouble with the law. Some call this experience a "jail-house conversion," where the criminal suddenly gets "religion" in an attempt to influence the judge, jury, and public. But one fact must always be kept in mind: knowing some religious clichés, memorizing certain portions of Scripture, and having one's name on a church roll does not bring a saving relationship with Jesus Christ. Only one thing truly saves a person: true repentance and faith in the Lord Jesus Christ. Nonetheless, a profession of faith, true or false, had nothing to do with the crime committed. This does not mean, of course, that there are not some genuine, saving experiences taking place in jails--and thank God for them. But it did not and does not do away with the need to pay the penalty for the evil act.

"Then Peter said unto them, Repent, and be baptized every one of you in the name of Jesus Christ for the remission of sins, and ye shall receive the gift of the Holy Ghost" (Acts 2:38).
"Repent ye therefore, and be converted, that your sins may be blotted out, when the times of refreshing shall come from the presence of the Lord" (Acts 3:19).
"For by grace are ye saved through faith; and that not of yourselves: *it is* the gift of God: Not of works, lest any man should boast" (Eph.2:8-9).

"Let the wicked forsake his way, and the unrighteous man his thoughts: and let him return unto the LORD, and he will have mercy upon him; and to our God, for he will abundantly pardon" (Is.55:7).

4. The cursing and malicious abuse of parents was to be punished by death (v.15). A child who hated his parents so much that he cursed them went far outside the boundaries of acceptable behavior, so far that the child was to be executed (v.15, 17). This may be shocking to the ears of some people in modern society. How could such a severe penalty as execution be justified in the abuse of parents, even if the abuse is malicious? Listen to these quotes by several of the great Biblical scholars and commentators:

⇒ George Bush says this:

"The parental... [relationship] is the... [center] of human society. God guards it with peculiar care. To violate that, is to violate all. Whoever tramples on that, shows that no relation has any sacredness in his eyes--that he is unfit to move among human relations who violates one so sacred and tender [as a parent]."[4]

⇒ The great Biblical scholar Matthew Henry says:

"The [evil] behaviour of children towards their parents is a very great provocation to God our common Father; and, if men do not punish it, he will. Those are perfectly lost to all virtue, and abandoned to all wickedness, [and] have broken through the bonds of [love,] reverence and duty to such a degree as...to abuse their own parents. What yoke will those bear that have shaken off this? Let children take heed of entertaining...any such thought or passions towards their parents as...contempt: for the righteous God searches the heart."[5]

⇒ The great Pulpit Commentary says:

"The severity of the law...strongly emphasises the dignity and authority of parents. There is no parallel to it in any other known code, though of course the patria potestas of the Roman father gave him the power of punishing a son who had struck him, capitally."[6]

⇒ The Expositor's Bible Commentary says:

"Parental authority is so highly valued in biblical law that striking and cursing parents was a criminal and capital offense. Verses 15 and 17 are illustrations of the fifth commandment. Notice that the father and mother are mentioned together, thereby stressing their basic equality."[7]

The malicious hatred and abuse of parents is a personal attack upon the authority of God, an attack that will not go unpunished. It was God who ordained the institution of the family. Within the family, God has established the order of authority throughout Scripture. In descending order...

• there is God

"One God and Father of all, who is above all, and through all, and in you all" (Eph.4:6).

• then the father

"For the husband is the head of the wife, even as Christ is the head of the church: and he is the saviour of the body" (Eph.5:23).

• then the mother

"Therefore as the church is subject unto Christ, so let the wives be to their own husbands in every thing" (Eph.5:24).

• then the child

"Children, obey your parents in the Lord: for this is right. Honour thy father and mother; (which is the first commandment with promise;) That it may be well with thee, and thou mayest live long on the earth" (Eph.6:1-3).

Any child who hated and maliciously attacked, abused, or murdered a parent was in effect also attacking God. The malicious attack upon a parent is declared by God to be the ultimate act of rebellion, the ultimate act of rejection and alienation. Such an act of ultimate rebellion and rejection is to be judged as a severe offense by men. It is so judged by God and will be severely punished by God in the judgment to come.

---

[4] George Bush. *Commentary on Exodus*. (Grand Rapids, MI: Kregel Publications, 1993), p.315.
[5] Matthew Henry. *Matthew Henry's Commentary*, Vol. 1, p.367.
[6] *Pulpit Commentary*, Vol.1, Exodus. Edited by H.D.M. Spence & Joseph S. Exell. (Grand Rapids, MI: Eerdmans Publishing Company, 1950), p.168.
[7] Frank E. Gaebelein. *The Expositor's Bible Commentary*, Vol. 2. (Grand Rapids, MI: Zondervan Publishing House, 1990), p.432.

Thought 1. How a child treats his parents is of critical importance to God. The child who constantly rebels against or abuses his parents will stand opposed to God. Modern society would do well to pay attention to this: the breakdown of society begins with the breakdown of the family. We have drifted a long way from the days of requiring the respect and obedience of our children. Much of modern society allows their children to dictate the schedules and even the standards by which they live. If parents would be firmer with their children from the beginning, teaching them the Word of God and His commandments, there would be far fewer children ever reaching the point where they would abuse their parents. Note what several Scriptures say:

"**For every one that curseth his father or his mother shall be surely put to death: he hath cursed his father or his mother; his blood shall be upon him**" (Lev.20:9).

"**If a man have a stubborn and rebellious son, which will not obey the voice of his father, or the voice of his mother, and that, when they have chastened him, will not hearken unto them: Then shall his father and his mother lay hold on him, and bring him out unto the elders of his city, and unto the gate of his place; And they shall say unto the elders of his city, This our son is stubborn and rebellious, he will not obey our voice; he is a glutton, and a drunkard. And all the men of his city shall stone him with stones, that he die: so shalt thou put evil away from among you; and all Israel shall hear, and fear**" (Dt.21:18-21).

"**Cursed be he that setteth light [dishonors] by his father or his mother. And all the people shall say, Amen**" (Dt.27:16).

"**There is a generation that curseth their father, and doth not bless their mother**" (Pr.30:11).

"**The eye that mocketh at his father, and despiseth to obey his mother, the ravens of the valley shall pick it out, and the young eagles shall eat it**" (Pr.30:17).

"**For the son dishonoureth the father, the daughter riseth up against her mother, the daughter in law against her mother in law; a man's enemies are the men of his own house**" (Mic.7:6).

"**For God commanded, saying, Honour thy father and mother: and, He that curseth father or mother, let him die the death**" (Mt.15:4).

5. The penalty for kidnapping was the death penalty (v.16). Moreover, when a person kidnaps another person...
- he abuses the victim
- he dehumanizes the victim
- he puts the victim at personal risk
- he robs the victim of his ability to make choices
- he breaks the heart of loved ones
- he often kills or causes the early death of the victim

Thought 1. God keeps an accurate account of abuse and will be swift to judge the kidnapper.

"**If a man be found stealing any of his brethren of the children of Israel, and maketh merchandise of him, or selleth him; then that thief shall die; and thou shalt put evil away from among you**" (Dt.24:7).
"**The LORD executeth righteousness and judgment for all that are oppressed**" (Ps.103:6).

6. The penalty for cursing one's parents was the death penalty (v.17). (See note, pt.4 above--Ex.21:15 for more discussion.)

7. Restitution was required for any injury caused by a quarrel or fight (v.18-19). The Scripture is clear in the area of restitution:
⇒ The attacker was to pay for all medical costs--until the person had completely recovered
⇒ The attacker was to pay for all lost time and income from employment

Thought 1. A society is far more just when the principle of *restitution* is legalized and enforced. Both the victims and the criminals are treated far more fairly when this law makes up the fabric of a society. The critical factor often forgotten by societies and nations is this: the answer to solving a crime problem is not to...
- legislate more laws
- build more prisons
- spend more money on a failed system

The answer to solving the problem of crime is one of...
- morality and justice that are enforced
- protecting the rights of the victim
- requiring people to be responsible for their actions
- establishing laws of restitution and enforcing them
- changing hearts, one by one

"**If a soul sin, and commit a trespass against the LORD, and lie unto his neighbour in that which was delivered him to keep, or in fellowship, or in a thing taken away by violence, or hath de-**

ceived his neighbour; Or have found that which was lost, and lieth concerning it, and sweareth falsely; in any of all these that a man doeth, sinning therein: Then it shall be, because he hath sinned, and is guilty, that he shall restore that which he took violently away, or the thing which he hath deceitfully gotten, or that which was delivered him to keep, or the lost thing which he found, Or all that about which he hath sworn falsely; he shall even restore it in the principal, and shall add the fifth part more thereto [pay interest]" (Lev.6:2-5).

"But if he [the thief] be found, he shall restore <u>sevenfold</u>; he shall give all the substance of his house" (Pr.6:31).

"If the wicked restore the pledge, give again that he had robbed, walk in the statutes of life, without committing iniquity; he shall surely live, he shall not die" (Ezk.33:15).

"And Zacchaeus stood, and said unto the Lord; Behold, Lord, the half of my goods I give to the poor; and if I have taken any thing from any man by false accusation, I restore him fourfold" (Lk.19:8).

8. There was a law against the beating of a slave to the point of injury (v.20-21; cp. pt.10, v.26-27). This remarkable law blazed a brand new thought into the mind of the ancient world. For the first time in history, the master was required to control his supervision of a slave. In supervising a slave, a master was not to be abusive. If the master was maliciously abusive and killed the slave, the master was to suffer the penalty of the law. The great <u>Pulpit Commentary</u> has an excellent explanation of this law, an exposition that is well worth quoting in full:

"In most ancient states the slave was the absolute property of his master, and might be ill-used to any extent, even killed, without the law in any way interfacing. It is said that the state of things was different in Egypt (Kalisch); but we have scarcely sufficient evidence on the point to be certain that the slave enjoyed there any real and efficient protection. At Athens, beyond a doubt, the law protected the life of the slave; and a very moderate amount of ill-treatment entitled a slave to bring an action. At Rome, on the contrary, 'the master could treat the slave as he pleased, could sell him, punish him, and put him to death' (Dict. of Greek & Rom. Antiq. p. 1036). And this was the ordinary state of the law, particularly in Oriental countries. The Mosaic legislation must be regarded as having greatly ameliorated [eased] the condition of the native slave population. Hebrew bondsmen it placed nearly upon a par with hired servants (Lev. xxv. 40); foreign slaves, whether prisoners taken in war, or persons bought in the market, it protected to a very great extent. By the law given in verses 26, 27, it largely controlled the brutality of masters, who had to emancipate their slaves if they did them any serious injury. By the law laid down in verse 20, it gave their lives the same protection, or nearly the same, as the lives of freemen. 'Smiting' was allowed as a discipline, without which slavery cannot exist; but such smiting as resulted in death was, as a general rule, punishable like any other homicide. The only exception was, if the slave did not die for some days (ver. 21). In that case the master was considered not to have intended the slave's death, and to be sufficiently punished by the loss of his property [the slave]."[8]

The Expositor's Bible Commentary is also worthy of quote:

"This law is unprecedented in the ancient world where a master could treat his slave as he pleased...this law is considered alongside the law in vv.26-27, which acted to control brutality against slaves at the point where it hurt the master...his pocketbook...a whole new statement of the value and worth of the personhood of the slave is introduced. Thus if the master struck a slave severely enough only to injure one of his members, he lost his total investment immediately in that the slave won total freedom; or if he struck severely enough to kill the slave immediately, he was tried for capital punishment (vv.18-19). The aim of this law was not to place the slave at the master's mercy but to restrict the master's power over him."[9]

<u>Thought 1</u>. There is a very practical lesson to learn from this law, a lesson that we all need to heed, that of controlling anger, the kind of anger that makes us want to strike out at people, whether slave, employee, child, or friend. The man who knows how to control his anger will be a conqueror in life. The man who fails to control his anger...
- will act foolishly
- will give in to hasty and rash decisions
- will lack discretion
- will be filled with rage and wrath
- will develop a low self-image
- will lose friends and be avoided

"Cease from anger, and forsake wrath: fret not thyself in any wise to do evil" (Ps.37:8).
"He that is soon angry dealeth foolishly: and a man of wicked devices is hated" (Pr.14:17).
"The discretion of a man deferreth his anger; and it is his glory to pass over a transgression" (Pr.19:11).
"Be not hasty in thy spirit to be angry: for anger resteth in the bosom of fools" (Eccl.7:9).
"But now ye also put off all these; anger, wrath, malice, blasphemy, filthy communication out of your mouth" (Col.3:8).

---
8 *Pulpit Commentary*, Vol.1, Exodus, p.168-169.
9 Frank E. Gaebelein. *The Expositor's Bible Commentary*, Vol. 2, p.434.

9. There was the law that governed the punishment due to someone who injured a pregnant woman (v.22-25). A pregnant woman is a very special vessel for carrying new life in her womb, life that is precious and priceless to God. The <u>Pulpit Commentary</u> again gives an excellent exposition of this law:

> "Women in all countries are apt to interfere in the quarrels of men, and run the risk of suffering injuries which proceed from accident rather than design....The Mosaic legislation sought to protect pregnant women from suffering this injury by providing, first, that if death resulted the offender should suffer death (ver.23); and, secondly, that if there were no further ill-result than the miscarriage itself, still a fine should be paid to be assessed by the husband of the injured woman with the consent of the judges (ver.22)."[10]

The outline points are self-explanatory: note how the law protected the precious and priceless life of the child (fetus) in the mother's womb:
⇒ If the injury caused a premature birth, the offender was to pay whatever the husband demanded and the court allowed
⇒ If the woman were seriously injured, the offender was to be equally punished
• Life for life, eye for eye
• Tooth for tooth, hand for hand, foot for foot
• Burn for burn, wound for wound, bruise for bruise (see <u>Deeper Study # 3</u>--Ex.21:24-25 for more discussion)

<u>The Expositor's Bible Commentary</u> asks an important question for society today.

> "Should the pregnant woman or her child die, the principle of *talio* is invoked, demanding 'life for life' (v.23). But why should this principle be invoked if it were an accidental fatality when v.13 exempted such a person from the death penalty? The answer is found in two facts.
> 1) the *talion principle* (vv.23-25) is a stereotype formula that states simply that the punishment must match, but not exceed, the damage done...
> 2) Numbers 35:31 permits a substitute to ransom all capital offenses in the OT except in the one case of willful and premeditated murder. Thus we conclude that the defendant must surrender to the deceased child's father or wife's husband the monetary value of each life (note v.30) if either or both were harmed. The *lex talionis* of vv.23^b-25 does impose a strict limit on the amount of damages anyone could collect; in modern terms it would read: car bumper for car bumper and car fender for car fender. No one was to try to get rich quick off such situations. Notice also that this was to be a rule of thumb for the judges, not an authorization of personal vendetta or private retaliation (cf. Lev.24:19-20; Deut.19:21)."[11]

<u>Thought 1</u>. In today's society, life is under violent attack. What was designed by God to be a place of safety and refuge for the unborn child--the womb--has become a place of grave danger. Millions of unborn babies--innocent, helpless, and defenseless--are being sinfully aborted every year. While species of nearly extinct animals are being preserved at all costs, the heinous act of abortion is being carried out, trivialized, and even approved of by governments worldwide.

What is God's priority? The same as it has always been--esteeming the value of human life above all else. What is God's view concerning babies who are in their mother's womb? The Scriptures tell us that God is actively at work in the womb of mothers.

> **"For thou hast possessed my reins: <u>thou hast covered me in my mother's womb</u>. I will praise thee; for I am fearfully and wonderfully made: marvellous are thy works; and that my soul knoweth right well. <u>My substance was not hid from thee, when I was made in secret, and curiously wrought in the lowest parts of the earth</u>. Thine eyes did see my substance, yet being unperfect; and in thy book all my members were written, which in continuance were fashioned, when as yet there was none of them" (Ps.139:13-16).**
> **"Thus saith the LORD that made thee, and formed thee from the womb, which will help thee; Fear not, O Jacob, my servant; and thou, Jesurun, whom I have chosen" (Is.44:2).**
> **"Thus saith the LORD, thy redeemer, and he that formed thee from the womb, I am the LORD that maketh all things; that stretcheth forth the heavens alone; that spreadeth abroad the earth by myself" (Is.44:24).**
> **"Before I formed thee in the belly I knew thee; and <u>before thou camest forth out of the womb I sanctified thee</u>, and I ordained thee a prophet unto the nations" (Jer.1:5).**
> **"And, behold, thou shalt conceive in thy womb, and bring forth a son, and shalt call his name JESUS" (Lk.1:31).**
> **"And it came to pass, that, when Elisabeth heard the salutation of Mary, the babe leaped in her womb; and Elisabeth was filled with the Holy Ghost" (Lk.1:41).**

10. If a slave were permanently injured by his master, he was to be immediately freed (v.26-27; cp. pt.8 above, v.20-21). This law kept the master from treating his slave as a money-making machine. It kept the master from driving his slave to continually produce in order to gain more and more money, from driving the slave to the point of injury--whether through exhaustive overwork or beatings. Again, the great <u>Pulpit Commentary</u> is worth quoting on this law:

---

[10] *Pulpit Commentary*, Vol.1, Exodus, p.169.
[11] Frank E. Gaebelein. *The Expositor's Bible Commentary*, Vol. 2, p.433.

"The general law of retaliation was not made to extend to slaves. For ordinary blows the slave was not thought entitled to compensation, any more than the child. They were natural incidents of his condition. In extremer cases, where he was permanently injured in an organ or a member, he was, however, considered to have ground of complaint and to deserve a recompense. But for him to revenge himself upon his master by inflicting the same on him was not to be thought of. It would have put the slave into a false position, have led to his prolonged ill-treatment, and have been an undue degradation of the master. Therefore, compulsory emancipation was made the penalty of all such aggravated assaults, even the slightest....

"The 'eye' seems to be selected as the most precious of our organs, the 'tooth' as that...which is of least consequence. The principle was that any permanent loss of any part of his frame entitled the slave to his liberty. A very considerable check must have been put on the brutality of masters by this enactment"[12]

Thought 1. Throughout society many of us hold positions of authority. Far too often we forget that with authority comes great responsibility. And when we forget to fulfill our responsibility, we usually abuse the power of our position. And when power is abused, those who are under our control usually catch the brunt of our frustration or anger (v.26-27). God has called every believer to be a good and faithful steward. To be a good and faithful steward...

- we must acknowledge that God Himself is the owner of all things
- we must act like managers not owners
- we must seek the best for God and others not for ourselves
- we must think about the possible consequences before we act
- we must keep an open heart for communication not a clenched fist for retaliation
- we must minister to others as Jesus would and not as our fallen natures desire

"And he called his ten servants, and delivered them ten pounds, and said unto them, Occupy till I come" (Lk.19:13).

"So then every one of us shall give account of himself to God" (Ro.14:12).

"Moreover it is required in stewards, that a man be found faithful" (1 Cor.4:2).

"O Timothy, keep that which is committed to thy trust, avoiding profane and vain babblings, and oppositions of science falsely so called" (1 Tim.6:20).

DEEPER STUDY #2

(21:13) Refuge, Cities of--Murder:

God established six Levitical cities that would serve as a refuge for people who *accidentally* killed another person (cp. Josh.20:7-8). Scripture identifies these six cites as...

- *Bezer*: located in the territory of the tribe of Reuben, east of the Jordan River's entrance into the Dead Sea
- *Golan*: located in the territory of the tribe of Manasseh, east of the Sea of Galilee
- *Hebron*: located in the territory of the tribe of Judah, approximately twenty miles south of Jerusalem
- *Kedesh*: located in the territory of the tribe of Naphtali, about fifteen miles north of the Sea of Galilee
- *Shechem*: located in the territory of the tribe of Ephraim, between Mt. Ebal and Mt. Gerizim
- *Ramoth*: located in the territory of the tribe of Gad, in the highlands of Giliad

The person who accidentally killed someone else was allowed to flee to a city of refuge for safety. He remained there until he could be tried by the judge of his own city (Num.35:22-25). These cities of refuge were a hedge of protection against the avenger of the person who was killed. If he were found innocent, he was then free to leave the city of refuge and return to his former life. If he were found guilty, the avenger or family of the victim could demand life for life or either accept some money or property payment as compensation for the death of their loved one. According to Scripture, the only way a manslayer could leave the city of refuge safely was after the death of the High Priest. (For further study, refer to Num.35:9-34, Dt.4:41-43, Dt.19:1-13, and Josh.20:1-9.)

"The LORD also spake unto Joshua, saying, Speak to the children of Israel, saying, Appoint out for you cities of refuge, whereof I spake unto you by the hand of Moses: That the slayer that killeth any person unawares and unwittingly may flee thither: and they shall be your refuge from the avenger of blood. And when he that doth flee unto one of those cities shall stand at the entering of the gate of the city, and shall declare his cause in the ears of the elders of that city, they shall take him into the city unto them, and give him a place, that he may dwell among them. And if the avenger of blood pursue after him, then they shall not deliver the slayer up into his hand; because he smote his neighbour unwittingly, and hated him not beforetime. And he shall dwell in that city, until he stand before the congregation for judgment, and until the death of the high priest that shall be in those days: then shall the slayer return, and come unto his own city, and unto his own house, unto the city from whence he fled. And they appointed Kedesh in Galilee in mount Naphtali, and Shechem in mount Ephraim, and Kirjath-arba, which is Hebron, in the mountain of Judah. And on the other side Jordan by Jericho eastward, they assigned Bezer in the wilderness upon the plain out of the tribe of Reuben, and Ramoth in Gilead out of the tribe of Gad, and Golan in Bashan out of the tribe of Manasseh" (Josh.20:1-8).

---

[12] *Pulpit Commentary*, Vol.1, Exodus, p.170.

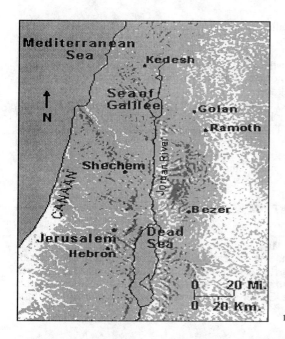

13

5 (21:28-32) **Law, Civil--Possessions--Stewardship--Animals, Control of**: there were the laws governing animal control. The purpose of these laws was to protect human life from animals, both violent and non-violent animals. Note how God makes men responsible for the injuries their animals cause to other people. These laws show the great value God places upon human life. Life is sacred to God; He has created man in His image, both male and female--every man, woman, boy, and girl (Gen.1:26-27). Therefore, every human life is to be cherished, safeguarded, and protected even from animals. People are to be responsible for their animals. Society is to establish *animal control laws* for its citizens.

LAWS GOVERNING ANIMAL CONTROL

OUTLINE	SCRIPTURE	SCRIPTURE	OUTLINE

5. Laws governing animal control
a. The non-violent animal that killed a person
  1) The animal: To be killed
  2) The owner: Not held responsible
b. The violent animal that killed a person because the owner did not keep it penned
  1) The animal: To be killed
 	
  2) The owner: Was to be executed or to pay a ran-
	28 If an ox gore a man or a woman, that they die: then the ox shall be surely stoned, and his flesh shall not be eaten; but the owner of the ox shall be quit. 29 But if the ox were wont to push with his horn in time past, and it hath been testified to his owner, and he hath not kept him in, but that he hath killed a man or a woman; the ox shall be stoned, and his owner also shall be put to death.	30 If there be laid on him a sum of money, then he shall give for the ransom of his life whatsoever is laid upon him. 31 Whether he have gored a son, or have gored a daughter, according to this judgment shall it be done unto him. 32 If the ox shall push a manservant or a maidservant; he shall give unto their master thirty shekels of silver, and the ox shall be stoned.	som if preferred by the injured family
			
			3) The same law applied if an animal killed a child
			
			c. The violent animal that killed a slave
			  1) The animal: To be killed
			  2) The owner: To pay a fee

---

1. There was the law that dealt with the non-violent animal that killed a person (v.28). The non-violent animal that killed a person was to be killed. The animal was to suffer the same fate that it had inflicted: death. Why? To prevent the animal from ever killing again. Note that the meat could not even be salvaged for sale or eating. The animal was counted accursed, for it had killed the most precious and valuable thing upon earth, a human being, a person made in the very image of God Himself (Gen.1:26-27). Note this fact also: the owner was not held responsible for the animal's violent behavior: the animal had always acted tame and peaceful so far as the owner knew.

2. However, the violent animal that killed a person because the owner did not keep it penned was a different matter (v.29). In this case the animal was violent and dangerous and the owner knew it. Moreover, the owner either failed to put the violent creature to death or did not keep a watch over the animal. The result was most tragic: due to the owner's neglect, the animal killed a person. Consequently...

- the animal was to be killed (v.30)
- the owner was to be executed or to pay a ransom if preferred by the injured family (v.30-31)
- the same law applied if an animal killed a child (v.32)

3. The violent animal that killed a slave was to be killed. The owner was to pay a fee to the master, pay the average price that it cost to purchase a slave (30 shekels of silver in that day).

Thought 1. It is important to note that the emphasis upon these laws is not merely economic. In fact, the stress is upon doing what is good and right, what is moral and just. The theme of *personal responsibility* is a major pillar of this law. Throughout every society there are people who seem to flee from accepting responsibility and blame when things go wrong. The believer must apply the same principle, the principle of taking personal responsibility for his life and for all that he possesses, including pets and livestock. The Owner of the universe places the animal life of the world in our hands. He holds us accountable...

- to manage and manage responsibly
- to protect and preserve not to ignore and neglect
- to be wise not foolish

No animal, no matter its value nor how much it is needed, is ever to be counted of more value than a human life. Owners are to take responsibility and society is to hold owners accountable for their pets and livestock.

"His lord said unto him, Well done, thou good and faithful servant: thou hast been faithful over a few things, I will make thee ruler over many things: enter thou into the joy of thy lord" (Mt.25:21).

"And God said, Let us make man in our image, after our likeness: and let them have dominion over the fish of the sea, and over the fowl of the air, and over the cattle, and over all the earth, and over every creeping thing that creepeth upon the earth" (Gen.1:26).

"And the LORD God took the man, and put him into the garden of Eden to dress it and to keep it....And out of the ground the LORD God formed every beast of the field, and every fowl of the air; and brought them unto Adam to see what he would call them: and whatsoever Adam called every living creature, that was the name thereof. And Adam gave names to all cattle, and to the fowl of the air, and to every beast of the field; but for Adam there was not found an help meet for him" (Gen.2:15, 19-20).

"And the fear of you and the dread of you shall be upon every beast of the earth, and upon every fowl of the air, upon all that moveth upon the earth, and upon all the fishes of the sea; into your hand are they delivered" (Gen.9:2).

"Thou madest him to have dominion over the works of thy hands; thou hast put all things under his feet" (Ps.8:6).

"For every kind of beasts, and of birds, and of serpents, and of things in the sea, is tamed, and hath been tamed of mankind" (Jas.3:7).

Thought 2. We are responsible not only for our lives but also for *our possessions*--whether it be an animal, an automobile, or some other item. Any slothfulness on our part could cause some serious accident. There is great wisdom in being careful and not foolish. In the wrong hands, "safe" things can become deadly, safe things such as...

- automobiles
- motorcycles
- knives
- poisonous chemicals
- loaded guns
- prescription drugs
- pets and livestock that are unpredictable, violent, or dangerous

One of the believer's greatest challenges is to be a good steward of what God has entrusted to his care.

"Moreover it is required in stewards, that a man be found faithful" (1 Cor.4:2).

"His lord said unto him, Well done, [thou] good and faithful servant: thou hast been faithful over a few things, I will make thee ruler over many things: enter thou into the joy of thy lord" (Mt.25:21).

1. Laws governing damage to other people's property
   a. Case 1: Loss caused by a person's negligence or carelessness
      1) To pay for the loss: Full restitution
      2) The damaged property (dead animal) became the negligent person's
   b. Case 2: Unpreventable loss caused by another person
      1) To sell the property (live animal)
      2) To divide the money & property (dead animal) equally
   c. Case 3: Preventable loss caused by lack of safety control
      1) To pay property for property: Animal for animal
      2) The lost or damaged property (dead animal) became the offender's

2. Laws governing theft: The stealing of property (livestock)
   a. Case 1: The thief sells or destroys the property: To pay back four- to fivefold
   b. Case 2: The thief is killed while breaking into one's property
      1) He is killed at night: The defender is not guilty
      2) He is killed during the day: The defender is guilty
   c. Case 3: The thief is caught after getting rid of the stolen goods: Must work (be enslaved) until fully repaid
   d. Case 4: The thief is caught with the property (live animal): To pay back double

3. Laws governing irresponsible oversight--the failure to exercise due diligence
   a. The case: Loss caused by failure of due caution--property is destroyed (by animals, machine, or whatever)
   b. The penalty: Full restitution

B. The Laws Governing Property Rights, Ex.21:33-22:15

33 And if a man shall open a pit, or if a man shall dig a pit, and not cover it, and an ox or an ass fall therein;
34 The owner of the pit shall make it good, and give money unto the owner of them; and the dead beast shall be his.
35 And if one man's ox hurt another's, that he die; then they shall sell the live ox, and divide the money of it; and the dead ox also they shall divide.
36 Or if it be known that the ox hath used to push in time past, and his owner hath not kept him in; he shall surely pay ox for ox; and the dead shall be his own.

CHAPTER 22

If a man shall steal an ox, or a sheep, and kill it, or sell it; he shall restore five oxen for an ox, and four sheep for a sheep.
2 If a thief be found breaking up, and be smitten that he die, there shall no blood be shed for him.
3 If the sun be risen upon him, there shall be blood shed for him; for he should make full restitution; if he have nothing, then he shall be sold for his theft.
4 If the theft be certainly found in his hand alive, whether it be ox, or ass, or sheep; he shall restore double.
5 If a man shall cause a field or vineyard to be eaten, and shall put in his beast, and shall feed in another man's field; of the best of his own field, and of the best of his own vineyard, shall he make restitution.
6 If fire break out, and catch in thorns, so that the stacks of corn, or the standing corn, or the field, be consumed therewith; he that kindled the fire shall surely make restitution.
7 If a man shall deliver unto his neighbour money or stuff to keep, and it be stolen out of the man's house; if the thief be found, let him pay double.
If the thief be not found, then the master of the house shall be brought unto the judges, to see whether he have put his hand unto his neighbour's goods.
9 For all manner of trespass, whether it be for ox, for ass, for sheep, for raiment, or for any manner of lost thing, which another challengeth to be his, the cause of both parties shall come before the judges; and whom the judges shall condemn, he shall pay double unto his neighbour.
10 If a man deliver unto his neighbour an ass, or an ox, or a sheep, or any beast, to keep; and it die, or be hurt, or driven away, no man seeing it:
11 Then shall an oath of the LORD be between them both, that he hath not put his hand unto his neighbour's goods; and the owner of it shall accept thereof, and he shall not make it good.
12 And if it be stolen from him, he shall make restitution unto the owner thereof.
13 If it be torn in pieces, then let him bring it for witness, and he shall not make good that which was torn.
14 And if a man borrow ought of his neighbour, and it be hurt, or die, the owner thereof being not with it, he shall surely make it good.
15.But if the owner thereof be with it, he shall not make it good: if it be an hired thing, it came for his hire.

4. Laws governing fire & burning control
   a. The case: Fire spreads & damages other property
   b. The penalty: Equal restitution

5. Laws governing deposits: Money or goods entrusted to the care of a trustee (neighbor) for safekeeping
   a. Case 1: A thief steals: Must pay back double
   b. Case 2: The trustee is suspect
      1) To be brought before the court
      2) To have his property searched
         • If the property or goods are found and claimed by both parties, the court is to judge between the two parties
         • The guilty party is to pay back double
   c. Case 3: Property is damaged (injured or dies) while under the care of a trustee (neighbor)
      1) The trustee is to take an oath that he is innocent
      2) The owner is to accept the oath
      3) The exception
         • If stolen from the trustee, is to make restitution
         • If damaged in an unpreventable way & the trustee can produce the evidence, he is innocent
   d. Case 4: Borrowed property is damaged (injured or dies)
      1) If the owner is not present, the borrower makes restitution
      2) If the owner is present, the borrower is not to pay
      3) If the property was rented, the rent money covers the loss

DIVISION VIII

THE LAW AND THE PROMISES OF GOD (THE MOSAIC COVENANT) (PART 3): THE CIVIL AND RELIGIOUS LAWS OF ISRAEL--HELPFUL PRINCIPLES TO GOVERN MAN AND SOCIETY, 21:1-24:18

B.   Laws Governing Property Rights, 21:33-22:15

EXODUS 21:33-22:15

(21:33-22:15) **Introduction**: Does man have the right to hold property or is all property to be held by the state? Scripture gives an unequivocal answer: man has the right to hold property. In fact, God has even put within man a desire to hold property and to seek possessions. By property is meant far more than just real estate; property refers to all possessions, all that man can possess ranging from the clothes on his back to the house in which he lives, the vehicle he drives, the animals he owns, the investments he has, the real estate to which he holds title. As stated, man has within his being the drive and motivation to possess and seek after property. Note this fact as well: all things are really owned by God. God is the *title-holder* of all property and goods. Man is only the *trustee*, the trustee *under God*. Everything that man possesses during his short time upon earth is a gift from God. The possessions are a trust that God puts into man's hands. The trust (the property, goods, possessions) is to be used, looked after, invested, and increased according to the person's ability. Simply stated, a person is to take what God gives him and use it to the best of his ability for the benefit of mankind--to meet the needs of a dying world lost and reeling under the terrible weight of suffering, evil, and death. Simply stated, man is to take what possessions he has and use them to meet the desperate needs of the world and use them to get the message of the glorious gospel of God's Son out. He is to use the God-given drive to secure possessions and property, use it to get more and more--all to increase the Kingdom of God upon earth. He is to sacrificially use his money and possessions to reach out to help those in need and to proclaim the glorious gospel of salvation to the world. This is: *Laws Governing Property Rights*, Ex.21:33-22:15.

1. Laws governing damage to other people's property (v.33-36).
2. Laws governing theft: the stealing of property (livestock) (Ch.22:1-4).
3. Laws governing irresponsible oversight--the failure to exercise due diligence (v.5).
4. Laws governing fire and burning control (v.6).
5. Laws governing deposits: money or goods entrusted to the care of a trustee (neighbor) for safekeeping (v.7-15).

1 (21:33-36) **Law--Property Rights--Restitution**: there were the laws governing loss or damage to other people's property. Millions of people suffer property loss every day. We all know what it is to have property damaged or destroyed by other people. Sometimes it is preventable; sometimes it is not. What is fair, just, and equitable when property is lost or damaged? Note how clearly the following applies to situations we face every day and how fair and just the law is.

Remember that the ancient world was primarily a farming, agricultural society. Life in an agrarian (rural) society was intricately woven with animals, the most important of which were the ox and donkey. A man's entire livelihood was dependent upon the health of his ox (horse, mule, donkey, camel). This point spells out how the law was to protect the rights of Israel's property owners. But the point in Scripture is applicable to any society: it spells out how the law should protect the property rights of us all.

LAWS GOVERNING DAMAGE TO OTHER PEOPLE'S PROPERTY

OUTLINE	SCRIPTURE	SCRIPTURE	OUTLINE

1. Laws governing damage to other people's property
a. Case 1: Loss caused by a person's negligence or carelessness
  1) To pay for the loss: Full restitution
  2) The damaged property (dead animal) became the negligent person's
	B. Laws Governing Property Rights, Ex.21:33-22:15
	
	33 And if a man shall open a pit, or if a man shall dig a pit, and not cover it, and an ox or an ass fall therein;
	34 The owner of the pit shall make it good, and give money unto the owner of them; and the dead beast shall be his.
		35 And if one man's ox hurt another's, that he die; then they shall sell the live ox, and divide the money of it; and the dead ox also they shall divide.
		36 Or if it be known that the ox hath used to push in time past, and his owner hath not kept him in; he shall surely pay ox for ox; and the dead shall be his own.
			b. Case 2: Unpreventable loss caused by another person
			  1) To sell the property (live animal)
			  2) To divide the money & property (dead animal) equally
			c. Case 3: Preventable loss caused by lack of safety control
			  1) To pay property for property: Animal for animal
			  2) The lost or damaged property (dead animal) became the offender's

1. Case 1: There was property loss caused by another person's *negligence* or *carelessness* (v.33-34). The law was to provide protection for the property owner--always. So often, because of a person's gross *carelessness* or *negligence*, property is damaged or even destroyed. In this particular example, an open pit was not covered and the animal fell in and died. The person at fault was required by law to pay for the loss of property. Once he had made payment, the lost property (dead animal) was his to keep.

2. Case 2: there was *unpreventable loss* of property caused by another person. If unpreventable damage was caused, both owners were instructed by the law...
   * to sell any undamaged or remaining property (live animal) and divide the profit equally between themselves
   * to divide the damaged property (dead animal) equally between themselves (v.35)

3. Case 3: there was *preventable* loss caused by lack of *safety controls*: the death caused by a known violent animal not kept penned (v.36). The law required the offending owner to pay for the lost property: property for property, animal for animal. But note: once the neglectful person had made payment for the loss, the damaged or lost property (the dead animal) became his. This was fair and just, for he had made full restitution by paying for the loss.

Thought 1. George Bush says this:

"The owners were to adjust the matter by selling the live ox [the undamaged or remaining property] and dividing the price equally between them, and also by making an equal division of the dead ox [damaged property]."[1]

---
[1] George Bush. *Commentary on Exodus*, p.322.

Thought 2. We must always be on guard against *negligence* and *carelessness*. If not, we will...
- cause accidents
- cause great damage to life and property
- cause heartache for others and grief for ourselves

The counter-balance for negligence is *diligence*. We must stay alert and be diligent at work, home, driving, operating machinery, cooking, storing chemicals--whatever we do, no matter what it is--we must guard against being careless and negligent.

> **"The slothful *man* roasteth not that which he took in hunting: but the substance of a diligent man *is* precious" (Pr.12:27).**
> **"A slothful man does not roast his prey, But the precious possession of a man *is* diligence" (Pr.12:27, NASB).**
> **"Cursed be he that doeth the work of the LORD deceitfully [negligently], and cursed be he that keepeth back his sword from blood" (Jer.48:10).**
> **"Not slothful in business" (Ro.12:11).**
> **"See then that ye walk circumspectly [carefully], not as fools, but as wise" (Eph.5:15).**
> **"And whatsoever ye do, do it heartily, as to the Lord, and not unto men" (Col.3:23).**

2 (22:1-4) **Law--Stealing--Theft--Restitution**: there were laws governing theft, the stealing of property. One of the principle purposes of criminal law is the protection of a person and his property, whether animal, machine, building, land, or any other possession. If a man's property is unprotected or threatened, he has no peace of mind. He feels insecure and unsafe knowing that some day, a thief might steal or damage the unprotected property and perhaps even threaten his life. This law gave clear principles to govern the cases of theft that would arise in the future.

LAWS GOVERNING THEFT: THE STEALING OF PROPERTY (LIVESTOCK)

OUTLINE	SCRIPTURE	SCRIPTURE	OUTLINE
	CHAPTER 22	3 If the sun be risen upon him, there shall be blood shed for him; for he should make full restitution; if he have nothing, then he shall be sold for his theft.	2) He is killed during the day: The defender is guilty
2. Laws governing theft: The stealing of property (livestock)	If a man shall steal an ox, or a sheep, and kill it, or sell it; he shall restore five oxen for an ox, and four sheep for a sheep.		c. Case 3: The thief is caught after getting rid of the stolen goods: Must work (be enslaved) until fully repaid
a. Case 1: The thief sells or destroys the property: To pay back four- to fivefold			
b. Case 2: The thief is killed while breaking into one's property	2 If a thief be found breaking up, and be smitten that he die, there shall no blood be shed for him.	4 If the theft be certainly found in his hand alive, whether it be ox, or ass, or sheep; he shall restore double.	d. Case 4: The thief is caught with the property (live animal: To pay back double
1) He is killed at night: The defender is not guilty			

1. The first case addressed situations where a thief stole then sold or destroyed the property (v.1). The law required him to repay the owner four to fivefold. Note: the thief was not allowed to just replace the stolen property (animal). He was dealt a hard blow, a blow so hard that it would make him think twice before ever stealing again: he had to repay either four or five times what he had stolen. Why? Because the punishment was to be *corrective and restorative*. The punishment was meant to stop the thief dead in his tracks, correct him and restore him as a productive citizen of society. *Legally forcing* a person to repay four to five times what he had stolen would certainly stop most people from stealing. Moreover, when theft is prevented (or decreased), assaults and murder are often prevented (or decreased). Note how the punishment would force a thief to work and work hard, helping to prevent welfare problems. This particular punishment was given to prevent thievery, to help build a strong and moral society.

Thought 1. George Bush says:

> "The protection of person and property from the force of the violent, and from the frauds of the dishonest, is one of the chief objects of all criminal law....The most obvious, appropriate...punishment for stealing is [this]...the thief should be compelled to restore many times the value of that which he had stolen."[2]

Thought 2. Ronald F. Youngblood says:

> "Restitution for a stolen ox was more costly than for a stolen sheep (v.1) because a trained ox was more valuable than a sheep...."[3]

Thought 3. The man who has his property stolen is put under a great disadvantage. What can...
- a mechanic do without his tools?
- a painter do without his brushes?
- a plumber do without his wrenches?

---

[2] George Bush. *Commentary on Exodus*, p.322.
[3] Ronald F. Youngblood. *Exodus*, p.106.

- a builder do without his hammer?
- a teacher do without his books?
- a surgeon do without his scalpel?
- a secretary do without her files?
- a butcher do without his cleaver?
- a scientist do without his lab?
- a farmer do without his plow?
- a salesman do without his products?
- a writer do without his pen?

There is sometimes a double-edged sword when a man's property is stolen: a man not only loses his *possessions*, but he sometimes loses his ability to work and earn a living for himself. And if a man can no longer work and earn a living, his whole family potentially faces economic disaster. The thief must therefore be severely punished: he must be punished severely enough to correct and restore him as a productive citizen of society.

"Let him that stole steal no more: but rather let him labour, working with his hands the thing which is good, that he may have to give to him that needeth" (Eph.4:28).
"Trust not in oppression, and become not vain in robbery [do not vainly hope in robbery, NASB]: if riches increase, set not your heart upon them" (Ps.62:10).

2. The second case dealt with a thief who was killed while breaking into another man's property (v.2-3). Two different situations or cases are given.
   a. The first situation happened at night. If the owner felt that his life was at risk, he was allowed to defend himself, and if necessary, kill the intruder. It is interesting to note the phrase "breaking up" or "breaking in." In a very literal sense the thief would break up the dried mud that held the wooden structure together. To break in, the thief would have to tear up the house by digging a hole in it. One can only imagine the emotions of an owner being awakened by the frightening sounds of someone digging. The noise would be as startling as someone breaking into our home or business.
   b. The second situation placed guilt on the defender if he killed the thief during daylight. The reason for the distinction was due to the usual intent of a thief during the daylight hours: he came to steal, not to physically harm the manager or owner of the property. It is only natural for a man to want to dispense justice immediately and harshly. The principle behind this law ensured that the punishment would fit the crime, perfect justice was to be executed: the thief was to receive exactly what he deserved, nothing less, but nothing more. Stealing during the day did not usually warrant the death penalty. Life, even the life of the thief, is priceless; therefore, an attempt should be made to redeem the thief. Whether or not the defender was justified in killing a daytime thief was left up to the courts and judges to decide. George Bush reminds us of the sanctity of life:

"God's code...teaches us to be tender of the lives of bad men."[4]

Thought 1. By no means is it easy to be tender to a thief (or any other bad person) who breaks into our property, especially when lawlessness, assault, violence, and rape are so rampant. But the Bible is clear about what we as believers are to do after we have faced life-threatening situations: we are to forgive, love, and pray for our enemies. This does not mean that justice is not to be executed: it should be. Justice should always be exercised and it must always be severe enough to be *corrective and restorative*. But we are always to forgive, love, and pray for our enemies.

"An act of self-defense against a thief who broke in at night (see Job 24:16) did not produce blood-guilt even if the thief died (v.2), but killing an intruder in broad daylight was not justifiable (v.3)."[5]

George Bush says:

"The case was directly the reverse provided the sun had risen, for then the presumption was that the thief's sole purpose was to steal and not to kill, and slaying was not the punishment for stealing."[6]

"But I say unto you, Love your enemies, bless them that curse you, do good to them that hate you, and pray for them which despitefully use you, and persecute you" (Mt.5:44).
"Therefore if thine enemy hunger, feed him; if he thirst, give him drink: for in so doing thou shalt heap coals of fire on his head" (Ro.12:20).

3. The third case dealt with a thief who was caught while he still had the property in his possession (v.4). The law forced him to pay the owner double. This case was not as severe as the first because the property could still be recovered by the owner. But note: the thief had to give up not only what he had stolen, but he had to reimburse the owner a double payment. Note how fair and just this punishment is, how *corrective and restorative* it is. Again, a thief would stop dead in his tracks if such a punishment was to be fully enforced upon him. The law was definitely a deterrent, a check, a restraint, a prevention against stealing, and in some cases against an intruder assaulting or murdering a victim.

---

[4] George Bush. *Commentary on Exodus*, p.323.
[5] Ronald F. Youngblood. *Exodus,* p.106.
[6] George Bush. *Commentary on Exodus*, p.323.

Matthew Henry says:

> "This law teaches us that fraud and injustice, so far from enriching men, will impoverish them: if we unjustly get and keep that which is another's, it will not only waste itself, but it will consume that which is our own."[7]

> "Thou shalt not steal" (Ex.20:15).
> "Better is a little with righteousness than great revenues without right" (Pr.16:8).
> "Not purloining [stealing], but showing all good fidelity; that they may adorn the doctrine of God our Saviour in all things" (Tit.2:10).
> "But let none of you suffer as a murderer, or as a thief, or as an evildoer, or as a busybody in other men's matters" (1 Pt.4:15).

3 (22:5) **Law--Property Damage--Restitution**: there were laws governing irresponsible oversight--the failure to exercise due diligence or due caution.

LAWS GOVERNING IRRESPONSIBLE OVERSIGHT--
THE FAILURE TO EXERCISE DUE DILIGENCE

OUTLINE	SCRIPTURE
3. **Laws governing irresponsible oversight--the failure to exercise due diligence** a. The case: Loss caused by failure of due caution--property destroyed (by animals, machine, or whatever) b. The penalty: Full restitution	5 If a man shall cause a field or vineyard to be eaten, and shall put in his beast, and shall feed in another man's field; of the best of his own field, and of the best of his own vineyard, shall he make restitution.

1. The case: loss caused by irresponsible oversight (v.5). The example used to govern future cases is this: a person fails to be careful and cautious; consequently, he damages someone's property. For example, an animal strays and eats or damages a neighbor's property. The animal does not know any better, but the animal's owner does know better. He knows that his animals must be watched over or fenced in to keep them from wandering over and damaging other people's property. Therefore, the owner must be responsible: exercise due diligence and caution to make sure he does not damage his neighbor's property. An owner is responsible for controlling his property: with ownership comes the demand of responsibility. The Expositor's Bible Commentary says:

> "Men are held responsible, not only for the harm they do, but also for the harm they occasion...even though they may not have purposely designed the damaged that ensued."[8]

2. The penalty for breaking this law was full restitution: the offender was to repay the victim with the very best from his own property. Note, the key part of the restitution was the requirement to give the *best*. The law did not allow a...
- repayment of second-hand goods
- repayment of goods that had less value

The law did not even allow the repayment of goods with equal value. Repayment was to be of the very best goods, the maximum amount.

> **Thought 1**. This law teaches a striking lesson: we are not only responsible for the harm we do throughout life, but for the harm we cause or allow. For example, we are responsible for the automobiles we drive, the machines we operate, and on and on. We must guard and take due caution to prevent harm. We must be diligent and actively seek to keep bad things from happening.

> "Not slothful in business" (Ro.12:11).
> "And let us not be weary in well doing: for in due season we shall reap, if we faint not. As we have therefore opportunity, let us do good unto all men" (Gal.6:9-10).

4 (22:6) **Law--Property Damage--Restitution**: there were laws governing fire or burning control. Wildfire! Men of every generation have had to cope with the damage that occurs from a fire that gets out of control. Some wildfires are caused by lightning. Others are due to people failing to carefully extinguish fires, such as campfires. Arsonists are another cause for the spread of damaging fires. This particular law addresses the fire that starts in one field and spreads to another. The law protected innocent property owners from fire damage caused by a neighbor's lack of burning control.

---

[7] Matthew Henry. *Matthew Henry's Commentary*, p.291.
[8] Frank E. Gaebelein. *The Expositor's Bible Commentary*, Vol. 2, p.437.

LAWS GOVERNING FIRE OR BURNING CONTROL

OUTLINE	SCRIPTURE
4. Laws governing fire or burning control a. The case: Fire spreads & damages other property b. The penalty: Equal restitution	6 If fire break out, and catch in thorns, so that the stacks of corn, or the standing corn, or the field, be consumed therewith; he that kindled the fire shall surely make restitution.

1. The case: loss caused by fire or lack of burning control (v.6). The example used is that of a fire spreading from one man's field into his neighbor's field. Setting fires in fields was not an uncommon or unnatural thing to do. In fact, a good fire would help prepare the soil for the next crop that was to be planted. The problem would come if the winds began to blow the fire out of control. The fire leapt over the thornbushes (or hedges) and rapidly consumed the neighbor's field.

2. The penalty was a fair one: equal restitution.

Thought 1. Millions of properties are damaged by fire every year. Note how fair and just the law is. The property owner is protected against loss caused by fire started by another person.

⑤ (22:7-15) **Law--Stewardship--Trustee**: there were laws governing deposits, money or goods entrusted to the care of a trustee (neighbor) for safekeeping. This particular law governed how money or goods were to be treated when given over to the care of another person. The great <u>Pulpit Commentary</u> says this:

"Deposition of property in the hands of a friend, to keep and guard, was a marked feature in the life of primitive societies, where investments were difficult, and bankers unknown. Persons about to travel, especially merchants...required some one to guard it [their property] in their absence. Refusals to return such deposits were rare,.... Sometimes, however, they took place....The penalty, if a man were cast in the suit, was...'He shall pay double.'"[9]

LAWS GOVERNING DEPOSITS: MONEY OR GOODS ENTRUSTED TO THE CARE OF A TRUSTEE (NEIGHBOR) FOR SAFE-KEEPING

OUTLINE	SCRIPTURE	SCRIPTURE	OUTLINE

5. Laws governing deposits: Money or goods entrusted to the care of a trustee (neighbor) for safekeeping
a. Case 1: A thief steals: Must pay back double
b. Case 2: The trustee is suspect
  1) To be brought before the court
 	
  2) To have his property searched
  • If the property or goods are found and claimed by both parties, the court is to judge between the two parties
  • The guilty party is to pay back double
 	
c. Case 3: Property is damaged (injured or dies) while under the care of a trustee (neighbor)
	7 If a man shall deliver unto his neighbour money or stuff to keep, and it be stolen out of the man's house; if the thief be found, let him pay double.
	8 If the thief be not found, then the master of the house shall be brought unto the judges, to see whether he have put his hand unto his neighbour's goods.
	9 For all manner of trespass, whether it be for ox, for ass, for sheep, for raiment, or for any manner of lost thing, which another challengeth to be his, the cause of both parties shall come before the judges; and whom the judges shall condemn, he shall pay double unto his neighbour.
	10 If a man deliver unto his neighbour an ass, or an ox, or a sheep, or any beast, to
		keep; and it die, or be hurt, or driven away, no man seeing it:
		11 Then shall an oath of the LORD be between them both, that he hath not put his hand unto his neighbour's goods; and the owner of it shall accept thereof, and he shall not make it good.
		12 And if it be stolen from him, he shall make restitution unto the owner thereof.
		13 If it be torn in pieces, then let him bring it for witness, and he shall not make good that which was torn.
		14 And if a man borrow ought of his neighbour, and it be hurt, or die, the owner thereof being not with it, he shall surely make it good.
		15 But if the owner thereof be with it, he shall not make it good: if it be an hired thing, it came for his hire.
			
			1) The trustee is to take an oath that he is innocent
			
			2) The owner is to accept the oath
			
			3) The exception
			• If stolen from the trustee, is to make restitution
			• If damaged in an unpreventable way & the trustee can produce the evidence, he is innocent
			d. Case 4: Borrowed property is damaged (injured or dies)
			1) If the owner is not present, the borrower makes restitution
			2) If the owner is present, the borrower is not to pay
			3) If the property was rented, the rent money covers the loss

1. In the first case a thief stole the deposit (v.7). If caught, he was required to pay double. Note again how the punishment would make any prospective thief think twice about the financial risk before he committed the crime. The law was *corrective and restorative*.

2. The second case was a little more complicated in that the trustee was the suspect (v.8-9). The law provided a very orderly progression of steps that would help to reveal the truth.

    a. First, if the goods were stolen and a hint of suspicion surrounded the custodian, the depositor and custodian would take their case before the judges.

---

b. Second, the home of the trustee was thoroughly searched for the stolen property or goods. If the goods were found in the home and claimed by both parties, the court would then judge between the two parties. If the court found the master of the house (the trustee) to be guilty, he was bound by the law to pay back double. Again, as in the first case, the threat of financial punishment was designed to make any thief think before stealing property or goods. It was designed to stop the crime before it began.

3. The third case involved property that was damaged or suffered total loss while under the care of a neighbor (v.10-13). The law required the trustee to take an oath that he was innocent and required the owner to accept the oath. There was an exception to this point of the law.

⇒ If the property or goods were stolen by a thief, the trustee was to make *equal* restitution (v.12). The property was in his care; he was therefore responsible for it.

⇒ If the property or goods were damaged by some unpreventable cause (such as being torn by wild animals) and the trustee could produce the evidence, he was innocent (v.13).

Apparently, laws similar to those seen in case number three (v.10-13) were in force as early as the patriarchal period which is recorded in Genesis 31:39.[10]

> **"That which was torn *of beasts* I brought not unto thee; I bare the loss of it; of my hand didst thou require it, *whether* stolen by day, or stolen by night" (Gen.31:39).**

4. The fourth case referred to property that was damaged or suffered loss while borrowed (such as an animal being injured or dying) (v.14-15). The law provided the following guidelines:

a. If the owner was not present, the borrower made restitution.

b. If the owner was present, the borrower was not to pay restitution. The owner was naturally responsible for his own property.

c. If the animal was hired, the hired money covered the loss. The modern-day equivalent would be this: if a man rented a machine from a company and the machine broke down while renting it, it would not be the renter's duty to replace the broken tool. The money he paid to rent the machine would cover the owner's risk of doing business.

Thought 1. The overriding principle behind these laws was as George Bush summarizes:

> "The more these statutes are examined, the more clearly does their reasonable, equitable, mild, and humane spirit appear."[11]

God's laws governing the property and goods of people had several purposes:

1) To protect the rights of the property owner.
2) To prevent people from damaging property either through negligence or deliberate action such as stealing or arson.
3) To serve as a deterrent, a check, a restraint, a prevention against any person stealing or damaging property either deliberately or through negligence.
4) To protect the thief from property owners and societies that might seek excessive revenge, going too far in exercising punishment (e.g., lynching or rioting).
5) To correct and restore the person who did steal.
6) To build a strong, moral, and just society by establishing laws that would arouse people…
   - to stay alert in order to prevent accidents and damage to property
   - to think twice before committing a crime
   - to correct and restore the person who did steal or cause some careless and irresponsible damage or loss to property

> **"Think not that I am come to destroy the law, or the prophets: I am not come to destroy, but to fulfil" (Mt.5:17).**
> **"Wherefore the law is holy, and the commandment holy, and just, and good" (Ro.7:12).**
> **"But we know that the law is good, if a man use it lawfully" (1 Tim.1:8).**

---

[10] Ronald F. Youngblood. *Exodus*, p.106.
[11] George Bush. *Commentary on Exodus*, p. 328.

	C. The Laws Governing Social & Moral Obligations, Ex.22:16-31	shall be widows, and your children fatherless.	
1. The law governing seduction or premarital sex a. If the woman's parents consent, the offender must marry her & pay a dowry b. If the woman's parents object to marriage, the offender must still pay the dowry **2. The law governing sorcerers: To be executed** **3. The law governing bestiality: To be executed** **4. The law governing idolatry: To be executed** **5. The law governing strangers** a. Must not oppress b. Reason: God's people were strangers in Egypt (the world) **6. The law governing the weak & helpless, such as widows & orphans** a. Must not take advantage of b. The reason: God will hear their cry & judge the oppressor	16 And if a man entice a maid that is not betrothed, and lie with her, he shall surely endow her to be his wife. 17 If her father utterly refuse to give her unto him, he shall pay money according to the dowry of virgins. 18 Thou shalt not suffer a witch to live. 19 Whosoever lieth with a beast shall surely be put to death. 20 He that sacrificeth unto any god, save unto the LORD only, he shall be utterly destroyed. 21 Thou shalt neither vex a stranger, nor oppress him: for ye were strangers in the land of Egypt. 22 Ye shall not afflict any widow, or fatherless child. 23 If thou afflict them in any wise, and they cry at all unto me, I will surely hear their cry; 24 And my wrath shall wax hot, and I will kill you with the sword; and your wives	25 If thou lend money to any of my people that is poor by thee, thou shalt not be to him as an usurer, neither shalt thou lay upon him usury. 26 If thou at all take thy neighbour's raiment to pledge, thou shalt deliver it unto him by that the sun goeth down: 27 For that is his covering only, it is his raiment for his skin: wherein shall he sleep? and it shall come to pass, when he crieth unto me, that I will hear; for I am gracious. 28 Thou shalt not revile the gods, nor curse the ruler of thy people. 29 Thou shalt not delay to offer the first of thy ripe fruits, and of thy liquors: the firstborn of thy sons shalt thou give unto me. 30 Likewise shalt thou do with thine oxen, and with thy sheep: seven days it shall be with his dam; on the eighth day thou shalt give it me. 31 And ye shall be holy men unto me: neither shall ye eat any flesh that is torn of beasts in the field; ye shall cast it to the dogs.	**7. The law governing loans to the needy** a. The law 1) Must not charge interest to the needy 2) Must not take any pledge of security, not even a simple cloak (coat): Being poor, he needs all he has (his cloak) to meet his basic needs b. The reason: God hears his cry & is compassionate **8. The law governing cursing God & rulers: Forbidden** **9. The law governing offerings to God: Must not hold back** a. To give the first fruit of the harvest b. To give the firstborn son c. To give the firstborn livestock: To give on the eighth day **10. The law governing livestock killed by wild animals** a. Must protect health (holiness) b. Must not eat unclean, unsafe meat

DIVISION VIII

THE LAW AND THE PROMISES OF GOD (THE MOSAIC COVENANT) (PART 3): THE CIVIL AND RELIGIOUS LAWS OF ISRAEL--HELPFUL PRINCIPLES TO GOVERN MAN AND SOCIETY, 21:1-24:18

C. Laws Governing Social and Moral Obligations, 22:16-31

(22:16-31) **Introduction--Law, Civil--Israel**: just and moral laws are an absolute essential for any nation to survive. The pages of history are littered with nations that have failed to enforce true justice and true morality. The result has been corruption, decay, ruin, and collapse. The greatest threat to any nation's survival is from within not from without. A nation of people--in fact, any body of people--can remain strong only if they exercise true justice and morality among themselves.

The humanists and secularists are wrong. History proves that without the truth of God--without true justice and morality--society suffers.
- ⇒ Society suffers from rampant immorality, broken marriages, and terrible sexual diseases.
- ⇒ Society suffers from a gross perversion of religion and the acceptance of the occult.
- ⇒ Society suffers from unnatural acts between humans and animals, pressing the edge of vile wickedness.
- ⇒ Society suffers from false worship (idolatry and the deception of people who follow false worship).
- ⇒ Society suffers from the mistreatment of those who are different, whether of a different nationality or just a stranger.
- ⇒ Society suffers from indifference toward the weak and the helpless, such as widows and orphans.
- ⇒ Society suffers from the greed of people who seek to enrich themselves to the neglect of the poor.
- ⇒ Society suffers from a complete lack of respect for leaders and for God.
- ⇒ Society suffers from people who hold back on God, not wanting to share their resources in meeting the desperate needs of people who suffer and are dying without Christ and God.
- ⇒ Society suffers from a people who are defiled, both spiritually and physically.

God loves the world, every person in every society and every nation of the world. Therefore, God revealed His law to the Israelites to show exactly how their society was to be governed, and to show all future societies the very spirit and principles that were to underlie their laws.

God gave His law to people who had to relate to each other. The God of Israel has a very important role to play in every society. This is the subject of this portion of God's Holy Word. It is: *Laws Governing Social and Moral Obligations,* Ex.22:16-31.

1. The law governing seduction or premarital sex (v.1-17).
2. The law governing sorcerers: to be executed (v.18).
3. The law governing bestiality: to be executed (v.19).
4. The law governing idolatry: to be executed (v.20).
5. The law governing strangers (v.21).
6. The law governing the weak and helpless, such as widows and orphans (v.22-24).
7. The law governing loans to the needy (v.25-27).
8. The law governing cursing God and rulers: forbidden (v.28).
9. The law governing offerings to God: must not hold back (v.29-30).
10. The law governing livestock killed by wild animals (v.31).

1 (22:16-17) **Israel, Law of--Obedience--Law, Moral--Sex, Premarital**: there was the law governing seduction or premarital sex. There are few things more sacred to God than the sexual relationship between husband and wife. Sex is a gift from God, a gift that is to be enjoyed in marriage, but only in marriage. God gave sex for at least two purposes:

⇒ First, God gave sex so that man and woman could propagate the human race. Note that this purpose eliminates--totally eliminates--a temporary relationship between man and woman: it necessitates a permanent, life-long relationship. Why? Because it takes nine months for a child to be born and years--many years--for a child to grow into adulthood, and both parents are needed to teach and nourish the child through those years. Moreover, both parents are needed to help teach and nourish grandchildren. Sex was the process chosen by God for reproduction, a process that takes years--a lifetime of years--for just one child. Sex was given by God for husband and wife and for husband and wife alone.

⇒ Second, God gave sex so that man and woman could develop the closest and most intimate relationship imaginable, so they could become so close that they would be as one flesh and one spirit. Note that this purpose also eliminates a temporary relationship between man and woman. It takes years and years of intimacy for a husband and wife to become as one flesh and one spirit. Sex is to be the unique experience of marriage and marriage alone.

These two purposes clearly show why God declares that sex outside of marriage is wrong, tragically wrong. Sex becomes perverted and loses its purpose when committed outside marriage. This is the reason God gave Israel a law governing seduction and premarital sex.

THE LAWS GOVERNING SEDUCTION OR PREMARITAL SEX

OUTLINE	SCRIPTURE
	C. Laws Governing Social & Moral Obligations, Ex.22:16-31
1. The law governing seduction or premarital sex a. If the woman's parents consent, the offender must marry her & pay a dowry b. If the woman's parents object to marriage, the offender must still pay the dowry	16 And if a man entice a maid that is not betrothed, and lie with her, he shall surely endow her to be his wife. 17 If her father utterly refuse to give her unto him, he shall pay money according to the dowry of virgins.

There are many men and women who seem to be on a personal mission to seduce any person who will give in and say yes to their sexual advances. The rules of this mission are rules of...
* selfishness
* unchecked lust
* instant self-gratification

Illicit sex probably causes more pain within the human heart than any other single thing, more hurt for men, women, and children. Illicit sex causes divorce, broken trust and relationships, financial loss, terrible emotional stress, unwanted pregnancy, and the slaughter of millions of unborn babies. On and on the list of painful, distressing examples could be given. This is the reason God gave the law governing seduction or premarital sex. If a man seduced a woman and went to bed with her, the law was specific, very specific:

1. The offender had to marry the woman and pay a dowry (the bride-price) to her parents if the woman's parents consented to the marriage. This dowry was not a set amount; the amount was determined by the social and economic status of her family.

2. The offender must still pay the dowry even if the woman's parents objected to the marriage. Note the understanding and compassion seen in this exception. A parent might object because of the critical differences between his or her daugh-

ter and the young man, or because the young man was unfit, immature, or irresponsible. The guilty party still had to pay for the injury he had inflicted upon the misled or violated victim.

Note the power the father held in this particular society. By his word, he had the power to bless or to curse any man who took advantage of his daughter. In other societies, the courts might have to assume the authority to enforce the law.

Thought 1. What would happen in today's society if a man and woman were required to marry each other because they had premarital sex? If the guilty had to pay a large amount of money for victimizing a person? Would men and women behave differently knowing that a huge sum of money was directly tied to their treating one another with respect and dignity? How can a man and woman keep themselves pure?

"Let nothing be done through strife or vainglory; but in lowliness of mind let each esteem other better than themselves. Look not every man on his own things, but every man also on the things of others" (Ph.2:3-4).

"Wherewithal [how] shall a young man cleanse his way? by taking heed thereto according to thy word....Thy word have I hid in mine heart, that I might not sin against thee" (Ps.119:9, 11).

Thought 2. Note a significant fact: neither the marriage nor the payment of money removed the guilt and coming judgment of God upon the two lawbreakers. Guilt and forgiveness of sin come only through confession of sin and repentance, only by turning to God and beginning to follow Him anew.

"I tell you, Nay: but, except ye repent, ye shall all likewise perish" (Lk.13:3).

"And the publican, standing afar off, would not lift up so much as [his] eyes unto heaven, but smote upon his breast, saying, God be merciful to me a sinner" (Lk.18:13).

"Repent ye therefore, and be converted, that your sins may be blotted out, when the times of refreshing shall come from the presence of the Lord" (Acts 3:19).

"Repent therefore of this thy wickedness, and pray God, if perhaps the thought of thine heart may be forgiven thee" (Acts 8:22).

"If my people, which are called by my name, shall humble themselves, and pray, and seek my face, and turn from their wicked ways; then will I hear from heaven, and will forgive their sin, and will heal their land" (2 Chron.7:14).

"Then Job answered the LORD, and said....Wherefore I abhor myself, and repent in dust and ashes" (Job 42:1, 6).

Thought 3. This law places a great honor upon parents. It stresses how children should respect and honor their parents even in seeking to be married. Children should seek the consent of their parents for marriage, and they should listen to the advice and counsel of their parents.

"My son, hear the instruction of thy father, and forsake not the law of thy mother" (Pr.1:8).

"Hearken unto thy father that begat thee, and despise not thy mother when she is old" (Pr.23:22).

"Children, obey your parents in the Lord: for this is right. Honour thy father and mother; (which is the first commandment with promise;) That it may be well with thee, and thou mayest live long on the earth" (Eph.6:1-3).

"Children, obey your parents in all things: for this is well pleasing unto the Lord" (Col.3:20).

2 (22:18) **Law, Civil--Israel, Law of--Sorcery--Witchcraft--Occult, The--Magic--Divination**: there was the law governing sorcerers: they were to be executed.

THE LAW GOVERNING SORCERERS: TO BE EXECUTED

OUTLINE	SCRIPTURE
2. The law governing sorcerers: To be executed	18 Thou shalt not suffer a witch to live.

Sorcery is a terrible and destructive evil. Why? How? By misleading and deceiving people. Sorcery claims to have contact with the spiritual world or with the basic force and energy of the universe; it claims to know the future and destiny of people and things. Sorcery misleads and deceives people by causing them to follow the false hopes and gods of sorcery. The result is a terrible evil, for people are misled and doomed to eternal death, doomed to separation from the only true and living God, Jehovah - Yahweh Himself.

Note: this law would also apply to witchcraft, astrology, palm-reading, mysticism, divination, fortune-telling, seances, and to the reading of the horoscope or the signs of the zodiac to foretell events in one's life. God knows how easy it is for a person to be led into this forbidden area of life and how it can destroy human life. The warning is blunt and to the point: a person who is a sorcerer is to be destroyed.

"There shall not be found among you any one that maketh his son or his daughter to pass through the fire, or that useth divination, or an observer of times, or an enchanter, or a witch, Or a charmer, or a consulter with familiar spirits, or a wizard, or a necromancer. For all that do these things are an abomination unto the LORD: and because of these abominations the LORD thy God doth drive them out from before thee" (Dt.18:10-12).

"And I will come near to you to judgment; and I will be a swift witness against the sorcerers, and against the adulterers, and against false swearers, and against those that oppress the hireling in his wages, the widow, and the fatherless, and that turn aside the stranger from his right, and fear not me, saith the LORD of hosts" (Mal.3:5).

"But the fearful, and unbelieving, and the abominable, and murderers, and whoremongers, and sorcerers, and idolaters, and all liars, shall have their part in the lake which burneth with fire and brimstone: which is the second death" (Rev.21:8).

3 (22:19) **Israel, Law of--Obedience--Law, Moral--Sex, Bestiality**: there was the law governing bestiality (sexual relations between a human being and an animal): the person was to be executed. Note the Scripture:

THE LAW GOVERNING BESTIALITY: TO BE EXECUTED

OUTLINE	SCRIPTURE
3. The law governing bestiality: To be executed	19 Whosoever lieth with a beast shall surely be put to death.

In the ancient world, bestiality was often involved in pagan worship, celebrating the fertility power of all living creatures. The very thought of bestiality is so detestable that it is barely imaginable. Bestiality is a detestable evil, disgusting and contemptible. Bestiality is a clear symptom of a much deeper problem, that of rebellion against God. This sexual pervert rejects the natural use of sex, the natural order given by God. Remember God has given us sex for two primary purposes:
⇒ to propagate the human race
⇒ to give intimacy and closeness, the most intimate way possible for husband and wife to grow together, to become as one body and one spirit

Bestiality rejects God's purpose for sex, rejects the natural use for sex. Thereby bestiality rejects God and rebels against God, rejects and rebels in the most deviating, detestable, disgusting, perverted way imaginable. Bestiality was absolutely not to be tolerated. The pervert was to be executed.

"Whosoever lieth with a beast shall surely be put to death" (Ex.22:19).
"Neither shalt thou lie with any beast to defile thyself therewith: neither shall any woman stand before a beast to lie down thereto: it is confusion" (Lev.18:23).
"And if a man lie with a beast, he shall surely be put to death: and ye shall slay the beast. And if a woman approach unto any beast, and lie down thereto, thou shalt kill the woman, and the beast: they shall surely be put to death; their blood shall be upon them" (Lev.20:15-16).
"Cursed be he that lieth with any manner of beast. And all the people shall say, Amen" (Dt.27:21).

Thought 1. Why would a human being, a person who was made in the image of God, stoop so low in depravity? One of the inherent principles of sin is that it pulls people down, not up. The weight of sin will never allow a sinner to gravitate upwards. This is why it is so important for all sexual perverts to take three immediate steps.
1) Sexual perverts must repent of sin.

"Then Peter said unto them, Repent, and be baptized every one of you in the name of Jesus Christ for the remission of sins, and ye shall receive the gift of the Holy Ghost" (Acts 2:38).
"Repent ye therefore, and be converted, that your sins may be blotted out, when the times of refreshing shall come from the presence of the Lord" (Acts 3:19).
"Repent therefore of this thy wickedness, and pray God, if perhaps the thought of thine heart may be forgiven thee" (Acts 8:22).

2) Sexual perverts must be cleansed from sin.

"If we confess our sins, he is faithful and just to forgive us our sins, and to cleanse us from all unrighteousness" (1 Jn.1:9).

3) Sexual perverts must resist the temptation to sin.

"There hath no temptation taken you but such as is common to man: but God is faithful, who will not suffer you to be tempted above that ye are able; but will with the temptation also make a way to escape, that ye may be able to bear it" (1 Cor.10:13).
"Submit yourselves therefore to God. Resist the devil, and he will flee from you. Draw nigh to God, and he will draw nigh to you. Cleanse your hands, ye sinners; and purify your hearts, ye double minded" (Jas.4:7-8).

4) Sexual perverts must reject, turn away from the prevalent practices of modern-day Canaanites (those who live carnal, fleshly, immoral lives).

"Wherefore God also gave them up to uncleanness through the lusts of their own hearts, to dishonour their own bodies between themselves: Who changed the truth of God into a lie, and worshipped and served the creature more than the Creator, who is blessed for ever. Amen. For this cause God gave them up unto vile affections: for even their women did change the natural use into that which is against nature: And likewise also the men, leaving the natural use of the woman, burned in their lust one toward another; men with men working that which is unseemly, and receiving in themselves that recompence of their error which was meet" (Ro.1:24-27).
"And even as they did not like to retain God in their knowledge, God gave them over to a reprobate mind, to do those things which are not convenient; Being filled with all unrighteousness, fornication, wickedness, covetousness, maliciousness; full of envy, murder, debate, deceit, malignity; whisperers, Backbiters, haters of God, despiteful, proud, boasters, inventors of evil things, disobedient to parents, Without understanding, covenantbreakers, without natural affection, implacable, unmerciful: Who knowing the judgment of God, that they which commit such things are worthy of death, not only do the same, but have pleasure in them that do them" (Ro.1:28-32).

Thought 2. George Bush says that God demanded the death penalty because it was a "monster of impurity":

"This was a crime of such crying enormity that the earth itself was defiled by bearing such a monster of impurity as its perpetrator."[1]

4 (22:20) **Idolatry--Law, Civil--Gods, False**: there was the law governing idolatry. The idolater was to be executed. Note the law:

THE LAW GOVERNING IDOLATRY: TO BE EXECUTED

OUTLINE	SCRIPTURE
4. The law governing idolatry: To be executed	20 He that sacrificeth unto any god, save unto the LORD only, he shall be utterly destroyed.

Why such a severe penalty? To teach man the seriousness of the offense. The most terrible offense a person can commit is that of high treason, of betrayal (cp. 2 Pt.2:20). When a person betrays his family, people, or nation, he has cast them away and turned away from them. The penalty for high treason in most nations has been execution.

Now think for a moment: there is only one living and true God, only one Sovereign Ruler and Master of the universe. Moreover, not only is He the Sovereign Ruler of the universe, He created everything, the entire universe. If a person commits high treason against Him, betraying God--hates Him so much that he actually turns away or denies God, creating false, imaginary gods to worship and serve--what kind of justice should God exercise upon that person? Again, the person who curses, rejects, and denies God--the person who hates the Creator and Ruler of the universe--what does he deserve? What judgment would be fair and equitable? What does true justice require? God told Israel: the worshipper of false gods is to be executed. The idolater condemns himself to death. Scripture declares this time and again.

"Take heed to yourselves, that your heart be not deceived, and ye turn aside, and serve other gods, and worship them; And then the LORD'S wrath be kindled against you, and he shut up the heaven, that there be no rain, and that the land yield not her fruit; and lest ye perish quickly from off the good land which the LORD giveth you" (Dt.11:16-17).
"For the wrath of God is revealed from heaven against all ungodliness and unrighteousness of men, who hold the truth in unrighteousness; Because that which may be known of God is manifest in them; for God hath showed it unto them. For the invisible things of him from the creation of the world are clearly seen, being understood by the things that are made, even his eternal power and Godhead; so that they are without excuse: Because that, when they knew God, they glorified him not as God, neither were thankful; but became vain in their imaginations, and their foolish heart was darkened. Professing themselves to be wise, they became fools, And changed the glory of the uncorruptible God into an image made like to corruptible man, and to birds, and fourfooted beasts, and creeping things....And even as they did not like to retain God in their knowledge, God gave them over to a reprobate mind, to do those things which are not convenient; Being filled with all unrighteousness, fornication, wickedness, covetousness, maliciousness; full of envy, murder, debate, deceit, malignity; whisperers, Backbiters, haters of God, despiteful, proud, boasters, inventors of evil things, disobedient to parents, Without understanding, covenantbreakers, without natural affection, implacable, unmerciful: Who knowing the judgment of God, that they which commit such things are worthy of death, not only do the same, but have pleasure in them that do them" (Ro.1:18-23, 28-32).
"Now the works of the flesh are manifest, which are these; Adultery, fornication, uncleanness, lasciviousness, Idolatry, witchcraft, hatred, variance, emulations, wrath, strife, seditions, heresies, Envyings, murders, drunkenness, revellings, and such like: of the which I tell you before, as I have also told you in time past, that they which do such things shall not inherit the kingdom of God" (Gal.5:19-21).
"But the fearful, and unbelieving, and the abominable, and murderers, and whoremongers, and sorcerers, and idolaters, and all liars, shall have their part in the lake which burneth with fire and brimstone: which is the second death" (Rev.21:8).

---

[1] George Bush. *Commentary on Exodus*, p.331.

5 (22:21) **Israel, Law of--Obedience--Law, Social--Hospitality--Oppression**: there was the law governing strangers or foreigners.

THE LAW GOVERNING STRANGERS

OUTLINE	SCRIPTURE
5. The law governing strangers a. Must not oppress b. Reason: God's people were strangers in Egypt (the world)	21 Thou shalt neither vex a stranger, nor oppress him: for ye were strangers in the land of Egypt.

What an unusual law, to require the citizens of a nation to accept and be kind to strangers, foreigners, immigrants, aliens, different nationalities; they were all to be treated with respect, dignity, and justice. How desperately the law is needed within all lands, for mistreatment of strangers is common among both adults and children. Strangers and foreigners are often ridiculed, rejected, and even oppressed. But this is not God's way: He even requires that His people love strangers and foreigners:

> **"But the stranger that dwelleth with you shall be unto you as one born among you, and thou shalt love him as thyself; for ye were strangers in the land of Egypt: I am the LORD your God" (Lev.19:34).**

1. The instructions of this law were clear: Israel was not to mistreat nor oppress a stranger.
2. The reason for this law was plain and simple: God's people had also been strangers in Egypt (the world). They knew the experience of being strangers, what it felt like to be mistreated and oppressed. As followers of God, they knew what it was to experience the rejection, ridicule, and persecution of Egypt (the world). Therefore, they were to be tender toward strangers, accept and receive them.

Thought 1. The lesson for believers is emphatic: we are never to mistreat or oppress a stranger or foreigner, much less anyone else. On the contrary, we are to accept them and help them, even love them.

> **"And if a stranger sojourn with thee in your land, ye shall not vex him. But the stranger that dwelleth with you shall be unto you as one born among you, and thou shalt love him as thyself; for ye were strangers in the land of Egypt: I am the LORD your God" (Lev.19:33-34).**
> **"Love ye therefore the stranger: for ye were strangers in the land of Egypt" (Dt.10:19).**
> **"The LORD preserveth the strangers; he relieveth the fatherless and widow: but the way of the wicked he turneth upside down" (Ps.146:9).**
> **"Owe no man any thing, but to love one another: for he that loveth another hath fulfilled the law. For this, Thou shalt not commit adultery, Thou shalt not kill, Thou shalt not steal, Thou shalt not bear false witness, Thou shalt not covet; and if there be any other commandment, it is briefly comprehended in this saying, namely, Thou shalt love thy neighbour as thyself" (Ro.13:8-9).**
> **"Be not forgetful to entertain strangers: for thereby some have entertained angels unawares" (Heb.13:2).**
> **"Use hospitality one to another without grudging" (1 Pt.4:9).**

Thought 2. Matthew Henry says that "Humanity is one of the laws of religion." We must, therefore, be tender and show compassion and concern to strangers. "Strangers...are known to God, and he preserves them."[2]

> **"The LORD preserveth the strangers; he relieveth the fatherless and widow: but the way of the wicked he turneth upside down" (Ps.146:9).**

6 (22:22-24) **Israel, Law of--Obedience--Law, Moral--Widows and Orphans, Treatment of**: there was the law governing the treatment of the weak and helpless, such as widows and orphans. The commandment of God is strong and issues a severe warning to the oppressor:

THE LAW GOVERNING WIDOWS AND ORPHANS

OUTLINE	SCRIPTURE
6. The law governing the weak & helpless, such as widows & orphans a. Must not take advantage of b. The reason: God will hear their cry & judge the oppressor	22 Ye shall not afflict any widow, or fatherless child. 23 If thou afflict them in any wise, and they cry at all unto me, I will surely hear their cry; 24 And my wrath shall wax hot, and I will kill you with the sword; and your wives

---

[2] Matthew Henry. *Matthew Henry's Commentary*, p.293.

1. This law warned people not to take advantage of the weak and helpless in society such as the widow and the orphan. These dear people are often weak and defenseless and are at the greatest risk in society. This law would apply to any person who is helpless, defenseless, unprotected, or vulnerable. But in most societies the two most helpless classes of people are the orphans and widows. Therefore, the civil law addresses these two as the representative case to govern society's treatment of the weak and helpless.
   a. The widow had depended upon the provision and protection of her husband, and now he was no longer there. But other men on the prowl would be. They would come to gain personal or sexual favors or to offer fraudulent business deals. She would be bombarded with all sorts of proposals and most likely would be ill-equipped to handle them.
   b. The orphan was in a more fragile position. Being a child meant that the orphan had little or no rights. He had no one to state his case or to speak out in his defense. He was alone, without the oversight of a parent to love and care for him.
2. The reason behind this law was clear: God cares for the weak and defenseless, for the widows and orphans. He would, therefore, hear their cry and judge the oppressor (v.23-24). If a person dared to break this law, the punishment was to be a perfect, righteous judgment. God warned the oppressor: he would suffer the judgment of God, a judgment comparable to dying and leaving behind a widow and children who would be fatherless.

Thought 1. Note three lessons.
1) God demands that we protect and provide for widows and orphans, not mistreat nor take advantage of them.

> "Thou shalt not pervert the judgment of the stranger, nor of the fatherless; nor take a widow's raiment to pledge: But thou shalt remember that thou wast a bondman in Egypt, and the LORD thy God redeemed thee thence: therefore I command thee to do this thing. When thou cuttest down thine harvest in thy field, and hast forgot a sheaf in the field, thou shalt not go again to fetch it: it shall be for the stranger, for the fatherless, and for the widow: that the LORD thy God may bless thee in all the work of thine hands. When thou beatest thine olive tree, thou shalt not go over the boughs again: it shall be for the stranger, for the fatherless, and for the widow. When thou gatherest the grapes of thy vineyard, thou shalt not glean it afterward: it shall be for the stranger, for the fatherless, and for the widow. And thou shalt remember that thou wast a bondman in the land of Egypt: therefore I command thee to do this thing" (Dt.24:17-22).
> "When thou hast made an end of tithing all the tithes of thine increase the third year, which is the year of tithing, and hast given it unto the Levite, the stranger, the fatherless, and the widow, that they may eat within thy gates, and be filled; Then thou shalt say before the LORD thy God, I have brought away the hallowed things out of mine house, and also have given them unto the Levite, and unto the stranger, to the fatherless, and to the widow, according to all thy commandments which thou hast commanded me: I have not transgressed thy commandments, neither have I forgotten them" (Dt.26:12-13).
> "Thus saith the LORD of hosts, the God of Israel, Amend your ways and your doings, and I will cause you to dwell in this place [God's presence]....If ye oppress not the stranger, the fatherless, and the widow, and shed not innocent blood in this place, neither walk after other gods to your hurt" (Jer.7:3, 6).
> "Thus saith the LORD; Execute ye judgment and righteousness, and deliver the spoiled out of the hand of the oppressor: and do no wrong, do no violence to the stranger, the fatherless, nor the widow, neither shed innocent blood in this place" (Jer.22:3).
> "And oppress not the widow, nor the fatherless, the stranger, nor the poor; and let none of you imagine evil against his brother in your heart" (Zech.7:10).
> "Pure religion and undefiled before God and the Father is this, To visit the fatherless and widows in their affliction, and to keep himself unspotted from the world" (Jas.1:27).

2) God declares that He is the husband and defender of the widow and the father of the orphan.

> "For thy Maker is thine husband; the LORD of hosts is his name; and thy Redeemer the Holy One of Israel; The God of the whole earth shall he be called" (Is.54:5).
> "A father of the fatherless, and a judge of the widows, is God in his holy habitation" (Ps.68:5).

3) God warns the oppressor of widows and orphans: the oppressor will face the fierce judgment of God.

> "And I will come near to you to judgment; and I will be a swift witness against the sorcerers, and against the adulterers, and against false swearers, and against those that oppress the hireling in his wages, the widow, and the fatherless, and that turn aside the stranger from his right, and fear not me, saith the LORD of hosts" (Mal.3:5).
> "But whoso shall offend one of these little ones which believe in me, it were better for him that a millstone were hanged about his neck, and [that] he were drowned in the depth of the sea" (Mt.18:6).
> "Woe unto you, scribes and Pharisees, hypocrites! for ye devour widows' houses, and for a pretence make long prayer: therefore ye shall receive the greater damnation" (Mt.23:14).

7 (22:25-27) <u>Law, Civil--Loans--Poverty--Society--Needy, The--Poor, The</u>: there was the law governing loans to the needy. Very simply, interest was not to be charged to the needy. This passage is not dealing with what the modern world calls commercial loans; it is dealing with...
- a neighbor becoming poverty-stricken
- some person within the community being poor due to a handicap or being unskilled and unable to find employment

THE LAW GOVERNING LOANS TO THE NEEDY

OUTLINE	SCRIPTURE	SCRIPTURE	OUTLINE
7. The law governing loans to the needy a. The law 1) Must not charge interest to the needy 2) Must not take any pledge of security, not even a simple cloak (coat): Being	25 If thou lend money to any of my people that is poor by thee, thou shalt not be to him as an usurer, neither shalt thou lay upon him usury. 26 If thou at all take thy neighbour's raiment to pledge, thou shalt deliver it	unto him by that the sun goeth down: 27 For that is his covering only, it is his raiment for his skin: wherein shall he sleep? and it shall come to pass, when he crieth unto me, that I will hear; for I am gracious.	poor, he needs all he has (his cloak) to meet his basic needs b. The reason: God hears his cry & is compassionate

1. The law was laid out in two main points:
   a. The person who loaned money to the needy was not to charge interest (v.25). Believers are to help the poor and minister to them, not make money off them. The poor need compassion not abuse. God has called believers to be people of compassion and mercy, people who see the needs of the world and do all they can to meet those needs. The true believer would never take advantage of a person's poverty: if a poor person needs money, the believer gives the poverty-stricken person whatever he can. He does not make a loan with interest to the poverty-stricken person; he reaches out in compassion and gives whatever he can to meet the need of the person. This is exactly what Christ taught: He instructed His followers to make loans to the poor and to count those loans as free gifts.

   > **"And if ye lend [to them] of whom ye hope to receive, what thank have ye? for sinners also lend to sinners, to receive as much again. But love ye your enemies, and do good, and lend, hoping for nothing again; and your reward shall be great, and ye shall be the children of the Highest: for he is kind unto the unthankful and [to] the evil" (Lk.6:34-35).**

   b. The person giving a loan to the poor must not take any pledge of security, not even a simple cloak (coat, poncho) (v.26-27). The poverty-stricken person needs all he has (his cloak) to meet his basic needs. For the poor man, the cloak was more than an overcoat: it was used for a blanket or bedding at night. Without it, the cold would quickly make its way deep into his bones. The point is clear: the believer is not to demand security when making loans to the poor, not to demand anything as security, not even something as simple as a cloak. The poverty-stricken person needs what little he has to survive.

2. The reason or purpose behind this law is encouraging: God hears the cry of the needy and is compassionate toward them (v.27). God truly cares for the poor and the needy, and He expects His people to care for them and to do all they can to meet their needs.

   <u>Thought 1</u>. Two clear lessons are gleaned from this law:
   1) Believers are to show compassion and care for the needy of this earth: do all they can to meet their needs.
   2) Believers are never to take advantage of the poor and needy, not by charging them interest on money loaned (given) to them.

   > **"And if thy brother be waxen poor, and fallen in decay with thee; then thou shalt relieve him: yea, though he be a stranger, or a sojourner; that he may live with thee. Take thou no usury [interest] of him, or increase: but fear thy God; that thy brother may live with thee. Thou shalt not give him thy money upon usury, nor lend him thy victuals for increase" (Lev.25:35-37).**
   > **"If there be among you a poor man of one of thy brethren within any of thy gates in thy land which the LORD thy God giveth thee, thou shalt not harden thine heart, nor shut thine hand from thy poor brother" (Dt.15:7).**
   > **"Thou shalt not lend upon usury to thy brother; usury [interest] of money, usury of victuals, usury of any thing that is lent upon usury: Unto a stranger thou mayest lend upon usury; but unto thy brother thou shalt not lend upon usury: that the LORD thy God may bless thee in all that thou settest thine hand to in the land whither thou goest to possess it" (Dt.23:19-20).**
   > **"And I was very angry when I heard their cry and these words. Then I consulted with myself, and I rebuked the nobles, and the rulers, and said unto them, Ye exact usury, every one of his brother. And I set a great assembly against them. And I said unto them, We after our ability have redeemed our brethren the Jews, which were sold unto the heathen; and will ye even sell your brethren? or shall they be sold unto us? Then held they their peace, and found nothing to answer. Also I said, It is not good that ye do: ought ye not to walk in the fear of our God because of the reproach of the heathen our enemies? I likewise, and my brethren, and my servants, might exact of them money and corn: I pray you, let us leave off this usury. Restore, I pray you, to them, even**

this day, their lands, their vineyards, their oliveyards, and their houses, also the hundredth part of the money, and of the corn, the wine, and the oil, that ye exact of them. Then said they, We will restore them, and will require nothing of them; so will we do as thou sayest. Then I called the priests, and took an oath of them, that they should do according to this promise" (Neh.5:6-12).

"They pluck the fatherless from the breast, and take a pledge of the poor" (Job 24:9).

"He that putteth not out his money to usury [for interest], nor taketh reward against the innocent. He that doeth these things shall never be moved" (Ps.15:5).

"He that by usury and unjust gain increaseth his substance, he shall gather it for him that will pity the poor" (Pr.28:8).

"He that hath not given forth upon usury, neither hath taken any increase, that hath withdrawn his hand from iniquity, hath executed true judgment between man and man" (Ezk.18:8; cp. v.13, 17).

"Hath given forth upon usury, and hath taken increase: shall he then live? he shall not live: he hath done all these abominations; he shall surely die; his blood shall be upon him" (Ezk.18:13).

"In thee have they taken gifts to shed blood; thou hast taken usury and increase, and thou hast greedily gained of thy neighbours by extortion, and hast forgotten me, saith the Lord GOD" (Ezk.22:12).

Thought 2. God hears the cry of anyone who hits rock bottom. God is always with the poor and poverty-stricken, there all the time, each step of the way. God is there to provide hope and help in the midst of the storm. We must always remember this fact: no matter where we are, God always knows where we are, what we need, and when we need it.

"Hear my prayer, O LORD, and let my cry come unto thee. Hide not thy face from me in the day *when* I am in trouble; incline thine ear unto me: in the day *when* I call answer me speedily" (Ps.102:1-2).

"For he satisfieth the longing soul, and filleth the hungry soul with goodness" (Ps.107:9).

"He raiseth up the poor out of the dust, *and* lifteth the needy out of the dunghill; That he may set *him* with princes, *even* with the princes of his people" (Ps.113:7-8).

"I love the LORD, because he hath heard my voice *and* my supplications. Because he hath inclined his ear unto me, therefore will I call upon *him* as long as I live. The sorrows of death compassed me, and the pains of hell got hold upon me: I found trouble and sorrow. Then called I upon the name of the LORD; O LORD, I beseech thee, deliver my soul. Gracious *is* the LORD, and righteous; yea, our God *is* merciful" (Ps.116:1-5).

"I called upon the LORD in distress: the LORD answered me, *and set me* in a large place. The LORD *is* on my side; I will not fear: what can man do unto me? The LORD taketh my part with them that help me: therefore shall I see *my desire* upon them that hate me. *It is* better to trust in the LORD than to put confidence in man. *It is* better to trust in the LORD than to put confidence in princes" (Ps.118:5-9).

"In my distress I cried unto the LORD, and he heard me" (Ps.120:1).

"The LORD *is* thy keeper: the LORD *is* thy shade upon thy right hand. The sun shall not smite thee by day, nor the moon by night. The LORD shall preserve thee from all evil: he shall preserve thy soul. The LORD shall preserve thy going out and thy coming in from this time forth, and even for evermore" (Ps.121:5-8).

"Our help *is* in the name of the LORD, who made heaven and earth" (Ps.124:8).

"Out of the depths have I cried unto thee, O LORD. Lord, hear my voice: let thine ears be attentive to the voice of my supplications" (Ps.130:1-2).

8 (22:28) **Israel, Law of--Obedience--Law, Moral--Cursing, God and Rulers:** there was the law governing the cursing of God and rulers. Simply stated, neither God nor rulers are ever to be cursed, not by any of us. A people who grumble, complain, curse, and speak evil always disturb the peace and keep people stirred up. If the rulers and God are the objects of the cursing and evil speaking, then the very foundation of the nation begins to crumble. Note the law:

THE LAW GOVERNING CURSING GOD
AND RULERS: FORBIDDEN

OUTLINE	SCRIPTURE
8. The law governing cursing God & rulers: Forbidden	28 Thou shalt not revile the gods, nor curse the ruler of thy people.

Respect for God and rulers is a must if a society is to live in peace. A nation of people who curses rulers is a nation that will soon crumble into a thousand broken pieces. A nation cannot survive unless its rulers are respected and honored. In addition, Scripture teaches that God as well as rulers must be respected and honored. God does not tolerate His name being cursed, not for long. Judgment is soon pronounced upon an evil speaking people. Moreover, rulers are set in place and given their authority under the sovereignty of God. Therefore, rulers--their office, their position--must be respected not cursed.

Note how important respect and honor are to God: the penalty for cursing rulers and God was death. Why so severe a penalty? Because cursing and evil speaking disturb the peace and can eventually lead to rebellion and insurrection. And the result of rebellion and insurrection is terrible suffering and death. God is the God of peace and reconciliation, not of evil speaking, disturbance, and war. Therefore, He demands respect and honor for both rulers and Himself. If not--if a person insists on malicious rebellion and insurrection against a ruler or God--the judgment is to be carried out.

Thought 1. The teaching of Scripture is clear:
1) We are to respect and pray for those in authority.

"Curse not the king, no not in thy thought; and curse not the rich in thy bedchamber: for a bird of the air shall carry the voice, and that which hath wings shall tell the matter" (Eccl.10:20).
"Then said Paul, I wist [knew] not, brethren, that he was the high priest: for it is written, Thou shalt not speak evil of the ruler of thy people" (Acts 23:5).
"Let every soul be subject unto the higher powers. For there is no power but of God: the powers that be are ordained of God" (Ro.13:1).
"I exhort therefore, that, first of all, supplications, prayers, intercessions, *and* giving of thanks, be made for all men; For kings, and *for* all that are in authority; that we may lead a quiet and peaceable life in all godliness and honesty" (1 Tim.2:1-2).
"Put them in mind to be subject to principalities and powers, to obey magistrates, to be ready to every good work" (Tit.3:1).
"Submit yourselves to every ordinance of man for the Lord's sake: whether it be to the king, as supreme; Or unto governors, as unto them that are sent by him for the punishment of evildoers, and for the praise of them that do well" (1 Pt.2:13-14).
"Honour all *men*. Love the brotherhood. Fear God. Honour the king" (1 Pt.2:17).
"Likewise also these *filthy* dreamers defile the flesh, despise dominion, and speak evil of dignities" (Jude 1:8).

2) We are not to curse and blaspheme the name of God, never speak evil of Him.

"Thou shalt not take the name of the LORD thy God in vain; for the LORD will not hold him guiltless that taketh his name in vain" (Ex.20:7).
"And ye shall not swear by my name falsely, neither shalt thou profane the name of thy God: I am the LORD" (Lev.19:12).
"And thou shalt speak unto the children of Israel, saying, Whosoever curseth his God shall bear his sin. And he that blasphemeth the name of the LORD, he shall surely be put to death, and all the congregation shall certainly stone him: as well the stranger, as he that is born in the land, when he blasphemeth the name of the LORD, shall be put to death" (Lev.24:15-16).
"But I say unto you, Swear not at all; neither by heaven; for it is God's throne: Nor by the earth; for it is his footstool: neither by Jerusalem; for it is the city of the great King. Neither shalt thou swear by thy head, because thou canst not make one hair white or black. But let your communication be, Yea, yea; Nay, nay: for whatsoever is more than these cometh of evil" (Mt.5:34-37).
"But above all things, my brethren, swear not, neither by heaven, neither by the earth, neither by any other oath: but let your yea be yea; and your nay, nay; lest ye fall into condemnation" (Jas.5:12).

9 (22:29-30) **Israel, Law of--Obedience--Law, Moral--Offerings--Stewardship:** there was the law governing man's offerings to God. The law was clear: a man was not to keep, not even hold back, the offering. He was not even to delay in giving his offering to God.

THE LAW GOVERNING OFFERINGS TO GOD:
MUST NOT HOLD BACK

OUTLINE	SCRIPTURE
9. The law governing offerings to God: Must not hold back a. To give the first fruit of the harvest b. To give the firstborn son c. To give the firstborn livestock: To give on the eighth day	29 Thou shalt not delay to offer the first of thy ripe fruits, and of thy liquors: the firstborn of thy sons shalt thou give unto me. 30 Likewise shalt thou do with thine oxen, and with thy sheep: seven days it shall be with his dam; on the eighth day thou shalt give it me.

The exhortation is clear: a person is not to hold back those things that belong to God. Three offerings were required of the Israelites:
1. The first fruit of the harvest was required: the crop had been planted, tended, and harvested by the sweat of the brow (v.29). And every farmer in every generation has had to cope with the same set of problems:
    a. Will the seed or plants or trees be good?
    b. Will enough rain fall to water the crops?
    c. Will some disease strike the crops?
    d. Will labor be available to harvest the crops on time?

231

The believer was to trust God through all, and when the harvest came, he was to give the very first of the fruit or harvest to God. Large or small, God was to receive the best of his crops.

2. The firstborn son of a family was required as part of the offering (v.29). (See outline and notes--Ex.13:1-16; <u>Deeper Study # 1</u>--Ex.13:13 for more discussion.) There is nothing more dear to parents than their children. Thus, the point was clear to God's people: the first and most joyful was to be given to God. Note that children were to be redeemed by a money payment.

> **"And every firstling of an ass thou shalt redeem with a lamb; and if thou wilt not redeem it, then thou shalt break his neck: and all the firstborn of man among thy children shalt thou redeem"** (Ex.13:13).
>
> **"And for those that are to be redeemed of the two hundred and threescore and thirteen of the firstborn of the children of Israel, which are more than the Levites; Thou shalt even take five shekels apiece by the poll, after the shekel of the sanctuary shalt thou take them: (the shekel is twenty gerahs:) And thou shalt give the money, wherewith the odd number of them is to be redeemed, unto Aaron and to his sons"** (Num.3:46-48).

3. The firstborn livestock was required as part of the offering (v.30). The livestock was to be given on the eighth day. A man's animals were an important commodity to his financial well-being, and a good ox was worth a lot of money. Nevertheless, the offering was to be made, no matter the sacrifice required.

Thought 1. The lesson of this law must be heeded by God's people. The desperate of the world are crying out for help. We must, therefore, obey God in our tithes and offerings. We must give and give, and we must give generously from a broken heart.

> **"Lay not up for yourselves treasures upon earth, where moth and rust doth corrupt, and where thieves break through and steal: But lay up for yourselves treasures in heaven, where neither moth nor rust doth corrupt, and where thieves do not break through nor steal: For where your treasure is, there will your heart be also"** (Mt.6:19-21).
>
> **"No man can serve two masters: for either he will hate the one, and love the other; or else he will hold to the one, and despise the other. Ye cannot serve God and mammon [money, possessions]. Therefore I say unto you, Take no thought for your life, what ye shall eat, or what ye shall drink; nor yet for your body, what ye shall put on....But seek ye first the kingdom of God, and his righteousness; and all these things shall be added unto you"** (Mt.6:24-25, 33).
>
> **"For what is a man profited, if he shall gain the whole world, and lose his own soul? or what shall a man give in exchange for his soul?"** (Mt.16:26).
>
> **"Will a man rob God? Yet ye have robbed me. But ye say, Wherein have we robbed thee? In tithes and offerings. Ye are cursed with a curse: for ye have robbed me, even this whole nation. Bring ye all the tithes into the storehouse, that there may be meat in mine house, and prove me now herewith, saith the LORD of hosts, if I will not open you the windows of heaven, and pour you out a blessing, that there shall not be room enough to receive it"** (Mal.3:8-10).
>
> **"Give, and it shall be given unto you; good measure, pressed down, and shaken together, and running over, shall men give into your bosom. For with the same measure that ye mete withal it shall be measured to you again"** (Lk.6:38).
>
> **"But this I say, He which soweth sparingly shall reap also sparingly; and he which soweth bountifully shall reap also bountifully. Every man according as he purposeth in his heart, so let him give; not grudgingly, or of necessity: for God loveth a cheerful giver"** (2 Cor.9:6-7).

10 (22:31) <u>Israel, Law of--Obedience--Law, Social--Law, Dietary</u>: there was the law governing livestock killed by wild animals. Note exactly what this law said:

THE LAW GOVERNING LIVESTOCK
KILLED BY WILD ANIMALS

OUTLINE	SCRIPTURE
10. The law governing livestock killed by wild animals	31 And ye shall be holy men unto me: neither shall ye eat any flesh that is torn of beasts in the field; ye shall cast it to the dogs.
a. Must protect health (holiness)	
b. Must not eat unclean, unsafe meat	

Holy or holiness means to be consecrated, sanctified, set apart to God; it means to be distinct and different from other things. God's people are to be holy people, people totally set apart to God. But note: holiness is to be *outward as well as inward*. This is the point of this law: people would know that followers of God did not eat livestock killed by wild animals. There was a health reason for abstaining from this practice. The blood of the livestock would not be totally drained: some blood would still be in the tissues. Consequently, the animal would be unclean and perhaps dangerous. The dead animal was to be cast to the dogs.

Thought 1. God's calling is the highest of callings, that of living pure and holy lives. God's people--those who truly believe and follow Him--are to be totally set apart to Him both in heart and in deed (conduct, behavior).

"Now therefore, if ye will obey my voice indeed, and keep my covenant, then ye shall be a peculiar treasure unto me above all people: for all the earth is mine: And ye shall be unto me a kingdom of priests, and an holy nation. These are the words which thou shalt speak unto the children of Israel" (Ex.19:5-6).

"For I am the LORD your God: ye shall therefore sanctify yourselves, and ye shall be holy; for I am holy: neither shall ye defile yourselves with any manner of creeping thing that creepeth upon the earth" (Lev.11:44).

"Sanctify yourselves therefore, and be ye holy: for I am the LORD your God" (Lev.20:7).

"And ye shall be holy unto me: for I the LORD am holy, and have severed you from other people, that ye should be mine" (Lev.20:26).

"I beseech you therefore, brethren, by the mercies of God, that ye present your bodies a living sacrifice, holy, acceptable unto God, which is your reasonable service. And be not conformed to this world: but be ye transformed by the renewing of your mind, that ye may prove what is that good, and acceptable, and perfect, will of God" (Ro.12:1-2).

"Be not thou therefore ashamed of the testimony of our Lord, nor of me his prisoner: but be thou partaker of the afflictions of the gospel according to the power of God; Who hath saved us, and called us with an holy calling, not according to our works, but according to his own purpose and grace, which was given us in Christ Jesus before the world began" (2 Tim.1:8-9).

"But as he which hath called you is holy, so be ye holy in all manner of conversation; Because it is written, Be ye holy; for I am holy" (1 Pt.1:15-16).

"But ye are a chosen generation, a royal priesthood, an holy nation, a peculiar people; that ye should show forth the praises of him who hath called you out of darkness into his marvellous light" (1 Pt.2:9).

	D. The Laws Governing Justice & Mercy In Court & Among Neighbors, Ex.23:1-9	that hateth thee lying under his burden, and wouldest forbear to help him, thou shalt surely help with him. 6 Thou shalt not wrest the judgment of thy poor in his cause. 7 Keep thee far from a false matter; and the innocent and righteous slay thou not: for I will not justify the wicked. 8 And thou shalt take no gift: for the gift blindeth the wise, and perverteth the words of the righteous. 9 Also thou shalt not oppress a stranger: for ye know the heart of a stranger, seeing ye were strangers in the land of Egypt.	you are to help him
1. The law governing slander: You must not bear a false report a. Not to help yourself b. Not to help a wicked person c. Not to help others plotting to do wrong d. Not to help a poor man by showing favoritism in a lawsuit **2. The law governing the treatment of enemies** a. If you find his lost property, you must return it b. If you find him needing help,	Thou shalt not raise a false report: put not thine hand with the wicked to be an unrighteous witness. 2 Thou shalt not follow a multitude to do evil; neither shalt thou speak in a cause to decline after many to wrest judgment: 3 Neither shalt thou countenance a poor man in his cause. 4 If thou meet thine enemy's ox or his ass going astray, thou shalt surely bring it back to him again. 5 If thou see the ass of him		**3. The law governing justice to the poor** a. Must not deny him justice b. Must not falsely charge him c. Must not put the innocent or honest person to death d. The reason: God will judge the unjust & immoral **4. The law governing bribery: You must not take bribes** a. Will blind the wise b. Will twist the words of the righteous **5. The law governing treatment of a stranger (foreigner)** a. Must not oppress him b. Reason: Bc. God's people know what it feels like to be strangers

DIVISION VIII

THE LAW AND THE PROMISES OF GOD (THE MOSAIC COVENANT) (PART 3): THE CIVIL AND RELIGIOUS LAWS OF ISRAEL--HELPFUL PRINCIPLES TO GOVERN MAN AND SOCIETY, 21:1-24:18

D.   The Law Governing Justice and Mercy In Court and Among Neighbors, Ex.23:1-9

(23:1-9) **Introduction**: one of society's most important institutions is its legal system. The courts of the land are to be a refuge for the truth and for justice. The purpose of a court of law is...
- to execute justice and truth (each equally important)
- to enforce protection and compassion
- to seek the complete truth, unshaded by bias
- to mediate between two parties with different interests and motives
- to be fair and just to all
- to reconcile two different positions, to bring peace between them, peace for the sake of both society and the parties

When the courts are governed by honorable men and women who rightly apply the law, a nation will prosper. However, a nation will quickly slide into moral and political chaos if the laws of the people are not administered fairly, justly. God warns both Israel and future generations of this very thing, to guard against judicial corruption. These are: *The Laws Governing Justice and Mercy in Court and Among Neighbors*, Ex.23:1-9.

1. The law governing slander: must not bear a false report (v.1-3).
2. The law governing one's enemies (v.4-5).
3. The law governing justice to the poor (v.6-7).
4. The law governing bribery: must not take bribes (v.8).
5. The law governing strangers (v.9).

1   (23:1-3) **Israel, Law of--Obedience--False Witness--Slander**: there was the law governing slander. A person must not bear false witness or report. A false report is a lie. This passage deals specifically with courtroom situations, but it is applicable to everyday events. A person is not to give a false report in court; he is never to lie in court. Neither is a person to give a false report in day to day conversations. He is never to lie as he walks throughout the day. In western courts, every witness who is called to the witness stand must agree to do one thing: "to tell the truth, the whole truth, and nothing but the truth, so help me God." The root of this universal principle, to tell the whole truth, is traceable to this important section of Scripture. Without the constraints of this law, men would be free to twist the truth and to fabricate lie after lie to their own advantage--all at the expense of innocent people.

THE LAW GOVERNING SLANDER: ONE MUST NOT BEAR A FALSE WITNESS

OUTLINE	SCRIPTURE	SCRIPTURE	OUTLINE
	D. The Law Governing Justice & Mercy In Court & Among Neighbors, Ex. 23:1-9	righteous witness. 2 Thou shalt not follow a multitude to do evil; neither shalt thou speak in a cause to decline after many to wrest judgment:	b. Not to help a wicked person c. Not to help others plotting to do wrong
1. The law governing slander: Must not bear a false report a. Not to help oneself	Thou shalt not raise a false report: put not thine hand with the wicked to be an un-	3 Neither shalt thou countenance a poor man in his cause.	d. Not to help a poor man by showing favoritism in a lawsuit

Frankly, without this law justice and fairness would be a joke, for people would be twisting the truth to get their way and to gain more and more of whatever they wanted. Moreover, the wealthy and powerful would be paying witnesses to testify for them. There would be no true justice, not without this law that governs slander and perjury, that prohibits false reports and lying in court, and in day to day experiences and conversations. The law governs four general cases that are to be applied to all situations.

1. Case 1: a person must not bear a false report, not even to help himself (v.1). Throughout life, we are all called upon to give an account for something we said or did. We have to give an account to a parent, teacher, neighbor, friend, fellow worker, boss, or judge. The situation is tense; emotions are strained; pressure and stress set in; nevertheless, we have to give an account. This law, the Word of God, tells us in no uncertain terms: we are not to give a false report, not even to help ourselves.

> "Wherefore putting away lying, speak every man truth with his neighbour: for we are members one of another" (Eph.4:25).
> "Lie not one to another, seeing that ye have put off the old man with his deeds" (Col.3:9).
> "The lip of truth shall be established for ever: but a lying tongue *is* but for a moment" (Pr.12:19).
> "A false witness shall not be unpunished, and *he that* speaketh lies shall not escape" (Pr.19:5).
> "A false witness shall not be unpunished, and he that speaketh lies shall perish" (Pr.19:9).
> "Thou shalt destroy them that speak leasing [lying]: the LORD will abhor the bloody and deceitful man" (Ps.5:6).
> "The getting of treasures by a lying tongue *is* a vanity tossed to and fro of them that seek death" (Pr.21:6).
> "For the rich men thereof are full of violence, and the inhabitants thereof have spoken lies, and their tongue *is* deceitful in their mouth" (Mic.6:12).
> "But the fearful, and unbelieving, and the abominable, and murderers, and whoremongers, and sorcerers, and idolaters, and all liars, shall have their part in the lake which burneth with fire and brimstone: which is the second death" (Rev.21:8).

The only hope for a liar is that he confess his sin, turn to Christ, and turn away from the habit of lying, learning always to tell the truth.

> "In whom we have redemption through his blood, the forgiveness of sins, according to the riches of his grace" (Eph.1:7).
> "If we confess our sins, he is faithful and just to forgive us *our* sins, and to cleanse us from all unrighteousness" (1 Jn.1:9).

2. Case 2: a person must not bear a false report for a wicked person (v.1). This law addresses people who are tempted to lock arms with evil people. Instead of standing up for the truth, there are some people who sear their conscience and wed themselves to a lie. Note how several different translations interpret this particular verse.

⇒ The New American Standard Bible says:

> "You shall not bear a false report; <u>do not join your hand</u> with a wicked man to be a malicious witness" (Ex.23:1).

⇒ The New International Version Bible says:

> "Do not spread false reports. <u>Do not help a wicked man</u> by being a malicious witness" (Ex.23:1).

⇒ The New Living Translation Bible says:

> "Do not pass along false reports. <u>Do not cooperate with evil people</u> by telling lies on the witness stand" (Ex.23:1).

Why would anyone want to cooperate with someone who is evil? Why would anyone want to protect an evil person by lying for him?
⇒ because of the promise of financial gain (bribery)
⇒ because of the risk of going against men of influence
⇒ because of a lack of moral strength and fortitude

Thought 1. The Bible warns against any association with evil people. If a person rejects God's warning, there are several things that are put at risk.
1) The believer's character is put at risk.

> "Be not deceived: evil communications [behavior, conduct] corrupt good manners [character]" (1 Cor.15:33).

"But now I have written unto you <u>not to keep company</u>, if any man that is called a brother be a fornicator, or covetous, or an idolater, or a railer, or a drunkard, or an extortioner; with such an one no not to eat" (1 Cor.5:11).

"Be ye not unequally yoked together with unbelievers: for what fellowship hath righteousness with unrighteousness? and what communion hath light with darkness?" (2 Cor.6:14).

"Be not thou envious against evil men, neither desire to be with them" (Pr.24:1).

2) The believer's path in life is put at risk.

"Blessed *is* the man that walketh not in the counsel of the ungodly, nor standeth in the way of sinners, nor sitteth in the seat of the scornful" (Ps.1:1).

"Enter not into the path of the wicked, and go not in the way of evil *men*" (Pr.4:14).

3. Case 3: A person must not bear a false report with people who plot to do wrong (v.2). People, individuals and groups, are always plotting to get more and more...

- by twisting the facts
- by manipulating situations
- by lying
- by exaggerating
- by hiding or camouflaging something
- by misleading people
- by cheating people
- by scheming
- by offering false opportunities

But the law is clear: a person is not to join with anyone in giving a false report--never, no matter what he stands to gain.

> **Thought 1**. The lesson is clear: we must never follow the crowd in lying, in giving a false report. In fact, God's Word is direct and straightforward: we must not follow the crowd to do any kind of evil, no matter what it is, no matter how much it may seem to benefit us.
>
> "Blessed is the man that walketh not in the counsel of the ungodly, nor standeth in the way of sinners, nor sitteth in the seat of the scornful" (Ps.1:1).
> "Enter not into the path of the wicked, and go not in the way of evil men" (Pr.4:14).
> "Be ye not unequally yoked together with unbelievers: for what fellowship hath righteousness with unrighteousness? and what communion hath light with darkness?" (2 Cor.6:14).
> "Wherefore come out from among them, and be ye separate, saith the Lord, and touch not the unclean thing; and I will receive you, And will be a Father unto you, and ye shall be my sons and daughters, saith the Lord Almighty" (2 Cor.6:17-18).

4. Case 4: a person must not bear a false report by showing favoritism to a poor man in a lawsuit (v.3). This case was to caution judges from becoming sentimental toward the poor man, from showing favoritism to him--all because he was in such dire need. No matter how desperate and touching a person's need is, a person's poverty is not to be the balance that influences a judge's decision. Poverty is never to be the balance that corrupts justice. Justice, the protection of the innocent, is the only glue that can ever hold a society together. People have to be protected and treated fairly for society to exist. Therefore--rich or poor, native or stranger, friend or foe--there is to be no bias in executing justice. A perverted justice is never right. It is always wrong.

> "Perverse disputings of men of corrupt minds, and destitute of the truth, supposing that gain is godliness: from such withdraw thyself" (1 Tim.6:5).
> "That which is altogether just shalt thou follow, that thou mayest live, and inherit the land which the LORD thy God giveth thee" (Dt.16:20).
> "Defend the poor and fatherless: do justice to the afflicted and needy" (Ps.82:3).
> "To do justice and judgment is more acceptable to the LORD than sacrifice" (Pr.21:3).
> "Thus saith the LORD, Keep ye judgment, and do justice: for my salvation is near to come, and my righteousness to be revealed" (Is.56:1).

[2] (23:4-5) **Law, Civil--Enemies, Treatment of--Retaliation--Revenge--Vengeance**: there was the law governing the treatment of enemies. Of all the laws ever written, the law governing enemies is one of the most peculiar. It is certainly one of the most difficult for people to understand. Note what this law says about the treatment of enemies:

THE LAW GOVERNING THE TREATMENT OF ENEMIES

OUTLINE	SCRIPTURE
2. The law governing treatment of enemies a. If you find his lost property, you must return it b. If you find him needing help, you are to help him	4 If thou meet thine enemy's ox or his ass going astray, thou shalt surely bring it back to him again. 5 If thou see the ass of him that hateth thee lying under his burden, and wouldest forbear to help him, thou shalt surely help with him.

1. If a person found lost property that belonged to his enemy, he was to return it (v.4). This is a difficult law for any person to obey. No matter who the person is, it is difficult to return lost property to an enemy. The tendency of the human heart is...

- to ignore the property (whether money or some possessions) and let the owner find it for himself
- to hide the property and make it even more difficult for the owner to find
- to destroy the property so that one's enemy could never recover it
- to steal the property and keep it for one's own use

But note the clear instructions of the law: the person was not allowed to keep nor to ignore the property of his enemy. On the contrary, he was to go the extra mile and personally take the property back to his enemy.

2. If a person saw an enemy who needed help, he was personally to go and help him (v.5). Think how tough this law was, how difficult it was to accept. Picture the scene: some enemy had spoken or done some evil thing against a person such as:

⇒ slandered or lied against him
⇒ stolen something from him
⇒ attacked or assaulted him or a loved one
⇒ mistreated or abused him in some way
⇒ damaged or destroyed some piece of property

Despite all this, if a person saw an enemy who needed help, he was personally to go and help him. This law presents a different idea to man than what man usually feels like doing. Man usually wants either to ignore or retaliate against his enemy. But the law is clear: man is to do good to his enemies.

Thought 1. We must always remember this fact: any person can be nice to someone who is nice. It is easy to love a friend, but an enemy is a different story altogether. The command to love our enemies is one of the major distinctives of the true followers of the living Lord. Scripture tells us this time and again:
⇒ We are to love our enemies.

> **"But I say unto you, Love your enemies, bless them that curse you, do good to them that hate you, and pray for them which despitefully use you, and persecute you" (Mt.5:44).**

⇒ We are to bless people who curse us.

> **"But I say unto you, Love your enemies, bless them that curse you, do good to them that hate you, and pray for them which despitefully use you, and persecute you" (Mt.5:44).**

⇒ We are to do good to people who hate us.

> **"But I say unto you, Love your enemies, bless them that curse you, do good to them that hate you, and pray for them which despitefully use you, and persecute you" (Mt.5:44).**

⇒ We are to pray for people who despitefully use us and persecute us.

> **"But I say unto you, Love your enemies, bless them that curse you, do good to them that hate you, and pray for them which despitefully use you, and persecute you" (Mt.5:44).**

⇁ We are not to rejoice when an enemy falls.

> **"Rejoice not when thine enemy falleth, and let not thine heart be glad when he stumbleth" (Pr.24:17).**

⇒ We are to give food and water to an enemy who is in need.

> **"If thine enemy be hungry, give him bread to eat; and if he be thirsty, give him water to drink" (Pr.25:21).**
> **"Therefore if thine enemy hunger, feed him; if he thirst, give him drink: for in so doing thou shalt heap coals of fire on his head" (Ro.12:20).**

⇒ We are to heap kindness upon the heads of our enemies.

> **"For thou shalt heap coals of fire upon his head, and the LORD shall reward thee" (Pr.25:22).**

3 (23:6-7) <u>Law, Civil--Justice--Poor, Treatment of--Israel, Law of</u>: there was the law governing justice to the poor. Since the beginning of history, every society has been flooded with poor people. There have always been people who can barely make ends meet: people who have little food, few clothes, and a shanty for housing, if any housing at all. But even more tragic than these are the millions who have literally nothing. They are so destitute that they die from starvation or from lack of shelter against the frigid weather or some natural catastrophe such as a cyclone or hurricane.

The poor are often the object of...
- overwork and low wages
- oversight and neglect
- manipulation and abuse
- prejudice and discrimination
- inadequate education and unskilled training
- theft and violence

But this law is direct and straightforward: there is to be justice for the poor. Society is to guarantee justice and fairness to the poor.

THE LAW GOVERNING JUSTICE TO THE POOR

OUTLINE	SCRIPTURE
3. The law governing justice to the poor a. Must not deny him justice b. Must not falsely charge him c. Must not put the innocent or honest person to death d. The reason: God will judge the unjust & immoral	6 Thou shalt not wrest the judgment of thy poor in his cause. 7 Keep thee far from a false matter; and the innocent and righteous slay thou not: for I will not justify the wicked.

No matter how rich or poor a man is, the law is to treat him with fairness and with dignity. There are four clear distinctives in this law:

1. The poor must not be denied justice (v.6). The lack of money is not to be held against the poor man in a court of law. In many societies the wealthy can buy justice; whereas, the poor man cannot even afford to defend himself. Unable to buy justice, he usually faces the full brunt of the law. This law was to assure justice to the poor.

2. The poor must not be falsely charged (v.7). Judges are to make certain that the facts support an indictment against a poor person for breaking the law. Why? When a man is falsely charged...
- he has to defend himself for something he did not do
- he can lose all he has, be forced into bankruptcy
- he loses his good name, and in many cases his employment
- he has to explain to friends and family the reasons for his innocence

3. The poor must not be put to death if they are innocent and honest (v.7). One of the greatest tragedies ever committed is when an innocent man is executed for a crime he did not commit. Great care is to be administered by the judges before sentencing a man to die. They must know--know without a doubt--that the man is guilty of the crime.

4. The reason: God will judge the unjust (v.7). This law was to ensure that justice was executed fairly without bias toward the poor. God promised swift judgment upon those who judged wrongly. God expects a great deal out of those who have been given trusted positions of authority.

"Ye shall do no unrighteousness in judgment: thou shalt not respect the person of the poor, nor honour the person of the mighty: but in righteousness shalt thou judge thy neighbour" (Lev.19:15).
"Defend the poor and fatherless: do justice to the afflicted and needy" (Ps.82:3).
"Whoso stoppeth his ears at the cry of the poor, he also shall cry himself, but shall not be heard" (Pr.21:13).
"The king that faithfully judgeth the poor, his throne shall be established for ever" (Pr.29:14).
"He judged the cause of the poor and needy; then it was well with him" (Jer.22:16).
"Prove all things; hold fast that which is good" (1 Th.5:21).

4 (23:8) **Israel, Law of--Obedience--Bribe - Bribery--Ethics--Honesty:** there was the law governing bribery. A person must not take bribes. The power of the bribe is one of most subtle, indirect attacks upon the character of people. A man who offers or accepts a bribe commits a terrible evil: he destroys society by destroying the justice system as well as the laws of society. He tragically weakens the moral strength that holds people together. Note the law:

THE LAW GOVERNING BRIBERY: ONE MUST NOT TAKE BRIBES

OUTLINE	SCRIPTURE
4. The law governing bribery: One must not take bribes a. Will blind the wise b. Will twist the words of the righteous	8 And thou shalt take no gift: for the gift blindeth the wise, and perverteth the words of the righteous.

Bribery is a very real temptation to some people. Bribery is a problem...
- because it is an easy way to make money
- because it appeals to a man's lust and pride
- because it is so "acceptable" in many business dealings

There are two serious consequences when a bribe is taken.

1. A bribe will blind the wise. The man who accepts a bribe will lose sight of true justice. His perspective will become warped beyond repair. This law was addressed specifically to judges, but it is a lesson for us all. The danger to society is clear: if the judge is bought off by a rich man, he makes a mockery of the law, a mockery of justice.

⇒ He causes people to ridicule authority. People mock the rulers and judges of society and the justice system itself.

⇒ He causes people to lose their trust in their rulers and in the human institutions of society (such as courts, businesses, and governments).

⇒ He causes people to ignore the clear instructions of the law and to become more lawless themselves.

Thought 1. When the bribe is treated as the "normal way of doing business," a society quickly unravels. Tragically, bribery is running rampant in today's society: buying influence from politicians, protection for businesses, contracts, jobs, cheaper prices, merchandise, and a host of other things that can fill the pockets and bank accounts of the evil and dishonest person. God hates bribery because of what it does to people.

1) Bribery seeks to destroy the lives of other people.

> "And the lords of the Philistines came up unto her, and said unto her, Entice him, and see wherein his [Sampson] great strength *lieth*, and by what *means* we may prevail against him, that we may bind him to afflict him: and we will give thee every one of us eleven hundred *pieces* of silver" (Judg.16:5).

> "If it please the king, let it be written that they may be destroyed: and I will pay ten thousand talents of silver to the hands of those that have the charge of the business, to bring *it* into the king's treasuries" (Esth.3:9).

> "And when they heard *it*, they were glad, and promised to give him money. And he [Judas] sought how he might conveniently betray him [Christ]" (Mk.14:11).

2) Bribery perverts judgment.

> "And his [Samuel's] sons walked not in his ways, but turned aside after lucre [money, gain], and took bribes, and perverted judgment" (1 Sam.8:3).

3) Bribery attempts to hide the truth.

> "And when they were assembled with the elders, and had taken counsel, they gave large money unto the soldiers [to lie about the resurrection of Christ]" (Mt.28:12).

4) Bribery presumes that even God and His power are for sale.

> "And when Simon saw that through laying on of the apostles' hands the Holy Ghost was given, he offered them money" (Acts 8:18).

2. A bribe will twist the words of the righteous. This consequence adds an ironic twist to those who accept a bribe. Even a righteous man can succumb to the temptation of bribery and destroy his witness. When a person accepts a bribe, his words are no longer accepted at face value; his word is no longer his bond. Everything he says, even when he is telling the truth, is suspect. We must never forget: a man's most precious possession is his word, the fact that people respect his word, that they believe him.

> "Moreover thou shalt provide out of all the people able men, such as fear God, men of truth, hating covetousness; and place *such* over them, *to be* rulers of thousands, *and* rulers of hundreds, rulers of fifties, and rulers of tens" (Ex.18:21).

> "Thou shalt not wrest judgment; thou shalt not respect persons, neither take a gift: for a gift doth blind the eyes of the wise, and pervert the words of the righteous" (Dt.16:19).

> "Wherefore now let the fear of the LORD be upon you; take heed and do *it*: for *there is* no iniquity with the LORD our God, nor respect of persons, nor taking of gifts" (2 Chron.19:7).

> "*He that* putteth not out his money to usury, nor taketh reward [a bribe] against the innocent. He that doeth these *things* shall never be moved" (Ps.15:5).

> "Gather not my soul with sinners, nor my life with bloody men: In whose hands *is* mischief, and their right hand is full of bribes" (Ps.26:9-10).

> "He that is greedy of gain troubleth his own house; but he that hateth gifts [bribes] shall live" (Pr.15:27).

> "The prince that wanteth understanding *is* also a great oppressor: *but* he that hateth covetousness shall prolong *his* days" (Pr.28:16).

> "The king by judgment establisheth the land: but he that receiveth gifts overthroweth it" (Pr.29:4).

> "In thee have they taken gifts to shed blood; thou hast taken usury and increase, and thou hast greedily gained of thy neighbours by extortion, and hast forgotten me, saith the Lord GOD" (Ezk.22:12).

"The heads thereof judge for reward, and the priests thereof teach for hire, and the prophets thereof divine for money: yet will they lean upon the LORD, and say, *Is* not the LORD among us? none evil can come upon us" (Mic.3:11).

5 (23:9) **Israel, Law of--Obedience--Strangers, Treatment of:** there was the law governing the treatment of strangers or foreigners. It is no accident that the issue of strangers comes up again so quickly. (See note--Ex.22:21 for more discussion.) God wanted Israel never to forget how hard it was being a stranger or foreigner in another land.

THE LAW GOVERNING TREATMENT OF A STRANGER

OUTLINE	SCRIPTURE
5. **The law governing treatment of a stranger (foreigner)** a. Must not oppress him b. Reason: Bc. God's people know what it feels like to be strangers	9 Also thou shalt not oppress a stranger: for ye know the heart of a stranger, seeing ye were strangers in the land of Egypt.

1. No person is to oppress a stranger or foreigner. The force of the word oppress (*lahas*) means to crush, to confine, to be pressed close.[1]

2. The reason is clearly stated: because God's people know what it feels like to be strangers. When the temptation crept up on the Israelites to oppress a stranger or foreigner, they were to remember the crushing feeling that ridicule and oppression causes. God had been faithful...

- to save them from being crushed by Pharaoh
- to deliver them from Egypt's oppression (a symbol of the world's oppression)
- to trust them with the fate of other strangers

This law was to be pressed into the depths of the Israelite's heart. Compassion and empathy were to be natural things for the Israelite on behalf of the stranger. They were to know exactly what to do: they were to help and do all they could to support the stranger.

Thought 1. We must learn through trials, disappointments, and heartaches, learn what it feels like to suffer, learn how to conquer all through the power of God. Then we must help those who are going through similar trials, disappointments, and heartaches. God allows us to walk through difficult times for the sake of other people, that we might be able to minister to them. The excellent Bible commentator George Bush states:

"Our trials and sorrows...[must] train us to [feel] a deep sympathy with those who are called to drink of the same bitter cup."[2]

"Blessed *be* God, even the Father of our Lord Jesus Christ, the Father of mercies, and the God of all comfort; Who comforteth us in all our tribulation, that we may be able to comfort them which are in any trouble, by the comfort wherewith we ourselves are comforted of God." (2 Cor. 1:3-4).

"But a certain Samaritan, as he journeyed, came where he was: and when he saw him, he had compassion *on him,* And went to *him,* and bound up his wounds, pouring in oil and wine, and set him on his own beast, and brought him to an inn, and took care of him" (Lk.10:33-34).

"I have showed you all things, how that so labouring ye ought to support the weak, and to remember the words of the Lord Jesus, how he said, It is more blessed to give than to receive" (Acts 20:35).

"We then that are strong ought to bear the infirmities of the weak, and not to please ourselves" (Ro.15:1).

"Bear ye one another's burdens, and so fulfil the law of Christ" (Gal.6:2).

"Wherefore comfort yourselves together, and edify one another, even as also ye do" (1 Th.5:11).

"Now we exhort you, brethren, warn them that are unruly, comfort the feebleminded, support the weak, be patient toward all *men*" (1 Th.5:14).

"Remember them that are in bonds, as bound with them; *and* them which suffer adversity, as being yourselves also in the body" (Heb.13:3).

---

[1] *The Hebrew-Greek Key Study Bible, New International Version.* Spiros Zodhiates, Th.D., Executive Editor. (Chattanooga, TN: AMG Publishers, 1996), p.1958.
[2] George Bush. *Commentary on Exodus,* p.342.

	E. The Laws Governing Religion: The Sabbath & Religious Feasts, Ex. 23:10-19	15 Thou shalt keep the feast of unleavened bread: (thou shalt eat unleavened bread seven days, as I commanded thee, in the time appointed of the month Abib; for in it thou camest out from Egypt: and none shall appear before me empty:)	a. The Feast of Unleavened Bread 1) Eat unleavened bread for seven days 2) Eat at the appointed time: The month of Abib when Israel was delivered from Egypt 3) A warning: Must not approach God empty-handed
1. The law governing the Sabbath a. Every 7th year was to be a Sabbath year 1) To let the land & vineyards lie unplowed & unused every Sabbath year 2) Reason: To let the land rest & to let the poor & wild animals secure food from the land b. Every 7th day was to be a Sabbath day 1) That man & animal may rest 2) That slave & strangers may be refreshed	10 And six years thou shalt sow thy land, and shalt gather in the fruits thereof: 11 But the seventh year thou shalt let it rest and lie still; that the poor of thy people may eat: and what they leave the beasts of the field shall eat. In like manner thou shalt deal with thy vineyard, and with thy oliveyard. 12 Six days thou shalt do thy work, and on the seventh day thou shalt rest: that thine ox and thine ass may rest, and the son of thy handmaid, and the stranger, may be refreshed.	16 And the feast of harvest, the firstfruits of thy labours, which thou hast sown in the field: and the feast of ingathering, which is in the end of the year, when thou hast gathered in thy labours out of the field. 17 Three times in the year all thy males shall appear before the Lord GOD.	b. The Feast of Harvest: To celebrate with the first fruits of harvest c. The Feast of Ingathering: To celebrate after the harvest was completed d. The persons responsible for celebrating the feasts: All the men
2. The basic religious law: Governs idolatry a. Must obey God b. Must not call upon false gods, never let their names be heard on your lips 3. The law governing the three annual feasts	13 And in all things that I have said unto you be circumspect: and make no mention of the name of other gods, neither let it be heard out of thy mouth. 14 Three times thou shalt keep a feast unto me in the year.	18 Thou shalt not offer the blood of my sacrifice with leavened bread; neither shall the fat of my sacrifice remain until the morning. 19 The first of the firstfruits of thy land thou shalt bring into the house of the LORD thy God. Thou shalt not seethe a kid in his mother's milk.	4. The law governing the Passover sacrifice a. Must not offer the sacrificial lamb with leaven in the house b. Must not keep the fat of the lamb until morning 5. The law governing one's offerings to God a. Must offer the best of one's firstfruit b. Must not take the offering away from God, away from the Giver of life

DIVISION VIII

THE LAW AND THE PROMISES OF GOD (THE MOSAIC COVENANT) (PART 3): THE CIVIL AND RELIGIOUS LAWS OF ISRAEL--HELPFUL PRINCIPLES TO GOVERN MAN AND SOCIETY, 21:1-24:18

E. Laws Governing Religion: The Sabbath and Religious Feasts, Ex. 23:10-19

(23:10-19) **Introduction**: religion is important to man. But it is critical that man follow the right religion. If he follows a false religion, he worships a false god and misses out on the true and living God, misses out...
- on God's care and provision throughout life
- on living eternally with God in the promised land of heaven.

The person who follows a false religion dooms himself. Man must, therefore, follow the true religion, follow the LORD God Himself, the only true and living God. This is the purpose of this Scripture, to give some clear-cut instructions on how to follow the right religion. God gives man: *Laws Governing Religion: The Sabbath and Religious Feasts*, Ex.23:10-19.
1. The law governing the Sabbath (v.10-12).
2. The basic religious law: governs idolatry (v.13).
3. The law governing the three annual feasts (v.14-17).
4. The law governing the Passover sacrifice (v.18).
5. The law governing one's offerings to God (v.19).

1 (23:10-12) **Law, Civil--Israel, Law of--Sabbath--Religion--Farming**: there was the law governing the Sabbath. Remember, the word "Sabbath" means to rest or cease from work. (See outline and notes--Ex.20:8-11 for more discussion.) There were to be two Sabbaths: the Sabbath year and the Sabbath day. Note the Scripture and outline:

EXODUS 23:10-19

THE LAW GOVERNING THE SABBATH

OUTLINE	SCRIPTURE	SCRIPTURE	OUTLINE
	E. The Laws Governing Religion: The Sabbath & Religious Feasts, Ex. 23:10-19	may eat: and what they leave the beasts of the field shall eat. In like manner thou shalt deal with thy vineyard, and with thy oliveyard.	used every sabbath year 2) Reason: To let the land rest & to let the poor & wild animals secure food from the land
1. The law governing the Sabbath	10 And six years thou shalt sow thy land, and shalt gather in the fruits thereof:	12 Six days thou shalt do thy work, and on the seventh day thou shalt rest: that thine ox and thine ass may rest, and	a. Every 7th day was to be a Sabbath day 1) That man & animal may rest
a. Every 7th year was to be a Sabbath year 1) To let the land & vineyards lie unplowed & un-	11 But the seventh year thou shalt let it rest and lie still; that the poor of thy people	the son of thy handmaid, and the stranger, may be refreshed.	2) That slave & strangers may be refreshed

1. Every seventh year was to be a Sabbath year (v.10-11). That is, Israel's land, the farms and vineyards, was to lie unplowed and unused every seventh year. The people were to farm for six years and then not touch the land on the seventh year, not for farming purposes. Imagine! There was to be an entire year of rest for the land, an entire year of rest for the land owner's farm. Such an idea among the nations has been unknown down through history--except in Israel.

This was one of the religious laws of Israel, the law of *The Sabbath Year*, a year of land rest, a year when all work on the land was to stop. But why? Why would God demand that Israel observe this religious law, the Sabbath year, that Israel let the land rest every seventh year? Scripture gives at least three reasons, two in these verses and one in Deuteronomy (see pt.c below).

  a. There was a need for the land to rest (v.11). Through the centuries farmers have learned about the problems of overusing land, such problems as...
   - plowing too deeply
   - destroying soil nutrients
   - failing to rotate crops

   Most likely, the farmers of the ancient world were not aware of these problems, certainly not all of them. But there was One who did know: the LORD God Himself. He knew that the land would produce more, be revitalized, and be better preserved by resting every seventh year. Therefore, He instituted *The Sabbath Year* as one of the religious laws of Israel.

  b. There was a great need for Israel to learn compassion for the poor; moreover, there was a great need for God's compassion to be demonstrated to the world (v.11). Note that this is clearly stated:

   "But the seventh year thou shalt let it rest and lie still; that the poor of thy people may eat: and what they leave the beasts of the field shall eat. In like manner thou shalt deal with thy vineyard, and with thy oliveyard" (v.11).

   The land was to lie unplowed and unused every seventh year. Whatever the land brought forth naturally was to be shared with the poor and with the wild animals of the fields and forests.

   Note God's enormous compassion for all of life, both human and animal life. Imagine! Setting aside all farm land for an entire year for the poor of the earth to harvest and store up food for their survival--without having to worry about trespassing or being threatened. What care and compassion for the poor of the earth! A compassion that God wanted Israel to learn and teach to the world.

  c. There was a need for Israel to set aside a special time for special worship and study of God's Holy Word.

   "And Moses commanded them, saying, At the end of every seven years [the Sabbath Year], in the solemnity of the year of release, in the feast of tabernacles, When all Israel is come to appear before the LORD thy God in the place which he shall choose, thou shalt read this law before all Israel in their hearing. Gather the people together, men, and women, and children, and thy stranger that is within thy gates, that they may hear, and that they may learn, and fear the LORD your God, and observe to do all the words of this law: And that their children, which have not known any thing, may hear, and learn to fear the LORD your God, as long as ye live in the land whither ye go over Jordan to possess it" (Dt.31:10-13).

   Note closely the above Scripture: the purpose of the Sabbath Year was to set aside a special time, a very special time...
   - for worship
   - for reading and studying the law, the Word of God

   The Sabbatical Year was to be a time of focused study and learning for children and foreigners and a time of focused review for the adults. The Word of God, His law, was to be the subject studied. The people were to learn to follow the LORD, to live as He commanded. To do this they had to know His Word, learn His commandments.

Thought 1. The <u>Pulpit Commentary</u> says this:

"Great difficulty was probably experienced in enforcing the law. Just as there were persons who wished to gather manna on the seventh day (ch. xvi. 27), so there would be many anxious to obtain in the seventh year something more from their fields than Nature would give them if left to herself. If the 'seventy years' of the captivity were intended exactly to make up for omissions of...the sabbatical year, we must suppose that between the time of the exodus and the destruction of Jerusalem by Nebuchadnezzar, the ordinance had been as often neglected as observed. (See 2 Chron. xxxvi. 21.)"[1]

Was Israel faithful in keeping the Sabbatical Year? Apparently not. Israel failed to keep the Sabbatical Year for century after century (for at least 490 years); consequently, God judged Israel by allowing the land to be taken away from the people. He allowed Babylon to conquer and relocate them for seventy years. By so doing, God gave the land all the *Sabbath rests* at one time. The land rested for seventy years during the judgment of the Babylonian captivity.

"Then shall the land enjoy her sabbaths, as long as it lieth desolate, and ye be in your enemies' land; even then shall the land rest, and enjoy her sabbaths. As long as it lieth desolate it shall rest; because it did not rest in your sabbaths, when ye dwelt upon it....The land also shall be left of them, and shall enjoy her sabbaths, while she lieth desolate without them: and they shall accept of the punishment of their iniquity: because, even because they despised my judgments, and because their soul abhorred my statutes" (Lev.26:34-35, 43).
"To fulfil the word of the LORD by the mouth of Jeremiah, until the land had enjoyed her sabbaths: for as long as she lay desolate she kept sabbath, to fulfil threescore and ten years" (2 Chron.36:21).

Again, the <u>Pulpit Commentary</u> says this:

"It was also intended that the Sabbatical year should be one of increased religious observance...the solemn reading of the law in the ears of the people at the Feast of Tabernacle 'in the year of release' (Deut. xxxi. 10)....That reading was properly preceded by a time of religious preparation (Neh. viii. 1-15), and would naturally lead on to further acts of a religious character, which might occupy a considerable period (*ibid*. chs. ix. and x.). Altogether, the year was a most solemn period, calling men to religious self-examination, to repentance, to the formation of holy habits, and tending to a general elevation among the people of the standard of holiness."[2]

Thought 1. There are three strong lessons for us in the *Sabbatical Year*.
1) We must obey God. God expects us to obey Him, no matter how strange His commandment may seem. The Sabbath year was a strange, unusual law--something unheard of among the nations and peoples of the earth. Nevertheless, the Sabbath year was the law of God, and there were strong reasons for the law. God knew what He was doing when He commanded His people to keep the Sabbatical year. And He knows what He is doing when He commands us to do certain things.

"Now therefore, if ye will obey my voice indeed, and keep my covenant, then ye shall be a peculiar treasure unto me above all people: for all the earth is mine" (Ex.19:5).
"This day the LORD thy God hath commanded thee to do these statutes and judgments: thou shalt therefore keep and do them with all thine heart, and with all thy soul" (Dt.26:16).
"This book of the law shall not depart out of thy mouth; but thou shalt meditate therein day and night, that thou mayest observe to do according to all that is written therein: for then thou shalt make thy way prosperous, and then thou shalt have good success" (Josh.1:8).
"Not every one that saith unto me, Lord, Lord, shall enter into the kingdom of heaven; but he that doeth the will of my Father which is in heaven" (Mt.7:21).

2) We must have compassion for the poor. The world reels in desperate need. We must be compassionate: give all we are and have to meet those needs.

"Jesus said unto him, If thou wilt be perfect, go [and] sell that thou hast, and give to the poor, and thou shalt have treasure in heaven: and come [and] follow me" (Mt.19:21).
"Only they would that we should remember the poor; the same which I [Paul] also was forward to do" (Gal.2:10).
"If there be among you a poor man of one of thy brethren within any of thy gates in thy land which the LORD thy God giveth thee, thou shalt not harden thine heart, nor shut thine hand from thy poor brother" (Dt.15:7).
"Blessed is he that considereth the poor: the LORD will deliver him in time of trouble" (Ps.41:1).

---

[1] *Pulpit Commentary*, Vol. 1, Exodus, p.201.
[2] *Pulpit Commentary*, Vol.1, Exodus, p.201.

"He that hath pity upon the poor lendeth unto the LORD; and that which he hath given will he pay him again" (Pr.19:17).

3)   We must set aside special times for special worship and study of God's Holy Word.

"These were more noble than those in Thessalonica, in that they received the word with all readiness of mind, and searched the scriptures daily, whether those things were so" (Acts 17:11).

"Study to show thyself approved unto God, a workman that needeth not to be ashamed, rightly dividing the word of truth" (2 Tim.2:15).

"All scripture is given by inspiration of God, and is profitable for doctrine, for reproof, for correction, for instruction in righteousness" (2 Tim.3:16).

"Not forsaking the assembling of ourselves together, as the manner of some is; but exhorting one another: and so much the more, as ye see the day approaching" (Heb.10:25).

"As newborn babes, desire the sincere milk of the word, that ye may grow thereby: If so be ye have tasted that the Lord is gracious" (1 Pt.2:2-3).

"Therefore also now, saith the LORD, turn ye even to me with all your heart, and with fasting, and with weeping, and with mourning" (Joel 2:12).

2. There was to be a Sabbath day every week (v.12). The Sabbath day is fully covered in the fourth commandment (see outline and notes--Ex.20:8-11 for discussion). Why is it repeated here? Because the civil laws of Israel are being covered throughout these chapters; and in this particular passage, the laws governing the Sabbath are being discussed. In order to have the two Sabbath laws together, there was a need to repeat the law governing the Sabbath day. Moreover, by stressing the Sabbath day of rest, there is a strong reminder not to forsake the fourth commandment (see outline and notes--Ex.20:8-11; Deeper Study # 2--Ex.20:8-11 for discussion).

"Remember the sabbath day, to keep it holy" (Ex.20:8).

"Blessed is the man that doeth this, and the son of man that layeth hold on it; that keepeth the sabbath from polluting it, and keepeth his hand from doing any evil" (Is.56:2).

"Not forsaking the assembling of ourselves together, as the manner of some is; but exhorting one another: and so much the more, as ye see the day approaching" (Heb.10:25).

2 (23:13) **Law, Civil--Gods, False--Idolatry:** there was the basic religious law, the law governing idolatry. Note the law:

THE BASIC RELIGIOUS LAW: GOVERNING IDOLATRY

OUTLINE	SCRIPTURE
2. The basic religious law: Governs idolatry a. Must obey God b. Must not call upon false gods, never let their names be heard on your lips	13 And in all things that I have said unto you be circumspect: and make no mention of the name of other gods, neither let it be heard out of thy mouth.

This is what we might call the basic law of God, the demand of God that underlies all the other laws and commandments of God. This most basic law includes two points:

1. God's people are to obey Him; they are to keep all His commandments. But note: more than just obeying and keeping God's commandments, they are to be *careful, cautious,* and *watchful* in obeying His commandments. They are to be diligent--always watching and being cautious, as careful as they can be--in obeying and keeping every law and commandment of God.

"O that there were such an heart in them, that they would fear me, and keep all my commandments always, that it might be well with them, and with their children for ever!" (Dt.5:29).

"This book of the law shall not depart out of thy mouth; but thou shalt meditate therein day and night, that thou mayest observe to do according to all that is written therein: for then thou shalt make thy way prosperous, and then thou shalt have good success" (Josh.1:8).

"He that hath my commandments, and keepeth them, he it is that loveth me: and he that loveth me shall be loved of my Father, and I will love him, and will manifest myself to him" (Jn.14:21).

"This is a faithful saying, and these things I will that thou affirm constantly, that they which have believed in God might be careful to maintain good works. These things are good and profitable unto men" (Tit.3:8).

"But whoso looketh into the perfect law of liberty, and continueth therein, he being not a forgetful hearer, but a doer of the work, this man shall be blessed in his deed" (Jas.1:25).

2. God's people must not call upon false gods, never even mention their names. The purpose of this law was to erase even the very name of false gods. Just think: if the name of a person or thing is never mentioned or uttered, it is soon forgotten and essentially remembered no more. It is wiped from the memory of people. But the opposite is also true: if the

names of people and things are constantly mentioned, the people and things become a part of human life. The more God's people talk and discuss false gods, the more some people will follow after false gods. There is only one living and true God, the LORD God Himself. Therefore, He and He alone is to be followed and worshipped. All other false gods should be forgotten, erased from the conversations and memories of men, for they are helpless in meeting the needs of people; and they lead people into eternal destruction. As far as possible, God's people are to forget false gods: they are not even to mention their names.

> "That ye come not among these nations, these that remain among you; neither make mention of the name of their gods, nor cause to swear by them, neither serve them, nor bow yourselves unto them: But cleave unto the LORD your God, as ye have done unto this day" (Josh.23:7-8).
> "Their idols are silver and gold, the work of men's hands. They have mouths, but they speak not: eyes have they, but they see not: They have ears, but they hear not: noses have they, but they smell not: They have hands, but they handle not: feet have they, but they walk not: neither speak they through their throat. They that make them are like unto them; so is every one that trusteth in them" (Ps.115:4-8).
> "For as he thinketh in his heart, so is he" (Pr.23:7).
> "For it is a shame even to speak of those things which are done of them in secret" (Eph.5:12).

3   **Law, Civil--Israel, Law of--Feasts, Religious--Unleavened Bread, Feast of--Harvest, Feast of--Ingathering, Feast of--Tabernacles, Feast of**: there was the law governing the three annual feasts. Three times a year, all the men of Israel were to make a pilgrimage to the Tabernacle to celebrate one of the feasts. Only some of the facts about the feasts are given here. Each is expanded in other Scriptures:

THE LAW GOVERNING THE THREE ANNUAL FEASTS

OUTLINE	SCRIPTURE	SCRIPTURE	OUTLINE

3. The law governing the three annual feasts
  a. The Feast of Unleavened Bread
    1) Eat unleavened bread for seven days
    2) Eat at the appointed time: The month of Abib when Israel was delivered from Egypt
    3) A warning: Must not approach God empty
	14 Three times thou shalt keep a feast unto me in the year.
	15 Thou shalt keep the feast of unleavened bread: (thou shalt eat unleavened bread seven days, as I commanded thee, in the time appointed of the month Abib; for in it thou camest out from Egypt: and none shall appear before me
		empty:)
		16 And the feast of harvest, the firstfruits of thy labours, which thou hast sown in the field: and the feast of ingathering, which is in the end of the year, when thou hast gathered in thy labours out of the field.
		17 Three times in the year all thy males shall appear before the Lord GOD.
			handed
			b. The Feast of Harvest: To celebrate with the first fruits of harvest
			c. The Feast of Ingathering: To celebrate after the harvest was completed
			d. The persons responsible for celebrating the feasts: All the men

The feasts celebrated both an *agricultural* and an *historical* event in the life of the nation. Each was connected to some harvest season and to some great historical event. No matter where they were nor how far away, every man of Israel was to travel to the Tabernacle and appear before God: he was to pray, give thanks, and remember the great mercy and grace of God...

- in giving the harvest of crops
- in delivering and guiding their nation throughout its history

1. There was the Feast of Unleavened Bread (v.15). The law governing the feast gives three clear instructions (see outline and notes--Ex.12:14-20 for more discussion):
⇒ The people were to eat unleavened bread for seven days.
⇒ The people were to celebrate the feast at the appointed time, during the month of Abib, celebrating their great deliverance from Egypt.
⇒ The people were to heed the warning of God: they must not approach Him empty-handed, that is, without an offering.

The Feast of Unleavened Bread began with the Passover and continued for seven days. There was to be a great worship service on the first day and another on the last day of the feast (Lev.23:5-8). As stated, the feast celebrated God's great deliverance of Israel from Egyptian slavery. The eating of unleavened bread was to remind the people of their quick, hasty exodus from Egypt. Unleavened bread symbolized the utter necessity of fleeing--quickly fleeing--the slavery of Egypt (the world), the utter necessity to immediately begin their march to the promised land of God (a symbol of heaven, of perfect righteousness). They did not even have time to let the yeast leaven the bread.

Note another fact: there was a stern warning from God concerning the feast. No man was to fail nor neglect to bring an offering of the barley harvest to God. God had done so much for His people; therefore, no person should come before God empty-handed, without a generous offering.

> "Every man shall give as he is able, according to the blessing of the LORD thy God which he hath given thee" (Dt.16:17).
> "Accept, I beseech thee, the freewill offerings of my mouth, O LORD, and teach me thy judgments" (Ps.119:108).

"Give, and it shall be given unto you; good measure, pressed down, and shaken together, and running over, shall men give into your bosom. For with the same measure that ye mete withal it shall be measured to you again" (Lk.6:38).

"Every man according as he purposeth in his heart, so let him give; not grudgingly, or of necessity: for God loveth a cheerful giver" (2 Cor.9:7).

2. There was the Feast of Harvest (v.16ᵃ). The Feast of Harvest was also called the *Feast of Weeks*, for it was held seven weeks after the Feast of Unleavened Bread (Ex.34:22). The Feast of Harvest was later called the *Day of Pentecost* because it was celebrated fifty days after the Feast of Unleavened Bread. The word "pentecost" is a Greek word meaning fifty (Lev.23:16; Acts 2:1; 20:16; 1 Cor.16:8). The feast celebrated the beginning of the law on Mt. Sinai, the very law under discussion in these particular chapters of Exodus. The Feast of Harvest was just that: it was a one-day festival that celebrated the *firstfruits* of the harvest (cp. Lev.23:15-22; Dt.16:9-11). The main ceremony was the offering to God of two loaves of leavened bread. The bread was made out of the flour from the wheat just gathered in, and it was called firstfruits of the harvest.[3] God was to receive the very best that man could offer from the harvest. The Feast of Harvest was a joyful, festive occasion, celebrating the wonderful harvest given by God.

Thought 1. The lesson to us is clear: we are to thank God for the harvest He gives us, for the income and blessings He pours out upon us. We are not to approach God empty-handed: we are to give God the tithes and offerings due Him.

"And as soon as the commandment came abroad, the children of Israel brought in abundance the firstfruits of corn, wine, and oil, and honey, and of all the increase of the fields; and the tithe of all things brought they in abundantly" (2 Chron.31:5).

"Honour the LORD with thy substance, and with the firstfruits of all thine increase: So shall thy barns be filled with plenty, and thy presses shall burst out with new wine" (Pr.3:9-10).

"Bring ye all the tithes into the storehouse, that there may be meat in mine house, and prove me now herewith, saith the LORD of hosts, if I will not open you the windows of heaven, and pour you out a blessing, that there shall not be room enough to receive it" (Mal.3:10).

3. There was the Feast of Ingathering or the Feast of Tabernacles (v.16ᵇ) (Lev.23:34; Dt.16:13; 31:10; Jn.7:2). This feast was more commonly called the Feast of Tabernacles because the people were commanded to make small *booths* or *lean-tos* to stay in during the time of the feast (Lev.23:42-43). The booths or lean-tos were to remind the people of their wilderness wanderings, of the forty years they had to live in tabernacles or tents as they journeyed to the promised land. The feast celebrated the harvest of the vines and orchards and lasted for either seven or eight days. Apparently the feast was discontinued during different periods of Israel's history; however, it was restored by Nehemiah (Neh.8:17).

4. Note the persons responsible for celebrating the feasts: all the able-bodied men of Israel (v.17). Not a man was exempted. As stated earlier, no matter where a man was nor how far away he was, he was required to attend the feasts. Why? Why would God make such a demand upon the men of Israel? God's purpose for these three national celebrations was threefold:
⇒ to bring the men together in a great spirit of unity and oneness, thereby building a strong, unified nation
⇒ to keep before the people the great blessings of God, His great deliverance and guidance day by day
⇒ to arouse the people to give thanks, to praise God and to give their tithes and offerings to Him

Thought 1. We grow through our association with other believers. The man who surrounds himself with other Christian believers has...
• the benefit of wisdom and counsel

"Without counsel purposes are disappointed: but in the multitude of counsellors they are established" (Pr.15:22).

• the benefit of encouragement and edification

"And let us consider one another to provoke unto love and to good works: Not forsaking the assembling of ourselves together, as the manner of some *is;* but exhorting *one another:* and so much the more, as ye see the day approaching" (Heb.10:24-25).

• the benefit of safety and protection

"Brethren, if a man be overtaken in a fault, ye which are spiritual, restore such an one in the spirit of meekness; considering thyself, lest thou also be tempted. Bear ye one another's burdens, and so fulfil the law of Christ" (Gal.6:1-2).

• the benefit of unity and common purpose

"Again I say unto you, That if two of you shall agree on earth as touching any thing that they shall ask, it shall be done for them of my Father which is in heaven" (Mt.18:19).

---
[3] *Pulpit Commentary*, Vol.1, Exodus, p.202.

- the benefit of worshipping God with like-minded people

> "If *there be* therefore any consolation in Christ, if any comfort of love, if any fellowship of the Spirit, if any bowels and mercies, Fulfil ye my joy, that ye be likeminded, having the same love, *being* of one accord, of one mind" (Ph.2:1-2).

4 (23:18) **Law, Civil--Feasts, Religious--Passover:** there was the law governing the Passover sacrifice. The Passover celebrated the greatest event in Israel's history, their great deliverance from Egyptian slavery. The Passover has been discussed in detail earlier, but it is listed here as part of the civil and religious law of the nation. (See outline and notes--Ex.12:1-13:16 for more discussion.) Two basic instructions are given:

THE BASIC LAW GOVERNING PASSOVER

OUTLINE	SCRIPTURE
4. The law governing the Passover sacrifice a. Must not offer the sacrificial lamb with leaven in the house b. Must not keep the fat of the lamb until morning	18 Thou shalt not offer the blood of my sacrifice with leavened bread; neither shall the fat of my sacrifice remain until the morning.

1. The people were not to offer (not kill) the sacrificial lamb with leaven in the house. Why? Because leaven is a symbol of evil, and God was delivering His people from the evil enslavement of Egypt (a type of the world). Note that God calls the sacrifice "my sacrifice." The Passover Lamb is a very special sacrifice; therefore, it is termed *God's Sacrifice*. What is so special about the *sacrificial lamb*? What does the lamb symbolize? God's Son, the Lord Jesus Christ. God's Son is the Lamb of God who takes away the sin of the world. Jesus Christ delivers God's people from the evil enslavement of the world, delivers God's people from sin. It was Jesus Christ whom the lamb symbolized.

> "The next day John seeth Jesus coming unto him, and saith, Behold the Lamb of God, which taketh away the sin of the world" (Jn.1:29).
> "Purge out therefore the old leaven, that ye may be a new lump, as ye are unleavened. For even Christ our passover is sacrificed for us" (1 Cor.5:7).
> "Now once in the end of the world hath he appeared to put away sin by the sacrifice of himself" (Heb.9:26).
> "So Christ was once offered to bear the sins of many; and unto them that look for him shall he appear the second time without sin unto salvation" (Heb.9:28).
> "And he is the propitiation [sacrifice] for our sins: and not for ours only, but also for the sins of the whole world" (1 Jn.2:2).

2. The term "fat" refers to the very best of the lamb. Earlier, God had instructed the people to eat *all* of the lamb (see note, pt.5--Ex.12:6-11). Now in giving the law, He stresses the point by being forceful in the description He uses: not even the fat--not even the best part--of the sacrificial lamb is to be kept. All of the lamb must be eaten.

Thought 1. The point is clear: a person cannot *eat* and take in only part of Christ. He must take all of Christ. A person must believe in the Lamb of God...

- believe that if he eats, takes in, all of the Lamb, God will deliver him from the sin and enslavement of the world.

> "The next day John seeth Jesus coming unto him, and saith, Behold the Lamb of God, which taketh away the sin of the world" (Jn.1:29).

5 (23:19) **Law, Civil--Israel, Law of--Offerings--Stewardship--Giving:** there was the law governing one's offerings to God. Note that the amount of one's offering is not the issue in this law: the issue is what part of one's harvest or resources is given to God:

THE BASIC LAW GOVERNING THE OFFERINGS TO GOD

OUTLINE	SCRIPTURE
5. The law governing one's offerings to God a. Must offer the best of one's firstfruit b. Must not take away from the Giver of life	19 The first of the firstfruits of thy land thou shalt bring into the house of the LORD thy God. Thou shalt not seethe a kid in his mother's milk.

1. The first part of this law is direct: a person must offer the best, the very first of his harvest or resources to God. The very first part of a man's income was to be given to God, not the last part. And note where the very first part was to be given: not to the poor or needy of the earth, but to the house of the Lord (the Tabernacle, the church). The house of the

Lord and its ministry was to be taken care of first; then with broken hearts and compassion, God's people were to reach out and meet the needs of the poor and needy of the earth.

"Honour the LORD with thy substance, and with the firstfruits of all thine increase: So shall thy barns be filled with plenty, and thy presses shall burst out with new wine" (Pr.3:9-10).

"Bring ye all the tithes into the storehouse, that there may be meat in mine house, and prove me now herewith, saith the LORD of hosts, if I will not open you the windows of heaven, and pour you out a blessing, that there shall not be room enough to receive it" (Mal.3:10).

"Upon the first day of the week let every one of you lay by him in store, as God hath prospered him, that there be no gatherings when I come" (1 Cor.16:2).

"Every man according as he purposeth in his heart, so let him give; not grudgingly, or of necessity: for God loveth a cheerful giver" (2 Cor.9:7).

2. The second part of this law is a warning: a person must not take the offering away from God, away from the Giver of life. The picture is that of a kid, a baby lamb or goat, that was being taken away from its mother who had given it life. The kid was being cooked in its mother's milk. The point is probably this: no person is to take the offering away from God, away from the Giver of life, the LORD God Himself. God is the great Giver of life, the One who gives the milk or sustenance to life. No person should ever take the offering of God and use it for any other thing in life, no matter how much of a delicacy or possession the thing may be.

Note: this is an important principle in the law of God. It is repeated three times in the law of Moses (Ex.34:16; Dt.14:21).

Thought 1. We have no right to take the offering that belongs to God. If we do, we are in fact stealing from God. The Bible emphatically warns the man who would steal from God.

"Will a man rob God? Yet ye have robbed me. But ye say, Wherein have we robbed thee? In tithes and offerings. Ye *are* cursed with a curse: for ye have robbed me, *even* this whole nation" (Mal.3:8-9).

"In thee have they taken gifts to shed blood; thou hast taken usury and increase, and thou hast greedily gained of thy neighbours by extortion, and hast forgotten me, saith the Lord GOD. Behold, therefore I have smitten mine hand at thy dishonest gain which thou hast made, and at thy blood which hath been in the midst of thee" (Ezk.22:12-13).

"But a certain man named Ananias, with Sapphira his wife, sold a possession, And kept back part of the price, his wife also being privy to it, and brought a certain part, and laid it at the apostles' feet. But Peter said, Ananias, why hath Satan filled thine heart to lie to the Holy Ghost, and to keep back part of the price of the land? Whiles it remained, was it not thine own? and after it was sold, was it not in thine own power? why hast thou conceived this thing in thine heart? thou hast not lied unto men, but unto God. And Ananias hearing these words fell down, and gave up the ghost: and great fear came on all them that heard these things. And the young men arose, wound him up, and carried him out, and buried him. And it was about the space of three hours after, when his wife, not knowing what was done, came in. And Peter answered unto her, Tell me whether ye sold the land for so much? And she said, Yea, for so much. Then Peter said unto her, How is it that ye have agreed together to tempt the Spirit of the Lord? behold, the feet of them which have buried thy husband are at the door, and shall carry thee out. Then fell she down straightway at his feet, and yielded up the ghost: and the young men came in, and found her dead, and, carrying her forth, buried her by her husband" (Acts 5:1-10).

"Nor thieves, nor covetous, nor drunkards, nor revilers, nor extortioners, shall inherit the kingdom of God" (1 Cor.6:10).

| 1. Reward 1: God's special Angel (messenger), His protection & guidance to the promised land

a. The believer's duty: To heed, obey, & not rebel against God's Angel (messenger)
1) Bc. He will not forgive
2) Bc. God's name is in Him
b. The promises of God: Are conditional--if His people fully obey
1) God will stand against the enemies of His people

2) God's Angel (messenger) will guide His people to the promised land
3) God will wipe out all enemies

2. Reward 2: God's special provision & blessing
a. The believer's obligation
1) You must not worship nor follow the false gods of other people
2) You must worship the LORD (Jehovah, Yahweh) & Him alone
b. The promises of God
1) God will bless the food, water & health of His people | F. The Conclusion of the Law, the Mosaic Covenant: The Rewards of Obedience, Ex. 23:20-33

20 Behold, I send an Angel before thee, to keep thee in the way, and to bring thee into the place which I have prepared.
21 Beware of him, and obey his voice, provoke him not; for he will not pardon your transgressions: for my name is in him.
22 But if thou shalt indeed obey his voice, and do all that I speak; then I will be an enemy unto thine enemies, and an adversary unto thine adversaries.
23 For mine Angel shall go before thee, and bring thee in unto the Amorites, and the Hittites, and the Perizzites, and the Canaanites, and the Hivites, and the Jebusites: and I will cut them off.
24 Thou shalt not bow down to their gods, nor serve them, nor do after their works: but thou shalt utterly overthrow them, and quite break down their images.
25 And ye shall serve the LORD your God, and he shall bless thy bread, and thy water; and I will take sickness away from the midst of thee. | 26 There shall nothing cast their young, nor be barren, in thy land: the number of thy days I will fulfil.
27 I will send my fear before thee, and will destroy all the people to whom thou shalt come, and I will make all thine enemies turn their backs unto thee.
28 And I will send hornets before thee, which shall drive out the Hivite, the Canaanite, and the Hittite, from before thee.
29 I will not drive them out from before thee in one year; lest the land become desolate, and the beast of the field multiply against thee.
30 By little and little I will drive them out from before thee, until thou be increased, and inherit the land.
31 And I will set thy bounds from the Red sea even unto the sea of the Philistines, and from the desert unto the river: for I will deliver the inhabitants of the land into your hand; and thou shalt drive them out before thee.
32 Thou shalt make no covenant with them, nor with their gods.
33 They shall not dwell in thy land, lest they make thee sin against me: for if thou serve their gods, it will surely be a snare unto thee. | 2) God will give many offspring & give a long, fulfilling life

3. Reward 3: God's conquering power & gift of the promised land
a. The promises of God
1) God will cause the enemies of His people to fear, become confused, & flee
2) God will send the hornet (some enemy, plague, or a symbol of the power of God) ahead of His people to drive out all enemies
3) God will carefully plan the deliverance of His people: Will defeat the enemies little by little
• To save the land
• To give the people time to multiply
4) God will give His people the promised land, a great land
• Stretching from the Red Sea to the Philistine Sea (Mediterranean)
• Stretching from the desert (southern border) to the river (northern border)

b. The believer's obligation: Total separation from unbelievers
1) You must make no covenants with unbelievers
2) You must not let unbelievers live with you
• Bc. of their influence
• Bc. of their false gods: Would be a snare to you |

DIVISION VIII

THE LAW AND THE PROMISES OF GOD (THE MOSAIC COVENANT) (PART 3): THE CIVIL AND RELIGIOUS LAWS OF ISRAEL--HELPFUL PRINCIPLES TO GOVERN MAN AND SOCIETY, 21:1-24:18

F. THE CONCLUSION OF THE LAW, THE MOSAIC COVENANT (PART 1): THE REWARDS OF OBEDIENCE, EX.23:20-33

(23:20-33) **Introduction**: picture the scene. Over three million people are camped around Mt. Sinai; hundreds of thousands are stretched out all across the desert floor surrounding the mountain--men, women, and children of all ages. Who are these people? The Israelites of ancient history, the Israelites who had been cruelly enslaved for over four hundred years by the Egyptians. But now they were freed, miraculously set free by the mighty hand of God. And here they were camped out before Mt. Sinai, the mountain that is known as the "mountain of God." Why? Because of the great event that had just taken place: God had just given His people...
- the Ten Commandments, the same Ten Commandments that are followed by God's people today
- the great civil laws that were to govern ancient Israel, the civil laws that hold so many lessons for us

God had one great expectation of His people: obedience. God's people were to...
- obey the Ten Commandments
- obey the civil laws of the nation

If God's people obeyed, the people would be greatly rewarded. Three extraordinary things would happen. This is the subject of this passage: *The Conclusion of the Law, the Mosaic Covenant: The Rewards of Obedience*, Ex. 23:20-33.
1. Reward 1: God's Angel (messenger), His protection and guidance to the promised land (v.20-23).
2. Reward 2: God's provision and blessing (v.24-26).
3. Reward 3: God's conquering power and gift of the promised land (v.27-33).

1 (23:20-23) **Lord, Angel of--The Angel Of the Lord--Protection--Guidance--Rewards--Obedience--Land, Promised--Promises**: the first reward is that of God's Angel, of His protection and guidance to the promised land. The people were on their way to the promised land of God. They had just been delivered from the evil bondage of Egypt (a symbol of the world). They were about to break camp and embark on the most amazing journey imaginable: that of journeying through the wilderness and desert country of the land that lay between Egypt (the world) and Canaan (the promised land, symbolizing heaven). The amazing journey is what is known among believers as the *wilderness wanderings*. (See note, **Division Overview**--Ex.13:17-18:27 for more discussion.) The journey of God's people to the promised land was to take about forty years, and the journey was to be arduous and difficult. Trial after trial and enemy after enemy were to attack God's people as they journeyed to their destination. They would often become worn and weary. They were going to need God's help, His protection and guidance in order to reach the promised land. This is the first great promise God makes to His people: He will protect and guide His people if they will just obey His commandments.

REWARD 1: GOD'S ANGEL (MESSENGER), HIS PROTECTION AND GUIDANCE TO THE PROMISED LAND

OUTLINE	SCRIPTURE	SCRIPTURE	OUTLINE
	F. The Conclusion of the Law, the Mosaic Covenant (Part 1): The Rewards of Obedience, Ex. 23:20-33	transgressions: for my name is in him. 22 But if thou shalt indeed obey his voice, and do all that I speak; then I will be an enemy unto thine enemies, and an adversary unto thine adversaries.	1) Bc. He will not forgive 2) Bc. God's name is in Him b. The promises of God: Are conditional—if His people fully obey 1) God will stand against the enemies of His people
1. Reward 1: God's special Angel (messenger), His protection & guidance to the promised land a. The believer's duty: To heed, obey, & not rebel against God's Angel (messenger)	20 Behold, I send an Angel before thee, to keep thee in the way, and to bring thee into the place which I have prepared. 21 Beware of him, and obey his voice, provoke him not; for he will not pardon your	23 For mine Angel shall go before thee, and bring thee in unto the Amorites, and the Hittites, and the Perizzites, and the Canaanites, and the Hivites, and the Jebusites: and I will cut them off.	2) God's Angel (messenger) will guide His people to the promised land 3) God will wipe out all enemies

Who is this Angel who protects and guides God's people? The word Angel means *messenger*. Note what verse 21 says about this messenger of God: He is to be obeyed and never rebelled against. Why? Because He has the authority and power to forgive sins and because the very name of God is in Him. This description is far, far too high to apply to an ordinary angel. This Angel, this messenger, must be the Lord God Himself, more particularly, the second person of the Godhead, the Lord Jesus Christ. He is the great messenger of the covenant, the covenant God has made with His people.

> "Behold, I will send my messenger, and he shall prepare the way before me: and the Lord, whom ye seek, shall suddenly come to this temple, even the messenger of the covenant, whom ye delight in: behold, he shall come, saith the LORD of hosts" (Mal.3:1. See note--Ex.3:1-3; **Deeper Study # 2**--Gen.16:7 for more discussion.)

1. Now, what is the believer's duty? Scripture is clear, very clear: God's people are to heed and obey the Angel (God's special messenger). They are not to rebel against him. Note that the Angel was to speak to God's people, giving them directions and guiding them step by step. They were to listen, to pay close attention to the directions. The idea is that of heeding, of being very careful, of making absolutely sure that a person obeyed and did exactly what God's special Angel said. God's people were never to rebel against His instructions, never strike out on their own, never do their own thing, never go their own way. If they did rebel and disobey God, the special Angel would not forgive their rebellion. And note, the Angel had the authority to forgive or not to forgive their sin: God's very name was in the Angel.

Thought 1. God speaks to us through His Word, the Holy Bible, and through His Holy Spirit. God guides us and directs us through the wilderness of this world as we journey to the promised land. Our duty is to listen, to do exactly what He says, to obey His Word and the leadership of His Spirit.

> "The LORD is my shepherd; I shall not want" (Ps.23:1).
> "Thou shalt guide me with thy counsel, and afterward receive me to glory" (Ps.73:24).
> "And thine ears shall hear a word behind thee, saying, This is the way, walk ye in it, when ye turn to the right hand, and when ye turn to the left" (Is.30:21).
> "And I will bring the blind by a way that they knew not; I will lead them in paths that they have not known: I will make darkness light before them, and crooked things straight. These things will I do unto them, and not forsake them" (Is.42:16).
> "In all their affliction he was afflicted, and the angel of his presence saved them: in his love and in his pity he redeemed them; and he bare them, and carried them all the days of old" (Is.63:9).
> "Behold, I will send my messenger, and he shall prepare the way before me: and the Lord, whom ye seek, shall suddenly come to this temple, even the messenger of the covenant, whom ye delight in: behold, he shall come, saith the LORD of hosts" (Mal.3:1).

"Howbeit when he, the Spirit of truth, is come, he will guide you into all truth: for he shall not speak of himself; but whatsoever he shall hear, [that] shall he speak: and he will shew you things to come" (Jn.16:13).

2. Now note the great promises of God. God's special Angel would guide and protect His people, but His protection and guidance were conditional. The people had to obey the angel, follow His directions and do exactly what He said. If God's people would follow His special Angel (messenger), then God would do three great things for them as they journeyed to the promised land.

   a. God would stand against the enemies of His people (v.22). An enemy of God's people is an enemy of God, for God's name is in His people. The person who stands against God's people stands against God and opposes God, for they oppose the witness of God in His people. Therefore, the person makes himself an enemy of God. But note: God promises to protect and secure the believer. If the believer will just obey God, God will stand against the enemies of the believer. God will protect and guide the believer from the enemies of this world.

   b. God's special Angel (messenger) would guide His people to the promised land (v.23). He will actually walk out ahead of the believer as the believer journeys day by day. God's special Angel will make sure, absolutely sure, that the believer reaches the promised land of God.

Thought 1. Most of us know where we want to go. If there really is such a place as the promised land of heaven, then we want to go there and live eternally with God in a perfect world. Our problem, however, is this: we just do not know how to get there. It is at this point that Jesus Christ enters: we get into heaven through Jesus Christ. Jesus Christ is our Guide, our Savior, our LORD who has already gone before us and prepared the way.

"Let not your heart be troubled: ye believe in God, believe also in me. In my Father's house are many mansions: if *it were* not so, I would have told you. I go to prepare a place for you. And if I go and prepare a place for you, I will come again, and receive you unto myself; that where I am, *there* ye may be also" (Jn.14:1-3).

"Jesus saith unto him, I am the way, the truth, and the life: no man cometh unto the Father, but by me" (Jn.14:6).

"For this is good and acceptable in the sight of God our Saviour; Who will have all men to be saved, and to come unto the knowledge of the truth. For there is one God, and one mediator between God and men, the man Christ Jesus; Who gave himself a ransom for all, to be testified in due time" (1 Tim.2:3-6).

"Seeing then that we have a great high priest, that is passed into the heavens, Jesus the Son of God, let us hold fast *our* profession" (Heb.4:14).

"For this God is our God for ever and ever: he will be our guide even unto death" (Ps.48:14).

"Thou shalt guide me with thy counsel, and afterward receive me to glory" (Ps.73:24).

   c. God would even wipe out the believer's enemies (v.23). This is a pronouncement of judgment upon the enemies of God's people. No one--no person, not even a spiritual being--can stop a true believer from reaching the promised land of God. God will destroy any person or being who opposes the believer, any person or being who tries to keep the believer from reaching the promised land of God. (See Deeper Study # 2--Ex.3:8 for discussion on the nations listed here.)

Thought 1. The magnitude of this promise is overwhelming. God promised to go *before* His people. If we really believed and lived what this verse is saying...

   * we would not go our own way
   * we would not run ahead of God
   * we would let God guide us

When we go our own way, when we get ahead of God and do not allow God to fight for us, we will always lose the battle. The cry of each heart should be, "O' God, deliver me from evil, from all those who stand against and oppose me."

"Surely he shall deliver thee from the snare of the fowler, and from the noisome pestilence" (Ps.91:3).

"And even to your old age I am he; and even to hoar [gray] hairs will I carry you: I have made, and I will bear; even I will carry, and will deliver you" (Is.46:4).

"Be not afraid of their faces: for I am with thee to deliver thee, saith the LORD" (Jer.1:8).

"He delivereth and rescueth, and he worketh signs and wonders in heaven and in earth, who hath delivered Daniel from the power of the lions" (Dan.6:27).

"There hath no temptation taken you but such as is common to man: but God is faithful, who will not suffer you to be tempted above that ye are able; but will with the temptation also make a way to escape, that ye may be able to bear it" (1 Cor.10:13).

"And the Lord shall deliver me from every evil work, and will preserve me unto his heavenly kingdom: to whom be glory for ever and ever. Amen" (2 Tim.4:18).

"The Lord knoweth how to deliver the godly out of temptations, and to reserve the unjust unto the day of judgment to be punished" (2 Pt.2:9).

2 (23:24-26) **Reward--Obedience--Promises--Idolatry--Gods, False**: the second reward is that of God's special provision and blessing. Note exactly what God says:

REWARD 2: GOD'S PROVISION AND BLESSING

OUTLINE	SCRIPTURE	SCRIPTURE	OUTLINE
2. Reward 2: God's special provision & blessing a. The believer's obligation 1) You must not worship nor allow the false gods of other people 2) You must worship the LORD (Jehovah, Yahweh) &	24 Thou shalt not bow down to their gods, nor serve them, nor do after their works: but thou shalt utterly overthrow them, and quite break down their images. 25 And ye shall serve the LORD your God, and he	shall bless thy bread, and thy water; and I will take sickness away from the midst of thee. 26 There shall nothing cast their young, nor be barren, in thy land: the number of thy days I will fulfil.	Him alone b. The promises of God 1) God will bless the bread, water & health of His people 2) God will bless the womb of mothers & give a long, fulfilling life

No matter how deep our need, God promises to provide for His people. God promises to provide every necessity of life. But again, the promise is conditional. God's people had an obligation to fulfill. Note the believer's obligation.

1. God's people had to follow and worship God and God alone.
⇒ They must never bow down and worship false gods.
⇒ They must never follow the practices of false gods.
⇒ They must demolish and crush the sacred stones of false gods.

This may seem harsh, a violent reaction toward other religions. But the following must always be remembered about the religion of the ancient Canaanite nations:

"The idolatries of the heathen were connected 'works of darkness,' which it is shameful even to speak of. The rites of Baal and Ashtoreth, of Chemosh, Molech, Rimmon, and the other Canaanite and Syrian deities were at once defiled by the abomination of human sacrifices, and polluted with the still more debasing evil of religious impurity. 'The sacrifice offered to Ashtoreth,' says Dr. Döllinger, 'consisted in the prostitution of women: the women submitted themselves to the visitors of the feast, in the temple of the goddess or the adjoining precinct. A legend told of Astarte (Ashtoreth) having prostituted herself in Tyre for ten years: and in many places matrons, as well as maidens, consecrated themselves for a length of time, or on the festivals of the goddess, with a view of propitiating her, or earning her favour as *hieroduli* of unchastity....In this way they went so far at last as to contemplate the abominations of unnatural lust as a homage rendered to the deity, and to exalt it into a regular cultus. The worship of the goddess at Aphaca in Lebanon was specially notorious in this respect. The temple in a solitary situation was, as Eusebius tells us, a place of evil-doing for such as chose to ruin their bodies in scandalous ways....Criminal intercourse with women, impurity, shameful and degrading deeds, were practised in the temple, where there was no custom and no law, and no honourable or decent human being could be found.' (*Jew and Gentile*, vol.i. pp. 428, 429; Darnell's translation.)

"**Thou shalt utterly overthrow them**. The heathen gods are identified with their images. These were to be torn from their bases, overthrown, and rolled in the dust for greater contempt and ignominy. They were then to be broken up and burnt, till the gold and the silver with which they were overlaid was calcined and could be stamped to powder. Nothing was to be spared that had been degraded by idolatry, either for its beauty or its elaborate workmanship, or its value. All was hateful to God, and was to be destroyed."[1]

2. Again, God's people had an obligation to worship God alone. There is only one true and living God, only one great Creator, only one Sovereign Lord and Majesty of the universe: the LORD God Himself (Jehovah, Yahweh). It is, therefore, only logical that He would demand that He and He alone be followed and worshipped. This was the condition to receiving the great promises of God. If God's people followed and worshipped Him--faithfully followed and worshipped Him--God promised to meet the basic necessities of life:
⇒ God would bless and provide the food, water, and health that His people needed.
⇒ God would give many offspring to His people and give them a long and fulfilling life.

Thought 1. Godly, righteous living makes the human body stronger and more vigorous, both mentally and physically. In addition to this, if we truly follow and worship God and Him alone, He promises to meet all the necessities of life. He promises to meet every need we have.

"But seek ye first the kingdom of God, and his righteousness; and all these things shall be added unto you" (Mt.6:33).
"These things have I spoken unto you, that my joy might remain in you, and [that] your joy might be full" (Jn.15:11).
"But my God shall supply all your need according to his riches in glory by Christ Jesus" (Ph.4:19).
"And ye shall serve the LORD your God, and he shall bless thy bread, and thy water; and I will take sickness away from the midst of thee" (Ex.23:25).

---

[1] *Pulpit Commentary*, Vol.1, Exodus, p.212.

"Bring ye all the tithes into the storehouse, that there may be meat in mine house, and prove me now herewith, saith the LORD of hosts, if I will not open you the windows of heaven, and pour you out a blessing, that there shall not be room enough to receive it" (Mal.3:10).

"Keep therefore the words of this covenant, and do them, that ye may prosper in all that ye do" (Dt.29:9).

"Then shalt thou prosper, if thou takest heed to fulfil the statutes and judgments which the LORD charged Moses with concerning Israel: be strong, and of good courage; dread not, nor be dismayed" (1 Chron.22:13).

"As long as he sought the LORD, God made him to prosper" (2 Chron.26:5).

"Blessed is the man that walketh not in the counsel of the ungodly, nor standeth in the way of sinners, nor sitteth in the seat of the scornful. But his delight is in the law of the LORD; and in his law doth he meditate day and night. And he shall be like a tree planted by the rivers of water, that bringeth forth his fruit in his season; his leaf also shall not wither; and whatsoever he doeth shall prosper" (Ps.1:1-3).

"Oh how great is thy goodness, which thou hast laid up for them that fear thee; which thou hast wrought for them that trust in thee before the sons of men!" (Ps.31:19).

3 (23:27-33) **Reward--Land, The Promised--Planning--Victory--Conquest--Separation**: the third reward is that of God's conquering power and the gift of the promised land. The goal of Israel was the promised land of God. But as they journeyed toward the promised land, they were to face enemy after enemy. They had one hope and only one hope: God's conquering power. They could reach the promised land only if God's power was with them. Note the great promise that God now makes to His people.

REWARD 3: GOD'S CONQUERING POWER AND THE GIFT OF THE PROMISED LAND

OUTLINE	SCRIPTURE	SCRIPTURE	OUTLINE

3. Reward 3: God's conquering power & gift of the promised land
a. The promises of God
  1) God will cause the enemies of His people to fear, become confused, & flee
  2) God will send the hornet (some enemy, plague, or a symbol of the power of God) ahead of His people to drive out all enemies
  3) God will carefully plan the deliverance of His people: Will defeat the enemies little by little
  • To save the land
 	
  • To give the people time to multiply
	27 I will send my fear before thee, and will destroy all the people to whom thou shalt come, and I will make all thine enemies turn their backs unto thee.
	28 And I will send hornets before thee, which shall drive out the Hivite, the Canaanite, and the Hittite, from before thee.
	29 I will not drive them out from before thee in one year; lest the land become desolate, and the beast of the field multiply against thee.
	30 By little and little I will drive them out from before
		thee, until thou be increased, and inherit the land.
		31 And I will set thy bounds from the Red sea even unto the sea of the Philistines, and from the desert unto the river: for I will deliver the inhabitants of the land into your hand; and thou shalt drive them out before thee.
		32 Thou shalt make no covenant with them, nor with their gods.
		33 They shall not dwell in thy land, lest they make thee sin against me: for if thou serve their gods, it will surely be a snare unto thee.
			4) God will give His people the promised land, a great land
			  • Stretching from the Red Sea to the Philistine Sea (Mediterranean)
			  • Stretching from the desert (southern border) to the river (northern border)
			
			b. The believer's obligation: Total separation from unbelievers
			  1) You must make no covenants with unbelievers
			  2) You must not let unbelievers live with you
			    • Bc. of their influence
			    • Bc. of their false gods: Would be a snare to you

1. God gave Israel four specific promises.
   a. God would cause the enemies of His people to fear, become confused, and flee (v.27). Note: it was not Israel's great ability to make weapons of mass-destruction that caused its enemies to fear. It was not their great bravery that sent chills into the inhabitants of Canaan. Note what Scripture later records:

> "And she [Rahab] said unto the men, I know that the LORD hath given you the land, and that your terror is fallen upon us, and that all the inhabitants of the land faint because of you. For we have heard how the LORD dried up the water of the Red sea for you, when ye came out of Egypt; and what ye did unto the two kings of the Amorites, that were on the other side Jordan, Sihon and Og, whom ye utterly destroyed. And as soon as we had heard these things, our hearts did melt, neither did there remain any more courage in any man, because of you: for the LORD your God, he is God in heaven above, and in earth beneath" (Josh.2:9-11).

   b. God would send the hornet (some enemy, plague, or symbol of the power of God) ahead of His people (v.28). Whatever this "hornet" was, it was very effective. As organized nations, the Hivites, Canaanites, and Hittites became a distant memory in the history of the world. The reference to the hornet occurs only here and in Dt.7:20 and Josh 24:12.
   c. God would carefully plan the deliverance of His people: He would defeat the enemies little by little (v.29). The reason for this procedure was to save the land and give Israel time to multiply population-wise. God had to make sure that the land would not waste away before Israel had a chance to inhabit it. A mass exodus of their enemies would have ruined the fields. The weeds, briars, wildlife, and animals would have taken over the land. On a more spiritual level, God knew that His people were in no position spiritually to assume control of the entire promised

land. In fact, Israel did not fully enjoy this promise until the kingdoms of David and Solomon--hundreds of years later.

    d. God would give His people the promised land, a great land (v.31). It was a land so great that:
        ⇒ it stretched from the Red Sea (Sea of Reeds) to the Philistine Sea (Mediterranean).
        ⇒ it stretched from the desert (southern border) to the river (northern border).
    Israel came close to possessing all the land promised here during the united kingdoms of David and Solomon.

  2. But again note: these promises were conditional. God's people were to live a life of spiritual separation, a life totally separated and different from their unbelieving neighbors. They were not to let unbelievers live with them...
- because of their sinful influence
- because of their false gods that would be a snare to God's people

God's people were not to expose themselves to the sin and evil, the immoral and unrighteous ways of unbelievers. Being around sin causes a person to become more and more insensitive to sin. The more a person is around immorality or exposes himself to immorality, the more he accepts the immoral ways of society. God knows this; therefore He demands that His people separate themselves from all unbelievers. The Expositor's Bible Commentary says this:

> "No covenant was to be made with these people (though the Gibeonites did succeed in making one, Josh 9:3-15). The potential snare of their gods, practices, and worship was too great; thus there was to be no peaceful co-existence between these nations and Israel in Canaan."[2]

Thought 1. God demands a *life of separation*, a *life of sanctification*: we are to separate ourselves as much as possible from the sin and evil of this world and live a *life of sanctification* before God.

> **"I beseech you therefore, brethren, by the mercies of God, that ye present your bodies a living sacrifice, holy, acceptable unto God, which is your reasonable service. And be not conformed to this world: but be ye transformed by the renewing of your mind, that ye may prove what is that good, and acceptable, and perfect, will of God" (Ro.12:1-2).**
> **"Wherefore come out from among them, and be ye separate, saith the Lord, and touch not the unclean thing; and I will receive you, And will be a Father unto you, and ye shall be my sons and daughters, saith the Lord Almighty" (2 Cor.6:17-18).**
> **"Proving what is acceptable unto the Lord. And have no fellowship with the unfruitful works of darkness, but rather reprove them" (Eph.5:10-11).**
> **"Love not the world, neither the things that are in the world. If any man love the world, the love of the Father is not in him. For all that is in the world, the lust of the flesh, and the lust of the eyes, and the pride of life, is not of the Father, but is of the world" (1 Jn.2:15-16).**
> **"Now we command you, brethren, in the name of our Lord Jesus Christ, that ye withdraw yourselves from every brother that walketh disorderly, and not after the tradition which he received of us" (2 Th.3:6).**
> **"Depart ye, depart ye, go ye out from thence, touch no unclean thing; go ye out of the midst of her; be ye clean, that bear the vessels of the LORD" (Is.52:11).**
> **"And with many other words did he testify and exhort, saying, Save yourselves from this untoward generation" (Acts 2:40).**

Thought 2. In today's society, there is a strong temptation for the believer to compromise and make a covenant with an unbeliever. The believer is playing with fire when he makes these critical errors of judgment:
    ⇒ There are covenants with a business partner who is lost.
    ⇒ There are covenants with a young man or lady who is lost, a covenant that far too often ends up in marriage, in being unequally yoked together.
    ⇒ There are covenants with a friend who is lost.

God has given clear instructions on how to avoid making a covenant with an unbeliever.

1) The believer is not to walk in the counsel of the ungodly.

> **"Blessed *is* the man that walketh not in the counsel of the ungodly, nor standeth in the way of sinners, nor sitteth in the seat of the scornful" (Ps.1:1).**

2) The believer is not walk in the path of the wicked.

> **"Enter not into the path of the wicked, and go not in the way of evil *men*" (Pr.4:14).**

3) The believer is not to keep company with a brother who is living a life of sin and rebellion.

> **"But now I have written unto you not to keep company, if any man that is called a brother be a fornicator, or covetous, or an idolater, or a railer, or a drunkard, or an extortioner; with such an one no not to eat" (1 Cor.5:11).**

---

[2]   Frank E. Gaebelein. *The Expositor's Bible Commentary*, Vol. 2, p.447.

4) The believer is not to be associated with evil talk.

"Be not deceived: evil communications corrupt good manners" (1 Cor.15:33).
"Proving what is acceptable unto the Lord. And have no fellowship with the unfruitful works of darkness, but rather reprove them" (Eph.5:10-11).

5) The believer is not to be unequally yoked with unbelievers.

"Be ye not unequally yoked together with unbelievers: for what fellowship hath righteousness with unrighteousness? and what communion hath light with darkness?" (2 Cor.6:14).

Thought 3. The best way to avoid falling into temptation is to avoid temptation. The believer has no business flirting with unbelievers and their false gods. Satan has a ready snare for any believer who seeks to stray away from an exclusive relationship with God.

"My son, if sinners entice thee, consent thou not" (Pr.1:10).
"Enter not into the path of the wicked, and go not in the way of evil *men*" (Pr.4:14).
"Neither yield ye your members *as* instruments of unrighteousness unto sin: but yield yourselves unto God, as those that are alive from the dead, and your members *as* instruments of righteousness unto God" (Ro.6:13).
"Lest Satan should get an advantage of us: for we are not ignorant of his devices" (2 Cor.2:11).
"But I fear, lest by any means, as the serpent beguiled Eve through his subtilty, so your minds should be corrupted from the simplicity that is in Christ" (2 Cor.11:3).
"For this cause, when I could no longer forbear, I sent to know your faith, lest by some means the tempter have tempted you, and our labour be in vain" (1 Th.3:5).
"Ye therefore, beloved, seeing ye know *these things* before, beware lest ye also, being led away with the error of the wicked, fall from your own stedfastness" (2 Pt.3:17).

1. **God's great call: Worship Him**
   a. Extended to all: Were represented in their leaders
   b. The limitation of God's call
      1) Must worship afar off: Acknowledge the great gulf between God & man
      2) Must know that only God's appointed mediator can approach God

2. **The 1st duty: Obedience--to make a total commitment to obey God**
   a. Moses declared God's law, God's Word, to the people
   b. The people's commitment: Would do all God said

3. **The 2nd duty: To seal one's commitment--to make a formal agreement (covenant) with God**
   a. Moses wrote God's law
   b. Moses confirmed the agreement, the covenant
      1) Built an altar & 12 pillars
      2) Moses sent young men to offer sacrifices upon the altar: Burnt offerings & peace (fellowship) offerings
      3) Moses sprinkled half the blood on the altar: Symbolized the people dedicating their lives (blood) to God
      4) Moses read the Book of the Covenant, the Law, to the people
      5) The people again declared their commitment: "We will obey God's Word"
      6) Moses sprinkled half the blood upon the people: Symbolized God offering His life (blood) to the people & binding them to Him, accepting them

G. The Climactic Adoption of the Law, the Mosaic Covenant: The Great Duty of Believers After Receiving the Law, the Word of God, Ex.24:1-18

And he said unto Moses, Come up unto the LORD, thou, and Aaron, Nadab, and Abihu, and seventy of the elders of Israel; and worship ye afar off.
2 And Moses alone shall come near the LORD: but they shall not come nigh; neither shall the people go up with him.
3 And Moses came and told the people all the words of the LORD, and all the judgments: and all the people answered with one voice, and said, All the words which the LORD hath said will we do.
4 And Moses wrote all the words of the LORD, and rose up early in the morning, and builded an altar under the hill, and twelve pillars, according to the twelve tribes of Israel.
5 And he sent young men of the children of Israel, which offered burnt offerings, and sacrificed peace offerings of oxen unto the LORD.
6 And Moses took half of the blood, and put it in basons; and half of the blood he sprinkled on the altar.
7 And he took the book of the covenant, and read in the audience of the people: and they said, All that the LORD hath said will we do, and be obedient.
8 And Moses took the blood, and sprinkled it on the people, and said, Behold the blood of the covenant, which the LORD hath made with you concerning all these words.

9 Then went up Moses, and Aaron, Nadab, and Abihu, and seventy of the elders of Israel:
10 And they saw the God of Israel: and there was under his feet as it were a paved work of a sapphire stone, and as it were the body of heaven in his clearness.
11 And upon the nobles of the children of Israel he laid not his hand: also they saw God, and did eat and drink.
12 And the LORD said unto Moses, Come up to me into the mount, and be there: and I will give thee tables of stone, and a law, and commandments which I have written; that thou mayest teach them.
13 And Moses rose up, and his minister Joshua: and Moses went up into the mount of God.
14 And he said unto the elders, Tarry ye here for us, until we come again unto you: and, behold, Aaron and Hur are with you: if any man have any matters to do, let him come unto them.
15 And Moses went up into the mount, and a cloud covered the mount.
16 And the glory of the LORD abode upon mount Sinai, and the cloud covered it six days: and the seventh day he called unto Moses out of the midst of the cloud.
17 And the sight of the glory of the LORD was like devouring fire on the top of the mount in the eyes of the children of Israel.
18 And Moses went into the midst of the cloud, and gat him up into the mount: and Moses was in the mount forty days and forty nights.

4. **The 3rd duty: To worship God**
   a. Moses & the leaders obeyed God: Went up to worship God
      1) Saw God (cp. 33:20)
      2) Saw the pavement under God's feet: As sapphire, clear & blue like the sky
      3) God's glory did not strike the leaders dead
   b. The leaders ate a covenant meal before God: Symbolized the people's commitment & covenant with God

5. **The 4th duty: To receive more and more of God's law, of God's Word**
   a. God called Moses farther up the mountain to stay in His presence a long time: To receive more of God's Word, more instruction
      1) Moses obeyed & took Joshua with him
      2) Moses did not neglect the people: He secured help in looking after the people-- left Aaron & Hur in charge
   b. God's cloud of glory covered the mountain
      1) Moses waited on the Lord (prayed & prayed) on the mountain for six days
      2) The voice of God finally spoke to Moses on the 7th day
      3) The spectacular sight of God's glory was like a consuming fire
      4) Moses got all alone with God: Experienced the glory of God & received more instructions from God--for forty days & nights

DIVISION VIII

THE LAW AND THE PROMISES OF GOD (THE MOSAIC COVENANT) (PART 3): THE CIVIL AND RELIGIOUS LAWS OF ISRAEL--HELPFUL PRINCIPLES TO GOVERN MAN AND SOCIETY, 21:1-24:18

G.   The Climactic Adoption of the Law, the Mosaic Covenant: The Great Duty of Believers After Receiving the Law, the Word of God, Ex.24:1-18

(24:1-18) **Introduction**: this is a climactic passage, the Scripture that graphically closes the giving of the law to Israel. But note: once a person has heard the law of God--heard the Word of God--that person becomes obligated to God. The one thing we must all realize is this: people by the millions own the Holy Bible, the Word of God, and many of them have read a passage here and there. Millions of others have heard the Word of God preached. But one thing is missing in the reading and hearing of most people: a sense of their obligation to God. Again, God is clear: once a person has received or heard His Word, that person has certain obligations, certain duties before God.

This was the situation with Israel. God had just given the law, His Holy Word, to Moses; and Moses was now ready to bring the Word of God to the people. But once they had received the Word, they would become obligated to God, strongly obligated. This is the subject of this passage: *The Climactic Adoption of the Law, the Mosaic Covenant: The Great Duty of Believers After Receiving the Law, the Word of God*, Ex.24:1-18.

1. God's great call: worship Him (v.1-2).
2. The 1st duty: obedience--to make a total commitment to obey God (v.3).
3. The 2nd duty: to seal one's commitment--to make a formal agreement (covenant) with God (v.4-8).
4. The 3rd duty: to worship God (v.9-11).
5. The 4th duty: to receive more and more of God's law, of God's Word (v.12-18).

1 (24:1-2) **Worship--Separation, From God--Barrier, Between God and Man--Man, Separation From God--Moses--Mediator**: there was God's great call for His people to worship Him. Remember, Moses was still up on Mt. Sinai in the presence of God. God had just given him...

- the Ten Commandments (19:1-20:26)
- the civil laws to govern Israel (21:1-23:19)
- the three great rewards or promises for obedience (23:20-23)

Now, God was ready for Moses to return to the people, to lead them to ratify the law, to adopt it as the law of the land. God expected two things from the people: obedience to the law and the faithful worship of God.

1. Note what God did right before Moses left His presence: God extended a call for Moses to return after Moses had given the law to the people. Moses was to come back up into God's presence for worship. But this time the call to worship was extended to all Israel. Moses was to bring the leaders of Israel, the representatives of the people, with him:

⇒ Aaron, and Nadab and Abihu, the two oldest sons of Aaron
⇒ The seventy elders or rulers of Israel

One of the most glorious events in the history of the world was about to take place: the giving of the Ten Commandments and the law to God's people. Consequently, God wanted and expected His people to obey the commandments and to worship Him in appreciation for the commandments and the law. Moses was, therefore, to return to God for worship after the law was ratified (formally accepted and sanctioned); and he was to bring the leaders of God's people with him.

2. But note: there was a limitation to God's call, two limitations. The leaders were to worship afar off, a great distance away from God's presence. Only Moses could come near and approach God.

Why did God lay these two restrictions upon the people? Obviously, to teach two necessary lessons.

a. God's people must know this fact: there is a great gulf between God and man, an impassable gulf. God is holy, righteous, and pure--perfect in all His being. But man is the very opposite. Man is unholy, unrighteous, and impure--imperfect (sinful and depraved) in his being.

God lives in the incorruptible world, the spiritual and heavenly world that is permanent and eternal, that never wastes away. Whereas, man lives in the corruptible world, the physical and earthly world that is running down and is temporal and wasting away.

There is a great gulf between God and man: man cannot enter God's presence. He cannot approach God nor enter heaven, not unless God Himself makes the way and shows man the way.

> "But your iniquities have separated between you and your God, and your sins have hid his face from you, that he will not hear" (Is.59:2).
>
> "But we are all as an unclean thing, and all our righteousnesses are as filthy rags; and we all do fade as a leaf; and our iniquities, like the wind, have taken us away" (Is.64:6).
>
> "And beside all this, between us and you there is a great gulf fixed: so that they which would pass from hence to you cannot; neither can they pass to us, that [would come] from thence" (Lk.16:26).
>
> "As it is written, There is none righteous, no, not one: There is none that understandeth, there is none that seeketh after God. They are all gone out of the way, they are together become unprofitable; there is none that doeth good, no, not one. Their throat is an open sepulchre; with their tongues they have used deceit; the poison of asps is under their lips: Whose mouth is full of cursing and bitterness: Their feet are swift to shed blood: Destruction and misery are in their ways: And the way of peace have they not known: There is no fear of God before their eyes" (Ro.3:10-18).
>
> "For all have sinned, and come short of the glory of God" (Ro.3:23).

b. God's people must know another fact as well: only God's appointed mediator can approach God. This was Moses: only Moses could come near God. This, of course, pointed toward Jesus Christ, the great mediator appointed by God to bridge the great gulf between God and man.

> "For there is one God, and one mediator between God and men, the man Christ Jesus; Who gave himself a ransom for all, to be testified in due time" (1 Tim.2:5-6).
>
> "Wherefore, holy brethren, partakers of the heavenly calling, consider the Apostle and High Priest of our profession, Christ Jesus; Who was faithful to him that appointed him, as also Moses was faithful in all his house" (Heb.3:1-2).

"Wherefore he is able also to save them to the uttermost that come unto God by him, seeing he ever liveth to make intercession for them" (Heb.7:25).

"But now hath he obtained a more excellent ministry, by how much also he is the mediator of a better covenant, which was established upon better promises" (Heb.8:6).

"And for this cause he is the mediator of the new testament, that by means of death, for the redemption of the transgressions that were under the first testament, they which are called might receive the promise of eternal inheritance" (Heb.9:15).

"For Christ is not entered into the holy places made with hands, which are the figures of the true; but into heaven itself, now to appear in the presence of God for us: Nor yet that he should offer himself often, as the high priest entereth into the holy place every year with blood of others; For then must he often have suffered since the foundation of the world: but now once in the end of the world hath he appeared to put away sin by the sacrifice of himself. And as it is appointed unto men once to die, but after this the judgment: So Christ was once offered to bear the sins of many; and unto them that look for him shall he appear the second time without sin unto salvation" (Heb.9:24-28).

"For Christ also hath once suffered for sins, the just for the unjust, that he might bring us to God, being put to death in the flesh, but quickened by the Spirit" (1 Pt.3:18).

"My little children, these things write I unto you, that ye sin not. And if any man sin, we have an advocate with the Father, Jesus Christ the righteous" (1 Jn.2:1).

DEEPER STUDY # 1

(24:1) **Nadab**: was Aaron and Elisheba's oldest son. He was in line to succeed his father Aaron as High Priest.

- Nadab was called to join his father and the seventy elders as they went up Mount Sinai to enter the presence of God (cp. Ex.24:1, 9-11).

"And he said unto Moses, Come up unto the LORD, thou, and Aaron, Nadab, and Abihu, and seventy of the elders of Israel; and worship ye afar off" (Ex.24:1).

- Nadab was ordained to be one of the original priests (cp. Ex.28:1; Lev.8:1-36).

"And take thou unto thee Aaron thy brother, and his sons with him, from among the children of Israel, that he may minister unto me in the priest's office, *even* Aaron, Nadab and Abihu, Eleazar and Ithamar, Aaron's sons" (Ex.28:1).

- Nadab tragically sinned against God with his brother Abihu by offering strange fire before the Lord. They were both consumed with God's fire of judgment (cp. Lev.10:1-2; Num.3:4).

"And Nadab and Abihu, the sons of Aaron, took either of them his censer, and put fire therein, and put incense thereon, and offered strange fire before the LORD, which he commanded them not. And there went out fire from the LORD, and devoured them, and they died before the LORD" (Lev.10:1-2).

Nadab's untimely death, along with Abihu, was a graphic picture for the other priests that they had to approach God exactly as He said, that they must never take lightly the holiness of God.

DEEPER STUDY # 2

(24:1) **Abihu**: was Aaron and Elisheba's second oldest son (cp. Ex.6:23; Num.3:2; 26:60; 1 Chron.6:3; 24:1).

- Abihu was called to join his father and the seventy elders as they went up Mount Sinai to enter the presence of God (cp. Ex.24:1, 9-11).

"And he said unto Moses, Come up unto the LORD, thou, and Aaron, Nadab, and Abihu, and seventy of the elders of Israel; and worship ye afar off" (Ex.24:1).

- Abihu was ordained as one of the original priests (cp. Ex.28:1; Lev.8:1-36).

"And take thou unto thee Aaron thy brother, and his sons with him, from among the children of Israel, that he may minister unto me in the priest's office, *even* Aaron, Nadab and Abihu, Eleazar and Ithamar, Aaron's sons" (Ex.28:1).

- Abihu tragically sinned against God with his brother Nadab by offering strange fire before the Lord. They were both consumed with God's fire of judgment (cp. Lev.10:1-2; Num.3:4).

"And Nadab and Abihu, the sons of Aaron, took either of them his censer, and put fire therein, and put incense thereon, and offered strange fire before the LORD, which he commanded them not. And there went out fire from the LORD, and devoured them, and they died before the LORD" (Lev.10:1-2).

2 (24:3) **Obedience--Commitment**: the very first duty of God's people is obedience--to make a total commitment to obey God. Picture the scene: Mt. Sinai is covered with a thick, bright cloud. All of a sudden, someone at the foot of the mountain notices an unclear shadow emerging more and more out of the foggy cloud, walking down the mountain. Soon the shadow is clearly seen: it is Moses! No doubt people began running all about the camp of the Israelites, shouting the news, "Moses is returning! Moses is returning!"

The leaders gathered at the foot of the mountain to greet Moses while all the people spread the news among themselves and anxiously began gathering together tribe by tribe--eagerly waiting to hear what Moses had to report. Two great events then took place.

1. Moses declared God's law, God's Word, to the people. Note that he shared "all" with the people. This means that he declared...
- the Ten Commandments (19:1-20:26)
- the civil laws to govern the nation (21:1-23:19)

2. The people committed themselves to keep the commandments and laws of God. In fact, note exactly what they said: they would do *everything* the LORD had said. What a moment of excitement and of enthusiasm, of being emotionally charged: hearing the law of God being proclaimed for the first time, the very laws that were to govern their nation. With one voice, in unison, they shouted out that they would do *everything* God had said. The people committed themselves--*totally committed themselves*--to follow God, to keep His commandments and laws.

Thought 1. The one thing God wants from us is obedience. God longs for us to keep His commandments, to do all He says.

"O that there were such an heart in them, that they would fear me, and keep all my commandments always, that it might be well with them, and with their children for ever!" (Dt.5:29).

"This day the LORD thy God hath commanded thee to do these statutes and judgments: thou shalt therefore keep and do them with all thine heart, and with all thy soul" (Dt.26:16).

"This book of the law shall not depart out of thy mouth; but thou shalt meditate therein day and night, that thou mayest observe to do according to all that is written therein: for then thou shalt make thy way prosperous, and then thou shalt have good success" (Josh.1:8).

"And Samuel said, Hath the LORD as great delight in burnt offerings and sacrifices, as in obeying the voice of the LORD? Behold, to obey is better than sacrifice, and to hearken than the fat of rams" (1 Sam.15:22).

"Not every one that saith unto me, Lord, Lord, shall enter into the kingdom of heaven; but he that doeth the will of my Father which is in heaven" (Mt.7:21).

"Therefore whosoever heareth these sayings of mine, and doeth them, I will liken him unto a wise man, which built his house upon a rock" (Mt.7:24).

"If ye keep my commandments, ye shall abide in my love; even as I have kept my Father's commandments, and abide in his love" (Jn.15:10).

"Blessed are they that do his commandments, that they may have right to the tree of life, and may enter in through the gates into the city" (Rev.22:14).

3 (24:4-8) **Obedience--Commitment--Covenant--Word of God--Scripture**: the second duty of God's people is to seal the commitment made to God. In Israel's case, Moses sealed the commitment by making a *formal agreement* (covenant) with God.

1. First, Moses carefully wrote down everything the LORD God said (v.4). No doubt God's Spirit quickened his memory to remember all that God had said (2 Pt.1:21; Jn.14:26). Perhaps Moses had also taken some notes up on the mountain when God was instructing him. Whatever the case, the Ten Commandments and law needed to be recorded so that God's people would always have God's Word available for study, understanding, and guidance.

"Study to show thyself approved unto God, a workman that needeth not to be ashamed, rightly dividing the word of truth" (2 Tim.2:15).

"All scripture is given by inspiration of God, and is profitable for doctrine, for reproof, for correction, for instruction in righteousness" (2 Tim.3:16).

"As newborn babes, desire the sincere milk of the word, that ye may grow thereby: If so be ye have tasted that the Lord is gracious" (1 Pt.2:2-3).

2. Second, Moses confirmed the agreement, the covenant, between God and the people. He sealed the commitment the people had made to God, sealed it by conducting a public service.
- a. Moses built an altar and twelve stone pillars at the foot of Mt. Sinai (v.4b). The altar was necessary in order to sacrifice the animals to God. The twelve stone pillars represented the twelve tribes of Israel (Josh.4:3, 5-9, 20; 1 Ki.18:31).
- b. Moses sent young men to offer sacrifices upon the altar (v.5). They sacrificed young bulls as burnt offerings and peace or fellowship offerings. (See note, Burnt Offerings--Gen.8:20; Deeper Study # 1--Gen.8:20 for more discussion.)
- c. Moses then took half the blood and sprinkled it on the altar (v.6). The blood symbolized that the life of the offerer was being sacrificed, given up, poured out, dedicated to God. In sprinkling the blood upon the altar, Moses was declaring that the people were asking God...
  - to accept them and their commitment
  - to forgive their sins
  - to receive them and their dedication as being genuinely given

259

d. Moses then took the Book of the Covenant or Law that he had written and read it to the people (v.7). Why? Because it was the very thing they were committing themselves to keep. In order to keep the law, they needed to hear it time and again. They needed to learn the Ten Commandments and the civil laws, keep them focused in their memories.

e. The people again declared their commitment: they would do everything the LORD had said (v.7ᵇ). But note: this time they added a more forceful declaration: "We will obey."

> **"I will never forget thy precepts: for with them thou hast quickened me" (Ps.119:93).**
> **"I am thy servant; give me understanding, that I may know thy testimonies" (Ps.119:125).**
> **"Thy testimonies are wonderful: therefore doth my soul keep them" (Ps.119:129).**
> **"The righteousness of thy testimonies is everlasting: give me understanding, and I shall live" (Ps.119:144).**

f. Moses sprinkled half the blood upon the people (v.8). Remembering that there were over two to three million Israelites, the leaders obviously helped Moses or else Moses sprinkled only the leaders and the people are seen as being represented in their leaders. The symbolic meaning of this act is graphic: the picture is that of God offering His forgiveness and acceptance to the people...

- because the people *believed* that the sacrifice secured God's forgiveness and acceptance
- because the people committed themselves to obey God's Word

Note what Moses did as he sprinkled the people: he cried out, "this blood confirms the covenant between you and God" (v.8).

Thought 1. The blood of the sacrifice is a symbol or picture of the Lord Jesus Christ. The blood of Christ confirms the covenant God has made with man. God forgives and accepts man--binds man to Himself--through the blood of Christ and only through the blood of Christ.

> **"For the life of the flesh is in the blood: and I have given it to you upon the altar to make an atonement for your souls: for it is the blood that maketh an atonement for the soul" (Lev.17:11).**
> **"For this is my blood of the new testament, which is shed for many for the remission of sins" (Mt.26:28).**
> **"Much more then, being now justified by his blood, we shall be saved from wrath through him" (Ro.5:9).**
> **"And, having made peace through the blood of his cross, by him to reconcile all things unto himself; by him, I say, whether they be things in earth, or things in heaven" (Col.1:20).**
> **"How much more shall the blood of Christ, who through the eternal Spirit offered himself without spot to God, purge your conscience from dead works to serve the living God?" (Heb.9:14).**
> **"And almost all things are by the law purged with blood; and without shedding of blood is no remission" (Heb.9:22).**
> **"Forasmuch as ye know that ye were not redeemed with corruptible things, as silver and gold, from your vain conversation received by tradition from your fathers; But with the precious blood of Christ, as of a lamb without blemish and without spot" (1 Pt.1:18-19).**
> **"But if we walk in the light, as he is in the light, we have fellowship one with another, and the blood of Jesus Christ his Son cleanseth us from all sin" (1 Jn.1:7).**
> **"And from Jesus Christ, who is the faithful witness, and the first begotten of the dead, and the prince of the kings of the earth. Unto him that loved us, and washed us from our sins in his own blood" (Rev.1:5).**

4 (24:9-11) **Worship--Glory, of God--God, Person--God, Holiness**: the third duty of God's people is to worship God.
1. Once the public service ended, Moses and the leaders obeyed God: they went up on Mt. Sinai to worship God (v.9). What these men experienced is one of the most amazing experiences described in all of Scripture. Three phenomenal facts are reported.

a. First, the leaders saw God (v.10). How could this be when Scripture says time and again that no person has ever seen God? No doubt what they saw was only a shadow, a faint resemblance of God. Scripture is clear: no person could ever see God in the splendor and brilliance of His glory and holiness. God's glory and holiness would consume and vaporize the person. This is exactly what Scripture declares:

> **"And he said, Thou canst not see my face: for there shall no man see me, and live" (Ex.33:20).**
> **"No man hath seen God at any time; the only begotten Son, which is in the bosom of the Father, he hath declared him" (Jn.1:18).**
> **"Who only hath immortality, dwelling in the light which no man can approach unto; whom no man hath seen, nor can see: to whom be honour and power everlasting. Amen" (1 Tim.6:16).**

b. Second, the leaders saw a dazzling pavement made of blue sapphire stone under God's feet (v.10ᵇ). The sapphire stone was as clear as the blue of the sky itself. What a beautiful sight this must have been: a glimpse of the splendor, brilliance, glory, and beauty of the spiritual world, of heaven itself, the very place where God Himself is. Note how Moses grasped after words to describe the scene, how inadequate human language is in describing the glory of heaven: he says that this *seemed to be* what it was; that it *was something like this*; that there *appeared to be* pavement made of brilliant blue sapphire stone. Moses and the leaders were unquestionably caught up in the glory and splendor of the sight, worshipping and praising God for all He is and for all He had done for His people.

    c. Third, God's glory did not strike the leaders dead (v.11). And again, it is emphasized that they *saw* God. The word "saw" (chazah) means an inward, spiritual, or prophetic vision.[1] It means to mentally see and contemplate with pleasure; to have a vision: beholding, looking, seeing something in one's mind.[2]

2. Note that the leaders ate a covenant meal before God. The meal symbolized the people's commitment and covenant with God. The meal sealed the covenant and commitment. It was probably during the meal and worship session that God revealed His glory to the leaders.

Thought 1. God calls us to come aside and worship Him. It is when we get all alone with God--away from the hustle and bustle of day-to-day activities--that God meets us and pours out His presence and glory upon us.

"Give unto the LORD the glory due unto his name; worship the LORD in the beauty of holiness" (Ps.29:2).

"O come, let us worship and bow down: let us kneel before the LORD our maker" (Ps.95:6).

"O worship the LORD in the beauty of holiness: fear before him, all the earth" (Ps.96:9).

"Exalt ye the LORD our God, and worship at his footstool; for he is holy" (Ps.99:5).

"God [is] a Spirit: and they that worship him must worship [him] in spirit and in truth" (Jn.4:24).

"And I saw another angel fly in the midst of heaven, having the everlasting gospel to preach unto them that dwell on the earth, and to every nation, and kindred, and tongue, and people, Saying with a loud voice, Fear God, and give glory to him; for the hour of his judgment is come: and worship him that made heaven, and earth, and the sea, and the fountains of waters" (Rev.14:6-7).

5 (24:12-18) **Law--Word of God--Glory, of God**: the fourth duty of God's people is to receive more and more of God's law, of God's Word.

1. God called Moses to come farther up the mountain and to prepare to stay for a long time. God was to give Moses the tablets of stone with more instruction, more laws and commands. Moses obeyed God and took Joshua with him (v.13).

But note: Moses did not neglect the people (v.14). Knowing that he was to be gone for a long time, he appointed Aaron and Hur to be in charge, to handle any dispute that might arise.

2. As Moses walked up the mountain, God's cloud of glory covered it. The wonderful, glorious presence of God (the Shekinah glory) settled on the mountain for six days. Now note the wonderful experience given to Moses, to this man who sought to receive more and more of God's Holy Word.

    a. Moses waited on the Lord, waited and waited day after day, and nothing happened. He waited for six long days--praying and praying (v.16).

    b. The voice of God finally called out to Moses on the seventh day (v.16[b]).

    c. The spectacular, awesome sight of God's glory looked like a consuming fire on top of the mountain (v.17). The Israelites, no doubt, stood in awe, utterly amazed and stricken with a sense of wonder and apprehension.

    d. Moses, God's dear servant, went up higher on the mountain, disappearing into the cloud. He went up to get alone with God (v.18). And he experienced the awesome glory of God and received more and more of God's Holy Word. Note how long he was in God's presence, for forty days and nights. Imagine being in God's holy presence and glory for forty days and nights! Imagine being fed the Word of God by God Himself for forty days and nights!

Thought 1. One of the great duties of believers is to get alone with God, to get alone for long periods of time, to seek more and more of God's holy presence and Word.

"But if from thence thou shalt seek the LORD thy God, thou shalt find him, if thou seek him with all thy heart and with all thy soul" (Dt.4:29).

"Seek the LORD and his strength, seek his face continually" (1 Chron.16:11).

"Seek ye the LORD while he may be found, call ye upon him while he is near" (Is.55:6).

"For thus saith the LORD unto the house of Israel, Seek ye me, and ye shall live" (Amos 5:4).

"Seek ye the LORD, all ye meek of the earth, which have wrought his judgment; seek righteousness, seek meekness: it may be ye shall be hid in the day of the LORD'S anger" (Zeph.2:3).

"And he spake a parable unto them to this end, that men ought always to pray, and not to faint" (Lk.18:1).

"These were more noble than those in Thessalonica, in that they received the word with all readiness of mind, and searched the scriptures daily, whether those things were so" (Acts 17:11).

"Study to show thyself approved unto God, a workman that needeth not to be ashamed, rightly dividing the word of truth" (2 Tim.2:15).

"As newborn babes, desire the sincere milk of the word, that ye may grow thereby: If so be ye have tasted that the Lord is gracious" (1 Pt.2:2-3).

---

[1] Frank E. Gaebelein. *The Expositor's Bible Commentary*, Vol. 2, p.450.
[2] James Strong. *Strong's Exhaustive Concordance of the Bible*. Hebrew number 2372.

Thought 2. Moses prayed for six days before he heard God speak. Many people quit praying if they do not get an immediate answer from God. Sometimes God does give quick answers to our prayers, but not always. We must patiently wait upon the Lord, persevere and endure in prayer.

"Ask, and it shall be given you; seek, and ye shall find; knock, and it shall be opened unto you" (Mt.7:7).

"And he spake a parable unto them to this end, that men ought always to pray, and not to faint" (Lk.18:1).

"Praying always with all prayer and supplication in the Spirit, and watching thereunto [being sleepless] with all perseverance and supplication for all saints" (Eph.6:18).

"Lead me in thy truth, and teach me: for thou art the God of my salvation; on thee do I wait all the day" (Ps.25:5).

"Wait on the LORD: be of good courage, and he shall strengthen thine heart: wait, I say, on the LORD" (Ps.27:14).

"My soul, wait thou only upon God; for my expectation is from him" (Ps.62:5).

"Behold, as the eyes of servants look unto the hand of their masters, and as the eyes of a maiden unto the hand of her mistress; so our eyes wait upon the LORD our God, until that he have mercy upon us" (Ps.123:2).

"Say not thou, I will recompense evil; but wait on the LORD, and he shall save thee" (Pr.20:22).

"But they that wait upon the LORD shall renew their strength; they shall mount up with wings as eagles; they shall run, and not be weary; and they shall walk, and not faint" (Is.40:31).

TYPES, SYMBOLS, AND PICTURES
(Exodus 24:1-18)

| The Law (Ex.24:12) | The law is a symbol of a schoolmaster or guardian who brings us to Jesus Christ.

"And the LORD said unto Moses, Come up to me into the mount, and be there: and I will give thee tables of stone, and a law, and commandments which I have written; that thou mayest teach them" (Ex.24:12). | One of the purposes for the law was to show a person that he is a law-breaker, that he is unrighteous, short of God's glory; therefore, a person needs a Savior.

Another way to say the same thing is this:
a. The law was to lead a person to Christ. The law does this by showing a person that he is utterly unable to secure righteousness by himself. (See outline & notes—Gal.3:23-25.)
b. We must look to Christ, the True Guardian, to bring us to God. Christ alone can give us righteousness and acceptance by God, that is, justification by faith.
c. Once Christ (faith in Him) has come, there is no need for the law nor for any other guardian. It is Christ and Christ alone who brings us face to face with God. | "But before faith came, we were kept under the law, shut up unto the faith which should afterwards be revealed. Wherefore the law was our schoolmaster to bring us unto Christ, that we might be justified by faith" (Gal.3:23-24).
"Therefore by the deeds of the law there shall no flesh be justified in his sight: for by the law is the knowledge of sin" (Ro.3:20).
"And by him all that believe are justified from all things, from which ye could not be justified by the law of Moses" (Acts 13:39).
"And be found in him, not having mine own righteousness, which is of the law, but that which is through the faith of Christ, the righteousness which is of God by faith" (Ph.3:9).
"Wherefore he is able also to save them to the uttermost that come unto God by him, seeing he ever liveth to make intercession for them. For such an high priest became us, who is holy, harmless, undefiled, separate from sinners, and made higher than the heavens" (Heb.7:25-26). |

DIVISION IX

THE TABERNACLE, ITS BLUEPRINT AND PRIESTHOOD: THE TRUE WAY TO APPROACH AND WORSHIP GOD, 25:1-31:18

(25:1-31:18) **DIVISION OVERVIEW--Tabernacle--Symbolism--Jesus Christ, Fulfills Symbolism**: the Tabernacle was the worship center of the Israelites during their *wilderness wanderings*. The Tabernacle was actually a large, beautiful, portable tent, built so it could be easily pitched and taken down.

1. The Tabernacle was the worship center of the Israelites for a long, long time: almost *five hundred years* from Moses to David--until Solomon's temple was built.

2. A large portion of God's Holy Word is dedicated to the Tabernacle: *fifty entire chapters*. Thirteen chapters in the book of Exodus discuss the Tabernacle and its priesthood. Eighteen chapters of Leviticus center on the sacrificial system of the Tabernacle. Two chapters of Deuteronomy are set aside for the study of the Tabernacle. In the New Testament, the Tabernacle is discussed in four of the thirteen chapters in the book of Hebrews, over 30% of the entire book. Note the proportion of Exodus given over to the study of the Tabernacle:
   ⇒ The deliverance of Israel from Egypt consists of fourteen chapters (1-14).
   ⇒ The wilderness wanderings from the Red Sea to Mount Sinai consist of only five chapters (15-19).
   ⇒ The giving of the Law consists of only five chapters (20-24).
   ⇒ The instructions, the construction, and the setting up of the Tabernacle consist of thirteen chapters (25-31 and 35-40).

3. The Tabernacle was the worship center for the Israelites, but it was also used by God as a great object lesson, as a great teaching tool. The Tabernacle was full of symbols, types, pictures, and shadows that point to spiritual truths for the believer. The symbolism of the Tabernacle is significant, very significant. However in looking at symbolic meanings, we must be careful to guard against the extreme of so many interpreters.
   ⇒ There are well known and respected commentaries that find specific meanings for everything mentioned in the Tabernacle. Often, it seems that these commentaries are making an attempt to force a meaning upon a particular term.
   ⇒ At the other end of the interpretation spectrum, there are just as many respected commentaries that focus only on the historical purpose of the Tabernacle. These commentaries acknowledge very few, if any, symbolic teachings from the Tabernacle.

What are we to make of these two extremes? It is the duty of every believer and sincere Bible scholar to be true to God's Word. The Bible is full of symbols, pictures, and shadows waiting to be studied and taught without having to make them up. It will be our goal...
   • to allow the Bible to speak for itself
   • to allow "Scripture to interpret Scripture"
   • to draw out useful, significant, and practical application
   • to study, with the Holy Spirit as our guide, the design that God showed Moses

4. God's Holy Spirit inspired Moses to write down *everything* that God's people would need in order to know how God wanted to be approached and worshipped. The Tabernacle and its priesthood were teaching tools for almost five hundred years. The Tabernacle was a picture, an object lesson, the focal point of life for God's people--from the time of Moses until Solomon's Temple. The people of that time could only faintly appreciate the message, the reality that stood behind the symbols and shadows. Israel had to settle for an abstract, imperfect Tabernacle that was made with human hands. The believer today has a much better perspective of the great plan of redemption that was spelled out in the Tabernacle. We are no longer limited to a mere shadow of the Tabernacle and its priesthood; we have the reality of the Tabernacle's message, the very person to whom the Tabernacle pointed, the Lord Jesus Christ, the Savior and Redeemer of the world.

> "Which are a shadow of things to come; but the body *is* of Christ" (Col.2:17).
> "Who serve unto the example and shadow of heavenly things, as Moses was admonished of God when he was about to make the tabernacle: for, See, saith he, *that* thou make all things according to the pattern showed to thee in the mount" (Heb.8:5).
> "*It was* therefore necessary that the patterns of things in the heavens should be purified with these; but the heavenly things themselves with better sacrifices than these. For Christ is not entered into the holy places made with hands, *which are* the figures of the true; but into heaven itself, now to appear in the presence of God for us....So Christ was once offered to bear the sins of many; and unto them that look for him shall he appear the second time without sin unto salvation" (Heb.9:23-24, 28).

"For the law having a shadow of good things to come, and not the very image of the things, can never with those sacrifices which they offered year by year continually make the comers thereunto perfect. For then would they not have ceased to be offered? because that the worshippers once purged should have had no more conscience of sins. But in those sacrifices there is a remembrance again made of sins every year. For it is not possible that the blood of bulls and of goats should take away sins. Wherefore when he cometh into the world, he saith, Sacrifice and offering thou wouldest not, but a body hast thou prepared me....Then said he, Lo, I come to do thy will, O God. He taketh away the first, that he may establish the second. By the which will we are sanctified through the offering of the body of Jesus Christ once for all. And every priest standeth daily ministering and offering oftentimes the same sacrifices, which can never take away sins: But this man, after he had offered one sacrifice for sins for ever, sat down on the right hand of God" (Heb.10:1-5, 9-12).

5. The Tabernacle symbolizes or pictures three major things. The symbols and pictures will be clearly seen as each portion of Scripture is studied.
   a. The Tabernacle symbolizes or pictures the ministry of Jesus Christ. The materials used to construct the Tabernacle are pictures of God's redemption in Jesus Christ. The various furnishings show God's great plan of salvation for the repentant sinner. The Tabernacle of Moses reveals every aspect of Jesus Christ and His work as the Word who became flesh and dwelt ("tabernacled") among us (Jn.1:14).
   b. The Tabernacle symbolizes or pictures the ministry of the church. The Tabernacle was a worship center in which God dwelt, and the Tabernacle stood as a witness to the world. So does the church. God's presence and witness dwell within the church in two ways:
   ⇒ God's Spirit dwells within believers.

   "What? know ye not that your body is the temple of the Holy Ghost which is in you, which ye have of God, and ye are not your own? For ye are bought with a price: therefore glorify God in your body, and in your spirit, which are God's" (1 Cor.6:19-20).

   ⇒ God's Spirit dwells among--within the very presence of--believers when two or three of them gather together.

   "For where two or three are gathered together in my name, there am I in the midst of them" (Mt.18:20).
   "Know ye not that ye [plural, referring to the church, the body or assembly of believers] are the temple of God, and that the Spirit of God dwelleth in you?" (1 Cor.3:16).
   "In whom ye [plural] also are builded together for an habitation of God through the Spirit" (Eph.2:22).

   c. The Tabernacle symbolizes or pictures the Christian believer, the person who truly follows God. The Tabernacle was the dwelling place for God's presence upon earth, standing as a strong witness to the LORD. The believer--his body--is the very temple of God, the sanctuary and dwelling place for the presence and witness of God upon earth.

   "I in them, and thou in me, that they may be made perfect in one; and that the world may know that thou hast sent me, and hast loved them, as thou hast loved me" (Jn.17:23).
   "What? know ye not that your body is the temple of the Holy Ghost which is in you, which ye have of God, and ye are not your own? For ye are bought with a price: therefore glorify God in your body, and in your spirit, which are God's" (1 Cor.6:19-20).
   "And what agreement hath the temple of God with idols? for ye are the temple of the living God; as God hath said, I will dwell in them, and walk in them; and I will be their God, and they shall be my people" (2 Cor.:16).
   "I am crucified with Christ: nevertheless I live; yet not I, but Christ liveth in me: and the life which I now live in the flesh I live by the faith of the Son of God, who loved me, and gave himself for me" (Gal.2:20).
   "To whom God would make known what is the riches of the glory of this mystery among the Gentiles; which is Christ in you, the hope of glory" (Col.1:27).
   "Your life is hid with Christ in God" (Col.3:3).

The excellent Bible expositor Stephen Olford says this about the Tabernacle's parallel to the Christian believer:

"In a remarkable way, the entire person of the Christian represents the three compartments of the Tabernacle. The body corresponds to the outer court: it is the outer and visible part of our personality; it is the place of sacrifice and cleansing (see Romans 12:1-2; 1 John 1:7,9). The soul answers to the holy place, and therefore is that aspect of our personality which worships and enjoys fellowship with other believers, eating at the table, walking in the light, and interceding in prayer. The spirit speaks of the believer's inner holy of holies--the deepest hidden life, the individual and personal communion of one sheltered under the blood (John 4:23; Romans 1:9); it is the place of spiritual victory. As such, the Tabernacle speaks of the whole ministry of the New Testament Christian."[1]

---
[1] Stephen Olford. *The Tabernacle, Camping With God.* (Neptune, NJ: Loizeaux Brothers, 1971), p.23.

6. There was the great purpose of the Tabernacle. The purpose of the Tabernacle was twofold.
   a. Its short-term purpose was to build God a sanctuary where God might be worshipped and be able to live among His people.

> **"And let them make me a sanctuary; that I may dwell among them" (Ex.25:8).**
> **"And there I will meet with thee, and I will commune with thee from above the mercy seat, from between the two cherubims which** *are* **upon the ark of the testimony, of all** *things* **which I will give thee in commandment unto the children of Israel" (Ex.25:22).**

   b. The long-term purpose of the Tabernacle was to arouse God's people to look at the promised Messiah who would come and fulfill every picture of the Tabernacle within Himself. Through the life of Jesus Christ, God's people would no longer have to settle for a pattern made with human hands. Jesus Christ is the true Tabernacle who came to Tabernacle--"camp out, dwell, live among"--people.

> **"And the Word was made flesh, and dwelt [tabernacled] among us, (and we beheld his glory, the glory as of the only begotten of the Father,) full of grace and truth" (Jn.1:14).**
> **"God, who at sundry times and in divers manners spake in time past unto the fathers by the prophets, Hath in these last days spoken unto us by** *his* **Son, whom he hath appointed heir of all things, by whom also he made the worlds; Who being the brightness of** *his* **glory, and the express image of his person, and upholding all things by the word of his power, when he had by himself purged our sins, sat down on the right hand of the Majesty on high" (Heb.1:1-3).**

7. The word "tabernacle" (mishkan) means dwelling place, a tent, a place of habitation, a residence. The root word means to *pitch a tent*. The picture of the tabernacle is graphic:
   ⇒ God literally pitched His tent, the tabernacle, among His people, the Israelites.
   ⇒ Jesus Christ pitched His tent, the tabernacle of His body, and He lived and dwelt among us.

8. The message of the tabernacle is graphically illustrated by expositor Stephen Olford. He says:

"The message of the tabernacle...can be summed up in a twofold proposition:
   "God's appearance to man in grace.
   "Man's approach to God in faith.
"It is of very great significance that in giving the instructions for the construction of the tabernacle, God begins with the ark and concludes with the brazen altar; whereas in the use of the tabernacle, man commences with the brazen altar and moves through to the holy of holies and ark of the covenant. That is the Christian gospel.
"Christianity is unique in that it is the only religion which claims that God has taken the initiative in revealing Himself to man. All other religions describe man's search after God. But having revealed Himself to man by leaving His throne and humbling Himself unto death--even the death of the cross--God has effected a plan of salvation for man to approach Him by faith. That simple way of salvation is beautifully illustrated in seven steps, which we shall consider in more detail later.
"For the present, let us note that the penitent sinner who comes by faith there is:
"a. *The Way of Introduction* - The gate of the outer court. Jesus said: 'Enter ye in at the strait gate...because strait is the gate, and narrow is the way, which leadeth unto life' (Matthew 7:13-14).
"b. *The Way of Reconciliation* - the brazen altar. 'God was in Christ, reconciling the world unto Himself....For He hath made Him to be sin for us, who knew son sin; that we might be made the righteousness of God in Him' (2 Corinthians 5:19, 21).
"c. *The Way of Separation* - the laver. Speaking to His disciples Jesus said: 'He that is washed needeth not save to wash his feet, but is clean every whit' (John 13:10). Later He said: 'Now ye are clean through the word which I have spoken unto you' (John 15:3).
"d. *The Way of Illumination* - the golden candlestick. Jesus said: 'I am the light of the world: he that followeth Me shall not walk in darkness, but shall have the light of life" (John 8:12).
"e. *The Way of Satisfaction* - the table of showbread. Jesus said: 'I am the bread of life: he that cometh to Me shall never hunger; and he that believeth on Me shall never thirst' (John 6:35).
"f. *The Way of Intercession* - the altar of incense. 'By Him therefore let us offer the sacrifice of praise to God continually, that is, the fruit of our lips giving thanks to His name' (Hebrews 13:15).
"g. *The Way of Communion* - the ark of the covenant. 'Truly our fellowship is with the Father, and with His Son Jesus Christ' (1 John 1:3)."[2]

---

[2] Stephen Olford. *The Tabernacle, Camping With God*, p.23-25.

PLEASE NOTE THE
RESOURCE CHART SECTION:

The following charts on the Tabernacle are given in the Resource Chart Section at the conclusion of Ex.40:1-38. This is done to keep from interrupting a person's study of the Scripture outlines and commentary. A study of the Charts will help the reader more fully grasp the meaning of the Tabernacle.

Chart 1: **THE PICTURE OF THE BELIEVER'S LIFE IN THE TABERNACLE**

Chart 2: **HOW CHRIST FULFILLED THE SYMBOLISM OF THE TABERNACLE**

Chart 3: **HOW CHRIST FULFILLED THE SYMBOLISM OF THE PRIESTHOOD**

DIVISION IX

THE TABERNACLE, ITS BLUEPRINT AND PRIESTHOOD: THE TRUE WAY TO APPROACH AND WORSHIP GOD, 25:1-31:18

A. The Materials Needed to Construct the Tabernacle: God's Call to Stewardship, to Give from a Willing Heart, 25:1-9

B. The Ark or Chest of God: the Symbol of the Very Throne and Presence of God, 25:10-22

C. The Table of Showbread: The Symbol of God Himself as the Bread of Life, 25:23-30

D. The Gold Lampstand, the Symbol of God Himself as the Light of the World, 25:31-40

E. The Tabernacle Itself: The Symbol of God Dwelling Among His People and of Man's Need to Approach God Exactly as God Dictates, Ex.26:1-37

F. The Altar of Burnt Offering, The Court of the Tabernacle, and The Lampstand: All Symbolizing The True Way to Approach God, Ex. 27:1-21

G. The Garments of the Priests: The Symbol of Bringing Dignity and Honor to the Name of God, Ex. 28:1-43

H. The Dedication, Consecration, and Ordination of the Priests: God's Qualifications for Leadership, Ex.29:1-46

I. The Altar of Incense: The Symbol of the Prayers and Communion of God's People Ascending to God: Ex.30:1-10

J. Other Instructions for the Tabernacle: Symbolizing Spiritual Health and Maturity, Ex.30:11-38

K. Other Instructions For the Tabernacle: Three Great Charges Given to Man, Ex.31:1-18

	IX. THE TABERNACLE, ITS BLUEPRINT AND PRIESTHOOD: THE TRUE WAY TO AP-PROACH AND WOR-SHIP GOD, EX.25:1-31:18	which ye shall take of them; gold, and silver, and brass, 4 And blue, and purple, and scarlet, and fine linen, and goats' hair, 5 And rams' skins dyed red, and badgers' skins, and shittim wood, 6 Oil for the light, spices for anointing oil, and for sweet incense, 7 Onyx stones, and stones to be set in the ephod, and in the breastplate.	a. Gold, silver, & bronze b. Blue, purple, & scarlet yarn, fine threaded linen, & goat hair c. Ram skins dyed red d. Badger (sea cow) skins e. Acacia wood f. Oil for light g. Spices for the anointing oil & for incense h. Onyx stones i. Gems to be set in the priests' ephod & breastpiece
	A. The Materials Needed to Construct the Tabernacle: God's Call to Stewardship, to Give from a Willing Heart, 25:1-9		

1. The architect of the tabernacle: God Himself
2. The supplier of the materials: The people
  a. Were to bring an offering
  b. Were to give willingly
3. The materials listed
	And the LORD spake unto Moses, saying,
	2 Speak unto the children of Israel, that they bring me an offering: of every man that giveth it willingly with his heart ye shall take my offering.
	3 And this is the offering
		8 And let them make me a sanctuary; that I may dwell among them.
		9 According to all that I show thee, after the pattern of the tabernacle, and the pattern of all the instruments thereof, even so shall ye make it.
			4. The purpose: to build a sanctuary so that God could dwell among His people
			5. The plan & design of the tabernacle: Dictated by God—God alone determines how a person is to approach Him

DIVISION IX

THE TABERNACLE, ITS BLUEPRINT AND PRIESTHOOD:
THE TRUE WAY TO APPROACH AND WORSHIP GOD, EX.25:1-31:18

A.   The Materials Needed to Construct the Tabernacle: God's Call to Stewardship, to Give from a Willing Heart, 25:1-9

(25:1-9) **Introduction--Man, Needs**: a place to meet God--this is one of the dire needs of man. When man is bombarded with the painful trials and sufferings of life, he needs the help that only God can give. He needs the help of God in facing the moments of...

- loneliness and despair
- emptiness and restlessness
- accident and disease
- suffering and pain
- hunger and thirst
- hopelessness and helplessness
- unemployment and poverty
- temptation and sin
- aging and dying

Man needs the presence and assurance of God all throughout life. He needs the security of God, to know that God loves and cares for him, that God is looking after him. But even more basic than all this, man needs the peace and reconciliation of God. Man needs to know that his sins are forgiven, that God accepts him and is going to receive him into heaven, life everlasting.

God knows that man has these needs. Therefore, God established a very special place for His people...
- a place where He could live among His people
- a place where a special manifestation of His presence would dwell
- a place where His people could come to Him for worship and help

That place was the Tabernacle. This is the focus of this passage: *The Materials Needed to Construct the Tabernacle: God's Call to Stewardship, to Give from a Willing Heart, Ex.25:1-9.*
1. The architect of the tabernacle: God Himself (v.1).
2. The supplier of the materials: the people (v.2).
3. The materials listed (v.3-7).
4. The purpose: to build a sanctuary so that God could dwell among His people (v.8).
5. The plan and design of the tabernacle: dictated by God—God alone determines how a person is to approach Him (v.9).

1 (25:1) **Tabernacle--Worship**: the architect of the Tabernacle was God Himself. When planning and constructing a building, the most important person is the architect. The architect is the person...
- who is the master builder
- who knows the science, rules, and principles of buildings and architecture
- who dreams and lays out the plan for the building
- who designs and works out the structure for the building
- who oversees and looks after the construction
- who inspects and approves the building

More than anyone else, the architect is responsible for the construction of a building. He determines whether a building stands or falls, functions or fails, is problem-free or loaded with problems, lasts or quickly needs repairs, brings joy to the users or arouses disappointment.

The Tabernacle was so important--so desperately needed by God's people--that God Himself chose to be the architect of the Tabernacle. He could not leave the design and structure of the Tabernacle in the hands of men. Why? Because the Tabernacle was...

- to be His dwelling place among men, the very place where God's presence was to be manifested among His people
- to be the special place where people would come to worship God
- to be the special place where people would learn about God

Only God knew what kind of building He needed and wanted for the manifestation of His presence, what kind of building He needed to receive man's worship, what kind of building He needed to teach people about Himself. No man knew. Therefore, God Himself had to be the architect of the Tabernacle.

"For this man [Christ Jesus] was counted worthy of more glory than Moses, inasmuch as he who hath builded the house hath more honour than the house" (Heb.3:3).

"O the depth of the riches both of the wisdom and knowledge of God! how unsearchable are his judgments, and his ways past finding out!" (Ro.11:33).

"One thing have I desired of the LORD, that will I seek after; that I may dwell in the house of the LORD all the days of my life, to behold the beauty of the LORD, and to inquire in his temple" (Ps.27:4).

"I was glad when they said unto me, Let us go into the house of the LORD" (Ps.122:1).

"And many people shall go and say, Come ye, and let us go up to the mountain of the LORD, to the house of the God of Jacob; and he will teach us of his ways, and we will walk in his paths: for out of Zion shall go forth the law, and the word of the LORD from Jerusalem" (Is.2:3).

2 (25:2) **Offerings--Stewardship--Giving--Gifts**: Who was to supply the materials to build the Tabernacle? The people. Moses was to take up offerings from the people, and the people were to give willingly and generously. The word for "offering" (terumah) has the idea of a present, a gift that is given sacrificially; the giving of a special gift, a valuable, costly gift.

Remember: the Israelites had been slaves in Egypt for about 400 years. As slaves, they had earned and accumulated little if any wealth. But now they had enough to give offerings to build the Tabernacle. Where had their wealth come from? From the Egyptians. Right before God freed the Israelites from Egypt, He had stirred within the Egyptians a desperate desire to get rid of the Israelites, a desperation so deep that they were willing to pay them just to get rid of them, willing to give their gold and silver and other wealth to the Israelites (Ex.11:2; 12:35-36). God had seen to it that the needs of His people were met. Thus they were now able to give offerings to build the Tabernacle.

The point is this: God had provided for the people. What they had was due to Him: they had money--gold, silver, and possessions--because God had moved upon the Egyptians to give them wealth. Now, they were to give some of the wealth back to Him:

⇒ give willingly
⇒ give sacrificially
⇒ give valuable, costly gifts

Thought 1. Note several important lessons.
1) Ultimately everything belongs to God. All that we have has come from Him.

"For every beast of the forest is mine, and the cattle upon a thousand hills" (Ps.50:10).
"The silver is mine, and the gold is mine, saith the LORD of hosts" (Hag.2:8).

2) The greatest thing we can give God is an undivided heart, totally yielded to Him.

"Lay not up for yourselves treasures upon earth, where moth and rust doth corrupt, and where thieves break through and steal: But lay up for yourselves treasures in heaven, where neither moth nor rust doth corrupt, and where thieves do not break through nor steal: For where your treasure is, there will your heart be also" (Mt.6:19-21).

"No man can serve two masters: for either he will hate the one, and love the other; or else he will hold to the one, and despise the other. Ye cannot serve God and mammon [money]" (Mt.6:24).

"And he said to [them] all, If any [man] will come after me, let him deny himself, and take up his cross daily, and follow me" (Lk.9:23).

3) Every person has something to offer to God. No matter how little a person may have, he has something that he can give to God.

"They gave after their ability unto the treasure of the work threescore and one thousand drams of gold, and five thousand pound of silver, and one hundred priests' garments" (Ezra 2:69).

"And I said unto them, We after our ability have redeemed our brethren the Jews, which were sold unto the heathen; and will ye even sell your brethren? or shall they be sold unto us? Then held they their peace, and found nothing *to answer*" (Neh.5:8).

"And there came a certain poor widow, and she threw in two mites, which make a farthing. And he called [unto him] his disciples, and saith unto them, Verily I say unto you, That this poor widow hath cast more in, than all they which have cast into the treasury" (Mk.12:42-43).

"Then the disciples, every man according to his ability, determined to send relief unto the brethren which dwelt in Judaea" (Acts 11:29).

4) We are to share with those who are in need.

"And all that believed were together, and had all things common; And sold their possessions and goods, and parted them to all *men,* as every man had need" (Acts 2:44-45).

"I have showed you all things, how that so labouring ye ought to support the weak, and to remember the words of the Lord Jesus, how he said, It is more blessed to give than to receive" (Acts 20:35).

"And a certain ruler asked him, saying, Good Master, what shall I do to inherit eternal life? And Jesus said unto him, Why callest thou me good? none [is] good, save one, [that is], God. Thou knowest the commandments, Do not commit adultery, Do not kill, Do not steal, Do not bear false witness, Honour thy father and thy mother. And he said, All these have I kept from my youth up. Now when Jesus heard these things, he said unto him, Yet lackest thou one thing: sell all that thou hast, and distribute unto the poor, and thou shalt have treasure in heaven: and come, follow me. And when he heard this, he was very sorrowful: for he was very rich. And when Jesus saw that he was very sorrowful, he said, How hardly shall they that have riches enter into the kingdom of God! For it is easier for a camel to go through a needle's eye, than for a rich man to enter into the kingdom of God" (Lk.18:18-25).

5) We are to give sacrificially, to give willingly and cheerfully.

"Neither was there any among them that lacked: for as many as were possessors of lands or houses sold them, and brought the prices of the things that were sold, And laid *them* down at the apostles' feet: and distribution was made unto every man according as he had need" (Acts 4:34-35).

"Every man according as he purposeth in his heart, *so let him give;* not grudgingly, or of necessity: for God loveth a cheerful giver" (2 Cor.9:7).

"Every man shall give as he is able, according to the blessing of the LORD thy God which he hath given thee" (Dt.16:17).

3 (25:3-7) **Tabernacle--Construction--Worship**: there were the materials for the Tabernacle. Throughout Scripture the Tabernacle is said to be full of rich symbolism, pointing in particular to Christ. Because of this...
- some writers strain to see a symbolic meaning or some type in everything
- other writers ignore and fail to point out the symbolism and types

When looking at symbolism and types, it is most important to always be true to Scripture. The Scripture must never be strained nor stretched to give some meaning that is not there. But on the other hand we must not be stubborn or opinionated when people see some symbolic meaning or type that is not specifically mentioned in Scripture. We must always keep this fact in mind: when a person looked at the Tabernacle, God wanted His people to think about certain spiritual truths. When a person saw the valuable metals and materials and the beautiful colors, God wanted the person's mind to focus upon spiritual things. There is, therefore, a richness of meaning and symbolism in the Tabernacle that is sometimes clear, although it is not specifically spelled out by Scripture. When the symbolic meaning is clear, it points the person to Christ and spiritual truth. Now, note the materials that were to be used in building the Tabernacle.
1. There was gold, silver, and bronze (v.3).
   a. Gold is a symbol of value, of the greatest and most precious value that can be possessed. In Scripture it is a symbol of the great value of the LORD Himself, of His deity and righteousness.

   "I counsel thee to buy of me gold [righteousness] tried in the fire, that thou mayest be rich; and white raiment, that thou mayest be clothed, and that the shame of thy nakedness do not appear; and anoint thine eyes with eyesalve, that thou mayest see" (Rev.3:18).
   "And thou shalt make a mercy seat of pure gold: two cubits and a half shall be the length thereof, and a cubit and a half the breadth thereof" (Ex.25:17).

   b. Silver is a symbol of redemption, of the soul being ransomed by the atonement money.

   "When thou takest the sum of the children of Israel after their number, then shall they give every man a ransom for his soul unto the LORD, when thou numberest them; that there be no plague among them, when thou numberest them. This they shall give, every one that passeth among them that are numbered, half a shekel after the shekel of the sanctuary: (a shekel is twenty gerahs:) an half shekel shall be the offering of the LORD. Every one that pas-

Bronze = Copper + Tin
Brass = Copper + Zinc **EXODUS 25:1-9**

seth among them that are numbered, from twenty years old and above, shall give an offering unto the LORD. The rich shall not give more, and the poor shall not give less than half a shekel, when they give an offering unto the LORD, to make an atonement for your souls. And thou shalt take the atonement money of the children of Israel, and shalt appoint it for the service of the tabernacle of the congregation; that it may be a memorial unto the children of Israel before the LORD, to make an atonement for your souls" (Ex.30:12-16).

"And those that are to be redeemed from a month old shalt thou redeem, according to thine estimation, for the money of five shekels, after the shekel of the sanctuary, which is twenty gerahs" (Num.18:16).

c. Bronze or copper is a symbol of the death of Christ, of His bearing the judgment of sin for man. This is seen in the brazen altar, the place where the lamb was slain as the sacrificial offering on behalf of the people.

"And thou shalt make his pans to receive his ashes, and his shovels, and his basons, and his fleshhooks, and his firepans: all the vessels thereof thou shalt make of brass" (Ex.27:3).

"And his feet like unto fine brass, as if they burned in a furnace; and his voice as the sound of many waters" (Rev.1:15).

2. There was blue, purple, and scarlet yarn and fine linen (v.4). This combination of colors was the main color scheme used in the Tabernacle. These main colors are mentioned about twenty-five times in the Book of Exodus alone.

a. Blue is the color of the heavens above; therefore, it is said to be the symbol of the heavenly character of Christ.

"For such an high priest became us, who is holy, harmless, undefiled, separate from sinners, and made higher than the heavens" (Heb.7:26).

b. Purple is the color of royalty; therefore, it is a symbol of Christ as the King of kings and LORD of lords.

"And they clothed him with purple, and platted a crown of thorns, and put it about his head, And began to salute him, Hail, King of the Jews!" (Mk.15:17-18).

"And he hath on his vesture and on his thigh a name written, KING OF KINGS, AND LORD OF LORDS" (Rev.19:16).

c. Scarlet (red) symbolizes sacrifice, picturing the entire scene of sacrifice and redemption. Jesus Christ is the Lamb of God, the One sacrificed to take away the sins of man.

"But Christ being come an high priest of good things to come, by a greater and more perfect tabernacle, not made with hands, that is to say, not of this building; Neither by the blood of goats and calves, but by his own blood he entered in once into the holy place, having obtained eternal redemption for us. For if the blood of bulls and of goats, and the ashes of an heifer sprinkling the unclean, sanctifieth to the purifying of the flesh: How much more shall the blood of Christ, who through the eternal Spirit offered himself without spot to God, purge your conscience from dead works to serve the living God?" (Heb.9:11-14).

"For when Moses had spoken every precept to all the people according to the law, he took the blood of calves and of goats, with water, and scarlet wool, and hyssop, and sprinkled both the book, and all the people, Saying, This is the blood of the testament which God hath enjoined unto you" (Heb.9:19-20).

"It was therefore necessary that the patterns of things in the heavens should be purified with these; but the heavenly things themselves with better sacrifices than these" (Heb.9:23).

"So Christ was once offered to bear the sins of many; and unto them that look for him shall he appear the second time without sin unto salvation" (Heb.9:28).

d. White linen symbolizes purity and righteousness, the purity, righteousness, and holiness of God and the purity and righteousness demanded by God.

"And to her was granted that she should be arrayed in fine linen, clean and white: for the fine linen is the righteousness of saints" (Rev.19:8).

"He that overcometh, the same shall be clothed in white raiment [righteousness]; and I will not blot out his name out of the book of life, but I will confess his name before my Father, and before his angels" (Rev.3:5).

"I counsel thee to buy of me gold tried in the fire, that thou mayest be rich; and white raiment [righteousness], that thou mayest be clothed [in righteousness], and that the shame of thy nakedness do not appear; and anoint thine eyes with eyesalve, that thou mayest see" (Rev.3:18).

"And round about the throne were four and twenty seats: and upon the seats I saw four and twenty elders sitting, clothed in white raiment [righteousness]; and they had on their heads crowns of gold" (Rev.4:4).

"After this I beheld, and, lo, a great multitude, which no man could number, of all nations, and kindreds, and people, and tongues, stood before the throne, and before the Lamb, clothed with white robes [righteousness], and palms in their hands" (Rev.7:9).

3. There was goat hair (izzim) (v.4) which was to be used for the tent's covering (see Ex.26:7). These curtains of goat hair were mostly likely black in color. A set of eleven curtains were joined together to make one great covering for the tent. There seems to be a direct symbolism between the goat hair and Christ's relationship to sin, pointing to Christ as the sin-bearer appointed by God to bear the sins of the world. Stephen Olford comments about the significance of the goat in Scripture:

"...the goat, in Scripture, is mentioned in connection with the sin offering and sinners. We read: 'Take ye a kid of the goats for a sin offering' (Leviticus 9:3). 'Take...two kids of the goats for a sin offering' on the great Day of Atonement (Leviticus 16:5-28). 'One kid of the goats for a sin offering unto the LORD shall be offered' (Numbers 28:15). 'He shall separate them one from another, as a shepherd divideth his sheep from the goats'--representing the saved and the unsaved at the judgment of the nations (Matthew 25:32). So it is fairly clear that the tent of goat's hair speaks of the Lord Jesus as the divine Sin-bearer."[1]

Thought 1: Jesus Christ became the "scapegoat" for the world. Instead of allowing the sting of sin to rest upon sinners, Jesus Christ offered Himself up as a Sacrifice, as the Substitute and Savior of the world, as the sin-bearer for the sins of all people of all generations.

"**Therefore will I divide him** *a portion* **with the great, and he shall divide the spoil with the strong; because he hath poured out his soul unto death: and he was numbered with the transgressors; and he bare the sin of many, and made intercession for the transgressors**" (Is.53:12).
"**Who gave himself for our sins, that he might deliver us from this present evil world, according to the will of God and our Father**" (Gal.1:4).
"**So Christ was once offered to bear the sins of many; and unto them that look for him shall he appear the second time without sin unto salvation**" (Heb.9:28).
"**Who his own self bare our sins in his own body on the tree, that we, being dead to sins, should live unto righteousness: by whose stripes ye were healed**" (1 Pt.2:24).
"**And ye know that he was manifested to take away our sins; and in him is no sin**" (1 Jn.3:5).
"**And from Jesus Christ,** *who is* **the faithful witness,** *and* **the first begotten of the dead, and the prince of the kings of the earth. Unto him that loved us, and washed us from our sins in his own blood**" (Rev.1:5).

4. There were ram skins dyed red (v.5). The Expositor's Bible Commentary describes these ram skins as *"skins that had all the wool removed and then were dyed red; it was like our morocco leather."* [2] The purpose of these tanned ram skins was to provide a protective covering for the tent. It was layered between the goat hair and the badger (or sea cow) skins. (For more discussion, see Ex.36:19.)
5. There were badger (sea cow) skins (v.5). The source of this outer covering for the Tabernacle probably came from the Red Sea.[3] This durable, weather-resistant skin was the ideal choice to protect the tent from the hot sun, the drenching rains, and the piercing dust storms that swept across the desert.
6. There was acacia wood (v.5). Acacia or Shittim was an area in the plains of Moab, slightly northeast of the Dead Sea. Acacia wood came from a tree that flourished in the wilderness. Acacia was an extremely hard wood that was a mixture of brown and orange in color. During the period of the Old Testament, the tree was very plentiful as it grew in groves next to fast-moving bodies of water. It was the craftsman's prime choice for furniture because of its durability. The Septuagint (the Greek translation of the Hebrew Old Testament) translates acacia as "incorruptible" wood.

Thought 1: In a world filled with corruption, Jesus Christ is the only person who is incorruptible. As the acacia tree speaks of durability and strength, Jesus Christ is the epitome of durability and strength. Jesus Christ is the only Man strong enough...
- to live a sinless life and take away our sins
- to defeat sin and death on the Cross

"**And ye know that he was manifested to take away our sins; and in him is no sin**" (1 Jn.3:5).
"**Who his own self bare our sins in his own body on the tree, that we, being dead to sins, should live unto righteousness: by whose stripes ye were healed**" (1 Pt.2:24).

7. There was oil for light (v.6). The oil was made by crushing the olives from olive trees. The oil would be needed to provide continuous light for the sanctuary with the golden lampstand (see Ex.27:20). Throughout Scripture, the olive tree is a symbol of fulness and fruitfulness, a choice tree among people. Thus the oil is a symbol of the fulness and fruitfulness of God's Spirit, a symbol of the anointing of God's Spirit.

"**But the anointing which ye have received of him abideth in you, and ye need not that any man teach you: but as the same anointing teacheth you of all things, and is truth, and is no lie, and even as it hath taught you, ye shall abide in him**" (1 Jn.2:27).
"**But the olive tree said unto them, Should I leave my fatness, wherewith by me they honour God and man, and go to be promoted over the trees?**" (Judg.9:9).

1 Stephen Olford. *The Tabernacle, Camping With God,* p.80-81.
2 Frank E. Gaebelein. *The Expositor's Bible Commentary*, Vol. 2, p.453.
3 ibid., Vol.2, p.453.

"But I am like a green olive tree in the house of God: I trust in the mercy of God for ever and ever" (Ps.52:8).

"The LORD called thy name, A green olive tree, fair, and of goodly fruit: with the noise of a great tumult he hath kindled fire upon it, and the branches of it are broken" (Jer.11:16).

"His branches shall spread, and his beauty shall be as the olive tree, and his smell as Lebanon" (Hos.14:6).

8. There were spices for the anointing oil and for incense (v.6. See Ex.30:22-25 for the list of ingredients that made the anointing oil. See Ex.30:34-38 for the four spices used in making the incense.)

9. There were onyx stones (v.7). These were semi-precious stones. The color of these stones is uncertain. The Scriptures are clear on their purpose: to be used on the priests' ephod and breastpiece. (See Ex.28:6-25 for more discussion on the purpose of these stones.) The Hebrew word for "onyx" (shoh-ham) comes from a root word meaning a flashing forth of splendor. The names of the twelve tribes of Israel were to be inscribed on the two onyx stones. The picture is this: in God's eyes, His people shine forth in splendor, as precious gems.

10. There were gems to be set in the priests' ephod and breastpiece (v.7).

4 (25:8) **Tabernacle--Worship--God, Presence of**: God had one main purpose for building the Tabernacle, that He might dwell in a very special way among His people.

The word "sanctuary" (miqdash) means a holy place, a hallowed place, a place sanctified or set apart for God. God wanted the Tabernacle to be a holy, hallowed place...

- a place sanctified or set apart for God
- a place looked upon as being where God dwelt in a very special way
- a place where God could live in a special way among His people
- a place where God met with people and people with God
- a place where people worshipped God, received the forgiveness of God, and committed their lives to God

Note that God took the initiative to build a relationship with Israel. God longs to be with His people, to fellowship and commune with them. How can He do this? By planning a special place where He can meet with people and people can come to meet with Him. In dealing with the ancient Israelites, that place was the Tabernacle, the sanctuary.

Thought 1. The believer's body is now the temple, the sanctuary of God. We are therefore to sanctify, to set apart our bodies to live holy and righteous lives. Our bodies are to be fit sanctuaries, "holy places" in which the Spirit of God can live. (See outline and notes for the church as the temple of God--1 Cor.3:16.)

"Know ye not that ye are the temple of God, and that the Spirit of God dwelleth in you? If any man defile the temple of God, him shall God destroy; for the temple of God is holy, which temple ye are" (1 Cor.3:16-17).

"And ye are Christ's; and Christ is God's" (1 Cor.3:23).

"What? know ye not that your body is the temple of the Holy Ghost which is in you, which ye have of God, and ye are not your own? For ye are bought with a price: therefore glorify God in your body, and in your spirit, which are God's" (1 Cor.6:19-20).

"Having therefore these promises, dearly beloved, let us cleanse ourselves from all filthiness of the flesh and spirit, perfecting holiness in the fear of God" (2 Cor.7:1).

"For I am the LORD that bringeth you up out of the land of Egypt, to be your God: ye shall therefore be holy, for I am holy" (Lev.11:45).

"That he would grant unto us, that we being delivered out of the hand of our enemies might serve him without fear, In holiness and righteousness before him, all the days of our life" (Lk.1:74-75).

"Follow peace with all men, and holiness, without which no man shall see the Lord" (Heb.12:14).

"But as he which hath called you is holy, so be ye holy in all manner of conversation; Because it is written, Be ye holy; for I am holy" (1 Pt.1:15-16).

5 (25:9) **Tabernacle--Worship**: the pattern or model of the Tabernacle was dictated by God. God alone determines how a person is to approach Him.

This is the first time the word "tabernacle" is used in Scripture. The word "tabernacle" (mishkan) means a dwelling place, a habitation, a residence, a tent. The picture is that of God pitching His tent among His people and living in a very special way with them. Note that the Tabernacle is God's tent, God's residence. The point is emphatic: since the Tabernacle is His residence, He alone has the right to plan and design the Tabernacle with all its furnishings. This is exactly what this verse says: "I will show you"--show you the plan and design.

Thought 1. The application is clear: the Tabernacle was the place where a person approached God, where a person came to meet God. God alone determines how a person is to approach Him. There is only one approach, only one way to God: that way is through His Son, the Lord Jesus Christ.

"For God so loved the world, that he gave his only begotten Son, that whosoever believeth in him should not perish, but have everlasting life. For God sent not his Son into the world to condemn the world; but that the world through him might be saved. He that believeth on him is not condemned: but he that believeth not is condemned already, because he hath not believed in the name of the only begotten Son of God" (Jn.3:16-18).

"Then Simon Peter answered him, Lord, to whom shall we go? thou [alone] hast the words of eternal life" (Jn.6:68).

"I said therefore unto you, that ye shall die in your sins: for if ye believe not that I am [he], ye shall die in your sins" (Jn.8:24).

"I am the door: by me if any man enter in, he shall be saved, and shall go in and out, and find pasture" (Jn.10:9).

"Jesus saith unto him, I am the way, the truth, and the life: no man cometh unto the Father, but by me" (Jn.14:6).

"Neither is there salvation in any other: for there is none other name under heaven given among men, whereby we must be saved" (Acts 4:12).

Thought 2. God has come to earth to dwell among us in the person of Jesus Christ. In Christ, God has come to. We can now meet God by coming to Christ, and God can meet us when we approach Him through Christ. People and God meet together in the sanctuary, the holy person of His Son, the Lord Jesus Christ.

"And the Word was made flesh, and dwelt among us, (and we beheld his glory, the glory as of the only begotten of the Father,) full of grace and truth" (Jn.1:14; cp. Jn.2:19-22).

"Jesus saith unto him, I am the way, the truth, and the life: no man cometh unto the Father, but by me" (Jn.14:6).

"Neither is there salvation in any other: for there is none other name under heaven given among men, whereby we must be saved" (Acts 4:12).

"For other foundation can no man lay than that is laid, which is Jesus Christ" (1 Cor.3:11).

"Wherefore he is able also to save them to the uttermost that come unto God by him, seeing he ever liveth to make intercession for them" (Heb.7:25).

"But Christ being come an high priest of good things to come, by a greater and more perfect tabernacle, not made with hands, that is to say, not of this building; Neither by the blood of goats and calves, but by his own blood he entered in once into the holy place, having obtained eternal redemption for us. For if the blood of bulls and of goats, and the ashes of an heifer sprinkling the unclean, sanctifieth to the purifying of the flesh: How much more shall the blood of Christ, who through the eternal Spirit offered himself without spot to God, purge your conscience from dead works to serve the living God?" (Heb.9:11-14).

TYPES, SYMBOLS, AND PICTURES
(Exodus 25:1-9)

Historical Term	Type or Picture (Scriptural Basis for Each)	Life Application for Today's Believer	Biblical Application for Today's Believer
Badger (sea cow) skins (Ex.25:5)	*The badger skins acted as a protective shield for the Tabernacle. This outer covering gave protection against the wind-swept desert sands, the beating sun, and the occasional rains. The protection of the badger skins against the harsh wilderness symbolized a protective separation from the world.* *"And he made a covering for the tent of rams' skins dyed red, and a covering of badgers' skins above that"* (Ex.36:19).	a. Jesus Christ protects the believer from the world. Christ protects us from the elements of... • emptiness • loneliness • fear • guilt • sin • evil • death b. Jesus Christ is our protective separation from the world. Jesus Christ protects us from the world's perils and temptations. Jesus Christ protects us... • by sanctifying us, setting us apart to God • by sanctifying us with His Word • by watching over us with loving eyes • by surrounding us with His presence	*"And be not conformed to this world: but be ye transformed by the renewing of your mind, that ye may prove what is that good, and acceptable, and perfect, will of God"* (Ro.12:2). *"I have given them thy word; and the world hath hated them, because they are not of the world, even as I am not of the world. I pray not that thou shouldest take them out of the world, but that thou shouldest keep them from the evil. They are not of the world, even as I am not of the world. Sanctify them through thy truth: thy word is truth"* (Jn.17:14-17). *"If ye were of the world, the world would love his own: but because ye are not of the world, but I have chosen you out of the world, therefore the world*

Historical Term	Type or Picture (Scriptural Basis for Each)	Life Application for Today's Believer	Biblical Application for Today's Believer
			hateth you" (Jn.15:19). *"No man that warreth entangleth himself with the affairs of this life; that he may please him who hath chosen him to be a soldier" (2 Tim.2:4).* *"By faith Moses, when he was come to years, refused to be called the son of Pharaoh's daughter; Choosing rather to suffer affliction with the people of God, than to enjoy the pleasures of sin for a season" (Heb.11:24-25).* *"Love not the world, neither the things that are in the world. If any man love the world, the love of the Father is not in him" (1 Jn.2:15).*
Onyx stones (Ex.25:7)	*The onyx stones were placed in the ephod that was worn by the High Priest as he ministered to the LORD in the Tabernacle. The onyx stones symbolized the High Priest representing and carrying the name of God's people before the LORD as their mediator and intercessor.* **"Onyx stones, and stones to be set in the ephod, and in the breastplate" (Ex.25:7).**	⇒ In God's eyes, His people shine forth in splendor, as precious, priceless gems. Jesus Christ, our great High Priest, always intercedes for us and carries the names of <u>believers</u> before God. But a person must bring his needs to Christ in order for Christ to act as our Mediator before God.	*"Wherefore he is able also to save them to the uttermost that come unto God by him, seeing he ever liveth to make intercession for them" (Heb.7:25).* *"Seeing then that we have a great high priest, that is passed into the heavens, Jesus the Son of God, let us hold fast our profession. For we have not an high priest which cannot be touched with the feeling of our infirmities; but was in all points tempted like as we are, yet without sin. Let us therefore come boldly unto the throne of grace, that we may obtain mercy, and find grace to help in time of need" (Heb.4:14-16).* *"Since thou wast precious in my sight, thou hast been honourable, and I have loved thee" (Is.43:4).* *"Now therefore, if ye will obey my voice indeed, and keep my covenant, then ye shall be a peculiar treasure unto me above all people: for all the earth is mine" (Ex.19:5).* *"For the LORD hath chosen Jacob unto himself, and Israel for his peculiar treasure" (Ps.135:4).*

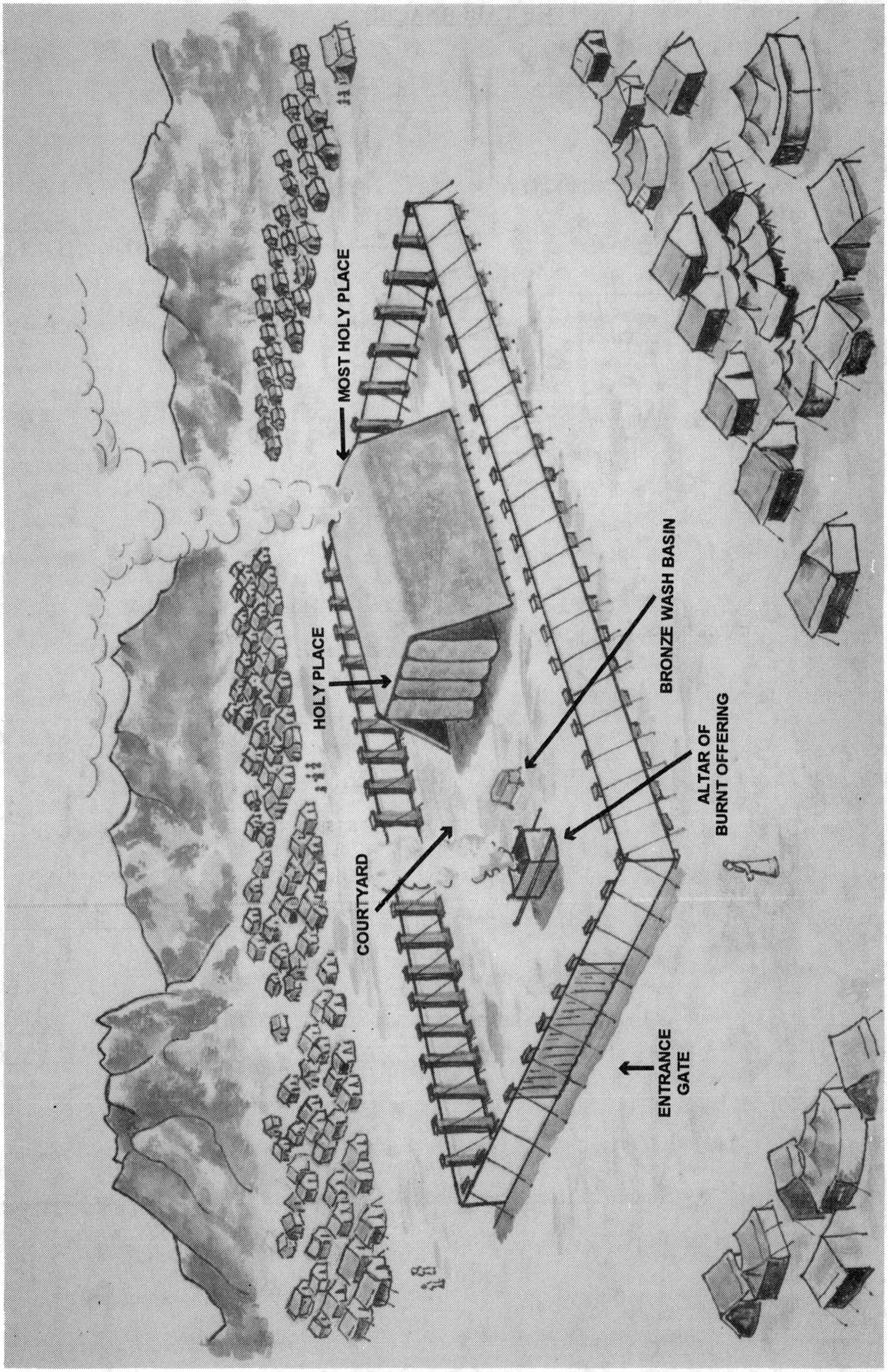

MOST HOLY PLACE

HOLY PLACE

COURTYARD

BRONZE WASH BASIN

ALTAR OF
BURNT OFFERING

ENTRANCE
GATE

THE TABERNACLE IN THE WILDERNESS

THE TABERNACLE

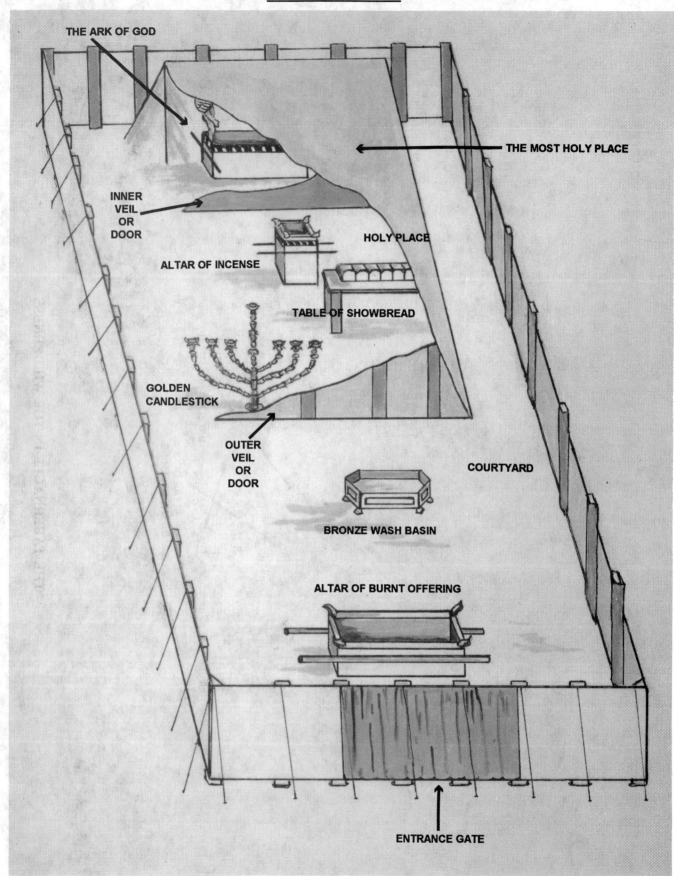

| 1. The Ark, the sacred throne & chest of God Himself
  a. To make it of acacia wood
  b. To make it 3¾' x 2¼' x 2¼' (1.1 meters by .07 meters by .07 meters)

  c. To overlay it with pure gold (inside & out) & to use a pure gold molding

  d. To cast four gold rings & attach them to the four corners of the Ark

  e. To make two poles of acacia wood & overlay them with gold
  f. To insert the poles into the gold rings on the Ark for the purpose of carrying it: The poles were never to be removed

  g. To put the Testimony of God, the Ten Commandments, into the Ark (cp. v.21)
2. The Mercy Seat or Atonement Cover for the Ark | **B. The Ark or Chest of God: The Symbol of the Very Throne and Presence of God, 25:10-22**

10 And they shall make an ark of shittim wood: two cubits and a half shall be the length thereof, and a cubit and a half the breadth thereof, and a cubit and a half the height thereof.
11 And thou shalt overlay it with pure gold, within and without shalt thou overlay it, and shalt make upon it a crown of gold round about.
12 And thou shalt cast four rings of gold for it, and put them in the four corners thereof; and two rings shall be in the one side of it, and two rings in the other side of it.
13 And thou shalt make staves of shittim wood, and overlay them with gold.
14 And thou shalt put the staves into the rings by the sides of the ark, that the ark may be borne with them.
15 The staves shall be in the rings of the ark: they shall not be taken from it.
16 And thou shalt put into the ark the testimony which I shall give thee.
17 And thou shalt make a mercy seat of pure gold: two | cubits and a half shall be the length thereof, and a cubit and a half the breadth thereof.
18 And thou shalt make two cherubims of gold, of beaten work shalt thou make them, in the two ends of the mercy seat.
19 And make one cherub on the one end, and the other cherub on the other end: even of the mercy seat shall ye make the cherubims on the two ends thereof.
20 And the cherubims shall stretch forth their wings on high, covering the mercy seat with their wings, and their faces shall look one to another; toward the mercy seat shall the faces of the cherubims be.
21 And thou shalt put the mercy seat above upon the ark; and in the ark thou shalt put the testimony that I shall give thee.
22 And there I will meet with thee, and I will commune with thee from above the mercy seat, from between the two cherubims which are upon the ark of the testimony, of all things which I will give thee in commandment unto the children of Israel. | a. To make it of pure gold
b. To make it 3¾' long by 2¼' wide (1.1 meters by .07 meters)
c. To make two cherubim at the two ends of the Mercy Seat
  1) To be made by hammering out the gold

  2) To hammer out one cherub at one end of the Mercy Seat & the other cherub at the other end

  3) To spread the wings of the cherubim upward, overshadowing the Mercy Seat
  4) To have the cherubim facing each other, looking toward the Mercy Seat

d. To place the Mercy Seat on top of the Ark
3. The purpose for the Ark
  a. To be the place where God's testimony (the 10 commandments) was kept, the place for special instruction
  b. To be the place where God met with His people
  c. To be the place where God's mercy was symbolized
  d. To be the place where God would instruct & guide His people |

DIVISION IX

THE TABERNACLE, ITS BLUEPRINT AND PRIESTHOOD: THE TRUE WAY TO APPROACH AND WORSHIP GOD, EX.25:1-31:18

B. The Ark or Chest of God: the Symbol of the Very Throne and Presence of God, 25:10-22

(25:10-22) **Introduction**: most of us have a place, or would like to have a place, where we can get all alone and be quiet, a place where we can think, work through problems, meditate, or pray. The place may be in any room, an office, a corner, a porch, a backyard, an alley, a field, a forest--it does not matter where. It is hallowed, meaningful ground to us.

    The Tabernacle was something like this to the Israelite believer, except even more. The Tabernacle was to be the place--the very special place--where God's people came to meet Him, seeking...

- His presence
- His help
- His forgiveness
- His strength
- His guidance

    This is what this passage is all about: it spells out the most important piece of furniture in the Tabernacle, that of the Ark of God, the symbol of the very presence and throne of God (1 Sam.4:4; 2 Sam.6:2). More than anything else, the Ark of God pictured the presence of God, His glory and mercy. The Tabernacle drew people to approach God for help, but it was knowing that the Ark of God, God's holy presence, sat in the midst of the Tabernacle that especially drew them. This is the subject of this important passage: *The Ark or Chest of God: the Symbol of the Very Throne of God,* Ex.25:10-22.

    1. The Ark, the sacred throne and chest of God Himself (v.10-16).
    2. The Mercy Seat or Atonement Cover for the Ark (v.17-21).
    3. The purpose for the Ark (v.21-22).

1 (25:10-16) <u>Ark--Ark of God--Ark of the Covenant--Ark of the Tabernacle--Commandments, The Ten</u>: there were the instructions to build the Ark of God, the sacred throne and chest of God Himself. The Ark was the most important piece of furniture in the Tabernacle. The Ark was to represent...

- the throne and presence of God Himself (1 Sam.4:4; 2 Sam.6:2)
- the Mercy Seat of God
- the place where the testimony of God, the Ten Commandments, was kept

Nothing could be any more important to the people than the Ark of God. Why? Because it was to be the very place where God Himself was to meet with them. God would rule and instruct them, have mercy and forgive them, guide and help them--all from the Ark. As they walked day by day through the *wilderness journey,* He would take care of them as they marched toward the promised land of God. The Ark of God was to become the most precious meeting place between God and His dear people. It was to be hallowed and holy ground, a very special place. This was to be especially true to the believer who loved God and was faithful in his worship of God.

The Ark was the centerpiece of the Tabernacle. Every part of the Tabernacle and every piece of furniture pointed toward and focused attention upon the Ark of God, the very place where God focused His presence. As long as the Tabernacle existed--in fact, up until Solomon's temple--God focused His presence upon the Ark of the Covenant. This is the reason the room where it was kept is called the *Holy of Holies* or *The Most Holy Place.*

Historically, the Ark of God was the most important piece of furniture to the Israelites. Its significance is emphasized in that it is mentioned over 200 times in the Bible. The Ark is called different names throughout Scripture:

⇒ The Ark (Ex.25:14)
⇒ The Ark of the LORD (1 Sam.4:6)
⇒ The Ark of God (1 Sam.4:18)
⇒ The Ark of the Testimony (referring to the great testimony of God given to man, the Ten Commandments) (Ex.25:22)
⇒ The Ark of the Covenant of God (referring to the great covenant of God made with man, the Ten Commandments) (Judg.20:27)
⇒ The Ark of the LORD God (1 Ki.2:26)

Now note the instructions for building the Ark, how detailed they are. The plan and design were exact, precise.
1. The Ark was to be made of acacia wood (v.10): a hard, durable wood, resistant to weather and insects.
2. The Ark was to be a box-like or chest-like structure: 3¾' long x 2¼' wide x 2¼' high (1.1 meters by .07 meters by .07 meters) (v.10).
3. The Ark was to be overlaid with pure gold both inside and out, and it was to have a gold molding around the rim (v.11).
4. The Ark was to have four gold rings attached to its four lower corners at the base of the ark (v.12).
5. The Ark was to have two strong poles made of acacia wood overlaid with gold (v.13).
6. The poles were to be slid into the gold rings on the Ark for the purpose of carrying it (v.14). And note: once inserted, the poles were never to be removed. They were a permanent part of the Ark of God.
7. The *Testimony of God*, the stone tablets of God's covenant (the Ten Commandments), was to be placed into the Ark.

Thought 1. The one thing we need throughout life is the presence of God. We need:
⇒ God's care and love
⇒ God's guidance and help
⇒ God's mercy and forgiveness
⇒ God's rule and instructions

"And, behold, I am with thee, and will keep thee in all places whither thou goest, and will bring thee again into this land; for I will not leave thee, until I have done that which I have spoken to thee of" (Gen.28:15).

"And he said, My presence shall go with thee, and I will give thee rest" (Ex.33:14).

"There shall not any man be able to stand before thee all the days of thy life: as I was with Moses, so I will be with thee: I will not fail thee, nor forsake thee" (Josh.1:5).

"When thou passest through the waters, I will be with thee; and through the rivers, they shall not overflow thee: when thou walkest through the fire, thou shalt not be burned; neither shall the flame kindle upon thee" (Is.43:2).

"For the mountains shall depart, and the hills be removed; but my kindness shall not depart from thee, neither shall the covenant of my peace be removed, saith the LORD that hath mercy on thee" (Is.54:10).

"For where two or three are gathered together in my name, there am I in the midst of them" (Mt.18:20).

"Lo, I am with you alway, [even] unto the end of the world. Amen" (Mt.28:20).

"I will not leave you comfortless: I will come to you" (Jn.14:18).

"Let your conversation [behavior, conduct] be without covetousness; and be content with such things as ye have: for he hath said, I will never leave thee, nor forsake thee" (Heb.13:5).

Thought 2. There are three arks mentioned in Scripture, and all three were used by God to save His people.
1) There was *Noah's ark*, the ark that God used to save Noah and his family from the terrible judgment of the flood. (See outline and notes--Gen.7:1-9 for more discussion.)
2) There was *Moses' ark*, the ark that God used to save baby Moses from the holocaust launched by Pharaoh against the newborn babies of the Israelites. (See outline and notes--Ex.2:1-10 for more discussion.)
3) There was the Ark of God, the Ark of the Covenant, that had the Mercy Seat sitting on top of it. The mercy of God was pictured (symbolized) as flowing out upon God's people, flowing out from the Mercy Seat. Salvation flowed out to the people from the presence and mercy of God, from the Mercy Seat and Ark of God.

> "And thou shalt put the mercy seat above upon the ark...And there I will meet with thee, and I will commune with thee from above the mercy seat, from between the two cherubims which are upon the ark of the testimony, of all things which I will give thee in commandment unto the children of Israel" (Ex.25:21-22).
>
> "And it shall come to pass, that whosoever shall call on the name of the Lord shall be saved" (Acts 2:21).
>
> "For whosoever shall call upon the name of the Lord shall be saved" (Ro.10:13).
>
> "For the grace of God that bringeth salvation hath appeared to all men, Teaching us that, denying ungodliness and worldly lusts, we should live soberly, righteously, and godly, in this present world; Looking for that blessed hope, and the glorious appearing of the great God and our Saviour Jesus Christ" (Tit.2:11-13).
>
> "The Lord is not slack concerning his promise, as some men count slackness; but is long-suffering to us, not willing that any should perish, but that all should come to repentance" (2 Pt.3:9).

2 (25:17-21) **Mercy, of God--Ark of God--Mercy Seat, The--Atonement--Atonement Cover, The**: there was the Mercy Seat or Atonement Cover for the Ark. The Hebrew word for "Mercy Seat" (kapporeth) means *covering* or *atonement*. The idea is that of the covering of sins, of atonement or reconciliation being made possible by the mercy of God. Forgiveness and reconciliation were made possible because the blood of the sacrifice (propitiation) was sprinkled upon the Mercy Seat once a year on the Day of Atonement.

The root word for "Mercy Seat" or "atonement cover" (kapporeth) comes from *kaphar* which means...
- to cover
- to make atonement, to reconcile
- to cleanse, forgive, pardon, purge away, put off
- to appease, placate, cancel, annul

This root word has a rich meaning in relation to the Mercy Seat.[1] It is at the Mercy Seat...
- that God covers man's sin
- that God cleanses, forgives, pardons, purges away, and puts off man's sin
- that God makes atonement and reconciles man to Himself
- that God's wrath is appeased, placated, canceled, annulled

The importance of the Mercy Seat in picturing the mercy of God cannot be overstressed. Various commentators say this:

The Pulpit Commentary says:

> "The truth is that *kapporeth*...never [has] any other sense than that of covering, or forgiving sins."[2]

The Expositor's Bible Commentary says:

> "The verb that lies behind the noun 'atonement' in the expression 'atonement cover' (v.17) means 'to ransom or deliver by means of a substitute....The LXX [Greek Septuagint Version] has 'propitiatory covering' or 'Mercy Seat,' as does Hebrews 9:5 (NIV mg.). This place of expiating the sins of mankind is an adumbration [sketchy picture] of Christ's propitiatory work...and is at the heart of our worship of the one who died for us."[3]

The NIV Study Bible says:

> "*Atonement*. Reconciliation, the divine act of grace whereby God draws to himself and makes 'at one' with him those who were once alienated from him. In the OT, the shed blood of sacrificial offerings effected atonement (see Lev 17:11 and note); in the NT, the blood of Jesus, shed once for all time, does the same (see Ro 3:25; 1Jn 2:2). atonement cover. See NIV text note; see also Lev 16:2 and note. That God's symbolic throne was capped with an atonement cover signified his great mercy toward his people--only such a God can be revered (see Ps 130:3-4)."[4]

1 James Strong. *Strong's Exhaustive Concordance of the Bible*, 3722, 3727.
2 *Pulpit Commentary*, Vol.1, Exodus, p.249.
3 Frank E. Gaebelein. *The Expositor's Bible Commentary*, Vol. 2, p.455.
4 *The NIV Study Bible*. (Grand Rapids, MI: The Zondervan Corporation, 1985), p.123.

F.B. Huey, Jr. says:

"'Mercy seat' comes from a word that means 'to cover,' hence 'to provide reconciliation, atonement'."[5]

Matthew Henry says:

"The mercy seat was the covering of the ark or chest, made of solid gold, exactly to fit the dimensions of the ark, v.17, 21. This *propitiatory covering*, as it might well be translated, was a type of Christ, the great propitiation, whose satisfaction fully answers the demands of the law, covers our transgressions, and comes between us and the curse we deserve. Thus he is the *end of the law for righteousness*."[6]

Maxie Dunnam says:

"The rendered 'mercy seat' really means 'a covering.' This makes special reference to the forgiveness and covering of transgression and sin by the slain blood of the lamb. The same word occurs in the Greek in the New Testament, where we are told by the apostle Paul that the Father sent Christ to be a propitiation through faith, by His blood and in the passing over of sin.
"But now the righteousness of God apart from the law is revealed, being witnessed by the Law and the Prophets, even the righteousness of God, through faith in Jesus Christ, to all and on all who believe. For there is no difference; for all have sinned and fall short of the glory of God, being justified freely by His grace through the redemption that is in Christ Jesus, whom God set forth as a propitiation by His blood, through faith, to demonstrate His righteousness, because in His forbearance God had passed over the sins that were previously committed...."
Rom. 3:21-25
"We might translate that 25th verse in this fashion: 'The redemption that is in Christ Jesus whom God set forth to be a mercy seat.'
"Isn't that a beautiful term? A seat of mercy. Is there a more beautiful term in our language? Let it hang on your lip--mercy--mercy--mercy. More than that, be immersed in the meaning of it, for that is the constant stream of love flowing from God--abundant mercy. Not wrath, not judgment, not indignation, but mercy is pouring forth from the eternal fountain in the heart of God.
"I'm not saying that there's not judgment. I'm not saying that God does not get indignant with our sloppy response to His call. I'm not saying that there isn't the demand of holiness and the expression of wrath in the character of God. I'm saying what the Bible says, that even before we reach that pinnacle of revelation as to who God is-- Jesus Christ hanging on a cross--we have the eternal mercy seat to show us God's nature."[7]

Paul the apostle says this:

"Whom God hath set forth to be a propitiation through faith in his blood, to declare his righteousness for the remission of sins that are past, through the forbearance of God" (Ro.3:25).

John the apostle says:

"Herein is love, not that we loved God, but that he loved us, and sent his Son to be the propitiation for our sins" (1 Jn.4:10).

Note the plan and design for constructing the Mercy Seat or Atonement Cover. Keep in mind that it was to be placed on top of the Ark, that it was to serve both as a *lid* to the Ark or Chest and as the Mercy Seat for God's Holy Presence.
1. The Mercy Seat was to be made of pure gold (v.17).
2. The Mercy Seat was to be oblong: the very same size as the Ark itself: 3¾' long x 2¼' wide (v.17).
3. There were to be two cherubim at the two ends of the Mercy Seat (v.18-20. The cherubim symbolized God's justice. Stephen F. Olford says this: "We meet them first in the very early chapters of the Bible, placed at the east of the Garden of Eden with a 'flaming sword which turned every way, to keep the way of the tree of life' (Genesis 3:24). It is true that the progressive revelation gives us more light on them, as we see them appearing again in such books as the prophecy of Ezekiel, and later the Revelation, but essentially they are messengers of judgment. Here on the mercy seat they stand poised to strike, were it not for the blood-sprinkled mercy seat."[8] (See Deeper Study # 2, Cherubim--Gen.3:24 for discussion.)

Note how the Mercy Seat was to be made:
⇒ To make it of pure gold
⇒ To make it 3¾' long by 2¼' wide (1.1 meters by .07 meters)
⇒ To make two cherubim at the two ends of the Mercy Seat
⇒ To be made by hammering out the gold
⇒ To hammer out one cherub at one end of the Mercy Seat and the other cherub at the other end
⇒ To spread the wings of the cherubim upward overshadowing the Mercy Seat
⇒ To have the cherubim facing each other, looking toward the Mercy Seat

5   F.B. Huey, Jr. *Exodus,* p.107.
6   Matthew Henry, *Matthew Henry's Commentary,* Vol. 1, p.383-384.
7   Maxie Dunnam. *Mastering The Old Testament, Volume 2: Exodus,* p.314.
8   Stephen F. Olford. *The Tabernacle. Camping with God,* p.139.

4. The Mercy Seat was to be placed on top of the Ark (v.21).

Thought 1. Our sin has separated us from God. There is a great gulf between God and man, a gulf so vast that it keeps us from reaching God. That gulf is sin. And sin condemns us to death. But there is hope, one hope: the *mercy of God*. This is the very reason God designed the Mercy Seat of the Ark, to proclaim the great *mercy of God*. Scripture says:

1) The mercy of God saves us.

> "Not by works of righteousness which we have done, but according to his mercy he saved us, by the washing of regeneration, and renewing of the Holy Ghost; Which he shed on us abundantly through Jesus Christ our Saviour; That being justified by his grace, we should be made heirs according to the hope of eternal life" (Tit.3:5-7).
> "But God, who is rich in mercy, for his great love wherewith he loved us, Even when we were dead in sins, hath quickened us together with Christ, (by grace ye are saved)....For by grace are ye saved through faith; and that not of yourselves: it is the gift of God: Not of works, lest any man should boast" (Eph.2:4-5, 8-9).

2) The mercy of God demands repentance for salvation.

> "And rend your heart, and not your garments, and turn unto the LORD your God: for he is gracious and merciful, slow to anger, and of great kindness, and repenteth him of the evil" (Joel 2:13).

3) The mercy of God is poured out upon those who fear Him.

> "But the mercy of the LORD is from everlasting to everlasting upon them that fear him, and his righteousness unto children's children" (Ps.103:17).
> "I am a companion of all them that fear thee, and of them that keep thy precepts. The earth, O LORD, is full of thy mercy: teach me thy statutes" (Ps.119:63-64).

4) The mercy of God sent His Son, Jesus Christ, to become the merciful and faithful High Priest, to make atonement for sin, and to deliver us from death.

> "Forasmuch then as the children are partakers of flesh and blood, he also himself likewise took part of the same; that through death he might destroy him that had the power of death, that is, the devil; And deliver them who through fear of death were all their lifetime subject to bondage. For verily he took not on him the nature of angels; but he took on him the seed of Abraham. Wherefore in all things it behoved him to be made like unto his brethren, that he might be a merciful and faithful high priest in things pertaining to God, to make reconciliation for the sins of the people" (Heb.2:14-17).

5) The mercy of God forgives our sin.

> "Who is a God like unto thee, that pardoneth iniquity, and passeth by the transgression of the remnant of his heritage? he retaineth not his anger for ever, because he delighteth in mercy" (Mic.7:18).

6) The mercy of God delivers us from the consuming trials of life day by day.

> "It is of the LORD'S mercies that we are not consumed, because his compassions fail not. They are new every morning: great is thy faithfulness" (Lam.3:22-23).

7) The mercy of God invites us to approach God in order to receive mercy and find help in time of need.

> "Let us therefore come boldly unto the throne of grace, that we may obtain mercy, and find grace to help in time of need" (Heb.4:16).

8) The mercy of God has no end; it reaches above the heavens.

> "For thy mercy is great above the heavens: and thy truth reacheth unto the clouds" (Ps.108:4).

3 (25:21-22) **Ark of God--Ark of the Covenant--Mercy, of God--Testimony, God's--Commandments, The Ten--Tabernacle**: there were four purposes for the Ark of God. Note how clearly God spelled out why He had planned and designed the Ark of the Covenant.

EXODUS 25:10-22

1. The Ark of God was to hold God's testimony, the two tablets of the covenant, that is, the Ten Commandments (v.21). The Ten Commandments are a very special covenant between God and man, the basic laws that are to govern man's life. So far as laws are concerned, man is above all to keep the Ten Commandments. Therefore, they were to be preserved and secured, contained in the very throne of God Himself. They were to be under His watchful care.

There were several other items kept in the Ark as well. These are not covered in this particular passage of Scripture, but they are noted here because this is the most complete and detailed coverage of the Ark of God.

a. There was the golden pot of the Manna.

> **"Which had the golden censer, and the ark of the covenant overlaid round about with gold, wherein was the golden pot that had manna, and Aaron's rod that budded, and the tables of the covenant" (Heb.9:4).**
> **"And Moses said unto Aaron, Take a pot, and put an omer full of manna therein, and lay it up before the LORD, to be kept for your generations. As the LORD commanded Moses, so Aaron laid it up before the Testimony, to be kept" (Ex.16:33-34; cp. Ex.16:11-31; Num.11:1-9).**

b. There was Aaron's rod or staff that budded.

> **"Which had the golden censer, and the ark of the covenant overlaid round about with gold, wherein was the golden pot that had manna, and Aaron's rod that budded, and the tables of the covenant" (Heb.9:4; cp. Num. Chapters 16 and 17).**

c. There was the Book of the Covenant (most likely the civil law of God).

> **"And he took the book of the covenant, and read in the audience of the people: and they said, All that the LORD hath said will we do, and be obedient" (Ex.24:7).**
> **"That Moses commanded the Levites, which bare the ark of the covenant of the LORD, saying, Take this book of the law, and put it in the side of the ark of the covenant of the LORD your God, that it may be there for a witness against thee" (Dt.31:25-26).**

2. The Ark was to be the place--the very special place--where God met with His people (v.22). In a very special way, God's presence dwelt above the Ark of the Covenant. The people knew this. Therefore, when they needed a special sense of God's presence--when they needed to feel a special closeness to God--they knew where to go. They could go to the Tabernacle, the ground surrounding the Tabernacle, to worship and seek forgiveness by offering sacrifice to the Lord.

Keep in mind that only the High Priest could enter the Holy of Holies and actually stand before the Ark of God. Moreover, he could only do this once a year on the Day of Atonement, when he offered the sacrifice for sins on behalf of all the people. However, the people did have access to God--access to a deep sense of God's presence--by coming to the ground surrounding the Tabernacle and offering a sacrifice or giving an offering to God.

The Tabernacle presented a graphic, vivid picture of God's Holy presence and, no doubt, aroused a deep, deep sense of God's presence within the believers who truly believed and loved God. Genuine believers would have visited the holy, hallowed ground often in order to meet God: to experience a deep sense of His holy presence and to seek His guidance and help.

3. The Ark was to be the place of mercy, the place where God's mercy was clearly pictured (v.22). Once a year on the Day of Atonement, the High Priest was to offer sacrifice and sprinkle the blood of the victim upon the Mercy Seat. The people were to learn this: they were to learn all about the Mercy Seat and the blood sprinkled upon it. They were to learn that the blood made atonement for their sins, reconciled them to God. They were to learn that the mercy of God was to be showered upon them because of the blood, because they believed and trusted the blood of the sacrifice to cover their sins. This was one of the great lessons to be learned, one of the purposes for the Ark of God.

Thought 1. There are two meaningful pictures seen in the Mercy Seat that covered the Ark of God.
1) There is the picture that points toward the finished work of Christ. The High Priest was never allowed to sit on the Mercy Seat, no matter how tired or weary he became. In fact, the priests were always working when in the Tabernacle. Their priestly work was never finished: they were continually offering sacrifice and ministering. But this was not true with Jesus Christ. When Jesus Christ offered Himself as the Perfect Sacrifice to God, His work was finished. His sacrifice for the sins of people was perfect: no other sacrifice was ever needed. Therefore, Christ was able to sit down on the right hand of God's throne. This is exactly what Scripture says:

> **"And every priest standeth daily ministering and offering oftentimes the same sacrifices, which can never take away sins: But this man, after he had offered one sacrifice for sins for ever, sat down on the right hand of God" (Heb.10:11-12).**
> **"For in that he died, he died unto sin once: but in that he liveth, he liveth unto God" (Ro.6:10).**
> **"Which he wrought in Christ, when he raised him from the dead, and set him at his own right hand in the heavenly places" (Eph.1:20).**
> **"And being found in fashion as a man, he humbled himself, and became obedient unto death, even the death of the cross. Wherefore God also hath highly exalted him, and given him a name which is above every name: That at the name of Jesus every knee should bow, of things in heaven, and things in earth, and things under the earth" (Ph.2:8-10).**

282

"Saying with a loud voice, Worthy is the Lamb that was slain to receive power, and riches, and wisdom, and strength, and honour, and glory, and blessing. And every creature which is in heaven, and on the earth, and under the earth, and such as are in the sea, and all that are in them, heard I saying, Blessing, and honour, and glory, and power, be unto him that sitteth upon the throne, and unto the Lamb for ever and ever" (Rev.5:12-13).

2) There is the picture that points toward God covering the law with His mercy. No person can keep the law, not perfectly. And perfection is required in order to live in God's holy presence. How then can we ever become acceptable to God, be allowed to live in heaven with Him? By His mercy. God's mercy has been given us through His Son, the Lord Jesus Christ. God gave His Son to be the *Perfect Sacrifice* for our sins. The mercy of God shown us in Jesus Christ covers the law, covers our sin, our failure to keep the law. When we trust Jesus Christ as our Savior, the mercy of God covers all the law--all the accusations of the law against us, all our failure to keep the law, all the guilt that gnaws at our hearts and convicts us.

"Therefore by the deeds of the law there shall no flesh be justified in his sight: for by the law is the knowledge of sin. But now the righteousness of God without the law is manifested, being witnessed by the law and the prophets; Even the righteousness of God which is by faith of Jesus Christ unto all and upon all them that believe: for there is no difference" (Ro.3:20-22).

"For all have sinned, and come short of the glory of God; Being justified freely by his grace through the redemption that is in Christ Jesus: Whom God hath set forth to be a propitiation through faith in his blood, to declare his righteousness for the remission of sins that are past, through the forbearance of God" (Ro.3:23-25).

"Moreover the law entered, that the offence might abound. But where sin abounded, grace [mercy] did much more abound: That as sin hath reigned unto death, even so might grace reign through righteousness unto eternal life by Jesus Christ our Lord" (Ro.5:20-21).

"But the scripture hath concluded all under sin, that the promise by faith of Jesus Christ might be given to them that believe. But before faith came, we were kept under the law, shut up unto the faith which should afterwards be revealed. Wherefore the law was our schoolmaster to bring us unto Christ, that we might be justified by faith. But after that faith is come, we are no longer under a schoolmaster. For ye are all the children of God by faith in Christ Jesus" (Gal.3:22-26).

"But when the fulness of the time was come, God sent forth his Son, made of a woman, made under the law, To redeem them that were under the law, that we might receive the adoption of sons" (Gal.4:4-5).

"And you, being dead in your sins and the uncircumcision of your flesh, hath he quickened together with him [Christ], having forgiven you all trespasses; Blotting out the handwriting of ordinances that was against us, which was contrary to us, and took it out of the way, nailing it to his cross" (Col.2:13-14).

4. The Ark was to be the place where God would instruct and guide His people (v.22). The Ark was to be the symbol of the throne of God. His divine presence was apparently to be manifested in a very special way right above the empty space of the Mercy Seat, right between the cherubim. From that position, God promised to speak to His people, to give them His commandments, instructions, and guidance.

When God's people needed help or guidance, they were to come to the Tabernacle. The Tabernacle was to become very, very special to God's people. Special because it was where God's presence was manifested in a very significant way. It was the place where they would be able to seek God's special care and help, His direction and guidance. No matter what the pain or suffering was--no matter how terrible the trial--God was ready and able to help His dear believer.

"But if from thence thou shalt seek the LORD thy God, thou shalt find him, if thou seek him with all thy heart and with all thy soul" (Dt.4:29).

"If my people, which are called by my name, shall humble themselves, and pray, and seek my face, and turn from their wicked ways; then will I hear from heaven, and will forgive their sin, and will heal their land" (2 Chron.7:14).

"The meek will he guide in judgment: and the meek will he teach his way" (Ps.25:9).

"For this God is our God for ever and ever: he will be our guide even unto death" (Ps.48:14).

"Thou shalt guide me with thy counsel, and afterward receive me to glory" (Ps.73:24).

"For we have not an high priest which cannot be touched with the feeling of our infirmities; but was in all points tempted like as we are, yet without sin. Let us therefore come boldly unto the throne of grace, that we may obtain mercy, and find grace to help in time of need" (Heb.4:15-16).

"Seek the LORD, and his strength: seek his face evermore" (Ps.105:4).

"I love them that love me; and those that seek me early shall find me" (Pr.8:17).

"Seek ye the LORD while he may be found, call ye upon him while he is near" (Is.55:6).

"For every one that asketh receiveth; and he that seeketh findeth; and to him that knocketh it shall be opened" (Lk.11:10).

TYPES, SYMBOLS, AND PICTURES
(Exodus 25:10-22)

Historical Term	Type or Picture (Scriptural Basis for Each)	Life Application for Today's Believer	Biblical Application for Today's Believer
Acacia wood (Ex.25:10)	*Acacia wood was a hard, durable wood that was resistant to insects and harsh weather. Acacia flourished in the wilderness and speaks of the incorruptibility and perfection of Jesus Christ.* **"And they shall make an ark** *of* **shittim [acacia] wood: two cubits and a half** *shall be* **the length thereof, and a cubit and a half the breadth thereof, and a cubit and a half the height thereof"** (Ex.25:10).	⇒ In a world filled with corruption, Jesus Christ is the One who is the epitome of durability and strength, the only One who is incorruptible. Therefore, the believer should call upon Christ for help in time of need and for strength in time of temptation. The believer should build his life upon Jesus Christ, the only foundation that will stand the test of time.	*"For he hath made him to be sin for us, who knew no sin; that we might be made the righteousness of God in him"* (2 Cor.5:21). *"For we have not an high priest which cannot be touched with the feeling of our infirmities; but was in all points tempted like as we are, yet without sin"* (Heb.4:15). *"For such an high priest became us, who is holy, harmless, undefiled, separate from sinners, and made higher than the heavens"* (Heb.7:26). *"And ye know that he was manifested to take away our sins; and in him is no sin"* (1 Jn.3:5). *"Who his own self bare our sins in his own body on the tree, that we, being dead to sins, should live unto righteousness: by whose stripes ye were healed"* (1 Pt.2:24).
The Ark or Chest (Ex.25:10-22; 40:20) See also Ex.35:12; 37:1-5; 39:35; 40:3, 20-21	*The Ark was the very special place where God's Holy presence was manifested.*	What the Ark of the Covenant taught:	
	a. The Ark was the symbol of God's presence. A very special manifestation of God's presence dwelt right above the Ark, right between the two cherubim.	a. God reveals His presence to believers in a very special way: • When people need a special sense of God's presence—when they need to feel a special closeness to God—they can go directly into the presence of God. They can worship and seek the Lord personally. How is this possible? Because of the great sacrifice of God's Son, the Lord Jesus Christ.	*"And he said, My presence shall go with thee, and I will give thee rest"* (Ex.33:14). *"When thou passest through the waters, I will be with thee; and through the rivers, they shall not overflow thee: when thou walkest through the fire, thou shalt not be burned; neither shall the flame kindle upon thee"* (Is.43:2).
	b. The Mercy Seat sat on top of the Ark; therefore, the Ark was a symbol of God's mercy.	b. God covers our lives with His mercy: • Believers are to understand that the blood shed upon the cross makes atonement for their sins, that the blood reconciles them to God. Believers are to learn that the mercy of	*"But the mercy of the LORD is from everlasting to everlasting upon them that fear him, and his righteousness unto children's children"* (Ps.103:17). *"But God, who is rich in mercy, for his great love wherewith he loved us, Even when we were dead in*

Historical Term	Type or Picture (Scriptural Basis for Each)	Life Application for Today's Believer	Biblical Application for Today's Believer
		God is to be showered upon them because of the blood, because they believe and trust the blood of the sacrifice (Jesus Christ) to cover their sins.	sins, hath quickened us together with Christ, (by grace ye are saved;) And hath raised us up together, and made us sit together in heavenly places in Christ Jesus" (Eph.2:4-6).
	c. The Ark was the symbol of the very throne of God. It was the place where the people sought the guidance and instruction of God.	c. God instructs and guides His people from His heavenly throne. From that position, God speaks to His people, gives them His commandments, instructions, and guidance; therefore, when God's people need help or guidance, they are to come directly to the throne of mercy, to come and find grace to help in time of need.	"The meek will he guide in judgment: and the meek will he teach his way" (Ps.25:9). "I will instruct thee and teach thee in the way which thou shalt go: I will guide thee with mine eye" (Ps.32:8). "For we have not an high priest which cannot be touched with the feeling of our infirmities; but was in all points tempted like as we are, yet without sin. Let us therefore come boldly unto the throne of grace, that we may obtain mercy, and find grace to help in time of need" (Heb.4:15-16).
	d. The Ark was the symbol of God's Law, holding the Ten Commandments.	d. God gave the Ten Commandments so we would know how to live and relate to God and to one another--so we would know how to how to build a just and peaceful society.	"For this is the love of God, that we keep his commandments: and his commandments are not grievous" (1 Jn.5:3). "Righteousness exalteth a nation: but sin is a reproach to any people" (Pr.14:34).
	e. The Ark was the symbol of Christ, of the very presence of God personally fulfilling every picture of the Ark. Remember, the word "tabernacle" means to dwell, to abide in the midst of.	e. How Christ fulfilled the symbolism of the Ark of God: ⇒ Jesus Christ promises to be with His people always	"For where two or three are gathered together in my name, there am I in the midst of them" (Mt.18:20). "Teaching them to observe all things whatsoever I have commanded you: and, lo, I am with you alway, even unto the end of the world. Amen" (Mt.28:20).
	"And they shall make an ark of shittim wood: two cubits and a half shall be the length thereof, and a cubit and a half the breadth thereof, and a cubit and a half the height thereof" (Ex.25:10). "And he took and put the testimony into the ark, and set the staves on the ark, and put the mercy seat above upon the ark" (Ex.40:20).	⇒ Jesus Christ shed His blood in order to have mercy upon us and to cleanse us from our sins.	"Who his own self bare our sins in his own body on the tree, that we, being dead to sins, should live unto righteousness: by whose stripes ye were healed" (1 Pt.2:24). "For Christ also hath once suffered for sins, the just for the unjust, that he might bring us to God, being put to death in the flesh, but quickened by the Spirit" (1 Pt.3:18). "Unto him that loved us, and washed us from our

Historical Term	Type or Picture (Scriptural Basis for Each)	Life Application for Today's Believer	Biblical Application for Today's Believer
			sins in his own blood" (Rev.1:5).
		⇒ Jesus Christ is the Good Shepherd, the One who leads, protects, and guides His people.	*"Go ye therefore, and teach all nations, baptizing them in the name of the Father, and of the Son, and of the Holy Ghost: Teaching them to observe all things whatsoever I have commanded you: and, lo, I am with you alway, [even] unto the end of the world. Amen"* (Mt.28:19-20). *"Let your conversation be without covetousness; and be content with such things as ye have: for he hath said, I will never leave thee, nor forsake thee"* (Heb.13:5).
		⇒ Jesus Christ kept the Law of the covenant that was kept in the Ark, kept the Law perfectly, without sin.	*"For we have not an high priest which cannot be touched with the feeling of our infirmities; but was in all points tempted like as we are, yet without sin"* (Heb.4:15).
Gold (Ex.25:17)	*A symbol of value, of the greatest worth there is: A symbol of the LORD Himself, of His deity and righteousness.* **"And thou shalt make a mercy seat of pure gold: two cubits and a half shall be the length thereof, and a cubit and a half the breadth thereof"** (Ex.25:17).	⇒ Jesus Christ is the greatest and most precious value that can be possessed. He is more precious and more valuable than gold. Above all else, a person should strive to have Jesus Christ in his life.	*"Unto me, who am less than the least of all saints, is this grace given, that I should preach among the Gentiles the unsearchable riches of Christ"* (Eph.3:8). *"Wherefore God also hath highly exalted him, and given him a name which is above every name: That at the name of Jesus every knee should bow, of things in heaven, and things in earth, and things under the earth"* (Ph.2:9-10). *"Riches and honour are with me; yea, durable riches and righteousness. My fruit is better than gold, yea, than fine gold; and my revenue than choice silver. I lead in the way of righteousness, in the midst of the paths of judgment: That I may cause those that love me to inherit substance; and I will fill their treasures"* (Pr.8:18-21).
The Mercy Seat (Ex.25:17-21; 25:22) See also Ex.; 35:12; 37:6-9; 39:35; 40:3, 20	*The Mercy Seat covered the Ark and symbolized at least three things:* *a. The Mercy Seat symbolized the very mercy of God Himself.*	What the Mercy Seat taught: a. God is not only holy and righteous, He is also merciful. God is the Sovereign Creator and Majesty who rules	*"And rend your heart, and not your garments, and turn unto the LORD your God: for he is gracious and merciful, slow to anger,*

Historical Term	Type or Picture (Scriptural Basis for Each)	Life Application for Today's Believer	Biblical Application for Today's Believer
		in mercy as well as in righteousness and holiness. The Mercy Seat symbolized that God has mercy upon all who truly come to Him, who truly believe and follow Him.	*and of great kindness, and repenteth him of the evil"* (Joel 2:13). *"Who is a God like unto thee, that pardoneth iniquity, and passeth by the transgression of the remnant of his heritage? he retaineth not his anger for ever, because he delighteth in mercy" (Mic. 7:18).*
	b. The Mercy Seat symbolized that God covered the Law with His mercy: Remember, the law (the Ten Commandments) was kept in the Ark under the Mercy Seat. The mercy of God covers the law and its charges against people, covers the transgressions of every person who trusts in Jesus Christ.	b. There was the picture that pointed toward God covering the law with His mercy. No person can keep the law, not perfectly. And perfection is required in order to live in God's holy presence. How then can we ever become acceptable to God, be allowed to live in heaven with Him? By His mercy. God's mercy has been given us through His Son, the Lord Jesus Christ. God gave His Son to be the *Perfect Sacrifice* for our sins. The mercy of God shown us in Jesus Christ covers the law, covers our sin, our failure to keep the law. When we trust Jesus Christ as our Savior, the mercy of God covers all the law—all the accusations of the law against us, all our failure to keep the law, all the guilt that gnaws at our hearts and convicts us.	*"Blessed be the God and Father of our Lord Jesus Christ, which according to his abundant mercy hath begotten us again unto a lively hope by the resurrection of Jesus Christ from the dead" (1 Pt. 1:3).* *"If any man serve me, let him follow me; and where I am, there shall also my servant be: if any man serve me, him will my Father honour" (Jn. 12:26).*
	c. The Mercy Seat symbolized the finished work of Christ. The High Priest was never allowed to sit on the Mercy Seat, no matter how tired or weary he became. In fact, the priests were always working when in the Tabernacle. Their priestly work was never finished: they were continually offering sacrifice and ministering. **"And thou shalt make a mercy seat of pure gold: two cubits and a half shall**	c. When Jesus Christ offered Himself as the Perfect Sacrifice to God, His work was finished. His sacrifice for the sins of people was perfect: no other sacrifice was ever needed. Therefore, Christ was able to sit down on the right hand of God's throne. Believers no longer have to offer sacrifices to God to atone for their sins. Christ has already satisfied God's requirement. It is because of the mercy of God in the sacrifice of	*"For all have sinned, and come short of the glory of God; Being justified freely by his grace through the redemption that is in Christ Jesus: Whom God hath set forth to be a propitiation [covering, sacrifice] through faith in his blood, to declare his righteousness for the remission of sins that are past, through the forbearance of God" (Ro. 3:23-25).* *"And every priest standeth daily ministering and offering oftentimes the same sacrifices, which can never take away sins: But this man, after he had of-*

Historical Term	Type or Picture (Scriptural Basis for Each)	Life Application for Today's Believer	Biblical Application for Today's Believer
	be the length thereof, and a cubit and a half the breadth thereof." (Ex.25:17). "And there I will meet with thee, and I will commune with thee from above the mercy seat, from between the two cherubims which *are* upon the ark of the testimony, of all *things* which I will give thee in commandment unto the children of Israel" (Ex.25:22).	His Son that we are cleansed once and for all from our sins.	*fered one sacrifice for sins for ever, <u>sat down</u> on the right hand of God"* (Heb.10:11-12). *"And being found in fashion as a man, he humbled himself, and became obedient unto death, even the death of the cross. Wherefore God also hath highly exalted him, and given him a name which is above every name: That at the name of Jesus every knee should bow, of things in heaven, and things in earth, and things under the earth"* (Ph.2:8-10).

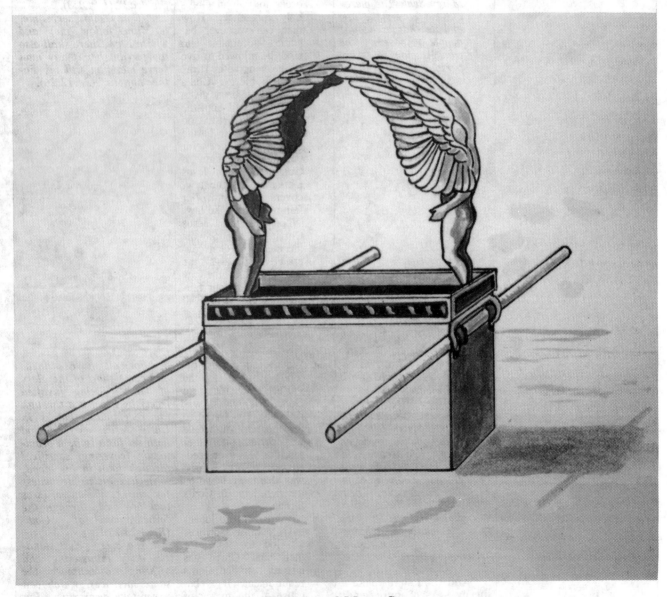

The Ark and Mercy Seat

	C. The Table of Show-bread: The Symbol of God Himself as the Bread of Life, 25:23-30	four rings of gold, and put the rings in the four corners that are on the four feet thereof.	1) Attach them to the four corners where the legs are
1. The Table's design & mate-rials a. To make it of acacia wood b. To make it 3' long & 1½' wide & 2¼' high (.9 meters x .5 meters x .7 meters) c. To overlay it with pure gold & make a gold molding	23 Thou shalt also make a table of shittim wood: two cubits shall be the length thereof, and a cubit the breadth thereof, and a cubit and a half the height thereof. 24 And thou shalt overlay it with pure gold, and make thereto a crown of gold round about.	27 Over against the border shall the rings be for places of the staves to bear the table. 28 And thou shalt make the staves of shittim wood, and overlay them with gold, that the table may be borne with them.	2) Place them close to the border or rim to hold the poles for carrying the ta-ble f. To make the poles of acacia wood & overlay them with gold: To be used to carry the table g. To make the dishes, plates, pictures, & bowls of gold: To be used in the offerings
d. To make a 3" gold border or trim	25 And thou shalt make unto it a border of an hand breadth round about, and thou shalt make a golden crown to the border thereof round about.	29 And thou shalt make the dishes thereof, and spoons thereof, and covers thereof, and bowls thereof, to cover withal: of pure gold shalt thou make them.	**2. The Table's purpose: To give the bread as an offering of thanksgiving & dependence upon God**
e. To make four gold rings	26 And thou shalt make for it	30 And thou shalt set upon the table showbread before me alway.	

DIVISION IX

THE TABERNACLE, ITS BLUEPRINT AND PRIESTHOOD: THE TRUE WAY TO APPROACH AND WORSHIP GOD, EX.25:1-31:18

C. The Table of Showbread: The Symbol of God Himself as the Bread of Life, 25:23-30

(25:23-30) **Introduction**: the gnawing pain of hunger, the need to feed oneself, is one of the strongest drives that a person has. As long as a person's hunger is fed, he can go on about his normal life. However if food is withheld for a long time, the body starves to death. Without food, a person becomes sick and eventually dies. Now note: physical hunger is a picture of spiritual hunger. When a person senses spiritual hunger, he seeks to satisfy that hunger. Spiritual hunger is a normal thing: God made the human heart to hunger and thirst after Him. But spiritual hunger becomes abnormal when man tries to satisfy his hunger with the things of the world...

- illicit sex
- partying
- sensual pleasures
- excessive possessions
- position and power
- money and property
- recognition and fame
- alcohol and drugs
- food and drink

The hunger of the human heart can be met by God and by God alone. This is what the Table of the Showbread is all about: it points a person to God as the provision of life, as the One who provides whatever is necessary to meet the hunger of man. This is the much needed lesson of this passage: *The Table of Showbread, The Symbol of God Himself as the Bread of Life*, Ex.25:23-30.

1. The Table's design and materials (v.23-29).
2. The Table's purpose: to give the bread as an offering of thanksgiving and dependence upon God (v.30).

1 (25:23-29) **Showbread, Table of--Tabernacle--Bread of Life**: there was the design and materials of the Table. The second piece of furniture to be built was the Table of Showbread. The word "showbread" (paneh) literally means two things:

⇒ The *Bread of the Face* referring to the face of God. The showbread was bread placed before the very face of God Himself.
⇒ The *Bread of the Presence* referring to the presence of God. The showbread was bread placed in the very presence of God Himself.

The Showbread is also called the *Holy Bread* or the *Consecrated Bread* (1 Sam.21:4-6). Obviously the Table of Showbread was the table upon which the bread of thanksgiving and dependence was placed. Note that the Table was not to sit in the Holy of Holies: it was to be placed in the Holy Place right outside the inner curtain of the Holy of Holies. It was to sit as it were right before the presence and face of God, which was behind the inner curtain. There was only one piece of furniture in the Holy of Holies, the Ark of God that symbolized the very throne of God itself. The arrangement of furniture in the two sanctuaries was to be this:

THE HOLY OF HOLIES OR THE MOST HOLY PLACE
The Ark of God with the Mercy Seat (25:10-22)

THE HOLY PLACE
The Table of Showbread (25:23-30)
The Lampstand (25:31-40)
The Altar of Incense (30:1-10)

Now note that the design for the Table of Showbread was planned by God Himself. The design was exact, precise.

1. The table was to be made of acacia wood: a hard and durable wood, resistant to insects, disease, and weather (v.23).
2. The table was to be quite small: 3' long & 1½' wide & 2¼' high (.9 meters x .5 meters x .7 meters) (v.23).
3. The table was to be overlaid with pure gold and have a gold molding running around it (v.24).
4. The table was to have a rim three inches wide around the top with a gold molding around it (v.25).
5. The table was to have four gold rings attached to the four corners where the legs were: to support the poles for carrying the table (v.26-27).
6. The poles to carry the table were to be made of acacia wood and be overlaid with gold (v.28).
7. The table's plates and dishes were to be made of gold as well as the pitchers and bowls that were to be used in pouring out drink offerings (v.29).

2 (25:30) **Table of Showbread--Tabernacle--Bread of Life**: the table's purpose was to hold the showbread, to present the showbread before the face of God, to present it as an offering of thanksgiving and dependence upon God. In order to get a complete picture of the showbread table, it is helpful to look at the Scripture that describes the showbread itself:

> "And thou shalt take fine flour, and bake twelve cakes thereof: two tenth deals shall be in one cake. And thou shalt set them in two rows, six on a row, upon the pure table before the LORD. And thou shalt put pure frankincense upon each row, that it may be on the bread for a memorial, even an offering made by fire unto the LORD. Every sabbath he shall set it in order before the LORD continually, being taken from the children of Israel by an everlasting covenant. And it shall be Aaron's and his sons'; and they shall eat it in the holy place: for it is most holy unto him of the offerings of the LORD made by fire by a perpetual statute" (Lev.24:5-9).

⇒ Twelve loaves of bread were to be made (v.5).
⇒ The loaves were to be made of choice flour, three quarts each (v.5).
⇒ The loaves were to be arranged in two rows of six each (v.6).
⇒ Some frankincense was to be sprinkled over each row and burned in place of the bread as *an offering* (v.7).
⇒ The bread was to be changed every Sabbath day (v.8).
⇒ The bread was to be laid out in behalf of the people as *an offering*, as a continuing part of the covenant (v.8).
⇒ The bread was to be eaten by the priest but only in a holy place, for the bread was an *offering made to the Lord* (v.9).

Now note the significant facts about the bread: twelve loaves of bread were to be made and they were to be presented to God as an offering. Where were they to be presented? On the Table of Showbread, in the very presence of God Himself, right before His face. The meaning and symbolism is obvious.

1. The twelve loaves of showbread represented an offering from each tribe of Israel, an offering of thanksgiving to God. Each tribe was represented as thanking God for the bread and food He provided, for meeting their physical needs.

> "When thou hast eaten and art full, then thou shalt bless the LORD thy God for the good land which he hath given thee" (Dt.8:10).
> "Enter into his gates with thanksgiving, and into his courts with praise: be thankful unto him, and bless his name" (Ps.100:4).
> "And when he had thus spoken, he took bread, and gave thanks to God in presence of them all: and when he had broken it, he began to eat" (Acts 27:35).
> "In every thing give thanks: for this is the will of God in Christ Jesus concerning you" (1 Th.5:18).

2. The twelve loaves also represented the people's dependence upon God. Note that the loaves sat in God's presence, before His very face. The people were to acknowledge their dependence upon God, acknowledge that they needed His provision. They needed His watchful eye upon the bread, upon them as His followers. They needed Him to continue to provide their bread and food, continue to look after and care for them. Their dependence upon God as the Provision of life was symbolized in the showbread as well as their offering of thanksgiving.

3. The twelve loaves also acknowledged their trust of God. By setting the bread before God, they were declaring their belief and trust that He would continue to meet their physical needs.

> "Blessed [are] they which do <u>hunger and thirst</u> after righteousness: for they shall be filled" (Mt.5:6).
> "But seek ye first the kingdom of God, and his righteousness; and all these things shall be added unto you" (Mt.6:33).
> "John answered and said, A man can receive nothing, except it be given him from heaven" (Jn.3:27).
> "I am the vine, ye [are] the branches: He that abideth in me, and I in him, the same bringeth forth much fruit: for without me ye can do nothing" (Jn.15:5).
> "But my God shall supply all your need according to his riches in glory by Christ Jesus" (Ph.4:19).

"But I am poor and needy; yet the Lord thinketh upon me: thou art my help and my deliverer; make no tarrying, O my God" (Ps.40:17).
"For he satisfieth the longing soul, and filleth the hungry soul with goodness" (Ps.107:9).
"[God] Who giveth food to all flesh: for his mercy endureth for ever. O give thanks unto the God of heaven: for his mercy endureth for ever" (Ps.136:25-26).

4. The showbread also pointed to Jesus Christ as the Bread of Life. Scripture declares that He is the Living Bread who came *out of* heaven to satisfy the hunger of a person's soul.

"For the bread of God is he which cometh down from heaven, and giveth life unto the world" (Jn.6:33).
"And Jesus said unto them, I am the bread of life: he that cometh to me shall never hunger; and he that believeth on me shall never thirst" (Jn.6:35).
"I am that bread of life" (Jn.6:48).
"This is the bread which cometh down from heaven, that a man may eat thereof, and not die. I am the living bread which came down from heaven: if any man eat of this bread, he shall live for ever: and the bread that I will give is my flesh, which I will give for the life of the world" (Jn.6:50-51).
"This is that bread which came down from heaven: not as your fathers did eat manna, and are dead: he that eateth of this bread shall live for ever" (Jn.6:58).

5. The showbread pointed to God Himself as the nourishment that man really needs. Far too often man tries to live his life apart from God's provision and presence. The culture of today says...
• to have it your way--where man is self-exalted
• to do it your way--where man is making his own path in life
• to go it alone--where man is cut off from the very One he needs

There is nothing that can replace man's need for God. It is God and God alone who truly nourishes and satisfies the hungry soul of man.

"I will abundantly bless her provision: I will satisfy her poor with bread" (Ps.132:15).
"The LORD is my shepherd; I shall not want. He maketh me to lie down in green pastures: he leadeth me beside the still waters. He restoreth my soul: he leadeth me in the paths of righteousness for his name's sake. Yea, though I walk through the valley of the shadow of death, I will fear no evil: for thou art with me; thy rod and thy staff they comfort me. Thou preparest a table before me in the presence of mine enemies: thou anointest my head with oil; my cup runneth over. Surely goodness and mercy shall follow me all the days of my life: and I will dwell in the house of the LORD for ever" (Ps.23:1-6).
"Oh how great is thy goodness, which thou hast laid up for them that fear thee; which thou hast wrought for them that trust in thee before the sons of men!" (Ps.31:19).
"With my soul have I desired thee in the night; yea, with my spirit within me will I seek thee early: for when thy judgments are in the earth, the inhabitants of the world will learn righteousness" (Is.26:9).
"But my God shall supply all your need according to his riches in glory by Christ Jesus" (Ph.4:19).
"And all Judah rejoiced at the oath: for they had sworn with all their heart, and sought him with their whole desire; and he was found of them: and the LORD gave them rest round about" (2 Chron.15:15).
"Blessed [are ye] that hunger now: for ye shall be filled. Blessed [are ye] that weep now: for ye shall laugh" (Lk.6:21).
"Blessed [are] they which do hunger and thirst after righteousness: for they shall be filled" (Mt.5:6).

6. The showbread pointed to the great need of people for the bread of God's presence and worship. A constant diet of unhealthy things will cause a person to become sick and unhealthy, things such as...

lust	jealousy	pride	envy	outbursts of anger
immorality	dissension	idolatry	gossip	drunkenness
apathy	laziness	impurity	sensuality	slothfulness
sorcery	disputes	enmities	strife	carousings

The bread of God's presence and worship is the only thing that will cause the soul to be healthy.

"And the LORD thy God will make thee plenteous in every work of thine hand, in the fruit of thy body, and in the fruit of thy cattle, and in the fruit of thy land, for good: for the LORD will again rejoice over thee for good, as he rejoiced over thy fathers" (Dt.30:9).
"They shall be abundantly satisfied with the fatness of thy house; and thou shalt make them drink of the river of thy pleasures" (Ps.36:8).

"I am feeble and sore broken: I have roared by reason of the disquietness of my heart. Lord, all my desire is before thee; and my groaning is not hid from thee. My heart panteth, my strength faileth me: as for the light of mine eyes, it also is gone from me" (Ps.38:8-10).

"Whom have I in heaven *but thee*? and *there is* none upon earth *that* I desire beside thee. My flesh and my heart faileth: *but* God *is* the strength of my heart, and my portion for ever" (Ps.73:25-26).

"Bless the LORD, O my soul: and all that is within me, bless his holy name. Bless the LORD, O my soul, and forget not all his benefits: Who forgiveth all thine iniquities; who healeth all thy diseases; Who redeemeth thy life from destruction; who crowneth thee with lovingkindness and tender mercies; Who satisfieth thy mouth with good things; so that thy youth is renewed like the eagle's" (Ps.103:1-5).

"Wherefore do ye spend money for that which is not bread? and your labour for that which satisfieth not? hearken diligently unto me, and eat ye that which is good, and let your soul delight itself in fatness" (Is.55:2).

"He that hath an ear, let him hear what the Spirit saith unto the churches; To him that overcometh will I give to eat of the tree of life, which is in the midst of the paradise of God" (Rev.2:7).

"He that hath an ear, let him hear what the Spirit saith unto the churches; To him that overcometh will I give to eat of the hidden manna, and will give him a white stone, and in the stone a new name written, which no man knoweth saving he that receiveth it" (Rev.2:17).

7. The showbread pointed to the bread that we all desperately need, the bread...
- that satisfies the hunger of our hearts
- that supplies our needs
- that provides for us
- that nourishes fellowship among us (cp. 1 Jn.1:3; Rev.3:20)

Note what Jesus Christ, the Son of God Himself, said about this bread:
⇒ It is "the true bread."

"Then Jesus said unto them, Verily, verily, I say unto you, Moses gave you not that bread from heaven; but my Father giveth you the true bread from heaven" (Jn.6:32).

⇒ It is "the living bread," the bread that causes a person to live forever.

"I am the living bread which came down from heaven: if any man eat of this bread, he shall live for ever: and the bread that I will give is my flesh, which I will give for the life of the world" (Jn.6:51).

⇒ It is "the bread of God."

"For the bread of God is he which cometh down from heaven, and giveth life unto the world" (Jn.6:33).

⇒ It is "the bread of life."

"And Jesus said unto them, I am the bread of life: he that cometh to me shall never hunger; and he that believeth on me shall never thirst" (Jn.6:35).
"I am that bread of life" (Jn.6:48).

Note what the disciples said about this bread.

"Then said they unto him, Lord, evermore give us this bread" (Jn.6:34).

8. The showbread pointed to the spiritual needs of man. This is seen in that the showbread sat in the Tabernacle itself, the very place where spiritual needs were met. This truth was dictated by both God and His Son, the Lord Jesus Christ.

"And he [God] humbled thee, and suffered thee to hunger, and fed thee with manna, which thou knewest not, neither did thy fathers know; that he might make thee know that man doth not live by bread only, but by every word that proceedeth out of the mouth of the LORD doth man live" (Dt.8:3).

"But he [Jesus Christ] answered and said, It is written, Man shall not live by bread alone, but by every word that proceedeth out of the mouth of God" (Mt.4:4).

TYPES, SYMBOLS, AND PICTURES
(Exodus 25:23-30)

Historical Term	Type or Picture (Scriptural Basis for Each)	Life Application for Today's Believer	Biblical Application for Today's Believer
The Table of Showbread (Ex.25:23-30; 40:22-23) See also Ex.35:13; 37:10-16; 39:36; 40:4, 22-23	*The purpose for the Table of Showbread was to be able to set the showbread before God.* *The Table of Showbread is the Symbol of God Himself as the Bread of Life. The showbread pointed to God Himself as the nourishment that a person really needs. Note that the loaves sat in God's presence, before His very face. The people were to acknowledge their dependence upon God, acknowledge that they needed His provision. They needed His watchful eye upon the bread, upon them as His followers. They needed Him to continue to provide their bread and food, to continue to look after and care for them. By setting the bread before God, they were declaring their belief and trust that He would continue to meet their needs.* **"Thou shalt also make a table of shittim wood: two cubits shall be the length thereof, and a cubit the breadth thereof, and a cubit and a half the height thereof" (Ex.25:23).** **"And he put the table in the tent of the congregation, upon the side of the tabernacle northward, without the vail. And he set the bread in order upon it before the LORD; as the LORD had commanded Moses" (Ex.40:22-23).**	What the Table of Showbread taught: God is the only One who can satisfy the spiritual hunger in a person's soul. God knows what a person needs in order to thrive; therefore God provides and cares for us, feeds the hunger of the believer's soul. Far too often, a person tries to live his life apart from God's provision and presence. But Scripture declares that Christ is the Living Bread that came *out of* heaven to satisfy the hunger of a person's soul. If a person attempts to satisfy his soul in any other way, the results will be empty and unsatisfying. Note this fact as well: God promises to meet the physical needs as well as the spiritual needs of the believer--if the believer will truly seek the kingdom of God and His righteousness above all else.	*"But my God shall supply all your need according to his riches in glory by Christ Jesus" (Ph.4:19; cp. Ps.23).* *"Thou preparest a table before me in the presence of mine enemies: thou anointest my head with oil; my cup runneth over" (Ps.23:5).* *"Oh how great is thy goodness, which thou hast laid up for them that fear thee; which thou hast wrought for them that trust in thee before the sons of men!" (Ps.31:19).* *"Trust in the LORD, and do good; so shalt thou dwell in the land, and verily thou shalt be fed" (Ps.37:3).* *"I am that bread of life" (Jn.6:48).* *"For the bread of God is he which cometh down from heaven, and giveth life unto the world" (Jn.6:33).* *"And Jesus said unto them, I am the bread of life: he that cometh to me shall never hunger; and he that believeth on me shall never thirst" (Jn.6:35).* *"But seek ye first the kingdom of God, and his righteousness; and all these things shall be added unto you" (Mt.6:33).*

The Table of Showbread

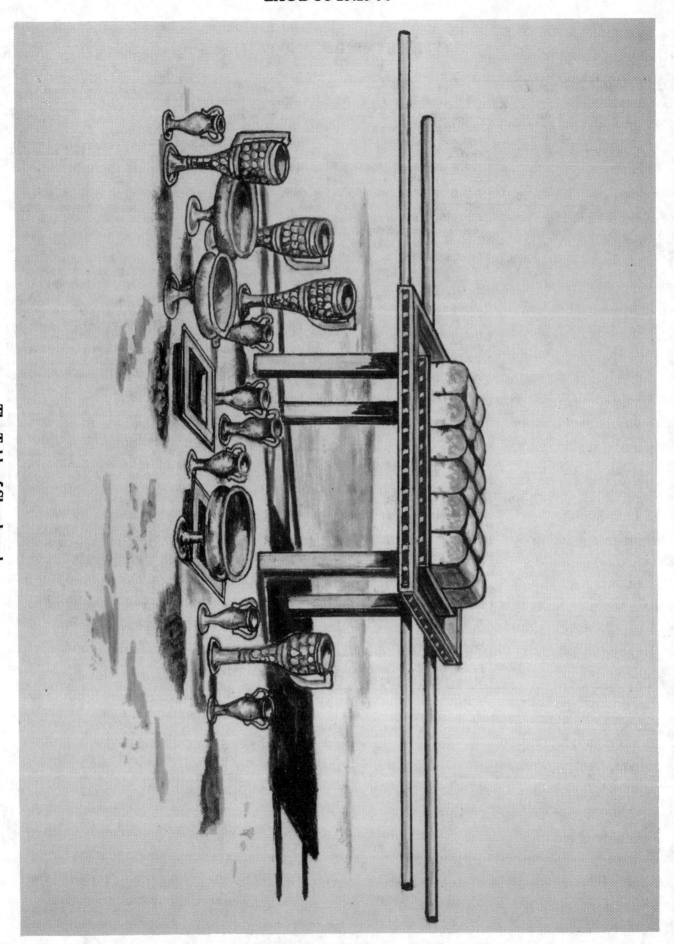

	D. The Gold Lampstand, the Symbol of God Himself as the Light of the World, 25:31-40	unto almonds, with their knops and their flowers.	like cups with buds & blossoms

1. The design & materials
a. To be made of pure gold, hammered out as one piece
  1) The center stem
  2) The branches with their flower-like cups, buds, & blossoms
b. To have six branches
  1) Three branches on each side
	31 And thou shalt make a candlestick of pure gold: of beaten work shall the candlestick be made: his shaft, and his branches, his bowls, his knops, and his flowers, shall be of the same.
	32 And six branches shall come out of the sides of it; three branches of the candlestick out of the one side, and three branches of the candlestick out of the other side:
		35 And there shall be a knop under two branches of the same, and a knop under two branches of the same, and a knop under two branches of the same, according to the six branches that proceed out of the candlestick.	d. To have one blossom under each pair of branches

2) Each branch was to have three cups shaped like almond flowers with buds & blossoms	33 Three bowls made like unto almonds, with a knop and a flower in one branch; and three bowls made like almonds in the other branch, with a knop and a flower: so in the six branches that come out of the candlestick. 34 And in the candlestick shall be four bowls made like	36 Their knops and their branches shall be of the same: all it shall be one beaten work of pure gold. 37 And thou shalt make the seven lamps thereof: and they shall light the lamps thereof, that they may give light over against it. 38 And the tongs thereof, and the snuffdishes thereof, shall be of pure gold. 39 Of a talent of pure gold shall he make it, with all these vessels. 40 And look that thou make them after their pattern, which was showed thee in the mount.	e. To hammer out the gold flower buds & branches as one piece with the Lampstand f. To make seven lamps for the Lampstand & set them so they would reflect light forward g. To make lampsnuffers & trays of pure gold to use with the lampstand h. To use 75 pounds of pure gold in the construction **2. The strict instructions & warning: To be made according to the pattern, the plan & design of God Himself**
c. To have a center stem with four similar almond flower-			

DIVISION IX

THE TABERNACLE, ITS BLUEPRINT AND PRIESTHOOD: THE TRUE WAY TO APPROACH AND WORSHIP GOD, EX.25:1-31:18

D. The Gold Lampstand, the Symbol of God Himself as the Light of the World, 25:31-40

(25:31-40) **Introduction**: spiritual darkness--is it a reality? Does it exist? Whether or not man acknowledges or recognizes it, spiritual darkness does indeed exist and is prevalent throughout the world. In every nation and every culture, millions of men and women are stumbling about in the darkness of this world. They are attempting to find the way through life on their own, yet they are stumbling about and falling ever more deeply into the abyss. Their hearts are crying out for some direction, some leading. But what they need--what we all need--is not anything the world has to offer, but the light of God, a clear picture showing how to reach God, the assurance that they are acceptable to God.

Yet the deep down assurance, the absolute certainty that they will live with God eternally, is missing. God knows this. God knows...

- that man's heart is blind and lacks assurance
- that man needs the way to God lit and lit brightly
- that man can never reach God unless God gives him light and shows man the way

This is what this passage is all about. This is: *The Gold (Lampstand, the Symbol of God Himself as the Light of the World*, Ex.25:31-40.
1. The design and materials (v.31-39).
2. The strict instructions and warning: to be made according to the pattern, the plan and design of God Himself (v.40).

1 (25:31-39) **Lampstand, The--Tabernacle--Light, Of the World--Jesus Christ, Light of the World**: the third piece of furniture was the Lampstand. The Lampstand was probably the most beautiful and ornate furniture in the Tabernacle. It was the first thing that captured the attention of the ministering priests as they entered the Sanctuary. Just imagine the experience of the priests who entered this room. The sense of smell quickly picked up the sweet scent of incense that filled the Holy Place. As the priests peered into the room without windows, a beautiful glow illuminated the Table of Showbread, the Altar of Incense, and the gold Lampstand. A sense of reverence and awe would have swept over their being as it would over any person entering such an atmosphere in the Holy Place of God.

1. The design and materials of the Lampstand were exact and precise (25:31-39). Again, God Himself designed the Lampstand. Human creativity had no part in designing this Lampstand, no part in designing anything in the Tabernacle. No person knew the perfect way to approach God; no person knew perfectly how to please God in his worship. God and God alone knew how He was to be approached and worshipped. Therefore, God and God alone had to design the Lampstand and the other furnishings that were to be used in worshipping Him.

a. The Lampstand was to be made of pure gold, hammered out as one piece (v.31). The entire Lampstand was to be of one piece of gold: the base and center stem, the flower-like lamp cups, buds, and blossoms.
b. The Lampstand was to have six branches (v.32-38).
⇒ Three branches were to be on each side (v.32).
⇒ Each branch was to have three cups shaped like almond flowers with buds and blossoms (v.33).

c. The Lampstand was to have four similar flower-like cups, one flower bud under each pair of branches (v.34).
d. The Lampstand was to have one blossom or bud under each pair of branches (v.35). All this means that the total number of ornaments was 69. Imagine 69 ornaments on one Lampstand. What beauty and splendor must have attracted the eye of the priest as he entered the Holy Place and saw the glowing, flickering flames arising from the seven light holders (six branches and the center stem). The impact of these ornaments can be better seen when glanced at in a chart:

BRANCH NUMBER	ORNAMENT #1: CUPS	ORNAMENT #2: BUDS	ORNAMENT #3: BLOSSOMS	TOTAL ORNAMENTS
#1 on the left side: 3 sets	3 Cups (gebia)	3 Buds (kaphtorim)	3 Blossoms (perahehah)	9
#2 on the left side: 3 sets	3 Cups (gebia)	3 Buds (kaphtorim)	3 Blossoms (perahehah)	9
#3 on the left side: 3 sets	3 Cups (gebia)	3 Buds (kaphtorim)	3 Blossoms (perahehah)	9
Central shaft: 4 sets	4 Cups (gebia)	7 Buds (kaphtorim)	4 Blossoms (perahehah)	15
#1 on the right side: 3 sets	3 Cups (gebia)	3 Buds (kaphtorim)	3 Blossoms (perahehah)	9
#2 on the right side: 3 sets	3 Cups (gebia)	3 Buds (kaphtorim)	3 Blossoms (perahehah)	9
#3 on the right side: 3 sets	3 Cups (gebia)	3 Buds (kaphtorim)	3 Blossoms (perahehah)	9
				TOTAL: 69

e. The decorations (flower buds) and branches were to be hammered out as one piece with the stem (v.36).
f. The seven lamps were to be made for the Lampstand and set so they would reflect the light forward (v.37).
g. The lampsnuffers and trays were to made of pure gold to use with the lampstand (v.38).
h. The Lampstand and the accessories would require 75 pounds of pure gold (v.39).

2 (25:40) **Lampstand, The--Tabernacle--Light--God, Light of the World--Jesus Christ, Light of the World**: note the strict instructions and warning given by God: the Lampstand was to be made according to the pattern, the plan and design of God Himself. This was a warning to Israel and to all succeeding generations as well, a warning that the Tabernacle and its furnishings...
• were only types of the real salvation and worship of God
• were only symbolic of how a person was to approach and worship God

A person must be sure, very sure, that he does not miss this truth, the reality lying behind the type and symbol. As Scripture says, these things were only shadows of good things to come:

"For the law having a shadow of good things to come, and not the very image of the things, can never with those sacrifices which they offered year by year continually make the comers thereunto perfect" (Heb.10:1).

What are the types and symbols, the shadows, the pictures seen in the Lampstand? There are at least four.
1. The Lampstand taught that a person needs light and illumination in order to know God and serve God. There were no windows, no opening (other than a closed door) within the Holy Place. The Holy Place would have been in complete darkness without the Lampstand. It was the Lampstand that gave light and illuminated the Holy Place so that the priests could serve God. Therefore, the light of the Lampstand...
• symbolized the need of man for light and illumination in order to know and serve God

2. The Lampstand pictures God's people (Israel) as the light of the world, as God's witness to the world. This is emphasized by Scripture itself:

"I the LORD have called thee in righteousness, and will hold thine hand, and will keep thee, and give thee for a covenant of the people, for a light of the Gentiles" (Is.42:6, cp. Zech.4:1-6).
"Ye are the light of the world. A city that is set on an hill cannot be hid" (Mt.5:14).
"For so hath the Lord commanded us, saying, I have set thee to be a light of the Gentiles, that thou shouldest be for salvation unto the ends of the earth" (Acts 13:47).

"For ye were sometimes darkness, but now are ye light in the Lord: walk as children of light" (Eph.5:8).

"That ye may be blameless and harmless, the sons of God, without rebuke, in the midst of a crooked and perverse nation, among whom ye shine as lights in the world" (Ph.2:15).

3. The Lampstand points to Jesus Christ as the Light of the world.

"The people that walked in darkness have seen a great light: they that dwell in the land of the shadow of death, upon them hath the light shined" (Is.9:2).

"In him was life; and the life was the light of men" (Jn.1:4).

"Then spake Jesus again unto them, saying, I am the light of the world: he that followeth me shall not walk in darkness, but shall have the light of life" (Jn.8:12).

"Then Jesus said unto them, Yet a little while is the light with you. Walk while ye have the light, lest darkness come upon you: for he that walketh in darkness knoweth not whither he goeth" (Jn.12:35).

"For God, who commanded the light to shine out of darkness, hath shined in our hearts, to give the light of the knowledge of the glory of God in the face of Jesus Christ" (2 Cor.4:6).

"Wherefore he saith, Awake thou that sleepest, and arise from the dead, and Christ shall give thee light" (Eph.5:14).

"And the city had no need of the sun, neither of the moon, to shine in it: for the glory of God did lighten it, and the Lamb is the light thereof" (Rev.21:23).

4. The Lampstand points to God as the Light of the world, the Light that shows man how to approach and worship Him. It was God who planned and designed the Lampstand, who showed the Israelites exactly how to approach and worship Him. He does the same for us.

"The LORD is my light and my salvation; whom shall I fear? the LORD is the strength of my life; of whom shall I be afraid?" (Ps.27:1).

"For the LORD God is a sun and shield: the LORD will give grace and glory: no good thing will he withhold from them that walk uprightly" (Ps.84:11).

"Thy sun shall no more go down; neither shall thy moon withdraw itself: for the LORD shall be thine everlasting light, and the days of thy mourning shall be ended" (Is.60:20).

"Rejoice not against me, O mine enemy: when I fall, I shall arise; when I sit in darkness, the LORD shall be a light unto me" (Mic.7:8).

"This then is the message which we have heard of him, and declare unto you, that God is light, and in him is no darkness at all. If we say that we have fellowship with him, and walk in darkness, we lie, and do not the truth: But if we walk in the light, as he is in the light, we have fellowship one with another, and the blood of Jesus Christ his Son cleanseth us from all sin" (1 Jn.1:5-7).

"And there shall be no night there; and they need no candle, neither light of the sun; for the Lord God giveth them light: and they shall reign for ever and ever" (Rev.22:5).

Thought 1. Jesus Christ is the true Lampstand. Christ came into the world to give light and illumination so that we might know and serve God. As the Light of the world, Christ fulfills the symbolism of the Lampstand. Christ and Christ alone is able to bring people out of the darkness of sin and death, giving them the light of salvation and eternal life.

1) The light of Christ is the true light, the only true light.

"The same [John the Baptist] came for a witness, to bear witness of the Light, that all *men* through him might believe. He was not that Light, but *was sent* to bear witness of that Light. *That* [Jesus Christ] was the true Light, which lighteth every man that cometh into the world" (Jn.1:7-9).

2) The light of Jesus Christ shines in the darkness and brings life to people.

"In him was life; and the life was the light of men. And the light shineth in darkness; and the darkness comprehended it not [can never extinguish it]" (Jn.1:4-5).

3) The light of Christ will keep people out of darkness and give them light.

"Then spake Jesus again unto them, saying, I am the light of the world: he that followeth me shall not walk in darkness, but shall have the light of life" (Jn.8:12).

4) The light of Christ is the only way for believing men to escape the darkness.

"I am come a light into the world, that whosoever believeth on me should not abide in darkness" (Jn.12:46).

5) The light of Christ brings the believer out of darkness into the marvelous light of God.

"But ye *are* a chosen generation, a royal priesthood, an holy nation, a peculiar people; that ye should show forth the praises of him who hath called you out of darkness into his marvelous light" (1 Pt.2:9).

6) The light of Christ is the only way a man can see and find his way to the Father.

"Jesus saith unto him, I am the way, the truth, and the life: no man cometh unto the Father, but by me" (Jn.14:6).

7) The light of Christ gives light to those who are spiritually asleep and dead.

"Wherefore he saith, Awake thou that sleepest, and arise from the dead, and Christ shall give thee light" (Eph.5:14).

8) The light of Christ brings life and immortality to people.

"But is now made manifest by the appearing of our Saviour Jesus Christ, who hath abolished death, and hath brought life and immortality to light through the gospel" (2 Ti.1:10).

9) The light of Christ makes people the children of light.

"Then Jesus said unto them, Yet a little while is the light with you. Walk while ye have the light, lest darkness come upon you: for he that walketh in darkness knoweth not whither he goeth. While ye have light, believe in the light, that ye may be the children of light. These things spake Jesus, and departed, and did hide himself from them" (Jn.12:35-36).

10) The light of Christ shines in the heart of the believer.

"For God, who commanded the light to shine out of darkness, hath shined in our hearts, to *give* the light of the knowledge of the glory of God in the face of Jesus Christ" (2 Cor.4:6).

11) The light of Christ is in the world.

"As long as I am in the world, I am the light of the world" (Jn.9:5).

12) The light of Christ has no darkness at all.

"This then is the message which we have heard of him [Christ], and declare unto you, that God is light, and in him is no darkness at all" (1 Jn.1:5).

13) The light of Christ will be the only light needed for the new Jerusalem.

"And the city had no need of the sun, neither of the moon, to shine in it: for the glory of God did lighten it, and the Lamb *is* the light thereof. And the nations of them which are saved shall walk in the light of it: and the kings of the earth do bring their glory and honour into it" (Rev.21:23-24).

TYPES, SYMBOLS, AND PICTURES
(Exodus 25:31-40)

Historical Term	Type or Picture (Scriptural Basis for Each)	Life Application for Today's Believer	Biblical Application for Today's Believer
The Gold Lampstand (Ex.25:31-40; 40:24) See also Ex.27:20-21; 35:14; 37:17-24; 39:37; 40:4, 25	*The Gold Lampstand provided the only light in the Holy Place. In the absence of light, darkness would have kept the priest from serving the LORD. The priest would have been helpless without light, unable to see his way, having to blindly feel his way around the Sanctuary. Thus the Lampstand pictures at least four things:* *a. The Lampstand symbol-*	a. The Lampstand pointed	*"The LORD is my light*

Historical Term	Type or Picture (Scriptural Basis for Each)	Life Application for Today's Believer	Biblical Application for Today's Believer
	ized God as the Light of the World.	to God as the Light of the world, the Light that shows a person how to approach and worship Him. It was God who planned and designed the Lampstand, who showed the Israelites exactly how to approach and worship Him. He does the same for us.	*and my salvation; whom shall I fear? the LORD is the strength of my life; of whom shall I be afraid?" (Ps.27:1).* *"This then is the message which we have heard of him, and declare unto you, that God is light, and in him is no darkness at all" (1 Jn.1:5).* *"For the LORD God is a sun and shield: the LORD will give grace and glory: no good thing will he withhold from them that walk uprightly" (Ps.84:11).*
	b. The Lampstand symbolized Jesus Christ as the Light of the World.	b. Jesus Christ is the true Lampstand. Christ came into the world to give light and illumination so that we might know and serve God. As the Light of the world, Christ fulfills the symbolism of the Lampstand. Christ and Christ alone is able to bring people out of the darkness of sin and death and give them the light of salvation and life, life now and forever.	*"The same [John the Baptist] came for a witness, to bear witness of the Light, that all men through him might believe. He was not that Light, but was sent to bear witness of that Light. That [Jesus Christ] was the true Light, which lighteth every man that cometh into the world" (Jn.1:7-9).* *"In him was life; and the life was the light of men. And the light shineth in darkness; and the darkness comprehended it not [can never extinguish it]" (Jn.1:4-5).* *"Then spake Jesus again unto them, saying, I am the light of the world: he that followeth me shall not walk in darkness, but shall have the light of life" (Jn.8:12).* *"I am come a light into the world, that whosoever believeth on me should not abide in darkness" (Jn.12:46).* *"Jesus saith unto him, I am the way, the truth, and the life: no man cometh unto the Father, but by me" (Jn.14:6).* *"For God, who commanded the light to shine out of darkness, hath shined in our hearts, to give the light of the knowledge of the glory of God in the face of Jesus Christ" (2 Cor.4:6).*
	c. The Lampstand symbolized believers, God's people, as the light of the world.	c. Believers are called to be the light of the world: they are to shine as God's witness to the world. In a world that is filled with darkness, God has placed His light in the hearts of	*"Ye are the light of the world. A city that is set on an hill cannot be hid" (Mt.5:14).* *"For ye were sometimes darkness, but now are ye light in the Lord: walk*

Historical Term	Type or Picture (Scriptural Basis for Each)	Life Application for Today's Believer	Biblical Application for Today's Believer
		His people. Every believer has the great responsibility to walk in the light so the world might see a witness of God's light.	*as children of light"* (Eph.5:8).
	d. *The Lampstand symbolized the Word of God, His Word that enables a person to know and serve God.* "And thou shalt make a candlestick of pure gold: of beaten work shall the candlestick be made: his shaft, and his branches, his bowls, his knops, and his flowers, shall be of the same" (Ex.25:31). "And he put the candlestick in the tent of the congregation, over against the table, on the side of the tabernacle southward" (Ex.40:24).	d. The believer must have light, the light of God's Word, in order to know God and serve God. The Word of God provides the believer light… • when he needs direction • when he needs wisdom • when he needs comfort • when he needs correction • when he needs anything from the infinite counsel of God.	*"Thy word is a lamp unto my feet, and a light unto my path"* (Ps.119:105). *"For the commandment is a lamp; and the law is light; and reproofs of instruction are the way of life"* (Pr. 6:23). *"All scripture is given by inspiration of God, and is profitable for doctrine, for reproof, for correction, for instruction in righteousness"* (2 Tim.3:16).

The Golden Lampstand With Its Lamps

1. It was to be a tent constructed of four coverings
  a. The 1st covering of fine linen: Pictured purity & righteousness
    1) The design: 10 curtains with cherubim
    2) The size
      • Each was to be about 42' long x 6' wide
      • Two groups of five curtains each were to be stitched together to make two long sets of curtains
    3) The loops & clasps to join & fasten the curtains together
      • To be blue material
      • To be sewed along the edges
      • To sew 50 loops on each curtain
      • To make 50 gold clasps: For fastening the curtains together, making the tabernacle a single tent
  b. The 2nd covering of goat hair: Pictured the need for a sin offering & for cleansing*DSI* (Num.28:15; Lev.16)
    1) The number: 11 curtains
    2) The size: Each was to be about 45' long x 6'wide
      • Five to be joined together into one set & six into another set
      • The 6th curtain: To be folded double at the front of the tent
    3) The loops & clasps
      • To sew 50 loops along the edge of both curtains

E. The Tabernacle Itself: The Symbol of God Dwelling Among His People & of Man's Need to Approach God Exactly as God Dictates, Ex.26:1-37

Moreover thou shalt make the tabernacle with ten curtains of fine twined linen, and blue, and purple, and scarlet: with cherubim of cunning work shalt thou make them. 2 The length of one curtain shall be eight and twenty cubits, and the breadth of one curtain four cubits: and every one of the curtains shall have one measure. 3 The five curtains shall be coupled together one to another; and other five curtains shall be coupled one to another. 4 And thou shalt make loops of blue upon the edge of the one curtain from the selvedge in the coupling; and likewise shalt thou make in the uttermost edge of another curtain, in the coupling of the second. 5 Fifty loops shalt thou make in the one curtain, and fifty loops shalt thou make in the edge of the curtain that is in the coupling of the second; that the loops may take hold one of another. 6 And thou shalt make fifty taches of gold, and couple the curtains together with the taches: and it shall be one tabernacle. 7 And thou shalt make curtains of goats' hair to be a covering upon the tabernacle: eleven curtains shalt thou make. 8 The length of one curtain shall be thirty cubits, and the breadth of one curtain four cubits: and the eleven curtains shall be all of one measure. 9 And thou shalt couple five curtains by themselves, and six curtains by themselves, and shalt double the sixth curtain in the forefront of the tabernacle. 10 And thou shalt make fifty loops on the edge of the one curtain that is outmost in the coupling, and fifty loops in the edge of the curtain which coupleth the second. 11 And thou shalt make fifty taches of brass, and put the taches into the loops, and couple the tent together, that it may be one. 12 And the remnant that remaineth of the curtains of the tent, the half curtain that remaineth, shall hang over the backside of the tabernacle. 13 And a cubit on the one side, and a cubit on the other side of that which remaineth in the length of the curtains of the tent, it shall hang over the sides of the tabernacle on this side and on that side, to cover it. 14 And thou shalt make a covering for the tent of rams' skins dyed red, and a covering above of badgers' skins. 15 And thou shalt make boards for the tabernacle of shittim wood standing up. 16 Ten cubits shall be the length of a board, and a cubit and a half shall be the breadth of one board. 17 Two tenons shall there be in one board, set in order one against another: thus shalt thou make for all the boards of the tabernacle. 18 And thou shalt make the boards for the tabernacle, twenty boards on the south side southward. 19 And thou shalt make forty sockets of silver under the twenty boards; two sockets under one board for his two tenons, and two sockets under another board for his two tenons. 20 And for the second side of the tabernacle on the north side there shall be twenty boards: 21 And their forty sockets of silver; two sockets under one board, and two sockets under another board. 22 And for the sides of the tabernacle westward thou shalt make six boards. 23 And two boards shalt thou make for the corners of the tabernacle in the two sides. 24 And they shall be coupled together beneath, and they shall be coupled together above the head of it unto one ring: thus shall it be for them

      • To make 50 bronze clasps: For fastening the curtains together, making the tabernacle a single tent
    4) The extra half sheet length of this first covering
      • To hang down at the rear of the tabernacle
      • To hang 18" extra over the sides of the tabernacle: To completely cover it
  c. The 3rd covering of ram skins dyed red: Pictured the blood
  d. The 4th covering of leather: Pictured a protective separation from the world

2. It was to be a tent hanging over wood framing (acacia wood): Symbolized stability, support, a strong foundation
  a. The size of each framing board: 15' long x 2¼' wide with two pegs set parallel to each other (for hooking to the base)
  b. The framing
    1) To make a wall, a frame of 20 boards on the south side
      • A foundation of 40 silver sockets or bases, 2 under each board
      • Joined together by pegs
    2) To make a wall frame of 20 boards on the north side: A foundation of 40 silver sockets, 2 sockets under each board
    3) To make a wall frame on the west of six boards
    4) To make a framing post of two boards for each corner
      • Joined together at the bottom
      • Joined together at the top, fitted into a single ring

- A total of 8 board frames & a foundation of 16 silver sockets, 2 under each board

  5) To make durable crossbars (acacia wood)
  - 5 crossbars for the south
  - 5 crossbars for the north
  - 5 crossbars for the west

  - The center crossbar was to run from end to end in the middle of the frames
  6) To cover the crossbars with gold & to make gold rings to hold the crossbars

  c. The strict instructions: To be exact—to build exactly according to plan, exactly as the design dictated
3. **It was to be a tent with a very special inner curtain, an inner veil: Symbolized God's majestic holiness & man's separation from God**
  a. A veil of great beauty & skill

both; they shall be for the two corners.

25 And they shall be eight boards, and their sockets of silver, sixteen sockets; two sockets under one board, and two sockets under another board.

26 And thou shalt make bars of shittim wood; five for the boards of the one side of the tabernacle,

27 And five bars for the boards of the other side of the tabernacle, and five bars for the boards of the side of the tabernacle, for the two sides westward.

28 And the middle bar in the midst of the boards shall reach from end to end.

29 And thou shalt overlay the boards with gold, and make their rings of gold for places for the bars: and thou shalt overlay the bars with gold.

30 And thou shalt rear up the tabernacle according to the fashion thereof which was showed thee in the mount.

31 And thou shalt make a vail of blue, and purple, and scarlet, and fine twined linen of cunning work: with cherubims shall it be made:

32 And thou shalt hang it upon four pillars of shittim wood overlaid with gold: their hooks shall be of gold, upon the four sockets of silver.

33 And thou shalt hang up the vail under the taches, that thou mayest bring in thither within the vail the ark of the testimony: and the vail shall divide unto you between the holy place and the most holy.

34 And thou shalt put the mercy seat upon the ark of the testimony in the most holy place.

35 And thou shalt set the table without the vail, and the candlestick over against the table on the side of the tabernacle toward the south: and thou shalt put the table on the north side.

36 And thou shalt make an hanging for the door of the tent, of blue, and purple, and scarlet, and fine twined linen, wrought with needlework.

37 And thou shalt make for the hanging five pillars of shittim wood, and overlay them with gold, and their hooks shall be of gold: and thou shalt cast five sockets of brass for them.

b. To hang with gold hooks on 4 posts of durable wood (acacia): Posts to stand on 4 silver sockets or bases

c. The purpose for the inner veil: To shield the ark of the testimony (covenant) from all else
  1) To separate the Holy Place from the Most Holy Place

  2) To separate the Mercy Seat from all else: Pictured separation, no access; man's desperate need for mercy
    - From the table: To be placed on the north side
    - From the lampstand: To be placed on the south side

4. **It was to be a tent with an outer curtain, a screen-like entrance: Symbolized the door into God's presence**
  a. *An entrance of great beauty & craftsmanship*
  b. *The hanging frame*
    1) Make gold hooks & 5 posts overlaid with gold
    2) Make 5 bronze bases for them

DIVISION IX

THE TABERNACLE, ITS BLUEPRINT AND PRIESTHOOD: THE TRUE WAY TO APPROACH AND WORSHIP GOD, EX.25:1-31:18

E.   The Tabernacle Itself: The Symbol of God Dwelling Among His People and of Man's Need to Approach God Exactly as God Dictates, Ex.26:1-37

(26:1-37) **Introduction**: note the magnitude of the following statement: the great Creator of the Universe--the Sovereign Lord and Majesty of all--wants to dwell among His people. God wants to dwell in a world...
- where many people ignore and scorn Him
- where many people curse and deny Him
- where many people have allowed sin to run rampant in their lives
- where people have even killed His Son, His only Son, the Lord Jesus Christ

The picture of the Tabernacle reveals God taking steps to give man a personal relationship with Himself. In having the Tabernacle built, it is important to note:
⇒ God was not cheapening Himself by dwelling among His people.
⇒ God was not demeaning His holy character by associating with sinful men.
⇒ God was not compromising His greatness by coming down to live with people.

The truth is this: by coming to earth to live with people, God was revealing His great compassion and love for people. In fact, God was teaching His people two basic things through the Tabernacle:
1. God loved His people and wanted to be with them, wanted to dwell and live among them.
2. God had to be approached by His people in the right way, exactly as God dictated.

God's master plan to dwell with His people is further revealed to Moses in this chapter. The design of the Tabernacle was a plan of great beauty and craftsmanship. The Tabernacle would soon become the most ornate portable place of worship in the world, designed by God Himself.

EXODUS 26:1-37

In seeking to understand the Tabernacle, we must do exactly what Stephen Olford, the excellent expositor of Scripture, says:

> "In seeking to interpret the Tabernacle, we must not dogmatize but humbly follow the method of the Holy Spirit as illustrated in the Epistle to the Hebrews. Referring there to the Tabernacle and the priesthood, He speaks of the 'shadow of heavenly things' (Hebrews 8:5); 'the patterns of things in the heavens' (Hebrews 9:23); 'the figures of the true' (Hebrews 9:24); 'a shadow of good things to come' (Hebrews 10:1). Thus it is clear that the Tabernacle was intended to signify spiritual realities. In other words, in the Tabernacle we see shadows, patterns, and figures of heavenly or spiritual things that are revealed in Christ."[1]

The Tabernacle itself is the subject of this most important passage of Scripture. This is: *The Tabernacle Itself: The Symbol of God Dwelling Among His People and of Man's Need to Approach God Exactly as God Dictates*, Ex.26:1-37.
1. It was to be a tent constructed of four coverings (v.1-14).
2. It was to be a tent hanging over wood framing (acacia wood): symbolized stability, support, a strong foundation (v.15-30).
3. It was to be a tent with a very special inner curtain, an inner veil: symbolized God's majestic holiness and man's separation from God (v.31-35).
4. It was to be a tent with an outer curtain, a screen-like entrance: symbolized the door into God's presence (v.36-37).

1 (26:1-14) **Tabernacle--Tent--Curtains--Covering of Tabernacle--Righteousness, of God**: the Tabernacle was a tent constructed of four coverings that were to serve as the roof and sides of the Tabernacle.

1. The first covering was made of ten linen curtains that served as the inside ceiling and walls (v.1-6). This inner covering would be what the priests would see as they ministered in the Holy Place and in the Most Holy Place. To behold such a striking beauty was the greatest of privileges, a privilege that no one else would have. Each trip inside the Tabernacle was an experience beyond description. It was a trip into the presence of the God of Abraham, Isaac, and Jacob, into the presence of the LORD God Himself (Jehovah, Yahweh). The curtains symbolized purity and righteousness. The priest who entered into the Tabernacle never lost sight of God's character. As he looked up and studied the curtains, he saw the blue, purple, and scarlet yarn--all twisted and sewn together to make the linen. He knew what the colors meant: the blue represented the heavenly nature of God, the purple His kingly nature, and the scarlet His humility in receiving and accepting man through sacrifice. The priest was bound to be caught up in the worship of God, in all that God is.

Moreover, as he worshipped God, the priest knew that his feeble act of worship was focused upon the One who was perfectly pure and absolutely righteous. As the priest gazed about the Holy Place, the light from the Lampstand illuminated the beautiful linen walls and ceiling, the Table, the Altar of Incense, and the Lampstand itself. Everything in the Sanctuary magnified God's glory and made even the most prideful man take note of how small he is when in the presence of a pure and righteous God. Note the facts about these unique curtains:
   a. The design of cherubim was embroidered on each curtain (v.1). With a background color of blue, purple, and scarlet, the curtains were without doubt breathtaking.
   b. The size of each curtain was to be about 42 feet long by 6 feet wide (v.2). Two groups of five curtains each were to be stitched together to make two sets of long curtains (v.3).
   c. The loops and clasps to join and fasten the curtains together were to be made of blue material and sewn along the edges (v.4). A total of 50 loops were to be sewn on each curtain (v.5). The curtains were fastened together by making 50 gold clasps that were inserted through the connecting loops. This made the Tabernacle a single tent (v.6).

Thought 1. Jesus Christ fulfilled the symbolism of these inner curtains by being the perfect embodiment of purity and righteousness.
1) Jesus Christ is the righteousness of believers just as the fine linen is a symbol of righteousness.

> "And to her was granted that she should be arrayed in fine linen, clean and white: for the **fine linen** is the righteousness of saints" (Rev.19:8).
> "But of him are ye in Christ Jesus, who of God is made unto us wisdom, and righteousness, and sanctification, and redemption" (1 Cor.1:30).
> "For he hath made him to be sin for us, who knew no sin; that we might be made the righteousness of God in him" (2 Cor.5:21).
> "But now the righteousness of God without the law is manifested, being witnessed by the law and the prophets; Even the righteousness of God which is by faith of Jesus Christ unto all and upon all them that believe: for there is no difference" (Ro.3:21-22).

2) Jesus Christ is righteous and pure, without sin.

> "For he hath made him to be sin for us, who knew no sin; that we might be made the righteousness of God in him" (2 Cor.5:21).
> "For we have not an high priest which cannot be touched with the feeling of our infirmities; but was in all points tempted like as we are, yet without sin" (Heb.4:15).
> "For such an high priest became us, who is holy, harmless, undefiled, separate from sinners, and made higher than the heavens" (Heb.7:26).

---
[1] Stephen F. Olford. *The Tabernacle, Camping with God*, p.21-22.
303

"But with the precious blood of Christ, as of a lamb without blemish and without spot" (1 Pt.1:19).
"And ye know that he was manifested to take away our sins; and in him is no sin" (1 Jn.3:5).

3) Jesus Christ loves righteousness.

"Thou [the Messiah] lovest righteousness, and hatest wickedness: therefore God, thy God, hath anointed thee with the oil of gladness above thy fellows" (Ps.45:7).

4) Jesus Christ is the Righteous Branch.

"Behold, the days come, saith the LORD, that I will raise unto David a righteous Branch, and a King shall reign and prosper, and shall execute judgment and justice in the earth" (Jer.23:5).

Thought 2. Whenever a believer enters into the presence of God, he is to focus upon two facts:
1) The fact that God is pure and righteous.

"According to thy name, O God, so *is* thy praise unto the ends of the earth: thy right hand is full of righteousness" (Ps.48:10).
"Clouds and darkness *are* round about him: righteousness and judgment *are* the habitation of his throne" (Ps.97:2).
"The LORD *is* righteous in all his ways, and holy in all his works" (Ps.145:17).
"In his days Judah shall be saved, and Israel shall dwell safely: and this *is* his name whereby he shall be called, THE LORD OUR RIGHTEOUSNESS" (Jer.23:6).

2) The fact that God demands righteousness, that any person who approaches and worships God must live a righteous life.

"For I say unto you, That except your righteousness shall exceed [the righteousness] of the scribes and Pharisees, ye shall in no case enter into the kingdom of heaven" (Mt.5:20).
"Awake to righteousness, and sin not; for some have not the knowledge of God: I speak this to your shame" (1 Cor.15:34).

2. The second covering was made of goat hair. This covering symbolized the need for the sin offering and for cleansing (v.7-13). It is significant that this outer curtain of goat hair was laid on top of the inner curtain. If the inner curtain is symbolic of purity and righteousness, then the place for the goat hair is most appropriate. It clearly pictures that a person's sins must be forgiven before he can approach the righteousness of God. The picture is this: as God gave Moses the pattern for the Tabernacle, it is important to note the sequence: from the inside out.
⇒ The first covering of linen: speaks of purity and righteousness.
⇒ The second covering of goat skin: speaks of the need for a sin offering and cleansing in order to approach the righteousness of God.

Most likely, this goatskin covering was black in color (see Song of Solomon 1:5). This covering of goat hair was coarse to touch, unlike the soft fine linen of the inner curtains. Contrasted with the beautiful blue, purple, and scarlet curtain that was embroidered with cherubim, the curtains of goat hair were not very appealing to view. Sin is never a pretty picture, but the curtains of goat hair speak of sacrifice, the fact that God forgives our sins through the blood of the sacrifice.
These are the facts that apply to the covering of goat hair:
a. The number of the curtains was eleven (v.7).
b. The size of each curtain was to be about 45 feet long by 6 feet wide (v.8). Five of the curtains were to be joined together into one set and six curtains into another set. The sixth curtain was to be folded double at the front of the tent (v.9).
c. The loops and clasps fastened the curtains together, making the curtains a single covering for the tent or Tabernacle. Note the instructions:
⇒ to sew 50 loops along the edge of both curtains
⇒ to make 50 bronze clasps for fastening the curtains together (v.10-11).
d. The extra half sheet length of this first covering was to hang down at the rear of the Tabernacle (v.12). The goat hair curtain was to hang 18 inches over the sides of the Tabernacle.

Thought 1. The Lord Jesus Christ is the One who took the blackness of sin upon Himself. He became the sin-offering for the sins of His people. (See Deeper Study # 1, Goats--Sin Offering--Ex.26:7-13 for more discussion.)

"Yet it pleased the LORD to bruise him; he hath put *him* to grief: when thou shalt make his soul an offering for sin, he shall see *his* seed, he shall prolong *his* days, and the pleasure of the LORD shall prosper in his hand" (Is.53:10).
"Therefore will I divide him *a portion* with the great, and he shall divide the spoil with the strong; because he hath poured out his soul unto death: and he was numbered with the transgressors; and he bare the sin of many, and made intercession for the transgressors" (Is.53:12).
"For he hath made him *to be* sin for us, who knew no sin; that we might be made the righteousness of God in him" (2 Cor.5:21).

"Who gave himself for our sins, that he might deliver us from this present evil world, according to the will of God and our Father" (Gal.1:4).

"And walk in love, as Christ also hath loved us, and hath given himself for us an offering and a sacrifice to God for a sweetsmelling savour" (Eph.5:2).

"Who his own self bare our sins in his own body on the tree, that we, being dead to sins, should live unto righteousness: by whose stripes ye were healed" (1 Pt.2:24).

"And from Jesus Christ, *who is* the faithful witness, *and* the first begotten of the dead, and the prince of the kings of the earth. Unto him that loved us, and washed us from our sins in his own blood" (Rev.1:5).

3. The third covering of ram skins symbolized the sacrificial blood. The ram skins had the wool removed and were then dyed red. Red, of course, is symbolic of the sacrificial blood.

Thought 1. The third covering of ram skins points to the sacrifice of Jesus Christ and His shed blood for sinners.

1) It is by the blood of Jesus Christ that our sins are forgiven.

"For this is my blood of the new testament, which is shed for many for the remission of sins" (Mt.26:28).

2) It is by the blood of Jesus Christ that He has purchased us.

"Take heed therefore unto yourselves, and to all the flock, over the which the Holy Ghost hath made you overseers, to feed the church of God, which he hath purchased with his own blood" (Acts 20:28).

3) It is by the blood of Jesus Christ that we are justified.

"Much more then, being now justified by his blood, we shall be saved from wrath through him" (Ro.5:9).

4) It is by the blood of Jesus Christ that our consciences are purged from dead works.

"How much more shall the blood of Christ, who through the eternal Spirit offered himself without spot to God, purge your conscience from dead works to serve the living God?" (Heb.9:14).

5) It is by the blood of Jesus Christ that we are cleansed from all sin.

"But if we walk in the light, as he is in the light, we have fellowship one with another, and the blood of Jesus Christ his Son cleanseth us from all sin" (1 Jn.1:7).

6) It is by the blood of Jesus Christ that we are freed from the power of sin.

"And from Jesus Christ, *who is* the faithful witness, *and* the first begotten of the dead, and the prince of the kings of the earth. Unto him that loved us, and washed us from our sins in his own blood" (Rev.1:5).

4. The outside covering was the covering of leather or of seal skins. The outer covering of leather was symbolic of a protective separation from the world.[2] It was the covering that kept the Tabernacle safe from the elements of the weather and the wilderness: the scorching sun, the torrential rains, the wind-blasted sand, and the wild animals. Moving from campsite to campsite, the Tabernacle obviously took a constant beating. The covering of leather protected the Tabernacle from the outside, from the elements of the world. In simple terms, it kept the bad things out (the world) and the good things in (the worship of God). Today, there are many things that the believer needs in order to have protective separation from the world.

Thought 1. The outer covering of leather is a picture of separation, of being protected from the world and the things in the world.
1) The believer needs protection from the pleasures of the world.

"Love not the world, neither the things *that are* in the world. If any man love the world, the love of the Father is not in him. For all that is in the world, the lust of the flesh, and the lust of the eyes, and the pride of life, is not of the Father, but is of the world" (1 Jn.2:15-16).

---

[2]   Frank E. Gaebelein. *The Expositor's Bible Commentary*, Vol. 2, p.459.

2) The believer needs protection from the unclean thing.

"Therefore if any man be in Christ, he is a new creature: old things are passed away; behold, all things are become new. And all things are of God, who hath reconciled us to himself by Jesus Christ, and hath given to us the ministry of reconciliation" (2 Cor.5:17-18).

3) The believer needs protection from the course or the path of the world.

"And you hath he quickened, who were dead in trespasses and sins; Wherein in time past ye walked according to the course of this world, according to the prince of the power of the air, the spirit that now worketh in the children of disobedience" (Eph.2:1-2).

4) The believer needs protection from the cares of the world.

"Therefore take no thought, saying, What shall we eat? or, What shall we drink? or, Wherewithal shall we be clothed? (For after all these things do the Gentiles seek:) for your heavenly Father knoweth that ye have need of all these things. But seek ye first the kingdom of God, and his righteousness; and all these things shall be added unto you. Take therefore no thought for the morrow: for the morrow shall take thought for the things of itself. Sufficient unto the day [is] the evil thereof" (Mt.6:31-34).

"He also that received seed among the thorns is he that heareth the word; and the care of this world, and the deceitfulness of riches, choke the word, and he becometh unfruitful" (Mt.13:22).

5) The believer needs protection from evil associations.

"But now I have written unto you not to keep company, if any man that is called a brother be a fornicator, or covetous, or an idolater, or a railer, or a drunkard, or an extortioner; with such an one no not to eat" (1 Cor.5:11).

"Be ye not unequally yoked together with unbelievers: for what fellowship hath righteousness with unrighteousness? and what communion hath light with darkness?" (2 Cor.6:14).

"Thou shalt not follow a multitude to do evil; neither shalt thou speak in a cause to decline after many to wrest judgment" (Ex.23:2).

"Blessed is the man that walketh not in the counsel of the ungodly, nor standeth in the way of sinners, nor sitteth in the seat of the scornful" (Ps.1:1).

"Enter not into the path of the wicked, and go not in the way of evil men" (Pr.4:14).

"Be not thou envious against evil men, neither desire to be with them" (Pr.24:1).

Thought 2. Jesus Christ fulfilled the symbolism of the outer cover. Jesus Christ is our protective separation from the world and from the coming wrath of God against the evil of the world. Jesus Christ protects us from the world's perils and temptations and from God's terrible wrath against the sins of the world.

1) Jesus Christ protects us by saving us from the wrath of God against sin and evil.

"For God so loved the world, that he gave his only begotten Son, that whosoever believeth in him should not perish, but have everlasting life" (Jn.3:16).

"Much more then, being now justified by his blood, we shall be saved from wrath through him" (Ro.5:9).

"Who gave himself for our sins, that he might deliver us from this present evil world, according to the will of God and our Father" (Gal.1:4).

2) Jesus Christ protects us by sanctifying us, setting us apart unto God.

"But of him are ye in Christ Jesus, who of God is made unto us wisdom, and righteousness, and sanctification, and redemption" (1 Cor.1:30).

"If a man therefore purge himself from these, he shall be a vessel unto honour, sanctified, and meet for the master's use, and prepared unto every good work" (2 Tim.2:21).

"Wherefore Jesus also, that he might sanctify the people with his own blood, suffered without the gate" (Heb.13:12).

"Elect according to the foreknowledge of God the Father, through sanctification of the Spirit, unto obedience and sprinkling of the blood of Jesus Christ: Grace unto you, and peace, be multiplied" (1 Pt.1:2).

3)	Jesus Christ protects us by sanctifying us with His Word.

"I have given them thy word; and the world hath hated them, because they are not of the world, even as I am not of the world. I pray not that thou shouldest take them out of the world, but that thou shouldest keep them from the evil. They are not of the world, even as I am not of the world. Sanctify them through thy truth: thy word is truth" (Jn.17:14-17).

4)	Jesus Christ protects us with His watchful eyes.

"For the eyes of the LORD run to and fro throughout the whole earth, to show himself strong in the behalf of *them* whose heart *is* perfect toward him. Herein thou hast done foolishly: therefore from henceforth thou shalt have wars" (2 Chron.16:9).

5)	Jesus Christ protects us by surrounding us.

"As the mountains *are* round about Jerusalem, so the LORD *is* round about his people from henceforth even for ever" (Ps.125:2).

6)	Jesus Christ protects us, even the hairs upon our head.

"But there shall not an hair of your head perish" (Lk.21:18).

DEEPER STUDY # 1
(Ex.26:7-13) **Goats--Sin Offering**: throughout Scripture, the goat is pictured as an animal used in the sin offering.

"Or if his sin, wherein he hath sinned, come to his knowledge; he shall bring his offering, a kid of the goats, a male without blemish: And he shall lay his hand upon the head of the goat, and kill it in the place where they kill the burnt offering before the LORD: it is a sin offering" (Lev.4:23-24).

"Or if his sin, which he hath sinned, come to his knowledge: then he shall bring his offering, a kid of the goats, a female without blemish, for his sin which he hath sinned" (Lev.4:28).

"And he shall bring his trespass offering unto the LORD for his sin which he hath sinned, a female from the flock, a lamb or a kid of the goats, for a sin offering; and the priest shall make an atonement for him concerning his sin" (Lev.5:6).

"And he brought the people's offering, and took the goat, which was the sin offering for the people, and slew it, and offered it for sin, as the first" (Lev.9:15).

"And Moses diligently sought the goat of the sin offering, and, behold, it was burnt: and he was angry with Eleazar and Ithamar, the sons of Aaron which were left alive, saying, Wherefore have ye not eaten the sin offering in the holy place, seeing it is most holy, and God hath given it you to bear the iniquity of the congregation, to make atonement for them before the LORD?" (Lev.10:16-17).

"And he shall take of the congregation of the children of Israel two kids of the goats for a sin offering, and one ram for a burnt offering" (Lev.16:5).

"And he shall take the two goats, and present them before the LORD at the door of the tabernacle of the congregation. And Aaron shall cast lots upon the two goats; one lot for the LORD, and the other lot for the scapegoat. And Aaron shall bring the goat upon which the LORD'S lot fell, and offer him for a sin offering. But the goat, on which the lot fell to be the scapegoat, shall be presented alive before the LORD, to make an atonement with him, and to let him go for a scapegoat into the wilderness" (Lev.16:7-10).

"Then shall he kill the goat of the sin offering, that is for the people, and bring his blood within the vail, and do with that blood as he did with the blood of the bullock, and sprinkle it upon the mercy seat, and before the mercy seat" (Lev.16:15).

"And he shall go out unto the altar that is before the LORD, and make an atonement for it; and shall take of the blood of the bullock, and of the blood of the goat, and put it upon the horns of the altar round about" (Lev.16:18).

"And when he hath made an end of reconciling the holy place, and the tabernacle of the congregation, and the altar, he shall bring the live goat: And Aaron shall lay both his hands upon the head of the live goat, and confess over him all the iniquities of the children of Israel, and all their transgressions in all their sins, putting them upon the head of the goat, and shall send him away by the hand of a fit man into the wilderness: And the goat shall bear upon him all their iniquities unto a land not inhabited: and he shall let go the goat in the wilderness" (Lev.16:20-22).

"And he that let go the goat for the scapegoat shall wash his clothes, and bathe his flesh in water, and afterward come into the camp. And the bullock for the sin offering, and the goat for the sin offering, whose blood was brought in to make atonement in the holy place, shall one carry forth without the camp; and they shall burn in the fire their skins, and their flesh, and their dung" (Lev.16:26-27).

> "Neither by the blood of goats and calves, but by his own blood he entered in once into the holy place, having obtained eternal redemption for us. For if the blood of bulls and of goats, and the ashes of an heifer sprinkling the unclean, sanctifieth to the purifying of the flesh" (Heb.9:12-13).
>
> "For when Moses had spoken every precept to all the people according to the law, he took the blood of calves and of goats, with water, and scarlet wool, and hyssop, and sprinkled both the book, and all the people" (Heb.9:19).
>
> "For it is not possible that the blood of bulls and of goats should take away sins" (Heb.10:4).

2 (26:15-30) **Tabernacle of Moses--Pattern--Frame**: the Tabernacle was to be a tent hanging over wood framing (acacia wood). The curtains and coverings would have been useless without the wood framing. The wood framing had a very practical purpose: to support the curtains and coverings. Instead of a solid wall of gold-covered boards, it is most likely that the Tabernacle was built like a trellis. A solid wall of boards would have blocked the inner linen curtains from being seen by the priests. Note the facts about the wood framing:

1. The size of each framing board was 15 feet long by 2¼ feet wide with two pegs set parallel to each other for hooking to the base (v.15-17).

2. The framing consisted of the following items with instructions:
    a. To make a wall, a frame of 20 boards on the south side (v.18). On the south side there was a foundation of 40 silver sockets or bases, two under each board which were joined together by pegs (v.19).
    b. To make a wall, a frame of 20 boards on the north side (v.20). Like the south side, the north side was to have a foundation of 40 silver sockets, two sockets under each board (v.21). Each one of the silver sockets required about 75 pounds of silver. Why did God want the foundation built of silver? Why not gold or bronze? Because silver is a symbol of the atonement: of reconciliation, ransom, or redemption. The silver was collected by taking up an offering that is actually called *atonement money* (Ex.30:11-16; 38:25-28). Each Israelite man gave *atonement money* in the form of silver. Each man gave the same amount of silver--rich and poor, famous and unknown, educated and uneducated. (See outline and notes--Ex.30:11-16; cp. Ex.38:25-28 for a more detailed study on the atonement money.)

Thought 1. The silver in the Tabernacle would be an ever-present reminder of man's need for atonement: for reconciliation with God, for redemption. The foundation of the Tabernacle would be a foundation of silver. This pictured a glorious truth: the foundation of the believer is to be redemption, reconciliation with God through His Son the LORD Jesus Christ. The great need for the foundation of redemption is clearly seen by looking at Israel's experience.

⇒ The Tabernacle was firmly planted in the shifting sands of the desert (a symbol of the world and its wilderness).

> "Therefore whosoever heareth these sayings of mine, and doeth them, I will liken him unto a wise man, which built his house upon a rock: And the rain descended, and the floods came, and the winds blew, and beat upon that house; and it fell not: for it was founded upon a rock" (Mt.7:24-25).

⇒ The Tabernacle was firmly planted under God's direction and care as He led His people from campsite to campsite.

> "Trust in the LORD with all thine heart; and lean not unto thine own understanding. In all thy ways acknowledge him, and he shall direct thy paths" (Pr.3:5-6).

⇒ The Tabernacle was firmly planted in God's ability to save helpless men.

> "For when we were yet without strength, in due time Christ died for the ungodly" (Ro.5:6).

    c. To make a wall frame of six boards on the west (v.22).
    d. To make a framing post of two boards for each corner (v.23)...
        • joined together at the bottom
        • joined together at the top, fitting into a single ring (v.24)
        • having a total of eight board frames and a foundation of sixteen silver sockets, two under each board (v.25)

    e. To make durable crossbars (acacia wood). There were to be...
        • 5 crossbars for the south (v.26)
        • 5 crossbars for the north (v.27)
        • 5 crossbars for the west (v.27)

The exact design as to how these crossbars were arranged on each of the three walls is unknown. What is known is that the center crossbar was to run from end to end in the middle of the frames (v.28).
    f. To cover the crossbars with gold and to make gold rings to hold the crossbars (v.29). The 15 crossbars served as a means of stability to the wood framing. Without the support of the crossbars, the Tabernacle would have been at

the mercy of every contrary wind. The Scripture gives no reason why God wanted five crossbars for each wall. What we do know and can apply in a most practical way is the purpose of the crossbars: to give stability and support.

Thought 1. The stability and support of the crossbars pictures the stability and support that Jesus Christ gives each believer.
1) Jesus Christ is our support, our eternal refuge.

"**The eternal God *is thy* refuge, and underneath *are* the everlasting arms: and he shall thrust out the enemy from before thee; and shall say, Destroy *them***" (Dt.33:27).

2) Jesus Christ holds us, sustains us with His right hand.

"**Thou hast also given me the shield of thy salvation: and thy right hand hath holden me up, and thy gentleness hath made me great**" (Ps.18:35).

3) Jesus Christ strengthens us, holds us up.

"**Fear thou not; for I *am* with thee: be not dismayed; for I *am* thy God: I will strengthen thee; yea, I will help thee; yea, I will uphold thee with the right hand of my righteousness**" (Is.41:10).

4) Jesus Christ delivers us.

"**And the Lord shall deliver me from every evil work, and will preserve *me* unto his heavenly kingdom: to whom *be* glory for ever and ever. Amen**" (2 Tim.4:18).

5) Jesus Christ preserves us, those who are faithful.

"**O love the LORD, all ye his saints: *for* the LORD preserveth the faithful, and plentifully rewardeth the proud doer**" (Ps.31:23).

3. The instructions were to be exact: the Tabernacle was to be built exactly according to plan, exactly as God's design dictated (v.30). God's plan is reinforced once again. No short-cuts were to be taken. No materials were to be replaced by other materials. No dimensions were to be adjusted. No man-made suggestions were to be submitted. The Tabernacle had to be built *exactly* as God commanded.

"**This book of the law shall not depart out of thy mouth; but thou shalt meditate therein day and night, that thou mayest observe to do according to all that is written therein: for then thou shalt make thy way prosperous, and then thou shalt have good success**" (Josh.1:8).
"**Not every one that saith unto me, Lord, Lord, shall enter into the kingdom of heaven; but he that doeth the will of my Father which is in heaven**" (Mt.7:21).
"**He that hath my commandments, and keepeth them, he it is that loveth me: and he that loveth me shall be loved of my Father, and I will love him, and will manifest myself to him**" (Jn.14:21).
"**If ye keep my commandments, ye shall abide in my love; even as I have kept my Father's commandments, and abide in his love....Ye are my friends, if ye do whatsoever I command you**" (Jn.15:10, 14).
"**Then Peter and the *other* apostles answered and said, We ought to obey God rather than men**" (Acts 5:29).

3 (26:31-35) **Tabernacle of Moses--Pattern--Inner Veil--Approaching God--Holiness**: the Tabernacle was to be a tent with a very special inner curtain or door, an inner veil. The *inner curtain* or *veil* symbolized God's majestic holiness and man's terrible separation from God. This special curtain or veil was made just like the inner covering of the Tabernacle that covered the Holy Place and the Most Holy Place. Note the facts as they are described by the Scripture:
1. It was a veil of great beauty made with remarkable skill (v.31). Like the inner curtain, it was made of fine linen. The same striking colors of blue, purple, and scarlet were a part of this veil. The embroidered cherubim were also worked into this veil.
2. It was to hang with gold hooks on four posts of durable wood (acacia). The posts were to stand on four silver sockets or bases (v.32).
3. The purpose for the inner veil was basically to shield the ark of the testimony (covenant) from all else.
   a. The inner veil was to separate the Holy Place from the Most Holy Place (v.33). This symbolized the majestic holiness and righteousness of God, the light of His perfection which no man can approach.

"**Who only hath immortality, dwelling in the light which no man can approach unto; whom no man hath seen, nor can see: to whom be honour and power everlasting. Amen**" (1 Tim.6:16).

b. The inner veil was to separate the Mercy Seat from all else. The veil symbolized the holiness of God, separation from the presence of God (v.34). Note what was to be separated from the Mercy Seat in the Most Holy Place:
⇒ The Table of Showbread: the table was to be placed on the north side in the Holy Place (v.35).
⇒ The Lampstand: the Lampstand was to be placed opposite the table on the south side (v.35).

Why was this necessary? The separation of the Mercy Seat from all else symbolized man's terrible separation from God, that man has no access to God, none whatsoever--not apart from God's mercy. God's mercy is an absolute essential if man's approach to God is to be acceptable. How do we know that God has mercy upon us? Because He sent His Son into the world...
• as the Bread of Life (pictured by the Table of Showbread. See outline and notes--Ex.25:22-30 for more discussion.)
• as the Light of the World (pictured by the Lampstand. See outline and notes--Ex.25:31-40 for more discussion.)

Note that the initiative for salvation (approaching God) is pictured as being taken by God and God alone. God reaches out in mercy, providing the bread of life and the light of the world. God reaches out from the Mercy Seat that sits in the Most Holy Place.

The *inner veil* is rich in symbolism as it speaks of Jesus Christ. Jesus Christ fulfilled the symbolism of the inner veil. Christ and Christ alone is the way to God, the way to know God and to experience the presence, fellowship, and communion of God. Remember what happened to the inner veil of the temple when Jesus Christ died on the cross: it was torn from top to bottom, symbolizing that God Himself acted, took the initiative, and tore the veil. The heavenly veil that kept man out of God's presence was torn by Christ when He suffered and died on the cross. We now have eternal access into the presence of God. The inner veil pictures at least the following lessons to the believer:
⇒ Fellowship and communion with God Himself is the supreme act of worship.
⇒ God is holy and righteous, far, far removed from man and his world--totally set apart and separated from the pollution and uncleanness of man.
⇒ God must be approached ever so carefully--in reverence, awe, and fear.
⇒ There is only one way to God, only one door into His presence.

"And, behold, the veil of the temple was rent in twain from the top to the bottom; and the earth did quake, and the rocks rent" (Mt.27:51).
"And the veil of the temple was rent in twain from the top to the bottom" (Mk.15:38).
"And the sun was darkened, and the veil of the temple was rent in the midst" (Lk.23:45).
"Which *hope* we have as an anchor of the soul, both sure and stedfast, and which entereth into that within the veil" (Heb.6:19).
"And after the second veil, the tabernacle which is called the Holiest of all" (Heb.9:3).
"Having therefore, brethren, boldness to enter into the holiest by the blood of Jesus, By a new and living way, which he hath consecrated for us, through the veil, that is to say, his flesh; And *having* an high priest over the house of God" (Heb.10:19-21).

4 (26:36-37) **Tabernacle of Moses--Pattern--Outer Curtain--Worship, Entrance into**: the Tabernacle was to be a tent with an outer curtain, a screen-like entrance. The center curtain symbolized the door into God's presence. This curtain divided the Holy Place from the courtyard of the Tabernacle. Note the facts:
1. It was an entrance of great beauty and craftsmanship (v.36). This curtain was identical to the inner curtain with one exception: there were no cherubim embroidered into the curtain.
2. The hanging frame was slightly different from that of the inner curtain's hanging frame.
a. There were to be gold hooks and five posts overlaid with gold (v.37). The inner curtain was hung on four posts overlaid with gold (cp. v.32).
b. There were to be five bronze bases or sockets for the posts (v.37). The poles for the inner curtain required only four bases of silver (cp. v.32). Note the change of metals for the bases from silver to bronze. Why? Most likely because sin offerings were made at the bronze altar, and before a person can offer acceptable worship, he must deal with his sins. There at the bronze altar, his sins were judged by God and God's wrath was satisfied. This is the foundation of man's worship, the blood that cleanses a person from sin. Therefore, the foundation sockets for the entrance to the Tabernacle were made of bronze: all to symbolize the need for cleansing in order to worship God. Simply stated, until a man has been forgiven for his sins, he can never enter into the presence of God. Once blood has been shed, man is invited to come and worship God.

Thought 1. Jesus Christ fulfilled the symbolism of this outer curtain. With His shed blood, He invites men to come through the door and worship God. The way to a deeper knowledge of God, to the deeper things of God, is through the Lord Jesus Christ and through Him alone. The lessons of the outer veil are these:
1) A person cannot just rush into the presence of a holy God; he cannot show disrespect to a holy God.
2) There is only one way into the presence of God.

"I am the door: by me if any man enter in, he shall be saved, and shall go in and out, and find pasture" (Jn.10:9).
"Jesus saith unto him, I am the way, the truth, and the life: no man cometh unto the Father, but by me" (Jn.14:6).

"Neither is there salvation in any other: for there is none other name under heaven given among men, whereby we must be saved" (Acts 4:12).

"By whom also we have access by faith into this grace wherein we stand, and rejoice in hope of the glory of God" (Ro.5:2).

"For there is one God, and one mediator between God and men, the man Christ Jesus; Who gave himself a ransom for all, to be testified in due time" (1 Tim.2:5-6).

3) There is a deeper knowledge of God: there is much more to knowing and experiencing God's presence than just making sacrifice and receiving forgiveness of sins. Remember: offerings for sin were made at the brazen altar in the courtyard. But there was more than this in knowing and worshipping God, more than just receiving forgiveness of sins. There was worship in the Holy Place and even in the inner sanctuary or Most Holy Place.

"And this is life eternal, that they might know thee the only true God, and Jesus Christ, whom thou hast sent" (Jn.17:3).

"But of him are ye in Christ Jesus, who of God is made unto us wisdom, and righteousness, and sanctification, and redemption" (1 Cor.1:30).

"But speaking the truth in love, may grow up into him in all things, which is the head, even Christ" (Eph.4:15).

"That I may know him, and the power of his resurrection, and the fellowship of his sufferings, being made conformable unto his death" (Ph.3:10).

"Therefore leaving the principles of the doctrine of Christ, let us go on unto perfection; not laying again the foundation of repentance from dead works, and of faith toward God" (Heb.6:1).

"As newborn babes, desire the sincere milk of the word, that ye may grow thereby: if so be ye have tasted that the Lord is gracious" (1 Pt.2:2-3).

"Whereby are given unto us exceeding great and precious promises: that by these ye might be partakers of the divine nature [of Jesus Christ], having escaped the corruption that is in the world through lust. And beside this, giving all diligence, add to your faith virtue; and to virtue knowledge; and to knowledge temperance; and to temperance patience; and to patience godliness; and to godliness brotherly kindness; and to brotherly kindness charity" (2 Pt.1:4-7).

"But grow in grace, and in the knowledge of our Lord and Saviour Jesus Christ. To him be glory both now and forever" (2 Pt.3:18).

THE TABERNACLE OF MOSES

SECTION OF THE TABERNACLE	WHAT IS TAUGHT	HOW CHRIST FULFILLED THE SYMBOLISM
The Sanctuary of the Tabernacle	What the Sanctuary (the walls and roof) taught: ⇒ There are different forms of worship, certain steps to take in approaching God. ⇒ There are some initial steps to take in approaching God before one approaches Him in the most intimate worship. ⇒ God is righteous and holy and completely separate from man, even from the religious who move about and minister in walls of religion. ⇒ God must be approached in reverence and awe and ever so carefully by men, even by the religious who are involved in His service.	How Christ fulfilled the symbolism of the Sanctuary (the walls and roof): *"By whom [Christ] also we have access by faith into this grace wherein we stand, and rejoice in hope of the glory of God" (Ro.5:2).* *"For through him we both have access by one Spirit unto the Father" (Eph.2:18).* *"In whom we have boldness and access with confidence by the faith of him" (Eph.3:12).* *"Let us draw near with a true heart in full assurance of faith, having our hearts sprinkled from an evil conscience, and our bodies washed with pure water" (Heb.10:22).* *"Wherefore we receiving a kingdom which cannot be moved, let us have grace [of our Lord Jesus Christ], whereby we may serve God acceptably with reverence and godly fear" (Heb. 12:28).*
The Outer Veil or Curtain Door (The Holy Place, The First Room, or Outer Sanctuary)	What the outer veil or door taught: ⇒ A person cannot just rush into the presence of God. God is holy; therefore; he cannot show disrespect to a holy God. ⇒ There is only one way into the deeper things of God.	How Christ fulfilled the symbolism of the outer veil: ⇒ The way to a deeper knowledge of God, to the deeper things of God, is through the Lord Jesus Christ and through Him alone.

SECTION OF THE TABERNACLE	WHAT IS TAUGHT	HOW CHRIST FULFILLED THE SYMBOLISM
The Outer Veil or Curtain Door (The Holy Place, The First Room, or Outer Sanctuary) (cont.)	⇒ There is a deeper knowledge of God, much more to knowing and experiencing God's presence than just making sacrifice and receiving forgiveness of sins. (Re-member: offerings for sin were made at the brazen altar in the courtyard. But there was more than this, more than forgiveness of sins, more necessary to really know and worship God. There was worship in the Holy Place and even in the inner sanctuary of God's presence, in the Most Holy Place or the Holy of Holies.)	*"And this is life eternal, that they might know thee the only true God, and Jesus Christ, whom thou hast sent"* (Jn.17:3). *"But of him are ye in Christ Jesus, who of God is made unto us wisdom, and righteousness, and sanctification, and redemption"* (1 Cor.1:30). *"But speaking the truth in love, may grow up into him in all things, which is the head, even Christ"* (Eph.4:15). *"That I may know him, and the power of his resurrection, and the fellowship of his sufferings, being made conformable unto his death"* (Ph.3:10). *"Therefore leaving the principles of the doctrine of Christ, let us go on unto perfection; not laying again the foundation of repentance from dead works, and of faith toward God"* (Heb.6:1). *"As newborn babes, desire the sincere milk of the word, that ye may grow thereby: if so be ye have tasted that the Lord is gracious"* (1 Pt.2:2-3).
The Inner Veil or Curtain Door, The Holy of Holies, or the Most Holy Place (The Inner Room or Inner Sanctuary)	What the Inner Veil or Curtain Door taught: ⇒ Fellowship and communion with God Himself is the supreme act of worship. ⇒ God is holy and righteous, far, far removed from man and his world—totally set apart and separated from the pollution and uncleanness of man. ⇒ God must be approached ever so carefully—in reverence, awe, and fear. ⇒ There is only one way to God, only one door into His presence.	How Christ fulfilled the symbolism of the veil: ⇒ Christ and Christ alone is the way to God, to knowing God and to experiencing the presence, fellowship and communion of God. *"Wherefore in all things it behooved him to be made like unto his brethren, that he might be a merciful and faithful high priest in things pertaining to God, to make reconciliation for the sins of the people"* (Heb. 2:17). *"Seeing then that we have a great high priest, that is passed into the heavens, Jesus the Son of God, let us hold fast our profession. For we have not an high priest which cannot be touched with the feeling of our infirmities; but was in all points tempted like as we are, yet without sin"* (Heb.4:14-15). *"[Christ] entereth into that within the veil; wither the forerunner is for us entered, even Jesus"* (Heb.6:19-20). *"For Christ is not entered into the holy places made with hands, which are the figures of the true; but into heaven itself, now to appear in the presence of God for us"* (Heb.9:24). *"Having therefore, breth-ren, boldness to enter into the holiest by the blood of Jesus, by a new and living way, which he hath consecrated for us, through the veil, that is to say, his flesh"* (Heb.10:19-20).

TYPES, SYMBOLS, AND PICTURES
(Exodus 26:1-37)

Historical Term	Type or Picture (Scriptural Basis for Each)	Life Application for Today's Believer	Biblical Application for Today's Believer
Fine threaded linen (Ex.26:1)	*Fine linen is clean and white; therefore, the linen symbolized the purity and righteousness of God. This fact is spelled out in Scripture:* **"Moreover thou shalt make the tabernacle with ten curtains of <u>fine twined linen</u>, and blue, and purple, and scarlet: with cherubims of cunning work shalt thou make them" (Ex.26:1).** **"And to her was granted that she should be arrayed in <u>fine linen, clean and white</u>: for the fine linen is the righteousness of saints" (Rev.19:8).**	a. God's righteousness is… • totally pure • totally righteous • totally holy b. The believer must strive to be more godly in all his ways, to be pure and righteous and holy… • in his heart (cp. Ps.24:4; Mt.5:8; 1 Tim.1:5) • in his soul (cp. 1 Pt. 1:22) • in his religion (cp. Jas.1:27)	*"He that overcometh, the same shall be clothed in white raiment; and I will not blot out his name out of the book of life, but I will confess his name before my Father, and before his angels" (Rev.3:5).* *"I counsel thee to buy of me gold tried in the fire, that thou mayest be rich; and white raiment, that thou mayest be clothed, and that the shame of thy nakedness do not appear; and anoint thine eyes with eyesalve, that thou mayest see" (Rev.3:18).* *"And round about the throne were four and twenty seats: and upon the seats I saw four and twenty elders sitting, clothed in white raiment; and they had on their heads crowns of gold" (Rev.4:4; cp.Rev.7:9).*
Blue (Ex.26:1)	*Blue, of course, is the color of the sky; therefore, blue is a symbol of the heavenly Person of Christ.* **"Moreover thou shalt make the tabernacle with ten curtains of fine twined linen, and <u>blue</u>, and purple, and scarlet: with cherubims of cunning work shalt thou make them" (Ex.26:1).**	⇒ Jesus Christ is the great High Priest… • who is made higher than the heavens • who is highly exalted • who has a name higher than any other being When a person looks upward toward the beautiful blue sky, he should remember… • to exalt Christ for who He is, for His deity • to praise and worship Christ for what He has done • to lift up prayers of intercession and supplication to the great High Priest, Jesus Christ	*"For such an high priest became us, who is holy, harmless, undefiled, separate from sinners, and made higher than the heavens" (Heb.7:26).* *"Wherefore God also hath highly exalted him, and given him a name which is above every name" (Ph.2:9).* *"He that cometh from above is above all: he that is of the earth is earthly, and speaketh of the earth: he that cometh from heaven is above all" (Jn.3:31).* *"Being made so much better than the angels, as he hath by inheritance obtained a more excellent name than they" (Heb.1:4).* *"I am Alpha and Omega, the beginning and the end, the first and the last" (Rev.22:13).* *"Jesus said unto them, If God were your Father, ye would love me: for I proceeded forth and came from God; neither came I of myself, but he sent me" (Jn.8:42).*

Historical Term	Type or Picture (Scriptural Basis for Each)	Life Application for Today's Believer	Biblical Application for Today's Believer
The Inner Curtains in the Sanctuary (Ex.26:1-6; 36:8-9) See also Ex.35:11; 36:8-13; 39:33; 40:19	*The Inner Curtains in the Sanctuary symbolized purity and righteousness. The Inner Curtains were made of brilliant colors and embroidered cherubim. Glancing at these, the High Priest was able to picture how pure, how holy, how perfect and righteous God is. The beauty and splendor of the Inner Curtains in the Sanctuary caused the High Priest to stand in awe of God's holy perfection.* **"Moreover thou shalt make the tabernacle with ten curtains of fine twined linen, and blue, and purple, and scarlet: with cherubims of cunning work shalt thou make them"** (Ex.26:1). **"And every wise hearted man among them that wrought the work of the tabernacle made ten curtains *of* fine twined linen, and blue, and purple, and scarlet: *with* cherubims of cunning work made he them. The length of one curtain *was* twenty and eight cubits, and the breadth of one curtain four cubits: the curtains *were* all of one size"** (Ex.36:8-9).	What the Inner Curtains in the Sanctuary taught: a. God is righteous and holy and completely distinct from any other being. In fact, God is so righteous and holy that there is a great gulf separating man from God. That gulf is caused by sin, by our coming so short of God's glory. It is sin that has caused the great divide and that makes God unapproachable. Man desperately needs someone, a mediator, who can bridge the great gulf or divide to God. That Someone, that Mediator, is Jesus Christ. b. God must be approached in reverence and awe and ever so carefully by men, even by the religious who are involved in His service.	*"For he hath made him to be sin for us, who knew no sin; that we might be made the righteousness of God in him"* (2 Cor.5:21). *"By whom [Christ] also we have access by faith into this grace wherein we stand, and rejoice in hope of the glory of God"* (Ro.5:2). *"In whom we have boldness and access with confidence by the faith of him"* (Eph.3:12). *"For there is one God, and one mediator between God and men, the man Christ Jesus; Who gave himself a ransom for all, to be testified in due time"* (1 Tim.2:5-6). *"And for this cause he is the mediator of the new testament, that by means of death, for the redemption of the transgressions that were under the first testament, they which are called might receive the promise of eternal inheritance"* (Heb.9:15). *"For Christ is not entered into the holy places made with hands, which are the figures of the true; but into heaven itself, now to appear in the presence of God for us"* (Heb.9:24). *"My little children, these things write I unto you, that ye sin not. And if any man sin, we have an advocate with the Father, Jesus Christ the righteous: And he is the propitiation for our sins: and not for ours only, but also for the sins of the whole world"* (1 Jn.2:1-2). *"Let all the earth fear the LORD: let all the inhabitants of the world stand in awe of him"* (Ps.33:8). *"God is greatly to be feared in the assembly of the saints, and to be had in reverence of all them that are about him"* (Ps.89:7). *"Stand in awe, and sin not: commune with your own heart upon your bed, and be still. Selah"* (Ps.4:4).

Historical Term	Type or Picture (Scriptural Basis for Each)	Life Application for Today's Believer	Biblical Application for Today's Believer
			"Wherefore we receiving a kingdom which cannot be moved, let us have grace, whereby we may serve God acceptably with reverence and godly fear" (Heb.12:28). *"And if ye call on the Father, who without respect of persons judgeth according to every man's work, pass the time of your sojourning here in fear [reverence]"* (1 Pt.1:17). *"Let all the earth fear the LORD: let all the inhabitants of the world stand in awe of him"* (Ps.33:8). *"God is greatly to be feared in the assembly of the saints, and to be had in reverence of all them that are about him"* (Ps.89:7). *"But the LORD is in his holy temple: let all the earth keep silence before him"* (Hab.2:20).
Goat Hair Covering (Ex.26:7)	*The covering of goat hair symbolized the need for the sin offering and for cleansing. The goat blood was shed, then its hair was used to cover the inner curtain (which symbolized righteousness).* *On the Day of Atonement, Aaron cast lots to decide which of the two goats brought as offerings should be sacrificed as a sin offering for the people. After killing one goat and sprinkling its blood on the altar, Aaron then returned to the live goat and laid both his hands upon its head. Aaron transferred the sin and wickedness of the Israelites to the goat's head. The live goat was then led outside the camp and turned loose.* **"And thou shalt make curtains of goats' hair to be a covering upon the tabernacle: eleven curtains shalt thou make"** (Ex. 26:7).	a. Jesus Christ became the *scapegoat* for the world (the One who carried the blackness of sin away from the camp, cp. Lev.16:5-28). b. Instead of allowing the sting of sin to rest upon sinners, Jesus Christ offered Himself up as a Sacrifice, as the Substitute and Savior of the world. A person has to approach God through the shed blood of Christ before he is counted righteous. A person's sin must be forgiven before he can approach the righteousness of God.	*"And one kid of the goats for a sin offering unto the LORD shall be offered, beside the continual burnt offering, and his drink offering"* (Num.28:15). *"Therefore will I divide him a portion with the great, and he shall divide the spoil with the strong; because he hath poured out his soul unto death: and he was numbered with the transgressors; and he bare the sin of many, and made intercession for the transgressors"* (Is.53:12). *"Who gave himself for our sins, that he might deliver us from this present evil world, according to the will of God and our Father"* (Gal.1:4). *"So Christ was once offered to bear the sins of many; and unto them that look for him shall he appear the second time without sin unto salvation"* (Heb.9:28; cp. 1 Pt.2:24; 1 Jn.3:5; Rev.1:5)
Ram skins dyed red (Ex.26:14)	*Red, the color of blood, was dyed into the ram's skin, symbolizing the sacrificial blood of Christ* **"And thou shalt make a covering for the tent of rams' skins dyed red, and**	⇒ A person must recognize that it is by the blood of Jesus Christ... • that he is cleansed from all sin • that his sins are forgiven	*"How much more shall the blood of Christ, who through the eternal Spirit offered himself without spot to God, purge your conscience from dead works to serve the living God?"* (Heb.9:14).

Historical Term	Type or Picture (Scriptural Basis for Each)	Life Application for Today's Believer	Biblical Application for Today's Believer
	a covering above *of badgers' skins*" (Ex.26:14).	• that he is freed from the power of sin • that He has been redeemed • that he is justified • that his conscience is purged from dead works	"*For this is my blood of the new testament, which is shed for many for the remission of sins*" (Mt.6:28). "*Take heed therefore unto yourselves, and to all the flock, over the which the Holy Ghost hath made you overseers, to feed the church of God, which he hath purchased with his own blood*" (Acts 20:28). "*Much more then, being now justified by his blood, we shall be saved from wrath through him*" (Ro. 5:9). "*But if we walk in the light, as he is in the light, we have fellowship one with another, and the blood of Jesus Christ his Son cleanseth us from all sin*" (1 Jn.1:7).
The Framework of the Tabernacle (the posts, bases, boards, and crossbars) (Ex.26:15-30; 36:31-33) See also Ex.36:20-34; 40:2, 17-18	*The Framework of the Tabernacle supported all the curtains and coverings. The foundation of the Tabernacle was firmly planted against the shifting sands of the desert (a symbol of the world and its wilderness). Without the support of the Framework, these hangings would have been useless; therefore, the Framework symbolized the picture of the stability and support that Jesus Christ gives the believer.* "And thou shalt make boards for the tabernacle of shittim wood standing up. Ten cubits shall be the length of a board, and a cubit and a half shall be the breadth of one board. Two tenons shall there be in one board, set in order one against another: thus shalt thou make for all the boards of the tabernacle" (Ex.26:15). "And he made bars of shittim wood; five for the boards of the one side of the tabernacle, And five bars for the boards of the other side of the tabernacle, and five bars for the boards of the tabernacle for the sides westward. And he made the middle bar to shoot through the boards from the one end to the other" (Ex.36:31-33).	⇒ By dying upon the cross and redeeming a person from his sins, Christ became the foundation of redemption for every believer. Christ is our support and stability, our assurance and security. However, a person must call upon Christ in order to receive the benefit of His support and stability. These blessings are not offered to those who curse, reject, and deny Christ.	"*Forasmuch as ye know that ye were not redeemed with corruptible things, as silver and gold, from your vain conversation received by tradition from your fathers; But with the precious blood of Christ, as of a lamb without blemish and without spot*" (1 Pt.1:18-19). "*Being confident of this very thing, that he which hath begun a good work in you will perform it until the day of Jesus Christ*" (Ph.1:6). "*For I know whom I have believed, and am persuaded that he is able to keep that which I have committed unto him against that day*" (2 Tim. 1:12). "*And the Lord shall deliver me from every evil work, and will preserve me unto his heavenly kingdom: to whom be glory for ever and ever. Amen*" (2 Tim. 4:18). "*Now unto him that is able to keep you from falling, and to present you faultless before the presence of his glory with exceeding joy, To the only wise God our Saviour, be glory and majesty, dominion and power, both now and ever. Amen*" (Jude 24-25).

Historical Term	Type or Picture (Scriptural Basis for Each)	Life Application for Today's Believer	Biblical Application for Today's Believer
The Inner Curtain or Veil (Ex.26:31-35; 36:35-36) See also Ex.35:12; 36:35-36; 39;34; 40:3, 21	*The Inner Veil divided the Most Holy Place from the Holy Place. Remember that the Ark of God, the very presence of God Himself, sat in the Most Holy Place. God used the Inner Veil to draw a clear line of separation between Himself and a person, between His holiness and man's sin. Thus the Inner Veil symbolized at least five things:*	What the Inner Veil or Curtain Door taught:	
	a. The Inner Veil symbolized the great separation between God and man.	a. God is holy and righteous, far, far removed from man and his world—totally set apart and separated from the pollution and uncleanness of man.	"If I regard iniquity in my heart, the Lord will not hear me" (Ps.66:18). "And there is none that calleth upon thy name, that stirreth up himself to take hold of thee: for thou hast hid thy face from us, and hast consumed us, because of our iniquitie" (Is.64:7). "They shall go with their flocks and with their herds to seek the LORD; but they shall not find him; he hath withdrawn himself from them" (Hos.5:6).
	b. The Inner Veil symbolized that God must be approached ever so carefully.	b. God must be approached ever so carefully—in reverence, awe, and fear.	"And now, Israel, what doth the LORD thy God require of thee, but to fear the LORD thy God, to walk in all his ways, and to love him, and to serve the LORD thy God with all thy heart and with all thy soul" (Dt.10:12). "Let us hear the conclusion of the whole matter: Fear God, and keep his commandments: for this is the whole duty of man" (Eccl.12:13). "But the LORD is in his holy temple: let all the earth keep silence before him" (Hab.2:20). "And if ye call on the Father, who without respect of persons judgeth according to every man's work, pass the time of your sojourning here in fear" (1 Pt.1:17).
	c. The Inner Veil symbolized that there is only one way into God's presence.	c. There is only one door into God's presence-- that door is Jesus Christ.	"For God so loved the world, that he gave his only begotten Son, that whosoever believeth in him should not perish, but have everlasting life" (Jn.3:16). "Then Simon Peter answered him, Lord, to whom shall we go? thou hast the words of eternal life" (Jn.6:68).

Historical Term	Type or Picture (Scriptural Basis for Each)	Life Application for Today's Believer	Biblical Application for Today's Believer
			"Jesus saith unto him, I am the way, the truth, and the life: no man cometh unto the Father, but by me" (Jn.14:6). *"Neither is there salvation in any other: for there is none other name under heaven given among men, whereby we must be saved"* (Acts 4:12).
	d. The Inner Veil symbolized the entrance into fellowship and communion with God.	d. God rewards those who diligently seek Him and who enter into His presence. He rewards them with the most wonderful fellowship and communion imaginable--with God Himself.	*"And it came to pass, that, while they communed together and reasoned, Jesus himself drew near, and went with them....And they said one to another, Did not our heart burn within us, while he talked with us by the way, and while he opened to us the scriptures?"* (Lk.24:15, 32). *"God is faithful, by whom ye were called unto the fellowship of his Son Jesus Christ our Lord"* (1 Cor.1:9). *"But without faith it is impossible to please him: for he that cometh to God must believe that he is, and that he is a rewarder of them that diligently seek him"* (Heb.11:6). *"That which we have seen and heard declare we unto you, that ye also may have fellowship with us: and truly our fellowship is with the Father, and with his Son Jesus Christ"* (1 Jn.1:3). *"Behold, I stand at the door, and knock: if any man hear my voice, and open the door, I will come in to him, and will sup with him, and he with me"* (Rev.3:20). *"Call unto me, and I will answer thee, and show thee great and mighty things, which thou knowest not"* (Jer.33:3).
	e. The Inner Veil symbolized the great need of man for a Savior, a Savior who could tear down the wall that separated man from God. **"And he made a vail of blue, and purple, and scarlet, and fine twined linen:** *with* **cherubims**	e. Jesus Christ fulfilled the symbolism of the Inner Veil. Remember what happened to the inner veil of the temple when Christ died on the cross: it was torn from top to bottom, symbolizing that God Himself acted, took the initiative, and tore the veil.	*"And, behold, the veil of the temple was rent in twain from the top to the bottom; and the earth did quake, and the rocks rent"* Mt.27:51). *"And the veil of the temple was rent in twain from the top to the bottom"* (Mk.15:38).

Historical Term	Type or Picture (Scriptural Basis for Each)	Life Application for Today's Believer	Biblical Application for Today's Believer
	made he it of cunning work. And he made thereunto four pillars *of* shittim *wood,* and overlaid them with gold: their hooks *were of* gold; and he cast for them four sockets of silver" (Ex.36:35-36).	The heavenly veil that kept a person out of God's presence was torn by Christ when He suffered and died on the cross. We now have eternal access into the presence of God. The door into God's presence is wide open.	"Wherefore in all things *it behooved him to be made like unto his brethren, that he might be a merciful and faithful high priest in things pertaining to God, to make reconciliation for the sins of the people"* (Heb.2:17). "Seeing then that we have a great high priest, that is passed into the heavens, Jesus the Son of God, let us hold fast our profession. For we have not an high priest which cannot be touched with the feeling of our infirmities; but was in all points tempted like as we are, yet without sin"* (Heb.4:14-15). "[Christ] entereth into that within the veil; wither the forerunner is for us entered, even Jesus"* (Heb.6:19-20). "For Christ is not entered into the holy places made with hands, which are the figures of the true; but into heaven itself, now to appear in the presence of God for us"* (Heb.9:24). "Having therefore, brethren, boldness to enter into the holiest by the blood of Jesus, by a new and living way, which he hath consecrated for us, through the veil, that is to say, his flesh"* (Heb.10:19-20).
The Outer Veil or Curtain Door (The Holy Place: The First Room or Outer Sanctuary) (Ex.26:36-37; 36:37-38) See also Ex.35:15; 39:38; 40:6, 29	*The Outer Veil shielded the Sanctuary (i.e., the Holy Place and the Most Holy Place) from the activity of the Courtyard. The Veil prevented people from seeing into the Holy Place to see the worship of God taking place inside the Sanctuary. God has dictated that any worship of Him must be done by coming into His presence, by entering the Holy Place through the Outer Veil, a symbol of the only entrance into God's presence.* "And thou shalt make an hanging for the door of the tent, of blue, and purple, and scarlet, and fine twined linen, wrought with needlework. And thou shalt make for the*	What the Outer Veil or Curtain Door taught: a. The Outer Veil pointed to Jesus Christ as the Way, the entrance into God's presence. Jesus Christ fulfilled the symbolism of this outer curtain. With His shed blood, He invites men to come through the door and worship God.	"Jesus saith unto him, I *am the way, the truth, and the life: no man cometh unto the Father, but by me"* (Jn.14:6). "Neither is there salvation in any other: for there is none other name under heaven given among men, whereby we must be saved"* (Acts 4:12). "By whom also we have access by faith into this grace wherein we stand, and rejoice in hope of the glory of God"* (Ro.5:2). "For by grace are ye saved through faith; and that not of yourselves: it is the gift of God"* (Eph.2:8). "Because strait is the gate, and narrow is the way, which leadeth unto*

Historical Term	Type or Picture (Scriptural Basis for Each)	Life Application for Today's Believer	Biblical Application for Today's Believer
	hanging five pillars of shittim wood, and overlay them with gold, and their hooks shall be of gold: and thou shalt cast five sockets of brass for them" (Ex.26:36-37). "And he made an hanging for the tabernacle door *of* blue, and purple, and scarlet, and fine twined linen, of needle-work; And the five pillars of it with their hooks: and he overlaid their chapiters and their fillets with gold: but their five sockets *were of* brass" (Ex.36:37-38).	b. Not just any person can come into the presence of God. Nor can a believer come into God's presence, into a deeper knowledge of God, in just any manner. God has spelled out exactly how He expects us to approach Him: through His Son Jesus Christ. The way to a deeper knowledge of God, to the deeper things of God, is through the Lord Jesus Christ and through Him alone.	*life, and few there be that find it*" (Mt.7:14). "*That I may know him, and the power of his resurrection, and the fellowship of his sufferings, being made conformable unto his death*" (Ph.3:10). "*And this is life eternal, that they might know thee the only true God, and Jesus Christ, whom thou hast sent*" (Jn.17:3). "*But of him are ye in Christ Jesus, who of God is made unto us wisdom, and righteousness, and sanctification, and redemption*" (1 Cor.1:30). "*But speaking the truth in love, may grow up into him in all things, which is the head, even Christ*" (Eph.4:15). "*Therefore leaving the principles of the doctrine of Christ, let us go on unto perfection; not laying again the foundation of repentance from dead works, and of faith toward God*" (Heb.6:1). "*As newborn babes, desire the sincere milk of the word, that ye may grow thereby: if so be ye have tasted that the Lord is gracious*" (1 Pt.2:2-3).

1. The Altar of Burnt Offering: Symbolized the need for atonement, for reconciliation with God

a. To make of acacia wood: 7½' x 7½' x 4½' high
b. To make a horn at each of the four corners: Make all one piece
c. To overlay the altar with bronze
d. To make all utensils of bronze
1) Ash buckets & shovels
2) Basins & meat hooks
3) Fire pans

e. To make a bronze grate
1) Make four bronze rings for each corner

2) Place the grate under the ledge, half way up the altar

f. To make poles of acacia wood
1) Overlay the poles with bronze
2) Insert the poles into the rings on each side to carry the altar

g. To make the altar hollow
h. The strict instructions: To build the altar exactly as designed

2. The Courtyard of the Tabernacle: Symbolized that God can be approached

a. The mandate: Build the Courtyard
b. The south side
1) To be 150' of linen curtains
2) To make 20 posts that fit into 20 bronze bases
3) To make silver hooks & bands attached to the posts

c. The north side
1) To be 150' of curtains

F. The Altar of Burnt Offering, The Court of the Tabernacle, & The Lampstand: All Symbolizing the True Way to Approach God, Ex. 27:1-21

And thou shalt make an altar of shittim wood, five cubits long, and five cubits broad; the altar shall be foursquare: and the height thereof shall be three cubits.
2 And thou shalt make the horns of it upon the four corners thereof: his horns shall be of the same: and thou shalt overlay it with brass.
3 And thou shalt make his pans to receive his ashes, and his shovels, and his basons, and his fleshhooks, and his firepans: all the vessels thereof thou shalt make of brass.
4 And thou shalt make for it a grate of network of brass; and upon the net shalt thou make four brasen rings in the four corners thereof.
5 And thou shalt put it under the compass of the altar beneath, that the net may be even to the midst of the altar.
6 And thou shalt make staves for the altar, staves of shittim wood, and overlay them with brass.
7 And the staves shall be put into the rings, and the staves shall be upon the two sides of the altar, to bear it.
8 Hollow with boards shalt thou make it: as it was showed thee in the mount, so shall they make it.
9 And thou shalt make the court of the tabernacle: for the south side southward there shall be hangings for the court of fine twined linen of an hundred cubits long for one side:
10 And the twenty pillars thereof and their twenty sockets shall be of brass; the hooks of the pillars and their fillets shall be of silver.
11 And likewise for the north side in length there shall be

hangings of an hundred cubits long, and his twenty pillars and their twenty sockets of brass; the hooks of the pillars and their fillets of silver.
12 And for the breadth of the court on the west side shall be hangings of fifty cubits: their pillars ten, and their sockets ten.
13 And the breadth of the court on the east side eastward shall be fifty cubits.
14 The hangings of one side of the gate shall be fifteen cubits: their pillars three, and their sockets three.
15 And on the other side shall be hangings fifteen cubits: their pillars three, and their sockets three.
16 And for the gate of the court shall be an hanging of twenty cubits, of blue, and purple, and scarlet, and fine twined linen, wrought with needlework: and their pillars shall be four, and their sockets four.
17 All the pillars round about the court shall be filleted with silver; their hooks shall be of silver, and their sockets of brass.
18 The length of the court shall be an hundred cubits, and the breadth fifty every where, and the height five cubits of fine twined linen, and their sockets of brass.
19 All the vessels of the tabernacle in all the service thereof, and all the pins thereof, and all the pins of the court, shall be of brass.
20 And thou shalt command the children of Israel, that they bring thee pure oil olive beaten for the light, to cause the lamp to burn always.
21 In the tabernacle of the congregation without the vail, which is before the testimony, Aaron and his sons shall order it from evening to morning before the LORD: it shall be a statute for ever unto their generations on the behalf of the children of Israel.

2) To have 20 posts that fit into 20 bronze bases
3) To have silver hooks and boards

d. The west end
1) To be 75' of curtains
2) To set 10 posts into 10 bases

e. The east end
1) To be 75' long

2) To include the entrance to the Courtyard, flanked by two curtains
• Each to be 22½' long
• Each to be supported by three posts set into three bases

f. The entrance itself: Make a curtain 30' long
• To be of fine linen
• To be decorated, embroidered in blue, purple, & scarlet yarn
• To be attached to four posts set in four bases
g. The posts of the Courtyard: To be connected by silver bands & hooks

h. The summary
1) The Courtyard: To be 150' x 75' with 7½' high curtain walls
• To be made of fine linen
• To have bronze bases supporting the walls
2) The articles used in the work of the Tabernacle, including the tent pegs: Must be bronze

3. The Lampstand of the Tabernacle: Symbolized that the way into God's presence is always open

a. A command
1) To provide pure olive oil to keep the light burning continually
2) To place the Lampstand right outside the inner curtain of the most Holy Place
3) To keep the lamps burning in the Lord's presence day & night
b. The great significance of this command: To be a permanent law--kept by all generations

DIVISION IX

THE TABERNACLE, ITS BLUEPRINT AND PRIESTHOOD: THE TRUE WAY TO APPROACH AND WORSHIP GOD, EX.25:1-31:18

F. The Altar of Burnt Offering, The Court of the Tabernacle, and The Lampstand: All Symbolizing the True Way to Approach God, Ex. 27:1-21

(27:1-21) **Introduction**: in the beginning of time, when God created Adam and Eve, there were no barriers between God and man. Man had a continuous, unbroken fellowship with God. Man obeyed God, obeyed Him perfectly. God was able to provide everything man needed, able to meet every need of man. But then it happened: man sinned, disobeyed, and rebelled against God. Man squandered the most important thing in the world: the care, fellowship, and guidance of God. At that very moment, the door into God's holy presence slammed shut. Man was banned from entering into God's presence and was destined to be separated from God forever.

But God had a plan for redemption, a plan that would allow man back into His presence again. It was a plan that took years to fulfill; nevertheless, God worked to carry out His plan down through the centuries. One of the first stages of God's plan was revealed in the construction of the Tabernacle. Through the Tabernacle, God allowed the Priests to stand in His presence for the people. But God's people were still far removed from experiencing the close, intimate presence of God, for they could not approach God personally; they had to approach Him through a mediator. But note: the Tabernacle was only a shadow of greater things to come. In God's perfect timing, He planned to send into the world the One Person who could open the door into God's presence, the One Person who could give open access to God anytime, anywhere. That Person is Jesus Christ. Christ alone is the way into God's presence. It is Jesus Christ who cut the path whereby sinful man can once again walk in the presence of God. It is Jesus Christ who fulfilled the symbolism as the door, the door that only He can open. Christ is the only door into the presence of God. This is the emphasis of this section of Scripture. This is: *The Altar of Burnt Offering, the Court of the Tabernacle, and the Lampstand: All Symbolizing the True Way to Approach God*, Ex.27:1-21.

1. The Altar of Burnt Offering: symbolized the need for atonement, for reconciliation with God (v.1-8).
2. The Courtyard of the Tabernacle: symbolized that God can be approached (v.9-19).
3. The Lampstand of the Tabernacle: symbolized that the way into God's presence is always open (v.20-21).

1 (27:1-8) **Tabernacle of Moses--Bronze Altar--Burnt Offering--Atonement--Reconciliation--Cross of Christ**: the Altar of Burnt Offering sat in the Courtyard of the Tabernacle. The altar symbolized the need for atonement, for reconciliation with God. As the believer entered into the great Tabernacle of God, the first thing he saw was the Altar of Burnt Offering. It was, no doubt, the focus of attention for all worshippers who entered the Tabernacle. But note: it was an altar for God's people only. The Altar of Burnt Offering was not for the use of anyone outside the family of God. The altar was where God met with His people--a people who needed to atone for their sins. This bronze altar must have been breathtaking to the observer. Blazing with a red hot fire, the altar was surrounded by priests who tended the constant sacrifices. The massive structure could not be ignored. Every man who entered through the gate had to acknowledge its presence, and the altar symbolized the need for atonement, for reconciliation with God through the sacrificial blood of the animal, the animal that was substituted for the life of the offerer. We must always remember this truth: before any man can have a relationship with God, he must come to grips with his need for atonement, for reconciliation with God through the sacrificial blood of the Savior, Jesus Christ. These are the facts of this sanctified altar:

1. The altar was to be made of acacia wood with the following dimensions: it was to be a square altar that was 7 1/2 feet wide by 7 1/2 feet long by 4 1/2 feet high (v.1). Like the other parts of the Tabernacle, acacia wood was chosen for its hardness and its durability. The wood was harder than oak or hickory. Modern wood products like plywood and particle board would have quickly become useless rubbish and ashes in comparison to acacia wood.

Thought 1. An atonement that does not last, a reconciliation with God that is not enduring, is of no value at all. The philosophies of the world offer many cheap alternatives to becoming right with God. The world teaches that a person can approach God and become acceptable to God...

- by doing the best he can
- by keeping the rules and rituals of religion
- by belonging to a certain religion or church and being faithful
- by believing in the god worshipped by all religions, who is said to be the same god no matter what he may be called
- by following certain men who claim to be prophets of God

The brazen altar declares a different message. Atonement, reconciliation with God--the forgiveness of sin--is necessary in order to approach and become acceptable to God. Man needs a Savior, a Savior who will sacrifice Himself for man. No person can approach God apart from the Savior. The life of the pure, perfect sacrifice has to be given and substituted for man. Blood has to be shed and substituted in order for man to stand acceptable before God. This is the only way of salvation, and Jesus Christ fulfills the message and symbol of the brazen altar.

"**The next day John seeth Jesus coming unto him, and saith, Behold the Lamb of God, which taketh away the sin of the world**" (Jn.1:29).

"**For if the blood of bulls and of goats, and the ashes of an heifer sprinkling the unclean, sanctifieth to the purifying of the flesh: How much more shall the blood of Christ, who through the eternal Spirit offered himself without spot to God, purge your conscience from dead works to serve the living God?**" (Heb.9:13-14).

"**And almost all things are by the law purged with blood; and without shedding of blood is no remission. It was therefore necessary that the patterns of things in the heavens should be purified with these; but the heavenly things themselves with better sacrifices than these. For Christ is not entered into the holy places made with hands, which are the figures of the true; but into heaven it-**

self, now to appear in the presence of God for us: Nor yet that he should offer himself often, as the high priest entereth into the holy place every year with blood of others; For then must he often have suffered since the foundation of the world: but now once in the end of the world hath he appeared to put away sin by the sacrifice of himself. And as it is appointed unto men once to die, but after this the judgment: So Christ was once offered to bear the sins of many; and unto them that look for him shall he appear the second time without sin unto salvation" (Heb.9:22-28; cp. Mt.26:28).

"Forasmuch as ye know that ye were not redeemed with corruptible things, as silver and gold, from your vain conversation received by tradition from your fathers; But with the precious blood of Christ, as of a lamb without blemish and without spot" (1 Pt.1:18-19).

"But if we walk in the light, as he is in the light, we have fellowship one with another, and the blood of Jesus Christ his Son cleanseth us from all sin" (1 Jn.1:7).

2. The altar was to be made with a horn at each of the four corners, made of one piece (v.2). The horns of the altar were symbolic of several truths.

   a. The horns symbolized the atoning power of the altar, symbolized the fact that God accepted the sacrifice as a substitute for the believer making the offering. This is seen in the ritual of the sacrifice: some of the blood was put on the horns before the rest was poured out at the base of the altar (Ex.29:12; Lev.4:7, 18, 25, 30, 34; 8:15; 9:9; 16:18).

   b. The horn symbolized God's *power and strength*.

> "And seven priests shall bear before the ark seven trumpets of rams' horns: and the seventh day ye shall compass the city seven times, and the priests shall blow with the trumpets. And it shall come to pass, that when they make a long *blast* with the ram's horn, *and* when ye hear the sound of the trumpet, all the people shall shout with a great shout; and the wall of the city shall fall down flat, and the people shall ascend up every man straight before him. And Joshua the son of Nun called the priests, and said unto them, Take up the ark of the covenant, and let seven priests bear seven trumpets of rams' horns before the ark of the LORD" (Josh.6:4-6).

> "The adversaries of the LORD shall be broken to pieces; out of heaven shall he thunder upon them: the LORD shall judge the ends of the earth; and he shall give strength unto his king, and exalt the horn of his anointed" (1 Sam.2:10).

> "All the horns of the wicked also will I cut off; *but* the horns of the righteous shall be exalted" (Ps.75:10).

> "For thou *art* the glory of their strength: and in thy favour our horn shall be exalted" (Ps.89:17).

> "But my faithfulness and my mercy *shall be* with him: and in my name shall his horn be exalted" (Ps.89:24).

> "He also exalteth the horn of his people, the praise of all his saints; *even* of the children of Israel, a people near unto him. Praise ye the LORD" (Ps.148:14).

   c. The horn symbolized God's *salvation*.

> "And Aaron shall make an atonement upon the horns of it once in a year with the blood of the sin offering of atonements: once in the year shall he make atonement upon it throughout your generations: it *is* most holy unto the LORD" (Ex.30:10).

> "And he slew *it;* and Moses took the blood, and put *it* upon the horns of the altar round about with his finger, and purified the altar, and poured the blood at the bottom of the altar, and sanctified it, to make reconciliation upon it" (Lev.8:15).

> "And he shall go out unto the altar that *is* before the LORD, and make an atonement for it; and shall take of the blood of the bullock, and of the blood of the goat, and put *it* upon the horns of the altar round about" (Lev.16:18).

> "And Hannah prayed, and said, My heart rejoiceth in the LORD, mine horn is exalted in the LORD: my mouth is enlarged over mine enemies; because I rejoice in thy salvation" (1 Sam.2:1).

> "God *is* the LORD, which hath showed us light: bind the sacrifice with cords, *even* unto the horns of the altar" (Ps.118:27).

> "And hath raised up an horn of salvation for us in the house of his servant David" (Lk.1:69).

   d. The horn symbolized God's *protection, security, sanctuary, help*.

> "The God of my rock; in him will I trust: *he is* my shield, and the horn of my salvation, my high tower, and my refuge, my saviour; thou savest me from violence" (2 Sam.22:3).

> "The LORD *is* my rock, and my fortress, and my deliverer; my God, my strength, in whom I will trust; my buckler, and the horn of my salvation, *and* my high tower" (Ps.18:2).

> "And Adonijah feared because of Solomon, and arose, and went, and caught hold on the horns of the altar" (1 Ki.1:50).

"Then tidings came to Joab: for Joab had turned after Adonijah, though he turned not after Absalom. And Joab fled unto the Tabernacle of the LORD, and caught hold on the horns of the altar" (1 Ki.2:28).

3. The altar was to be overlaid (covered) with bronze (v.2). Overlaying the altar with bronze was an absolute necessity to prevent its consumption by the blazing fires that burned continuously upon the altar. And God was clear in His instructions: the fire must never be allowed to go out.

"The fire shall ever be burning upon the altar; it shall never go out" (Lev.6:13).

It is interesting to note God's scientific wisdom in planning the altar, the fact that the altar was built to withstand the tremendous heat. Stephen Olford comments:

"The wood overlaid with brass [bronze] constituted a fireproof combination. Only comparatively recently has it been discovered by scientists what an ingenious, fire-resisting invention is hard wood overlaid with copper and hermetically [airtight] sealed. How wonderfully this combination speaks of the Person of our Lord Jesus Christ, who endured the fires of Calvary without being consumed; like the bush which Moses saw in the wilderness which burned with fire but was not destroyed (Exodus 3:1-5). Peter, quoting from Psalm 16, expresses this plainly in his Pentecostal sermon when he declares: 'Thou wilt not...suffer thine Holy One to see corruption' (Acts 2:27)."[1]

Thought 1. Jesus Christ is the only person who could have endured the cross. Anyone else would have been consumed instantly, consumed by the blazing wrath of God judging sin.

"And he bearing his cross went forth into a place called *the place* of a skull, which is called in the Hebrew Golgotha" (Jn.19:17).
"And being found in fashion as a man, he humbled himself, and became obedient unto death, even the death of the cross" (Ph.2:8).
"Looking unto Jesus the author and finisher of *our* faith; who for the joy that was set before him endured the cross, despising the shame, and is set down at the right hand of the throne of God" (Heb.12:2).

1) Jesus Christ endured the suffering of the cross that we might be saved from our sins.

"So Christ was once offered to bear the sins of many; and unto them that look for him shall he appear the second time without sin unto salvation" (Heb.9:28).
"For Christ also hath once suffered for sins, the just for the unjust, that he might bring us to God, being put to death in the flesh, but quickened by the Spirit" (1 Pt.3:18).

2) Jesus Christ endured the suffering of the cross that we might be set free from the curse of the Law.

"Christ hath redeemed us from the curse of the law, being made a curse for us: for it is written, Cursed *is* every one that hangeth on a tree" (Gal.3:13).

3) Jesus Christ endured the suffering of the cross that we might be healed.

"But he *was* wounded for our transgressions, *he was* bruised for our iniquities: the chastisement of our peace *was* upon him; and with his stripes we are healed" (Is.53:5).
"Who his own self bare our sins in his own body on the tree, that we, being dead to sins, should live unto righteousness: by whose stripes ye were healed" (1 Pt.2:24).

4. All of the utensils were to be made of bronze (v.3):
   a. The ash buckets and shovels. The buckets were used to carry the ashes from the altar to a place outside the camp (Lev.6:10-11). The shovels were apparently used to collect the burned out embers from the altar.
   b. The basins and meat hooks. The basins were used to collect the blood of the sacrifice which was either sprinkled inside the Sanctuary or poured out at the base of the altar. The meat hooks were most likely three-pronged forks that adjusted the sacrifice upon the altar.
   c. The fire pans. The fire pans held the living coals of the divine fire whenever the altar was being cleaned or moved from campsite to campsite (see Lev.6:13; 9:24). The fire pans were also used to carry hot coals from the altar of incense inside the Holy Place (cp. Lev.10:1; 16:12).
5. A bronze grate was to be made (v.4). Special instructions were given for its construction:
   a. Make four bronze rings for each corner.
   b. Place the grate under the ledge, half way up the altar.
6. Two poles were to be made of acacia wood. They were to be overlaid with bronze. These poles were then inserted into the four rings when the altar was carried (v.6-7).
7. The altar was to be made hollow (v.8).
8. Note the strict instructions: the altar was to be built exactly as designed (v.8).

---

[1] Stephen Olford. *The Tabernacle, Camping With God*, p.93-94.

Thought 1. What kind of altar would man have designed? What kind of altar would man build to secure the favor of God, to become acceptable to God? Man's altar would be...

- an altar of religion and ritual
- an altar of works and good deeds
- an altar of doing good and feeling good
- an altar of money and gifts
- an altar that requires no sacrifice
- an altar that allowed doing one's own thing
- an altar that allowed going one's own way
- an altar of self-help and self-esteem
- an altar of ego-boosters and self-image

Thank God He did not trust the design of the altar to man. But He assigned this great task to His Son, the Lord Jesus Christ, who is the Lamb of God.

> **"And walk in love, as Christ also hath loved us, and hath given himself for us an offering and a sacrifice to God for a sweetsmelling savour" (Eph.5:2).**
> **"And being found in fashion as a man, he humbled himself, and became obedient unto death, even the death of the cross" (Ph.2:8).**
> **"For God so loved the world, that he gave his only begotten Son, that whosoever believeth in him should not perish, but have everlasting life" (Jn.3:16).**
> **"For Christ also hath once suffered for sins, the just for the unjust, that he might bring us to God, being put to death in the flesh, but quickened by the Spirit" (1 Pt.3:18).**

Thought 2. The Altar of Burnt Offering taught several things:
⇒ Substitutionary sacrifice is necessary for the forgiveness of sins.
⇒ There is no forgiveness without the shedding of the blood of the sacrifice.
⇒ There is no way to approach God--to be saved--other than through the death of a substitute.

Jesus Christ fulfilled the symbolism of the bronze altar.

1) It is Jesus Christ who is the Lamb of God.

> **"The next day John seeth Jesus coming unto him, and saith, Behold the Lamb of God, which taketh away the sin of the world!" (Jn.1:29).**

2) It is Jesus Christ who is the Lamb brought to the slaughter.

> **"He was oppressed, and he was afflicted, yet he opened not his mouth: he is brought as a lamb to the slaughter, and as a sheep before her shearers is dumb, so he openeth not his mouth" (Is.53:7).**

3) It is Jesus Christ who is the Passover Lamb sacrificed for us.

> **"Purge out therefore the old leaven, that ye may be a new lump, as ye are unleavened. For even Christ our passover is sacrificed for us" (1 Cor.5:7).**

4) It is Jesus Christ who gave His life as a ransom.

> **"[I] give my life a ransom for many" (Mk.10:45).**

5) It is Jesus Christ who laid down His life for us.

> **"Hereby perceive we the love of God, because he laid down his life for us: and we ought to lay down our lives for the brethren" (1 Jn.3:16).**

2 (27:9-19) **Tabernacle of Moses--Courtyard--Approaching God**: the Courtyard of the Tabernacle symbolized that God can be approached. The Courtyard served several purposes, all of which were important in the building of the Tabernacle. Remember the over-all purpose of the Tabernacle: to be a place where God could dwell with *His* people, a place where people could approach and worship God. The Courtyard served as a hedge between the outside world and the presence of a holy God. A clear line was drawn between the world and God's presence.

The Courtyard was a guard against any unlawful approach. The Tabernacle of God was the holiest site on earth, and not just anyone could enter its sanctified grounds. Only believers, true believers, were to enter. The Courtyard was a protection against wild animals wandering into the Tabernacle. The Courtyard revealed one clear and distinct truth: the only way to enter God's presence is through *one* entrance, *one* gate or door. These are the facts about the Courtyard:

1. The mandate was to build the Courtyard (v.9). God wanted to ensure the safety of the holy furnishings of the Tabernacle by having His people build a protective hedge around the Tabernacle.

2. The south side was to be built with these exact specifications (v.9-10):
⇒ to be 150 feet of linen curtains
⇒ to make 20 posts to fit into 20 bronze bases
⇒ to make silver hooks and bands attached to the posts

3. The north side was to be built with these exact specifications (v.11):
   ⇒ to be 150 feet of linen curtains
   ⇒ to make 20 posts to fit into 20 bronze bases
   ⇒ to make silver hooks and bands
4. The west end was to be built with these exact specifications (v.12):
   ⇒ to be 75 feet of curtains
   ⇒ to set 10 posts into 10 bases
5. The east end was also to be 75 feet long (v.13). Included in the east end was the one and only Courtyard entrance, but note: the entrance (door) to the Tabernacle was large, large enough to receive any person. The entrance was flanked by two curtains. Note their specifications:
   ⇒ Each was to be 22½ feet long.
   ⇒ Each was to be supported by 3 posts set into 3 bases (v.14-15).
6. The entrance (door) was to be constructed with one door and only one door (v.16). The curtain was to be 30 feet long and was to be made of fine linen. This curtain was to be decorated, embroidered in blue, purple, and scarlet yarn--the same set of brilliant colors throughout the inner curtains of the sanctuary. The curtain was to be attached to 4 posts set in 4 bases.
7. The posts of the Courtyard were to be connected by silver bands and hooks (v.17).
8. The summary reinforces what has just been revealed to Moses (v.18-19):
   a. The Courtyard was to be 150 feet by 75 feet with 7½ foot curtain walls made of fine linen. These walls were to be supported by bronze bases.
   b. The articles used in the work of the Tabernacle, including the tent pegs, had to be bronze.

Thought 1. The walls of the Courtyard teach at least three lessons:
   ⇒ The walls of linen symbolized the righteousness and holiness of God. He is so righteous and holy, so white and pure, that He is set apart from the world.
   ⇒ When a person looks at God, he must see that God dwells in righteousness and holiness. When a person looked at the walls they were to be reminded that God was holy.
   ⇒ When a person approaches God, he must approach Him in reverence and awe, adoration and worship. He must praise and thank God, that God allows him to enter His presence.

Jesus Christ fulfilled the symbolism of the walls of the Courtyard. Jesus Christ is the righteousness of God.

"But now the righteousness of God without the law is manifested, being witnessed by the law and the prophets; Even the righteousness of God which is by faith of Jesus Christ unto all and upon all them that believe: for there is no difference" (Ro.3:21-22).
"For he hath made him to be sin for us, who knew no sin; that we might be made the righteousness of God in him" (2 Cor.5:21).

Thought 2. The door or gate into the Tabernacle taught at least two things:
   ⇒ There is only one way to enter God's presence; there are not many ways as most men think and practice.
   ⇒ God has to be approached if a man wishes to live eternally. No person shall ever live with God unless he approaches God exactly as God dictates.

Jesus Christ fulfilled the symbolism of the door or gate.
   ⇒ Jesus Christ is the door, the only door, into God's presence. A man has to approach God through Jesus Christ, through Him and Him alone.

"I am the door: by me if any man enter in, he shall be saved, and shall go in and out, and find pasture" (Jn.10:9).

   ⇒ Jesus Christ is the way, the only way, that a man can approach and come to the Father.

"Jesus saith unto him, I am the way, the truth, and the life: no man cometh unto the Father, but by me" (Jn.14:6).

3 (27:20-21) **Tabernacle of Moses--Lampstand--Light**: the Lampstand of the Tabernacle symbolized that the way into God's presence is always open. Placed in the Holy Place, the Lampstand was the vessel that illuminated the priest's view. Without the Lampstand, the tent would have been a dark, unknown mystery. For the human heart, darkness causes...
   • stumbling about   • false teaching
   • fear   • false worship
   • confusion   • loneliness
   • helplessness   • emptiness
   • hopelessness

The Lampstand illuminated the way into God's presence, showed people how to walk into His presence. Note the instructions:
1. A command was given to provide pure olive oil to keep the light burning continually (v.20). The lamp of God was to give brilliant, bright, pure light. The source of this light was from the pure olive oil. The oil came from unripened olives

that were beaten not crushed. Olives that were beaten or pounded apparently produced a light that was smokeless (or with very little smoke). The Lampstand was to be placed right outside the inner curtain of the Most Holy Place (v.21). This Lampstand was to provide its light continually in the presence of the Lord, both day and night. To keep this command required the constant attention of the priests who would trim the wicks and replenish the olive oil.

2. Note that this command was to be a permanent law--kept by all generations. This is significant: God's light is for all generations, for every man, woman, and child throughout history.

⇒ When the light of God is hidden from men, the darkness brings destruction and death.
⇒ When God's light is shielded from the acts of sinful men, their hearts become hardened.
⇒ When God's light is extinguished, people follow after false gods.

This is not only a command for Israel, this is also a command for believers today. The light of God must be kept burning or else the world will be lost in darkness.

Thought 1. Jesus Christ is the true light and His light is never extinguished. His light is always burning...
- to show a person how to approach God and secure His approval
- to show a person how to face the trials of life, no matter how severe the trial
- to show a person how to solve the serious problems of life

"In him was life; and the life was the light of men" (Jn.1:4).
"*That* was the true Light, which lighteth every man that cometh into the world" (Jn.1:9).
"Then spake Jesus again unto them, saying, I am the light of the world: he that followeth me shall not walk in darkness, but shall have the light of life" (Jn.8:12).
"For God, who commanded the light to shine out of darkness, hath shined in our hearts, to *give* the light of the knowledge of the glory of God in the face of Jesus Christ" (2 Cor.4:6).
"And the city had no need of the sun, neither of the moon, to shine in it: for the glory of God did lighten it, and the Lamb *is* the light thereof" (Rev.21:23).
"And there shall be no night there; and they need no candle, neither light of the sun; for the Lord God giveth them light: and they shall reign for ever and ever" (Rev.22:5).

Thought 2. Throughout Scripture oil is a symbol of the Holy Spirit. We must be filled with God's Spirit so the world can see Christ and His great love for them. The challenge for every believer is to have a life marked by the fulness of God's Spirit.

1) The believer who is filled with God's Spirit bears a strong witness of love, joy, and peace.

"And be not drunk with wine, wherein is excess; but be filled with the Spirit" (Eph.5:18).
"But the fruit of the Spirit is love, joy, peace, longsuffering, gentleness, goodness, faith, meekness, temperance: against such there is no law" (Gal.5:22-23).

2) The believer who is filled with God's Spirit is a light for all the world to see.

"Ye are the light of the world. A city that is set on an hill cannot be hid" (Mt.5:14).
"That ye may be blameless and harmless, the sons of God, without rebuke, in the midst of a crooked and perverse nation, among whom ye shine as lights in the world" (Ph.2:15).

THE TABERNACLE OF MOSES

SECTION OF THE TABERNACLE	WHAT IS TAUGHT	HOW CHRIST FULFILLED THE SYMBOLISM
The Brazen Altar in the Courtyard, 27:1-8	What the altar taught: ⇒ Substitutionary sacrifice is necessary for the forgiveness of sins. ⇒ There is no forgiveness without the shedding of the blood of a sacrifice. ⇒ There is no way to approach God--to be saved--other than through the death of a substitute.	How Christ fulfilled the symbolism of the brazen altar: "*[I] give my life a ransom for many*" (Mk.10:45). "*He was oppressed, and he was afflicted, yet he opened not his mouth: he is brought as a lamb to the slaughter, and as a sheep before her shearers is dumb, so he openeth not his mouth*" (Is.53:7). "*The next day John seeth Jesus coming unto him, and saith, Behold the Lamb of God, which taketh away the sin of the world!*" (Jn.1:29). "*Purge out therefore the old leaven, that ye may be a new lump, as ye are unleavened. For even Christ our passover is sacrificed for us*" (1 Cor.5:7). "*But with the precious blood of*

SECTION OF THE TABERNACLE	WHAT IS TAUGHT	HOW CHRIST FULFILLED THE SYMBOLISM
The Brazen Altar in the Courtyard, 27:1-8 (cont.)		*Christ, as of a lamb without blemish and without spot" (1 Pt.1:19).* *"Hereby perceive we the love of God, because he laid down his life for us: and we ought to lay down our lives for the brethren" (1 Jn.3:16).*
The Walls of the Tabernacle, 27:9-19	What the Walls taught: ⇒ The wall of white linen symbolized the righteousness and holiness of God. He is so righteous and holy, so white and pure, that He is set apart from the world. ⇒ When a person looks at God, he must see that He dwells in righteousness and holiness. (When a person looked at white walls, they were to be reminded that God was holy.) ⇒ When a person approaches God, he must approach Him in reverence and awe, adoration and worship. He must praise and thank God that God allows him to enter His presence.	How Christ fulfilled the symbolism of the Walls: *"For he hath made him to be sin for us, who knew no sin; that we might be made the <u>righteousness</u> of God in him" (2 Cor.5:21).* *"And that ye put on the new man [Christ], which after God is created in <u>righteousness</u> and true holiness" (Eph.4:24).* *"And have put on the new man, which is renewed in knowledge after the image of him that created him" (Col.3:10).*
The Only Door or Gate into the Tabernacle, 27:16	What the Door or Gate taught: ⇒ There is only one way to enter God's presence; there are not many ways as most men think and practice. ⇒ God has to be approached if a man wishes to live eternally. No person shall ever live with God unless he approaches God exactly as God dictates.	How Christ fulfilled the symbolism of the Door or Gate: ⇒ Jesus Christ is the door, the only door, that a man can enter to be saved. ⇒ Jesus Christ is the way, the only way, that a man can come to the Father. *"I am the door: by me if any man enter in, he shall be saved, and shall go in and out, and find pasture" (Jn.10:9).* *"Jesus saith unto him, I am the way, the truth, and the life: no man cometh unto the Father, but by me" (Jn.14:6).*

TYPES, SYMBOLS, AND PICTURES
(Exodus 27:1-21)

Historical Term	Type or Picture (Scriptural Basis for Each)	Life Application for Today's Believer	Biblical Application for Today's Believer
The Horns of the Altar (Ex.27:2) See also The Altar of Burnt Offering—Ex.27:1-8; 35:16; 38:1-7; 39:39; 40:6, 29 See also The Altar of Incense—Ex.30:1-10; 35:15; 37:25-29; 39:38; 40:5, 26-27	*The Altar of Burnt Offering and the Altar of Incense both had horns on each corner. In the whole of Scripture, the horns of both altars are symbolic of four different things:* *a. Horn throughout Scripture is symbolic of power and strength. Therefore, the Horns of the Altar are symbolic of God's power and strength.* *"But thou art holy, O thou that inhabitest the praises of Israel" (Ps.22:3).* *"But my faithfulness and my mercy shall be*	a. God alone has the power and strength to deliver His people through all the trials and temptations of life.	*"And Aaron shall make an atonement upon the horns of it once in a year with the blood of the sin offering of atonements: once in the year shall he make atonement upon it throughout your generations: it is most holy unto the LORD" (Ex.30:10).* *"For the life of the flesh is in the blood: and I have given it to you upon the al-*

Historical Term	Type or Picture (Scriptural Basis for Each)	Life Application for Today's Believer	Biblical Application for Today's Believer
	with him: and in my name shall his horn be exalted" (Ps.89:24). "But my horn shalt thou exalt like the horn [power] of an unicorn: I shall be anointed with fresh oil" (Ps.92:10). "There will I make the horn [power] of David to bud: I have ordained a lamp for mine anointed" (Ps.132:17).		tar to make an atonement for your souls: for it is the blood that maketh an atonement for the soul" (Lev.17:11). "And not only so, but we also joy in God through our Lord Jesus Christ, by whom we have now received the atonement" (Ro.5:11).
	b. The Horns of the Altar are symbolic of the sacrificial and atoning (reconciling) power of the altar. This is seen in that the altar was the place of sacrifice.	b. Today, God accepts the sacrifice of Jesus Christ as the substitute for the believer's offering. Jesus Christ Himself is the atoning (reconciling) power that reconciles the believer to God. But note: a person must first call upon the name of the Lord to receive this atoning, reconciling power.	"And he said, The LORD is my rock, and my fortress, and my deliverer" (2 Sam. 22:2). "He delivered me from my strong enemy, and from them which hated me: for they were too strong for me" (Ps.18:17). "I sought the LORD, and he heard me, and delivered me from all my fears" (Ps.34:4). "For thou hast delivered my soul from death: wilt not thou deliver my feet from falling, that I may walk before God in the light of the living?" (Ps.56:13). "And even to your old age I am he; and even to hoar [gray] hairs will I carry you: I have made, and I will bear; even I will carry, and will deliver you" (Is.46:4). "Who delivered us from so great a death, and doth deliver: in whom we trust that he will yet deliver us" (2 Cor.1:10). "Notwithstanding the Lord stood with me, and strengthened me; that by me the preaching might be fully known, and that all the Gentiles might hear: and I was delivered out of the mouth of the lion" (2 Tim. 4:17).
	c. The Horns of the Altar are symbolic of God's salvation.	c. God's salvation can be experienced by every person who cries out to the LORD and who pleads for salvation (cp. Ex.30:10; Ps.118:27; Lk.1:69).	"The LORD is my light and my salvation; whom shall I fear? the LORD is the strength of my life; of whom shall I be afraid?" (Ps.27:1). "But the salvation of the righteous is of the LORD: he is their strength in the time of trouble" (Ps.37:39). "Behold, God is my salvation; I will trust, and not

Historical Term	Type or Picture (Scriptural Basis for Each)	Life Application for Today's Believer	Biblical Application for Today's Believer
			be afraid: for the LORD JEHOVAH is my strength and my song; he also is become my salvation" (Is.12:2). *"The LORD thy God in the midst of thee is mighty; he will save, he will rejoice over thee with joy; he will rest in his love, he will joy over thee with singing"* (Zeph.3:17).
	d. The Horns of the Altar are symbolic of God's protection, security, sanctuary, and help **"And thou shalt make the horns of it upon the four corners thereof: his horns shall be of the same: and thou shalt overlay it with brass"** (Ex.27:2).	d. God has promised to hold His people close to His heart and to watch over them, to lead and guide them as they journey to the promised land of heaven. God has promised to provide <u>everything</u> that His dear people need (cp. 2 Sam.22:3; Ps.18:2; 1 Ki.2:28).	*"The God of my rock; in him will I trust: he is my shield, and the horn of my salvation, my high tower, and my refuge, my saviour; thou savest me from violence"* (2 Sam.22:3). *"For in the time of trouble he shall hide me in his pavilion: in the secret of his tabernacle shall he hide me; he shall set me up upon a rock"* (Ps.27:5). *"Thou art my hiding place; thou shalt preserve me from trouble; thou shalt compass me about with songs of deliverance"* (Ps.32:7). *"In the fear of the LORD is strong confidence: and his children shall have a place of refuge"* (Pr.14:26). *"The name of the LORD is a strong tower: the righteous runneth into it, and is safe"* (Pr.18:10).
Brass (bronze or copper) (Ex.27:2-3)	*Brass was the only metal durable enough to withstand the consuming fires upon the altar. Brass is a symbol of Jesus Christ. Jesus Christ is the only Person able to bear the consuming fire of God's judgment against sin, the only Person able to bear the judgment of sin for a person.* **"And thou shalt make the horns of it upon the four corners thereof: his horns shall be of the same: and thou shalt overlay it with brass. And thou shalt make his pans to receive his ashes, and his shovels, and his basons, and his fleshhooks, and his firepans: all the vessels thereof thou shalt make of brass"** (Ex.27:2-3).	⇒ A person cannot even imagine the magnitude of God's wrath against sin. Nor can any person bear the wrath. Therefore, it is essential that an individual call upon Christ to bear the wrath of coming judgment against him. No person will escape eternal damnation unless he genuinely turns to Christ.	*"And his feet like unto fine brass, as if they burned in a furnace; and his voice as the sound of many waters"* (Rev.1:15). *"But he was wounded for our transgressions, he was bruised for our iniquities: the chastisement of our peace was upon him; and with his stripes we are healed"* (Is.53:5). *"But we see Jesus, who was made a little lower than the angels for the suffering of death, crowned with glory and honour; that he by the grace of God should taste death for every man"* (Heb.2:9).

EXODUS 27:1-21

Historical Term	Type or Picture (Scriptural Basis for Each)	Life Application for Today's Believer	Biblical Application for Today's Believer
The Courtyard Walls (Ex.27:9-19) See also Ex.35:17; 36:20-34; 38:9-20; 39:33, 40; 40:8, 33	*The Courtyard Walls were walls of linen. Throughout Scripture, fine linen is described as clean and white, speaking of the righteousness of God.* *The Courtyard Walls symbolized the righteousness and holiness of God. God is so holy and righteous, so white and pure, that He is set apart--totally set apart --from the world.* **"The length of the court shall be an hundred cubits, and the breadth fifty every where, and the height five cubits of fine twined linen, and their sockets of brass" (Ex.27:18).**	What the Courtyard Walls taught: ⇒ When a person looks at God, he is to remember that God is holy, that God dwells in righteousness and holiness. Therefore, when a person approaches God, he must approach Him in reverence and awe, adoration and worship. He must praise and thank God, that God allows him to enter His presence.	*"Exalt the LORD our God, and worship at his holy hill; for the LORD our God is holy" (Ps.99:9).* *"That he would grant unto us, that we being delivered out of the hand of our enemies might serve him without fear, In holiness and righteousness before him, all the days of our life" (Lk.1:74-75).* *"Having therefore these promises, dearly beloved, let us cleanse ourselves from all filthiness of the flesh and spirit, perfecting holiness in the fear of God" (2 Cor.7:1).* *"By him therefore let us offer the sacrifice of praise to God continually, that is, the fruit of our lips giving thanks to his name" (Heb.13:15).* *"But ye are a chosen generation, a royal priesthood, an holy nation, a peculiar people; that ye should shew forth the praises of him who hath called you out of darkness into his marvellous light" (1 Pt.2:9).*
The Door or Gate (Ex.27:16) See also 35:17; 38:18-19; 39:40; 40:33	*There was an opening to the Tabernacle Courtyard. It was a Door that was clearly marked and accessible to any person, large or small, rich or poor who would accept the invitation to enter. However, there was only one Door to enter God's presence. The Door or Gate symbolized at least two things:* a. *The Door symbolized the great invitation of God, that God invites a person to enter His presence. But note: there is only one door, only one entrance into God's presence.*	What the Door or Gate taught: a. There is only one way, one door, to enter God's presence. Jesus Christ is that door. There are not many ways as most men think and practice.	*"I am the door: by me if any man enter in, he shall be saved, and shall go in and out, and find pasture" (Jn.10:9).* *"By whom also we have access by faith into this grace wherein we stand, and rejoice in hope of the glory of God" (Ro.5:2).* *"Having therefore, brethren, boldness to enter into the holiest by the blood of Jesus, By a new and living way, which he hath consecrated for us, through the veil, that is to say, his flesh" (Heb.10:19-20).*

Historical Term	Type or Picture (Scriptural Basis for Each)	Life Application for Today's Believer	Biblical Application for Today's Believer
	b. The Door symbolized that God has to be approached exactly as God dictates. "And for the gate of the court *shall be* an hanging of twenty cubits, *of* blue, and purple, and scarlet, and fine twined linen, wrought with needlework: *and* their pillars *shall be* four, and their sockets four" (Ex.27:16).	b. God has to be approached exactly as He dictates. No person shall ever live with God unless he approaches God in the right way, through His Son, the Lord Jesus Christ.	*"Jesus saith unto him, I am the way, the truth, and the life: no man cometh unto the Father, but by me" (Jn.14:6).* *"For through him [Christ] we both have access by one Spirit unto the Father" (Eph.2:18).* *"Then said Jesus unto them again, Verily, verily, I say unto you, I am the door of the sheep" (Jn.10:7).*
Oil for light (Ex.27:20-21)	*The Priest was to tend to the Lampstand and keep it supplied with oil so the light would never burn out. The oil symbolized the Holy Spirit, the presence of the Holy Spirit in the life of the follower of God.* "And thou shalt command the children of Israel, that they bring thee pure oil olive beaten for the light, to cause the lamp to burn always. In the tabernacle of the congregation without the vail, which *is* before the testimony, Aaron and his sons shall order it from evening to morning before the LORD: *it shall be* a statute for ever unto their generations on the behalf of the children of Israel" (Ex.27:20-21).	⇒ Jesus Christ promised the believer that the Holy Spirit would always be present, always leading and guiding God's people to the true light of Jesus Christ. The Holy Spirit will... • show a person how to approach God and secure His approval • show a person how to face the trials of life, no matter how severe the trial • show a person how to solve the serious problems of life	*"And I will put my spirit within you, and cause you to walk in my statutes, and ye shall keep my judgments, and do them" (Ezk.36:27).* *"And I will pray the Father, and he shall give you another Comforter, that he may abide with you for ever; Even the Spirit of truth; whom the world cannot receive, because it seeth him not, neither knoweth him: but ye know him; for he dwelleth with you, and shall be in you" (Jn.14:16-17).* *"But ye are not in the flesh, but in the Spirit, if so be that the Spirit of God dwell in you. Now if any man have not the Spirit of Christ, he is none of his" (Ro.8:9).* *"Know ye not that ye are the temple of God, and that the Spirit of God dwelleth in you?" (1 Cor.3:16).* *"Thou preparest a table before me in the presence of mine enemies: thou anointest my head with oil; my cup runneth over" (Ps.23:5).* *"Thou hast loved righteousness, and hated iniquity; therefore God, even thy God, hath anointed thee with the oil of gladness above thy fellows" (Heb.1:9; cp.Jas.5:14).*

The Altar of Burnt Offering or Brazen Altar

1. The call of the priests
a. The source of the call: God--God Himself called Aaron & his sons
b. The purpose of the call
   1) To set the priests apart from all other people
   2) To serve God
c. The symbol of the High Priests' special call: His clothing--to stir dignity & honor for God's call & for the High Priest's office
   1) Skilled people were appointed to make the special garments

   2) The garments
      • A chestpiece or breast-piece
      • An ephod
      • A robe
      • A woven tunic
      • A turban
      • A sash

   3) The materials
      • Yarn: Gold, blue, purple, & scarlet
      • Fine linen
2. The ephod: A sleeveless, coat-like garment
a. The materials
      • Yarn: Gold, blue, purple, & scarlet
      • Fine linen
b. The design
   1) To be in 2 pieces, front & back, joined by 2 straps at the shoulder
   2) To have a sash or waist-band: Made of the same materials

   3) To take 2 onyx stones & engrave Israel's tribes on them

      • Six names on one stone & six names on the other stone: In the order of their birth

      • Engrave just as a gem-cutter engraves a seal

G. The Garments of the Priests: The Symbol of Bringing Dignity & Honor to the Name of God, Ex.28:1-43

And take thou unto thee Aaron thy brother, and his sons with him, from among the children of Israel, that he may minister unto me in the priest's office, even Aaron, Nadab and Abihu, Eleazar and Ithamar, Aaron's sons.
2 And thou shalt make holy garments for Aaron thy brother for glory and for beauty.
3 And thou shalt speak unto all that are wise hearted, whom I have filled with the spirit of wisdom, that they may make Aaron's garments to consecrate him, that he may minister unto me in the priest's office.
4 And these are the garments which they shall make; a breastplate, and an ephod, and a robe, and a broidered coat, a mitre, and a girdle: and they shall make holy garments for Aaron thy brother, and his sons, that he may minister unto me in the priest's office.
5 And they shall take gold, and blue, and purple, and scarlet, and fine linen.
6 And they shall make the ephod of gold, of blue, and of purple, of scarlet, and fine twined linen, with cunning work.
7 It shall have the two shoulderpieces thereof joined at the two edges thereof; and so it shall be joined together.
8 And the curious girdle of the ephod, which is upon it, shall be of the same, according to the work thereof; even of gold, of blue, and purple, and scarlet, and fine twined linen.
9 And thou shalt take two onyx stones, and grave on them the names of the children of Israel:
10 Six of their names on one stone, and the other six names of the rest on the other stone, according to their birth.
11 With the work of an engraver in stone, like the engravings of a signet, shalt

thou engrave the two stones with the names of the children of Israel: thou shalt make them to be set in ouches of gold.
12 And thou shalt put the two stones upon the shoulders of the ephod for stones of memorial unto the children of Israel: and Aaron shall bear their names before the LORD upon his two shoulders for a memorial.
13 And thou shalt make ouches of gold;
14 And two chains of pure gold at the ends; of wreathen work shalt thou make them, and fasten the wreathen chains to the ouches.
15 And thou shalt make the breastplate of judgment with cunning work; after the work of the ephod thou shalt make it; of gold, of blue, and of purple, and of scarlet, and of fine twined linen, shalt thou make it.
16 Foursquare it shall be being doubled; a span shall be the length thereof, and a span shall be the breadth thereof.
17 And thou shalt set in it settings of stones, even four rows of stones: the first row shall be a sardius, a topaz, and a carbuncle: this shall be the first row.
18 And the second row shall be an emerald, a sapphire, and a diamond.
19 And the third row a ligure, an agate, and an amethyst.
20 And the fourth row a beryl, and an onyx, and a jasper: they shall be set in gold in their inclosings.
21 And the stones shall be with the names of the children of Israel, twelve, according to their names, like the engravings of a signet; every one with his name shall they be according to the twelve tribes.
22 And thou shalt make upon the breastplate chains at the ends of wreathen work of pure gold.
23 And thou shalt make upon the breastplate two rings of gold, and shalt put the two rings on the two ends of the breastplate.
24 And thou shalt put the two wreathen chains of gold

• Mount the stones in gold settings

• Fasten the stones to the shoulder pieces of the ephod
c. The purpose of the ephod & stones: To symbolize that the priest represents & carries the name of God's people before the Lord
d. The design continued
   1) Make all settings gold
   2) Make two chains of pure gold: Attach to the settings

3. The breastpiece or chestpiece: A pouch-like garment used to determine God's will
a. The basic materials: The same as the ephod garment

b. The design
   1) To be 9" square, folded double, forming a pouch

   2) To attach four rows of precious stones on it
      • The 1st row of stones

      • The 2nd row of stones

      • The 3rd row of stones

      • The 4th row of stones
      • To set the stones in gold

      • To number 12 stones, one for each of the 12 tribes of Israel
      • To engrave the names of the 12 tribes on the stones as a seal

   3) To attach the chestpiece to the ephod
      • Make braided chains of pure gold
      • Make two gold rings: Attach to the top corners of the chestpiece--for the gold cords to go through--tie the cords to the gold settings on the shoulder pieces

of the ephod garment

- Make 2 more gold rings: Attach to the other two ends of the chestpiece--on the inside next to the ephod garment
- Make 2 more gold rings: Attach to the ephod garment near the sash

- Tie the rings of the chestpiece to the rings of the ephod with blue cord: To hold the two securely together

c. The purpose for the chestpiece
1) To symbolize that the High Priest represents & carries the names of God's people upon his heart, that he represents them before the Lord continually

2) To hold the urim & thummim (probably two stones or lots) next to the High Priest's heart: Symbolizes the High Priest seeking God's will for the people

4. The robe of the ephod: A long, sleeveless, solid blue robe
a. Make an opening for the head in the center: Reinforce the opening with a woven collar so it will not tear

b. Make pomegranates out of yarn: Blue, purple, scarlet yarn
1) Attach them to the hem of the robe with gold bells between them

the two rings which are on the ends of the breastplate.
25 And the other two ends of the two wreathen chains thou shalt fasten in the two ouches, and put them on the shoulderpieces of the ephod before it.
26 And thou shalt make two rings of gold, and thou shalt put them upon the two ends of the breastplate in the border thereof, which is in the side of the ephod inward.
27 And two other rings of gold thou shalt make, and shalt put them on the two sides of the ephod underneath, toward the forepart thereof, over against the other coupling thereof, above the curious girdle of the ephod.
28 And they shall bind the breastplate by the rings thereof unto the rings of the ephod with a lace of blue, that it may be above the curious girdle of the ephod, and that the breastplate be not loosed from the ephod.
29 And Aaron shall bear the names of the children of Israel in the breastplate of judgment upon his heart, when he goeth in unto the holy place, for a memorial before the LORD continually.
30 And thou shalt put in the breastplate of judgment the Urim and the Thummim; and they shall be upon Aaron's heart, when he goeth in before the LORD: and Aaron shall bear the judgment of the children of Israel upon his heart before the LORD continually.
31 And thou shalt make the robe of the ephod all of blue.
32 And there shall be an hole in the top of it, in the midst thereof: it shall have a binding of woven work round about the hole of it, as it were the hole of an habergeon, that it be not rent.
33 And beneath upon the hem of it thou shalt make pomegranates of blue, and of purple, and of scarlet, round about the hem thereof; and bells of gold between them

round about:
34 A golden bell and a pomegranate, a golden bell and a pomegranate, upon the hem of the robe round about.
35 And it shall be upon Aaron to minister: and his sound shall be heard when he goeth in unto the holy place before the LORD, and when he cometh out, that he die not.
36 And thou shalt make a plate of pure gold, and grave upon it, like the engravings of a signet, HOLINESS TO THE LORD.
37 And thou shalt put it on a blue lace, that it may be upon the mitre; upon the forefront of the mitre it shall be.
38 And it shall be upon Aaron's forehead, that Aaron may bear the iniquity of the holy things, which the children of Israel shall hallow in all their holy gifts; and it shall be always upon his forehead, that they may be accepted before the LORD.
39 And thou shalt embroider the coat of fine linen, and thou shalt make the mitre of fine linen, and thou shalt make the girdle of needlework.
40 And for Aaron's sons thou shalt make coats, and thou shalt make for them girdles, and bonnets shalt thou make for them, for glory and for beauty.
41 And thou shalt put them upon Aaron thy brother, and his sons with him; and shalt anoint them, and consecrate them, and sanctify them, that they may minister unto me in the priest's office.
42 And thou shalt make them linen breeches to cover their nakedness; from the loins even unto the thighs they shall reach:
43 And they shall be upon Aaron, and upon his sons, when they come in unto the tabernacle of the congregation, or when they come near unto the altar to minister in the holy place; that they bear not iniquity, and die: it shall be a statute for ever unto him and his seed after him.

2) Alternate the pomegranates & bells

c. The symbolic purpose:
1) To sound forth the intercessory ministry of the High Priest
2) To sound forth the acceptance of the offering of the High Priest, that he had not been stricken dead

5. The gold medallion worn on the turban: A headdress cloth or cap
a. To be engraved with these words: HOLY TO THE LORD
b. To be attached to the front of the turban by a blue cord

c. The purpose
1) To symbolize that the High Priest bore the guilt for the shortcomings & errors of the people
2) To symbolize that the people must seek the acceptance of a holy God

6. The final instructions governing the clothing
a. The turban & tunic (a long coat-like garment): Make of fine linen
b. The sash (worn around the waist): To be embroidered
c. The clothing for the other priests
1) To be tunics, sashes, & headdresses
2) The purpose: To set them apart for dignity & respect
d. The priests were to be clothed in the special garments, then ordained

e. The linen underclothing
1) To be worn next to the body, covering the priest from the waist to the thigh

2) Always to be worn when serving God
3) The purpose
- To cover their nakedness (modesty & purity)
- To keep from arousing God's anger & judgment against immodesty & immorality

DIVISION IX

THE TABERNACLE, ITS BLUEPRINT AND PRIESTHOOD:
THE TRUE WAY TO APPROACH AND WORSHIP GOD, EX.25:1-31:18

G.   The Garments of the Priests: The Symbol of Bringing Dignity and Honor to the Name of God, Ex. 28:1-43

(28:1-43) **Introduction**: respect, dignity, and honor are virtues missing in today's society. Few people show respect and honor to others, even to those in the highest positions of rule and authority. Tragically, the reason is often because those in authority live such deceptive and immoral lives. They destroy the honor due their position.

This must never be so with the people of God. Whatever believers do reflects upon the name of God. And God deserves the highest respect, the highest dignity and honor. Therefore, believers must live lives that demand respect, dignity, and honor. When people look upon a believer, the life of the believer must point people to God, to God's willingness to forgive and help them. The believer's life must stir people to respect and honor God. This is the subject of this passage: *The Garments of the Priests: The Symbol of Bringing Dignity and Honor to the Name of God,* Ex. 28:1-43.

1. The call of the priests (v.1-5).
2. The ephod: a sleeveless, coat-like garment (v.6-14).
3 The breastpiece or chestpiece: a pouch-like garment used to determine God's will (v.15-30).
4. The robe of the ephod: a long, sleeveless, solid blue robe (v.31-35).
5. The gold medallion worn on the turban: a headdress cloth or cap (v.36-38).
6. The final instructions governing the clothing (v.39-43).

1 (28:1-5) **Tabernacle of Moses--Priesthood, Call of**: there was the call of the priests. God called and set apart Aaron and his sons to serve Him in a special way. God selected these men from the masses of humanity to serve Him and Him alone. Note the details of this call:
1. The source of the call was God. God Himself called Aaron and his sons (v. 1). It was God who took the initiative and did the calling. The idea to serve God as a priest did not come from Moses nor from Aaron and his sons. The idea was God's alone. When God calls a person, any person, it is...

- God who *makes* the choice
- God who *equips* His choice
- God who *empowers* His choice
- God who *sends forth* His choice

2. The purpose of the call was to set the priests apart from all other people, to set them apart so they could serve God. Note the call was given so that they could "serve God as priests" (v.1). Scripture says that their work included five activities:

⇒ They were to offer gifts and sacrifices for sin.

"For every high priest taken from among men is ordained for men in things pertaining to God, that he may offer both gifts and sacrifices for sins" (Heb.5:1).
"Who needeth not daily, as those high priests, to offer up sacrifice, first for his own sins, and then for the people's: for this he did once, when he offered up himself" (Heb.7:27).

⇒ They were to show compassion for the ignorant and for people going astray.

"Who can have compassion on the ignorant, and on them that are out of the way; for that he himself also is compassed with infirmity" (Heb.5:2).

⇒ They were to teach the people.

"And Ezra the priest brought the law before the congregation both of men and women, and all that could hear with understanding, upon the first day of the seventh month....And Nehemiah, which is the Tirshatha, and Ezra the priest the scribe, and the Levites that taught the people, said unto all the people, This day is holy unto the LORD your God; mourn not, nor weep. For all the people wept, when they heard the words of the law" (Neh.8:2, 9).

⇒ They were to be representatives of God, mediators between God and man.

"And he shall bring his trespass offering unto the LORD, a ram without blemish out of the flock, with thy estimation, for a trespass offering, unto the priest: And the priest shall make an atonement for him before the LORD: and it shall be forgiven him for any thing of all that he hath done in trespassing therein" (Lev.6:6-7).
"For on that day shall the priest make an atonement for you, to cleanse you, that ye may be clean from all your sins before the LORD" (Lev.16:30).

⇒ They were to pray and make strong intercession for the people.

> "Aaron shall bear their names [of God's people] before the LORD upon his two shoulders for a memorial" (Ex.28:12).
> "And they truly were many priests [who made intercession], because they were not suffered to continue by reason of death: But this man, because he continueth ever, hath an unchangeable priesthood. Wherefore he is able also to save them to the uttermost that come unto God by him, seeing he ever liveth to make intercession for them" (Heb.7:23-25).

Thought 1. The greatest privilege in all the world is to be called by God to serve God. Note what Scripture says about God's call.

1) The call of God is made possible because of the gospel.

> "Whereunto he called you by our gospel, to the obtaining of the glory of our Lord Jesus Christ" (2 Th.2:14).

2) The call of God is a call to salvation, a holy calling, not based upon a man's ministry but upon God's very own purpose.

> "Who hath saved us, and called *us* with an holy calling, not according to our works, but according to his own purpose and grace, which was given us in Christ Jesus before the world began" (2 Tim.1:9).

3) The call of God is a heavenly calling.

> "Wherefore, holy brethren, partakers of the heavenly calling, consider the Apostle and High Priest of our profession, Christ Jesus" (Heb.3:1).

4) The call of God is a call to the kingdom and glory of God, His eternal glory.

> "But the God of all grace, who hath called us unto his eternal glory by Christ Jesus, after that ye have suffered a while, make you perfect, stablish, strengthen, settle *you*" (1 Pt.5:10).
> "That ye would walk worthy of God, who hath called you unto his kingdom and glory" (1 Th.2:12)

5) The call of God involves a glorious hope.

> "The eyes of your understanding being enlightened; that ye may know what is the hope of his calling, and what the riches of the glory of his inheritance in the saints" (Eph.1:18).

6) The call of God requires a person to walk worthy of God.

> "That ye would walk worthy of God, who hath called you unto his kingdom and glory" (1 Th.2:12).

7) The call of God demands faithfulness, personal responsibility.

> "I therefore, the prisoner of the Lord, beseech you that ye walk worthy of the vocation wherewith ye are called" (Eph.4:1).
> "Moreover it is required in stewards, that a man be found faithful" (1 Cor.4:2).

8) The call of God demands careful diligence.

> "Wherefore the rather, brethren, give diligence to make your calling and election sure: for if ye do these things, ye shall never fall" (2 Pt.1:10).

9) The call of God is a high calling, the ultimate goal for life.

> "I press toward the mark for the prize of the high calling of God in Christ Jesus" (Ph.3:14).

10) The call of God is unique, personal, individual, one of a kind.

> "For ye see your calling, brethren, how that not many wise men after the flesh, not many mighty, not many noble, *are called*" (1 Cor.1:26).

3. The symbol of the High Priest's special call was his clothing. The purpose of his clothing was to stir dignity and honor for God's call and for the Priestly office. The charge was to make holy garments for a man who would personally minister to a holy God. Note the special instructions for making these holy garments:

a. Skilled people were appointed to make the special garments (v.3). Note that they were equipped for their work by God Himself, equipped with special wisdom and ability.
b. The garments were...
- a chestpiece or breastpiece
- an ephod
- a robe
- a woven tunic
- a turban
- a sash (v.4)
c. The materials that were used were gold thread that was embroidered into the garments and multicolored yarn (blue, purple, and scarlet) that was spun and made a part of the garments along with fine linen (v.5).

Thought 1. When the High Priest *put on* these holy garments, it lent dignity to his work. In the same sense, when the believer *puts on holy garments* it also lends dignity to his work for the Lord.
⇒ The believer is to put on Christ.

"For as many of you as have been baptized into Christ have put on Christ" (Gal.3:27).

⇒ The believer is to put on the new man.

"And that ye put on the new man, which after God is created in righteousness and true holiness" (Eph.4:24).
"And have put on the new man, which is renewed in knowledge after the image of him that created him" (Col.3:10).

⇒ The believer is to put on the armor of God, the whole armor.

"Put on the whole armour of God, that ye may be able to stand against the wiles of the devil" (Eph.6:11).

⇒ The believer is to put on the armor of light.

"The night is far spent, the day is at hand: let us therefore cast off the works of darkness, and let us put on the armour of light" (Ro.13:12).

⇒ The believer is to put on love.

"And above all these things put on charity, which is the bond of perfectness" (Col.3:14).

⇒ The believer is to put on compassion, kindness, humility, gentleness, and patience.

"Put on therefore, as the elect of God, holy and beloved, bowels of mercies, kindness, humbleness of mind, meekness, longsuffering" (Col.3:12).

⇒ The believer is to put on incorruption and immortality.

"For this corruptible must put on incorruption, and this mortal must put on immortality. So when this corruptible shall have put on incorruption, and this mortal shall have put on immortality, then shall be brought to pass the saying that is written, Death is swallowed up in victory" (1 Cor.15:53-54).

2 (28:6-14) **Tabernacle of Moses--Priesthood--Ephod--Prayer, Intercessory**: there was the ephod, a sleeveless, coat-like garment. This was the first garment to be made.
1. The ephod was made of the following materials: gold thread made from thin gold sheets cut into thin, thread-like wires (see Ex.39:3); yarn that was blue, purple, and scarlet (v.6); and fine linen.
2. The design of the ephod was spelled out with these instructions:
a. It was to be in two pieces, front and back, joined by two straps at the shoulder (v.7).
b. It was to have a sash or waistband that was made of the same materials (v.8).
c. It was to have two onyx stones that had Israel's 12 tribes engraved on them (v.9). Six names were to be engraved on each stone in the order of their birth (v.10). Each stone was to be engraved just as a gemcutter engraves a seal (v.11). The maker of the ephod was to mount the stones in gold settings and then fasten the stones to the shoulder pieces of the ephod (v.11-12).
3. The purpose of the ephod and stones was to symbolize that the priest represented and carried the name of God's people before the Lord as their *mediator and intercessor* (v.12).
4. The design for the ephod continued with two final points of instruction:
a. To make all settings gold (v.13).
b. To make two chains of pure gold and attach these to the settings (v.14).

Thought 1. Jesus Christ is the One who represents and carries the name of every believer before the LORD God. Jesus Christ is our *Mediator and Intercessor*. No matter what our burden, no matter how heavy or terrifying the burden may be, we can cast it upon Christ. Christ will relieve us, strengthen us, give us peace and rest from the burden. The heavy burdens of the soul need to be freely cast upon His strong, never-failing shoulders. There is no burden that can ever weigh Him down.

> "Come unto me, all *ye* that labour and are heavy laden, and I will give you rest. Take my yoke upon you, and learn of me; for I am meek and lowly in heart: and ye shall find rest unto your souls. For my yoke *is* easy, and my burden is light" (Mt.11:28-30).
> "Who is he that condemneth? It is Christ that died, yea rather, that is risen again, who is even at the right hand of God, who also maketh intercession for us" (Ro.8:34).
> "Wherefore in all things it behooved him to be made like unto his brethren, that he might be a merciful and faithful high priest in things pertaining to God, to make reconciliation for the sins of the people. For in that he himself hath suffered being tempted, he is able to succour them that are tempted" (Heb.2:17-18).
> "For we have not an high priest which cannot be touched with the feeling of our infirmities; but was in all points tempted like as we are, yet without sin. Let us therefore come boldly unto the throne of grace, that we may obtain mercy, and find grace to help in time of need" (Heb.4:15-16).
> "Wherefore he is able also to save them to the uttermost that come unto God by him, seeing he ever liveth to make intercession for them" (Heb.7:25).
> "Casting all your care upon him; for he careth for you" (1 Pt.5:7).

3 (28:15-30) **Tabernacle of Moses--Breastpiece--Will of God**: there was the breastpiece or chestpiece, a pouch-like garment used to determine God's will. The breastpiece was an ornate square piece of cloth made of the same materials as the ephod. These are the instructions as to how it was to be made:
1. The basic materials were the same as the ephod garment (v.15).
2. The design of the breastpiece or chestpiece is outlined for simplicity:
   a. To be 9" square, folded double, forming a pouch (v.16).
   b. To have attached 4 rows of precious stones on it, which numbered a total of 12 (v.17-20). Each one of the 12 stones was attached to a gold setting (v.21). The 12 stones represented the 12 tribes of Israel and were identified by engraving the names of the 12 tribes on the stones as a seal (v.21).
   c. To attach the chestpiece to the ephod--permanently.
   • Make braided chains of pure gold
   • Make 2 gold rings: attach to the top corners of the chestpiece--for the gold cords to go through--tie the cords to the gold settings on the shoulder pieces of the ephod garment
   • Make 2 more gold rings: attach to the other 2 ends of the chestpiece--on the inside next to the ephod garment
   • Make 2 more gold rings: attach to the ephod garment near the sash
   • Tie the rings of the chestpiece to the rings of the ephod with blue cord: to hold the 2 securely together

3. The purpose for the chestpiece or breastpiece was twofold:
   a. To symbolize that the High Priest represented and carried the names of God's people upon his heart, that he represented them before the Lord continually (v.29).

Thought 1. Jesus Christ knows us by name, everyone of us. Christ does not know us as a number, a statistic, or a program goal. He knows each one of us individually and personally. This means that Jesus Christ cares for us. He cares about the trials, temptations, and sufferings that afflict us.

> "But now thus saith the LORD that created thee, O Jacob, and he that formed thee, O Israel, Fear not: for I have redeemed thee, I have called thee by thy name; thou art mine" (Is.43:1).
> "Casting all your care upon him; for he careth for you" (1 Pt.5:7).
> "But I am poor and needy; yet the Lord thinketh upon me: thou art my help and my deliverer; make no tarrying, O my God" (Ps.40:17).
> "Fear thou not; for I am with thee: be not dismayed; for I am thy God: I will strengthen thee; yea, I will help thee; yea, I will uphold thee with the right hand of my righteousness" (Is.41:10).
> "When thou passest through the waters, I will be with thee; and through the rivers, they shall not overflow thee: when thou walkest through the fire, thou shalt not be burned; neither shall the flame kindle upon thee" (Is.43:2).

b. The second purpose of the chestpiece was to hold the urim and thummim (probably two stones or lots) next to the High Priest's heart (v.30). This symbolized the High Priest seeking God's will for the people. The Hebrew word for *urim* is uncertain. It means either *lights* or *curse*. *Thummim* means perfection. What these two stones looked like and how they were used is not known. Some scholars feel they were used as dice or lots, that they were cast upon the ground with a decision being made based upon which stone turned up a certain way. However this seems unlikely; it is just contrary to the way God works throughout Scripture. God reveals His will. He does not base it upon the turn of stones like dice. Perhaps the <u>Expositor's Bible Commentary</u> is closer to the truth:

"Perhaps they only symbolized the special revelation open to the high priest rather than being the necessary means of achieving that information."[1]

Imagine the scene as the High Priest entered into the Holy Place. The urim and thummim reminded him and the people that God would speak and give His direction to His people. The High Priest was there on behalf of the people of God; therefore, God would hear and answer him. God would make His will and direction known to the High Priest. How? God would speak and move upon the heart of the High Priest.

Thought 1. We are to pray and seek God's face for the needs of others. The world reels under the weight of suffering and evil, of death and judgment to come. The only hope is God. God's help is needed. We must therefore seek His face, seek Him day and night.

"But if from thence thou shalt seek the LORD thy God, thou shalt find him, if thou seek him with all thy heart and with all thy soul" (Dt.4:29).

"Seek the LORD and his strength, seek his face continually" (1 Chron.16:11).

"He shall call upon me, and I will answer him: I *will be* with him in trouble; I will deliver him, and honour him" (Ps.91:15).

"Seek ye the LORD while he may be found, call ye upon him while he is near" (Is.55:6).

"And it shall come to pass, that before they call, I will answer; and while they are yet speaking, I will hear" (Is.65:24).

"Call unto me, and I will answer thee, and show thee great and mighty things, which thou knowest not" (Jer.33:3).

"And I say unto you, Ask, and it shall be given you; seek, and ye shall find; knock, and it shall be opened unto you" (Lk.11:9).

"And he spake a parable unto them to this end, that men ought always to pray, and not to faint" (Lk.18:1).

"Praying always with all prayer and supplication in the Spirit, and watching thereunto with all perseverance and supplication for all saints" (Eph.6:18).

4 (28:31-35) **Tabernacle of Moses--Priesthood--Robe of the Ephod**: there was the robe of the ephod, a long, sleeveless, solid blue robe. These are the instructions that were given:

1. Make an opening for the head in the center. The opening was to be reinforced with a woven collar so it would not tear (v.32).

2. Make pomegranates out of yarn in the colors of blue, purple, and scarlet (v.33). These pomegranates of yarn were attached to the hem of the robe with gold bells between them. The pattern was a pomegranate and a bell alternated at the hem of the robe (v.34).

3. The symbolic purpose of the robe was twofold:

   a. The first symbol was to sound forth the *intercessory ministry* of the High Priest (v.35). Before the High Priest could minister before the Lord, he had to slip on this robe. After he was fully dressed in the priestly garments, the tinkling of the bells marked his every step. The sound of the bells told the people where he was as he carried their names before the LORD. As he ministered in their behalf, they could follow his intercessory ministry as he moved about the various rituals of worship. As he carried out a particular ritual, the people would obviously meditate and pray over the truth symbolized by the ritual. The pomegranate fruit, traditionally known for its beautiful flower and fertility, symbolized the beauty and fruitfulness of the priest's intercessory ministry.

   b. The second symbol was to sound forth a wonderful fact: that *God accepted the offering* of the High Priest, that he had not been stricken dead (v.35). The sound of the bells let the people know that he was alive and ministering on their behalf. Every time the High Priest went into the Holy Place, there was always the chance that his offering would not be acceptable to God. When a Holy God is approached by an unholy offering, death is always the final consequence (always spiritual death; sometimes physical death).

Thought 1. Jesus Christ is the great High Priest who fulfills the intercessory ministry of the High Priest. Jesus Christ intercedes for us at the throne of God, and His intercessory ministry never stops.

⇒ Jesus Christ makes intercession for us at the right hand of God.

"Who *is* he that condemneth? *It is* Christ that died, yea rather, that is risen again, who is even at the right hand of God, who also maketh intercession for us" (Ro.8:34).

⇒ Jesus Christ lives forever and makes intercession for those He has saved.

"Wherefore he is able also to save them to the uttermost that come unto God by him, seeing he ever liveth to make intercession for them" (Heb.7:25).

⇒ Jesus Christ makes intercession for the sinner.

"Therefore will I divide him *a portion* with the great, and he shall divide the spoil with the strong; because he hath poured out his soul unto death: and he was numbered with the transgressors; and he bare the sin of many, and made intercession for the transgressors" (Is.53:12).

---

[1] Frank E. Gaebelein. *Expositor's Bible Commentary*, Vol.2, p.467.

⇒ Jesus Christ makes intercession for those who are weak and ready to fail.

>"But I have prayed for thee, that thy faith fail not: and when thou art converted, strengthen thy brethren" (Lk.22:32).

⇒ Jesus Christ makes intercession even for His enemies.

>"Then said Jesus, Father, forgive them; for they know not what they do. And they parted his raiment, and cast lots" (Lk.23:34).

⇒ Jesus Christ makes intercession for the church, for all believers throughout all generations.

>"I pray for them: I pray not for the world, but for them which thou hast given me; for they are thine" (Jn.17:9).

Thought 2. Jesus Christ offered Himself to God in five significant ways:
1) Jesus Christ offered Himself as the perfect offering of righteousness, as the Just for the unjust.

>"For Christ also hath once suffered for sins, the just for the unjust, that he might bring us to God, being put to death in the flesh, but quickened by the Spirit" (1 Pt.3:18).

2) Jesus Christ offered Himself as the perfect sacrifice, as the Lamb of God.

>"The next day John seeth Jesus coming unto him, and saith, Behold the Lamb of God, which taketh away the sin of the world" (Jn.1:29).

3) Jesus Christ offered Himself as the perfect High Priest, as the One who intercedes for man.

>"But this man, because he continueth ever, hath an unchangeable priesthood. Wherefore he is able also to save them to the uttermost that come unto God by him, seeing he ever liveth to make intercession for them" (Heb.7:24-25).

4) Jesus Christ offered Himself as the resurrected Savior, as the One who lives forevermore.

>"For I delivered unto you first of all that which I also received, how that Christ died for our sins according to the scriptures; And that he was buried, and that he rose again the third day according to the scriptures" (1 Cor.15:3-4).
>"For the Lord himself shall descend from heaven with a shout, with the voice of the archangel, and with the trump of God: and the dead in Christ shall rise first: Then we which are alive and remain shall be caught up together with them in the clouds, to meet the Lord in the air: and so shall we ever be with the Lord" (1 Th.4:16-17).

5) Jesus Christ offered Himself as the exalted Lord, as the One who is seated at the right hand of God.

>"So then after the Lord had spoken unto them, he was received up into heaven, and sat on the right hand of God" (Mk.16:19).
>"Hereafter shall the Son of man sit on the right hand of the power of God" (Lk.22:69).
>"[The power of God] which he wrought in Christ, when he raised him from the dead, and set *him* at his own right hand in the heavenly *places*" (Eph.1:20).
>"Wherefore God also hath highly exalted him, and given him a name which is above every name" (Ph.2:9).
>"Saying with a loud voice, Worthy is the Lamb that was slain to receive power, and riches, and wisdom, and strength, and honour, and glory, and blessing" (Rev.5:12).

5 (28:36-38) **Tabernacle of Moses--Priesthood--Garments, Gold Medallion on Turban**: there was the gold medallion worn on the turban (a headdress cloth or cap). The gold medallion was the most significant piece of the turban. Note the special instructions for the gold medallion:
1. The gold medallion was to be engraved with these words: HOLY TO THE LORD (v.36). What a great proclamation to wear! It is important to note where this medallion was to be worn: on the forehead, right where it would attract attention. It was probably the first item to attract people.

Thought 1. What a great difference in the behavior of believers if "HOLY TO THE LORD" were strapped to their foreheads. Pressed next to the mind, the gold medallion would be a constant reminder for the believer to live a holy life. Yet this is the very thing we must do, do mentally, do diligently. We must live holy lives.
1) We must put no worthless thing before our eyes.

>"I will set no wicked thing before mine eyes: I hate the work of them that turn aside; it shall not cleave to me" (Ps.101:3).

2) We must guard and restrain our tongues.

"**Keep thy tongue from evil, and thy lips from speaking guile [deceit]**" (Ps.34:13).

3) We must think only upon things that are pure and holy.

"**Finally, brethren, whatsoever things are true, whatsoever things are honest, whatsoever things are just, whatsoever things are pure, whatsoever things are lovely, whatsoever things are of good report; if there be any virtue, and if there be any praise, think on these things**" (Ph.4:8).

4) We must live lives that are HOLY TO THE LORD.

"**For I *am* the LORD that bringeth you up out of the land of Egypt, to be your God: ye shall therefore be holy, for I *am* holy**" (Lev.11:45).
"**Having therefore these promises, dearly beloved, let us cleanse ourselves from all filthiness of the flesh and spirit, perfecting holiness in the fear of God**" (2 Cor.7:1).
"**And that ye put on the new man, which after God is created in righteousness and true holiness**" (Eph.4:24).
"**Follow peace with all *men,* and holiness, without which no man shall see the Lord**" (Heb.12:14).
"**Because it is written, Be ye holy; for I am holy**" (1 Pt.1:16).
"***Seeing* then *that* all these things shall be dissolved, what manner *of persons* ought ye to be in *all* holy conversation and godliness**" (2 Pt.3:11).

2. The gold medallion was to be attached to the front of the turban by a blue cord (v.37).
3. The purpose of the medallion was twofold:
   a. To symbolize that the High Priest bore the guilt for the shortcomings and errors of the people as they presented their offerings to God (v.38). The people came short--ever so short--of the glory and holiness of God.
   b. To symbolize that the people must seek the acceptance of a holy God (v.38).

Thought 1. Two strong lessons are seen in the medallion and its purposes.
1) Jesus Christ bore the guilt for the shortcomings and errors of us all. Man needs a perfect, sinless Sacrifice, and Jesus Christ is that sacrifice.

"**But he *was* wounded for our transgressions, *he was* bruised for our iniquities: the chastisement of our peace *was* upon him; and with his stripes we are healed**" (Is.53:5).
"**But God commendeth his love toward us, in that, while we were yet sinners, Christ died for us**" (Ro.5:8).
"**[Christ] who gave himself for our sins, that he might deliver us from this present evil world, according to the will of God and our Father**" (Gal.1:4).
"**Christ hath redeemed us from the curse of the law, being made a curse for us: for it is written, Cursed *is* every one that hangeth on a tree**" (Gal.3:13).
"**And walk in love, as Christ also hath loved us, and hath given himself for us an offering and a sacrifice to God for a sweetsmelling savour**" (Eph.5:2).
"**Who gave himself for us, that he might redeem us from all iniquity, and purify unto himself a peculiar people, zealous of good works**" (Tit.2:14).
"**Who his own self bare our sins in his own body on the tree, that we, being dead to sins, should live unto righteousness: by whose stripes ye were healed**" (1 Pt.2:24).
"**For Christ also hath once suffered for sins, the just for the unjust, that he might bring us to God, being put to death in the flesh, but quickened by the Spirit**" (1 Pt.3:18).

2) We must seek the acceptance of God by approaching God through Christ and through Christ alone.

"**For God so loved the world, that he gave his only begotten Son, that whosoever believeth in him should not perish, but have everlasting life**" (Jn.3:16).
"**For I came down from heaven, not to do mine own will, but the will of him that sent me**" (Jn.6:38).
"**I said therefore unto you, that ye shall die in your sins: for if ye believe not that I am [he], ye shall die in your sins**" (Jn.8:24).
"**Jesus saith unto him, I am the way, the truth, and the life: no man cometh unto the Father, but by me**" (Jn.14:6).
"**Neither is there salvation in any other: for there is none other name under heaven given among men, whereby we must be saved**" (Acts 4:12).
"**For other foundation can no man lay than that is laid, which is Jesus Christ**" (1 Cor.3:11).

6 (28:39-43) **Tabernacle of Moses--Priesthood. Garments**: there were the final instructions governing clothing. Note the exact instructions that God gave to Moses:
1. The turban and tunic (a long coat-like garment) were to be made of fine linen (v.39).
2. The sash (worn around the waist) was to be embroidered (v.39).

3. The clothing for the other priests was not as ornate as the High Priest's clothes, but the clothes still had to meet the same criteria: they had to be made according to God's pattern. The other priests were to have tunics, sashes, and head-dresses (v.40). The purpose of their clothing was to set their call and office apart for dignity and respect (v.41).
4. The priests were to be clothed in the special garments, then ordained (v.41). (See outline and notes--Ex.29:1-46 for discussion on the ordination of the priests.)
5. The linen underclothing was the final garment to be made.
  a. It was to be worn next to the body, covering the priest from the waist to the thigh (v.42).
  b. It was always to be worn when serving God (v.43).
  c. The purpose of the linen underclothing was to cover their nakedness (modesty and purity) as they climbed the steps of the altar. God's anger and judgment are aroused against immodesty and immorality (v.43).

Thought 1. It has become quite fashionable for people to do good works in the name of God. And yet, so many things are done in God's name that are worldly, carnal, and selfish. We who serve the Lord must not bring shame and embarrassment to the cause of Christ by living immoral and immodest lives. In the service of Christ, there is no room for the flesh, for man's sinful nature, not for the believer who wants to be a faithful follower of Christ.

1) The faithful believer must forsake all and follow Christ.

"Then said Jesus unto his disciples, If any *man* will come after me, let him deny himself, and take up his cross, and follow me" (Mt.16:24).
"If any *man* come to me, and hate not his father, and mother, and wife, and children, and brethren, and sisters, yea, and his own life also, he cannot be my disciple" (Lk.14:26).
"So likewise, whosoever he be of you that forsaketh not all that he hath, he cannot be my disciple" (Lk.14:33).

2) The faithful believer must abide in God's Word.

"Then said Jesus to those Jews which believed on him, If ye continue in my word, *then* are ye my disciples indeed" (Jn.8:31).
"Study to show thyself approved unto God, a workman that needeth not to be ashamed, rightly dividing the word of truth" (2 Tim.2:15).

3) The faithful believer must bear fruit, much fruit.

"Herein is my Father glorified, that ye bear much fruit; so shall ye be my disciples" (Jn.15:8).
"But the fruit of the Spirit is love, joy, peace, longsuffering, gentleness, goodness, faith, Meekness, temperance: against such there is no law" (Gal.5:22-23).

4) The faithful believer must live a life that is godly and above reproach.

"For this is the will of God, even your sanctification, that ye should abstain from fornication" (1 Th.4:3).
"Teaching us that, denying ungodliness and worldly lusts, we should live soberly, righteously, and godly, in this present world; Looking for that blessed hope, and the glorious appearing of the great God and our Saviour Jesus Christ" (Tit.2:12-13).

TYPES, SYMBOLS, AND PICTURES
(Exodus 28:1-43)

Historical Term	Type or Picture (Scriptural Basis for Each)	Life Application for Today's Believer	Biblical Application for Today's Believer
The Sash (Ex.28:4; 39:29) See also Ex.28:39	*The multi-colored sash of fine linen was symbolic of truth, the truth of God's Word. It is comparable to the belt of truth in the armor of God that the believer is to put on (Eph.6:14). The Word of God enlightens and wraps together everything in the believer's spiritual wardrobe.* "**And these are the garments which they shall make; a breastplate, and**	What the Sash taught: ⇒ Jesus Christ is the Truth, the Living Word of God. It is the Word of God that holds everything together. ⇒ A person needs help and support in life because he does not have the strength to conquer the terrible trials and temptations of life, the trials and temptations that drag him ever downward toward the	*"Jesus saith unto him, I am the way, the truth, and the life: no man cometh unto the Father, but by me" (Jn.14:6). "Stand therefore, having your loins girt about with truth, and having on the breastplate of righteousness" (Eph.6:14). "Sanctify them through thy truth: thy word is truth" (Jn.17:17). "All scripture is given by inspiration of God, and is*

Historical Term	Type or Picture (Scriptural Basis for Each)	Life Application for Today's Believer	Biblical Application for Today's Believer
	an ephod, and a robe, and a broidered coat, a mitre, and a girdle [sash]: and they shall make holy garments for Aaron thy brother, and his sons, that he may minister unto me in the priest's office" (Ex.28:4). "And a girdle [sash] of fine twined linen, and blue, and purple, and scarlet, of needlework; as the LORD commanded Moses" (Ex.39:29).	grave and eternal separation from God. Only the living Word of God can strengthen and hold us together as we walk through life.	profitable for doctrine, for reproof, for correction, for instruction in righteousness" (2 Tim.3:16). "For the word of God is quick, and powerful, and sharper than any twoedged sword, piercing even to the dividing asunder of soul and spirit, and of the joints and marrow, and is a discerner of the thoughts and intents of the heart" (Heb.4:12).
Purple (Ex.28:5-6)	Purple is the color of royalty; therefore, purple is a symbol of Christ as the King of kings and LORD of lords "And they shall take gold, and blue, and purple, and scarlet, and fine linen. And they shall make the ephod of gold, of blue, and of purple, of scarlet, and fine twined linen, with cunning work" (Ex.28:5-6).	⇒ Jesus Christ is the King of kings and LORD of lords, the Sovereign Ruler and Majesty of the Universe. A person needs to give Christ the honor and praise He deserves, the respect and thanksgiving that is due Him as his Savior and Deliverer. Nothing less is acceptable.	"And they clothed him with purple, and platted a crown of thorns, and put it about his head, And began to salute him, Hail, King of the Jews!" (Mk.15:17-18). "And he hath on his vesture and on his thigh a name written, KING OF KINGS, AND LORD OF LORDS" (Rev.19:16). "And from Jesus Christ, who is the faithful witness, and the first begotten of the dead, and the prince of the kings of the earth. Unto him that loved us, and washed us from our sins in his own blood" (Rev.1:5). "These shall make war with the Lamb, and the Lamb shall overcome them: for he is Lord of lords, and King of kings: and they that are with him are called, and chosen, and faithful" (Rev.17:14).
The Ephod (Ex.28:4, 6-14; 39:6-7) See also Ex.39:2-7	The Ephod symbolized that the priest represented and carried the names of God's people before the Lord. "And they shall make the ephod of gold, of blue, and of purple, of scarlet, and fine twined linen, with cunning work" (Ex.28:6). "And they wrought onyx stones inclosed in ouches of gold, graven, as signets are graven, with the names of the children of Israel. And he put them on the shoulders of the ephod, that they should be stones for a memorial to the children of Israel; as the LORD commanded Moses" (Ex.39:6-7).	What the Ephod taught: ⇒ A person cannot represent himself before God because he is a sinner. A person needs an Advocate, an Intercessor, a Mediator, a Savior who can approach God legally and perfectly. A person cannot do any of this; therefore, a person needs Someone who can. That person is the Lord Jesus Christ. ⇒ No matter what our burden, no matter how heavy or terrifying our trial, God knows us, knows us personally. He knows all about our burdens and trials--all because Christ represents us and carries our	"Come unto me, all ye that labour and are heavy laden, and I will give you rest. Take my yoke upon you, and learn of me; for I am meek and lowly in heart: and ye shall find rest unto your souls. For my yoke is easy, and my burden is light" (Mt.11:28-30). "Who is he that condemneth? It is Christ that died, yea rather, that is risen again, who is even at the right hand of God, who also maketh intercession for us" (Ro.8:34). "For we have not an high priest which cannot be touched with the feeling of our infirmities; but was in all points tempted like as we are, yet without sin. Let us therefore come boldly unto

Historical Term	Type or Picture (Scriptural Basis for Each)	Life Application for Today's Believer	Biblical Application for Today's Believer
		names before the Father.	*the throne of grace, that we may obtain mercy, and find grace to help in time of need" (Heb.4:14-15).* *"Casting all your care upon him; for he careth for you" (1 Pt.5:7).*
Scarlet (Ex.28:15)	*Scarlet, a bright color of red, symbolizes sacrifice. Therefore, scarlet pictures the entire scene of sacrifice and redemption through Jesus Christ* **"And thou shalt make the breastplate of judgment with cunning work; after the work of the ephod thou shalt make it; of gold, of blue, and of purple, and of <u>scarlet</u>, and of fine twined linen, shalt thou make it" (Ex.28:15).**	⇒ Jesus Christ is the Lamb of God, the One who was sacrificed to take away the sins of the world and to redeem mankind. It is only through the shed blood of Jesus Christ that we are saved and delivered.	*"So Christ was once offered to bear the sins of many; and unto them that look for him shall he appear the second time without sin unto salvation" (Heb.9:28).* *"But Christ being come an high priest of good things to come, by a greater and more perfect tabernacle, not made with hands, that is to say, not of this building; Neither by the blood of goats and calves, but by his own blood he entered in once into the holy place, having obtained eternal redemption for us. For if the blood of bulls and of goats, and the ashes of an heifer sprinkling the unclean, sanctifieth to the purifying of the flesh: How much more shall the blood of Christ, who through the eternal Spirit offered himself without spot to God, purge your conscience from dead works to serve the living God?" (Heb.9:11-14; cp.9:19-20; 9:23).*
The Breastpiece or Chestpiece (Ex.28:4, 15-20; 28:29) See also Ex.39:8-21	*The Breastpiece was a garment that was worn close to the heart of the High Priest. The purpose for the chestpiece was twofold:* *a. First, to symbolize that the High Priest represents and carries the names of God's people upon his heart, that he represents them before the Lord continually (28:29).*	What the Breastpiece or Chestpiece taught: a. This is a strong picture of the love of God: how much God loves His people. He loves us so much that He keeps us ever so close to His heart, keeps us continually before His face. God is not a God who is... • removed from the feelings of His people • calloused in His heart when His people are suffering • too busy to listen to the desperate cries of those who need His help God is never caught	*"Before I formed thee in the belly I knew thee; and before thou camest forth out of the womb I sanctified thee, and I ordained thee a prophet unto the nations" (Jer.1:5).* *"Behold, God is mine helper: the Lord is with them that uphold my soul" (Ps.54:4).* *"The LORD is nigh unto them that are of a broken heart; and saveth such as be of a contrite spirit" (Ps.34:18).* *"I know thy works: behold, I have set before thee an open door, and no man can shut it: for thou hast a little strength, and hast kept my word, and hast not de-*

Historical Term	Type or Picture (Scriptural Basis for Each)	Life Application for Today's Believer	Biblical Application for Today's Believer
		off guard by the circumstances that come our way. God knows and God cares.	nied my name" (Rev.3:8). "But even the very hairs of your head are all numbered. Fear not therefore: ye are of more value than many sparrows" (Lk.12:7).
	b. The second purpose of the chestpiece was to hold the urim and thummim (probably two stones or lots) next to the High Priest's heart (28:30). This symbolized the High Priest seeking God's will for the people. Imagine the scene as the High Priest entered into the Holy Place. He was there on behalf of the people of God and would not leave until God had made His will clear. "And thou shalt make the breastplate of judgment with cunning work; after the work of the ephod thou shalt make it; of gold, of blue, and of purple, and of scarlet, and of fine twined linen, shalt thou make it" (Ex.28:15). "And Aaron shall bear the names of the children of Israel in the breastplate of judgment upon his heart, when he goeth in unto the holy place, for a memorial before the LORD continually" (Ex.28:29).	b. Jesus Christ is our great High Priest who represents and carries our names upon His heart and before the Lord God continually. Jesus Christ wants the very best for us. He prays for us, seeking nothing less than God's perfect will for us.	"I pray for them [believers]: I pray not for the world, but for them which thou hast given me; for they are thine" (Jn.17:9). "Wherefore he is able also to save them to the uttermost that come unto God by him, seeing he ever liveth to make intercession for them [believers]" (Heb.7:25).
The Robe of the Ephod (Ex.28:4, 31-35) See also Ex.39:22-26	The Robe of the Ephod was worn by the High Priest as he entered through the Veil and ministered to the Lord in the Sanctuary. The Robe of the Ephod was symbolic of two things: a. The Robe of the Ephod symbolized the sounding forth of the intercessory ministry of the High Priest. b. The Robe of the Ephod	What the Robe of the Ephod taught: a. Jesus Christ is our great High Priest who sounds forth the intercessory ministry of the High Priest. His intercession never ends, never stops. This is a strong lesson for us: we too must pray without ceasing. We must become intercessors--great intercessors -- for our loved ones and for the lost of the world. b. We should rejoice in	"Seek the LORD and his strength, seek his face continually" (1 Chron.16:11). "Evening, and morning, and at noon, will I pray, and cry aloud: and he shall hear my voice" (Ps.55:17). "Praying always with all prayer and supplication in the Spirit, and watching thereunto with all perseverance and supplication for all saints" (Eph.6:18). "But this man, because he continueth ever, hath an unchangeable priesthood.

Historical Term	Type or Picture (Scriptural Basis for Each)	Life Application for Today's Believer	Biblical Application for Today's Believer
	symbolized the sounding forth of a wonderful fact: that God accepted the offering of the High Priest, that he had not been stricken dead. **"And thou shalt make the robe of the ephod all of blue. And there shall be an hole in the top of it, in the midst thereof: it shall have a binding of woven work round about the hole of it, as it were the hole of an habergeon, that it be not rent"** (Ex.28:31-32).	the fact that the sacrifice made by Jesus Christ was perfectly acceptable to God the Father. Once we have been saved, we no longer have to worry about being judged guilty or condemned to die.	*Wherefore he is able also to save them to the uttermost that come unto God by him, seeing he ever liveth to make intercession for them"* (Heb.7:24-25). *"The next day John seeth Jesus coming unto him, and saith, Behold the Lamb of God, which taketh away the sin of the world"* (Jn.1:29). *"Wherefore God also hath highly exalted him, and given him a name which is above every name"* (Ph.2:9). *"Who is he that condemneth? It is Christ that died, yea rather, that is risen again, who is even at the right hand of God, who also maketh intercession for us"* (Ro.8:34).
The Gold Medallion or Diadem (Ex.28:36-38; 39:30-31)	*The Gold Medallion was attached with a blue ribbon to the head of the High Priest and was the crowning piece of the High Priest's wardrobe. The words "HOLINESS TO THE LORD" were written upon the Medallion.* a. *The Gold Medallion symbolized that the High Priest bore the guilt for the shortcomings of the people.*	What the Gold Medallion taught: a. We are ever so short of the glory and holiness of God. We desperately need Someone to bear the guilt for our shortcoming. That person is Jesus Christ. It is Jesus Christ who bore the guilt for the shortcomings and errors of the people. A person needs a perfect sacrifice, and that Sacrifice is Jesus Christ, who died upon the cross for our sins.	*"Who gave himself for us, that he might redeem us from all iniquity, and purify unto himself a peculiar people, zealous of good works"* (Tit.2:14). *"For Christ also hath once suffered for sins, the just for the unjust, that he might bring us to God, being put to death in the flesh, but quickened by the Spirit"* (1 Pt. 3:18).
	b. *The Gold Medallion symbolized that the people must seek the acceptance of a holy God.* **"And thou shalt make a plate of pure gold, and grave upon it, like the engravings of a signet, HOLINESS TO THE LORD."** (Ex.28:36) **"And they made the plate of the holy crown of pure gold, and wrote upon it a writing, like to the en-**	b. We are guilty of sin. Our sin indicts us and places us at the mercy of a holy and righteous Judge. God beckons each person to come to Him on the basis of the merit of Christ and His righteousness. We must seek the approval of God by approaching God through Christ and Christ alone.	*"Jesus saith unto him, I am the way, the truth, and the life: no man cometh unto the Father, but by me"* (Jn.14:6). *"Neither is there salvation in any other: for there is none other name under heaven given among men, whereby we must be saved"* (Acts 4:12).

Historical Term	Type or Picture (Scriptural Basis for Each)	Life Application for Today's Believer	Biblical Application for Today's Believer
	gravings of a signet, HOLINESS TO THE LORD. And they tied unto it a lace of blue, to fasten *it* on high upon the mitre; as the LORD commanded Moses" (Ex.39:30-31).		
The Linen Turbans and Tunics (Ex.28:4, 39; 39:27-28)	*Linen is symbolic of righteousness. The Linen Turban and Tunic (a long coat-like garment that essentially covered the whole body) were symbolic of putting on God's righteousness.* "And thou shalt embroider the coat of fine linen, and thou shalt make the mitre of fine linen, and thou shalt make the girdle of needlework" (Ex.28:39). "And they made coats *of* fine linen *of* woven work for Aaron, and for his sons, And a mitre *of* fine linen, and goodly bonnets *of* fine linen, and linen breeches *of* fine twined linen" (Ex.39:27-28).	What the Linen Turbans & Tunics taught: ⇒ If a person wishes to live in God's presence, he must put on the righteousness of Christ. A person is depraved and totally inadequate, having no righteousness of his own. Therefore, a person cannot walk before God or serve God unless he puts on the righteousness of Christ.	"For he hath made him to be sin for us, who knew no sin; that we might be made the righteousness of God in him" (2 Cor.5:21). *"I put on righteousness, and it clothed me: my judgment was as a robe and a diadem" (Job 29:14).* *"I will greatly rejoice in the LORD, my soul shall be joyful in my God; for he hath clothed me with the garments of salvation, he hath covered me with the robe of righteousness, as a bridegroom decketh himself with ornaments, and as a bride adorneth herself with her jewels" (Is.61:10).* *"But of him are ye in Christ Jesus, who of God is made unto us wisdom, and righteousness, and sanctification, and redemption" (1 Cor.1:30).* *"But we are all as an unclean thing, and all our righteousnesses are as filthy rags; and we all do fade as a leaf; and our iniquities, like the wind, have taken us away" (Is.64:6).*
The Linen Headband (Ex.28:40) See also Ex.39:28	*The Linen Headband symbolized the need for a person to subject his mind and his thoughts to God and His righteousness. (Remember, the linen pictures the righteousness of God.)* "And for Aaron's sons thou shalt make coats, and thou shalt make for them girdles, and bonnets shalt thou make for them, for glory and for beauty" (Ex.28:40).	What the Linen Headband taught: ⇒ It is Jesus Christ who has established His Lordship over every thought, every idea, every agenda of a person. The believer must willingly submit his mind and will, his thoughts and agenda to God.	"Teach me to do thy will; for thou art my God: thy spirit is good; lead me into the land of uprightness" (Ps.143:10). *"I beseech you therefore, brethren, by the mercies of God, that ye present your bodies a living sacrifice, holy, acceptable unto God, which is your reasonable service. And be not conformed to this world: but be ye transformed by the renewing of your mind, that ye may prove what is that good, and acceptable, and perfect, will of God" (Ro.12:1-2).* *"Not with eyeservice, as menpleasers; but as the servants of Christ, doing the will of God from the heart" (Eph.6:6).* *"Casting down imaginations, and every high thing*

Historical Term	Type or Picture (Scriptural Basis for Each)	Life Application for Today's Believer	Biblical Application for Today's Believer
			that exalteth itself against the knowledge of God, and bringing into captivity every thought to the obedience of Christ" (2 Cor. 10:5).
The Linen Underclothing (Ex.28:42-43) See also Ex.39:28	*The Linen Underclothing was worn next to the body, covering the priests from the waist to the thigh. It was always to be worn when serving God. The purpose of the Linen Underclothing was to cover their nakedness (modesty) as they climbed the steps of the altar. Thus, the Linen Underclothing symbolized the covering of the believer's spiritual nakedness before God.* **"And thou shalt make them linen breeches to cover their nakedness; from the loins even unto the thighs they shall reach: And they shall be upon Aaron, and upon his sons, when they come in unto the tabernacle of the congregation, or when they come near unto the altar to minister in the holy** *place;* **that they bear not iniquity, and die:** *it shall be* **a statute for ever unto him and his seed after him"** **(Ex.28:42-43).**	What the Linen Underclothing taught: ⇒ The person who is without Christ is spiritually naked; he is exposed and shamed. We must all put on the Lord Jesus Christ and His righteousness, making no provision for the flesh. ⇒ It is Jesus Christ who covers a person with His righteousness, protecting a person from exposure and shame before God and people.	*"Knowing this, that our old man is crucified with him, that the body of sin might be destroyed, that henceforth we should not serve sin" (Ro.6:6).* *"But put ye on the Lord Jesus Christ, and make not provision for the flesh, to fulfil the lusts thereof" (Ro.13:14).* *"And have put on the new man, which is renewed in knowledge after the image of him that created him" (Col.3:10).* *"Teaching us that, denying ungodliness and worldly lusts, we should live soberly, righteously, and godly, in this present world" (Tit.2:12).*

LINEN TURBAN

GOLD MEDALLION

LINEN HEADBAND

BREAST PIECE OR CHESTPIECE

SASH

EPHOD

LINEN UNDERCLOTHING (UNDERNEATH)

ROBE OF THE EPHOD

LINEN TUNIC

HIGH PRIEST

H. The Dedication, Conse-
cration, & Ordination of
the Priests: God's
Qualifications for Lead-
ership, Ex.29:1-46

1. **The call for a dedication**
   service
   a. To consecrate the priests
   b. To secure the items needed
      1) A young bull & two rams
         with no defect
      2) Unleavened bread, cakes,
         & wafers: Made with
         wheat flour & oil

   c. To present the items to the
      Lord

2. **The moral cleansing, to wash**
   the priests with water: A
   ceremonial washing--sym-
   bolized spiritual cleansing

3. **The putting on of the holy**
   clothes: Symbolized the
   clothing of righteousness
   a. The tunic
   b. The robe of the ephod
   c. The ephod itself
   d. The chestpiece
   e. The sash
   f. The turban & the sacred dia-
      dem

4. **The anointing: Symbolized**
   being anointed with the Spirit
   & power of God

5. **The permanence & security of**
   the Priesthood
   a. To dress Aaron's sons: Sym-
      bolic of righteousness
   b. The emphatic truth: The
      priest's ordination was per-
      manent, forever

6. **The judicial cleansing: The sac-**
   rifice of a bull as the sin offering
   a. To have the priests lay their
      hands on the bull's head: Sym-
      bolized identification, trans-
      ferring their sins to the animal
   b. To slaughter it before the
      LORD: Symbolized ap-
      peasement, substitution
      (substituting the animal to
      bear God's judgment)
   c. To apply blood to the horns
      & base of the altar: Symbol-
      ized the sanctification of the
      place (worship center) as
      well as the worshipper
   d. To burn the fat & choice

And this is the thing that thou shalt do unto them to hallow them, to minister unto me in the priest's office: Take one young bullock, and two rams without blemish,

2 And unleavened bread, and cakes unleavened tempered with oil, and wafers unleavened anointed with oil: of wheaten flour shalt thou make them.

3 And thou shalt put them into one basket, and bring them in the basket, with the bullock and the two rams.

4 And Aaron and his sons thou shalt bring unto the door of the tabernacle of the congregation, and shalt wash them with water.

5 And thou shalt take the garments, and put upon Aaron the coat, and the robe of the ephod, and the ephod, and the breastplate, and gird him with the curious girdle of the ephod:

6 And thou shalt put the mitre upon his head, and put the holy crown upon the mitre.

7 Then shalt thou take the anointing oil, and pour it upon his head, and anoint him.

8 And thou shalt bring his sons, and put coats upon them.

9 And thou shalt gird them with girdles, Aaron and his sons, and put the bonnets on them: and the priest's office shall be theirs for a perpetual statute: and thou shalt consecrate Aaron and his sons.

10 And thou shalt cause a bullock to be brought before the tabernacle of the congregation: and Aaron and his sons shall put their hands upon the head of the bullock.

11 And thou shalt kill the bullock before the LORD, by the door of the tabernacle of the congregation.

12 And thou shalt take of the blood of the bullock, and put it upon the horns of the altar with thy finger, and pour all the blood beside the bottom of the altar.

13 And thou shalt take all the

fat that covereth the inwards, and the caul that is above the liver, and the two kidneys, and the fat that is upon them, and burn them upon the altar.

14 But the flesh of the bullock, and his skin, and his dung, shalt thou burn with fire without the camp: it is a sin offering.

15 Thou shalt also take one ram; and Aaron and his sons shall put their hands upon the head of the ram.

16 And thou shalt slay the ram, and thou shalt take his blood, and sprinkle it round about upon the altar.

17 And thou shalt cut the ram in pieces, and wash the inwards of him, and his legs, and put them unto his pieces, and unto his head.

18 And thou shalt burn the whole ram upon the altar: it is a burnt offering unto the LORD: it is a sweet savour, an offering made by fire unto the LORD.

19 And thou shalt take the other ram; and Aaron and his sons shall put their hands upon the head of the ram.

20 Then shalt thou kill the ram, and take of his blood, and put it upon the tip of the right ear of Aaron, and upon the tip of the right ear of his sons, and upon the thumb of their right hand, and upon the great toe of their right foot, and sprinkle the blood upon the altar round about.

21 And thou shalt take of the blood that is upon the altar, and of the anointing oil, and sprinkle it upon Aaron, and upon his garments, and upon his sons, and upon the garments of his sons with him: and he shall be hallowed, and his garments, and his sons, and his sons' garments with him.

22 Also thou shalt take of the ram the fat and the rump, and the fat that covereth the inwards, and the caul above the liver, and the two kidneys, and the fat that is upon them, and the right shoulder; for it is a ram of consecration:

23 And one loaf of bread, and one cake of oiled bread, and one wafer out of the basket of the unleavened bread that is before the LORD:

parts on the altar; but to take the bad--the flesh, hide, & waste--outside the camp & burn
   1) Symbolized that sin (the bad)
      had to be taken out of the camp,
      away from the worshipper
   2) Symbolized the sin offer-
      ing: The taking away of
      sin by the sacrifice of one
      (Jesus Christ) for another

7. **The total dedication of life:**
   The sacrifice of a ram as the
   burnt offering
   a. To lay their hands on its head
   b. To slaughter it & sprinkle
      blood on all sides of the altar

   c. To cut the ram into pieces &
      wash the inner parts & legs

   d. To burn all the parts on the
      altar so the pleasing aroma
      would ascend up toward
      heaven: Symbolized that
      God accepted the person's
      sacrifice & dedication

8. **The consecration to service:**
   The sacrifice of a second ram
   a. To lay their hands on its
      head
   b. To slaughter it & put some
      blood...
      1) On the tip of the right ear:
         Setting it apart to listen
      2) On the thumb of the right
         hand: Setting it apart to do
         good
      3) On the big toe of the right
         foot: Setting it apart to
         walk in the ways of God
      4) On all sides of the altar
   c. To mix some blood &
      anointing oil & sprinkle it on
      the priests & their clothes
   d. The purpose: Symbolized
      full consecration to the serv-
      ice of God

9. **The commitment to give God**
   the best: The ceremony of two
   wave offerings
   a. The first wave offering
      1) To cut away the fat &
         choice parts from the ram
         of ordination

      2) To take one loaf of un-
         leavened bread, one cake,
         & one wafer from the bas-
         ket

3) To put all these into the hands of the priests: Were to lift them up & wave them before the LORD as a wave offering

4) To burn the items upon the altar as a pleasing aroma to the LORD: Symbolized the pleasure, acceptance of the LORD

b. The second wave offering: To take the breast & shoulder of the ram, lift & wave it before the LORD

1) To sanctify--set apart as holy--the parts of the ram that belong to the priests

2) To always give these parts to the priests when making fellowship offerings (thanksgiving or peace offerings)

10. There was to be the passing down of the ordination clothes of the High Priest
a. To be worn in the ordination service by the succeeding descendant
b. To be worn seven days

11. There was a type of communion or fellowship meal
a. To boil the ram's meat

b. To hold a type of communion meal among the priests at the door of the tabernacle
1) To eat the ram's meat along with the bread in the basket
2) To eat the meat & bread sacrificed for their atonement: No one else was allowed to eat

3) To burn any sacrificial meat or bread left over: Not to be eaten, because it is holy (set apart to God)

24 And thou shalt put all in the hands of Aaron, and in the hands of his sons; and shalt wave them for a wave offering before the LORD.
25 And thou shalt receive them of their hands, and burn them upon the altar for a burnt offering, for a sweet savour before the LORD: it is an offering made by fire unto the LORD.
26 And thou shalt take the breast of the ram of Aaron's consecration, and wave it for a wave offering before the LORD: and it shall be thy part.
27 And thou shalt sanctify the breast of the wave offering, and the shoulder of the heave offering, which is waved, and which is heaved up, of the ram of the consecration, even of that which is for Aaron, and of that which is for his sons:
28 And it shall be Aaron's and his sons' by a statute for ever from the children of Israel: for it is an heave offering: and it shall be an heave offering from the children of Israel of the sacrifice of their peace offerings, even their heave offering unto the LORD.
29 And the holy garments of Aaron shall be his sons' after him, to be anointed therein, and to be consecrated in them.
30 And that son that is priest in his stead shall put them on seven days, when he cometh into the tabernacle of the congregation to minister in the holy place.
31 And thou shalt take the ram of the consecration, and seethe his flesh in the holy place.
32 And Aaron and his sons shall eat the flesh of the ram, and the bread that is in the basket, by the door of the tabernacle of the congregation.
33 And they shall eat those things wherewith the atonement was made, to consecrate and to sanctify them: but a stranger shall not eat thereof, because they are holy.
34 And if ought of the flesh of the consecrations, or of the bread, remain unto the morning, then thou shalt burn the remainder with fire: it shall not be eaten, because it

is holy.
35 And thus shalt thou do unto Aaron, and to his sons, according to all things which I have commanded thee: seven days shalt thou consecrate them.
36 And thou shalt offer every day a bullock for a sin offering for atonement: and thou shalt cleanse the altar, when thou hast made an atonement for it, and thou shalt anoint it, to sanctify it.
37 Seven days thou shalt make an atonement for the altar, and sanctify it; and it shall be an altar most holy: whatsoever toucheth the altar shall be holy.
38 Now this is that which thou shalt offer upon the altar; two lambs of the first year day by day continually.
39 The one lamb thou shalt offer in the morning; and the other lamb thou shalt offer at even:
40 And with the one lamb a tenth deal of flour mingled with the fourth part of an hin of beaten oil; and the fourth part of an hin of wine for a drink offering.
41 And the other lamb thou shalt offer at even, and shalt do thereto according to the meat offering of the morning, and according to the drink offering thereof, for a sweet savour, an offering made by fire unto the LORD.
42 This shall be a continual burnt offering throughout your generations at the door of the tabernacle of the congregation before the LORD: where I will meet you, to speak there unto thee.
43 And there I will meet with the children of Israel, and the tabernacle shall be sanctified by my glory.
44 And I will sanctify the tabernacle of the congregation, and the altar: I will sanctify also both Aaron and his sons, to minister to me in the priest's office.
45 And I will dwell among the children of Israel, and will be their God.
46 And they shall know that I am the LORD their God, that brought them forth out of the land of Egypt, that I may dwell among them: I am the LORD their God.

12. There was the repetition of the ordination ceremony: To be repeated seven days
a. The stress: Obedience

b. To sacrifice a bull every day: As a sin offering
c. To purify & anoint the altar for seven days

1) Would make it holy (set apart to God)
2) Would make whatever touched it holy

13. There were the morning & evening sacrifices
a. To offer two one-year old lambs each day
1) One in the morning
2) One in the evening

b. To offer the first lamb with two quarts of flour mixed with one quart of olive oil & wine: As a drink offering

c. To offer the second lamb with the same items
d. The effect upon the LORD
1) Is a pleasing aroma & sacrifice to the LORD
2) Satisfies the fire (holiness) of the LORD

e. The critical importance of the morning & evening sacrifice: To be observed forever, throughout all generations
f. The results of the daily sacrifice
1) The Lord would meet & speak to His messenger (Moses)
2) The Lord would meet & speak to the people
3) The Lord would sanctify the tabernacle with His glory
4) The Lord would sanctify (set apart as holy) the tabernacle, altar, & the priests--all to His service

5) The LORD would dwell among His people & be their God
6) The people would know that the LORD is the God who delivers & sets them free

DIVISION IX

THE TABERNACLE, ITS BLUEPRINT AND PRIESTHOOD: THE TRUE WAY TO APPROACH AND WORSHIP GOD, EX.25:1-31:18

H. **The Dedication, Consecration, and Ordination of the Priests: God's Qualifications for Leadership, Ex.29:1-46**

(29:1-46) **Introduction**: people need good leaders. A great shortage of qualified leaders is confronting the world today. Serious cracks have arisen in the major institutions of society, cracks caused by a lack of qualified leaders.

⇒ There is a scarcity of good, diligent husbands, wives, children, and parents.
⇒ There is a scarcity of good, diligent business leaders.
⇒ There is a scarcity of good, diligent political leaders.
⇒ There is a scarcity of good, diligent church leaders.
⇒ There is a scarcity of good, diligent employers and employees.
⇒ There is a scarcity of good, diligent managers.
⇒ There is a scarcity of good, diligent teachers and students.

Tragically, the qualifications for leadership have become so diluted that almost anyone can become a leader. Today, a person can become a leader because he has...

- some money
- some popularity
- some heightened self-image
- some professional image
- some social standing
- some personal charisma
- some political position
- some claim to fame

Good leadership is a critical need for God's people. This is the reason God has established a lofty standard for leadership. To become one of God's leaders, a person has to be...

- forgiven by God
- dedicated to God
- consecrated by God
- prepared by God
- called by God

This is the purpose of this section of Scripture, to show how God places a person into service for Him. It is: *The Dedication, Consecration, and Ordination of the Priest: God's Qualifications for Leadership*, Ex.29:1-46.

1. The call for a dedication service (v.1-3).
2. The moral cleansing, to wash the priests with water: a ceremonial washing--symbolized spiritual cleansing (v.4).
3. The putting on of the holy clothes: symbolized the clothing of righteousness (v.5-6).
4. The anointing: symbolized being anointed with the Spirit and power of God (v.7).
5. The permanence and security of the Priesthood (v.8-9).
6. The judicial cleansing: the sacrifice of a bull as the sin offering (v.10-14).
7. The total dedication of life: the sacrifice of a ram as the burnt offering (v.15-18).
8. The consecration to service: the sacrifice of a second ram (v.19-21).
9. The commitment to give God the best: the ceremony of two wave offerings (v.22-28).
10. There was to be the passing down of the ordination clothes of the High Priest (v.29-30).
11. There was a type of communion or fellowship meal (v.31-34).
12. There was the repetition of the ordination ceremony: to be repeated seven days (v.35-37).
13. There were the morning and evening sacrifices (v.38-46).

1 (29:1-3) **Priesthood--Ordination--Consecration--Services, Dedication--Tabernacle**: there was the call for a Dedication Service. It was now time for Aaron and his sons to be publicly ordained and installed as the official priests for Israel. Note the word *dedicate* or *consecrate* (qadash): it means to sanctify, to set apart to God. The point is to publicly take Aaron and his sons and set them apart to God, set them apart before the people in a public service. Focus the attention of the people upon the fact that these men are to serve as their priests, the ministers of God among them. In preparation for the service, God told Moses two things.

1. Moses was to secure the items needed for the various offerings (v.1).
   a. He was to secure a young bull and two rams with no defect (v.1). Note the requirement that the animals have *no defect*. The sacrifice had to be *perfect*. This type was fulfilled in Jesus Christ, the perfect, sinless Lamb of God (Jn.1:29).
   b. He was to secure unleavened bread, cakes, and wafers that were made with wheat, flour, and oil (v.1). Remember, leavened bread is a symbol of evil and unleavened bread a symbol of righteousness. The picture is striking: the priests were to partake of, to take in righteousness. (See outline and notes--Ex.12:14-20 for more discussion.)
2. Moses was to present the items to the Lord (v.3).

Thought 1. A person called by God to serve His people should be publicly set apart, ordained to God's service. The people's attention should be focused upon the fact...
- that this person has been called by God to serve God's people
- that this person is to serve and minister to them as God's appointed servant

"Ye have not chosen me, but I have chosen you, and ordained you, that ye should go and bring forth fruit, and [that] your fruit should remain: that whatsoever ye shall ask of the Father in my name, he may give it you" (Jn.15:16).

"He saith unto him the third time, Simon, [son] of Jonas, lovest thou me? Peter was grieved because he said unto him the third time, Lovest thou me? And he said unto him, Lord, thou knowest all things; thou knowest that I love thee. Jesus saith unto him, Feed my sheep" (Jn.21:17).

"But the Lord said unto him, Go thy way: for he is a chosen vessel unto me, to bear my name before the Gentiles, and kings, and the children of Israel" (Acts 9:15).

"Take heed therefore unto yourselves, and to all the flock, over the which the Holy Ghost hath made you overseers, to feed the church of God, which he hath purchased with his own blood" (Acts 20:28).

"Feed the flock of God which is among you, taking the oversight thereof, not by constraint, but willingly; not for filthy lucre, but of a ready mind" (1 Pt.5:2).

"And I will give you pastors according to mine heart, which shall feed you with knowledge and understanding" (Jer.3:15).

"And I will set up shepherds over them which shall feed them: and they shall fear no more, nor be dismayed, neither shall they be lacking, saith the LORD" (Jer.23:4).

2 (29:4) **Cleansing--Washing--Forgiveness--Ceremony--Ritual**: there was moral cleansing. Note that this is a special cleansing that takes place after the call to consecration. This is an *immediate, initial cleansing*. When God calls a person to consecration, the person is immediately to seek to be *morally cleansed* by the Lord. Note how God symbolized this moral cleansing for Aaron and his sons: they were to be publicly washed with water before the Tabernacle, washed in the presence of God's people.

Thought 1. The person who serves God must be clean, morally pure, cleansed from all filthiness of the flesh and spirit.

"Having therefore these promises, dearly beloved, let us cleanse ourselves from all filthiness of the flesh and spirit, perfecting holiness in the fear of God" (2 Cor.7:1).

"If a man therefore purge himself from these, he shall be a vessel unto honour, sanctified, and meet for the master's use, and prepared unto every good work" (2 Tim.2:21).

"Draw nigh to God, and he will draw nigh to you. Cleanse your hands, ye sinners; and purify your hearts, ye double minded" (Jas.4:8).

"Help us, O God of our salvation, for the glory of thy name: and deliver us, and purge away our sins, for thy name's sake" (Ps.79:9).

"Wash you, make you clean; put away the evil of your doings from before mine eyes; cease to do evil" (Is.1:16).

3 (29:5-6) **Priesthood--Clothing--Righteousness--Symbols**: there was the putting on of the holy clothes. Aaron was to be dressed in the priestly clothing:
⇒ the tunic   ⇒ the chestpiece
⇒ the robe of the ephod   ⇒ the sash
⇒ the ephod itself   ⇒ the turban and the sacred diadem

Thought 1. Scripture says that believers are to be clothed with the righteousness of Jesus Christ, to put on--clothe themselves with--the new man. This is the picture seen in Aaron putting on the holy clothes. The minister of God must put on Christ, put on the new man, the new nature of God. He must be clothed with righteousness.

"But put ye on the Lord Jesus Christ, and make not provision for the flesh, to fulfil the lusts thereof" (Ro.13:14).

"And that ye put on the new man, which after God is created in righteousness and true holiness" (Eph.4:24).

"And have put on the new man, which is renewed in knowledge after the image of him that created him" (Col.3:10).

"Put on therefore, as the elect of God, holy and beloved, bowels of mercies, kindness, humbleness of mind, meekness, longsuffering" (Col.3:12).

"Let thy priests be clothed with righteousness; and let thy saints shout for joy" (Ps.132:9).

"I will greatly rejoice in the LORD, my soul shall be joyful in my God; for he hath clothed me with the garments of salvation, he hath covered me with the robe of righteousness, as a bridegroom decketh himself with ornaments, and as a bride adorneth herself with her jewels" (Is.61:10).

4 (25:7) **Anointing--Oil--Priesthood--Holy Spirit**: there was the anointing with oil. The oil is a symbol of the Holy Spirit and of God's appointment and power. The priest, the servant of God, was appointed by God; therefore, he was to be anointed with the Spirit and power of God.

Thought 1. No minister can serve God apart from God's anointing, the anointing of God's Spirit and power.

"But ye shall receive power, after that the Holy Ghost is come upon you: and ye shall be witnesses unto me both in Jerusalem, and in all Judaea, and in Samaria, and unto the uttermost part of the earth" (Acts 1:8).

"How God anointed Jesus of Nazareth with the Holy Ghost and with power: who went about doing good, and healing all that were oppressed of the devil; for God was with him" (Acts 10:38).

"But the fruit of the Spirit is love, joy, peace, longsuffering, gentleness, goodness, faith, Meekness, temperance: against such there is no law" (Gal.5:22-23).

"Be filled with the Spirit" (Eph.5:18).

"But truly I am full of power by the spirit of the LORD, and of judgment, and of might, to declare unto Jacob his transgression, and to Israel his sin" (Mic.3:8).

5 (25:8-9) **Priesthood--Security**: there was the permanence and security of the priesthood. Both Aaron and his sons were to be dressed in their priestly clothing. This, too, was symbolic of righteousness.

Note the emphatic truth declared: the priest's call and ordination were permanent, forever.

Thought 1. Two strong lessons are seen in the permanence of God's call and ordination.

1) The minister and servant of God is called and ordained forever. He is forever responsible to serve God faithfully.

"And he called his ten servants, and delivered them ten pounds, and said unto them, Occupy till I come" (Lk.19:13).

"Moreover it is required in stewards, that a man be found faithful" (1 Cor.4:2).

"Therefore, my beloved brethren, be ye stedfast, unmoveable, always abounding in the work of the Lord, forasmuch as ye know that your labour is not in vain in the Lord." (1 Cor.15:58).

2) The office of priesthood was established forever by God. All believers are made priests of God; all believers are called to be representatives of God upon earth.

"And ye shall be unto me a kingdom of priests, and an holy nation. These are the words which thou shalt speak unto the children of Israel" (Ex.19:6).

"But ye shall be named the Priests of the LORD: men shall call you the Ministers of our God: ye shall eat the riches of the Gentiles, and in their glory shall ye boast yourselves" (Is.61:6).

"Ye also, as lively stones, are built up a spiritual house, an holy priesthood, to offer up spiritual sacrifices, acceptable to God by Jesus Christ" (1 Pt.2:5).

"And [Christ] hath made us kings and priests unto God and his Father; to him be glory and dominion for ever and ever. Amen" (Rev.1:6).

6 (29:10-14) **Sacrifices--Sacrificial System--Bull--Burnt Offering**: there was the judicial cleansing. A bull was to be sacrificed as the sin offering for Aaron and his sons. No person could serve God until he was cleansed and forgiven by God. Cleansing was based upon the atonement, upon being reconciled to God through the shed blood of the sacrifice. The sacrifice of the *sin offering* is rich with symbolic meaning. Note the clear instructions of God.

1. Moses was to have the priests lay their hands on the bulls head. This act symbolized *identification*, transferring their sins to the animal (v.10). The animal became the sin-bearer: the animal was to bear the judgment of God against sin, bear the judgment for the believer. This act of identification pointed toward Jesus Christ as the sin-bearer of the world.

"All we like sheep have gone astray; we have turned every one to his own way; and the LORD hath laid on him the iniquity of us all" (Is.53:6).

"So Christ was once offered to bear the sins of many; and unto them that look for him shall he appear the second time without sin unto salvation" (Heb.9:28).

"Who his own self bare our sins in his own body on the tree, that we, being dead to sins, should live unto righteousness: by whose stripes ye were healed" (1 Pt.2:24).

"And ye know that he was manifested to take away our sins; and in him is no sin" (1 Jn.3:5).

2. Moses was to slaughter the bull before the LORD. This act symbolized appeasement, substitution, substituting the animal to bear God's judgment (v.11). God's wrath toward sin can only be appeased by a sacrifice. During Old Testament history, God used animal sacrifice to point toward Christ. But the only sacrifice that has ever satisfied God's eternal wrath was the Lamb who was slaughtered on the cross. He and He alone was the *perfect sacrifice* who could atone for sin and pay the penalty demanded by God's holy righteousness.

"For when we were yet without strength, in due time Christ died for the ungodly" (Ro.5:6).

"But God commendeth his love toward us, in that, while we were yet sinners, Christ died for us. Much more then, being now justified by his blood, we shall be saved from wrath through him" (Ro.5:8-9).

"For if, when we were enemies, we were reconciled to God by the death of his Son, much more, being reconciled, we shall be saved by his life. And not only so, but we also joy in God through our Lord Jesus Christ, by whom we have now received the atonement" (Ro.5:10-11).

"Who gave himself for our sins, that he might deliver us from this present evil world, according to the will of God and our Father" (Gal.1:4).

"Who gave himself for us, that he might redeem us from all iniquity, and purify unto himself a peculiar people, zealous of good works" (Tit.2:14).

3. Moses was to apply blood to the horns and base of the altar. This symbolized the sanctification of the place (worship center) as well as the worshipper (v.12).

Thought 1. The shed blood of Christ is a constant reminder of His great love for His people. The cross without His blood is powerless, empty, and worthless. It is the blood of Christ that sanctified or set apart the altar of the cross as holy. And it is the blood of Christ that sanctifies or sets apart the believer as holy.

> "For this is my blood of the new testament, which is shed for many for the remission of sins" (Mt.26:28).
> "How much more shall the blood of Christ, who through the eternal Spirit offered himself without spot to God, purge your conscience from dead works to serve the living God?" (Heb.9:14).
> "But if we walk in the light, as he is in the light, we have fellowship one with another, and the blood of Jesus Christ his Son cleanseth us from all sin" (1 Jn.1:7).
> "And from Jesus Christ, *who is* the faithful witness, *and* the first begotten of the dead, and the prince of the kings of the earth. Unto him that loved us, and washed us from our sins in his own blood" (Rev.1:5).
> "And they sung a new song, saying, Thou art worthy to take the book, and to open the seals thereof: for thou wast slain, and hast redeemed us to God by thy blood out of every kindred, and tongue, and people, and nation" (Rev.5:9).

4. Moses was to burn the fat and choice parts on the altar, but he was to take the bad--the flesh, skin, and waste--outside the camp and burn it (v.13-14). This symbolized that sin (the bad) had to be taken out of the camp, away from the worshipper. It also symbolized the sin offering: the taking away of sin by the sacrifice of one (Jesus Christ) for another.

Thought 1. It was Jesus Christ who fulfilled this symbol by His own death on the cross: He was crucified outside the walls of Jerusalem on Calvary.

> "Wherefore Jesus also, that he might sanctify [cleanse, purify, set apart] the people with his own blood, suffered without [outside the city] the gate" (Heb.13:12).
> "For he hath made him *to be* sin for us, who knew no sin; that we might be made the righteousness of God in him" (2 Cor.5:21).
> "Who gave himself for our sins, that he might deliver us from this present evil world, according to the will of God and our Father" (Gal.1:4).
> "Who gave himself for us, that he might redeem us from all iniquity, and purify unto himself a peculiar people, zealous of good works" (Tit.2:14).

7 (29:15-18) **Sacrifices - Sacrificial System--Priesthood--Ram--Burnt Offering**: there was the total dedication of life. Note that Aaron and his sons were to take a *whole ram* and sacrifice it to the LORD. This symbolized total dedication, the dedication of the priest's whole life to the LORD. Note the instructions that God gave Moses for this burnt offering of the ram:
1. The priests were to lay their hands on its head (v.15).
2. The priests were to slaughter it and sprinkle blood on all sides of the altar (v.16).
3. The priests were to cut the ram into pieces and wash the inner parts and legs (v.17).
4. The priests were to burn all the parts--the entire ram--on the altar so the pleasing aroma would ascend toward heaven (v.18). This symbolized that God accepted the person's sacrifice and dedication. God seeks and longs for people to give all they are and have to Him.

Thought 1. Believers are priests before the LORD, His representatives upon earth (1 Pt.2:5, 9). God's priests, God's people, must be willing to climb upon the altar and become a living sacrifice to God. God has no use for those...
- who want to go their own way
- who have their own agenda
- who have their own plans and programs

We must dedicate our entire beings to the Lord; we must make a total dedication to Christ. Nothing less than the dedication of our total being, of all our faculties, constitutes the *"entire ram" being laid upon the altar* (v.18).

> "I beseech you therefore, brethren, by the mercies of God, that ye present your bodies a living sacrifice, holy, acceptable unto God, which is your reasonable service. And be not conformed to this world: but be ye transformed by the renewing of your mind, that ye may prove what is that good, and acceptable, and perfect, will of God" (Ro.12:1-2).
> "And he said to [them] all, If any [man] will come after me, let him deny himself, and take up his cross daily, and follow me" (Lk.9:23).
> "So likewise, whosoever he be of you that forsaketh not all that he hath, he cannot be my disciple" (Lk.14:33).
> "Ye also, as lively stones, are built up a spiritual house, an holy priesthood, to offer up spiritual sacrifices, acceptable to God by Jesus Christ" (1 Pt.2:5).
> "But ye are a chosen generation, a royal priesthood, an holy nation, a peculiar people; that ye should show forth the praises of him who hath called you out of darkness into his marvellous light" (1 Pt.2:9).
> "My son, give me thine heart, and let thine eyes observe my ways" (Pr.23:26).

8 (29:19-21) <u>Sacrifices - Sacrificial System--Priesthood--Ram--Ministry--Consecration--Service</u>: there was the consecration to service symbolized by the sacrifice of a second ram. The instructions given by God are full of lessons for the believer.
1. The priests were to lay their hands on its head (v.19).
2. The priests were to slaughter the ram and put some blood...
   - on the tip of the right ear: setting it apart to listen (v.20)
   - on the thumb of the right hand: setting it apart to touch and do only righteous things (v.20)
   - on the big toe of the right foot: setting it apart to walk in the ways of God (v.20)
   - on all sides of the altar (v.20)

Thought 1. The priests of God (believers) are to be totally consecrated to the service of God. *Consecration* means that we are to be sanctified, purified, set apart totally to serving God.
1) Our ears are to be sanctified, purified, set apart to God. We are to guard what we listen to and hear, guard the...
   - music
   - conversations
   - films
   - jokes

Our ears are to be totally consecrated to God. We must be constantly listening to God and to the cries and needs of people.

> "Blessed is the man that heareth me, watching daily at my gates, waiting at the posts of my doors" (Pr.8:34).
> "Wherefore, my beloved brethren, let every man be swift to hear, slow to speak, slow to wrath" (Jas.1:19).
> "And they shall turn away their ears from the truth, and shall be turned unto fables" (2 Tim.4:4).

2) Our fingers must be used to do good, to do only righteous deeds.

> "Bear ye one another's burdens, and so fulfil the law of Christ" (Gal.6:2).
> "As we have therefore opportunity, let us do good unto all men, especially unto them who are of the household of faith" (Gal.6:10).
> "Serve the LORD with fear, and rejoice with trembling" (Ps.2:11).

3) Our feet are to be consecrated to walk in the ways of God.

> "I therefore, the prisoner of the Lord, beseech you that ye walk worthy of the vocation wherewith ye are called" (Eph.4:1).
> "This I say then, Walk in the Spirit, and ye shall not fulfil the lust of the flesh" (Gal.5:16).
> "But if we walk in the light, as he is in the light, we have fellowship one with another, and the blood of Jesus Christ his Son cleanseth us from all sin" (1 Jn.1:7).
> "And now, Israel, what doth the LORD thy God require of thee, but to fear the LORD thy God, to walk in all his ways, and to love him, and to serve the LORD thy God with all thy heart and with all thy soul" (Dt.10:12).

3. Some blood and anointing oil were to be sprinkled on the priests and their clothes (v.21). This command seems a bit strange. Why would God have His priests adorned in such splendid clothing only to *ruin* them with spots of blood and oil? Remember what this ram symbolized--a consecration to service. God's priests were not called to an easy task, never to get dirty, never to become involved in the sufferings and problems of people. The blood and the oil addressed the very purpose for the priests: to serve God and to serve His people, no matter how terrible the suffering or difficult the problem.

Thought 1. Far too many believers do not want to become soiled by the broken lives of people. Seeking some title or lofty position has become the norm for many believers. Getting dirty hands while ministering to the desperate needs of fallen people is offensive, repugnant, and vile to the person who does not want to get involved. God has a far different idea in mind for those who truly want to serve Him.

> "They that sow in tears shall reap in joy" (Ps.126:5).
> "And whosoever shall give to drink unto one of these little ones a cup of cold *water* only in the name of a disciple, verily I say unto you, he shall in no wise lose his reward" (Mt.10:42).
> "Even as the Son of man came not to be ministered unto, but to minister, and to give his life a ransom for many" (Mt.20:28).
> "For whether *is* greater, he that sitteth at meat, or he that serveth? *is* not he that sitteth at meat? but I am among you as he that serveth" (Lk.22:27).
> "Who, being in the form of God, thought it not robbery to be equal with God: But made himself of no reputation, and took upon him the form of a servant, and was made in the likeness of men" (Ph.2:6-7).

4. The purpose for slaughtering the second ram was to symbolize full consecration to the service of God.

"And now, Israel, what doth the LORD thy God require of thee, but to fear the LORD thy God, to walk in all his ways, and to love him, and to serve the LORD thy God with all thy heart and with all thy soul" (Dt.10:12).

"Serve the LORD with fear, and rejoice with trembling" (Ps.2:11).

"With good will doing service, as to the Lord, and not to men" (Eph.6:7).

"Wherefore we receiving a kingdom which cannot be moved, let us have grace, whereby we may serve God acceptably with reverence and godly fear" (Heb.12:28).

9 (29:22-28) **Wave Offering--Priesthood--Commitment**: there was the commitment to give God the best. This was symbolized in the observance of two wave offerings.

1. There was the first wave offering (v.22-25). The order of this first ceremony was unique.
   a. Moses was to cut away the fat and choice parts from the ram of ordination (v.22).
   b. Moses was to take one loaf of unleavened bread, one cake, and one wafer from the basket (v.23).
   c. Moses was to put all these into the hands of the priests. Then they were to lift them up and wave them before the LORD as a wave offering (v.24). The meaning of the original language comes from the original root (nuph) that translates wave as "*to shake, agitate, move to and fro, or up and down.*"[1] This was a ceremony that required a physical act on the part of the priests. It required a personal involvement, an open show of thanksgiving to God. The Expositor's Bible Commentary adds more clarity to the form of this wave offering:

   > "The waving was not from side to side but toward the altar and back, showing that the sacrifice was given to God and then received back by the priest for his use (cf. Lev.7:30; 23:20). Everything that had been waved except the 'breast of the ram' was then to be burned on the altar."[2]

   d. Moses was to burn the items upon the altar as a burnt offering of pleasing aroma to the LORD, which symbolized the pleasure and acceptance of the LORD (v.25).

2. There was the second wave offering (v.26-28). Moses was to take the breast and shoulder of the ram, lift and wave it before the LORD (v.26). God gave him two specific reasons for this:
   a. To sanctify--set apart as holy--the parts of the rams that belong to the priests (v.27).
   b. To always give these parts to the priests when making fellowship offerings (thanksgiving or peace offerings) (v.28).

   Thought 1. Note that only the choice parts were offered to God. Only the very best should ever be offered to God. Only the very best pleases Him. What is the best that we can give to God? What are the things that please God the most?

   ⇒ God is pleased when we give Him our bodies.

   > "I beseech you therefore, brethren, by the mercies of God, that ye present your bodies a living sacrifice, holy, acceptable unto God, which is your reasonable service. And be not conformed to this world: but be ye transformed by the renewing of your mind, that ye may prove what is that good, and acceptable, and perfect, will of God" (Ro.12:1-2).
   > "What? know ye not that your body is the temple of the Holy Ghost which is in you, which ye have of God, and ye are not your own? For ye are bought with a price: therefore glorify God in your body, and in your spirit, which are God's" (1 Cor.6:19-20).

   ⇒ God is pleased when we obey Him.

   > "And Samuel said, Hath the LORD as great delight in burnt offerings and sacrifices, as in obeying the voice of the LORD? Behold, to obey is better than sacrifice, and to hearken than the fat of rams" (1 Sam.15:22).

   ⇒ God is pleased when we are faithful to Him.

   > "His lord said unto him, Well done, *thou* good and faithful servant: thou hast been faithful over a few things, I will make thee ruler over many things: enter thou into the joy of thy lord" (Mt.25:21).

   ⇒ God is pleased when His people introduce a sinner to the *good news* of the gospel.

   > "But ye shall receive power, after that the Holy Ghost is come upon you: and ye shall be witnesses unto me both in Jerusalem, and in all Judaea, and in Samaria, and unto the uttermost part of the earth" (Acts 1:8).
   > "Go, stand and speak in the temple to the people all the words of this life" (Acts 5:20).

---

[1] George Bush. *Commentary on Exodus*, p. 482.
[2] Frank E. Gaebelein. *The Expositor's Bible Commentary*, Vol.2, p.470.

"For I am not ashamed of the gospel of Christ: for it is the power of God unto salvation to every one that believeth; to the Jew first, and also to the Greek" (Ro.1:16).

⇒ God is pleased when His people do good and share with those in need.

"But to do good and to communicate forget not: for with such sacrifices God is well pleased" (Heb.13:16).

10 (29:29-30) **Tabernacle of Moses--Priesthood, Clothes--High Priest**: there was to be the passing down of the ordination clothes of the High Priest. These treasured garments would not be the sole possession of only one owner.
1. The ordination clothes were to be worn by the succeeding son in the ordination service (v.29).
2. The ordination clothes were to be worn for seven days (v.30). Often the number seven is seen in Scripture as perfection or completeness. The command for the clothes to be worn for seven days could be symbolic of the priest's perfection, that he was consecrating himself totally and completely to the LORD'S service.

"I beseech you therefore, brethren, by the mercies of God, that ye present your bodies a living sacrifice, holy, acceptable unto God, which is your reasonable service. And be not conformed to this world: but be ye transformed by the renewing of your mind, that ye may prove what is that good, and acceptable, and perfect, will of God" (Ro.12:1-2).
"And thou shalt love the LORD thy God with all thine heart, and with all thy soul, and with all thy might" (Dt.6:5).

11 (29:31-34) **Tabernacle of Moses--Priesthood--Communion--Fellowship**: there was a type of communion or fellowship meal. Rooted deeply in the sacrificial system was the idea of feasts. The Hebrew calendar is filled with various sacrifices and feasts (see Deeper Study # 1, Calendar, Hebrew--Ex.12:1-2 for more information). Note the details of this particular meal:
1. Moses was to boil the ram's meat in the holy place (v.31). This was most probably done in the courtyard of the Tabernacle.
2. Moses was to hold a type of communion meal among the priests at the door of the tabernacle (v.32).
   a. The priests were to eat the ram's meat along with the bread in the basket (v.32).
   b. The priests were to eat the meat and bread sacrificed for their atonement. This was a meal that no one else was allowed to eat because the food had been sanctified, set apart as holy to the Lord (v.33).
   c. The priests were to burn any sacrificial meat or bread left over. It was not to be eaten because it was holy (set apart to God) (v.34).

Thought 1. Jesus Christ invites His people to come, eat, and commune with Him.

"Wherefore do ye spend money for *that which is* not bread? and your labour for *that which* satisfieth not? hearken diligently unto me, and eat ye *that which is* good, and let your soul delight itself in fatness" (Is.55:2).
"And Jesus said unto them, I am the bread of life: he that cometh to me shall never hunger; and he that believeth on me shall never thirst" (Jn.6:35).
"I am the living bread which came down from heaven: if any man eat of this bread, he shall live for ever: and the bread that I will give is my flesh, which I will give for the life of the world" (Jn.6:51).
"Behold, I stand at the door, and knock: if any man hear my voice, and open the door, I will come in to him, and will sup with him, and he with me" (Rev.3:20).

12 (29:35-37) **Tabernacle of Moses--Priesthood, Ordination**: there was the repetition of the ordination ceremony that was to be repeated for seven days.
1. The stress was obedience--to do everything God commanded (v.35).
2. Moses was to sacrifice a bull every day as a sin offering to God (v.36).
3. Moses was to purify and anoint the altar for seven days for the following great purposes (v.36):
   a. It would make it holy (set apart to God) (v.37).
   b. It would make whatever touched it holy (v.37).

Thought 1. It is Jesus Christ who is holy, set apart to God. It is Jesus Christ who makes every sinful heart He touches holy.

"That he would grant unto us, that we being delivered out of the hand of our enemies [by Christ] might serve him without fear, In holiness and righteousness before him, all the days of our life" (Lk.1:74-75).
"Wherefore come out from among them, and be ye separate, saith the Lord, and touch not the unclean thing; and I will receive you, And will be a Father unto you, and ye shall be my sons and daughters, saith the Lord Almighty. Having therefore these promises, dearly beloved, let us cleanse ourselves from all filthiness of the flesh and spirit, perfecting holiness in the fear of God" (2 Cor.6:17-7:1).
"But as he which hath called you is holy, so be ye holy in all manner of conversation; Because it is written, Be ye holy; for I am holy" (1 Pt.1:15-16).

"But ye are a chosen generation, a royal priesthood, an holy nation, a peculiar people; that ye should show forth the praises of him who hath called you out of darkness into his marvellous light" (1 Pt.2:9).

13 (29:38-46) <u>Tabernacle of Moses--Priesthood--Sacrifices, Morning and Evening</u>: there were the morning and evening sacrifices. The final charge in this portion of Scripture contains the *daily* offerings, the morning and evening sacrifices.

1. The priests were to offer two one-year old lambs each day, one in the morning and one in the evening (v.38-39). These offerings were not to replace the other sacrifices; they were in addition to the others. The morning and evening sacrifices set the tone for the worship of God's people: they were to worship morning until night--all day, every day.

> <u>Thought 1</u>. We need to be renewed in the morning before we begin our day and at night before we retire to sleep. This is the clear message from Scripture.

> > "And they rose up in the <u>morning early</u>, and worshipped before the LORD, and returned, and came to their house to Ramah: and Elkanah knew Hannah his wife; and the LORD remembered her" (1 Sam.1:19).
> > "And it was so, when the days of *their* feasting were gone about, that Job sent and sanctified them, and rose up <u>early in the morning</u>, and offered burnt offerings *according* to the number of them all: for Job said, It may be that my sons have sinned, and cursed God in their hearts. Thus did Job continually" (Job 1:5).
> > "My voice shalt thou hear in the morning, O LORD; in the morning will I direct *my prayer* unto thee, and will look up" (Ps.5:3).
> > "Evening, and morning, and at noon, will I pray, and cry aloud: and he shall hear my voice" (Ps.55:17).
> > "From the rising of the sun unto the going down of the same the LORD'S name *is* to be praised" (Ps.113:3).
> > "Seven times a day do I praise thee because of thy righteous judgments" (Ps.119:164).
> > "And in the morning, rising up a great while before day, he went out, and departed into a solitary place, and there prayed" (Mk.1:35).
> > "Night and day praying exceedingly that we might see your face, and might perfect that which is lacking in your faith" (1 Th.3:10).
> > "Now she that is a widow indeed, and desolate, trusteth in God, and continueth in supplications and prayers night and day" (1 Tim.5:5).

2. The priests were to offer the first lamb with two quarts of flour mixed with one quart of olive oil and wine. It was a drink offering (v.40).
3. The priests were to offer the second lamb with the same items (v.41).
4. The effect upon the LORD would be twofold:
   a. It would be a pleasing aroma and sacrifice to the LORD (v.41).
   b. It would satisfy the fire (holiness) of the LORD (v.41).
5. The critical importance of the morning and evening sacrifice was the heartbeat of the believer's daily relationship with God. It was to be observed forever, throughout all generations (v.42).
6. If God's people were faithful in keeping the daily sacrifice--keeping it with a genuine, trusting heart--the results would be phenomenal.

   a. The Lord would meet and speak to His messenger (Moses), guiding and giving him direction (v.42).

> > "Thou shalt guide me with thy counsel, and afterward receive me to glory" (Ps.73:24).
> > "And thine ears shall hear a word behind thee, saying, This is the way, walk ye in it, when ye turn to the right hand, and when ye turn to the left" (Is.30:21).
> > "He that hath my commandments, and keepeth them, he it is that loveth me: and he that loveth me shall be loved of my Father, and I will love him, and will manifest myself to him" (Jn.14:21).

   b. The Lord would meet and speak to the people (v.43).

> <u>Thought 1</u>. God has promised to speak to His people in a voice they know, in a way that they can understand.

> > "My sheep hear my voice, and I know them, and they follow me" (Jn.10:27).
> > "God, who at sundry times and in divers manners spake in time past unto the fathers by the prophets, Hath in these last days spoken unto us by *his* Son, whom he hath appointed heir of all things, by whom also he made the worlds" (Heb.1:1-2).
> > "All scripture is given by inspiration of God, and is profitable for doctrine, for reproof, for correction, for instruction in righteousness" (2 Tim.3:16).

   c. The Lord would sanctify the Tabernacle (place of worship) with His glory (v.44).

EXODUS 29:1-46

Thought 1. The Christian believer (his body and life) is the Tabernacle that God has sanctified with His glory.

"And I will put my spirit within you, and cause you to walk in my statutes, and ye shall keep my judgments, and do *them*" (Ezk.36:27).
"Know ye not that ye are the temple of God, and *that* the Spirit of God dwelleth in you?" (1 Cor.3:16).
"What? know ye not that your body is the temple of the Holy Ghost *which is* in you, which ye have of God, and ye are not your own?" (1 Cor.6:19).
"I am crucified with Christ: nevertheless I live; yet not I, but Christ liveth in me: and the life which I now live in the flesh I live by the faith of the Son of God, who loved me, and gave himself for me" (Gal.2:20).
"To whom God would make known what *is* the riches of the glory of this mystery among the Gentiles; which is Christ in you, the hope of glory" (Col.1:27).
"That good thing which was committed unto thee keep by the Holy Ghost which dwelleth in us" (2 Tim.1:14).
"And he that keepeth his commandments dwelleth in him, and he in him. And hereby we know that he abideth in us, by the Spirit which he hath given us" (1 Jn.3:24).

d. The Lord would sanctify (set apart as holy) the Tabernacle, altar, and the priests--all to His service (v.44).

Thought 1. The goal of every believer should be to serve God, to be useful to God. God only uses those whom He sanctifies (makes holy), and He only sanctifies (makes holy) those whom He can use.

"Sanctify them through thy truth: thy word is truth" (Jn.17:17).
"But of him are ye in Christ Jesus, who of God is made unto us wisdom, and righteousness, and sanctification, and redemption" (1 Cor.1:30).
"That he might sanctify and cleanse it with the washing of water by the word" (Eph.5:26).
"If a man therefore purge himself from these, he shall be a vessel unto honour, sanctified, and meet for the master's use, *and* prepared unto every good work" (2 Tim.2:21).
"By the which will we are sanctified through the offering of the body of Jesus Christ once *for all*" (Heb.10:10).
"Wherefore Jesus also, that he might sanctify the people with his own blood, suffered without the gate" (Heb.13:12).

e. The Lord would dwell among His people and be their God (v.45).

Thought 1. There is a twofold blessing in this promise:
1) God will dwell among His people. God will live with them, care for them, love them.

"And, behold, I *am* with thee, and will keep thee in all *places* whither thou goest, and will bring thee again into this land; for I will not leave thee, until I have done *that* which I have spoken to thee of" (Gen.28:15).
"When thou passest through the waters, I *will be* with thee; and through the rivers, they shall not overflow thee: when thou walkest through the fire, thou shalt not be burned; neither shall the flame kindle upon thee" (Is.43:2).

2) God will be *their* God. God will be their Father, their Lord, their Savior.

"I have redeemed thee, I have called thee by thy name; thou art mine" (Is.43:1).

f. The people would know that the LORD is the God who delivers and sets them free (v.46).

Thought 1. Jesus Christ is the only One who can deliver us from the bondage of sin and set us free.

"The Spirit of the Lord GOD *is* upon me [Jesus Christ]; because the LORD hath anointed me to preach good tidings unto the meek; he hath sent me to bind up the brokenhearted, to proclaim liberty to the captives, and the opening of the prison to *them that are* bound" (Is.61:1).
"And ye shall know the truth, and the truth shall make you free" (Jn.8:32).
"For the wages of sin is death; but the gift of God is eternal life through Jesus Christ our Lord" (Ro.6:23).
"*There is* therefore now no condemnation to them which are in Christ Jesus, who walk not after the flesh, but after the Spirit. For the law of the Spirit of life in Christ Jesus hath made me free from the law of sin and death" (Ro.8:1-2).

	I. The Altar of Incense: The Symbol of the Prayers & Communion of God's People Ascending to God, Ex.30:1-10	staves of shittim wood, and overlay them with gold.	wood overlaid with gold
1. The design and materials a. To be made of acacia wood (symbolized the perfection of Christ's intercession) b. To be square: 18" x 18" x 3' high c. To have horns on each corner, carved from the same piece of wood (symbolized the power of God in answer to prayer) d. To be overlaid with gold & to have a gold molding (a symbol of deity, of the most valuable, prized possession)	And thou shalt make an altar to burn incense upon: of shittim wood shalt thou make it. 2 A cubit shall be the length thereof, and a cubit the breadth thereof; foursquare shall it be: and two cubits shall be the height thereof: the horns thereof shall be of the same. 3 And thou shalt overlay it with pure gold, the top thereof, and the sides thereof round about, and the horns thereof; and thou shalt make unto it a crown of gold round about.	6 And thou shalt put it before the vail that is by the ark of the testimony, before the mercy seat that is over the testimony, where I will meet with thee. 7 And Aaron shall burn thereon sweet incense every morning: when he dresseth the lamps, he shall burn incense upon it. 8 And when Aaron lighteth the lamps at even, he shall burn incense upon it, a perpetual incense before the LORD throughout your generations. 9 Ye shall offer no strange incense thereon, nor burnt sacrifice, nor meat offering; neither shall ye pour drink offering thereon.	g. To place the altar just outside the inner curtain opposite the Ark of the Covenant & its cover, the Mercy Seat (symbolized how prayer brings people near God) **2. The purpose of the altar** a. To have the High Priest burn incense every morning when he tended the lamps & every evening when he lit them b. To be a permanent incense ascending up to the LORD (symbolized the permanent intercession of Christ & that we should pray always, morning & evening) **3. The holiness of the altar** a. Never to allow the altar to be desecrated nor misused
e. To attach two gold rings on each side to hold the two poles used to carry the altar (a symbol that prayer is not limited to one geographical location: People are to pray everywhere) f. To make the poles of acacia	4 And two golden rings shalt thou make to it under the crown of it, by the two corners thereof, upon the two sides of it shalt thou make it; and they shall be for places for the staves to bear it withal. 5 And thou shalt make the	10 And Aaron shall make an atonement upon the horns of it once in a year with the blood of the sin offering of atonements: once in the year shall he make atonement upon it throughout your generations: it is most holy unto the LORD.	b. To purify the altar by placing on its horns some blood from the atoning sacrifice: To be done once a year (symbolized that we can only approach God through the intercessory ministry, the atoning sacrifice of Christ) c. The reason: Because the altar was holy to the LORD

DIVISION IX

THE TABERNACLE, ITS BLUEPRINT AND PRIESTHOOD:
THE TRUE WAY TO APPROACH AND WORSHIP GOD, EX.25:1-31:18

I. The Altar of Incense: The Symbol of the Prayers and Communion of God's People Ascending to God, Ex.30:1-10

(30:1-10) **Introduction**: God answers prayer. When we face severe problems, trouble, or crises, God answers prayer. When we face terrible trial or temptation, God answers prayer. When we face sickness, disease, or accident, God answers prayer. When we face pain, suffering, terminal illness, or death, God answers prayer. When we face the difficult times of life--if we pray, cry out to God from the depths of our heart--God hears and answers our prayers. When we need comfort, guidance, assurance, security, companionship, friendship--God hears and answers our prayers. He meets our need always. This is the significance and purpose of the Altar of Incense. The Altar was used to offer up the most pleasing and acceptable aroma that can be imagined. This symbolized the pleasure and acceptance of God, that He was pleased with the aroma and accepted the offering being made. What was the offering? Prayer, the prayers of His dear people. The Altar of Incense symbolized the prayers of God's dear people ascending up to God. This is the subject of this important portion of Scripture: *The Altar of Incense: The Symbol of the Prayers and Communion of God's People Ascending to God,* Ex.30:1-10.

1. The design and materials of the altar (v.1-6).
2. The purpose of the altar (v.7-8).
3. The holiness of the altar (v.9-10).

1 (30:1-6) **Tabernacle of Moses--Altar of Incense--Prayer--Intercession**: there was the design and the materials of the Altar of Incense. The incense on the altar was to burn continuously, symbolizing two significant things:

⇒ the unbroken intercession of Jesus Christ for us
⇒ the prayers and communion of God's people ascending to God

Note again: God Himself is the One who designed this altar. The altar was to be made like every other piece of furniture in the Tabernacle, made according to God's perfect plan and design. These are the details for its construction:

1. The Altar of Incense was to be made of acacia wood (v.1). We have already noted the quality of acacia wood and how it speaks of incorruptibility, the incorruption and perfection of Jesus Christ (see note--Ex.25:5). Jesus Christ is the One who intercedes for us, who stands between God and us and makes us acceptable to God. The intercession of Christ is not corrupt in any way; His intercession is perfect. He makes us acceptable to God.

"Wherefore he is able also to save them to the uttermost that come unto God by him, seeing he ever liveth to make intercession for them. For such an high priest became us, who is holy, harmless, undefiled, separate from sinners, and made higher than the heavens; Who needeth not daily, as those high priests, to offer up sacrifice, first for his own sins, and then for the people's: for this he did once, when he offered up himself" (Heb.7:25-27).

2. The Altar of Incense was to be square: 18 inches by 18 inches by 3 feet high (v.2).

3. The Altar of Incense was to have horns on each corner, carved from the same piece of wood (v.2). Horns are symbolic of God's power and strength, God's salvation, protection, security, sanctuary, and help.

Thought 1. Note the strong lesson seen in the symbol of the horns. The horns are symbolic of God's power and strength. God's power and strength are available to help us in times of desperate need, times of...

- pain and anguish
- loneliness and emptiness
- accident and disease
- temptation and sin
- bankruptcy and loss
- hunger and poverty
- suffering and death
- broken trust and desertion

The Altar of Incense reminds us that God has the power and strength to deliver us through all trials, no matter how terrible.

"And he said unto me, My grace is sufficient for thee: for my strength is made perfect in weakness. Most gladly therefore will I rather glory in my infirmities, that the power of Christ may rest upon me" (2 Cor.12:9).

"And the Lord shall deliver me from every evil work, and will preserve me unto his heavenly kingdom: to whom be glory for ever and ever. Amen" (2 Tim.4:18).

"So that we may boldly say, The Lord is my helper, and I will not fear what man shall do unto me" (Heb.13:6).

"The LORD is my shepherd; I shall not want. He maketh me to lie down in green pastures: he leadeth me beside the still waters. He restoreth my soul: he leadeth me in the paths of righteousness for his name's sake. Yea, though I walk through the valley of the shadow of death, I will fear no evil: for thou art with me; thy rod and thy staff they comfort me. Thou preparest a table before me in the presence of mine enemies: thou anointest my head with oil; my cup runneth over. Surely goodness and mercy shall follow me all the days of my life: and I will dwell in the house of the LORD for ever" (Ps.23:1-6).

"The LORD is my strength and my shield; my heart trusted in him, and I am helped: therefore my heart greatly rejoiceth; and with my song will I praise him" (Ps.28:7).

"But I am poor and needy; yet the Lord thinketh upon me: thou art my help and my deliverer; make no tarrying, O my God" (Ps.40:17).

"Fear thou not; for I *am* with thee: be not dismayed; for I *am* thy God: I will strengthen thee; yea, I will help thee; yea, I will uphold thee with the right hand of my righteousness" (Is.41:10).

"And even to your old age I am he; and even to hoar [gray] hairs will I carry you: I have made, and I will bear; even I will carry, and will deliver you" (Is.46:4).

4. The Altar of Incense was to be overlaid with gold and have a gold molding (v.3). Just like the other holy pieces of furniture in the sanctuary, the altar was covered with pure gold. The most precious of metals was God's choice for building this altar of intercession. Remember, gold is a symbol of deity, a symbol of the most precious possession, God Himself. The golden Altar of Incense points to the LORD Jesus Christ...

- Who is the most precious possession a person can have
- Who is the *Perfect Intercessor*, the One who *lives* forever to make intercession, to passionately pray for the people of God

"Wherefore he is able also to save them to the uttermost that come unto God by him, seeing he ever liveth to make intercession for them" (Heb.7:25).

The purpose for the gold molding was to keep the burning coals from falling off the altar and burning out on the desert floor. What was the origin of the fire that was kept in the altar? The live coals came from the altar of burnt offerings, the altar which symbolized the need for atonement with God. No effectual prayers can be offered to God unless a sacrifice has been offered to satisfy the righteous and just nature of a holy God. As the priests ministered at the Altar of Incense, the gold molding and hot coals reminded them of several things:

⇒ They were reminded of God's righteous and just nature and of His blazing judgment against sin.

⇒ They clearly saw the hot coals that burned red with heat.

⇒ They were reminded of God's wonderful mercy and grace that invited them to approach His holy throne.

⇒ They were reminded of their reason for being at the altar: to intercede for the desperate needs of a sinful people who needed the help of God.

Thought 1. Our prayers should always be fervent, hot as the coals on the altar. Prayer is not an occasion for complacency and lethargy but for the deep cry of the human spirit to touch the living God!

"*The righteous* cry, and the LORD heareth, and delivereth them out of all their troubles. The LORD *is* nigh unto them that are of a broken heart; and saveth such as be of a contrite spirit" (Ps.34:17-18).

"I waited patiently for the LORD; and he inclined unto me, and heard my cry" (Ps.40:1).

"As the hart panteth after the water brooks, so panteth my soul after thee, O God. My soul thirsteth for God, for the living God: when shall I come and appear before God?" (Ps.42:1-2).

"O God, thou *art* my God; early will I seek thee: my soul thirsteth for thee, my flesh longeth for thee in a dry and thirsty land, where no water is" (Ps.63:1).

"My soul followeth hard after thee: thy right hand upholdeth me" (Ps.63:8).

5. The Altar of Incense was to have two gold rings attached to each side. The rings were to hold the two poles used in carrying the altar (v.4).

6. The Altar of Incense was to have two poles made of acacia wood overlaid with gold (v.5). The altar, like the rest of the Tabernacle, was designed to be moved. The Altar of Incense, of prayer, was to go with God's people whenever and wherever they traveled. This points to a beautiful, meaningful fact about prayer. Prayer is not limited to a single geographical location on the earth. God's people are to pray wherever they go, anyplace, anywhere, all the time.

"Pray without ceasing" (1 Th.5:17).

"I will therefore that men pray every where, lifting up holy hands, without wrath and doubting" (1 Tim.2:8).

7. God told Moses to place the altar just outside the inner curtain. It was to be opposite the Ark of the Covenant and its cover, the Mercy Seat (v.6). The location of the altar is significant. How close to the inner curtain was the altar placed? No one knows, but what is known is that the altar was *just outside* the curtain. It was very, very close to the presence of God. This is the great blessing of intercessory prayer: intercessory prayer...

- is close to the veil
- is close to the very throne of God
- is close to the glory of God
- is close to the place where God's eternal mercy and grace reside
- is close to the door of answered prayer
- is close to the most intimate fellowship and communion with God imaginable

Thought 1. The one thing we are to seek above all else is to be near God, to fellowship and commune with Him in an unbroken sense of His presence.

"I have set the LORD always before me: because he is at my right hand, I shall not be moved" (Ps.16:8).

"The LORD is nigh unto them that are of a broken heart; and saveth such as be of a contrite spirit" (Ps.34:18).

"But it is good for me to draw near to God: I have put my trust in the Lord GOD, that I may declare all thy works" (Ps.73:28).

"The LORD is nigh unto all them that call upon him, to all that call upon him in truth" (Ps.145:18).

"Let us draw near with a true heart in full assurance of faith, having our hearts sprinkled from an evil conscience, and our bodies washed with pure water" (Heb.10:22).

"Draw nigh to God, and he will draw nigh to you. Cleanse your hands, ye sinners; and purify your hearts, ye double minded" (Jas.4:8).

Thought 2. The inner curtain that had once separated the Altar of Incense and the Ark of God's presence was torn down, torn from top to bottom by God Himself. God ripped it open through the death of His Son, the Lord Jesus Christ. The way into God's presence is now open. We are now invited to come boldly and worship God at the Throne of Grace.

"Let us therefore come boldly unto the throne of grace, that we may obtain mercy, and find grace to help in time of need" (Heb.4:16).

[2] (30:7-8) **Altar of Incense--Prayer--Intercession--Tabernacle**: the purpose for the altar was twofold.

1. The altar was to be the place where sweet incense was offered up to the LORD every morning and evening. The High Priest burned incense every morning when he tended the lamps and every evening when he lit them (v.7). This symbolized the critical importance of praying every morning and evening.

2. The Altar of Incense was to be the place where a permanent incense ascended up to the LORD (v.8). This symbolized two things.

  a. There is the symbol of the permanent intercession of Jesus Christ. Jesus Christ is living forever--in the very presence of God--to make intercession for us. He died and arose from the dead for us for this very purpose: to stand before God as the great Intercessor for us. (The following is taken from the Thompson Chain Reference Bible, the General Index # 1783.)[1]

---

[1] *The New Thompson Chain Reference Bible.* (Indianapolis, IN: B.B. Kirkbride Bible Co., Inc., 1964.)

⇒ Jesus Christ intercedes for sinners

"Therefore will I divide him a portion with the great, and he shall divide the spoil with the strong; because he hath poured out his soul unto death: and he was numbered with the transgressors; and he bare the sin of many, and made intercession for the transgressors" (Is.53:12).

⇒ Jesus Christ intercedes for weak believers

"But I have prayed for thee, that thy faith fail not: and when thou art converted, strengthen thy brethren" (Lk.22:32).

⇒ Jesus Christ intercedes for His enemies

"Then said Jesus, Father, forgive them; for they know not what they do. And they parted his raiment, and cast lots" (Lk.23:34).

⇒ Jesus Christ intercedes for the church

"I pray for them: I pray not for the world, but for them which thou hast given me; for they are thine" (Jn.17:9).

⇒ Jesus Christ intercedes for God to accept us

"Who is he that condemneth? It is Christ that died, yea rather, that is risen again, who is even at the right hand of God, who also maketh intercession for us" (Ro.8:34).

⇒ Jesus Christ intercedes for our salvation

"Wherefore he is able also to save them to the uttermost that come unto God by him, seeing he ever liveth to make intercession for them" (Heb.7:25).

⇒ Jesus Christ intercedes for the Holy Spirit to abide with us

"And I will pray the Father, and he shall give you another Comforter, that he may abide with you for ever" (Jn.14:16).

b. There is the symbol that believers are to pray morning and evening, to pray always, to develop an unbroken communion with God, to never cease being in a spirit of prayer.

"Seek the LORD and his strength, seek his face continually" (1 Chron.16:11).
"Ask, and it shall be given you; seek, and ye shall find; knock, and it shall be opened unto you" (Mt.7:7).
"And he spake a parable unto them to this end, that men ought always to pray, and not to faint" (Lk.18:1).
"Praying always with all prayer and supplication in the Spirit, and watching thereunto with all perseverance and supplication for all saints" (Eph.6:18).
"Pray without ceasing" (1 Th.5:17).

3 (30:9-10) **Incense, Altar of--Prayer--Intercession--Tabernacle**: the holiness of the Altar of Incense set it apart as a very special piece of furniture. Note how forcefully God stressed the holiness of the altar.

1. The priests were never to allow the altar to be desecrated nor misused (v.9). Any foreign thing that was placed on the altar was a direct affront to God. Prayer is holy to God. It is more intimate than any physical relationship experienced by people. Adding anything to His ordained plan for intercession and prayer was sin.

2. Once a year Aaron was to purify the altar by placing on its horns some blood from the atoning sacrifice (the blood of the sin offering) (v.10). For the Altar of Incense to have any lasting significance, it had to be directly connected to the blood that was shed on the altar of burnt offerings. Why? Because the prayers of believers have to be directly connected to the shed blood of Christ.

⇒ It is at the altar of prayer where we plead the power of Christ's blood to cleanse and accept us.
⇒ It is at the altar of prayer where we stand in Christ's atonement.
⇒ It is at the altar of prayer where we go behind the inner curtain, in Christ's name, and experience the wonderful presence and glory of God Himself.

3. Why was this altar to be purified? Because the altar was most holy to the LORD (v.10). Prayer is a very serious thing to God. How He longs for people who will stand before the holy altar and offer an incense that is pleasing to Him. How He longs for people who will live holy lives and pray seeking His face continually.

The Altar of Incense is *most holy* to the LORD because it represents the *Intercessory Ministry*, the *atoning sacrifice* of Christ. Nothing is as dear to the heart of God as His Son, the Lord Jesus Christ. God wanted Christ to die for us, to die as the atoning sacrifice for our sins. This Jesus Christ did. He died for us, died in obedience to God's will. Because He obeyed God--did what God the Father wanted--nothing touches the heart of God like the *Intercessory Ministry*, the atoning sacrifice, of His Son.

Thus God has taken the *Intercessory Ministry*, the *atoning sacrifice,* of His dear Son and made it holy: sanctified it, set it apart as very special in the eternal plan of redemption.

⇒ By the *Intercessory Ministry* of Christ, He stands forth as our eternal Mediator, making us acceptable to God.

"Jesus saith unto him, I am the way, the truth, and the life: no man cometh unto the Father, but by me" (Jn.14:6).

"For there is one God, and one mediator between God and men, the man Christ Jesus; Who gave himself a ransom for all, to be testified in due time" (1 Tim.2:5-6).

"And for this cause he is the mediator of the new testament, that by means of death, for the redemption of the transgressions that were under the first testament, they which are called might receive the promise of eternal inheritance" (Heb.9:15).

"For Christ is not entered into the holy places made with hands, which are the figures of the true; but into heaven itself, now to appear in the presence of God for us" (Heb.9:24).

"My little children, these things write I unto you, that ye sin not. And if any man sin, we have an advocate with the Father, Jesus Christ the righteous: And he is the propitiation for our sins: and not for ours only, but also for the sins of the whole world" (1 Jn.2:1-2).

⇒ By the *Intercessory Ministry* of Christ, the door into God's presence is opened. We now have access into God's presence--anytime, anyplace--through prayer.

"I am the door: by me if any man enter in, he shall be saved, and shall go in and out, and find pasture" (Jn.10:9).

"Hitherto have ye asked nothing in my name: ask, and ye shall receive, that your joy may be full" (Jn.16:24).

"By whom also we have access by faith into this grace wherein we stand, and rejoice in hope of the glory of God" (Ro.5:2).

"For through him we both have access by one Spirit unto the Father" (Eph.2:18).

"In whom we have boldness and access with confidence by the faith of him" (Eph.3:12).

"Let us draw near with a true heart in full assurance of faith, having our hearts sprinkled from an evil conscience, and our bodies washed with pure water" (Heb.10:22).

TYPES, SYMBOLS, AND PICTURES
(Exodus 30:1-10)

Historical Term	Type or Picture (Scriptural Basis for Each)	Life Application for Today's Believer	Biblical Application for Today's Believer
The Altar of Incense (Ex.30:1-10; 40:26-27) See also Ex.35:15; 37:25-29; 39:38; 40:5	*The Altar of Incense filled the Sanctuary with a sweet-smelling incense. Twice a day, in the morning and evening, the High Priest burned incense in the Altar. The message of the Altar is at least two things:* *a. The intercession of the High Priest symbolized a permanent intercession, an intercession that never quits.*	What the Altar of Incense taught: a. Christ as our great High Priest is always praying and living in an unbroken communion with God the Father, interceding for God's people.	*"I pray for them: I pray not for the world, but for them which thou hast given me; for they are thine" (Jn.17:9). "Who is he that condemneth? It is Christ that died, yea rather, that is risen again, who is even at the right hand of God, who also maketh intercession for us" (Ro.8:34). "Seeing then that we have a great high priest [Intercessor], that is passed into the heavens, Jesus the Son of God, let us hold fast our profession. For we have not an high priest which cannot be touched with the feeling of our infirmities; but was in all points tempted like as we are, yet without sin" (Heb.4:14-15). "Wherefore he is able also to save them to the uttermost that come unto God by him, seeing he ever*

Historical Term	Type or Picture (Scriptural Basis for Each)	Life Application for Today's Believer	Biblical Application for Today's Believer
	b. *The Altar of Incense symbolized the prayers and unbroken communion of God's people ascending up to God and pleasing Him.* "And thou shalt make an altar to burn incense upon: of shittim wood shalt thou make it" (Ex.30:1). "And he put the golden altar in the tent of the congregation before the vail: And he burnt sweet incense thereon; as the LORD commanded Moses" (Ex.40:26-27).	b. Believers are to pray morning and evening, to pray always, to develop an unbroken communion with God, to never cease being in a spirit of prayer.	liveth to make intercession for them" (Heb.7:25). "Seek the LORD and his strength, seek his face continually" (1 Chron.16:11). "Ask, and it shall be given you; seek, and ye shall find; knock, and it shall be opened unto you" (Mt.7:7). "Watch and pray, that ye enter not into temptation: the spirit indeed is willing, but the flesh is weak" (Mt.26:41). "Hitherto have ye asked nothing in my name: ask, and ye shall receive, that your joy may be full" (Jn.16:24). "Praying always with all prayer and supplication in the Spirit, and watching thereunto with all perseverance and supplication for all saints" (Eph.6:18). "Pray without ceasing" (1 Th.5:17).

The Altar Of Incense

1. The raising of money for the Tabernacle offering: Symbolized the ransom paid for one's life
a. To pay a ransom tax every time a census was taken
   1) Would be a reminder of God's redemption
   2) Would assure God's protection: Erase any chance of God's judgment or plague
b. To pay one fifth of an ounce of silver

c. To include every person 20 years old & above

d. To be the same amount for both rich & poor: Because it is an offering to make atonement for the soul

e. The purpose of the offering (tax)
   1) A material purpose: To take care of the Tabernacle
   2) A spiritual purpose: To be a memorial pointing to the atonement or ransom being paid for one's life
2. The bronze wash basin: Symbolized the washing, cleansing, & forgiveness of sin
a. To make the bronze basin with a bronze pedestal
b. To place it between the Tabernacle & altar: Fill with water
c. The purpose: For the priests to wash their hands & feet
   1) When they entered the Tabernacle
   2) When they approached the altar to make sacrifice

d. The warning: Must wash or die
e. The importance of the washing & cleansing: Was a permanent law for all generations

J. Other Instructions for the Tabernacle: Symbolizing Spiritual Health & Maturity, Ex.30:11-38

11 And the LORD spake unto Moses, saying,
12 When thou takest the sum of the children of Israel after their number, then shall they give every man a ransom for his soul unto the LORD, when thou numberest them; that there be no plague among them, when thou numberest them.
13 This they shall give, every one that passeth among them that are numbered, half a shekel after the shekel of the sanctuary: (a shekel is twenty gerahs:) an half shekel shall be the offering of the LORD.
14 Every one that passeth among them that are numbered, from twenty years old and above, shall give an offering unto the LORD.
15 The rich shall not give more, and the poor shall not give less than half a shekel, when they give an offering unto the LORD, to make an atonement for your souls.
16 And thou shalt take the atonement money of the children of Israel, and shalt appoint it for the service of the tabernacle of the congregation; that it may be a memorial unto the children of Israel before the LORD, to make an atonement for your souls.
17 And the LORD spake unto Moses, saying,
18 Thou shalt also make a laver of brass, and his foot also of brass, to wash withal: and thou shalt put it between the tabernacle of the congregation and the altar, and thou shalt put water therein.
19 For Aaron and his sons shall wash their hands and their feet thereat:
20 When they go into the tabernacle of the congregation, they shall wash with water, that they die not; or when they come near to the altar to minister, to burn offering made by fire unto the LORD:
21 So they shall wash their hands and their feet, that they die not: and it shall be a statute for ever to them, even to

him and to his seed throughout their generations.
22 Moreover the LORD spake unto Moses, saying,
23 Take thou also unto thee principal spices, of pure myrrh five hundred shekels, and of sweet cinnamon half so much, even two hundred and fifty shekels, and of sweet calamus two hundred and fifty shekels,
24 And of cassia five hundred shekels, after the shekel of the sanctuary, and of oil olive an hin:
25 And thou shalt make it an oil of holy ointment, an ointment compound after the art of the apothecary: it shall be an holy anointing oil.
26 And thou shalt anoint the tabernacle of the congregation therewith, and the ark of the testimony,
27 And the table and all his vessels, and the candlestick and his vessels, and the altar of incense,
28 And the altar of burnt offering with all his vessels, and the laver and his foot.
29 And thou shalt sanctify them, that they may be most holy: whatsoever toucheth them shall be holy.
30 And thou shalt anoint Aaron and his sons, and consecrate them, that they may minister unto me in the priest's office.
31 And thou shalt speak unto the children of Israel, saying, This shall be an holy anointing oil unto me throughout your generations.
32 Upon man's flesh shall it not be poured, neither shall ye make any other like it, after the composition of it: it is holy, and it shall be holy unto you.
33 Whosoever compoundeth any like it, or whosoever putteth any of it upon a stranger, shall even be cut off from his people.
34 And the LORD said unto Moses, Take unto thee sweet spices, stacte, and onycha, and galbanum; these sweet spices with pure frankincense: of each shall there be a like weight:
35 And thou shalt make it a perfume, a confection after the art of the apothecary, tempered together, pure and holy:

3. The anointing oil: Symbolized God's appointment to service & the Holy Spirit
a. To blend these choice spices
   1) 12½ pounds of pure myrrh
   2) 6¼ pounds of cinnamon
   3) 6¼ pounds of sweet cane

   4) 12½ pounds of cassia
   5) 1 gallon of olive oil

b. To mix & blend into a holy anointing oil

c. To use the oil to anoint
   • The Tabernacle & its furnishings
   • The Ark of the Covenant
   • The table & its utensils
   • The Lampstand & its accessories
   • The Altar of Incense
   • The Altar of Burnt Offering & its utensils
   • The wash basin with its stand
d. The purpose:
   1) To sanctify the Tabernacle & its furnishings: That all be holy
   2) To anoint the priests: To sanctify them for the ministry

e. The importance of the anointing oil
   1) Always to be God's holy anointing oil

   2) Never to be misused...
      • By pouring it on the ordinary person, someone not chosen by God
      • By making it for one's own use
f. The warning: If ever misused, that person shall be cut off from the community

4. The sweet incense: Symbolized the pleasing & acceptable aroma of prayer to God
a. The instructions
   1) To gather sweet spices, the same amount of each
   2) To blend & refine the spices using the techniques of a perfumer
b. The importance of the incense
   1) To be made a pure & holy incense

2) To be put in front of the Ark of the Covenant, the very place where God meets people 3) To be counted most holy 4) To be distinctive, the only incense made this way:	36 And thou shalt beat some of it very small, and put of it before the testimony in the tabernacle of the congregation, where I will meet with thee: it shall be unto you most holy. 37 And as for the perfume which thou shalt make,	ye shall not make to yourselves according to the composition thereof: it shall be unto thee holy for the LORD. 38 Whosoever shall make like unto that, to smell thereto, shall even be cut off from his people.	Made exclusively for the Lord, treated as holy c. The warning: To judge any person who makes an incense like it: To be cut off

DIVISION IX

THE TABERNACLE, ITS BLUEPRINT AND PRIESTHOOD:
THE TRUE WAY TO APPROACH AND WORSHIP GOD, EX.25:1-31:18

J. Other Instructions for the Tabernacle: Symbolizing Spiritual Health and Maturity, Ex.30:11-38

(30:11-38) **Introduction**: What makes a person spiritually healthy and mature? Four strong pictures are seen in this passage. To be spiritually healthy and mature, a believer…
- must be a giving person
- must be a morally pure person
- must be an anointed person, a person anointed by God for service
- must be a prayer warrior, an intercessor

These four pictures were also given to Israel in the wilderness. Note that these pictures center around the Tabernacle. If the Israelites were going to have spiritual health, these same four pictures had to become a part of their daily walk with the Lord. This is the subject of this section of Scripture. This is: *Other Instructions for the Tabernacle: Symbolizing Spiritual Health and Maturity,* Ex.30:11-38.
1. The raising of money for the Tabernacle offering: symbolized the ransom paid for one's life (v.11-16).
2. The bronze wash basin: symbolized the washing, cleansing, and forgiveness of sin (v.17-21).
3. The anointing oil: symbolizing God's appointment to service and the Holy Spirit (v.22-33).
4. The sweet incense: symbolized the pleasing and acceptable aroma of prayer to God (v.34-38).

1 (30:11-16) **Tabernacle of Moses--Offering--Ransom--Atonement**: there was the raising of money for the Tabernacle offering. Note that the raising of money is inserted by Moses between the discussion of the Altar of Incense and the bronze wash basin. This seems like an odd place to insert such information. What place does money have in the ministry of the Tabernacle? Why would God tell Moses to insert the raising of money in this portion of Scripture? There was a practical reason in relation to the Altar of Incense. We can pray and pray for God to meet the needs of His people, but God usually does not hear our prayers unless we have committed all we are and have to Him. God usually does not meet our needs if we are hoarding and not giving to meet the needs of others.

This passage declares a much needed lesson to us: prayer (the Altar of Incense) is available to us, and God will hear and answer our prayer. But we must be giving to the cause and work of God if we expect God to hear our prayers.

> **"The liberal soul shall be made fat: and he that watereth shall be watered also himself" (Pr.11:25).**
> **"He that hath a bountiful eye shall be blessed; for he giveth of his bread to the poor" (Pr.22:9).**
> **"And if thou draw out thy soul to the hungry, and satisfy the afflicted soul; then shall thy light rise in obscurity, and thy darkness be as the noonday" (Is.58:10).**
> **"Bring ye all the tithes into the storehouse, that there may be meat in mine house, and prove me now herewith, saith the LORD of hosts, if I will not open you the windows of heaven, and pour you out a blessing, that there shall not be room enough to receive it" (Mal.3:10).**
> **"Give, and it shall be given unto you; good measure, pressed down, and shaken together, and running over, shall men give into your bosom. For with the same measure that ye mete withal it shall be measured to you again" (Lk.6:38).**
> **"But this I say, He which soweth sparingly shall reap also sparingly; and he which soweth bountifully shall reap also bountifully" (2 Cor.9:6).**

Following are the facts concerning the raising of money for the Tabernacle:
1. The people were to pay a ransom tax (as an offering) every time a census was taken. This would be a constant reminder of God's redemption, the redemption of His precious people. Obedience in paying this tax would assure God's protection and erase any chance of God's judgment or plague. (v.12). Taking this census was no small thing, for hundreds of thousands of people needed to be counted. Why would Israel periodically need to take a census? For military and other public services. The leaders, just as in any other nation, needed to know how many men were available for their armed forces, how many men were old enough to fight in the event of a national crisis. Note what God says about the census: if the people believed God and were faithful in their worship, they would pay the tax willingly. If they were not faithful in their worship, they of course would become negligent in their duties, one of which would be paying the tax to keep up the

Tabernacle. God promised the people: if they were faithful, He would not judge (plague) them. But God also warned the people: if they were unfaithful, He would send a plague upon them.

2. Each person counted under the census was to pay one fifth of an ounce of silver as the tax or offering to the LORD (v.13).

3. The census was to include every person twenty years old and above (v.14).

4. The offering was to be the same amount for both the rich and the poor (v.15). Why was this? Because it was an offering to make atonement for one's life. An abundance of wealth will not secure a person's reconciliation with God, his place in the promised land (symbolic of heaven). Neither will a life of austere poverty. Everyone is equal in God's eyes: everyone is a sinner; everyone needs to be saved in the same way. Everyone needs to be redeemed by the blood of Jesus Christ.

⇒ Rich or poor, no one is righteous enough to save himself.

"As it is written, There is none righteous, no, not one" (Ro.3:10).

⇒ Rich or poor, no one is justified enough to save himself.

"Therefore by the deeds of the law there shall no flesh be justified in his sight: for by the law *is* the knowledge of sin" (Ro.3:20).

⇒ Rich or poor, no one can afford the cost of eternal life. Only Jesus Christ can pay the debt of sin.

"For the wages of sin *is* death; but the gift of God *is* eternal life through Jesus Christ our Lord" (Ro.6:23).

5. The purpose for the offering (tax) was twofold.

a. The offering had a material purpose: to take care of the needs of the Tabernacle (v.16).

Thought 1. It is the responsibility of God's people to take care of the needs of the church and of believers. It is not the responsibility of the political leaders in government, nor is it the task of unbelievers.

"Bring ye all the tithes into the storehouse, that there may be meat in mine house, and prove me now herewith, saith the LORD of hosts, if I will not open you the windows of heaven, and pour you out a blessing, that there shall not be room enough to receive it" (Mal.3:10).

"Honour the LORD with thy substance, and with the firstfruits of all thine increase" (Pr.3:9).

"Every man shall give as he is able, according to the blessing of the LORD thy God which he hath given thee" (Dt.16:17).

"Freely ye have received, freely give" (Mt.10:8).

"Jesus said unto him, If thou wilt be perfect [saved], go [and] sell that thou hast, and give to the poor, and thou shalt have treasure in heaven: and come [and] follow me" (Mt.19:21).

"For it hath pleased them of Macedonia and Achaia to make a certain contribution for the poor saints which are at Jerusalem. It hath pleased them verily; and their debtors they are. For if the Gentiles have been made partakers of their spiritual things, their duty is also to minister unto them in carnal things" (Ro.15:26-27).

"Upon the first day of the week let every one of you lay by him in store, as God hath prospered him, that there be no gatherings when I come" (1 Cor.16:2).

"Every man according as he purposeth in his heart, so let him give; not grudgingly, or of necessity: for God loveth a cheerful giver" (2 Cor.9:7).

b. The offering had a spiritual purpose: to be a memorial pointing to the atonement being made for the believer (v.16). The offering was to remind God's people of the rewards for obeying God. God had blessed them abundantly in so many ways:

⇒ He had delivered them from slavery in Egypt (the world)

⇒ He was going to lead them to Canaan (the Promised Land, a symbol of heaven)

⇒ He had bought them--ransomed, redeemed them--and now they were His people, God's very own possession. The silver tax was a reminder to Israel: they had been redeemed (bought) by God. Therefore, they owed *everything* to God. They were no longer their own.

Thought 1. When we say "yes" to Jesus Christ, we are redeemed, bought by His blood. Therefore, we are to give all we are and have to Him.

⇒ We are to give our material possessions to Christ.

"Jesus said unto him, If thou wilt be perfect [saved], go *and* sell that thou hast, and give to the poor, and thou shalt have treasure in heaven: and come *and* follow me" (Mt.19:21).

⇒ We are to give our hopes and dreams to Christ.

> **"Then Jesus beholding him loved him, and said unto him, One thing thou lackest: go thy way, sell whatsoever thou hast, and give to the poor, and thou shalt have treasure in heaven: and come, take up the cross, and follow me" (Mk.10:21).**

⇒ We are to give our very lives to Christ.

> **"For to me to live *is* Christ, and to die *is* gain" (Ph.1:21).**
> **"That I may know him, and the power of his resurrection, and the fellowship of his sufferings, being made conformable unto his death" (Ph.3:10).**

2 (30:17-21) **Tabernacle of Moses--Bronze Wash Basin--Sanctification--Holiness**: there was the bronze wash basin. The second major piece of furniture in the courtyard of the Tabernacle was the bronze wash basin. The materials for the bronze basin came from the free-will offerings of the women (see Ex.38:8). Made from polished bronze mirrors, the bronze wash basin played a very significant role in the priest's service to God. These are the facts:
1. The builder was to make the bronze basin with a bronze pedestal (v.18).
2. The bronze basin was to be placed between the Tabernacle and the Altar of Burnt Offering (v.18). This was the logical place for the basin. Before a priest could go into the Holy Place and Most Holy Place, his first order of business was at the Altar of Burnt Offering. Blood had to be shed. A sacrifice had to be offered to appease the righteousness and justice of God. A portion of the blood was sprinkled on the bronze wash basin, symbolizing that it was where the priest was cleansed. No one could approach God…
- unless a sacrifice had been offered
- unless blood had been shed
- unless he had been sanctified and set apart by the blood of the sacrifice

The bronze wash basin was the next step in following the path of holiness, of entering into the presence of God.
3. The sole purpose of the bronze wash basin was for the priests to wash their hands and feet (v.19). They were to wash when they entered the Tabernacle and when they approached the altar to make a sacrifice. A man of God cannot minister with hands that have not been washed and cleansed, nor can he walk about ministering for the Lord until his feet have been cleansed (v.20).

Thought 1. There are many sins that entangle a believer. We must constantly be on guard and wash regularly and faithfully by coming to Christ, the Perfect Sacrifice who alone can wash and cleanse us from sin.

> **"I will wash mine hands in innocency: so will I compass thine altar, O LORD" (Ps.26:6).**
> **"Wash you, make you clean; put away the evil of your doings from before mine eyes; cease to do evil" (Is.1:16).**
> **"Depart ye, depart ye, go ye out from thence, touch no unclean *thing;* go ye out of the midst of her; be ye clean, that bear the vessels of the LORD" (Is.52:11).**
> **"Wash away thy sins, calling on the name of the Lord" (Acts 22:16).**
> **"In whom we have redemption through his blood, the forgiveness of sins, according to the riches of his grace" (Eph.1:7).**
> **"Having therefore these promises, dearly beloved, let us cleanse ourselves from all filthiness of the flesh and spirit, perfecting holiness in the fear of God" (2 Cor.7:1).**
> **"If a man therefore purge himself from these, he shall be a vessel unto honour, sanctified, and meet for the master's use, and prepared unto every good work" (2 Tim.2:21).**
> **"Draw nigh to God, and he will draw nigh to you. Cleanse your hands, ye sinners; and purify your hearts, ye double minded" (Jas.4:8).**
> **"If we confess our sins, he is faithful and just to forgive us *our* sins, and to cleanse us from all unrighteousness" (1 Jn.1:9).**

4. The warning was stark and blunt: the priests must wash or die (v.21). God is holy and He will not allow any person to bring sin into His presence. Their very lives depended upon obedience. The priests could not afford to skip this station and go into the Tabernacle. They could not afford to forget and wash later. God was serious, very serious: a person had to be washed and cleansed before approaching Him and before serving Him.

Thought 1. God is always serious about holiness. There are no exceptions.

> **"Having therefore these promises, dearly beloved, let us cleanse ourselves from all filthiness of the flesh and spirit, perfecting holiness in the fear of God" (2 Cor.7:1).**
> **"*Seeing* then *that* all these things shall be dissolved, what manner *of persons* ought ye to be in *all* holy conversation and godliness" (2 Pt.3:11).**
> **"Who shall not fear thee, O Lord, and glorify thy name? for *thou* only *art* holy: for all nations shall come and worship before thee; for thy judgments are made manifest" (Rev.15:4).**
> **"Who *is* like unto thee, O LORD, among the gods? who *is* like thee, glorious in holiness, fearful *in* praises, doing wonders?" (Ex.15:11).**

"For I *am* the LORD that bringeth you up out of the land of Egypt, to be your God: ye shall therefore be holy, for I *am* holy" (Lev.11:45).

"Exalt the LORD our God, and worship at his holy hill; for the LORD our God *is* holy" (Ps.99:9).

"And one cried unto another, and said, Holy, holy, holy, *is* the LORD of hosts: the whole earth *is* full of his glory" (Is.6:3).

5. The importance of the washing and cleansing cannot be overstressed: it was made a permanent law for all generations (v.21). The need to be cleansed from defilement was not a problem just for Aaron and his sons. Every believer--in every generation, in every culture--must be washed and cleansed from the defilement of sin.

Thought 1. God will cleanse us; this is His promise if we will only cry out for cleansing.

"Simon Peter saith unto him, Lord, not my feet only, but also my hands and my head" (Jn.13:9).

"Husbands, love your wives, even as Christ also loved the church, and gave himself for it; That he might sanctify and cleanse it with the washing of water by the word" (Eph.5:25-26).

"How much more shall the blood of Christ, who through the eternal Spirit offered himself without spot to God, purge your conscience from dead works to serve the living God?" (Heb.9:14).

"But if we walk in the light, as he is in the light, we have fellowship one with another, and the blood of Jesus Christ his Son cleanseth us from all sin" (1 Jn.1:7).

"Who can understand his errors? cleanse thou me from secret faults" (Ps.19:12).

"Wash me throughly from mine iniquity, and cleanse me from my sin" (Ps.51:2).

"Purge me with hyssop, and I shall be clean: wash me, and I shall be whiter than snow" (Ps.51:7).

"Help us, O God of our salvation, for the glory of thy name: and deliver us, and purge away our sins, for thy name's sake" (Ps.79:9).

"Come now, and let us reason together, saith the LORD: though your sins be as scarlet, they shall be as white as snow; though they be red like crimson, they shall be as wool" (Is.1:18).

3 (30:22-33) **Tabernacle of Moses--Priesthood--Anointing Oil**: there was the anointing oil. The anointing oil symbolized the special call and appointment of God and the Holy Spirit, His equipping of a person for the service of God. Note these carefully worded instructions:

1. Moses was to collect and blend these choice spices.
    a. Myrrh: 12½ pounds of pure myrrh (v.23).
    b. Cinnamon: 6¼ pounds of cinnamon (v.23).
    c. Sweet cane: 6¼ pounds of sweet cane (v.23).
    d. Cassia: 12½ pounds of cassia (v.24).
    e. Olive oil: one gallon of olive oil (v.24).
2. The ingredients were to be mixed and blended into a holy anointing oil (v.25).
3. The end result would be a unique, special oil that would be used to anoint the Tabernacle and its priests (v.26-28). The oil was to be used to anoint...
    • the Tabernacle and its furnishings
    • the Ark of the Covenant
    • the Table and its utensils
    • the Lampstand and its accessories
    • the Altar of Incense
    • the Altar of Burnt Offering and its utensils
    • the wash basin with its stand

4. The purpose of the anointing oil was twofold.
    a. To sanctify the Tabernacle and its furnishings: that all be holy (v.29).
    b. To anoint the priests and sanctify them for the ministry (v.30).
5. The importance of the anointing oil was stressed (v.31-32). It was to be used as God's holy anointing oil and God's alone. It was never to be misused by pouring it on an ordinary person, someone not chosen and appointed by God. It was never to be misused by making it for one's own use. The anointing oil belonged to God and it was to be used for His purpose alone.
6. The stern warning was given: if the oil was ever misused, that person was to be cut off from the community (v.34).

Thought 1. The anointing is not man's to give. The anointing is God's. It is God who chooses, who calls, who appoints and gives His Holy Spirit. It is God who chooses to anoint and set apart both objects and people.
1) God does anoint things; He does set things apart for His service, set them apart as being needed for some very special purpose.

"And thou shalt offer every day a bullock *for* a sin offering for atonement: and thou shalt cleanse the altar, when thou hast made an atonement for it, and thou shalt anoint it, to sanctify it" (Ex.29:36).

"And thou shalt anoint the tabernacle of the congregation therewith, and the ark of the testimony" (Ex.30:26).

"And thou shalt anoint the altar of the burnt offering, and all his vessels, and sanctify the altar: and it shall be an altar most holy" (Ex.40:10).

"And he sprinkled thereof upon the altar seven times, and anointed the altar and all his vessels, both the laver and his foot, to sanctify them" (Lev.8:11).

"And it came to pass on the day that Moses had fully set up the tabernacle, and had anointed it, and sanctified it, and all the instruments thereof, both the altar and all the vessels thereof, and had anointed them, and sanctified them" (Num.7:1).

2) God does anoint people; He does call and appoint people, setting people apart to serve Him. God gives His Spirit to people, equipping them in a very special way for His service.

"And Moses took of the anointing oil, and of the blood which *was* upon the altar, and sprinkled *it* upon Aaron, *and* upon his garments, and upon his sons, and upon his sons' garments with him; and sanctified Aaron, *and* his garments, and his sons, and his sons' garments with him" (Lev.8:30).

"Then Samuel took a vial of oil, and poured *it* upon his head, and kissed him, and said, *Is it* not because the LORD hath anointed thee *to be* captain over his inheritance?" (1 Sam.10:1).

"Then Samuel took the horn of oil, and anointed him in the midst of his brethren: and the Spirit of the LORD came upon David from that day forward. So Samuel rose up, and went to Ramah" (1 Sam.16:13).

"And Zadok the priest took an horn of oil out of the tabernacle, and anointed Solomon. And they blew the trumpet; and all the people said, God save king Solomon" (1 Ki.1:39).

4 (30:34-38) **Tabernacle of Moses--Priesthood--Incense**: there was the sweet incense. The sweet incense was prepared for worshipping God and for no other purpose. The incense was to be burned on the Gold Altar of Incense and was to fill the Tabernacle with the most pleasing aroma that can be imagined. This symbolized the pleasure of God, that He was pleased to see the prayers of His people and that He accepted their prayers.
1. Note the instructions for making the incense.
   a. To gather sweet spices, the same amount of each (v.34). There were resin droplets, mollusk scent, galbanum, and pure frankincense.
   b. To blend and refine the spices using the techniques of a perfumer (v.35).
2. Note the importance of the incense.
   a. The incense was to be made a pure and holy incense (v.35).
   b. The incense was to be put in front of the Ark of the Covenant, the very place where God meets people (v.36). This symbolized the prayers of God's people, and prayer is very special and precious to God. Prayer is communion and fellowship with God. Therefore the sweet aroma of the incense was to ascend up right next to the presence of God, the Ark of God.
   c. The incense was to be counted most holy (v.36).
   d. The incense was to be distinctive, the only incense made this way. It was to be made exclusively for the Lord and to be treated as holy (v.37).
3. Note the warning given by God: any person who made an incense like this incense was to be judged, cut off, excommunicated from the group, exiled from the nation (v.38).

Thought 1. Picture the pleasing aroma of the incense rising up and filling the Tabernacle of worship. The incense with its pleasing aroma is a picture of...
   • the believer's prayers ascending up to God
   • God being pleased with the prayers of His people, receiving them, accepting and answering them

1) Remember God hearing the prayer of Gideon.

"And Gideon said unto God, Let not thine anger be hot against me, and I will speak but this once: let me prove, I pray thee, but this once with the fleece; let it now be dry only upon the fleece, and upon all the ground let there be dew. And God did so that night: for it was dry upon the fleece only, and there was dew on all the ground" (Judg.6:39-40).

2) Remember God hearing the prayer of Hannah.

"For this child I prayed; and the LORD hath given me my petition which I asked of him" (1 Sam.1:27).

3) Remember God hearing the prayer of Samuel.

"And Samuel took a sucking lamb, and offered it for a burnt offering wholly unto the LORD: and Samuel cried unto the LORD for Israel; and the LORD heard him. And as Samuel was offering up the burnt offering, the Philistines drew near to battle against Israel: but the LORD thundered with a great thunder on that day upon the Philistines, and discomfited them; and they were smitten before Israel" (1 Sam.7:9-10).

4) Remember God hearing the prayer of Solomon.

"**And the LORD said unto him, I have heard thy prayer and thy supplication, that thou hast made before me: I have hallowed this house, which thou hast built, to put my name there for ever; and mine eyes and mine heart shall be there perpetually**" **(1 Ki.9:3).**

5) Remember God hearing the prayer of Elijah.

"**Hear me, O LORD, hear me, that this people may know that thou art the LORD God, and that thou hast turned their heart back again. Then the fire of the LORD fell, and consumed the burnt sacrifice, and the wood, and the stones, and the dust, and licked up the water that was in the trench**" **(1 Ki.18:37-38).**

6) Remember God hearing the prayer of Hezekiah.

"**Now therefore, O LORD our God, I beseech thee, save thou us out of his hand, that all the kingdoms of the earth may know that thou art the LORD God, even thou only**" **(2 Ki.19:19).**

7) Remember God hearing the prayer of Jehoshaphat.

"**And it came to pass, when the captains of the chariots saw Jehoshaphat, that they said, It is the king of Israel. Therefore they compassed about him to fight: but Jehoshaphat cried out, and the LORD helped him; and God moved them to depart from him**" **(2 Chron.18:31).**

8) Remember God hearing the prayer of Ezra.

"**So we fasted and besought our God for this: and he was intreated of us**" **(Ezra 8:23).**

9) Remember God hearing the prayer of Zacharias, John the Baptist's father.

"**But the angel said unto him, Fear not, Zacharias: for thy prayer is heard; and thy wife Elisabeth shall bear thee a son, and thou shalt call his name John**" **(Lk.1:13).**

10) Remember God hearing the prayers of the disciples and early believers.

"**And when they had prayed, the place was shaken where they were assembled together; and they were all filled with the Holy Ghost, and they spake the word of God with boldness**" **(Acts 4:31).**

11) Remember God's promise to us all.

"**He shall call upon me, and I will answer him: I will be with him in trouble; I will deliver him, and honour him**" **(Ps.91:15).**
"**And it shall come to pass, that before they call, I will answer; and while they are yet speaking, I will hear**" **(Is.65:24).**

12) Remember God's promise to those who ask in the name of Christ.

"**Hitherto have ye asked nothing in my name: ask, and ye shall receive, that your joy may be full**" **(Jn.16:24).**

13) Remember God's promise to those who abide in Him.

"**If ye abide in me, and my words abide in you, ye shall ask what ye will, and it shall be done unto you**" **(Jn.15:7).**

14) Remember God's promise to those who persevere in prayer.

"**And I say unto you, Ask, and it shall be given you; seek, and ye shall find; knock, and it shall be opened unto you**" **(Lk.11:9).**

TYPES, SYMBOLS, AND PICTURES
(Exodus 30:11-38)

Historical Term	Type or Picture (Scriptural Basis for Each)	Life Application for Today's Believer	Biblical Application for Today's Believer
Silver (Ex.30:16)	*Silver is a symbol of redemption. The LORD literally required His people to pay "atonement money" (one fifth of an ounce of silver) to maintain the temple. This*	⇒ God has bought us, ransomed us, redeemed us through His Son, the Lord Jesus Christ. Now we are His people, God's very own pos-	"*For ye are bought with a price: therefore glorify God in your body, and in your spirit, which are God's*" *(1 Cor.6:20).* "*In whom we have re-*

Historical Term	Type or Picture (Scriptural Basis for Each)	Life Application for Today's Believer	Biblical Application for Today's Believer
	"atonement money" symbolizing the ransom paid for one's life. **"And thou shalt take the atonement money of the children of Israel, and shalt appoint it for the service of the tabernacle of the congregation; that it may be a memorial unto the children of Israel before the LORD, to make an atonement for your souls"** (Ex.30:16; cp.30:12-15).	session. The silver tax is a reminder to the believer: we owe *everything* to God. We are no longer our own. He has redeemed us through Christ; therefore, we belong to Him.	*demption through his blood, the forgiveness of sins, according to the riches of his grace" (Eph.1:7).* *"Giving thanks unto the Father, which hath made us meet to be partakers of the inheritance of the saints in light: Who hath delivered us from the power of darkness, and hath translated us into the kingdom of his dear Son: In whom we have redemption through his blood, even the forgiveness of sins" (Col.1:12-14).* *"Teaching us that, denying ungodliness and worldly lusts, we should live soberly, righteously, and godly, in this present world; Looking for that blessed hope, and the glorious appearing of the great God and our Saviour Jesus Christ; Who gave himself for us, that he might redeem us from all iniquity, and purify unto himself a peculiar people, zealous of good works" (Tit.2:12-14).* *"Forasmuch as ye know that ye were not redeemed with corruptible things, as silver and gold, from your vain conversation received by tradition from your fathers; But with the precious blood of Christ, as of a lamb without blemish and without spot: Who verily was foreordained before the foundation of the world, but was manifest in these last times for you, Who by him do believe in God, that raised him up from the dead, and gave him glory; that your faith and hope might be in God. Seeing ye have purified your souls in obeying the truth through the Spirit unto unfeigned love of the brethren, see that ye love one another with a pure heart fervently" (1 Pt.1:18-22).*
The Bronze Wash Basin (Ex.30:17-21; 38:8) See also Ex.35:16; 39:39; 40:7, 30-32	*The Bronze Wash Basin was placed just outside the Sanctuary for the purpose of cleansing. The priests used the Wash Basin to wash the blood, soot, and dirt from their hands and feet before they entered the Sanctuary and when they approached*	What the Wash Basin taught:	

Historical Term	Type or Picture (Scriptural Basis for Each)	Life Application for Today's Believer	Biblical Application for Today's Believer
	the Altar to make a sacrifice. a. The Bronze Wash Basin symbolized that a person must be cleansed before he can enter God's presence and before he can be saved.	a. The Wash Basin is a picture of our great need to be cleansed. A person *cannot enter* God's presence before he is cleansed and made pure. God cleanses us and forgives our sins through the blood of His Son, the Lord Jesus Christ, through His death and His death alone.	*"For all have sinned, and come short of the glory of God; Being justified freely by his grace through the redemption that is in Christ Jesus: Whom God hath set forth to be a propitiation through faith in his blood, to declare his righteousness for the remission of sins that are past, through the forbearance of God"* (Ro.3:23-25). *"Then Peter said unto them, Repent, and be baptized every one of you in the name of Jesus Christ for the remission of sins, and ye shall receive the gift of the Holy Ghost"* (Acts 2:38).
	b. The Bronze Wash Basin symbolized a person's need to be cleansed before he can serve God.	b. The shed blood of Christ allows the believer to effectively serve God. A person cannot serve God until he is cleansed and made pure; made a clean vessel.	*"Not by works of righteousness which we have done, but according to his mercy he saved us, by the washing of regeneration, and renewing of the Holy Ghost"* (Tit.3:5; cp. Tit.2:14). *"Flee fornication. Every sin that a man doeth is without the body; but he that committeth fornication sinneth against his own body"* (1 Cor.6:18).
	c. The Bronze Wash Basin symbolized a person's need to be cleansed as he continually served God. **"And the LORD spake unto Moses, saying, Thou shalt also make a laver of brass, and his foot also of brass, to wash withal: and thou shalt put it between the tabernacle of the congregation and the altar, and thou shalt put water therein"** (Ex.30:17). **"And he made the laver** *of* **brass, and the foot of it** *of* **brass, of the looking-glasses of** *the women* **assembling, which assembled** *at* **the door of the tabernacle of the congregation"** (Ex.38:8).	c. The blood of Jesus Christ continues to wash the believer from the corruption of daily sin. We need to be washed, cleansed, and purified with His cleansing blood in order to *continually serve* God.	*"How much more shall the blood of Christ, who through the eternal Spirit offered himself without spot to God, purge your conscience from dead works to serve the living God?"* (Heb.9:14). *"Draw nigh to God, and he will draw nigh to you. Cleanse your hands, ye sinners; and purify your hearts, ye double minded"* (Jas.4:8). *"If we confess our sins, he is faithful and just to forgive us our sins, and to cleanse us from all unrighteousness"* (1 Jn.1:9; cp. 1 Jn.3:2-3).

Historical Term	Type or Picture (Scriptural Basis for Each)	Life Application for Today's Believer	Biblical Application for Today's Believer
Anointing oil (Ex.30:23-33)	*Oil is a type of the Holy Spirit throughout Scripture. In this particular case, the anointing oil symbolized the special call and appointment of God, the anointing of the Holy Spirit, and His equipping of a person for the service of God.* **"Take thou also unto thee principal spices, of pure myrrh five hundred** *shekels,* **and of sweet cinnamon half so much,** *even* **two hundred and fifty** *shekels,* **and of sweet calamus two hundred and fifty** *shekels"* **(Ex.30:23).**	⇒ The anointing of the Holy Spirit for service comes from God. The anointing is not man's to give. It is God who chooses, who calls, who appoints, and who gives His Holy Spirit.	*"Now he which stablisheth us with you in Christ, and hath anointed us, is God"* (2 Cor.1:21). *"But ye have an unction [an anointing] from the Holy One, and ye know all things"* (1 Jn.2:20). *"But the anointing which ye have received of him abideth in you, and ye need not that any man teach you: but as the same anointing teacheth you of all things, and is truth, and is no lie, and even as it hath taught you, ye shall abide in him"* (1 Jn.2:27). *"It is the spirit that quickeneth; the flesh profiteth nothing: the words that I speak unto you, they are spirit, and they are life"* (Jn.6:63). *"Howbeit when he, the Spirit of truth, is come, he will guide you into all truth: for he shall not speak of himself; but whatsoever he shall hear, that shall he speak: and he will show you things to come"* (Jn.16:13). *"But ye shall receive power, after that the Holy Ghost is come upon you: and ye shall be witnesses unto me both in Jerusalem, and in all Judaea, and in Samaria, and unto the uttermost part of the earth"* (Acts 1:8). *"For as many as are led by the Spirit of God, they are the sons of God"* (Ro.8:14).
Incense for the Golden Altar of Incense (Ex.30:35-36)	*Incense possesses a unique quality that dissolves away all other odors. As the incense burned on the Golden Altar, the Tabernacle was filled with the most pleasing aroma that can be imagined. The incense symbolized the sweet fragrance of Christ before God and the pleasure and acceptance of God concerning the prayers of His people.* **"And thou shalt make it a perfume [incense], a confection after the art of the apothecary, tempered together, pure** *and* **holy: And thou shalt beat** *some* **of it very small, and put of**	⇒ The most pleasing aroma a believer can offer up to God is that of his prayers and that of placing his trust and hope in the saving grace of God, in the sacrifice of Jesus Christ. Like the incense that drifted continually up to God, our prayers should be constantly ascending up and pleasing God.	*"He shall call upon me, and I will answer him: I will be with him in trouble; I will deliver him, and honour him"* (Ps.91:15). *"And I say unto you, Ask, and it shall be given you; seek, and ye shall find; knock, and it shall be opened unto you"* (Lk.11:9). *"If ye abide in me, and my words abide in you, ye shall ask what ye will, and it shall be done unto you"* (Jn.15:7). *"Hitherto have ye asked nothing in my name: ask, and ye shall receive, that your joy may be full"* (Jn.16:24).

Historical Term	Type or Picture (Scriptural Basis for Each)	Life Application for Today's Believer	Biblical Application for Today's Believer
	it before the testimony in the tabernacle of the congregation, where I will meet with thee: it shall be unto you most holy" (Ex.30:35-36).		*"Praying always with all prayer and supplication in the Spirit, and watching thereunto with all perseverance and supplication for all saints" (Eph. 6:18).* *"Pray without ceasing" (1 Th.5:17).*

The Bronze Wash Basin

K. Other Instructions For the Tabernacle: Three Great Charges Given to Man, Ex.31:1-18

1. The charge to build the Tabernacle: The appointmet of craftsmen

a. The superintendent: Bezalel
   1) His call: Chosen by God
   2) His heritage
   3) His equipping by God
      • Filled with God's Spirit
      • Given skill & ability
      • Given knowledge in crafts
   4) His skill & ability
      • To work in metal
      • To work in setting stone
      • To work in woodwork
      • To work in many crafts

b. The assistant superintendent: Oholiab:
   1) His heritage
   2) His equipping by God

c. The equipping of other craftsmen by God: Given skill to make everything
   1) The Tabernacle
   2) The Ark of the Covenant & the Mercy Seat
   3) The other furnishings
   4) The table & its utensils
   5) The gold Lampstand
   6) The Altar of Incense
   7) The altar of burnt offering & its utensils
   8) The basin & stand
   9) The beautifully stitched, holy garments for the pries

And the LORD spake unto Moses, saying,
2 See, I have called by name Bezaleel the son of Uri, the son of Hur, of the tribe of Judah:
3 And I have filled him with the spirit of God, in wisdom, and in understanding, and in knowledge, and in all manner of workmanship,
4 To devise cunning works, to work in gold, and in silver, and in brass,
5 And in cutting of stones, to set them, and in carving of timber, to work in all manner of workmanship.
6 And I, behold, I have given with him Aholiab, the son of Ahisamach, of the tribe of Dan: and in the hearts of all that are wise hearted I have put wisdom, that they may make all that I have commanded thee;
7 The tabernacle of the congregation, and the ark of the testimony, and the mercy seat that is thereupon, and all the furniture of the tabernacle,
8 And the table and his furniture, and the pure candlestick with all his furniture, and the altar of incense,
9 And the altar of burnt offering with all his furniture, and the laver and his foot,
10 And the cloths of service, and the holy garments for Aaron the priest, and the garments of his sons, to minister in the priest's office,
11 And the anointing oil, and sweet incense for the holy place: according to all that I have commanded thee shall they do.
12 And the LORD spake unto Moses, saying,
13 Speak thou also unto the children of Israel, saying, Verily my sabbaths ye shall keep: for it is a sign between me and you throughout your generations; that ye may know that I am the LORD that doth sanctify you.
14 Ye shall keep the sabbath therefore; for it is holy unto you: every one that defileth it shall surely be put to death: for whosoever doeth any work therein, that soul shall be cut off from among his people.
15 Six days may work be done; but in the seventh is the sabbath of rest, holy to the LORD: whosoever doeth any work in the sabbath day, he shall surely be put to death.
16 Wherefore the children of Israel shall keep the sabbath, to observe the sabbath throughout their generations, for a perpetual covenant.
17 It is a sign between me and the children of Israel for ever: for in six days the LORD made heaven and earth, and on the seventh day he rested, and was refreshed.
18 And he gave unto Moses, when he had made an end of communing with him upon mount Sinai, two tables of testimony, tables of stone, written with the finger of God.

   10) The anointing oil
   11) The special incense
d. The purpose & warning of God: To make everything just as God commanded

2. The charge to keep the Sabbath day

a. The commandment: Must keep while working on the Tabernacle
   1) Because it is a sign of the covenant between God & man forever
   2) Because it reminds man that God is the LORD: The One who makes us holy, sets us apart

b. The warning
   1) To be observed, kept holy
   2) To be judged if violated
      • To be executed if desecrate the Sabbath
      • To be cut off if work on the Sabbath

c. The importance to God
   1) Man has been given 6 days to work & one day to rest
   2) The Sabbath is counted holy by God
   3) If defiled, to be executed

d. The commandment is a perpetual covenant
   1) A sign between God & His people (Israel) forever
   2) The reason: Because God worked--He created heaven & earth in six days, but He rested on the Sabbath day

3. The charge to keep the 10 com.

a. The great gift of God to man: The two tablets of God's testimony, the 10 commandments
b. Their extreme value: Written by the finger of God Himself

DIVISION IX

THE TABERNACLE, ITS BLUEPRINT AND PRIESTHOOD: THE TRUE WAY TO APPROACH AND WORSHIP GOD, EX.25:1-31:18

K.   Other Instructions For the Tabernacle: Three Great Charges Given to Man, Ex.31:1-18

(31:1-18) **Introduction**: the heart-cry of every human being is for purpose, meaning, and significance in life. All over the world, people are asking questions such as:
   ⇒ "What am I living for?"
   ⇒ "What is the sense of all this?"
   ⇒ "Am I making a difference?"
Far too often, the questions are quickly answered by feelings of emptiness and loneliness, a sense of helplessness, disappointment, depression, even despair and hopelessness. People find themselves trapped in an endless cycle of futility and emptiness. They live a life where nothing lasts, not for long. And tragically, in far too many lives, when the winds of time blow across their graves, nothing lasting will be found.

This is not so for the Christian believer who follows God, who takes the great charges of God and obeys them. It is the charges of God and obedience to them that brings purpose, meaning, and significance...

- to the rich and the poor
- to the educated and the uneducated
- to the profound and the simple
- to the weak and the strong
- to the sick and the healthy

God's great charges stir us to serve God, and when we serve God, we experience a deep, rich fulfillment. When we serve God, God gives us...

- a deep sense of satisfaction and completion
- a deep sense of purpose, meaning, and significance
- a deep sense of assurance and security, the assurance and security of being His, of being loved by God and of living forever

This is the picture of this present Scripture: *Other Instructions For the Tabernacle: Three Great Charges Given to Man*, Ex.31:1-18.
1. The charge to build the Tabernacle: the appointmet of craftsmen (v.1-11).
2. The charge to keep the Sabbath day (v.12-17).
3. The charge to keep the 10 commandments (v.18).

1 (31:1-11) **Tabernacle--Construction--Bezalel--Uri--Hur--Holy Spirit--Equipping--Skill--Ability--Oholiab--Dan, Tribe of--Judah, Tribe of--Craftsmen**: there was the appointment of craftsmen, the people who were charged to build the Tabernacle and all of its furnishings. Remember, God had just finished giving Moses the blueprint, the pattern for the Tabernacle's design. The Tabernacle's blueprints were waiting for the construction superintendent to be appointed, waiting for God to appoint the man He wanted to build the Tabernacle. This is the story of what happens when God calls a man to serve Him.
1. The man appointed superintendent was Bezalel. Who was Bezalel, the man appointed to oversee the construction of the Tabernacle of God, the very place where God Himself was to dwell among His people? Who was given such a privilege as this?
Bezalel had been born in slavery, raised in Egypt as a slave. He had obviously grown up toiling and laboring long, hard days, even to the point of utter exhaustion. He had known the hardness, the cruelty, and the savagery of slavery. But through it all, he had apparently learned trade after trade and skill after skill. He had obviously been a slave to several Egyptian craftsmen and businessmen and learned the crafts well. Note what Scripture says about Bezalel.
   a. God Himself appointed Bezalel to be superintendent of the construction. The name Bezalel means "under the shadow of God," under God's protection and guidance. The picture is graphic: God had been protecting and guiding Bezalel throughout his life as an Egyptian slave...
      - protecting him from serious harm
      - guiding and preparing him, making sure he learned the skills necessary to serve God in the future--the skills necessary to build the Tabernacle of God

The point to see is that God Himself actually chose and appointed the man who was to serve Him as superintendent of the Tabernacle. The Hebrew actually says that God called "him by name." God knew Bezalel, knew Him personally, knew His name.

Thought 1. When God calls a person to service, He always calls the person by *name*. God's appointment is a *personal* call, an appointment that is always framed in God's love for His dear people. God knew that Bezalel was His man for the job before the foundation of the earth. God knew Bezalel even when he was still in his mother's womb. The God of the universe, the Creator of all things, knew Bezalel *personally*. The call of God is not an impersonal, bureaucratic, faceless procedure. The call of God goes right to the heart of the man, setting him apart to serve God's dear people.

"O LORD, thou hast searched me, and known *me*. Thou knowest my downsitting and mine uprising, thou understandest my thought afar off. Thou compassest my path and my lying down, and art acquainted *with* all my ways. For *there is* not a word in my tongue, *but*, lo, O LORD, thou knowest it altogether. Thou hast beset me behind and before, and laid thine hand upon me" (Ps.139:1-5).
"But now thus saith the LORD that created thee, O Jacob, and he that formed thee, O Israel, Fear not: for I have redeemed thee, I have called thee <u>by thy name</u>; thou art mine" (Is.43:1).
"Then the word of the LORD came unto me, saying, Before I formed thee in the belly I knew thee; and before thou camest forth out of the womb I sanctified thee, *and* I ordained thee a prophet unto the nations" (Jer.1:4-5).
"He that dwelleth in the secret place of the most High shall abide under the shadow of the Almighty. I will say of the LORD, He is my refuge and my fortress: my God; in him will I trust" (Ps.91:1-2).
"Ye have not chosen me, but I have chosen you, and ordained you, that ye should go and bring forth fruit, and [that] your fruit should remain: that whatsoever ye shall ask of the Father in my name, he may give it you" (Jn.15:16).

b. Note the godly heritage, the godly upbringing of Bezalel (v.2). His godly heritage is suggested by three facts.
⇒ His father's name was Uri which means *light*. The word *light* always refers to positive facts: the light of knowledge, understanding, wisdom, sight, or the light of God. Being descendants of Abraham, they knew about the great promises of God, the promise of the promised land and the promise of the promised seed, the Savior and Messiah of the world. Therefore, Uri was probably given his name because of the hope for the light and promises of God.
⇒ His grandfather's name was Hur which means *free*. This obviously refers to the hope of being freed from Egyptian slavery, being freed to journey to the promised land of God.
⇒ His tribe was the tribe of Judah which means *praise*. This refers to the praise due God. Judah led the way when the Tabernacle was moved from campsite to campsite.

Thought 1. A godly heritage can never be overstressed. Children and adults alike need godly parents and grand-parents. We all need a godly heritage. And we need to be godly parents if we have children. We all need to build a godly heritage for our families and for the earth.

"For thou, O God, hast heard my vows: thou hast given me the heritage of those that fear thy name" (Ps.61:5).
"Thy word have I hid in mine heart, that I might not sin against thee" (Ps.119:11).
"And now, brethren, I commend you to God, and to the word of his grace, which is able to build you up, and to give you an inheritance [a godly heritage] among all them which are sanctified" (Acts 20:32).
"To open their eyes, and to turn them from darkness to light, and from the power of Satan unto God, that they may receive forgiveness of sins, and inheritance [a godly heritage] among them which are sanctified by faith that is in me" (Acts 26:18).
"Giving thanks unto the Father, which hath made us meet to be partakers of the inheritance [a godly heritage] of the saints in light" (Col.1:12).

c. Note the equipping of Bezalel: he was filled with God's Spirit (v.3). When God calls a person to service, the person is not left by himself to do the work. God fills the person with His Spirit, and the Holy Spirit equips the person. In Bezalel's case, he was...
• given special skill and ability
• given special knowledge in all kinds of crafts
d. His skill and ability were to work in several areas (v.4-5). He was equipped...
• to design and work in metals: gold, silver, and bronze
• to design and work in cutting and setting stones
• to design and work in woodwork
• to design and work in many crafts

Thought 1. When God calls a person, He equips the person to serve Him. The person is not left to himself, not left to do the work of God in his own strength. God fills him with the Holy Spirit and gives the person whatever skill and abilities are needed to do the work.

"And unto one he gave five talents, to another two, and to another one; to every man according to his several ability; and straightway took his journey" (Mt.25:15).
"Having then gifts differing according to the grace that is given to us, whether prophecy, let us prophesy according to the proportion of faith; Or ministry, let us wait on our ministering: or he that teacheth, on teaching; Or he that exhorteth, on exhortation: he that giveth, let him do it with simplicity; he that ruleth, with diligence; he that showeth mercy, with cheerfulness" (Ro.12:6-8).
"Now there are diversities of gifts, but the same Spirit. And there are differences of administrations, but the same Lord. And there are diversities of operations, but it is the same God which worketh all in all" (1 Cor.12:4-6).
"And he gave some, apostles; and some, prophets; and some, evangelists; and some, pastors and teachers; For the perfecting of the saints, for the work of the ministry, for the edifying of the body of Christ" (Eph.4:11-12).

2. The man appointed to be the assistant superintendent was Oholiab (v.6). His name means either "tent of the father" or "the (divine) father is my tent."[1] Note the suggestion: God had been covering, protecting, and looking after Oholiab just like He had Bezalel. God had been preparing him for future service.
a. Oholiab was from the tribe of Dan (v.6). Throughout Scripture, the citizens of Dan are seen to be a rough, rude, war-like people. Some generations later, Hiram, the chief craftsman for the ornamental work on Solomon's temple, was to be from the tribe of Dan (2 Chron.2:14). The nature of both men seems to be anything other than artistic. Oholiab definitely goes against the grain of his heritage and stands out as an artist who can be used mightily by God. The point is just this: both men show how a person can go against the grain of his heritage and stand out as a strong, gifted servant of God and society.

---
[1] Frank E. Gaebelein. *The Expositor's Bible Commentary*, Vol.2, p.475.

b. Note that God called Oholiab and equipped him for his work. He equipped him to be the helper, the assistant superintendent, in building the Tabernacle of God, the very place where God was to dwell among His people.

3. The other craftsmen were also equipped by God, given the skill to make everything (v.6-11). They were appointed to work under the direct supervision of Bezalel and Oholiab. The building of the Tabernacle was to be Israel's most important construction project; therefore, it would take workmen who were willing to follow the leadership of Bezalel and Oholiab. When God's people come together and work it must be done according to the design of God and in complete unity. As a result of their commitment to the LORD and to His blueprint, the Tabernacle would soon be built. This great task included...

- the Tabernacle
- the Ark of the Covenant and the Mercy Seat
- the other furnishings
- the Table and its utensils
- the gold Lampstand
- the Altar of Incense
- the Altar of Burnt Offering and its utensils
- the basin and stand
- the beautifully stitched, holy garments for the priests
- the anointing oil and the the special incense

4. There was the purpose and warning of God: to make everything just as God had commanded (v.11). God had left nothing to chance, nothing that could be misunderstood. God had called together a group of craftsmen who had to place their own pride aside and do things God's way. The blueprint was now complete: any changes--any additions or deletions from God's Master Plan--were forbidden. God did not call these men into service for their own wisdom and worldly ingenuity. He called these men to do exactly what He had called and prepared them to do: build the Tabernacle of God according to the design that was shown to Moses.

Thought 1. The warning of God is clear: we are to live just as He says, obey His commandments, His Word. We must not try to add to nor take away from His commandments. Yet so many of us do. We add our reasoning to what God says by rationalizing and asking questions such as:

⇒ Does God really want me to forgive someone who has hurt me so deeply and caused so much pain and suffering?

"**And when ye stand praying, forgive, if ye have ought against any: that your Father also which is in heaven may forgive you your trespasses. But if ye do not forgive, neither will your Father which is in heaven forgive your trespasses**" (Mk.11:24-26).

⇒ Is Jesus Christ really the true way to heaven? The only way?

"**Jesus saith unto him, I am the way, the truth, and the life: no man cometh unto the Father, but by me**" (Jn.14:6).

⇒ Does God really want me to deny myself, my rights, my own ideas and personal agenda?

"**But seek ye first the kingdom of God, and his righteousness; and all these things shall be added unto you**" (Mt.6:33).
"**And he said to** them **all, If any** man **will come after me, let him deny himself, and take up his cross daily, and follow me. For whosoever will save his life shall lose it: but whosoever will lose his life for my sake, the same shall save it. For what is a man advantaged, if he gain the whole world, and lose himself, or be cast away?**" (Lk.9:23-25).

⇒ Does God really want my money? When I am so far in debt, does God really expect me to tithe?

"**Bring ye all the tithes into the storehouse, that there may be meat in mine house, and prove me now herewith, saith the LORD of hosts, if I will not open you the windows of heaven, and pour you out a blessing, that** there shall **not** be room **enough** to receive it" (Mal.3:10).

⇒ Does God really mean what He says? Are His commandments, His Word, really that important?

"**For I testify unto every man that heareth the words of the prophecy of this book, If any man shall add unto these things, God shall add unto him the plagues that are written in this book: And if any man shall take away from the words of the book of this prophecy, God shall take away his part out of the book of life, and out of the holy city, and** from **the things which are written in this book**" (Rev.22:18-19).

2 (31:12-17) **Sabbath--Covenant--Tabernacle, The--Sign--Obedience**: there were the charges to keep the Sabbath day.
In the beginning stages of this ambitious construction project, the people were excited, very excited. They were so excited that they were obviously ready to work around the clock, seven days a week. But note carefully God's instructions to Moses.

1. The commandment to keep the Sabbath had to be kept while everyone was working on the Tabernacle (v.13). Why did God require His people to *slow down* the production schedule in order to keep the Sabbath?

    a. They were to keep the Sabbath because the Sabbath is a sign of the covenant between God and man, a perpetual sign of the covenant. This is important to note: God is here establishing the Sabbath as a sign of the covenant between Himself and man. Keeping the Sabbath is one of the Ten Commandments; therefore if a person keeps the Sabbath--actually sets a whole day aside for God and rest--he will most likely be seeking to obey God in all the other commandments. The importance of the Sabbath is seen in these facts:

      ⇒ The Sabbath day had been set aside as a day for rest and worship since creation. (See outline and notes--Gen.2:1-3 for more discussion.)

      ⇒ The Sabbath day was given as a law to the nation of Israel before any other law (Ex.16:23).

      ⇒ The Sabbath day was given as one of the Ten Commandments, a part of the moral law of God (see outline and notes--Ex.20:8-11 for more discussion).

      ⇒ The Sabbath day was even given as one of the civil and judicial laws of Israel (see outline and notes--Ex.23:10-12 for more discussion).

      ⇒ The Sabbath day is here made a part of the religious and ceremonial law of Israel. Moreover, it is set up as the very sign of the covenant between God and His people, the sign that declares the very special relationship between God and those who follow and obey Him.

    It is easy for people to forget the special relationship between God and His people. The Sabbath is to be a constant reminder that man and God have a very unique relationship, a relationship that must not be taken for granted, a relationship that must be cultivated and treasured. The Sabbath day has been given by God to help keep the relationship (covenant) between Himself and man alive.

    b. They were to keep the Sabbath because it reminds man that God is the LORD, the only living and true God, the One who makes us holy, who sets us apart to be His people and to live pure and righteous lives. By keeping the Sabbath, it would be a keen reminder that the One who revealed the blueprints for the Tabernacle was the One who was to be worshipped and loved. A day was to be set aside that would be devoted to focusing upon the LORD and His great call to us, that we are to be His holy people, set apart to live pure and righteous lives and to inherit the promised land of God.

2. Note that God gave a warning, a warning to keep this commandment (v.14).

    a. It was to be observed and kept holy. "Holy" means set apart, sanctified, consecrated, kept pure and righteous. The Sabbath day is to be set apart as a very special day, as the day belonging to God and man, a day for the worship of God and for the rest and relaxation of man.

    b. The person who violated this commandment was to be judged harshly.

      ⇒ He was to be executed if the Sabbath was desecrated, that is, if he did any evil thing on the Sabbath or refused to honor and keep the Sabbath.

      ⇒ If he worked on the Sabbath, he was to be cut off from his people, cut off from fellowshipping and living among the people of God.

3. The Sabbath is important to God (v.15). He has given man six days to work and one day to rest. The Sabbath is counted holy by God. If any man defiled the Sabbath, he was to be executed. This seems a bit harsh when viewed through the eyes of modern man. Why is God so serious about the Sabbath? God is serious about the Sabbath because it is holy to God. The God who lives above space and time knows several facts:

    ⇒ God knows that man needs both work and rest, that man needs to work six days a week, but he needs--absolutely needs--to rest on the Sabbath day.

    ⇒ God knows that man needs both work and worship, that man needs to sense purpose and meaning in his life and work, that purpose and meaning are found in God and in God alone, in knowing that one is working and living for a higher cause than just for what this world offers. Man needs to know that he serves the LORD God Himself and that he is going to be rewarded with the promised land of God.

    ⇒ God knows that man will most likely keep the other laws if he keeps the Sabbath day. Why? If man obeys God by setting aside a whole day for true worship and rest, committing to God one full day out of every seven, he will most likely seek to obey God in all things.

    The converse is also true and the point is most graphic: if the Sabbath day is not kept, and if people thereby will break all the laws of God, society crumbles. And no society can survive, not for long, not apart from God. This is the reason for the strict penalty against the violators of the Sabbath day.

4. Note that the commandment is a perpetual covenant (v.16-17). The Sabbath was to be sign between God and His people forever. Why was this a perpetual covenant? Because God worked and created heaven and earth in six days, but He rested on the Sabbath day. The commandment to keep the Sabbath day stretches from the creation to the end of the world, covering all people of all generations.

    Thought 1. The Sabbath day was not to be a temporary commandment made for Israel alone. It was to be a continuous, perpetual commandment. The Sabbath day was made for all generations of men, made for every man, woman, and child upon earth.

    "And he said unto them, The Sabbath was made for man, and not man for the Sabbath" (Mk.2:27).

    "For in six days the LORD made heaven and earth, the sea, and all that in them is, and rested the seventh day: wherefore the LORD blessed the Sabbath day, and hallowed it [for all people]" (Ex.20:11).

Thought 2. When businesses have to operate seven days a week, what are the employees of these businesses to do about worship and rest? Two very practical things must be done throughout the remaining generations of history:

⇒ The church must provide other services throughout the week for worship and rest, provide them for people who have to work Saturday or Sunday.

⇒ People who work on the regular day of worship and rest must still worship God and rest at the alternate services and days scheduled by the church.

"Not forsaking the assembling of ourselves together, as the manner of some is; but exhorting one another: and so much the more, as ye see the day approaching" (Heb.10:25).

"And he came to Nazareth, where he had been brought up: and, as <u>his custom</u> was, he went into the synagogue on the sabbath day, and stood up for to read" (Lk.4:16).

"But when they departed from Perga, they came to Antioch in Pisidia, and went into the synagogue on the sabbath day, and sat down" (Acts 13:14).

3 (31:18) <u>Tabernacle of Moses--Commandments, The Ten</u>: there was the charge to keep the Ten Commandments. God gave a great gift to man: the two tablets of God's testimony, the Ten Commandments themselves. The very foundation of God's law was given to Moses, the great Lawgiver of Israel. The value of these tables was *priceless*. They were conceived by God, written by the finger of God, crafted by God, and transmitted by God to His people. The mention of these tablets at this time of the Tabernacle's blueprints is a graphic reminder, a reminder that God cannot be worshipped if God's law and Word are not close at hand.

Thought 1. Man is to obey God's great gift, His commandments and His Word. We are to live righteous and pure lives, bearing witness that God does save and does lead people to the promised land of heaven.

"But the hour cometh, and now is, when the true worshippers shall worship the Father in spirit and in truth: for the Father seeketh such to worship him. God *is* a Spirit: and they that worship him must worship *him* <u>in spirit</u> and <u>in truth</u>" (Jn.4:23-24).

"Sanctify them through thy truth: thy word is truth" (Jn.17:17).

"Search the scriptures; for in them ye think ye have eternal life: and they are they which testify of me" (Jn.5:39).

"He that hath my commandments, and keepeth them, he it is that loveth me: and he that loveth me shall be loved of my Father, and I will love him, and will manifest myself to him" (Jn.14:21).

"If ye keep my commandments, ye shall abide in my love; even as I have kept my Father's commandments, and abide in his love" (Jn.15:10).

"These were more noble than those in Thessalonica, in that they received the word with all readiness of mind, and searched the scriptures daily, whether those things were so" (Acts 17:11).

"All scripture is given by inspiration of God, and is profitable for doctrine, for reproof, for correction, for instruction in righteousness" (2 Tim.3:16).

DIVISION X

THE GOLDEN CALF AND MOSES' GREAT INTERCESSION: THE BREAKING AND RENEWAL OF THE COVENANT BETWEEN GOD AND ISRAEL, 32:1-34:35

(32:1-34:35) **DIVISION OVERVIEW--Israel--Nation, Founding of--Covenant, Broken**: If a people were ever to experience a high moment, this was the perfect moment. Never before had a people been so privileged as Israel. Never before had God so blessed a people. Just imagine a people who had recently experienced so much:

⇒ The Israelites had just been liberated, set free after 400 years of slavery.
⇒ Their nation was being born, the nation of Israel. They were soon to be given a homeland, their very own country, the land of Canaan that is known today as Palestine.
⇒ Moreover, and just as important as any of the above events, the Israelites had been chosen by God to be His followers, the people of God.

They had been chosen to be God's witnesses to the other nations of the earth, witnessing that there is only One true and living God. In fact, at this very moment Moses was up on Mount Sinai receiving the civil and religious laws of God, the very laws that were to form them into a nation and govern them as a people. We know from the preceding chapters (Ex.19-31) that God had just completed giving Moses the Ten Commandments, the civil and religious laws, and the instructions for constructing the Tabernacle, the place where God's very own presence was to dwell in a very special way upon earth. Moses was almost ready to come down from the mountain and share all with the people, forming them into a nation ruled by law, the laws that had actually been given by God Himself. The people were about ready to be formed into the great nation of Israel and begin their final march to the promised land, the land that was to become their homeland. This should have been one of the most joyful, celebrated, momentous occasions in the history of Israel.

But abruptly, a catastrophic tragedy struck. A sad, terrible, and shocking thing happened. The people broke their covenant with God: just when one of the greatest blessings in their lives was about to take place, the people broke their promise and commitment to God. The Israelites turned away from God: they lost their faith and trust in Him, denied, rejected, and rebelled against Him. Instead of trusting God and waiting upon Him, the people chose to take matters into their own hands, do their own thing, and go their own way. They gave up on Moses and decided to strike out on their own for the promised land. They turned away from trusting God for guidance and decided to trust their own wisdom and the gods of their own imaginations. This is the story of the next three chapters, the sad, terrible tragedy of the golden calf.

DIVISION X

THE GOLDEN CALF AND MOSES' GREAT INTERCESSION: THE BREAKING AND RENEWAL OF THE COVENANT BETWEEN GOD AND ISRAEL, 32:1-34:35

A. The Golden Calf--The Breaking of the Covenant Between God and Man : A Picture of Man's Corrupt Heart and Rebellion Against God, Ex.32:1-35
B. The Threat of Separation From God and Moses' Great Intercession: The Essentials for Repentance and Renewal After Sinning, Ex.33:1-23
C. The Renewal of the Covenant Between God and Man: The Steps to Renewal, Ex.34:1-35

X. THE GOLDEN CALF & MOSES' GREAT INTERCESSION: THE BREAKING & RENEWAL OF THE COVENANT BETWEEN GOD & ISRAEL, Ex.32:1-34:35

A. The Golden Calf--The Breaking of the Covenant Between God & Man: A Picture of Man's Corrupt Heart & Rebellion Against God, Ex.32:1-35

1. The causes of terrible sin
a. Caused by impatience: Tired of waiting for the promised land
b. Caused by pressure from a crowd
c. Caused by suggesting evil to a weak leader
d. Caused by disobeying God's commandments
e. Caused by believing that deliverance is of man not of God
f. Caused by believing in false gods
g. Caused by giving in to or fearing the crowd: Aaron made an idol

   1) He made it from the gold of the people's earrings

   2) He molded it into the shape of a golden calf
   3) He presented it to the people as their god: They proclaimed it to be the god who had saved & delivered them
h. Caused by false worship: Aaron built an altar in honor of the LORD
   1) He built an altar before the golden calf
   2) He planned a dedication to the LORD
   3) The people offered sacrifices to God
i. Caused by indulging in food, drink, partying, & illicit sex
2. The great intercession for terrible sinners
a. God saw the terrible sin & was very angry
   1) Told Moses to go to his people: God was disowning them
   2) Charged the people...
    • With being corrupt
    • With being quick to turn away from His commandments

And when the people saw that Moses delayed to come down out of the mount, the people gathered themselves together unto Aaron, and said unto him, Up, make us gods, which shall go before us; for as for this Moses, the man that brought us up out of the land of Egypt, we wot not what is become of him.
2 And Aaron said unto them, Break off the golden earrings, which are in the ears of your wives, of your sons, and of your daughters, and bring them unto me.
3 And all the people brake off the golden earrings which were in their ears, and brought them unto Aaron.
4 And he received them at their hand, and fashioned it with a graving tool, after he had made it a molten calf: and they said, These be thy gods, O Israel, which brought thee up out of the land of Egypt.
5 And when Aaron saw it, he built an altar before it; and Aaron made proclamation, and said, To morrow is a feast to the LORD.
6 And they rose up early on the morrow, and offered burnt offerings, and brought peace offerings; and the people sat down to eat and to drink, and rose up to play.
7 And the LORD said unto Moses, Go, get thee down; for thy people, which thou broughtest out of the land of Egypt, have corrupted themselves:
8 They have turned aside quickly out of the way which I commanded them: they have made them a molten calf, and have worshipped it, and have sacrificed thereunto, and said, These be thy

gods, O Israel, which have brought thee up out of the land of Egypt.
9 And the LORD said unto Moses, I have seen this people, and, behold, it is a stiff-necked people:
10 Now therefore let me alone, that my wrath may wax hot against them, and that I may consume them: and I will make of thee a great nation.
11 And Moses besought the LORD his God, and said, LORD, why doth thy wrath wax hot against thy people, which thou hast brought forth out of the land of Egypt with great power, and with a mighty hand?
12 Wherefore should the Egyptians speak, and say, For mischief did he bring them out, to slay them in the mountains, and to consume them from the face of the earth? Turn from thy fierce wrath, and repent of this evil against thy people.
13 Remember Abraham, Isaac, and Israel, thy servants, to whom thou swarest by thine own self, and saidst unto them, I will multiply your seed as the stars of heaven, and all this land that I have spoken of will I give unto your seed, and they shall inherit it for ever.
14 And the LORD repented of the evil which he thought to do unto his people.
15 And Moses turned, and went down from the mount, and the two tables of the testimony were in his hand: the tables were written on both their sides; on the one side and on the other were they written.
16 And the tables were the work of God, and the writing was the writing of God, graven upon the tables.
17 And when Joshua heard the noise of the people as they shouted, he said unto Moses, There is a noise of war in the camp.
18 And he said, It is not the voice of them that shout for mastery, neither is it the voice of them that cry for being overcome: but the noise of them that sing do I hear.
19 And it came to pass, as soon as he came nigh unto

   • With false worship
   • With proclaiming that salvation & deliverance are found in others
   • With being a stubborn, rebellious people

b. God threatened judgment
   1) To destroy them
   2) To fulfill His covenant promise to Abraham in a different way: Through Moses' descendants not Abraham's
c. The strong intercession of God's servant, Moses: Made four pleas
   1) For God to remember that He had saved & delivered His people: He had a special relationship with them, a covenant relationship
   2) For God to preserve His honor & trust in the eyes of the world, to keep His name from being falsely charged with evil
   3) For God to turn from His fierce anger & not destroy His people

   4) For God to remember His great promises (given to the ancient Patriarchs: Abraham, Isaac, & Jacob)
    • That He would cause believers to number as the stars
    • That He would give believers the promised land forever
   5) The result of the intercession: God withdrew His threat of annihilation
3. The righteous anger against terrible sin
a. Moses turned & went down the mountain: Carried the two tablets of God's testimony (the Ten Commandments)
   1) Written on both sides
   2) Written by God (cp. 31:18; 34:28)

b. The noise of the revelry: Was so loud it could be heard up on the mountain
   1) Joshua thought it was war cries
   2) Moses simply stated that it was the noise of singing & partying

c. The sight of the wickedness, of seeing the false worship &

partying: Hotly angered Moses 1) He cast the tablets down & broke them 2) He burned the golden calf • Ground it to powder • Scattered it on the water • Made the people drink the water **4. The shameful excuses of terrible sin** a. Moses confronted Aaron: Asked him to explain b. Aaron's four excuses: He blamed the people & Moses 1) He accused the people of being set, prone to do evil 2) He accused the people of forcing him to sin & commit the evil 3) He accused Moses of being gone too long 4) He suggested a miracle had happened in molding the golden calf or more likely he was mocking Moses, rebelling against his leadership **5. The righteous judgment of terrible sin** a. Moses saw that the people had cast off all restraint, were running wild, out of control: Were a joke to their enemies b. Moses challenged the people: Take a stand for the LORD 1) Join him 2) The Levites rallied to him c. Moses declared the judgment God had pronounced: Execution of the guilty	the camp, that he saw the calf, and the dancing: and Moses' anger waxed hot, and he cast the tables out of his hands, and brake them beneath the mount. 20 And he took the calf which they had made, and burnt it in the fire, and ground it to powder, and strawed it upon the water, and made the children of Israel drink of it. 21 And Moses said unto Aaron, What did this people unto thee, that thou hast brought so great a sin upon them? 22 And Aaron said, Let not the anger of my lord wax hot: thou knowest the people, that they are set on mischief. 23 For they said unto me, Make us gods, which shall go before us: for as for this Moses, the man that brought us up out of the land of Egypt, we wot not what is become of him. 24 And I said unto them, Whosoever hath any gold, let them break it off. So they gave it me: then I cast it into the fire, and there came out this calf. 25 And when Moses saw that the people were naked; (for Aaron had made them naked unto their shame among their enemies:) 26 Then Moses stood in the gate of the camp, and said, Who is on the LORD'S side? let him come unto me. And all the sons of Levi gathered themselves together unto him. 27 And he said unto them, Thus saith the LORD God of Israel, Put every man his sword by his side, and go in and out from gate to gate throughout the camp, and slay every man his brother, and every man his companion, and every man his neighbour. 28 And the children of Levi did according to the word of Moses: and there fell of the people that day about three thousand men. 29 For Moses had said, Consecrate yourselves to day to the LORD, even every man upon his son, and upon his brother; that he may bestow upon you a blessing this day. 30 And it came to pass on the morrow, that Moses said unto the people, Ye have sinned a great sin: and now I will go up unto the LORD; peradventure I shall make an atonement for your sin. 31 And Moses returned unto the LORD, and said, Oh, this people have sinned a great sin, and have made them gods of gold. 32 Yet now, if thou wilt forgive their sin-; and if not, blot me, I pray thee, out of thy book which thou hast written. 33 And the LORD said unto Moses, Whosoever hath sinned against me, him will I blot out of my book. 34 Therefore now go, lead the people unto the place of which I have spoken unto thee: behold, mine Angel shall go before thee: nevertheless in the day when I visit I will visit their sin upon them. 35 And the LORD plagued the people, because they made the calf, which Aaron made.	1) Called upon the Levites to arm themselves 2) Called upon them to execute every evil person: Even their own family members 3) The Levites obeyed: Executed 3000 evil people d. Moses declared that the obedience of the Levites had set them apart to the LORD, for His service **6. The just plea for forgiveness of terrible sin** a. The guilt of all the people: The innocent had failed to stop the rebellious crowd b. The need: Atonement for sin c. The intercession of Moses 1) Confessed the sin of the people 2) Pleaded for forgiveness of their sin 3) Cried out, if God would not forgive their sin, then blot him out of God's book **7. The sure judgment of terrible sin: The sinner must be & will be blotted out of God's book** **8. The just chastisement of terrible sin** a. The LORD's charge to Moses: To lead the people to the promised land b. The LORD's promise: His angel would guide them c. The LORD's just chastisement • The judgment pronounced • The judgment executed: A plague

DIVISION X

THE GOLDEN CALF AND MOSES' GREAT INTERCESSION: THE BREAKING AND RENEWAL OF THE COVENANT BETWEEN GOD AND ISRAEL, Ex.32:1-34:35

A. **The Golden Calf--The Breaking of the Covenant Between God and Man: A Picture of Man's Corrupt Heart and Rebellion Against God, Ex.32:1-35**

(32:1-35) **Introduction**: man's heart is sinful, corrupt, depraved. No person is sinless; no person can keep from sinning. All have sinned and come short of the glory of God (Ro.3:23). This passage shows how wicked--desperately wicked--man's heart really is. This is not a pretty picture nor an enjoyable subject, but it is a true picture; therefore it must be faced. A terrible situation can be corrected only as it is seen and faced. This is the reason we must face the sinful, corrupt nature of our hearts, so that we can correct that part of our nature that is so destructive.

Keep in mind what Israel had just experienced within the previous few months. They had witnessed God miraculously delivering them...

- from Egyptians slavery
- through the Red Sea
- through hunger and thirst during the beginning of their desert journey

They had seen the glory and power of God descend upon Mt. Sinai in a cloud, and they had received the law of God from God Himself through His servant Moses, their leader. And not only this, they had made a covenant, a commitment to follow and obey God and His commandments with their whole heart. Moreover, they had made a commitment to build a portable worship center, the Tabernacle, where the very presence of God could abide with them as they journeyed to the promised land. The scene for the present Scripture is just this: over the past few months they had just experienced all of the above and much more, and now they were camped at the foot of Mt. Sinai waiting for Moses to return with God's design for the Tabernacle. Six weeks had passed--six long weeks--since Moses had climbed up the mountain into the cloud of God's glory and power. What now begins to take place vividly exposes what is stated above: the sinful, corrupt nature of man's heart. God's people broke their covenant, their agreement with God. They broke their commitment to follow and obey God. Breaking one's commitment to God is so serious that God drops all other work in order to deal with the situation. God broke off His consultation with Moses--abruptly broke off giving His instructions to build the Tabernacle. He had to stop in order to deal with the terrible sin of Israel. The situation was so serious that three complete chapters of Holy Scripture are given over to dealing with the terrible sin. This is the subject of the present chapter: *The Golden Calf and Moses' Great Intercession: The Breaking of the Covenant Between God and Man : A Picture of Man's Corrupt Heart and Rebellion Against God*, Ex.32:1-35.

1. The causes of terrible sin (v.1-6).
2. The great intercession for terrible sinners (v.7-14).
3. The righteous anger against terrible sin (v.15-20).
4. The shameful excuses of terrible sin (v.21-24).
5. The righteous judgment of terrible sin (v.25-29).
6. The just plea for forgiveness of terrible sin (30-32).
7. The sure judgment of terrible sin: the sinner must be and will be blotted out of God's book (v.33-34).
8. The just chastisement of terrible sin (v.35).

1 (32:1-6) **Calf, The Golden--Idolatry--Revelry--Indulgence--Sin--Worship, False--Immorality--Heart, Corrupt--Mob--Humanism--Gods, False**: What causes terrible sin? The causes are clearly seen in what now happens to the Israelites: they lost faith in God, turned away from God, taking their lives and destiny into their own hands. They broke the Ten Commandments, the very commandments that had just been given to them by God Himself. Note the causes of their terrible sin. These are the very causes of terrible sin in any person's life.

1. Terrible sin is caused by impatience (v.1). Remember the Israelites were on their way to the promised land of Canaan. They had stopped at Mt. Sinai so that Moses and their leaders, under the direction of God, could formulate the laws that were to govern them as a nation. Moses had gone up on the mountain to pray and seek God's will, the very laws and commandments that were to govern God's people. But that had been six weeks ago--six long weeks--and Moses had not returned. Neither had he sent Joshua to bring them up to date on the progress, nor to inform them why there was such a long delay. Note the Scripture: Moses had been up on the mountain so long that the people did not know what had happened to him. The speculation was twofold:

⇒ Either Moses and Joshua had been killed...
⇒ or Moses had forsaken them and the cause of God, the seeking after the promised land. Some, no doubt, speculated that he had returned to his ranching business with his father-in-law, Jethro.

The people just had no idea what had happened to Moses. Six weeks is a long time to wait without any progress report. The people were speculating, surely Moses would have sent some report by now if he were still up on the mountain. The people were imagining, questioning, and becoming more and more restless until finally impatience gripped them; they jumped to the conclusion that something had happened to Moses, that he was not returning. Therefore they had to take matters into their own hands: they themselves would have to take charge and resume their journey to the promised land, and it was time to go. They had been at Mt. Sinai long enough. Their speculation, questioning, restlessness, and impatience led to the terrible sin they were about to commit.

2. Terrible sin is caused by pressure from a crowd (v.1). Aaron had been left in charge of the people while Moses was up on the mountain. Scripture indicates that a crowd went to Aaron insisting that he take charge and that they make preparation to begin the journey to the promised land. Note, another man had been left in charge of the people along with Aaron, but there is no mention of him whatsoever. His name was Hur. Jewish tradition says he was killed by a mob of people because he stood against the terrible sin they were about to commit. Pressure, strong pressure, was being put upon Aaron to go along with the crowd. Pressure from a crowd can cause terrible sin.

3. Terrible sin is caused by suggesting evil to a weak leader (v.1). Aaron was weak, tragically weak, throughout this whole episode. He did not have the backbone to stand up for God, to stand against the pressure of the crowd. He gave in; he crumbled. Note the Scripture: he made an idol to represent the LORD.

⇒ He made it from the gold of the people's earrings (v.3).
⇒ He molded it into the shape of a golden calf (v.4).
⇒ He presented the golden calf to the people as their god, and the people committed a terrible, terrible sin: they proclaimed the gold calf to be the god who had saved and delivered them (v.4).

4. Terrible sin is caused by believing in false gods (v.1). Note what the people requested of Aaron: that he make them an image of some god who would guide them to the promised land of Canaan. Remember, the majority of people in that day believed in many gods just as the majority of people today believe in many gods. They wanted the help of God, His

strength and power as they resumed their journey to the promised land. And they felt that the image, the representation of some strong, powerful animal, would help them secure and focus upon the help and guidance of God. Therefore they asked Aaron to mold them an image representing the power and strength of God, an idol strong and powerful enough to get them to the promised land. Believing in false gods leads to terrible sin.

5. Terrible sin is caused by disobeying God's commandments (v.1). Believing in false gods and worshipping idols are violations of the first two commandments of God. There is only one true and living God, and man is to believe Him and Him alone. Moreover, man is never to make an image or idol of God, neither follow after an image or idol in seeking the help of God. To do these things is a direct violation of the first two great commandments of God. Disobeying God's commandments causes terrible sin.

6. Terrible sin is caused by believing deliverance is of man not God (v.1). Note, the people credited Moses with having delivered and saved them from Egyptian slavery. How quickly they had forgotten the glorious deliverance of the LORD God Himself, the glorious salvation of the only living and true God:

⇒ His glorious deliverance through the terrifying plagues of Egypt
⇒ His glorious deliverance from Egyptian slavery
⇒ His glorious deliverance through the Red Sea
⇒ His glorious provision of water through their wilderness journey in the desert
⇒ His glorious provision of manna (bread) and quail day by day
⇒ His wonderful guidance by the pillar of cloud by day and the pillar of fire by night
⇒ His wonderful demonstration of glory and power in the awesome, terrifying cloud that settled upon Mt Sinai

Again, how quickly the Israelites had forgotten the deliverance and salvation of the LORD God Himself. Here they were attributing their deliverance and salvation to a mere man, even if that man was Moses. How typical of the humanistic philosophy of every generation, believing that deliverance and salvation rest in the hands of man himself. This belief causes terrible sin.

7. Terrible sin is caused by giving in to and fearing the crowd (v.2). Aaron gave in to the crowd and caused a terrible, terrible sin. Note that the crowd began to proclaim that the idols were the very gods who had delivered and saved them from Egyptian slavery (v.4). There were over three thousand of the Israelites who were leading this rebellion against God and His commandments (cp. v.28). Some of the ringleaders were, most likely, Egyptian converts who had left with the Israelites when they fled Egypt. The point to see is this: Aaron had given in to the pressure of the crowd, and now a terrible sin was being committed. Over three thousand people were rebelling against God and His commandments: they were following false gods and proclaiming those gods to be the savior of Israel. All this because Aaron had given in to the crowd, failed to stand up for God and His commandments. Now, there was the threat that thousands upon thousands of God's people could be misled about His glorious deliverance from Egyptian slavery. Giving in to the crowd can lead to terrible sin.

8. Terrible sin is caused by false worship (v.5-6). When Aaron saw so many people following and turning to the false god as their savior and guide, he apparently knew he was in trouble. This is clearly seen in what he did next: he built an altar and announced throughout the whole nation that there would be a festival held to the LORD the next day. Note that this festival was to be in the name of the LORD God Himself, Jehovah - Yahweh. Aaron was obviously being severely convicted by God's Spirit for the terrible sin he had committed. Apparently, he himself had built the altar to make sacrifices to the LORD and was planning to use the festival to try to focus the people's attention back upon the LORD.

But it was too late: the golden calf had already been built and the terrible sin had already been committed in the hearts of the people. Note that the people rose early and sacrificed both burnt offerings and fellowship offerings to the LORD. But in the eyes of the LORD the offerings were not to Him but to the golden calf. The offerings of the sacrifices were unacceptable to the LORD, for the people's attention was focused upon the golden calf, the false god to whom they were looking as their savior. Their offerings and sacrifices were profession only, false professions. False worship causes a terrible sin.

9. Terrible sin is caused by indulging in food, drink, partying, and illicit sex (v.6). The festival got out of hand. The Hebrew word for play or revelry (tsachaq) has the idea of loose conduct, the kind of loose behavior that happens when a person has been drinking or taking drugs. The word has the idea of crude language and laughter, of playing around, of sexual misconduct, of engaging in a wild dancing party or a wild drinking party. The picture is that of a festival breaking out into wild drinking, lewd dancing, and immoral behavior (cp. v.25). Indulgence in food, drink, and dancing leads to loose behavior and terrible sin.

Thought 1. God warns us against terrible sin.

"For the wrath of God is revealed from heaven against all ungodliness and unrighteousness of men, who hold the truth in unrighteousness....Being filled with all unrighteousness, fornication, wickedness, covetousness, maliciousness; full of envy, murder, debate, deceit, malignity; whisperers, backbiters, haters of God, despiteful, proud, boasters, inventors of evil things, disobedient to parents, Without understanding, covenantbreakers, without natural affection, implacable, unmerciful: Who knowing the judgment of God, that they which commit such things are worthy of death, not only do the same, but have pleasure in them that do them" (Ro.1:18, 29-32).

"Know ye not that the unrighteous shall not inherit the kingdom of God? Be not deceived: neither fornicators, nor idolaters, nor adulterers, nor effeminate, nor abusers of themselves with mankind, nor thieves, nor covetous, nor drunkards, nor revilers, nor extortioners, shall inherit the kingdom of God. And such were some of you: but ye are washed, but ye are sanctified, but ye are justified in the name of the Lord Jesus, and by the Spirit of our God" (1 Cor.6:9-11).

"Now the works of the flesh are manifest, which are these; Adultery, fornication, uncleanness, lasciviousness, idolatry, witchcraft, hatred, variance, emulations, wrath, strife, seditions, heresies, envyings, murders, drunkenness, <u>revellings</u>, and such like: of the which I tell you before, as I have also told you in time past, that they which do such things shall not inherit the kingdom of God" (Gal.5:19-21).

"For the time past of our life may suffice us to have wrought the will of the Gentiles, when we walked in lasciviousness, lusts, excess of wine, revellings, banquetings, and abominable idolatries: Wherein they think it strange that ye run not with them to the same excess of riot, speaking evil of you: Who shall give account to him that is ready to judge the quick and the dead" (1 Pt.4:3-5).

"For the wages of sin is death" (Ro.6:23).

"The soul that sinneth, it shall die" (Ezk.18:20).

2 **(32:7-14) Intercession--Prayer--Judgment**: there is the picture of great intercession for terrible sin.

1. God saw the terrible sin and was angry, very angry (v.7). God is not blind; He sees everything that a person does, and He saw the terrible sin being committed by the Israelites.

   a. God abruptly stopped the conference He was having with Moses. He shut the meeting down. God abruptly faced Moses and shocked him to the core: He told Moses to go to "his [Moses'] people." God was disowning the people. He changed the pronoun: He did not call them "My people" as He had done in the past (Ex.3:7-10; 5:1; 7:4; 7:16; 8:1; 8:20; 8:21; 8:22; 8:23; 9:1; 9:13; 9:17; 10:3; 10:4). From the first they had been called God's people, but not now. Their terrible sin had separated them from the LORD. And their sin was so terrible God was ready to disown them.

   b. Note the charge God brought against the people.
      ⇒ God charged them with being "corrupt" (sihet) (v.7). The word means running to destruction, ruin, waste, perishing. This is the same destructive word used to describe the terrible sin of the people in Noah's day. (See note--Gen.6:11-12 for more discussion.)
      ⇒ God charged the people with being quick to turn away from His commandments (v.8). God had just given them His commandments. Moreover, they had made a covenant, an agreement with God: they had committed themselves to obey God, to keep His commandments. But here they were, quickly turning away. The picture is that of walking in one direction then quickly whipping around and running in the opposite direction.
      ⇒ God charged the people with false worship (v.8). He saw the idol they had made. But even more tragic, He saw the people bow before the idol and sacrifice to it.
      ⇒ God charged the people with proclaiming a false message: that deliverance and salvation are of man not God (v.8). God saw the crowd of three thousand plus declaring that it was the false gods who had delivered them (represented by the strength and power of the golden calf). He saw their rebellion, apostasy, unbelief.
      ⇒ God charged the people with being stiff-necked: a stubborn, hard, stiff, impudent, obstinate people; a people unwilling to hear the commandments of God; a people unwilling to turn away from the lusts of the flesh and from the pride of life (cp. 1 Jn.2:15-16).

2. God had no choice: He had to deal with the people. God threatened judgment (v.10).

   a. Note what He said to Moses: "Moses, leave me alone so that my anger may burn...[and] destroy them." But observe: Moses was not bothering God, not speaking to God. Moses was standing there shocked at the abrupt ending to the conference with God and the severe charges of terrible sin against the people. Why then did God pronounce His judgment with the words, "Moses, leave me alone"?

   God was doing two things: God was drawing Moses into prayer, into intercessory prayer for the people. Only intercession could save them. Thereby God was teaching the awesome importance of intercessory prayer.
      ⇒ God was placing the intercession of Moses between the people and Himself. Moses stood as the intercessor between God and the people. Thereby Moses was to picture (symbolize) the great Intercessor, the Lord Jesus Christ.

   "Who is he that condemneth? It is Christ that died, yea rather, that is risen again, who is even at the right hand of God, who also maketh intercession for us" (Ro.8:34).
   "Wherefore in all things it behooved him to be made like unto his brethren, that he might be a merciful and faithful high priest in things pertaining to God, to make reconciliation for the sins of the people" (Heb.2:17; cp. Heb.2:14-15).
   "Wherefore he is able also to save them to the uttermost that come unto God by him, seeing he ever liveth to make intercession for them" (Heb.7:25).

   b. God then utterly shocked Moses: He threatened to fulfill His covenant promised to Abraham in a different way. (See outline and notes--Gen.12:1-3 for more discussion.) God would build a nation of people through Moses' descendants not through Abraham's (v.10).

   This was all it took: Moses was in shock, utterly dumbfounded, but he could remain silent no longer. God's purpose to move Moses into intercessory prayer had worked.
      ⇒ Moses did not want the people to face the terrifying judgment of God, did not want the people destroyed.
      ⇒ Moses did not want the covenant of God altered. He wanted the promise to Abraham to be fulfilled through Abraham's descendants.

3. Moses went to prayer. He began to intercede, to ask--seek--knock at the door of God's heart (v.11-14). Moses made four strong pleas.

   a. Moses asked God to remember that He had saved and delivered His people, that He had a special relationship with them, a covenant relationship (v.11). Note that Moses declared that the people were "Your [God's] people." He cried out, "You, O God, are the One who brought them out of slavery: You, O God, saved and delivered them. Remember all You did--the mighty works--for them."

b. Moses asked God to preserve God's own honor and trust in the eyes of the world (the Egyptians): that God keep His name from being slandered, falsely charged with evil (v.12). If God wiped the people out after saving and delivering them, what would the world say? They would declare that the God of the Israelites is weak, vengeful, and evil.

c. Moses asked God to turn from His fierce anger and not destroy the people (v.12).

d. Moses asked God to remember His great promises to the ancient patriarchs, to Abraham, Isaac, and Israel (Jacob) (v.13). What were the promises?

⇒ That God would cause Abraham's descendants to number as the stars in the sky.

⇒ That God would give the promised land to His people, give it to them as an inheritance forever.

e. Note that Moses' intercessory prayer was answered. God relented, withdrew His threat to destroy all the people (v.14).

Thought 1. Prayer--intercessory prayer--is an absolute essential for the salvation and deliverance of people. There is no question, the lack of intercessory prayer is the reason more people...

• are not reached for Christ	• are not saved from judgment
• are not making decisions for Christ	• are not delivered from temptation and sin

We must intercede for our loved ones and for the lost of the world. We must constantly go before the LORD and ask--seek--knock--cry--beg--plead.

"**Ask, and it shall be given you; seek, and ye shall find; knock, and it shall be opened unto you**" (Mt.7:7).

"**Elias was a man subject to like passions as we are, and he prayed earnestly that it might not rain: and it rained not on the earth by the space of three years and six months**" (Jas.5:17).

"**But if from thence thou shalt seek the LORD thy God, thou shalt find him, if thou seek him with all thy heart and with all thy soul**" (Dt.4:29).

"**And ye shall seek me, and find me, when ye shall search for me with all your heart**" (Jer.29:13).

"**For thus saith the LORD unto the house of Israel, Seek ye me, and ye shall live**" (Amos 5:4).

"**Seek ye the LORD, all ye meek of the earth, which have wrought his judgment; seek righteousness, seek meekness: it may be ye shall be hid in the day of the LORD'S anger**" (Zeph.2:3).

3 (32:15-20) **Anger--Calf, The Golden**: there is the picture of righteous anger against terrible sin.

1. After his intercessory prayer, Moses turned and went down the mountain. Note that he carried the two tablets of God's testimony, the Ten Commandments, with him (v.15-16). This is the only passage that tells us the tablets were written on both sides (v.15) and that they were the work of God (v.16). Another passage tells us they were written by the finger of God (Ex.31:18); however another passage says that Moses himself wrote on the tablets the words of the covenant, the Ten Commandments (Ex.34:28). This simply means that God inspired Moses to write the commandments: the Author of the commandments is the LORD God Himself.

2. The noise of the partying and revelry was so loud that it could be heard up on the mountain (v.17-18). Note that Joshua thought it was the cry of battle, but Moses informed him that it was the noise of singing and partying. Remember, God had just informed Moses about the terrible sin the people were committing (v.7-8).

3. The sight of the wickedness, of seeing the false worship and partying, hotly angered Moses (v.19-20). As he approached the camp, Moses saw it all: the calf, the dancing, the drinking, the intoxication of some, and the unclean, immoral misconduct of all. Note what Moses did.

a. Moses cast the tablets down and broke them (v.19). This was obviously done in anger, hot anger. But it was also a deliberate act, symbolizing that the people were undeserving of God's holy commandments. They had broken God's covenant, their agreement and commitment to obey God's Holy Word. They therefore would not receive the written copy of it.

b. Moses burned the golden calf (v.20). He ground it to powder, scattered it on the water, and note: he made the people drink the water. This was most likely a deliberate act to symbolize that the people's disobedience, immorality, and idolatry had made them unclean, corrupting and contaminating their whole being.

Thought 1. There is a justified anger, a righteous anger, that strikes out against sin. Such an anger against the sin and evil of this world should be aroused within all of us more and more. We should be angry against the sin and evil that destroys our loved ones, friends, and the other people of the world created by the very hand of God Himself.

"**Be ye angry, and sin not: let not the sun go down upon your wrath**" (Eph.4:26).

"**And found in the temple those that sold oxen and sheep and doves, and the changers of money sitting: And when he had made a scourge of small cords, he drove them all out of the temple, and the sheep, and the oxen; and poured out the changers' money, and overthrew the tables; And said unto them that sold doves, Take these things hence; make not my Father's house an house of merchandise. And his disciples remembered that it was written, The zeal of thine house hath eaten me up**" (Jn.2:14-17).

"**For he put on righteousness as a breastplate, and an helmet of salvation upon his head; and he put on the garments of vengeance for clothing, and was clad with zeal as a cloke**" (Is.59:17).

4 (32:21-24) **Excuses--Shame--Embarrassment--Sin**: there were the shameful excuses of terrible sin.

1. Moses confronted Aaron and asked him to explain his behavior (v.21). Remember Aaron had been left in charge of the people. He was therefore the first to give an account for the terrible sin. Initially Aaron was not one of the ringleaders of the crowd, but he became *the leader* once he had given in to the pressure from the crowd. Aaron deserved to be cut off

from God, severely chastised and disciplined, perhaps even destroyed because of his part in the terrible sin. Note that Moses accused him of having led the people into such great sin (v.21). Only one thing saved him: a very special time of intercession. At some point, Moses got alone with God and interceded just for Aaron (Dt.9:20).

2. What then happened was tragic: Aaron made excuse after excuse, blaming the people and Moses for the terrible sin (v.22-24). He did what is so common among people: he blamed others for his misbehavior and failure. He attempted to lay the fault at the feet of others, to transfer his own guilt upon others. (See note--Gen.3:10-13 for Adam blaming Eve and Eve blaming the serpent for their terrible sin.) Note the four excuses used by Aaron.

   a. Aaron accused the people of being set and prone to do evil (v.22).
   b. Aaron accused the people of forcing him to sin and commit the evil (v.23).
   c. Aaron accused Moses of being gone too long (v.23). He related how the people became uneasy, wondering and questioning what had happened to Moses, why he had been gone so long without at least some report being sent to them informing them of Moses' delay.
   d. Aaron suggested that a miracle had happened in molding the golden calf or most likely, he was mocking Moses, rebelling against his leadership (v.24). The thought of a miracle happening in the way described here seems very far-fetched, in particular thinking that a person would believe this. Moreover, when a person is facing an accuser, it is *most unlikely* that he would offer such a ridiculous idea, expecting Moses to believe it. Remember, Aaron's life had just been threatened. (See note, pt.2--Ex.32:1-6 for more discussion.) In his mind, he was probably thinking he had done the best he could under such circumstances. Therefore, he was fed up with Moses' questioning and misunderstanding of the situation. Thus, he mocked Moses to end the conversation.

Thought 1. We must not make excuses for our sin. We must confess and repent of them. God has provided salvation--the forgiveness of our sins--but we must be honest and quit blaming others. We must do exactly what Scripture says: repent and confess our sins.

> "And saying, Repent ye: for the kingdom of heaven is at hand" (Mt.3:2).
>
> "I tell you, Nay: but, except ye repent, ye shall all likewise perish" (Lk.13:3).
>
> "Then Peter said unto them, Repent, and be baptized every one of you in the name of Jesus Christ for the remission of sins, and ye shall receive the gift of the Holy Ghost" (Acts 2:38).
>
> "Repent ye therefore, and be converted, that your sins may be blotted out, when the times of refreshing shall come from the presence of the Lord" (Acts 3:19).
>
> "Repent therefore of this thy wickedness, and pray God, if perhaps the thought of thine heart may be forgiven thee" (Acts 8:22).
>
> "If we confess our sins, he is faithful and just to forgive us our sins, and to cleanse us from all unrighteousness" (1 Jn.1:9).
>
> "If my people, which are called by my name, shall humble themselves, and pray, and seek my face, and turn from their wicked ways; then will I hear from heaven, and will forgive their sin, and will heal their land" (2 Chron.7:14).
>
> "Let the wicked forsake his way, and the unrighteous man his thoughts: and let him return unto the LORD, and he will have mercy upon him; and to our God, for he will abundantly pardon" (Is.55:7).
>
> "But if the wicked will turn from all his sins that he hath committed, and keep all my statutes, and do that which is lawful and right, he shall surely live, he shall not die" (Ezk.18:21).

5 **(32:25-29) Judgment--Sin--Levites**: there was the righteous judgment of terrible sin. The leader, Aaron, had just been dealt with. Now it was time for the people to be confronted.

1. Moses had seen that the people had cast off all restraint, that they had been running wild, totally out of control morally (v.25). And tragically they had become a joke to their enemies. The Hebrew word for *naked* or *out of control* (para) means to expose, uncover, and loosen all restraints; to get out of control. The people, at least some of the people, had apparently stripped themselves and were engaging in immoral and sexual misconduct--all due to the wild partying, drinking, and dancing.

2. Moses took a position at the entrance to the camp and shouted out to the partying crowd, shouted out for all to take a stand for the LORD (v.26). Decisive action was needed, and Moses challenged the people to take this decisive action. Tragically, only the Levites from among the partying crowd rallied to him.

3. Moses then declared the judgment upon the people. But note: it was the judgment that God had pronounced not Moses. The guilty were to be executed (v.27). Moses called upon the Levites themselves to execute every evil person, even their own family members. Note that the Levites obeyed, and three thousand evil, rebellious people were executed (v.28).

Thought 1. God is holy, pure, and righteous. Therefore, He executes justice upon people.

> "Also unto thee, O Lord, belongeth mercy: for thou renderest to every man according to his work" (Ps.62:12).
>
> "I the LORD search the heart, I try the reins, even to give every man according to his ways, and according to the fruit of his doings" (Jer.17:10).
>
> "For the Son of man shall come in the glory of his Father with his angels; and then he shall reward every man according to his works" (Mt.16:27).
>
> "When the Son of man shall come in his glory, and all the holy angels with him, then shall he sit upon the throne of his glory: And before him shall be gathered all nations: and he shall separate them one from another, as a shepherd divideth [his] sheep from the goats: And he shall set the sheep on his right hand, but the goats on the left....Then shall he say also unto them on the left

hand, Depart from me, ye cursed, into everlasting fire, prepared for the devil and his angels" (Mt.25:31-33, 41).

"Marvel not at this: for the hour is coming, in the which all that are in the graves shall hear his voice, And shall come forth; they that have done good, unto the resurrection of life; and they that have done evil, unto the resurrection of damnation" (Jn.5:28-29).

"For we must all appear before the judgment seat of Christ; that every one may receive the things done in his body, according to that he hath done, whether it be good or bad" (2 Cor.5:10).

"And I saw the dead, small and great, stand before God; and the books were opened: and another book was opened, which is the book of life: and the dead were judged out of those things which were written in the books, according to their works" (Rev.20:12).

"And, behold, I come quickly; and my reward is with me, to give every man according as his work shall be" (Rev.22:12).

4. Moses then declared that the obedience of the Levites had set them apart to the LORD for His service (v.29). Some of the Levites were apparently forced to execute family members. In the words of The Expositor's Bible Commentary:

"A necessary part of consecration is being obedient to the Lord's command, which always results in his blessings (v.29). The Levites wholeheartedly followed God (Josh.14:8) and counted other ties of kinship as nothing in comparison (Deut.33:9)."[1]

Thought 1. God demands first place in our lives. The true follower of God will put God first, even above family members. No person can truly follow God who does not put Him first in his life.

"Then Peter began to say unto him, Lo, we have left all, and have followed thee" (Mk.10:28).

"And he said to [them] all, If any [man] will come after me, let him deny himself, and take up his cross daily, and follow me" (Lk.9:23).

"If any [man] come to me, and hate not his father, and mother, and wife, and children, and brethren, and sisters, yea, and his own life also, he cannot be my disciple. And whosoever doth not bear his cross, and come after me, cannot be my disciple" (Lk.14:26-27).

"So likewise, whosoever he be of you that forsaketh not all that he hath, he cannot be my disciple" (Lk.14:33).

"Yea doubtless, and I count all things but loss for the excellency of the knowledge of Christ Jesus my Lord: for whom I have suffered the loss of all things, and do count them but dung, that I may win Christ" (Ph.3:8).

6 (32:30-32) **Prayer--Intercession**: there was the plea, the great intercession for forgiveness of terrible sin. This is one of the most descriptive pictures of intercession for sinners in all of Scripture. (See outline and notes--Gen.18:16-33 for Abraham's great intercession on behalf of Sodom and Gomorrha.)

1. Note that all of the people were guilty of the terrible sin, even those who had not actually taken part in the revelry and partying. God had spared them because they had not been actively involved; nevertheless, they were guilty of the sin. Why? Because they had failed to stop the sinful, rebellious crowd (v.30). The citizens of any nation are responsible for stopping the rampage of sinful, evil people. Sin and evil can be restrained only when good people step forth, taking a stand for God and righteousness.

2. The people stood in great need, that of atonement for their sins (v.30). Note what Moses announced to the people: he was going to become their intercessor; he was going to go before the LORD and seek His face, begging God to forgive the people. The people needed atonement (reconciliation), and the servant of God was going to seek the face of the LORD...
* for reconciliation between the people and God
* for forgiveness of sins

3. Now, note the great intercession of Moses (v.31-32).
a. Moses confessed the terrible sin of the people (v.31). He spelled out their sin before the LORD, confessing that they had committed the terrible sin of idolatry, of creating man-made gods.
b. Moses pleaded for the forgiveness of their sin (v.32).
c. Moses cried out for the people: If God would not forgive their sin, then blot him out of God's book (v.32). Scripture teaches that God records the names of believers in a book that is kept in heaven. The book is called...
* the Book of the Living

"Let them be blotted out of the book of the living, and not be written with the righteous" (Ps.69:28).

"And it shall come to pass, that he that is left in Zion, and he that remaineth in Jerusalem, shall be called holy, even every one that is written among the living in Jerusalem" (Is.4:3).

* the Book of Life

"He that overcometh, the same shall be clothed in white raiment; and I will not blot out his name out of the book of life, but I will confess his name before my Father, and before his angels" (Rev.3:5).

---

[1] Frank E. Gaebelein. *The Expositor's Bible Commentary*, Vol.2, p.480.

"And I saw the dead, small and great, stand before God; and the books were opened: and another book was opened, which is the book of life: and the dead were judged out of those things which were written in the books, according to their works" (Rev.20:12, cp. Rev.21:27; 22:19).

Thought 1. The love of Moses for his people is a dynamic example to us. His love for the Israelites was as great as Paul's love.

"I say the truth in Christ, I lie not, my conscience also bearing me witness in the Holy Ghost, That I have great heaviness and continual sorrow in my heart. For I could wish that myself were accursed from Christ for my brethren, my kinsmen according to the flesh" (Ro.9:1-3).

Again, what an unbelievable example for us. When we are gripped with a passion for the lost--for our family, friends, and neighbors--then we will go before God and seek His face in intercessory prayer. We will pray as never before for others, pleading for their atonement (reconciliation), crying out for God to forgive their sins.

"And I say unto you, Ask, and it shall be given you; seek, and ye shall find; knock, and it shall be opened unto you" (Lk.11:9).
"Praying always with all prayer and supplication in the Spirit, and watching thereunto with all perseverance and supplication for all saints" (Eph.6:18).
"He shall call upon me, and I will answer him: I will be with him in trouble; I will deliver him, and honour him" (Ps.91:15).
"And it shall come to pass, that before they call, I will answer; and while they are yet speaking, I will hear" (Is.65:24).
"And ye shall seek me, and find me, when ye shall search for me with all your heart" (Jer.29:13).

7 (32:33) **Judgment--Responsibility, Personal**: there is the picture of the sure judgment of terrible sin. Note exactly what God replied to Moses: every person pays for his own sin. Each person is responsible and accountable for what he alone has done. No person is responsible for what someone else has done.
God declares: "Whosoever hath sinned against me, him will I blot out of my book" (v.33).

"Also unto thee, O Lord, belongeth mercy: for thou renderest to <u>every man</u> according to his work" (Ps.62:12).
"I the LORD search the heart, I try the reins, even to give <u>every man</u> according to his ways, and according to the fruit of his doings" (Jer.17:10).
"For the Son of man shall come in the glory of his Father with his angels; and then he shall reward <u>every man</u> according to his works" (Mt.16:27).
"For we must all appear before the judgment seat of Christ; that every one may receive the things done in his body, according to that he hath done, whether it be good or bad" (2 Cor.5:10).
"And if ye call on the Father, who without respect of persons judgeth according to every man's work, pass the time of your sojourning here in fear" (1 Pt.1:17).
"And, behold, I come quickly; and my reward is with me, to give every man according as his work shall be" (Rev.22:12).

8 (32:34-35) **Chastisement--Judgment**: there was the chastisement of terrible sin.
1. God charged Moses to go, lead the people to the promised land (v.34).
2. God gave a great promise to Moses, the promise that God's very own angel would guide them as they journeyed to the promised land (v.34). In the past the Lord Himself had led the people, but now Moses and an angel were to lead them (cp. Ex.12:42, 51; 13:17; 15:13, 22). The Lord would, however, chastise the people for their terrible sin (v.34-35). Note that He announced the chastisement and that the chastisement took place sometime later (v.35). The chastisement was executed in the form of some plague.

Thought 1. God chastises and disciplines His people when they sin. God loves us; therefore He sets out to correct us when we go astray. Chastisement is always for the believer's good: to keep us from harming, damaging, injuring ourselves; to keep us from bringing shame and embarrassment upon ourselves, our family, our friends, our neighbors, and God.

"Thou shalt also consider in thine heart, that, as a man chasteneth his son, so the LORD thy God chasteneth thee" (Dt.8:5).
"Blessed is the man whom thou chastenest, O LORD, and teachest him out of thy law" (Ps.94:12).
"My son, despise not the chastening of the LORD; neither be weary of his correction: For whom the LORD loveth he correcteth; even as a father the son in whom he delighteth" (Pr.3:11-12).
"Every branch in me that beareth not fruit he taketh away: and every [branch] that beareth fruit, he purgeth it, that it may bring forth more fruit" (Jn.15:2).
"And ye have forgotten the exhortation which speaketh unto you as unto children, My son, despise not thou the chastening of the Lord, nor faint when thou art rebuked of him: For whom the Lord loveth he chasteneth, and scourgeth every son whom he receiveth" (Heb.12:5-6; cp. Heb.12:7-11).
"As many as I love, I rebuke and chasten: be zealous therefore, and repent" (Rev.3:19).

1. Essential 1: Hearing God's call & God's warning--the warning that sin causes God to withdraw His personal presence

a. God's call: To proceed on the journey to the promised land

b. God's promise of a limited presence & limited guidance: Would not guide them Himself but would send an angel to guide & conquer their enemies

c. God's threat & warning: To withdraw His personal presence
 1) Because the people were stubborn & sinful
 2) Because He would not be able to withhold His holy & just wrath

2. Essential 2: Repentance

a. The people mourned & repented: Stripped off their jewelry (sign of worldliness)
 1) Because of God's charge, that they were stubborn & sinful
 2) Because of God's warning of judgment
 3) Because God had demanded them to repent: To strip off their jewelry (a sign of worldliness & of mourning for sin)

b. The people obeyed: Repented

3. Essential 3: Understanding that God does withdraw His presence, does chastise His people

a. Symbolized by Moses taking a tent (a worship center) outside the camp: Concerned believers sought the Lord there

b. Moses continually went to the tent to seek the Lord
 1) The people's deep concern & reverence when Moses went to seek the LORD: Rose & stood at the entrance of their tents
 2) The pillar of cloud (the LORD's presence) would descend at the entrance: The Lord talked with Moses

B. The Threat of Separation From God & Moses' Great Intercession: The Essentials for Repentance & Renewal After Sinning, Ex.33:1-23

And the LORD said unto Moses, Depart, and go up hence, thou and the people which thou hast brought up out of the land of Egypt, unto the land which I sware unto Abraham, to Isaac, and to Jacob, saying, Unto thy seed will I give it:
2 And I will send an angel before thee; and I will drive out the Canaanite, the Amorite, and the Hittite, and the Perizzite, the Hivite, and the Jebusite:
3 Unto a land flowing with milk and honey: for I will not go up in the midst of thee; for thou art a stiffnecked people: lest I consume thee in the way.
4 And when the people heard these evil tidings, they mourned: and no man did put on him his ornaments.
5 For the LORD had said unto Moses, Say unto the children of Israel, Ye are a stiffnecked people: I will come up into the midst of thee in a moment, and consume thee: therefore now put off thy ornaments from thee, that I may know what to do unto thee.
6 And the children of Israel stripped themselves of their ornaments by the mount Horeb.
7 And Moses took the tabernacle, and pitched it without the camp, afar off from the camp, and called it the Tabernacle of the congregation. And it came to pass, that every one which sought the LORD went out unto the tabernacle of the congregation, which was without the camp.
8 And it came to pass, when Moses went out unto the tabernacle, that all the people rose up, and stood every man at his tent door, and looked after Moses, until he was gone into the tabernacle.
9 And it came to pass, as Moses entered into the tabernacle, the cloudy pillar descended, and stood at the door of the tabernacle, and

the LORD talked with Moses.
10 And all the people saw the cloudy pillar stand at the tabernacle door: and all the people rose up and worshipped, every man in his tent door.
11 And the LORD spake unto Moses face to face, as a man speaketh unto his friend. And he turned again into the camp: but his servant Joshua, the son of Nun, a young man, departed not out of the tabernacle.
12 And Moses said unto the LORD, See, thou sayest unto me, Bring up this people: and thou hast not let me know whom thou wilt send with me. Yet thou hast said, I know thee by name, and thou hast also found grace in my sight.
13 Now therefore, I pray thee, if I have found grace in thy sight, show me now thy way, that I may know thee, that I may find grace in thy sight: and consider that this nation is thy people.
14 And he said, My presence shall go with thee, and I will give thee rest.
15 And he said unto him, If thy presence go not with me, carry us not up hence.
16 For wherein shall it be known here that I and thy people have found grace in thy sight? is it not in that thou goest with us? so shall we be separated, I and thy people, from all the people that are upon the face of the earth.
17 And the LORD said unto Moses, I will do this thing also that thou hast spoken: for thou hast found grace in my sight, and I know thee by name.
18 And he said, I beseech thee, show me thy glory.
19 And he said, I will make all my goodness pass before thee, and I will proclaim the name of the LORD before thee; and will be gracious to whom I will be gracious, and will show mercy on whom I will show mercy.
20 And he said, Thou canst not see my face: for there shall no man see me, and live.
21 And the LORD said, Behold, there is a place by me,

3) The people, deeply concerned, stood at their tent doors and worshipped when they saw the pillar of cloud at the door of the worship center
4) The LORD would speak with Moses face to face
5) When Moses returned to camp, his young aide, Joshua, would stay & pray & guard the worship center

4. Essential 4: Intercession for restoration & renewal, for God's full presence & guidance

a. Moses' bold requests
 1) Asks who is going to help him
 2) Asks God for renewed assurance
 • That God knows him by name
 • That he pleases God
 3) Asks God to teach him God's ways: That he might know & please God
 4) Asks God to remember that Israel is His people

b. God's promise: His presence & rest (the rest of reaching the promised land)

c. Moses' emphasis: God's presence was an absolute necessity
 1) Was necessary to reach the promised land
 2) Was necessary to show God's grace & approval
 3) Was necessary to show that God's people were distinctive

d. God's strong reassurance of His presence. Because of Moses' intercession & his close relationship with God

5. Essential 5: Pleading to know the LORD more & more

a. Moses' bold but humble request: Show me your glory

b. The Lord promised even more
 1) To reveal His goodness
 2) To reveal His name, the LORD, to Moses
 3) To reveal His sovereignty: He would have mercy & compassion as He willed & reveal His glory to Moses

c. The LORD's restriction: No man can see His face & live (because of His blazing holiness & purity)

d. The LORD answered Moses' prayer: Showed Moses His back

1) Had Moses stand on a nearby rock 2) Put Moses in a cleft in a rock 3) Covered Moses with His hand	and thou shalt stand upon a rock: 22 And it shall come to pass, while my glory passeth by, that I will put thee in a clift of the rock, and will cover	thee with my hand while I pass by: 23 And I will take away mine hand, and thou shalt see my back parts: but my face shall not be seen.	4) Removed His hand & allowed Moses to see His back

DIVISION X

THE GOLDEN CALF AND MOSES' GREAT INTERCESSION:
THE BREAKING AND RENEWAL OF THE COVENANT
BETWEEN GOD AND ISRAEL, Ex.32:1-34:35

B. **The Threat of Separation From God and Moses' Great Intercession: The Essentials for Repentance and Renewal After Sinning, Ex.33:1-23**

(33:1-23) **Introduction**: sin separates a person from God. God is holy, pure, and righteous; therefore, God can have nothing to do with sin. He has to judge and condemn sin. His holy nature demands it. But even more than this, God is love; He is merciful and gracious. God has to exercise His love toward man. Therefore, God has to execute justice on behalf of all who have been hurt and wronged by other people. God has to execute justice upon all the sinners and evil people upon earth. This is the reason for the coming day of judgment, the reason why God must execute justice upon earth.

This was the experience of the Israelites. They had just sinned, broken their commitment to God, disobeyed and rejected God. They had broken the Ten Commandments; consequently the judgment of God was about to fall upon Israel. But Moses had gone before God in behalf of Israel: he had prayed and prayed, asking God to forgive Israel. The present passage shows Moses still before God, still seeking God to forgive and restore His people into His favor. This is the important subject of this passage: *The Threat of Separation From God and Moses' Great Intercession: The Essentials for Repentance and Renewal After Sinning*, Ex.33:1-23.

1. Essential 1: hearing God's call and God's warning--the warning that sin causes Him to withdraw His personal presence (v.1-3).
2. Essential 2: repentance (v.4-6).
3. Essential 3: understanding that God does withdraw His presence, does chastise His people (v.7-11).
4. Essential 4: intercession for restoration and renewal, for God's full presence and guidance (v.12-17).
5. Essential 5: pleading to know the LORD more and more (v.18-23).

[1] (33:1-3) **Sin, Results of--Restoration--Renewal--Warning--Guidance--Protection--God, Presence of--Judgment**: the first essential to restoration is clear: a person must hear God's call and God's warning, the warning that sin causes God to withdraw His presence.

1. Note God's call: God told Moses to leave Mt. Sinai and proceed to the promised land (v.1). God had made a promise to Abraham, Isaac, and Jacob: if they believed God, really believed and followed God, He would give them the glorious inheritance of the promised land, a land that flowed with milk and honey, a land that would give them rest from all their enemies (a symbol of heaven).

God always fulfills His promise. Man may be unfaithful, but God is faithful (2 Tim.2:13). Man may break his commitment to God, but God does not break His commitment to man. The Israelites had committed a terrible, deplorable sin: they had sinned and broken the covenant, their commitment to God.

They had turned away from God, turned back to the world, to its false worship and drunkenness, dancing and immorality. And the judgment of God was about to fall upon them. But Moses had interceded for the people. He had prayed long and hard for God to forgive their terrible sin (Ex.32:30-34). God had heard Moses' prayer and forgiven their sin. Now it was time for them to get up and once again begin their journey to the promised land.

2. But note what God promised: a *limited presence* and a *limited guidance* (v.2). God would no longer guide them Himself. God would send a guardian angel to guide His people, but His *personal presence* would no longer dwell in their midst and guide them.

This news was obviously a shock, a frightening shock to Moses and the Israelites. From the beginning, God's very own presence had guided them as they journeyed to the promised land. God's presence had been symbolized in the pillar of cloud by day and the pillar of fire by night. But now, the pillar of cloud was obviously to be removed, no longer guiding and protecting them (cp. Ex.13:21-22; 14:19-20).

3. Note why God could no longer grant them His *personal presence*, why He could no longer give them His unlimited presence and guidance (v.3). And note, this stands as a threat and warning from God: He would withdraw His presence, His personal guidance and protection...

- because the people were stubborn and sinful: stiff-necked, hard, and disobedient.
- because God could not stand the presence of sin. His holiness--His righteousness and purity--is just. Therefore, when a person sins, God has to execute justice.

The people were a stiff-necked, stubborn people. As they journeyed to the promised land, the likelihood was that they were going to continue to sin, continue to disobey and turn away from God. If the very special presence of God--the special manifestation of God's presence--were dwelling in their midst, God's holiness and righteousness would strike immediately and execute justice. The people would be destroyed.

Thought 1. Sin separates us from God. When we continue in sin, God's presence is no longer *alive* within our hearts and lives. We become dull and lose the sense of His presence, of His guidance and care.

"If I regard iniquity in my heart, the Lord will not hear me" (Ps.66:18).

"But your iniquities have separated between you and your God, and your sins have hid his face from you, that he will not hear" (Is.59:2).

"And there is none that calleth upon thy name, that stirreth up himself to take hold of thee: for thou hast hid thy face from us, and hast consumed us, because of our iniquities" (Is.64:7).

"They shall go with their flocks and with their herds to seek the LORD; but they shall not find him; he hath withdrawn himself from them" (Hos.5:6).

"Quench not the Spirit" (1 Th.5:19).

"Now the just shall live by faith: but if any man draw back, my soul shall have no pleasure in him. But we are not of them who draw back unto perdition; but of them that believe to the saving of the soul" (Heb.10:38-39).

"For if after they have escaped the pollutions of the world through the knowledge of the Lord and Saviour Jesus Christ, they are again entangled therein, and overcome, the latter end is worse with them than the beginning" (2 Pt.2:20).

2 (33:4-6) **Repentance--Mourning--Worldliness**: the second essential for restoration is an absolute essential, that of repentance. The news that a mere angel would lead them, that God Himself--His personal presence--would no longer guide them, distressed the Israelites. They become deeply concerned, worried, and troubled over the news. They knew that things were not right--not fully right--in their relationship with God. Note what happened:

1. The people began to mourn and repent (v.4-5). Their repentance is symbolized in that they wore no jewelry. Jewelry was apparently a symbol of worldliness, a sign of being fleshly and carnal, that a person was seeking to attract attention to one's flesh. Three reasons are given for the people's repentance (v.5).

⇒ They heard God's charge, that they were stiff-necked and sinful.

⇒ They heard God's warning of judgment, that if they continued to sin, He would destroy them.

⇒ They heard God's demand for repentance, that they strip off their jewelry (a sign of worldliness), that they symbolize true repentance and mourning for their sin.

2. Note how this point is restressed: the people stripped off their jewelry. They obeyed God: they repented (v.6).

Thought 1. Repentance is essential to restoration. When we sin, we must repent.

⇒ We must not remain stiff-necked and sinful.

⇒ We must hear God's warning: if we continue to sin, His judgment will fall upon us.

⇒ We must hear God's demand for repentance: we must strip off all signs of worldliness.

"If my people, which are called by my name, shall humble themselves, and pray, and seek my face, and turn from their wicked ways; then will I hear from heaven, and will forgive their sin, and will heal their land" (2 Chron.7:14).

"Let the wicked forsake his way, and the unrighteous man his thoughts: and let him return unto the LORD, and he will have mercy upon him; and to our God, for he will abundantly pardon" (Is.55:7).

"But if the wicked will turn from all his sins that he hath committed, and keep all my statutes, and do that which is lawful and right, he shall surely live, he shall not die" (Ezk.18:21).

"Cast away from you all your transgressions, whereby ye have transgressed; and make you a new heart and a new spirit: for why will ye die, O house of Israel?" (Ezk.18:31).

"Therefore also now, saith the LORD, turn ye even to me with all your heart, and with fasting, and with weeping, and with mourning" (Joel 2:12).

"And saying, Repent ye: for the kingdom of heaven is at hand" (Mt.3:2).

"I tell you, Nay: but, except ye repent, ye shall all likewise perish" (Lk.13:3).

"Then Peter said unto them, Repent, and be baptized every one of you in the name of Jesus Christ for the remission of sins, and ye shall receive the gift of the Holy Ghost" (Acts 2:38).

"Repent ye therefore, and be converted, that your sins may be blotted out, when the times of refreshing shall come from the presence of the Lord" (Acts 3:19).

"Repent therefore of this thy wickedness, and pray God, if perhaps the thought of thine heart may be forgiven thee" (Acts 8:22).

"And the times of this ignorance God winked at; but now commandeth all men every where to repent" (Acts 17:30).

3 (33:7-11) **Chastisement--Judgment**: the third essential for restoration must be understood: a person must understand that God does chastise His people when they sin. God does withdraw His presence. When a person sins, he loses his sensitivity to God's presence. He loses his deep sense of God's guidance, assurance, care, protection, and security. God begins to seem far, far away--unreachable.

This was what happened to the Israelites. God had threatened to chastise them because of their terrible sin. God loved the Israelites just as He loves us. Consequently, when they sinned, He had to chastise them--to correct and discipline them. God's way of bringing chastisement was by withdrawing His presence.

1. This was symbolized by Moses taking a tent outside the camp and declaring that it was to be the worship center of Israel (v.7). It was called the "Tent of Meeting," the place where the believer was to meet God. The point: God's presence

397

was to be outside the camp, away from the people, not inside the camp, not among the people. Concerned believers--those who really wanted to seek after the Lord--had to go outside the camp to seek Him.

2. Note what Moses did: he *continually* went to the tent to seek the LORD (v.8). His concern over God's chastisement, over God's withdrawal of His presence, drove Moses to seek the LORD. Picture what Scripture now says:

   a. The people were also deeply concerned. They showed unusual reverence. When Moses entered the "Tent of Meeting," every man rose up and stood at the door of his tent. Picture the scene. Several million people stopping whatever they were doing, walking over to their doors and standing there in a moment of prayer and silence while their mediator, Moses, approached God on their behalf.

   b. As Moses entered the "Tent of Meeting," the pillar of cloud (the Lord's presence) descended and hovered at the entrance to the tent (v.9). And the LORD discussed the situation with Moses while Moses prayed and sought the LORD.

   c. Note what the people did while Moses was in the tent: they were so concerned that they stood at the doors of their tents and worshipped the LORD (v.10). They too sought the LORD for full restoration, for the restoration...
      * of God's personal presence
      * of God's guidance, care, and assurance
      * of God's protection and security

   d. Scripture says an amazing thing: God would actually speak with Moses face to face, just as a man speaks to his friend (v.11; cp. Num.12:8; Dt.34:10). Imagine this! What glorious experiences Moses had with God. These times were obviously special revelations to Moses, special manifestations of God's presence and voice. Remember the great call God had given Moses, the awesome task Moses had: leading God's people out of slavery, organizing and establishing them into a nation, and leading them through the wilderness journey for 40 years, 40 long, hard years. Moses needed special experiences, very special encounters with God. His call and task were probably the most difficult call and task ever assigned to a man. The truth of this statement is seen by thinking through the awesome, even terrifying task pictured in Exodus, Leviticus, Numbers, and Deuteronomy.

   e. Note that Joshua always stayed behind to pray and guard the worship center after Moses left (v.11). Moses made it a habit to expose Joshua to the presence of God. He had taken Joshua up the mountain with him, and now he placed Joshua into the *only* tent where God's presence was manifested.

Thought 1. We must understand one thing: God chastises us when we sin. God loves us, loves us with a perfect love; therefore, when we sin, God sets out to discipline and correct us. God's chastisement is not for the purpose of punishment: it is to discipline and correct us, to keep us from harming and destroying ourselves. Because of this, God will always chastise us when we sin. God will always discipline and correct us because He loves us and wants the very best for us.

"Thou shalt also consider in thine heart, that, as a man chasteneth his son, so the LORD thy God chasteneth thee" (Dt.8:5).

"Blessed is the man whom thou chastenest, O LORD, and teachest him out of thy law" (Ps.94:12).

"My son, despise not the chastening of the LORD; neither be weary of his correction: For whom the LORD loveth he correcteth; even as a father the son in whom he delighteth" (Pr.3:11-12).

"Every branch in me that beareth not fruit he taketh away: and every [branch] that beareth fruit, he purgeth it, that it may bring forth more fruit" (Jn.15:2).

"For this cause many are weak and sickly among you, and many sleep. For if we would judge ourselves, we should not be judged. But when we are judged, we are chastened of the Lord, that we should not be condemned with the world" (1 Cor.11:30-32).

"And ye have forgotten the exhortation which speaketh unto you as unto children, My son, despise not thou the chastening of the Lord, nor faint when thou art rebuked of him: For whom the Lord loveth he chasteneth, and scourgeth every son whom he receiveth" (Heb.12:5-6).

4 (33:12-17) **Intercession--Prayer--Restoration--Renewal**: the fourth essential for restoration is intercession, spending time in focused, diligent prayer, wrestling with God--asking, seeking, knocking, begging, crying out to God. Once the believer has sinned, the only way for him to be fully restored--the only way he can regain a full sense of God's presence and guidance--is by intercession. The believer must seek God's face for forgiveness and restoration.

Moses was concerned, very concerned, about the chastisement of God. He felt that he and the people could never reach the promised land without God's very own presence leading them. He was not satisfied with second best; he wanted the best. He was not satisfied with an angel; he wanted God.

⇒ Moses did not want the presence of an angel; he wanted God's presence.
⇒ Moses did not want the guidance of an angel; he wanted God's guidance.
⇒ Moses did not want the protection of an angel; he wanted God's protection.

Moses did the only thing he could. Moses took up the arm of intercession. Moses went before God and prayed. He prayed as he had never done before. He interceded and interceded; he stayed before God until God heard and met his need.

1. Note what Moses asked, the four bold requests he made (v.12-13).
   a. He asked God who was going to help him (v.12).

b. He asked God for renewed assurance...
- the assurance that God knew him by name--in a very, very personal way
- the assurance that he (Moses) pleased God (v.13)

c. He asked God to teach him the ways of God (v.13). And note why Moses wanted to know the ways of God: that he might know and please God more and more.

d. He asked God to remember that the Israelites were His very own people (v.13). God had created the Israelites as a nation of believers by calling Abraham...
- to bear the descendants
- to teach them the ways of God

Here they were now camped at the foot of Mt. Sinai having just committed the terrible sin of rejecting God. They were now facing the terrible withdrawal of God's presence. Moses wanted God to remember that Israel was His nation of people, the very people God had wanted to be His followers and witnesses upon earth.

2. What was God's response? God gave Moses a great promise, the promise of His very own presence and of rest: "I will go with you and give you rest" (v.14). God forgave the sin of His people and restored His full presence. God promised to lead His people to the promised land, to lead them to the land of rest He had promised. By "rest" is meant...
- a spiritual rest, the assurance and security of God's guidance and protection day by day
- a saving and redeeming rest, the deliverance from all their enemies, both spiritual and physical
- an eternal rest, the rest of living forever with God in the promised land

"And he said, My presence shall go with thee, and I will give thee rest" (Ex.33:14).

"Blessed be the LORD, that hath given rest unto his people Israel, according to all that he promised: there hath not failed one word of all his good promise, which he promised by the hand of Moses his servant" (1 Ki.8:56).

"And I said, Oh that I had wings like a dove! for then would I fly away, and be at rest" (Ps.55:6).

"Return unto thy rest, O my soul; for the LORD hath dealt bountifully with thee" (Ps.116:7).

"To whom he said, This is the rest wherewith ye may cause the weary to rest; and this is the refreshing: yet they would not hear" (Is.28:12).

"Take my yoke upon you, and learn of me; for I am meek and lowly in heart: and ye shall find rest unto your souls" (Mt.11:29).

"For we which have believed do enter into rest, as he said, As I have sworn in my wrath, if they shall enter into my rest: although the works were finished from the foundation of the world" (Heb.4:3).

"And I heard a voice from heaven saying unto me, Write, Blessed are the dead which die in the Lord from henceforth: Yea, saith the Spirit, that they may rest from their labours; and their works do follow them" (Rev.14:13).

3. Note Moses' emphasis as he prayed: God's presence was an absolute necessity (v.15-16). Why?
a. Because they could not reach the promised land without God's very own presence, without His very own guidance and protection (v.15). Note that Moses was so desperate for God's presence that he felt he just could not go on unless God met his need. (How desperately we need to learn this truth.)
b. Because God's presence demonstrated God's grace and approval (v.16). How could Moses and Israel be a witness for God unless God was with them, guiding and protecting them? God had to grant His presence, His guidance and protection, in order for the world to know that God was the LORD, the only living and true God.
c. Because God's presence showed that God's people were distinctive, that they were the true believers, that they followed the only true and living God (v.16).

4. Note how forcefully God met Moses' need: God gave strong reassurance of His presence (v.17). And note why: because of Moses' intercession and because of his close relationship with God.

Thought 1. Prayer changes things. Intercession--strong, strong prayer--attracts God and moves the heart of God. God will meet the need of the person who truly seeks the face of God, who will not let God go until God meets his need. This is the teaching of Holy Scripture.

"But if from thence thou shalt seek the LORD thy God, thou shalt find him, if thou seek him with all thy heart and with all thy soul" (Dt.4:29).

"He shall call upon me, and I will answer him: I will be with him in trouble; I will deliver him, and honour him" (Ps.91:15).

"Then shalt thou call, and the LORD shall answer; thou shalt cry, and he shall say, Here I am. If thou take away from the midst of thee the yoke, the putting forth of the finger, and speaking vanity" (Is.58:9).

"And it shall come to pass, that before they call, I will answer; and while they are yet speaking, I will hear" (Is.65:24).

"Ask, and it shall be given you; seek, and ye shall find; knock, and it shall be opened unto you" (Mt.7:7).

"If ye abide in me, and my words abide in you, ye shall ask what ye will, and it shall be done unto you" (Jn.15:7).

"Hitherto have ye asked nothing in my name: ask, and ye shall receive, that your joy may be full" (Jn.16:24).

"Is any among you afflicted? let him pray. Is any merry? let him sing psalms" (Jas.5:13).

Thought 2. Moses is a type of Christ in his *intercession* for Israel. He stood before God as Israel's *mediator*, Israel's *intercessor*. He pleaded with God for God to forgive the sins of the people and to restore the full measure of His presence to the people. Again, Moses is a type of Christ in his intercessory ministry.

> "Therefore will I divide him a portion with the great, and he shall divide the spoil with the strong; because he hath poured out his soul unto death: and he was numbered with the transgressors; and he bare the sin of many, and made intercession for the transgressors" (Is.53:12).
>
> "For there is one God, and one mediator between God and men, the man Christ Jesus; Who gave himself a ransom for all, to be testified in due time" (1 Tim.2:5-6).
>
> "Wherefore he is able also to save them to the uttermost that come unto God by him, seeing he ever liveth to make intercession for them" (Heb.7:25).
>
> "My little children, these things write I unto you, that ye sin not. And if any man sin, we have an advocate with the Father, Jesus Christ the righteous: And he is the propitiation for our sins: and not for ours only, but also for the sins of the whole world" (1 Jn.2:1-2).

5 (33:18-23) **Knowledge, of God--Growth, Spiritual--Intercession--Maturity**: the fifth essential for restoration is spiritual growth, that of pleading to know God more and more. What Moses did was heart-warming and touching, causing the heart of the genuine believer to reach out for the very thing Moses was craving: that of experiencing more and more of God's glory, that of knowing God more and more.

1. Moses made a bold but humble request: he asked God to show him His glory (v.18). Moses wanted...
   - a greater knowledge of God
   - a closer, warmer fellowship with God
   - a more intimate communion with God
   - a deeper experience of God's glory

Moses wanted more and more of God in his life. He wanted a bond, a oneness, a unity with God that just grew and grew.

2. Note what God said to such a hunger and craving after Him: the LORD promised even more than what was asked (v.19).
   a. The LORD promised to reveal His goodness to Moses (v.19). By "goodness" is meant all that God is: His love, mercy, grace, and even His holiness and justice. When God executes justice and judgment upon evil, He is good. He is good because He rights the wrongs and evil done to people and to His own name. The person who seeks to know more and more of God will receive just what God promised Moses: a revelation of God's goodness.
   b. The LORD promised to reveal His name to Moses (v.19). God's name is the LORD (Jehovah, Yahweh), the God of revelation, salvation, deliverance, and redemption; the God who is the great "I AM," the very source, essence, energy, and force of Being itself. (See <u>Deeper Study # 1</u>, <u>God - LORD</u>--Ex.3:14-15 for more discussion.)
   The person who seeks to know more and more of the LORD will learn the name of the LORD in all its meaning, learn that God is the LORD, the great "I AM" of revelation, salvation, deliverance, and redemption; that He is the great Creator and Sustainer of the universe.
   c. The LORD promised to show mercy and compassion upon His people, to reveal Himself as He wills (v.19). God was telling Moses that He would have compassion upon him and reveal Himself as Moses requested. Note: this verse is a declaration of God's sovereignty, to have mercy and compassion as He wills. (See note--Ro.9:15-18 for more discussion.)

3. There was to be one restriction in Moses' (or anyone else's) request to see God's glory: no person could see God's face and live (v.20). God's blazing holiness, His righteousness and purity, would consume a person--far, far quicker than the intense energy and brilliance of the sun. Therefore, God would not allow Moses nor anyone else in the universe to see His face.

4. But note: God did answer Moses' prayer (v.21-23). God would show Moses what he could bear, as much of His glory as Moses needed. What Moses experienced was so wonderful that he could describe it only as Scripture states in these three simple verses:
   ⇒ God told Moses to stand on a particular rock (v.21).
   ⇒ God put Moses in a cleft of a rock (v.22).
   ⇒ God covered Moses with the very hand of God Himself (v.22).
   ⇒ God removed His hand at some point and Moses saw some faint, hazy image of God's back (v.23).

The reference to God's "hand" and "back" are what is called <u>anthropomorphisms</u>. The word simply means describing God and the experiences of God in a way that man can understand.

Thought 1. We must seek to know the LORD more and more. We must constantly seek...
   - a greater knowledge of the LORD
   - a stronger belief and understanding of the LORD
   - a clear, warmer fellowship with Him
   - a more intimate communion with Him
   - a deeper experience of His glory

> "Ye are my witnesses, saith the LORD, and my servant whom I have chosen: that ye may <u>know</u> and <u>believe</u> me, and <u>understand</u> that I am he: before me there was no God formed, neither shall there be after me" (Is.43:10).

"But let him that glorieth glory in this, that he understandeth and knoweth me, that I am the LORD which exercise lovingkindness, judgment, and righteousness, in the earth: for in these things I delight, saith the LORD" (Jer.9:24).

"Then shall we know, if we follow on to know the LORD: his going forth is prepared as the morning; and he shall come unto us as the rain, as the latter and former rain unto the earth" (Hos.6:3).

"Jesus answered them, and said, My doctrine is not mine, but his that sent me. If any man will do his will, he shall know of the doctrine, whether it be of God, or [whether] I speak of myself" (Jn.7:16-17).

"Then said Jesus to those Jews which believed on him, If ye continue in my word, [then] are ye my disciples indeed; And ye shall know the truth, and the truth shall make you free" (Jn.8:31-32).

"And this is life eternal, that they might know thee the only true God, and Jesus Christ, whom thou hast sent" (Jn.17:3).

"That I may know him, and the power of his resurrection, and the fellowship of his sufferings, being made conformable unto his death" (Ph.3:10).

"That ye might walk worthy of the Lord unto all pleasing, being fruitful in every good work, and increasing in the knowledge of God; Strengthened with all might, according to his glorious power, unto all patience and longsuffering with joyfulness" (Col.1:10-11).

"All scripture is given by inspiration of God, and is profitable for doctrine, for reproof, for correction, for instruction in righteousness" (2 Tim.3:16).

"Therefore leaving the principles of the doctrine of Christ, let us go on unto perfection; not laying again the foundation of repentance from dead works, and of faith toward God" (Heb.6:1).

"As newborn babes, desire the sincere milk of the word, that ye may grow thereby: If so be ye have tasted that the Lord is gracious" (1 Pt.2:2-3).

"But grow in grace, and in the knowledge of our Lord and Saviour Jesus Christ. To him be glory both now and for ever. Amen" (2 Pt.3:18).

1. Step 1—responding to God's call to come back into His presence: God called Moses to return to His presence

a. To prepare to receive a second copy of God's law, His Word: To chisel two stone tablets

b. To meet God in the morning on Mt. Sinai: The very special place where God's presence was symbolized

c. To meet God alone: No person, not even an animal, was to be present to distract

d. God's servant responded & obeyed: Did everything God said

2. Step 2—seeking & experiencing God's presence afresh

a. God revealed Himself & proclaimed His name

1) He is the LORD, the LORD

2) He is merciful & gracious

3) He is slow to anger

4) He abounds in love & is faithful

5) He shows love to thousands by forgiving wickedness, rebellion, & sin

6) He executes righteousness & justice: He punishes the guilty & the children of the guilty to the third & fourth generations

b. Moses bowed & worshipped & prayed

1) For God's guidance

2) For God's forgiveness

3) For God to accept His people as His very special possession & inheritance

3. Step 3—making a renewed covenant with God, a renewed commitment to obey God

a. God's part

1) To do great works for His people—as a witness to the

C. The Renewal of the Covenant Between God & Man: The Steps to Renewal, Ex.34:1-35

And the LORD said unto Moses, Hew thee two tables of stone like unto the first: and I will write upon these tables the words that were in the first tables, which thou brakest.

2 And be ready in the morning, and come up in the morning unto mount Sinai, and present thyself there to me in the top of the mount.

3 And no man shall come up with thee, neither let any man be seen throughout all the mount; neither let the flocks nor herds feed before that mount.

4 And he hewed two tables of stone like unto the first; and Moses rose up early in the morning, and went up unto mount Sinai, as the LORD had commanded him, and took in his hand the two tables of stone.

5 And the LORD descended in the cloud, and stood with him there, and proclaimed the name of the LORD.

6 And the LORD passed by before him, and proclaimed, The LORD, The LORD God, merciful and gracious, long-suffering, and abundant in goodness and truth,

7 Keeping mercy for thousands, forgiving iniquity and transgression and sin, and that will by no means clear the guilty; visiting the iniquity of the fathers upon the children, and upon the children's children, unto the third and to the fourth generation.

8 And Moses made haste, and bowed his head toward the earth, and worshipped.

9 And he said, If now I have found grace in thy sight, O Lord, let my Lord, I pray thee, go among us; for it is a stiffnecked people; and pardon our iniquity and our sin, and take us for thine inheritance.

10 And he said, Behold, I make a covenant: before all thy people I will do marvels, such as have not been done in all the earth, nor in any nation: and all the people

---

among which thou art shall see the work of the LORD: for it is a terrible thing that I will do with thee.

11 Observe thou that which I command thee this day: behold, I drive out before thee the Amorite, and the Canaanite, and the Hittite, and the Perizzite, and the Hivite, and the Jebusite.

12 Take heed to thyself, lest thou make a covenant with the inhabitants of the land whither thou goest, lest it be for a snare in the midst of thee:

13 But ye shall destroy their altars, break their images, and cut down their groves:

14 For thou shalt worship no other god: for the LORD, whose name is Jealous, is a jealous God:

15 Lest thou make a covenant with the inhabitants of the land, and they go a whoring after their gods, and do sacrifice unto their gods, and one call thee, and thou eat of his sacrifice;

16 And thou take of their daughters unto thy sons, and their daughters go a whoring after their gods, and make thy sons go a whoring after their gods.

17 Thou shalt make thee no molten gods.

18 The feast of unleavened bread shalt thou keep. Seven days thou shalt eat unleavened bread, as I commanded thee, in the time of the month Abib: for in the month Abib thou camest out from Egypt.

19 All that openeth the matrix is mine; and every firstling among thy cattle, whether ox or sheep, that is male.

20 But the firstling of an ass thou shalt redeem with a lamb: and if thou redeem him not, then shalt thou break his neck. All the firstborn of thy sons thou shalt redeem. And none shall appear before me empty.

21 Six days thou shalt work, but on the seventh day thou shalt rest: in earing time and in harvest thou shalt rest.

22 And thou shalt observe the feast of weeks, of the firstfruits of wheat harvest, and the feast of ingathering at the year's end.

23 Thrice in the year shall all

---

lost (wonders, miracles)

2) To demand obedience of His people

3) To defeat the enemies of His people (all who stand in their way as they journey to the promised land)

b. The believer's part: Receiving & obeying God's commandment

1) Must live a life of separation, not become associated or tied to unbelievers: Will be a snare

2) Must not worship false gods

• To destroy their altars

• Because God's name is "Jealous": He is passionate over His people

3) Must absolutely live a life of separation, not make alliances with unbelievers

• Because of their evil influence: Will lead to spiritual adultery, the worship of false gods

• Because of their influence to intermarry, leading believers to intermarry

4) Must make no idols whatsoever

5) Must celebrate the Passover: Keep the Feast of Unleavened Bread

• To eat seven days

• To celebrate God's great deliverance from Egypt (a symbol of the world)

6) Must always give the firstborn to God

• To give the first of every herd & flock

• To give & redeem a substitute lamb for a donkey

• To give & redeem a substitute lamb for a son

7) Must keep the Sabbath: Must keep even during the busiest season

8) Must keep & celebrate the religious Feasts: The Feast of Weeks & the Feast of Ingathering

9) Must have all the men

appear before God three times a year
- To keep the annual religious feasts
- God's promise: Would protect His people from their enemies while they were worshipping Him

10) Must guard the Passover
- Not to use leavened bread, bread with yeast
- Not to leave overnight

11) Must bring the firstfruits to the house of God
12) Must not cook a young goat in its mother's milk

4. Step 4--knowing the importance of the special commandments of God: The Ten Commandments themselves
a. They are the basis of God's covenant
b. They are so important that Moses did not sleep or eat while receiving the law
c. They are so important that they are set apart & entitled the Ten Commandments

5. Step 5--going forth to proclaim God's Word
a. God's servant was prepared:

your men children appear before the Lord GOD, the God of Israel.
24 For I will cast out the nations before thee, and enlarge thy borders: neither shall any man desire thy land, when thou shalt go up to appear before the LORD thy God thrice in the year.
25 Thou shalt not offer the blood of my sacrifice with leaven; neither shall the sacrifice of the feast of the passover be left unto the morning.
26 The first of the firstfruits of thy land thou shalt bring unto the house of the LORD thy God. Thou shalt not seethe a kid in his mother's milk.
27 And the LORD said unto Moses, Write thou these words: for after the tenor of these words I have made a covenant with thee and with Israel.
28 And he was there with the LORD forty days and forty nights; he did neither eat bread, nor drink water. And he wrote upon the tables the words of the covenant, the Ten Commandments.
29 And it came to pass, when Moses came down from mount Sinai with the two tables of testimony in Moses' hand, when he came down from the mount, that Moses wist not that the skin of his face shone while he talked with him.
30 And when Aaron and all the children of Israel saw Moses, behold, the skin of his face shone; and they were afraid to come nigh him.
31 And Moses called unto them; and Aaron and all the rulers of the congregation returned unto him: and Moses talked with them.
32 And afterward all the children of Israel came nigh: and he gave them in commandment all that the LORD had spoken with him in mount Sinai.
33 And till Moses had done speaking with them, he put a vail on his face.
34 But when Moses went in before the LORD to speak with him, he took the vail off, until he came out. And he came out, and spake unto the children of Israel that which he was commanded.
35 And the children of Israel saw the face of Moses, that the skin of Moses' face shone: and Moses put the vail upon his face again, until he went in to speak with him.

He had been in the presence of the LORD--symbolized by the radiance of his face

1) The people were afraid to come near him

2) Moses called them to him
b. God's servant declared God's commandments to the leaders
c. God's servant declared God's commandments to the people

d. God's servant covered his face with a veil after declaring God's commandments
e. God's servant removed the veil when he entered God's presence
f. God's servant received a new radiance from God every time he entered God's presence
1) The people saw God's radiance upon Moses' face every time he spoke
2) Moses wore the veil when not communing with God

DIVISION X

THE GOLDEN CALF AND MOSES' GREAT INTERCESSION: THE BREAKING AND RENEWAL OF THE COVENANT BETWEEN GOD AND ISRAEL, Ex.32:1-34:35

C. The Renewal of the Covenant Between God and Man: The Steps to Renewal, Ex.34:1-35

(34:1-35) **Introduction--Starting Over--New Beginning--New Life**: one of man's greatest needs is to know this one truth: he can start all over again; he can make a new beginning; he can have a brand new life. No matter how terrible the sin or shame, how horrible the failure or devastation, how tragic the suffering or pain, how helpless or hopeless the situation--no matter what the problem or trial--man can start all over again. He can have a new beginning for one simple reason: God loves him and cares for him. God wants to take care of him and look after him, delivering him through the trials that confront him. This is the subject of this great passage, a subject that offers the greatest hope to us all: we can start all over again. This is: *The Renewal of the Covenant Between God and Man: The Steps to Renewal*, Ex.34:1-35
1. Step 1--responding to God's call to come back into His presence: God called Moses to return to His presence (v.1-4).
2. Step 2--seeking and experiencing God's presence afresh (v.5-9).
3. Step 3--making a renewed covenant with God, a renewed commitment to obey God (v.10-26).
4. Step 4--knowing the importance of the special commandments of God: the Ten Commandments themselves (v.27-28).
5. Step 5--going forth to proclaim God's Word (v.29-35).

1 (34:1-4) **Starting Over--Restoration--Renewal--New Beginning--Beginning Again--New Life**: when starting over, the first step is to respond to God's call, to come back into His presence. God called Moses to return to His presence. Note that the invitation to come was extended to Moses by God. There is a special significance to this invitation, one that is easily overlooked. The invitation was to Moses and to him alone. Remember, Moses was the mediator between God and

Israel. It was through Moses that God had revealed His law to His people, and through Moses that He revealed His plans for the Tabernacle. And now it was through Moses that God was renewing His covenant with His people. This is a clear picture of how Jesus Christ is our Mediator. Jesus Christ is the One who renews God's covenant with us. It is Jesus Christ who enters God's presence for us, who makes us acceptable to God.

> "Jesus saith unto him, I am the way, the truth, and the life: no man cometh unto the Father, but by me" (Jn.14:6).
> "Neither is there salvation in any other: for there is none other name under heaven given among men, whereby we must be saved" (Acts 4:12).
> "For *there is* one God, and one mediator between God and men, the man Christ Jesus" (1 Tim.2:5).
> "But now hath he obtained a more excellent ministry, by how much also he is the mediator of a better covenant, which was established upon better promises" (Heb.8:6).
> "And for this cause he is the mediator of the new testament, that by means of death, for the redemption of the transgressions that were under the first testament, they which are called might receive the promise of eternal inheritance" (Heb.9:15).
> "For Christ is not entered into the holy places made with hands, which are the figures of the true; but into heaven itself, now to appear in the presence of God for us" (Heb.9:24).
> "My little children, these things write I unto you, that ye sin not. And if any man sin, we have an advocate with the Father, Jesus Christ the righteous" (1 Jn.2:1).

God called Moses to come back into His presence for a very specific reason: to receive the second copy of God's law, the Ten Commandments (Ex.20:1-19; 31:18; 32:15-16, 19). Remember, Moses had cast the first copy of tablets to the ground in anger when he was descending the mountain and saw the people committing their terrible sin (Ex.32:19). But Moses and the people had cried out to God for forgiveness and they had repented of their sin. Furthermore, Moses had spent days in intercession, begging God to restore the people fully and completely, just as strongly as they were before. Moses had pleaded for the full manifestation of God's presence among the people. God had heard the prayers and intercession of Moses and the people. God had forgiven their sin and accepted their repentance. But one thing was still lacking: the law of God, the Ten Commandments. The Ten Commandments were the very basis of the covenant between God and man. In order to start over, the law had to be rewritten and given to the people. Now note what happened.

1. God told Moses to prepare to receive the second copy of God's law, of His Ten Commandments (v.1). God told Moses to chisel out two stone or slate tablets. They were thin and small, for Moses was able to carry them by hand.
2. God told Moses to climb the mountain in the morning to meet with God (v.2).
3. God told Moses to come alone (v.3). No person, not even Joshua, was to reenter God's presence with Moses. Not even an animal was to be anywhere near, not even grazing in front of the mountain.
4. Note that Moses responded to and obeyed God's call. He did everything God said. Moses did not selectively obey God, doing only those things that were convenient or easy to do. Moses obeyed God...

- obeyed when he prepared himself to receive God's law, His Word, again
- obeyed when he met God early in the morning on Mount Sinai
- obeyed when he met God alone

Thought 1. The very first step in starting over, in seeking a new beginning with God, is clearly seen in this passage. A person must respond to God's call to return to His presence. A person must get into God's presence and seek the LORD.

> "Ask, and it shall be given you; seek, and ye shall find; knock, and it shall be opened unto you" (Mt.7:7).
> "Hitherto have ye asked nothing in my name: ask, and ye shall receive, that your joy may be full" (Jn.16:24).
> "If my people, which are called by my name, shall humble themselves, and pray, and seek my face, and turn from their wicked ways; then will I hear from heaven, and will forgive their sin, and will heal their land" (2 Chron.7:14).
> "Seek the LORD, and his strength: seek his face evermore" (Ps.105:4).
> "Seek ye the LORD while he may be found, call ye upon him while he is near" (Is.55:6).
> "And ye shall seek me, and find me, when ye shall search for me with all your heart" (Jer.29:13).

Thought 2. Note that Moses met God early in the morning (v.2, 4). Any person who wants to be useful to God must be willing to start the day early. The day becomes much too short if the mornings are wasted away with laziness or slumber. The believer who truly seeks God arises early, spending a quiet devotional time with God, and then gets busy taking care of his duties for the day.

⇒ Abraham rose up early and worked for God.

> "And Abraham rose up early in the morning, and saddled his ass, and took two of his young men with him, and Isaac his son, and clave the wood for the burnt offering, and rose up, and went unto the place of which God had told him" (Gen.22:3).

⇒ Jacob rose up early and worked for God.

"And Jacob rose up early in the morning, and took the stone that he had put *for* his pillows, and set it up *for* a pillar, and poured oil upon the top of it" (Gen.28:18).

⇒ Moses rose up early and worked for God.

"And the LORD said unto Moses, Rise up early in the morning, and stand before Pharaoh; lo, he cometh forth to the water; and say unto him, Thus saith the LORD, Let my people go, that they may serve me" (Ex.8:20).

"And the LORD said unto Moses, Rise up early in the morning, and stand before Pharaoh, and say unto him, Thus saith the LORD God of the Hebrews, Let my people go, that they may serve me" (Ex.9:13).

"And Moses wrote all the words of the LORD, and rose up early in the morning, and builded an altar under the hill, and twelve pillars, according to the twelve tribes of Israel" (Ex.24:4).

"And he hewed two tables of stone like unto the first; and Moses rose up early in the morning, and went up unto mount Sinai, as the LORD had commanded him, and took in his hand the two tables of stone" (Ex.34:4).

⇒ Joshua rose up early and worked for God.

"And Joshua rose early in the morning; and they removed from Shittim, and came to Jordan, he and all the children of Israel, and lodged there before they passed over" (Josh.3:1).

"And Joshua rose early in the morning, and the priests took up the ark of the LORD" (Josh.6:12).

"And Joshua rose up early in the morning, and numbered the people, and went up, he and the elders of Israel, before the people to Ai" (Josh.8:10).

⇒ Samuel's parents rose up early and worked for God.

"And they rose up in the morning early, and worshipped before the LORD, and returned, and came to their house to Ramah: and Elkanah knew Hannah his wife; and the LORD remembered her" (1 Sam.1:19).

⇒ Samuel rose up early and worked for God.

"And when Samuel rose early to meet Saul in the morning, it was told Samuel, saying, Saul came to Carmel, and, behold, he set him up a place, and is gone about, and passed on, and gone down to Gilgal" (1 Sam.15:12).

⇒ David rose up early and worked for God.

"And David rose up early in the morning, and left the sheep with a keeper, and took, and went, as Jesse had commanded him; and he came to the trench, as the host was going forth to the fight, and shouted for the battle" (1 Sam.17:20).

⇒ David and his men rose up early and worked for God.

"Wherefore now rise up early in the morning with thy master's servants that are come with thee: and as soon as ye be up early in the morning, and have light, depart. So David and his men rose up early to depart in the morning, to return into the land of the Philistines. And the Philistines went up to Jezreel" (1 Sam.29:10-11).

⇒ Job rose up early and worked for God.

"And it was so, when the days of *their* feasting were gone about, that Job sent and sanctified them, and rose up early in the morning, and offered burnt offerings *according* to the number of them all: for Job said, It may be that my sons have sinned, and cursed God in their hearts. Thus did Job continually" (Job 1:5).

⇒ Jesus Christ rose up early and worked for God.

"And in the morning, rising up a great while before day, he went out, and departed into a solitary place, and there prayed" (Mk.1:35).

"And early in the morning he came again into the temple, and all the people came unto him; and he sat down, and taught them" (Jn.8:2).

⇒ Jesus' disciples rose up early and worked for God.

"And very early in the morning the first *day* of the week, they came unto the sepulchre at the rising of the sun" (Mk.16:2).
"Now upon the first *day* of the week, very early in the morning, they came unto the sepulchre, bringing the spices which they had prepared, and certain *others* with them" (Lk.24:1).

⇒ The apostles rose up early and worked for God.

"And when they heard *that,* they entered into the temple early in the morning, and taught. But the high priest came, and they that were with him, and called the council together, and all the senate of the children of Israel and sent to the prison to have them brought" (Acts 5:21).

2 (34:5-9) **God, Nature--Attributes, of God--Intercession--Prayer--Spiritual Experience**: when starting over, the second step is to seek and experience God's presence afresh. When Moses reached the top of Mount Sinai, the cloud of God descended and covered the mountain. Scripture says that God's presence was in the cloud and that God gave Moses one of the deepest spiritual experiences ever granted a person.

1. God revealed Himself and proclaimed His name, *the LORD* (v.5-7). Remember, in ancient history the name of a person stood for all that a person is and does. All that God is and all that God does--His character, nature, person--are wrapped up in God's name, *the LORD*. Note how God describes His name, how He defines His name, what He says His name stands for. This is what God proclaimed to Moses; this is the deep spiritual experience God gave to His dear servant.
   a. God is *the LORD, the LORD* (v.5). God passed in front of Moses proclaiming Himself to be "the LORD, the LORD" (Jehovah, Yahweh). The word has at least three significant meanings:
      ⇒ "LORD" means "I AM THAT I AM," the very essence of Being, the energy, force, and source of Being. (See <u>Deeper Study # 1</u>--Ex.3:14-15 for more discussion.)
      ⇒ "LORD" means the God of salvation, deliverance, and redemption. (See note--Gen.2:4; <u>Deeper Study # 4</u>--Ex.4:10-11; note--Ex.6:1-5 for more discussion.)
      ⇒ "LORD" means the God of revelation, the God who reveals Himself and the truth to man. (See <u>Deeper Study # 4</u>--Ex.4:10-11 for more discussion.)

   God was proclaiming all this to Moses and He declares the same message to us. God proclaims His name to us, for His name has never changed. God is the LORD (Jehovah - Yahweh):
      ⇒ The great "I AM THAT I AM"
      ⇒ The great God of salvation, deliverance, and redemption
      ⇒ The great God of revelation who reveals Himself and the truth to us
   b. God is merciful (compassionate) and gracious (v.5). The name of God, *the LORD*, means...
      • the very nature of God is that of mercy, compassion, and grace
      • the very nature of God reaches out in mercy and in compassion and grace

   The very name of God tells us that He has compassion for us when we need help--any kind of help--and that He wants to have mercy upon us and pour out the riches of His grace upon us. God proclaimed this to Moses and He declares the same message to us. His name, *the LORD*, tells us that God is merciful (compassionate) and gracious
   c. God is long-suffering, slow to anger (v.5). The very name, *the LORD*, means that God is long-suffering, that He suffers a long time before taking action against sin and evil, suffers a long time before executing justice and judgment upon sinful people. God is long-suffering, not wanting any person to perish.
   d. God abounds in goodness. The very name and character of the LORD God point to and are wrapped in goodness and faithfulness. When thoughts of God fill our minds, they usually focus upon His goodness and faithfulness--which have never failed, never run out, never expired.
   e. God shows mercy and love to thousands by forgiving wickedness, rebellion, and sin (v.7). The name of God, *the LORD*, means that God is merciful and loving; therefore, He forgives all kinds of wrong. God forgives...
      • iniquities
      • transgressions
      • sin, no matter what the sin is
      • all wickedness and evil
      • rebellion against Him and His commandments
      • corruption

   No matter what a person has done or how terrible the evil, God shows mercy and love by withholding His justice and judgment, giving a person time to repent and seek Him. And God forgives thousands, forgives because His name is *the LORD*. God is the God of mercy and love.
   f. God executes righteousness and justice: He punishes the guilty and the children of the guilty to the third and fourth generations (v.7). God's name, *the LORD*, means that God is righteous and just, that He does execute justice and judgment upon the wicked, the rebellious, and the sinful of the world. (See note, pt.2--Ex.20:5-6 for more discussion.)

EXODUS 34:1-35

The above six character traits and attributes are a description of God's name, a description of what God's name--*the LORD*--means. God revealed Himself and proclaimed His glorious name to Moses. When we see or hear God's name--*the LORD*--we can know...

- that God is *the LORD, the LORD*
- that God is *merciful and gracious*
- that God is *long-suffering, slow to anger*
- that God shows *mercy and love* to thousands by forgiving wickedness, rebellion, and sin
- that God *executes justice*, that He punishes the guilty and the children of the guilty for generations

This is the nature of God. This is the very name of God, *the LORD*. The revelation of God's name was the deep spiritual experience given to Moses.

2. Now, note what Moses did after God revealed His name and His nature: Moses immediately fell to the ground, prostrating himself before the Lord in worship and prayer (v.8-9). He asked God for three very specific things, the very same requests he had already been making of God. Moses was doing just what the LORD Jesus Christ was to reveal when He came to earth: that we should ask, seek, and knock when we face desperate need, and God will hear us.

⇒ Moses prayed for God's guidance, that the Lord Himself would lead him and God's people to the promised land.
⇒ Moses prayed for God's forgiveness. He could not get away from the fact that he and the people were short, ever so short, of God's glory, that they were stiff-necked--sinful and depraved--always standing in need of God's forgiveness.
⇒ Moses prayed for God to accept His people as God's very special possession and inheritance. Moses wanted God to attach Himself so closely to His people that He would never cast them off, holding them ever so dear to His heart. He wanted God to make them eternally secure in Himself, to claim them as His very own people, His very own possession and inheritance.

Thought 1. When starting over--when seeking a new beginning, when wanting a brand new start in life--we must seek and experience God's presence afresh. We must seek *the LORD*, seek all that He is and does, seek Him in all His fulness.

1) When starting over, we must learn and understand that God is the LORD, the only living and true God, the great Creator and Sustainer of the universe (v.5).

"Hear, O Israel: The LORD our God is one LORD: And thou shalt love the LORD thy God with all thine heart, and with all thy soul, and with all thy might" (Dt.6:4-5).
"Thou, even thou, art LORD alone; thou hast made heaven, the heaven of heavens, with all their host, the earth, and all things that are therein, the seas, and all that is therein, and thou preservest them all; and the host of heaven worshippeth thee" (Neh.9:6).
"Ye are my witnesses, saith the LORD, and my servant whom I have chosen: that ye may know and believe me, and understand that I am he: before me there was no God formed, neither shall there be after me. I, even I, am the LORD; and beside me there is no saviour" (Is.43:10-11).
"Through faith we understand that the worlds were framed by the word of God, so that things which are seen were not made of things which do appear" (Heb.11:3).

2) When starting over, we must learn and understand that God is merciful and gracious (v.6).

"For we have not an high priest which cannot be touched with the feeling of our infirmities; but was in all points tempted like as we are, yet without sin. Let us therefore come boldly unto the throne of grace, that we may obtain mercy, and find grace to help in time of need" (Heb.4:15-16).
"Who is a God like unto thee, that pardoneth iniquity, and passeth by the transgression of the remnant of his heritage? he retaineth not his anger for ever, because he delighteth in mercy" (Mic.7:18).

3) When starting over, we must learn and understand that God is long-suffering, slow to anger (v.6).

"The Lord is not slack concerning his promise, as some men count slackness; but is long-suffering to us, not willing that any should perish, but that all should come to repentance" (2 Pt.3:9).

4) When starting over, we must learn and understand that God abounds in goodness and truth (v.6).
(a) God overflows with goodness.

"O taste and see that the LORD is good: blessed is the man that trusteth in him" (Ps.34:8).
"The LORD is good, a strong hold in the day of trouble; and he knoweth them that trust in him" (Nah.1:7).

(b) God overflows with truth.

> "And ye shall know the truth, and the truth shall make you free" (Jn.8:32).
> "And now, O Lord GOD, thou art that God, and thy words be true, and thou hast promised this goodness unto thy servant" (2 Sam.7:28).

5) When starting over, we must learn and understand that God shows mercy and love to thousands by forgiving their wickedness, rebellion, and sin (v.7).

> "In whom we have redemption through his blood, the forgiveness of sins, according to the riches of his grace" (Eph.1:7).
> "If we confess our sins, he is faithful and just to forgive us our sins, and to cleanse us from all unrighteousness" (1 Jn.1:9).

6) When starting over, we must learn and understand that God executes righteousness and justice, that He punishes the guilty and the children of the guilty for generations (v.7).

> "Also unto thee, O Lord, belongeth mercy: for thou renderest to every man according to his work" (Ps.62:12).
> "And to you who are troubled rest with us, when the Lord Jesus shall be revealed from heaven with his mighty angels, In flaming fire taking vengeance on them that know not God, and that obey not the gospel of our Lord Jesus Christ" (2 Th.1:7-8).
> "And as it is appointed unto men once to die, but after this the judgment" (Heb.9:27).
> "The Lord knoweth how to deliver the godly out of temptations, and to reserve the unjust unto the day of judgment to be punished" (2 Pt.2:9).

3 (34:10-26) <u>Covenant--Commitment--Restoration--Renewal--Starting Over--New Beginning--New Life</u>: when starting over, the third step is to make a renewed covenant with God, a renewed commitment to obey Him. Note the unbelievable love of God. The people had committed a terrible, appalling sin. They had broken the Ten Commandments; they had disobeyed and rejected God. But here God is seen reaching out, taking the initiative to renew the covenant between Himself and the people, seeking to reestablish their relationship. To do this, the terms of the covenant, of the relationship, had to be recovered.

1. Note God's part in renewing the relationship, the covenant with His people (v.10-11).
    a. God promised to do great works (wonders, miracles) for His people (v.10). And note why: that His people and the mighty works might be a great witness to the lost. God had chosen the Israelites to be His witnesses upon the earth, His missionary force to reach the lost of the world. He was, therefore, promising to do mighty works through them so that they would be dynamic witnesses to the power of God, His power to save and deliver man from the evils of this world.

> "Ye are my witnesses, saith the LORD, and my servant whom I have chosen: that ye may know and believe me, and understand that I am he: before me there was no God formed, neither shall there be after me" (Is.43:10).
> "For the Son of man is come to seek and to save that which was lost" (Lk.19:10; cp. Jn.20:21).
> "Ye have not chosen me, but I have chosen you, and ordained you, that ye should go and bring forth fruit, and [that] your fruit should remain: that whatsoever ye shall ask of the Father in my name, he may give it you" (Jn.15:16).
> "And ye also shall bear witness, because ye have been with me from the beginning" (Jn.15:27).
> "Then said Jesus to them again, Peace [be] unto you: as [my] Father hath sent me, even so send I you" (Jn.20:21).

    b. God demanded the obedience of His people (v.11). God is the only living and true God, the sovereign Lord and Majesty of the universe; therefore He has the right to demand obedience. In establishing a relationship with man, a covenant, the right to demand obedience belongs to the Sovereign Ruler, to Him and Him alone. In starting over, in making a new beginning with God, God demands obedience.
    c. God promised to defeat the enemies of His people, to defeat all who stood in their way as they journeyed to the promised land (v.11). Once again, God promised to drive out the inhabitants of the land of Canaan. No enemy would be allowed to stop His people from reaching the promised land. All who stood against God's people--all who tried to entice, ensnare, enslave, defeat, or destroy--would themselves be defeated and destroyed. (See Deeper Study # 2--Ex.3:8 for more discussion.)

Thought 1. God promises to defeat all enemies who stand against the believer, all who try to stop the believer from reaching the promised land of heaven. God has given the believer victory through Jesus Christ. Jesus Christ has triumphed over our most fearsome enemies.

1) Jesus Christ has conquered the enemy of sin for the believer.

> "For I delivered unto you first of all that which I also received, how that Christ died for our sins according to the scriptures" (1 Cor.15:3).

"Who gave himself for our sins, that he might deliver us from this present evil world, according to the will of God and our Father" (Gal.1:4).

"So Christ was once offered to bear the sins of many; and unto them that look for him shall he appear the second time without sin unto salvation" (Heb.9:28).

"Who his own self bare our sins in his own body on the tree, that we, being dead to sins, should live unto righteousness: by whose stripes ye were healed" (1 Pt.2:24).

"And ye know that he was manifested to take away our sins; and in him is no sin" (1 Jn.3:5).

2) Jesus Christ has conquered the enemy of death for the believer.

"For he must reign, till he hath put all enemies under his feet. The last enemy that shall be destroyed is death" (1 Cor.15:25-26).

"O death, where is thy sting? O grave, where is thy victory? The sting of death is sin; and the strength of sin is the law. But thanks be to God, which giveth us the victory through our Lord Jesus Christ" (1 Cor.15:55-57).

"But we see Jesus, who was made a little lower than the angels for the suffering of death, crowned with glory and honour; that he by the grace of God should taste death for every man" (Heb.2:9).

"Forasmuch then as the children are partakers of flesh and blood, he also himself likewise took part of the same; that through death he might destroy him that had the power of death, that is, the devil; And deliver them who through fear of death were all their lifetime subject to bondage" (Heb.2:14-15).

"He will swallow up death in victory; and the Lord GOD will wipe away tears from off all faces; and the rebuke of his people shall he take away from off all the earth: for the LORD hath spoken it" (Is.25:8).

3) Jesus Christ has defeated the enemy of our soul, Satan himself, for the believer.

"Now is the judgment of this world: now shall the prince of this world be cast out" (Jn.12:31).

"Hereafter I will not talk much with you: for the prince of this world cometh, and hath nothing in me" (Jn.14:30).

"And the God of peace shall bruise Satan under your feet shortly. The grace of our Lord Jesus Christ be with you. Amen" (Ro.16:20).

"Forasmuch then as the children are partakers of flesh and blood, he also himself likewise took part of the same; that through death he might destroy him that had the power of death, that is, the devil" (Heb.2:14).

"He that committeth sin is of the devil; for the devil sinneth from the beginning. For this purpose the Son of God was manifested, that he might destroy the works of the devil" (1 Jn.3:8).

4) Jesus Christ has conquered the world for the believer.

"For whatsoever is born of God overcometh the world: and this is the victory that overcometh the world, even our faith. Who is he that overcometh the world, but he that believeth that Jesus is the Son of God?" (1 Jn.5:4-5).

5) Jesus Christ has conquered every enemy--no matter how fierce or terrible--for the believer

"Who shall separate us from the love of Christ? shall tribulation, or distress, or persecution, or famine, or nakedness, or peril, or sword?...Nay, in all these things we are more than conquerors through him that loved us. For I am persuaded, that neither death, nor life, nor angels, nor principalities, nor powers, nor things present, nor things to come, Nor height, nor depth, nor any other creature, shall be able to separate us from the love of God, which is in Christ Jesus our Lord" (Ro.8:35, 37-39).

2. Note the believer's part in renewing the relationship, the covenant with God (v.12-26). The believer's duties to God listed here had been covered before when the covenant was first established. But in starting over, in making a new beginning, it was necessary to review the duties of the believer. There needed to be a written record of what God expected in order to maintain a good relationship with Him. The Israelites were no different than anyone else: they needed a written record of the law, of the covenant, a constant reminder of their duties toward God.

a. The people were to live a life of separation, never becoming associated or tied to unbelievers (v.12). Note why: lest they be influenced by the sinful, worldly ways of unbelievers. God's people must never be unequally yoked with unbelievers, not in anything.

"But now I have written unto you not to keep company, if any man that is called a brother be a fornicator, or covetous, or an idolater, or a railer, or a drunkard, or an extortioner; with such an one no not to eat" (1 Cor.5:11).

"Be ye not unequally yoked together with unbelievers: for what fellowship hath righteousness with unrighteousness? and what communion hath light with darkness?" (2 Cor.6:14).

"Wherefore come out from among them, and be ye separate, saith the Lord, and touch not the unclean thing; and I will receive you, And will be a Father unto you, and ye shall be my sons and daughters, saith the Lord Almighty" (2 Cor.6:17-18).

"And have no fellowship with the unfruitful works of darkness, but rather reprove them" (Eph.5:11).

"Love not the world, neither the things that are in the world. If any man love the world, the love of the Father is not in him. For all that is in the world, the lust of the flesh, and the lust of the eyes, and the pride of life, is not of the Father, but is of the world" (1 Jn.2:15-16).

"Thou shalt not follow a multitude to do evil; neither shalt thou speak in a cause to decline after many to wrest judgment" (Ex.23:2).

"Be not thou envious against evil men, neither desire to be with them" (Pr.24:1).

"Depart ye, depart ye, go ye out from thence, touch no unclean thing; go ye out of the midst of her; be ye clean, that bear the vessels of the LORD" (Is.52:11).

b. The people were not to worship false gods, the gods of unbelievers (v.13-14). The instructions were clear: they were to allow no false gods, no false worship in their midst. They were to destroy the altars of other gods and of false worship. Why? Because one of God's names—one of the names by which God is known--is Jealous (quanna). This unique name is reserved solely for God. Note that it is mentioned twice in this verse, emphasizing God's great love and passion for His people. God is far more jealous over the believer than a husband is over his wife. The Expositor's Bible Commentary says this: "This particular word is used only of God, occurring but five times in the O.T., and illustrates the parallel between idolatry and adultery."[1]

God is jealous whenever one of His dear people flirts with another god. God hates idolatry and false worship. God forbids idolatry and false worship. (See note--Ex.20:3 for more discussion.)

"Take heed to yourselves, that your heart be not deceived, and ye turn aside, and serve other gods, and worship them" (Dt.11:16).

"I am the LORD: that is my name: and my glory will I not give to another, neither my praise to graven images" (Is.42:8).

"Little children, keep yourselves from idols. Amen" (1 Jn.5:21).

c. The people were to live lives of absolute separation, never making an alliance nor any permanent tie with unbelievers (v.15-16). Why was God so strict with this command? Because of evil influence. God knows that no believer is strong enough to resist the worldly influence of unbelievers if he is always associated with them. He knows that the worldly ways of unbelievers will eventually wear down the resistance of the believer. The believer will eventually commit spiritual adultery, that is, turn away from God to the gods of this world (the attractions, possessions, and pleasures of the world). Note that God also knows another fact: alliances and permanent associations with unbelievers will lead to intermarriage with unbelievers (v.16). God knows how difficult it is for believers to remain pure and untainted; how difficult it is to always be alert against the lust of the flesh, the lust of the eyes, and the pride of life (1 Jn.2:15-16). God knows how difficult it is to continually be growing and maturing in Christ. He knows that a believer needs the constant help of other believers, in particular the help of a spouse and other family members.

"Thou shalt not follow a multitude to do evil; neither shalt thou speak in a cause to decline after many to wrest judgment" (Ex.23:2).

"Take heed to thyself, lest thou make a covenant with the inhabitants of the land whither thou goest, lest it be for a snare in the midst of thee" (Ex.34:12).

"Blessed is the man that walketh not in the counsel of the ungodly, nor standeth in the way of sinners, nor sitteth in the seat of the scornful" (Ps.1:1).

"Be ye not unequally yoked together with unbelievers: for what fellowship hath righteousness with unrighteousness? and what communion hath light with darkness?" (2 Cor.6:14).

d. The people were to make no idols whatsoever (v.17). Note how God stresses this prohibition time and time again: man is to have nothing whatsoever to do with idols and false worship. (See outline and notes--Ex.20:4-6 for more discussion.)

"For thou shalt worship no other god: for the LORD, whose name is Jealous, is a jealous God" (Ex.34:14).

"Ye shall make you no idols nor graven image, neither rear you up a standing image, neither shall ye set up any image of stone in your land, to bow down unto it: for I am the LORD your God" (Lev.26:1).

"Forasmuch then as we are the offspring of God, we ought not to think that the Godhead is like unto gold, or silver, or stone, graven by art and man's device" (Acts 17:29).

e. The people must celebrate the Passover: keep the Feast of Unleavened Bread (v.18). Note that they were to eat unleavened bread for seven days and celebrate God's great deliverance from Egypt (a symbol of the world). (See outline and notes--Ex.12:14-20 for more discussion.)

---

[1] Frank E. Gaebelein. *The Expositor's Bible Commentary*, Vol.2, p.486.

f. The people were to give the firstborn to God (v.19-20).
  ⇒ They were to give the first of every herd and flock (v.19).
  ⇒ They were to give and redeem a substitute lamb for a donkey (v.20).
  ⇒ They were to give and redeem a substitute lamb for their own sons (v.20).

Giving is important to God, for it shows the true heart of a person. The person who truly loves God will give all that he *is and has* to God. Everything beyond the necessities of life are desperately needed to meet the dire needs of the suffering and lost of the world. Note what God says: "No one is to appear before me empty-handed" (v.20).

"Every man shall give as he is able, according to the blessing of the LORD thy God which he hath given thee" (Dt.16:17).
"Honour the LORD with thy substance, and with the firstfruits of all thine increase" (Pr.3:9).
"Then the disciples, every man according to his ability, determined to send relief unto the brethren which dwelt in Judaea" (Acts 11:29).
"Upon the first day of the week let every one of you lay by him in store, as God hath prospered him, that there be no gatherings when I come" (1 Cor.16:2).
"For if there be first a willing mind, it is accepted according to that a man hath, and not according to that he hath not" (2 Cor.8:12).

g. The people were to keep the Sabbath day even during the busiest season of their work (v.21). (See outline and notes--Ex.31:12-17; also see note--Ex.20:8-11 for more discussion.)
h. The people were to keep and celebrate all the religious feasts, the Feast of Weeks and the Feast of Ingathering. The Feast of Weeks refers to Pentecost which took place seven weeks after the Passover. The Feast of Ingathering refers to the Feast of Tabernacles. (See outline and notes--Ex.23:14-17; Heb.12:1-2 for more discussion.)

"LORD, I have loved the habitation of thy house, and the place where thine honour dwelleth" (Ps.26:8).
"One thing have I desired of the LORD, that will I seek after; that I may dwell in the house of the LORD all the days of my life, to behold the beauty of the LORD, and to inquire in his temple" (Ps.27:4).
"O come, let us worship and bow down: let us kneel before the LORD our maker" (Ps.95:6).
"O worship the LORD in the beauty of holiness: fear before him, all the earth" (Ps.96:9).

i. The people were to have all the men appear before God three times a year (v.23-24). The men were to take the lead in keeping the religious feasts. This demand required a strong commitment by the men, for it meant they would have to leave behind their wives, children, jobs, and property in order to come and worship God. This meant that their loved ones and everything they possessed would be exposed to their ungodly neighbors, to the assault, theft, and attack by their ungodly neighbors. But note God's promise: He would protect His people from their ungodly neighbors while they were worshipping Him (v.24). God would either keep the thoughts of assault and attack out of their minds or else prevent the acts in some way.

"For the eyes of the LORD run to and fro throughout the whole earth, to show himself strong in the behalf of them whose heart is perfect toward him. Herein thou hast done foolishly: therefore from henceforth thou shalt have wars" (2 Chron.16:9).
"The angel of the LORD encampeth round about them that fear him, and delivereth them" (Ps.34:7).
"He shall cover thee with his feathers, and under his wings shalt thou trust: his truth shall be thy shield and buckler" (Ps.91:4).

j. The people were to guard the Passover (v.25). The Passover was the most important feast for the Israelites. Therefore God wanted them to observe the Passover in the right way. They were never to profane the feast by using leavened bread, bread with yeast. Neither were they to leave any of the Passover meal overnight. (See outlines and notes--Ex.12:1-13; 12:14-20 for more discussion.)
k. They were to bring the firstfruits to the house of God (v.26). (See outline and notes--Ex.22:29-30 for more discussion.)

"Bring ye all the tithes into the storehouse, that there may be meat in mine house, and prove me now herewith, saith the LORD of hosts, if I will not open you the windows of heaven, and pour you out a blessing, that there shall not be room enough to receive it" (Mal.3:10).
"Upon the first day of the week let every one of you lay by him in store, as God hath prospered him, that there be no gatherings when I come" (1 Cor.16:2).

l. The people were not to cook a young goat in its mother's milk (v.26). (See note, pt.2--Ex.23:19.)

Thought 1. When starting over, when seeking to make a new beginning with God, a person must make a renewed covenant with God, a renewed commitment to obey Him. This is man's part in seeking a renewed relationship with God: obedience. A man must obey God in order to have a right relationship with God. A man must keep the commandments of God in order to please God, to be acceptable to Him.

> "This day the LORD thy God hath commanded thee to do these statutes and judgments: thou shalt therefore keep and do them with all thine heart, and with all thy soul" (Dt.26:16).
>
> "This book of the law shall not depart out of thy mouth; but thou shalt meditate therein day and night, that thou mayest observe to do according to all that is written therein: for then thou shalt make thy way prosperous, and then thou shalt have good success" (Josh.1:8).
>
> "And Samuel said, Hath the LORD as great delight in burnt offerings and sacrifices, as in obeying the voice of the LORD? Behold, to obey is better than sacrifice, and to hearken than the fat of rams" (1 Sam.15:22).
>
> "Not every one that saith unto me, Lord, Lord, shall enter into the kingdom of heaven; but he that doeth the will of my Father which is in heaven" (Mt.7:21).
>
> "He that hath my commandments, and keepeth them, he it is that loveth me: and he that loveth me shall be loved of my Father, and I will love him, and will manifest myself to him" (Jn.14:21).
>
> "Jesus answered and said unto him, If a man love me, he will keep my words: and my Father will love him, and we will come unto him, and make our abode with him" (Jn.14:23).

4 **(34:27-28) Commandments, The Ten--Intercession--Starting Over--Devotions**: when starting over, the fourth step is to know the importance of the special commandments of God, the Ten Commandments themselves.

1. The Ten Commandments are the basis of God's covenant, of His relationship to man (v.27). The Ten Commandments are the very basis of civilization, of human life itself. Review the Ten Commandments and note how they are the very foundation of human order, decency, and respect. Without the principles and rules of the Ten Commandments, human life and civilization would be utter chaos. Therefore, if a person wishes to start over with God, to establish a renewed relationship with God, he must learn the importance of the Ten Commandments.

2. The Ten Commandments are so important that Moses did not sleep or eat while receiving the law (v.28). Note what Scripture says: Moses was up on the mountain for *forty days and forty nights* without eating bread or drinking water. He was in deep prayer and communion with God, receiving the Ten Commandments and the civil law that were to govern the Israelites as a nation. God obviously sustained Moses during the forty days and forty nights, miraculously taking care of him during this intense communion and fellowship with God.

3. The Ten Commandments are so important that they are set apart and entitled, *the Ten Commandments* (v.28). Throughout Scripture God has given many instructions or decrees, but there are ten very specific commandments He has given. These specific Ten Commandments are given this very distinct name in order to set them apart from all other commandments. This is noteworthy and significant: this means that man must pay very special attention to the Ten Commandments. He must obey these Ten Commandments above all others commandments. The Ten Commandments are the very basis of his relationship with God, the very basis of the covenant and agreement between himself and God. Man must, therefore, make a strong commitment throughout life to keep *the Ten Commandments*.

> "Now therefore, if ye will obey my voice indeed, and keep my covenant, then ye shall be a peculiar treasure unto me above all people: for all the earth is mine" (Ex.19:5).
>
> "And all the people answered together, and said, All that the LORD hath spoken we will do. And Moses returned the words of the people unto the LORD" (Ex.19:8).
>
> "O that there were such an heart in them, that they would fear me, and keep all my commandments always, that it might be well with them, and with their children for ever!" (Dt.5:29).
>
> "Not every one that saith unto me, Lord, Lord, shall enter into the kingdom of heaven; but he that doeth the will of my Father which is in heaven" (Mt.7:21).
>
> "Blessed are they that do his commandments, that they may have right to the tree of life, and may enter in through the gates into the city" (Rev.22:14).

5 **(34:29-35) Proclamation--Witnessing--Preaching--Word of God--Veil, of Moses**: when starting over, the fifth step is going forth to proclaim God's Word. God's dear servant Moses had sought the Lord for forty days and forty nights, and God had met his every need. God had given him the Word of God that was to be carried to the people. It was now time for him to go forth and proclaim the great commandments of God to the people. Note these facts about God's servant.

1. God's servant was prepared: he had been in the presence of the Lord--symbolized by the radiance of God's glory upon his face (v.29-31). God's dear servant had remained and refused to leave God's presence until he had received God's Word. It was essential--absolutely essential--that he stay in God's presence until he had the message of God, the message that God wanted proclaimed to His dear people. Note an astonishing fact: Moses had stayed in the presence of God so long, waiting for the message of God, that the glory of God had actually permeated his being. The glory of God was actually radiated (garan) as a bright light upon his face. It is critical to note why: because he had spoken with the Lord, actually been in the presence of the Lord, for so long. Note that the radiating light of God's glory upon Moses' face is referred to three times (v.29, 30, 35). A fact should be noted about this experience of Moses: he had been spending day after day in intercessory prayer...

- seeking the forgiveness of sins
- seeking the presence of God
- seeking to know and understand the Lord and His ways more and more

Keep in mind that these sessions of intercessory prayer took place prior to Moses' spending forty days and forty nights in God's presence. The point is this: intercessory prayer--spending day after day seeking God--obviously led Moses into a deep, intense communion with God, a communion so intense that God just imparted some of His glory into the very being of Moses. (What a glorious lesson for us: to seek God so much that He has to impart His glory into our very being, so much so that His glory radiates upon our face.) Moses experienced, apparently to a greater degree, just what Scripture says all believers are to experience: he beheld as in a glass the glory of the Lord and was changed into the same image from glory to glory (2 Cor.3:18).

The fact to keep in mind is this: Moses was spiritually prepared to proclaim the message of God to the people. But note the reaction of the people, even of Aaron: when they saw that Moses' face was radiant, they were afraid to come near him (v.30). But in humility and meekness, Moses called them to come near and receive the message of God (v.31).

2. God's servant declared God's commandments *to the leaders* (v.31).

3. God's servant faithfully declared God's commandments *to the people* (v.32). Note that Moses declared all the commandments the Lord had given him on Mount Sinai. God's servant must always proclaim God's Word to the people.

> "And they taught in Judah, and had the book of the law of the LORD with them, and went about throughout all the cities of Judah, and taught the people" (2 Chron.17:9).
>
> "For we cannot but speak the things which we have seen and heard" (Acts 4:20).
>
> "Go, stand and speak in the temple to the people all the words of this life" (Acts 5:20).
>
> "We having the same spirit of faith, according as it is written, I believed, and therefore have I spoken; we also believe, and therefore speak" (2 Cor.4:13).
>
> "And the things that thou hast heard of me among many witnesses, the same commit thou to faithful men, who shall be able to teach others also" (2 Tim.2:2).
>
> "These things speak, and exhort, and rebuke with all authority. Let no man despise thee" (Tit.2:15).

4. God's servant covered his face with a veil after declaring God's commandments (v.33). There is a hint as to why God allowed His glory to be radiated upon Moses' face. The people needed such a miraculous event in order to strengthen their faith in God and His commandments. When Moses declared the commandments of God to the people, they knew that the commandments were the Word of God. They knew because of the miraculous glory that was radiating from Moses' face. Their faith in God and in His Word was thereby strengthened.

Thought 1. Moses' experience with the glory of God was the very opposite experience of Christ. Jesus Christ experienced the glory of God upon the mount of transfiguration (Mt.17:2). Scripture declares that the whole body of Jesus Christ radiated the glory of God as brightly as the sun itself, that His clothing was white and glistering (Lk.9:29). But when Christ came down from the mount, He laid aside that glory. His face did not shine nor radiate the glory of God. He willingly laid aside the glory, made sure that the glory was not radiating through His being. Why? Because it is necessary that believers walk by faith not by sight (2 Cor.5:7).

5. God's servant removed the veil when he entered God's presence (v.34). Note that the veil was removed from Moses' face only on two occasions: when he was proclaiming the Word of God and when he was praying and seeking the face of the Lord. This is the picture of a great truth: when a person seeks the face of God or proclaims the Word of God, there is to be nothing--no mask, no counterfeit, no deception--between him and God. There is to be nothing, absolutely nothing, covering his face or the truth of his heart from God. The person is to approach God with an open face and heart, approach Him in truth and spirit.

6. God's servant received a new radiance from God every time he entered God's presence (v.34-35). The picture being painted is this: before proclaiming the Word of God to the people, Moses prepared himself. He sought the face of the Lord every time he was to address the people. And God gave him more and more of His glory to radiate upon his face. When Moses walked before the people to proclaim the Word of God, they saw that his face was radiating the glory of God, that he had been in the presence of God and was ready to present God's message to them.

Thought 1. When starting over, when making a new beginning, the last step in our journey is to go forth and proclaim God's Holy Word to a lost and dying world, to a world that is reeling under the heavy weight of terrible need and suffering.

> "Come and hear, all ye that fear God, and I will declare what he hath done for my soul" (Ps.66:16).
>
> "Ye are my witnesses, saith the LORD, and my servant whom I have chosen: that ye may know and believe me, and understand that I am he: before me there was no God formed, neither shall there be after me. I, even I, am the LORD; and beside me there is no saviour" (Is.43:10-11).
>
> "I will mention the lovingkindnesses of the LORD, and the praises of the LORD, according to all that the LORD hath bestowed on us, and the great goodness toward the house of Israel, which he hath bestowed on them according to his mercies, and according to the multitude of his lovingkindnesses" (Is.63:7).
>
> "Then they that feared the LORD spake often one to another: and the LORD hearkened, and heard it, and a book of remembrance was written before him for them that feared the LORD, and that thought upon his name" (Mal.3:16).
>
> "For we cannot but speak the things which we have seen and heard" (Acts 4:20).
>
> "Go, stand and speak in the temple to the people all the words of this life. And when they heard that, they entered into the temple early in the morning, and taught. But the high priest

came, and they that were with him, and called the council together, and all the senate of the children of Israel and sent to the prison to have them brought" (Acts 5:20-21).

"And he said, The God of our fathers hath chosen thee, that thou shouldest know his will, and see that Just One, and shouldest hear the voice of his mouth. For thou shalt be his witness unto all men of what thou hast seen and heard" (Acts 22:14-15).

"We having the same spirit of faith, according as it is written, I believed, and therefore have I spoken; we also believe, and therefore speak" (2 Cor.4:13).

"These things speak, and exhort, and rebuke with all authority. Let no man despise thee" (Tit.2:15).

Thought 2. Paul uses the veil that covered Moses' face to illustrate two great truths.

1) Scripture declares that Moses wore the veil so the Israelites would not see the glory of the law fading away (2 Cor.3:7-18). This means that the dispensation of law was to pass and fade away, that it was to be replaced by the greater splendor of the dispensation of the Spirit. The point is simply this: the work of Jesus Christ was a far greater and more glorious work than the work of the law. Through the work of Christ, His death and resurrection, we are saved and given life eternal. Our sins are forgiven and we are given the inheritance of living with God forever and ever.

"For God so loved the world, that he gave his only begotten Son, that whosoever believeth in him should not perish, but have everlasting life" (Jn.3:16).

"Forasmuch then as the children are partakers of flesh and blood, he also himself likewise took part of the same; that through death he might destroy him that had the power of death, that is, the devil; And deliver them who through fear of death were all their lifetime subject to bondage" (Heb.2:14-15).

"Wherefore he is able also to save them to the uttermost that come unto God by him, seeing he ever liveth to make intercession for them" (Heb.7:25).

"So Christ was once offered to bear the sins of many; and unto them that look for him shall he appear the second time without sin unto salvation" (Heb.9:28).

"Who his own self bare our sins in his own body on the tree, that we, being dead to sins, should live unto righteousness: by whose stripes ye were healed" (1 Pt.2:24).

"For Christ also hath once suffered for sins, the just for the unjust, that he might bring us to God, being put to death in the flesh, but quickened by the Spirit" (1 Pt.3:18).

2) Scripture declares that the veil of Moses symbolizes the blindness of Israel in reading the Scriptures (2 Cor.3:7-18). When Israel reads the Scripture, they are spiritually blind: they do not see the true glory of God that He has given to the world, that is, His Son, the Lord Jesus Christ. The veil of spiritual blindness that covers their eyes can be removed only through Christ, the Son of God Himself, the true Messiah and Savior of the world. Jesus Christ alone is the Light of the world; His Light alone can remove the veil of blindness that covers men's eyes.

"The people that walked in darkness have seen a great light: they that dwell in the land of the shadow of death, upon them hath the light shined" (Is.9:2).

"In him was life; and the life was the light of men" (Jn.1:4).

"Then spake Jesus again unto them, saying, I am the light of the world: he that followeth me shall not walk in darkness, but shall have the light of life" (Jn.8:12).

"Then Jesus said unto them, Yet a little while is the light with you. Walk while ye have the light, lest darkness come upon you: for he that walketh in darkness knoweth not whither he goeth" (Jn.12:35).

"For God, who commanded the light to shine out of darkness, hath shined in our hearts, to give the light of the knowledge of the glory of God in the face of Jesus Christ" (2 Cor.4:6).

"Wherefore he saith, Awake thou that sleepest, and arise from the dead, and Christ shall give thee light" (Eph.5:14).

"And the city had no need of the sun, neither of the moon, to shine in it: for the glory of God did lighten it, and the Lamb [Jesus Christ] is the light thereof" (Rev.21:23).

TYPES, SYMBOLS, AND PICTURES
(Exodus 34:1-35)

Historical Term	Type or Picture (Scriptural Basis for Each)	Life Application for Today's Believer	Biblical Application for Today's Believer
Moses' Veil (Ex.34:35)	*When Moses came down the mountain after spending time in God's presence, his face shone. After the people saw him, Moses placed a veil over his face. There are two clear symbols seen in Moses' Veil:*	What Moses' Veil taught:	*"For God so loved the world, that he gave his only begotten Son, that whosoever believeth in him should not perish, but have everlasting life" (Jn.3:16).* *"Forasmuch then as the children are partakers of*

Historical Term	Type or Picture (Scriptural Basis for Each)	Life Application for Today's Believer	Biblical Application for Today's Believer
	a. Moses' Veil symbolized the fading glory of the law.	a. The work of Jesus Christ is a far greater and more glorious work than the work of the law. Through the work of Christ, His death and resurrection, we are saved and given life eternal. Our sins are forgiven and we are given the inheritance of living with God forever and ever.	*flesh and blood, he also himself likewise took part of the same; that through death he might destroy him that had the power of death, that is, the devil; And deliver them who through fear of death were all their lifetime subject to bondage" (Heb.2:14-15).* "*Wherefore he is able also to save them to the uttermost that come unto God by him, seeing he ever liveth to make intercession for them" (Heb.7:25).*
	b. Moses' Veil symbolized the spiritual blindness of Israel in reading the Scriptures, that they are unable to understand the truth of Scripture that Jesus Christ is the true Messiah and Savior of the world. **"And the children of Israel saw the face of Moses, that the skin of Moses' face shone: and Moses put the vail upon his face again, until he went in to speak with him" (Ex.34:35).**	b. Christ alone is the Light of the world, the Light who can remove the veil of blindness that covers men's eyes.	"*The people that walked in darkness have seen a great light: they that dwell in the land of the shadow of death, upon them hath the light shined" (Is.9:2).* "*In him was life; and the life was the light of men" (Jn.1:4).* "*Then spake Jesus again unto them, saying, I am the light of the world: he that followeth me shall not walk in darkness, but shall have the light of life" (Jn.8:12).* "*Then Jesus said unto them, Yet a little while is the light with you. Walk while ye have the light, lest darkness come upon you: for he that walketh in darkness knoweth not whither he goeth" (Jn.12:35).*

DIVISION XI

THE TABERNACLE, ITS CONSTRUCTION AND DEDICATION: THE PEOPLE OBEY GOD, 35:1-40:38

(35:1-40:38) **DIVISION OVERVIEW--Tabernacle**: this division completes the great story of Exodus, the story of God's great deliverance and redemption of His people. The construction of the Tabernacle is the subject of these concluding chapters. Reading through the chapters is often felt to be uninteresting and even unimportant. Why? Because most of the material covered here has already been covered earlier:

⇒ Chapters 25-31 covered God's design and instructions for building the Tabernacle.
⇒ Chapters 35-40 now cover the actual construction of the Tabernacle.

The two passages are almost identical except for switching from the future to the past tense. There are very few changes. Therefore the reader could feel there is no need to reread the account, that he can pass over the account of the actual construction without missing anything. But this should not be. God has deliberately had the account included in His Holy Word, had the actual construction included for at least three very specific purposes.

1. Man must approach God correctly, exactly as God dictates. This is the great lesson of the Tabernacle, the great symbolic meaning of the Tabernacle. The Tabernacle shows man...

- that he must approach God through the sacrifice of the lamb
- that God is holy and righteous and dwells in the Most Holy Place, dwells behind the inner veil of holiness
- that God sits upon the Mercy Seat, that His very throne is a throne of mercy

On and on the lessons of the Tabernacle could be listed--all declaring that man must approach God exactly as God says. God cannot accept man apart from the blood of the sacrificial lamb. This truth must be emphasized time and time again. This is the first great purpose for repeating the material given in these chapters, the reason why Holy Scripture covers the actual construction of the Tabernacle. We must read the account time and again, noting how *exact* the design was and how *carefully* everything was constructed. All this points to the fact...

- that we must be *exact* in our approach and worship of God, approaching and worshipping Him exactly as He dictatesc
- that we must be *careful* in our approach and worship of God, again being careful to approach and worship Him exactly as He says

2. The actual construction of the Tabernacle emphasizes *obedience*, the obedience of God's dear servant (Moses) and God's dear people. Both Moses and the people built the Tabernacle exactly as God designed. Their obedience is deliberately stressed. This is seen in two very clear passages: Chapters 39 and 40. Note the sevenfold repetition in each of the passages, the forceful stress upon the fact that God's people did exactly "as the LORD [Yahweh] commanded Moses."

⇒ Note chapter 39.

> "And of the blue, and purple, and scarlet, they made cloths of service, to do service in the holy place, and made the holy garments for Aaron; **as the LORD commanded Moses**" (Ex.39:1).
>
> "And the curious girdle of his ephod, that was upon it, was of the same, according to the work thereof; of gold, blue, and purple, and scarlet, and fine twined linen; **as the LORD commanded Moses**" (Ex.39:5).
>
> "And he put them on the shoulders of the ephod, that they should be stones for a memorial to the children of Israel; **as the LORD commanded Moses**" (Ex.39:7).
>
> "And they did bind the breastplate by his rings unto the rings of the ephod with a lace of blue, that it might be above the curious girdle of the ephod, and that the breastplate might not be loosed from the ephod; **as the LORD commanded Moses**" (Ex.39:21).
>
> "A bell and a pomegranate, a bell and a pomegranate, round about the hem of the robe to minister in; **as the LORD commanded Moses**" (Ex.39:26).
>
> "And a girdle of fine twined linen, and blue, and purple, and scarlet, of needlework; **as the LORD commanded Moses**" (Ex.39:29).
>
> "And they tied unto it a lace of blue, to fasten it on high upon the mitre; **as the LORD commanded Moses**" (Ex.39:31).

⇒ Note chapter 40.

> "And he spread abroad the tent over the tabernacle, and put the covering of the tent above upon it; <u>as the LORD commanded Moses</u>" (Ex.40:19).
> "And he brought the ark into the tabernacle, and set up the vail of the covering, and covered the ark of the testimony; <u>as the LORD commanded Moses</u>" (Ex.40:21).
> "And he set the bread in order upon it before the LORD; <u>as the LORD had commanded Moses</u>" (Ex.40:23).
> "And he lighted the lamps before the LORD; <u>as the LORD commanded Moses</u>" (Ex.40:25).
> "And he burnt sweet incense thereon; <u>as the LORD commanded Moses</u>" (Ex.40:27).
> "And he put the altar of burnt offering by the door of the tabernacle of the tent of the congregation, and offered upon it the burnt offering and the meat offering; <u>as the LORD commanded Moses</u>" (Ex.40:29).
> "When they went into the tent of the congregation, and when they came near unto the altar, they washed; <u>as the LORD commanded Moses</u>" (Ex.40:32).

The lesson is clear: the people of God obeyed God exactly as He dictated. They built the Tabernacle according to God's design so they could approach and worship God precisely as He dictated.

3. The third purpose for recording the actual building of the Tabernacle is of vital importance: God wanted man to know that He is, above all else, *loving* and *faithful*, merciful and forgiving. And God will dwell in the midst of His people if they will only obey Him, approach Him as He says. All this is symbolized in the Tabernacle.

Remember, the golden calf tragedy had just occurred. The people had just failed God, miserably failed Him. They had rejected God and chosen a man-made worship over the true worship of God. They had broken the Ten Commandments, broken the covenant, their commitment to God.

In recording the actual construction of the Tabernacle--after the terrible sin of the people--God is stressing this great lesson: He is loving and faithful, merciful and forgiving. Once man has repented and confessed his sin, God will actually come and dwell among His people. Despite man's terrible depravity, if man will truly approach God as God dictates, God will still prove faithful: He will...

- forgive man's sin
- restore man
- renew His covenant with man
- give man a new start, a new beginning
- dwell in the midst of man

Note that it takes six chapters to cover the actual construction and dedication of the Tabernacle. The space given to the construction, six chapters out of forty, stresses the importance that God places upon the Tabernacle and the three purposes described above. This is the reason we must never pass over these chapters, feeling they are unimportant.

The details of the Tabernacle design have already been discussed in chapters 25-31. Therefore, the reader can turn back to this parallel passage for a discussion of the design. Because of this, our approach in discussing the construction will be to focus upon the outline and the practical application of the Tabernacle--the pictures, symbols, and types--the meaning that the Tabernacle holds for us in our day and time.

PLEASE NOTE THE
RESOURCE CHART SECTION:

The following charts on the Tabernacle are given in the Resource Chart Section at the conclusion of Ex.40:1-38. This is done to keep from interrupting a person's study of the Scripture outlines and commentary. A study of the Charts will help the reader more fully grasp the meaning of the Tabernacle.

Chart 1: THE PICTURE OF THE BELIEVER'S LIFE IN THE TABERNACLE

Chart 2: HOW CHRIST FULFILLED THE SYMBOLISM OF THE TABERNACLE

Chart 3: HOW CHRIST FULFILLED THE SYMBOLISM OF THE PRIESTHOOD

DIVISION XI

THE TABERNACLE, ITS CONSTRUCTION AND DEDICATION: THE PEOPLE OBEY GOD, 35:1-40:38

A. The Preparations for Building the Tabernacle: The Call to Give Sacrificially, Ex.35:1-35

B. The Construction of the Tabernacle: The Excitement of Building for God, Ex.36:1-38

C. The Building of the Furnishings For the Tabernacle (Part 1): Learning the Only Way to Approach God, Ex.37:1-29

D. The Building of the Furnishings For the Tabernacle (Part 2): Learning the Only Way to Approach God, Ex.38:1-31

E. The Making of the Garments For the Priests: Being Clothed in Righteousness, Ex.39:1-43

F. The Assembly and Dedication of the Tabernacle, the Center of Worship: Experiencing the Presence of the Lord, Ex.40:1-38

EXODUS 35:1-35

XI. THE TABERNACLE, ITS CONSTRUCTION & DEDICATION: THE PEOPLE OBEY GOD, 35:1-40:38

A. The Preparations for Building the Tabernacle: The Call to Give Sacrificially, Ex.35:1-35

1. **The call: Everyone is called to have a part in building the Tabernacle (worship center)**

2. **The most important instruction: Keep the Sabbath while building**
   a. To work six days, but keep the Sabbath: As a holy day & day of rest
   b. The importance stressed
      1) To execute violators
      2) To start no fires on the Sabbath

3. **The offerings to build the Tabernacle**
   a. The privilege of giving was presented to everyone
   b. The offerings were to be given freely, only by willing hearts
      1) The metals
      2) The fabrics
      3) The (animal) skins
      4) The wood
      5) The oil, spices, & sweet incense
      6) The stones & gems for the ephod & breastpiece

4. **The challenge to the skilled workers: To come & make everything**
   a. The Tabernacle itself (symbolized God dwelling among His people & man's need to approach God as God dictates)
   b. The Ark & Mercy Seat & Veil (symbolized the presence, mercy, & holiness of God)
   c. The Table of Showbread (pointed to Christ as the Bread of Life)
   d. The Lampstand (pointed to Christ as the Light of the world)

And Moses gathered all the congregation of the children of Israel together, and said unto them, These are the words which the LORD hath commanded, that ye should do them.
2 Six days shall work be done, but on the seventh day there shall be to you an holy day, a sabbath of rest to the LORD: whosoever doeth work therein shall be put to death.
3 Ye shall kindle no fire throughout your habitations upon the sabbath day.
4 And Moses spake unto all the congregation of the children of Israel, saying, This is the thing which the LORD commanded, saying,
5 Take ye from among you an offering unto the LORD: whosoever is of a willing heart, let him bring it, an offering of the LORD; gold, and silver, and brass,
6 And blue, and purple, and scarlet, and fine linen, and goats' hair,
7 And rams' skins dyed red, and badgers' skins, and shittim wood,
8 And oil for the light, and spices for anointing oil, and for the sweet incense,
9 And onyx stones, and stones to be set for the ephod, and for the breastplate.
10 And every wise hearted among you shall come, and make all that the LORD hath commanded;
11 The tabernacle, his tent, and his covering, his taches, and his boards, his bars, his pillars, and his sockets,
12 The ark, and the staves thereof, with the mercy seat, and the vail of the covering,
13 The table, and his staves, and all his vessels, and the showbread,
14 The candlestick also for the light, and his furniture, and his lamps, with the oil for the light,

15 And the incense altar, and his staves, and the anointing oil, and the sweet incense, and the hanging for the door at the entering in of the tabernacle,
16 The altar of burnt offering, with his brasen grate, his staves, and all his vessels, the laver and his foot,
17 The hangings of the court, his pillars, and their sockets, and the hanging for the door of the court,
18 The pins of the tabernacle, and the pins of the court, and their cords,
19 The cloths of service, to do service in the holy place, the holy garments for Aaron the priest, and the garments of his sons, to minister in the priest's office.
20 And all the congregation of the children of Israel departed from the presence of Moses.
21 And they came, every one whose heart stirred him up, and every one whom his spirit made willing, and they brought the LORD'S offering to the work of the tabernacle of the congregation, and for all his service, and for the holy garments.
22 And they came, both men and women, as many as were willing hearted, and brought bracelets, and earrings, and rings, and tablets, all jewels of gold: and every man that offered offered an offering of gold unto the LORD.
23 And every man, with whom was found blue, and purple, and scarlet, and fine linen, and goats' hair, and red skins of rams, and badgers' skins, brought them.
24 Every one that did offer an offering of silver and brass brought the LORD'S offering: and every man, with whom was found shittim wood for any work of the service, brought it.
25 And all the women that were wise hearted did spin with their hands, and brought that which they had spun, both of blue, and of purple, and of scarlet, and of fine linen.
26 And all the women whose heart stirred them up in wis-

e. The Altar of Incense (symbolized the prayers ascending up & pleasing God)
f. The outer veil or door (symbolized that God can be approached only through one door, Jesus Christ)
g. The Altar of Burnt Offering (symbolized the need for atonement, reconciliation with God)
h. The bronze wash basin (symbolized the cleansing & forgiveness of sin)
i. The walls (curtains) of the courtyard (symbolized sacrifice)
j. The entrance veil (curtain) (symbolized that God can be approached & spiritual separation)
k. The tent pegs & ropes (symbolized Christ, the binding strength of believers)
l. The clothing for the priests (symbolized bringing dignity & honor to the name of God)

5. **The response of the people to God's call & challenge**

   a. Every person—who was willing & whose heart was stirred—brought an offering to the LORD

   b. Every person who was willing—both men & women—brought gold jewelry as an offering: Presented it as a wave offering to the LORD

   c. Everyone who had colored linen & animal skins brought them as an offering

   d. Everyone who had silver or bronze brought it as an offering to the LORD

   e. Every skilled woman who could sew & spin prepared the curtains
      1) Brought the linen curtains
      2) Brought the goats' hair

419

f. Every leader made his contribution
  1) Brought the stones & gems for the ephod & breastpiece
  2) Brought spices & oil for the light & anointing oil for the incense
 	
g. The glorious fact restated & stressed: All the men & women who were willing gave the LORD freewill offerings for the work
 	
6. **The superintendent & his associate: Chosen by God**
  a. The general superintendent: Bezalel
 	
    1) God filled him with the Spirit
	dom spun goats' hair.
	27 And the rulers brought onyx stones, and stones to be set, for the ephod, and for the breastplate;
	28 And spice, and oil for the light, and for the anointing oil, and for the sweet incense.
	29 The children of Israel brought a willing offering unto the LORD, every man and woman, whose heart made them willing to bring for all manner of work, which the LORD had commanded to be made by the hand of Moses.
	30 And Moses said unto the children of Israel, See, the LORD hath called by name Bezaleel the son of Uri, the son of Hur, of the tribe of Judah;
	31 And he hath filled him with the spirit of God, in
		wisdom, in understanding, and in knowledge, and in all manner of workmanship;
		32 And to devise curious works, to work in gold, and in silver, and in brass,
		33 And in the cutting of stones, to set them, and in carving of wood, to make any manner of cunning work.
		34 And he hath put in his heart that he may teach, both he, and Aholiab, the son of Ahisamach, of the tribe of Dan.
		35 Them hath he filled with wisdom of heart, to work all manner of work, of the engraver, and of the cunning workman, and of the embroiderer, in blue, and in purple, in scarlet, and in fine linen, and of the weaver, even of them that do any work, and of those that devise cunning work.
			2) God filled him with intelligence, knowledge, & skill in construction
			    • In designing metal objects
			    • In cutting & setting stones
			    • In woodworking
			    • In all kinds of craftsmanship
			  b. The associate superintendent: Oholiab
			    1) He & Bezalel were both equipped by God to teach others
			    2) Both were filled by God, filled with skill to do all kinds of work
			    • As craftsmen, designers, embroiderers, & weavers
			    • As master craftsmen & designers

DIVISION XI

THE TABERNACLE, ITS CONSTRUCTION AND DEDICATION:
THE PEOPLE OBEY GOD, Ex.35:1-40:38

A.   The Preparations for Building the Tabernacle: The Call to Give Sacrificially, Ex.35:1-35

(35:1-35) **Introduction**: what does it take to build a successful business? The person who wants to make his business successful has to do several things:
- ⇒ He must be willing to invest significant sums of money.
- ⇒ He must be willing to invest significant amounts of time.
- ⇒ He must be willing to ask other talented and resourceful people to help him.
- ⇒ He must be willing to make any sacrifice, to do whatever it takes to make his business a success.

These principles are true for anyone who wants to succeed in the business world. But they should be even more true in the believer's service for the LORD. How much sacrifice does God require of those who profess and serve Him? What does God expect from His people? What kind of sacrifice does it take to make a successful church or ministry? God expects a full and total sacrifice from any person who follows Him. Note what Scripture says:

> **"And he said to [them] all, If any [man] will come after me, let him deny himself, and take up his cross daily, and follow me" (Lk.9:23).**

There are no short-cuts in serving God. There is no way to circumvent or go around the commitment God requires. This portion of Scripture speaks directly to the person whom God has called to serve Him. It is: *The Preparations for Building the Tabernacle: The Call to Give Sacrificially*, Ex.35:1-35
1. The call: everyone is called to have a part in building the Tabernacle (worship center) (v.1).
2. The most important instruction: keep the Sabbath (v.2-3).
3. The offerings to build the Tabernacle (v.4-9).
4. The challenge to the skilled workers: to come and make everything (v.10-19).
5. The response of the people to God's call and challenge (v.20-29).
6. The two supervisors or managers: chosen by God (v.30-35).

1 (35:1) **Call of God--Christian Service--Church Work**: there was the call: everyone was called to have a part in building the Tabernacle (worship center). Moses called a meeting of all the people; not a single person was left out nor considered unimportant. The call of God to build the worship center went to every person. And note: the call to build the Tabernacle was the command of God. The call was not to be altered or changed whatsoever. The call was to go out to every person, and every person was to *respond* and *obey* the call.

Thought 1. Every believer is called to build God's church here upon earth. Every believer is to become personally involved in the building of the LORD's church. This is not the sole responsibility of a select few nor the privileged right of the rich and powerful. Those who love God have been called to have a part in building God's church and Kingdom here upon earth.

> "For unto whomsoever much is given, of him shall be much required: and to whom men have committed much, of him they will ask the more" (Lk.12:48).
> "Ye have not chosen me, but I have chosen you, and ordained you, that ye should go and bring forth fruit, and [that] your fruit should remain: that whatsoever ye shall ask of the Father in my name, he may give it you" (Jn.15:16).
> "I have glorified thee on the earth: I have finished the work which thou gavest me to do" (Jn.17:4).
> "For we are labourers together with God: ye are God's husbandry, ye are God's building" (1 Cor.3:9).
> "Therefore, my beloved brethren, be ye stedfast, unmoveable, always abounding in the work of the Lord, forasmuch as ye know that your labour is not in vain in the Lord" (1 Cor.15:58).
> "We then, as workers together with him, beseech you also that ye receive not the grace of God in vain" (2 Cor.6:1).
> "If any man speak, let him speak as the oracles of God; if any man minister, let him do it as of the ability which God giveth: that God in all things may be glorified through Jesus Christ, to whom be praise and dominion for ever and ever. Amen" (1 Pt.4:11).
> "If ye be willing and obedient, ye shall eat the good of the land" (Is.1:19).

2 (35:2-3) <u>Sabbath--Rest--Commandments, The Ten--Work--Obedience</u>: there was the most important instruction: keep the Sabbath while building the Tabernacle. Remember, the Sabbath was the sign of the covenant between God and man. If a person was committed to God--if he had made a covenant, an agreement to follow God--he kept the Sabbath. The Sabbath was the sign, the symbol, that he had made a covenant with God.

The Israelites faced a problem. They were very excited about building the Tabernacle. There was the danger that their excitement might cause them to keep right on working, forgetting the Sabbath. They might feel the Tabernacle was so important that they should just keep right on working seven days a week. But God says, "No." The Tabernacle is important: it is the work of God. But keeping the Sabbath, resting and worshipping God one day a week, is more important. Therefore keep the Sabbath. Above all else, rest and worship God one full day a week. Note the clear instructions of Scripture:

1. The believer is to work six days but keep the Sabbath as a holy day and a day of rest (v.2). There is nothing here about a three-day weekend set aside for personal indulgences. There is no mention here of over-working, no mention of working seven days a week. What is noted is this:

⇒ Man is to work six days, to work very hard.
⇒ Man is to set aside the seventh day of the week as a special day. The Sabbath is to be treated as a holy day and a day when man rests from his labor.

2. The importance of the Sabbath is stressed. Violators of the Sabbath were to be executed (v.2). Anyone who got so caught up in his work and forgot the Lord was to be put to death. Even lighting a fire in the home on the Sabbath was emphatically prohibited (v.3). The lighting of a fire probably referred to a person having to work by cooking and cleaning up after meals.

Thought 1. Man would have a far healthier and more fruitful life if he learned how to work extremely hard six days a week and then rested and worshipped on the Sabbath day. Somehow in the extremes of life, periods of work and rest have both been warped and abused.

1) God has commanded man to work and to work hard.

> "And the LORD God took the man, and put him into the garden of Eden to dress it and to keep it" (Gen.2:15).
> "In all labour there is profit: but the talk of the lips *tendeth* only to penury [poverty]" (Pr.14:23).
> "Whatsoever thy hand findeth to do, do *it* with thy might; for *there is* no work, nor device, nor knowledge, nor wisdom, in the grave, whither thou goest" (Eccl.9:10).
> "Let him that stole steal no more: but rather let him labour, working with his hands the thing which is good, that he may have to give to him that needeth" (Eph.4:28).
> "And whatsoever ye do in word or deed, do all in the name of the Lord Jesus, giving thanks to God and the Father by him" (Col.3:17).
> "And whatsoever ye do, do it heartily, as to the Lord, and not unto men" (Col.3:23).
> "Now them that are such we command and exhort by our Lord Jesus Christ, that with quietness they work, and eat their own bread" (2 Th.3:12).

2) God has commanded man to keep the Sabbath, to rest and worship one day a week.

> "Six days thou shalt do thy work, and on the seventh day thou shalt rest: that thine ox and thine ass may rest, and the son of thy handmaid, and the stranger, may be refreshed" (Ex.23:12).
> "Six days may work be done; but in the seventh is the sabbath of rest, <u>holy to the LORD</u>: whosoever doeth *any* work in the sabbath day, he shall surely be put to death" (Ex.31:15).

"Six days thou shalt work, but on the seventh day thou shalt rest: in earing time and in harvest thou shalt rest" (Ex.34:21).

"Six days shall work be done: but the seventh day *is* the sabbath of rest, **an holy convocation;** ye shall do no work *therein:* it *is* the sabbath of the LORD in all your dwellings" (Lev.23:3).

"And he came to Nazareth, where he had been brought up: and, as **his custom** was, he went into the synagogue on the sabbath day, and stood up for to read" (Lk.4:16; cp. Mt.12:9; Mk.1:2).

"Not forsaking the assembling of ourselves together, as the manner of some is; but exhorting one another: and so much the more, as ye see the day approaching" (Heb.10:25).

Thought 2. Should a believer keep the Sabbath today? Rest and worship one day a week? What if he breaks it? Will God judge him and take his life? There is a principle in this portion of Scripture that every believer must face: we must never get so busy that we forget the LORD. God knows us better than we do; therefore He knows how easily we slip into bad habits. God will not strike us down and kill us if we fail to keep the Sabbath, but we will be destroying ourselves. Those who break the Sabbath and forget about God will slip off into a life of sin, rebellion, and a loss of communion with God. Moreover, if a person works seven days a week, he weakens and eventually damages his body.

"And it came to pass, *that* there went out *some* of the people on the seventh day for to gather, and they found none. And the LORD said unto Moses, How long refuse ye to keep my commandments and my laws?" (Ex.16:27-28).

"Ye shall keep the sabbath therefore; for it *is* holy unto you: every one that defileth it shall surely be put to death: for whosoever doeth *any* work therein, that soul shall be cut off from among his people" (Ex.31:14).

"But the house of Israel rebelled against me in the wilderness: they walked not in my statutes, and they despised my judgments, which *if* a man do, he shall even live in them; and my sabbaths they greatly polluted: then I said, I would pour out my fury upon them in the wilderness, to consume them" (Ezk.20:13).

"Thou hast despised mine holy things, and hast profaned my sabbaths" (Ezk.22:8).

3 (35:4-9) **Offerings to God--Tithes--Stewardship**: there were the offerings to build the Tabernacle. There can be no building for God unless the people of God are willing to contribute their tithes and offerings, their talents and spiritual gifts to the LORD. Why does God, the Sovereign LORD and Majesty of the universe, want our resources? Because God wants us to be co-workers along with Him. Being a co-worker means that we labor and serve with God, that we bear witness with God, bear witness to a lost and dying world.

"For we are labourers together with God: ye are God's husbandry, ye are God's building" (1 Cor.3:9).

"We then, as workers together with him, beseech you also that ye receive not the grace of God in vain" (2 Cor.6:1).

Note two significant points.

1. The privilege of giving was presented to everyone (v.4). Everyone was given the opportunity to make an offering to God. Everyone was to have a part in building the Tabernacle, to feel they had a very special part in contributing to God's house of worship. The financial burden of the church is not to be placed upon the backs of the leadership and the *faithful few*. Everyone is to have a part in the support of the church.

2. The offerings were to be given freely, only by willing hearts (v.5). Note that God did not levy a tax to build the Tabernacle. When dealing with the financial support of the church and the mission to reach the world for Christ, God does not use a heavy hand with us. He does not lay a heavy financial yoke upon us; He does not burden us with a large financial obligation. God leaves the giving up to us; He wants us to judge what is right. God wants us to give freely, willingly, cheerfully. Note what the people offered in the building of the Tabernacle:

   a. They gave the right kind of metals (v.5).
   b. They gave the right kind of fabrics (v.6).
   c. They gave the right kind of animal skins (v.7).
   d. They gave the right kind of wood (v.7).
   e. They gave the right kind of oil, spices, and sweet incense (v.8).
   f. They gave the right kind of stones and gems for the ephod and breastpiece (v.9).

Thought 1. God looks for people who are not stingy and greedy. God has no use for a person who gives with a clenched fist. God wants a cheerful giver, one who gives willingly and cheerfully. God wants people to consider every offering, every contribution, as an eternal investment with great dividends.

"Every man *shall give* as he is able, according to the blessing of the LORD thy God which he hath given thee" (Dt.16:17).

"Then the people rejoiced, for that they offered willingly, because with perfect heart they offered willingly to the LORD: and David the king also rejoiced with great joy" (1 Chron.29:9).

"And I said unto them, Ye *are* holy unto the LORD; the vessels *are* holy also; and the silver and the gold *are* a freewill offering unto the LORD God of your fathers" (Ezra 8:28).

"Honour the LORD with thy substance, and with the firstfruits of all thine increase" (Pr.3:9).

"Freely ye have received, freely give" (Mt.10:8).

"Every man according as he purposeth in his heart, *so let him give;* not grudgingly, or of necessity: for God loveth a cheerful giver" (2 Cor.9:7).

Thought 2. Too many believers are making generous contributions to things that have no eternal value. Contributions are being made...
- to multi-million dollar buildings that are used only one to three times a week, only two to six hours a week
- to programs that add to the already large indulgences of a materialistic people
- to ministries which exist solely for the financial benefit of the employed staff

The needs are too great and the funds are too precious for believers to misuse the offerings given to the LORD. The world reels under the weight of desperate need, and the needs must be met by the church. (See note--Lk.9:4 for more discussion.)

"Go ye therefore, and teach all nations, baptizing them in the name of the Father, and of the Son, and of the Holy Ghost: Teaching them to observe all things whatsoever I have commanded you: and, lo, I am with you alway, *even* unto the end of the world. Amen" (Mt.28:18-20).
"And he said unto them, Go ye into all the world, and preach the gospel to every creature" (Mk.16:15).
"For the Son of man is come to seek and to save that which was lost" (Lk.19:10).
"Then said Jesus to them again, Peace [be] unto you: as [my] Father hath sent me, even so send I you" (Jn.20:21).

Thought 3. The people were obedient in their giving. Note: they did not bring anything that was not on God's list of materials. God's people gave exactly what God wanted from them.

4 (35:10-19) **Tabernacle--Ark--Mercy Seat--Inner Veil--Table of Showbread--Lampstand--Altar of Incense--Outer Veil--Altar of Burnt Offering--Courtyard, The Walls of--The Entrance Veil--The Priesthood, Clothing of-- Symbols of the Tabernacle**: there was the challenge to the skilled workers: come and make everything. The time had finally come to make the Tabernacle and all its furnishings. The time had come to show man exactly how God is to be approached and worshipped. It is easy to take for granted Israel's unique place in history. It is easy to assume...
- that they had been worshipping God in the right way for many years
- that they had always known how to approach God.

But Israel had not always been faithful; Scripture is clear about this. Like the believers of today, they needed to be taught that there is only one living and true God and only one way to approach Him: through the blood of the sacrificial lamb. This was being symbolized in the Tabernacle. God was using the Tabernacle to teach this great truth; therefore the people needed to know the symbolism behind each piece of furniture. They needed to know how this eternal truth--that there is only one living and true God and only one way to approach Him--applied to their lives. In order to get the whole truth in the Tabernacle, it was critically important that the skilled workers make *everything* just as God designed, adding nothing, changing nothing, and leaving nothing out, not a single thing. Leaving even one thing out would have created a gap in God's truth for His people.

Note the carefully worded command to the skilled workers: to come and make everything the LORD commanded, make everything exactly as God designed (v.10-19).
1. The workers were to make the *Tabernacle* itself. The Tabernacle symbolized God's dwelling among His people and man's need to approach God as God dictates (v.11). Man desperately needed to learn how to approach God. The Tabernacle was to teach man how to approach Him, that there is only one door, one way into God's holy presence. (See outline and notes--Ex.26:1-37 for more discussion.)

"Jesus saith unto him, I am the way, the truth, and the life: no man cometh unto the Father, but by me" (Jn.14:6).
"For this is good and acceptable in the sight of God our Saviour; Who will have all men to be saved, and to come unto the knowledge of the truth. For there is one God, and one mediator between God and men, the man Christ Jesus; Who gave himself a ransom for all, to be testified in due time" (1 Tim.2:3-6).

2. The workers were to make the *Ark and the Mercy Seat and the Inner Veil.*
⇒ The Ark symbolized the presence of God. It symbolized the very throne of God, the place where the presence of God dwelt in a very special way. A very special manifestation of God's presence hovered right above the Ark. (See outline and notes--Ex.25:10-22 for more discussion.)
⇒ The Mercy Seat sat upon the Ark and was the actual seat of the Ark. It symbolized the mercy of God, that God sat upon His throne to execute both justice and mercy. (See outline and note--Ex.25:17-21 for more discussion.)
⇒ The Inner Veil symbolized the blazing holiness and righteousness of God, that He dwells in pure holiness and righteousness, so pure that He is totally separated from man, so pure that man cannot look upon God without being totally extinguished. (See note--Ex.26:31-35 for more discussion.)

The High Priest alone was allowed to enter the Holy of Holies, and he could enter only once a year. He appeared before God once a year to offer up the sacrificial blood of the lamb as the atonement--as the reconciliation and substitute--for the sins of the people. This, of course, pointed to Jesus Christ, the Lamb of God who takes away the sin of the world.

a. By taking away our sin, Jesus Christ makes us righteous in Himself, makes it possible for God to count us justified, righteous in Christ.

> "Therefore being justified by faith, we have peace with God through our Lord Jesus Christ" (Ro.5:1).
> "And such were some of you: but ye are washed, but ye are sanctified, but ye are justified in the name of the Lord Jesus, and by the Spirit of our God" (1 Cor.6:11).
> "For he hath made him to be sin for us, who knew no sin; that we might be made the righteousness of God in him" (2 Cor.5:21).

b. By taking away our sin, Jesus Christ reconciles us to God and brings us into the presence of God, making us acceptable to Him.

> "The next day John seeth Jesus coming unto him, and saith, Behold the Lamb of God, which taketh away the sin of the world" (Jn.1:29).
> "Who his own self bare our sins in his own body on the tree, that we, being dead to sins, should live unto righteousness: by whose stripes ye were healed" (1 Pt.2:24).
> "For Christ also hath once suffered for sins, the just for the unjust, that he might bring us to God, being put to death in the flesh, but quickened by the Spirit" (1 Pt.3:18).

3. The workers were to make the *Table of Showbread*. The Table pointed to Christ as the Bread of Life (v.13). Man will always have a deep hunger that only Jesus Christ can satisfy. Only Christ, the Bread of Life, can fill man's hungry soul. (See outline and notes--Ex.25:23-30 for more discussion.)

> "For the bread of God is he which cometh down from heaven, and giveth life unto the world" (Jn.6:33).
> "And Jesus said unto them, I am the bread of life: he that cometh to me shall never hunger; and he that believeth on me shall never thirst" (Jn.6:35).
> "I am that bread of life" (Jn.6:48).
> "This is the bread which cometh down from heaven, that a man may eat thereof, and not die. I am the living bread which came down from heaven: if any man eat of this bread, he shall live for ever: and the bread that I will give is my flesh, which I will give for the life of the world" (Jn.6:50-51).
> "This is that bread which came down from heaven: not as your fathers did eat manna, and are dead: he that eateth of this bread shall live for ever" (Jn.6:58).

4. The workers were to make the *Lampstand*. The Lampstand pointed to Christ as the Light of the world (v.14). In a world darkened by sin and evil, Jesus Christ is the Light of the world. He points man to the light of life and righteousness, both now and eternally. (See outline and notes--Ex.25:31-40 for more discussion.)

> "Then spake Jesus again unto them, saying, I am the light of the world: he that followeth me shall not walk in darkness, but shall have the light of life" (Jn.8:12).
> "I am come a light into the world, that whosoever believeth on me should not abide in darkness" (Jn.12:46).
> "Wherefore he saith, Awake thou that sleepest, and arise from the dead, and Christ shall give thee light" (Eph.5:14).
> "But is now made manifest by the appearing of our Saviour Jesus Christ, who hath abolished death, and hath brought life and immortality to light through the gospel" (2 Tim.1:10).

5. The workers were to make the *Altar of Incense*. This Altar symbolized the prayers of God's people ascending up to God and pleasing Him. There was an incense always burning upon the Altar, always ascending up as a sweet aroma, filling the Tabernacle of God. This symbolized that God's people were to walk in unbroken prayer, always lifting up the sweet aroma of prayer to God. (See outline and note--Ex.30:1-10 for more discussion.)

> "Seek the LORD and his strength, seek his face continually" (1 Chron.16:11).
> "And he spake a parable unto them to this end, that men ought always to pray, and not to faint" (Lk.18:1).
> "Praying always with all prayer and supplication in the Spirit, and watching thereunto with all perseverance and supplication for all saints" (Eph.6:18).
> "Pray without ceasing" (1 Th.5:17).

6. The workers were to make the *Outer Veil or Door*. This symbolized that God can be approached--but only *one way*, only through *one door*. The way, the door into God's presence, is Jesus Christ (v.15). The world claims that there are many ways to God. But Scripture declares that there is only one approach to God, only one way, only one door: the LORD Jesus Christ Himself. (See outline and note--Ex.26:36-37 for more discussion.)

> "I am the door: by me if any man enter in, he shall be saved, and shall go in and out, and find pasture" (Jn.10:9).

"Jesus saith unto him, I am the way, the truth, and the life: no man cometh unto the Father, but by me" (Jn.14:6).

"Neither is there salvation in any other: for there is none other name under heaven given among men, whereby we must be saved" (Acts 4:12).

"By whom also we have access by faith into this grace wherein we stand, and rejoice in hope of the glory of God" (Ro.5:2).

"For there is one God, and one mediator between God and men, the man Christ Jesus; Who gave himself a ransom for all, to be testified in due time" (1 Tim.2:5-6).

7. The workers were to make the *Altar of Burnt Offering*. This altar symbolized the need for atonement, for reconciliation with God (v.16). Every man needs to be reconciled to God. Jesus Christ is the Lamb of God who takes away the sin of the world and reconciles man to God. The atoning sacrifice of Jesus Christ has forevermore made man right with God. (See outline and note--Ex.27:1-8 for more discussion.)

"The next day John seeth Jesus coming unto him, and saith, Behold the Lamb of God, which taketh away the sin of the world" (Jn.1:29).

"And that he might reconcile both unto God in one body by the cross, having slain the enmity thereby" (Eph.2:16).

"And, having made peace through the blood of his cross, by him to reconcile all things unto himself; by him, I say, whether they be things in earth, or things in heaven" (Col.1:20).

"For if the blood of bulls and of goats, and the ashes of an heifer sprinkling the unclean, sanctifieth to the purifying of the flesh: How much more shall the blood of Christ, who through the eternal Spirit offered himself without spot to God, purge your conscience from dead works to serve the living God?" (Heb.9:13-14).

"Forasmuch as ye know that ye were not redeemed with corruptible things, as silver and gold, from your vain conversation received by tradition from your fathers; But with the precious blood of Christ, as of a lamb without blemish and without spot" (1 Pt.1:18-19).

"For Christ also hath once suffered for sins, the just for the unjust, that he might bring us to God, being put to death in the flesh, but quickened by the Spirit" (1 Pt.3:18).

8. The workers were to make the *Bronze Wash Basin* (v.16). This symbolized the washing away of sin, the cleansing and forgiveness of sin. (See notes--Ex.30:17-21; 38:3 for more discussion.) The wash basin symbolized Jesus Christ, His cleansing us from sin through His shed blood.

"In whom we have redemption through his blood, the forgiveness of sins, according to the riches of his grace" (Eph.1:7).

"But if we walk in the light, as he is in the light, we have fellowship one with another, and the blood of Jesus Christ his Son cleanseth us from all sin" (1 Jn.1:7).

"If we confess our sins, he is faithful and just to forgive us our sins, and to cleanse us from all unrighteousness" (1 Jn.1:9).

"Unto him that loved us, and washed us from our sins in his own blood" (Rev.1:5).

9. The workers were to make the *Walls or Curtains* of the Courtyard. The walls symbolized the need for sacrificial blood and separation from the world. Animals had to be slaughtered to provide the skins and hair for the tent coverings. The slaughtering of the animals was a natural picture of the need for sacrificial blood in approaching God. The coverings also provided a barrier, a wall of separation between God's presence and the world. In order to enter God's presence, man had to leave the world behind and enter the Tabernacle wall through the blood of the sacrificed lamb. All this, of course, pointed toward the blood of Jesus Christ that was to be sacrificed and shed for man. (See outline and note--Ex.26:1-14 for more discussion.)

a. The walls symbolized the blood of the sacrifice that had to be made for man.

"Much more then, being now justified by his blood, we shall be saved from wrath through him" (Ro.5:9).

"Who gave himself for our sins, that he might deliver us from this present evil world, according to the will of God and our Father" (Gal.1:4).

"For if the blood of bulls and of goats, and the ashes of an heifer sprinkling the unclean, sanctifieth to the purifying of the flesh: How much more shall the blood of Christ, who through the eternal Spirit offered himself without spot to God, purge your conscience from dead works to serve the living God?" (Heb.9:13-14).

"Forasmuch as ye know that ye were not redeemed with corruptible things, as silver and gold, from your vain conversation received by tradition from your fathers; But with the precious blood of Christ, as of a lamb without blemish and without spot" (1 Pt.1:18-19).

"Who his own self bare our sins in his own body on the tree, that we, being dead to sins, should live unto righteousness: by whose stripes ye were healed" (1 Pt.2:24).

"But if we walk in the light, as he is in the light, we have fellowship one with another, and the blood of Jesus Christ his Son cleanseth us from all sin" (1 Jn.1:7).

"Unto him that loved us, and washed us from our sins in his own blood" (Rev.1:5).

b. The walls symbolized the need for separation from the world.

> "Wherefore come out from among them, and be ye separate, saith the Lord, and touch not the unclean thing; and I will receive you, And will be a Father unto you, and ye shall be my sons and daughters, saith the Lord Almighty" (2 Cor.6:17-18).
> "Love not the world, neither the things that are in the world. If any man love the world, the love of the Father is not in him. For all that is in the world, the lust of the flesh, and the lust of the eyes, and the pride of life, is not of the Father, but is of the world" (1 Jn.2:15-16).

10. The workers were to make the *Entrance Door or Outer Veil* (Curtain). The Outer Door symbolized that God can be approached (v.17). God's invitation is strong, and it is wide open. God's invitation is universal, open to every man, woman, and child upon earth: "whosover will" may come. It is a door of welcome, of divine invitation, of calling repentant sinners to Himself. (See outline and notes--Ex.26:36-37; pt.6--Ex.27:16 for more discussion.)

> "Look unto me, and be ye saved, all the ends of the earth: for I am God, and there is none else" (Is.45:22).
> "Ho, every one that thirsteth, come ye to the waters, and he that hath no money; come ye, buy, and eat; yea, come, buy wine and milk without money and without price" (Is.55:1).
> "In the last day, that great [day] of the feast, Jesus stood and cried, saying, If any man thirst, let him come unto me, and drink" (Jn.7:37).
> "For whosoever shall call upon the name of the Lord shall be saved" (Ro.10:13).
> "And the Spirit and the bride say, Come. And let him that heareth say, Come. And let him that is athirst come. And whosoever will, let him take the water of life freely" (Rev.22:17).

11. The workers were to make the *Tent Stakes or Pegs* and their *ropes*. These pointed to Jesus Christ as the eternal, infinite love of God (v.18). The stakes and cords upheld the posts or pillars of the Tabernacle. It is Jesus Christ who upholds the pillars of the church. It is through the ministry of Jesus Christ that people are bound together in love. It is through His love that unity is realized.

> "Little children, yet a little while I am with you. Ye shall seek me: and as I said unto the Jews, Whither I go, ye cannot come; so now I say to you. A new commandment I give unto you, That ye love one another; as I have loved you, that ye also love one another" (Jn.13:33-34).
> "And this is his commandment, That we should believe on the name of his Son Jesus Christ, and love one another, as he gave us commandment" (1 Jn.3:23).

12. The workers were to make the *clothing* for the priests. The priests' clothing symbolized bringing dignity and honor to the name of God (v.19). By wearing the priestly garments, the priests were constantly reminded that they were serving God, the Sovereign LORD and Majesty of the universe. (See outline and note--Ex.28:1-43 for more discussion.)

> "Let a man so account of us, as of the ministers of Christ, and stewards of the mysteries of God. Moreover it is required in stewards, that a man be found faithful" (1 Cor.4:1-2).
> "What? know ye not that your body is the temple of the Holy Ghost which is in you, which ye have of God, and ye are not your own? For ye are bought with a price: therefore glorify God in your body, and in your spirit, which are God's" (1 Cor.6:19-20).
> "Therefore, my beloved brethren, be ye stedfast, unmoveable, always abounding in the work of the Lord, forasmuch as ye know that your labour is not in vain in the Lord" (1 Cor.15:58).
> "As every man hath received the gift, even so minister the same one to another, as good stewards of the manifold grace of God" (1 Pt.4:10).

5 (35:20-29) **Obedience--Call of God--Stewardship--Offerings**: there was the response of the people to God's call and challenge. God offers an infinite number of opportunities for believers to serve Him. In fact, God brings a daily challenge to the believer who wants to serve Him. Note how the people responded to God's call and challenge:

1. Everyone who was willing and whose heart was stirred brought his offering to the LORD (v.20-21). Millions of people heard the call and responded to the challenge. But note: not everyone responded to this great challenge. Some of the people held back. Not everyone had a heart willing to give. Not everyone brought his offering to the LORD.

Thought 1. We often miss an opportunity to be used by God. Why? Because we do not get involved. We refuse to serve in the church; we refuse to give and support God's work; we keep silent and do not bear witness to the saving grace of Christ.

> "For the Son of man shall come in the glory of his Father with his angels; and then he shall reward every man according to his works" (Mt.16:27).
> "Now he that planteth and he that watereth are one: and every man shall receive his own reward according to his own labour" (1 Cor.3:8).
> "But this *I say*, He which soweth sparingly shall reap also sparingly; and he which soweth bountifully shall reap also bountifully" (2 Cor.9:6).
> "And, behold, I come quickly; and my reward *is* with me, to give every man according as his work shall be" (Rev.22:12).

2. Everyone who was willing--both men and women--brought their gold jewelry and presented it as a wave offering to the LORD (v.22). The genuine believers were not selfish; they were not attached to the things of the world; they did not hoard their possessions or wealth. They gave *willingly* to the LORD. Their act of giving their gifts as a wave offering was a symbolic act saying, "LORD, here it is--all of it. We give it to You freely, confessing that You mean far more to us than gold."

Thought 1. The most liberated men on earth are those who are not owned by their possessions. The liberated man knows that nothing is as valuable as his relationship with God.

"But thou shalt remember the LORD thy God: for *it is* he that giveth thee power to get wealth, that he may establish his covenant which he sware unto thy fathers, as *it is* this day" (Dt.8:18).
"There is that maketh himself rich, yet *hath* nothing: *there is* that maketh himself poor, yet *hath* great riches" (Pr.13:7).
"Every man also to whom God hath given riches and wealth, and hath given him power to eat thereof, and to take his portion, and to rejoice in his labour; this *is* the gift of God" (Eccl.5:19).
"Lay not up for yourselves treasures upon earth, where moth and rust doth corrupt, and where thieves break through and steal" (Mt.6:19).
"[Moses] esteeming the reproach of Christ greater riches than the treasures in Egypt: for he had respect unto the recompence of the reward" (Heb.11:26).

3. Everyone who had colored linen and animal skins brought them as an offering (v.23). The task of building the Tabernacle required precious materials like gold and gems. The Tabernacle also needed more common things like the skins of animals. No gift was too large or too small. Everything was needed in order to build what God wanted: a place where He could dwell with His people, a place that was set apart for the people to pray, worship, and seek His face.

Thought 1. God does not love a person because he can afford to give more to the work of God than someone else. Neither does God love the poor man just because he is poor. God loves us all. When it comes to giving, God is more interested in the heart behind the gift and in how much we keep than in how much we give.

"And Jesus sat over against the treasury, and beheld how the people cast money into the treasury: and many that were rich cast in much. And there came a certain poor widow, and she threw in two mites, which make a farthing. And he called *unto him* his disciples, and saith unto them, Verily I say unto you, That this poor widow hath cast more in, than all they which have cast into the treasury: For all *they* did cast in of their abundance; but she of her want did cast in all that she had, *even* all her living" (Mk.12:41-44).

4. Everyone who had silver or bronze brought it as an offering to the LORD (v.24).
5. Every skilled woman who could sew and spin prepared the curtains (v.25). These talented women brought the linen curtains and the curtains of goat hair (v.26).
6. Every leader made his contribution as he brought stones and gems for the ephod and breastpiece (v.27). These leaders also brought spices and oil for the light and anointing oil for the incense (v.28).
7. The glorious fact is restated and stressed: all the men and women who were willing gave the LORD freewill offerings for the work (v.29).

Thought 1. We are to give and support the work of God, but we are to give willingly and cheerfully.

"Bring ye all the tithes into the storehouse, that there may be meat in mine house, and prove me now herewith, saith the LORD of hosts, if I will not open you the windows of heaven, and pour you out a blessing, that there shall not be room enough to receive it" (Mal.3:10).
"Honour the LORD with thy substance, and with the firstfruits of all thine increase" (Pr.3:9).
"The liberal soul shall be made fat: and he that watereth shall be watered also himself" (Pr.11:25).
"Give, and it shall be given unto you; good measure, pressed down, and shaken together, and running over, shall men give into your bosom. For with the same measure that ye mete withal it shall be measured to you again" (Lk.6:38).
"I have showed you all things, how that so labouring ye ought to support the weak, and to remember the words of the Lord Jesus, how he said, It is more blessed to give than to receive" (Acts 20:35).
"But this I say, He which soweth sparingly shall reap also sparingly; and he which soweth bountifully shall reap also bountifully" (2 Cor.9:6).

6 (35:30-35) **Call of God--Chosen--Bezalel--Oholiab--Management--Supervisors**: there were the two supervisors or managers who were chosen by God. There is no higher calling and no greater responsibility given by God than to be a leader of His people. On this great construction project, God called two men to set the pace for the others to follow. God called two men who were able to communicate with others the master plan of God's design for the Tabernacle. God called two men who were willing to stick to the task at hand and not be swayed or corrupted by their own ideas. God called two men that He could use.

1. There was the general superintendent named Bezalel (v.30). Note his special qualifications, the qualifications needed to build the Tabernacle:
   a. God filled him with the Holy Spirit (v.31).
   b. God filled him with intelligence, knowledge, and skill in construction (v.31). Bezalel was able to design metal objects (v.32) and able to cut and set precious stones (v.33). Bezalel was gifted by God in woodworking and in all kinds of craftsmanship (v.33). Bezalel was chosen and set apart by God for the most important building project in Israel's history. God chose a man and gave him the necessary skills to build the Tabernacle exactly as it was designed.

2. There was the associate superintendent named Oholiab (v.34-35). He willingly served as a support to Bezalel. Oholiab had no desire to usurp Bezalel nor to buck his authority. Oholiab was committed to God, committed to using his gifts to the fullest of his ability, committed to the building of the Tabernacle. Note these facts:
   a. Oholiab and Bezalel were both equipped by God to teach others.
   b. Both were filled by the Holy Spirit of God, filled with skill to do all kinds of work.
   c. They were skilled to work as craftsmen, designers, embroiderers, and weavers.
   d. They were skilled as master craftsmen and designers.

God had everything and everyone in the right place. He had given Moses the blueprint, the pattern and design. He had called the people to give and they had responded. He had called the two supervisors to come and lead the way. The only thing that remained was the actual construction itself. The Tabernacle was soon to become a reality.

Thought 1. We should never fear nor shrink back from serving God. God will never call us to a task without first equipping us to do it. God equips us to serve Him, always equips us. He gives us exactly what we need to serve Him. Moreover, He runs ahead of us and strengthens us to follow Him.

> "And unto one he gave five talents, to another two, and to another one; to every man according to his several ability; and straightway took his journey" (Mt.25:15).
> "Ye have not chosen me, but I have chosen you, and ordained you, that ye should go and bring forth fruit, and [that] your fruit should remain: that whatsoever ye shall ask of the Father in my name, he may give it you" (Jn.15:16).
> "For as we have many members in one body, and all members have not the same office: So we, being many, are one body in Christ, and every one members one of another. Having then gifts differing according to the grace that is given to us, whether prophecy, let us prophesy according to the proportion of faith; Or ministry, let us wait on our ministering: or he that teacheth, on teaching; Or he that exhorteth, on exhortation: he that giveth, let him do it with simplicity; he that ruleth, with diligence; he that showeth mercy, with cheerfulness" (Ro.12:4-8).
> "Now there are diversities of gifts, but the same Spirit. And there are differences of administrations, but the same Lord. And there are diversities of operations, but it is the same God which worketh all in all. But the manifestation of the Spirit is given to every man to profit withal" (1 Cor.12:4-7).
> "For we are his workmanship, created in Christ Jesus unto good works, which God hath before ordained that we should walk in them" (Eph.2:10).
> "And he gave some, apostles; and some, prophets; and some, evangelists; and some, pastors and teachers; For the perfecting of the saints, for the work of the ministry, for the edifying of the body of Christ" (Eph.4:11-12).
> "I can do all things through Christ which strengtheneth me" (Ph.4:13).
> "For God hath not given us the spirit of fear; but of power, and of love, and of a sound mind" (2 Tim.1:7).

1. The summons to skilled management & workers
a. To acknowledge one important fact: Their skills & abilities were from God
b. To build the Tabernacle exactly as God designed

c. To begin work: All were summoned, all who were gifted by the LORD & willing to serve Him

2. The overwhelming faithfulness of the people in giving
a. The offerings were passed out to the workmen
b. The offerings continued to be brought by the people morning after morning

c. The offerings overflowed so much they had to be stopped
1) The workmen told Moses they had enough materials

2) Moses had to stop the offerings

• Instructed the people not to bring any more offerings

• Had more than enough to do the work

3. The inside covering of fine linen: Pictured the purity & righteousness of God
a. The material: Ten curtains of fine linen

b. The size:
1) Each was to be 42' long x 6' wide

2) Two long sets were to be made by joining together five curtains in each set

---

B. The Construction of the Tabernacle: The Excitement of Building for God, Ex.36:1-38

Then wrought Bezaleel and Aholiab, and every wise hearted man, in whom the LORD put wisdom and understanding to know how to work all manner of work for the service of the sanctuary, according to all that the LORD had commanded.
2 And Moses called Bezaleel and Aholiab, and every wise hearted man, in whose heart the LORD had put wisdom, even every one whose heart stirred him up to come unto the work to do it:
3 And they received of Moses all the offering, which the children of Israel had brought for the work of the service of the sanctuary, to make it withal. And they brought yet unto him free offerings every morning.
4 And all the wise men, that wrought all the work of the sanctuary, came every man from his work which they made;
5 And they spake unto Moses, saying, The people bring much more than enough for the service of the work, which the LORD commanded to make.
6 And Moses gave commandment, and they caused it to be proclaimed throughout the camp, saying, Let neither man nor woman make any more work for the offering of the sanctuary. So the people were restrained from bringing.
7 For the stuff they had was sufficient for all the work to make it, and too much.
8 And every wise hearted man among them that wrought the work of the tabernacle made ten curtains of fine twined linen, and blue, and purple, and scarlet: with cherubims of cunning work made he them.
9 The length of one curtain was twenty and eight cubits, and the breadth of one curtain four cubits: the curtains were all of one size.
10 And he coupled the five curtains one unto another: and the other five curtains he

---

coupled one unto another.
11 And he made loops of blue on the edge of one curtain from the selvedge in the coupling: likewise he made in the uttermost side of another curtain, in the coupling of the second.
12 Fifty loops made he in one curtain, and fifty loops made he in the edge of the curtain which was in the coupling of the second: the loops held one curtain to another.
13 And he made fifty taches of gold, and coupled the curtains one unto another with the taches: so it became one tabernacle.
14 And he made curtains of goats' hair for the tent over the tabernacle: eleven curtains he made them.
15 The length of one curtain was thirty cubits, and four cubits was the breadth of one curtain: the eleven curtains were of one size.
16 And he coupled five curtains by themselves, and six curtains by themselves.
17 And he made fifty loops upon the uttermost edge of the curtain in the coupling, and fifty loops made he upon the edge of the curtain which coupleth the second.
18 And he made fifty taches of brass to couple the tent together, that it might be one.
19 And he made a covering for the tent of rams' skins dyed red, and a covering of badgers' skins above that.
20 And he made boards for the tabernacle of shittim wood, standing up.
21 The length of a board was ten cubits, and the breadth of a board one cubit and a half.
22 One board had two tenons, equally distant one from another: thus did he make for all the boards of the tabernacle.
23 And he made boards for the tabernacle; twenty boards for the south side southward:
24 And forty sockets of silver he made under the twenty boards; two sockets under one board for his two tenons, and two sockets under another board for his two tenons.
25 And for the other side of the tabernacle, which is to-

---

c. The loops & clasps
1) Made the loops of blue material: Made them along the edge of the end curtains of the two sets

2) Made 50 loops on each set: Made them to match one another

3) Made 50 gold clasps: To join the two sets together
4) Joined the Tabernacle together as a unit

4. The three outer coverings of the Tabernacle: Symbolized sacrifice
a. The 11 curtains of goat hair: Pictured the need for a sin offering, for cleansing
1) The size:
• Each was 45' long x 6' wide

• Five were joined together to make one set & six into another set
2) The loops: Made 50 along the edge of the end curtains of each set

3) The clasps: Made 50 to join the two sets & tent together
b. The covering of ram skins dyed red: Pictured the blood
c. The covering of leather: Pictured a protective separation from the world

5. The frame: Symbolized stability, support, a strong foundation
a. The size of each framing board: 15' high x 2¼' wide
1) Made two pegs on each framing board (for hooking to the base)
2) Made all framing boards this way

b. The framing
1) Made a wall, a frame of 20 boards, for the south side
• A foundation of 40 silver sockets or bases
• 2 under each board

2) Made a wall of 20 boards for the north side

• A foundation of 40 sockets • Two under each board 3) Made a wall frame of 6 boards for the west side • Made a framing post of two boards for each corner: Joined together at the bottom & at the top, fitted into a single ring • Made for the west side: A total of 8 board frames & a foundation of 16 silver sockets, 2 under each board 4) Made strong, durable crossbars • 5 crossbars for the south • 5 crossbars for the north • 5 crossbars for the west	ward the north corner, he made twenty boards, 26 And their forty sockets of silver; two sockets under one board, and two sockets under another board. 27 And for the sides of the tabernacle westward he made six boards. 28 And two boards made he for the corners of the tabernacle in the two sides. 29 And they were coupled beneath, and coupled together at the head thereof, to one ring: thus he did to both of them in both the corners. 30 And there were eight boards; and their sockets were sixteen sockets of silver, under every board two sockets. 31 And he made bars of shittim wood; five for the boards of the one side of the tabernacle, 32 And five bars for the boards of the other side of the tabernacle, and five bars for the boards of the tabernacle for the sides westward.	33 And he made the middle bar to shoot through the boards from the one end to the other. 34 And he overlaid the boards with gold, and made their rings of gold to be places for the bars, and overlaid the bars with gold. 35 And he made a vail of blue, and purple, and scarlet, and fine twined linen: with cherubims made he it of cunning work. 36 And he made thereunto four pillars of shittim wood, and overlaid them with gold: their hooks were of gold; and he cast for them four sockets of silver. 37 And he made an hanging for the tabernacle door of blue, and purple, and scarlet, and fine twined linen, of needlework; 38 And the five pillars of it with their hooks: and he overlaid their chapiters and their fillets with gold: but their five sockets were of brass.	• The center crossbar was made to run from end to end in the middle of the frames • Covered the crossbars with gold & made gold rings to hold the crossbars 6. **The inner veil: Symbolized God's majestic holiness & man's separation from God** a. The materials b. The four posts: Made of acacia wood & overlaid with gold c. The hooks: Made of gold d. The bases or sockets: Made of silver 7. **The outer veil: Symbolized the door into God's presence** a. The materials b. The five posts: Made hooks for the curtains 1) Overlaid the tops & bands with gold 2) Made 5 bronze sockets or bases for them

DIVISION XI

THE TABERNACLE, ITS CONSTRUCTION AND DEDICATION: THE PEOPLE OBEY GOD, Ex.35:1-40:38

B.   The Construction of the Tabernacle: The Excitement of Building for God, Ex.36:1-38

(36:1-38) **Introduction**: how to spend one's time is one of the most important decisions a man makes, a decision he makes every day of his life. All kinds of things compete for his attention. There is the call of...

- family
- work
- business
- friendships
- entertainment
- hobbies and recreation
- church programs
- civic obligations and programs

Often it is the least important things that require the bulk of our time. Tragically, many people waste much of their time, pouring their lives into things that will not last, things that are more recreational than beneficial and productive, things that are wasteful and unprofitable, even sinful and evil.

God is concerned, very concerned, about how we use our time. God wants His people to use their time worshipping and serving Him by meeting the desperate needs of the world. God wants His people to invest their time in reaching people for Him and in building up His kingdom. There is nothing more exciting or more thrilling for the Christian believer than to be involved in the work of building God's kingdom upon earth. God invites us to get involved, to be an active participant in His great design for the universe, in building His church and kingdom upon earth. This is the subject of this Scripture: *The Construction of the Tabernacle: The Excitement of Building for God*, Ex.36:1-38.

1. The summons to skilled management and workers (v.1-2).
2. The unbelievable faithfulness of the people in giving (v.3-7).
3. The inside covering of fine linen: pictured purity and righteousness (v.8-13).
4. The three outer coverings of the Tabernacle: symbolized sacrifice (v.14-19).
5. The frame: symbolized stability, support, a strong foundation (v.20-34).
6. The inner veil: symbolized God's majestic holiness and man's separation from God (v.35-36).
7. The outer veil: symbolized the door into God's presence (v.37-38).

☐1 (36:1-2) **Work for God--Bezalel--Oholiab--Skills--Talents--Gifts--Obedience**: there was the summons to skilled management and workers. There comes a time--after all the preparation, the study, the search for workers, and the gathering of materials--to build. The time had come for God's people to put into action the plan of God. The design for the great worship center had been given to Moses and passed along to these skilled managers and workers. What a tragedy it

430

would have been to have everything in place except the workers. No matter how much money had been collected, no matter how detailed the blueprints were, no matter how great the vision of the leaders was, if there were no one to do the work, all would have been lost.

Thought 1. This is the cry of the heart of God: for workers who are willing to use His resources. He has supplied almost everything that is needed for the harvest of souls. There is only one thing lacking: workers, laborers for the harvest.

> **"Then saith he unto his disciples, The harvest truly *is* plenteous, but the labourers *are* few; Pray ye therefore the Lord of the harvest, that he will send forth labourers into his harvest" (Mt.9:37-38).**

1. The skilled managers and workers were to acknowledge one important fact: their skills and abilities were from God (v.1). God was the source of their unique skills, and every worker was to know this: their abilities were directly traceable to God and God alone.

> **"Every good gift and every perfect gift is from above, and cometh down from the Father of lights, with whom is no variableness, neither shadow of turning" (Jas.1:17).**
> **"Now there are diversities of gifts, but the same Spirit. And there are differences of administrations, but the same Lord. And there are diversities of operations, but it is the same God which worketh all in all" (1 Cor.12:4-6).**

2. The skilled managers and workers were to build the Tabernacle exactly as God had designed (v.1). These people were given one of the greatest building projects in all of history: that of building the Tabernacle of God, the very place where God was going to dwell among His people. God trusted these workers with His dwelling place. God placed within their hands a hallowed trust, the trust that the workers would construct the Tabernacle exactly as He had designed.

Thought 1. God calls and chooses us because He counts us trustworthy. God trusts the believer to be faithful. It is up to us to be trustworthy, to be faithful.

> **"And he called his ten servants, and delivered them ten pounds, and said unto them, Occupy till I come" (Lk.19:13).**
> **"Moreover it is required in stewards, that a man be found faithful" (1 Cor.4:2).**
> **"Therefore, my beloved brethren, be ye stedfast, unmoveable, always abounding in the work of the Lord, forasmuch as ye know that your labour is not in vain in the Lord" (1 Cor.15:58).**
> **"And I thank Christ Jesus our Lord, who hath enabled me, for that he counted me faithful, putting me into the ministry" (1 Tim.1:12).**
> **"O Timothy, keep that which is committed to thy trust, avoiding profane and vain babblings, and oppositions of science falsely so called" (1 Tim.6:20).**

3. The skilled managers and workers were to begin work: all were summoned, all who were gifted by the LORD and willing to serve Him (v.2). Imagine the scene: the cream of the community, the artists, the craftsmen, the skilled people of the nation of Israel were assembled for this great task. The workers came from different tribes to work on the Tabernacle.
⇒ Each person had a unique experience with God. God called each worker individually and personally.
⇒ Each person was given a special gift by God, a very special skill and ability.
⇒ God was able to take this wide representation of people and mold them into a single working unit with one goal in mind: to build the Tabernacle of God.
Everyone was willing to lay down his or her artistic talents and offer them at the feet of God. Personal pride was surrendered as these people yielded their wills to God and to God's plan.

> **"I beseech you therefore, brethren, by the mercies of God, that ye present your bodies a living sacrifice, holy, acceptable unto God, which is your reasonable service" (Ro.12:1).**
> **"For we are labourers together with God: ye are God's husbandry, ye are God's building" (1 Cor.3:9).**
> **"What? know ye not that your body is the temple of the Holy Ghost which is in you, which ye have of God, and ye are not your own? For ye are bought with a price: therefore glorify God in your body, and in your spirit, which are God's" (1 Cor.6:19-20).**
> **"We then, as workers together with him, beseech you also that ye receive not the grace of God in vain" (2 Cor.6:1).**
> **"Serve the LORD with fear, and rejoice with trembling" (Ps.2:11).**
> **"If ye be willing and obedient, ye shall eat the good of the land" (Is.1:19).**

2 (36:3-7) **Faithfulness--Stewardship--Giving--Offerings--Abundance**: there was the unbelievable faithfulness of the people in giving. The hearts of the people were touched and touched deeply as they gave willingly. There was an enormous sense of excitement in being a part of something so very special. Note the experience of the people as they gave:
1. The offerings were passed out to the workmen (v.3). The people made sure that their offerings were going to the right place.

Thought 1. Sometimes monies are given to the Lord's work but wind up in the wrong places. It does not take long for the cost of administration to soak up the gift of the giver. Instead of meeting the needs of the people for which the gifts were intended, the funds are generated to satisfy the never-ending appetite of the fund-raising machine. In addition to extravagant administrative costs, monies are sometimes...

- misused
- wasted
- stolen
- hoarded
- left unused

"He that is greedy of gain troubleth his own house; but he that hateth gifts shall live" (Pr.15:27).

"Whoso stoppeth his ears at the cry of the poor, he also shall cry himself, but shall not be heard" (Pr.21:13).

"He that giveth unto the poor shall not lack: but he that hideth his eyes shall have many a curse" (Pr.28:27).

"He that loveth silver shall not be satisfied with silver; nor he that loveth abundance with increase: this is also vanity" (Eccl.5:10).

"There is a sore evil which I have seen under the sun, namely, riches kept for the owners thereof to their hurt" (Eccl.5:13).

"But a certain man named Ananias, with Sapphira his wife, sold a possession, And kept back part of the price, his wife also being privy to it, and brought a certain part, and laid it at the apostles' feet. But Peter said, Ananias, why hath Satan filled thine heart to lie to the Holy Ghost, and to keep back part of the price of the land? Whiles it remained, was it not thine own? and after it was sold, was it not in thine own power? why hast thou conceived this thing in thine heart? thou hast not lied unto men, but unto God. And Ananias hearing these words fell down, and gave up the ghost: and great fear came on all them that heard these things" (Acts 5:1-5).

"Your gold and silver is cankered; and the rust of them shall be a witness against you, and shall eat your flesh as it were fire. Ye have heaped treasure together for the last days" (Jas.5:3).

2. The offerings continued to be brought by the people morning after morning (v.3).
3. The offerings overflowed so much they had to be stopped. Why? Because the generosity of the people was simply overwhelming (v.4-7). The workmen told Moses they had enough materials, so Moses had to restrain the people from bringing more offerings. He simply instructed the people not to bring any more offerings: they had more than enough to do all the work. Note: the workmen showed a great deal of integrity and accountability: it would have been very easy for them to line their own pockets with the excess offerings. They could have taken advantage of the generosity of the people and become wealthy. They could have become corrupted, but they did not. They refused to profit off their work for the Lord.

Thought 1. The church is not a place for profiteering or greed, nor is it just a place to seek a profession, or job, or some financial security. The funds, the tithes and offerings of God's people, are to support the ministry of the church. The resources of the church are to be used...

- to meet the desperate needs of a suffering world
- to carry the gospel to a lost and dying world

"No man can serve two masters: for either he will hate the one, and love the other; or else he will hold to the one, and despise the other. Ye cannot serve God and mammon" (Mt.6:24).

"For what is a man advantaged, if he gain the whole world, and lose himself, or be cast away?" (Lk.9:25).

"And he said unto them, Take heed, and beware of covetousness: for a man's life consisteth not in the abundance of the things which he possesseth. And he spake a parable unto them, saying, The ground of a certain rich man brought forth plentifully: And he thought within himself, saying, What shall I do, because I have no room where to bestow my fruits? And he said, This will I do: I will pull down my barns, and build greater; and there will I bestow all my fruits and my goods. And I will say to my soul, Soul, thou hast much goods laid up for many years; take thine ease, eat, drink, *and* be merry. But God said unto him, *Thou* fool, this night thy soul shall be required of thee: then whose shall those things be, which thou hast provided? So *is* he that layeth up treasure for himself, and is not rich toward God" (Lk.12:15-21).

Thought 2. God's people are to give and give sacrificially in order to meet the desperate needs of the world. This is the clear declaration of Scripture.

"Jesus said unto him, If thou wilt be perfect, go [and] sell that thou hast, and give to the poor, and thou shalt have treasure in heaven: and come [and] follow me" (Mt.19:21).

"Sell that ye have, and give alms; provide yourselves bags which wax not old, a treasure in the heavens that faileth not, where no thief approacheth, neither moth corrupteth" (Lk.12:33).

"Neither was there any among them that lacked: for as many as were possessors of lands or houses sold them, and brought the prices of the things that were sold, And laid them down at the apostles' feet: and distribution was made unto every man according as he had need" (Acts 4:34-35).

"I have showed you all things, how that so labouring ye ought to support the weak, and to remember the words of the Lord Jesus, how he said, It is more blessed to give than to receive" (Acts 20:35).

"But this I say, He which soweth sparingly shall reap also sparingly; and he which soweth bountifully shall reap also bountifully" (2 Cor.9:6).

"The liberal soul shall be made fat: and he that watereth shall be watered also himself" (Pr.11:25).

3 (36:8-13) **Tabernacle, Inside Covering--Curtains--Symbols of Purity and Righteousness**: there was the inside covering of fine linen which pictured the purity and righteousness of God. This beautiful covering actually formed the inside walls and ceiling of the Tabernacle, and the inside covering was constantly before the face of the priests as they ministered to the Lord in the Tabernacle. It was a constant reminder that God is pure and righteous. These are the facts of the inside covering of fine linen:

1. The material consisted of ten curtains of fine linen (v.8).

2. The size of each curtain was to be 42 feet long by 6 feet wide (v.9). One group of five curtains was to be joined together to make one set and another five curtains joined together to make the second set (v.10).

3. The loops were made of blue material and were made along the edge of the end curtains of the two sets, 50 loops per set (v.11). The loops were made to match one another (v.12). Fifty gold clasps were made. These joined the two sets together, thereby joining the Tabernacle together as a unit (v.13). (See outline and notes--Ex.26:1-6 for more discussion.)

Thought 1. No matter where the priests looked, they saw the inside covering of the Tabernacle. They were bound to soak in the great symbolism of the curtains, that God is pure and righteous. This is the great truth we all need to learn and remember: God is pure and righteous.

⇒ We need to remember that the very name of God is righteousness.

"In his days Judah shall be saved, and Israel shall dwell safely: and this *is* his name whereby he shall be called, THE LORD OUR RIGHTEOUSNESS" (Jer.23:6).

⇒ We need to remember that God is righteous in *all* His ways.

"The LORD *is* righteous in all his ways, and holy in all his works" (Ps.145:17).

⇒ We need to remember that God's right hand is full of righteousness.

"According to thy name, O God, so *is* thy praise unto the ends of the earth: thy right hand is full of righteousness" (Ps.48:10).

⇒ We need to remember that we can only approach God with a pure (righteous) heart.

"Who shall ascend into the hill of the LORD? or who shall stand in his holy place? He that hath clean hands, and a pure heart; who hath not lifted up his soul unto vanity, nor sworn deceitfully" (Ps.24:3-4).
"Blessed *are* the pure in heart: for they shall see God" (Mt.5:8).

⇒ We need to remember to keep ourselves pure.

"Lay hands suddenly on no man, neither be partaker of other men's sins: keep thyself pure" (1 Tim.5:22).

⇒ We need to remember to purify our souls by obeying the truth.

"Seeing ye have purified your souls in obeying the truth through the Spirit unto unfeigned love of the brethren, *see that ye* love one another with a pure heart fervently" (1 Pt.1:22).

⇒ We need to remember to seek God's righteousness before anything else.

"But seek ye first the kingdom of God, and his righteousness; and all these things shall be added unto you" (Mt.6:33).

4 (36:14-19) **Tabernacle, the Outer Coverings--Goat Hair--Ram Skins--Leather--Symbols of Cleansing, the Blood of Christ, Separation from the World**: there were the three outer coverings of the Tabernacle. In general, the outer coverings symbolized sacrifice and separation from the world. However, each of the three coverings also had a specific symbolic meaning.

1. The first outer covering was the eleven curtains of goat hair. Each curtain was 45 feet long and 6 feet wide. Five of the curtains were joined together to make one set and six curtains were joined together to make another set. 50 loops were

made along the edge of the end curtains of each set. In addition, 50 clasps were made to join the two sets and tent together--making one entire curtain.

The goat was sometimes offered as a *sin offering*. Therefore, the goat skins pictured the need for a *sin offering* and *cleansing*. The first inner curtain discussed in note 3 above symbolized God's purity and righteousness. God's perfect holiness cannot be mixed with man's sin. There has to be a sin offering if the righteous wrath of God is going to be satisfied.

Thought 1. Three great lessons can be learned from the covering of goat skins. Keep in mind that the goat skin covering symbolized the need for a sin offering and for cleansing. Therefore the covering of goat skins was placed on top of the inner curtain of linen, symbolizing that a sin offering was covering the worshipper as he approached the righteousness and purity of God.

1) If there is no sin offering, if there is no cleansing, the consequences are catastrophic!

   (a) Uncleansed sinners are miserable in their sin.

> **"Fools because of their transgression, and because of their iniquities, are afflicted" (Ps.107:17).**
>
> **"The way of transgressors *is* hard" (Pr.13:15).**
>
> **"Tribulation and anguish, upon every soul of man that doeth evil, of the Jew first, and also of the Gentile" (Ro.2:9).**
>
> **"Destruction and misery *are* in their ways" (Ro.3:16).**
>
> **"Go to now, *ye* rich men, weep and howl for your miseries that shall come upon *you*" (Jas.5:1).**

   (b) Uncleansed sinners are never freed from sin's bondage.

> **"His own iniquities shall take the wicked himself, and he shall be holden with the cords of his sins" (Pr.5:22).**
>
> **"Jesus answered them, Verily, verily, I say unto you, Whosoever committeth sin is the servant of sin" (Jn.8:34).**
>
> **"For I perceive that thou art in the gall of bitterness, and *in* the bond of iniquity" (Acts 8:23).**
>
> **"Know ye not, that to whom ye yield yourselves servants to obey, his servants ye are to whom ye obey; whether of sin unto death, or of obedience unto righteousness?" (Ro.6:16).**
>
> **"But I see another law in my members, warring against the law of my mind, and bringing me into captivity to the law of sin which is in my members. O wretched man that I am! who shall deliver me from the body of this death?" (Ro.7:23-24).**

   (c) Uncleansed sinners are always hiding their secret sins, trying to protect their reputations from exposure.

> **"And they heard the voice of the LORD God walking in the garden in the cool of the day: and Adam and his wife <u>hid themselves</u> from the presence of the LORD God amongst the trees of the garden" (Gen.3:8).**
>
> **"When I saw among the spoils a goodly Babylonish garment, and two hundred shekels of silver, and a wedge of gold of fifty shekels weight, then I coveted them, and took them; and, behold, they *are* <u>hid</u> in the earth in the midst of my tent, and the silver under it" (Josh.7:21).**
>
> **"And the children of Israel did <u>secretly</u> *those* things that *were* not right against the LORD their God, and they built them high places in all their cities, from the tower of the watchmen to the fenced city" (2 Ki.17:9).**
>
> **"Who can understand *his* errors? cleanse thou me from secret *faults*" (Ps.19:12).**
>
> **"Thou hast set our iniquities before thee, our secret *sins* in the light of thy countenance" (Ps.90:8).**
>
> **"He that covereth his sins shall not prosper: but whoso confesseth and forsaketh *them* shall have mercy" (Pr.28:13).**
>
> **"Woe unto them that seek deep to hide their counsel from the LORD, and their works are in the dark, and they say, Who seeth us? and who knoweth us?" (Is.29:15).**
>
> **"Woe to the rebellious children, saith the LORD, that take counsel, but not of me; and that cover with a covering, but not of my spirit, that they may add sin to sin" (Is.30:1).**
>
> **"Then said he unto me, Son of man, hast thou seen what the ancients of the house of Israel <u>do in the dark</u>, every man in the chambers of his imagery? for they say, The LORD seeth us not; the LORD hath forsaken the earth" (Ezk.8:12).**
>
> **"For it is a shame even to speak of those things which are done of them in secret" (Eph.5:12).**

   (d) Uncleansed sinners are dead in their sins.

> **"The man that wandereth out of the way of understanding shall remain in the congregation of the dead" (Pr.21:16).**
>
> **"The soul that sinneth, it shall die" (Ezk.18:20).**
>
> **"Then Jesus said unto them, Verily, verily, I say unto you, Except ye eat the flesh of the Son of man, and drink his blood, ye have no life in you" (Jn.6:53).**

"And you *hath he quickened,* who were dead in trespasses and sins" (Eph.2:1).
"Wherefore he saith, Awake thou that sleepest, and arise from the dead, and Christ shall give thee light" (Eph.5:14).
"And you, being dead in your sins and the uncircumcision of your flesh, hath he quickened together with him, having forgiven you all trespasses" (Col.2:13).
"Therefore let us not sleep, as do others; but let us watch and be sober" (1 Th.5:6).

2) The perfect sin offering has now been made--once for all. That sin offering was Jesus Christ. Jesus Christ died for the sins of men.

"For this is my blood of the new testament, which is shed for many for the remission of sins" (Mt.26:28).
"In whom we have redemption through his blood, the forgiveness of sins, according to the riches of his grace" (Eph.1:7).
"Who his own self bare our sins in his own body on the tree, that we, being dead to sins, should live unto righteousness: by whose stripes ye were healed" (1 Pt.2:24).
"But if we walk in the light, as he is in the light, we have fellowship one with another, and the blood of Jesus Christ his Son cleanseth us from all sin" (1 Jn.1:7).
"Unto him that loved us, and washed us from our sins in his own blood" (Rev.1:5).

3) Since Jesus Christ has made the perfect sin offering, a way has been made to cleanse the sin of man's darkened heart. Once a person's heart is cleansed and his sins forgiven, some wonderful things happen to him.
(a) The person who has been cleansed is forgiven all his sin, forgiven every sin he has ever committed.

"Thou hast forgiven the iniquity of thy people, thou hast covered all their sin" (Ps.85:2).

(b) The person who has been cleansed experiences the mercy of God.

"Who *is* a God like unto thee, that pardoneth iniquity, and passeth by the transgression of the remnant of his heritage? he retaineth not his anger for ever, because he delighteth *in* mercy" (Mic.7:18).

(c) The person who has been cleansed is cleansed from all unrighteousness.

"If we confess our sins, he is faithful and just to forgive us *our* sins, and to cleanse us from all unrighteousness" (1 Jn.1:9).

(d) The person who has been cleansed is made alive.

"And you, being dead in your sins and the uncircumcision of your flesh, hath he quickened together with him, having forgiven you all trespasses" (Col.2:13).

(e) The person who has been cleansed receives the gift of the Holy Spirit.

"Then Peter said unto them, Repent, and be baptized every one of you in the name of Jesus Christ for the remission of sins, and ye shall receive the gift of the Holy Ghost" (Acts 2:38).

(f) The person who has been cleansed has his conscience purified for service to God.

"How much more shall the blood of Christ, who through the eternal Spirit offered himself without spot to God, purge your conscience from dead works to serve the living God?" (Heb.9:14).

(g) The person who has been cleansed is given a close bond of fellowship with other believers.

"But if we walk in the light, as he is in the light, we have fellowship one with another, and the blood of Jesus Christ his Son cleanseth us from all sin" (1 Jn.1:7).

(h) The person who has been cleansed lives with God forever: he never dies.

"But we see Jesus, who was made a little lower than the angels for the suffering of death, crowned with glory and honour; that he by the grace of God should taste death for every man" (Heb.2:9).
"Forasmuch then as the children are partakers of flesh and blood, he also himself likewise took part of the same; that through death he might destroy him that had the power of death, that is, the devil; And deliver them who through fear of death were all their lifetime subject to bondage" (Heb.2:14-15).
"Who his own self bare our sins in his own body on the tree, that we, being dead to sins, should live unto righteousness: by whose stripes ye were healed" (1 Pt.2:24).

2. The second outer covering was made of ram skins dyed red (v.19). The red covering, of course, pictured...
* the blood that had to be shed
* the sacrifice that had to be made in order to approach God
* the necessity to cover the Tabernacle with the sacrifice, the place where man and God met

The ram skins were symbolic of the shed blood of Jesus Christ. He is the Perfect Sacrifice, the Perfect Lamb of God who died for the sins of mankind. Jesus Christ is the sinless, perfect Man who died to redeem us from our sins. The point is this:

⇒ God's *Perfect Holiness and Righteousness* demands justice; demands that the penalty of sin be paid; demands that the people who curse, deny, reject, disobey, and rebel against God be judged. What is the judgment? Death, eternal separation from God.

⇒ The Son of God, Jesus Christ, is the *Perfect Sacrifice*, the *Perfect Lamb* of God who died for the sin of man. His death is the Perfect, Ideal death. As the Perfect and Ideal death, His death can cover and stand for every person's death. The person who trusts Jesus Christ, who trusts the shed blood of Jesus Christ to cover his sins, becomes acceptable to God. God forgives the person's sin--counts his sin as having already been paid for in the death of Jesus Christ, the *Perfect Sacrifice*, the *Perfect Lamb of God*. As the *Perfect and Ideal Man*, He died for the sins of *the whole world, the entire universe*; therefore any person who approaches God through Jesus Christ becomes acceptable to God.

Thought 1. This is what the ram skins dyed red pictured, that the blood had to be shed, the sacrifice had to be made in order to cover the Tabernacle, the place where man and God met. Man becomes acceptable to God through the shed blood of Jesus Christ, through His death and only through His death. Note what Holy Scripture declares:

1) God sent His Son, the Lord Jesus Christ, to this lost and dying world to save us.

"**For unto you is born this day in the city of David a Saviour, which is Christ the Lord**" (Lk.2:11).
"**For the Son of man is come to seek and to save that which was lost**" (Lk.19:10).
"**For God so loved the world, that he gave his only begotten Son, that whosoever believeth in him should not perish, but have everlasting life. For God sent not his Son into the world to condemn the world; but that the world through him might be saved**" (Jn.3:16-17).
"**This** *is* **a faithful saying, and worthy of all acceptation, that Christ Jesus came into the world to save sinners; of whom I am chief**" (1 Tim.1:15).

2) Jesus Christ died as our substitute.

"**But he** *was* **wounded** <u>for our transgressions</u>, *he was* **bruised for our iniquities: the chastisement of our peace** *was* **upon him; and with his stripes we are healed**" (Is.53:5).
"**For he hath** <u>made him *to be* sin for us</u>, **who knew no sin; that we might be made the righteousness of God in him**" (2 Cor.5:21).
"**Christ hath redeemed us from the curse of the law, being** <u>made a curse for us</u>: **for it is written, Cursed** *is* **every one that hangeth on a tree**" (Gal.3:13).
"**But we see Jesus, who was made a little lower than the angels for the suffering of death, crowned with glory and honour; that he by the grace of God should** <u>taste death for every man</u>" (Heb.2:9).
"**For Christ also hath once suffered for sins, the** <u>just for the unjust</u>, **that he might bring us to God, being put to death in the flesh, but quickened by the Spirit**" (1 Pt.3:18; cp. 1 Cor.5:7; Gal.1:4; Eph.5:2; Tit.2:14; 1 Jn.3:16).

3) Jesus Christ took upon Himself the full weight of our sin.

"**Therefore will I divide him** *a portion* **with the great, and he shall divide the spoil with the strong; because he hath poured out his soul unto death: and he was numbered with the transgressors; and he bare the sin of many, and made intercession for the transgressors**" (Is.53:12).
"**So Christ was once offered to bear the sins of many; and unto them that look for him shall he appear the second time without sin unto salvation**" (Heb.9:28).
"**Who his own self bare our sins in his own body on the tree, that we, being dead to sins, should live unto righteousness: by whose stripes ye were healed**" (1 Pt.2:24).
"**And ye know that he was manifested to take away our sins; and in him is no sin**" (1 Jn.3:5).

4) Jesus Christ came as the Perfect Lamb of God, the Perfect Sacrifice for us.

"**All we like sheep have gone astray; we have turned every one to his own way; and the LORD hath laid on him the iniquity of us all. He was oppressed, and he was afflicted, yet he opened not his mouth: he is brought as a lamb to the slaughter, and as a sheep before her shearers is dumb, so he openeth not his mouth**" (Is.53:6-7).
"**The next day John seeth Jesus coming unto him, and saith, Behold the Lamb of God, which taketh away the sin of the world**" (Jn.1:29).

"Purge out therefore the old leaven, that ye may be a new lump, as ye are unleavened. For even Christ our passover is sacrificed for us" (1 Cor.5:7).

"Forasmuch as ye know that ye were not redeemed with corruptible things, as silver and gold, from your vain conversation received by tradition from your fathers; But with the precious blood of Christ, as of a lamb without blemish and without spot" (1 Pt.1:18-19).

5) Jesus Christ deliberately chose to die for us, willingly sacrificed Himself for us.

"I am the good shepherd: the good shepherd giveth his life for the sheep" (Jn.10:11).

"And that he died for all, that they which live should not henceforth live unto themselves, but unto him which died for them, and rose again" (2 Cor.5:15).

"For ye know the grace of our Lord Jesus Christ, that, though he was rich, yet for your sakes he became poor, that ye through his poverty might be rich" (2 Cor.8:9).

"Who gave himself for our sins, that he might deliver us from this present evil world, according to the will of God and our Father" (Gal.1:4).

"And walk in love, as Christ also hath loved us, and hath given himself for us an offering and a sacrifice to God for a sweetsmelling savour" (Eph.5:2).

"Who gave himself for us, that he might redeem us from all iniquity, and purify unto himself a peculiar people, zealous of good works" (Tit.2:14).

"Hereby perceive we the love *of God,* because he laid down his life for us: and we ought to lay down *our* lives for the brethren" (1 Jn.3:16).

6) Jesus Christ both suffered for us and died for us--all to redeem us from our sins.

"I gave my back to the smiters, and my cheeks to them that plucked off the hair: I hid not my face from shame and spitting" (Is.50:6).

"But he *was* wounded for our transgressions, *he was* bruised for our iniquities: the chastisement of our peace *was* upon him; and with his stripes we are healed" (Is.53:5).

"And at the ninth hour Jesus cried with a loud voice, saying, Eloi, Eloi, lama sabachthani? which is, being interpreted, My God, my God, why hast thou forsaken me?" (Mk.15:34).

"Saying, Father, if thou be willing, remove this cup from me: nevertheless not my will, but thine, be done. And there appeared an angel unto him from heaven, strengthening him. And being in an agony he prayed more earnestly: and his sweat was as it were great drops of blood falling down to the ground" (Lk.22:42-44; cp. Heb.12:3-4).

"In his humiliation his judgment was taken away: and who shall declare his generation? for his life is taken from the earth" (Acts 8:33).

"For when we were yet without strength, in due time Christ died for the ungodly" (Ro.5:6).

"For I delivered unto you first of all that which I also received, how that Christ died for our sins according to the scriptures" (1 Cor.15:3).

"[Jesus Christ] who, being in the form of God, thought it not robbery to be equal with God: But made himself of no reputation, and took upon him the form of a servant, and was made in the likeness of men. And being found in fashion as a man, he humbled himself, and became obedient unto death, even the death of the cross" (Ph.2:6-8).

"But we see Jesus, who was made a little lower than the angels for the suffering of death, crowned with glory and honour; that he by the grace of God should taste death for every man" (Heb.2:9).

"For it became him, for whom *are* all things, and by whom *are* all things, in bringing many sons unto glory, to make the captain of their salvation perfect through sufferings" (Heb.2:10).

"Forasmuch then as the children are partakers of flesh and blood, he also himself likewise took part of the same; that through death he might destroy him that had the power of death, that is, the devil; And deliver them who through fear of death were all their lifetime subject to bondage" (Heb.2:14-15).

"Wherefore Jesus also, that he might sanctify the people with his own blood, suffered without the gate" (Heb.13:12).

"For Christ also hath once suffered for sins, the just for the unjust, that he might bring us to God, being put to death in the flesh, but quickened by the Spirit" (1 Pt.3:18).

"And they sung a new song, saying, Thou art worthy to take the book, and to open the seals thereof: for thou wast slain, and hast redeemed us to God by thy blood out of every kindred, and tongue, and people, and nation" (Rev.5:9).

3. The third outer covering was made of leather, probably the skins of sea cows (v.19). This covering was the top covering, the covering that protected all the other coverings, that protected the Tabernacle and its furnishings from the weather and any other potential damage from the outside. This protective covering pictured a protective separation from the world.

Thought 1. As the believer walks throughout life day by day, he needs to be on guard lest he become spoiled by the world. The threat of worldliness is a very real danger to us all. The world can quickly stain the heart of even the most mature believer. We cannot go it alone and survive in the world. We need God's love and care, His protection and guidance. Only He can protect us and guide us as we walk through the world day by day. What dangers are there in the world? What is it in the world that threatens us?

EXODUS 36:1-38

1) There is the danger of being contaminated by the unclean things of the world, of touching things forbidden by the Lord.

> "Depart ye, depart ye, go ye out from thence, touch no unclean *thing;* go ye out of the midst of her; be ye clean, that bear the vessels of the LORD" (Is.52:11).
> "Wherefore come out from among them, and be ye separate, saith the Lord, and touch not the unclean thing; and I will receive you, And will be a Father unto you, and ye shall be my sons and daughters, saith the Lord Almighty" (2 Cor.6:17-18).

2) There is the danger of loving the world and the things of the world too much.

> "Set your affection on things above, not on things on the earth" (Col.3:2).
> "Love not the world, neither the things *that are* in the world. If any man love the world, the love of the Father is not in him. For all that is in the world, the lust of the flesh, and the lust of the eyes, and the pride of life, is not of the Father, but is of the world" (1 Jn.2:15-16).
> "No man that warreth entangleth himself with the affairs of *this* life; that he may please him who hath chosen him to be a soldier" (2 Tim.2:4).

3) There is the danger of falling in love with the pleasures of sin.

> "By faith Moses, when he was come to years, refused to be called the son of Pharaoh's daughter; Choosing rather to suffer affliction with the people of God, than to enjoy the pleasures of sin for a season" (Heb.11:24-25).
> "And have no fellowship with the unfruitful works of darkness, but rather reprove *them*" (Eph.5:11).

4) There is the danger of being caught up in the friendship of the world, of giving in to its sexual and immoral ways.

> "Ye adulterers and adulteresses, know ye not that the friendship of the world is enmity with God? whosoever therefore will be a friend of the world is the enemy of God" (Jas.4:4).

5) There is the danger of being caught up and enslaved by worldly lusts.

> "Teaching us that, denying ungodliness and worldly lusts, we should live soberly, righteously, and godly, in this present world; Looking for that blessed hope, and the glorious appearing of the great God and our Saviour Jesus Christ" (Tit.2:12-13).

6) There is the danger of being ensnared by the deceitfulness of the world.

> "He also that received seed among the thorns is he that heareth the word; and the care of this world, and the deceitfulness of riches, choke the word, and he becometh unfruitful" (Mt.13:22).

7) There is the danger of being consumed with the ways of the world and cares of this life, of being caught off guard.

> "And take heed to yourselves, lest at any time your hearts be overcharged with surfeiting, and drunkenness, and cares of this life, and [so] that day come upon you unawares" (Lk.21:34).

8) There is the danger of forgetting the godly, righteous things one has been taught and giving in to the influence of the world.

> "And they rejected his statutes, and his covenant that he made with their fathers, and his testimonies which he testified against them; and they followed vanity, and became vain, and went after the heathen that were round about them, concerning whom the LORD had charged them, that they should not do like them" (2 Ki.17:15).

9) There is the danger of being led into sin by getting caught up with the wrong crowd.

> "Thou shalt not follow a multitude to do evil; neither shalt thou speak in a cause to decline after many to wrest judgment" (Ex.23:2).
> "Depart from me, ye evildoers: for I will keep the commandments of my God" (Ps.119:115).
> "Now we command you, brethren, in the name of our Lord Jesus Christ, that ye withdraw yourselves from every brother that walketh disorderly, and not after the tradition which he received of us" (2 Th.3:6).

438

10) There is the danger of being conformed to the world, of allowing one's mind to be captivated by the things of the world instead of the things of God.

> **"And be not conformed to this world: but be ye transformed by the renewing of your mind, that ye may prove what is that good, and acceptable, and perfect, will of God" (Ro.12:2).**

11) There is the danger of returning to the world because of ridicule and persecution.

> **"If ye were of the world, the world would love his own: but because ye are not of the world, but I have chosen you out of the world, therefore the world hateth you" (Jn.15:19).**

12) There is the danger of following the false gods and worship of the world.

> **"Take heed to thyself that thou be not snared by following them, after that they be destroyed from before thee; and that thou inquire not after their gods, saying, How did these nations serve their gods? even so will I do likewise" (Dt.12:30).**

13) There is the danger of losing one's soul.

> **"For what is a man profited, if he shall gain the whole world, and lose his own soul? or what shall a man give in exchange for his soul?" (Mt.16:26).**

5 (36:20-34) **Tabernacle, Frame of--Symbols of Stability, Support, a Strong Foundation**: there was the frame of the Tabernacle. The frame symbolized stability, support, a strong foundation. The curtains and outer coverings would have been absolutely useless without the frame, and the beautiful and ornate furnishings of the Tabernacle would have been at the mercy of the desert's weather. Without the frame, the Tabernacle's message would have been impossible to see, the message...
- that God is holy and righteous but also merciful and loving
- that man must approach God in the exact and precise way He designed: through the sacrificial blood of the lamb
- that man is to live a life of separation from the world, a righteous life of prayer and fellowship with God

Without the frame, there would have been no tent, no sanctuary, no Most Holy Place in which God could dwell.
1. The size of each framing board was 15 feet high by 2¼ feet wide. It was made with two pegs on each framing board for hooking to the base. Each framing board was to be made the same way (v.21-22).
2. Note the following facts about the framing of the Tabernacle.
   ⇒ The workers made a wall, a frame of 20 boards, for the south side. This wall was supported by a foundation of 40 silver sockets or bases--two under each board (v.23-24).
   ⇒ The workers made an identical wall and then supported it in the same fashion as the south side (v.25-26).
   ⇒ The workers then made the west side, a wall frame of six boards. This west wall also included a framing post of two boards for each corner that were joined together at the bottom and joined together at the top, fitted into a single ring (v.27-29). For the west side, a total of eight board frames and a foundation of sixteen silver sockets were made, two under each board (v.30).
   ⇒ The builders also made strong, durable crossbars: five for the south, five for the north, and five for the west walls (v.31-32). There was also a center crossbar that was made to run from end to end in the middle of the frames (v.33). Each one of the crossbars was covered with gold. Gold rings were made to hold the crossbars (v.34).

Thought 1. One of the strongest messages of the Tabernacle is the symbolism of the frame. The frame was the foundation, the support that held up and stabilized the tent or Tabernacle. Jesus Christ is the foundation of the believer's life, the support that holds up and stabilizes the believer as he journeys to the promised land of heaven. Jesus Christ gives the believer stability. He gives the believer support. The New Testament tells us that the passages in the Old Testament that refer to the Rock or Stone are prophecies pointing to the Messiah, the Lord Jesus Christ Himself (1 Pt.2:6).
1) Jesus Christ is the foundation of life, the very Rock upon which we must build our lives.
   (a) Jesus Christ is the Rock, the Cornerstone, a sure foundation.

> **"Wherefore also it is contained in the scripture, Behold, I lay in Sion a chief corner stone, elect, precious: and he that believeth on him shall not be confounded" (1 Pt.2:6).**
> **"Therefore thus saith the Lord GOD, Behold, I lay in Zion for a foundation a stone, a tried stone, a precious corner *stone,* a sure foundation: he that believeth shall not make haste" (Is.28:16).**

   (b) Jesus Christ is the Rock, the only foundation that will last.

> **"For other foundation can no man lay than that is laid, which is Jesus Christ. Now if any man build upon this foundation gold, silver, precious stones, wood, hay, stubble" (1 Cor.3:10-12).**

(c) Jesus Christ is the Rock of our salvation.

"O come, let us sing unto the Lord: let us make a joyful noise to the rock of our salvation" (Ps.95:1).

(d) Jesus Christ is the Rock that gives us a firm place to stand.

"He brought me up also out of an horrible pit, out of the miry clay, and set my feet upon a rock, *and* established my goings" (Ps.40:2).

(e) Jesus Christ is the Rock that protects us from the storms of life.

"Therefore whosoever heareth these sayings of mine, and doeth them, I will liken him unto a wise man, which built his house upon a rock: And the rain descended, and the floods came, and the winds blew, and beat upon that house; and it fell not: for it was founded upon a rock" (Mt.7:24-25).

(f) Jesus Christ is the Rock that protects us from all enemies.

"And he said, The Lord *is* my rock, and my fortress, and my deliverer; The God of my rock; in him will I trust: *he is* my shield, and the horn of my salvation, my high tower, and my refuge, my saviour; thou savest me from violence" (2 Sam.22:2-3).

(g) Jesus Christ is the Rock who will never bring shame to us.

"As it is written, Behold, I lay in Sion a stumblingstone and rock of offence: and whosoever believeth on him shall not be ashamed" (Ro.9:33).

(h) Jesus Christ is the Rock that stands firm and makes us eternally secure.

"Nevertheless the foundation of God standeth sure, having this seal, The Lord knoweth them that are his. And, Let every one that nameth the name of Christ depart from iniquity" (2 Tim.2:19).

(i) Jesus Christ is the Rock upon which the church is built.

"And I say also unto thee, That thou art Peter, and upon this rock I will build my church; and the gates of hell shall not prevail against it" (Mt.16:18).

(j) Jesus Christ is a Rock like no other.

"How should one chase a thousand, and two put ten thousand to flight, except their Rock had sold them, and the Lord had shut them up? For their rock *is* not as our Rock, even our enemies themselves *being* judges" (Dt.32:30-31).

2) Jesus Christ is faithful, as strong as a rock: He gives us strong support and stabilizes us as we walk day by day throughout life.
(a) Jesus Christ is faithful to forgive us our sins.

"If we confess our sins, he is faithful and just to forgive us our sins, and to cleanse us from all unrighteousness" (1 Jn.1:9).
"Unto him that loved us, and washed us from our sins in his own blood" (Rev.1:5).

(b) Jesus Christ is faithful to reconcile us with God.

"Wherefore in all things it behooved him to be made like unto his brethren, that he might be a merciful and faithful high priest in things pertaining to God, to make reconciliation for the sins of the people" (Heb.2:17).

(c) Jesus Christ is faithful to strengthen and protect us from evil.

"But the Lord is faithful, who shall stablish you, and keep *you* from evil" (2 Th.3:3).

(d) Jesus Christ is faithful to deliver us from temptation.

"There hath no temptation taken you but such as is common to man: but God *is* faithful, who will not suffer you to be tempted above that ye are able; but will with the temptation also make a way to escape, that ye may be able to bear *it*" (1 Cor.10:13).

(e) Jesus Christ is faithful to keep us from wavering in our faith.

> "Let us hold fast the profession of *our* faith without wavering; (for he is faithful that promised)" (Heb.10:23).

(f) Jesus Christ is faithful to help us even if we fail to trust and believe.

> "If we believe not, yet he abideth faithful: he cannot deny himself" (2 Tim.2:13).

3) God Himself is faithful, as strong as a rock in helping us as we walk throughout life day by day.
   (a) God is faithful to keep His promises to believers.

> "Know therefore that the LORD thy God, he is God, the faithful God, which keepeth covenant and mercy with them that love him and keep his commandments to a thousand generations" (Dt.7:9).
> "Blessed be the LORD, that hath given rest unto his people Israel, according to all that he promised: there hath not failed one word of all his good promise, which he promised by the hand of Moses his servant " (1 Ki.8:56).

(b) God is faithful to all generations of people.

> "I will sing of the mercies of the LORD for ever: with my mouth will I make known thy faithfulness to all generations" (Ps.89:1).

(c) God is faithful to grant the fellowship of His Son, Jesus Christ our Lord.

> "For this cause we also, since the day we heard it, do not cease to pray for you, and to desire that ye might be filled with the knowledge of his will in all wisdom and spiritual understanding" (Col.1:9).

(d) God is faithful to give refuge and fulfill the hope that He has set before us.

> "That by two immutable things, in which it was impossible for God to lie, we might have a strong consolation, who have fled for refuge to lay hold upon the hope set before us" (Heb.6:18).

(e) God is faithful in that He will keep and secure our souls until the end.

> "And the Lord shall deliver me from every evil work, and will preserve me unto his heavenly kingdom: to whom be glory for ever and ever. Amen" (2 Tim.4:18).
> "Wherefore let them that suffer according to the will of God commit the keeping of their souls to him in well doing, as unto a faithful Creator" (1 Pt.4:19).

6 (36:35-36) **Tabernacle of Moses--Inner Veil--Holiness of God--Separation--Symbolic of God's Holiness and Man's Separation from God**: there was the inner veil that separated the Most Holy Place from the rest of the Tabernacle. Remember the Most Holy Place was where the Ark or throne of God sat. The veil shielded and separated the Ark of God--His presence, His holiness and mercy--from everything else. Therefore, the Inner Veil symbolized God's majestic holiness and man's separation from God. Note the facts about the construction of the veil:
1. The materials: the veil was made of beautiful colored yarn and elegant linen. Skilled workers embroidered cherubim in the veil (v.35).
2. The four posts: were made of acacia wood and overlaid with gold (v.36).
3. The hooks: were made of gold (v.36).
4. The bases or sockets: were made of silver (v.36).

Thought 1. There are at least three symbolic lessons gleaned from the Inner Veil.
1) God is holy.

> "Who *is* like unto thee, O LORD, among the gods? who *is* like thee, glorious in holiness, fearful *in* praises, doing wonders?" (Ex.15:11).
> "Exalt the LORD our God, and worship at his holy hill; for the LORD our God *is* holy" (Ps.99:9).
> "And one cried unto another, and said, Holy, holy, holy, *is* the LORD of hosts: the whole earth *is* full of his glory" (Is.6:3).
> "So will I make my holy name known in the midst of my people Israel; and I will not *let* them pollute my holy name any more: and the heathen shall know that I *am* the LORD, the Holy One in Israel" (Ezk.39:7).
> "*Thou art* of purer eyes than to behold evil, and canst not look on iniquity: wherefore lookest thou upon them that deal treacherously, *and* holdest thy tongue when the wicked devoureth *the man that is* more righteous than he?" (Hab.1:13).

"And the four beasts had each of them six wings about *him;* and *they were* full of eyes within: and they rest not day and night, saying, Holy, holy, holy, Lord God Almighty, which was, and is, and is to come" (Rev.4:8).

"Who shall not fear thee, O Lord, and glorify thy name? for *thou* only *art* holy: for all nations shall come and worship before thee; for thy judgments are made manifest" (Rev.15:4).

2) Man is sinful and separated from God's holy presence. The blackness of sin has covered his heart, marring the image of God within him, destroying his perfect relationship with God. Sin is the opposite of God's holy presence: sin is on one end of the spectrum and God's holiness is on the other end. The two will never be compatible.

"As it is written, There is none righteous, no, not one: There is none that understandeth, there is none that seeketh after God. They are all gone out of the way, they are together become unprofitable; there is none that doeth good, no, not one. Their throat is an open sepulchre; with their tongues they have used deceit; the poison of asps is under their lips: Whose mouth is full of cursing and bitterness: Their feet are swift to shed blood: Destruction and misery are in their ways: And the way of peace have they not known: There is no fear of God before their eyes" (Ro.3:10-18).

"For all have sinned, and come short of the glory of God" (Ro.3:23).

"If we say that we have no sin, we deceive ourselves, and the truth is not in us" (1 Jn.1:8).

"And GOD saw that the wickedness of man was great in the earth, and that every imagination of the thoughts of his heart was only evil continually" (Gen.6:5).

"Who can say, I have made my heart clean, I am pure from my sin?" (Pr.20:9).

"But your iniquities have separated between you and your God, and your sins have hid his face from you, that he will not hear" (Is.59:2).

"But we are all as an unclean thing, and all our righteousnesses are as filthy rags; and we all do fade as a leaf; and our iniquities, like the wind, have taken us away" (Is.64:6).

"And there is none that calleth upon thy name, that stirreth up himself to take hold of thee: for thou hast hid thy face from us, and hast consumed us, because of our iniquities" (Is.64:7).

"They shall go with their flocks and with their herds to seek the LORD; but they shall not find him; he hath withdrawn himself from them" (Hos.5:6).

3) Jesus Christ has bridged the great gulf between God's holiness and man's sin. He is the Entrance, the Veil, that man must enter to approach God and become acceptable to God. We can now approach God through the veil of Jesus Christ.

"Jesus, when he had cried again with a loud voice, yielded up the ghost. And, behold, the veil of the temple [the Inner Veil] was rent in twain from the top to the bottom; and the earth did quake, and the rocks rent" (Mt.27:50-51).

"I am the door: by me if any man enter in, he shall be saved, and shall go in and out, and find pasture" (Jn.10:9).

"Jesus saith unto him, I am the way [door, veil], the truth, and the life: no man cometh unto the Father, but by me" (Jn.14:6).

"Which *hope* [the hope of heaven, of being accepted by God] we have as an anchor of the soul, both sure and stedfast, and which entereth into that within the veil; Whither the forerunner is for us entered, even Jesus, made an high priest for ever after the order of Melchisedec" (Heb.6:19-20).

"Having therefore, brethren, boldness to enter into the holiest by the blood of Jesus, By a new and living way, which he hath consecrated for us, through the veil, that is to say, his flesh; And having an high priest over the house of God; Let us draw near with a true heart in full assurance of faith, having our hearts sprinkled from an evil conscience, and our bodies washed with pure water" (Heb.10:19-22).

7 (36:37-38) **Tabernacle of Moses--Outer Veil--Symbolic of the Presence of God**: there was the Outer Veil that symbolized the door into God's presence. The pathway from the Courtyard to the Holy Place was marked off by the Outer Veil. The Outer Veil was the only passageway into the presence of God. There was no other way. It was made of the same material as the beautiful Inner Veil and lacked only the embroidered cherubim (v.37). Five posts with hooks were made to hold the Outer Veil. The tops of the posts and their bands were overlaid with gold. Five bronze sockets or bases were made for the posts (v.38).

Thought 1. The Outer Veil is symbolic of the door that leads into God's presence. In the most gracious act imaginable, God has provided a way for man to enter into His presence. Man no longer has to guess about God. Man no longer has to stumble and grope about in the dark, wondering if there is a God, and if there is, how to find Him. God is not way off in outer space, someplace unreachable and undiscoverable. God has revealed Himself to us in the person of His Son, the Lord Jesus Christ. The door into God's presence is none other than Jesus Christ Himself.

1) Jesus Christ came to earth to show us the way to God.

"Verily, verily, I say unto you, He that entereth not by the door into the sheepfold, but climbeth up some other way, the same is a thief and a robber. But he that entereth in by the door is the shepherd of the sheep" (Jn.10:1-2).

"Then said Jesus unto them again, Verily, verily, I say unto you, I am the door of the sheep" (Jn.10:7).

"I am the door: by me if any man enter in, he shall be saved, and shall go in and out, and find pasture" (Jn.10:9).

"Jesus saith unto him, I am the way, the truth, and the life: no man cometh unto the Father, but by me" (Jn.14:6).

2) Jesus Christ came to earth to give us life, life abundant and life eternal, a life filled with love, joy, and peace.

"I am come that they might have life, and that they might have *it* more abundantly" (Jn.10:10).

"Hitherto have ye asked nothing in my name: ask, and ye shall receive, that your joy may be full" (Jn.16:24).

"Therefore being justified by faith, we have peace with God through our Lord Jesus Christ: By whom also we have access by faith into this grace wherein we stand, and rejoice in hope of the glory of God" (Ro.5:1-2).

"And God *is* able to make all grace abound toward you; that ye, always having all sufficiency in all *things,* may abound to every good work" (2 Cor.9:8).

"But the fruit of the Spirit is love, joy, peace, longsuffering, gentleness, goodness, faith, Meekness, temperance: against such there is no law. And they that are Christ's have crucified the flesh with the affections and lusts. If we live in the Spirit, let us also walk in the Spirit" (Gal.5:22-25).

"Now unto him that is able to do exceeding abundantly above all that we ask or think, according to the power that worketh in us" (Eph.3:20).

"But my God shall supply all your need according to his riches in glory by Christ Jesus" (Ph.4:19).

"And the Lord shall deliver me from every evil work, and will preserve me unto his heavenly kingdom: to whom be glory for ever and ever. Amen" (2 Tim.4:18).

(Please note: The Types, Symbols, and Pictures for this outline can be found at the end of Chapter 26, where they are initially discussed.)

1. The Ark of God: Symbolized the throne & presence of God
a. The material: Acacia wood
b. The size: 3¾' long x 2¼' wide x 2¼' high

c. The covering: Overlaid with gold, both inside & out, with a gold molding

d. The four gold rings: Were fastened to its four corners

e. The carrying poles
1) Made of acacia wood & overlaid with gold
2) Were inserted into the rings for carrying the Ark

2. The Mercy Seat: Symbolized the atonement, reconciliation, mercy of God
a. The material: Pure gold
b. The size: 3¾' wide x 2¼' high
c. The two cherubim, one at each end
1) Made them by hammering out the gold of the Mercy Seat
2) Made them at the two ends of the Mercy Seat
3) Made them one piece with the Mercy Seat

4) Made their wings upward overshadowing the Mercy Seat
5) Made them facing one another & looking down on the Mercy Seat

3. The Table of Showbread: Symbolized God as the Bread of Life
a. The material: Acacia wood
b. The size: 3' long x 1½' wide x 2¼' high
c. The covering: Overlaid with pure gold

d. The 3" rim or trim: Made of gold

e. The four rings

C. The Building of the Furnishings For the Tabernacle (Part 1): Learning the Only Way to Approach God, Ex.37:1-29

And Bezaleel made the ark of shittim wood: two cubits and a half was the length of it, and a cubit and a half the breadth of it, and a cubit and a half the height of it:
2 And he overlaid it with pure gold within and without, and made a crown of gold to it round about.
3 And he cast for it four rings of gold, to be set by the four corners of it; even two rings upon the one side of it, and two rings upon the other side of it.
4 And he made staves of shittim wood, and overlaid them with gold.
5 And he put the staves into the rings by the sides of the ark, to bear the ark.
6 And he made the mercy seat of pure gold: two cubits and a half was the length thereof, and one cubit and a half the breadth thereof.
7 And he made two cherubims of gold, beaten out of one piece made he them, on the two ends of the mercy seat;
8 One cherub on the end on this side, and another cherub on the other end on that side: out of the mercy seat made he the cherubims on the two ends thereof.
9 And the cherubims spread out their wings on high, and covered with their wings over the mercy seat, with their faces one to another; even to the mercy seatward were the faces of the cherubims.
10 And he made the table of shittim wood: two cubits was the length thereof, and a cubit the breadth thereof, and a cubit and a half the height thereof:
11 And he overlaid it with pure gold, and made thereunto a crown of gold round about.
12 Also he made thereunto a border of an handbreadth round about; and made a crown of gold for the border thereof round about.
13 And he cast for it four

rings of gold, and put the rings upon the four corners that were in the four feet thereof.
14 Over against the border were the rings, the places for the staves to bear the table.
15 And he made the staves of shittim wood, and overlaid them with gold, to bear the table.
16 And he made the vessels which were upon the table, his dishes, and his spoons, and his bowls, and his covers to cover withal, of pure gold.
17 And he made the candlestick of pure gold: of beaten work made he the candlestick; his shaft, and his branch, his bowls, his knops, and his flowers, were of the same:
18 And six branches going out of the sides thereof; three branches of the candlestick out of the one side thereof, and three branches of the candlestick out of the other side thereof:
19 Three bowls made after the fashion of almonds in one branch, a knop and a flower; and three bowls made like almonds in another branch, a knop and a flower: so throughout the six branches going out of the candlestick.
20 And in the candlestick were four bowls made like almonds, his knops, and his flowers:
21 And a knop under two branches of the same, and a knop under two branches of the same, and a knop under two branches of the same, according to the six branches going out of it.
22 Their knops and their branches were of the same: all of it was one beaten work of pure gold.
23 And he made his seven lamps, and his snuffers, and his snuffdishes, of pure gold.
24 Of a talent of pure gold made he it, and all the vessels thereof.
25 And he made the incense altar of shittim wood: the length of it was a cubit, and the breadth of it a cubit; it was foursquare; and two cubits was the height of it; the horns thereof were of the same.
26 And he overlaid it with pure gold, both the top of it,

1) Made of gold & fastened to the four corners

2) Made for carrying the table

f. The two carrying poles: Made of acacia wood overlaid with gold

g. The utensils:
1) Made the plates, dishes, bowls, & pitchers of gold
2) Made for the pouring out of the drink offerings

4. The Lampstand: Symbolized God as the Light of the world
a. The material
1) Used pure hammered gold
2) Made of one piece: The base, shaft, lamp cups, buds, & blossoms
b. The six branches
1) Made three branches on each side of the center shaft or stem

2) Made three cups shaped like almond flowers with buds & blossoms for each branch

3) Made four similar almond flower-like cups on the center shaft or stem

4) Made one blossom under each pair of branches

5) Hammered out all the decorations & branches as one piece with the Lampstand
c. The seven lamps & accessories
1) Made of pure gold
2) Made from 75 pounds of pure gold

5. The Altar of Incense: Symbolized the prayers & communion of God's people ascending up to God & pleasing Him
a. The material: Acacia wood
b. The size: 18" x 18" x 3' high

c. The covering: Overlaid with pure gold--the top, sides,

| horns, & molding | and the sides thereof round about, and the horns of it: also he made unto it a crown of gold round about. | to bear it withal. | e. The carrying poles: Made of acacia wood & overlaid with gold |
| d. The gold rings: Two were placed on each side for carrying the Altar | 27 And he made two rings of gold for it under the crown thereof, by the two corners of it, upon the two sides thereof, to be places for the staves | 28 And he made the staves of shittim wood, and overlaid them with gold. 29 And he made the holy anointing oil, and the pure incense of sweet spices, according to the work of the apothecary. | f. The anointing oil & fragrant incense: Made by skilled perfumers |

DIVISION XI

THE TABERNACLE, ITS CONSTRUCTION AND DEDICATION: THE PEOPLE OBEY GOD, 35:1-40:38

C. The Building of the Furnishings for the Tabernacle (Part 1): Learning the Only Way to Approach God, Ex.37:1-29

(37:1-29) **Introduction**: there is a saying that declares "ignorance is bliss." While this may sometimes be true in trivial matters, ignorance is not bliss if it keeps a person from progressing, moving ahead, succeeding or embracing a much needed truth. This is certainly true when dealing with the LORD, the only living and true God, the great Creator and Sustainer of the universe. A person who is ignorant about God suffers a great handicap. A person who cannot relate to God...

- has no concept about how *holy and awesome* God is
- has no idea how *merciful and loving* God is
- has no answer for the emptiness and loneliness he feels in his heart
- has no solution for the meaningless tasks of life
- has no direction or guide as he walks through the dark days of life
- has no power outside himself
- has no hope at the end of this life
- has no assurance--absolute certainty--of living eternally

The greatest challenge faced by man is just this: to learn how to relate to God. But note: the task of learning about God is too great for man alone. Therefore, God has provided the way to learn about Him, the way to approach Him. This is the subject of this section of Scripture: *The Building of the Furnishings for the Tabernacle (Part 1): Learning the Only Way to Approach God, Ex.37:1-29.*

1. The Ark of God: symbolized the throne and presence of God (v.1-5).
2. The Mercy Seat: symbolized the atonement, reconciliation, mercy of God (v.6-9).
3. The Table of Showbread: symbolized God as the Bread of Life (v.10-16).
4. The Lampstand: symbolized God as the Light of the world (v.17-24).
5. The Altar of Incense: symbolized the prayers and communion of God's people ascending up to God and pleasing Him (v.25-29).

1 (37:1-5) **Tabernacle of Moses--Ark of God--Throne of God--Presence of God**: there was the Ark of God that symbolized the throne and presence of God. (See outline and notes--Ex.25:10-16; 25:21-22 for more discussion.) It was Bezalel who was given the great privilege of making the Ark of God. Bezalel was God's choice to make the piece of furniture that would serve as a constant reminder of God's presence among His people. The Ark or throne of God was made of acacia wood and was 3¾ feet long by 2¼ feet wide by 2¼ feet high (v.1). It was overlaid with pure gold, both inside and out, with a gold molding (v.2). Bezalel made four gold rings that were fastened to the Ark's four corners (v.3). He then made two poles of acacia wood that were overlaid with gold (v.4). These poles were then inserted into the rings for carrying the Ark (v.5).

Thought 1. How important is the throne of God? The throne of God was the place where God promised to meet with His people and instruct them. The throne of God is the place where we all are to come, fall down and prostrate ourselves, casting our very lives upon the Sovereign King and Majesty of the universe. The Scriptures have much to say about the throne of God.

1) The description of the throne of God.
   (a) God's throne is a great white throne.

   "And I saw a great white throne, and him that sat on it, from whose face the earth and the heaven fled away; and there was found no place for them" (Rev.20:11).

   (b) God's throne is a high, glorious throne.

   "And I will fasten him as a nail in a sure place; and he shall be for a glorious throne to his father's house" (Is.22:23).

445

"And Jesus said unto them, Verily I say unto you, That ye which have followed me, in the regeneration when the Son of man shall sit in the throne of his glory, ye also shall sit upon twelve thrones, judging the twelve tribes of Israel" (Mt.19:28).

"When the Son of man shall come in his glory, and all the holy angels with him, then shall he sit upon the throne of his glory" (Mt.25:31).

"A glorious high throne from the beginning is the place of our sanctuary" (Jer.17:12).

(c) God's throne is like a fiery flame.

"I beheld till the thrones were cast down, and the Ancient of days did sit, whose garment was white as snow, and the hair of his head like the pure wool: his throne was like the fiery flame, and his wheels as burning fire" (Dan.7:9).

(d) God's throne is surrounded by a rainbow.

"And he that sat was to look upon like a jasper and a sardine stone: and there was a rainbow round about the throne, in sight like unto an emerald" (Rev.4:3).

(e) God's throne is a place of lightning, thunderclaps, voices, and fire.

"And out of the throne proceeded lightnings and thunderings and voices: and there were seven lamps of fire burning before the throne, which are the seven Spirits of God" (Rev.4:5).

(f) God's throne has a sea of glass in front of it and is surrounded by twenty-four seats, with elders sitting upon the seats.

"And before the throne there was a sea of glass like unto crystal: and in the midst of the throne, and round about the throne, were four beasts full of eyes before and behind" (Rev.4:6).

"And round about the throne were four and twenty seats: and upon the seats I saw four and twenty elders sitting, clothed in white raiment; and they had on their heads crowns of gold" (Rev.4:4).

(g) God's throne has a pure river, clear as crystal, that flows from it and from the Lamb. It is the water of life.

"And he showed me a pure river of water of life, clear as crystal, proceeding out of the throne of God and of the Lamb" (Rev.22:1).

2) The purpose of the throne of God.
   (a) God's throne is the place where God Himself sits as the Sovereign Lord and Majesty of the universe.

"To him that overcometh will I grant to sit with me in my throne, even as I also overcame, and am set down with my Father in his throne" (Rev.3:21).

"And he came and took the book out of the right hand of him that sat upon the throne" (Rev.5:7).

"At that time they shall call Jerusalem the throne of the LORD; and all the nations shall be gathered unto it, to the name of the LORD, to Jerusalem: neither shall they walk any more after the imagination of their evil heart" (Jer.3:17).

"God reigneth over the heathen: God sitteth upon the throne of his holiness" (Ps.47:8).

   (b) God's throne is the place where God is worshipped and praised.

"The four and twenty elders fall down before him that sat on the throne, and worship him that liveth for ever and ever, and cast their crowns before the throne, saying, Thou art worthy, O Lord, to receive glory and honour and power: for thou hast created all things, and for thy pleasure they are and were created" (Rev.4:10-11).

"And the four and twenty elders and the four beasts fell down and worshipped God that sat on the throne, saying, Amen; Alleluia. And a voice came out of the throne, saying, Praise our God, all ye his servants, and ye that fear him, both small and great" (Rev.19:4-5).

"And when those beasts give glory and honour and thanks to him that sat on the throne, who liveth for ever and ever" (Rev.4:9).

"And every creature which is in heaven, and on the earth, and under the earth, and such as are in the sea, and all that are in them, heard I saying, Blessing, and honour, and glory, and power, be unto him that sitteth upon the throne, and unto the Lamb for ever and ever" (Rev.5:13).

"After this I beheld, and, lo, a great multitude, which no man could number, of all nations, and kindreds, and people, and tongues, stood before the throne, and before the Lamb, clothed with white robes, and palms in their hands; And cried with a loud voice, saying, Salvation to our God which sitteth upon the throne, and unto the Lamb. And all the angels stood round about the throne, and about the elders and the four beasts, and fell before the throne on their faces, and worshipped God" (Rev.7:9-11).

"And before the throne there was a sea of glass like unto crystal: and in the midst of the throne, and round about the throne, were four beasts full of eyes before and behind" (Rev.4:6).

"And they sung as it were a new song before the throne, and before the four beasts, and the elders: and no man could learn that song but the hundred and forty and four thousand, which were redeemed from the earth" (Rev.14:3).

(c) God's throne is the place where judgment and justice (the wrath of God) are executed.

"But the LORD shall endure for ever: he hath prepared his throne for judgment" (Ps.9:7).

"Justice and judgment are the habitation of thy throne: mercy and truth shall go before thy face" (Ps.89:14).

"Of the increase of his government and peace there shall be no end, upon the throne of David, and upon his kingdom, to order it, and to establish it with judgment and with justice from henceforth even for ever. The zeal of the LORD of hosts will perform this" (Is.9:7).

"Clouds and darkness are round about him: righteousness and judgment are the habitation of his throne" (Ps.97:2).

"And said to the mountains and rocks, Fall on us, and hide us from the face of him that sitteth on the throne, and from the wrath of the Lamb" (Rev.6:16).

(d) God's throne is the place where mercy and grace, provision and comfort flow out.

"And in mercy shall the throne be established: and he shall sit upon it in truth in the tabernacle of David, judging, and seeking judgment, and hasting righteousness" (Is.16:5).

"Let us therefore come boldly unto the throne of grace, that we may obtain mercy, and find grace to help in time of need" (Heb.4:16).

"For the Lamb which is in the midst of the throne shall feed them, and shall lead them unto living fountains of waters: and God shall wipe away all tears from their eyes" (Rev.7:17).

(e) God's throne is the place where the prayers of saints are directed.

"Therefore are they before the throne of God, and serve him day and night in his temple: and he that sitteth on the throne shall dwell among them" (Rev.7:15).

"And another angel came and stood at the altar, having a golden censer; and there was given unto him much incense, that he should offer it with the prayers of all saints upon the golden altar which was before the throne" (Rev.8:3).

(f) God's throne is the place where believers are accepted by God, where no deceit or fault is found in them.

"And in their mouth was found no guile: for they are without fault before the throne of God" (Rev.14:5).

(g) God's throne is the place where all things are made new.

"And he that sat upon the throne said, Behold, I make all things new. And he said unto me, Write: for these words are true and faithful" (Rev.21:5).

3) The location of the throne of God.
  (a) God's throne is in Heaven.

"The LORD is in his holy temple, the LORD'S throne is in heaven: his eyes behold, his eyelids try, the children of men" (Ps.11:4).

"The LORD hath prepared his throne in the heavens; and his kingdom ruleth over all" (Ps.103:19).

"Thus saith the LORD, The heaven is my throne, and the earth is my footstool: where is the house that ye build unto me? and where is the place of my rest?" (Is.66:1).

"But I say unto you, Swear not at all; neither by heaven; for it is God's throne" (Mt.5:34).

"And he that shall swear by heaven, sweareth by the throne of God, and by him that sitteth thereon" (Mt.23:22).

"Heaven is my throne, and earth is my footstool: what house will ye build me? saith the Lord: or what is the place of my rest?" (Acts 7:49).

"And immediately I was in the spirit: and, behold, a throne was set in heaven, and one sat on the throne" (Rev.4:2).

(b) God's throne will be in the new Jerusalem of the new heavens and earth.

"And I saw a new heaven and a new earth: for the first heaven and the first earth were passed away; and there was no more sea. And I John saw the holy city, new Jerusalem, coming down from God out of heaven, prepared as a bride adorned for her husband....And there shall be no more curse: but the throne of God and of the Lamb shall be in it; and his servants shall serve him" (Rev.21:1-2; 22:3).

4) The security and permanence of the throne of God.

"Thy throne, O God, is for ever and ever: the sceptre of thy kingdom is a right sceptre" (Ps.45:6).
"But unto the Son he saith, Thy throne, O God, is for ever and ever: a sceptre of righteousness is the sceptre of thy kingdom" (Heb.1:8).
"His seed shall endure for ever, and his throne as the sun before me" (Ps.89:36).
"Thy throne is established of old: thou art from everlasting" (Ps.93:2).

5) The relationship of Jesus Christ to the throne of God.
(a) God's throne is where Jesus Christ sits next to His Father.

"Looking unto Jesus the author and finisher of our faith; who for the joy that was set before him endured the cross, despising the shame, and is set down at the right hand of the throne of God" (Heb.12:2).

(b) God's throne is the place where Jesus Christ sits as the slain Lamb of God.

"And I beheld, and, lo, in the midst of the throne and of the four beasts, and in the midst of the elders, stood a Lamb as it had been slain, having seven horns and seven eyes, which are the seven Spirits of God sent forth into all the earth" (Rev.5:6).

(c) God's throne is the place where Jesus Christ sits as our great High Priest.

"Now of the things which we have spoken this is the sum: We have such an high priest, who is set on the right hand of the throne of the Majesty in the heavens" (Heb.8:1).

(d) God's throne is the place where Jesus Christ, the Lion of Judah, sits with the seven seals of judgment.

"And I saw in the right hand of him that sat on the throne a book written within and on the backside, sealed with seven seals" (Rev.5:1).

2 (37:6-9) **Tabernacle of Moses--Mercy Seat--Atonement Cover--Mercy--Forgiveness**: there was the Mercy Seat or Atonement Cover for the Ark. (See outline and note--Ex.25:17-21 for more discussion.) Note what it is that sets God's throne apart from the thrones of men: the covering. God's holy throne is covered by mercy, by the merciful heart of a God who grants forgiveness to sinners. Every aspect of the Mercy Seat symbolizes and speaks of mercy and forgiveness, atonement and reconciliation. The Mercy Seat was made of pure gold, symbolic of deity (v.6). Remember, only God has the authority to forgive a man's sin.

"When Jesus saw their faith, he said unto the sick of the palsy, Son, thy sins be forgiven thee. But there were certain of the scribes sitting there, and reasoning in their hearts, Why doth this *man* thus speak blasphemies? who can forgive sins but God only? And immediately when Jesus perceived in his spirit that they so reasoned within themselves, he said unto them, Why reason ye these things in your hearts? Whether is it easier to say to the sick of the palsy, *Thy* sins be forgiven thee; or to say, Arise, and take up thy bed, and walk? But that ye may know that the Son of man hath power on earth to forgive sins, (he saith to the sick of the palsy,) I say unto thee, Arise, and take up thy bed, and go thy way into thine house. And immediately he arose, took up the bed, and went forth before them all; insomuch that they were all amazed, and glorified God, saying, We never saw it on this fashion" (Mk.2:5-12).

The size of the Mercy Seat was a perfect fit for the Ark. It was exactly 3¼ feet wide and 2¼ feet high (v.6). At each end of the Mercy Seat was a cherubim (v.7). These cherubim were made by hammering out the gold and being made of one piece with the Mercy Seat (v.8). Their wings were made upward, overshadowing the Mercy Seat (v.9). Bezalel made them facing one another and looking down on the Mercy Seat (v.9).

Thought 1. The Mercy Seat or Atonement Cover is symbolic of God's great mercy, of atonement and reconciliation with Him, of His willingness to forgive sinners. What impact does God's mercy have upon the believer?

1) God's mercy causes us to repent, to turn away from sin and toward God.

"**And rend your heart, and not your garments, and turn unto the LORD your God: for he *is* gracious and merciful, slow to anger, and of great kindness, and repenteth him of the evil**" (Joel 2:13).

2) God's mercy forgives our sins.

"**Who *is* a God like unto thee, that pardoneth iniquity, and passeth by the transgression of the remnant of his heritage? he retaineth not his anger for ever, because he delighteth *in* mercy**" (Mic.7:18).

3) God's mercy saves us.

"**Not by works of righteousness which we have done, but according to his mercy he saved us, by the washing of regeneration, and renewing of the Holy Ghost**" (Tit.3:5).

4) God's mercy saves us from being consumed by God's fierce judgment.

"***It is of* the LORD'S mercies that we are not consumed, because his compassions fail not. *They are* new every morning: great *is* thy faithfulness**" (Lam.3:22-23).

5) God's mercy cannot be measured.

"**For thy mercy *is* great above the heavens: and thy truth *reacheth* unto the clouds**" (Ps.108:4).

6) God's mercy will last forever.

"**But the mercy of the LORD *is* from everlasting to everlasting upon them that fear him, and his righteousness unto children's children**" (Ps.103:17).

3 (37:10-16) **Tabernacle of Moses--Table of Showbread--Bread of Life**: there was the Table of Showbread that symbolized God as the Bread of Life. (See outline and notes--Ex.25:23-30 for more discussion.) Only God can satisfy a man's constant craving to fill his empty heart. Located in the Holy Place behind the Outer Veil, the Table of Showbread pointed to one of man's most important needs: the need to feed his hunger for God. The Table was made of acacia wood and was 3 feet long by 1½ feet wide by 2¼ feet high (v.10).

After the Table was built, it was then covered with pure gold (v.11). On the top of the Table a three inch gold rim or trim ran along the edge of the Table (v.12). Four rings were made of gold and fastened to the four corners of the Table (v.13). This enabled the Table to be carried with two acacia poles that were covered with gold (v.13-15). The utensils used with the Table were also made of gold. They included plates, dishes, bowls, and pitchers. These were used for the pouring out of drink offerings (v.16).

Thought 1. God feeds us spiritually, satisfies the gnawing hunger within our hearts. When we come to God for spiritual food, He feeds and satisfies us.

1) We are satisfied with good things.

"**Who satisfieth thy mouth with good *things; so that* thy youth is renewed like the eagle's**" (Ps.103:5).
"**For he satisfieth the longing soul, and filleth the hungry soul with goodness**" (Ps.107:9).

2) We are satisfied within our souls.

"**My soul shall be satisfied as *with* marrow and fatness; and my mouth shall praise *thee* with joyful lips**" (Ps.63:5).

3) We are filled to the brim with joy.

"**These things have I spoken unto you, that my joy might remain in you, and [that] your joy might be full**" (Jn.15:11).

4) We are filled with the fulness of God Himself.

"**And to know the love of Christ, which passeth knowledge, that ye might be filled with all the fulness of God**" (Eph.3:19).

5) We are filled with the knowledge of God's will and with wisdom.

"For this cause we also, since the day we heard it, do not cease to pray for you, and to desire that ye might be filled with the knowledge of his will in all wisdom and spiritual understanding" (Col.1:9).

6) We are nourished by the LORD even during the barren and unfruitful times of life.

"And the LORD shall guide thee continually, and satisfy thy soul in drought, and make fat thy bones: and thou shalt be like a watered garden, and like a spring of water, whose waters fail not" (Is.58:11).

7) We are filled with an overflowing cup even when opposed by enemies.

"Thou preparest a table before me in the presence of mine enemies: thou anointest my head with oil; my cup runneth over" (Ps.23:5).

8) We shall be satisfied when we see God's face.

"As for me, I will behold thy face in righteousness: I shall be satisfied, when I awake, with thy likeness" (Ps.17:15).

4 (37:17-24) **Tabernacle of Moses--Lampstand--Light--Symbolic of the Light of the World--Shine**: there was the Lampstand that symbolized God as the Light of the world. One of the most significant attributes of God is light. Without God's light, the world would be lost in darkness. No one could see the way: the purpose, meaning, and significance of life. Light helps men see the way and the truth, what life is all about. Light shines on God's handiwork, showing everyone His power and might in the lives of men.

1. The actual Lampstand itself was made of one piece of pure hammered gold. This one piece of gold made the base, the shaft, the six branches, the lamp cups, the bud, and the blossoms (v.17).

2. The six branches were made with three branches on each side of the center shaft or stem (v.18). Three cups shaped like almond flowers with buds and blossoms for each branch were made (v.19). On the center staff or stem, four similar almond flower-like cups were made (v.20). One blossom under each pair of branches was made (v.21). The builders of the Lampstand hammered out all the decorations and branches--all as one piece forming the Lampstand (v.22).

3. The seven lamps and accessories were made of pure gold (v.23). The Lampstand, the lamps, and all the accessories were made from 75 pounds of pure gold (v.24).

Thought 1. The Lampstand illuminated anyone who entered into the Holy Place of the Tabernacle. Thus it is with the believer. When the believer enters the presence of God, the Light of God shines upon the believer. The believer becomes God's light to the world.

1) Note what Scripture says about God's light.

(a) God's light demands that we believe and trust in the light.

"While ye have light, believe in the light, that ye may be the children of light. These things spake Jesus, and departed, and did hide himself from them" (Jn.12:36).

(b) The light of God eliminates fear within us.

"The LORD is my light and my salvation; whom shall I fear? the LORD is the strength of my life; of whom shall I be afraid?" (Ps.27:1).

(c) God's light shows us the way even when darkness is all around.

"Rejoice not against me, O mine enemy: when I fall, I shall arise; when I sit in darkness, the LORD shall be a light unto me" (Mic.7:8).

(d) God's light demands that we work for God while we can.

"I must work the works of him that sent me, while it is day: the night cometh, when no man can work" (Jn.9:4).

(e) God's light will never burn out; it lasts forever.

"Thy sun shall no more go down; neither shall thy moon withdraw itself: for the LORD shall be thine everlasting light, and the days of thy mourning shall be ended" (Is.60:20).

(f) The light of God shines through us to the world.

"And the Gentiles shall come to thy light, and kings to the brightness of thy rising" (Is.60:3).
"Ye are the light of the world. A city that is set on an hill cannot be hid" (Mt.5:14).

"For so hath the Lord commanded us, *saying,* I have set thee to be a light of the Gentiles, that thou shouldest be for salvation unto the ends of the earth" (Acts 13:47).

"For ye were sometimes darkness, but now *are ye* light in the Lord: walk as children of light" (Eph.5:8).

"That ye may be blameless and harmless, the sons of God, without rebuke, in the midst of a crooked and perverse nation, among whom ye shine as lights in the world" (Ph.2:15).

"Ye are all the children of light, and the children of the day: we are not of the night, nor of darkness" (1 Th.5:5).

2) Note what Scripture says about the light of Jesus Christ.
   a)   The light of Jesus Christ is the True light.

"*That* was the true Light, which lighteth every man that cometh into the world" (Jn.1:9).

"Again, a new commandment I write unto you, which thing is true in him and in you: because the darkness is past, and the true light now shineth" (1 Jn.2:8).

   b)   Jesus Christ is the Light of the world and His light eliminates all darkness.

"Then spake Jesus again unto them, saying, I am the light of the world: he that followeth me shall not walk in darkness, but shall have the light of life" (Jn.8:12).

   c)   The light of Jesus Christ gives life to men.

"In him was life; and the life was the light of men" (Jn.1:4).

   d)   The light of Jesus Christ shines in our hearts, giving us the knowledge of God.

"For God, who commanded the light to shine out of darkness, hath shined in our hearts, to *give* the light of the knowledge of the glory of God in the face of Jesus Christ" (2 Cor.4:6).

   e)   The light of Jesus Christ gives light to those who live in darkness, to those who live in the shadow of death.

"To give light to them that sit in darkness and *in* the shadow of death, to guide our feet into the way of peace" (Lk.1:79).

   f)   The light of Jesus Christ is a great light.

"The people which sat in darkness saw great light; and to them which sat in the region and shadow of death light is sprung up" (Mt.4:16; cp. Is.9:2).

   g)   The light of Jesus Christ will illuminate the New Jerusalem.

"And the city had no need of the sun, neither of the moon, to shine in it: for the glory of God did lighten it, and the Lamb *is* the light thereof" (Rev.21:23).

5 (37:25-29) **Tabernacle of Moses--Altar of Incense--Prayer--Intercession**: there was the Altar of Incense. The Altar of Incense was made of acacia wood that was 18 inches square and 3 feet high (v.25). The altar was covered with pure gold including the top, sides, horns, and molding (v.26). Two gold rings were made and placed on each side for carrying the Altar (v.27). The carrying poles were made of acacia wood and overlaid with gold (v.28). The anointing oil and fragrant incense were made by skilled perfumers (v.29).

The Altar of Incense symbolized the prayers and communion of God's people ascending up to God and pleasing Him. (See outline and notes--Ex.30:1-10 for more discussion.) Prayer is the most powerful tool God gives His people, but unfortunately it is the least used. There are believers who know the importance of prayer but seldom pray. Why? Why do more believers not pray as they should? Remember the subject of this portion of Scripture: *Learning the Only Way to Approach God.* Many people do not pray simply because they have never learned how to approach God.

Thought 1. The Altar was small in stature but by no means was it small in importance. The job of the priest was incomplete and unfinished if he bypassed the Altar of Incense. His job included prayer as well as tending to the Lampstand and the Table of Showbread. Sometimes we become so busy that we forget to tend to the Altar of Incense; we get so caught up in life that we forget to pray. This Altar is too important to overlook, too important to ignore. This Altar symbolized the prayers and communion of God's people ascending up to God and pleasing Him. The lesson is forceful: we must pray: we must intercede at the Altar of Incense.

•   We must call upon the name of the LORD.

"I will offer to thee the sacrifice of thanksgiving, and will call upon the name of the LORD" (Ps.116:17).

"For then will I turn to the people a pure language, that they may all call upon the name of the LORD, to serve him with one consent" (Zeph.3:9).

"For whosoever shall call upon the name of the Lord shall be saved" (Ro.10:13).

- We must pray and make an eternal deposit with God.

  "And when he had taken the book, the four beasts and four *and* twenty elders fell down before the Lamb, having every one of them harps, and golden vials full of odours, which are the prayers of saints" (Rev.5:8).
  "And another angel came and stood at the altar, having a golden censer; and there was given unto him much incense, that he should offer *it* with the prayers of all saints upon the golden altar which was before the throne" (Rev.8:3).

- We must seek God and His strength continually.

  "Seek the LORD and his strength, seek his face continually" (1 Chron.16:11).

- We must watch and pray, resisting temptation.

  "Watch and pray, that ye enter not into temptation: the spirit indeed *is* willing, but the flesh *is* weak" (Mt.26:41).

- We must not give up, but continue to stand in prayer.

  "And he spake a parable unto them *to this end,* that men ought always to pray, and not to faint" (Lk.18:1).

- We must make our request in the name of Jesus Christ.

  "Hitherto have ye asked nothing in my name: ask, and ye shall receive, that your joy may be full" (Jn.16:24).

- We must pray by the power and with the help of the Holy Spirit.

  "Likewise the Spirit also helpeth our infirmities: for we know not what we should pray for as we ought: but the Spirit itself maketh intercession for us with groanings which cannot be uttered. And he that searcheth the hearts knoweth what *is* the mind of the Spirit, because he maketh intercession for the saints according to *the will of* God" (Ro.8:26-27).
  "Praying always with all prayer and supplication in the Spirit, and watching thereunto with all perseverance and supplication for all saints" (Eph.6:18).

- We must pray always.

  "Pray without ceasing" (1 Th.5:17).

- We must pray in humility.

  "If my people, which are called by my name, shall humble themselves, and pray, and seek my face, and turn from their wicked ways; then will I hear from heaven, and will forgive their sin, and will heal their land" (2 Chron.7:14).

- We must pray with our whole heart.

  "And ye shall seek me, and find *me,* when ye shall search for me with all your heart" (Jer.29:13).

- We must pray with unshakable faith.

  "Therefore I say unto you, What things soever ye desire, when ye pray, believe that ye receive *them,* and ye shall have *them*" (Mk.11:24).
  "And this is the confidence that we have in him, that, if we ask any thing according to his will, he heareth us" (1 Jn.5:14).

- We must pray with fervent energy.

  "Confess *your* faults one to another, and pray one for another, that ye may be healed. The effectual fervent prayer of a righteous man availeth much" (Jas.5:16).

- We must do those things that are pleasing to God.

  "And whatsoever we ask, we receive of him, because we keep his commandments, and do those things that are pleasing in his sight" (1 Jn.3:22).

1. The Altar of Burnt Offering: Symbolized the need for atonement, reconciliation with God
a. The material: Acacia wood
b. The size: 7½' x 7½' x 4½' high
c. The horns
   1) Made a horn at each of the four corners—all of one piece
   2) Was overlaid with bronze
d. The utensils: Made of bronze

e. The grate: Made of bronze
   1) Placed under the ledge halfway up the altar
   2) Made 4 bronze rings for each corner: To hold the carrying poles

f. The carrying poles
   1) Made of acacia wood & overlaid with bronze
   2) Were inserted into the rings for carrying the altar
g. The altar was made hollow

2. The Bronze Wash Basin: Symbolized the washing, cleansing, forgiveness of sin
a. Made with a bronze stand
b. Made from mirrors given by the women who served the LORD

3. The Courtyard: Symbolized that God can be approached
a. The south side
   1) Made 150' of linen curtains
   2) Made 20 posts that set into 20 bronze bases
   3) Made silver hooks & bands to hold the curtains

b. The north side
   1) Made 150' long
   2) Made 20 posts that were set into 20 bronze bases
   3) Made silver hooks & bands

c. The west end
   1) Made 75' of curtains
   2) Made 10 posts & 10 bases

D. The Building of the Furnishings For the Tabernacle (Part 2): Learning the Only Way to Approach God, Ex.38:1-31

And he made the altar of burnt offering of shittim wood: five cubits was the length thereof, and five cubits the breadth thereof; it was foursquare; and three cubits the height thereof.
2 And he made the horns thereof on the four corners of it; the horns thereof were of the same: and he overlaid it with brass.
3 And he made all the vessels of the altar, the pots, and the shovels, and the basons, and the fleshhooks, and the firepans: all the vessels thereof made he of brass.
4 And he made for the altar a brasen grate of network under the compass thereof beneath unto the midst of it.
5 And he cast four rings for the four ends of the grate of brass, to be places for the staves.
6 And he made the staves of shittim wood, and overlaid them with brass.
7 And he put the staves into the rings on the sides of the altar, to bear it withal; he made the altar hollow with boards.
8 And he made the laver of brass, and the foot of it of brass, of the lookingglasses of the women assembling, which assembled at the door of the tabernacle of the congregation.
9 And he made the court: on the south side southward the hangings of the court were of fine twined linen, an hundred cubits:
10 Their pillars were twenty, and their brasen sockets twenty; the hooks of the pillars and their fillets were of silver.
11 And for the north side the hangings were an hundred cubits, their pillars were twenty, and their sockets of brass twenty; the hooks of the pillars and their fillets of silver.
12 And for the west side were hangings of fifty cubits, their pillars ten, and their

sockets ten; the hooks of the pillars and their fillets of silver.
13 And for the east side eastward fifty cubits.
14 The hangings of the one side of the gate were fifteen cubits; their pillars three, and their sockets three.
15 And for the other side of the court gate, on this hand and that hand, were hangings of fifteen cubits; their pillars three, and their sockets three.
16 All the hangings of the court round about were of fine twined linen.
17 And the sockets for the pillars were of brass; the hooks of the pillars and their fillets of silver; and the overlaying of their chapiters of silver; and all the pillars of the court were filleted with silver.
18 And the hanging for the gate of the court was needlework, of blue, and purple, and scarlet, and fine twined linen: and twenty cubits was the length, and the height in the breadth was five cubits, answerable to the hangings of the court.
19 And their pillars were four, and their sockets of brass four; their hooks of silver, and the overlaying of their chapiters and their fillets of silver.
20 And all the pins of the tabernacle, and of the court round about, were of brass.
21 This is the sum of the tabernacle, even of the tabernacle of testimony, as it was counted, according to the commandment of Moses, for the service of the Levites, by the hand of Ithamar, son to Aaron the priest.
22 And Bezaleel the son of Uri, the son of Hur, of the tribe of Judah, made all that the LORD commanded Moses.
23 And with him was Aholiab, son of Ahisamach, of the tribe of Dan, an engraver, and a cunning workman, and an embroiderer in blue, and in purple, and in scarlet, and fine linen.
24 All the gold that was occupied for the work in all the work of the holy place, even the gold of the offering, was twenty and nine talents, and

   3) Made silver hooks & bands

d. The east end: 75' wide

e. The curtained walls on each side of the entrance
   1) Made one side 22½' long with 3 posts & 3 bases
   2) Made the other side 22½' long with 3 posts & 3 bases

f. The curtains of the Courtyard: Made of fine linen

g. The posts & bases
   1) The bases: Made of bronze
   2) The hooks & bands on each post: Made of silver
   3) The tops of the posts & the bands to hold up the curtains: Made of solid silver

h. The entrance (door) to the Courtyard
   1) Made of linen & embroidered with blue, purple, & scarlet yarn
   2) Made 30' long x 7½' high: Just like the Courtyard curtained walls

   3) Made 4 posts & set into 4 bronze bases
   4) Made hooks & bands of silver & overlaid the top of the posts with silver

i. The tent pegs for the Tabernacle & Courtyard: Made of bronze

4. The inventory used in building the Tabernacle: Pictured the faithfulness of God's people
a. The compilers of the figures: The Levites
b. The recorder: Ithamar, son of Aaron
c. The superintendent of the construction: Bezalel
   1) His heritage
   2) His faithfulness: Made everything the LORD commanded
d. The assistant superintendent: Oholiab
   1) His heritage
   2) His skill

e. The gifts of gold
   1) Taken up through a wave offering
   2) Totaled 2200 pounds

			75 pounds for each base

f. The gifts of silver
1) Totaled about 7545 pounds

seven hundred and thirty shekels, after the shekel of the sanctuary. 25 And the silver of them that were numbered of the congregation was an hundred talents, and a thousand seven hundred and threescore and fifteen shekels, after the shekel of the sanctuary:

dred talents, a talent for a socket.
28 And of the thousand seven hundred seventy and five shekels he made hooks for the pillars, and overlaid their chapiters, and filleted them.

4) About 45 pounds of silver was used to make the bands & hooks & to overlay the posts

2) Was collected through the census tax or ransom tax
• Was 1/15 of an ounce of silver
• Was collected from every man 20 years or older, a total of 603,550 men

26 A bekah for every man, that is, half a shekel, after the shekel of the sanctuary, for every one that went to be numbered, from twenty years old and upward, for six hundred thousand and three thousand and five hundred and fifty men.

29 And the brass of the offering was seventy talents, and two thousand and four hundred shekels.
30 And therewith he made the sockets to the door of the tabernacle of the congregation, and the brasen altar, and the brasen grate for it, and all the vessels of the altar,

g. The gifts of bronze
1) Totaled about 5310 pounds

2) Used to make all the bases
• For the posts at the entrance to the Tabernacle
• For the Bronze Altar & its utensils
• For the surrounding Courtyard
• For the curtain at the entrance of the Courtyard

3) About 7500 pounds of silver was used to make the 100 bases for the sanctuary walls & for the posts supporting the inner curtain: About

27 And of the hundred talents of silver were cast the sockets of the sanctuary, and the sockets of the vail; an hundred sockets of the hun-

31 And the sockets of the court round about, and the sockets of the court gate, and all the pins of the tabernacle, and all the pins of the court round about.

3) Used to make all the tent pegs

DIVISION XI

THE TABERNACLE, ITS CONSTRUCTION AND DEDICATION: THE PEOPLE OBEY GOD, 35:1-40:38

D. **The Building of the Furnishings For the Tabernacle (Part 2): Learning the Only Way to Approach God, Ex.38:1-31**

(38:1-31) **Introduction**: What is the greatest problem that confronts man? Is it possible to even designate one problem as being the greatest problem? Yes. The greatest problem facing man today is the same problem that has confronted man down through the centuries.
⇒ How does man approach God, approach Him so that God accepts Him?

This is the greatest problem facing man. How can we say this? Because a person's eternal destiny is determined--entirely determined--by how he approaches God.
⇒ If a person denies, questions, or neglects God, just has little or nothing to do with God, or if a person approaches God in the wrong way, then he is doomed to what the Bible calls hell, a life of eternal separation from God.
⇒ If a person believes God and approaches God in the right way, then God pours out the greatest of blessings: love, joy, peace, reconciliation, forgiveness of sin, power, a sound mind, eternal life--the greatest virtues known to man.

Think of this: the greatest things known to man--the greatest virtues and gifts--are given to a person when that person approaches God in such a way that God accepts that person. But note: the key is to approach God in the right way. And Scripture makes an astounding declaration: there is only one way to approach God, and that way is narrow. Tragically, only a few walk in the narrow way. What is the right way? This is the subject of this passage: *The Building of the Furnishings For the Tabernacle (Part 2): Learning the Only Way to Approach God,* Ex.38:1-31.
1. The Altar of Burnt Offering: symbolized the need for atonement, reconciliation with God (v.1-7).
2. The Bronze Wash Basin: symbolized the washing, cleansing, forgiveness of sin (v.8).
3. The Courtyard: symbolized that God can be approached (v.9-20).
4. The inventory used in building the Tabernacle: pictured the faithfulness of God's people (v.21-31).

1 (38:1-7) **Tabernacle, The--Altar of Burnt Offering--Atonement--Reconciliation**: there was the Altar of Burnt Offering that symbolized the need for atonement and reconciliation with God. (See outline and note--Ex.27:1-8 for more discussion.) There it sat--the blazing Altar consuming every sacrifice placed upon it--just inside the entrance of the Courtyard. No one could ignore it. No one could walk by it without being stirred by its vicarious ministry, the ministry of substituting the life of an animal for one's sins, for one's own life. Thereby, one became reconciled and acceptable to God. No one could escape the strong pull of the Altar that was a symbol of the cross, the cross of our LORD and Savior, Jesus Christ. These are the facts about how this Altar was built:
1. The Altar was made of acacia wood (v.1).
2. The size of the Altar was 7½ feet square and 4½ feet high (v.1).

3. The horns of the Altar were made at each of the four corners--all of one piece (v.2). The entire Altar was overlaid with bronze (v.2).

4. The utensils were made of bronze (v.3).

5. The grate was made of bronze and placed under the ledge half-way up the Altar (v.4). Four bronze rings for carrying the Altar were made for the corners (v.5). These rings held the carrying poles.

6. The carrying poles were made of acacia wood, overlaid with bronze, and inserted into the rings for carrying the Altar (v.6-7).

7. The Altar was made hollow (v.7).

Thought 1. The Altar of Burnt Offering symbolized the great need of man for atonement, the great need for reconciliation with God.

1) Scripture declares that we need the atonement, need to be reconciled with God.

   (a) Our sins have separated us from God.

       "But your iniquities have separated between you and your God, and your sins have hid his face from you, that he will not hear" (Is.59:2).

       "And there is none that calleth upon thy name, that stirreth up himself to take hold of thee: for thou hast hid thy face from us, and hast consumed us, because of our iniquities" (Is.64:7).

       "If I regard iniquity in my heart, the Lord will not hear me" (Ps.66:18).

   (b) Our forsaking God has separated us from God.

       "The LORD is with you, while ye be with him; and if ye seek him, he will be found of you; but if ye forsake him, he will forsake you" (2 Chron.15:2).

       "The hand of our God is upon all them for good that seek him; but his power and his wrath is against all them that forsake him" (Ezra 8:22).

       "And I will utter my judgments against them touching all their wickedness, who have forsaken me, and have burned incense unto other gods, and worshipped the works of their own hands" (Jer.1:16).

       "For my people have committed two evils; they have forsaken me the fountain of living waters, and hewed them out cisterns, broken cisterns, that can hold no water" (Jer.2:13).

   (c) Our wicked works have separated us from God.

       "And you, that were sometime alienated and enemies in your mind by wicked works" (Col.1:21).

   (d) Our worldly walk and life have separated us from God.

       "Wherein in time past ye walked according to the course of this world, according to the prince of the power of the air, the spirit that now worketh in the children of disobedience: Among whom also we all had our conversation in times past in the lusts of our flesh, fulfilling the desires of the flesh and of the mind; and were by nature the children of wrath, even as others" (Eph.2:2-3).

   (e) Our rejection of Christ has separated us from God.

       "That at that time ye were without Christ, being aliens from the commonwealth of Israel, and strangers from the covenants of promise, having no hope, and without God in the world" (Eph.2:12).

   (f) Our lusts have separated us from God.

       "So I gave them up unto their own hearts' lust: and they walked in their own counsels" (Ps.81:12).

       "Wherefore God also gave them up to uncleanness through the lusts of their own hearts, to dishonour their own bodies between themselves" (Ro.1:24).

   (g) Our unfaithfulness has separated us from God.

       "They shall go with their flocks and with their herds to seek the LORD; but they shall not find him; he hath withdrawn himself from them. They have dealt treacherously [been unfaithful] against the LORD: for they have begotten strange children: now shall a month devour them with their portions" (Hos.5:6-7).

2) Scripture declares that God reconciles us to Himself by Jesus Christ and only by Jesus Christ.

"But God commendeth his love toward us, in that, while we were yet sinners, Christ died for us. Much more then, being now justified by his blood, we shall be saved from wrath through him. For if, when we were enemies, we were reconciled to God by the death of his Son, much more, being reconciled, we shall be saved by his life. And not only so, but we also joy in God through our Lord Jesus Christ, by whom we have now received the atonement [reconciliation]" (Ro.5:8-11).

"And all things are of God, who hath reconciled us to himself by Jesus Christ, and hath given to us the ministry of reconciliation And all things are of God, who hath reconciled us to himself by Jesus Christ, and hath given to us the ministry of reconciliation" (2 Cor.5:18).

"But now in Christ Jesus ye who sometimes were far off are made nigh by the blood of Christ" (Eph.2:13).

"And that he might reconcile both [Jew and Gentile] unto God in one body by the cross, having slain the enmity thereby" (Eph.2:16).

"And, having made peace through the blood of his cross, by him to reconcile all things unto himself; by him, I say, whether they be things in earth, or things in heaven. And you, that were sometime alienated and enemies in your mind by wicked works, yet now hath he reconciled In the body of his flesh through death, to present you holy and unblameable and unreproveable in his sight" (Col.1:20-22).

"Wherefore in all things it behooved him to be made like unto his brethren, that he might be a merciful and faithful high priest in things pertaining to God, to make reconciliation for the sins of the people" (Heb.2:17).

Thought 2. Note where the Altar of Burnt Offering was *not* placed: it was not placed *outside* the Courtyard, outside the gate or entrance. The Altar of Burnt Offering was placed *inside* the walls of the Courtyard. It is only *inside* the Tabernacle that atonement can be applied to man's sinful heart. It is only *inside* the Tabernacle that reconciliation can be made with God. It is only *inside* the walls of the Tabernacle that the power of sin can be annulled by the cross.

"And the Word was made flesh, and dwelt [or tabernacled] among us, (and we beheld his glory, the glory as of the only begotten of the Father,) full of grace and truth" (Jn.1:14).

Every part, every aspect, every detail of the Tabernacle pointed to the Person of Jesus Christ and His work of redemption. The Tabernacle is a clear picture of reconciliation: the Tabernacle pictures the only way a person can be reconciled to God. He must be *in Christ*. There is no benefit, there is no blessing, there is no salvation for the person who does not approach God *in Christ*. Note the great benefits of being *in Christ*:
1) If we are in Christ, we receive the greatest gifts and blessings imaginable.

⇒ In Christ, a person will never be separated from the love of God.

"Who shall separate us from the love of Christ? shall tribulation, or distress, or persecution, or famine, or nakedness, or peril, or sword?...Nay, in all these things we are more than conquerors through him that loved us. For I am persuaded, that neither death, nor life, nor angels, nor principalities, nor powers, nor things present, nor things to come, Nor height, nor depth, nor any other creature, shall be able to separate us from the love of God, which is in Christ Jesus our Lord" (Ro.8:35, 37-39).

⇒ In Christ, a person is sanctified.

"Unto the church of God which is at Corinth, to them that are sanctified in Christ Jesus, called *to be* saints, with all that in every place call upon the name of Jesus Christ our Lord, both theirs and ours" (1 Cor.1:2).

⇒ In Christ, a person receives wisdom, righteousness, sanctification, and redemption.

"But of him are ye in Christ Jesus, who of God is made unto us wisdom, and righteousness, and sanctification, and redemption" (1 Cor.1:30).

⇒ In Christ, a person becomes a child of God by faith.

"For ye are all the children of God by faith in Christ Jesus" (Gal.3:26).

⇒ In Christ, a person has access to all the blessings of God.

"Blessed *be* the God and Father of our Lord Jesus Christ, who hath blessed us with all spiritual blessings in heavenly *places* in Christ" (Eph.1:3).

⇒ In Christ, a person is raised up to sit with Christ in heavenly places.

"**And hath raised** *us* **up together, and made** *us* **sit together in heavenly** *places* **in Christ Jesus" (Eph.2:6).**

⇒ In Christ, a person is brought near God by the blood of Christ.

"**But now in Christ Jesus ye who sometimes were far off are made nigh by the blood of Christ" (Eph.2:13).**

⇒ In Christ, a person becomes a partaker of God's promise.

"**That the Gentiles should be fellowheirs, and of the same body, and partakers of his promise in Christ by the gospel" (Eph.3:6).**

⇒ In Christ, a person will be made perfect.

"**Whom we preach, warning every man, and teaching every man in all wisdom; that we may present every man perfect in Christ Jesus" (Col.1:28).**

⇒ In Christ, a person receives the promise of life.

"**Paul, an apostle of Jesus Christ by the will of God, according to the promise of life which is in Christ Jesus" (2 Tim.1:1).**

⇒ In Christ, a person will experience His peace.

"**Peace I leave with you, my peace I give unto you: not as the world giveth, give I unto you. Let not your heart be troubled, neither let it be afraid" (Jn.14:27).**
"**These things I have spoken unto you, that in me ye might have peace. In the world ye shall have tribulation: but be of good cheer; I have overcome the world" (Jn.16:33).**
"**Greet ye one another with a kiss of charity. Peace** *be* **with you all that are in Christ Jesus. Amen" (1 Pt.5:14).**

2) If we are in Christ, we are changed: saved, delivered, redeemed, and set free.

⇒ In Christ, a person is justified by His grace.

"**Being justified freely by his grace through the redemption that is in Christ Jesus" (Ro.3:24).**

⇒ In Christ, a person is free from condemnation.

"*There is* **therefore now no condemnation to them which are in Christ Jesus, who walk not after the flesh, but after the Spirit. For the law of the Spirit of life in Christ Jesus hath made me free from the law of sin and death" (Ro.8:1-2).**

⇒ In Christ, a person is made alive.

"**For as in Adam all die, even so in Christ shall all be made alive" (1 Cor.15:22).**

⇒ In Christ, a person becomes a new creation.

"**Therefore if any man** *be* **in Christ,** *he is* **a new creature: old things are passed away; behold, all things are become new" (2 Cor.5:17).**
"**For in Christ Jesus neither circumcision availeth any thing, nor uncircumcision, but a new creature" (Gal.6:15).**

⇒ In Christ, a person is reconciled to God.

"**To wit, that God was in Christ, reconciling the world unto himself, not imputing their trespasses unto them; and hath committed unto us the word of reconciliation" (2 Cor.5:19).**

⇒ In Christ, a person is saved by Him.

"**Who hath saved us, and called** *us* **with an holy calling, not according to our works, but according to his own purpose and grace, which was given us in Christ Jesus before the world began" (2 Tim.1:9).**

"Therefore I endure all things for the elect's sakes, that they may also obtain the salvation which is in Christ Jesus with eternal glory" (2 Tim.2:10).

"And that from a child thou hast known the holy scriptures, which are able to make thee wise unto salvation through faith which is in Christ Jesus" (2 Tim.3:15).

3) If we are in Christ, we are to go forth conquering and triumphing for God.

⇒ In Christ, a person will triumph.

"Now thanks *be* unto God, which always causeth us to triumph in Christ, and maketh manifest the savour of his knowledge by us in every place" (2 Cor.2:14).

⇒ In Christ, a person is created to do good works.

"For we are his workmanship, created in Christ Jesus unto good works, which God hath before ordained that we should walk in them" (Eph.2:10).

⇒ In Christ, a person presses on toward the high calling of God.

"I press toward the mark for the prize of the high calling of God in Christ Jesus" (Ph.3:14).

⇒ In Christ, a person is able to give thanks for all the experiences of life.

"In every thing give thanks: for this is the will of God in Christ Jesus concerning you" (1 Th.5:18).

2 (38:8) **Tabernacle of Moses--Bronze Wash Basin--Washing--Cleansing--Forgiveness--Mirror--Word of God**: there was the Bronze Wash Basin that symbolized the washing away of sin, the cleansing and forgiveness of sin. (See outline and note--Ex.30:17-21 for more discussion.) This Bronze Wash Basin was made with a bronze stand and with mirrors given by the women who served the LORD. This important furnishing was placed between the Altar of Burnt Offering and the Outer Veil. A priest could not minister to the LORD without first being cleansed, without being washed, without being forgiven of his sin.

Thought 1.The Wash Basin was a symbol of Christ. God cleanses us and forgives our sins through the blood of His Son, the Lord Jesus Christ, through His death and His death alone.

"For this is my blood of the new testament, which is shed for many for the remission of sins" (Mt.26:28).

"Then Peter said unto them, Repent, and be baptized every one of you in the name of Jesus Christ for the remission of sins, and ye shall receive the gift of the Holy Ghost" (Acts 2:38).

"Him hath God exalted with his right hand to be a Prince and a Saviour, for to give repentance to Israel, and forgiveness of sins" (Acts 5:31).

"Be it known unto you therefore, men and brethren, that through this man is preached unto you the forgiveness of sins" (Acts 13:38).

"For all have sinned, and come short of the glory of God; Being justified freely by his grace through the redemption that is in Christ Jesus: Whom God hath set forth to be a propitiation through faith in his blood, to declare his righteousness for the remission of sins that are past, through the forbearance of God" (Ro.3:23-25).

"In whom we have redemption through his blood, the forgiveness of sins, according to the riches of his grace" (Eph.1:7).

"In whom we have redemption through his blood, even the forgiveness of sins" (Col.1:14).

"[Christ] who gave himself for us, that he might redeem us from all iniquity, and purify unto himself a peculiar people, zealous of good works" (Tit.2:14).

"Neither by the blood of goats and calves, but by his own blood he entered in once into the holy place, having obtained eternal redemption for us. For if the blood of bulls and of goats, and the ashes of an heifer sprinkling the unclean, sanctifieth to the purifying of the flesh: How much more shall the blood of Christ, who through the eternal Spirit offered himself without spot to God, purge your conscience from dead works to serve the living God?" (Heb.9:12-14).

"And almost all things are by the law purged with blood; and without shedding of blood is no remission" (Heb.9:22).

"So Christ was once offered to bear the sins of many; and unto them that look for him shall he appear the second time without sin unto salvation" (Heb.9:28).

"But if we walk in the light, as he is in the light, we have fellowship one with another, and the blood of Jesus Christ his Son cleanseth us from all sin" (1 Jn.1:7).

"If we confess our sins, he is faithful and just to forgive us our sins, and to cleanse us from all unrighteousness" (1 Jn.1:9).

"Unto him that loved us, and washed us from our sins in his own blood" (Rev.1:5).

"All we like sheep have gone astray; we have turned every one to his own way; and the LORD hath laid on him the iniquity of us all" (Is.53:6).

Thought 2. It is easy for a person to think more highly of himself than he really should. Spiritual pride is a subtle thing that can attach itself to any person. A person can become puffed up and prideful because of...

- abilities
- social status
- success
- money
- position
- education
- beauty
- strength
- knowledge
- honor
- charisma
- skill
- eloquence
- fame

We constantly need to be reminded of who we are--redeemed sinners who need to be regularly washed, cleansed, and forgiven of our sin. What does God use to remind us of who we are? We are reminded of who we are when we see our depraved condition mirrored in God's Word.

"But be ye doers of the word, and not hearers only, deceiving your own selves. For if any be a hearer of the word, and not a doer, he is like unto a man beholding his natural face in a glass: For he beholdeth himself, and goeth his way, and straightway forgetteth what manner of man he was. But whoso looketh into the perfect law of liberty, and continueth *therein*, he being not a forgetful hearer, but a doer of the work, this man shall be blessed in his deed" (Jas.1:22-25).

1) We are sinful, everyone of us.
   (a) The Old Testament declares the tragic fact.

   "And GOD saw that the wickedness of man was great in the earth, and that every imagination of the thoughts of his heart was only evil continually" (Gen.6:5).
   "There were they in great fear, where no fear was: for God hath scattered the bones of him that encampeth against thee: thou hast put them to shame, because God hath despised them" (Ps.53:3).
   "Who can say, I have made my heart clean, I am pure from my sin?" (Pr.20:9).
   "For there is not a just man upon earth, that doeth good, and sinneth not" (Eccl.7:20).
   "But we are all as an unclean thing, and all our righteousnesses are as filthy rags; and we all do fade as a leaf; and our iniquities, like the wind, have taken us away" (Is.64:6).

   (b) The New Testament declares the tragic fact.

   "As it is written, There is none righteous, no, not one: There is none that understandeth, there is none that seeketh after God. They are all gone out of the way, they are together become unprofitable; there is none that doeth good, no, not one. Their throat is an open sepulchre; with their tongues they have used deceit; the poison of asps is under their lips: Whose mouth is full of cursing and bitterness: Their feet are swift to shed blood: Destruction and misery are in their ways: And the way of peace have they not known: There is no fear of God before their eyes. Now we know that what things soever the law saith, it saith to them who are under the law: that every mouth may be stopped, and all the world may become guilty before God" (Ro.3:10-19).
   "For all have sinned, and come short of the glory of God" (Ro.3:23).
   "For we ourselves also were sometimes foolish, disobedient, deceived, serving divers lusts and pleasures, living in malice and envy, hateful, and hating one another" (Tit.3:3).
   "If we say that we have no sin, we deceive ourselves, and the truth is not in us" (1 Jn.1:8).
   "And we know that we are of God, and the whole world lieth in wickedness" (1 Jn.5:19).

2) We must be washed and cleansed from sin. Everyone of us must be forgiven our sins in order to be acceptable to God.

   "Be it known unto you therefore, men and brethren, that through this man is preached unto you the forgiveness of sins: And by him all that believe are justified [counted acceptable] from all things, from which ye could not be justified by the law of Moses" (Acts 13:38-39).
   "To the praise of the glory of his grace, wherein he hath made us accepted in the beloved. In whom we have redemption through his blood, the forgiveness of sins, according to the riches of his grace" (Eph.1:6-7).
   "If we say that we have fellowship with him, and walk in darkness, we lie, and do not the truth: But if we walk in the light, as he is in the light, we have fellowship one with another, and the blood of Jesus Christ his Son cleanseth us from all sin. If we say that we have no sin, we deceive ourselves, and the truth is not in us. If we confess our sins, he is faithful and just to forgive us our sins, and to cleanse us from all unrighteousness. If we say that we have not sinned, we make him a liar, and his word is not in us" (1 Jn.1:6-10).
   "My little children, these things write I unto you, that ye sin not. And if any man sin, we have an advocate [One who pleads that we be acceptable] with the Father, Jesus Christ the righteous: And he is the propitiation for our sins: and not for ours only, but also for the sins of the whole world" (1 Jn.2:1-2).
   "I have blotted out, as a thick cloud, thy transgressions, and, as a cloud, thy sins: return unto me; for I have redeemed thee" (Is.44:22).

459

"Let the wicked forsake his way, and the unrighteous man his thoughts: and let him return unto the LORD, and he will have mercy upon him; and to our God, for he will abundantly pardon" (Is.55:7).

3 (38:9-20) **Tabernacle of Moses--Courtyard--Walls--Curtains--Posts--Bases--Bronze--Approaching God**: there was the Courtyard that symbolized this great truth: God can be approached. (See outline and note--Ex.27:9-19 for more discussion.)

Who is like the LORD God? There is none like Him. God is the Eternal LORD and Majesty of the universe, the great Creator and Sustainer of the universe. God is Sovereign, ruling over all. God is Omnipresent, all seeing, present everywhere. God is omnipotent, all powerful. God is omniscient, all knowing and all wise. God is holy, perfect in righteousness and purity. How can One who is so high and lifted up be approached by people, people who are...

- unholy and unrighteous?
- weak and feeble?
- limited in their understanding?

It would have been impossible for people to approach God. God knew this. But in the most amazing and wonderful way possible, God made a way for people to come to Him. In the middle of the wilderness, God had His people build a Courtyard that would be a visible symbol that God could be approached. Note the facts of its construction:

1. The south side was made of 150 feet of linen curtains (v.9). Twenty posts were made and set into 20 bronze bases (v.10). Silver hooks and bands were made to hold the curtains (v.10).

2. The north side was made of 150 feet of linen curtains. Like the south side, 20 posts were made and set into 20 bronze bases. Silver hooks and bands were made to hold the curtains (v.11).

3. The west end of the Courtyard was made of 75 feet of linen curtains. Ten posts and 10 bases were made along with silver hooks that held the curtains (v.12).

4. The east end was made of 75 feet of linen curtains (v.13).

5. The curtained walls on each side of the entrance were made with one side 22½ feet long and the other side also 22½ feet. Three posts and 3 bases were made for each side of the entrance (v.14-15).

6. All the curtains of the Courtyard were made of fine linen (v.16).

7. All the posts and bases were made of bronze while all the hooks and bands were made of silver (v.17). The tops of the posts and bands that were to hold up the curtains were made of silver (v.17).

8. The entrance or door to the Courtyard was made of linen and embroidered with blue, purple, and scarlet yarn. It was made 30 feet long and 7½ feet high--just like the Courtyard curtained walls (v.18). The builders made four posts and set them into four bronze bases. Hooks and bands of silver were made and the top of each post was overlaid with silver (v.19).

9. The tent pegs for the Tabernacle and Courtyard were made of bronze (v.20).

Thought 1. God has invited man to come and approach Him. This great invitation of God to sinful man is found throughout Scripture:

1) There is the great invitation of God to *come* to Him. These verses might be titled "*The 'Come' Invitations of God.*"

(a) "Come and enter" the ark of salvation; come and escape the judgment of God. This is symbolized in the invitation of God given to Noah.

"And the LORD said unto Noah, Come thou and all thy house into the ark; for thee have I seen righteous before me in this generation" (Gen.7:1).

(b) "Come" for the cleansing from sin.

"Come now, and let us reason together, saith the LORD: though your sins be as scarlet, they shall be as white as snow; though they be red like crimson, they shall be as wool" (Is.1:18).

(c) "Come" and have your spiritual hunger and thirst satisfied.

"Ho, every one that thirsteth, come ye to the waters, and he that hath no money; come ye, buy, and eat; yea, come, buy wine and milk without money and without price" (Is.55:1).

(d) "Come" for the rest of your soul.

"Come unto me, all [ye] that labour and are heavy laden, and I will give you rest" (Mt.11:28).

(e) "Come" to the great marriage feast of the Lord.

"Again, he sent forth other servants, saying, Tell them which are bidden, Behold, I have prepared my dinner: my oxen and [my] fatlings [are] killed, and all things [are] ready: come unto the marriage" (Mt.22:4).

(f) "Come" to the great supper of God in heaven.

> "And sent his servant at supper time to say to them that were bidden, Come; for all things are now ready" (Lk.14:17).

(g) "Come" to Christ and drink the water of life

> "And the Spirit and the bride say, Come. And let him that heareth say, Come. And let him that is athirst come. And whosoever will, let him take the water of life freely" (Rev.22:17).

2) There are the results of accepting God's great invitation, the results of *coming* to God.
   (a) The person who comes to God will live.

> "Incline your ear, and come unto me: hear, and your soul shall live; and I will make an everlasting covenant with you, *even* the sure mercies of David" (Is.55:3).

   (b) The person who comes to God will be secure, never rejected, never cast out by Jesus Christ.

> "All that the Father giveth me shall come to me; and him that cometh to me I will in no wise cast out" (Jn.6:37).

   (c) The person who comes to God will receive rest.

> "Come unto me, all *ye* that labour and are heavy laden, and I will give you rest" (Mt.11:28).

   (d) The person who comes to God will have his thirst quenched by the Lord Jesus.

> "In the last day, that great *day* of the feast, Jesus stood and cried, saying, If any man thirst, let him come unto me, and drink" (Jn.7:37).

   (e) The person who comes to God will be raised up on the last day to live eternally with God.

> "No man can come to me, except the Father which hath sent me draw him: and I will raise him up at the last day" (Jn.6:44).

   (f) The person who comes to God does so only by God's will.

> "And he said, Therefore said I unto you, that no man can come unto me, except it were given unto him of my Father" (Jn.6:65).

---

4 (38:21-31) **Tabernacle of Moses--Materials--Inventory--Levites--Ithamar--Bezalel**: there was the inventory used in building the Tabernacle. (See outline and note--Ex.25:1-9 for more discussion.) A list of the inventory shows how faithful God's people were in their labor for God. Note that Moses, always the precise writer, summarized everything that went into building the Tabernacle. This master checklist itemized every important detail.

1. The compilers of the figures were the Levites (v.21).
2. The recorder of the figures was Ithamar, son of Aaron (v.21).
3. The superintendent of the construction was Bezalel, a man with a rich heritage: son of Uri and grandson of Hur. Bezalel was a member of the tribe of Judah (v.22). Bezalel was a faithful man. He made everything the LORD commanded (v.22).
4. Bezalel's assistant superintendent was Oholiab, the son of Ahisamach, of the tribe of Dan. Oholiab was a craftsman who was skilled at engraving, designing, and embroidering (v.23).
5. There were the offerings of gold that were taken up through a wave offering. The total amount of gold given to build the Tabernacle was 2,200 pounds (v.24).
6. There were the offerings of silver that totaled about 7,545 pounds. The silver was collected through the census tax or ransom tax. This tax was 1/15 of an ounce of silver and was collected from every man 20 years or older, a total of 603,550 men (v.25-26). About 7,500 pounds of silver was used to make the 100 bases for the sanctuary walls and for the posts supporting the inner curtain (about 75 pounds for each base) (v.27). About 45 pounds of silver was used to make the bands and hooks as well as overlay the posts (v.28).
7. There were the gifts of bronze that totaled about 5,310 pounds (v.29). The bronze was used to make all the bases...
   - for the posts at the entrance to the Tabernacle
   - for the Bronze Altar and its utensils
   - for the surrounding Courtyard
   - for the curtain at the entrance of the Courtyard (v.30-31)

The bronze was also used to make all the tent pegs for the Tabernacle and for the Courtyard (v.31).

Thought 1. Note two lessons.

1) We must be faithful in our labor for the Lord: work and work hard; be diligent and zealous. We must do our best to complete the work of God upon earth, to finish the task He has given us to do.

"Jesus saith unto them, My meat is to do the will of him that sent me, and to finish his work" (Jn.4:34).

"Say not ye, There are yet four months, and [then] cometh harvest? behold, I say unto you, Lift up your eyes, and look on the fields; for they are white already to harvest" (Jn.4:35).

"I have glorified thee on the earth: I have finished the work which thou gavest me to do" (Jn.17:4).

"But none of these things move me, neither count I my life dear unto myself, so that I might finish my course with joy, and the ministry, which I have received of the Lord Jesus, to testify the gospel of the grace of God" (Acts 20:24).

"For we are labourers together with God: ye are God's husbandry, *ye are* God's building" (1 Cor.3:9).

"Therefore, my beloved brethren, be ye stedfast, unmoveable, always abounding in the work of the Lord, forasmuch as ye know that your labour is not in vain in the Lord" (1 Cor.15:58).

"We then, *as* workers together *with him,* beseech *you* also that ye receive not the grace of God in vain" (2 Cor.6:1).

"Wherefore I put thee in remembrance that thou stir up the gift of God, which is in thee by the putting on of my hands" (2 Tim.1:6).

"I have fought a good fight, I have finished *my* course, I have kept the faith" (2 Tim.4:7).

"Whatsoever thy hand findeth to do, do it with thy might; for there is no work, nor device, nor knowledge, nor wisdom, in the grave, whither thou goest" (Eccl.9:10).

2) God will always supply what is needed to do His work.

"But ye shall receive power, after that the Holy Ghost is come upon you: and ye shall be witnesses unto me both in Jerusalem, and in all Judaea, and in Samaria, and unto the uttermost part of the earth" (Acts 1:8).

"And with great power gave the apostles witness of the resurrection of the Lord Jesus: and great grace was upon them all" (Acts 4:33).

"And God is able to make all grace abound toward you; that ye, always having all sufficiency in all things, may abound to every good work" (2 Cor.9:8).

"Now unto him that is able to do exceeding abundantly above all that we ask or think, according to the power that worketh in us" (Eph.3:20).

"But my God shall supply all your need according to his riches in glory by Christ Jesus" (Ph.4:19).

"And I thank Christ Jesus our Lord, who hath enabled me, for that he counted me faithful, putting me into the ministry" (1 Tim.1:12).

"For God hath not given us the spirit of fear; but of power, and of love, and of a sound mind" (2 Tim.1:7).

"But truly I am full of power by the spirit of the LORD, and of judgment, and of might, to declare unto Jacob his transgression, and to Israel his sin" (Mic.3:8).

"Then he answered and spake unto me, saying, This is the word of the LORD unto Zerubbabel, saying, Not by might, nor by power, but by my spirit, saith the LORD of hosts" (Zech.4:6).

(Please note: The Types, Symbols, and Pictures for this outline can be found at the end of Chapter 30, where they are initially discussed.)

1. The sacred garments, the garments of service: Symbolized the dignity & honor of God's call
a. Made from blue, purple, & scarlet yarn
b. Made for ministering
c. Made as God commanded

2. The ephod: Symbolized that the priest represented & carried the names of God's people before the Lord
a. The material: Yarn & linen
b. The method of securing
1) Hammered out thin sheets of gold
2) Cut thin strands & worked them into the yarn & linen
c. The shoulder pieces: Made & attached to two corners

d. The waistband: Made one piece with the ephod
1) Made of the yarn & linen
2) Made exactly as God commanded

e. The two onyx stones
1) Mounted in gold filigree settings
2) Engraved the names of Israel's tribes on them
3) Fastened the stones on the shoulder pieces of the ephod

3. The breastpiece or chestpiece, a pouch-like garment: Symbolized that the priest represented & carried the names of God's people upon his heart & before the Lord continually
a. The materials: Gold, yarn, & linen
b. The design
1) Made square, folded double
2) Attached four rows of precious stones to it
   • The 1st row of stones

   • The 2nd row of stones

   • The 3rd row of stones

   • The 4th row of stones
3) The stones were mounted in gold

E. The Making of the Garments For the Priests: Being Clothed in Righteousness, Ex.39:1-43

And of the blue, and purple, and scarlet, they made cloths of service, to do service in the holy place, and made the holy garments for Aaron; as the LORD commanded Moses.

2 And he made the ephod of gold, blue, and purple, and scarlet, and fine twined linen.

3 And they did beat the gold into thin plates, and cut it into wires, to work it in the blue, and in the purple, and in the scarlet, and in the fine linen, with cunning work.

4 They made shoulderpieces for it, to couple it together: by the two edges was it coupled together.

5 And the curious girdle of his ephod, that was upon it, was of the same, according to the work thereof; of gold, blue, and purple, and scarlet, and fine twined linen; as the LORD commanded Moses.

6 And they wrought onyx stones inclosed in ouches of gold, graven, as signets are graven, with the names of the children of Israel.

7 And he put them on the shoulders of the ephod, that they should be stones for a memorial to the children of Israel; as the LORD commanded Moses.

8 And he made the breastplate of cunning work, like the work of the ephod; of gold, blue, and purple, and scarlet, and fine twined linen.

9 It was foursquare; they made the breastplate double: a span was the length thereof, and a span the breadth thereof, being doubled.

10 And they set in it four rows of stones: the first row was a sardius, a topaz, and a carbuncle: this was the first row.

11 And the second row, an emerald, a sapphire, and a diamond.

12 And the third row, a ligure, an agate, and an amethyst.

13 And the fourth row, a beryl, an onyx, and a jasper: they were inclosed in ouches

of gold in their inclosings.

14 And the stones were according to the names of the children of Israel, twelve, according to their names, like the engravings of a signet, every one with his name, according to the twelve tribes.

15 And they made upon the breastplate chains at the ends, of wreathen work of pure gold.

16 And they made two ouches of gold, and two gold rings; and put the two rings in the two ends of the breastplate.

17 And they put the two wreathen chains of gold in the two rings on the ends of the breastplate.

18 And the two ends of the two wreathen chains they fastened in the two ouches, and put them on the shoulderpieces of the ephod, before it.

19 And they made two rings of gold, and put them on the two ends of the breastplate, upon the border of it, which was on the side of the ephod inward.

20 And they made two other golden rings, and put them on the two sides of the ephod underneath, toward the forepart of it, over against the other coupling thereof, above the curious girdle of the ephod.

21 And they did bind the breastplate by his rings unto the rings of the ephod with a lace of blue, that it might be above the curious girdle of the ephod, and that the breastplate might not be loosed from the ephod; as the LORD commanded Moses.

22 And he made the robe of the ephod of woven work, all of blue.

23 And there was an hole in the midst of the robe, as the hole of an habergeon, with a band round about the hole, that it should not rend.

24 And they made upon the hems of the robe pomegranates of blue, and purple, and scarlet, and twined linen.

25 And they made bells of pure gold, and put the bells between the pomegranates upon the hem of the robe, round about between the pomegranates;

4) There were 12 stones, one for each of the 12 tribes
5) The name of a different tribe was engraved on each of the 12 stones

c. Attached the chestpiece to the ephod
1) Made braided chains of pure gold
2) Made two gold settings & rings: Fastened the rings to two corners of the chestpiece

3) Fastened the two gold chains to the rings of the chestpiece & the other ends of the chains to the two settings: Attached them to the shoulder pieces

4) Made two more gold rings: Attached them to the other two ends of chestpiece—on the inside next to the ephod garment

5) Made two more gold rings: Attached them to the ephod garment next to the sash

6) Tied the rings of the chestpiece to the rings of the ephod with blue cord: To hold the two together

4. The robe of the ephod: Symbolized the prayer ministry of the High Priest
a. The material
b. The opening for the head: Was reinforced with a woven collar so it would not tear

c. The pomegranates & bells
1) Made yarn & linen in the shape of pomegranates: Attached to the hem

2) Made gold bells: Attached around the hem between the pomegranates

d. The purpose: Was worn for ministering—as the LORD commanded
e. The symbolic purpose: To sound forth the intercessory ministry of the High Priest
5. **The other garments for the priests: Symbolized putting on God's righteousness**
a. Made tunics of fine linen
b. Made the turban of fine linen
c. Made linen headbands
d. Made linen underwear
e. Made the sash

f. Made all exactly as the LORD had commanded
6. **The gold medallion or diadem: Symbolized that the High Priest bore the guilt for the shortcomings of the people**
a. Engraved with the words: HOLY TO THE LORD
b. Attached to the front of the turban with a blue cord
c. Made exactly as the LORD commanded
7. **The work on the Tabernacle was completed**
a. The construction: Was built exactly as the LORD commanded

b. The presentation to Moses
1) The tent & its furnishings

2) The coverings
3) The inner curtain: Enclosed the Holy of Holies

26 A bell and a pomegranate, a bell and a pomegranate, round about the hem of the robe to minister in; as the LORD commanded Moses.
27 And they made coats of fine linen of woven work for Aaron, and for his sons,
28 And a mitre of fine linen, and goodly bonnets of fine linen, and linen breeches of fine twined linen,
29 And a girdle of fine twined linen, and blue, and purple, and scarlet, of needlework; as the LORD commanded Moses.
30 And they made the plate of the holy crown of pure gold, and wrote upon it a writing, like to the engravings of a signet, HOLINESS TO THE LORD.
31 And they tied unto it a lace of blue, to fasten it on high upon the mitre; as the LORD commanded Moses.
32 Thus was all the work of the tabernacle of the tent of the congregation finished: and the children of Israel did according to all that the LORD commanded Moses, so did they.
33 And they brought the tabernacle unto Moses, the tent, and all his furniture, his taches, his boards, his bars, and his pillars, and his sockets,
34 And the covering of rams' skins dyed red, and the covering of badgers' skins, and the

vail of the covering,
35 The ark of the testimony, and the staves thereof, and the mercy seat,
36 The table, and all the vessels thereof, and the showbread,
37 The pure candlestick, with the lamps thereof, even with the lamps to be set in order, and all the vessels thereof, and the oil for light,
38 And the golden altar, and the anointing oil, and the sweet incense, and the hanging for the tabernacle door,
39 The brasen altar, and his grate of brass, his staves, and all his vessels, the laver and his foot,
40 The hangings of the court, his pillars, and his sockets, and the hanging for the court gate, his cords, and his pins, and all the vessels of the service of the tabernacle, for the tent of the congregation,
41 The cloths of service to do service in the holy place, and the holy garments for Aaron the priest, and his sons' garments, to minister in the priest's office.
42 According to all that the LORD commanded Moses, so the children of Israel made all the work.
43 And Moses did look upon all the work, and, behold, they have done it as the LORD had commanded, even so had they done it: and Moses blessed them.

4) The Ark of the Covenant & the Mercy Seat
5) The Table of Showbread with its utensils & the bread
6) The gold lampstand with its accessories & oil
7) The gold altar with its oil & incense
8) The entrance curtain
9) The bronze altar with its grating, poles, & utensils
10) The wash basin & pedestal
11) The courtyard curtains with their support posts, bases, & all the accessories
12) The courtyard curtain for the entrance & all the articles used in the Tabernacle
13) The priestly garments: The sacred garments worn by the High Priest & the other priests

c. The final inspection
1) The builders had built the Tabernacle exactly as God had designed
2) Moses inspected the work & saw the faithfulness, excellent work: Was built exactly as God had designed
3) Moses blessed them

DIVISION XI

THE TABERNACLE, ITS CONSTRUCTION AND DEDICATION: THE PEOPLE OBEY GOD, 35:1-40:38

E. The Making of the Garments For the Priests: Being Clothed in Righteousness, Ex.39:1-43

(39:1-43) **Introduction**: it has been said that *clothes make the man*. In other words, what a person wears says a lot about the image he presents to others--whether he intends to present the image or not. If a person is always sloppy, an impression of being unkempt or unclean is presented. If a person goes to the other extreme and openly flaunts his expensive clothes, he presents an image of pride. In the same sense, how a believer is dressed in his spiritual clothing makes the man. The believer who continues to wear the sinful nature, the flesh, projects an image of one who does not care about his testimony. The believer who "puts on" his religious rituals presents an image of self-righteousness or of being religious. The believer who "puts on" his knowledge projects an image of spiritual pride. God wants His people to wear the right spiritual clothing.

"Put on therefore, as the elect of God, holy and beloved, bowels of mercies, kindness, humbleness of mind, meekness, longsuffering" (Col.3:12).

Note that each of these traits concern behavior, spiritual qualities of character. What does God have to say about what His people wear? This is the subject of this portion of Scripture. God made it clear: the person who is going to serve Him has to put on the right garments. He has to wear clothing that brings dignity to what he is doing: serving and working for the LORD. This is: *The Making of the Garments for the Priests: Being Clothed in Righteousness*, Ex.39:1-43.

1. The sacred garments, the garments of service: symbolized dignity and honor for God's call (v.1).
2. The ephod: symbolized that the priest represented and carried the names of God's people before the Lord (v.2-7).
3. The breastpiece or chestpiece, a pouch-like garment: symbolized that the priest represented and carried the names of God's people upon his heart and before the Lord continually (v.8-21).
4. The robe of the ephod: symbolized the prayer ministry of the High Priest (v.22-26).
5. The other garments for the priests: symbolized putting on God's righteousness (v.27-29).
6. The gold medallion or diadem: symbolized that the High Priest bore the guilt for the shortcomings of the people (v.30-31).
7. The work on the Tabernacle was completed (v.32-43).

1 (39:1) **The Priesthood--Garments--Service--Call of God--Dignity--Honor--Obedience**: there were the sacred garments of service. The sacred garments symbolized the dignity and honor of God's call. (See outline and note--Ex.28:1-5 for more discussion.) Note the particular facts about these special clothes: the garments were made from blue, purple, and scarlet yarn. These were no ordinary garments: their sole purpose was for ministering in the Holy Place. The garments were made just as God commanded.

Thought 1. There is no greater call than the call of God. When God calls the believer into service, the believer has a unique opportunity, an opportunity...
* to minister in the sanctuary, the church of God Himself
* to give his life in service to the LORD God of the universe
* to receive some of the greatest blessings of God
* to experience a deep sense of purpose and fulfillment throughout life
* to minister to people in their deepest needs, when they need help the most
* to preach and teach the unsearchable riches of Christ
* to reach people for Christ, snatching them from an eternity of hell and saving them for heaven
* to lead people to life--life abundant and life eternal--all through Christ

"And whosoever will be chief among you, let him be your servant: Even as the Son of man came not to be ministered unto, but to minister, and to give his life a ransom for many" (Mt.20:27-28).

"Go ye therefore, and teach all nations, baptizing them in the name of the Father, and of the Son, and of the Holy Ghost: Teaching them to observe all things whatsoever I have commanded you: and, lo, I am with you alway, [even] unto the end of the world. Amen" (Mt.28:19-20).

"And he said unto them, Go ye into all the world, and preach the gospel to every creature" (Mk.16:15).

"For the Son of man is come to seek and to save that which was lost" (Lk.19:10; cp. Jn.20:21).

"Then said Jesus to them again, Peace [be] unto you: as [my] Father hath sent me, even so send I you" (Jn.20:21).

"He saith unto him the third time, Simon, [son] of Jonas, lovest thou me? Peter was grieved because he said unto him the third time, Lovest thou me? And he said unto him, Lord, thou knowest all things; thou knowest that I love thee. Jesus saith unto him, Feed my sheep" (Jn.21:17).

"Take heed therefore unto yourselves, and to all the flock, over the which the Holy Ghost hath made you overseers, to feed the church of God, which he hath purchased with his own blood" (Acts 20:28).

"For we preach not ourselves, but Christ Jesus the Lord; and ourselves your servants for Jesus' sake" (2 Cor.4:5).

"Feed the flock of God which is among you, taking the oversight thereof, not by constraint, but willingly; not for filthy lucre, but of a ready mind" (1 Pt.5:2).

2 (39:2-7) **The Priesthood--Ephod--People of God--Representation**: there was the ephod. The ephod symbolized that the priest represented and carried the names of God's people before the Lord. (See outline and note--Ex.28:6-14 for more discussion.) Remember, God had created the nation of ancient Israel through the seed (descendants) of Abraham. God had created Israel to be His witnesses to a lost and dying world. In an act of His sovereign will, God had selected the Israelites to be His chosen people. This fact was symbolized with the ephod. Note the facts about how it was made:
1. The ephod was made of blue, purple and scarlet yarn and fine linen (v.2).
2. The ephod was made by hammering out thin sheets of gold that were cut into thin strands. The strands were then worked into the yarn and linen (v.3).
3. The shoulder pieces were made and attached to the two corners of the ephod (v.4).
4. The waistband was made as one piece with the ephod and was made of the multi-colored yarn and linen. The waistband was made exactly as God commanded (v.5).
5. The two onyx stones were mounted in gold filigree settings. The names of Israel's twelve tribes were engraved on the stones (v.6). The stones were then fastened to the shoulder pieces of the ephod (v.7). Again, this was done just as the Lord commanded Moses.

Thought 1. When the High Priest went before the LORD, the names of God's people were carried with him. Why is this significant for the believer?

1) God wants a personal relationship with His dear people. He wants, He desires, He longs for a personal relationship with each one of us. He wants us coming into His presence constantly, coming to worship, fellowship, and commune, seeking His guidance and help.

"For where two or three are gathered together in my name, there am I in the midst of them" (Mt.18:20).

"God is faithful, by whom ye were called unto the fellowship of his Son Jesus Christ our Lord" (1 Cor.1:9).

"Let us draw near with a true heart in full assurance of faith, having our hearts sprinkled from an evil conscience, and our bodies washed with pure water" (Heb.10:22).

"Draw nigh to God, and he will draw nigh to you" (Jas.4:8).

"That which we have seen and heard declare we unto you, that ye also may have fellowship with us: and truly our fellowship is with the Father, and with his Son Jesus Christ" (1 Jn.1:3).

"Behold, I stand at the door, and knock: if any man hear my voice, and open the door, I will come in to him, and will sup [fellowship] with him, and he with me" (Rev.3:20).

"The LORD is nigh unto them that are of a broken heart; and saveth such as be of a contrite spirit" (Ps.34:18).

"But it is good for me to draw near to God: I have put my trust in the Lord GOD, that I may declare all thy works" (Ps.73:28).

"The LORD is nigh unto all them that call upon him, to all that call upon him in truth" (Ps.145:18).

"When thou passest through the waters, I will be with thee; and through the rivers, they shall not overflow thee: when thou walkest through the fire, thou shalt not be burned; neither shall the flame kindle upon thee" (Is.43:2).

2) God knows every believer by name: He knows the name of every one of us. We are His sons and daughters, part of the adopted family of God.

"Notwithstanding in this rejoice not, that the spirits are subject unto you; but rather rejoice, because your names are written in heaven" (Lk.10:20).

"But as many as received him, to them gave he power to become the sons of God, even to them that believe on his name" (Jn.1:12).

"To him the porter openeth; and the sheep hear his voice: and he calleth his own sheep by name, and leadeth them out" (Jn.10:3).

"Wherefore come out from among them, and be ye separate, saith the Lord, and touch not the unclean thing; and I will receive you, And will be a Father unto you, and ye shall be my sons and daughters, saith the Lord Almighty" (2 Cor.6:17-18).

"But when the fulness of the time was come, God sent forth his Son, made of a woman, made under the law, To redeem them that were under the law, that we might receive the adoption of sons. And because ye are sons, God hath sent forth the Spirit of his Son into your hearts, crying, Abba, Father" (Gal.4:4-6).

"He that overcometh, the same shall be clothed in white raiment; and I will not blot out his name out of the book of life, but I will confess his name before my Father, and before his angels" (Rev.3:5).

"Fear not: for I have redeemed thee, I have called thee by thy name; thou art mine" (Is.43:1).

3 (39:8-21) **The Priesthood--Breastpiece or Chestpiece--Heart of God**: there was the breastpiece or chestpiece, a pouch-like garment. (See outline and note--Ex.28:15-30 for more discussion.) The chestpiece symbolized that the priest represented and carried the names of God's people upon his heart and before the Lord continually. The fact that the chestpiece was worn upon the High Priest's heart was significant. He was to hold God's people ever so near and dear to his heart, constantly praying and upholding them before the LORD and ministering to them as needed. The breastpiece or chestpiece was fashioned in the following way:

1. The materials in the chestpiece were gold, blue, purple, and scarlet yarn and fine linen (v.8).
2. The design of the chestpiece was as follows:
   a. The chestpiece was made square and folded double (v.9).
   b. There were four rows of precious stones attached to it (v.10-13).
      ⇒ The first row held a ruby, a topaz, and a beryl.
      ⇒ The second row held a turquoise, a sapphire, and an emerald.
      ⇒ The third row held a jacinth, an agate, and an amethyst.
      ⇒ The fourth row held a chrysolite, an onyx, and a jasper.
   c. The precious stones were mounted in gold filigree settings (v.13).
   d. The twelve stones symbolized each of the twelve tribes of Israel.
   e. The name of a different tribe was engraved on each of the twelve stones (v.14).
3. The chestpiece was then attached to the ephod. This was done by making braided chains of pure gold (v.15). Two gold settings were made along with two gold rings. The rings were fastened to the two corners of the chestpiece (v.16). Then the two gold chains were fastened to the rings of the chestpiece and the other ends of the chains to the two settings.

This attached them to the shoulder pieces (v.17-18). Two more gold rings were made and attached to the other two ends of the chestpiece--on the inside next to the ephod garment (v.19). An additional two rings were made and attached to the ephod garment next to the sash (v.21). The rings on the chestpiece were then tied together with the rings of the ephod, tied with blue cord. This final act held the two garments together (v.21).

Thought 1. The chestpiece symbolized that the priest represented and carried the names of God's people upon his heart and before the Lord continually. This is a strong picture of how much we mean to God, just how dear we are to Him. God loves us, and keeps us ever so close to His heart.
1) God knows us personally and intimately.

"For thou hast possessed my reins: thou hast covered me in my mother's womb. I will praise thee; for I am fearfully *and* wonderfully made: marvelous *are* thy works; and *that* my soul knoweth right well. My substance was not hid from thee, when I was made in secret, *and* curiously wrought in the lowest parts of the earth. Thine eyes did see my substance, yet being unperfect; and in thy book all *my members* were written, *which* in continuance were fashioned, when *as yet there was* none of them" (Ps.139:13-16).
"Fear not: for I have redeemed thee, I have called thee by thy name; thou art mine" (Is.43:1).
"Before I formed thee in the belly I knew thee; and before thou camest forth out of the womb I sanctified thee, *and* I ordained thee a prophet unto the nations" (Jer.1:5).
"I am the good shepherd, and know my *sheep,* and am known of mine" (Jn.10:14).

2) God knows our every need.

"Be not ye therefore like unto them: for your Father knoweth what things ye have need of, before ye ask him" (Mt.6:8).
"Therefore take no thought, saying, What shall we eat? or, What shall we drink? or, Wherewithal shall we be clothed? (For after all these things do the Gentiles seek:) for your heavenly Father knoweth that ye have need of all these things" (Mt.6:31-32).
"But my God shall supply all your need according to his riches in glory by Christ Jesus" (Ph.4:19).
"And he said, My presence shall go with thee, and I will give thee rest" (Ex.33:14).
"The eternal God is thy refuge, and underneath are the everlasting arms: and he shall thrust out the enemy from before thee; and shall say, Destroy them" (Dt.33:27).
"But I *am* poor and needy; *yet* the Lord thinketh upon me: thou *art* my help and my deliverer; make no tarrying, O my God" (Ps.40:17).
"Behold, God *is* mine helper: the Lord *is* with them that uphold my soul" (Ps.54:4).
"For thou hast been a strength to the poor, a strength to the needy in his distress, a refuge from the storm, a shadow from the heat, when the blast of the terrible ones is as a storm against the wall" (Is.25:4).
"When thou passest through the waters, I will be with thee; and through the rivers, they shall not overflow thee: when thou walkest through the fire, thou shalt not be burned; neither shall the flame kindle upon thee" (Is.43:2).

3) God knows the pain of every lonely, hurting heart.

"And, behold, I am with thee, and will keep thee in all places whither thou goest, and will bring thee again into this land; for I will not leave thee, until I have done that which I have spoken to thee of" (Gen.28:15).
"The LORD *is* nigh unto them that are of a broken heart; and saveth such as be of a contrite spirit" (Ps.34:18).
"For the LORD loveth judgment, and forsaketh not his saints; they are preserved for ever: but the seed of the wicked shall be cut off" (Ps.37:28).
"As one whom his mother comforteth, so will I comfort you" (Is.66:13).
"Fear thou not; for I am with thee: be not dismayed; for I am thy God: I will strengthen thee; yea, I will help thee; yea, I will uphold thee with the right hand of my righteousness" (Is.41:10).
"And even to your old age I am he; and even to hoar [gray] hairs will I carry you: I have made, and I will bear; even I will carry, and will deliver you" (Is.46:4).
"Let not your heart be troubled: ye believe in God, believe also in me" (Jn.14:1).
"Blessed *be* God, even the Father of our Lord Jesus Christ, the Father of mercies, and the God of all comfort" (2 Cor.1:3).

4) God knows everything that we do for Him.

"I know thy works: behold, I have set before thee an open door, and no man can shut it: for thou hast a little strength, and hast kept my word, and hast not denied my name" (Rev.3:8).

"He revealeth the deep and secret things: he knoweth what is in the darkness, and the light dwelleth with him" (Dan.2:22).

5) God knows the most minute details of our lives, even our thoughts.

"Casting all your care upon him; for he careth for you" (1 Pt.5:7).

"And thou, Solomon my son, know thou the God of thy father, and serve him with a perfect heart and with a willing mind: for the LORD searcheth all hearts, and understandeth all the imaginations of the thoughts: if thou seek him, he will be found of thee; but if thou forsake him, he will cast thee off for ever" (1 Chron.28:9).

"The LORD hath been mindful of us: he will bless us; he will bless the house of Israel; he will bless the house of Aaron" (Ps.115:12).

"I the LORD search the heart, I try the reins, even to give every man according to his ways, and according to the fruit of his doings" (Jer.17:10).

"Can any hide himself in secret places that I shall not see him? saith the LORD. Do not I fill heaven and earth? saith the LORD" (Jer.23:24).

"But even the very hairs of your head are all numbered. Fear not therefore: ye are of more value than many sparrows" (Lk.12:7).

"And again, The Lord knoweth the thoughts of the wise, that they are vain" (1 Cor.3:20).

4 (39:22-26) **The Priesthood--The Robe of the Ephod--Prayer--Intercession**: there is the robe of the ephod. The ephod symbolized the prayer ministry of the High Priest. (See outline and note--Ex.28:31-35.) Just imagine someone who has a personal relationship with the Ruler of a nation (a President or King, or a Premier). Suppose this person was *your* advocate, your personal representative who brought all your needs before the Ruler. Think what the Ruler could do for you, how much he could do to meet your needs and enrich your life.

This was the exact situation with Israel. God's people could not approach God on their own. Christ had not yet come. Therefore, they did not have the personal, intimate relationship with God that is now possible. The Israelites needed someone who could stand in their place, someone who could speak on their behalf. When the High Priest put on the robe of the ephod, the people knew what he was about to do. He was about to approach God and plead the concerns of every man, woman, and child. This is how the robe of the ephod was made:

1. The material of the robe was made by a weaver who used only blue cloth (v.22).

2. The opening for the head was reinforced with a woven collar so it would not tear when the High Priest pulled the robe over his head (v.23).

3. The pomegranates and bells were made and attached to the hem of the robe. The pomegranates were made of blue, purple, and scarlet yarn and fine linen (v.24). The bells were made of gold and attached around the hem of the robe between the pomegranates (v.25).

4. The purpose of the robe was to wear for ministering--as the LORD commanded. Its symbolic purpose was to sound forth the intercessory ministry of the High Priest (v.26).

Thought 1. Jesus Christ is our advocate, our High Priest who lives to make intercession for us. He loves us. He cares for us. He prays for us. He carries our needs before the Sovereign Majesty of the universe, the LORD God Himself (Jehovah - Yahweh).

1) Jesus Christ prays for the sinner, that he would forsake his sin and be saved.

"Therefore will I divide him *a portion* with the great, and he shall divide the spoil with the strong; because he hath poured out his soul unto death: and he was numbered with the transgressors; and he bare the sin of many, and made intercession for the transgressors" (Is.53:12).

2) Jesus Christ prays for those who hate and reject Him even as He prayed for those who crucified Him.

"But I say unto you, Love your enemies, bless them that curse you, do good to them that hate you, and pray for them which despitefully use you, and persecute you" (Mt.5:44).

"Then said Jesus, Father, forgive them; for they know not what they do. And they parted his raiment, and cast lots" (Lk.23:34).

3) Jesus Christ prays for all unbelievers, for all who are condemned.

"Who shall lay any thing to the charge of God's elect? *It is* God that justifieth. Who *is* he that condemneth? *It is* Christ that died, yea rather, that is risen again, who is even at the right hand of God, who also maketh intercession for us" (Ro.8:33-34).

4) Jesus Christ prays for those whom He saves.

"Wherefore he is able also to save them to the uttermost that come unto God by him, seeing he ever liveth to make intercession for them" (Heb.7:25).

5) Jesus Christ prays for those who belong to Him, for those who believe and follow Him.

> "I pray for them: I pray not for the world, but for them which thou hast given me; for they are thine" (Jn.17:9).

6) Jesus Christ prays for the believers of every generation.

> "Neither pray I for these alone, but for them also which shall believe on me through their word" (Jn.17:20).

7) Jesus Christ prays for those who need His comfort and care.

> "And I will pray the Father, and he shall give you another Comforter, that he may abide with you for ever" (Jn.14:16).

8) Jesus Christ prays for those who are weak and frail in their faith.

> "But I have prayed for thee, that thy faith fail not: and when thou art converted, strengthen thy brethren" (Lk.22:32).

9) Jesus Christ prays for those who are facing strong temptations.

> "And when he was at the place, he said unto them, Pray that ye enter not into temptation. And he was withdrawn from them about a stone's cast, and kneeled down, and prayed" (Lk.22:40-41).

10) Jesus Christ prays for our protection against the power of evil.

> "I pray not that thou shouldest take them out of the world, but that thou shouldest keep them from the evil" (Jn.17:15).

5 (39:27-29) **The Priesthood--Garments--Tunic--Turban--Headbands--Underwear--Sash--Obedience**: there were the other garments for the priests. The priestly garments were symbolic of putting on God's righteousness. (See outline and note--Ex.28:39-43 for more discussion.) Tunics of fine linen were made by a weaver (v.27). Turbans were made of fine linen, as well as the headbands (v.28). The undergarments were made of fine twisted linen (v.28). The sash for each priest was made of fine linen and multi-colored yarn (v.29). All of these garments were made exactly as the LORD commanded Moses (v.29).

Thought 1. The turbans and tunics were long coat-like garments that essentially covered the whole body. They are therefore symbolic of putting on God's righteousness. Those who minister in God's name must bear His righteousness. Anything less than God's righteousness is totally insufficient.

> "I put on righteousness, and it clothed me: my judgment *was* as a robe and a diadem" (Job 29:14).
> "Let thy priests be clothed with righteousness; and let thy saints shout for joy" (Ps.132:9).
> "I will also clothe her priests with salvation: and her saints shall shout aloud for joy" (Ps.132:16).
> "I will greatly rejoice in the LORD, my soul shall be joyful in my God; for he hath clothed me with the garments of salvation, he hath covered me with the robe of righteousness, as a bridegroom decketh *himself* with ornaments, and as a bride adorneth *herself* with her jewels" (Is.61:10).
> "But of him are ye in Christ Jesus, who of God is made unto us wisdom, and righteousness, and sanctification, and redemption" (1 Cor.1:30).
> "For he hath made him *to be* sin for us, who knew no sin; that we might be made the righteousness of God in him" (2 Cor.5:21).

Thought 2. The linen headbands were of course worn on the head. They were symbolic of the believer's mind and will being subjected to God. The believer is to willingly submit his will, his thoughts, and his own personal agenda to God.

> "I delight to do thy will, O my God: yea, thy law *is* within my heart" (Ps.40:8).
> "Teach me to do thy will; for thou *art* my God: thy spirit *is* good; lead me into the land of uprightness" (Ps.143:10).
> "I beseech you therefore, brethren, by the mercies of God, that ye present your bodies a living sacrifice, holy, acceptable unto God, *which is* your reasonable service. And be not conformed to this world: but be ye transformed by the renewing of your mind, that ye may prove what is that good, and acceptable, and perfect, will of God" (Ro.12:1-2).
> "Casting down imaginations, and every high thing that exalteth itself against the knowledge of God, and bringing into captivity every thought to the obedience of Christ" (2 Cor.10:5).

"Not with eyeservice, as menpleasers; but as the servants of Christ, doing the will of God from the heart" (Eph.6:6).

Thought 3. The linen underwear was symbolic of covering the believer's spiritual nakedness. The person who is without Christ in his life will be exposed and shamed. We must put on the Lord Jesus Christ and make no provision for the flesh.

"He shall put on the holy linen coat, and he shall have the linen breeches upon his flesh, and shall be girded with a linen girdle, and with the linen mitre shall he be attired: these *are* <u>holy garments</u>; therefore shall he wash [symbolic of spiritual cleansing] his flesh in water, and *so* <u>put them on</u>" (Lev.16:4).
"Knowing this, that our old man is crucified with *him,* that the body of sin might be destroyed, that henceforth we should not serve sin" (Ro.6:6).
"But <u>put ye on</u> the Lord Jesus Christ, and make not provision for the flesh, to *fulfil* the lusts *thereof*" (Ro.13:14).
"And that ye <u>put on</u> the new man, which after God is created in righteousness and true holiness" (Eph.4:24).
"And have <u>put on</u> the new *man,* which is renewed in knowledge after the image of him that created him" (Col.3:10).

Thought 4. The multi-colored sash of fine linen was symbolic of truth, the truth of God's Word. It is comparable to the *belt of truth* in the armor of God that the believer is to put on (Eph.6:14). The Word of God enlightens and wraps everything in the believer's spiritual wardrobe together. It is the Word of God that holds everything together.

"And ye shall know the truth, and the truth shall make you free" (Jn.8:32).
"Sanctify them through thy truth: thy word is truth" (Jn.17:17).
"But these are written, that ye might believe that Jesus is the Christ, the Son of God; and that believing ye might have life through his name" (Jn.20:31).
"For whatsoever things were written aforetime were written for our learning, that we through patience and comfort of the scriptures might have hope" (Ro.15:4).
"Wherefore take unto you the whole armour of God, that ye may be able to withstand in the evil day, and having done all, to stand. Stand therefore, having <u>your loins girt about with truth</u>, and having on the breastplate of righteousness" (Eph.6:13-14).
"All scripture is given by inspiration of God, and is profitable for doctrine, for reproof, for correction, for instruction in righteousness: That the man of God may be perfect, throughly furnished unto all good works" (2 Tim.3:16-17).
"For the word of God is quick, and powerful, and sharper than any twoedged sword, piercing even to the dividing asunder of soul and spirit, and of the joints and marrow, and is a discerner of the thoughts and intents of the heart" (Heb.4:12).

6 (39:30-31) **The Priesthood--Gold Medallion--Diadem--Guilt**: there was the gold medallion or diadem. The medallion symbolized that the High Priest bore the guilt for the shortcomings of the people. The sacred diadem had these words engraved upon it: HOLY TO THE LORD (v.30). These powerful words summarized the High Priest's entire wardrobe. These words were the crowning glory of the High Priest, declaring that he was to be completely set apart for God's purpose. The High Priest was sanctified, consecrated, set apart for the sole purpose of declaring that he was bringing honor and glory to God. The High Priest was challenged...

- to the high standard of holiness
- to the high call of personal sacrifice
- to the high service of God and His dear people

This medallion was attached to the front of the linen turban with a blue cord (v.31). The gold medallion or diadem was made exactly as the LORD commanded Moses (v.31).

Thought 1. We need a High Priest who not only bears the guilt of our shortcomings, but a High Priest who can take away the guilt and condemnation of sin. Scripture declares that Jesus Christ is our great High Priest.

1) As our great High Priest, Jesus Christ took our sins upon Himself.

"Therefore will I divide him *a portion* with the great, and he shall divide the spoil with the strong; because he hath poured out his soul unto death: and he was numbered with the transgressors; and he bare the sin of many, and made intercession for the transgressors" (Is.53:12).
"So Christ was once offered to bear the sins of many; and unto them that look for him shall he appear the second time without sin unto salvation" (Heb.9:28).
"Who his own self bare our sins in his own body on the tree, that we, being dead to sins, should live unto righteousness: by whose stripes ye were healed" (1 Pt.2:24).
"And ye know that he was manifested to take away our sins; and in him is no sin" (1 Jn.3:5).

2) As our great High Priest, Jesus Christ became the sacrifice for our sins, once for all.

"Who gave himself for our sins, that he might deliver us from this present evil world, according to the will of God and our Father" (Gal.1:4).

"And walk in love, as Christ also hath loved us, and hath given himself for us an offering and a sacrifice to God for a sweetsmelling savour" (Eph.5:2).

"Who gave himself for us, that he might redeem us from all iniquity, and purify unto himself a peculiar people, zealous of good works" (Tit.2:14).

"For then must he often have suffered since the foundation of the world: but now once in the end of the world hath he appeared to put away sin by the sacrifice of himself. And as it is appointed unto men once to die, but after this the judgment: So Christ was once offered to bear the sins of many; and unto them that look for him shall he appear the second time without sin unto salvation" (Heb.9:26-28).

"By the which will we are sanctified through the offering of the body of Jesus Christ once *for all*. (Heb.10:10).

"Hereby perceive we the love *of God*, because he laid down his life for us: and we ought to lay down *our* lives for the brethren" (1 Jn.3:16).

"Unto him that loved us, and washed us from our sins in his own blood" (Rev.1:5).

3) As our great High Priest, Jesus Christ makes reconciliation for our sins.

"Wherefore in all things it behooved him to be made like unto *his* brethren, that he might be a merciful and faithful high priest in things *pertaining* to God, to make reconciliation for the sins of the people" (Heb.2:17).

4) As our great High Priest, Jesus Christ is touched with the feelings of our weaknesses.

"Seeing then that we have a great high priest, that is passed into the heavens, Jesus the Son of God, let us hold fast *our* profession. For we have not an high priest which cannot be touched with the feeling of our infirmities; but was in all points tempted like as *we are, yet* without sin" (Heb.4:14-15).

5) As our great High Priest, Jesus Christ has us brought eternal salvation.

"So also Christ glorified not himself to be made an high priest; but he that said unto him, Thou art my Son, to day have I begotten thee....And being made perfect, he became the author of eternal salvation unto all them that obey him" (Heb.5:5, 9).

6) As our great High Priest, Jesus Christ has brought us the great hope of heaven, of living forever in God's presence.

"Which hope [of heaven] we have as an anchor of the soul, both sure and stedfast, and which entereth into that within the veil; Whither the forerunner is for us entered, *even* Jesus, made an high priest for ever after the order of Melchisedec" (Heb.6:19-20).

7) As our great High Priest, Jesus Christ brings us the forgiveness of sin.

"For such an high priest became us, *who is* holy, harmless, undefiled, separate from sinners, and made higher than the heavens; Who needeth not daily, as those high priests, to offer up sacrifice, first for his own sins, and then for the people's: for this he did once, when he offered up himself" (Heb.7:26-27).

8) As our great High Priest, Jesus Christ sits at the right hand of God for us.

"Now of the things which we have spoken *this is* the sum: We have such an high priest, who is set on the right hand of the throne of the Majesty in the heavens" (Heb.8:1).

9) As our great High Priest, Jesus Christ brings us an abundance of good things.

"But Christ being come an high priest of good things to come, by a greater and more perfect tabernacle, not made with hands, that is to say, not of this building" (Heb.9:11).

10) As our great High Priest, Jesus Christ gives us access into God's presence.

"And *having* an high priest [Jesus Christ] over the house of God; Let us draw near with a true heart in full assurance of faith, having our hearts sprinkled from an evil conscience, and our bodies washed with pure water" (Heb.10:21-22).

11) As our great High Priest, Jesus Christ saves us to the uttermost, completely, permanently, and forever.

"But this man, because he continueth ever, hath an unchangeable priesthood. Wherefore he is able also to save them to the uttermost that come unto God by him, seeing he ever liveth to make intercession for them" (Heb.7:24-25).

7 (39:32-43) <u>Tabernacle of Moses--Construction--Faithfulness--Obedience--Dedication</u>: the work on the Tabernacle was complete. Finally, the long-awaited time had come. The Tabernacle of God was built and completed by His people.

1. The construction of the Tabernacle was built exactly as the LORD commanded (v.32). Note several things:
   a. All of the work was done. Nothing was left incomplete.
   b. The Israelites (God's people) did the work. God did not entrust this important project to unbelievers.
   c. The Israelites did everything just as the LORD commanded Moses. There was no human input or changes to the plans for the Tabernacle. They followed the instructions exactly, completely, and entirely.

<u>Thought 1</u>. God counts only those things that last as being successful. If we do things God's way, the work will always be complete. God wants us to have a lasting impact upon the lives of those whom we touch with the gospel.

"Herein is my Father glorified, that ye bear much fruit; so shall ye be my disciples" (Jn.15:8).
"Ye have not chosen me, but I have chosen you, and ordained you, that ye should go and bring forth fruit, and *that* your fruit should remain: that whatsoever ye shall ask of the Father in my name, he may give it you" (Jn.15:16).

<u>Thought 2</u>. It should be the cry of every human heart to obey the Lord. We should all seek to know the ways of God, to learn what He wants us to do. And we should obey Him with perfect trust and confidence.

"O that there were such an heart in them, that they would fear me, and keep all my commandments always, that it might be well with them, and with their children for ever!" (Dt.5:29).
"Therefore whosoever heareth these sayings of mine, and doeth them, I will liken him unto a wise man, which built his house upon a rock" (Mt.7:24).
"Jesus answered and said unto him, If a man love me, he will keep my words: and my Father will love him, and we will come unto him, and make our abode with him" (Jn.14:23).
"But whoso looketh into the perfect law of liberty, and continueth *therein,* he being not a forgetful hearer, but a doer of the work, this man shall be blessed in his deed" (Jas.1:25).
"Blessed *are* they that do his commandments, that they may have right to the tree of life, and may enter in through the gates into the city" (Rev.22:14).

2. The workers who built the Tabernacle and made the priest's garments brought them all to Moses.
   a. They brought the tent and its furnishings (v.33).
   b. They brought the coverings for the tent (v.34).
   c. They brought the inner curtains that enclosed the Holy of Holies (v.34).
   d. They brought the Ark of the Covenant and the Mercy Seat with its poles (v.35).
   e. They brought the Table of Showbread with its utensils and the bread (v.36).
   f. They brought the gold Lampstand with its accessories and oil (v.37).
   g. They brought the gold Altar with its oil and incense (v.38).
   h. They brought the entrance curtain (v.38).
   i. They brought the bronze altar with its grating, poles, and utensils (v.39).
   j. They brought the wash basin and pedestal (v.39).
   k. They brought the courtyard curtains with their support posts, bases, and all the accessories (v.40).
   l. They brought the courtyard curtain for the entrance and all the articles used in the Tabernacle (v.40).
   m. They brought the priestly garments: the sacred garments worn by the High Priest and the other priests (v.41).

3. The final inspection was now at hand. The builders had constructed the Tabernacle exactly as God had designed (v.42). Moses, the man who had been given the blueprints, inspected the work and saw the faithfulness and the excellent work done by the workers. Everything was built exactly as God had designed (v.43). After his thorough inspection, Moses blessed the workers and offered up prayers to God on their behalf (v.43).

<u>Thought 1</u>. We are to be faithful to our work. No matter what our call or profession is, we are to work and work hard, being diligent and zealous, doing the very best job we can. We are to be faithful.
Note that Moses was given the responsibility to inspect the quality of the work. He did not just "rubber stamp" the whole undertaking. Moses carefully inspected the finished project. Whenever God places His people in places of great responsibility, He expects them to be diligent, to manage in His name. We are to be faithful, working ever so diligently and doing a good job.

"And he said unto him, Well, thou good servant: because thou hast been faithful in a very little, have thou authority over ten cities" (Lk.19:17).
"Therefore, my beloved brethren, be ye stedfast, unmoveable, always abounding in the work of the Lord, forasmuch as ye know that your labour is not in vain in the Lord" (1 Cor.15:58).
"And whatsoever ye do in word or deed, do all in the name of the Lord Jesus, giving thanks to God and the Father by him" (Col.3:17).
"And whatsoever ye do, do it heartily, as to the Lord, and not unto men" (Col.3:23).
"Wherefore I put thee in remembrance that thou stir up the gift of God, which is in thee by the putting on of my hands" (2 Tim.1:6).

"Wherefore the rather, brethren, give diligence to make your calling and election sure: for if ye do these things, ye shall never fall" (2 Pt.1:10).

"Wherefore, beloved, seeing that ye look for such things, be diligent that ye may be found of him in peace, without spot, and blameless" (2 Pt.3:14).

"Be thou faithful unto death, and I will give thee a crown of life" (Rev.2:10).

"And, behold, I come quickly; and my reward *is* with me, to give every man according as his work shall be" (Rev.22:12).

"So we laboured in the work: and half of them held the spears from the rising of the morning till the stars appeared" (Neh.4:21).

"Whatsoever thy hand findeth to do, do it with thy might; for there is no work, nor device, nor knowledge, nor wisdom, in the grave, whither thou goest" (Eccl.9:10).

TYPES, SYMBOLS, AND PICTURES
(Exodus 39:1-43)

Historical Term	Type or Picture (Scriptural Basis for Each)	Life Application for Today's Believer	Biblical Application for Today's Believer
The precious stones for the breastpiece (Ex.39:10-14)	*Twelve precious stones were attached to the breastpiece that was worn close to the heart of the High Priest. These stones symbolized that the High Priest represented and carried the names of God's people (all of God's people, all twelve tribes) upon His heart, that He represented them before the Lord continually.* "And they set in it four rows of stones: *the first row was* a sardius, a topaz, and a carbuncle: this *was* the first row. And the second row, an emerald, a sapphire, and a diamond. And the third row, a ligure, an agate, and an amethyst. And the fourth row, a beryl, an onyx, and a jasper: *they were* inclosed in ouches of gold in their inclosings. And the stones *were* according to the names of the children of Israel, twelve, according to their names, *like* the engravings of a signet, every one with his name, according to the twelve tribes" (Ex.39:10-14).	⇒ Jesus Christ, as the great High Priest, keeps His people, all His people, close to His heart. He is always mindful of what His people are going through and what they need from Him. We are like precious gems to Him, gems that He lovingly and tenderly cares for.	*"Casting all your care upon him; for he careth for you"* (1 Pt.5:7). *"But I am poor and needy; yet the Lord thinketh upon me: thou art my help and my deliverer; make no tarrying, O my God"* (Ps.40:17). *"Fear thou not; for I am with thee: be not dismayed; for I am thy God: I will strengthen thee; yea, I will help thee; yea, I will uphold thee with the right hand of my righteousness"* (Is.41:10). *"Fear not: for I have redeemed thee, I have called thee by thy name; thou art mine. When thou passest through the waters, I will be with thee; and through the rivers, they shall not overflow thee: when thou walkest through the fire, thou shalt not be burned; neither shall the flame kindle upon thee"* (Is.43:1-2).

(Please note: other Types, Symbols, and Pictures for this outline can be found at the end of Chapter 28, where they are initially discussed.)

F. The Assembly & Dedication of the Tabernacle, the Center of Worship: Experiencing the Presence of the Lord, Ex.40:1-38

1. The instructions of the Lord

a. The Tabernacle: To be assembled on the 1st day of the first month

b. The furnishings to be set in place
   1) The Ark of the Testimony
   2) The curtain to shield the Ark
   3) The Table of Showbread & its utensils
   4) The Lampstand & its lamps

   5) The Gold Altar of Incense: Put in front of the Ark of Testimony
   6) The curtain for the entrance to the Tabernacle
   7) The Altar of Burnt Offering: Put in front of the entrance

   8) The Wash Basin: Put between the Tent of Meeting & the Altar & fill with water

   9) The Courtyard
   10) The curtain at the entrance to the Courtyard

c. The dedication of the Tabernacle & its furnishings
   1) Anoint the Tabernacle & its furnishings: Make them holy (set apart to God)

   2) Anoint the Altar of Burnt Offering & its utensils: Make them holy

   3) Anoint the Wash Basin & pedestal: Consecrate them

d. The consecration of the priests
   1) Bring the priests to the entrance of the Tabernacle and wash them
   2) Dress the High Priest in sacred clothing: Anoint & consecrate him

   3) Bring his sons & dress them in tunics

   4) Anoint his sons
   5) The purpose: To anoint

And the LORD spake unto Moses, saying,

2 On the first day of the first month shalt thou set up the tabernacle of the tent of the congregation.

3 And thou shalt put therein the ark of the testimony, and cover the ark with the vail.

4 And thou shalt bring in the table, and set in order the things that are to be set in order upon it; and thou shalt bring in the candlestick, and light the lamps thereof.

5 And thou shalt set the altar of gold for the incense before the ark of the testimony, and put the hanging of the door to the tabernacle.

6 And thou shalt set the altar of the burnt offering before the door of the tabernacle of the tent of the congregation.

7 And thou shalt set the laver between the tent of the congregation and the altar, and shalt put water therein.

8 And thou shalt set up the court round about, and hang up the hanging at the court gate.

9 And thou shalt take the anointing oil, and anoint the tabernacle, and all that is therein, and shalt hallow it, and all the vessels thereof: and it shall be holy.

10 And thou shalt anoint the altar of the burnt offering, and all his vessels, and sanctify the altar: and it shall be an altar most holy.

11 And thou shalt anoint the laver and his foot, and sanctify it.

12 And thou shalt bring Aaron and his sons unto the door of the tabernacle of the congregation, and wash them with water.

13 And thou shalt put upon Aaron the holy garments, and anoint him, and sanctify him; that he may minister unto me in the priest's office.

14 And thou shalt bring his sons, and clothe them with coats:

15 And thou shalt anoint them, as thou didst anoint

their father, that they may minister unto me in the priest's office: for their anointing shall surely be an everlasting priesthood throughout their generations.

16 Thus did Moses: according to all that the LORD commanded him, so did he.

17 And it came to pass in the first month in the second year, on the first day of the month, that the tabernacle was reared up.

18 And Moses reared up the tabernacle, and fastened his sockets, and set up the boards thereof, and put in the bars thereof, and reared up his pillars.

19 And he spread abroad the tent over the tabernacle, and put the covering of the tent above upon it; as the LORD commanded Moses.

20 And he took and put the testimony into the ark, and set the staves on the ark, and put the mercy seat above upon the ark:

21 And he brought the ark into the tabernacle, and set up the vail of the covering, and covered the ark of the testimony; as the LORD commanded Moses.

22 And he put the table in the tent of the congregation, upon the side of the tabernacle northward, without the vail.

23 And he set the bread in order upon it before the LORD; as the LORD had commanded Moses.

24 And he put the candlestick in the tent of the congregation, over against the table, on the side of the tabernacle southward.

25 And he lighted the lamps before the LORD; as the LORD commanded Moses.

26 And he put the golden altar in the tent of the congregation before the vail:

27 And he burnt sweet incense thereon; as the LORD commanded Moses.

28 And he set up the hanging at the door of the tabernacle.

29 And he put the altar of burnt offering by the door of the tabernacle of the tent of the congregation, and offered upon it the burnt offering and the meat offering; as the LORD commanded Moses.

30 And he set the laver be-

the priesthood for all generations (set apart)

2. The obedience of Moses: He did everything God commanded

a. Set up the Tabernacle on the first day of the first month in the 2nd year

   1) Constructed the bases, frames, crossbars, & posts

   2) Spread the tent over the Tabernacle & put the covering over the tent:
   3) Did just as God commanded

b. Placed the Testimony (Ten Com.) in the Ark: Attached the poles & placed the Mercy Seat on the top of the Ark

c. Placed the Ark in the Tabernacle
   1) Hung the inner curtain
   2) Shielded the Ark of Testimony
   3) Did just as God commanded

d. Placed the Table in the Tent of Meeting
   1) Set it on the north side outside the curtain

   2) Set the bread before the Lord
   3) Did just as God commanded

e. Placed the Lampstand in the Tabernacle
   1) Set it opposite the Table on the south side
   2) Set up the lamps before the Lord
   3) Did just as God commanded

f. Placed the Altar of Incense in the Tent of Meeting in front of the curtain
   1) Burned incense on it
   2) Did just as God commanded

g. Put up the curtain at the entrance

h. Set the Altar of Burnt Offering near the entrance to the Tabernacle
   1) Offered burnt offerings & grain offerings
   2) Did just as God commanded

i. Placed the Wash Basin be-

tween the Tent of Meeting & the Altar 1) Put water in it 2) Used it to symbolically wash their hands & feet: Before entering the Tent of Meeting or approaching the Altar 3) Did just as God commanded j. Set up the Courtyard around the Tabernacle & the Altar & put up the entrance curtain to the Courtyard k. Moses finished the work **3. The response of the Lord** a. He covered & filled the Tabernacle with His glorious & awesome presence, with the cloud of His glory	tween the tent of the congregation and the altar, and put water there, to wash withal. 31 And Moses and Aaron and his sons washed their hands and their feet thereat: 32 When they went into the tent of the congregation, and when they came near unto the altar, they washed; as the LORD commanded Moses. 33 And he reared up the court round about the tabernacle and the altar, and set up the hanging of the court gate. So Moses finished the work. 34 Then a cloud covered the tent of the congregation, and the glory of the LORD filled the tabernacle.	35 And Moses was not able to enter into the tent of the congregation, because the cloud abode thereon, and the glory of the LORD filled the tabernacle. 36 And when the cloud was taken up from over the tabernacle, the children of Israel went onward in all their journeys: 37 But if the cloud were not taken up, then they journeyed not till the day that it was taken up. 38 For the cloud of the LORD was upon the tabernacle by day, and fire was on it by night, in the sight of all the house of Israel, throughout all their journeys.	1) Moses could not enter the Tabernacle 2) The fact re-emphasized: The awesome glory of the LORD filled the Tabernacle b. He guided the Israelites 1) If the cloud lifted from above the Tabernacle, the Israelites marched 2) If the cloud did not lift, the Israelites stayed put c. He gave the cloud to hang over the Tabernacle by day & a fire within the cloud by night 1) Gave it as a testimony: So all Israel could see it 2) Gave it during all the wilderness journey

DIVISION XI

THE TABERNACLE, ITS CONSTRUCTION AND DEDICATION: THE PEOPLE OBEY GOD, 35:1-40:38

F. The Assembly and Dedication of the Tabernacle, the Center of Worship: Experiencing the Presence of the Lord, Ex.40:1-38

(40:1-38) **Introduction**: man is made to worship God. When man fails to worship God--fails to worship God in the right way--his soul becomes empty, void of purpose. Man's soul begins to hunger and thirst after purpose, after meaning and significance. The only way a person's soul can be filled and fruitful is to worship God in the right way. If there is any one message man needs to heed, it is the truth just stated: "The only way a person's soul can be filled and fruitful is to worship God and to worship God in the right way." This is the reason God gave the Tabernacle to Israel, so they could worship Him and He could dwell among them...

- filling them with the fulness of life
- guiding and protecting them as they journeyed to the promised land

But there was another reason why God gave the Tabernacle to Israel: He wanted the Tabernacle to be a picture, a shadow of Christ. He wanted us to look at the Tabernacle and seek out its fulfillment in Christ. God intended that the Tabernacle of Moses benefit not only the people of Moses' day, but us as well. Now, even today, the lessons and symbolism of the Tabernacle speak to the hearts of believers. The ministry of Jesus Christ leaps from the Tabernacle, its priesthood, and all of its furnishings--leaps and causes us to focus our worship upon God. This is the subject of this final portion of Scripture from the book of Exodus. It is the great climax to one of the most exciting stories in all of Scripture: *The Assembly and Dedication of the Tabernacle, the Center of Worship: Experiencing the Presence of the Lord,* Ex.40:1-38.

1. The instructions of the Lord (v.1-15).
2. The obedience of Moses: he did everything God commanded (v.16-33).
3. The response of the Lord (v.34-38).

[1] (40:1-15) **Commandments--Instructions--Word of God--Tabernacle of Moses--Priesthood**: there were the instructions of the Lord to assemble the Tabernacle and get everything ready for worship. The history of Israel peaked during this *momentous occasion*. For about four hundred years the Israelites had lived as slaves in Egypt (a symbol of the world). But they had come a long, long way in a short, short time. It had been only two years earlier that they had been enslaved and were crying out to God for relief in their sufferings (cp. Ex.2:23). And imagine this: it had been just one year earlier when God had delivered His people from the bondage of slavery with a mighty display of His awesome power. And what a year it had been for Israel. In the course of the year, Israel had been journeying through the wilderness and had experienced...

- God's miraculous guidance through the pillar of cloud, His guidance by day and by night (Ex.13:17-22)
- God's pushing back the waters of the Red Sea (Ex.14:1-31)
- God's chastisement as they complained, grumbled, and murmured at the bitter waters of Marah (Ex.15:22-27)
- God's provision of food as they grumbled and did not believe the Lord (Ex.16:1-36)
- God's provision of water from the rock (Ex.17:1-7)
- God's victory during the war with the Amalekites (Ex.17:8-16)
- God's administration as He set their affairs in order (Ex.18:1-27)

EXODUS 40:1-38

- God's challenge as He gave the law to Moses (Ex.19:1-24:18)
- God's pattern as He showed Moses the plans for the Tabernacle (Ex.25:1-31:18)
- God's judgment as they rebelled against Him by making the golden calf (Ex.32:1-35)
- God's mercy as Moses interceded for them (Ex.33:1-23)
- God's renewal of His covenant with them (Ex.34:1-35)
- God's call to build the Tabernacle, the worship center (Ex.35:1-39:43)

1. Now, God told Moses to assemble the Tabernacle: on the first day of the first month of a brand new year (v.2; cp. v.17). All the experiences of the past year taught Israel one great truth: God is the God of *new beginnings*. A person can start all over again, have a brand new life through the power of God. Establishing the Tabernacle was no different. This new beginning would be a symbolic reminder to God's people of *new beginnings*. The same God who created the heavens and the earth is also the One who gave His people a brand new start--from slavery to freedom, from lawlessness to law, from a land of idolatry to a Tabernacle where God was to dwell with His people and receive their worship.

2. Note that all the furnishings were now to be set in place. Note the order of these items:
   a. The Tabernacle itself, the Tent of Meeting (v.2).
   b. The Ark of God, the Ark that contained the Testimony of God (the Ten Commandments) (v.3).
   c. The curtain to shield the Ark (v.3).
   d. The Table of Showbread and its utensils (v.4).
   e. The Lampstand and its lamps (v.4).
   f. The Gold Altar of Incense was to be put in front of the Ark of Testimony (v.5).
   g. The curtain for the entrance to the Tabernacle (v.5).
   h. The Altar of Burnt Offering was to be put in front of the entrance to the Tabernacle (v.6).
   i. The Wash Basin was to be put between the Tent of Meeting and the Altar and then filled with water (v.7).
   j. The Courtyard (v.8).
   k. The curtain at the entrance to the Courtyard (v.8).

3. God then gave Moses instructions on the dedication of the Tabernacle and its furnishings. Moses was instructed to anoint the Tabernacle and its furnishings: to make them holy, to set them apart for God (v.9). Moses was also told to anoint the Altar of Burnt Offering and its utensils for the purpose of making them holy (v.10). He was also instructed to anoint the Wash Basin and pedestal, consecrating them (v.13).

4. God then gave Moses instructions on the consecration of the priests. Moses was to bring the priests to the entrance of the Tabernacle and wash them with water (v.12). After washing, Moses was to dress the High Priest in sacred clothing and anoint and consecrate him (v 13). God instructed Moses to bring in Aaron's sons and dress them in tunics and then anoint them for service, just as he had anointed Aaron (v.14-15). The purpose for this instruction was to anoint the priesthood as an institution, as a permanent, lasting ministry down through all generations. Those who followed the original priests, Aaron and his sons, were to be set apart for service to God just as they were (v.15).

Thought 1. Note three lessons gleaned from the instructions of God to set up the Tabernacle.
1) God is the God of *new beginnings*. The assembly of the Tabernacle shows us that God gave His people a brand new start. God had delivered Israel from slavery in Egypt (a symbol of the world) to this point in their lives, the point of freedom, the freedom to set up the Tabernacle of God and the freedom to worship God. Moreover, God had forgiven their terrible sin of the golden calf, the terrible sin of rejecting God and breaking His commandments. God had not rejected them but forgiven them. The proof of His forgiveness, proof that He had not rejected them, is seen in His instructions to build the Tabernacle. By instructing them to set up the Tabernacle, God was giving them a new beginning, a new start, a new life with Him.

God is the God of *new beginnings*. A person can start all over again, can have a brand new life through the power of God, through the Person who came to earth to dwell among us, the Son of God Himself, the Lord Jesus Christ. When we receive Christ, we experience the power and the presence of the LORD.

> "A new heart also will I give you, and a <u>new spirit</u> will I put within you: and I will take away the stony heart out of your flesh, and I will give you an heart of flesh" (Ezk.36:26).
> "But as many as received him, to them gave he <u>power to become</u> the sons of God, even to them that believe on his name: Which were born, not of blood, nor of the will of the flesh, nor of the will of man, but of God" (Jn.1:12-13).
> "Jesus answered and said unto him, Verily, verily, I say unto thee, Except a man be <u>born again</u>, he cannot see the kingdom of God" (Jn.3:3).
> "Therefore if any man be in Christ, he is a <u>new creature</u>: old things are passed away; behold, all things are become new" (2 Cor.5:17).
> "And that ye put on the <u>new man</u>, which after God is created in righteousness and true holiness" (Eph.4:24).
> "Being <u>born again</u>, not of corruptible seed, but of incorruptible, by the word of God, which liveth and abideth for ever" (1 Pt.1:23).
> "Whosoever believeth that Jesus is the Christ is <u>born of God</u>: and every one that loveth him that begat loveth him also that is begotten of him" (1 Jn.5:1).

2) Every material thing we have should be dedicated to God, set apart for His purposes. Moses was told to anoint the Tabernacle and all its furnishings, to dedicate and consecrate everything to God. We too must dedicate and consecrate everything we have to God. If we cannot consecrate a material possession to God, then that item has become more important to us than God. What are the things that become so important to us, more important than God

Himself? What are the things that cause such a struggle within our souls, that make us hesitate to set them apart for God? There is...

- money
- clothes
- cars
- profession
- position
- property
- houses
- business
- recreation
- hobbies
- toys
- music, movies
- televisions, stereos

On and on the list could go, but God's Word is clear: we must never allow our material possessions to rob us of our relationship with God. We must offer everything to God with open hands of submission and not clenched fists of greed. When we obey, we experience the presence of the LORD.

"No man can serve two masters: for either he will hate the one, and love the other; or else he will hold to the one, and despise the other. Ye cannot serve God and mammon [money]" (Mt.6:24).

"For what is a man advantaged, if he gain the whole world, and lose himself, or be cast away?" (Lk.9:25).

"But they that will be rich fall into temptation and a snare, and *into* many foolish and hurtful lusts, which drown men in destruction and perdition. For the love of money is the root of all evil: which while some coveted after, they have erred from the faith, and pierced themselves through with many sorrows" (1 Tim.6:9-10).

"This know also, that in the last days perilous times shall come. For men shall be lovers of their own selves, covetous, boasters, proud, blasphemers, disobedient to parents, unthankful, unholy" (2 Tim.3:1-2).

3) We must dedicate and consecrate ourselves to God as well as our material possessions. Moses was told to anoint and consecrate the priests, Aaron and his sons. God demands that we also be set apart to His service, that we dedicate and consecrate ourselves to Him and His great cause. When we obey, we experience the presence of the LORD.

"And he said to [them] all, If any [man] will come after me, let him deny himself, and take up his cross daily, and follow me" (Lk.9:23).

"I beseech you therefore, brethren, by the mercies of God, that ye present your bodies a living sacrifice, holy, acceptable unto God, which is your reasonable service. And be not conformed to this world: but be ye transformed by the renewing of your mind, that ye may prove what is that good, and acceptable, and perfect, will of God" (Ro.12:1-2).

"What? know ye not that your body is the temple of the Holy Ghost which is in you, which ye have of God, and ye are not your own? For ye are bought with a price: therefore glorify God in your body, and in your spirit, which are God's" (1 Cor.6:19-20).

"And I thank Christ Jesus our Lord, who hath enabled me, for that he counted me faithful, putting me into the ministry" (1 Tim.1:12).

"My son, give me thine heart, and let thine eyes observe my ways" (Pr.23:26).

2 (40:16-33) **Tabernacle of Moses--Obedience--Faithfulness**: there was the obedience of Moses; he did everything God commanded. This is one of the major points and themes of this chapter: obedience to God. Moses did everything just as the LORD commanded. Note that his obedience is mentioned eight times, after each major step of setting up the Tabernacle (v.16, 19, 21, 23, 25, 27, 29, 32). The wisdom behind God's choice of Moses is seen time and again in this portion of Scripture. God did not need...

- a man who wavered back and forth
- a man who might or might not follow instructions
- a man who might or might not finish the job

God needed a man just like Moses, a man who would be faithful and obey Him, a man who would follow instructions. God needed a man who would do exactly what God said. Moses was such a man.

1. Moses set up the Tabernacle exactly according to God's instructions: on the first day of the first month in the second year of their wilderness wanderings (v.17-19). Moses constructed the bases, the frames, the crossbars, and the posts (v.18). He then spread the tent over the Tabernacle and put the covering over the tent. Note that he did all this just as God commanded (v.19).

Thought 1. It is very significant that the Tabernacle was the first thing God had Moses set up. Before God's glory could come, before His presence could dwell with men, before sacrifices could be made for sins, the Tabernacle had to be built. This was also true of Jesus Christ. Before He went to the cross and made an atonement for our sins, before He put His glory in us, Christ was born and came to "tabernacle" (dwell) with us. According to Strong's Concordance, Jesus Christ figuratively "encamped" with us. Jesus Christ resided with us "as God did in the Tabernacle of old, a symbol of protection and communion."[1] There had to be a Tabernacle in place before God could do anything else.

---

[1] James Strong. *Strong's Exhaustive Concordance of the Bible.*

"And the Word was made flesh, and <u>dwelt among us</u>, (and we beheld his glory, the glory as of the only begotten of the Father,) full of grace and truth" (Jn.1:14).
"Therefore the Lord himself shall give you a sign; Behold, a virgin shall conceive, and bear a son, and shall call his name Immanuel" (Is.7:14).
"For unto us a child is born, unto us a son is given: and the government shall be upon his shoulder: and his name shall be called Wonderful, Counsellor, The mighty God, The everlasting Father, The Prince of Peace" (Is.9:6).
"And, behold, thou shalt conceive in thy womb, and bring forth a son, and shalt call his name JESUS" (Lk.1:31).

2. Moses then placed the Testimony [the Ten Commandments] in the Ark, attached the poles, and placed the Mercy Seat on the top (v.20). Note once again the great importance of these furnishings: the Ark and the Mercy Seat were the center for the worship of God. A special manifestation of God's presence and glory rested right above the Ark and Mercy Seat. The Ark symbolized God's presence: His rule and reign and His mercy. The fact that mercy flowed out from the presence of God is significant: this meant that man could find the mercy and help of God by coming into God's presence, by coming to the Tabernacle. The Mercy Seat pointed to the perfect demonstration of God's mercy and grace, the giving of His Son to die for the sins of the world.

"Let us therefore come boldly unto the throne of grace, that we may obtain mercy, and find grace to help in time of need" (Heb.4:16).
"For the grace of God that bringeth salvation hath appeared to all men" (Tit.2:11).
"Not by works of righteousness which we have done, but according to his mercy he saved us, by the washing of regeneration, and renewing of the Holy Ghost; Which he shed on us abundantly through Jesus Christ our Saviour" (Tit.3:5-6).

3. Moses placed the Ark in the Tabernacle (v.21). He then hung the inner curtain and shielded the Ark of Testimony just as God commanded (v.21). As everyone looked on, imagine the emotions that filled the hearts of the people. This would be the *last time* that Bezalel, the builder of the Ark, would ever see the Ark again. The crowning achievement of his life was being forever hid from his sight. The other workers looked on, marveling at the beauty of the gold-covered chest. For them it would also be a final gaze as Moses hid the Ark from view. From now on, as long as the Ark remained in the Holy of Holies, only one man would be able to see the Ark and live: the High Priest. Note that Moses did all this just as God commanded (v.21).

Thought 1. It is through the ministry of Jesus Christ, our great High Priest, that we now have access to the very throne of God. In His name we come through the veil and gaze upon the glory of God.

"And, behold, the veil of the temple was rent in twain from the top to the bottom; and the earth did quake, and the rocks rent" (Mt.27:51).
"I am the door: by me if any man enter in, he shall be saved, and shall go in and out, and find pasture" (Jn.10:9).
"Therefore being justified by faith, we have peace with God through our Lord Jesus Christ" (Ro.5:1)
"Which *hope* [the hope of heaven and of God's acceptance] we have as an anchor of the soul, both sure and stedfast, and which entereth into that within the veil" (Heb.6:19).
"For through him we both have access by one Spirit unto the Father" (Eph.2:18).
"In whom we have boldness and access with confidence by the faith of him" (Eph.3:12).
"By a new and living way, which he hath consecrated for us, through the veil, that is to say, his flesh, By a new and living way, which he hath consecrated for us, through the veil, that is to say, his flesh" (Heb.10:19-20).

4. Moses placed the Table of Showbread in the Tent of Meeting or Tabernacle (v.22-23). He set it on the north side outside the inner curtain (v.22). Moses then set the bread before the Lord (v.23). All of this Moses did just as God commanded him (v.23).

"Then Jesus said unto them, Verily, verily, I say unto you, Moses gave you not that bread from heaven; but my Father giveth you the true bread from heaven. For the bread of God is he which cometh down from heaven, and giveth life unto the world. Then said they unto him, Lord, evermore give us this bread. And Jesus said unto them, I am the bread of life: he that cometh to me shall never hunger; and he that believeth on me shall never thirst" (Jn.6:32-35).
"I am the living bread which came down from heaven: if any man eat of this bread, he shall live for ever: and the bread that I will give is my flesh, which I will give for the life of the world" (Jn.6:51).

5. Moses placed the Lampstand in the Tabernacle and set it opposite the Table on the south side (v.24). (See outline and notes--Ex.25:31-40 for more discussion.) He set up the lamps before the Lord. Moses did all this just as God commanded (v.25). Remember, up to this point there was no light in the Tabernacle. The only light was coming through the entrance into the Holy Place. What had been set up so far could not be clearly seen, not the Tabernacle and its coverings, not the Ark and the Mercy Seat, not the inner curtain, and not the Table of Showbread. By this stage, the Holy Place was full of shadows. But after Moses lit the lamps before the Lord, the Holy Place was filled with light. This is the quality of light: it

always melts the dark shadows and fills the void with rays of light. The Lampstand pointed to the coming of the Lord Jesus Christ, the Light of the world.

> "Then spake Jesus again unto them, saying, I am the light of the world: he that followeth me shall not walk in darkness, but shall have the light of life" (Jn.8:12).
> "I am come a light into the world, that whosoever believeth on me should not abide in darkness" (Jn.12:46).
> "This then is the message which we have heard of him, and declare unto you, that God is light, and in him is no darkness at all" (1 Jn.1:5).

6. Moses placed the Altar of Incense in the Tent of Meeting in front of the curtain (v.26). He burned incense on it just as God commanded him to do (v.27). The Altar of Incense pointed to Jesus Christ as the great Intercessor and Mediator who represents us before God and makes our prayers acceptable to God.

> "Hitherto have ye asked nothing in my name: ask, and ye shall receive, that your joy may be full" (Jn.16:24).
> "Who is he that condemneth? It is Christ that died, yea rather, that is risen again, who is even at the right hand of God, who also maketh intercession for us" (Ro.8:34).
> "Wherefore he is able also to save them to the uttermost that come unto God by him, seeing he ever liveth to make intercession for them" (Heb.7:25).
> "By him therefore let us offer the sacrifice of praise to God continually, that is, the fruit of our lips giving thanks to his name" (Heb.13:15).

7. Moses put up the curtain at the entrance (v.28). This curtain divided the Tent of Meeting from the Courtyard. This curtain shielded the Holy Place and prevented people from gazing into its holy sanctuary. The curtain pointed to Jesus Christ who made a new and living way into God's presence, who made it possible for us to approach and worship God in spirit and in truth.

> "Having therefore, brethren, boldness to enter into the holiest by the blood of Jesus, By a new and living way, which he hath consecrated for us, through the veil, that is to say, his flesh" (Heb.10:19-20).
> "God [is] a Spirit: and they that worship him must worship [him] in spirit and in truth" (Jn.4:24).
> "Jesus saith unto him, I am the way, the truth, and the life: no man cometh unto the Father, but by me" (Jn.14:6).

8. Moses set the Altar of Burnt Offering near the entrance to the Tabernacle (v.29). Once he had set it up, Moses offered burnt offerings and grain offerings to the Lord (v.29); once again Moses was careful to set this up just as God commanded (v.29). The Altar of Burnt Offering pointed to Jesus Christ as the Perfect Sacrifice for sin, as the Lamb of God who takes away the sins of the world.

> "The next day John seeth Jesus coming unto him, and saith, Behold the Lamb of God, which taketh away the sin of the world" (Jn.1:29).
> "Forasmuch as ye know that ye were not redeemed with corruptible things, as silver and gold, from your vain conversation received by tradition from your fathers; But with the precious blood of Christ, as of a lamb without blemish and without spot" (1 Pt.1:18-19).

9. Moses placed the Wash Basin between the Tent of Meeting and the Altar. He put water in it after he had set up the basin (v.30). The Wash Basin was used by Moses, Aaron, and his sons to wash their hands and feet before entering the Tent of Meeting or approaching the Altar (v.30-32). Moses did this just as God commanded. Remember, the washing symbolized spiritual cleansing and forgiveness of sins. (See outline and note--Ex.30:17-21 for more discussion.) The Wash Basin pointed to Jesus Christ as the One who cleanses us from sin.

> "In whom we have redemption through his blood, the forgiveness of sins, according to the riches of his grace" (Eph.1:7).
> "Who his own self bare our sins in his own body on the tree, that we, being dead to sins, should live unto righteousness: by whose stripes ye were healed" (1 Pt.2:24).

10. Moses finished the work (v.33). Note Moses' final act: he hung the curtain that was the entrance into the Tabernacle, the one curtain or one door that stood for (symbolized) God's invitation for man to enter His presence.

Keep in mind that Moses could have quit and walked away but he did not. Moses was faithful to God: he finished the work. Moreover, he did everything just as God commanded.

Thought 1. Two strong lessons can be gleaned from the obedience of Moses.
1) We must obey God.

> "This day the LORD thy God hath commanded thee to do these statutes and judgments: thou shalt therefore keep and do them with all thine heart, and with all thy soul" (Dt.26:16).

"This book of the law shall not depart out of thy mouth; but thou shalt meditate therein day and night, that thou mayest observe to do according to all that is written therein: for then thou shalt make thy way prosperous, and then thou shalt have good success" (Josh.1:8).

"But if ye will not obey the voice of the LORD, but rebel against the commandment of the LORD, then shall the hand of the LORD be against you, as it was against your fathers" (1 Sam.12:15).

"And Samuel said, Hath the LORD as great delight in burnt offerings and sacrifices, as in obeying the voice of the LORD? Behold, to obey is better than sacrifice, and to hearken than the fat of rams" (1 Sam.15:22).

"Not every one that saith unto me, Lord, Lord, shall enter into the kingdom of heaven; but he that doeth the will of my Father which is in heaven" (Mt.7:21).

"Therefore whosoever heareth these sayings of mine, and doeth them, I will liken him unto a wise man, which built his house upon a rock" (Mt.7:24).

"And to you who are troubled rest with us, when the Lord Jesus shall be revealed from heaven with his mighty angels, In flaming fire taking vengeance on them that know not God, and that obey not the gospel of our Lord Jesus Christ: Who shall be punished with everlasting destruction from the presence of the Lord, and from the glory of his power" (2 Th.1:7-9).

"How shall we escape, if we neglect so great salvation; which at the first began to be spoken by the Lord, and was confirmed unto us by them that heard him" (Heb.2:3).

"Blessed are they that do his commandments, that they may have right to the tree of life, and may enter in through the gates into the city" (Rev.22:14).

2) We must finish and conclude what God gives us to do. We must never quit, but endure and persevere to the end, completing the race and work set before us.

"But none of these things move me, neither count I my life dear unto myself, so that I might finish my course with joy, and the ministry, which I have received of the Lord Jesus, to testify the gospel of the grace of God" (Acts 20:24).

"Therefore, my beloved brethren, be ye stedfast, unmoveable, always abounding in the work of the Lord, forasmuch as ye know that your labour is not in vain in the Lord" (1 Cor.15:58).

"And let us not be weary in well doing: for in due season we shall reap, if we faint not" (Gal.6:9).

"For I am now ready to be offered, and the time of my departure is at hand. I have fought a good fight, I have finished my course, I have kept the faith" (2 Tim.4:6-7).

"Wherefore seeing we also are compassed about with so great a cloud of witnesses, let us lay aside every weight, and the sin which doth so easily beset us, and let us run with patience the race that is set before us" (Heb.12:1).

"Wherefore gird up the loins of your mind, be sober, and hope to the end for the grace that is to be brought unto you at the revelation of Jesus Christ" (1 Pt.1:13).

"Behold, I come quickly: hold that fast which thou hast, that no man take thy crown" (Rev.3:11).

"The righteous also shall hold on his way, and he that hath clean hands shall be stronger and stronger" (Job 17:9).

3 (40:34-38) **Tabernacle of Moses--Glory of God--Guidance**: there was the response of the Lord. In one of the greatest manifestations of God's power in all of Scripture, God's glory came to the Tabernacle and filled it. Note how God responded to the completion of the Tabernacle.

1. God covered and filled the Tabernacle with His glorious and awesome presence, with the cloud of His glory (v.34). Remember the pillar of cloud that God had used to lead Israel through the wilderness wanderings: this was the cloud of God's glory, the Shekinah glory, the cloud that descended upon the Tabernacle. However, there was one difference in this event: a far greater display of God's glory descended upon the Tabernacle. How do we know this? Because Moses was not able to enter the Tabernacle. Remember Mt. Sinai, when the cloud of God's glory descended upon it (Ex.19:18-20); and remember Moses' tent that had been set up for worship, when God's glory covered it (Ex.33:7-11). Moses was able to stand before God's glory in both cases, but not now, not when God's glory filled the Tabernacle. Scripture declares...

- that God is light

"This then is the message which we have heard of him, and declare unto you, that God is light, and in him is no darkness at all" (1 Jn.1:5).

- that God is a consuming fire

"For our God is a consuming fire" (Heb.12:29; cp. Dt.4:23-25).

Just as the pillar of cloud descended upon the Tabernacle, there was obviously a burst of light that broke forth from the Holy of Holies, a burst of light...

- that broke forth in all the splendor, radiance, brightness, and illumination of God's presence

The glory of God broke forth in the brightest light imaginable. The light of God's nature was shining so brightly that Moses could not enter without being blinded and consumed. God was giving His people a very special manifestation of His presence. His awesome presence was to remain in the Most Holy Place right above the throne of God, right between the two golden cherubim on the Mercy Seat. God's presence and glory were to give direction and lead His dear people to the promised land.

2. Note how God guided the Israelites with the cloud of His glory. If the cloud lifted from above the Tabernacle, the Israelites marched in the direction of the cloud (v.36). If the cloud did not lift, the Israelites stayed put (v.37).

3. Note this wonderful fact: God gave the cloud to hang over the Tabernacle by day and a fire within the cloud by night. God gave it as a testimony so that all of Israel could see it. By seeing the cloud they would know that God was with them, guiding and protecting them as they journeyed to the promised land. Note that God was faithful to the very end: He led His dear people to the very end; He gave the cloud during all the wilderness journey (v.38). For the next thirty-eight years, this cloud would be a constant companion to God's people as they wandered in the wilderness. God led them until they reached their eternal destination, the promised land of God.

"And on the day that the tabernacle was reared up the cloud covered the tabernacle, *namely,* the tent of the testimony: and at even there was upon the tabernacle as it were the appearance of fire, until the morning. So it was alway: the cloud covered it *by day,* and the appearance of fire by night. And when the cloud was taken up from the tabernacle, then after that the children of Israel journeyed: and in the place where the cloud abode, there the children of Israel pitched their tents. At the commandment of the LORD the children of Israel journeyed, and at the commandment of the LORD they pitched: as long as the cloud abode upon the tabernacle they rested in their tents. And when the cloud tarried long upon the tabernacle many days, then the children of Israel kept the charge of the LORD, and journeyed not. And *so* it was, when the cloud was a few days upon the tabernacle; according to the commandment of the LORD they abode in their tents, and according to the commandment of the LORD they journeyed. And *so* it was, when the cloud abode from even unto the morning, and *that* the cloud was taken up in the morning, then they journeyed: whether *it was* by day or by night that the cloud was taken up, they journeyed. Or *whether it were* two days, or a month, or a year, that the cloud tarried upon the tabernacle, remaining thereon, the children of Israel abode in their tents, and journeyed not: but when it was taken up, they journeyed. At the commandment of the LORD they rested in the tents, and at the commandment of the LORD they journeyed: they kept the charge of the LORD, at the commandment of the LORD by the hand of Moses" (Num.9:15-23).

God's promise to be with His dear people, to give His wonderful presence to His people, was now a reality. God's promise to guide and protect His dear people was now at hand. God's promise to live and dwell among His dear people was now beginning. Without question they would reach the promised land of God. Nothing--no enemy, no force of nature, no form of evil--would be able to stand against them, not victoriously. God's people would be triumphant. All because God now dwelt among them and lived in their midst. God guided and protected them until their final destination was reached, the destination of the promised land of God.

Thought 1. What caused the glory of God to fill the Tabernacle? What stirred God to give His people this special experience, this very special manifestation of His presence? Obedience. When we obey God--keep His commandments and do exactly what He says--God gives us a very special and very deep sense of His presence. Moreover, when we have a very special need, God gives us a most special manifestation of His glory. All because we obey Him.

1) When Moses obeyed the LORD and built a place for Him, God filled the Tabernacle with His presence and glory.

"Then a cloud covered the tent of the congregation, and the glory of the LORD filled the tabernacle. And Moses was not able to enter into the tent of the congregation, because the cloud abode thereon, and the glory of the LORD filled the tabernacle" (Ex.40:34-35).

2) When Solomon obeyed the LORD and built a place for Him, God filled the Temple with His presence and glory.

"And it came to pass, when the priests were come out of the holy *place,* that the cloud filled the house of the LORD, So that the priests could not stand to minister because of the cloud: for the glory of the LORD had filled the house of the LORD" (1 Ki.8:10-11).

3) When the Christian believer obeys the LORD and builds a place for Him, God fills the heart of the believer with His presence and glory.

"He that hath my commandments, and keepeth them, he it is that loveth me: and he that loveth me shall be loved of my Father, and I will love him, and will **manifest** myself to him" (Jn.14:21).
"Jesus answered and said unto him, If a man love me, he will keep my words: and my Father will love him, and we will come unto him, and make our abode with him" (Jn.14:23).
"If ye keep my commandments, ye shall abide in my love; even as I have kept my Father's commandments, and abide in his love" (Jn.15:10).
"And when the day of Pentecost was fully come, they were all with one accord in one place. And suddenly there came a sound from heaven as of a rushing mighty wind, and it filled all the house where they were sitting. And there appeared unto them cloven tongues like as of

fire, and it sat upon each of them. And they were all filled with the Holy Ghost, and began to speak with other tongues, as the Spirit gave them utterance" (Acts 2:1-4).

"Know ye not that ye are the temple of God, and *that* the Spirit of God dwelleth in you?" (1 Cor.3:16).

"What? know ye not that your body is the temple of the Holy Ghost which is in you, which ye have of God, and ye are not your own? For ye are bought with a price: therefore glorify God in your body, and in your spirit, which are God's" (1 Cor.6:19-20).

"And what agreement hath the temple of God with idols? for ye are the temple of the living God; as God hath said, I will dwell in them, and walk in *them;* and I will be their God, and they shall be my people" (2 Cor.6:16).

"Now therefore, if ye will obey my voice indeed, and keep my covenant, then ye shall be a peculiar treasure unto me above all people: for all the earth is mine" (Ex.19:5).

Thought 2. The glory of God was so brilliant and intense that Moses was unable to draw near God's presence. But what Moses could not do in that he was weak through the flesh, Jesus Christ did. Jesus Christ was obedient to God, obedient in the absolute sense. He never disobeyed God, not once. He was sinless and perfect before God. Therefore, He was able to enter God's presence, not only for Himself but for every man, woman, and child throughout all the ages. He is the Perfect, Ideal Man. Therefore He is able to stand before God as the Perfect, Ideal Man, able to stand before God in our behalf, as our High Priest, our Representative, our Intercessor, our Advocate (attorney). Jesus Christ opened up a new and living way into God's presence for us. Note this wonderful and glorious declaration of Scripture:

1) Through Christ, we can approach God in a new and living way.

"Having therefore, brethren, boldness to enter into the holiest by the blood of Jesus, By a new and living way, which he hath consecrated for us, through the veil, that is to say, his flesh [through His death upon the cross]" (Heb.10:19-20).

2) Through Christ we are acceptable to God and saved to the uttermost.

"Wherefore he is able also to save them to the uttermost that come unto God by him, seeing he ever liveth to make intercession for them" (Heb.7:25).

"For Christ is not entered into the holy places made with hands, which are the figures of the true; but into heaven itself, now to appear in the presence of God for us" (Heb.9:24).

3) Through Christ we shall inherit the promised land of heaven, living with God forever and ever.

"For we know that if our earthly house of this tabernacle were dissolved [our flesh], we have a building of God, an house not made with hands, eternal in the heavens" (2 Cor.5:1).

"For our conversation [citizenship] is in heaven; from whence also we look for the Saviour, the Lord Jesus Christ: Who shall change our vile body, that it may be fashioned like unto his glorious body, according to the working whereby he is able even to subdue all things unto himself" (Ph.3:20-21).

"Blessed be the God and Father of our Lord Jesus Christ, which according to his abundant mercy hath begotten us again unto a lively hope by the resurrection of Jesus Christ from the dead, To an inheritance incorruptible, and undefiled, and that fadeth not away, reserved in heaven for you" (1 Pt.1:3-4).

TYPES, SYMBOLS, AND PICTURES
(Exodus 40:1-38)

Historical Term	Type or Picture (Scriptural Basis for Each)	Life Application for Today's Believer	Biblical Application for Today's Believer
The Altar of Burnt Offering [The brazen altar] (Ex.40:29) See also Ex.27:1-8; 35:16; 38:1-7; 39:39; 40:6	*The Altar of Burnt Offering was the most prominent furnishing in the Courtyard. The animal sacrifices offered to God were consumed on the Altar, consumed in a blazing, roaring fire. The picture of the Altar was graphic: unless there was a blood sacrifice for sins, there was no forgiveness.*	What the Altar taught:	*"For we have not an high priest which cannot be touched with the feeling of our infirmities; but was in all points tempted like as we are, yet without sin" (Heb.4:15).*
	a. The Altar of Burnt Offering symbolized the work of the Lord's	a. Substitutionary sacrifice is necessary for the forgiveness of sins.	*"Forasmuch as ye know that ye were not redeemed with corruptible things, as silver and gold, from your vain conversation received by tradition from your fathers; But with the precious blood of Christ, as of a*

Historical Term	Type or Picture (Scriptural Basis for Each)	Life Application for Today's Believer	Biblical Application for Today's Believer
	cross, the death of a Perfect Sacrifice who was acceptable to God.	There is no forgiveness without the shedding of the blood of a sacrifice, the sacrifice of God's very own Son, the Lord Jesus Christ.	*lamb without blemish and without spot"* (1 Pt. 1:18-19). *"Who did no sin, neither was guile found in his mouth....Who his own self bare our sins in his own body on the tree, that we, being dead to sins, should live unto righteousness: by whose stripes ye were healed"* (1 Pt.2:22, 24).
	b. *The Altar of Burnt Offering symbolized man's need for atonement, for reconciliation with God.* **"And he put the altar of burnt offering** *by* **the door of the tabernacle of the tent of the congregation, and offered upon it the burnt offering and the meat offering; as the** LORD **commanded Moses"** (Ex.40:29).	b. There is no way to approach God--to be saved and reconciled--other than through the death of a substitute. A person is hopelessly lost and cannot save himself from the bondage of sin. The only way a person can be saved is to be ransomed, to be bought with a price. Someone had to come forth and stand before God, offering Himself as the ransom, the price for our lives. That Someone was the Lord Jesus Christ Himself. God saved us by sacrificing His Son for us; and His Son, the Lord Jesus Christ, willingly laid down His life for us.	*"But he was wounded for our transgressions, he was bruised for our iniquities: the chastisement of our peace was upon him; and with his stripes we are healed"* (Is.53:5). *"For God so loved the world, that he gave his only begotten Son, that whosoever believeth in him should not perish, but have everlasting life"* (Jn.3:16). *"Christ hath redeemed us from the curse of the law, being made a curse for us: for it is written, Cursed is every one that hangeth on a tree"* (Gal.3:13). *"For Christ also hath once suffered for sins, the just for the unjust, that he might bring us to God, being put to death in the flesh, but quickened by the Spirit"* (1 Pt.3:18).

(Please note: other Types, Symbols, and Pictures for this outline can be found at the end of Chapters 25:10-22; 25:23-30; and 30:1-10, where they are initially discussed.)

RESOURCE CHART SECTION

Chart 1: THE PICTURE OF THE BELIEVER'S LIFE IN THE TABERNACLE

Chart 2: HOW CHRIST FULFILLED THE SYMBOLISM OF THE TABERNACLE

Chart 3: HOW CHRIST FULFILLED THE SYMBOLISM OF THE PRIESTHOOD

CHART 1

THE PICTURE OF
THE BELIEVER'S LIFE
IN THE TABERNACLE

(The Seven Essential Steps of the Believer's Life or Walk)

The Tabernacle gives a descriptive picture of the believer's life. Seven *essential steps* are symbolized, picturing the believer's life as he walks day by day, marching toward the promised land of heaven. All seven steps are based upon the LORD God Himself, upon His Person, His holiness, and His mercy. His holiness demanded the life of the sinner, but His mercy accepted the sacrifice of a substitute. Through faith in this simple picture of the Tabernacle, a person can approach God and become acceptable to Him, can begin his walk or pilgrimage to the promised land of God, to heaven itself.

Note the facts about the seven essential steps:

⇒ A person must approach each step in proper sequence. It is important to note that God's design for the Tabernacle began from the inside and moved outward. God began with the Ark, the place where God's very presence dwelt, and ended with the Altar of Burnt Offering. This is the way of *grace*. This is looking at the Tabernacle from *God's perspective*. However, as man approached God he started from the outside of the Tabernacle. Man started by entering the only door into the Tabernacle and walking up to the Altar of Burnt Offering. He concluded his journey at the Ark and Mercy Seat where the High Priest approached the presence of God in his behalf. This is the way of *faith*. This is looking at the Tabernacle from *man's perspective*.

⇒ The believer must experience each step listed below as he follows God to the promised land of heaven. The gospel of Jesus Christ cannot be watered down with an easy "believism." There are no short-cuts between the cross (the Altar of Burnt Offering) and the Throne of God (the Ark and Mercy Seat). Man must *experience* each symbol, each step on the march to the promised land. Anything less than this is not the true gospel.

⇒ The most important step is the first one. This is where a person's journey must begin: at the door.

<u>Please note</u>: This chart is useful in helping a seeker or a new believer understand the gospel of Jesus Christ. As you lead a person through the great foundational truths found in this chart, remember…

- to fully grasp the *purpose* of each furnishing. This will help you explain the furnishing and what it did.
- to fully grasp the practical *meaning* of each symbol. All Biblical truth must be joined with practical Biblical application.

STEP #1	THE PURPOSE OF THE FURNISHING OF THE TABERNACLE	THE PRACTICAL MEANING OF THE SYMBOL	SUPPORTING SCRIPTURE
GOD'S INVITATION TO MAN	The Gate of the Outer Courtyard ⇒ There was only one gate into the Tabernacle. The purpose for this gate was to invite man to come into the presence of God. The only way for the person to approach God was to walk through the gate of the Outer Courtyard. **"And for the gate of the court *shall be* an hanging of twenty cubits, *of* blue, and purple, and scarlet, and fine twined linen, wrought with needlework: *and* their pillars *shall be***	*God invites man to enter His presence: any person who will believe in and completely trust Jesus Christ will be welcomed into God's presence.* ⇒ The gate into the Tabernacle taught at least two things: 1. There is only one way to enter God's presence; there are not many ways as most men think and practice. 2. God has to be approached in a very specific way, in God's perfect way. No person shall ever live with God unless he approaches	*"Enter ye in at the strait gate: for wide is the gate, and broad is the way, that leadeth to destruction, and many there be which go in thereat: Because strait is the gate, and narrow is the way, which leadeth unto life, and few there be that find it"* *(Mt. 7:13-14).*

	four, and their sockets four" (Ex.27:16).	God in the right way. Jesus Christ is the right way to God. **"For God so loved the world, that he gave his only begotten Son, that <u>whosoever believeth in him</u> should not perish, but have everlasting life"** (Jn.3:16).	

STEP #2	THE PURPOSE OF THE FURNISHING OF THE TABERNACLE	THE PRACTICAL MEANING OF THE SYMBOL	SUPPORTING SCRIPTURE
GOD'S RECONCILIATION OF MAN	The Altar of Burnt Offering ⇒ The purpose of the Altar was to meet man's need for atonement or reconciliation with God through the sacrifice of the lamb. **"And thou shalt set the altar of the burnt offering before the door of the tabernacle of the tent of the congregation"** (Ex.40:6).	*Jesus Christ is the Lamb of God who was sacrificed on the cross for the sins of mankind. Jesus Christ reconciles man to God by His death on the cross.* ⇒ The true altar upon which the Lamb was slain for the sins of the believer was the cross of Jesus Christ. **"The next day John seeth Jesus coming unto him, and saith, Behold the Lamb of God, which taketh away the sin of the world"** (Jn.1:29). **"Wherefore in all things it behooved him to be made like unto *his* brethren, that he might be a merciful and faithful high priest in things *pertaining* to God, <u>to make reconciliation for the sins of the people</u>"** (Heb.2:17).	**"Forasmuch as ye know that ye were not redeemed with corruptible things, as silver and gold, from your vain conversation received by tradition from your fathers; But with the precious blood of Christ, as of a lamb without blemish and without spot"** (1 Pt.1:18-19). **"For he hath made him to be sin for us, who knew no sin; that we might be made the righteousness of God in him"** (2 Cor.5:21).

STEP #3	THE PURPOSE OF THE FURNISHING OF THE TABERNACLE	THE PRACTICAL MEANING OF THE SYMBOL	SUPPORTING SCRIPTURE
THE BELIEVER'S SANCTIFICATION: HIS WASHING AND CLEANSING, THE FORGIVENESS OF HIS SIN	The Bronze Wash Basin ⇒ The purpose of the Wash Basin was for the priests to wash off the blood, soot, and dirt from their hands and feet. **"Thou shalt also make a laver *of* brass, and his foot *also of* brass, to wash *withal:* and thou shalt put it between the tabernacle of the congregation and the altar, and thou shalt put water therein. For Aaron and his sons shall wash their hands and their feet thereat: When they go into the tabernacle of the congregation, they**	*God has sanctified the believer by washing and cleansing him, by forgiving his sin through the blood of Christ.* ⇒ The Word of God declares that we must be washed with the cleansing blood of Jesus Christ. It is the Word of God that reminds us of our need: that we must be… • sanctified • purified We must, therefore, study the Word of God in order to become more and more sanctified, more and more set apart to God.	**"Wherewithal shall a young man cleanse his way? by taking heed thereto according to thy word"** (Ps.119:9). **"Sanctify them through thy truth: thy word is truth"** (Jn.17:17). **"That he might sanctify and cleanse it with the washing of water by the word"** (Eph.5:26). **"But be ye doers of the word, and not hearers only, deceiving your own selves. For if any be a hearer of the word, and not a doer, he is like unto a man beholding his natural face in a glass: For he beholdeth himself, and goeth his way,**

THE BELIEVER'S LIFE IN THE TABERNACLE

	shall wash with water, that they die not; or when they come near to the altar to minister, to burn offering made by fire unto the LORD: So they shall wash their hands and their feet, that they die not: and it shall be a statute for ever to them, *even* to him and to his seed throughout their generations" (Ex.30:18-21).	"Now <u>ye are clean</u> through the word which I have spoken unto you" (Jn.15:3).	*and straightway forgetteth what manner of man he was. But whoso looketh into the perfect law of liberty, and continueth therein, he being not a forgetful hearer, but a doer of the work, this man shall be blessed in his deed"* (Jas.1:22-25). *"Study to show thyself approved unto God, a workman that needeth not to be ashamed, rightly dividing the word of truth"* (2 Tim.2:15). *"All scripture is given by inspiration of God, and is profitable for doctrine, for reproof, for correction, for instruction in righteousness"* (2 Tim.3:16).

STEP #4	THE PURPOSE OF THE FURNISHING OF THE TABERNACLE	THE PRACTICAL MEANING OF THE SYMBOL	SUPPORTING SCRIPTURE
THE BELIEVER'S WALK WITH GOD	The Lampstand ⇒ The purpose of the Lampstand was to illuminate the Holy Place, to show the High Priest he needed God's light in order to know… • how to know God • how to serve God • how to walk before God "And thou shalt make the seven lamps thereof: and they shall light the lamps thereof, that they may give light over against it" (Ex.25:37).	*The believer's heart is filled with God's guiding light. God as the Light of the world shows the believer how to walk with God.:* ⇒ It is God who provides the light that burns perpetually, that dissolves all darkness from the life of the believer. "Then spake Jesus again unto them, saying, <u>I am the light of the world</u>: he that followeth me shall not walk in darkness, but shall have the light of life" (Jn.8:12). "That was the true Light, which lighteth every man that cometh into the world" (Jn.1:9). "Again, a new commandment I write unto you, which thing is true in him and in you: because the darkness is past, and the true light now shineth" (1 Jn.2:8).	*"The LORD is my light and my salvation; whom shall I fear? the LORD is the strength of my life; of whom shall I be afraid?"* (Ps.27:1). *"The people that walked in darkness have seen a great light: they that dwell in the land of the shadow of death, upon them hath the light shined"* (Is.9:2). *"For God, who commanded the light to shine out of darkness, hath shined in our hearts, to give the light of the knowledge of the glory of God in the face of Jesus Christ"* (2 Cor.4:6). *"And the city had no need of the sun, neither of the moon, to shine in it: for the glory of God did lighten it, and the Lamb is the light thereof"* (Rev.21:23).

STEP #5	THE PURPOSE OF THE FURNISHING OF THE TABERNACLE	THE PRACTICAL MEANING OF THE SYMBOL	SUPPORTING SCRIPTURE
THE BELIEVER'S NOURISHMENT (FOOD FOR THE SOUL)	The Table of Showbread ⇒ The Table's purpose was to hold the showbread, to present the showbread before the face of God, to present it as an offering of thanksgiving and dependence upon God.	*The believer's spiritual hunger is satisfied with God who is the bread of life* ⇒ Jesus Christ is the fulfillment of the Showbread. Jesus Christ is the Bread of Life who nourishes the believer's soul by giving the believer eternal joy, satis-	*"And he humbled thee, and suffered thee to hunger, and fed thee with manna, which thou knewest not, neither did thy fathers know; that he might make thee know that man doth not live by bread only, but by every word that pro-*

		faction, and fulfillment.	ceedeth out of the mouth of the LORD doth man live" (Dt. 8:3).
	"And thou shalt set upon the table showbread before me alway" (Ex. 25:30).	"And Jesus said unto them, <u>I am the bread of life</u>: he that cometh to me shall never hunger; and he that believeth on me shall never thirst" (Jn.6:35). "For he satisfieth the longing soul, and filleth the hungry soul with goodness" (Ps.107:9). "And the LORD shall guide thee continually, and satisfy thy soul in drought, and make fat thy bones: and thou shalt be like a watered garden, and like a spring of water, whose waters fail not" (Is.58:11).	"These things have I spoken unto you, that my joy might remain in you, and [that] your joy might be full" (Jn.15:11). "My soul shall be satisfied as with marrow and fatness; and my mouth shall praise thee with joyful lips" (Ps.63:5). "For the bread of God is he which cometh down from heaven, and giveth life unto the world" (Jn.6:33; cp. Jn.10:10).

STEP #6	THE PURPOSE OF THE FURNISHING OF THE TABERNACLE	THE PRACTICAL MEANING OF THE SYMBOL	SUPPORTING SCRIPTURE
THE BELIEVER'S INTERCESSION, HIS PRAYER LIFE	The Altar of Incense ⇒ The purpose for the altar was twofold: 1. The altar was to be the place where sweet incense was offered up to the LORD every morning and evening. 2. The Altar of Incense was to be the place where a permanent incense ascended up to the LORD. "And Aaron shall burn thereon sweet incense every morning: when he dresseth the lamps, he shall burn incense upon it. And when Aaron lighteth the lamps at even, he shall burn incense upon it, a perpetual incense before the LORD throughout your generations" (Ex.30:7-8).	The believer's prayers are to ascend up to God and be as consistent and common as breathing. ⇒ The believer's prayer life is to be an unending communion and intercession with God "And <u>whatsoever we ask</u>, we receive of him, because we keep his commandments, and do those things that are <u>pleasing in his sight</u>" (1 Jn.3:22). "Pray without ceasing" (1 Th.5:17). "Praying always with all prayer and supplication in the Spirit, and watching thereunto with all perseverance and supplication for all saints" (Eph.6:18).	"And another angel came and stood at the altar, having a golden censer; and there was given unto him much incense, that he should offer it with the prayers of all saints upon the golden altar which was before the throne" (Rev.8:3). "Seek the LORD and his strength, seek his face continually" (1 Chron.16:11). "And he spake a parable unto them to this end, that men ought always to pray, and not to faint" (Lk.18:1). "Hitherto have ye asked nothing in my name: ask, and ye shall receive, that your joy may be full" (Jn.16:24). "And ye shall seek me, and find me, when ye shall search for me with all your heart" (Jer.29:13).

STEP #7	THE PURPOSE OF THE FURNISHING OF THE TABERNACLE	THE PRACTICAL MEANING OF THE SYMBOL	SUPPORTING SCRIPTURE
THE BELIEVER'S COMMUNION AND FELLOWSHIP WITH GOD	The Inner Veil, The Ark and The Mercy Seat ⇒ The purpose of the Inner Veil was to separate the Holy Place from the Most Holy Place. The Most Holy Place was where the presence of God was manifested in a very special way. "And thou shalt hang up the vail under the taches, that thou mayest	The ultimate goal for every believer should be to experience an intimate communion with the God of all mercy and grace ⇒ The Ark and Mercy Seat is the place where the believer's most intimate moments of communion are spent with God, spent in His most Holy presence "Let us therefore come boldly unto the throne of	"Now of the things which we have spoken this is the sum: We have such an high priest, who is set on the right hand of the throne of the Majesty in the heavens" (Heb.8:1). "Looking unto Jesus the author and finisher of our faith; who for the joy that was set before him endured the cross, despising the shame, and is set down at the right hand of the throne of God" (Heb.12:2).

bring in thither within the vail the ark of the testimony: and the vail shall divide unto you between the holy *place* and the most holy" (Ex.26:33).

⇒ The Purpose of the Ark and Mercy Seat was...
- to be the place where God's testimony (the Ten Commandments) was kept, the place where God was to give very special instructions to His people
- to be the place where God met with His people
- to be the place of mercy, the place where God's mercy was symbolized
- to be the place where God would instruct & guide His people

"And there I will meet with thee, and I will commune with thee from above the mercy seat, from between the two cherubims which *are* upon the ark of the testimony, of all *things* which I will give thee in commandment unto the children of Israel" (Ex.25:22).

grace, that we may <u>obtain mercy</u>, and <u>find grace</u> to help in time of need" (Heb.4:16).

"That which we have seen and heard declare we unto you, that ye also may have fellowship with us: and truly our fellowship *is* with the Father, and with his Son Jesus Christ" (1 Jn.1:3).

"Who *is* a God like unto thee, that pardoneth iniquity, and passeth by the transgression of the remnant of his heritage? he retaineth not his anger for ever, because he delighteth *in* mercy" (Mic.7:18).

"To him that overcometh will I grant to sit with me in my throne, even as I also overcame, and am set down with my Father in his throne" (Rev.3:21).

"And the four and twenty elders and the four beasts fell down and worshipped God that sat on the throne, saying, Amen; Alleluia. And a voice came out of the throne, saying, Praise our God, all ye his servants, and ye that fear him, both small and great" (Rev.19:4-5).

CHART 2

HOW CHRIST FULFILLED THE SYMBOLISM OF THE TABERNACLE

(See Deeper Study--Heb.9:11-14 for more discussion)

I. **THE SYMBOLIC LESSONS CONCERNING THE ARK OR CHEST,** Ex.25:10-22; 35:12; 37:1-5; 39:35; 40:3, 20-21

II. **THE SYMBOLIC LESSONS CONCERNING THE MERCY SEAT,** Ex.25:17-21; 35:12; 37:6-9; 39:35; 40:3, 20

III. **THE SYMBOLIC LESSONS CONCERNING THE TABLE OF SHOWBREAD,** Ex.25:23-30; 35:13; 37:10-16; 39:36; 40:4, 22-23

IV. **THE SYMBOLIC LESSONS CONCERNING THE LAMPSTAND,** Ex.25:31-40; 27:20-21; 35:14; 37:17-24; 39:37; 40:4, 24-25

V. **THE SYMBOLIC LESSONS CONCERNING THE SANCTUARY,** Ex.26:1-30; 35:17-18, 23, 25-26; 36:8-34; 39:33-34; 40:17-19

VI. **THE SYMBOLIC LESSONS CONCERNING THE INNER VEIL,** Ex.26:31-35; 35:12; 36:35-36; 39:34; 40:3, 21

VII. **THE SYMBOLIC LESSONS CONCERNING THE OUTER VEIL,** Ex.26:36-37; 35:15; 36:37-38; 39:38; 40:5, 22

VIII. **THE SYMBOLIC LESSONS CONCERNING THE BRAZEN ALTAR,** Ex.27:1-8; 35:16; 38:1-7; 39:39; 40:6, 29

IX. **THE SYMBOLIC LESSONS CONCERNING THE WALLS OF THE TABERNACLE,** Ex.27:9-19; 35:17; 36:20-34; 38:9-20; 39:33, 40; 40:8, 33

X. **THE SYMBOLIC LESSONS CONCERNING THE DOOR OR GATE,** Ex.27:16; 35:17; 38:18-19; 39:40; 40:8, 33

XI. **THE SYMBOLIC LESSONS CONCERNING THE ALTAR OF INCENSE,** Ex.30:1-10; 35:15; 37:25-29; 39:38; 40:5, 26-27

XII. **THE SYMBOLIC LESSONS CONCERNING THE BRONZE WASH BASIN,** Ex.30:17-21; 35:16; 38:8; 39:39; 40:7, 30-32

HOW CHRIST FULFILLED THE SYMBOLISM OF THE TABERNACLE

I. THE SYMBOLIC LESSONS CONCERNING THE ARK OR CHEST,
Ex.25:10-22; 35:12; 37:1-5; 39:35; 40:3, 20-21

THE FACTS CONCERNING THE ARK	WHAT IS TAUGHT BY THE ARK OR CHEST	HOW CHRIST FULFILLED THE SYMBOLISM
1. The facts: a. The Ark was made of acacia wood (v.10): a hard, durable wood, resistant to weather and insects. b. The Ark was a box-like or chest-like structure: 3¾' long x 2¼' wide x 2¼' high (1.1 meters by .07 meters by .07 meters) (v.10). c. The Ark was overlaid with pure gold both inside and out, and it had a gold molding around the rim (v.11). d. The Ark had four gold rings attached to its four lower corners, at the base of the ark (v.12). e. The Ark had two strong poles made of acacia wood overlaid with gold (v.13). f. The poles were slid into the gold rings on the Ark for the purpose of carrying it (v.14). And note: once inserted, the poles were never removed. They were a permanent part of the Ark of God. g. The *Testimony of God* (the stone tablets of God's covenant, the Ten Commandments) was put into the Ark. h. The Ark actually contained three items: the tables of the law or Ten Commandments (Ex.25:16f; Dt.9:9; 10:5), the golden pot of manna (Ex.16:32-34), and Aaron's rod (Num.17:1-11).	2. What the Ark of the Covenant taught: a. The Ark was the place--the very special place--where God met with His people (v.22). God's presence was manifested in a very special way above the Ark of the Covenant. The people knew this. Therefore, when they needed a special sense of God's presence--when they needed to feel a special closeness to God--they knew where to go. They went to the Tabernacle, the ground surrounding the Tabernacle, worshipping and seeking forgiveness by offering sacrifice to the Lord. b. The Ark was the place of mercy, the place where God's mercy was clearly pictured (v.22). God's mercy was pictured in the Mercy Seat that sat upon the Ark. (See The Mercy Seat--next chart.) The people were to learn all about the Mercy Seat and the blood sprinkled upon it. They were to learn that the blood made atonement for their sins, reconciled them to God. They were to learn that the mercy of God was to be showered upon them because of the blood, because they believed and trusted the blood of the sacrifice to cover their sins. c. The Ark was the place where God instructed and guided His people (v.22). The Ark was to be the symbol of the throne of God. His divine presence was apparently manifested in a very special way right above the empty space of the Mercy Seat, right between the cherubim. From that position, God promised to speak to His people, to give them His commandments, instructions, and guidance; therefore, when God's people needed help or guidance, they were to come to the Tabernacle. d. The Ark of God held God's testimony, the two tablets of the covenant, that is, the Ten Commandments (v.21). Therefore, man is to keep the Ten Commandments.	3. How Christ fulfilled the symbolism of the Ark of the Covenant: a. Jesus Christ promised to be with His people always. "For where two or three are gathered together in my name, there am I in the midst of them" (Mt.18:20). "Teaching them to observe all things whatsoever I have commanded you: and, lo, I am with you alway, *even* unto the end of the world. Amen" (Mt.28:20). b. Jesus Christ shed His own blood and sprinkled it on the Mercy Seat, washing us from our sins. "Who his own self bare our sins in his own body on the tree, that we, being dead to sins, should live unto righteousness: by whose stripes ye were healed" (1 Pt.2:24). "For Christ also hath once suffered for sins, the just for the unjust, that he might bring us to God, being put to death in the flesh, but quickened by the Spirit" (1 Pt.3:18). "Unto him that loved us, and washed us from our sins in his own blood" (Rev.1:5). c. Jesus Christ is the Good Shepherd, the One who leads, protects, and guides His people, the precious sheep of His pasture. "I am the good shepherd: the good shepherd giveth his life for the sheep" (Jn.10:11). d. Jesus Christ kept the Law of the covenant that was kept in the Ark, kept the Law perfectly, without sin. "For we have not an high priest which cannot be touched with the feeling of our infirmities; but was in all points tempted like as *we are, yet* without sin" (Heb.4:15).

II. THE SYMBOLIC LESSONS CONCERNING THE MERCY SEAT,
Ex.25:17-21; 35:12; 37:6-9; 39:35; 40:3, 20

THE FACTS CONCERNING THE MERCY SEAT	WHAT IS TAUGHT BY THE MERCY SEAT	HOW CHRIST FULFILLED THE SYMBOLISM

1. The facts:
 	
Note the plan and design for the Mercy Seat or Atonement Cover. Keep in mind that it was placed on top of the Ark, that it served both as a *lid* to the Ark or Chest and as the Mercy Seat for God's Holy Presence.
  a. The Mercy Seat was made of pure gold (v.17).
  b. The Mercy Seat was oblong: the very same size as the Ark itself: 3¾' long x 2¼' wide (v.17).
  c. There was to be a cherubim at each end of the Mercy Seat (v.18-20). Note how the Mercy Seat was made:
    1) It was made of pure gold
    2) It was 3¾' long by 2¼' wide (1.1 meters by .07 meters)
    3) It had a cherubim at each end of the Mercy Seat
    4) It was made by hammering out the gold
    5) One cherub was hammered out at one end of the Mercy Seat & the other cherub at the other end
    6) The wings of the cherubim were spread upward overshadowing the Mercy Seat
    7) The cherubim faced each other, looking toward the Mercy Seat
  d. The Mercy Seat was placed on top of the Ark (v.21).
	2. What the Mercy Seat taught:
	  a. There was the picture that points toward the *finished work* of Christ. The High Priest was never allowed to sit on the Mercy Seat, no matter how tired or weary he became. In fact, the priests were always working when in the Tabernacle. Their priestly work was never finished: they were continually offering sacrifice and ministering.
	  b. There was the picture that pointed toward God covering the law with His mercy. No person can keep the law, not perfectly. And perfection is required in order to live in God's holy presence. How then can we ever become acceptable to God, be allowed to live in heaven with Him? By His mercy. God's mercy has been given us through His Son, the Lord Jesus Christ. God gave His Son to be the *Perfect Sacrifice* for our sins. The mercy of God shown us in Jesus Christ covers the law, covers our sin, our failure to keep the law. When we trust Jesus Christ as our Savior, the mercy of God covers all the law--all the accusations of the law against us, all our failure to keep the law, all the guilt that gnaws at our hearts and convicts us
		3. How Christ fulfilled the symbolism of the Mercy Seat:
		  a. When Jesus Christ offered Himself as the *Perfect Sacrifice* to God, His work was finished. His sacrifice for the sins of people was perfect: no other sacrifice was ever needed. Therefore, Christ was able to sit down on the right hand of God's throne.
		  b. God's mercy has been given us through His Son, the Lord Jesus Christ. God gave His Son to be the *Perfect Sacrifice* for our sins. The mercy of God shown us in Jesus Christ covers the law, covers our sin, our failure to keep the law. When we trust Jesus Christ as our Savior, the mercy of God covers all the law--all the accusations of the law against us, all our failure to keep the law, all the guilt that gnaws at our hearts and convicts us
		
		"For all have sinned, and come short of the glory of God; Being justified freely by his grace through the redemption that is in Christ Jesus: Whom God hath set forth to be a propitiation through faith in his blood, to declare his righteousness for the remission of sins that are past, through the forbearance of God" (Ro.3:23-25).
		"And every priest standeth daily ministering and offering oftentimes the same sacrifices, which can never take away sins: But this man, after he had offered one sacrifice for sins for ever, <u>sat down</u> on the right hand of God" (Heb.10:11-12).
		"And being found in fashion as a man, he humbled himself, and became obedient unto death, even the death of the cross. Wherefore God also hath highly exalted him, and given him a name which is above every name: That at the name of Jesus every knee should bow, of things in heaven, and things in earth, and things under the earth" (Ph.2:8-10).

III. THE SYMBOLIC LESSONS CONCERNING THE TABLE OF SHOW-BREAD, Ex.25:23-30; 35:13; 37:10-16; 39:36; 40:4, 22-23

THE FACTS CONCERNING THE TABLE OF SHOWBREAD	WHAT IS TAUGHT BY THE TABLE OF SHOWBREAD	HOW CHRIST FULFILLED THE SYMBOLISM
1. The facts: a. The table was made of acacia wood: a hard and durable wood, resistant to insects, disease, and weather (v.23). b. The table was quite small: 3' long & 1½' wide & 2¼' high (.9 meters x .5 meters x .7 meters) (v.23). c. The table was overlaid with pure gold and had a gold molding that ran around it (v.24). d. The table had a rim three inches wide around the top with a gold molding around it (v.25). e. The table had four gold rings attached to the four corners where the legs were: to support the poles for carrying the table (v.26-27). f. The poles to carry the table were made of acacia wood and overlaid with gold (v.28). g. The table's plates and dishes were made of gold as well as the pitchers and bowls that were used in pouring out drink offerings (v.29).	2. What the Table of Showbread taught: a. The twelve loaves of showbread represented an offering from each tribe of Israel, an offering of thanksgiving to God. Each tribe was represented as thanking God for the bread and food He provided, for meeting their physical needs. b. The twelve loaves also represented the people's dependence upon God. Note that the loaves sat in God's presence, before His very face. The people were to acknowledge their dependence upon God, acknowledge that they needed His provision. They needed His watchful eye upon the bread, upon them as His followers. They needed Him to continue to provide their bread and food, continue to look after and care for them. Their dependence upon God as the Provision of life was symbolized in the showbread as well as their offering of thanksgiving. c. The twelve loaves also acknowledged their trust in God. By setting the bread before God, they were declaring their belief and trust that He would continue to meet their physical needs. d. The showbread also pointed to Jesus Christ as the Bread of Life. Scripture declares that He is the Living Bread that came *out of* heaven to satisfy the hunger of a person's soul. e. The showbread pointed to God Himself as the nourishment that man really needs. Far too often, man tries to live his life apart from God's provision and presence. f. The showbread pointed to the great need of people for the bread of God's presence and worship. A constant diet of unhealthy things will cause a person to become sick and unhealthy. g. The showbread pointed to the bread that we all desperately need, the bread… • that satisfies the hunger of our hearts • that supplies our needs • that provides for us • that nourishes fellowship among us (cp. 1 Jn.1:3; Rev.3:20) h. The showbread pointed to the spiritual needs of man. This is seen in that the showbread sat in the Tabernacle itself, the very place where spiritual needs were met. This truth was dictated by both God and His Son, the Lord Jesus Christ.	3. How Christ fulfilled the symbolism of the table of showbread: ⇒ Jesus Christ is the Bread of Life, the nourishment upon which man must feed in order to know and worship God. "I am that bread of life" (Jn.6:48). "For the bread of God is he which cometh down from heaven, and giveth life unto the world" (Jn.6:33). "And Jesus said unto them, I am the bread of life: he that cometh to me shall never hunger; and he that believeth on me shall never thirst" (Jn.6:35). "This is the bread which cometh down from heaven, that a man may eat thereof, and not die. I am the living bread which came down from heaven: if any man eat of this bread, he shall live for ever: and the bread that I will give is my flesh, which I will give for the life of the world" (Jn.6:50-51). "This is that bread which came down from heaven: not as your fathers did eat manna, and are dead: he that eateth me, even he shall live by me" (Jn.6:58).

IV. THE SYMBOLIC LESSONS CONCERNING THE LAMPSTAND,
Ex.25:31-40; 27:20-21; 35:14; 37:17-24; 39:37; 40:4, 24-25

THE FACTS CONCERNING THE LAMPSTAND	WHAT IS TAUGHT BY THE LAMPSTAND	HOW CHRIST FULFILLED THE SYMBOLISM
1. The facts: The design and materials of the Lampstand were exact and precise (25:31-39). Again, God Himself designed the Lampstand. Human creativity had no part in designing this item, no part in designing anything in the Tabernacle. No person knew the perfect way to approach God; no person knew perfectly how to please God in his worship. God and God alone knew how He was to be approached and worshipped. Therefore, God and God alone had to design the Lampstand and the other furnishings that were to be used in worshipping Him. a. The Lampstand was made of pure gold, hammered out as one piece (v.31). The entire Lampstand was of one piece of gold: the base and center stem, the flower-like lamp cups, buds, and blossoms. b. The Lampstand had six branches (v.32-38). ⇒ Three branches were on each side (v.32). ⇒ Each branch had three cups shaped like almond flowers with buds and blossoms (v.33). c. The Lampstand had four similar flower-like cups, one flower bud under each pair of branches (v.34). d. The Lampstand had one blossom or bud under each pair of branches (v.35). All this means that the total number of ornaments was 69. Imagine 69 ornaments on one Lampstand. What beauty and splendor must have attracted the eye of the priest as he entered the Holy Place and saw the glowing, flickering flames arising from the seven light holders (six branches and the center stem). e. The decorations (flower buds) and branches were hammered out as one piece with the stem (v.36). f. The seven lamps were made for the Lampstand and set so they would reflect the light forward (v.37). g. The Lampstand and the accessories required 75 pounds of pure gold (v.39).	2. What the Lampstand taught: a. The Lampstand taught that a person needs light and illumination in order to know God and serve God. b. The Lampstand pictures God's people (Israel) as the light of the world, as God's witness to the world. c. The Lampstand points to Jesus Christ as the Light of the world. d. The Lampstand points to God as the Light of the world, the Light that shows man how to approach and worship Him. It was God who planned and designed the Lampstand, who showed the Israelites exactly how to approach and worship Him. He does the same for us.	3. How Christ fulfilled the symbolism of the Lampstand: ⇒ Jesus Christ is the true Lampstand. Christ came into the world to give light and illumination so that we might know and serve God. As the Light of the world, Christ fulfills the symbolism of the Lampstand. Christ and Christ alone is able to bring people out of the darkness of sin and death and give them the light of salvation and eternal life. "The same [John the Baptist] came for a witness, to bear witness of the Light, that all *men* through him might believe. He was not that Light, but *was sent* to bear witness of that Light. *That* [Jesus Christ] was the true Light, which lighteth every man that cometh into the world" (Jn.1:7-9). "In him was life; and the life was the light of men. And the light shineth in darkness; and the darkness comprehended it not [can never extinguish it]" (Jn.1:4-5). "Then spake Jesus again unto them, saying, I am the light of the world: he that followeth me shall not walk in darkness, but shall have the light of life" (Jn.8:12). "I am come a light into the world, that whosoever believeth on me should not abide in darkness" (Jn.12:46). "Jesus saith unto him, I am the way, the truth, and the life: no man cometh unto the Father, but by me" (Jn.14:6). "For God, who commanded the light to shine out of darkness, hath shined in our hearts, to *give* the light of the knowledge of the glory of God in the face of Jesus Christ" (2 Cor.4:6).

V. THE SYMBOLIC LESSONS CONCERNING THE SANCTUARY,
Ex.26:1-30; 35:17-18, 23, 25-26; 36:8-34; 39:33-34; 40:17-19

THE FACTS CONCERNING THE SANCTUARY	WHAT IS TAUGHT BY THE SANCTUARY	HOW CHRIST FULFILLED THE SYMBOLISM
1. The facts: A. The Tabernacle was a tent constructed of four coverings that were to serve as the roof and sides of the Tabernacle. a. The *first covering* was made of ten *linen curtains* that served as the inside ceiling and walls (v.1-6). This inner covering was what the priests saw as they ministered in the Holy Place and in the Most Holy Place. To behold such a striking beauty was the greatest of privileges, a privilege that no one else had. Note the facts about these unique curtains: 1) The design of cherubim was embroidered on each curtain (v.1). With a background color of blue, purple, and scarlet, the curtains were without doubt breathtaking. 2) The size of each curtain was about 42 feet long by 6 feet wide (v.2). Two groups of five curtains each were stitched together to make two sets of long curtains (v.3). 3) The loops and clasps to join and fasten the curtains together were made of blue material and sewn along the edges (v.4). A total of fifty loops was to be sewn on each curtain (v.5). The curtains were fastened together by making fifty gold clasps that were inserted through the connecting loops. This made the Tabernacle a single tent (v.6). b. The *second covering* was made of *goat hair*. These are the facts that apply to the covering of goat hair: 1) The number of the curtains was eleven (v.7). 2) The size of each curtain was about 45 feet long by 6 feet wide (v.8). Five of the curtains were joined together into one set and six curtains into another set. The sixth curtain was to be folded double at the front of the tent (v.9). 3) The loops and clasps fastened the curtains together, making the curtains a single covering for the tent or Tabernacle. Note how they were made: ⇒ Fifty loops were sewn along the edge of both curtains	2. What the Sanctuary taught: A. The four coverings of the Tabernacle Tent a. There are different forms of worship, certain steps to take in approaching God. b. There are some initial steps to take in approaching God before one approaches Him in the most intimate worship. c. God is righteous and holy and completely separate from man, even from the religious who move about and minister within the walls of religion. d. God must be approached in reverence and awe and ever so carefully by men, even by the religious who are involved in His service.	3. How Christ fulfilled the symbolism of the Sanctuary: A. The symbol of the coverings of the Tabernacle Tent a. *The Inner Curtains:* Christ is pure and righteous; therefore, Christ fulfilled the symbolism of these inner curtains by being the perfect embodiment of purity and righteousness. **"For he hath made him to be sin for us, who knew no sin; that we might be made the righteousness of God in him" (2 Cor.5:21).** b. *The Covering of Goat Hair:* Christ, being perfectly pure and righteous, was able to become the sin-offering for the sins of His people. The goat hair was probably black (cp. Song of Solomon 1:5). Therefore, Christ fulfilled the symbolism of the goat covering by taking the blackness of sin upon Himself. (See note, pt.2--Ex.26:1-4 for more discussion.) **"Who his own self bare our sins in his own body on the tree, that we, being dead to sins, should live unto righteousness: by whose stripes ye were healed" (1 Pt.2:24).** c. *The Covering of Ram Skin Dyed Red:* Christ willingly shed His blood for mankind. Therefore, the third covering of ram skins *dyed red* points to the sacrificial blood of Jesus Christ that was shed for man. **"For this is my blood of the new testament, which is shed for many for the remission of sins" (Mt.26:28).** d. *The Outside Leather Covering:* Christ is our protective separation from the world and from the coming wrath of God against the evil of the world; therefore, Christ fulfilled the symbolism of the outer cover. Just as the outer covering protected the Tabernacle from the elements of the world, Jesus Christ protects us from the world's perils and temptations and from God's terrible wrath against the sins of the world.

THE FACTS CONCERNING THE SANCTUARY	WHAT IS TAUGHT BY THE SANCTUARY	HOW CHRIST FULFILLED THE SYMBOLISM
⇒ Fifty bronze clasps were made for fastening the curtains together (v.10-11). 4) The extra half sheet length of this first covering hung down at the rear of the Tabernacle (v.12). The goat hair curtain hung 18 inches over the sides of the Tabernacle. c. The *third covering of ram skins* symbolized the sacrificial blood. The ram skins had the wool removed and were then dyed red. Red, of course, is symbolic of the sacrificial blood. d. The *outside covering* was the covering of *leather or of seal skins*. It was the covering that kept the Tabernacle safe from the elements of the weather and the wilderness: the scorching sun, the torrential rains, the wind-blasted sand, and the wild animals. Moving from campsite to campsite, the Tabernacle obviously took a constant beating. The covering of leather protected the Tabernacle from the outside, from the elements of the world.		"Who gave himself for our sins, that he might deliver us from this present evil world, according to the will of God and our Father" (Gal.1:4).
B. The Tabernacle was a tent hanging over wood framing (acacia wood). Note the facts about the wood framing: a. The size of each framing board was 15 feet long by 2¼ feet wide with two pegs set parallel to each other for hooking to the base (v.15-17). b. The framing consisted of the following items: 1) A wall, a frame of twenty boards on the south side (v.18). On the south side there was a foundation of forty silver sockets or bases, two under each board which were joined together by pegs (v.19). 2) A wall, a frame of twenty boards on the north side (v.20). Like the south side, the north side had a foundation of forty silver sockets, two sockets under each board (v.21). Each one of the silver sockets required about seventy-five pounds of silver. 3) A wall frame of six boards on the west (v.22). 4) A framing post of two boards for each corner (v.23)... • that was joined together at the bottom • that was joined together at the top, fitted into a single ring (v.24) • that had a total of eight board frames and a foundation of	B. The Foundation of the Tabernacle tent: The Redemption and Stability of Christ a. The foundation of the Tabernacle was firmly planted... • in the shifting sands of the desert (a symbol of the world and its wilderness) • under God's direction and care as He led His people from campsite to campsite • in God's ability to save helpless men b. The 15 crossbars served as a means of stability to the wood framing. Without the support of the crossbars, the Tabernacle would have been at the mercy of every contrary wind. The Scripture gives no reason why God wanted five crossbars for each wall. What we do know and can apply in a most practical way is the purpose of the crossbars: to give stability and support.	B. The Foundation of the Tabernacle tent: The Redemption and Stability of Christ a. *The foundation of the Tabernacle:* Christ fulfilled the symbolism of the foundation of the Tabernacle. How? By dying upon the cross and redeeming man from his sins. By this act, Christ became the foundation of redemption for every believer. The silver in the Tabernacle was an ever-present reminder of man's need for atonement: for reconciliation with God, for redemption. The foundation of the Tabernacle was a foundation of silver. This pictured a glorious truth: the foundation of the believer is redemption, reconciliation with God through His Son the LORD Jesus Christ. "And thou shalt take the atonement money of the children of Israel, and shalt appoint it for the service of the tabernacle of the congregation; that it may be a memorial unto the children of Israel before the LORD, to make an <u>atonement</u> for your souls" (Ex.30:16). "Forasmuch as ye know that ye were not redeemed with corruptible things, as silver and gold, from your vain conversation received by tradition from your fathers; But with the precious blood of Christ, as of a lamb without blemish and without spot" (1 Pt.1:18-19).

THE FACTS CONCERNING THE SANCTUARY	WHAT IS TAUGHT BY THE SANCTUARY	HOW CHRIST FULFILLED THE SYMBOLISM
sixteen silver sockets, two under each board (v.25) 5) Fifteen durable crossbars (acacia wood). There were... • Five crossbars for the south (v.26) • Five crossbars for the north (v.27) • Five crossbars for the west (v.27) The exact design as to how these crossbars were arranged on each of the three walls is unknown. What is known is that the center crossbar ran from end to end in the middle of the frames (v.28). 6) The crossbars were covered with gold and gold rings were made to hold the crossbars (v.29). The fifteen crossbars served as a means of stability to the wood framing.		b. Christ fulfilled the stability and support symbolized in the crossbars. Christ fulfilled the symbolism... • by being our support, our eternal refuge "The eternal God *is thy* refuge, and underneath *are* the everlasting arms: and he shall thrust out the enemy from before thee; and shall say, Destroy *them*" (Dt.33:27). • by holding us up, by sustaining us with His right hand "Thou hast also given me the shield of thy salvation: and thy right hand hath holden me up, and thy gentleness hath made me great" (Ps.18:35). • by strengthening and helping us "Fear thou not; for I *am* with thee: be not dismayed; for I *am* thy God: I will strengthen thee; yea, I will help thee; yea, I will uphold thee with the right hand of my righteousness" (Is.41:10). • by delivering us "And the Lord shall deliver me from every evil work, and will preserve *me* unto his heavenly kingdom: to whom *be* glory for ever and ever. Amen" (2 Tim.4:18). • by preserving us "O love the LORD, all ye his saints: *for* the LORD preserveth the faithful, and plentifully rewardeth the proud doer" (Ps.31:23).

VI. THE SYMBOLIC LESSONS CONCERNING THE INNER VEIL, Ex.26:31-35; 35:12; 36:35-36; 39:34; 40:3, 21

THE FACTS CONCERNING THE INNER VEIL	WHAT IS TAUGHT BY THE INNER VEIL	HOW CHRIST FULFILLED THE SYMBOLISM
1. The facts: a. It was a veil of great beauty made with remarkable skill (v.31). Like the inner curtain, it was made of fine linen. The same striking colors of blue, purple, and scarlet were a part of this veil. The embroidered cherubim were also worked into this veil. b. It was hung with gold hooks on four posts of durable wood (acacia). The posts stood on four silver sockets or bases (v.32). c. The purpose for the inner veil was basically to shield the ark of God from all else. 1) The inner veil was to separate	2. What the Inner Veil or Curtain Door taught: a. God is holy and righteous, far, far removed from man and his world--totally set apart and separated from the pollution and uncleanness of man. b. God must be approached ever so carefully--in reverence, awe, and fear. c. There is only one way to God, only one door into His presence. d. Fellowship and communion with God Himself is the supreme act of worship.	3. How Christ fulfilled the symbolism of the veil: ⇒ The *inner veil* is rich in symbolism as it speaks of Jesus Christ. Christ fulfilled the symbolism of the inner veil. Christ and Christ alone is the way to God, the way to know God and to experience the presence, fellowship, and communion of God. Remember what happened to the inner veil of the temple when Christ died on the cross: it was torn from top to bottom, symbolizing that God Himself acted, took the initiative, and tore the veil. The heavenly veil that kept man out

the Holy Place from the Most Holy Place (v.33). This symbolized the majestic holiness and righteousness of God, the light of His perfection which no man can approach.

2) The inner veil separated the mercy seat from all else. The veil symbolized the holiness of God, separation from the presence of God (v.34). Note what was separated from the Mercy Seat in the Most Holy Place:

⇒ The Table of Showbread: the table was placed on the north side in the Holy Place (v.35).

⇒ The Lampstand: the Lampstand was placed opposite the table on the south side (v.35).

of God's presence was torn by Christ when He suffered and died on the cross. We now have eternal access into the presence of God. The door into God's presence is wide open.

"Wherefore in all things it behooved him to be made like unto his brethren, that he might be a merciful and faithful high priest in things pertaining to God, to make reconciliation for the sins of the people" (Heb.2:17).

"Seeing then that we have a great high priest, that is passed into the heavens, Jesus the Son of God, let us hold fast our profession. For we have not an high priest which cannot be touched with the feeling of our infirmities; but was in all points tempted like as we are, yet without sin" (Heb.4:14-15).

"[Christ] entereth into that within the veil; wither the forerunner is for us entered, even Jesus" (Heb.6:19-20).

"For Christ is not entered into the holy places made with hands, which are the figures of the true; but into heaven itself, now to appear in the presence of God for us" (Heb.9:24).

"Having therefore, brethren, boldness to enter into the holiest by the blood of Jesus, by a new and living way, which he hath consecrated for us, through the veil, that is to say, his flesh" (Heb.10:19-20).

VII. THE SYMBOLIC LESSONS CONCERNING THE OUTER VEIL, Ex.26:36-37; 35:15; 36:37-38; 39:38; 40:5, 22

THE FACTS CONCERNING THE OUTER VEIL	WHAT IS TAUGHT BY THE OUTER VEIL	HOW CHRIST FULFILLED THE SYMBOLISM
1. The facts: a. It was an entrance of great beauty and craftsmanship (v.36). This curtain was identical to the inner curtain with one exception: there were no cherubim embroidered into the curtain. b. The hanging frame was slightly different from that of the inner curtain's hanging frame. 1) There were gold hooks and five posts overlaid with gold (v.37). The inner curtain was hung on four posts overlaid with gold (cp. v.32). 2) There were five bronze bases or sockets for the posts (v.37). The poles for the inner curtain required only four bases of silver (cp. v.32). Note the change of metals for the bases from silver to bronze. Why? Most likely because sin offerings were made at the bronze altar,	2. What the Outer Veil or Curtain Door taught: a. A person cannot just rush into the presence of a holy God; he cannot show disrespect to a holy God. b. There is only one way into the deeper things of God. c. There is a deeper knowledge of God, much more to knowing and experiencing God's presence than just making sacrifice and receiving forgiveness of sins. (Remember: offerings for sin were made at the brazen altar in the courtyard. But there was more than this, more than forgiveness of sins, in knowing and worshipping God. There was worship in the Holy Place and even in the inner sanctuary of God's presence, in the Most Holy Place or the Holy of Holies.)	3. How Christ fulfilled the symbolism of the veil: ⇒ Jesus Christ fulfilled the symbolism of this outer curtain. With His shed blood, He invites men to come through the door and worship God. The way to a deeper knowledge of God, to the deeper things of God, is through the Lord Jesus Christ and through Him alone. "And this is life eternal, that they might know thee the only true God, and Jesus Christ, whom thou hast sent" (Jn.17:3). "But of him are ye in Christ Jesus, who of God is made unto us wisdom, and righteousness, and sanctification, and redemption" (1 Cor.1:30). "But speaking the truth in love, may grow up into him in all things, which is the head, even Christ"

		(Eph.4:15).
and before a person can offer acceptable worship, he must deal with his sins. There at the bronze altar, his sins were judged by God, and God's wrath was satisfied. This is the foundation of man's worship, the blood that cleanses a person from sin. Therefore, the foundation sockets for the entrance to the Tabernacle were made of bronze: all to symbolize the need for cleansing in order to worship God. Simply stated, until a man has been forgiven for his sins, he can never enter into the presence of God. Once blood has been shed, man is invited to come and worship God.		"That I may know him, and the power of his resurrection, and the fellowship of his sufferings, being made conformable unto his death" (Ph.3:10). "Therefore leaving the principles of the doctrine of Christ, let us go on unto perfection; not laying again the foundation of repentance from dead works, and of faith toward God" (Heb.6:1). "As newborn babes, desire the sincere milk of the word, that ye may grow thereby: if so be ye have tasted that the Lord is gracious" (1 Pt.2:2-3).

VIII. THE SYMBOLIC LESSONS CONCERNING THE BRAZEN ALTAR,
Ex.27:1-8; 35:16; 38:1-7; 39:39; 40:6, 29

THE FACTS CONCERNING THE BRAZEN ALTAR (THE ALTAR OF BURNT OFFERING)	WHAT IS TAUGHT BY THE BRAZEN ALTAR	HOW CHRIST FULFILLED THE SYMBOLISM
1. The facts: a. The altar was made of acacia wood with the following dimensions: it was a square altar that was 7½ feet wide by 7½ feet long by 4½ feet high. b. Like the other parts of the Tabernacle, acacia wood was chosen for its hardness and for its durability. c. The altar was made with a horn at each of the four corners, made of one piece. d. The altar was overlaid (covered) with bronze. e. All of the utensils were made of bronze f. The Altar was to have a bronze grate g. The Altar had poles of acacia wood that were overlaid with bronze. These poles were then inserted into the four rings when the altar was carried. h. The altar was made hollow.	2. What the Altar taught: a. Substitutionary sacrifice is necessary for the forgiveness of sins. b. There is no forgiveness without the shed blood of a sacrifice. c. There is no way to approach God--to be saved--other than through the death of a substitute.	3. How Christ fulfilled the symbolism of the Brazen Altar: a. Christ is the Lamb of God. "The next day John seeth Jesus coming unto him, and saith, Behold the Lamb of God, which taketh away the sin of the world!" (Jn.1:29). b. Christ is the Lamb brought to the slaughter. "He was oppressed, and he was afflicted, yet he opened not his mouth: he is brought as a lamb to the slaughter, and as a sheep before her shearers is dumb, so he openeth not his mouth" (Is.53:7). c. Christ is our Passover sacrificed for us. "Purge out therefore the old leaven, that ye may be a new lump, as ye are unleavened. For even Christ our passover is sacrificed for us" (1 Cor.5:7). d. Christ gave His life as a ransom. "[I] give my life a ransom for many" (Mk.10:45). e. Christ laid down His life for us. "Hereby perceive we the love of God, because he laid down his life for us: and we ought to lay down our lives for the brethren" (1 Jn.3:16).

IX. THE SYMBOLIC LESSONS CONCERNING THE WALLS OF THE TABERNACLE, Ex.27:9-19; 35:17; 36:20-34; 38:9-20; 39:33, 40; 40:8, 33

THE FACTS CONCERNING THE WALLS	WHAT IS TAUGHT BY THE WALLS	HOW CHRIST FULFILLED THE SYMBOLISM
1. The facts: a. A mandate had been given to build the courtyard (v.9). God had wanted to ensure the safety of the holy vessels of the Tabernacle by having His people build a protective hedge around the Tabernacle. b. The south side was built with these exact specifications (v.9-10): ⇒ 150 feet of linen curtains ⇒ 20 posts that fit into 20 bronze bases ⇒ silver hooks and bands attached to the posts c. The north side was built with these exact specifications (v.11): ⇒ 150 feet of linen curtains ⇒ 20 posts that fit into 20 bronze bases ⇒ silver hooks and bands d. The west end was built with these exact specifications (v.12): ⇒ 75 feet of curtains ⇒ 10 posts set into ten bases e. The east end was 75 feet long (v.13). Included in the east end was the one and only courtyard entrance. This entrance was flanked by two curtains. Note their specifications: ⇒ Each was 22½ feet long ⇒ Each was supported by 3 posts set into three bases (v.14-15). f. The entrance itself (v.16). This was the only door into the Tabernacle. The curtain was 30 feet long and was made of fine linen. This curtain was decorated, embroidered in blue, purple, and scarlet yarn. The same set of brilliant colors was used throughout the inner curtains of the sanctuary. This curtain was attached to four posts set in four bases. g. The posts of the courtyard were connected by silver bands and hooks (v.17). h. The Courtyard was 150 feet long by 75 feet wide with 7½ feet high curtain walls that were made of fine linen. These walls were supported by bronze bases. i. The articles used in the work of the Tabernacle, including the tent pegs, were bronze.	2. What the Walls taught: a. The walls of linen symbolized the righteousness and holiness of God. He is so righteous and holy, so white and pure, that He is set apart from the world. b. When a person looks at God, he must see that God dwells in righteousness and holiness. When a person looked at the walls of the Tabernacle, he was to be reminded that God was holy. c. When a person approaches God, he must approach Him in reverence and awe, adoration and worship. He must praise and thank God, that God allows him to enter His presence.	3. How Christ fulfilled the symbolism of the Walls: ⇒ Christ is the righteousness of God. "But now the righteousness of God without the law is manifested, being witnessed by the law and the prophets; Even the righteousness of God which is by faith of Jesus Christ unto all and upon all them that believe: for there is no difference" (Ro.3:21-22). "For he hath made him to be sin for us, who knew no sin; that we might be made the righteousness of God in him" (2 Cor.5:21). "And that ye put on the new man [Christ], which after God is created in righteousness and true holiness" (Eph.4:24). "And have put on the new man, which is renewed in knowledge after the image of him that created him" (Col.3:10).

X.   THE SYMBOLIC LESSONS CONCERNING THE DOOR OR GATE, Ex.27:16; 35:17; 38:18-19; 39:40; 40:8, 33

THE FACTS CONCERNING THE DOOR OR GATE	WHAT IS TAUGHT BY THE DOOR OR GATE	HOW CHRIST FULFILLED THE SYMBOLISM
1. The facts: Included in the east end was the one and only Courtyard entrance, but note: the entrance (door) to the Tabernacle was large, large enough to receive any person. a. The Door was on the east side. b. The Door was 30 feet wide and 7½ feet high. c. The Door was made out of fine twined linen woven together by needlework. This curtain was decorated, embroidered in blue, purple, and scarlet yarn--the same set of brilliant colors throughout the inner curtains of the sanctuary. d. The curtain was attached to four posts set in four bases.	2. What the Door or Gate taught: a. There is only one way to enter God's presence; there are not many ways as most men think and practice. b. God has to be approached. No person shall ever live with God unless he approaches God.	3. How Christ fulfilled the symbolism of the Door or Gate: a. Jesus Christ is the door, the only door, that a man can enter to be saved. **"I am the door: by me if any man enter in, he shall be saved, and shall go in and out, and find pasture" (Jn.10:9).** b. Jesus Christ is the way, the only way by which a man can come to the Father. **"Jesus saith unto him, I am the way, the truth, and the life: no man cometh unto the Father, but by me" (Jn.14:6).**

XI. THE SYMBOLIC LESSONS CONCERNING THE ALTAR OF INCENSE, Ex.30:1-10; 35:15; 37:25-29; 39:38; 40:5, 26-27

THE FACTS CONCERNING THE ALTAR OF INCENSE	WHAT IS TAUGHT BY THE ALTAR OF INCENSE	HOW CHRIST FULFILLED THE SYMBOLISM
1. The facts: a. The Altar of Incense was made of acacia wood (v.1). b. The Altar of Incense was square: 18 inches by 18 inches by 3 feet high (v.2). c. The Altar of Incense had horns on each corner, carved from the same piece of wood (v.2). Horns are symbolic of God's power, strength, salvation, protection, security, sanctuary, and help. d. The Altar of Incense was overlaid with gold and had a gold molding (v.3). Just like the other holy pieces of furniture in the sanctuary, the altar was covered with pure gold. e. The Altar of Incense had two gold rings attached to each side. The rings held the two poles used in carrying the altar (v.4). f. The Altar of Incense had two poles made of acacia wood overlaid with gold (v.5). The altar, like the rest of the Tabernacle, was designed to be moved. g. God told Moses to place the altar just outside the inner curtain. It was opposite the Ark of the Covenant and its cover, the Mercy Seat (v.6).	2. What the Altar of Incense taught: a. The altar was the place where sweet incense was offered up to the LORD every morning and evening. The High Priest burned incense every morning when he tended the lamps and every evening when he lit them (v.7). This symbolized the critical importance of praying every morning and evening. b. The Altar of Incense had a permanent incense ascending up to the LORD (v.8). This symbolized two things. 1) There is the symbol of the permanent intercession of Jesus Christ. Jesus Christ is living forever--in the very presence of God--to make intercession for us. He died and arose from the dead for this very purpose: to stand before God as the great Intercessor for us. 2) There is the symbol that believers are to pray morning and evening, to pray always, to develop an unbroken communion with God, never to cease being in a spirit of prayer.	3. How Christ fulfilled the symbolism of the Altar: a. Christ is always praying, living and walking in an unbroken communion with God the Father. b. Christ intercedes for God's people. **"I pray for them: I pray not for the world, but for them which thou hast given me; for they are thine" (Jn.17:9).** **"Who is he that condemneth? It is Christ that died, yea rather, that is risen again, who is even at the right hand of God, who also maketh intercession for us" (Ro.8:34).** **"Seeing then that we have a great high priest [Intercessor], that is passed into the heavens, Jesus the Son of God, let us hold fast our profession. For we have not an high priest which cannot be touched with the feeling of our infirmities; but was in all points tempted like as we are, yet without sin" (Heb.4:14-15).** **"Wherefore he is able also to save them to the uttermost that come unto God by him, seeing he ever liveth to make intercession for them" (Heb.7:25).**

XII. THE SYMBOLIC LESSONS CONCERNING THE BRONZE WASH BASIN, Ex.30:17-21; 35:16; 38:8; 39:39; 40:7, 30-32

THE FACTS CONCERNING THE BRONZE WASH BASIN	WHAT IS TAUGHT BY THE BRONZE WASH BASIN	HOW CHRIST FULFILLED THE SYMBOLISM
1. The facts: a. The size is not given. b. The builder made the Bronze Basin with a bronze pedestal (v.18). c. The Bronze Basin was placed between the Tabernacle and the Altar of Burnt Offering (v.18). d. The sole purpose of the Bronze Wash Basin was for the priests to wash their hands and feet (v.19). They were to wash when they entered the Tabernacle and when they approached the altar to make a sacrifice. e. The warning was clear and blunt: the priests must wash or die (v.21). f. The importance of the washing and cleansing cannot be over-stressed: it was made a permanent law for all generations (v.21).	2. What the Wash Basin taught: a. A person *cannot enter God's presence* before he is cleansed and made pure. b. A person *cannot serve God* until he is cleansed and made pure. c. A person must be continually cleansed and made pure in order to *continually serve God*.	3. How Christ fulfilled the symbolism of the Bronze Wash Basin: ⇒ The Wash Basin was a symbol of Christ. God cleanses us and forgives our sins through the blood of His Son, the Lord Jesus Christ, through His death and His death alone. "For this is my blood of the new testament, which is shed for many for the remission of sins" (Mt.26:28). "Then Peter said unto them, Repent, and be baptized every one of you in the name of Jesus Christ for the remission of sins, and ye shall receive the gift of the Holy Ghost" (Acts 2:38). "Him hath God exalted with his right hand to be a Prince and a Saviour, for to give repentance to Israel, and forgiveness of sins" (Acts 5:31). "Be it known unto you therefore, men and brethren, that through this man is preached unto you the forgiveness of sins" (Acts 13:38). "For all have sinned, and come short of the glory of God; Being justified freely by his grace through the redemption that is in Christ Jesus: Whom God hath set forth to be a propitiation through faith in his blood, to declare his righteousness for the remission of sins that are past, through the forbearance of God" (Ro.3:23-25). "In whom we have redemption through his blood, the forgiveness of sins, according to the riches of his grace" (Eph.1:7). "In whom we have redemption through his blood, even the forgiveness of sins" (Col.1:14). "[Christ] who gave himself for us, that he might redeem us from all iniquity, and purify unto himself a peculiar people, zealous of good works" (Tit.2:14).

CHART 3

HOW CHRIST FULFILLED
THE SYMBOLISM OF
THE PRIESTHOOD

I. THE SYMBOLIC LESSONS CONCERNING THE GARMENTS OF THE PRIEST-HOOD

    A. THE SASH, Ex.28:4; 39:29

    B. THE EPHOD, Ex.28:4, 6-14; 39:2-7

    C. THE BREASTPIECE OR CHESTPIECE, Ex.28:4, 15-30; 39:8-21

    D. THE ROBE OF THE EPHOD, Ex.28:4, 31-35; 39:22-26

    E. THE GOLD MEDALLION OR DIADEM, Ex.28:36-38; 39:30-31

    F. THE LINEN TURBANS AND TUNICS, Ex.28:4, 39; 39:27-28

    G. THE LINEN HEADBAND, Ex.28:40; 39:28

    H. THE LINEN UNDERCLOTHING, Ex.28:42-43; 39:28

II. THE SYMBOLIC LESSONS CONCERNING THE ORDINATION OF THE PRIEST-HOOD

    A. THE CEREMONIAL WASHING, Ex.29:4

    B. THE JUDICIAL CLEANSING, Ex.29:10-14

    C. THE TOTAL DEDICATION OF LIFE: THE SACRIFICE OF THE FIRST RAM AS THE BURNT OFFERING, Ex.29:15-18

    D. THE CONSECRATION TO SERVICE: THE SACRIFICE OF A SECOND RAM, Ex.29:19-21

    E. THE COMMITMENT TO GIVE GOD THE BEST: THE CEREMONY OF TWO WAVE OFFERINGS, Ex.29:22-28

I. THE SYMBOLIC LESSONS CONCERNING THE GARMENTS OF THE PRIESTHOOD

A. THE SASH, Ex.28:4; 39:29

THE FACTS CONCERNING THE SASH	WHAT IS TAUGHT BY THE SASH	HOW CHRIST FULFILLED THE SYMBOLISM
1. The Facts: ⇒ The sash for each priest was made of fine linen and multi-colored yarn	2. What the Sash taught: a. The multi-colored sash of fine linen was symbolic of truth, the truth of God's Word. It is comparable to the belt of truth in the armor of God that the believer is to put on (Eph.6:14). b. The Word of God enlightens and wraps together everything in the believer's spiritual wardrobe. c. It is the Word of God that holds everything together.	3. How Christ fulfilled the symbolism of the Sash: a. Jesus Christ fulfilled the symbolism of the Sash by being the Truth, the Living Word of God. "Stand therefore, having your loins girt about with truth, and having on the breastplate of righteousness" (Eph.6:14). "Sanctify them through thy truth: thy word is truth" (Jn.17:17). b. Jesus Christ is the One who holds everything and everyone together-- all by His Word. "For by him were all things created, that are in heaven, and that are in earth, visible and invisible, whether they be thrones, or dominions, or principalities, or powers: all things were created by him, and for him: And he is before all things, and by him all things consist" (Col.1:16-17).

B. THE EPHOD, Ex.28:4, 6-14; 39:2-7

THE FACTS CONCERNING THE EPHOD	WHAT IS TAUGHT BY THE EPHOD	HOW CHRIST FULFILLED THE SYMBOLISM
1. The facts: a. The materials of the ephod consisted of gold thread that had been made from thin gold sheets cut into thin, thread-like wires (See Ex.39:3). The ephod also consisted of yarn that was blue, purple, and scarlet (v.6). The final type of material in the ephod was fine linen. b. The design of the ephod was spelled out with these exact instructions: 1) It was in two pieces, front and back, joined by two straps at the shoulder (v.7). 2) It had a sash or waistband made of the same materials as the ephod (v.8). 3) It had two onyx stones that had Israel's twelve tribes engraved on them (v.9). Six names were engraved on each stone in the order of their birth (v.10). Each stone was engraved just as a gemcutter engraves a seal (v.11). The maker of the ephod mounted the stones in gold settings and then fastened the	2. What the Ephod taught: ⇒ The Ephod symbolized that the priest represented and carried the names of God's people before the Lord.	3. How Christ fulfilled the symbolism of the Ephod: ⇒ Jesus Christ is the One who represents and carries the name of believers before the Father. No matter what our burden, no matter how heavy or terrifying, we can cast it upon Christ. He will relieve us, strengthen us, and give us peace and rest from the burden. "Come unto me, all ye that labour and are heavy laden, and I will give you rest. Take my yoke upon you, and learn of me; for I am meek and lowly in heart: and ye shall find rest unto your souls. For my yoke is easy, and my burden is light" (Mt.11:28-30). "Who is he that condemneth? It is Christ that died, yea rather, that is risen again, who is even at the right hand of God, who also maketh intercession for us" (Ro.8:34). "Wherefore in all things it behooved him to be made like unto his brethren, that he might be a merciful and faithful high priest in things

stones to the shoulder pieces of the ephod (v.11-12).		pertaining to God, to make reconciliation for the sins of the people. For in that he himself hath suffered being tempted, he is able to succour them that are tempted" (Heb.2:17-18).

C. THE BREASTPIECE OR CHESTPIECE, Ex.28:4, 15-30; 39:8-21

THE FACTS CONCERNING THE BREASTPIECE OR CHESTPIECE	WHAT IS TAUGHT BY THE BREASTPIECE OR CHESTPIECE	HOW CHRIST FULFILLED THE SYMBOLISM
1. The Facts: a. The basic materials were the same as the ephod garment (v.15). b. The design was a 9 inch square, folded double, forming a pouch (v.16). On the breastpiece were attached four rows of precious stones which numbered a total of twelve (v.17-20). Each one of these twelve stones was attached to a gold setting (v.21). The twelve stones represented the twelve tribes of Israel and were identified by engraving the names of the twelve tribes on the stones as a seal (v.21). The chestpiece was then permanently attached to the ephod. The maker of the chestpiece made braided cords of pure gold (v.22). The chestpiece also had two gold rings which were attached to the top corners of the chestpiece--for the gold cords to go through. Then the cords were tied to the gold settings on the shoulder pieces of the ephod garment (v.23-25). Two more gold rings were made and attached to the other two ends of the chestpiece--on the inside next to the ephod garment (v.26). The final two gold rings were made and attached to the ephod garment near the sash (v.27). To hold the breastpiece and ephod together, the rings of the chestpiece were tied to the rings of the ephod with blue cord. This blue cord held both garments securely together (v.28).	2. What the Breastpiece or Chestpiece taught: ⇒ The purpose for the chestpiece was twofold: a. First, to symbolize that the High Priest represents and carries the names of God's people upon his heart, that he represents them before the Lord continually (v.29). b. The second purpose of the chestpiece was to hold the urim and thummim (probably two stones or lots) next to the High Priest's heart (v.30). This symbolized the High Priest seeking God's will for the people. Imagine the scene as the High Priest entered into the Holy Place. He was there on behalf of the people of God.	3. How Christ fulfilled the symbolism of the Breastpiece or Chestpiece: ⇒ Jesus Christ is our great High Priest who represents and carries the names of believers upon His heart and before the Lord continually. This is a strong picture of the love of God: how much God loves His people. He loves us so much that He keeps us ever so close to His heart, continually before His face. "Before I formed thee in the belly I knew thee; and before thou camest forth out of the womb I sanctified thee, and I ordained thee a prophet unto the nations" (Jer.1:5). "Behold, God is mine helper: the Lord is with them that uphold my soul" (Ps.54:4). "The LORD is nigh unto them that are of a broken heart; and saveth such as be of a contrite spirit" (Ps.34:18). "I know thy works: behold, I have set before thee an open door, and no man can shut it: for thou hast a little strength, and hast kept my word, and hast not denied my name" (Rev.3:8). "But even the very hairs of your head are all numbered. Fear not therefore: ye are of more value than many sparrows" (Lk.12:7).

D. THE ROBE OF THE EPHOD, Ex.28:4, 31-35; 39:22-26

THE FACTS CONCERNING THE ROBE OF THE EPHOD	WHAT IS TAUGHT BY THE ROBE OF THE EPHOD	HOW CHRIST FULFILLED THE SYMBOLISM
1. The Facts: ⇒ It was a long sleeveless solid blue robe. These are the facts about its construction: a. An opening was made in the center of the robe for the head. The maker reinforced the opening with a woven collar so it would not tear (v.32).	2. What the Robe of the Ephod taught: ⇒ The symbolic purpose of the robe was twofold: a. To sound forth the intercessory ministry of the High Priest (v.35). Before the High Priest would minister before the Lord, he would slip this robe over his head. After he was fully dressed in the priestly gar-	3. How Christ fulfilled the symbolism of the Robe of the Ephod: a. Jesus Christ is our great High Priest who sounds forth the intercessory ministry of the High Priest. His intercession never ends, never stops. "But this man, because he continueth ever, hath an unchangeable

b. Pomegranates were made out of yarn in the colors of blue, purple, and scarlet (v.33). These pomegranates of yarn were attached to the hem of the robe with gold bells between them. The pattern alternated the pomegranates and bells at the hem of the robe (v.34).

ments, the tinkling of the golden bells would mark his every step. The sound of the bells told the people where he was as he carried their names before the LORD. As he ministered in their behalf, they could follow his intercessory ministry as he moved about the various rituals of worship. As he carried out a particular ritual, the people would obviously meditate and pray over the truth symbolized by the ritual.

b. To sound forth that God had accepted the offering of the High Priest, that the High Priest had not been stricken dead (v.35). The sound of the bells let the people know that he was alive and ministering on their behalf. Every time the High Priest went into the Holy Place, there was always the chance that his offering would be unacceptable to God. When a Holy God is approached by an unholy offering, death is always the final consequence (always spiritual death; sometimes physical death).

priesthood. Wherefore he is able also to save them to the uttermost that come unto God by him, seeing he **ever liveth** to make intercession for them" (Heb.7:24-25).

b. As the great Intercessor, Jesus Christ offered Himself to God...
• as the perfect offering, the Lamb of God
• as the resurrected Lord and Christ, the One who lives forever more
• as the perfect High Priest, the One who intercedes for man

"The next day John seeth Jesus coming unto him, and saith, Behold the Lamb of God, which taketh away the sin of the world" (Jn.1:29).
"Wherefore God also hath highly exalted him, and given him a name which is above every name" (Ph.2:9).
"Who *is* he that condemneth? *It is* Christ that died, yea rather, that is risen again, who is even at the right hand of God, who also maketh intercession for us" (Ro.8:34).
"Therefore will I divide him a portion with the great, and he shall divide the spoil with the strong; because he hath poured out his soul unto death: and he was numbered with the transgressors; and he bare the sin of many, and made intercession for the transgressors" (Is.53:12).

E.   THE GOLD MEDALLION OR DIADEM, Ex.28:36-38; 39:30-31

THE FACTS CONCERNING THE GOLD MEDALLION	WHAT IS TAUGHT BY THE GOLD MEDALLION	HOW CHRIST FULFILLED THE SYMBOLISM
1. The facts: The gold medallion was worn on the turban, the headdress cloth or cap. The gold medallion was most significant, the crowning piece of the priestly garments. Note the special instructions for the gold medallion: a. It was engraved with these words: HOLY TO THE LORD (v.36). It is important to note where this medallion was to be worn: on the forehead of the High Priest. What a great proclamation to wear such inspiring words as a testimony to the LORD: HOLY TO THE LORD. b. It was attached to the front of the turban by a blue cord (v.37).	2. What the Gold Medallion taught: There was a twofold symbol: ⇒ The Gold Medallion symbolized that the High Priest bore the guilt for the shortcomings of the people. ⇒ The Gold Medallion symbolized that the people must seek the acceptance of a holy God.	3. How Jesus Christ fulfilled the symbolism of the Gold Medallion: a. It is Jesus Christ who bore the guilt for the shortcomings and errors of the people. Man needs a perfect Sacrifice. Jesus Christ is that sacrifice "Who gave himself for us, that he might redeem us from all iniquity, and purify unto himself a peculiar people, zealous of good works" (Tit.2:14). "For Christ also hath once suffered for sins, the just for the unjust, that he might bring us to God, being put to death in the flesh, but quickened by the Spirit" (1 Pt. 3:18). b. We must seek the approval of God by approaching God through Christ and Christ alone. "Jesus saith unto him, I am the

		way, the truth, and the life: no man cometh unto the Father, but by me" (Jn.14:6). "Neither is there salvation in any other: for there is none other name under heaven given among men, whereby we must be saved" (Acts 4:12).

F.   THE LINEN TURBANS AND TUNICS, Ex.28:4, 39; 39:27-28

THE FACTS CONCERNING THE LINEN TURBANS & TUNICS	WHAT IS TAUGHT BY THE LINEN TURBANS & TUNICS	HOW CHRIST FULFILLED THE SYMBOLISM
1. The Facts: The turban and tunic (a long coat-like garment) were to be made of fine linen (v.39).	2. What the Linen Turbans and Tunics taught: ⇒ The turban and tunic (a long coat-like garment essentially covering the whole body) are symbolic of putting on God's righteousness. Those who minister in God's name must bear His righteousness. Anything less than God's righteousness is totally insufficient.	3. How Jesus Christ fulfilled the symbolism of the Linen Turbans and Tunics: ⇒ It is Jesus Christ who is the righteousness of God. "I put on righteousness, and it clothed me: my judgment was as a robe and a diadem" (Job 29:14). "I will greatly rejoice in the LORD, my soul shall be joyful in my God; for he hath clothed me with the garments of salvation, he hath covered me with the robe of righteousness, as a bridegroom decketh himself with ornaments, and as a bride adorneth herself with her jewels" (Is.61:10). "But of him are ye in Christ Jesus, who of God is made unto us wisdom, and righteousness, and sanctification, and redemption" (1 Cor.1:30). "For he hath made him to be sin for us, who knew no sin; that we might be made the righteousness of God in him" (2 Cor.5:21).

G.   THE LINEN HEADBAND, Ex.28:40; 39:28

THE FACTS CONCERNING THE LINEN HEADBAND	WHAT IS TAUGHT BY THE LINEN HEADBAND	HOW CHRIST FULFILLED THE SYMBOLISM
1. The Facts: Linen headbands were made for the priests (v.28).	2. What the Linen Headband taught: ⇒ The linen headbands were of course worn on the head. They were symbolic of the believer's mind and will being subjected to God. The believer is to willingly submit his will, his thoughts, and his own personal agenda to God.	3. How Christ fulfilled the symbolism of the Linen Headband: ⇒ It is Jesus Christ who has established His Lordship over every thought, every idea, every scheme of man. "Teach me to do thy will; for thou art my God: thy spirit is good; lead me into the land of uprightness" (Ps.143:10). "I beseech you therefore, brethren, by the mercies of God, that ye present your bodies a living sacrifice, holy, acceptable unto God, which is your reasonable service. And be not conformed to this world: but be ye transformed by the renewing of your mind, that ye may prove what is that good, and acceptable, and perfect, will of God" (Ro.12:1-2). "Not with eyeservice, as menpleasers; but as the servants of Christ, doing the will of God from

		the heart" (Eph.6:6). "Casting down imaginations, and every high thing that exalteth itself against the knowledge of God, and bringing into captivity <u>every thought</u> to the obedience of Christ" (2 Cor. 10:5).

H.   THE LINEN UNDERCLOTHING, Ex.28:42-43; 39:28

THE FACTS CONCERNING THE LINEN UNDERCLOTHING	WHAT IS TAUGHT BY THE LINEN UNDERCLOTHING	HOW CHRIST FULFILLED THE SYMBOLISM
1. The Facts: The undergarments were made of fine twisted linen (v.28).	2. What the Linen Underclothing taught: ⇒ The linen underwear was symbolic of covering the believer's spiritual nakedness. The person who is without Christ is exposed and shamed. We must all put on the Lord Jesus Christ and make no provision for the flesh.	3. How Christ fulfilled the symbolism of the Linen Underclothing: ⇒ It is Jesus Christ who covers man with His righteousness, protecting man from exposure and shame before God and man. "Knowing this, that our old man is crucified with him, that the body of sin might be destroyed, that henceforth we should not serve sin" (Ro.6:6). "But put ye on the Lord Jesus Christ, and make not provision for the flesh, to fulfil the lusts thereof" (Ro.13:14). "And have put on the new man, which is renewed in knowledge after the image of him that created him" (Col.3:10). "Teaching us that, denying ungodliness and worldly lusts, we should live soberly, righteously, and godly, in this present world" (Tit.2:12).

II. THE SYMBOLIC LESSONS CONCERNING THE ORDINATION CEREMONY OF THE PRIESTHOOD

A.   THE CEREMONIAL WASHING, Ex.29:4

THE FACTS CONCERNING THE CEREMONIAL WASHING	WHAT IS TAUGHT BY THE CEREMONIAL WASHING	HOW CHRIST FULFILLED THE SYMBOLISM
1. The Facts: The priests were presented and washed with water (a ceremonial washing): this washing was a onetime, once-for-all cleansing, the only time they were washed by Moses. Remember, Moses stood as the mediator between the people and God until the ordination of Aaron. As mediator, Moses spoke and acted for God in appointing the priests.	2. What the Ceremonial Washing taught: a. This washing symbolized spiritual cleansing, a onetime, once-for-all cleansing. It symbolized the moment of salvation and regeneration, of being eternally saved, and the removal of uncleanness and sin (v.4). b. The person who serves God must be clean, morally pure, cleansed from all filthiness of the sinful nature and spirit.	3. How Christ fulfilled the symbolism of the Ceremonial Washing: ⇒ This washing speaks of what Christ has done for all believers. He has washed us and pronounced us "clean" (Jn. 15:3). Christ has made us clean: He has regenerated us, eternally saved us. "Having therefore these promises, dearly beloved, let us cleanse ourselves from all filthiness of the flesh and spirit, perfecting holiness in the fear of God" (2 Cor.7:1). "Help us, O God of our salvation, for the glory of thy name: and deliver us, and purge away our sins, for thy name's sake" (Ps.79:9).

<table>
<tr><td></td><td></td><td>"Wash you, make you clean; put away the evil of your doings from before mine eyes; cease to do evil" (Is.1:16).

"If a man therefore purge himself from these, he shall be a vessel unto honour, sanctified, and meet for the master's use, and prepared unto every good work" (2 Tim.2:21).

"Draw nigh to God, and he will draw nigh to you. Cleanse your hands, ye sinners; and purify your hearts, ye double minded" (Jas.4:8).</td></tr>
</table>

B. THE JUDICIAL CLEANSING, Ex.29:10-14

THE FACTS CONCERNING THE JUDICIAL CLEANSING	WHAT IS TAUGHT BY THE JUDICIAL CLEANSING	HOW CHRIST FULFILLED THE SYMBOLISM
1. The Facts: a. The priests laid their hands on the bull's head b. The priests slaughtered the bull before the LORD c. The priests applied blood to the horns and base of the altar d. The priests took the bad--the flesh, skin, and waste--outside the camp to burn	2. What the Judicial Cleansing taught: a. The act of the priest's laying their hands on the head of the bull symbolized identification, transferring their sins to the animal. b. The slaughter of the bull before the LORD symbolized appeasement and substitution, the substituting of the animal to bear God's judgment. c. The taking of the bad outside the camp... • Symbolized that sin (the bad) had to be taken out of the camp, away from the worshipper. • Symbolized the sin offering: the taking away of sin by the sacrifice of one (Jesus Christ) for another.	3. How Christ fulfilled the Judicial Cleansing: a. God accepted the blood of the sacrifice as payment for the sins of the believer. God accepted the faith of the believer and counted him righteous (forgiven) when he identified with the sacrificed animal. b. God's wrath toward sin can only be appeased by a sacrifice. The only sacrifice that has ever satisfied God's eternal wrath was the Lamb who was slaughtered on the cross. c. It was Jesus Christ who fulfilled this symbol of taking the bad (sinful, evil) outside the camp. He fulfilled the symbol by His own death on the cross when He was *crucified outside* the walls of Jerusalem on Calvary. "For when we were yet without strength, in due time Christ died for the ungodly" (Ro.5:6). "For this is my blood of the new testament, which is shed for many for the remission of sins" (Mt. 26:28). "But God commendeth his love toward us, in that, while we were yet sinners, Christ died for us. Much more then, being now justified by his blood, we shall be saved from wrath through him. For if, when we were enemies, we were reconciled to God by the death of his Son, much more, being reconciled, we shall be saved by his life. And not only so, but we also joy in God through our Lord Jesus Christ, by whom we have now received the atonement" (Ro.5:8-11). "For he hath made him to be sin for us, who knew no sin; that we might be made the righteousness of God in him" (2 Cor. 5:21). (cp.Tit.2:14; Heb.9:14; Heb.13:12)

C. THE TOTAL DEDICATION OF LIFE: THE SACRIFICE OF THE FIRST RAM AS THE BURNT OFFERING, Ex.29:15-18

THE FACTS CONCERNING THE FIRST RAM & ITS SACRIFICE	WHAT IS TAUGHT BY THE FIRST RAM & ITS SACRIFICE	HOW CHRIST FULFILLED THE SYMBOLISM
1. The Facts: a. The priests were to lay their hands on the ram's head (v.15). b. The priests were to slaughter the ram and sprinkle blood on all sides of the altar (v.16). c. The priests were to cut the ram into pieces and wash the inner parts and legs (v.17). d. The priests were to burn all the parts on the altar so the pleasing aroma would ascend up toward heaven (v.18).	2. What the sacrifice of the First Ram taught: a. The act of the priest's laying their hands on the head of the bull symbolized identification, transferring their sins to the animal. b. God accepted the person's sacrifice and dedication.	3. How Christ fulfilled the symbolism of the First Ram and its sacrifice: a. God accepted the blood of the sacrifice as payment for the sins of the believer. God accepted the faith of the believer and counted him righteous (forgiven) when he identified with the sacrificed animal. b. God accepted Christ's sacrifice and dedication on behalf of every believer. c. Christ gave His life willingly, unconditionally, that men might come to know the truth and spend eternity with God. **"But he was wounded for our transgressions, he was bruised for our iniquities: the chastisement of our peace was upon him; and with his stripes we are healed. All we like sheep have gone astray; we have turned every one to his own way; and the LORD hath laid on him the iniquity of us all" (Is.53:5-6).** **"Yet it pleased the LORD to bruise him; he hath put him to grief: when thou shalt make his soul an offering for sin, he shall see his seed, he shall prolong his days, and the pleasure of the LORD shall prosper in his hand" (Is.53:10).** **"Who gave himself for our sins, that he might deliver us from this present evil world, according to the will of God and our Father" (Gal.1:4).** **"And walk in love, as Christ also hath loved us, and hath given himself for us an offering and a sacrifice to God for a sweetsmelling savour" (Eph.5:2).** **"And they sung a new song, saying, Thou art worthy to take the book, and to open the seals thereof: for thou wast slain, and hast redeemed us to God by thy blood out of every kindred, and tongue, and people, and nation" (Rev.5:9).**

D. THE CONSECRATION TO SERVICE: THE SACRIFICE OF A SECOND RAM, Ex.29:19-21

THE FACTS CONCERNING THE SECOND RAM & ITS SACRIFICE	WHAT IS TAUGHT BY THE SECOND RAM & ITS SACRIFICE	HOW CHRIST FULFILLED THE SYMBOLISM
1. The Facts: a. The priests laid their hands on its head (v.19). b. The priests slaughtered the ram and put some blood...	2. What the sacrifice of the Second Ram taught: a. A person is to believe God, to trust that He accepts and forgives the person who truly believes and	3. How Christ fulfilled the symbolism of the Second Ram and its sacrifice: ⇒ Jesus Christ was fully consecrated to the service of God: He obeyed His Father perfectly.

• on the tip of the right ear: setting it apart to listen (v.20). • on the thumb of the right hand: setting it apart to touch and do only righteous things (v.20). • on the big toe of the right foot: setting it apart to walk in the ways of God (v.20). • on all sides of the altar (v.20). c. The priests mixed some blood and anointing oil and sprinkled the mixed oil and blood on the priests and their clothes (v.21).	identifies with the sacrificed animal. b. The purpose symbolized full consecration to the service of God. ⇒ A person is to dedicate and sanctify (set apart) his ears to God ⇒ A person is to dedicate and sanctify (set apart) his fingers to do good ⇒ A person is to dedicate and sanctify (set apart) his feet to walk in the ways of God	He dedicated Himself--His entire body--to do His Father's will. **"But that the world may know that I love the Father; and as the Father gave me commandment, even so I do. Arise, let us go hence" (Jn.14:31).** **"If ye keep my commandments, ye shall abide in my love; even as I have kept my Father's commandments, and abide in his love" (Jn.15:10).** **"For as by one man's disobedience many were made sinners, so by the obedience of one shall many be made righteous" (Ro.5:19).** **"Though he were a Son, yet learned he obedience by the things which he suffered" (Heb.5:8).** **"Then said he, Lo, I come to do thy will, O God. He taketh away the first, that he may establish the second" (Heb.10:9).**

E. THE COMMITMENT TO GIVE GOD THE BEST: THE CEREMONY OF TWO WAVE OFFERINGS, Ex.29:22-28

THE FACTS CONCERNING THE TWO WAVE OFFERINGS	WHAT IS TAUGHT BY THE TWO WAVE OFFERINGS	HOW CHRIST FULFILLED THE SYMBOLISM
1. The Facts: a. The fat and choice parts were to be cut away from the ram of ordination (v.22). b. One loaf of unleavened bread, one cake, and one wafer from the basket (v.23) were to be taken by the priests. They were then to lift them up and wave them before the LORD as a wave offering (v.24). c. After waving them before the LORD, these items were to be burned upon the altar as a burnt offering of pleasing aroma to the LORD (v.25). d. The breast and shoulder of the ram were also to be lifted and waved before the LORD (v.26). God gave two specific reasons for this: 1) To sanctify--set apart as holy-- the parts of the rams that belonged to the priests (v.27). 2) To stress that these parts were to be given to the priests when making fellowship offerings [thanksgiving or peace offerings] (v.28).	2. What the Ceremony of the Two Wave Offerings taught: ⇒ Note that only the choice parts were given to God. The two Wave Offerings symbolized that only the very best should ever be offered to God. Only the very best pleases Him. God accepts only the very best.	3. How Christ fulfilled the symbolism of the Two Wave Offerings: ⇒ Jesus Christ gave only the very best to His Father. Therefore, God the Father was well pleased with Jesus Christ in all things. Everything that Christ said, thought, and did was acceptable to the LORD. **"And lo a voice from heaven, saying, This is my beloved Son, in whom I am well pleased" (Mt.3:17).** **"While he yet spake, behold, a bright cloud overshadowed them: and behold a voice out of the cloud, which said, This is my beloved Son, in whom I am well pleased; hear ye him" (Mt.17:5).** **"And there came a voice from heaven, saying, Thou art my beloved Son, in whom I am well pleased" (Mk.1:11).** **"And the Holy Ghost descended in a bodily shape like a dove upon him, and a voice came from heaven, which said, Thou art my beloved Son; in thee I am well pleased" (Lk.3:22).** **"For he received from God the Father honour and glory, when there came such a voice to him from the excellent glory, This is my beloved Son, in whom I am well pleased" (2 Pt.1:17).**

INDEX

OUTLINE AND SUBJECT INDEX

REMEMBER: When you look up a subject & turn to the Scripture reference, you have not only the Scripture, you have an outline & a discussion (commentary) of the Scripture & subject.

This is one of the GREAT VALUES of The Preacher's Outline & Sermon Bible®. Once you have all the volumes, you will have not only what all other Bible indexes give you, that is, a list of all the subjects & their Scripture references, BUT you will also have...

- An outline of every Scripture & subject in the Bible.
- A discussion (commentary) on every Scripture & subject.
- Every subject supported by other Scriptures or cross references.

DISCOVER THE GREAT VALUE for yourself. Quickly glance below to the very first subject of the Index of Exodus. It is:

AARON
Dedication of. **A.** as High Priest.   Ex.29:1-46; 40:12-13

Turn to the reference. Glance at the Scripture & outline of the Scripture, then read the commentary. You will immediately see the GREAT VALUE of the INDEX of The Preacher's Outline & Sermon Bible®.

OUTLINE & SUBJECT INDEX

AARON
Dedication of. A. as High Priest. 29:1-46; 40:12-13
Discussed.
A. saw God. 24:9-11
God told Moses to bring A. up the mountain with him. 19:24
Had to be anointed with oil. Reason for. 30:30
Had to worship from afar. Reasons for. 24:1-2
Excuses to Moses. List.
Accused Moses of being gone too long. 32:23
Accused the people of being set & prone to do evil. 32:22
Accused the people of forcing him to sin & commit evil. 32:23
Suggested that a miracle had happened in molding the golden calf. 32:24
Family of.
Children. Nadab, Abihu, Eleazar, Ithamar. 28:1
Wife. Elisheba. 24:1, D.S.#1
Garments of. High Priest.
Breastpiece or chestpiece. 28:15-30; 39:8-21
Ephod. 28:6-14; 39:2-7
Gold medallion. 28:36; 39:30-31
Headband. 28:40; 39:27-29
Robe of the ephod. 28:31-35; 39:22-26
Sash. 28:39-40; 39:27-29
Tunic. 28:39-40; 39:27-29
Turban. 28:39-40; 39:27-29
Underclothing. 28:42; 39:27-29
Nature. Weak. Aaron gave in to the crowd & caused a terrible sin. 32:1-2
Work - Ministry of. As High Priest.
To burn incense on the Altar of Incense. 30:7-8
To keep the lamps burning. 27:21
To look after the people while Moses was away. 24:12-18
To purify the altar by placing blood on its horns. 30:10
To serve as the High Priest. 28:1-3
To wash his hands & feet at the Bronze Wash Basin. 30:17-21

ABIDE - ABIDING (See IN CHRIST)

ABIHU
Discussed. Aaron & Elisheba's second oldest son. 24:1, D.S.#2

ABILITY
Discussed. God gives the person whatever skills & a. are needed to do the work. 31:4-5, Thgt.1

ABORTION (See MURDER)
Discussed.
The needs of the mother who has aborted her child. 20:13, D.S.#1, pt.4
What the Bible says about the creation of man & the unborn baby in the womb. 20:13, D.S.#1, pt.1
What the medical profession says about the unborn child in the mother's womb. 20:13, D.S.#1, pt.2
When the unborn child becomes a human being. 20:13, D.S.#1, pt.3
Meaning. The killing of unborn babies. 20:13, D.S.#1

ABRAHAM
Example of. A. rose up early & worked for God. 34:2,4
Promises to. Discussed. 19:5-6, D.S.#1

ABRAHAMIC COVENANT (See COVENANT, ABRAHAMIC)

ABUNDANT - ABUNDANCE (See OFFERINGS)

ACACIA
Geographical area. 25:5

ACACIA WOOD
Discussed. 25:5; 30:1
Type - Symbol of. The incorruptibility & perfection of Jesus Christ. 25:5, pt.6, Thgt. 1; Intro.VI, pt.5

ACCESS
Available. Only one way to approach God. 25:9

ADAM
Fact. Originally no barriers between God & A. & Eve. 27:1-21

ADULTERY - ADULTERESS
Benefits of not committing a. 20:14, D.S.#2
Caused by - Is committed.
By any one of five acts. 20:17, D.S.#3, pt.3
List. 20:14, Note 2
Christ & His teaching concerning a. & man's family. 20:14, D.S.#3
Consequences of committing a. 20:14, D.S.#1
Fact. A. is not the unforgivable sin. 20:14, D.S.#3, pt.5
Kinds of a. Mental a. Desiring & lusting. 20:14, Note 2, pt.1c
Meaning. Expanded by Christ. 20:14, Note 2, pt.2
Protection from a. List. 20:14, Note 3
Seriousness of.
Corrupts sex. 20:14, Note 2, pt.3
Discussed. Impact upon society. Intro. 20:14

AGNOSTIC-AGNOSTICISM
Discussed. Commandment directed to the a. Intro. 20:3

ALTAR OF BURNT OFFERING (See TABERNACLE)
Chart. How Christ fulfilled the symbolism of the Tabernacle. Resource Chart 2, VIII
Construction of.
Discussed. 38:1-7
Instructions for construction. 27:1-8; 38:1-7
Set up. 40:29
Fact. The bronze & wood were a fireproof combination. 27:1-8, pt.3
Horns of the A. Type - Symbol of. 27:1-8, pt.2; Intro. VI, pt.19
How Christ fulfilled the symbolism of the A. Resource Chart 2, VIII
Location of.
Inside the walls of the Tabernacle. 38:1-7; Thgt. 2
Near the entrance of the Tabernacle. 40:29
Meaning. 27:1-8, pt.8, Thgt. 2
Question. What kind of a. would man have designed? 27:1-8, pt.8, Thgt. 1

INDEX

Type - Symbol of.
Man's need for atonement, reconciliation with God. 27:1-8, Thgt.1d;
35:16; 38:1-7; Intro. VI, pt.41
The work of the cross.
What is taught by the **A**. Resource Chart
2, VIII

ALTAR OF INCENSE (See **TABERNA-
CLE**)
Chart. How Christ fulfilled the symbol-
ism of the Tabernacle. Resource Chart
2, XI
Construction of.
Discussed. 37:25-29
Instructions for construction. 30:1-10;
37:25-29
Set up. 40:26-27
Discussed.
Burning coals. 30:3
Gold molding. 30:3
Holiness of the **a**. 30:9-10
Horns. 30:2
How Christ fulfilled the symbolism of the
A. Resource Chart 2, XI
Intercessor. (See **JESUS CHRIST**, Me-
diator; Priesthood of)
Christ is the Perfect Intercessor. 30:1-
6, pt.4
Who Christ intercedes for. 30:7-8
Location of. Just outside the inner curtain
(veil). 30:6; 40:26-27
Purpose.
To have a permanent incense ascend-
ing to the LORD. 30:8
To offer up incense to the LORD
every morning & evening. 30:7
Type - Symbol of.
A permanent intercession of the High
Priest. 30:1-10; 35:14; 37:25-29;
Intro. VI, pt.34
The prayers & communion of God's
people ascending to God. 30:1-10;
35:14; 37:25-29; Intro. VI, pt.34
What is taught by the Altar of **I**. Re-
source Chart 2, XI

ANGEL OF THE LORD
Believer's duty. To heed & obey God's
special messenger. 23:20-23, pt.1
Fact. The **A**. had the authority to forgive
or not to forgive sin. 23:20-23, pt.1
Purpose. To protect & guide God's people. 23:20-23
Type - Symbol of. God's very name was
in the **A**. 23:20-23, pt.1
Work of. To serve as God's messenger.
23:20-23

ANGELS (See **ANGEL OF THE LORD**)

ANGER
Caused by. List. 20:13, Note 2, Thgt.2
Discussed. 20:13, Note 2, pt.7
Fact. There is a justified **a**. 20:13, Note
2, pt.7
Kinds.
Justified. 20:13, Note 2, pt.7
Righteous. 32:15-20
The **a**. that broods, that is selfish.
20:13, Note 2, pt.7a
The **a**. that curses. 20:13, Note 2,
pt.7c
The **a**. that holds contempt (raca).
20:13, Note 2, pt.7b

Results of.
The man who fails to control his **a**.
21:12-27, pt.8, Thgt.1

ANIMALS
Control of. Discussed.
Laws to protect human life from dan-
gerous **a**. 21:28-32
Livestock killed by wild **a**. 22:31

ANOINT - ANOINTING
Discussed. 29:7
Duty.
To anoint the Altar of Burnt Offering
& its utensils. 30:26-28
To anoint the Altar of Incense. 30:26-
28
To anoint the Ark of the Covenant.
30:26-28
To anoint the Lampstand & its acces-
sories. 30:26-28
To anoint the priests & sanctify them
for the ministry. 30:30
To anoint the Tabernacle & its furnish-
ings. 30:26-28
To anoint the Table & its utensils.
30:26-28
To anoint the Wash Basin with its
stand. 30:26-28
To sanctify the Tabernacle & its fur-
nishings; to make holy. 30:29
Essential. God's **a**. No minister can serve
God apart from God's **a**. 29:7
Instructions for **a**. To **a**. with oil. 29:7
Warning. The **a**. is not man's to give; it
belongs to God. 30:22-33, Thgt. 1
What God **a**.
People. 30:22-33, Thgt. 1
Things. 30:22-33, Thgt. 1

ANTHROPOMORPHISMS
Examples.
God's back. 33:18-23, pt.4
God's hand. 33:18-23, pt.4
Meaning. 33:18-23, pt.4

APOSTLE - APOSTLES
Example of. The **a**. rose up early &
worked for God. 34:2,4

APPROACH - APPROACHABLE
Discussed.
God is near enough for us to speak to
Him, to have a personal relationship
with Him. 20:2
Instructions on how God was to be **a**.
Three lessons. 20:23-26
Many do not pray because they do not
understand how to **a**. God. 37:25-29
The great lesson of the Tabernacle.
35:1-40:18
Facts.
A great gulf exists between God &
man. 19:11-16, pt.2; 19:16-25, pt.2;
20:18, Thgt.1; 20:18; 24:1-2
God's appointed mediator alone can
approach God. 24:1-2
We must be exact & careful in our **a**.
& worship of God. 35:1-40:18
To God.
Must be **a**. ever so carefully--in rever-
ence, awe, & fear. 26:31-35
Our Mediator, Jesus Christ, ap-
proaches God for us. 20:19

The Ten Commandments teach man
how God is to be **a**. & worshipped.
20:23-26
Type - Symbol of. The Courtyard of the
Tabernacle symbolized that God can be
approached. 27:9-19; Intro. VI, pt.21;
Resource Chart 2, IX

ARCHITECT
Description of God. 25:1
Why God had to be the Tabernacle's **a**.
25:1

ARGUE - ARGUMENTS
Discussed. Restitution required for any
injury caused by a quarrel or fight.
21:18-19

ARK
Meaning of the three arks mentioned in
Scripture. 25:10-16, Thgt. 2

ARK OF GOD
Chart. How Christ fulfilled the symbol-
ism of the Tabernacle. Resource Chart
2, I
Construction of.
Discussed. 25:10-16; 25:21-22; 37:1-
5; 40:20
Instructions for construction. 25:10-
16; 25:21-22; 37:1-5
Set up. 40:20-21
Facts.
Held the Testimony [the Ten Com-
mandments]. 40:20
Mentioned over 200 times in the Bi-
ble. 25:10-16
How Christ fulfilled the symbolism of the
A. Resource Chart 2, I
Names of. 25:10-16
Placement of. 40:20-21
Purpose of. Four purposes listed. 25:21-
22
Throne of. (See **THRONE**)
Type - Symbol of.
Christ fulfilling every picture of the
Ark. 25:10-22; 35:10-19; 37:1-5;
40:20; Intro. VI, pt.6
Divine instruction & guidance. The
throne & presence of God. 25:10-
22; 35:10-19; 37:1-5; 40:20; Intro.
VI, pt.6
God's law holding the Ten Com-
mandments. 25:10-22; 35:10-19;
37:1-5; 40:20; Intro. VI, pt.6
God's mercy covered the Mercy Seat.
25:10-22; 35:10-19; 37:1-5; 40:20;
Intro. VI, pt.6
God's special presence revealed.
25:10-22; 35:10-19; 37:1-5; 40:20;
Intro. VI, pt.6
What is taught by the **A**. Resource Chart
2, I

ARK OF THE COVENANT OF GOD
(See **ARK OF GOD**)

ARK OF THE LORD (See **ARK OF
GOD**)

ARK OF THE LORD GOD (See **ARK OF
GOD**)

ARK OF THE TABERNACLE (See **ARK
OF GOD**)

514

ARK OF THE TESTIMONY (See **ARK OF GOD**)

ARMOR OF GOD
Discussed. 39:27-29, Thgt. 4

ART
Religious **a**. Questions about. 20:4-5, pt.1,c

ASSURANCE (See **SECURITY**)

ASTROLOGY (See **SORCERER - SORCERY**)

ATHEIST - ATHEISM
Fact. Has cut himself off from God. Intro. 20:3

ATONEMENT
Discussed. How the Tabernacle offering was to make **a**. for one's life. 30:11-16
Fact. Man needs the **a**. 38:1-7, Thgt. 1
Meaning. 25:17-21

ATONEMENT COVER, The (See **MERCY SEAT**)
Meaning. 25:17-21

ATONEMENT MONEY (See **SILVER**)
Fact. Each Israelite man gave atonement money in the form of silver. 26:15-30, pt.2b; 30:11-16; Intro. VI, pt.35

AUTHORITY
Of man. Over those under his control. 21:12-27, pt.10, Thgt.1
Of the family.
God. 21:12-27, pt.4
The child. 21:12-27, pt.4
The father. 21:12-27, pt.4
The mother. 21:12-27, pt.4

AVENGE - AVENGING
Discussed.
Law of victim protection. 21:24-25, D.S.#3
Refuge, Cities of. 21:13, D.S.#2

AWE (See **HOLINESS, OF GOD; REVERENCE; FEAR, OF GOD**)
Duty. We must reverence & fear God's holiness. 19:11-16, Thgt. 1

BACKSLIDING (See **DISOBEDIENCE**)

BADGER SKINS
Chart. How Christ fulfilled the symbolism of the Tabernacle. Resource Chart 2, V
Construction of.
Described. 26:14, pt.4; 36:19
Discussed. 25:5; 36:19
Instructions for construction. 26:14, pt.4
Set up. 40:19
Type - Symbol of. A picture of separation, of being protected from the world. 26:14, pt.4, Thgt. 1; 36:19; Intro. VI, pt.3

BARRIER (See **GULF**)
Between God & man. Two different worlds. 24:1-2

BASES (See **TABERNACLE**)

BEARING FALSE WITNESS (See **LYING**)

BELIEF - BELIEVING - BELIEFS (See **FAITH**)
Essential - Importance of. In God & God alone. 20:3

BELIEVER - BELIEVERS
Duty - Work.
Duty in relation to God.
To get alone with God for long periods of time. 24:12-18, Thgt. 1
To seek first the kingdom of God & His righteousness. 20:17, D.S.#3, pt.4
To seek more & more of God's holy presence & Word. 24:12-18, Thgt. 1
Duty in relation to others.
Must have no part with any verbal abuse against God's people. 20:13, D.S.#5, pt.6
Must never cheat his neighbor. 20:17, D.S.#3, pt.1
Essentials. Work, rest, & worship. Intro. 20:8
Life - Walk - Behavior. The Believer's Life. Discussed. 19:5-6, D.S.#1, pt.2
Names - Titles.
Name is carried by the High Priest before the LORD. 28:6-14; 39:2-7; Intro. VI, pt.26; Resource Chart 3, I:B
Name is known by God. 28:6-14; 39:2-7; Intro. VI, pt.26; Resource Chart 3, I:B
Picture of the believer's life in the Tabernacle. Chart. Resource Chart 1
Position. What God has promised to the **b**. The bread, water, & health of His people. 23:24-26

BENEFITS
Verses. List of.
To those who keep the first commandment. 20:3, DS #2
To those who keep the second commandment. 20:4-6, D.S.#2
To those who keep the third commandment. 20:7, D.S.#2
To those who keep the fourth commandment. 20:11, D.S.#3
To those who keep the fifth commandment. 20:12, D.S.#2
To those who keep the sixth commandment. 20:13, D.S.#4
To those who keep the seventh commandment. 20:14, D.S.#2
To those who keep the eighth commandment. 20:15, D.S.#2
To those who keep the ninth commandment. 20:16, D.S.#2
To those who keep the tenth commandment. 20:17, D.S.#2

BESTIALITY
Discussed. 22:19
Judgment of. To be executed. 22:19
Warning to. Sexual perverts. 22:19, Thgt. 1

BEZALEL
Described as.
A faithful man. Made everything the LORD commanded. 38:21-31
Skilled manager. 36:1-2

Discussed. His final glimpse of the Ark. 40:1-15, pt.3
Equipped. List. 31:4-5; 35:32-33
Fact. God filled **B**. with intelligence, knowledge, & skill in construction. 35:31
Life.
Family heritage. 31:2
Tribe of Judah. 31:2
Meaning of **B**. Under the shadow of God. 31:1-11, pt.1a
Ministry of. Call.
God called **B**. by name. 31:1-11, pt.1a
Overseer of the building of the Tabernacle. 31:1-11, pt.1
Spiritual experiences of. Filled with God's Spirit. 31:3; 35:31

BIBLE (See **WORD OF GOD**)

BLASPHEMY (See **CURSING; SWEARING**)
Caused by.
Belief in false gods. 20:3
Taking God's name in vain. 20:7
Worshipping false gods. 20:4-6

BLESSINGS (See **BELIEVER**, Position; **REWARD; SALVATION**, Results)
What God has promised the believer. The bread, water, & health of His people. 23:24-26

BLIND - BLINDNESS
Type - Symbol of. Moses' veil symbolized Israel's blindness. 34:35; Intro. VI, pt.39

BLOOD (See **JESUS CHRIST**, Blood of)

BLUE, Color of
Type - Symbol of. The heavenly character of Christ. 25:4; Intro. VI, pt.12

BOAST - BOASTING (See **PRIDE**)

BODY OF CHRIST
Discussed. The Tabernacle is a symbol of the body of Christ. 25:1-31:18

BONDAGE (See **SLAVERY**)

BOOK OF LIFE (See **LIFE, BOOK OF**)

BOOK OF THE LIVING
Fact. Records the names of believers. 32:30-32, pt.3c

BRASS (See **BRONZE**)

BRAZEN ALTAR (See **ALTAR OF BURNT OFFERING**)

BREAD (See **SHOWBREAD**)

BREAD OF LIFE (See **SHOWBREAD**)

BREASTPIECE (See **CHESTPIECE; HIGH PRIEST**)

BRIBE - BRIBERY
Results of. List. 23:8

BRONZE
Fact.
Overlaid the Altar of Burnt Offering. 27:1-8, pt.3

INDEX

The primary metal in the Courtyard of the Tabernacle. 38:9-20
Type - Symbol of. The death of Christ. 25:3; Intro. VI, pt.20

BRONZE ALTAR (See **ALTAR OF BURNT OFFERING, THE**)

BRONZE WASH BASIN (See **WASH BASIN, BRONZE**)

BROTHERHOOD (See **UNITY**)

BUILD - BUILDERS - BUILDING (See **TABERNACLE**)
Of the Tabernacle.
Bezalel was the superintendent. 31:1-11
God was the architect of the Tabernacle. 25:1
Oholiab was the assistant superintendent. 31:1-11

BULL
Sacrifice of. 29:10-11
Type - Symbol of. Christ as the sin-bearer of the world. 29:10-11

BURNT OFFERING
Discussed. Instructions given. 29:10-11; 29:15-18
Duty. To give all that we are & all that we have to God. 29:15-18
Meaning. 29:15-18
Type - Symbol of.
Christ as the sin-bearer of the world. 29:10-11
God accepting the person's sacrifice & dedication. 29:15-18

BUSINESS
Discussed. What it takes to build a successful b. Intro. 35:1-35

CALF, THE GOLDEN (See **IDOLS - IDOLATRY**)
Described as. A picture of man's corrupt heart & rebellion against God. 32:1-35
Facts.
Moses burned it, ground it into powder, scattered it on the water, made the people drink the water 32:20
The people proclaimed the g. c. to be the god who had saved & delivered them. 32:4
Source - Origin.
Aaron made it from the gold of the people's earrings. 32:3
Aaron molded it into the shape of a golden calf. 32:4
Type - Symbol of.
Man's corrupt heart & rebellion against God. 32:7-10
The people's contamination, disobedience, idolatry, immorality. 32:20

CALL - CALLED (See **DISCIPLE - DISCIPLES**)
Duty.
Demands faithfulness, personal responsibility. 28:1-5, pt.2, Thgt. 1
Demands great & careful diligence. 28:1-5, pt.2, Thgt. 1
Requires a person to walk worthy of God. 28:1-5, pt.2, Thgt. 1
To worship God. 24:1-2
Nature of.

A glorious call & hope. 28:1-5, pt.2, Thgt. 1
A heavenly calling. 28:1-5, pt.2, Thgt. 1
A high calling, ultimate goal for life. 28:1-5, pt.2, Thgt. 1
A holy calling. 28:1-5, pt.2, Thgt. 1
An eternal call. 28:1-5, pt.2, Thgt. 1
God always calls a person by name. 31:1-11, pt.1, Thgt. 1
Limited.
Unique, one of a kind. 28:1-5, pt.2, Thgt. 1
A great gulf between God & man. 24:1-2
God's appointed Mediator alone can approach God. 24:1-2
Of God.
Every believer is c. to build God's church here upon the earth. 35:1
Fact. No greater c. than the c. of God. 39:1
Source. God.
He always takes the initiative & does the calling. 28:1
He calls & always equips. 31:4-5, Thgt. 1
Made possible because of the gospel. 28:1-5, pt.2, Thgt. 1
No greater c. 39:1
To what. (See **CALL, Purpose**)
To be representatives of God, mediators between God & man. 28:1
To offer gifts & sacrifices for sin. 28:1
To pray & make strong intercession for the people. 28:1
To set the priests apart from all other people so they could serve God. 28:1
To show compassion for the ignorant & to people going astray. 28:1
To teach the people. 28:1

CANDLESTICK, THE GOLD (See **LAMPSTAND, THE GOLD**)

CAPITAL PUNISHMENT
Discussed. 20:13, Note 2

CARNAL - CARNALITY (See **FLESH**)

CEREMONIAL WASHING (See **PRIESTHOOD; CLEAN**)
How Christ fulfilled the symbolism of the C.W. Resource Chart 3, II:A
Type - Symbol of.
A person being washed in order to be saved by God. Resource Chart 3, II:A
A person being washed in order to serve God. Resource Chart 3, II:A
What is taught by the C.W. Resource Chart 3, II:A

CEREMONY - CEREMONIAL LAW (See **LAW, The; COVENANT, MOSAIC**)
Defined as. The commandments governing the sacrificial system. Div.VI, Overview
Discussed.
Annual feasts.
Harvest. 23:16
Ingathering. 23:16
Unleavened bread. 23:15

Idolatry. 23:13
Moral cleansing. 29:4
Offerings to God. 23:19
Passover. 23:18
The two Sabbaths. 23:10-12

CHARMS (See **OCCULT; IDOLATRY**)
List of lucky c. 20:4-5, pt.1c

CHART
How Christ fulfilled the symbolism of the Priesthood. Resource Chart 3
How Christ fulfilled the symbolism of the Tabernacle. Resource Chart 2
Listed.
Christ & His teaching concerning the Ten Commandments.
His t. concerning adultery & man's family. 20:14, D.S.#3;
His t. concerning false gods. 20:3, D.S.#3;
His t. concerning God's name. 20:7, D.S.#3;
His t. concerning man's parents. 20:12, D.S.#3;
His t. concerning man's word & character. 20:16, D.S.#3;
His t. concerning murder. 20:13, D.S.#5;
His t. concerning our neighbor's property. 20:17, D.S.#3
His t. concerning stealing. 20:15, D.S.#3;
His t. concerning the Sabbath Day. 20:8-11, D.S.#4;
His t. concerning the worship of God. 20:4-6, D.S.#3;
Lampstand ornaments. 25:31-39
The Great "I AM's" of God & Christ. 20:2, D.S.#1
The picture of the believer's life in the Tabernacle. Resource Chart 1
Types, Symbols, Pictures. Complete chart of. Intro. VI, pts.1-41

CHASTISEMENT - CHASTISED (See **CHURCH DISCIPLINE; DISCIPLINE**)
Response to.
Stirred to seek the LORD. 33:8
Stirred to worship the LORD. 33:10
Type - Symbol of. God withdraws His presence. 33:7-11
Verses. List of. 33:7-11, Thgt. 1
Why a believer is c.
Because God loves him. 33:7-11
To correct & discipline him. 33:7-11
To keep us from harming ourselves & others. 32:34-35

CHERUBIM
Construction of.
Discussed. 25:17-21; 37:6-9
Overshadowed the Mercy Seat. 25:17-21; 37:6-9

CHEST OF GOD (See **ARK OF GOD**)

CHESTPIECE (See **HIGH PRIEST**)
Chart. How Christ fulfilled the symbolism of the Tabernacle. Resource Chart 3, I:C
Discussed. 28:15-30; 39:8-21
How Christ fulfilled the symbolism of the c. Resource Chart 3, I:C
Instructions for making c. 28:15-30; 39:8-21

516

What is forbidden by this commandment? 20:14, Note 2
What is the decision required by this commandment? 20:14, Note 3
Who is to obey? *You.* 20:14, Note 1
Ten Commandments: #8, Never steal.
Benefits of keeping this commandment. 20:15, DS #2
Consequences of breaking this commandment. 20:15, DS #1
How long to obey? *Always.* 20:15, Note 1
What is forbidden by this commandment? 20:15, Note 2
What is the decision required by this commandment? 20:15, Note 3
Who is to obey? *You.* 20:15, Note 1
Ten Commandments: #9, Never lie or speak falsely against anyone.
Benefits of keeping this commandment. 20:16, DS #2
Consequences of breaking this commandment. 20:16, DS #1
How long to obey? *Always.* 20:16, Note 1
What is forbidden by this commandment? 20:16, Note 2
What is the decision required by this commandment? 20:16, Note 3
Who is to obey? *You.* 20:16, Note 1
Ten Commandments: #10, Never covet.
Benefits of keeping this commandment. 20:17, DS #2
Consequences of breaking this commandment. 20:17, DS #1
How long to obey? *Always.* 20:17, Note 1
What is forbidden by this commandment? 20:17, Note 2
What is the decision required by this commandment? 20:17, Note 3
Who is to obey? *You.* 20:17, Note 1
Duty.
Must keep the Ten Commandments. 31:18
Must learn the importance of the Ten Commandments. 34:27-28
Facts.
Moses received the second copy of the Ten Commandments. 34:1-4
Repeated in the New Testament. Div.VII, Overview, pt.4
The Bible does not number the Ten Commandments. (Done by different commentators) Div.VII, Overview, pt.3
The Ten Commandments are the great gift of God to man. 31:18
The Ten Commandments are the very basis of man's relationship with God. 34:27-28
The Ten Commandments were kept in the Ark of God. 25:16; 25:21-22
Universal. The Ten Commandments are timeless & universal. Div.VII, Overview, pt.7
Form.
All Ten Commandments are stated as moral absolutes. Div.VII, Overview, pt.6a
All Ten Commandments are written in the second person singular, *"you."* Div.VII, Overview, pt.6b
Eight of the Ten Commandments are stated negatively. Div.VII, Overview, pt.6c

The first four commandments concern man's relationship to God. Div.VII, Overview, pt.6d
The last six commandments concern man's relationship to others. Div.VII, Overview, pt.6d
Two of the Ten Commandments are stated positively. Div.VII, Overview, pt.6c
Jesus Christ. His teaching concerning the Ten Commandments. Div.VII, Overview, pt.9
His t. concerning adultery & man's family. 20:14, D.S.#3;
His t. concerning false gods. 20:3, D.S.#3;
His t. concerning God's name. 20:7, D.S.#3;
His t. concerning man's parents. 20:12, D.S.#3;
His t. concerning man's word & character. 20:16, D.S.#3;
His t. concerning murder. 20:13, D.S.#5;
His t. concerning our neighbor's property. 20:17, D.S.#3
His t. concerning stealing. 20:15, D.S.#3;
His t. concerning the Sabbath Day. 20:8-11, D.S.#4;
His t. concerning the worship of God. 20:4-6, D.S.#3;
Listed.
Commandment 1: Never believe in false gods. 20:3
Commandment 2: Never make nor worship false gods. 20:4-6
Commandment 3: Never misuse God's name, never use vulgarity. 20:7
Commandment 4: Never fail to remember the Sabbath, to keep it holy. 20:8-11
Commandment 5: Never dishonor parents. 20:12
Commandment 6: Never kill. 20:13
Commandment 7: Never commit adultery or immorality. 20:14
Commandment 8: Never steal. 20:15
Commandment 9: Never lie or speak falsely against anyone. 20:16
Commandment 10: Never covet anything that belongs to a neighbor. 20:17
Results of.
Great influence upon Western culture. Div.VII, Overview, pt.1
Not keeping the Sabbath. 35:2-3, Thgt. 2
Why God gave the Ten Commandments to man.
To reveal man's need for a mediator. 20:19
To reveal the glorious majesty & holiness of God. 20:18
To teach how God is to be approached & worshipped. 20:23-26
To teach that God alone is the LORD. 20:22
To test man. 20:20-21

COMMIT - COMMITMENT (See **DEDICATION - DEVOTION**)
Call to c.
To give God the best. 29:22-28

To make a renewed **c**. to obey God. 34:10-11
To make a total **c**. to God. 24:3
To seal one's **c**. to God. 24:4-8
Described. As a formal agreement (covenant) with God. 24:4-8

COMMUNICATE - COMMUNICATING
Fact. God **c**. with man. 20:1, Note 2

COMMUNION (See **FEASTS, RELIGIOUS; FELLOWSHIP MEAL**)

COMPLAIN - COMPLAINING
Caused by. Impatience. 32:1-6, pt.1

CONDITION - CONDITIONAL
Fact. The Israelites had to obey God in order to receive the blessings & promises of the covenant. Div.VI, Overview

CONFESS - CONFESSION (See **RESTORATION**)

CONQUEST
Discussed. God promised to give His people the promised land. 23:27-33

CONSECRATION (See **COMMITMENT; CROSS, DAILY; DEDICATION; HEART**)
Discussed.
How the people were to sanctify & **c**. themselves. 19:10
How the priests were to sanctify & **c**. themselves. 29:1-46
Meaning. 29:19-21
Of whom - Of what.
The burnt offering of the first ram. 29:15-18
The repetition of the ordination ceremony. 29:35-37
The sacrifice of the second ram. 29:19-21
Type - Symbol of. Full **c**. to the service of God. 29:19-21; Resource Chart 3, II:D

CONSEQUENCE - CONSEQUENCES
Warning. Verses. List of.
The **c**. of a false worship. 20:4-6, D.S.#1
The **c**. of committing adultery. 20:14, D.S.#1
The **c**. of coveting. 20:17, D.S.#1
The **c**. of failing to honor your father & your mother. 20:12, D.S.#1
The **c**. of failing to keep the Sabbath & to keep it holy. 20:11, D.S.#2
The **c**. of having other gods, of believing in other gods. 20:3, D.S.#1
The **c**. of killing another person. 20:13, D.S.#3
The **c**. of lying. 20:16, D.S.#1
The **c**. of misusing God's name. 20:7, D.S.#1
The **c**. of stealing. 20:15, D.S.#1

CONSTRUCTION (See **TABERNACLE**)

CONTENTION (See **ARGUE**)

CONVERSION (See **RENEW - RENEWAL**)

INDEX

DESIRE (See **LUST**)
Bad & evil **d**. The power of **d**. Discussed. Intro. 20:17

DEVOTION - DEVOTIONS (See **COMMITMENT; COMMUNION; QUIET TIME**)
Example of. Moses met God early in the morning. 34:2,4

DIADEM (See **MEDALLION, GOLD**)

DIGNITY (See **PRIESTHOOD, Call of**)

DISCIPLE - DISCIPLES (See **APOSTLES; BELIEVERS; DISCIPLESHIP; LABORERS; MINISTERS**)
Example of. Jesus' **d**. rose up early & worked for God. 34:2,4

DISCIPLESHIP (See **DISCIPLE - DISCIPLES**)

DISCIPLINE (See **CHASTISEMENT - CHASTISED**)

DISCRIMINATION (See **FAVORITISM**)

DISOBEDIENCE (See **BACKSLIDING; OBEDIENCE; SIN; TRANSGRESSION; UNBELIEF**)
Discussed. Warnings against making any idol or worshipping any false god. 20:4-5; 20:4-6, D.S.#1

DIVISION (See **ARGUE**)

DIVORCE
Caused by. Adultery & sexual immorality. 20:14, D.S.#3, pt.4
Discussed. Three unions are broken. 20:14, D.S.#3, pt.4

DOOR (See **ENTRANCE GATE; VEIL, INNER; VEIL, OUTER**)

DOWRY
Discussed. Hebrew females sold for marriage. 21:7-11

DRESS (See **CLOTHING**)

DRUNKENNESS
Results. In immorality. 32:1-6, pt.9

DWELL - DWELLING
Purpose of the Tabernacle. That God would have a place to **d**. 25:1-31:18

EAGLES
Symbol of deliverance. 19:1-4

EAT - EATING
Described. As partying, drinking, carousing. 32:1-6, pt.9

EDIFY - EDIFICATION
How a man **e**. a woman. By reaching her for Christ & building her up in the eyes of the world. 21:7-11, Thgt.4

EGYPT
Type - Symbol of. The world. Intro. 19:1-25; 34:18; 40:1-15

EMBARRASS - EMBARRASSED - EMBARRASSMENT
Caused by. Terrible sin. 32:21-24
Characteristic - Trait of. What a person does when **e**. Not accepting responsibility for sin but making excuses for sin. 32:21-24

EMPLOYEE - EMPLOYER - EMPLOYMENT (See **WORK, PHYSICAL OR SECULAR**)

ENEMIES
Duty toward.
To help one's **e**. 23:4-5
To love one's **e**. 23:4-5, Thgt. 1
To protect the property of one's **e**. 23:4-5

ENEMIES OF GOD
Judgment & the end of. Shall be defeated by God. 23: 23; 34:10-11

ENTRANCE GATE (See **TABERNACLE**)
Chart. How Christ fulfilled the symbolism of the Tabernacle. Resource Chart 2, X
Construction of.
Discussed. 38:18-19
Instructions for construction. 26:36-37; 27:16, pt.6
Set up. 40:33
How Christ fulfilled the symbolism of the **g**. Resource Chart 2, X
Type - Symbol of.
God has to be approached. 27:16; 35:17; 38:18-19; 39:40; 40:33; Intro. VI, pt.22
God's invitation to man to enter His presence. 27:16; 35:17; 38:18-19, 39:40; 40:33; Intro. VI, pt.22
What is taught by the **g**. Resource Chart 2, X

ENVY
Answer to - Deliverance from. Crucifying the flesh with its affections & lusts; refusing to covet what belongs to a neighbor. 20:17

EPHOD (See **PRIESTHOOD; HIGH PRIEST**)
Chart. How Christ fulfilled the symbolism of the Tabernacle. Resource Chart 3, I:B
Discussed. 28:6-14; 39:2-7
How Christ fulfilled the symbolism of the **e**. Resource Chart 3, I:B
Instructions for making **e**. 28:6-14; 39:2-7
Purpose of. 28:6-14; 39:2-7
Type - Symbol of. Jesus Christ is the One who represents & carries the name of every believer before the LORD God. 28:6-14, Thgt. 1; 39:2-7; Intro. VI, pt.26
What is taught by the **e**. Resource Chart 3, I:B

EQUIPPING
Discussed. The role of the Holy Spirit. 31:4-5

ETERNAL LIFE

Assurance of. Promised to all who keep the Ten Commandments.
To those who keep the first commandment. 20:3, DS #2
To those who keep the second commandment. 20:4-6, D.S.#2
To those who keep the third commandment. 20:7, D.S.#2
To those who keep the fourth commandment. 20:11, D.S.#3
To those who keep the fifth commandment. 20:12, D.S.#2
To those who keep the sixth commandment. 20:13, D.S.#4
To those who keep the seventh commandment. 20:14, D.S.#2
To those who keep the eighth commandment. 20:15, D.S.#2
To those who keep the ninth commandment. 20:16, D.S.#2
To those who keep the tenth commandment. 20:17, D.S.#2

ETHICS
Duty. Must not take bribes. 23:8

EVE
Fact. Originally no barriers between God & Adam & Eve. 27:1-21

EVERLASTING LIFE (See **ETERNAL LIFE**)

EXCUSES
Duty. We must not make **e**. for our sin. 32:21-24, Thgt. 1
List. Aaron's **e**. to Moses.
Accused Moses of being gone too long. 32:23
Accused the people of being set & prone to do evil. 32:22
Accused the people of forcing him to sin & commit the evil. 32:23
Suggested that a miracle had happened in molding the golden calf. 32:24

FAITH (See **BELIEVER**)
Discussed. Seven essential steps involved in the believer's life. Resource Chart 1

FAITH, THE CHRISTIAN (See **FAITH**)

FAITHFUL - FAITHFULNESS
Duty.
Of all believers.
To be **f**. in our work. 39:32-43
To be **f**. in small matters as well as large matters. 20:15, D.S.#3, pt.5
To build the Tabernacle exactly as God had designed. 36:1, pt.2
Example of.
Bezalel made everything God commanded. 38:21-31
Moses did everything God commanded. 40:16-33
The perfect obedience of the people in building the Tabernacle. 39:32-43
The unbelievable **f**. of people in giving. 36:3-7

FALSE WITNESS (See **LIE - LYING - LIAR**)

FAMILY - FAMILIES (See **FATHERS; MOTHERS; PARENTS**)
Children. (See **CHILDREN**)

520

INDEX

Fact. The first institution formed upon earth. Intro. 20:12
Failures - Dangers facing the **f**. Disintegration. 20:12, Note 2
Discussed.
   Mothers are to be honored just as much as fathers. 20:12, Note 3, pt.2
   The divine order of obedience. God first, then our parents. 20:12, Note 3
Duty.
   Children. To honor father & mother. 20:12
   Parents. To teach their children how to honor parents. 20:12, Note 3, pt.4
Meaning. Discussed.
   Honoring parents. 20:12, Note 3
   Obeying parents. 20:12, Note 3, pt.5
Results. Of honoring parents. 20:12, Note 3, pt.3; 20:12, Note 4
Warning. To parents. Never abuse a child. 20:12, Note 3, pt.5

FARMER - FARMING
Discussed. Treatment of the land during the Sabbath year. 23:10-12

FATHER - FATHERS
Duty toward one's **f**. To honor him.
   By accepting the true faith of one's **f**., belief in God's Son. 20:12, Note 3, pt.1
   By being wise, never foolish. 20:12, Note 3, pt.1
   By having a testimony of pure & right behavior. 20:12, Note 3, pt.1
   By honoring & respecting all persons. 20:12, Note 3, pt.1
   By listening to the instructions of one's **f**. 20:12, Note 3, pt.1
   By never despising him when he is old. 20:12, Note 3, pt.1
   By obeying & respecting one's **f**. 20:12, Note 3, pt.1
   By reverencing him when he is old. 20:12, Note 3, pt.1

FAVORITISM
Discussed. Do not show **f**. to a poor man in a lawsuit. 23:1-3, pt.4

FEAR
Kinds.
   Godly **f**. 20:20-21
   Respectful, honoring **f**. 20:20-21
   Tormenting **f**. 20:20-21
   Of God. Duty. We must reverence & **f**. His holiness. 19:11-16, Thgt. 1

FEAST OF HARVEST (WEEKS) (See PENTECOST)
Discussed. 23:16, pt.2
Fact. Refers to Pentecost. 34:22
Purpose. To celebrate the beginning of the law on Mt. Sinai. 23:16

FEAST OF INGATHERING - FEAST OF TABERNACLES
Discussed. 23:16, pt.3
Mentioned. 34:22

FEAST OF PASSOVER (See PASSOVER)

FEAST OF UNLEAVENED BREAD
Discussed. 34:18
Duty.

To celebrate the feast at the appointed time. 23:15
To eat unleavened bread for seven days. 23:15
To heed the warning of God: must not approach Him empty-handed. 23:15

FEASTS, RELIGIOUS
Annual **f**.
   Celebrated both an agricultural & an historical event in the life of the nation. 23:14-17
   Purpose.
      To arouse the people to give thanks, praise, & offerings to God. 23:17, pt.4
      To build unity. 23:17, pt.4
      To keep before the people's minds God's great blessings. 23:17, pt.4
Discussed. Communion or fellowship meal.
Instructions. 29:31-34
Kinds.
   Harvest. 23:16; 34:22
   Ingathering. 23:16; 34:22
   Passover. 23:18
   Unleavened bread. 23:15; 34:18

FEED - FEEDING, SPIRITUAL (See SHOWBREAD)

FELLOWSHIP MEAL (See FEASTS, RELIGIOUS)

FIDELITY (See MARRIAGE)

FINE THREADED LINEN
Type - Symbol of. The purity & righteousness of God. 26:1; Intro. VI, pt.11

FIRST DAY OF THE WEEK (See SABBATH)

FLESH - FLESHLY LUSTS (See LUST)

FOOD (See EAT - EATING)

FORGIVENESS, HUMAN (See ENEMIES)

FORGIVENESS, SPIRITUAL
Duty. To be forgiven of our sin. 38:8
Fact. Every aspect of the Mercy Seat speaks of mercy & **f**. 37:6-9
How one receives. By being morally cleansed by the Lord. 29:4

FORNICATION (See IMMORALITY)
Caused by. (See IMMORALITY)
Discussed. How a person becomes sexually impure. 20:14, Note 2, pt.1

FOUNDATION, SPIRITUAL (See FRAME, TABERNACLE'S)

FRAME, TABERNACLE'S (See TABERNACLE)
Chart. How Christ fulfilled the symbolism of the Tabernacle. Resource Chart 2, V:B
Construction of.
   Discussed. 36:20-34
   Described. 26:15-30; 36:20-34
   Instructions for construction. 26:15-30; 36:20-34
   Set up. 40:17-18

Type - Symbol of.
   The foundation of the Tabernacle. 36:31-33; Intro. VI, pt.16
   The stability & support that Christ gives each believer. 36:20-34, Thgt. 1; Intro. VI, pt.16

FULNESS, SPIRITUAL (See SATISFACTION, SPIRITUAL)

GARMENT - GARMENTS (See CLOTHING)
Chart. How Christ fulfilled the symbolism of the Priesthood. Resource Chart 3, I
Kinds of.
   Breastpiece or chestpiece. 28:15-30; 39:8-21; Intro. VI, pt.28; Resource Chart 3, I:C
   Ephod. 28:6-14; 39:2-7; Intro. VI, pt.26; Resource Chart 3, I:B
   Gold medallion. 28:36-38; 39:30-31; Intro. VI, pt.30; Resource Chart 3, I:E
   Headbands. 28:40; 39:27-29; Intro. VI, pt.32; Resource Chart 3, I:G
   Robe of the ephod. 28:31-35; 39:22-26; Intro. VI, pt.29; Resource Chart 3, I:D
   Sash. 28:40; 39:27-29; Intro. VI, pt.24; Resource Chart 3, I:A
   Tunic. 28:40-41; 39:27-29; Intro. VI, pt.31; Resource Chart 3, I:F
   Turban. 28:40-41; 39:27-29; Intro. VI, pt.31; Resource Chart 3, I:F
   Underclothing. 28:42-43; 39:27-29; Intro. VI, pt.33; Resource Chart 3, I:H
Type - Symbol of. The priesthood. Bringing dignity & honor to the name of God. 28:1-43; 39:1

GATE (See ENTRANCE GATE; VEIL)

GIFT - GIFTS OF GOD & CHRIST
G. of God. The ability to work for God is a **g**. from God. 36:2

GIVE - GIVING (See CROSS, DAILY - SELF-DENIAL; STEWARDSHIP; WORKS)
Discussed.
   The basic law governing the offerings to God. 23:19
   The challenge to give. 36:3-7, Thgt. 2
Facts - Principles.
   Every person has something to offer to God. 25:2, Thgt. 1
   The greatest thing we can give God is an undivided heart. 25:2, Thgt. 1
   Ultimately everything belongs to God. 25:2, Thgt. 1
How to give.
   Must give sacrificially. 25:2
   Must give willingly. 25:2
   Must share with those in need. 25:2, Thgt. 1
Verses. List of. 36:3-7, Thgt. 2

GLORY OF GOD
Described.
   God's **g**. came to the Tabernacle & filled it. 40:34-38
   So brilliant & intense that Moses was unable to draw near God's presence. 40:34-38
   The leaders saw God's glory. 24:9-11

INDEX

Facts.
God is the very embodiment of majestic glory & holiness. 20:18
God showed Moses only what he could endure. 33:21-23
Pillar of cloud & fire. (See **PILLAR OF CLOUD & FIRE**)
Why God's glory filled the Tabernacle. Because of the obedience of the people. 40:34-38

GLORYING IN MAN (See **PRIDE**)

GOAT HAIR COVERING
Chart. How Christ fulfilled the symbolism of the Tabernacle. Resource Chart 2, V:B
Construction of.
Discussed. 25:4; 36:14-18
Instructions for construction. 26:1-14, pt.2
Type - Symbol of.
Christ as the divine Sin-bearer. 25:4; Intro. VI, pt.14
The need for a sin offering. 36:14-18; Intro. VI, pt.14

GOATS--SIN OFFERING (See **SACRIFICE**)
Discussed.
Deeper Study. 26:7-13
Three great lessons learned from the covering of goat skins. 36:14-18, Thgt. 1

GOD
Described.
As Creator of the universe. Intro. 20:3
As Spirit. 20:4-5, pt.2b
As Supreme Being. 20:3
What Moses & his leaders saw.
A shadow of God. 24:10, pt.1
Brilliant blue sapphire stone under God's feet. 24:10, pt.1
What Moses saw. God's back. 33:18-23
Duty toward.
Must never misuse God's name. 20:7
To hallow God's name. 20:7, Note 5
Existence of. Intro. 20:3
Basis of. The Ten Commandments. 20:1
Face of God: no other gods before His face. 20:3
Fact. Has spoken to man & given man the Ten Commandments. 20:22
Forgiveness of. All kinds of wrongs. List of. 34:7
Holiness of. No man can see all of God's holiness & live. 24:9-11
Love of.
For believers.
God knows everything that we do for Him. 39:8-21, Thgt. 1
God knows our every need. 39:8-21, Thgt. 1
God knows the most minute details of our lives, even our thoughts. 39:8-21, Thgt. 1
God knows the pain of every lonely, hurting heart. 39:8-21, Thgt. 1
God knows us personally. 39:8-21, Thgt. 1
God's great love.

Desires a personal, loving relationship with His people. 20:2, Note 4
Verses. List of. 20:2, Note 4
Names - Titles
Deliverer. 20:2, Note 5
Jehovah, Yahweh. 20:2, Note 3; Intro. 20:3
Savior. 20:2, Note 5
The LORD. Meaning of. 20:2, Note 3; 34:5-9
Nature of.
What God is like - Attributes.
Abounds in goodness. 34:6
Executes justice. 34:7
God is holy. 36:35-36, Thgt. 1
Longsuffering. (See **LONGSUFFERING**) 34:5
Loving. 34:7
Merciful. (See **MERCY**, God's) 34:5
Gracious. (See **GRACE**) 34:5
Revealed - revelation of. Is revealed by His name. 34:5-7, pt.1
Person of. God cannot be described in human language. 24:9-11
Presence of.
List of benefits. 25:10-16, Thgt. 1
Warning. Can be withdrawn because of sin. 33:1-3
Sovereignty of. To have mercy & compassion as He wills. 33:19
Warning.
Must not use God's name in a careless, irreverent way. 20:7, Note 3, pt.3
Only One True & Living God. Believe only in Him. Intro. 20:3

GODLY - GODLINESS (See **RIGHTEOUS - RIGHTEOUSNESS**)

GODS, FALSE
Christ & His teaching concerning false gods. 20:3, D.S.#3
Discussed.
Atrocities. 23:24-26, pt.1
Belief in. Causes terrible sin. 32:1-6, pt.4
The law governing idolatry. 23:13
Names of. Mentioned.
Ashtoreth. 23:24-26, pt.1
Baal. 23:24-26, pt.1
Chemosh. 23:24-26, pt.1
Molech. 23:24-26, pt.1
Rimmon. 23:24-26, pt.1
Number worshipped by people: innumerable. Intro. 20:4-6

GOLD
Symbol of value. 25:3
Type - Symbol of. The LORD Himself, of His deity & righteousness. Intro. VI, pt.7

GOLD MEDALLION (See **MEDALLION, GOLD**)

GOLDEN CALF (See **CALF, THE GOLDEN; IDOLS - IDOLATRY**)

GOSPEL
Discussed. Seven essential steps of the believer's life. Resource Chart 1

GOVERNMENT (See **SOCIETY**)
Kinds.

Righteous **g**. 21:1-24:18, Div.VIII Overview
Theocracy. 21:1-24:18, Div.VIII Overview

GRACE
Discussed. Seven essential steps involved in the believer's life. Resource Chart 1
Fact. God is gracious. 34:5-9

GRATE, BRONZE (See **ALTAR OF BURNT OFFERING**)

GREED (See **COVET - COVETOUSNESS**)
Results. Brings judgment. 20:17, D.S.#1

GROWTH, SPIRITUAL - MATURITY
Assured.
God promises to reveal Himself to His people. 33:19
God promises to reveal His goodness. 33:19
God promises to reveal His name. 33:19
Essential. For restoration. 33:18-23
Need for.
A closer, warmer fellowship with God. 33:18
A deeper experience of God's glory. 33:18
A greater knowledge of God. 33:18
A more intimate communion with God. 33:18
Verses. List of. 33:18-23, Thgt. 1

GUIDANCE
Conditional **g**. Must obey. 23:20-23, pt.2
Discussed. Promise of **g**. 23:20-23; 25:21-22
Source.
The Ark. 25:10-22
The Cloud of God's glory. 40:34-38
Warning. Can be limited because of sin. 33:1-3

GUILT
Discussed. What the High Priest bore for the shortcomings of people. 39:30-31

GULF
Discussed. A great **g**. between God & man. 19:11-16, pt.2; 19:16-25, pt.2; 20:18,Thgt. 1; 20:18; Ex.24:1-2

HATE - HATRED (See **RETALIATION**)

HEADBAND (See **CLOTHES**)
How Christ fulfilled the symbolism of the **h**. Resource Chart 3, I:G
Instruction for making. 28:40; 39:28
Type - Symbol of. The believer's mind & will being subjected to God. 39:27-29, Thgt. 2; Intro. VI, pt.32
What is taught by the **h**. Resource Chart 3, I:G

HEART
Discussed. What darkness causes in the human **h**. 27:20-21
Kinds of. Corrupt. 32:1-6
Of God. God's people are upon His **h**. & before the Lord continually. 39:8-21

HELP - HELPING (See **GIVE - GIVING**)

INDEX

HERITAGE
Discussed. We all need to build a godly
h. for our families & for the earth.
31:1-11, pt.1b

HIGH PRIEST
Clothing of the High Priest.
Charge to the believer. To put on holy
garments. 28:5, pt.3, Thgt. 1
Discussed.
The passing down of the ordination
clothes. 29:29-30
The symbol of his special call. 28:3
Materials to be used. 28:5
List of garments. Intro. VI; Resource
Chart 3
Breastpiece or chestpiece. 28:3;
28:15-30; 39:8-21
Ephod. 28:4; 28:6-14; 39:2-7
Gold medallion. 28:36; 39:30-31
Headband. 28:4; 28:40; 39:27-29
Robe of the ephod. 28:4; 28:31-35;
39:22-26
Sash. 28:4; 28:39-40; 39:27-29
Tunic. 28:39-40; 39:27-29
Turban. 28:4; 28:39-40; 39:27-29
Underclothing. 28:42; 39:27-29
Ordination of. 29:1-46

HIGH PRIESTHOOD (See **JESUS
CHRIST**, Priesthood of)

HIRAM
Discussed. The chief craftsman for the
ornamental work on Solomon's temple.
31:6

HOLY - HOLINESS
Facts.
God is always serious about h. 30:17-
21, pt.4
God is h. 36:35-36, Thgt. 1
Meaning. 20:8, D.S.#1
Of God.
Discussed. A call to reverence & to
fear God's h. presence. 19:11-16
Facts.
The Ten Commandments were
given to reveal God's h. 20:18
There is a gulf that separates God &
man. 19:11-16, pt.2; 19:16-25,
pt.2; 20:18; Thgt. 1; 24:1-2
Type - Symbol of. The inner veil sym-
bolized God's majestic h. & man's
separation from God. 36:35-36; In-
tro. VI, pt.17; Resource Chart 2, VI
Purpose of.
The bronze wash basin. To cleanse the
priest. 30:17-21
The inner veil. To separate God's h.
from man. 26:31-35

HOLY OF HOLIES (See **TABERNA-
CLE**)
Fact. Contained only one piece of furniture: the Ark of God & Mercy Seat.
25:23-29

HOLY PLACE, THE (See **TABERNA-
CLE**)
Fact. Contained three pieces of furniture.
25:23-29

HOLY SPIRIT
Discussed. God fills the man He calls
with the Holy Spirit & gives him what-

ever skills & abilities are needed to do
the work. 31:1-11, pt.1d
Type - Symbol of.
Anointing oil. Intro. VI, pt.23
Oil for light. Intro. VI, pt.37

HONEST - HONESTY
Duty - Essential.
Must not profit from the offerings
given to support the ministry of the
church. 36:3-7, pt.3
Must not take bribes. 23:8
Results. Thirteen benefits of being h.
20:15, D.S.#2

HONOR - HONORED
Discussed. The call of God is an h. 39:1
Meaning. To esteem & value as precious.
20:12, Note 3, pt.6
Warning. Neither God nor rulers are ever
to be cursed. 22:28

HOREB, MOUNT (See **SINAI, MOUNT**)

HORN--HORNS (See **ALTAR OF BURNT
OFFERING; ALTAR OF INCENSE**)
Purpose of. How God's power & strength
are available to help in times of need.
30:1-6, pt.3
Type - Symbol of.
Atoning power of the altar. 27:1-8,
pt.2; Intro. VI, pt.19
God's power & strength. 27:1-8, pt.2;
Intro. VI, pt.19
God's protection, security, sanctuary,
help. 27:1-8, pt.2; Intro. VI, pt.19
God's salvation. 27:1-8, pt.2; Intro.
VI, pt.19

HUMANISM - HUMANIST (See **UNBE-
LIEF; WORLDLINESS**)
Warning to. Causes terrible sin. 32:1-6,
pt.6

HUNGER, SPIRITUAL (See **SATIS-
FACTION, SPIRITUAL**)
Answer to.
Being in God's presence & worship-
ping Him. Intro. VI, pt.9; Resource
Chart 2, III
Christ as the Bread of Life. 25:30;
35:13; 37:10-16; Intro. VI, pt.9; Re-
source Chart 2, III
God as the Bread of Life. 25:30; Intro.
VI, pt.9; Resource Chart 2, III
God nourishing man's hungry soul.
25:23-30; 35:13; 37:10-16; Intro. VI,
pt.9; Resource Chart 2, III

HUR
Discussed. Grandfather of Bezalel. 31:2
Meaning. 31:2

HUSBAND
Duty.
To cleave to his wife. 21:7-11, Thgt. 2
To honor his wife. 21:7-11, Thgt. 2
To know what his wife needs. 21:7-
11, Thgt. 2
To love his wife as much as Christ
loved the church. 21:7-11, Thgt. 2
Facts.
God will be a h. to the woman who is
abandoned by her h. 21:7-11, Thgt.
2, 3
H. is head of the wife & children.
21:12-27, pt.4

HYPOCRISY (See **LIE - LIAR - LYING**)

"I AM"
Chart. The Great "I AM's" of God &
Christ. 20:2, D.S.#1
God's declaration to unbelieving man.
20:3
Meaning. 20:2, Note 3

IDENTIFY - IDENTIFYING
Duty. To i. with the sacrifice. To transfer
sins. 29:10-14

IDLE - IDLENESS (See **LAZY - LAZI-
NESS**)

IDOL - IDOLS - IDOLATRY
Benefits of *not* worshipping i. 20:4-6,
DS #2
Consequences of worshipping i. 20:4-6,
DS #1
Creation of man's imagination & hands.
20:3
Description of. 20:3
Discussed.
Religious art: questions about. 20:4-5,
pt.1c
The laws governing i. 23:13
Duty.
Never to call upon false gods. 23:13
To obey God only. 23:13
Effects upon. Children. 20:4-5, pt.2-3
Fact. I. cause terrible sin. 32:1-6
Forbidden. List. 20:3
Judgment of. To be executed. 22:20
Meaning of. 20:3
Prohibited. 20:4-5; 23:24-26

IGNORANCE - IGNORANT
About God. Caused by. Man.
Some believe in many gods. Intro.
20:3
Some believe in the wrong god. Intro.
20:3
Some deny God. Intro. 20:3
Some question God's existence. Intro.
20:3

IMAGE OF GOD
Jesus Christ is the only image acceptable
to God. 20:4 5, pt.1, Thgt. 2

IMAGINATION, MAN'S
Wrong to picture God with man's i.
20:4-5, pt.2

IMMORALITY (See **ADULTERY;
LUST**)
Caused by.
A lack of teaching & training. 20:14,
Note 2, pt.3
Coldness. 20:14, Note 2, pt.3
Getting too close & becoming at-
tracted to a person. 20:14, Note 2,
pt.3
Ignoring or denying God & His Word.
20:14, Note 2, pt.3
Ignoring right vs. wrong. 20:14, Note
2, pt.3
Living in a dream or fantasy world.
20:14, Note 2, pt.3
Not guarding against loneliness, emp-
tiness, or the disappointment in one's
spouse or loved one. 20:14, Note 2,
pt.3

523

Summarized by five categories.
Anger, hostility, or the seeking of revenge. 20:14, Note 2, pt.3
Corrupt moral standards or a lack of moral standards. 20:14, Note 2, pt.3
Inflated ego or by a lack of self-esteem or self-worth. 20:14, Note 2, pt.3
Liberal moral standards. 20:14, Note 2, pt.3
The need for companionship. 20:14, Note 2, pt.3
Unsatisfying, inadequate sex with a spouse. 20:14, Note 2, pt.3
Effects upon society. Intro. 20:14
Example of. The golden calf. 32:1-6
Meaning. Of the word adultery. 20:14, Note 2, pt.1
Source of. The human heart. 20:14, D.S.#3, pt.3

IMMORTALITY (See ETERNAL LIFE)

IMPURITY (See ADULTERY; FORNICATION; IMMORALITY; LUST)

IN CHRIST
Benefits of. List of 21 blessings. 38:1-7; Thgt. 2

INCARNATION (See JESUS CHRIST)
How. Jesus Christ dwelt (tabernacled) with us. 25:1-31:18, Div.IX, Overview

INCENSE
Discussed. 30:34-38
Importance.
To be counted most holy. 30:36
To be made a pure & holy i. 30:35
To be made exclusively for the Lord & to be treated as holy. 30:37
To be put in front of the Ark of the Covenant. 30:36
Instructions for making i. 30:34-38
Type - Symbol of.
God being pleased with the prayers of His people. 30:34-38, Thgt. 1; Intro. VI, pt.38
The believer's prayers ascending up to God. 30:34-38, Thgt. 1; Intro. VI, pt.38
Warning. God will judge, cut off, & exile any offender who does not treat the i. as holy. 30:38

INCONSISTENCY - INCONSISTENT
Example of. Aaron. 32:1-35

INCORRUPTION (See WORLD)

INDULGE - INDULGENCE
Described as. A cause for terrible sin. 32:6

INFLUENCE
Evil i. The i. of idolatry is passed down from the parents to their children. 20:4-5, pt.2, 3
Good i. (See TESTIMONY)

INIQUITY (See SIN)

INSTRUCTIONS (See TABERNACLE)

Discussed. Three lessons gleaned from the i. of God to set up the Tabernacle. 40:1-15

INTEGRITY (See HONEST - HONESTY)

INTERCESSION (See PRAYER)
Duty.
To be near God; to fellowship & commune with Him in an unbroken sense & knowledge of His presence. 30:1-6, pt.7, Thgt.1
To pray: we must intercede at the Altar of Incense. 37:25-29
Essential.
For the forgiveness of terrible sin. 32:7-14; 33:12-17
For the salvation & deliverance of people. 32:11-14, pt.3e
Example.
Four bold requests. 33:12-17
Four strong pleas. 32:11-14
Purpose.
For forgiveness of sin. 32:30-32
For reconciliation between the people & God. 32:30-32
Result.
God answered Moses' prayer. 33:18-23, pt.4
God gave Moses a great promise. 33:14
Of Jesus Christ. (See JESUS CHRIST, Intercession; Mediator; Priesthood of)
As the great High Priest. 28:31-35, Thgt. 1
Who Christ i. for. 30:7-8; 39:22-26
Verses. List of. 32:11-14, pt.3, Thgt.1

INTOXICATION (See DRUNKENNESS)

INVENTORY (See TABERNACLE)
List of. Inventory in the Tabernacle.
The gifts of bronze. 38:29
The offerings of gold. 38:24
The offerings of silver. 38:25-27
Personnel in charge of.
Assistant Superintendent of the construction. Oholiab 38:23
Compilers of the figures. Levites. 38:21
Recorder of the figures. Ithamar, son of Aaron. 38:21
Superintendent of the construction. Bezalel. 38:22

INVITATION (See CALL; COME; DECISION)
Extended by God.
To come & have one's spiritual hunger & thirst satisfied. 38:9-20, Thgt. 1
To come & enter the ark of salvation to escape God's judgment. 38:9-20, Thgt. 1
To come for the cleansing of sin. 38:9-20, Thgt. 1
To come for the rest of one's soul. 38:9-20, Thgt. 1
To come to Christ & drink the water of life. 38:9-20, Thgt. 1
To come to the great marriage feast of the Lord. 38:9-20, Thgt. 1
To come to the great supper of God in heaven. 38:9-20, Thgt. 1
Fact. The person who comes to God does so only by God's will. 38:9-20, Thgt. 1

ISRAEL
Chosen by God. To enter into a covenant with God. 19:1-4
History. Experiences in the wilderness. 40:1-15
Laws of. (See CEREMONIAL LAWS; LAW, CIVIL)

ITHAMAR
Discussed. Son of Aaron was the recorder of the building figures for the Tabernacle. 38:21-31

JACOB
Example of. J. rose up early & worked for God. 34:2,4

JEALOUSY
Discussed. God is j. 20:5-6, pt. 1
Meaning. 34:13-14

JESUS CHRIST
Chart. How Christ fulfilled the symbolism of the Priesthood. Resource Chart 3
Chart. How Christ fulfilled the symbolism of the Tabernacle. Resource Chart 2
Blood of. Results. Man becomes acceptable to God. 36:19
Cross of. The only person who could have endured the c. 27:1-8, pt.3, Thgt. 1
Death of. God reconciled us to Himself by the death of Christ. 38:1-7
Example of. J. rose up early & worked for God. 34:2,4
Intercession of Jesus Christ. (See JESUS CHRIST, Intercessor; Mediator; Priesthood of)
As the great High Priest. 28:31-35, Thgt. 1
Who Christ intercedes for. 30:7-8; 39:22-26
Light of the world. Discussed. 25:31-39
Mediator.
Approaches God for us. 20:19, Thgt. 1
Makes us acceptable to God. 34:1-4
Renews God's covenant with us. 34:1-4
Priesthood of. As the great High Priest. 28:31-35, Thgt. 1
Relationship. To the Sabbath. 20:8-11, D.S.#4, pt.4-12
Teaching.
His t. concerning adultery & man's family. 20:14, D.S. #3
His t. concerning false gods. 20:3, D.S. #3
His t. concerning God's Name. 20:7, D.S. #3
His t. concerning man's parents. 20:12, D.S. #3
His t. concerning man's word & character. 20:16, D.S. #3
His t. concerning murder. 20:13, D.S. #5
His t. concerning our neighbor's property. 20:17, D.S. #3
His t. concerning stealing. 20:15, D.S. #3
His t. concerning the Sabbath Day. 20:8-11, D.S. #4
His t. concerning the worship of God. 20:4-6, D.S. #3
Type - Symbol of. The Priesthood. How Christ fulfilled the symbolism.
Breastpiece or Chestpiece. Christ represents & carries the names of be-

lievers upon His heart. 28:15-30; 39:8-21; Intro. VI, pt.28; Resource Chart 3, I:C

Ceremonial Washing. Christ has pronounced us clean, regenerated, eternally saved. 29:4; Resource Chart 3, II:A

Ceremony of Two Wave Offerings. Christ gave only the very best to His Father. 29:22-28; Resource Chart 3, II:E

Ephod. Christ carries our every burden before the Father. 28:6-14; 39:2-7; Intro. VI, pt.26; Resource Chart 3, I:B

Gold Medallion. Christ bore the guilt for our shortcomings. 28:36-38; 39:30-31; Intro. VI, pt.30; Resource Chart 3, I:E

Judicial Cleansing. Christ sacrificed His life & took sin out of the camp. 29:10-14; Resource Chart 3, II:B

Linen Headband. Christ has established His Lordship over all. 28:40; 39:28 Intro. VI, pt.32; Resource Chart 3, I:G

Linen Turbans & Tunics. Christ is the righteousness of God. 28:39; 39:27-28 Intro. VI, pt.31; Resource Chart 3, I:F

Linen Underclothing. Christ covers man with His righteousness, protecting man from exposure & shame before God & man. 28:42-43; 39:28; Intro. VI, pt.33; Resource Chart 3, I:H

Robe of the Ephod.
Christ's intercession for us never stops. 28:31-35; 39:22-26

Christ offered Himself up to God as the Perfect Offering. 28:31-35; 39:22-26 Intro. VI, pt.29; Resource Chart 3, I:D

Sacrifice of the First Ram. God accepted Christ's sacrifice & dedication. 29:15-18; Resource Chart 3, II:C

Sacrifice of the Second Ram. Christ was fully consecrated to the service of God. 29:19-21; Resource Chart 3, II:D

Sash.
Christ is the Truth, the Living Word Of God. 28:4; 39:29; Resource Chart 3, I:A

Christ is the One who holds everything & everyone together. 28:4; 39:29; Intro. VI, pt.24; Resource Chart 3, I:C

Type - Symbol of. The Tabernacle. How Christ fulfilled the symbolism.
Altar of Burnt Offering.
Christ gave His life for us. 27:1-8; 38:1-7; Intro. VI, pt.41; Resource Chart 2, VIII

Christ is our Passover, sacrificed for us. 27:1-8; 38:1-7 Intro. VI, pt.41; Resource Chart 2, VIII

Christ is the Lamb brought to slaughter. 27:1-8; 38:1-7; Intro. VI, pt.41; Resource Chart 2, VIII

Christ is the Lamb of God. 27:1-8; 38:1-7; Intro. VI, pt.41; Resource Chart 2, VIII

Christ laid down His life for us. 27:1-8; 38:1-7 Intro. VI, pt.28; Resource Chart 2, VIII

Altar of Incense.
Christ intercedes for God's people. 30:1-10; 37:25-29 Intro. VI, pt.34; Resource Chart 2, XI

Christ is always praying & living in an unbroken fellowship with God. 30:1-10; 37:25-29 Intro. VI, pt.34; Resource Chart 2, XI

Ark.
Christ fulfilled every picture of the Ark. 25:10-22; 37:1-5 Intro. VI, pt.6; Resource Chart 2, I

Christ is the Good Shepherd who leads, guides, & protects. 25:10-22; 37:1-5 Intro. VI, pt.6; Resource Chart 2, I

Christ kept the law of the covenant perfectly, without sin. 25:10-22; 37:1-5; Intro. VI, pt.6; Resource Chart 2, I

Christ promised to be with His people always. 25:10-22; 37:1-5 Intro. VI, pt.6; Resource Chart 2, I

Christ shed His own blood & sprinkled it on the Mercy Seat. 25:10-22; 37:1-5 Intro. VI, pt.6; Resource Chart 2, I

Bronze Wash Basin. God cleanses us & forgives us of our sins through the blood of Christ. 30:17-21; 38:8; Intro. VI, pt.36; Resource Chart 2, XII

Door or Gate.
Christ is the only way by which a man can come to the Father. 27:16; 38:18-19 Intro. VI, pt.22; Resource Chart 2, X

Christ is the only door that a man can enter & be saved. 27:16; 38:18-19; Intro. VI, pt.22; Resource Chart 2, X

Inner Veil. Christ gives us eternal access into the presence of God. 26:31-35; 36:35-36; Intro. VI, pt.17; Resource Chart 2, VI

Lampstand.
Jesus Christ is the Light of the World. 25:40, Thgt. 1; Ex.25:40, Thgt. 1; 27:20-21; 37:17-24; Intro. VI, pt.10; Resource Chart 2, IV

Jesus Christ is the true Lampstand. 25:40, Thgt. 1; 27:20-21; 37:17-24; Intro. VI, pt.10; Resource Chart 2, IV Chart

Mercy Seat.
Christ & His blood cover the law & our failure to keep the law. 25:17-21; 37:6-9; Intro. VI, pt.8; Resource Chart 2, II

Christ is the Perfect Sacrifice to God. 25:17-21; 37:6-9; Intro. VI, pt.8; Resource Chart 2, II

Outer Veil. Christ invites man to come & worship God on the basis of His shed blood. 26:36-37; 36:37-38; Intro. VI, pt.18; Resource Chart 2, VII

Sanctuary.
Christ became the sin-offering for man. 26:1-30; 36:8-34 Intro. VI, pt.14; Resource Chart 2, V

Christ is our foundation, our redemption & stability. 26:1-30; 36:8-34; Intro. VI, pt.16, 35; Resource Chart 2, V

Christ is our protective separation from the world. 26:1-30; 36:8-34; Intro. VI, pt.3; Resource Chart 2, V

Christ is the perfect embodiment of purity & righteousness. 26:1-30; 36:8-34 Intro. VI, pt.13; Resource Chart 2, V

Christ sacrificially shed His blood for man. 26:1-30; 36:8-34; Intro. VI, pt.15; Resource Chart 2, V

Table of Showbread. Christ is the Bread of Life. 25:23-30; 37:10-16; Intro. VI, pt.9; Resource Chart 2, III

Walls of the Tabernacle. Christ is the righteousness of God. 27:9-19; 36:20-34; 38:9-20; Intro. VI, pt.21; Resource Chart 2, IX

Work of - Ministry.
His work in destroying Satan & evil spirits. To destroy the power of the devil. 34:10-11

His work in meeting man's need for life, both abundant & eternal.
Through Christ we are acceptable to God & saved to the uttermost. 40:34-38, Thgt. 2

Through Christ, we can approach God in a new & living way. 40:34-38, Thgt. 2

Through Christ we shall inherit the promised land ofheaven, living with God forever & ever. 40:34-38, Thgt. 2

To give us life, a life filled with love, joy, & peace. 36:37-38

To show us the way to God. 36:37-38

To stand with & strengthen believers. 36:20-34, Thgt. 1

His work in relation to the High Priesthood, the Mediator & Intercessor.
To be touched with the feelings of our weaknesses. 39:30-31, Thgt. 1

To become the sacrifice for our sins, once for all. 39:30-31, Thgt. 1

To bring a permanent forgiveness of sin for us. 39:30-31, Thgt. 1

To bring eternal salvation to us. 39:30-31, Thgt. 1

To bring us an abundance of good things. 39:30-31, Thgt. 1

To bring us the great hope of heaven. 39:30-31, Thgt. 1

To give us access into God's presence. 39:30-31, Thgt. 1

To make reconciliation for our sins. 39:30-31, Thgt. 1

To save us to the uttermost. 39:30-31, Thgt. 1

To sit at the right hand of God for us. 39:30-31, Thgt. 1

To take upon Himself our sins. 39:30-31, Thgt. 1

His work in securing righteousness & dying for man.
To become sin for man. 34:10-11

To conquer death. 34:10-11

To conquer every enemy for the believer. 34:10-11

To conquer the world for the believer. 34:10-11

JEWS (See **ISRAEL**)

JOB
Example of. **J.** rose up early & worked for God. 34:2,4

INDEX

A school guardian or master. Div.VI,
  Overview, pt.6c; Ex.22:7-15, pt.4;
  Intro. VI., pt.2
A shadow. Div.VI, Overview, pt.6e
A yoke. Div.VI, Overview, pt.6b
God's Word. 24;12-18
Good. 22:7-15, pt.4
Holy. 22:7-15, pt.4
Letters written on stones. Div.VI,
  Overview, pt.6d
Perfect. 22:7-15, pt.4
Spiritual. 22:7-15, pt.4
Duty. Must study & learn God's Word.
  21:1
Discussed.
  Deposits. 22:7-15
  Fire or burning control. 22:6
  Justice & mercy in court & among
    neighbors. 23:1-9
  Property damage. 22:5
  Property rights. 21:33-36
  Theft, the stealing of property. 22:1-4
Fulfilled by Jesus Christ. Div.VI, Over-
  view, pt.7; Ex.20:3; 22:7-15, pt.4
Kinds.
  Ceremonial & ritual l. (See CERE-
    MONIAL LAW; RITUAL)
  Civil l. (See LAW, CIVIL)
  Religious l. (See CEREMONIAL
    LAW; RITUAL)
Obeyed by Jesus Christ. Div.VI, Over-
  view, pt.7
Of Israel. (See CEREMONIAL LAW;
  LAW, CIVIL; ISRAEL; RITUAL)
Purpose of the l.
  To arouse people to seek both life &
    the promised land. Div.VI, Over-
    view, pt.4h
  To be a guide who would lead people
    to Christ. Div.VI, Overview, pt.4g
  To mark believers as the priests of
    God. Div.VI, Overview, pt.4b
  To mark believers as the true followers
    of God. Div.VI, Overview, pt.4a
  To show man how to live a peaceful &
    productive life upon earth. Div.VI,
    Overview, pt.4i
  To show man that he can never be jus-
    tified by the l. Div.VI, Overview,
    pt.4d
  To show man that he is sinful. Div.VI,
    Overview, pt.4c
  To show man that he needed a Media-
    tor to approach God. Div.VI, Over-
    view, pt.4f
  To show man that he needs a Savior
    who can deliver him from the curse
    & penalty of the l. Div.VI, Over-
    view, pt.4e
Type - Symbol of. A schoolmaster or
  guardian who brings us to Christ. Intro.
  VI, pt.2
What the l. cannot & does not do.
  It cannot give life to man. Div.VI,
    Overview, pt.5g
  It cannot justify a person from sin.
    Div.VI, Overview, pt.5e
  It cannot make a person perfect.
    Div.VI, Overview, pt.5d
  It cannot make a person righteous.
    Div.VI, Overview, pt.5f
  It cannot save a person because no
    person can keep the law. Div.VI,
    Overview, pt.5c
  It could not be a permanent covenant.
    Div.VI, Overview, pt.5b

It does not replace nor void the great
  promises of God. Div.VI, Overview,
  pt.5a

LAWLESSNESS
Discussed.
  People have become desensitized &
    hardened to l. Intro. 20:13
  The media focuses upon l. Intro. 20:13
Example of. Israel. 32:1-35

LAZY - LAZINESS
Warning. 20:9-10

LEADERS - LEADERSHIP
Essentials. 29:1-46
Problem.
  Shortage of. A scarcity of good l.
    29:1-46
  Wrong qualifications for l. 29:1-46

LEATHER (See BADGER SKINS)

LEND - LENDING
Discussed.
  Borrowed property that is damaged.
    22:14-15
  Loans to the poor. 22:25-27

LEVI, TRIBE OF - LEVITE - LEVITES
Work - Function of.
  Commanded to execute judgment
    upon rebellious people. 32:25-29,
    pt.3-4
  Compiled the building figures of the
    Tabernacle. 38:21-31

LIE - LIAR - LYING (See DECEPTION)
Benefits of *not* lying. 20:16, D.S.#2
Christ & His teaching concerning man's
  word & lying. 20:16, D.S.#3
Discussed. Three terrible effects upon
  people. 20:16, Note 2, pt.3
Duty. To protect or guard oneself from l.
  20:16, Note 3.
Fact.
  Causes pain & suffering for other
    people. 20:16, Note 2, pt.4
  Is common to everyone. Intro. 20:16
  Is usually shared with loved ones &
    good friends. 20:16, Note 2, pt.4
  Judgment of. Is judged by God. 20:16,
    Note 2, pt.4
Kinds of - How one lies.
  Charges & criticism. 20:16, Note 2,
    pt.2
  Deception. 20:16, Note 2, pt.2
  Exaggeration & flattery. 20:16, Note
    2, pt.2
  Rumor, gossip, or tale-bearing. 20:16,
    Note 2, pt.2
  Slander. 20:16, Note 2, pt.2
  Suggestive hints or insinuations.
    20:16, Note 2, pt.2
  Unlimited ways. List. 20:16, Note 2,
    pt.2
Meaning.
  Includes all forms of false speech.
    20:16, Note 1
  That which is false, untrue. 20:16,
    Note 2, pt.1
Results. Consequences of l. 20:16,
  D.S.#1
Source. Satan is the father of lies. 20:16,
  Note 2, pt.5; D.S.#3, pt.3

LIFE (See SALVATION)

LIFE, BOOK OF
Fact. Records the names of believers.
  32:30-32, pt.3c

LIFE, SANCTITY OF
Duty.
  To respect the sanctity of life. 20:13,
    D.S.#4
  To teach the sanctity of life & the
    brotherhood of man. 20:13, Note 3
Results. Ten benefits to the person who
  respects the sanctity of life. 20:13,
  D.S.#4

LIGHT (See LAMPSTAND)
Fact. Jesus Christ is the true light & His
  light is never extinguished. 27:20-21,
  Thgt. 2
Source.
  Christ. Seven unique qualities of
    Christ's l. 37:17-24, Thgt. 1, pt.2
  God. Six characteristics of God's l.
    37:17-24, Thgt. 1, pt.1

LIGHT OF THE WORLD (See LAMP-STAND)

LINEN (See FINE THREADED LINEN)

LOANS
Duty.
  Must not charge interest to the needy.
    22:25-27
  Must not take any pledge from the
    needy. 22:25-27

LONGSUFFERING (See GOD, Nature of)
Fact. What God is like: God is l. 34:5

LORD, THE
Meaning. 20:2; 34:5-9

LOST, THE
Described. In spiritual darkness. 25:31-40

LOYAL - LOYALTY (See DEDICA-TION)
Example of. Oholiab was l. to Bezalel.
  35.30-35

LUST
Fourteen demands that forbid lusting or
  coveting. 20:17, Note 3

MAJESTY
Of God. (See GLORY OF GOD)
Discussed. 20:18

MAN (See JUDGMENT; LUST; SIN;
Related Subjects)
Needs of m.
  Discussed. Only God can truly nourish
    & satisfy the hungry soul of man.
    25:30, pt.5
  List. Intro. 25:1-9
Separation from God. great gulf between
  God & m. 19:16-25, pt.2; 20:18, Thgt.
  1; 24:1-2
Value - Worth of m. (See GOD, Love of)
  Created in the image & likeness of
    God. 20:13, Note 2, pt.1

INDEX

INDEX

PARENTS (See FAMILY & Related
Subjects)
Christ & His teaching concerning man's
p. 20:12, D.S.#3
Discussed. Consequences of p. idolatry
upon children. 20:5-6, pt.2-3
Disobedience to. An attack upon the
authority of God. 21:15, 17
Meaning.
Honoring p. 20:12, Note 3
Obeying p. 20:12, Note 3, pt.5

PARTIALITY (See FAVORITISM)

PARTYING
Results. In terrible sin. 32:1-6, pt.9

PASSOVER
Discussed. The law governing the P.
sacrifice. 23:18
Duty. To keep the Feast of Unleavened
Bread. 34:18

PATTERN (See TABERNACLE)

PAUL, THE APOSTLE
Love of. For Israel. 32:30-32, Thgt. 1

PEER PRESSURE
Example of.
Men who had to stand up to the ma-
jority of people.
Elijah. 23:1-3, pt.3, Thgt. 1
Noah. 23:1-3, pt.3, Thgt. 1
Men who succumbed to peer pres-
sure.
Aaron. 32:1-2
Pilate. 23:1-3, pt.3, Thgt. 1
Fact. One of the most difficult things to
resist. 23:1-3, pt.3, Thgt. 1
Results - Effects of. Aaron gave in to the
crowd & caused a terrible sin. 32:1-2

PENTECOST (See FEAST OF HAR-
VEST)
Meaning. Fifty. 23:16

PEOPLE OF GOD (See BELIEVER)

PERFECT - PERFECTION (See
WORKS, GOOD)

PERJURY (See PROFANITY)
Discussed. Bearing false witness. 20:16,
Note 2
Examples of.
Before a business partner. 20:7,
D.S.#3, pt.1
Before a judge or jury. 20:7, D.S.#3,
pt.1
Before a neighbor. 20:7, D.S.#3, pt.1
Before a wife or husband. 20:7,
D.S.#3, pt.1
Before any person. 20:7, D.S.#3, pt.1

PERSECUTION - PERSECUTORS
By whom.
Family. Reasons. 20:13, D.S.#5, pt.3
Religionists. 20:13, D.S.#5, pt.4
Secular & religious leaders. 20:13,
D.S.#5, pt.6
The world. 20:13, D.S.#5, pt.5
Kinds - Methods - Types.
Abuse. 20:13, D.S.#5, pt.5
Attack. 20:13, D.S.#5, pt.5
Criticism. 20:13, D.S.#5, pt.5

Imprisonment. 20:13, D.S.#5, pt.5
Martyrdom. 20:13, D.S.#5, pt.5
Murder. 20:13, D.S.#5, pt.3,4,5
Opposed. 20:13, D.S.#5, pt.5
Questioned. 20:13, D.S.#5, pt.5
Ridicule. 20:13, D.S.#5, pt.5
Slander. 20:16, D.S.#3, pt.5
Torture. 20:13, D.S.#5, pt.5
Purpose of - Why believers are p.
Are identified with Christ. 20:13,
D.S.#5, pt.3
Because religionists are deceived.
Think they know God but do not.
20:13, D.S.#5, pt.4
Warning -Predicted. Is to be expected.
20:13, D.S.#5, pt.5

PILLAR OF CLOUD & FIRE (See
GLORY OF GOD)
Discussed. 40:34-38

PLAN - PLANS - PLANNING
Discussed. God will carefully p. the deliverance of His people. 23:27-33,
pt.1c

POLYGAMY (See MARRIAGE)
Discussed. God tolerated but did not
condone p. 21:10, D.S.#2

POLYTHEISM - POLYTHEIST
Commandment directed to the p. 20:3,
pt. 3

POOR - POVERTY (See NEED - NE-
CESSITIES)
Duty - Essential.
Must not deny the p. justice. 23:6-7
Must not falsely charge the p. 23:6-7
Must not put the innocent or honest
person to death. 23:6-7
Fact. God will judge the person who has
judged the p. wrongly. 23:6-7

POSSESSIONS (See MATERIALISM;
WEALTH; WORLDLINESS)
Discussed. Society is to establish animal
control laws for its citizens. 21:28-32

POSTS (See TABERNACLE)

PRAY - PRAYER - PRAYING
Duty.
To intercede at the Altar of Incense.
Thirteen instructions on how to p.
37:25-29
To p. & seek God's face for the needs
of others. 28:15-30, pt.3
To patiently wait upon the Lord, per-
severe & endure in p. 24:12-18,
Thgt. 2
Discussed. The robe of the ephod.
39:22-26
Examples of.
The p. of Elijah. 30:34-38, Thgt. 1
The p. of Ezra. 30:34-38, Thgt. 1
The p. of Gideon. 30:34-38, Thgt. 1
The p. of Hannah. 30:34-38, Thgt. 1
The p. of Hezekiah. 30:34-38, Thgt. 1
The p. of Jehoshaphat. 30:34-38,
Thgt. 1
The p. of Samuel. 30:34-38, Thgt. 1
The p. of Solomon. 30:34-38, Thgt. 1
The p. of the disciples & early be-
lievers. 30:34-38, Thgt. 1

The p. of Zacharias, John the Bap-
tist's father. 30:34-38, Thgt. 1
Intercessory. Christ is our Mediator &
Intercessor. 28:6-14, Thgt. 1
Kinds of p.
Fervent. 30:1-6, pt.4
In Jesus' name. 30:34-38, Thgt. 1
Intercessory. 28:6-14; 32:30-32
Persevering. 30:34-38, Thgt. 1
Of Jesus Christ. (See JESUS CHRIST,
Intercessor; Mediator; Priesthood of)
As the great High Priest. 28:31-35,
Thgt. 1
List of. Who Christ prays for. 39:22-
26, Thgt. 1
Results - Work of.
Attracts God & moves the heart of
God. 33:12-17, Thgt. 1
Changes things. 33:12-17, Thgt. 1
When to pray.
After committing terrible sin. 32:7-14
All the time. 30:1-6, pt.6
Where to pray. Anywhere. 30:1-6, pt.6

PRECIOUS STONES FOR THE
CHESTPIECE
Type - Symbol of. The High Priest representing & carrying the names of
God's people upon His heart, that He
represents them before the LORD
continually. 39:10-14; Intro. VI, pt.40

PREGNANT - PREGNANCY
Discussed.
God's view concerning babies who
are in their mother's womb. 21:12-
27, pt. 9, Thgt.1
Protection of law given to p. women
who are injured. 21:22-26

PREJUDICE (See FAVORITISM)

PREPARE - PREPARATION (See
COMMITMENT; CROSS - SELF-
DENIAL;
DEDICATION; DEVOTION)
Fact. God will never call us to a task
without first equipping us to do it.
35:30-35, Thgt. 1
Verses. List of. 35:30-35, Thgt. 1

PRESENCE OF GOD
Comes by.
Close relationship with God. 33:17
Intercession. 33:17
Example.
At the Ark of God. 37:1-5
At the top of Mt. Sinai. 20:18
The Tabernacle. A place where God
could dwell with His people. 25:8
Fact. The door that leads into God's
presence is Jesus Christ. 36:37-38
Needed.
To demonstrate God's grace & ap-
proval. 33:15-16, pt.3
To reach the promised land. 33:15-
16, pt.3
To show that God's people are dis-
tinctive. 33:15-16, pt.3
Source of. In the cloud. 34:5-9
Special manifestation. Promise made.
19:7-9
Strong reassurance. Proof of. 33:17
Warning. Can be withdrawn because of
sin. 33:1-3

531

INDEX

PRIDE (See **BOASTING; GLORYING IN MAN; SELF-SUFFICIENCY**)
Caused by. Discussed. 38:8, Thgt. 2

PRIEST - PRIESTS (See **HIGH PRIEST**)

PRIESTHOOD (See **HIGH PRIEST**)
Call of. Discussed. 28:1-5
  Anointing of. Type - Symbol of. The special call & appointment of God. 30:22-33
  Permanence & security of the **p.** 29:8-9
  Purpose of. To set apart to serve God. 28:1, pt.2
  Source of. God. 28:1, pt.1
  The opportunity for service. 39:1
Chart. How Christ fulfilled the symbolism of the Priesthood. Resource Chart 3
Consecration of. Discussed. 40:12-15
Clothing of High Priest.
  Charge to the believer. To put on holy garments. 28:5, pt.3, Thgt. 1
  Chestpiece (See **CHESTPIECE**)
  Discussed.
    The passing down of the ordination clothes. 29:29-30
    The symbol of his special call. 28:3
  Ephod. (See **EPHOD**).
  Gold Medallion. (See **MEDALLION, GOLD**)
  List of garments. 28:3-4
  Making of. 39:1-43
  Materials to be used. 28:5
  Robe of the Ephod. (See **ROBE OF EPHOD**)
  Type - Symbol of. Bringing dignity & honor to the name of God. 35:19; 39:1
Duty. (See **CALL**, Purpose)
  To be representatives of God, mediators between God & man. 28:1
  To give God the best. 29:22-28
  To offer gifts & sacrifices for sin. 28:1
  To pray & make strong intercession for the people. 28:1
  To show compassion for the ignorant & to people going astray. 28:1
  To teach the people. 28:1
  To walk worthy of God. 28:1-5, pt.2, Thgt. 1
Nature of.
  A glorious call & hope. 28:1-5, Thgt. 1
  A heavenly calling. 28:1-5, pt.2, Thgt. 1
  A high calling, ultimate goal for life. 28:1-5, pt.2, Thgt. 1
  A holy calling. 28:1-5, pt.2, Thgt. 1
  An eternal call. 28:1-5, pt.2, Thgt. 1
  Demands faithfulness, personal responsibility. 28:1-5, pt.2, Thgt. 1
  Demands great & careful diligence. 28:1-5, pt.2, Thgt. 1
  Unique, one of a kind. 28:1-5, pt.2, Thgt. 1
Work - Ministry of.
  Consecration to service. 29:19-21; Resource Chart 3, II:D
  Judicial cleansing. 29:10-11; Resource Chart 3, II:B
  Total dedication of life. 29:15-18; Resource Chart 3, II:C

PROCLAMATION (See **PREACHING; WITNESSING; WORD OF GOD**)
Duty.
  To be spiritually prepared to share. 34:29-31
  To declare God's commandments to leaders. 34:31
  To declare God's commandments to people. 34:32

PROFANITY (See **CURSING; VAIN**)
Example of. George Washington's stand against **p.** 20:7, Note 3, pt.4
How a person takes God's name in **v.**
  By false swearing. 20:7, Note 3, pt.2
  By hypocrisy. 20:7, Note 3, pt.4
  By profanity & vulgarity. 20:7, Note 3, pt.1
  By using God's name in some irreverent way. 20:7, Note 3, pt.3
Meaning. 20:7, Note 3, pt.1
Results of.
  Corrupts the language of a nation & people. 20:7, Note 3, Thgt.1
  Destroys the ability of people to continue to grow & increase the quality of their lives, society, & nation. 20:7, Note 3, Thgt.1
  Destroys the moral strength & esteem of a people for one another. 20:7, Note 3, Thgt.1
  Destroys the source of respect between people. 20:7, Note 3, Thgt.1

PROMISE - PROMISES (See **REWARD**)
Promises to the believer.
  God's blessing. 23:24-26
  God's guidance. 23:20-23
  God's protection. 23:20-23
  God's special provision. 23:24-26
Surety of. Guaranteed & assured. 23:27-31
To whom God makes **p.** To the obedient.
  Must demolish & break their sacred stones (idols) to pieces. 23:24-26, pt.1
  Must never bow down & worship false gods. 23:24-26, pt.1
  Must never follow the practices of false gods. 23:24-26, pt.1

PROMISED LAND (See **LAND, THE PROMISED**)

PROPER USE OF GOD'S NAME
Christ & His teaching concerning God's name. 20:7, D.S.#3
Discussed. Nine benefits. 20:7, D.S.#2

PROPERTY
Damage to. Discussed.
  Causes.
    Irresponsible oversight. 22:5
    Lack of safety controls. 21:36
    Negligence. 21:33-34
    Unpreventable. 21:35
    Fields burned. 22:6
    Other people's **p.** 21:33-36
Discussed.
  Caring for a neighbor's money or goods. 22:7-15
  How a person is to respond to someone who steals his **p.** 22:1-4, pt.2, 3

Essential. A person's **p.** must be protected from being stolen. 20:15, Note 2, pt.3
Fact. God owns all **p.** 22:1-4
P. rights. 22:33-36
Stolen.
  Effect upon the person whose **p.** is stolen. 22:1-4, Thgt. 3
  Laws to protect the person & his **p.** 22:1-4

PROPITIATION (See **RECONCILE - RECONCILIATION**)

PROTECT - PROTECTION
Conditional **p.**
  Because of sin. 33:1-3
  Must obey. 23:20-23, pt.2
Source.
  God's special angel or messenger. 23:20-23
  The pillar of cloud. 40:36-38

PURE - PURITY (See **MORALS - MORALITY**)
Discussed. How to keep from committing sexual sin. Seventeen instructions. 20:14, Note 3
Duty.
  To be sanctified, consecrated, set apart for God. 19:10
  To live **p.**, holy lives. 20:14, Note 3

PURPLE, Color of
Type - Symbol of. Christ as the King of kings & LORD of lords. 25:4; Intro. VI, pt.25

PURPOSE (See **CALL - CALLED; MISSION**)
Earthly **p.** vs. spiritual **p.** Intro. 31:1-18

QUARREL - QUARRELING
Discussed. Restitution required for any injury caused by a **q.** or fight. 21:18-19

QUIET TIME
Example of. Moses met God early in the morning. 34:2,4

RAGE (See **ANGER**)

RAM
Discussed. Sacrificed to the LORD. 29:15-18; 29:19-21; Resource Chart 3, II:C, D
Type - Symbol of.
  Consecration to service. 29:19-21; Resource Chart 3, II:D
  Total dedication. 29:15-18; Resource Chart 3, II:C

RAM SKINS
Construction of. 36:19
  Discussed. 25:5; 36:19
  Instructions for construction. 26:14
  Set up. 40:19
Type - Symbol of. The sacrifice of Jesus Christ & His shed blood for sinners. 26:14; 36:19; Intro. VI, pt.15

RANSOM
Discussed. **R.** tax. 30:11-16

532

INDEX

REBELLION (seditions) (See **UNBE-LIEF**)
Against God.
Children attacking & abusing their parents. 21:15, 17
The Golden Calf. 32:1-35

RECONCILE - RECONCILIATION
(See **JESUS CHRIST**, Death of)
Discussed. God r. us to Himself by Jesus Christ. 38:1-7
Duty. To be r. with God. 38:1-7
Source. Christ's blood. 27:1-8, pt.1, Thgt.1

REDEEM - REDEMPTION (See **RANSOM**)

REFUGE, CITIES OF
List of. 21:13, D.S.#2

REGENERATION (See **SALVATION**)

REJECTION (See **REBELLION**)

RELIGION (See **CEREMONY**)
Discussed.
The law governing the offerings to God. 23:19
The law governing the Passover sacrifice. 23:18
The Sabbath year as a religious observance. 23:10-12
Warning against r. Not all have the same God. Intro. 20:3, pt.4

RELIGIONISTS (See **RELIGION**)

RENEW - RENEWAL
Duty. Must be renewed after sin. 33:1-3
Essential. Intercession, strong diligent prayer. 33:12-17

REPENT - REPENTANCE
Example of - Illustrated. The people stripped off their jewelry. 33:4-6, Thgt. 1
Source of r.
Hearing God's charge. 33:5
Hearing God's demand for r. 33:5
Hearing God's warning of judgment. 33:5
Type - Symbol of. Jewelry. A symbol of worldliness. 33:4-6
Verses. List of. 33:4-6

REPRESENT - REPRESENTATION
Discussed. The High Priest went before the LORD with the names of God's people. 39:2-7

RESPECT (See **HONOR; OBEDIENCE**)

RESPONSIBILITY (See **BELIEVERS**, Duty; **MINISTERS**, Duty; & Related Subjects)
Discussed. With authority comes great r. 21:12-27, pt.10, Thgt.1
Duty. You are to obey. 20:3, 4-6, 7, 8-11, 12, 13, 14, 15, 16, 17 (all under pt.1)
Personal. Everyone is accountable for his own sin & his alone. 32:33

REST - RELAXATION, PHYSICAL
Duty. To work six days a week but keep the Sabbath as a holy day & as a day of r. 35:2-3
Essential. Time for r. 20:11

REST, SPIRITUAL & ETERNAL
Verses. List of. 33:12-17, pt.2

RESTITUTION
Discussed. Purpose of. 21:12-27, pt.7
Duty.
To make full r. 22:5, 6
To pay for all lost time & lost income from employment. 21:12-27, pt.7
To pay for all medical costs. 21:12-27, pt.7
Examples of. Reasons to pay r.
Damage to other people's property. 21:33-36
Damaging fire. 22:6
Irresponsible oversight. 22:5
Stealing other people's property. 22:1-4
Results. Effect upon society. 21:12-27, pt.7, Thgt.1

RESTORATION (See **FORGIVENESS; REPENTANCE; SALVATION**)
Discussed. Five essentials for r. after sinning. 33:1-23
Fact. Man must experience r. after he sins. 33:1-3
How a believer is r.
Must hear God's call & warning. 33:1-3
Must repent. 33:4-6
Must seek God's face for forgiveness & r. 33:12-17
Must understand that God does chastise His people when they sin. 33:7-11
Must want to know God more & more. 33:18-23

RETALIATION (See **VENGEANCE**)
Discussed. The law of victim protection. 21:24-25, D.S.#3
Duty. To love our enemies. 23:4-5

REVEALED - REVELATION
The revelation of God. God has revealed Himself in the Ten Commandments. 20:22

REVELRY
Meaning of. 32:1-6, Note 1, pt.9

REVENGE (See **RETALIATION**)

REVERENCE (See **HONOR**, of God; **WORSHIP**)
Duty. How God is to be reverenced.
To acknowledge & respect His holy presence. 19:12-13
To be ready to meet Him. 19:11
To sanctify, consecrate oneself. 19:14
To totally focus upon Him. 19:15
To use God's name correctly. 20:7, Note 3, pt.3
Of God. Discussed. 19:11-16

REWARD
Discussed. The r. for obedience. 23:20-33
What the rewards are.

Rewards dealing with the personal relationship between God & believers.
God's Angel (messenger). 23:20-23
God's blessing. 23:24-26
God's conquering power & gift of the promised land. 23:27-33
God's guidance. 23:20-23
God's protection. 23:20-23
God's special provision. 23:24-26
The choice property of God. 19:6, Thgt.
The personal possession of God. 19:6, Thgt. 1
The precious treasure of God. 19:6, Thgt. 1
Will be a holy, sanctified, pure, righteous, consecrated people to God. 19:6, Thgt. 1
Rewards dealing with work or position or rule. Being made kings & priests. 19:6, Thgt. 1

RICH - RICHES (See **TREASURE, SPIRITUAL**)
Discussed. No security in storing the world's treasures. 20:15, D.S.#3, pt.3
Warning. Craving material possessions will leave a man empty. 20:15, D.S.#3, pt.4

RIGHTEOUS - RIGHTEOUSNESS (See **JUSTICE**)
Benefits to a righteous society.
God will bless the city that is filled with righteous people. Div.VIII, pt.10
God will bless the nation who claims Him. He will claim them for His very own inheritance. Div.VIII, pt.10
God will exalt a righteous nation. Div.VIII, pt.10
God will exalt the nation that diligently listens to His voice. Div.VIII, pt.10
God will make a righteous nation a great nation. Div.VIII, pt.10
God will protect the city that trusts in Him. Div.VIII, pt.10
God will spare a society from judgment if righteousness is found within its borders. Div.VIII, pt.10
Duty - Essential. To be clothed with the r. of Christ. 29:5-6
Of God.
God's right hand is full of r. 36:8-13, Thgt. 1
God is r. in all His ways. 36:8-13, Thgt. 1
Man is to seek God's r. before anything else. 36:8-13, Thgt. 1
The very name of God is r. 36:8-13, Thgt. 1
Type - Symbol of.
The inner curtains.
Fine threaded linen. The purity & r. of God. 26:1; Intro. VI, pt.11
Jesus Christ is r. & pure, without sin. 26:1-14, Thgt. 1
Jesus Christ is the r. of believers. 26:1-14, Thgt. 1
The inner curtains symbolized purity & r. 26:1-14; Intro. VI, pt.13; Resource Chart 2, V

533

INDEX

The Linen Headband. Man subjecting his mind & thoughts to God & His **r**. 28:40; 39:28; Intro. VI, pt.32

The Linen Turban & Tunic. Putting on God's **r**. 28:29; 39:27-28; Intro. VI, pt.31

The Linen Underclothing. Covering our nakedness with Christ's **r**. 28:42-43; 39:28; Intro. VI, pt.33

RITUAL (See **CEREMONY; RELIGION**)

ROBE OF THE EPHOD (See **HIGH PRIEST**)

Chart. How Christ fulfilled the symbolism of the Priesthood. Resource Chart 3, I:D

Discussed. 28:31-35; 39:22-26

Fulfillment in Jesus Christ.
As our advocate. 39:22-26, Thgt. 1
As the High Priest who fulfills the intercessory ministry. 28:31-35, Thgt. 1
Offered Himself to God in five significant ways. 28:31-35, Thgt. 2

How Christ fulfilled the symbolism of the **r**. Resource Chart 3, I:D

Instructions for making the **r**. 28:31-35; 39:22-26

Purpose of.
To sound forth God's acceptance of the High Priest's offering. 28:31-35; 39:26
To sound forth the intercessory ministry of the High Priest. 28:31-35; 39:26

Type - Symbol of.
The fact that God accepted the offering of the High Priest. 28:31-35; 39:22-26; Intro. VI, pt.29
The prayer ministry of the High Priest. 28:31-35; 39:22-26; Intro. VI, pt.29

What is taught by the **r**. Resource Chart 3, I:D

RULERS
Duty toward. To be respected. 22:28

SABBATH - SUNDAY
Christ & His teaching concerning the Sabbath Day. 20:8-11, D.S.#4

Discussed.
Christ is the Lord of the **S**. 20:8-11, D.S.#4, pt.1
S. is for all generations of men, women, & children. 20:8, Thgt.1
Jesus Christ made it His custom to worship God with other believers on the **S**. 20:4-6, D.S.#3, pt.5
Laws governing the **S**. & religious feasts. 23:10-19
The **S**. was made for man. 20:8-11, D.S.#4, pt.2
Why God required His people to slow down the production schedule. 31:13

Duty.
Not to do any work on the seventh day. 20:10; 35:2-3
To keep the **S**. while building the Tabernacle. 35:2-3
To set aside the seventh day as a holy day, a day of rest & worship. 20:11, Note 4

To work six days, but only six days. 20:9; 35:2-3
You are to keep the **S**. 20:8, Note 1

Facts.
Was a perpetual covenant. 31:16-17
Was given as a law to the nation of Israel before any other law. 31:13, pt.1a
Was given as one of the civil & judicial laws of Israel. 31:13, pt.1a
Was given as one of the Ten Commandments, the moral law. 31:13, pt.1a
Was given for our good. 20:8, pt.4, Thgt.1; 20:11, Note 5, Thgt.1
Was set aside as a day of rest & worship since creation. 31:13, pt.1a
Was the sign of the covenant between God & His people. 31:13, pt.1a

History of Sunday. Why most believers worship on Sunday. 20:8, pt.2b

Kinds.
S. day. 23:12
S. year. (See **SABBATH YEAR, THE**) 23:10-11

Meaning. 20:8, Note 3

Purpose of.
Three reasons for the **S**. year. 23:10-11, pt.1
Why the **S** is to be kept. Two strong reasons. 20:11, Note 3

Results. Of keeping the **S**.
Benefits. List of seven benefits. 20:11, D.S.#3
Man would have a far healthier & more fruitful life. 35:2-3, Thgt. 1

Type - Symbol of. The Sabbath rest & worship point to the Lord Jesus Christ. 20:11, Thgt. 1; Intro. VI, pt.1

Warning. Judgment.
Consequences of breaking the **S**. 20:11, D.S.#2
To be kept holy or harsh judgment would come. 20:15; 35:2-3
To be kept holy or the person would destroy himself. 35:2-3, Thgt. 2

Working on the **S**. Discussed. 20:8, Note 3; 31:16-17; 20:8-11, D.S.#4, pt.3

SABBATH YEAR, THE
Broken - Violated. Israel failed to keep the Sabbath Year. 23:10-11, Thgt. 1

Discussed. 23:10-11

Purpose of.
To give the land rest. 23:10-11, pt.1a
To learn compassion for the poor. 23:10-11, pt.1b
To set aside a special time for special worship & study of God's Word. 23:10-11, pt.1c

SACRIFICE (See **COMMIT - COMMITMENT**)

SACRIFICE OF THE FIRST RAM (See **DEDICATION; PRIESTHOOD**)
How Christ fulfilled the symbolism of the **S**. Resource Chart 3, II:C

Type - Symbol of.
God accepting the person's sacrifice & total dedication of life. 29:15-18
God being pleased with faith.

What is taught by the **S**. Resource Chart 3, II:C

SACRIFICE OF THE SECOND RAM (See **CONSECRATION; PRIESTHOOD**)
How Christ fulfilled the symbolism of the **S**. Resource Chart 3, II:D

Type - Symbol of.
Full consecration to the service of God. 29:19-21
The identification with the sacrificial animal.

What is taught by the **S**. Resource Chart 3, II:D

SACRIFICES - SACRIFICIAL SYSTEM
Morning & evening. Discussed. 29:38-46

What was **s**.
A bull. 29:10-11
A goat. 26:7-13
First ram. 29:15-18
Second ram. 29:19-21

SALVATION - SAVED (See **DELIVERANCE; REDEMPTION**; Related Subjects)
Deliverance of. From the evil & tragedies of this world. 20:2, Note 5
Results. What God has promised to believers.
The bread, water, & health of His people. 23:24-26

SAMUEL
Example of.
S. rose up early & worked for God. 34:2,4
S's. parents rose up early & worked for God. 34:2,4

SANCTIFY - SANCTIFICATION
Discussed. How the people were to **s**. & consecrate themselves. 19:10
Duty. To be on guard & wash regularly. 30:17-21, pt.3, Thgt.1
Meaning. 19:10

SANCTUARY
Chart. How Christ fulfilled the symbolism of the Tabernacle. Resource Chart 2, V
Identified as - Refers to.
Christ's body. 25:9, Thgt. 2
God indwelling the believer. 25:8, Thgt. 1
The Tabernacle itself. 26:1-37
Meaning. 25:8
What is taught by the **s**. Resource Chart 2, V

SAND
What the foundation of the Tabernacle was firmly built upon. 26:15-30, Thgt. 1

SASH (See **CLOTHING**)
Chart. How Christ fulfilled the symbolism of the Priesthood. Resource Chart 3, I:A
Instructions for making. 28:39; 39:29
Type - Symbol of.
The Word of God that girds up a believer. Intro. VI, pt.24
Truth, the truth of God's Word. 39:27-29, Thgt. 4; Intro. VI, pt.24
What is taught by the **S**. Resource Chart 3, I:A

534

INDEX

SATAN
Names & titles.
  Accuser. 20:16, D.S.#1
  Father of lies. 20:16, D.S.#1

SATISFACTION, SPIRITUAL
Discussed. Involves eight things. 37:10-16, Thgt. 1

SAVIOR (See JESUS CHRIST)

SCAPEGOAT
Type - Symbol of. Jesus Christ. 25:3-7, Thgt. 1

SCARLET, Color of
Type - Symbol of. Sacrifice & redemption through the Lamb of God. 25:4; Intro. VI, pt.27

SCHOOLMASTER (See LAW, The)

SCRIPTURE (See WORD OF GOD)

SEA COW (See BADGER SKINS)

SECULAR - SECULARISM - SECULARISTS
Definition of. Intro. 20:3, pt.1

SECURITY
Christ & His teaching concerning man's s. 20:17, D.S.#3
Fact. God wants man to feel secure & protected. 20:17, Note 2

SEE - SEEING (See SPIRITUAL SIGHT)
Moses & his leaders *saw* God. Meaning. 24:9-11, pt.1c
Moses saw God's back. 33:18-23

SELF-SUFFICIENCY (See PRIDE)

SEPARATE - SEPARATION (See SANCTIFICATION; WORLDLINESS)
Duty.
  Must make no covenants with unbelievers. 23:32-33
  Must not let unbelievers live with you. 23:32-33
Essential. To be sanctified, consecrated, set apart for God. 19:10
From God.
  A great gulf s. God from man. 19:11-16, pt.2; 19:16-25, pt.2; 20:18,Thgt. 1; 20:18; Ex.24:1-2 Ex.24:1-2
  Only God's appointed mediator can approach God. 24:1-2
  What separates us from God is sin. 33:1-3, Thgt. 1
Principles to govern s.
  Not to be associated with evil talk. 23:27-33, Thgt. 2
  Not to be unequally yoked with unbelievers. 23:27-33, Thgt. 2
  Not to keep company with a brother who is living a life of sin & rebellion. 23:27-33, Thgt. 2
  Not to walk in the counsel of the ungodly. 23:27-33, Thgt. 2
  Not to walk in the path of the wicked. 23:27-33, Thgt. 2
Type - Symbol of. The inner veil: God's majestic holiness & man's separation

from God. 36:35-36; Intro. VI, pt.19; Resource Chart 2, VI

SEPTUAGINT
Mentioned. 25:5, point 6; 25:17-21

SERVANT (See BELIEVER; SLAVE - SLAVERY)

SERVE - SERVICE (See MINISTRY)

SERVICES, DEDICATION
Discussed.
  Of the Priesthood. 29:1-3
  Of the Tabernacle. 29:1-3

SET APART (See CONSECRATION; SANCTIFICATION; SEPARATION)

SEX (See ADULTERY; FORNICATION; IMMORALITY; LUST; Related Subjects)
Abstinence. Reason for. 19:15
Kinds.
  Bestiality (See BESTIALITY)
  Premarital s. Judgment of. 22:16-17
Problems with illicit s. List. 20:14, Note 2, pt.4a
Purpose. Twofold. 20:14, Note 2, pt.4, 22:16-17
Warning.
  Adultery is forbidden. 20:14, Note 2
  To sexual perverts. 22:19, Thgt. 1

SEX, ILLICIT (See ADULTERY; IMMORALITY)
Caused by. (See IMMORAL - IMMORALITY)
Discussed. How a person becomes sexually impure. 20:14, Note 2, pt.1

SHAME - SHAMEFUL (See GUILT)
Caused by. Terrible sin. 32:21-24

SHEWBREAD (See SHOWBREAD; SHOWBREAD, TABLE OF)

SHINE (See LAMPSTAND; LIGHT)

SHITTIM (See ACACIA; ACACIA WOOD)

SHOWBREAD
Discussed. 25:30
Fact. What Jesus Christ said about this bread. 25:30, pt.7
Represented - Meaning of.
  Dependence upon God. 25:30
  Each tribe of Israel. 25:30
  God's presence & worship. 25:30
  God Himself as the nourishment that man really needs. 25:30
  Jesus Christ as the Bread of Life. 25:30
  The bread that we all desperately need. 25:30
  The spiritual needs of man. 25:30
  Trust of God. 25:30
Type - Symbol of.
  God as the Bead of Life. 25:23-30; 37:10-16; Intro. VI, pt.9; Resource Chart 2, III
  Jesus Christ as the Bread of Life. 25:30; Intro. VI, pt.9; Resource Chart 2, III

SHOWBREAD, TABLE OF
Chart. How Christ fulfilled the symbolism of the Tabernacle. Resource Chart 2, III
Construction of.
  Discussed. 37:10-16
  Instructions for construction. 25:23-30; 37:10-16
  Set up. 40:22-23
How Christ fulfilled the symbolism of the Table. Resource Chart 2, III
Presented to Moses. 39:36
Type - Symbol of.
  Being in God's presence & worshipping Him. Intro. VI, pt.9
  Christ as the Bread of Life. 25:30; 35:13; 37:10-16; Intro. VI, pt.9
  God as the Bread of Life. 25:30; Intro. VI, pt.9
  God nourishing man's hungry soul. 25:23-30; 35:13; 37:10-16; Intro. VI, pt.9
What is taught by the Table. Resource Chart 2, III

SILVER
Discussed. The foundation of the Tabernacle. 26:15-30, pt.2, Thgt.1
Fact. Atonement money. Given by each man in the form of s. 26:15-30, pt.2b; 30:11-16
Type - Symbol of. Redemption, ransom. 25:3; 30:11-16; Intro. VI, pt.35

SIN - SINS - SINNER
Caused by - Source of sin.
  By believing deliverance is of man not God. 32:1, pt.6
  By believing in false gods. 32:1, pt.4
  By coveting anything that belongs to one's neighbor. 20:17, Note 2
  By disobeying God's commandments. 32:1, pt.5
  By false worship. 32:5-6, pt.8
  By giving in to & fearing the crowd. 32:2, pt.7
  By impatience. 32:1, pt.1
  By indulging in food, drink, partying, & illicit sex. 32:6, pt.9
  By pressure from a crowd. 32:1, pt.2
  By suggesting evil to a weak leader. 32:1, pt.3
Deliverance. Through the work of Christ.
  Makes us righteous in Himself. 35:10-19, pt.2a
  Reconciles us to God. 35:10-19, pt.2b
Duty. Must not make excuses for our s. 32:21-24
Kinds of s.
  Adultery. 20:14, D.S.#1
  Coveting. 20:17, D.S.#1
  Failing to honor your father & your mother. 20:12, D.S.#1
  Failing to keep the Sabbath & to keep it holy. 20:11, D.S.#2
  False worship. 20:4-6, D.S.#1
  Having other gods, of believing in other gods. 20:3, D.S.#1
  Killing another person. 20:13, D.S.#3
  Lying. 20:16, D.S.#1
  Misusing God's name. 20:7, D.S.#1
  Stealing. 20:15, D.S.#1
Results of sin.

Judgment against.
  Adultery. 20:14, D.S.#1
  Coveting. 20:17, D.S.#1
  Failing to honor your father &
    your mother. 20:12, D.S.#1
  Failing to keep the Sabbath & to
    keep it holy. 20:11, D.S.#2
  False worship. 20:4-6, D.S.#1
  Having other gods, of believing in
    other gods. 20:3, D.S.#1
  Idolatry or worshipping false gods.
    20:5-6
  Killing another person. 20:13,
    D.S.#3
  Lying. 20:16, D.S.#1
  Misusing God's name. 20:7,
    D.S.#1
  Must face the judgment of God.
    20:5-6, pt.2
  Stealing. 20:15, D.S.#1
  Will be judged in righteousness.
    32:25-29
Warning. Sin causes God to withdraw
  His presence. 33:1-3

SIN OFFERING (See **GOATS**)

SINAI, MOUNT (See **CITIES - AREAS**)
  Discussed. 19:1-4; 19:16-25; 24:12-18;
    31:18; 32:1, 15; 34:2, 29, 32
  Map of. 19:16-25

SINNER - SINNERS (See **MAN; SIN**)

SKILLS
  Discussed.
    God gives the person whatever s. &
      abilities are needed to do the work.
      31:4-5, Thgt.1
    Workers were gifted by the LORD
      with s. 36:1-2

SLANDER - SLANDERING
  Discussed. A form of lying. 20:16, Note
    2, pt.2
  Duty. Must not bear false witness or re-
    port. 23:1-3

SLAVE - SLAVERY
  Discussed.
    Economic realities of the ancient
      world. 21:2-6
    Laws to protect the s. 21:12-27, pt.8, 10
  Facts.
    Why God permits s. 21:2-6
    Why some Hebrews became s. 21:2-6
  History of. 21:2-6
  Purpose. Why God did not demand the
    elimination of s. all at once. 21:2-6
  Treatment of. The rights of Hebrew
    slaves. 21:2-6

SLOTHFUL (See **LAZY - LAZINESS**)

SOCIETY (See **WORLD**)
  Corrupt s. Discussed. Intro. 20:12

SORCERER - SORCERY
  Error of. Misleads & deceives people.
    22:18
  Judgment of. To be destroyed. 22:18

SOVEREIGNTY (See **GOD; JESUS
CHRIST**)
  Discussed. God's eternal existence.
    20:1, Note 1

SPEAK - SPEECH (See **TONGUE**)
  Discussed. Profanity's effect upon soci-
    ety. Intro. 20:7
  Warning.
    Men are responsible for every word
      they speak. 20:16, D.S.#3, pt.2
    Our words will either justify or con-
      demn us. 20:16, D.S.#3, pt.4

SPEECH, FALSE (See **LYING**)

SPIRITUAL EXPERIENCE (See
GLORY)
  Example of. Moses.
    Caught up in God's glory on Mt. Si-
      nai. 19:16-25
    Continually went to the tent to seek
      the LORD. 33:8
    Could not enter the Tabernacle.
      40:34-35
    God personally spoke to Moses.
      "And the LORD said [or spake,
      KJV] to **M**." 19:9-10, 21; 20:22;
      24:12; 25:1; 30:11, 17, 34; 31:1,
      12; 32:7, 9, 33; 33:1, 11, 17; 34:1,
      27; 40:1
    God revealed Himself & proclaimed
      His name, *the LORD*. 34:5-9, pt.1
    God spoke to **M**. face to face. 33:7-11
    Had a close relationship with God.
      Reason for. 33:12-17, Thgt.1
    Saw God's back. 33:18-23
    Saw God. 24:9-11
    Veil of **M**. 34:29-35
    Wanted to know God more & more.
      33:18-33
    Was in God's presence & glory for
      forty days & nights. 24:12-18

SPIRITUAL SIGHT (See **KNOW -
KNOWING - KNOWLEDGE**)

STABILITY (See **FRAMEWORK OF
THE TABERNACLE**)

STARTING OVER (See **NEW BEGIN-
NING; RENEWAL; RESTORATION**)
  Source - How to secure.
    Go forth to proclaim God's Word.
      34:29-35
    Know the importance of the Ten
      Commandments. 34:27-28
    Make a renewed commitment to obey
      God. 34:10-26
    Respond to God's call to come back
      into His presence. 34:1-4
    Seek & experience God's presence
      afresh. 34:5-9

STEALING
  Benefits of *not* s. 20:15, D.S.#2
  Christ & His teaching concerning s.
    20:15, D.S.#3
  Discussed.
    A heart problem. 20:15, Note 2, pt.2
    Laws governing theft. 22:1-4
    S. from God. 20:15, Note 2, pt.4
  Duty. Must not steal. 20:15, Note 3
  Facts.
    One of the most common crimes. In-
      tro. 20:15
    S. was the first sin committed.
      By Ananias & Sapphira that de-
        filed the early church. 20:15,
        Note 2, pt.2

By Israel after entering Canaan.
  20:15, Note 2, pt.2
By the human race. 20:15, Note 2,
  pt.2
List. Things that are stolen. 20:15, Note
  2, pt.4
Meaning. To take & keep something
  that belongs to another person. 20:15,
  Note 2, pt.1
Results.
  Consequences of s. 20:15, D.S.#1
  S. threatens the very foundation of
    society itself. Intro. 20:15
Source. Satan is the greatest thief of all.
  20:15; D.S.#1, #3
Who stealing is a sin against.
  God. 20:15, Note 2, pt.4
  Society. 20:15, Note 2, pt.4
  The people stolen from. 20:15, Note
    2, pt.4

STEWARDSHIP (See **GIVE - GIVING;
OFFERING; STEWARD; TITHE**)
  Discussed.
    Laws governing deposits. 22:7-15
    The basic law governing the offerings
      to God. 23:19
    The proper use of offerings. 36:3-7
  Duty.
    To be a cheerful giver. 35:4-9
    To be responsible for our lives & our
      possessions. 21:28-32, pt.2, Thgt.1
    To give all we are & have to Christ.
      30:11-16, pt.5
    To take care of the needs of the
      church & of believers. 30:11-16,
      pt.5

STRANGERS
  Discussed. Treatment of. Not to be op-
    pressed. 23:9

STRONG FOUNDATION (See **FRAME-
WORK OF THE TABERNACLE**)

STUMBLING BLOCK (See **INFLU-
ENCE, Evil**)

**SUBJECTION - SUBMIT - SUBMIS-
SION**
  Believers are to be subject to God. The
    believer's mind & will are to be sub-
    jected to God. 39:27-29, Thgt. 2; In-
    tro. VI, pt.32; Resource Chart 3, I:G

SUBSTITUTION (See **JESUS CHRIST**)

SUFFERING (See **PERSECUTION**)

SUICIDE (See **MURDER**)
  Discussed.
    Different views of s. 20:13, D.S.#2
    Why a person should never commit s.
      20:13, D.S.#2
  Duty toward suicidal people & their
    families. To minister. 20:13, D.S.#2

SUNDAY (See **SABBATH - SUNDAY**)

SUPERSTITION (See **SORCERER -
SORCERY**)

SUPPORT (See **FRAMEWORK OF
THE TABERNACLE**)

SWEARING (See **CURSING**)

INDEX

INDEX

INDEX

TRIALS -TRIBULATION (See **TEST - TESTING**)

TRUSTEE
Duty. To be a good steward of money or goods entrusted for safe-keeping. 22:7-15

TRUTH
Duty. To be spoken in love & kindness. 20:16, Note 2, pt.8
Fact. The very foundation or basis of society is t. 20:16, Note 2, pt.7
Verses. List of . God is the source of truth. 20:16, Note 2, pt.6

TRUTHFULNESS
Fifteen benefits of being truthful. 20:16, D.S.#2

TUNIC (See **CLOTHING**)
Chart. How Christ fulfilled the symbolism of the Priesthood. Resource Chart 3, I:F
Instructions for making. 28:39; 39:27
Type - Symbol of. Putting on God's righteousness. 39:27-29, Thgt. 1; Intro. VI, pt.31
What is taught by the t. Resource Chart 3, I:F

TURBAN (See **CLOTHING**)
Chart. How Christ fulfilled the symbolism of the Priesthood. Resource Chart 3, I:F
Instructions for making. 28:39; 39:28
Type - Symbol of. Putting on God's righteousness. 39:27-29, Thgt. 1; Intro. VI, pt.31
What is taught by the t. Resource Chart 3, I:F

UNBELIEF (See **DISOBEDIENCE; SIN**)

UNBORN, THE (See **ABORTION**)

UNDERCLOTHING (See **CLOTHING**)
Chart. How Christ fulfilled the symbolism of the Priesthood. Resource Chart 3, I:H
Instructions for making. 28:42-43; 39:28
Purpose. To cover the nakedness of the priests as they climbed the steps of the altar. 28:43
Type - Symbol of. Covering the believer's spiritual nakedness. 39:27-29, Thgt. 3; Intro. VI, pt.33
What is taught by the u. Resource Chart 3, I:H

UNDERSTANDING (See **SEE - SEEING**)

UNDERWEAR (See **UNDERCLOTHING; CLOTHING**)

UNITY
Source - Comes by. Believers are unified by working together according to the design of God. 31:6-11, pt.3

UNLEAVENED BREAD, FEAST OF (See **FEASTS**)

URI
Discussed. Father of Bezalel. 31:2
Meaning. 31:2

UTENSILS (See **ALTAR OF BURNT OFFERING; TABLE OF SHOW-BREAD**)
Accessories.
For Altar of Burnt Offering. 38:3
For Lampstand. 31:8; 37:23
For Table. 31:8; 37:16
List.
Bronze u. for the Altar of Burnt Offering. 27:1-8, pt.4
Gold u. for the Table of Showbread. 37:16

VAIN (See **PROFANITY**)
Meaning of. Taking God's name in v. 20:7, Note 3

VEIL, ENTRANCE DOOR (See **ENTRANCE GATE; TABERNACLE**)

VEIL, INNER (See **TABERNACLE**)
Chart. How Christ fulfilled the symbolism of the Tabernacle. Resource Chart 2, VI
Construction of.
Discussed. 36:35-36
Instructions for construction. 26:31-35; 35-36
Set up. 40:21
Discussed. Four lessons for the believer. 26:31-35, pt.3b
Fact. Was later torn down from top to bottom by God. 30:6, Thgt. 2
How Christ fulfilled the symbolism of the v. Resource Chart 2, VI
Type - Symbol of.
God must be approached carefully. 26:31-35; 36:35-36; Intro. VI, pt.17
Only one way into God's presence. 26:31-35; 36:35-36; Intro. VI, pt.17
The entrance into fellowship & communion with God. 26:31-35; 36:35-36; Intro. VI, pt.17
The separation between Holy God & sinful man. 26:31-35; 36:35-36; Intro. VI, pt.17
What was taught by the v. Resource Chart 3, VI

VEIL, MOSES'
Discussed. 34:33-35
Illustration of. Discussed. 34:33-35, Thgt. 2
Type - Symbol of.
The results of a man spending time with God. 34:35; Intro. VI, pt.39
The spiritual blindness of Israel. 34:35: Intro. VI, pt.39

VEIL, OUTER (See **TABERNACLE**)
Chart. How Christ fulfilled the symbolism of the Tabernacle. Resource Chart 2, VII
Construction of.
Discussed. 36:37-38
Instructions for construction. 26:36-37; 36:37-38
Set up. 40:28
Described. 26:36-37; 36:37-38

Discussed. The lessons of the outer veil. 26:36-37, pt.2, Thgt. 1
How Christ fulfilled the symbolism of the v. Resource Chart 2, VII
Type - Symbol of.
Entrance into worship, into experiencing God in deeper ways. 26:36-37; 36:37-38; Intro. VI, pt.18
Reverence for God. 26:36-37; 36:37-38; Intro. VI, pt.18
What the v. taught. Resource Chart 2, VII

VENGEANCE
Duty. To love our enemies not take v. 23:4-5

VICARIOUS SUFFERINGS AND DEATH OF CHRIST (See **JESUS CHRIST**, Death)

VICTORY - VICTORIOUS LIVING
Source of. God. 23:27-33

VIOLENCE
Discussed.
Laws governing v. 21:12-27
People have become desensitized & hardened to v. Intro. 20:13

VOCATION (See **BUSINESS; WORK, PHYSICAL OR SECULAR**)

VULGARITY (See **CURSING; PROFANITY; SPEECH; SWEARING; TONGUE**)
Discussed. Two reasons why God forbids v. 20:7, Note 4

WALK, BELIEVER'S (See **BELIEVER**)
Picture of the believer's life in the Tabernacle. Chart. Resource Chart 1

WALLS (See **COURTYARD; TABERNACLE**)
How Christ fulfilled the symbolism of the w. Resource Chart 2, IX
Type - Symbol of. The righteousness & holiness of God. Intro. VI, pt.21
What is taught by the w. Resource Chart 2, IX

WARFARE (See **ARMOR OF GOD**)

WARN - WARNING
The warning to believers.
For not keeping the Ten Commandments.
False worship. 20:4-6, D.S.#1
Committing adultery. 20:14, D.S.#1
Coveting. 20:17, D.S.#1
Failing to honor your father & your mother. 20:12, D.S.#1
Failing to keep the Sabbath & to keep it holy. 20:11, D.S.#2
Having other gods, of believing in other gods. 20:3, D.S.#1
Killing another person. 20:13, D.S.#3
Lying. 20:16, D.S.#1
Misusing God's name. 20:7, D.S.#1
Stealing. 20:15, D.S.#1
Sin causes God to withdraw His presence. 33:1-3

539

WASH BASIN, BRONZE
Chart. How Christ fulfilled the symbolism of the Tabernacle. Resource Chart 2, XII
Construction of.
  Discussed. 38:8
  Instructions for construction. 30:17-21; 38:8
  Set up. 40:30
Discussed. 30:17-21; 35:16; 38:8; 39:9; 40:7; 40:30-32
How Christ fulfilled the symbolism of the w. Resource Chart 2, XII
Importance. Washing & cleansing was made a permanent law for all generations. 30:21
Placement of. Between the Tent of Meeting & the Altar. 40:30
Purpose.
  For the priests to wash their hands & feet. 30:19; 40:30
  To constantly remind us of who we are--redeemed sinners. 38:8, Thgt. 2
Type - Symbol of.
  A person's need to be cleansed as he continually served God. 35:16; 38:8; Intro. VI, pt.36
  A person's need to be cleansed before he can enter God's presence. 35:16; 38:8; Intro. VI, pt.36
  A person's need to be cleansed before he can serve God. 35:16; 38:8; Intro. VI, pt.36
Warning.
  The priest must wash or die. 30:17-21, pt.4
  We must constantly be on guard & wash regularly. 30:17-21, pt.3
What is taught by the w. Resource Chart 2, XII

WASHED - WASHING, SPIRITUAL (See **CLEAN - CLEANSING; PURE - PURITY**)
Discussed. Aaron & his sons were to be publicly w. before the Tabernacle. 29:4
Duty. To be washed & cleansed from sin. 38:8
Type - Symbol of. The bronze wash basin symbolized the w. away of sin. 38:8; Intro. VI, pt.36; Resource Chart 2, XII

WAVE OFFERING
Discussed. Instructions. 29:22-28
Fact. Should offer God the best of what we have. 29:22-28, Thgt. 1
How Christ fulfilled the symbolism of the w.o. Resource Chart 3, II:E
Meaning. 29:22-28, pt.1c
Type - Symbol of.
  The commitment to give God the best. 29:22-28
  The pleasure & acceptance of the LORD. 29:25
What is taught by the w.o. Resource Chart 3, II:E

WEALTH (See **RICH - RICHES**)

WHITE LINEN (See **TABERNACLE**)
Type - Symbol of. Purity, righteousness, holiness of God. 25:4; Intro. VI, pt.11

WIDOW
Discussed. Treatment of. 22:22-24

WIFE - WIVES (See **WOMEN**)

WILL OF GOD (See **OBEY - OBEDIENCE**)
Discussed. The purpose of the breast-piece or chestpiece. 28:15-30

WITCHCRAFT (See **SORCERER - SORCERY**)

WITNESS - WITNESSING (See **PROCLAMATION; TESTIMONY**)

WITNESS, FALSE
Discussed. How Scripture defines a false witness.
  A person who breathes out lies. 20:16, Note 2, pt.1
  A person who deceives. 20:16, Note 2, pt.1
  A person who shares a false report. 20:16, Note 2, pt.1

WOMAN - WOMEN
Discussed.
  God's care for w. 21:7-11, Thgt.1
  Treatment of. Laws governing the Hebrew female sold for marriage. 21:7-11
Duty toward.
  It is the man's responsibility to treat all w. fairly. 21:7-11, Thgt.3
  It is the man's responsibility to care for the w. 21:7-11, Thgt.2
  It is the man's responsibility to defend the w. 21:7-11, Thgt.4
Fact. God is actively at work in the wombs of pregnant w. 21:12-27, pt.9, Thgt.1
Warning. Penalty for harming a pregnant w. 21:12-27, pt.9

WORD OF GOD
Basis of the Ten Commandments. 20:1
Duty towards.
  To obey. 24:4-8
  To receive more & more of God's law, of God's Word. 24:12-18
Facts.
  God has spoken to man. 20:22
  Reminds us of our depraved condition. 38:8

WORDS (See **TONGUE**)

WORK FOR GOD
Discussed. The need to put into action the plan of God. 36:1-2
Essential.
  Everyone must surrender personal pride & work together. 36:2
  We must do our best to complete the work of God upon earth. 38:21-31, Thgt. 1
Example of. People who rose up early & worked for God. 34:1-4, Thgt. 1
Fact. God will always supply what is needed to do His work. 38:21-31, Thgt. 1
Source. All skills & abilities are from God. 36:1, pt.1

WORK, PHYSICAL OR SECULAR
Discussed. 20:9-10
Duty. To work six days, to work diligently. 20:8, pt.4
Purpose of. For the benefit of others. 20:8, pt.4

WORKS, GOOD (See **MAN; PERFECT - PERFECTION**)
Duty.
  Must abide in God's Word. 28:39-43
  Must bear much fruit. 28:39-43
  Must forsake all & follow Christ. 28:39-43
  Must live a life that is godly & above reproach. 28:39-43

WORLD (See **INCORRUPTION**)
Warning. Against the dangers of the w. 36:19, Thgt. 1

WORLDLINESS
Symbolized - Typed by. Jewelry was apparently a symbol of w. 33:4-6

WORSHIP
Christ & His teaching concerning the w. of God. 20:4-6, D.S.#3
Definition of. Intro. 20:4-6
Discussed. The Ten Commandments teach man how God is to be approached & w. 20:23-26
Duty.
  To assemble together with other believers. 20:4-6, D.S.#3, pt.5
  To be a true worshipper of God. 20:4-6, D.S.#3, pt.3
  To set aside the seventh day as a day of w. 20:11
  To w. God. 24:1-2; 24:9-11
  To w. morning until night--all day, every day. 29:38-46, pt.1
Entrance into. Christ invites men to come through the door & w. Him. 26:36-37, Thgt. 1
Example of. Moses fell to the ground, prostrating himself before the Lord in w. & prayer. 34:5-9, pt.2
Fact. Impossible to w. if God's law & Word are not close at hand. 31:18
How long God is to be w.: Forever. 20:4
Instructions on how God was to be w. Three lessons. 20:23-26
What God demands. Intro. 20:4-6
Who is to w.: You. 20:4.

WORSHIP, FALSE
Results of.
  Causes terrible sin. 32:5-6
  List of consequences. 20:4-6, D.S.#1
What men worship. Intro. 20:4-6

WRATH OF GOD (See **JUDGMENT**)

WRATH OF MAN (See **ANGER**)

ZODIAC
Mentioned. A form of idolatry. 20:4-5, pt.1c

INDEX

HEBREW WORD STUDIES

IN THE BOOK OF EXODUS

HEBREW WORD STUDIES
IN THE BOOK OF EXODUS

<u>REMEMBER</u>: When you look up an English word, this word study chart will give you the following information:
- ⇒ The English word in alphabetical order followed by the Hebrew word
- ⇒ The concordance reference numbers for three different translations
- ⇒ The Scripture reference and <u>The Preacher's Outline & Sermon Bible</u>® (POSB) reference
- ⇒ The Hebrew meaning of the word

Every Hebrew word that has been discussed in Exodus Part II has been placed into this chart for your convenience. To further assist you in your study, we have included the concordance numbers for Strong's (KJV), the New American Standard (NASB) and the New International Version (NIV). These reference numbers are located beneath each Hebrew word. The reader will notice that in some spellings of the Hebrew word there are several different renditions offered. This is due to the choices of each commentator gleaned in the research for Exodus. The *first spelling* is always found in the POSB commentary. Any spellings that follow come either from <u>Strong's Exhaustive Concordance of the Bible</u>,[1] the <u>NASB Greek/Hebrew Dictionary and Concordance</u>,[2] or the <u>NIV Exhaustive Concordance</u>[3].

<u>DISCOVER THE GREAT VALUE</u> for yourself. Quickly glance below to the very first English word. Turn to the reference. Glance at the Scripture and outline of the Scripture, then read the commentary. Note how the word is used and defined in the context of the Scripture. You will immediately see the GREAT VALUE of the HEBREW WORD STUDIES INDEX of <u>The Preacher's Outline & Sermon Bible</u>®.

ENGLISH WORD	HEBREW WORD	POSB REFERENCE	THE HEBREW MEANS...
1. Adultery	naap or naaph *5003 KJV *5003 NASB *5537 NIV	20:14, note 2, pt.1	⇒ To debase, to corrupt oneself sexually, to make oneself impure sexually, to have sex outside of marriage.
2. Before me	alpamaya or paniym or pa-nim or paneh *6440 KJV *6440 NASB *6584 + 7156 NIV	20:3, note 3	⇒ Literally before my face, against my face, in hostility toward me, in my presence, in my sight. ⇒ It means that man is to set no god... • *before* the LORD God • *beside* the LORD God • *in the presence* of the LORD God • *in the face* of the LORD God
3. Bezalel	Betsalel *1212 KJV *1212 NASB *1295 NIV	31:1-11, note 1	⇒ Under the shadow of God.
4. Corrupt	sihet or shachath *7843 KJV *7843 NASB *8845 NIV	32:7-14, note 2	⇒ Running to destruction, ruin, waste, perishing. ⇒ This is the same word used to describe the terrible sin of the people in Noah's day (Gen.6:11).

---

[1] James Strong. *Strong's Exhaustive Concordance of the Bible*.
[2] *The NASB Greek/Hebrew Dictionary and Concordance*. (La Habra, CA: The Lockman Foundation, 1988).
[3] *NIV Exhaustive Concordance*. (Grand Rapids, MI: Zondervan Corporation, 1990).

INDEX OF HEBREW WORDS

ENGLISH WORD	HEBREW WORD	POSB REFERENCE	THE HEBREW MEANS...
5. Covet	hamad or chamad *2530 KJV *2530 NASB *2773 NIV	20:17, note 2, pt.1	⇒ To desire, crave, want, long for, thirst for, lust after. ⇒ Coveting is a neutral word; that is, coveting can be good as well as bad, legitimate as well as illegitimate.
6. Fear	1st use of fear = yare *3372 KJV *3372a NASB *3707 NIV (*afraid*) 2nd use of fear = yirah *3374 KJV *3374 NASB *3711 NIV	20:20-21, note 3	⇒ First use of fear: A tormenting fear, the fear that defeats a person, that keeps a person from acting and doing what he should. ⇒ Second use of fear: A respectful, honoring fear, the fear of God that arouses a person to reverence and obey God.
7. Guiltless	waqah or naqah *5352 KJV *5352 NASB *5927 NIV	20:7, note 4, pt.2	⇒ To count as clear or free from blame. God will not count us clean or pure, innocent or guiltless. God will not acquit us, not let us go unpunished.
8. Holy	qados or qadash or qodesh *6942 KJV *6942 NASB *7727 NIV	D.S.#1, Ex.20:8; 29:1-3, note 1	⇒ Sanctified, separated, set apart, devoted, dedicated, consecrated, hallowed, honored, made sacred. ⇒ It means to be pure, clean and free from all pollution and defilement, totally free from sin and evil. ⇒ It means to be totally different and distinct from anything else, from all that is in the world with all its corruption.
9. Honor	kabed or kabad *3513 KJV *3513 NASB *3877 NIV	20:12, note 3	⇒ To respect, esteem, and highly regard our parents. ⇒ To reverence our parents.
10. Hur	Chur *2354 KJV *2354 NASB *2581 NIV	31:1-11, note 1	⇒ Free
11. Jealous	quanna or qanna *7067 KJV *7067 NASB *7862 NIV	34:10-26, note 3	⇒ It means red in the face, implying that God is fiercely possessive of his followers. This unique name is reserved solely for God. ⇒ "This particular word is used only of God, oc-

ENGLISH WORD	HEBREW WORD	POSB REFERENCE	THE HEBREW MEANS...
			curring but five times in the O.T., and illustrates the parallel between idolatry and adultery." [4]
12. Judah	Yehudah *3063 KJV *3063 NASB *3373 NIV	31:1-11, note 1	⇒ It means to give thanks and praise. ⇒ This word is a proper noun that is used to name individual people (including Jacob's son), a tribe, and a region in Palestine.
13. Judgments	mispatim or mishpat *4941 KJV *4941 NASB *5477 NIV	21:1, note 1	⇒ It means to govern with justice. God gave "the judgments" or the laws to judge civil disputes
14. Kill or killing	rasah or ratsach *7523 KJV *7523 NASB *8357 NIV (*murder*)	20:13, note 2, pt.2	⇒ Premeditated, planned, deliberate, intentional, unauthorized murder.
15. LORD	Jehovah - Yahweh Yhvh *3068 KJV *3068 NASB *3378 NIV	20:2, note 3; D.S.#1-- Ex.20:2; 34:5-9, note 2	⇒ This name of God means that He is the great I AM, I AM THAT I AM (Ex.3:14). ⇒ It means that God is the Essence, Force, and Energy of Being, the Self-existent One. ⇒ It means that God is the God of salvation, deliverance, and redemption. ⇒ It means that God is the God of revelation.
16. Lying (false witness)	sheqer *8267 KJV *8267 NASB *9214 NIV (*false testimony*)	20:16, note 2	⇒ That which is false, untrue. ⇒ It is untruthfulness, deception, misrepresentation, exaggeration.
17. Mercy Seat	kapporeth *3727 KJV *3727 NASB *4114 NIV (*atonement cover*)	25:17-21, note 2	⇒ Covering or atonement ⇒ The idea refers to the covering of sins, of atonement or reconciliation being made possible by the mercy of God. ⇒ The root word for "Mercy Seat" or "atonement cover" comes from *kaphar* which means... ⇒ to cover ⇒ to make atonement ⇒ to cleanse, forgive, pardon, purge away, put off ⇒ to appease, placate, cancel, annul

---

[4] Frank E. Gaebelein. *The Expositor's Bible Commentary*, p.486.

INDEX OF HEBREW WORDS

ENGLISH WORD	HEBREW WORD	POSB REFERENCE	THE HEBREW MEANS...
18. Naked or out of control	para *6544 KJV *6544a NASB *7277 NIV	32:25-29, note 5	⇒ To expose, uncover, and loosen all restraints; to get out of control.
19. Oholiab	Oholiab *171 KJV *171 NASB *190 NIV	31:1-11, note 1	⇒ Tent of the father or the (divine) father is my tent.
20. Onyx	shoh-ham or shoham *7718 KJV *7718 NASB *8732 NIV	25:3-7, note 3, pt.9	⇒ A flashing forth of splendor.
21. Oppress	lahas or lachats *3905 KJV *3905 NASB *4315 NIV	23:9, note 5	⇒ To crush, to confine, to press closely.
22. Play or revelry	tsachaq *6711 KJV *6711 NASB *7464 NIV	32:1-6, note 1	⇒ The idea of loose conduct, the kind of loose behavior that happens when a person has been drinking or taking drugs. ⇒ The word has the idea of crude language and laughter, of playing around, of sexual misconduct, of engaging in a wild dancing or drinking party. ⇒ The picture is that of a festival breaking out into wild drinking, lewd dancing, and immoral behavior.
23. Remember	zakar *2142 KJV *2142 NASB *2349 NIV	20:8-10, note 2	⇒ You must remember-- remember to the point of *keeping* and *observing*-- the day of rest and worship (it is a strong, strong imperative).
24. Sabbath	shabbath *7676 KJV *7676 NASB *8701 NIV	20:8-10, note 2	⇒ To rest, to repose, to cease. ⇒ It means to cease from work, to rest from work.
25. Sanctuary	miqdash or miqqedash *4720 KJV *4720 NASB *5219 NIV	25:8, note 4	⇒ A holy place, a hallowed place, a place sanctified or set apart for God.
26. Saw (the verb)	chazah *2372 KJV *2372 NASB *2600 NIV	24:9-11, note 4	⇒ An inward, spiritual, or prophetic vision. ⇒ It means to mentally see and contemplate with pleasure; to have a vi-

INDEX OF HEBREW WORDS

ENGLISH WORD	HEBREW WORD	POSB REFERENCE	THE HEBREW MEANS...
			sion: beholding, looking, seeing something in one's mind.
27. Showbread	lechem = bread *3899 KJV *3899 NASB *4312 NIV paneh or panim = presence *6440 KJV *6440 NASB *7156 NIV	25:23-29, note 1; See also 25:30	⇒ Literally means two things: ⇒ The *Bread of the Face* referring to the face of God. The showbread was placed before the very face of God Himself. ⇒ The *Bread of the Presence* referring to the presence of God. The showbread was bread placed in the very presence of God Himself.
28. Stealing	ganab *1589 KJV *1589 NASB *1704 NIV	20:15, note 2, pt.1	⇒ To take and keep something that belongs to another person.
29. Tabernacle	mishkan *4908 KJV *4908 NASB *5438 NIV	25:9, note 5	⇒ A dwelling place, a habitation, a residence, a tent. ⇒ The picture is that of God pitching His tent among His people and living in a very special way with them.
30. Thummim	Tummim *8550 KJV *8550 NASB *9460 NIV	28:15-30, note 3	⇒ The best meaning of this word is perfection, with the idea of completeness and integrity (BDB[5]).
31. Treasure	sequallah or segullah *5459 KJV *5459 NASB *6035 NIV	19:5-9, note 2	⇒ Select, choice, prized, precious, something held dear
32. Uri	Uri *221 KJV *221 NASB *247 NIV	31:1-11, note 1	⇒ Light or "fiery" (BDG[6]).
33. Urim	Urim *224 KJV *224 NASB *242 NIV	28:15-30, note 3	⇒ Either lights or curse
34. Vain	lassaw or shav or shawv *7723 KJV *7723 NASB *2021 + 4200 + 5951 + 8736 NIV (*misuse*)	20:7, note 3 (first use of the word in verse 7)	⇒ Empty, meaningless, thoughtless, senseless, frivolous, worthless, groundless. ⇒ It means using God's name in a thoughtless and insincere way.

---

[5] Francis Brown. *The New Brown-Driver-Briggs-Gesenius Hebrew-English Lexicon*, page 1070
[6] ibid., page 22

ENGLISH WORD	HEBREW WORD	POSB REFERENCE	THE HEBREW MEANS...
35. Vain (the root of the word)	shawu or shav or shawv *7723 KJV *7723 NASB *2021 + 4200 + 5951 + 8736 NIV (*misuses*)	20:7, note 3 (second use of the word in verse 7)	⇒ Has the idea of a vapor that fades and vanishes away, a vapor that is meaningless and worthless. ⇒ It also has the idea of a tempest, a storm, a tornado that is erratic, that jumps here and there, that causes senseless destruction and total devastation
36. Wave [offering]	nuph or tenuphah (from nuph) *8573 KJV *8573 NASB *5677 NIV	29:22-28, note 9	⇒ To shake, agitate, move to and fro, or up and down.

PURPOSE STATEMENT

LEADERSHIP MINISTRIES WORLDWIDE

exists to equip ministers, teachers, and laymen in their
understanding, preaching, and teaching of God's Word
by publishing and distributing worldwide
The Preacher's Outline & Sermon Bible®
and related *Outline* Bible materials,
to reach & disciple men, women, boys, and girls for Jesus Christ.

•MISSION STATEMENT•

1. To make the Bible so understandable - its truth so clear and plain - that men
   and women everywhere, whether teacher or student, preacher or hearer,
   can grasp its Message and receive Jesus Christ as Savior; and...
2. To place the Bible in the hands of all who will preach and teach God's Holy
   Word, verse by verse, precept by precept, regardless of the individual's
   ability to purchase it.

The *Outline* Bible materials have been given to LMW for printing and especially
distribution worldwide at/below cost, by those who remain anonymous. One fact,
however, is as true today as it was in the time of Christ:

• The Gospel is free, but the cost of taking it is not •

LMW depends on the generous gifts of Believers with a heart for Him and a love and
burden for the lost. They help pay for the printing, translating, and placing *Outline*
Bible materials in the hands and hearts of those worldwide who will present God's
message with clarity, authority and understanding beyond their own.

LMW was incorporated in the state of Tennessee in July 1992 and received IRS 501(c) 3 non-
profit status in March 1994. LMW is an international, nondenominational mission organization.
All proceeds from USA sales, along with donations from donor partners, go 100% into under-
writing our translation and distribution projects of *Outline* Bible materials to preachers,
church & lay leaders, and Bible students around the world.

8/97

© 1997. Leadership Ministries Worldwide

PO Box 21310 - Chattanooga, TN 37424 • (423) 855-2181 • FAX (423) 855-8616
• E-Mail 74152.616@compuserve.com — Web site: http://www.outlinebible.org •

**Publisher &
Distributor of...**

The
Preacher's
Outline
&
Sermon
Bible

Sharing the OUTLINED BIBLE with the World!

For Information about any of the above, kindly FAX, E-Mail, Call, or Write

Please PRAY 1 Minute/Day for LMW!

PO Box 21310, Chattanooga, TN 37424 • (423) 855-2181 • FAX (423) 855-8616
• E-Mail- outlinebible@compuserve.com — www.outlinebible.org •

LEADERSHIP
MINISTRIES
WORLDWIDE

The
Preacher's
Outline
&
Sermon
Bible

Sharing

The

OUTLINED

BIBLE

With the World!

The Beaches *of*
Delaware
and historic Sussex County

Beach buddies Ben Fleming of Annapolis, Maryland, Andrew Topel of Chadds Ford, Pennsylvania and
Zach Zimmer of North Potomac, Maryland make waves and treasured memories in Rehoboth Beach.

Kevin Fleming

text by Nancy E. Lynch

ISBN 0-9662423-2-7

Bathed in the colors of dawn, Rehoboth Beach awakens to the new day's first footprints and yesterday's sandcastle masterpiece (preceding pages). The morning solitude soon will be washed away, replenished by summer throngs making tracks to claim the sandy playground. Anchored along Sussex County's 25-mile Atlantic coastline, First State beaches dominate as Delaware's most popular destination. Millions of visitors swell populations from Lewes to Fenwick Island, depositing more than $400 million into local resorts that bask in unprecedented prosperity.

Rehoboth Beach, nicknamed the "Nation's Summer Capital" for the seasonal influx of visitors from Washington, D.C., remains the flagship of family fun where crowds overflow the boardwalk and jam the beach (following pages) waiting for ocean-launched Independence Day fireworks.

Spinning a shadow, Jim Powell (left) pedals his reproduction 1890s pennyfarthing long before summer pedestrians clog Rehoboth's mile-long boardwalk, which was first built in 1873, the year Methodists converted scrub pine barrens to a camp meeting site. "I call it 'my time,'" says Powell, a Lewes resident who annually vacations with family just two miles away in Rehoboth. "The beaches are quite different from the mountains of West Virginia where I grew up. Around here, going to the beach is the thing to do. I like to get to the boardwalk early to watch the sunrise and the dolphins. For me, it's a time to reflect, to clear my head and appreciate nature."

Beach furniture is big business oceanside where umbrellas sprout daily at Henlopen Acres Beach Club. Seasonal workers, like local Jonathan Ross (above), seat hundreds of Rehoboth Beach sun worshippers every summer day. "I like working on the beach and meeting people," says Ross, who also rents umbrellas and body boards from the Baltimore Avenue beach shack where he works. "The job offers a very good salary – I put about half away for college – and after work, I meet my friends and we surf. It's a good way to end a great day."

Family fun in Rehoboth Beach brings summer smiles to Doug Burdin and his son, Daniel, (above) of Oakton, Virginia and Glen Dodson and his daughter, Abigail, of Gaithersburg, Maryland while a young beach-goer (preceding pages) prefers to stake out his island in the sun. "Rehoboth's a place I'm comfortable with," says Burdin. "My family started coming here when I was a kid, maybe 30 years ago. The beaches are clean, people are friendly. It's a nice family place."

Mastering broken waves at the East Coast
Skimboarding Championships, an annual event in
Dewey Beach since 1980, requires speed, agility,
balance, lightning reaction and a boatload of
daredevil tricks. Skimmer Jamie Celano sometimes
sprints up to 50 yards on the beach before
throwing his high-density foam board on a
broken wave – the skim – and riding it out to
execute gravity-defying moves. An average ride
lasts 10 seconds or less. "Beaches here are set up
perfect. Dewey is world-famous for its shore
breaks," says event founder Harry Wilson.
"There's deep water right up to the beach and big
waves dump hard."

Volleyball spikes in popularity each summer in Rehoboth Beach. "It's probably one of our most important sports," says Tim Bamforth, the city's summer recreation director. "It's mostly pick-up games, but there's diehard volleyball too." Tournaments decide the best players at the city's day recreation area off Hickman Street and at its four busy night courts off Baltimore Avenue where players tip off from 7 to 11 p.m. Sand soccer, basketball, whiffle ball and tether ball also compete for free time at this two-block beach playground. During spring and fall seasons, Mid-Atlantic Volleyball holds court with its First Rites of Summer and Mayor's Cup weekend tournaments that draw hundreds of amateurs to 70 nets stretched along a mile of beach.

With true grit, a Rehoboth Beach Patrol member muscles a team landline rescue (above) as competitors sprint in the annual Lifeguard Olympics, a grueling test of the best from Delaware, Maryland and New Jersey patrols. "We're one of the safest beaches on the East Coast," Rehoboth Beach Patrol captain Jate Walsh says. "Since 1921, we've had thousands of saves and only two tragedies. For the volume of people coming to the beach, it's a great record."

Ravaged by nor'easters, Rehoboth Beach's landmark sign sports a fresh face. Dolle's sweetens all seasons with saltwater taffy and caramel popcorn, staples since 1927 when business partners Thomas Pachides and Rudolph Dolle opened the boardwalk confectionery. Third-generation owner Tom Ibach turns out "tons of both" from original family recipes.

Today's mile-square city (preceding pages) reigns as Delaware's premier resort famous for its beaches, tax-free shopping and fine dining.

The beach is a hot destination for Halie Murray-Davis (following pages) as she rolls into Rehoboth with a smile.

Promoting cooperation and understanding within Rehoboth Beach's diverse population fulfills CAMP Rehoboth director Steve Elkins. "The acronym means 'Create A More Positive Rehoboth.' Primarily we promote the inclusion of gays and lesbians into the greater community," says Elkins, the openly gay co-founder of the non-profit organization with artist Murray Archibald, his partner of 20 years. "We're pioneers of a sort. Rehoboth's climate has changed dramatically and we've helped make a smoother transition by giving the city a forum to talk about change," he says. "We're not Key West and we're not Provincetown and we don't want to be. Most of us come to Rehoboth because we like the inclusiveness and the embracing quality. We feel we're helping the community live up to its biblical name, 'room for all.' Gays and lesbians are more comfortable being open here." Every Labor Day weekend, CAMP Rehoboth sponsors Sundance, a sold-out, two-day fund-raiser that nets more than $100,000 for AIDS programs and gay and lesbian concerns. CAMP Rehoboth also seeks common ground with area medical and religious sectors and works to ensure sensitivity by area law enforcement agencies in their handling of harassment issues. Elkins also publishes the 15-issue *Letters From CAMP Rehoboth* magazine. "I think Rehoboth is one of the best places to live," he says. "When you put a face on the individual segments of the community and humanize it, when you put some heart into it, you find our stories as citizens of this community are much more similar than different."

Artistic prodigy Abraxas sketches in Cape
Henlopen State Park near the World War II
watchtower he popularized in his oil painting
"Lookout." Famous at 23 for "First Light," his
Cape Henlopen Lighthouse study, the Lewes artist
commands up to $30,000 for his landscapes and
portraits. "I enhance realism, painting possibilities
other people don't usually see," he says. "I want to
enlighten, to bring beauty back into art."

Detecting Delaware's maritime past spawns many
successful hunts along Sussex County shores. For
centuries, the state's Atlantic coastline and Delaware
Bay harbored some of early America's highest
concentrations of shipping – and shipwrecks. Marine
archeologist Dale Clifton, owner of Fenwick Island's
DiscoverSea Museum, displays the area's largest
collection of local shipwreck artifacts, including
(above) a signal cannon, a 1641 spoon, Irish and
British halfpennies, a gold bar and an 1815
proclamation coin. State regulations allow the
collection of artifacts on state park beaches east of the
ocean's dune line but on no other state owned or
managed lands.

  Darrell O'Connor of Wilmington (following pages)
creates his own beach treasure during a sandcastle
contest in Rehoboth Beach.

Harper Cullen of Rehoboth Beach yields to a sea gull's sunset craving for Grotto pizza on the boardwalk as his brother, Barratt, dives unimpeded into a bucket of Thrasher's french fries. Golden links in the resort's commercial food chain, Grotto devours 1,200 tons of cheddar cheese, 200 tons of flour and 45,000 gallons of pizza sauce annually at its 10 Sussex County restaurants. Employing a secret cooking technique perfected by Joe Thrasher in 1929, Thrasher's three Rehoboth stands fry 325,000 pounds of Idaho Russet potatoes in 20 tons of premium peanut oil every year.

Always a good ride, family-owned Funland in Rehoboth Beach amuses vacationers daily from Mother's Day to the weekend after Labor Day. Operated since 1962 by four generations of Fasnachts and hundreds of "Funlanders" – a high school and college student work force – the busy one-acre boardwalk amusement park offers 18 rides like the Sea Dragon (right), 12 Skee Ball alleys, 100 video games and no set closing time. Natalie Vietro (above) of Aldan, Pennsylvania is a big winner.

Snaking and sliding through summer, asphalt and aqua attractions at Jungle Jim's Adventure World in Rehoboth Beach and White Water Mountain in Midway elbow the beaches for prime-time patronage. "We're having a ball," says Cindy Forestieri (right) of Milton with her nephew C.J. Willey of Rock Hall, Maryland. "Going out to play is something we adults don't do that much."

Seven days a week, shoppers rally for bargain bragging rights at nearby Rehoboth Outlets, ranked among the nation's top 12 most popular outlet destinations. "Two things work together to draw two million people here," says Rehoboth Outlets' marketing manager Lana O'Hollaren. "One is the variety available with 140 stores, the other is tax-free shopping. We're the only outlet center in Delaware and the largest on the Delmarva Peninsula."

By land or by sea, fishing lures anglers to Sussex County's bounty of bluefish, rockfish, tautog, flounder and sea trout. Sport fishermen troll the popular Baltimore Canyon 50 to 70 miles out for tuna, marlin, wahoo and other migratory big game fish. Tracks temporarily etched in sand, a surf fisherman (preceding pages) tests the waters at Delaware Seashore State Park where year-round casting is permitted.

Angling for fair winds, Hobie Cat 16s square off for the North American Continental Championships on Rehoboth Bay (following pages). The week-long fall event, co-hosted by the Rehoboth Bay Sailing Association and local Hobie Cat Fleet 106, attracted about 70 world-class teams from America, Canada, Mexico and the Caribbean and is a qualifier for both U.S. and Canadian Pan Am Hobie 16 sailing teams.

The Lewes & Rehoboth Canal, authorized by the U.S. River and Harbor Act of 1912 as part of the federal inland waterway system, links Delaware and Rehoboth Bays and once served as a busy conduit for barges loaded with local produce. Today, the canal provides safe harbor for commercial fishing boats (preceding pages) and private boats that dock in Lewes, Delaware's oldest town.

Pallbearers lead a Memorial Day funeral procession on the 200th anniversary of the sinking of H.M. brig DeBraak, a two-masted British Royal Navy warship, lost during a 1798 squall in the Delaware Bay off Cape Henlopen. The consecration service and burial of crew remains recovered in 1984 were officiated by a British Royal Navy chaplain at Zwaanendael Museum in Lewes where DeBraak uniforms, shoes, caps and Captain James Drew's mourning ring are on view.

Had the DeBraak sailed 36 years later, the Delaware Breakwater's granite barrier off Lewes might have provided protection from sometimes treacherous bay waters. The breakwater's East End Light (preceding pages), which replaced an earlier beacon, guided mariners from 1885 until its 1996 decommission by the U.S. Coast Guard.

Awash in history, Cape Henlopen (following pages) projects its strategic location between the Delaware Bay and the Atlantic Ocean, a spit of geography prominent in Lewes' seafaring and military past. Native Americans inhabited the area centuries before Englishman Henry Hudson sailed here in 1609. Cape Henlopen saw duty during World War II as Fort Miles, a U.S. Army base protecting the shipping lanes of the Delaware Bay and River. Today, its more than 4,000 acres comprise Cape Henlopen State Park, Delaware's largest.

With the Harbor of Refuge Lighthouse standing watch on Lewes' outer breakwater, the Cape May-Lewes Ferry Delaware slices through the Delaware Bay to the New Jersey shore, clocking the 17-mile crossing in 70 minutes. Plying the bay since 1964, the fleet of five motor vessels has shuttled more than 25 million passengers and their vehicles between historic Lewes and Victorian Cape May. More than transportation, the Cape May-Lewes Ferry system has evolved into a destination, offering Family Fun Cruises and promotional tie-ins at each port. Flagship is the five-deck MV Twin Capes, refurbished for $27 million in 1996.

Door to the past, the circa 1700 Rabbit's Ferry House is the gateway to the Lewes Historical Society Complex which preserves 18th century Lewes. The post-and-beam farmhouse was moved from nearby Rabbit's Ferry in 1967 to the three-acre complex at Third and Shipcarpenter streets. A milkhouse (above) is part of the historic village. Keeper of the city's multinational heritage, the 600-member historical society organized in 1962 also conserves the 1665 Ryves Holt House, said to be Delaware's oldest and named for the chief justice of the "Three Lower Counties on Delaware." The 1730s Cannonball House Marine Museum, the 1884 U.S. Life Saving Station boat house and the 1938 lightship Overfalls are also under the society's care. "Our mission is to preserve and interpret our history through buildings and architecture for future generations," says historical society president George Elliott. "Many members give their time as docents and volunteer for house tours, fund-raisers and craft fairs. They're very dedicated to the cause of the society."

In peak form, conditioned athletes swim to raise more than a quarter of a million dollars for children with life-threatening illnesses during Bethany Beach's annual Make-A-Wish Sea Colony Triathlon. The 15-year tradition pushes area athletes to their limits in a 1.5K ocean swim, 36K bike and 10K run.

A century ago, Christians, too, faced physical tests settling swampy and mosquito-infested Mud Neck as a religious retreat. Renamed in a 1901 national contest, Mud Neck became Bethany Beach and their chosen spot forbade drinking, gambling and amusement rides. Although Bethany Beach (preceding pages) is now a family destination, second only to Rehoboth Beach in popularity, it is still considered one of Delaware's quiet resorts.

Not all sun and fun, oceanfront living proved risky for South Bethany residents during winter nor'easters that savaged the shoreline in 1998. Back-to-back storms eroded foundations, denuded Ocean Drive, uprooted sewers and felled utility lines (left). Delaware Department of Transportation workers assess damage in Dewey Beach where life on the edge exacted a similar toll. While devastating, these tempests wither before the Great Storm of 1962, Delaware's most destructive. The unpredicted March nor'easter pummeled the coast for 72 hours. Winds gusted to 80 miles an hour and huge waves, fed by unusually high tides, nearly wiped out Rehoboth Beach. The storm of '62 left seven dead and property damage totaling $22 million.

Silver Lake laps Rehoboth Beach's southern boundary and attracts select homeowners willing to pay sky-high prices for premium locations. "Unimproved lots have sold in excess of $1.4 million," says veteran Rehoboth real estate agent Allison Bateman. "With the lake on one side and the ocean on the other, it's an unparalleled location." Other Rehoboth real estate is more affordable. "You can buy fixer-upper summer cottages maybe five blocks from the beach for under $200,000," she says. "There's such a variety here."

Able to energize crowds with a single song, Love Seed Mama Jump rocks The Bottle and Cork in Dewey Beach. The local band has become known nationally and has been an opener for the Beach Boys and Matchbox 20.

"We're a high energy pop rock'n'roll band," says dynamic lead singer Rick Arzt, who credits the group's decade-old chemistry to "mutual respect, our love for making music and the energy we create together." The sky's the limit for him, guitarist Will Stack and Brian Gore, bass guitarist Pete Wiedmann, drummer Paul Voshell and percussionist David James. "We'd like," Arzt adds, "to be rock stars on a global basis."

Summer's last blast in Bethany Beach (preceding pages) sounds a sorrowful note as the Grim Reaper leads the resort's traditional boardwalk New Orleans-style jazz funeral on Labor Day. Revelry replaces mourning after spontaneous bandstand eulogies set sail to summertime.

Visiting more than 30 local venues, thousands fall for the music at the Rehoboth Beach Autumn Jazz Festival, an October high note since 1989. Jazz legend Maynard Ferguson (left) blows his own horn outside the loop at a Midway steakhouse.

Parading parking meters in Rehoboth Beach's Sea Witch Halloween Festival signal the end to the summer nightmare of tens of thousands of people jockeying daily for 2,200 metered parking spots. The resort's largest source of tourist revenue, metered parking collects more than a million dollars each year, about a fifth of the annual budget – all in quarters. Nearby, a good witch casts a spell of serenity at this popular autumn event.

Hot wheels drive 130,000 spectators to the U.S. 13 Dragway and Delaware International Speedway north of Delmar each year. The family-owned 132-acre motor sports complex takes second place behind the beaches as Sussex County's top attraction. The National Hot Rod Association's southernmost Division I track, the quarter-mile dragway hosts NHRA regional finals. March to October purses for weekly elapsed time races total about $200,000. Racing four stock car divisions on its half-mile clay oval from April to November, the speedway pays more than $400,000 in winnings every year. Drag racing draws more participants, stock cars more spectators.

Regional inhabitants for more than 10,000 years, Native Americans survive today in Delaware as Nanticokes, "people of the tidal waters," in the Riverdale area near Millsboro. "We're an endangered species with a long, proud history," says assistant chief Charles C. "Little Owl" Clark IV, an artist and writer. "There are only about 1,000 of us and about 75 percent live in lower Delaware." The Nanticokes celebrate their heritage with a September powwow that brings together 60 other tribes from across the nation and Canada. Dancing, drumming and storytelling sated with succotash, fry bread and Indian tacos highlight the two-day event revived in 1977. "The powwow went into a lull in the 1940s. Many men joined the service – the modern way of becoming a warrior – in World War II," Clark says. "The civil rights movement opened doors for Native Americans. After assimilation, it was OK to be an Indian. We looked for ways to re-establish and coalesce various aspects of our culture into one event." Powwows maintain the Nanticoke Indian Museum's trove of authentic arrowheads, stone tools, pottery and extensive Native American library. Thousands attend the Nanticoke powwow, one of the East Coast's largest and recipient of the Governor's Tourism Award in 1995. "We try to educate people and want them to leave with a better understanding of native culture," Clark says. "We live and die, bleed and cry like everyone else."

Soybeans, viewed in a new light as a heart-healthy legume, are Delaware's largest cash crop with seven million bushels harvested every year. Oil is extracted in Sussex from soybeans like these near Bridgeville before further refining out-of-state. Soybean meal remains as feed for local poultry and livestock.

An oilseed crop like soybeans, sunflowers (following pages) near Milton receive an August insecticide dusting for leafhoppers from veteran agriculture pilot Allen Chorman. Airborne in his 600-horsepower Thrush, Chorman sprays up to 90,000 acres annually, ridding them of weeds, insects and disease.

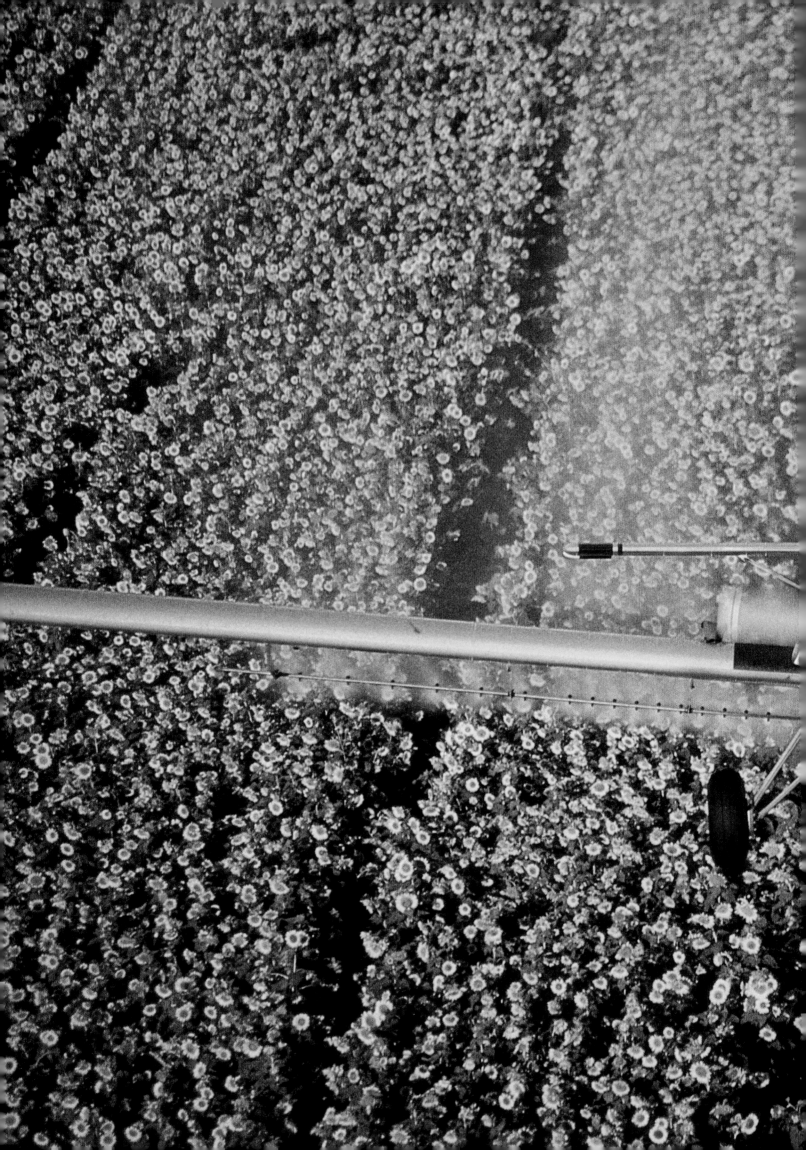

A young farmer puts the pedal to the metal at a
mini-tractor pull near Milford during Delaware
Plow Days, an agrarian retrospective sponsored
each spring by the First State Coon Hunters Association.
 Demonstrating that old ways endure, an Amish
farmer breaks ground with his draft team
(preceding pages). The three-day event also
features a night coon dog hunt, a mule show, an
antique tractor pull and a vintage carriage auction.
An outdoor toilet (following pages), once known as
"a necessary," is also reminiscent of days past.
"We get a lot of old-timers who bring their
grandchildren and tell 'em they used to farm that
way," says Coon Hunters Association past
president Dave Wilkins, who donates the use of his
family farm for Plow Days. "A lot of people aren't
used to seeing riding mules or draft horses
plowing. They can't believe it."

All ages truck to sales at the Laurel Auction Market where Delmarva growers meet East Coast buyers and brokers at The Block. Incorporated in 1940 on 12 dusty acres as the Southern Delaware Truck Growers' Association, the 1,500-member cooperative grosses about $3 million each summer from watermelons, cantaloupes and vegetables.

Roots run deep for lifelong farmers Brad Hickman (above) of Selbyville and Delmus Hickman of Ocean View who are unrelated but share a love of their agrarian heritage. On Sundays, Brad airs his family's restored 1927 Chevrolet one-ton pick-up that hauled chickens, ducks and guineas to Philadelphia during the Depression.

Delmus harvests truck crops in front of his 1947 corncrib. "I got a real mom-and-pop operation," he says. "I put my vegetables on a picnic bench under an umbrella in front of my house. That's my store."

"The more you eat, the more you want," promises Clara Williams, "Berry Boss" at Ryan's Berry Farm & Orchard, a 138-acre spread of reclaimed swampland near Frankford. Delaware's largest blueberry grower, Ryan's annually yields 200,000 pounds of the potassium-rich fruit. More than 50,000 customers pick 16 varieties of blueberries seven days a week from mid-June through July. "I keep 'em happy by telling 'em where the best berries are, yes indeedy," says Williams, culling experience from more than 50 summers in the patch she helped plant. "Clara's infamous," owner Tom Ryan says. "People come all the way from New York just to see her." Despite the draw, 64 million pounds of watermelons a year far outweigh blueberries as Delaware's top fruit crop, followed by apples, cantaloupes, peaches and strawberries.

Apples stem a nearly year-round growing season at T.S. Smith & Sons, a four-generation diversified farm business in Bridgeville. One of Delaware's two commercial apple growers, T.S. Smith wholesales most of its nine-variety crop out-of-state for processing as applesauce, apple butter, cider, juice and vinegar.

Arthur Johnson (right) rakes some of the 20 million pounds of green beans Draper King Cole cans yearly under hundreds of labels at its 28-acre Milton food processing complex. Although the company contracts for the vegetable in seven states, half the harvest grows on the fertile Delmarva Peninsula.

Come fall, tenant Brenda Johnson stores black walnuts in Paul Pepper's 1942 broiler house near Selbyville (following pages). "No one wants to crack walnuts anymore," laments Pepper. "I'll put 'em in there for the squirrels. We used to dry 'em til they were crispy, run 'em through a corn sheller then tap 'em with a hammer. Now people go to a store and buy 'em in a package."

All smiles, Sam Calagione lofts a keg of beer
behind the bottling line of Dogfish Head Craft
Brewery in Lewes. Delaware's first brewpub and
only microbrewery distributes its best seller Shelter
Pale Ale and other "eccentric beers" from Virginia
to Massachusetts to Pittsburgh. "The majority of
sales are on Delmarva," says Calagione, Dogfish
Head president. "We have no aspirations of
becoming national and want to be known as
Delaware's brewery." Dogfish Head uses no corn,
rice or extracts in its non-pasteurized products.
"We use higher quality ingredients, like 100
percent barley grown in Delaware and the
difference, we believe, is in the taste of the beer."

With six acres of her family's alfalfa farm near
Lewes under vine, a disarming but determined
Peggy Raley (following pages) convinced the
Delaware General Assembly in 1991 to pass
legislation to allow wineries in the state. Two years
later, she opened Nassau Valley Vineyards and
remains proprietor of Delaware's only winery. "I love
wine. It's part of the history of civilization," she
says of the gift of the grape. Raley produces 3,000
cases of eight varieties of wine annually, rating her
semisweet Meadow's Edge White most popular.
"If the product I put on your table allows you to
break bread and toast the lives around you and let
go of all your daily worries, then I've done my job."

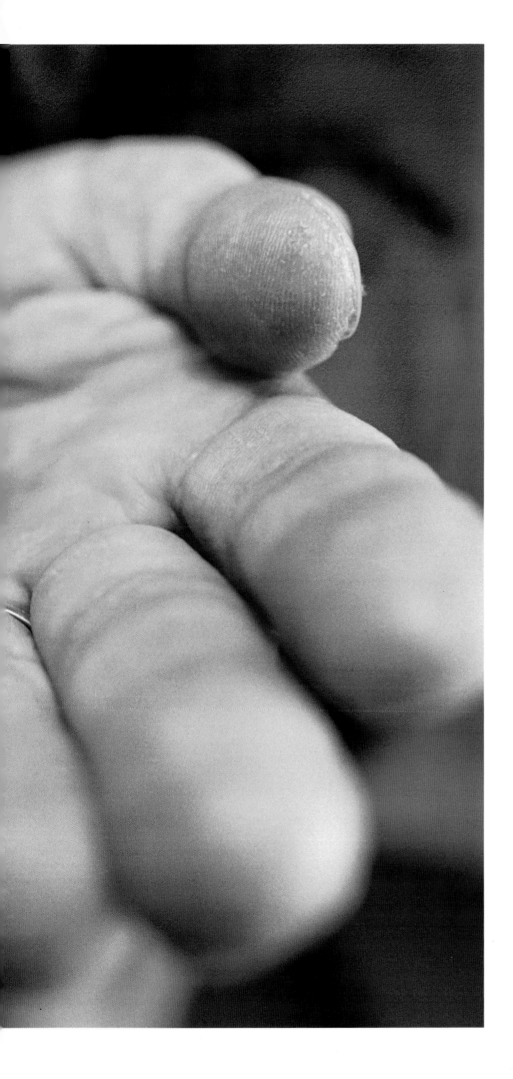

Near Seaford, Gray O'Bier (preceding pages) shovels corn at Hearn & Rawlins Flour Mill. Delaware's last grist mill custom-grinds about four tons of poultry and livestock feed each week for area farmers on its hammer mill and stone-grinds 3,000 pounds of yellow and white corn meal, bagging most of it for scrapple houses. Rebuilt after fire razed it in 1879, the mill on Hearn's Pond also is equipped with steel rollers that weekly process 9,500 pounds of soft red winter wheat into white and whole wheat flour, sold locally under the "White Dove" label.

Hours after hatching, baby chicks board a bus to be dropped off at a contract grower's poultry house. In the next 45 to 52 days, the time it takes a chicken to be ready for market, each bird eats two pounds of feed for every pound it weighs. "Chicken is the most efficient animal to convert grain protein into meat protein," says Charles C. "Chick" Allen III, president of Seaford-based Allen Family Foods.

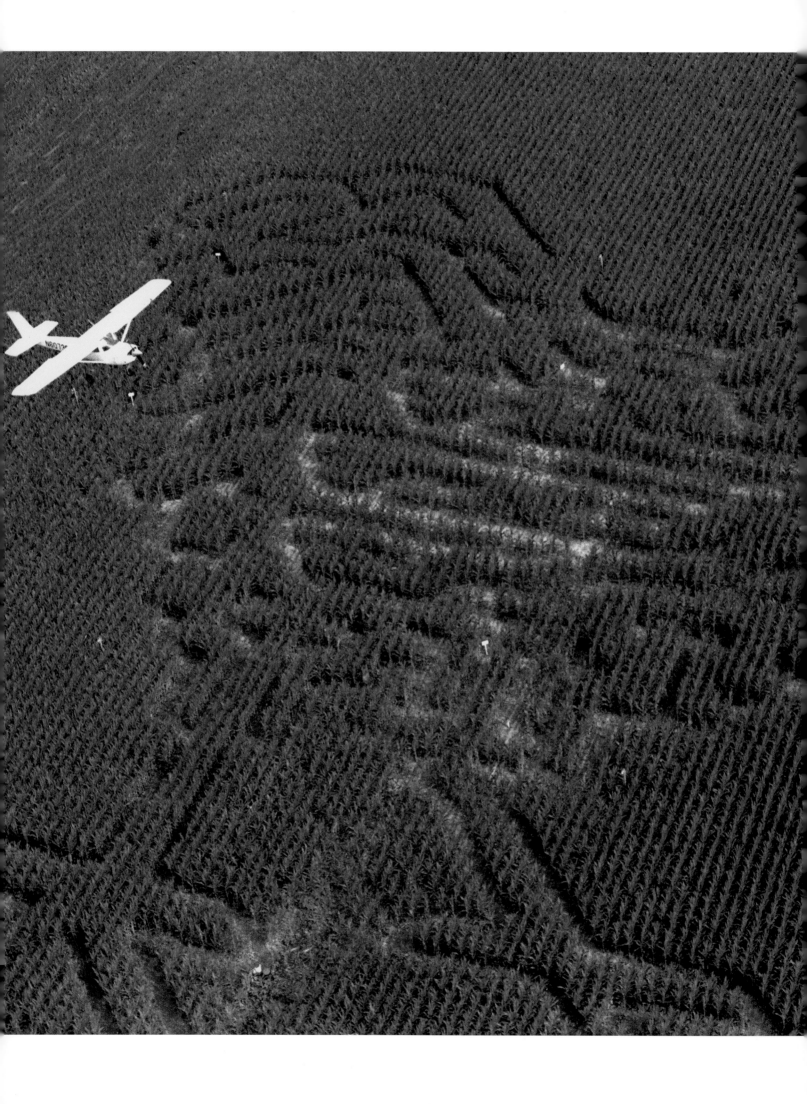

Symbolic of Sussex County's high-flying chicken industry, Magee's Maize Maze in Williamsville was visited by 10,000 people. "I thought a five-acre chicken would be pretty neat," says Danny Magee who needed a county permit to operate the maze which changes themes every year. "As you went through, there were 12 different questions relating to the poultry industry, so it was an education process too. We had a lot of fun with it." Magee raises 80,000 broilers and farms 1,400 acres owned by his family for five generations.

"I herd 'em up and run 'em into a pen. Then we catch seven, sometimes five or six, at a time by one leg," says professional chicken catcher Richard Parker (following pages) as he works a Mountaire poultry house near Millsboro. The gang of six catchers will cage the house's entire population of 21,000 birds in three to four hours. And move on to the next house. "All I think about is getting the chickens to the plant and going home," Parker says. "I always try to do a good job so the farmer will be happy."

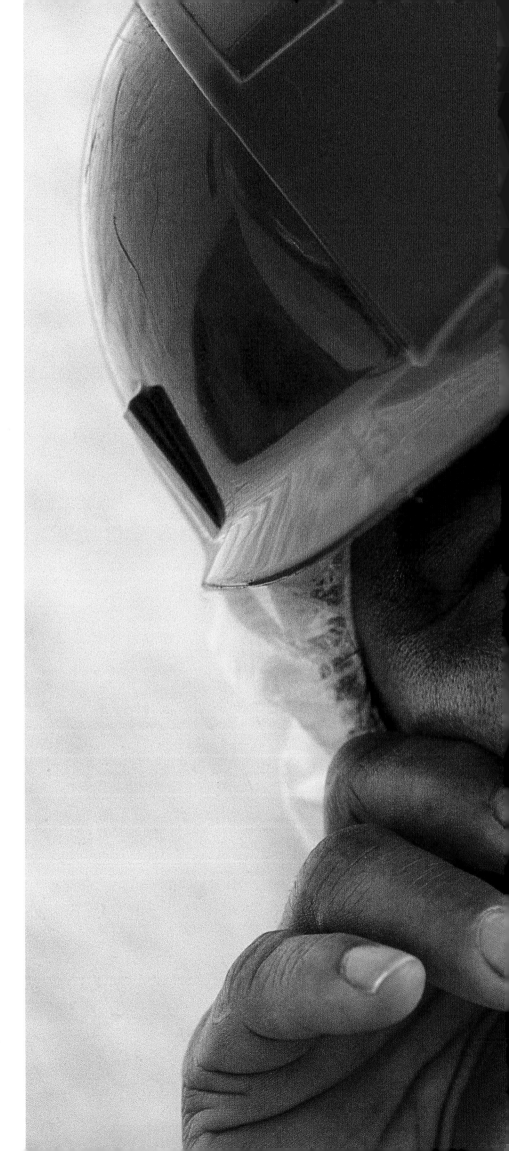

Chickens rule the roost in Sussex, the nation's top poultry-producing county and, increasingly, foreign workers like Maximino Rodriguez of El Salvador flock to employment opportunities far from home. "We are a stronger company for our diversity which is reflected in our management and is evident in our values," says Dave Tanner, director of Human Resources for Mountaire Farms. "It goes beyond the workplace to the family. We provide English as a second language course and recently made a large donation to a child care center that provides outreach services to new immigrant families." Nearly 15 percent of Mountaire's workforce immigrated to Delaware, mostly from Central America and also from Korea, Vietnam and Laos. "The reason they're coming in," Tanner says, "is because we provide good, safe working conditions and opportunity for advancement, good pay and good benefits." In addition to Mountaire, Allen Family Foods, Perdue Farms, Townsends and Tyson Foods also hire foreign workers in their processing plants. Together, these companies, backed by 669 growers countywide, produce 189 million birds annually, about three percent of the country's total broiler production.

No one remembers when chicken first came off the grill at the Greenwood barbecue (following pages). But everyone knows the Greenwood Volunteer Fire Company and the Greenwood VFW do chicken right. Patrons pile into a pole-shed flanked by picnic tables on the U.S. 13 median to purchase 2,000 platters every summer weekend. "I eat a whole lot more smoke cooking chicken than I do fighting a fire," says David Haymond (right) as he and David Warner baste chicken halves with a special sauce. Ingredients are a closely guarded secret.

"You don't walk out hungry," pledges Jim Tennefoss, owner of Jimmy's Grille in Bridgeville where 2,000 patrons a day dig into plates heaped with home cooking. From secret-recipe pancakes to 75 dinner entrees, Jimmy's caters to crowds, seated 275 at a time and served by a staff of 65. "Everything's cooked to order," Tennefoss says. "We have the fastest turnover of any restaurant." Here, waitress Christy Willey rushes another meal from kitchen to table. Diners applaud Jimmy's bountiful portions, reasonable prices and quick service by devouring 10,000 pounds of chicken, 3,000 pounds of beef and more than a ton of potatoes weekly. And 150 to 200 pies daily. "It's simple food," Tennefoss says of his cash-only restaurant that needs no advertising. "I only serve what I like." Including his mother's yeast rolls. "We have big eaters here. I like putting out good food," he adds. "And nobody does it like we do."

A curious concoction of pig snouts, jowls, tongues, livers, hearts, cornmeal, flour and special seasonings, scrapple is Sussex County's signature side dish. RAPA Scrapple in Bridgeville is the largest of Delaware's four purveyors and processes up to 48,000 pounds daily for markets in five states and Washington, D.C. Varieties of RAPA's one- and two-pound scrapple bricks include "Our Original," "Hot & Spicy," "With Bacon" and beef scrapple. Of Pennsylvania Dutch origin, the breakfast staple is sliced, fried and often finished with ketchup, mustard or maple syrup. Founded in 1926 by brothers Ralph and Paul Adams, RAPA was sold in 1981 to a Wisconsin company. Ernest Lofland (left), one of 44 employees, stirs a 1,000-pound-capacity stainless steel pot in the company's cavernous kitchen. Each October, RAPA celebrates its culinary coup by co-sponsoring the Apple Scrapple Festival with local orchard owners T.S. Smith & Sons. Highlight is the scrapple carving contest. "There are two things you don't want to know about Delaware," quips one local. "What goes into politics and what goes into scrapple."

Competitive pumpkin hurling attracts international media attention and plants 15,000 spectators in a Sussex County soybean field. "Where else can you see pumpkins fly?" asks Carol Ostasewski (left), secretary of the 300-member Punkin Chunkin Association. Dubbed "Delaware's home-grown insanity," the World Championship Punkin Chunk germinated in 1985 after a Lewes blacksmith, a Harbeson plumber and a Georgetown well driller got their gourds together. Today, teams chunk for best distance — and charity.

Colorful roadside enterprises like Joyce Bishop's hand-made cartoon character whirligigs, tended by her son, Felix Rodriguez of Lewes (above), relieve the tedium of travel to Delaware beaches. "We make ones that stick in the ground and ones that swing in the trees," says Bishop, who fashions the white pine windmills during the winter months with her sister. "We set $20 apiece on 'em," she says, "so everybody can afford to buy 'em."

Flush with pride, Esther Groves has her own roadside curiosity. "I call it a flower hopper. People going to the beaches stop and take pictures. They never seen anything like it," she says, holding her foster child, Taylor Lynn Smith, over the recycled planter near Milford. "Couldn't get nobody to move it so I pulled it over here with my riding mower. It just come on my mind what to do with it. Got yellow and beige hoppers too. I like odd things."

The Miss Delaware Scholarship Pageant bestows the state's most-coveted crown every June in Rehoboth Beach. A jubilant Jody Michelle Kelly (above) hugs sister Tracy after winning the contest's 57th tiara. Dressed in their finest head-to-toe, teenage girls bare their feet at Laurel High School's prom while Little Miss Millsboro hopefuls (following pages) contend with nervous butterflies before judging begins.

History reigns over Georgetown on Return Day,
a biennial balm for healing political wounds,
when winners and losers parade together two
days after November elections. Voters' first
opportunity more than 200 years ago to hear
poll results in the county seat, the uniquely
Delaware event — now a mandated half-day
holiday in Sussex County — survives as a festive
forum for political reconciliation. Party leaders
symbolically bury the hatchet and crowds
averaging 30,000 feed on free ox sandwiches.
Return Day crier Layton Johnson, Georgetown's
longest-serving mayor, prepares to read the results
from the Sussex County Courthouse balcony
overlooking The Circle.

A ticket to ride Delaware's last cable-operated ferry is priceless for the 200-yard crossing of the scenic Nanticoke River at Woodland near Seaford. The 65-foot Virginia C., better known as the Woodland Ferry, carries up to four vehicles at a time from 7 a.m. to sunset year-round, weather permitting. While the ferry master guides the open-ended steel vessel along the submerged cable from an elevated engine house, crewman Donny Tingle swabs the deck en route. Placed on the National Register of Historic Places in 1973, the ferry is operated by the state Department of Transportation, owner since 1935. A transport of some sort has negotiated the Nanticoke at this site since 1793 when the General Assembly granted Isaac and Betty Cannon exclusive permission to operate Cannon's Ferry.

PASSENGERS ARE NOT
· TO LEAVE BOAT UNTIL ·
CHAIN IS REMOVED

Officiating at a baptism, Pastor Charles Holland immerses one of his New Hope Assembly Church members in the still waters of Trap Pond near Laurel. "They separate from their sinful life," Holland explains. "When they come to the baptism and say they accept Christ in their lives that excites me and makes me feel spiritually elevated."

Four generations of Lesia Jones's family also receive a spiritual lift from summer gatherings at Carey's Camp (preceding pages), one of the few remaining active camp meetings and among the Methodist Church's oldest institutions. Erected in 1888 in an oak grove west of Millsboro, the camp's 47 clapboard "tents" encircle a cross-shaped open-air tabernacle. Turn-of-the-century farm families once gathered by the wagonload to socialize for two weeks before the corn harvest. Now open to any denomination, the camp welcomes guest ministers, choirs and speakers for daily services and classes. Attendance has topped 1,000 in past sessions. "Being with family and friends is important," says Jones, 37, a lifelong attendee. "It's a time for relaxing and fellowship. It's a lot of fun."

No cross too heavy, retired Episcopal minister Dick Swartout frequents Old Christ Church near Laurel, built in 1771-1772 as a "chapel of ease" or branch church of Stepney Parish, Maryland. The rare, unaltered pre-Revolutionary building remains without electricity, heat or plumbing. Its two-tiered pulpit, 43 box pews and east wall chancel – all of heart pine – are architecturally unparalleled. Maintained and administered since 1922 by the Old Christ Church League, the building is owned by St. Philip's Episcopal Church in Laurel and is open Sunday afternoons from April to October and July 4. "There's a special feeling you get when you walk in that says this is a holy place," Swartout says. "Think of how many prayers have been prayed here."

137

Suspended in seasonal limbo, an early frost clings to maple leaves near Georgetown. Sunset washes over fall foliage (preceding pages), shadowing farmland east of Milford where earth tones contrast with a monochromatic creek meandering toward the Delaware Bay. An ethereal Trussum Pond (following pages), home of one of the northernmost stands of bald cypress trees, waits out winter within Trap Pond State Park in southwestern Sussex County.

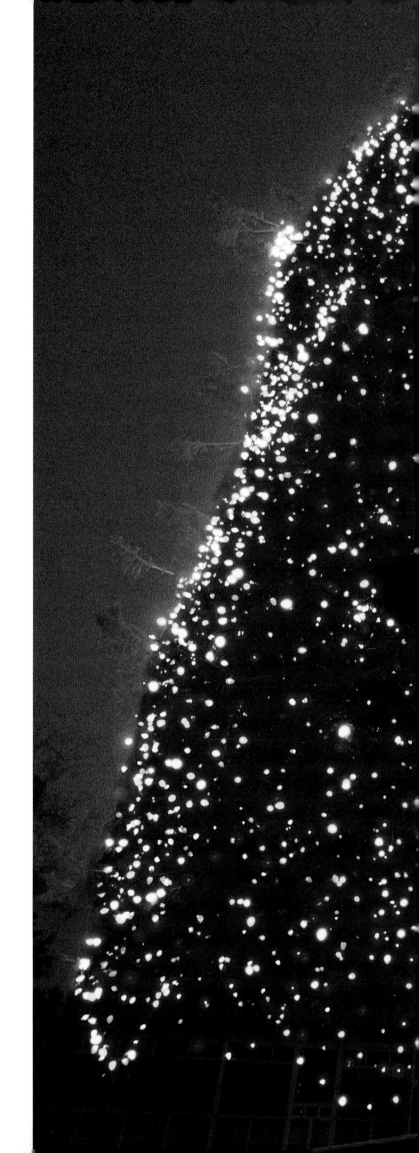

Rehoboth Beach mayor Sam Cooper decks his live 51-foot Norway spruce with 4,375 homemade lights, a Yule tradition his grandfather started in the 1940s. Cooper, a volunteer fireman, borrows the fire company's aerial truck for the two-day stringing task. "I don't enjoy putting the lights on it," he says, "but I do enjoy the feeling people get from it, particularly the kids."

Kim Hastings (above) waters some of the 33,000 poinsettias she and husband Jeff grow from cuttings at Jeff's Greenhouses in Bethel. No one in Sussex or Kent counties sells more of the holiday flower, available at Jeff's in nine varieties.

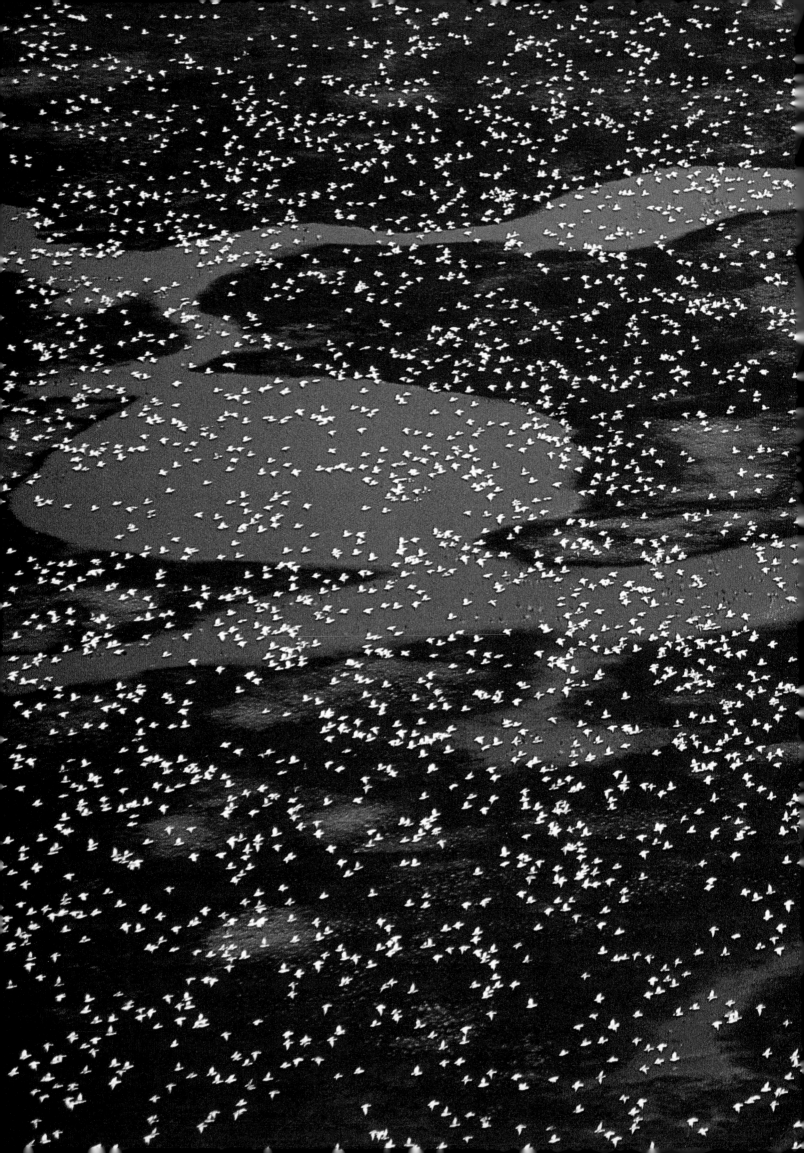

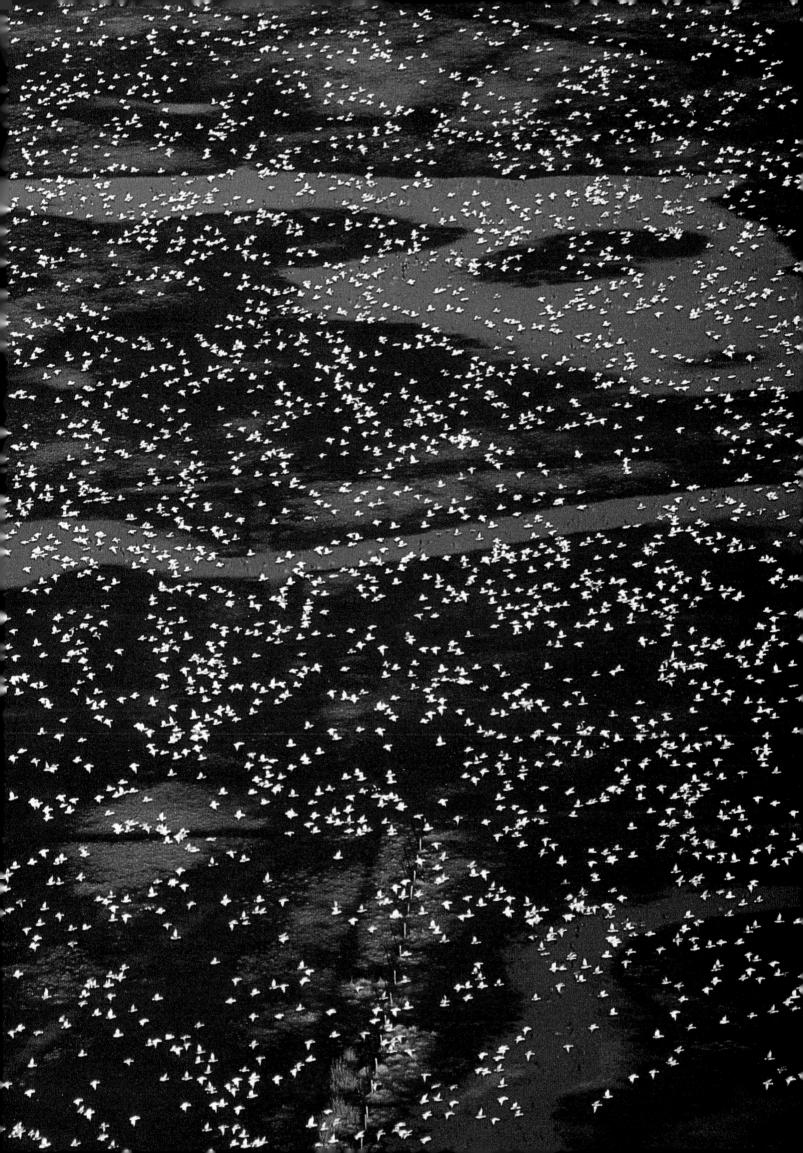

Watching for waterfowl, John G. "Roger" Townsend IV hunts on family lands along Black Hog Gut in the Great Marsh between Prime Hook and Lewes. "This is the first place I went duck hunting when I was about nine or so with my uncle, Joe Crowley," recalls Townsend, vice president of J.G. Townsend Jr. and Company, a Georgetown frozen vegetable business. The family-owned company began as a cannery purchased by his great-grandfather in 1928 and farms about half its 11,100 acres, reserving the rest for timber and real estate. "It's getting tougher and tougher in Sussex County to find lands to hunt because there are more people and more interest in the outdoors," Townsend says. "I grew up with hunting and like the ambiance of seeing the sunrise, setting decoys out, watching a good dog work and the camaraderie of friends. It's such a nice feeling."

Second reapers of corn and soybean fields, snow geese (preceding pages) fly from Prime Hook National Wildlife Refuge near Broadkill Beach in search of grains and grasses. Rare in Delaware before the 1970s, now nearly 300,000 migrate each fall from Canadian breeding grounds, often destroying valuable crops and fragile wetlands in their wake.

While fish-eating osprey (above) commonly nest along Sussex County's shorelines, great blue herons stake out fishing rights with a territorial display on Rehoboth Beach's Silver Lake, an oceanside freshwater oasis designated decades ago by the state as a waterfowl refuge.

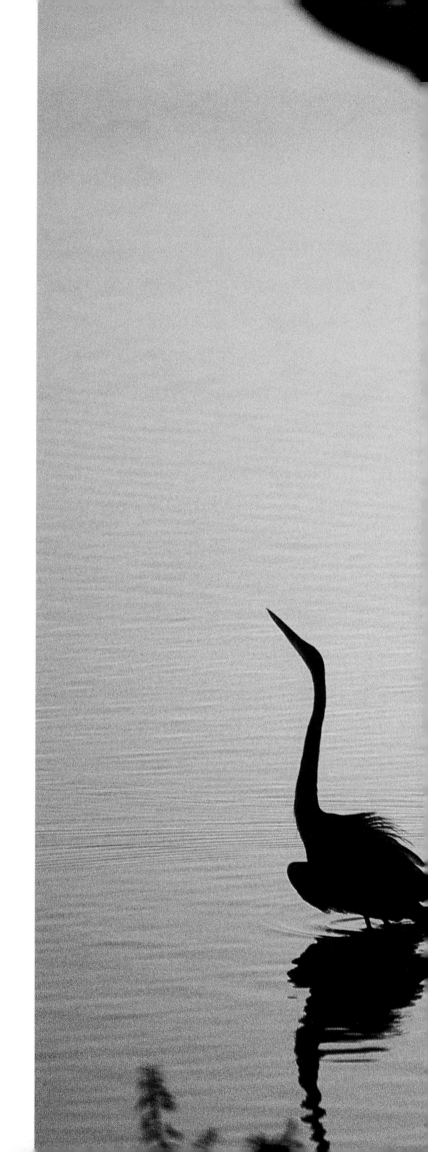

Quail Jones (preceding pages) unwinds outside
Signs of the Past, a converted 1930s poultry
feedhouse near Georgetown where he sells
antiques, glass, collectibles and his specialty, old
advertising signs. "Condition's a great part of their
value," he says of his 300-plus collection of mostly
metal signs, rated good to "near mint" and tagged
$20 to $2,000. "Old signs have nice graphics and
brilliant colors. They're works of art. The
excitement is finding something I've never seen."

Milton resident Chip Hunsicker (left) spruces up
at his Atlantic Street Victorian home of authentic
"competition yellow" and "election blue." In
1995, he fled Baltimore with bride Maura, a
Milton native. "We were tired of crime and not
knowing our neighbors and had an opportunity to
move to slower, lower Delaware. It was a shock at
first," he recalls. "But now I can't imagine living
anywhere else."

Frankford innkeeper Ray Davis (following pages)
agrees. "A lot of our guests like the beach but not
the crowds," he says, relaxing with his retriever
Nikki on the wraparound veranda of the 1870s
Captain Ebe T. Chandler House. "We're close
enough so they can spend the day at the beach yet
come back here to peace and quiet. Frankford's a
nice small town."

Summer crowds long gone, winter whitewashes Rehoboth Beach.

Portfolio Books
Post Office Box 156 • Rehoboth Beach, Delaware 19971
800.291.7600

Color scans by Baltimore Color Plate, Towson, Maryland
History consultant Hazel D. Brittingham • Proofreading by Ken Mammarella and J.L. Miller

Printed and bound in Korea by DNP America

No remedy for the faint of heart, Milton family practitioner and master balloonist
Dr. Charles Wagner (preceding pages) prescribes sunrise ballooning over Indian River Bay.